The European Union and You

Understand the EU

The Constitution

The Reform Treaty*

and the Arguments

Text of the EU Constitution

Text of the Laeken Declaration

Text of the Mandate for the Reform Treaty

* Also known as the Treaty of Lisbon

The European Union and You

Understand the EU

The Constitution

The Reform Treaty*

and the Arguments

Text of the EU Constitution

Text of the Laeken Declaration

Text of the Mandate for the Reform Treaty

David Roberts

Saxon Books

* Also known as the Treaty of Lisbon

The European Union and You

ISBN 978-0-9528969-4-4
Published by Saxon Books
London Road, Burgess Hill, RH15 9RN UK
Websites: www.saxonbooks.co.uk and www.warpoetry .co.uk

Printed and bound in Great Britain by Biddles Ltd, Kings Lynn.

Acknowledgements

I am grateful to all who have helped me to produce this book including officers of the European Union who have responded thoughtfully to my numerous queries. I am especially grateful to John Byng, Peter Golden and Francis Clark-Lowes who read early drafts of parts of the book and provided painstaking, thought-provoking and detailed commentaries. I am also grateful to Paul Roberts for his research, book design, cover, charts, maps and advice, John Bedford for proof reading our original texts, and Julie Roberts for her patience and valuable suggestions.

David Roberts

Copyright

Contents

List of tables

Maps and diagrams

Note on articles mentioned in this book

References throughout this book to specific articles are those of the Constitution, unless otherwise indicated.

Part One

Crisis of Confidence in the European Union

"The Union stands at a crossroads, a defining moment in its existence." – European leaders' Laeken Declaration, 15 December 2001.

"The European Union is facing a crisis of political legitimacy at a moment of major global change. . . Opinion polls show eroding support for European integration throughout the European Union." - Siim Kallas, Vice-President of the European Commission, 20 October 2005.[1]

Europe is united - but do its citizens love the EU?

There is no doubt that most British people love the rest of Europe. In 2004 they made 50,000,000 visits to mainland Europe. Three hundred thousand British people work there. One and a quarter million[2] have set up home there. Approximately half of all UK foreign trade is with "Europe". From time to time much of Britain is united with the rest of Europe in a passion for football. British people are impressed by the art, culture, achievements and lifestyles of fellow Europeans.

Britain and the British are enthusiastically part of Europe and would be outraged if it ever happened that Europeans put up trade barriers against us, or made it difficult for us to travel there to trade, or holiday or enjoy the friendship of our European neighbours.

Therefore this book is not about the question of whether the British people should be "in Europe", or work in peaceful co-operation with Europeans, or trade with Europeans, or even consider themselves to be Europeans. All this can be assumed. For virtually all British people these questions do not arise. What is of concern to the British and all European citizens, is the nature of the political system which has been invisibly constructed, little by little, over half a century, which controls large elements of the lives of 480,000,000 European citizens.

This system has evolved through a series of treaties and is now most comprehensively expressed in the 2004 European Constitution[3] and the repackaged versions of this which were devised in 2007. What is the nature of the political system that now confronts EU citizens? What are the facts? What are the issues? Do current plans resolve the problems facing the EU? What are the alternatives that may replace or modify current plans? These are the key concerns of this book.

Europe - time for change

There is evidence of widespread dissatisfaction both in Britain and among our European neighbours with the political institutions and policies that are developing control over the people of Europe. In 2005, referendums in France and the Netherlands rejected the Constitution by substantial majorities. There was significant disaffection with the Constitution in all EU member states. Earlier referendums in Ireland (which at first rejected the *Nice Treaty*), Denmark (which at first rejected the *Maastricht Treaty*), and Norway (which twice rejected membership) are indicative of popular feeling.

By 2001 European leaders were already so worried about criticisms of the functioning of the European Union and institutional failings that they set out their concerns in a document, *The Future of the European Union,*[4] which is printed later in this chapter.

When the European Project ran into a barrier of rejection, uncertainty and doubt the European Union paused in a rare period of reflection and self-examination. It might have been a time for new approaches, changed institutions and modified policies. But the European Union seems set to continue along its present line of development, increasingly passing power and control to Brussels, becoming more remote and dictatorial, whilst leaving unsolved the present problems, confusions and potential for political stalemate, economic decline and social unrest.

However, there are alternative approaches to the political organisation of Europe. The EU[5] could find more decentralised, more democratic, open, legitimate and accountable ways for member states of the Union to co-operate. A greater democratic engagement with eurocitizens might help to harness their enthusiasm, energy and creativity and enable them to prosper and advance the sustainability and well-being of the people of Europe and the world.

If EU leaders persist in transferring power from member states to Brussels without improving democratic accountability they may be faced with some form of revolt which may lead to a less centralised, less formal association of free states. This may come about as member states engage in piecemeal policy revision and disengagement.

A redirection of the European Union or its disintegration are the critical and historic possibilities now confronting the leaders of Europe. European leaders are unlikely to be able to continue to meet behind closed doors and take increasing power to themselves unchallenged. The 480 million citizens of the European Union are likely to wish to play a role in influencing the path Europe takes in coming years.

European leaders at the crossroads 2001-2007 and beyond

Awareness of widespread disaffection prompted the writing of the Laeken Declaration, the European Constitution and six years of reflection

Which way now for Europe?[6]

Reform of the EU has been under discussion for many years and EU institutions themselves as well as critics from outside the institutions have put forward their complaints and proposals. Each of the treaties which have developed the European Union from its original association of six states has aimed not only to expand the scope of its powers, but to improve the effectiveness of the way it worked.

The *Treaty of Nice* had been signed on 26 February 2001 and had not even come into force when the fifteen heads of EU member states, the European Council, met in Laeken, Belgium, in December 2001 to review their own concerns and the widespread unease. The Conference produced a declaration outlining what it considered were the strengths of the EU and presenting a list of numerous problem areas - questions which it considered needed answers and remedies. The document, *The Future of the European Union*, (also known as *The Laeken Declaration*)[7] is a key document in understanding the European Union in the twenty-first century. Whilst recognising that many things needed to change within the European Union and identifying some directions in which policies ought to move the leaders refrained from suggesting specific answers. They seemed conscious that the European Union had reached an historic impasse. They summarised their position in these words, "The Union stands at a crossroads, a defining moment in its existence."

The Laeken Declaration called for many popular and important reforms and changes of direction. It called for more transparency, more democracy, more clarity, more simplicity, more efficiency, for devolution and less centralisation of powers (subsidiarity - laws passed as close to citizens as possible), less rules, regulations and red tape, the guarding of state parliaments' rights to make laws in certain areas, and the avoidance of "a creeping expansion of the competence of the Union" and creating an EU superstate. It proclaimed the need for peace, justice and human rights.

Many serious criticisms, including the running sore of EU corruption, the dissatisfaction with agricultural policies, fisheries policies, transport policies, plans to increase arms spending, the EU army, and nuclear policy were not in the Laeken mandate.

To examine the problems and come up with proposed solutions the Council appointed one of the EU's elder statesmen to lead a convention. "In order to pave the way for the next Intergovernmental Conference . . . the European Council has decided to convene a Convention . . . It will be the task of that Convention to consider the key issues arising for the Union's future development and try to identify the various possible responses. The European Council has appointed Mr V. Giscard d'Estaing as Chairman of the Convention."[8]

Valery Giscard d'Estaing put together a team of people to consider the issues. This team took a great deal of evidence. It met many times and produced, as its response to the questions, a draft Constitution. This was delivered to the ministers in Rome on 18 July 2003. Giscard d'Estaing pointed to a key development that the Constitution would bring about. "With this Constitution, Europe is taking a decisive step towards political union." After further discussions and amendments the leaders accepted the Constitution.

At the signing ceremony of the final version of the Constitution in Rome on 24 October 2004, Silvio Berlusconi, Prime Minister of Italy and President of the European Council,[9] said, "Europe has at last acquired a Constitution based on the twofold and indivisible consensus of the citizens and Member States."

The consensus proved to be lacking in two founding states of the EU. On 29 May 2005 the French rejected the Constitution in a referendum. The Netherlands did the same on 1 June.

On 18 June the EU heads of state responded to the crisis by calling for a period of reflection. "We have noted the outcome of the referendums in France and the Netherlands... Citizens have ... expressed concerns and worries which need to be taken into account. Hence the need for us to reflect together on this situation... We have agreed to come back to this matter in the first half of 2006 to make an overall assessment of the national debates and agree on how to proceed.[10]

One year later, at the June 2006 meeting of EU heads of state, they decided to extend the period of reflection into 2008. President of the European Council, Austria's Federal Chancellor Wolfgang Schüssel, said at a press briefing on 15 June, " We had a very interesting discussion on how to proceed on the *Constitutional Treaty* as well as on integration and migration. These themes will remain on the agenda over the next few years... The presidency during the first six months of 2007 will present a report following consultations with the Member States to take stock of the state of discussions and examine future possible developments. Future decisions will be based on this report. The decisive steps should be taken in the second half of 2008 at the latest."[11]

In fact, following a two-day meeting behind closed doors, EU leaders announced on 23 June 2007 that they had reached agreement on "the way forward". The "way forward" was, they decided, to stand still, keeping the substance of the Constitution but in a repackaged form. Really, they had decided to remain at the crossroads indefinitely.

Setting back the European Union - D'Estaing's Convention

The Convention chaired by Valery Giscard d'Estaing set the European Union back several years. The task it was given was to explore the issues identified by European leaders in the *Laeken Declaration* in December 2001 (reflect on them) and come up with proposals for consideration – a starting point for discussions. The Convention's task had been clearly spelled out:

> The Convention will consider the various issues. It will draw up a final document which may comprise either different options, indicating the

> degree of support which they received, or recommendations if consensus is achieved. Together with the outcome of national debates on the future of the Union, *the final document will provide a starting point for discussions* at the Intergovernmental Conference, which will take the ultimate decision.[12]

Rather than put forward a range of proposals for consideration the Convention decided it would take the final decision about what to do and set out its conclusions in the elaborate form of a constitution, probably the longest the world has ever seen. In presenting the draft constitution Giscard d'Estaing asked for there to be no changes. He claimed that "Re-opening it, even in part, would cause it to unravel".[13]

This constitution might with benefit have been rejected by European leaders. It was not what they had asked for. There should have been a range of proposals for reform for EU leaders to consider. As an alternative, the convention's self-chosen response, a constitution, might have been short, easily comprehended, and focused and practical in the changes it proposed. But it did not propose remedies for some of the most critical problems identified by Europe's leaders. For example, whilst advocating transparency the constitution itself conceals many of the crucial, contentious issues, and pressing concerns. It barely touched on institutional secrecy. Whilst advocating efficiency and simplicity it is a vast, complex, and often incomprehensible document which sometimes proposes bewilderingly complex procedures and variations on procedures. The major issue of lack of democratic accountability is not answered. Nothing is done to ensure some areas of decision-making are reserved to member states. Leaders had clearly stated that "What they [citizens] expect is . . . not a European superstate," yet D'Estaing boasted that the Constitution took a decisive step towards making the European Union into a single state. If the Convention had addressed even the inadequate requirements of *The Laeken Declaration* then the EU would have been set on the way to becoming significantly more democratic and in tune with popular opinion across Europe.

With the rejection of the Constitution by two member states European Union leaders have been forced back to a consideration of the original problems, although many deny this, insisting that the Constitution is the answer they have been looking for and that eventually the citizens of Europe will accept it.

Preparing the Constitution – difficulties and complaints

The Constitution was prepared and offered as the solution to problems EU leaders identified. That being the case why were there so few attempts to solve problems and why were so many offered solutions so unsatisfactory?[14]

The failings of the Constitution may be partly explained by the haste and pressure under which its authors worked. Yet the authors appear to have gone to great lengths to do a thorough and workmanlike job, as they explain below. The Convention acquired a vast number of suggestions and comments. Were its members capable, in a short time, of assimilating and assessing such an enormous inflow of ideas and information? Was it humanly possible to respond adequately to such a plethora of advice? Could discussions and decision taking have been better managed? Certainly some of those present thought so. Here are three accounts of what happened.

Views of the President of the Convention

The authors of the European constitution list the following as elements of the work of the Convention which prepared the Constitution:

- They worked for seventeen months.
- The Convention's meetings were open to the public.
- There were 52 days of plenary sessions at which 1,800 interventions were heard.
- There were eleven working groups, and three discussion circles.
- Convention members provided 386 written contributions to the Convention as a whole, and 773 to working groups, and discussion circles.
- The Praesidium met on 50 occasions and submitted 52 papers to the Convention.
- Members of the Praesidium chaired the working groups and discussion circles and presented their reports to the Convention.
- They received 1,264 contributions from NGOs, the business community, academia and others.
- Meetings were organised with churches, think tanks, NGOs, youth organisations and representatives of local and regional organizations.
- Members from candidate countries "participated fully in the Convention's proceedings."

Summarised from a report issued on 18 July 2003 and signed by the chairman of the Convention, Valéry Giscard d'Estaing.[15]

Views of Gisela Stuart

> The Convention brought together a self-selected group of the European political elite, many of whom have their eyes on a career at a European level, which is dependent on more and more integration and who see national governments and parliaments as an obstacle. Not once in the sixteen months I spent on the Convention did representatives question whether deeper integration is what the people of Europe want, whether it serves their best interests or whether it provides the best basis for a sustainable structure for an expanding Union. The debates focused solely on where we could do more at European Union level. None of the existing policies were questioned.
>
> - Gisela Stuart, British Labour MP, member of the Convention.[16]

Eight other members of the Convention produced a summary of the Constitution's failures to meet the requirements of the Laeken Declaration:

Text of Minority report from members of the Convention - The failures of the Convention[17]

> The draft EU Constitution was never drafted through normal democratic methods.
>
> The applicant countries [ten countries were about to join the EU] were treated as observers in the Praesidium and had no real say.
>
> Only three political families were represented in the powerful Praesidium which drafted the tunnel vision text.

The members were refused the right to have their amendments translated, distributed, discussed and voted upon.
The Convention had no members for that half of the population which rejected the *Maastricht Treaty* in France or the *Nice Treaty* in Ireland.
Not one single Eurosceptic or Eurorealist person was allowed to observe or participate in the Praesidium, nor any of its assisting secretariats.
Giscard [d'Estaing] did not allow democracy and normal voting in the Convention. The draft constitution runs counter to all democratic principles.
We want a new draft from a much more representative Convention, democratic in content and democratic in procedures.

Laeken's Lost Missions

As members of the Convention, we cannot endorse the draft European Convention. It does not meet the requirements of *The Laeken Declaration* of December 2001. Laeken says 'The Union must be brought closer to its citizens.' The transfer of more decision making from member states to the Union, concerning criminal justice matters and new areas of domestic policy, will make the Union more remote.

Laeken adds that 'the division of competences be made more transparent.' But the new category of 'shared competences' gives no assurance about how power is to be shared, particularly as member states will be forbidden to legislate in these areas if the Union decides to act. The EU court in Luxembourg will decide on any doubt.

Laeken describes the Union as 'behaving too bureaucratically.' The draft Constitution fails to address the 97,000 accumulated pages of the acquis communautaire, and proposes a new legal instrument, the 'Non Legislative Act,' whereby the non-elected Commission can pass binding laws.

Laeken calls for the 'European institutions to be less unwieldy and rigid.' But the Constitution gives more power to all the existing EU institutions and creates a Europe of Presidents, with more jobs for politicians and less influence for the people.

Laeken highlights the importance of national parliaments, and the *Nice Treaty* 'stressed the need to examine their role in European integration.' National Parliaments lose influence relative to the Commission, the European Parliament and the European Council. Their proposed new role in 'ensuring' compliance with the subsidiarity principle is in reality no more than a request which the Commission can ignore. Not one competence will be returned to member states.

Laeken calls for 'more transparency and efficiency' in the Union. The Constitution concentrates more executive and budgetary power in the very EU institutions which have been the subject of repeated and continuing scandals over mismanagement, waste and fraud.

Laeken suggests the possibility of a constitution: 'The question ultimately arises as to whether this simplification and reorganisation might not lead in the long run to the adoption of a constitutional text of the Union.' The suggestion that the existing intergovernmental Treaties be transformed into a new European Constitution was rapidly seized upon, but without any study of either the alternatives on offer or the long-term consequences of such an act.

Lastly, Laeken's overriding aim was a Democratic Europe. The draft Constitution creates a new centralised European state, more powerful, more remote, with more politicians, more bureaucracy, and a wider gap between the rulers and the ruled.

The *EURATOM treaty* was brought into the Constitution in the last moment without any working group having the time to revise it."

Signatories:
William Abitbol (Alternate Member) European Parliament
Jens-Peter Bonde (Member) European Parliament
Per Dalgaard (Alternate Member) Denmark - Parliament
John Gormley (Alternate Member) Ireland - Parliament
David Heathcoat-Amory (Member) - UK - Parliament
Esko Seppanen (Alternate Member) European Parliament
Peter Skaarup (Member) Denmark - Parliament
Jan Zahradil (Member) Czech Republic – Parliament

Members of the Convention.

[END OF REPORT]

The signatories to the above statement have produced a short alternative to the Constitution, *The Europe of Democracies*, which is printed towards the end of this book, starting on page 367.

EU leaders prepare to stand still

On 23 June 2007 the leaders of the EU maintained their collective amnesia about the problems they had identified at Laeken in 2001. They reached an agreement on how to pursue their 2004 plans for running Europe. In essence they agreed to drop the word "Constitution" and reformulate almost all its provisions in existing EU treaties. They remained at the crossroads with essentially the same plan that failed so dramatically in 2005.

This is discussed in *Part Five, The Reform Treaty - the Constitution Repackaged.*

The Text of EU Document SN 273/01
The Future of the European Union
(*The Laeken Declaration*)

15 December 2001

[A statement produced by a meeting of the European Council – the leaders of the fifteen member states of the European Union - convened in Laeken, Belgium, to discuss reform of the EU]

I. Europe at a crossroads

For centuries, peoples and states have taken up arms and waged war to win control of the European continent. The debilitating effects of two bloody wars and the weakening of Europe's position in the world brought a growing realisation that only peace and concerted action could make the dream of a strong, unified Europe come true. In order to banish once and for all the demons of the past, a start was made with a coal and steel community. Other economic activities, such as agriculture, were subsequently added in. A genuine single market was eventually established for goods, persons, services and capital, and a single currency was added in 1999. On 1 January 2002 the euro is to become a day-to-day reality for 300 million European citizens.

The European Union has thus gradually come into being. In the beginning, it was more of an economic and technical collaboration. Twenty years ago, with the first direct elections to the European Parliament, the Community's democratic legitimacy, which until then had lain with the Council alone, was considerably strengthened. Over the last ten years, construction of a political union has begun and co-operation been established on social policy, employment, asylum, immigration, police, justice, foreign policy and a common security and defence policy.

The European Union is a success story. For over half a century now, Europe has been at peace. Along with North America and Japan, the Union forms one of the three most prosperous parts of the world. As a result of mutual solidarity and fair distribution of the benefits of economic development, moreover, the standard of living in the Union's weaker regions has increased enormously and they have made good much of the disadvantage they were at.

Fifty years on, however, the Union stands at a crossroads, a defining moment in its existence. The unification of Europe is near. The Union is about to expand to bring in more than ten new Member States, predominantly Central and Eastern European, thereby finally closing one of the darkest chapters in European history: the Second World War and the ensuing artificial division of Europe. At long last, Europe is on its way to becoming one big family, without bloodshed, a real transformation clearly calling for a different approach from fifty years ago, when six countries first took the lead.

The democratic challenge facing Europe

At the same time, the Union faces twin challenges, one within and the other beyond its borders.

Within the Union, the European institutions must be brought closer to its citizens. Citizens undoubtedly support the Union's broad aims, but they do not always see a connection between those goals and the Union's everyday action. They want the European institutions to be less unwieldy and rigid and, above all, more efficient and open. Many also feel that the Union should involve itself more with their particular concerns, instead of intervening, in every detail, in matters by their nature better left to Member States' and regions' elected representatives. This is even perceived by some as a threat to their identity. More importantly, however, they feel that deals are all too often cut out of their sight and they want better democratic scrutiny.

Europe's new role in legitimacy, which until then had lain with the Council alone, was considerably strengthened. Over the last ten years, construction of a political union has begun and cooperation been established on social policy, employment, asylum, immigration, police, justice, foreign policy and a common security and defence policy.

The European Union is a success story. For over half a century now, Europe has been at peace. Along with North America and Japan, the Union forms one of the three most prosperous parts of the world. As a result of mutual solidarity and fair distribution of the benefits of economic development, moreover, the standard of living in the Union's weaker regions has increased enormously and they have a globalised world

Beyond its borders, in turn, the European Union is confronted with a fast-changing, globalised world. Following the fall of the Berlin Wall, it looked briefly as though we would for a long while be living in a stable world order, free from conflict, founded upon human rights. Just a few years later, however, there is no such certainty. The eleventh of September has brought a rude awakening. The opposing forces have not gone away: religious fanaticism, ethnic nationalism, racism and terrorism are on the increase, and regional conflicts, poverty and under-development still provide a constant seedbed for them.

What is Europe's role in this changed world? Does Europe not, now that it is finally unified, have a leading role to play in a new world order, that of a power able both to play a stabilising role worldwide and to point the way ahead for many countries and peoples? Europe as the continent of humane values, the Magna Carta, the Bill of Rights, the French Revolution and the fall of the Berlin Wall; the continent of liberty, solidarity and above all diversity, meaning respect for others' languages, cultures and traditions. The European Union's one boundary is democracy and human rights. The Union is open only to countries which uphold basic values such as free elections, respect for minorities and respect for the rule of law.

Now that the Cold War is over and we are living in a globalised, yet also highly fragmented world, Europe needs to shoulder its responsibilities in the governance of globalisation. The role it has to play is that of a power resolutely doing battle against all violence, all terror and all fanaticism, but which also does not turn a blind eye to the world's heartrending injustices. In short, a power wanting to change the course of world affairs in such a way as to benefit not just the rich countries but also the poorest. A power seeking to set globalisation within a moral framework, in other words to anchor it in solidarity and sustainable development.

The expectations of Europe's citizens

The image of a democratic and globally engaged Europe admirably matches citizens' wishes. There have been frequent public calls for a greater EU role in justice and security, action against cross-border crime, control of migration flows and reception of asylum seekers and refugees from far-flung war zones. Citizens also want results in the fields of employment and combating poverty and social exclusion, as well as in the field of economic and social cohesion. They want a common approach on environmental pollution, climate change and food safety, in short, all transnational issues which they instinctively sense can only be tackled by working together. Just as they also want to see Europe more involved in foreign affairs, security and defence, in other words, greater and better coordinated action to deal with trouble spots in and around Europe and in the rest of the world.

At the same time, citizens also feel that the Union is behaving too bureaucratically in numerous other areas. In coordinating the economic, financial and fiscal environment, the basic issue should continue to be proper operation of the internal market and the single currency, without this jeopardising Member States' individuality. National and regional differences frequently stem from history or tradition. They can be enriching. In other words, what citizens understand by "good governance" is opening up fresh opportunities, not imposing further red tape. What they expect is more results, better responses to practical issues and not a European superstate or European institutions inveigling their way into every nook and cranny of life.

In short, citizens are calling for a clear, open, effective, democratically controlled Community approach, developing a Europe which points the way ahead for the world. An approach that provides concrete results in terms of more jobs, better quality of life, less crime, decent education and better health care. There can be no doubt that this will require Europe to undergo renewal and reform.

2. Challenges and Reforms in a Renewed Union

The Union needs to become more democratic, more transparent and more efficient. It also has to resolve three basic challenges: how to bring citizens, and primarily the young, closer to the European design and the European institutions, how to organise politics and the European political area in an enlarged Union and how to develop the Union into a stabilising factor and a model in the new, multipolar world. In order to address them a number of specific questions need to be put.

A better division and definition of competence in the European Union

Citizens often hold expectations of the European Union that are not always fulfilled. And vice versa - they sometimes have the impression that the Union takes on too much in areas where its involvement is not always essential. Thus the important thing is to clarify, simplify and adjust the division of competence between the Union and the Member States in the light of the new challenges facing the Union. This can lead both to restoring tasks to the Member States and to assigning new missions to the Union, or to the extension of existing powers, while constantly bearing in mind the equality of the Member States and their mutual solidarity.

A first series of questions that needs to be put concerns how the division of competence can be made more transparent. Can we thus make a clearer distinction between three types of competence: the exclusive competence of the Union, the competence of the Member States and the shared competence of the Union and the Member States? At what level is competence exercised in the most efficient way? How is the principle of subsidiarity to be applied here? And should we not make it clear that any powers not assigned by the Treaties to the Union fall within the exclusive sphere of competence of the Member States? And what would be the consequences of this?

The next series of questions should aim, within this new framework and while respecting the "acquis communautaire", to determine whether there needs to be any reorganisation of competence. How can citizens' expectations be taken as a guide here? What missions would this produce for the Union? And, vice versa, what tasks could better be left to the Member States? What amendments should be made to the Treaty on the various policies? How, for example, should a more coherent common foreign policy and defence policy be developed? Should the Petersberg tasks be updated? Do we want to adopt a more integrated approach to police and criminal law cooperation? How can economic-policy coordination be stepped up? How can we intensify cooperation in the field of social inclusion, the environment, health and food safety? But then, should not the day-to-day administration and implementation of the Union's policy be left more emphatically to the Member States and, where their constitutions so provide, to the regions? Should they not be provided with guarantees that their spheres of competence will not be affected?

Lastly, there is the question of how to ensure that a redefined division of competence does not lead to a creeping expansion of the competence of the Union or to encroachment upon the exclusive areas of competence of the Member States and, where there is provision for this, regions. How are we to ensure at the same time that the European dynamic does not come to a halt? In the future as well the Union must continue to be able to react to fresh challenges and developments and must be able to explore new policy areas. Should Articles 95 and 308 of the Treaty be reviewed for this purpose in the light of the "acquis jurisprudentiel"?

Simplification of the Union's instruments

Who does what is not the only important question; the nature of the Union's action and what instruments it should use are equally important. Successive amendments to the Treaty have on each occasion resulted in a proliferation of instruments, and directives have gradually evolved towards more and more detailed legislation. The key question is therefore whether the Union's various instruments should not be better defined and whether their number should not be reduced.

In other words, should a distinction be introduced between legislative and executive measures? Should the number of legislative instruments be reduced: directly applicable rules, framework legislation and non-enforceable instruments (opinions, recommendations, open coordination)? Is it or is it not desirable to have more frequent recourse to framework legislation, which affords the Member States more room for manoeuvre in achieving policy objectives? For which areas of competence are open coordination and mutual recognition the most appropriate instruments? Is the principle of proportionality to remain the point of departure?

More democracy, transparency and efficiency in the European Union

The European Union derives its legitimacy from the democratic values it projects, the aims it pursues and the powers and instruments it possesses. However, the European project also derives its legitimacy from democratic, transparent and efficient institutions. The national parliaments also contribute towards the legitimacy of the European project. The declaration on the future of the Union, annexed to the *Treaty of Nice*, stressed the need to examine their role in European integration. More generally, the question arises as to what initiatives we can take to develop a European public area.

The first question is thus how we can increase the democratic legitimacy and transparency of the present institutions, a question which is valid for the three institutions.

How can the authority and efficiency of the European Commission be enhanced? How should the President of the Commission be appointed: by the European Council, by the European Parliament or should he be directly elected by the citizens? Should the role of the European Parliament be strengthened? Should we extend the right of co-decision or not? Should the way in which we elect the members of the European Parliament be reviewed? Should a European electoral constituency be created, or should constituencies continue to be determined nationally? Can the two systems be combined? Should the role of the Council be strengthened? Should the Council act in the same manner in its legislative and its executive capacities? With a view to greater transparency, should the meetings of the Council, at least in its legislative capacity, be public? Should citizens have more access to Council documents? How, finally, should the balance and reciprocal control between the institutions be ensured?

A second question, which also relates to democratic legitimacy, involves the role of national parliaments. Should they be represented in a new institution, alongside the Council and the European Parliament? Should they have a role in areas of European action in which the European Parliament has no competence? Should they focus on the division of competence between Union and Member States, for example through preliminary checking of compliance with the principle of subsidiarity?

The third question concerns how we can improve the efficiency of decision-making and the workings of the institutions in a Union of some thirty Member States. How could the Union set its objectives and priorities more effectively and ensure better implementation? Is there a need for more decisions by a qualified majority? How is the co-decision procedure between the Council and the European Parliament to be simplified and speeded up? What of the six-monthly rotation of the Presidency of the Union? What is the future role of the European Parliament? What of the future role and structure of the various Council formations? How should the coherence of European foreign policy be enhanced? How is synergy between the High Representative and the competent Commissioner to be reinforced? Should the external representation of the Union in international fora be extended further?

Towards a Constitution for European citizens

The European Union currently has four Treaties. The objectives, powers and policy instruments of the Union are currently spread across those Treaties. If we are to have greater transparency, simplification is essential.

Four sets of questions arise in this connection. The first concerns simplifying the existing Treaties without changing their content. Should the distinction between the Union and the Communities be reviewed? What of the division into three pillars?

Questions then arise as to the possible reorganisation of the Treaties. Should a distinction be made between a basic treaty and the other treaty provisions? Should this distinction involve separating the texts? Could this lead to a distinction between the amendment and ratification procedures for the basic treaty and for the other treaty provisions?

Thought would also have to be given to whether the Charter of Fundamental Rights should be included in the basic treaty and to whether the European Community should accede to the European Convention on Human Rights.

The question ultimately arises as to whether this simplification and reorganisation might not lead in the long run to the adoption of a constitutional text in the Union. What might the basic features of such a constitution be? The values which the Union cherishes, the fundamental rights and obligations of its citizens, the relationship between Member States in the Union?

3. Convening of a convention on the future of Europe

In order to pave the way for the next Intergovernmental Conference as broadly and openly as possible, the European Council has decided to convene a Convention composed of the main parties involved in the debate on the future of the Union. In the light of the foregoing, it will be the task of that Convention to consider the key issues arising for the Union's future development and try to identify the various possible responses.

The European Council has appointed Mr V. Giscard d'Estaing as Chairman of the Convention and Mr G. Amato and Mr J.L. Dehaene as Vice-Chairmen.

Composition

In addition to its Chairman and Vice-Chairmen, the Convention will be composed of 15 representatives of the Heads of State or Government of the Member States (one from each Member State), 30 members of national parliaments (two from each Member State), 16 members of the European Parliament and two Commission representatives. The accession candidate countries will be fully involved in the Convention's proceedings. They will be represented in the same way as the current Member States (one government representative and two national parliament members) and will be able to take part in the proceedings without, however, being able to prevent any consensus which may emerge among the Member States.

The members of the Convention may only be replaced by alternate members if they are not present. The alternate members will be designated in the same way as full members.

The Praesidium of the Convention will be composed of the Convention Chairman and Vice-Chairmen and nine members drawn from the Convention (the representatives of all the governments holding the Council Presidency during the Convention, two national parliament representatives, two European Parliament representatives and two Commission representatives).

Three representatives of the Economic and Social Committee with three representatives of the European social partners; from the Committee of the Regions: six representatives (to be appointed by the Committee of the Regions from the regions, cities and regions with legislative powers), and the European Ombudsman will be invited to attend as observers. The Presidents of the Court of Justice and of the Court of Auditors may be invited by the Praesidium to address the Convention.

Length of proceedings

The Convention will hold its inaugural meeting on 1 March 2002, when it will appoint its Praesidium and adopt its rules of procedure. Proceedings will be completed after a year, that is to say in time for the Chairman of the Convention to present its outcome to the European Council.

Working methods

The Chairman will pave the way for the opening of the Convention's proceedings by drawing conclusions from the public debate. The Praesidium will serve to lend impetus and will provide the Convention with an initial working basis.

The Praesidium may consult Commission officials and experts of its choice on any technical aspect which it sees fit to look into. It may set up ad hoc working parties.

The Council will be kept informed of the progress of the Convention's proceedings. The Convention Chairman will give an oral progress report at each European Council meeting, thus enabling Heads of State or Government to give their views at the same time.

The Convention will meet in Brussels. The Convention's discussions and all official documents will be in the public domain. The Convention will work in the Union's eleven working languages.

Final document

The Convention will consider the various issues. It will draw up a final document which may comprise either different options, indicating the degree of support which they received, or recommendations if consensus is achieved.

Together with the outcome of national debates on the future of the Union, the final document will provide a starting point for discussions in the Intergovernmental Conference, which will take the ultimate decisions.

Forum

In order for the debate to be broadly based and involve all citizens, a Forum will be opened for organisations representing civil society (the social partners, the business world, non-governmental organisations, academia, etc.). It will take the form of a structured network of organisations receiving regular information on the Convention's proceedings. Their contributions will serve as input into the debate. Such organisations may be heard or consulted on specific topics in accordance with arrangements to be established by the Praesidium.

Secretariat

The Praesidium will be assisted by a Convention Secretariat, to be provided by the General Secretariat of the Council, which may incorporate Commission and European Parliament experts.

[On 28 January 2002 the General Affairs Council agreed a budget for the Convention of 10.5 million euros (approximately £7.2 million) for ten months.]

[END OF EU TEXT: *THE FUTURE OF THE EUROPEAN UNION*]

Notes

1 Europa press release. Reference: SPEECH/05/628. Date: 20/10/2005.

2 Source: Institute for Policy Research, 2006.

3 At this moment (October 2007) it is expected that the *Reform Treaty* will be signed in December in Lisbon. It is then expected to change its name to the *Lisbon Treaty* or *the Treaty of Lisbon*. This treaty is not a text of either the Constitution or the treaties which govern or will govern the operation of the European Union. It is a set of instructions for modifying two existing treaties. Until these modifications have been carried out the most accurate and up to date text describing the operation of the EU is the Constitution of 2004. It is an official account of the EU. Certain aspects of the Constitution's arrangements were modified in June 2007 and the main changes are described in part five of this book.

4 This is a key document in understanding the European Union.

5 In this book the term *European Union* and *EU* are used to denote the association of states in Europe which adopted the name *European Union* in the *Maastricht Treaty* which came into force on 1 November 1993. It is also used to denote this association of states in its earlier permutations when it had different names, more limited powers and fewer members - *The European Coal and Steel Community, The European Atomic Energy Community, The European Community (also known as the Common Market)* - up to the present association of twenty-seven states.

6 This topic is explored more fully in the chapters *The Constitution's Ideas, Major Issues,* and *Alternative Plans for EU Development*

7 Starts on page 17.

8 *Laeken Declaration* 15 December 2001

9 Political leaders of member states take turns to be the president of the European Council. The office is held for a period of six months. See *Institutions* in the *Nuts and Bolts* chapter.

10 Brussels, 18 June 2005 Ref. SN 117/05 2, Declaration by the heads of state or government of the member states of the European Union on the ratification of *The Treaty Establishing a Constitution for Europe*. European Council, 16 and 17 June 2005.

11 http://www.eu2006.at/en/News/Press_Releases/June/1506schuessel. htm l?null

12 Emphasis added. *The Future of the European Union* (*Laeken Declaration*) 15 December 2001.

13 Rome Declaration 18 July 2003.

14 Detailed discussion of the failings of the Constitution will take up much of this book, especially in part four, *The Constitution's Ideas*, and part six *Major Issues*.

15 Report from the Convention Presidency to the President of the European Union, Brussels 18 July 2003. EU ref 851/03.

16 *The Making of Europe's Constitution*, Fabian Society, London, 2003. From www.free-europe.org

17 EU document reference: CONV 851/03 (ANNEX III)

Part Two

Development of the European Union

"I believe that for the first time in history, certainly in the history of the last centuries, countries want to renounce part of their sovereignty, voluntarily and without compulsion, in order to transfer sovereignty to a supranational structure." - Konrad Adenaur, Chancellor of West Germany, 12 July 1952.

"The electorate and not Members of Parliament nor the Government are the ultimate source of parliamentary authority, sovereignty and democracy, all of which Members of Parliament and members of the Government merely hold on trust subject to re-election at a general election." - William Cash, MP, in a draft report proposed to the House of Commons European Scrutiny Committee, 9 October 2007.

How plans for European co-operation and unity developed

In modern times numerous thinkers have proposed ways of uniting the warring states of Europe.

Perhaps the first leading politician to take up the idea was a German armaments minister, Walter Rathenau, who, in 1914 proposed an immediate end to the First World War and the creation of a European economic system combining Germany, Austria, France, and Belgium.

In 1930 the French Prime Minister and Nobel Peace Prize winner, Aristide Briand, developed ideas which he put to the League of Nations[1] in a "memorandum on the organisation of a regime of European Federal Union." Although he talked of federation what he seemed to have in mind was collective decision-making rather than federation in the current sense of the word. "It is on the level of absolute sovereignty and of complete political independence that the understanding between European nations must be brought about... European political co-operation should be directed towards the following essential object: a federation based on the idea of union and not of unity - that is a federation elastic enough to respect the independence of national sovereignty[2] of each state while guaranteeing to all the benefits of collective solidarity in the settlement of the political questions affecting the destiny of the European commonwealth or that of one of its members."

He considered there was a need in his proposed Federal Union, for "a representative and responsible body in the shape of a regular institution known as the European Conference composed of representatives for the European governments." This is similar to the EU's present European Council or the Council of Ministers.

There was also, in his view, "the need for an executive body in the form of a permanent political committee composed only of a certain number of members of the European Conference which would act both as the research Committee and as the executive body of the European Union." This has some resemblance to today's EU Commission.

If a separate "executive body" existed with any powers of independent action, as Briand described, then whenever it took over an area in which it would have exclusive power to take action then the independence of member states would correspondingly be reduced. Briand seems not to have grasped that his proposal was for reducing the independence and sovereignty of member states. To this day, many people maintain that giving the EU exclusive rights to make decisions in certain areas of policy does not reduce the independence or sovereignty of member states.

It may be that because the executive was directed to work along guidelines agreed by member states he thought this would keep power in the hands of the member states. Today this is manifestly not the case. The EU has great powers to overrule the governments of its member states.

In his memorandum Briand explained that there was "a need for laying down in advance the essential principles which shall determine the general conceptions of the European Committee and guide it in the enquiries which it makes for the purpose of preparing the program of the European organisation." Today the treaties and the proposed European Constitution provide a framework within which today's executive, the Commission, is required to work.

European states learn to co-operate with Marshall Aid

After the Second World War the $12,500,000,000 of Marshall Aid from the USA came to Europe with conditions attached. The European states had to work together in agreeing the share-out of the funds which were to be made available. (And these were to be available only to countries dismantling trade barriers and taking action to increase their own production.) These years provided a learning experience for European states, which had so recently been destroying one another, in the benefits of co-operation. The organisation they set up in April 1948 to handle the finances and reconstruction work was the Organisation for European Economic Co-operation (OEEC) which has continued, after it had completed this task in 1952, as the Organisation for Security and Co-operation in Europe (OSCE).

Co-operating for European security

In 1949 the North Atlantic Treaty Organisation (NATO) treaty was signed by European states, the USA and Canada "to safeguard the freedom, common heritage and civilisation of its peoples, founded on the principles of democracy, individual liberty and law." For more than 50 years sovereign states have worked together on the basis that joint action only goes ahead when all member states are in agreement. There is no loss of sovereignty and no body within NATO to over-rule, or dictate to any Member. In April 1999, at the meeting of NATO leaders to celebrate its fiftieth anniversary, it changed its basic aims and charter from being a purely defensive organisation concerned with the security of its member states to one that was prepared to take military action anywhere in the world, and if necessary to go "out-of-area" in support of its members' interests.

Co-operating in the Council of Europe - the other "united Europe"

The Council of Europe (which is an entirely separate organisation from the European Union with its European Council) was established by the *Treaty of London* (1949). This was signed by ten states. Its aim was "to achieve a greater unity between its members." It has no executive powers over Member States. It researches and discusses issues and promotes ideas and policies by persuasion. It has produced the *European Convention on Human Rights* and the *European Charter*. Most importantly it has set up the *European Court of Human Rights*. Today 46 European States are members with a total population of 800,000,000 citizens.

Starting the process of centralising European power

Briand had been unclear about the political implications of a European Union, but his fellow countrymen, the financier and administrative genius, Jean Monnet, consciously set out to achieve political ends through administrative arrangements. He was the man whose ideas created the European Union by formulating the ideas and procedures which inaugurated and guided its development. Substantial power would be invested in a committee of experts and administrators.

He had played a major role in co-ordinating the war efforts of Britain and France in both world wars and in 1945 was appointed Planning Commissioner in charge of the reconstruction of France. He had witnessed Germany's rebuilding after the First World War - an economic recovery which enabled it to start the Second World War. He was deeply concerned with creating a peaceful world and had, at the age of only 31, been the first deputy Secretary General of the League of Nations. He feared that Germany would rise again and re-arm. "France will be trapped again . . . and this will lead inevitably to her being effaced." (Memo to Robert Schuman and George Bidault, 4 May 1950.)

His answer was to embark on a process of European unification. He appreciated that a direct proposal to this effect would be totally unacceptable - even though he had brilliantly convinced Charles de Gaulle and Winston Churchill, during the Second World War, that Britain and France should unite into a single state. The approach he proposed was to begin with the unification of the French and German coal and steel industries - and to offer to include any other European countries that might wish to join. The great significance of this starting point was that these industries, under a supranational common control, could no longer be developed for the purpose of rearmament since all members would have a large share of control over what they all did. In addition, they were key to the industrial regeneration of Europe. He knew, and both German and French leaders appreciated and welcomed this, that neither France nor Germany, represented on the governing committee, would agree to any increase in production that would enable rearmament in either country to take place.

Taking power little by little - the Monnet/Schuman plan

Once one element of co-operation had been accepted and a supranational body controlled it, with a corresponding but undetected diminution of Member states' sovereignty, the plan was to move on to include other areas of economic or political control. Each step would be so small that there would be no mass opposition to it. So, little by little, power would shift from member states to a central governing body until after many years a state called Europe would be built with the old state parliaments becoming mainly channels for enacting the directives of the central authority. A limited range of policy areas would remain in the exclusive control of state parliaments. Parliamentary debates in many policy areas would be about the adaptation and fine-tuning of the directives (or framework laws) issued from the European authority. Since the *Maastricht Treaty* of 1993 a principle of subsidiarity has been introduced into the EU whereby decisions, including law-making must be taken or enacted at the lowest possible level. However, the procedure devised for operating the subsidiarity requirement appear to be unsatisfactory for reasons explained elsewhere but particularly in the *Major Issues* chapter.

Monnet's plan was brilliant but contained a fatal flaw: there was no role for democracy.

His ideas were presented to the world by French Foreign Secretary, Robert Schuman, in one of the EU's most important founding documents, the *Schuman Declaration* of 9 May 1950. It explained how the proposed coal and steel community would be the first step in the Federation of Europe and the foundation for their economic unification.

> Europe will not be made all at once or according to a single plan. It will be built through concrete achievements which first create a de facto solidarity. The French government proposes that action be taken immediately on one limited and decisive point. It proposes that Franco-German production of coal and steel as a whole be placed under a common High Authority, within the framework of an organisation open to the participation of the other countries of Europe.
>
> The pooling of coal and steel production should immediately provide for the setting up of common foundations for economic development as a first step in the federation of Europe, and will change the destiny of those regions which have long been devoted to the manufacture of munitions of war, of which they have been the most constant victims.
>
> The Solidarity and production thus established will make it plain that any war between France and Germany becomes not merely unthinkable, but materially impossible. The setting up of this powerful productive unit. . . will play a true foundation for their economic unification. . .
>
> By pooling basic production and by instituting a new High Authority, whose decisions will bind France, Germany and other member countries, this proposal will lead to the realisation of the first concrete foundation of a European federation indispensable to the preservation of peace.

The gradualist approach to European integration continues to the present. See *European Union by stealth* in the *Major Issues* section and *Functionalism and Neo-functionalism* in the *Euroterminology chapter in part three.*

Giving away sovereignty

The West Germans were keen to show they had given up warlike ambitions. The Schuman plan was enthusiastically welcomed by West German Chancellor, Konrad Adenauer. Other countries were also enthusiastic. *The Treaty of Paris*, establishing the European Coal and Steel Community, was signed by France, Germany, Italy, Belgium, the Netherlands and Luxembourg on 18 April 1951. It came into effect on 10 August 1952. Jean Monnet was its first president.

A month before this, on 12 July 1952, Adenaur spelled out what he saw as the exceptional significance of the setting up of the European Coal and Steel Community.

> I believe that for the first time in history, certainly in the history of the last centuries, countries want to renounce part of their sovereignty, voluntarily and without compulsion, in order to transfer sovereignty to a supranational structure.

These six states worked successfully together and, with American help, for many years enjoyed increasing prosperity.

The story of the European treaties from 1952 onwards, together with the European Constitution, is the story of the progressive transfer of sovereignty from member states to the central power of, what eventually became known as, the

European Union, in Brussels. It is a complex story of the enormous benefits of peaceful co-operation and the disasters brought about by non-democratic decision-making, public deception, bureaucratic arrogance, confusion, corruption and lack of transparency, accountability and public debate. Problems have descended on the European Union like a freezing fog. We are searching for the road to a viable future.

How European Treaties developed the power of the European Union

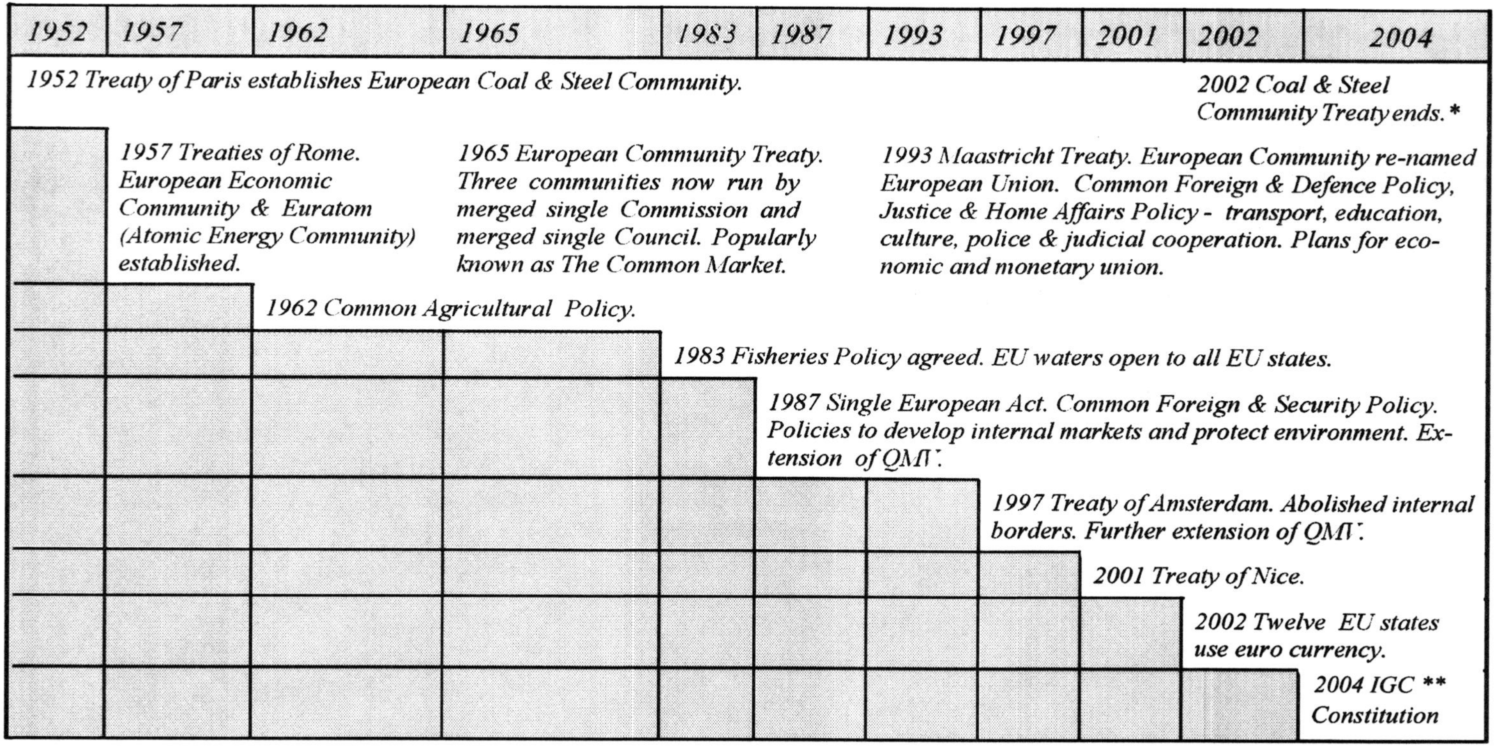

1952	1957	1962	1965	1983	1987	1993	1997	2001	2002	2004

1952 Treaty of Paris establishes European Coal & Steel Community.

2002 Coal & Steel Community Treaty ends. *

1957 Treaties of Rome. European Economic Community & Euratom (Atomic Energy Community) established.

1965 European Community Treaty. Three communities now run by merged single Commission and merged single Council. Popularly known as The Common Market.

1993 Maastricht Treaty. European Community re-named European Union. Common Foreign & Defence Policy, Justice & Home Affairs Policy - transport, education, culture, police & judicial cooperation. Plans for economic and monetary union.

1962 Common Agricultural Policy.

1983 Fisheries Policy agreed. EU waters open to all EU states.

1987 Single European Act. Common Foreign & Security Policy. Policies to develop internal markets and protect environment. Extension of QMV.

1997 Treaty of Amsterdam. Abolished internal borders. Further extension of QMV.

2001 Treaty of Nice.

2002 Twelve EU states use euro currency.

*2004 IGC ** Constitution*

* Its work transferred to the European Union.

** Inter-Governmental Conference finalised the Constitution. EU leaders signed it.

European Union Key Dates

1693 Englishman William Penn (founder of Pennsylvania) advocated the setting up of a European Parliament backed by a European army.

1795 German philosopher Emanuel Kant proposed a "federation of free states."

1863 Pierre Joseph Proudhon advocated a Federal Europe.

1914 Walter Rathenau, who was in charge of Germany's procurement of raw materials throughout the First World War, proposed in a letter to the Chancellery on 10th October 1914, that Germany should make peace immediately based on Germany's evacuation of Belgium, reconciliation with France and the creation of a European Economic System combining Germany, Austria, France and Belgium.

1926 Austrian Count Richard Coudenove Kalergi proposed ideas for a Pan-European Union - an idea supported by Einstein, Thomas Mann, Freud, Adenaur and others.

1929 French politician, Aristide Briand, proposes the establishment of a "European Federal Union".

1945 French administrator Jean Monnet works out ideas by which European countries, especially France and Germany, can work peacefully together. Devises, as a first step, the European Coal and Steel Community and a gradual approach to centralising power.

1946 Winston Churchill proposes a United States of Europe.

1949 French Foreign Minister, Robert Schuman, puts forward Monnet's ideas in the "Schuman Plan." West German Chancellor, Konrad Adenaur, enthusiastically welcomes the plan.

1952 Founding of the ECSC, the European Coal and Steel Community.

1957 *Treaty of Rome* established the EEC, the European Economic Community, also known as the Common Market. (The *Treaty of Rome* is also known as *The Treaty Establishing the European Community*. It has gone through many revisions, most recently by *The Treaty of Nice*, 2001, and *The Accession Treaty*, 2003.) *The Euratom Treaty* (the second *Treaty of Rome*) established EURATOM, the European Atomic Energy Community. Founder members of both communities were West Germany, France, Belgium, Italy, Luxembourg and the Netherlands.

1962 CAP, Common Agricultural Policy established.

1967 European Community established by merging the EEC, the ECSC and EURATOM.

1973 Britain, Ireland, and Denmark join.

1979 First direct elections to the European Parliament. EMS, the European Monetary System introduced.

1981 Greece becomes the tenth member.

1983 Fisheries policy agreed. EU waters' 200 mile limit open to all EU states.

1986 Spain and Portugal join.

1987 *Single European Act.* Firmer commitment to develop the internal market. Steps towards a common Foreign and Security Policy. Concerns for environment expressed. QMV (Qualified Majority Voting. See *Euroterminology* in *Part 3*) developed. The Erasmus programme set up to help young Europeans study in other European countries.

1989 9th of November, Berlin Wall dismantling begins.

1990 On the unification of East and West Germany the former East Germany becomes a member of the EU. Signing of *Schengen Agreement* which would abolish border checks between most EU countries.

1991 In December the European Council approves the *Maastricht Treaty,* the treaty on European Union. It lays the basis for a common foreign and security policy, closer cooperation on justice and home affairs and the creation of an economic and monetary union, including a single currency.
The inter-governmental cooperation in these fields added to the existing Community system is set to become the European Union (EU). The UK Conservative Government secures opt out clauses on a single currency and the "social chapter" which sought to improve living standards, employer/employee relations, health and safety at work etc.

1992 The *Maastricht Treaty* (signed 7 Feb) laid basis for common foreign and security policy, closer cooperation on domestic matters and economic and monetary union including common currency. Detailed plans for the free movement of goods, services, people and capital within the EU.

1993 Following difficulties in the ratification process. The *Maastricht Treaty* comes into effect 1November. The European Community becomes the European Union.

1995 Austria, Finland and Sweden join the EU. Norway rejects the idea of joining the EU. Partnership with the countries of North Africa launched.

1997 Britain accepts the social chapter of the *Maastricht Treaty*. *Amsterdam Treaty* signed. It set measures to have an effective Common Foreign and Security policy to include a fast response European military capability. The European Parliament is given powers to legislate "in co-decision"with the Council of Ministers on issues including employment, social policy health, transport and the environment. Abolition of security checks at borders between most EU countries incorpoprated into the treaty. Exceptions UK and Ireland. Arrangements agreed to co-ordinate and co-operate on matters of immigration, asylum, and law enforcement. Further extension of QMV.

1998 Agreement reached on a new common currency, the euro. Austria, Belgium, Finland, France, Germany, Ireland, Italy, Luxembourg, the Netherlands, Portugal and Spain meet the requirements for adopting the single currency on 1 January 1999. Greece to join later.
31 December, fixed and irrevocable exchange rates are set between the currencies that are to be replaced by the euro.

1999 On 1 January trading begins in the Euro currency in eleven European countries. The European Central Bank assumes responsibility for the monetary policy of the EU. *Amsterdam Treaty* comes into force 1 May.
March, NATO bombs Yugoslavia. Aggressors include 14 current (2007) EU countries who are members of NATO- Britain, France, Germany, Spain, Hungary, Netherlands, Belgium, Czech Republic, Poland, Denmark, Italy, Luxembourg, Portugal and Greece.
June, the European Council decides to ask a Convention to draw up a *European Charter of Fundamental Rights*. October the Tampere European Council decides to make the EU an area of freedom, security and justice.

2000 Nice Summit regarding EU decision making system. Further extension of QMV.

2001 After acrimonious discussions *The Treaty of Nice* is signed changing the EU's decision-making system to cope with the increased number of members anticipated in the next few years. European Prosecution Service set up. In December EU leaders issue the *Laeken Declaration* identifying serious problems and calling for answers to widespread problems within the EU. They announce the setting up of a Convention with a remit to propose remedies.

2002 January, Euro notes and coins come into use in eleven EU states. May, all 15 EU member states simultaneously ratify the *Kyoto Protocol* - the world-wide agreement to reduce air pollution. The Seville European Council reaches agreement on an EU asylum and immigration policy. Talks on the possible admission of Turkey to the EU begin. European Coal and Steel Community ends and its work is transferred to the European Union.

2003 *Athens Treaty* agreeing to the addition of ten new members to the EU. Inter-governmental conference (convention) established by *Laeken,* starts to consider how to deal with serious problems concerning the working of the EU. The conference decides to draw up a European Constitution which will replace the existing EU treaties.

2004 1 May, EU expands by the addition of ten new members: Latvia, Lithuania, Estonia, Poland, the Czech Republic, Slovakia, Slovenia, Hungary, Malta, and the Greek controlled half of Cyprus. Total membership is now 25 states with a total population of 450,000,000 people. The Convention on the Future of Europe fails to answer many of the questions it was set. It presents the European Constitution as its answer. Constitution of the European Union signed on 29 October. New Constitution ratified by Lithuania in November and Hungary in December.

2005 New Constitution ratified by the governments of Austria, Belgium, Greece, Italy, Slovakia, Latvia, Slovenia and Germany by parliamentary vote. People of Spain and Luxembourg back the Constitution in referendums. People of France (29 May) and the Netherlands (1June) reject the Constitution in referendums. June, European Council decides to postpone referendums in other countries planning to put the Constitution to their people. A "period of reflection" is called for. Austria opposes start of entry negotiations with Turkey but reluctantly gives in.

2006 May, Finnish parliament decides by a large majority to support the European Constitution and not have a referendum on the subject.
June, EU leaders call for more reflection. Hope to conclude reflection in 2008.

2007 1 January Bulgaria and Romania join EU, their parliaments having ratified the Constitution .
25 March. Fiftieth anniversary of the founding of the European Community from which the European Union developed (*Treaty of Rome,* 1957). At that time there were six member states.
23 June, EU leaders abandon the term "Constitution" and other words which suggest that the EU may be acting like a state, and agree a "Draft IGC Mandate" which will say how the new ideas of the Constitution will be integrated into existing treaties.

The Treaties

Key points of the treaties that direct the European Union

The significance of the EU treaties and the European Constitution – the European Union and You

This section sets out the main elements of the treaties of the European Union (and the earlier organisations which operated until they were transformed into the EU). These treaties are the blueprints for the EU's operation. They established its institutions, powers, and procedures. Not only this, they set out the policies, the actual political programmes which it pursues - matters of immense significance to the lives of everyone in Europe. The price of food, the rate of unemployment, the state of the environment, trade, levels of prosperity, privatisation, immigration control, freedom of movement, crime, the building of transport networks, education, the health service, culture, currency, relationships with member states and the rest of the world, war and peace - all of these and more come under the powerful influence of the EU.

Initially, over half a century ago, the purposes and plans were very clear. Since then the range of powers leading EU politicians have transferred from their home governments to the European Union have increased substantially. European power is now exercised primarily by the Commission, political heads of EU states (acting as the European Council), their own ministers meeting in Brussels as The Council, and by the European Parliament. As a result European treaties have become evermore complex. Added to this, successive amendments to treaties, re-numbering of articles and double naming and renaming of treaties can make it difficult to follow what is going on. The treaties, and now the Constitution, seem almost designed to create confusion and deny the ordinary citizen any understanding of what the EU is about. The following may prove helpful.

The main treaties

The beginning of the European Union was the European Coal and Steel Community which was established by the *Treaty of Paris* 1952. Its aims are described in the previous chapter.

In 1957 the organisation became the European Economic Community. The Treaties of Rome set out the changes. *The Treaty of Rome* (1957) has been renamed *The Treaty Establishing the European Economic Community.* The second EU Treaty signed in Rome in 1957 was the *Treaty Establishing the European Atomic Energy Community* (EURATOM). (The *Treaty of Rome* is discussed below.)

The EU treaties up to 1992 were consolidated into the *Treaty on European Union (1992).* This treaty is better known as the *Maastricht Treaty.*

The *Maastricht Treaty* of 1992 has been modified and developed by the *Treaty of Amsterdam (1997)* and by the *Treaty of Nice (2001)*. (The *Treaty of Amsterdam* renumbered the existing articles of the *Treaty on European Union/ Maastricht*. Details of all three of these treaties are summarised below.)

Other important EU treaties are:

- *The Merger Treaty*, signed 8 April 1965. Entered into force 1 July 1967. Also known as the *European Community Treaty*. This merged the European Coal and Steel Community, the European Economic Community and the European Atomic Energy Community. It amalgamated their governing institutions into a single Commission and a single Council.
- *The Budgetary Treaty 1970*, signed 22 April 1970. Entered into force 1 January 1971. It gave the European Parliament the final decision on one aspect of European spending "non-compulsory expenditure".
- *The Budgetary Treaty, 1975*, signed 22 July 1975. Entered into force 1 June 1977. This gave the European Parliament the power to reject the budget as a whole and it created the European Court of Auditors to examine the Community's accounts to attempt to ensure that finances had been properly managed and recorded.
- *The Single European Act 1987* (See below.)
- *The Schengen Agreement 1985, 1990, 1997* (became part of the *Treaty of Amsterdam*. See below.)
- *The Acts of Accession, 1973, 1981, 1986, 1995, 2004, 2005* - the Treaties which enabled new states to join. The last of these was to admit Bulgaria and Romania and the act, though signed, has not been ratified (2006).

Treaty of Rome 1957

This established the European Economic Community and was signed by Germany, France, Italy, The Netherlands, Belgium, and Luxembourg. The direc-tion it established has been followed through for over half a century.

Even though this treaty was signed by only six countries its opening statement referred to a determination "to lay the foundation of ever closer union among the peoples of Europe." The Community was open for other states to join. The treaty spoke of the desire of the founding states:

> "to ensure the economic and social progress of their countries by common action to eliminate the barriers which divide Europe," and "the essential objective of . . . the constant improvement of the living and working conditions of their peoples."

And the desire

> "to strengthen the unity of their economies and to ensure their harmonious development by reducing the differences existing between the various regions and the backwardness of the less favoured regions,
>
> to contribute, by means of a common commercial policy, to the progressive abolition of restrictions on international trade,
>
> to confirm the solidarity which binds Europe and the overseas countries
>
> to ensure the development of their prosperity, in accordance with the principles of the *Charter of the United Nations*,

to preserve and strengthen peace and liberty."

The key concerns of the Community are expressed in articles 2 and 3.

Article 2

The Community shall have as its task, by establishing a common market and progressively approximating the economic policies of Member States, to promote throughout the Community a harmonious development of economic activities, a continuous and balanced expansion, an increase in stability, an accelerated raising of the standard of living and closer relations between the States belonging to it.

Article 3

For the purposes set out in Article 2, the activities of the Community shall include, as provided in this Treaty and in accordance with the timetable set out therein

- a the elimination, as between Member States, of customs duties and of quantitative restrictions on the import and export of goods, and of all other measures having equivalent effect;
- b the establishment of a common customs tariff and of a common commercial policy towards third countries;
- c the abolition, as between Member States, of obstacles to freedom of movement for persons, services and capital;
- d the adoption of a common policy in the sphere of agriculture;
- e the adoption of a common policy in the sphere of transport;
- f the institution of a system ensuring that competition in the common market is not distorted;
- g the application of procedures by which the economic policies of Member States can be co-ordinated and disequilibria in their balances of payments remedied;
- h the approximation of the laws of Member States to the extent required for the proper functioning of the common market;
- i the creation of a European Social Fund in order to improve employment opportunities for workers and to contribute to the raising of their standard of living;
- j the establishment of a European Investment Bank to facilitate the economic expansion of the Community by opening up fresh resources;
- k the association of the overseas countries and territories in order to increase trade and to promote jointly economic and social development."

After bitter negotiations the Common Agricultural Policy was agreed in January 1962.

Treaty of the Elysée

The *Treaty of the Elysée,* 1963, is related to the operation of the EU. It was an agreement between the two largest members of the European Economic Community, France and West Germany, to consult each other before making any major foreign policy decision.

The Single European Act

Signed on 17 and 28 February 1986. Entered into force 1 July 1987.

After almost thirty years of operation this act made major changes to *The Treaty of Rome*. It was an important step towards the aim of creating a single European state. Article One of the treaty proclaimed, "the European Communities and European political co-operation shall have as their objective to contribute together to making concrete progress towards European unity."

The act set out the policies needed to achieve an internal market with the removal of all restrictions on the movement of goods, services, capital and people (labour) - with consequent reductions in control by member states. The aim was to complete changes by the last day of 1992.

Agreement was reached on Structural Funds, a huge kitty which the EU distributed to the European Agricultural Guidance and Guarantee Fund, the European Regional Development Fund and the European Social Fund.

Qualified majority voting was introduced in Council decision-making in matters relating to the single market, thus ending the veto rights of states in this area. Other areas of policy were already subject to QMV. Some 300 jealously guarded trade restrictions would fall to QMV.

The act also introduced the idea of "European political co-operation." This is a misleading term which actually referred only to foreign policy. It meant that leaders agreed to consult together on foreign policy matters and hope to achieve "agreed positions" or common policies – a step of practical value in itself and potentially another important step towards becoming a single European state.

European leaders asserted, in the act, that they, in their periodic European Council meetings took the major decisions and set the strategic guidelines of the EU.

Social policy was developed to bring to a common standard social rights in the spheres of health and worker security, research and development and environmental protection. Achieving decent standards in these spheres goes somewhat against the idea of free trade and shows something of the dichotomy of thinking in EU planners' minds.

The Treaty on European Union (The Maastricht Treaty)

Signed 7 February 1992. Entered into force 1 November 1993.

This Treaty accelerated the move towards unification of the states of Europe. The European Community was renamed the European Union. Article two of the Treaty states, "this treaty marks a new stage in the process of creating an ever closer union among the peoples of Europe."

The principal aim of European Community action since 1952 had been trade and financial *co-operation*. This treaty made a huge leap, taking the practical steps needed to bring about economic and monetary union.

It also took another major step by expanding its areas of action. New euro-terminology was introduced, the so-called "three pillars" that would build the state of Europe. (This terminology has been dropped in the Constitution.) The pillars are areas in which the EU would assume power to direct. Namely,

1 The community - the basis of this being the existing trade arrangements;
2 New development: Common Foreign and Security Co-operation;
3 New development: Justice and Home Affairs.

In the new areas, at this stage, decision-making was to be intergovernmental - meaning that no decision could be taken without unanimous agreement, and at this stage no directives could be issued in this area. The Commission, European Parliament and the European Court of Justice were given no powers to act in these areas. The intergovernmental arrangements foreshadow the handing of direct powers to Brussels at some later time.

In the community pillar decisions on more topics would be taken by qualified majority voting. The bolder step was the creation of a detailed plan and timetable to bring about the single market announced in the *Single European Act*. Countries would take steps to converge key aspects of their economies - controlling inflation, exchange rates and interest rates, and strictly limiting budget deficits - all this leading to economic and monetary union with a single currency (named in Madrid in 1995 as the euro).

The establishment of a European Central Bank was planned for the turn-of-the-century to control the currency, fix exchange rates etc. (This has been established in Frankfurt.)

The Treaty declared that citizens of member states were now additionally "European citizens." European passports now show this dual citizenship.

The Treaty gave the new European Union powers to act in areas of culture, education, and the building of major road and rail transport networks (here called "Trans European networks" or "TENS"). The powers taken by the Single European Act in setting environmental standards, industrial policy and research and development were extended.

Powers of the European Parliament were extended.

The cohesion fund was established. From the funds paid in by all euro-taxpayers financial help could be given to poorer regions to achieve a more equal economic balance within the EU.

The European Court of Justice was given the right to fine member states if they broke EU laws or directives.

The idea of subsidiarity[3] was re-affirmed.

Europol[4] was established.

Eleven of the twelve member states agreed on the "Social Chapter". The dissenting state was the UK. The treaty set out employment rights – workers' rights to a decent workplace, proper health and safety standards, free movement throughout the EC, "equitable" remuneration, sex equality, a maximum number of hours per working week, free association in trade unions and collective bargaining, professional training, a minimum working age of 16, minimum pension rights, protection for disabled workers, unemployment benefit and a requirement of management to consult workers in certain situations. These matters in the opinion of Margaret Thatcher, would be likely to add to labour costs and were, in any case, matters for individual states to decide for themselves. It was eventually agreed that Britain would "opt out" of these requirements which were put to the end of the treaty in a special "chapter." (Tony Blair signed up to the Social Chapter for Britain in 1997.)

It was agreed that the EU would build a common defence.

The Commission was given the official title of "Commission of the European Communities". The opportunity was missed to give it a more up-to-date title - "Commission of the European Union"

The Committee of the Regions was established.[5]

Hesitant ratification process suggested disquiet

The slow moves to ratify the treaty suggest the difficulty politicians had in convincing parliaments and peoples of its value. *The Maastricht Treaty* was opposed by many Europeans. Parliamentary ratification in the UK was achieved with difficulty. The French held a referendum and accepted the treaty by only a tiny majority, and in Denmark the Danes rejected the treaty in a referendum. This led to negotiations of changes applicable only to the Danes. A referendum a year after the first saw the Danes accepting the treaty by a small margin.

The Schengen Agreement 1985, 1990, 1997

This is the understanding between a number of countries which first abolished many internal border controls within Europe. The aim was to allow free movement of goods and persons within the member countries without border checks or controls, but with external borders with non-member countries strengthened. The first intergovernmental agreement was signed in 1985 and an updated version, The *Schengen Agreement,* was signed (in the Luxembourg village of Schengen) in 1990 by Belgium, France, Germany, Luxembourg, and the Netherlands. Part of the agreement was to harmonise visa requirements and eventually have a common visa for all Schengen countries. The countries would share a list of people considered undesirable. Police forces would have the right of pursuit across borders. The countries would co-operate in matters regarding excise duties and customs payments and share records on these matters through the establishment of a common database on Eurocitizens, later to cause concern about its size, use and security.

The UK and Ireland opposed these arrangements, being convinced that there would be problems in controlling terrorists, drug traffickers, illegal immigrants, and animal borne diseases.

In 1997 the *Schengen Agreement* was incorporated into the *Treaty of Amsterdam* with opt-outs for Ireland and the UK. Two countries from outside the EU joined the Schengen Area: Iceland and Norway.

In spite of the *Schengen Agreement* border checks occur in many places where they are theoretically abolished.

The Treaty of Amsterdam

Signed 2 October 1997. Entered into force 1 May 1999.

The main aims of the new treaty were:

- to develop an organisation capable of effective decision-making when the EU had expanded from having 15 member states to having 25 and more,
- to make the EU more democratic,
- to extend EU powers and influence into areas traditionally the preserve of member states (human rights, freedom, law and order, crime and punishment and data protection),

- to increase the role of the EU in common foreign and security matters,
- to modify the idea of subsidiarity,
- eliminate border controls and deal with immigration
- to make institutional changes.

1. EU decision-making

It was obvious that unanimity in decision-making would rarely be achieved and that a system of majority voting would have to be extended to more areas. In fact, sixteen more areas came within this system including: public health, equal opportunities and treatment of the sexes, customs co-operation, employment, anti fraud measures, and data protection.

Areas in which decision making had been intergovermental in the justice and home affairs area in the *Maastricht Treaty* now became a matter for EU control whereby decisions taken might overrule the views of some member states.

2. Democracy

The European Parliament was given the right of co-decision (with the Council) in the passing of EU laws in certain spheres of activity. If either did not approve of a law then it would not be passed. It was also given the power to veto member states' choice of president of the Commission.[6]

Qualified Majority Voting was extended to more areas. This increased the likelihood of a state being overruled by a majority of states and so having to accept laws passed against its will. (This replaced unanimous decision-making in these areas.)

Some states would be allowed to take decisions and act together in certain circumstances, regardless of what other states thought, thereby introducing a "two-speed Europe" with one grouping set free from the voting power of the other group. This would inevitably leave some states sidelined but perhaps open to the possibility of being seriously affected, as for example, if a new grouping became involved in military action.

3. Citizens' rights – extension of EU powers and concerns

The treaty declared the EU aim of "creating an area of freedom, security and justice". The EU was now concerned with "fundamental rights". The core purpose of the European project had always been trade and prosperity. The new concerns might be interpreted either as taking steps towards controlling more of the functions of member states or as an attempt to give the EU a human face. Suddenly not trade but human rights were the core aim.

The treaty gave the Council power to take action to combat discrimination based on sex, racial or ethnic origin, religion or belief, disability, age or sexual orientation.

The "Community" would meet to collaborate on issues of employment and unemployment.

With the need to keep records on all European citizens for the purpose of external border control, data protection, to limit the sharing of such information, was called for.

By this treaty EU leaders gave the EU powers to deal with organised crime and EU corruption and fraud. Europol was given an increased role in working in co-operation with police forces, judicial authorities and customs authorities to fight against terrorism, organised crime, money laundering, human trafficking, drug trafficking, offences against children, racism and xenophobia. Minimum penalties for these matters were set out. It was agreed to ease (for the police) extradition procedures. The idea of a future "harmonisation" of criminal law across the EU was suggested for the future.

Ideas which, in the *Maastricht Treaty*, had come under the heading of "Justice and Home Affairs" were now listed under "Police and Judicial Co-operation in Criminal Matters."

The Treaty demands (rather vaguely and ineffectually) that a high level of human health protection must be built into all "community" policies and actions.

It also requires a high level of consumer protection. All documents of EU institutions must be accessible to all EU citizens. (This has not been achieved yet. See *Transparency* in the *Major Issues* section.)

4. Common Foreign and Security Policy

The treaty aimed to develop more power and influence in the world for the EU.

It was agreed that the EU would work out common policies, and strategies in foreign affairs. The EU would carry out "Petersburg tasks" - humanitarian aid and peace keeping.

The EU would appoint a person to represent it in the international arena - the "High Representative for the Common, Foreign and Security Policy." The man appointed on 1 October 1999 was Xavier Solana, the man who, as Secretary-General of NATO, had been a key player in the NATO (and, in the main, EU) illegal bombing of Yugoslavia only a few months earlier that year. (See *Major Issues* section.)

5. Modifying subsidiarity

By the time that the *Maastricht Treaty* was being written some member states, particularly the UK, were becoming very concerned about the increasingly rapid removal of powers from some of them and their transfer to one or other central EU decision-making authority.

To allay fears the idea of subsidiarity was developed. This meant that decisions (including law making) would be taken as close to the people who would be affected as possible. The EU would only act if it was not possible to achieve a desired result with purely local or national decision-making. States were able to bring those issues which they could not deal with alone, such as international crime, to the EU for joint action.

But the *Treaty of Amsterdam* gave powers to EU decision-making bodies which reduced the range of topics on which member states could take decisions for themselves.

The treaty also made several things clear:

a European law always overrules laws passed by member states and there would be no return of any powers to member states once the EU had acted in any particular sphere.

b The right of initiative of national governments to bring cross-border issues to the EU for joint decision was to be removed.
c Only the EU Commission would have the right to propose legislation. The Commission's idea of the need to act was what counted above those of state governments.

6. Immigration and border control

The *Schengen Agreement* was incorporated into the treaty and it was agreed that internal frontier controls would be abolished except for the UK and Ireland.

EU bodies would now control
- Immigration
- External borders
- Visas
- Asylum

But with certain opt-outs for the UK and Ireland.

7. Institutional changes

- Membership of the European Parliament was limited to 700 MEPs[7]
- The European Parliament was given the right to approve the Commission president (nominated by member states)
- The Commission president was given the duty of formulating the Commission's political guidelines
- The EU Court of Justice had its role expanded to deal with human rights, (apparently duplicating the work of the European Court of Human Rights set up by the Council of Europe) immigration, asylum, visas and co-operation with European police
- The Court of Auditors was given new powers.

The Treaty of Nice

Signed 26 February 2001. Entered into force 1 February 2003.

Main developments
- Fundamental aims of the EU may be changed without a further treaty, state parliament's approval or referendum. A few dozen senior ranking EU office holders might do it. All that is required is the permission of the European Central Bank and the unanimous vote of the Council.
- Rules established for the setting up of Europe-wide political parties.
- The European Parliament - maximum membership increased to 732.
- The Commission - various proposals for limiting the number of Commissioners.
- Commission President chosen by QMV (qualified majority voting). The choice is subject to the approval of the European Parliament.
- Commission President given power to fire individual Commissioners.
- New and complicated rules developed for QMV.

- Member States lost their rights to veto decisions in some 40 new areas as QMV is extended.
- Election of the High Representative for the Common Foreign and Security Policy.
- Some aspects of the making of international agreements.
- Measures relating to visas, asylum and immigration.
- In certain circumstances, agreements relating to the Structural Funds.
- Unanimity - this is still required, for example in the field of defence and foreign affairs, but the treaty gave it a new definition. Previously, and outside the EU, unanimity means all present vote in agreement. Now EU decisions may be regarded as unanimous when there is "constructive abstention." This means that a state - for example a neutral country - which may disapprove of military action - may abstain in order to demonstrate its disapproval, but the decision will be taken regardless, as if all have agreed.
- Enhanced co-operation. New rules for greater integration and unification of part of the EU. Any group of eight or more member states can work as a single body on a project so long as they do so as a last resort, and that this action furthers EU aims, respects existing EU laws and competences, respects the rights and obligations of non-participating members, does not undermine the internal market or economic and social cohesion, and remains open to other member states joining the club.
- Social Protection Committee established.
- The administration of justice begins to move away from the control of member states.
- EU-wide co-operation in the field of criminal law and a new EU prosecution agency, Eurojust, are established.
- European Council meetings, after the accession of the eighteenth member state, to be held only in Brussels.

The European Constitution, signed 29 October 2004, blueprint for Europe's future

The core treaties of the EU were amalgamated into the European Constitution (2004) which was planned to come into force on 1 November 2006 and replace earlier EU treaties. This document contained plans to change the way the EU works. It extended the powers it exercises over member states. New policy areas were to come under direct EU supervision. Through a new system of "shared competences" a way would have been opened for more and more power to pass to Brussels. Although national parliaments would, for the time being, control defence policy, the foreign policy section demanded that national policies should conform to EU policies, and it contained a mechanism whereby a simple vote by the European Council could pass all control of defence to the EU subject to the ratification of member state parliaments. The Constitution would have, in principle, allowed disengagement. New provisions within the Constitution were being implemented before it had been ratified by all the member states. Eighteen member states ratified it. The official response to its rejection by the voters of Holland and France was to inaugurate "a period of reflection".

Draft Intergovernmental Conference Mandate for the Reform Treaty, 23 June 2007

Cutting short the "period of reflection", on 23 June 2007, EU leaders agreed a detailed mandate for The *Reform Treaty*. The *Reform Treaty* is a treaty to re-write two other treaties. Leaders decided to integrate the innovations of the Constitution into the Treaty on the European Union and the Treaty Establishing the European Community. When the two treaties have been revised the Treaty on European Union will keep its name. The Treaty Establishing the European Community will be renamed "Treaty on the Functioning of the Union".

Modifications to the Constitution are discussed in Part Five.

Notes

1 The League of Nations was the association of states (1919 to 1945) which came together in a failed attempt to bring about world peace. A forerunner of the United Nations.

2 Sovereignty is one of the most important concepts in the political arrangements of the European Union. Basically it is the ability of a state to act independently, take its own decisions. See *Euroterminology* and the discussions in *Major Issues*.

3 Subsidiarity means taking decisions at the lowest possible level. See *Euroterminology* and *Major Issues*.

4 Europol: European police force. See *Euroterminology*.

5 A committee set up primarily to advise the Commission on matters of regional development.

6 For descriptions of these and other EU bodies see the *Institutions* in *Part Three - Nuts and Bolts*.

7 See *Acronyms* in *Part Three - Nuts and Bolts* for the numerous acronyms used in the European Institutions.

For details of how to obtain the full texts of EU treaties see *Sources of Information*.

Note on articles mentioned in this book

References throughout this book to specific articles are those of the Constitution, unless otherwise indicated.

Growth of "EU" membership over 50 years

1957	1973	1981	1986	1995	2004	07
16 years	8 years	5 yrs	9 years	9 years	3 years	1 yr
France, West Germany, Italy, Holland, Belgium, Luxembourg **6 members**	Plus Britain Ireland Denmark **Total:** **9 members**	Plus Greece **Total:10 members**	Plus Spain and Portugal 1990 East Germany joined West Germany. **Total:** **12 members**	Plus Austria Finland Sweden **Total:** **15 members**	Plus Lithuania Latvia Estonia Poland Czech - Republic Slovakia Slovenia Hungary Malta Greek - Cyprus **Total: 25 members**	Plus Rumania and Bulgaria. **Total 27 members.**

The EU (including its earlier form as the EEC) has existed since 1957. In the first half of its life it had ten members or fewer. In the first 47 years there were 15 members or fewer. Growth has been very rapid in recent years. (Chart is approximately to scale.) See *Key Dates*.

Part Three

Nuts and bolts of the EU system

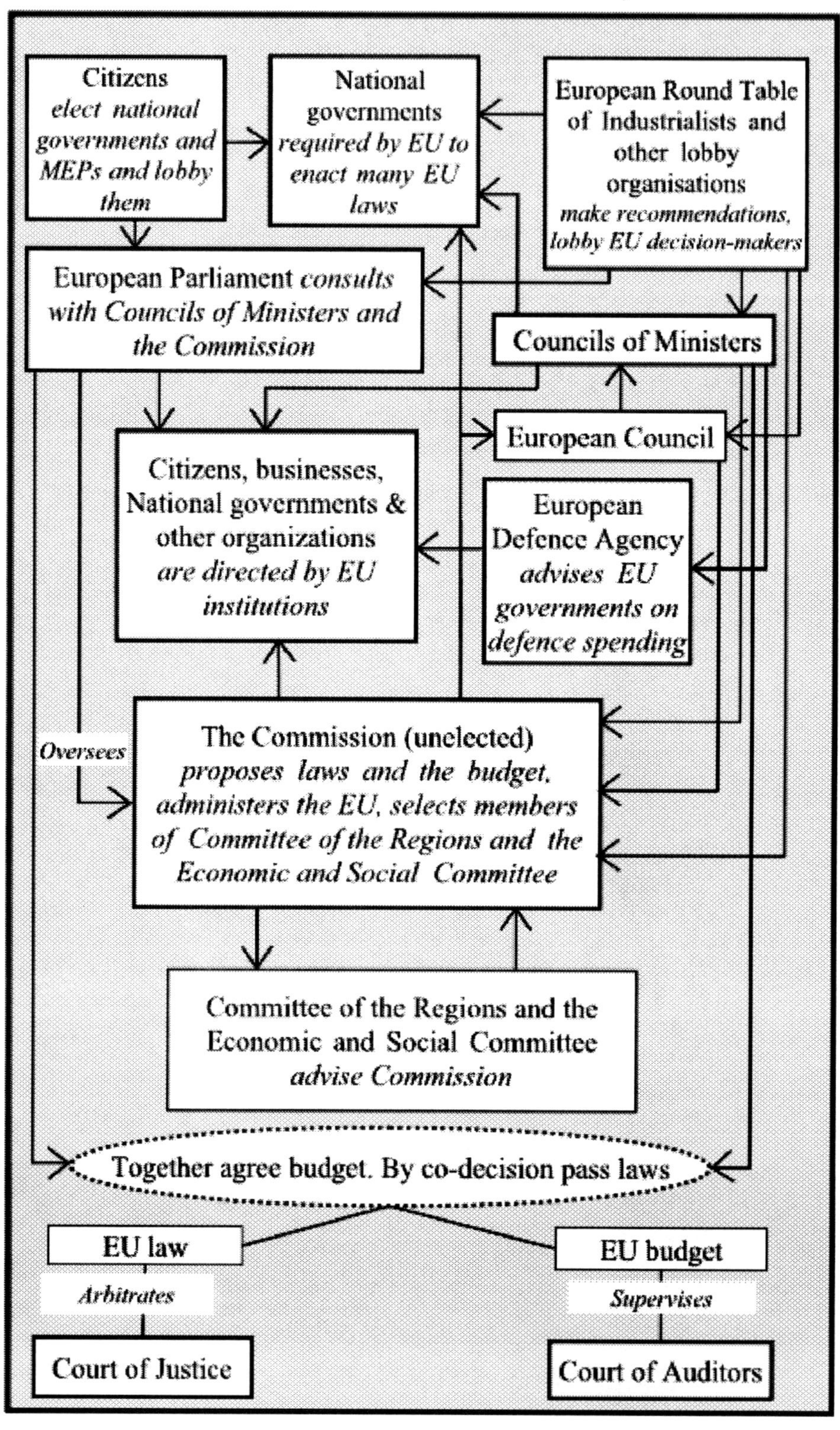
Who does what - Some of the main links in the EU power structure
Citizens elect national governments and MEPs and lobby them
National governments required by EU to enact many EU laws
European Round Table of Industrialists and other lobby organisations make recommendations, lobby EU decision-makers
European Parliament consults with Councils of Ministers and the Commission
Councils of Ministers
European Council
Citizens, businesses, National governments & other organizations are directed by EU institutions
European Defence Agency advises EU governments on defence spending
Oversees
The Commission (unelected) proposes laws and the budget, administers the EU, selects members of Committee of the Regions and the Economic and Social Committee
Committee of the Regions and the Economic and Social Committee advise Commission
Together agree budget. By co-decision pass laws
EU law
EU budget
Arbitrates
Supervises
Court of Justice
Court of Auditors

The 27 member states of the European Union (2007)

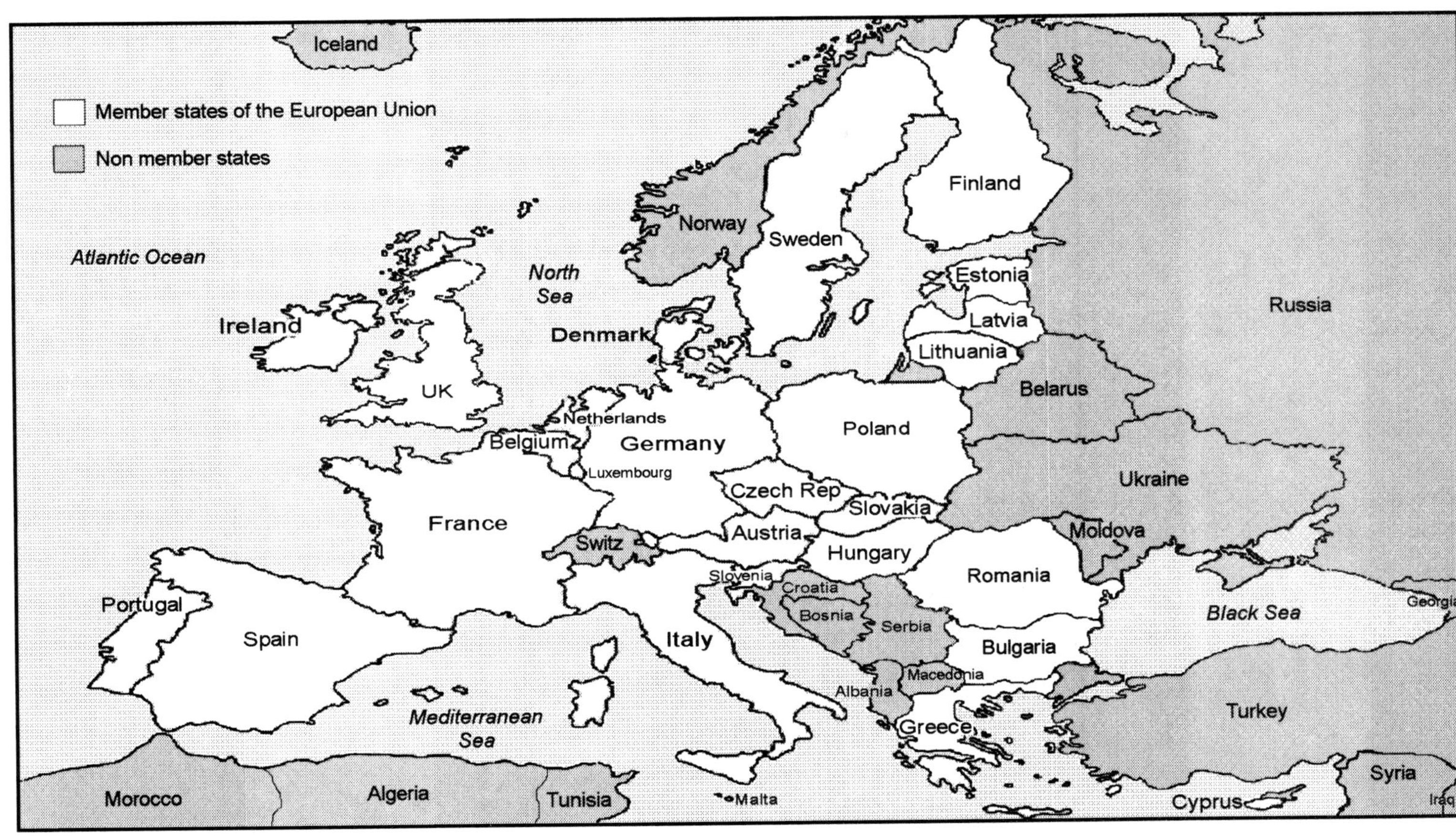

Member Countries of the European Union

Austria
Belgium
Bulgaria
Cyprus
Czech Republic
Denmark
Estonia
Finland
France
Germany
Greece
Hungary
Ireland
Italy
Latvia
Lithuania
Luxembourg
Malta
Poland
Portugal
Romania
Slovakia
Slovenia
Spain
Sweden
The Netherlands
United Kingdom

Other European countries

Albania
Andorra
Belarus
Bosnia-Herzegovina
Iceland
Liechtenstein
Moldova
Monaco
Norway
Russia
San Marino
Serbia
Montenegro
Switzerland
Ukraine
Vatican City

Applicant countries (as at 2007)

Croatia
Turkey
Former Yugoslav Republic of Macedonia

NATO
Members of North Atlantic Treaty Organisation

Founding members (1949)

Belgium
Canada
Denmark
France
Iceland
Italy
Luxembourg
Netherlands
Norway
Portugal
United Kingdom
United States

Countries that joined after the initial foundation

Greece (1952)
Turkey (1952)
West Germany (1955, joined by East Germany 1990)
Spain (1982)

Former Eastern Bloc states that joined after the end of the Cold War

1999:
Czech Republic
Hungary
Poland

2004:
Bulgaria
Estonia
Latvia
Lithuania
Romania
Slovakia
Slovenia

Population of EU Countries shown as a percentage of EU total (2006)

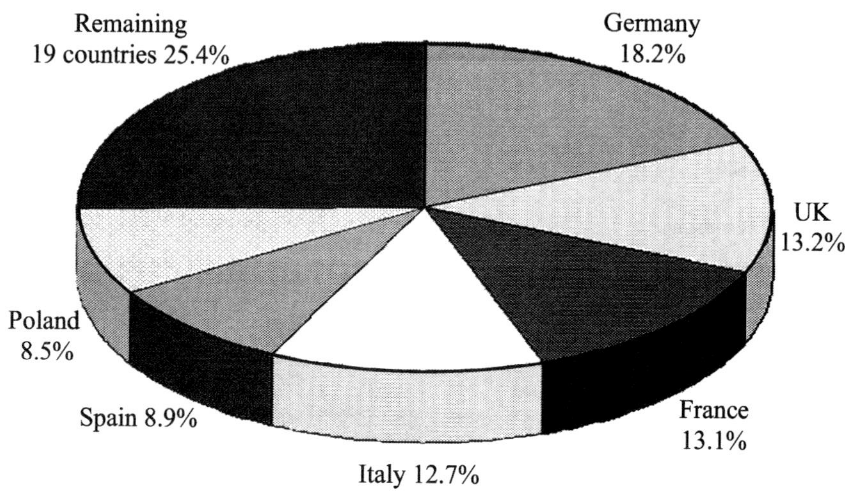

Seats in the European Parliament & percentage of E U population 2006 (25 members)

Country	Seats (2004 - 2009)	% of EU Population (2006)
Germany	99	18.17%
United Kingdom	78	13.18%
France	78	13.06%
Italy	78	12.75%
Spain	54	8.89%
Poland	54	8.53%
Romania	33	Joined 1 January 2007
Netherlands	27	3.54
Greece	24	2.33
Portugal	24	2.27

(continued)

Seats in the European Parliament
(Continuation)

Country	Seats (2004 - 2009)	% of E U Population(2006)
Belgium	24	2.27
Czech Republic	24	2.27
Hungary	24	2.25
Sweden	19	1.96
Austria	18	1.79
Bulgaria	17	Joined 1 January 2007
Slovakia	14	1.19
Denmark	14	1.18
Finland	13	1.14
Ireland	13	0.85
Lithuania	13	0.77
Latvia	9	0.52
Slovenia	7	0.44
Estonia	6	0.30
Cyprus	6	0.17
Luxembourg	6	0.10
Malta	5	0.09

The number of seats was revised downwards for most states on 1 January 2007, when Bulgaria and Romania joined the EU.

EU Key Indicators

Country	Gross Domestic Product £ Billions 2004	GDP EU rank	Gross Domestic Product per capita 2004 in £	GDP Per Capita EU rank
Austria	160.36	9	19,616	8
Belgium	196.87	7	18,899	9
Bulgaria	13.32	22	1,712	27
Cyprus	8.66	24	11,674	14
Czech Rep	59.3	16	5,810	19
Denmark	133.39	11	24,687	3
Estonia	6.37	26	4,702	21
Finland	103.32	13	19,765	6
France	1,128.13	3	18,101	11
Germany	1,500.9	1	18,193	10
Greece	114.52	12	10,351	15
Hungary	55.97	17	5,537	20
Ireland	100.35	14	24,721	2
Italy	944.43	4	16,234	12
Latvia	7.59	25	3,280	25
Lithuania	12.33	23	3,587	24
Luxembourg	18.36	20	40,497	1
Malta	2.97	27	7,402	18
Netherlands	333.1	6	20,466	5
Poland	138.69	10	3,633	23
Portugal	97.57	15	9,290	16
Romania	41.36	18	1,908	26
Slovakia	17.84	21	8,931	17
Slovenia	23.03	19	4,278	22
Spain	571.27	5	13,381	13
Sweden	191.16	8	21,255	4
U. K.	1,178.85	2	19,702	7
Turkey *	203.84		2745	
Norway **	145.34		32,132	

EU Key Indicators

Country	Population Millions 2004	Unemployment % of total labour force 2004	Balance of payments in £ billion 2004	Balance of Payments 2004 as % of GDP
Austria	8.09	4.8	1.7	0.2
Belgium	10.4	8.4	5.3	3.4
Bulgaria	8	12	-3	-5.8
Cyprus	0.73	4.6	-2.24	-5.7
Czech Rep	10.21	8.3	-0.54	-6.1
Denmark	5.40	5.5	5.03	2.3
Estonia	1.35	9.7	-1.09	-12.7
Finland	5.22	8.8	6.94	5.0
France	59.90	9.6	-4.28	-0.4
Germany	82.55	9.5	102.82	3.7
Greece	11.05	10.5	-17.27	-6.2
Hungary	10.12	6.1	-1.63	-8.6
Ireland	4.02	4.5	21.35	-0.6
Italy	57.48	8	5.98	-0.9
Latvia	2.32	10.4	-1.56	-13.0
Lithuania	3.45	11.4	-1.29	-7.7
Luxembourg	0.45	5.1	-1.9	10.5
Malta	0.40	7.3	-0.48	-9.5
Netherlands	16.26	4.6	23.53	8.9
Poland	38.19	19	-3.13	-4.2
Portugal	10.48	6.7	-10.2	-7.3
Romania	22	7.6	-3.67	-8.4
Slovakia	5.38	18.2	-0.82	-3.4
Slovenia	2.0	6.3	-0.68	-2.1
Spain	40.98	10.7	-36.45	-5.3
Sweden	8.97	6.3	18.8	6.8
U. K.	59.52	4.7	-61.06	-1.7
Turkey	71	10.3	-13.06	-5.2
Norway	4.48	4.4	18.36	13.8

EU Key Indicators

Country	Corporate tax rate % 2005	Top personal tax rate % 2005	Military Spending £ Millions 2002	Military Spending as % of GDP	Energy Imports MTOE 2002	Energy import dependency 2002 %
Austria	25	50	1,152	0.8	20.27	66
Belgium	34	50	2,304	1.3	45.34	76.4
Bulgaria	15	24	256	2.5	8.65	45.93
Cyprus	10	30	240	2.4	2.57	100
Czech Rep	26	32	960	2.1	10.89	26.6
Denmark	28	59	1728	1.6	- 8.52	- 41.1
Estonia	24	24	63	1.6	1.49	100
Finland	26	52	1,344	1.4	18.8	52.6
France	33.8	48.1	25,728	2.5	132.9	50.3
Germany	38.6	42	21,312	1.5	209.52	60.5
Greece	32	40	4,160	4.4	23.21	70.7
Hungary	17.5	38	640	1.8	14.64	58.2
Ireland	12.5	42	486	0.6	13.66	89.3
Italy	37.3	45	16,384	1.9	153.02	86.7
Latvia	15	25	149	1.8	2.42	54.6
Lithuania	15	33	158	1.8	3.75	42.7
Luxembourg	30.4	39	131	0.9	3.94	99
Malta	35	35	17	0.7	1.32	100
Netherlands	31.5	52	4,928	1.6	31.29	33.8
Poland	19	40	2,304	1.9	10.05	11.3
Portugal	27.5	40	1,088	2.3	22.5	84.2
Romania	16	16	704	2.3	9.12	25.51
Slovakia	19	19	297	2	12.12	65.3
Slovenia	25	50	211	1.5	3.44	49.9
Spain	35	45	5,568	1.2	107.4	78.3
Sweden	28	56.5	2,688	1.7	19.76	37.5
U. K.	30	40	23,872	2.4	- 28.95	- 12.8
Turkey	20	35	5,888	5.1	51.19	67.82
Norway **	28/78	28	2,304	1.9	-206	-765

EU Key indicators - sources and explanations

These statistics give some indication of the great variations in economic, social and military conditions that exist across the European Union.

Turkey has been included as a very important country which already has a special economic relationship with the EU and is an applicant state. Norway also has a strong relationship with the EU without being a member.

Where money values in sources were originally expressed in euros or other currencies these have been converted to British pounds. Euros have been converted at the rate of one euro to £0 .68.

Gross domestic product £ billions 2004

Source: *European Union Energy & Transport in Figures 2004,* European Commission Directorate-General for Energy and Transport in co-operation with Eurostat.
http://europa.eu.int/comm/dgs/energy_transport/figures/pocketbook/index_en.htm. See also http://epp.eurostat.cec.eu.Int/pls/portal

Population millions 2004

Figures source: *Energy & Transport in Figures 2004* European Commission Directorate-General for Energy and Transport.

Unemployment rate 2004

The 2004 figures are from *Europe in Figures - Eurostat Yearbook 2006-07.* This states, "Unemployment rates represent unemployed persons as a percentage of the labour force: the labour force is the total number of people employed and unemployed; unemployed persons comprise persons aged 15-74 . . ."

Balance of payments (current account balance) 2004

These were taken from *Europe in Figures - Eurostat Yearbook 2006-07.*

* Figures for Turkey are from economist.com/countries. Turkey's figures relate to 2006 and we converted them from US dollars to UK pounds at the 1 December 2006 rate using the Bank of Canada online Ten Year Currency Converter.

** Statistics for Norway are from the website of the Norwegian government, norway.no, *Statistics Norway.* Norwegian krone were converted using the Bank of Canada online Ten Year Currency Converter as at 2 December 2004.

Corporate tax rates 2005

Figures are from Eurostat, the Statistical Office of the European Communities, *Eurostat News Release,* 134/2005, 21 October 2005. The exceptions are as follows: Bulgaria's tax rates refer to 2006 and were found at worldwide-tax.com. Romania's tax rates relate to 2007 and were found at the website of the Federation of International Trade Associations, fita.org. **Norwegian tax rates are from the Norwegian government's website and refer to 2007. The 78% corporate tax rate is for oil companies only. Turkish tax rates are from the economist.com and for 2007.

Military spending

Military spending and military spending as percentage of GDP 2002 statistics are based on a CRS report for the US Congress, *Comparison of US and foreign military spending: Data from selected public sources,* 28 January 2004. CRS points out that military spending statistics are "inherently unreliable".

Energy imports and Energy Import Dependency 2002

These are expressed in MTOE, millions of tons of oil equivalent. Source: *European Union Energy & Transport in Figures 2004.*

Acronyms used by the European Union

ACP	Trade co-operation body comprising EU and African, Caribbean and Pacific countries
ALDE	A grouping of members of the European Parliament - Alliance of Liberal and Democrats for Europe
ASEAN	Association of South East Asian Nations - Brunei, Indonesia, Malaysia, the Philippines, Singapore, Vietnam and Thailand.
ASP	Agreement on Social Policy
CAP	Common Agricultural Policy
CEEP	EU-wide small businesses' group
CFP	Common Fisheries Policy
CFSP	Common Foreign and Security Policy
CMO	Common Market Organisation (under the CAP)
COREPER	Committee of Member States' Permanent Representatives
COPS	(French acronym for) Political and Security Committee
COSI	Standing Committee on Internal Security
CP	Common Position (an agreement adopted by Council)
CTP	Common Transport Policy
DG	Directorate General (a division of the Commission)
EAC	European Astronauts Centre in Cologne, Germany
EAGGF	European Agricultural Guidance and Guarantee Fund
EBA	European Border Agency
EC	European Community
ECB	European Central Bank
ECHR	European Convention on Human Rights
ECJ	European Court of Justice
Ecofin	Economic and Finance Council
ECOSOC	Economic and Social Committee
ECSC	European Coal and Steel Community
ECU	European Currency Unit
ECR	European Court Report
EEA	European Economic Area
EEB	European Environmental Board
EEC	European Economic Community

EESC	European Economic and Social Committee
EFA	A grouping of members of the European Parliament - Greens and European Free Alliance
EFTA	European Free Trade Area
EIB	European Investment Bank
EIF	European Investment Fund
EMS	European Monetary System
EMU	European Monetary Union
ENP	European Neighbourhood Policy - a policy aimed at including EU neighbouring countries
EP	European Parliament
EPP - ED	A grouping of members of the European Parliament - the European People's Party (Christian Democrats) and European Democrats.
EPSCO	Employment, Social Policy, Health and Consumer Affairs Council
ERDF	European Regional Development Fund
ESA	European Space Agency
ESDP	European Security and Defence Policy
ESC	Economic and Social Committee
ESCB	European System of Central Banks
ESF	European Social Fund
ESIF	European Security and Intelligence Force
ESTEC	European Space Research and Technology Centre in Noordwijk in the Netherlands
ESOC	European Space Operations Centre in Darmstadt, Germany
ESRIN	The European Space Agency Centre for Earth Observation in Frascati, Italy
ETUC	European Trade Union Council
ETUI	European Trade Union Institute
EU	European Union
EUMS	European Union Military Staff
EUMC	European Union Military Committee
Euratom	European Atomic Energy Community
Eures	European Employment Service
EUL/NGL	A grouping of members of the European Parliament - European United Left and the Nordic Green Alliance
Europol	EU police force
EYC	Education, Youth and Culture Council
FIFG	Financial Instrument for Fisheries Guidance
GAERC	General Affairs and External Relations Council
GATT	General Agreement on Tariffs and Trade

GDP	Gross Domestic Product
GMES	Global Monitoring for Enviroment and Security - an ESA satellite project
GNI	Gross National Income (of the EU)
GNP	Gross National Product
GSP	Generalised System of Preferences (under external trade rules)
IGC	Intergovernmental Conference
ILO	International Labour Organisation
IMF	International Monetary Fund
IND/DEM	A grouping of members of the European Parliament - Independence/Democracy Group
Inter-reg III	Structural fund for CEE applicant countries
JHA	Justice and Home Affairs
LIFE	EU fund to support nature conservation projects
Lingua	EU language education programme, now defunct
MAGP	Multi-annual Guidance Programme (under CFP)
MEP	Member of the European Parliament
MEPP	Middle East Peace Process
Mercosur	Latin American economic community
MNCs	Multinational Corporations
NAFTA	North American Free Trade Area
NATO	North Atlantic Treaty Organisation
NGO	Non-governmental organisation
NI	A grouping of members of the European Parliament - *Non-inscrit:* independent Member of European Parliament
OECD	Organisation for Economic Co-operation and Development
OLAF	The EU's anti-fraud office
PA	Palestinian Authority
PES	A grouping of members of the European Parliament 'Party of European Socialists': centre-left group in the EP
PCTF	Police Chiefs Task Force
PSC	Political and Security Committee
QMV	Qualified Majority Voting
R&D	Research and Development
SAP	Structural adjustment programme
SEA	Single European Act
SEM	Single European Market
SCA	Special Committee on Agriculture
SCIFA	Strategic Committee on Immigration, Frontiers and Asylum
SitCen	Joint Situation Centre
SMEs	Small and Medium Sized Enterprises

SMUS	Alternative term - Small and Medium Undertakings
Socrates	EU education programme
TAC	Total Allowable Catch (under the CFP)
TEC	Treaty Establishing the European Community
TENs	Trans European Networks
TEU	Treaty on European Union - the 'Maastricht Treaty'
TTE	Transport, Telecommunications and Energy Council
UEN	A grouping of members of the European Parliament - Union for Europe of the Nations
UNCTAD	United Nations Council for Trade and Development
UNHCR	United Nations High Commission for Refugees
UNICE	EU-wide employers' group
UNRWA	United Nations Relief and Works Agency - The UN's special agency set up in 1949 to serve the needs of Palestinians in refugee camps in the Middle East. It still operates in the West Bank and Gaza Strip, Lebanon, Jordan and Syria.
VAT	Value added tax
WEU	Western European Union
WTO	World Trade Organisation

Two-letter abbreviations used for EU states since 2004

Austria	AT	Latvia	LV
Belgium	BE	Lithuania	LT
Bulgaria	BG	Luxembourg	LU
Cyprus	CY	Malta	MT
Czech Republic	CZ	Netherlands	NL
Denmark	DK	Poland	PL
Estonia	EE	Portugal	PT
Finland	FI	Romania	RO
France	FR	Spain	ES
Germany	DE	Slovakia	SK
Greece	EL	Slovenia	SI
Hungary	HU	Sweden	SE
Ireland	IE	United Kingdom	UK
Italy	IT		

European Union Institutions

Advisory bodies

In an attempt by EU decision makers to keep in touch with the people of Europe two bodies have been set up to advise the European Parliament, the Council and the Commission.

They are

- The Committee of the Regions (selected from elected representatives of regional and local bodies across the EU) and
- The Economic and Social Committee (consisting of "representatives of organisations of employers, of the employed, and of other parties representative of civil society, notably in socio-economic, civic, professional and cultural areas."

Members of these committees, who are selected by the Commission, are required to be independent and work in the best interest of the EU.

EU decision makers are also advised by a very large number of official committees including COREPER and its subsidiaries, and committees of the European Parliament. They consult eurobarometer. In addition they may be influenced by the hundreds of lobbying organisations permanently set up in Brussels and by any eurocitizen.

See, Committee of the Regions, Economic and Social Committee, COREPER, below, and *Major Issues – Lobbying*. Also articles 32, 386-392.

Agriculture and Fisheries Council

Note: See *Council* below for a general account of the role and structure of EU Councils.

This Council is concerned with the biggest area of EU control. Almost half of all EU spending goes on agriculture. For a discussion of the policies, their aims, successes and failures please see the *Major Issues* chapter.

The Council meets once a month and brings together the Ministers for Agriculture and Fisheries and the European Commissioners responsible for agriculture and rural development, fisheries and maritime affairs, as well as consumer health and protection.

The proceedings of the Agriculture and Fisheries Council are prepared by 12 working parties spanning 45 subdivisions according to products (for example, the Working Party on Arable Crops (Rice)) or areas (for example, the Working Party on Agrimonetary Questions). The papers prepared by these sub-committees are then studied either by COREPER or by the Special Committee on Agriculture (SCA) before being forwarded to the Council. COREPER usually deals with fisheries and food safety issues and issues related to the funding of agriculture.

The EU's own explanation of the decision-making procedure for Agriculture and Fisheries is as follows. "Qualified majority – 232 votes out of 321 (Art. 205 of the TEC, amended by Art. 12 of the Act of Accession, OJ L 236/2003, p. 36) – which takes account of the weighting of votes within the Council is required when adopting legislative acts whose legal basis is Article 37 or Articles 152 and

153. The minority needed to block the adoption of an act is therefore 90 votes."

"The parliamentary procedure varies depending on the policies in question: Parliament's opinion is purely advisory and does not legally bind the Council when acts are based on Article 37; on the other hand, the opinion is legally binding for the Council when acts are based on Articles 152 and 153 of the TEC." (TEC is the *Treaty Establishing the European Community*, as ammended by the *Treaty of Nice,* 2003.)[1]

Committee, Article 36

A committee of representatives of member states who deal with policing, justice and home affairs matters within the COREPER setup. A more transparent/helpful title might be The police, justice and home affairs committee.[2]

Committee, Article 133

This is a committee of officials from member states who advise the Commission on international trade negotiations involving tariff amendments, customs and trade provisions and protective measures. It works as part of COREPER. See Foreign Affairs Council. A more transparent name for this committee might be The trade, customs and tariffs committee.

The Commission

The EU Commission is immensely powerful and important within the European Union. It is the executive body of the EU. It is responsible for the administration of the EU and has powers of independent initiative and decision making. Its forerunner was the High Authority of the Coal and Steel Community. It is currently established under articles 155- 163 of the *Treaty of Rome* as amended by the *Treaty of Nice* in articles numbered 211-219.

The Commission's main function is to "promote the general interest of the Union and take appropriate initiatives to that end." It ensures the application of the treaties/Constitution and enforces existing laws and regulations. It has the prime responsibility and right to propose and draft new laws for approval by the Council of Ministers and the European Parliament. When the Commission sets out to enforce EU law the final authority on such matters is the European Court of Justice. The Commission represents the European Union in negotiations with other countries in all matters except foreign and security policy. It plans and proposes the budget (which then has to be approved by the European Parliament and the Council). It is then responsible for the allocation and spending of the money (over 100 billion euros each year) and the running of the EU's programmes.

It is currently headed by 27 appointed (unelected) commissioners - one from each member state and it employs a staff of 27,000 people. Commissioners are effectively appointed by prime ministers and presidents of their countries who are free to propose any of their friends or associates to these top positions in the EU. Nominations have to be approved by the Council but this is usually just a formality. Commissioners serve for five years. The Council will include friends or associates of the presidents and prime ministers. The procedure cannot be said to be open or rigorous and is certainly not democratic. (See *Major Issues*.)

The Constitution will change the number of Commissioners. The simple arrangement of one Commissioner per member state will be changed to a system of having a number of Commissioners equivalent to two thirds of the number of member states. States will take it in turn not to have a commissioner.

Each commissioner specialises in a policy area, for example, trade or the environment, and is committed to working in the interest of the entire Union not his or her own country. Commissioners are forbidden from taking instructions from any organisation or entity. "The Commission shall be completely independent." Also, "The Commission shall neither seek nor take instructions from any government or other institution, body, office, or entity." (Constitution, article 26/7. Also, *Treaty Establishing the European Community*, article 213.) The Commission takes advice from the public through opinion polls (see "eurobarometer") and advisory committees which the Commission has itself appointed. The Commission is lobbied very lavishly and systematically by various organisations.

The Commission does not work from a publicly stated policy agenda which has been approved by the EU electorate. But in spite of the requirement not to take instructions from any body it actually works in co-operation with the European Council and the Council. It quietly, secretly gets on with the job of running the EU according to its own understanding of what needs to be done, mostly out of reach of scrutiny by the media, the public and public censure. Eurocitizens may not like what the Commission does, but there is nothing we can do about it. We will never get a chance to vote for an alternative party or alternative policies.

Nevertheless, the Commissioners are not invulnerable. Fraud within the Commission was a serious problem within this completely independent body. According to the rules the Commissioners are accountable to the EU Parliament which has the power to sack the entire commission, but not individuals. This offers undue protection to a "ministry" within the Commission whose policies may be disastrous and to individual commissioners who may be unsatisfactory in the eyes of the Parliament. Yet things were so bad in 1999 that the whole Commission would have been sacked over allegations of fraud at the highest level had they not prevented this by quickly resigning en masse.

Since then, the continuing failure of the Court of Auditors, year after year, to agree the accounts of the Commission does not inspire confidence that the EU, administered by the Commission, is in safe hands.

Under the Constitution the Commission itself or the Council may take steps to remove individual Commissioners. Which particular formulation of the Council is not specified – making it possible for any formulation of the Council to take a decision on an urgent issue. Article 349 states, "If any member of the Commission no longer fulfils the conditions required for the performance of his or her duties or if he or she has been guilty of serious misconduct, the Court of Justice may, on application by the Council, acting by a simple majority, or by the Commission, compulsorily retire him or her." The "conditions required for the performance of his or her duties" include "neither seeking nor taking instructions from any government, or any other body," and refraining from "actions incompatible with their duties." Commissioners may engage in no other occupation "whether gainful or not" and must behave with "integrity and discretion".

The European Council proposes a President of the Commission to direct the Commission's work and represent it. The European Parliament approves (or otherwise) the suggested candidate. He or she appoints Commission Vice-Presidents (in addition to the Minister for Foreign Affairs - from 2009).

See *Major Issues – Lobbying, Decision Makers - Commission,* and articles 26, 27, 28, 47, 325, 337, 340, 347, 349, 352, 397.

Comitology

The following explanation is taken directly from the main web site of the European Union.

> Under the *Treaty Establishing the European Community,* it is for the Commission to implement legislation at Community level. In practice, each legislative instrument specifies the scope of the implementing powers granted to the Commission and how the Commission is to use them. Frequently, the treaty will also make provision for the Commission to be assisted by a committee in accordance with a procedure known as 'comitology'.
>
> The committees which are forums for discussion, consist of representatives from Member States and are chaired by the Commission. They enable the Commission to establish a dialogue with national administrations before adopting implementing measures. The Commission ensures that they reflect as far as possible the situation in each country in question.
>
> The procedures which govern relations between the Commission and the committees are based on models set out in a Council Decision ("comitology" Decision), adopted on 13 July 1987. In order to take into account the changes in the Treaty - and, in particular, Parliament's new position under the codecision procedure - but also to reply to criticisms that the Community system is too complex, the 1987 Decision has been replaced by a new Council Decision of 28 June 1999.
>
> This latest Decision ensures that Parliament can keep an eye on the implementation of legislative instruments adopted under the codecision procedure. Parliament can express its disapproval of measures proposed by the Commission or, where appropriate, by the Council, which, in Parliament's opinion, go beyond the implementing powers provided for in the legislation.
>
> The Decision clarifies the criteria to be applied to the choice of committee and simplifies the operational procedures. The committees can be divided into the following categories:
>
> advisory committees: they give their opinions to the Commission which must take account of them. This procedure is generally used when the matters under discussion are not very sensitive politically.
>
> management committees: where the measures adopted by the Commission are not consistent with the committee's opinion, the Commission must communicate them to the Council which can take a different decision. This procedure is used in particular for measures relating to the management of the common agricultural policy, fisheries, and the main Community programmes.

regulatory committees: the Commission can only adopt implementing measures if it obtains the approval by the Member States meeting within the committee. In its absence, the proposed measure is referred back to the Council. The Commission finally adopts the implementing measure if the Council does not reach agreement. This procedure is used for measures relating to protection of the health or safety of persons, animals and plants and measures amending non-essential provisions of the basic legislative instruments.

Several innovations in the new "comitology" Decision enhance the transparency of the committee system to the benefit of Parliament and the general public: committee documents will be more readily accessible to the citizen. Committee documents are also registered in a public register. With the com-puterisation of decision-making procedures, the aim is to publish the full texts of non-confidential documents transmitted to Parliament on the Internet."

Committee of the Regions

Created by the *Maastricht Treaty* in 1992, the Committee of the Regions (CoR) is an advisory body which enables regional and local authorities to voice their views during the decision-making process of the European Union. It consists of 317 representatives who, to qualify for membership, must be elected to local or regional authorities within member states. The Constitution sets maxi-mum membership at 350. The committee is consulted by the Council, Parliament and the Commission in areas affecting local and regional interests, such as education, youth, culture, health and social and economic cohesion, the envi-ronment, the Social Fund, vocational training, cross-border co-operation and transport. It may also issue opinions on its own initiative.

Members of the Committee are selected by the Commission. The Council approves the list. Members serve for five years.

See articles 386-388.

Committee of Permanent Representatives

See COREPER.

Competitiveness Council(s)

Officially this Council merges three previous Councils: Internal Market, Industry, and Research. Their purposes are linked by the common aim of im-proving the competitiveness of European industry. However, depending on the items on the agenda, this Council is composed of European Affairs Ministers, or Industry Ministers, or Research Ministers. In reality, it remains three Councils. It meets about five or six times a year.

It reviews analyses provided by the Commission on competitiveness issues and gives its views on how competitiveness issues can be properly taken into account in all policy initiatives which have an impact on enterprise.

The Competitiveness Council is concerned with three main areas:

1 The internal market where the prime aim is to ensure that persons and goods can move freely. The Council is concerned with public procurement, free provision of services and establishment, free movement of goods, intellectual and industrial property rights, competition and company law.
2 In industrial policy the Council is concerned to ensure the competitiveness of the Union's industry through speeding up the adjustment of industry to structural changes, encouraging an environment favourable to initiative and to the development of enterprises throughout the Union, particularly small and medium-sized enterprises, encouraging an environment favourable to co-operation between enterprises and fostering better exploitation of the industrial potential of the policies of innovation, research and technological development. The Council has been involved in crises when major industries have been in steep decline. Its concern was to bring about restructuring in such a way as to prevent distortions of competition (ie by controlling/prohibiting state subsidy).
3 The Council believes that Scientific Research and Technological Development is playing an ever larger role in the process of economic development. Its main aim is the strengthening of the scientific and technological bases of European industry and of its international competitiveness, by combining research resources in certain key areas and priority technologies. It developed the Sixth Framework Programme (2002-2006). This is the Union's main instrument for the funding of research in Europe.

The Competitiveness Council legislates, mostly by qualified majority, in co-decision with the European Parliament.

COREPER

This is an important and powerful organisation within the European Union. It is the Committee of Permanent Representatives of the Governments of the Member States. It consists of the Ambassadors to the EU and meets at least once a week. Their task, officially, is to prepare the work of the Council and carry out tasks given to it by the Council. That is all existing treaties and the Constitution tell us. They are also there to further the views and interests of their own governments. (The acronym COREPER is from the French version of the name of the committee - Comité des représentants permanents.)

COREPER's work consists primarily of preparing the agendas for meetings of the Council, and (something which gives them great power), draft decisions or options for decisions.

Like the Council, COREPER meets in a whole variety of configurations, bringing in senior civil servants expert in their particular field, according to the topic under discussion. The committee has two levels of operation: COREPER I and COREPER II. COREPER II is the more senior level and deals with Common Foreign and Security Policy, economic affairs and police and judicial co-operation. COREPER I deals with other matters which include internal market policy legislation, agriculture, and environmental protection.

COREPER is assisted in its work by a further 250 or so committees and working groups consisting of delegates (specialists from the various ministries) from the member states. Some of these sub-committees have significant power themselves, for example, the Co-ordinating Committee responsible for preparing work in the area of police and judicial co-operation in criminal matters and the Political and Security Committee. Other committees include the Article 36 Committee, the Economic and Financial Committee, the Article 133 Committee, and the Special Committee on Agriculture. There may be in the region of two and a half thousand people in semi-permanent negotiation preparing decisions for the various Councils of Ministers. (This figure is an extrapolation from very limited information available. The real figure may be quite different.)

The sub-committees discuss issues and if agreement is reached they draft decisions to be approved by one of the Councils of Ministers. Their work is passed up to more senior people of the Permanent Committee. When there is agreement a draft decision is placed on the Ministers' agenda as an "A" point with the expectation that it would be agreed without discussion in the Council. More contentious issues are debated until most states are in agreement and then such issues are passed up to the relevant Council in the hope of resolution and decision. When agreement cannot be reached by COREPER matters are often passed over to the Commission or on to the European Council for decision. Alternatively the matters are passed back to the originating committee for further consideration.

Senior figures from COREPER (as well as representatives of the Commission) attend the Councils of Ministers. On rare occasions the Ministers themselves do not attend.

See *Political and Security Committee*, *Treaty Establishing the European Community* article 207 and the Constitution, articles 24/5 and 344.

COSI

COSI is the Standing Committee on Internal Security. It is a major committee responsible for police, internal security and border security including the operation of immigration and asylum policy. It was in the process of being set up in 2005 on the basis of article 261 of the unratified European Constitution. This authorised the establishment of a committee "within the Council in order to ensure that operational co-operation on internal security is promoted and strengthened within the Union. . . . The European Parliament and national parliaments shall be kept informed of the proceedings."

Its members include the chair persons of the Article 36 Committee, the Strategic Committee on Immigration, the Strategic Committee on Frontiers and Asylum, and representatives of the Commission, Europol, Eurojust, the Police Chiefs' Task Force, the Joint Situation Centre, and the European Border Agency.

The Committee itself has considered that its rules should be other than that described in the Constitution and has proposed that it should "prepare decisions of the Council" rather than being "a day-to-day tool for operational co-operation."

The Article 36 committee considered that COSI should have legislative powers [EU paper 6626/05]. COSI, because it works in an EU security field, will work in secret, allowing no access to its documents - a matter of concern to all who believe in open and accountable government.

See *Major Issues - Transparency.*

Council of the European Union

See the Council.

The Council

This apparently simple term is one of the most confusing in the EU vocabulary. The Council is also known as the Council of Ministers or the Council of the European Union. (Not to be confused with the Council of Europe or the European Council! See below.) Mostly it is known simply as "the Council."

"The Council" appears to denote a single body of people since it is a singular noun. This belief may be furthered by reference to the Constitution, articles 342 to 346, which describe the work of "the Council." The Constitution gives the clear impression that there are currently only 27 members of this single body. Article 23 states "The Council shall consist of a representative of each Member State at Ministerial level."

In fact, there is not one Council but many. The Constitution conceals the true number. Article 24 which claims to describe "the configurations of the Council of Ministers" mentions only "the General affairs Council" and the "Foreign Affairs Council." (To add to the confusion these two Councils are often referred to as a single Council. See below.)

What is the true number of Councils? Currently, according to the EU web site dedicated to "the Council of the European Union" there are nine distinct Councils with distinctive roles and personnel. One of these operates with two distinct bodies of Ministers and two others operate with three distinct bodies of Ministers. On the official web site this is explained as the nine meeting in different configurations to discuss different topics. If all the variations are acknowledged there are a total of fourteen different Councils. With the three general names for "the Council" this makes seventeen names for what is usually presented as a single body made up of 27 members. The true membership of "the Council" in all its forms is in the region of 375 Ministers.

The nine configurations of the Council acknowledged on the official web site are:

- The Economic and Financial Affairs Council (also known as ECOFIN)
- The Justice and Home Affairs Council (JHA, also known as the Co-operation in the fields of Justice and Home Affairs Council)
- The Employment, Social Policy, Health and Consumer Affairs Council
- The Competitiveness Council
- The Transport, Telecommunications and Energy Council
- The Agriculture Council (also known as The Agriculture and Fisheries Council)
- The Environment Council
- The Education, Youth and Culture Council
- The General Affairs Council (also known as the Foreign Affairs Council or the General Affairs Council or the General Affairs and External Relations Council. - The last of these names for this Council appears on The Council of Ministers web site. It is not used in the Constitution. However, its operation is not as simple as this account may have made it seem. See separate entry on this Council below.)

If we stick to the EU's suggestion in treaties and the Constitution that there is only one Council we can say that the Council is the Union's main decision-making and law making institution and directly represents the governments of the member states. It consists of ministers appointed in some way by the governments of the member states "who carry the authority to take decisions on behalf of their governments". At present (2007) each member state is normally represented by one minister at any of the council meetings. Meetings usually consist of 27 members. The ministers who attend each meeting vary according to the topic under discussion. Ministers of Agriculture attend the Agriculture Council meetings, and so on. In practice meetings are rarely attended by senior national ministers with the result that "non-controversial" issues are decided by lower ranking officials whilst difficult issues often get passed on to the European Council or the Foreign Affairs Council or, more often, the Commission to decide.

The Council of Ministers ("the Council" in whatever permutation) has the power to make two types of EU laws (currently called directives and regulations) and, in co-decision with the European Parliament, approve the budget. In many instances the European Parliament must also approve proposed laws for them to come into force. (See chapter on *Euroterminology – Law-making* and *Laws/rulings/ decisions/acts of the European Union.*)

Voting on some matters, for example, taxation, need unanimous agreement. Foreign affairs also require unanimity but this requirement is being eroded by matters of policy and procedure discussed in *Major Issues*. In Eurospeak "unanimity" does not mean that everyone present agrees with a proposal. (See *Unanimity*, in the *Euroterminology* chapter.) Other matters are decided by majority or qualified majority voting. (Also see *Euroterminology* chapter, and *Agriculture Council* above.)

The Council will play the main role in initiating and directing negotiations leading to treaties. The final agreement on conclusion of negotiations is subject to complex and varied procedures set out in article 3.

Since the Council in its various permutations consists of fourteen distinct sets of people it would be more accurate to refer to "the Councils" rather than "the Council".

See *COREPER* and articles of the Constitution which refer to this topic: 23, 24, 25, 325, and 342-346. See also *Major Issues - Transparency.*

The Council of Ministers

See the Council.

The Council of Europe

This is not an EU institution. See the *Euroterminology* chapter. It should not be confused with the European Council.

See below.

Court of Auditors

The body set up to examine the accounts of the European Union and to ensure that the accounts show sound financial management, and are correct and proper records of lawful receipts and legitimate spending. For eleven consecutive years it has announced that the accounts of the European Union are unsatisfactory.

See article 31, 384, 385, *OLAF* (below) and discussion in *Major issues*, the section on the *Common Agricultural Policy.*

Defence Agency

See *European Defence Agency.*

The Economic and Financial Affairs Council (also known as ECOFIN)

This Council is mainly concerned with economic policy co-ordination, economic surveillance, monitoring of Member States' budgetary policy and public finances, the euro (legal, practical and international aspects), financial markets and capital movements and economic relations with third countries. It decides mainly by qualified majority, in consultation or co-decision with the European Parliament, with the exception of fiscal matters which are decided by unanimity.

The Ecofin Council also prepares and adopts every year, together with the European Parliament, the annual budget of the European Union which is about 100 billion euros (approximately £70 billion).

The Eurogroup normally meets the day before the Ecofin meeting to deal with issues relating to the Economic and Monetary Union (EMU). This grouping meets informally and does not consider itself a separate Council in its own right.

When the Ecofin Council examines issues related to the euro and EMU only the Eurogroup members take part in the vote.

See *Council* above.

Economic and Financial Committee

This is the EU's financial watchdog. See article 192.

The Economic and Social Committee

This committee advises the European Parliament, the Commission, and the Council. It consists of representatives of organisations of employers, of the employed, and of other parties representative of civil society, notably in socio-economic, civic, professional and cultural areas. Members are expected to work with complete independence. Members are selected by the Commission. The list is approved by the Council.

See article 32 and 386-392.

Education, Youth and Culture Council

This Council meets three or four times a year. It aims to develop "quality education" within the EU, implement vocational training policy and contribute to the "flowering of Member States' cultures, bringing the common cultural heritage to the fore."

It has done important work towards the mutual recognition of educational qualifications across the European Union. It supports the teaching of European languages, encourages the mobility of teachers and students across Europe, seeks to improve "vocational training with a view to facilitating the integration of their citizens into the labour market, their adaptation to industrial change and their possible vocational retraining." It also wants to stimulate artistic and literary creation.

Legislation decisions must be unanimous on cultural affairs but are otherwise taken by qualified majority voting and are subject to the support of the European Parliament - co-decision procedure.

See the *Council* above.

Employment, Social Policy, Health and Consumer Affairs Council

This Council meets around four times a year to discuss employment, social protection, consumer protection, health and equal opportunities. It aims to raise the standard of living and quality of life of its citizens, notably through high-quality jobs and high levels of social protection, health protection and protection of consumers' interests, while at the same time guaranteeing equal opportunities for all its citizens.

In these fields, decisions are taken with the European Parliament. The Council usually decides by qualified majority, under the co-decision procedure.[3] Social Security is an exception and decisions must be unanimous on this topic.

It adopts European rules to harmonise or co-ordinate national laws, in particular on working conditions including workers' health and safety (See *Euroterminology - Working time directive*), social security, employee participation in the running of companies, strengthening of national policies to prevent illness and combat the major health scourges and protection of consumers' rights.

Since employment and social protection polices remain the responsibility of the Member States, the Community's contribution is confined to setting common objectives for all the Member States, analysing measures taken at national level and making recommendations to the Member States.

Within the Council, and in particular in the framework of the Employment Committee and the Social Protection Committee, Member States can exchange ideas and information or share the results of their own experiences.

See the *Council* above.

Energy Council

See *Transport, Telecommunications and Energy Council* below.

Environment Council

This Council meets about four times a year. Its purpose is to guide the EU into policies that will ensure the wise use of finite and natural resources and protect the environment and human health in the long term. The Council works on the precautionary principle (see the *Euroterminology* chapter). It believes that it is better to prevent problems rather than try to solve problems after they have grown to major proportions, and that pollution should be prevented at source. Polluters should pay for the solution of the problems they create.

The Environment Council's legislation is passed only with the agreement of the European Parliament –

the co-decision procedure.

See *Major Issues – Energy and the Environment* and the *Council* above.

EU government

See Government of the European Union, below.

EURATOM

This is the EU organisation set up by the *EURATOM Treaty* of 1957. Its purpose was "to create the conditions necessary for the development of a powerful nuclear industry" (Preamble). It is dedicated to "the speedy establishment and growth of nuclear industries" (article 1). Its continuing existence and funding by the EU tax payer is in conflict with the Constitution's commitment to renewable energy.

See *Major Issues - Energy*, and Protocol 36.

Euro Army and Eurocorps

Officially there is no such thing as a Euro army, but for some time military forces belonging to individual member states have been at the disposal of the European Union. In 1990 an experimental Franco-German brigade was set up. In May 1992 a military force known as Eurocorps was proposed by Chancellor Kohl of Germany and President Mitterrand of France. With headquarters in Strasbourg the force was under the command of a German general. It was soon joined by forces from Belgium, Luxembourg and Spain and became operational in November 1995 with about 50,000 troops.

In December 1998 Tony Blair and Jack Chirac met at St Malo in France. They decided that "Europe must have the capacity for autonomous action, backed up by credible military forces, the means to decide to use them, and a readiness to do so." In Toulouse in May 1999 France and Germany agreed that the Eurocorps might become a Rapid Reaction Force. It was intended that it should act as an alternative to NATO when NATO, if prevented by the United States, was unwilling to take action that the European Union considered necessary. The plan was endorsed by the Helsinki Council in December 1999.

Initially sixty thousand troops from a number of EU countries were to make up the European Union Rapid Reaction Force. These troops were to be mission-ready within 60 days and able to be sent up to 2,500 miles to deal with "humanitarian crises, crisis management and peacekeeping." These purposes could become controversial since there may be grounds for dispute about whether troops in a region are "occupying enemy troops" or a genuine "peace-keeping force". Iraq provides an example of this sort of contentious issue.

In November 2000 the fifteen member states of the European Union committed themselves to supply 100,000 troops, 400 aircraft and 100 ships to the new European Defence Force. Britain's commitment was 24,000 troops, 72 combat aircraft and eighteen warships. The EU planned that the force should have an EU Military Staff Committee at Chiefs of Defence level, a military staff organisation (actually established on 11 June 2001), a strategic planning unit, a satellite centre, and an Institute of Security Studies. [4]

Although at the disposal of the European Union these troops are regarded as under the control of the individual states from which they come. The forces remain within their own countries until called for by the EU. They first saw action in a "police" mission in Bosnia in 2003 and peace-keeping in the former Yugoslav Republic of Macedonia. Three subsequent operations have been undertaken.

In April 2004 EU Defence Ministers agreed that by 2007 the EU should be able to use nine battle groups, each consisting of fifteen hundred troops deployable within two weeks. They signed up to the goal of greatly increasing their military hardware by purchasing transport planes, unmanned aircraft and precision guided missiles by 2010.[5]

Presumably these forces which are already acting together already train together. With a central command set up the natural progression is for this force to begin to exist as an independent unit away from its many home bases and so become a truly European Union Army.

See the discussion on defence in the *Major Issues* chapter, *Petersberg Tasks* in *Euroterminology* chapter, *Political and Security Committee* and *Western European Union* (below), *European Defence Agency* (above), and article 312.

Eurogroup

States of the European Union whose currency is the euro. Also, the committee formed of finance ministers from these states.

See *Economics and Financial Affairs Council.*

Eurobarometer

Since 1973 the Commission has been measuring and analysing trends in public opinion in all the member states and in the candidate countries. It believes that knowing what the general public thinks is important in helping it to draft its legislative proposals, take decisions and evaluate its work. Eurobarometer uses both opinion polls and focus groups. Its surveys lead to the publication of around 100 reports every year. For further information go to the Eurobarometer web site.[6]

Eurojust

Eurojust is the European Prosecution Agency, an organisation set up by the EU in 2002 to assist and encourage investigations of serious cross-border crime. It is a permanent network of judicial authorities. It hosts meetings of prosecutors and investigators dealing with specific types of crime or particular cases. It works with the European Judicial Network, Europol, and the European Anti Fraud Office (OLAF). It is based in the Hague.

See article 273 and the discussion under *Major Issues - Area of Freedom, Security and Justice.*

Euroland

The twenty-seven member states of the European Union.

Europa

The name of the EU's main official web site. http://europa.eu.int/
See *Sources of Information* chapter, for other EU web addresses.

European Central Bank

The purpose of the European Central Bank, together with national central banks, is to conduct the monetary policy of the eurozone within the Union. It aims to maintain price stability and support the general economic policies of the Union. The decision making body of the central bank is independent, so much so that no official or office holder of the EU may seek to influence it. MEPs are silenced. This effectively abolishes freedom of speech in regard to the activities of the bank, placing it above official and democratic criticism. It operates in its official language which is English.

See article 30, 326, 382,383, and *Major Issues – Charter of Fundamental Rights – Rights removed by the EU Constitution - Free speech).*

The European Community

This is a name for what was originally called the 'European Economic Community' (EEC), Also known as The Common Market. Since the *Maastricht Treaty* and now, with many new members, it is known as the European Union. People still talk of the European Community when they mean the European Union. They also talk of Community Law when they mean the law of the European Union.

The European Council

The European Council makes the major policy decisions of the European Union. It consists of the most senior politicians of the 27 states of the European Union: prime ministers or presidents. They are supported at its meetings by their Foreign Secretaries. The President of the Commission attends with one of his/her Vice-Presidents. The President of the European Council is the leader of the state which holds the presidency of the Council of Ministers. (States take turns to "hold the presidency." When they do this the ministers from the country holding the presidency chair the various permutations of the Council too.)

States hold the presidency for six months, but the Constitution would extend the period to two and a half years.

The European Council meets quarterly in Brussels unless there is a special need to meet more often. Its role is to guide the political direction and the priorities of the European Union. Generally decisions are by consensus. The European Council cannot pass laws.

In the last one and a half decades it has made momentous decisions including the writing and acceptance of a series of treaties which have furthered the integration of EU states (including the introduction of the euro). The convention established following the European Council's *Laeken Declaration* failed to deal adequately with the issues it raised, yet the European Council members readily accepted and signed the new European Constitution which the convention produced. The European Council is also responsible for the enlargement of the European Union with the admission of many new European States.

The sessions of the European Council take place in secret. The public is not admitted to its meetings and they are not televised. Verbatim records are not available to the public and minutes may possibly be obtained if a lengthy procedure is gone through.[7] A report of *Conclusions* is made available. These reports record points of agreement only.

The European Council is not to be confused with The Council (which is also known as the Council of the European Union or the Council of Ministers – see above.). Nor should the European Council be confused with the non-EU institution, The Council of Europe.

See articles 20-22, 24/4, 25, 27, 28, 29 and 341 (and *Euroterminology - Presidency* and *The Council of Europe*).

European Court of Justice

The Court of Justice of the European Union consists of the Court of Justice, the General Court and specialised courts. Its task is to ensure that European Union law is observed through the proper interpretation and application of EU treaties and laws. Once ratified the Constitution will replace the treaties as the basis for many decisions.

The ECJ has two principal functions:

- to check whether instruments of the European institutions and of governments are compatible with the Treaties;
- to give rulings, at the request of a national court, on the interpretation or the validity of provisions contained in Community law.

It rules on actions brought by a Member State, an institution or a natural or legal person.

It may also rule in other cases provided for in the Constitution. It will insist on the primacy of EU law over national laws and promote centralisation and integration because it has to be guided by existing treaties and, if ratified, the EU Constitution - which call for increasing integration and centralisation.

See articles 29, 325, 353-381 and *Major Issues.*

European Defence Agency

The EU organisation set up to advise EU states what weaponry they should buy to keep up with the latest technological developments in military hardware. It has the effect of promoting the arms industry. The agency's recommendations appear to be based on knowledge of the catalogue of the latest developments in weapons technology and not on the basis of careful assessments of threats and the military preparations needed to deal with perceived threats. The setting up of the Defence Agency will be authorised by the Constitution when/if it is ratified, but the organisation has been set up without waiting for this formality.

The European Defence Agency was established by a charter on 12 July 2004 without attracting much media attention. (Its founding document is not actually called a charter. It goes by the name of, *Council Joint Action 2004/551/CFSP* and can be found on the Europa web site.) It has Javier Solana, the current (June 2006) EU High Representative for the Common Foreign and Security Policy in charge. He is the link with the Council of Ministers. The European Defence Agency is answerable to the Council and has to work within guidelines set by the

Council. Its first year budget was set at 20,000,000 euros and it anticipated having a staff of seventy by early 2005. The "Steering Board" of the agency consists of appointees of each participating government plus a representative of the Commission. Twenty-four member states are involved: the exception is Denmark. The Defence Agency has set up four directorates to further certain aims. This move takes transparency and visibility one stage further away from the people of Europe. The citizens of Europe are not likely to know what they are discussing or what decisions they may be taking.

The budget for the agency does not come from general EU funding which might be examined by the European Parliament, but from direct payments by states, the amounts to be decided by the agency itself. Paragraph 8 of article 13 of its charter states, "Revenue shall consist of: (a) miscellaneous revenue; (b) contributions payable by the Member States participating in the Agency based on the gross national income (GNI) scale."

See Major Issues - Defence and Transparency. Also articles 41/3 and 311.

European External Action Service

This is a new bureaucracy to be set up by the Constitution, article 296, the EU's own Foreign Office. Before getting under way the European Parliament will be consulted and the Commission must give its consent.

European Investment Bank

This bank was set up as an EU institution under the *Treaty of Rome*. Its role is to finance capital investments which are EU defined priorities. Most money goes to help develop Europe's poorer regions. Significant borrowers include Italy, Britain, Spain and Portugal. It also provides development aid to states around the world especially in Africa. It is the largest borrower and lender on international financial markets.

European Parliament

This is the only democratically elected *international* body in the world, and the only directly elected EU institution. Parliament currently has 736 members. (The permitted maximum is 750.)

The European Parliament is significantly different from the parliaments of member states. Members are not elected to carry through policies spelt out in party programmes and the executive of the European Union is not drawn from their ranks. MEPs are elected as individuals and are required to act independently. However, once elected MEPs are encouraged to form political groupings and operate as groups within the parliament. But there is no "party in power" and no "opposition". MEPs cannot be elected to carry through a specific set of policies because by the parliament's own rules MEPs cannot receive a binding mandate, and in any case, they have no powers to initiate any policies. (Rule 2 of the Rules of Procedure of the European Parliament states, "Members of the European Parliament shall exercise their mandate independently. They shall not be bound by any instructions and shall not receive a binding mandate." The Commission, not the leaders of the winning political grouping in the European Parliament, initiates legislation in the EU.

The existence of the European parliament does not make the EU a democratic state. The best one can say of the European Parliament is that it provides some democratic influence or input into some important areas of EU decision making and can act as an important modifier or brake on legislation in many policy areas.

Its work is split between three cities: not conducive to convenient administration, or economic or environmentally sound use of resources. It meets as a parliament in Brussels and Strasbourg and has administrative offices in Luxembourg.

Each year the European Parliament meets as a full parliament for just 60 days - twelve four-day plenary sessions in Strasbourg and six additional two-day plenary sessions in Brussels. Each month it sets aside two weeks for meetings of parliamentary committees and inter-parliamentary delegations, meetings with Commissioners etc, and one week for political group meetings. Four weeks a year MEPs concentrate exclusively on constituency work.

There are currently seven parliamentary groups within the European Parliament. MEPs who do not belong to a parliamentary group are listed as independent (non inscrit). The number of groups may be about to change (2006). The British Conservative Party is negotiating the creation of a new grouping of members of the European Parliament committed to a more decentralised European Union with stronger links with America. Conservative leader, David Cameron, dislikes the federalist views of the European Peoples' Party (EPP) and wants to remove the 27 Conservative MEPs from this group. Some of these Conservative MEPs are hostile to this proposal and point out that they have a manifesto commitment to remain within the EPP grouping till 2009.

The broad policies of the European parliamentary groups are set out below.

In its earliest days Parliament was only a discussion forum, but now has some direct power in conjunction with the Council of Ministers on legislation and the EU budget, but most significantly it has no power to initiate laws or policies. It can veto the budget and the passing of laws in certain policy areas. On taxation and some other matters it may only give an opinion. It is a watchdog on the European Commission and has the ultimate right to dismiss it in its entirety.

MEPs can have considerable influence on much of the EU's legislation. They may also influence the Commission or Council in informal meetings and by putting questions at question time, or asking for written answers. They can also petition the Commission and/or Council with what is called a "declaration" which is similar to an Early Day Motion in the British parliament and is open for signature by all MEPs. Any MEPs may suggest amendments and speak on any matter relating to any text before a committee, ask questions, and raise points of order.

There are twenty-five standing (permanent) committees (details below) where Commission proposals for legislation are examined prior to presentation to the whole parliament. Each committee appoints a rapporteur to draw up a report on it, setting out recommended amendments. Groups of MEPs band together to promote special concerns in what are called inter-groups. When reports are agreed they are placed before the whole parliament.

If the report is accepted by the Parliament it passes to the Council and Commission for consideration. When considering legislation one of four different procedures will apply which controls how many times a proposal is examined and voted on. The influence of the EU Parliament varies according to which procedure applies to a particular issue.

Constituents may have direct contact with their MEPs to express their wishes and put their concerns.

See *European Parliament standing committees* and *European Parliament political groups,* below, *EU Decision-makers - European Parliament. See also Major Issues – Democratic Deficit*, article 20, and *Euroterminology - Brussels, Strasbourg* and *Luxembourg.*

European Parliament political groups

Members of the European Parliament all have political agendas and philosophies which they seek to apply to proposals put before them and which they seek to promote when they have contact with decision-makers. They were elected as members of dozens of political parties across the EU but in order to bring some coherence to their activities they come together to work in seven political groups. Under the parliament's rules of procedure each of these political groups is funded by Parliament to equip itself with a secretariat appointed by the group. Each political group is allocated a share of speaking time in plenary sessions in proportion to the size of the group. Similarly each group is allocated a proportionate share of posts within parliament – for example, committee chair-persons, vice presidents, rapporteurs. The MEPs who do not join a recognised group are regarded as independents or non-attached MEPs and are known as non-inscrits (NI). They, too, receive a budget to fund a secretariat.

Often the parties within the seven groups have programmes which vary significantly at times from the general programmes outlined in the following pages. Two of the groups are particularly large and tend to dominate parliament

European People's Party and the European Democrats

The largest group is the EPP-ED, the European People's Party (Christian Democrats) and the European Democrats with 266 members. These are centre-right-wing parties and include the British Conservatives.

The EPP-ED say that all their member parties:

> "work together to resist the political priorities of the left in Europe and to advance the goal of a more competitive and democratic Europe, closer to its citizens."

Since the left also claim to want a more democratic Europe closer to its citizens readers will have to judge for themselves which side seems more committed to these popular aims. The EPP-ED proclaim their belief in an EU based on:

> "the primacy of law and respect for fundamental rights, on the application of the principle of subsidiarity and an efficient sharing out of power, and on independent democratic institutions, in order to ensure that future progress serves the common interest of all Europeans. As members of the EPP-ED Group, we believe in a Europe of values, united, open, more humane and embracing diversity.
>
> We want a Europe which creates opportunity and wealth within a single market, competitive at world level, and which at the same time promotes the

well-being of everybody, not only in Europe, but also in the rest of the world, in accordance with the principle of sustainable development."

The EPP-ED have stated their priorities for the current parliamentary session until 2009.
These include:

- "making the EU more competitive by concentrating on knowledge, tele-communications and technology-based activities, and making qualitatively superior products
- investing far more in research, encouraging innovation and individual motivation
- developing education and life-long learning
- implementing the Lisbon strategy
- encouraging entrepreneurship and reducing regulations
- having more flexible labour laws and lower, simpler taxation
- developing transport networks
- promoting subsidiarity/local responsibility in regional development
- promoting clean energy, renewable energy and developing nuclear energy
- encouraging higher birth rates
- improving agriculture, the quality of food, and sustainable fisheries
- combating terrorism, illegal immigration and international crime
- preserving peace, security, common values, respect for human rights and the rule of law
- eventually integrating the countries of Southeast Europe into the EU and increasing co-operation with the Ukraine, Moldova, Belarus and Russia
- developing transatlantic ties
- developing EU military capacities
- developing a European defence policy
- achieving the eradication of poverty everywhere
- developing global trade which is also fair
- making the WTO more accountable
- eradicating fraud and financial mismanagement within the EU."

Party of European Socialists

The second largest group is the PES - Party of European Socialists – with 201 members - a centre-left grouping which includes British Labour MEPs and the German SPD (Socialist Democratic Party) MEPs.

According to the PES manifesto for the 2004 election the PES has five priorities:

- Boost Europe's growth, fight poverty and create more and better jobs;
- Bring the European Union closer to its citizens;
- Manage migration and pursue social integration;
- Build a more secure, sustainable, peaceful and just world;
- Promote Europe as an area of democracy and equality.

They stated that "three principles should guide us in the achievement of our manifesto commitments and shape what Europe delivers to its citizens in this political term. These principles are prosperity; equality; solidarity."

The development of greater employment through increased growth based on sustainable energy sources and greater use of renewables is a major aim. The PDS favours "affordable, accessible and high quality public services." It aims to advance equality – especially between men and women and to combat violence against women and children and human trafficking

The PES web site includes the following statements:

> "Europe suffers from persistently low growth, which jeopardises the social democratic aim of full employment, higher living standards and high quality public services. EU enlargement has now made Europe into the largest economy in the world. This must now be used to the advantage of each of our economies.
>
> EU member states are of a Single Market that has generated a high degree of economic interdependence and prosperity. We have the tools at our disposal to use this economic interdependence for the creation of more and better jobs as well as raising our actual and potential growth. . .
>
> As a world region, Europe must face up to the challenge of climate change through the gradual shift towards sustainable energy sources. The move towards renewable energy is an imperative and should take place through a strong and consistent commitment to achieving clearly-defined targets.
>
> If Europe is to be prosperous in the long-term, growth, investment and sustainability must be mutually reinforcing."

In the aim of creating sustainable prosperity within Europe, the PES calls for:

- "A multi-annual European Growth and Investment Strategy for more and better jobs. One of the challenges facing the European Union is how to increase the means for research, innovation and training.
- A common effort of member states and European institutions for the dou-bling of the target for renewable energy. . .

> The PES Election Manifesto expressed our commitment to strengthen the European Social Model and defend workers' rights by reinforcing European social legislation as well to ensure affordable, accessible and high-quality public services.
>
> Services of general interest, essential as they are to the wellbeing of all citizens, are central to the values and objectives of social democracy. These services - including health, education, social care – are the foundations for social cohesion and equality of opportunity within our societies.
>
> In light of the current drive for an internal market in services, the PES wishes to ensure that the appropriate legal framework is established for services of general interest in the European Union. The PES is committed to protecting the special values and features of public services - including universal service obligations, guaranteed quality and continuity of service, consumer rights and affordability. The PES will reflect on and consult on the best ways of ensuring that these special values are preserved."

The Alliance of Liberals and Democrats for Europe

The ALDE group, the Alliance of Liberals and Democrats for Europe, has 89 members. They campaigned for a Yes vote to the proposed EU Constitution believing that "it builds liberty, democracy and security across our continent, and helps Europe to stand on its own feet in world affairs." By mid 2006 their position had changed. Neil Corlett, their spokesperson, said "We still support some form of constitutional text but an improved one that is hopefully much shorter and clearer as we believe that the current text has run its course in terms of ratification."[8]

This is their views on the European Union:

> "Individually the countries of Europe are too small to guarantee their peoples' security and welfare. The choice they face is to try and hold out in defence of a scale of things that no longer matches the times, or to pool their resources within the larger, stronger, more competitive entity that is the European Union. For the EU Member States there can be no future without Europe and no future outside Europe. Only by joining forces can we defend and uphold our values, both within the Union and beyond its boundaries, furthering our common and more specific interests and taking up the global challenges together – proactively, not reactively.
>
> Europe must be built not only as a Union of States based on diplomacy, but also by a democratic community of peoples.
>
> We are committed to unlocking the potential of our Union, by building on the fundamental principles of freedom, democracy, solidarity, the rule of law, respect for human rights, free enterprise and equal opportunities.
>
> *First, by promoting peace, through a Union in the federal tradition that respects our diverse cultural, local and linguistic identities, and is open to all European States which comply with the criteria for membership.*
>
> A Union that can finally vote with a qualified majority system in order to fully exercise the European sovereignty in compliance with the principle of subsidiarity.
>
> The ratification and entry into force of the European Constitution is in this respect essential.
>
> *Second, by making the EU a global player bridging the gap between its economic and political dimension: Europe must speak with one voice in world affairs.*
>
> This is why we fully support a Common Foreign and Security Policy which aims to promote a new era of peace, democracy and security, notably in the Mediterranean area.
>
> To this end, the perspective of a hard core in defence policy should be supported within an effective multilateral framework.
>
> Finally, the EU's leverage in international trade and financial frameworks should be extended.
>
> *Third, by opening up, democratising, making more accountable and strengthening the institutions of the European Union, also by identifying forms of participation and dialogue able to bring into the European debate those who at the moment feel excluded.*
>
> To this end, media pluralism is crucial. Furthermore, to foster common European experiences and the sense of belonging to a single continent-wide commu-

nity, language training and exchange among students, trainees and volunteers should be stimulated.

Fourth, since Europe is a union of minorities, by guaranteeing the fundamental rights of all European citizens and removing all forms of discrimination.

In our common fight against international crime and terrorism, we will always remain vigilant against any erosion of personal freedom. A Europe of security and justice for all is also a Europe that extends these rights to those who justly seek asylum or a new life here. To that effect, the Union needs to strengthen protection of the common external borders and to harmonise asylum policy. Europe has to develop a common strategy to manage legal immigration and coordinate action against illegal immigration, and to firmly combat any form of racism and xenophobia within Europe. The protection of minorities is the essence of democracy.

The Area of Freedom, Security and Justice should be deepened. Intercultural dialogue should be promoted and deepened further.

Fifth, believing that the aim of society must be the self-fulfilment of each individual, by promoting education at all levels.

Support for scientists and researchers, technology transfer, investments in information, eco-friendly technologies and R&D networks on a European basis are essential.

Sixth, by strengthening economic governance after the introduction of the Euro.

A common economic policy must aim to create prosperity, competitiveness and jobs, and keep the European social model viable, by modernising the European economy and fostering an innovative society. In this framework, we must reform Europe's economy to secure a stable and competitive climate for businesses to invest in innovation and create jobs, to facilitate labour mobility, and to achieve a real single and liberalised market.

An effective single market implies also the reduction of the bureaucratic impact of its implementation.

Seventh, by ensuring value for money for taxpayers, rooting out fraud wherever it is found, tackling unnecessary bureaucracy; by reforming the system of own resources to make it more transparent, progressive and fair.

Eighth, by making Europe the world leader in environmental protection.

This means seeking common solutions to our common environmental, public health problems, consumers protection and food safety. Europe must commit to cleaner, safer forms of energy and embrace renewable resource use. The Union should work for the achievement of the targets set out in the Kyoto Protocol for reductions in greenhouse gas emissions and for the launch of a follow-up to Kyoto.

Environmental and security policies should lay at the core of the Union's co-operation with its neighbours.

Ninth, by making globalisation work for everyone.

We recognise that globalisation has had together with positive effects also some negative ones. To overcome the negative effects, Europe must promote sustainable development through a more generous and targeted aid policy, and must give through the multilateral trading system the world's poorest nations access to our markets to escape the poverty trap.

Tenth, by ensuring a full recognition and enhancement of the role of Europe's regions, particularly those with legislative powers, and by building a structural policy which develops the potential of Europe's most needy regions.

EU resources should be used to mobilise additional investments, and cohesion funds should be focused on the poorest regions. The Union cannot afford that any of its region lags behind.

For a balanced development at home and abroad, it is necessary to rethink and reform the Union's Common Agricultural Policy.

The European Union's achievements to date are impressive - half a century of peace, prosperity and stability; instead of fighting each other, Europe's nations harness their collective genius and goodwill to a common enterprise and provide opportunity for our citizens. . .

United, our alliance of Liberals and Democrats is committed to realizing the dream of a political and democratic Union for our unified continent."

Greens/European Free Alliance

The EGP/EFA has 42 members in the European Parliament.
They state their key aims as to:

"Build a society respectful of fundamental human rights and environmental justice: the rights to self-determination, to shelter, to good health, to education, to culture, and to a high quality of life;
Increase freedom within the world of work, not only by tackling unemployment but also by widening people's choices, releasing human creative potential;
Deepen democracy by decentralisation and direct participation of people in decision-making that concerns them, and by enhancing openness of government in Council and Commission, and making the Commission fully answerable to Parliament;
Build a European Union of free peoples based on the principle of subsidiarity who believe in solidarity with each other and all the peoples of the world;
Re-orientate the European Union, which currently over-emphasises its economic conception at the expense of social, cultural and ecological values."

The Greens/European Free Alliance state that they are working for :

"Economic and social reforms to make development sustainable for both human beings and the natural world;
A democratic process linking trade, security, economic and social issues to environmental, cultural and democratic rights;
High ecological, social and democratic standards to ensure the quality of life;
Solidarity, guaranteed human and citizen's rights for everybody, including people who have come from non-EU countries;
A foreign policy designed to resolve problems by peaceful means rather than by military force;

Improved structures for democratic participation in political decision-making, involving NGOs, Trade Unions, citizens and civic authorities at all levels, with measures to ensure equal participation of women;
Guaranteed equal rights and opportunities, as well as cultural and linguistic diversity;
A policy of employment and redistribution of work with special attention to gender issues, in order to end the existing unbalanced division of labour and share the workload more fairly between women and men, ensuring that women are fully able to take part in the formal labour market as well as in political life.
Each Party in the Group reserves the right to interpret the common principles in the light of its own specific manifesto commitments."

The Confederal Group of the European United Left and the Nordic Green Left

The EUL/NGL (sometimes written as GUE/NGL) has 41 members in the European Parliament. The group describes its composition this way:

> "The group now combines two subgroups: the European United Left and the Nordic Green Left. . . The membership represents 16 different European communist, left and socialist parties. In terms of size the German (Linkspartei. PDS) and Italian national delegations are most important with seven MEPs respectively, followed by the Czech delegation with six MEPs. Other delegations vary between one and four MEPs. The Group also has four associate member parties, two of which are from non-EU member states Norway and Switzerland. This diversity can lead to different approaches over some questions. For the group it is important that each component party retains its own identity and policies while pooling their efforts in pursuit of common political objectives."

The group describes itself as "a forum for co-operation betweenleft-wing parties." The Group seeks to build "Another Europe: a social, peaceful, democratic, feminist, ecological Europe in solidarity with all the peoples of the world."

The chairman of the group is French Communist Francis Wurtz, who says:

> "The European Union and the European Parliament has long been criticised for its remoteness from the citizen. Part of this is due to language and distance but much of it is institutional and political. It is vital that those of us on the left, with a vision of a different Europe - for growth and employment, solidarity and high social standards, openness and democracy, fairness in our dealings with the developing countries and respect for the global environment - get our message across that Europe can, and must be, about something other than cutbacks and unemployment. In an increasingly interdependent world, Europe, with the right political will, has the capacity to change the circumstances of ordinary people for the better."

He also thinks Europe can play an essential role in the international arena, contributing to the building of bridges between civilisations.

> "But to enable such an ambition to become credible would imply breaking free from those who, while behaving as masters of the world, are actually

leading it to the brink of the clash. And it also implies the implementation of the same international law in all states, without exception, particularly in the Middle East - an open wound, and an endless source of the poison of despair."

This group is:

"firmly committed to European integration, although in a different form from the existing model. We want to see integration based on fully democratic institutions with a priority commitment to ensuring a new model of development aimed at tackling the most serious issues facing us. For us, these are: large-scale and increasing unemployment; ensuring respect for the environment; creating a common social area that provides equal rights at the highest level for all citizens; and, meeting the needs of those who are forced by poverty in their countries of origin (for which Europe bears a heavy responsibility) to seek their livelihood in the Union. We want a Europe that operates on a basis of complete solidarity in order to bring ever closer the real parameters of the economies of each Member State and, accordingly, we oppose the efforts of the most powerful countries to impose their policies on everyone else.

We want to see a different Europe, without the democratic deficit and free from the neo-liberal monetarist policies that go with it. . .

In order to deepen its ties of friendship, solidarity and co-operation with the other countries of Europe, the Union should strive to strengthen the OSCE, where instruments should be developed capable of addressing problems of joint security, while disbanding all those structures which, like NATO and the WEU, are a hangover from the political blocs of the Cold War. A secure peace cannot be guaranteed by military instruments but rather by ensuring that democracy gains a firm hold throughout the world and, above all, by reducing the huge gap separating the 'centre' from the 'periphery' , which is the main cause of instability and excessive concentrations of power, as well as large-scale migration, racism and xenophobia. With this in view, it is vital that the European Union correct its Eurocentric approach and its current model of development (which will only serve to increase disparities and results in serious environmental, social and political risks) and develop a policy in all international fora aimed at reforming all those international financial and political institutions which were founded in the 1950s and have today become inadequate and biased spokesmen for themselves, rather than representative of, all the peoples of the Earth. In so doing, emphasis should be placed on mutual efforts to achieve a balance between everyone's common concerns, rather than the current tendency to seek to bring the South in line with the North."

Union for a Europe of Nations

The UEN has 30 members in the European Parliament. They oppose the idea of ever increasing integration, ever increasing Federalism and want to see a Europe of freely co-operating independent states.

They state that their value is derived from respect for the individual as the basis of European civilisation. Their commitment is to liberty, Solidarity and equality between individuals, and human rights. For their tradition, sovereignty, democracy and the identities of European peoples are important.

UEN seeks to protect the vulnerable, the environment, traditional ways of life; it seeks to promote equal opportunities in education; values the family as the basic unit of society; believes in the sanctity of life and opposes the exclusively materialistic concept of society.

UEN supports the single market, workers' rights, the UN, and NATO, OSCE, generosity towards developing nations and co-operation with America on shared international problems.

The Independence/Democracy Group

This grouping, the IND/DEM group, with 29 MEPs, was set up in July 2004. Its members are united in opposing the European Constitution and this is their main goal. The group incorporates EU critics, eurosceptics and "eurorealists". The group opposes all forms of centralisation. Some members of the group, including the United Kingdom Independence Party, advocate the complete withdrawal of their country from the EU.

The independence/democracy group supports democracy, transparency and the sovereign independence of Nations co-operating freely together. On 18 October 2005 they issued the following seven point statement:

> "The Independence and Democracy Group of Members of the European Parliament considers the Constitution for Europe legally dead and shall resist any attempts at imposing such projects, as a whole or piecemeal, upon sovereign countries. In accordance with the political principles of freedom, democracy, and respect of national differences enshrined in the IND/DEM Constitutive Charter of 20 July 2004, we:
>
> 1 Call on the EU Member States to take advantage of the rejection of the Constitution for Europe to develop a new basis for transparent, democratic and accountable co-operation between sovereign countries to be approved by national referendums where appropriate;
> 2 Respect the right of individual Member States to withdraw from the European Union and support the right not to participate in any of its ventures such as the Euro-zone, and establish alternative, friendly relationships.
> 3 Advise other Member States and their citizens to reclaim their full rights and competencies in accordance with their national constitutions;
> 4 Reject any obligatory EU foreign, border and judicial policy and any other EU jurisdiction in areas of Member States' sovereignty;
> 5 Stress the need for a fair and open debate without preordained conclusions about the future of the EU within each Member State, and oppose the misuse of Member States' financial contribution to the European Union's budget for one-sided institutional propaganda;
> 6 Oppose attempts to centralise powers at the EU level;
> 7 Insist on involvement of voters and national parliaments in all stages of the legislative process, and oppose any legislation by non-elected bureaucrats."

Non-attached members/Independents

There are 37 non-attached (NI) MEPs. They are mostly politicians from the far right and include the Austrian Freedom Party, the French National Front, and the Democratic Unionist Party (Northern Ireland and UK). There are also two leftwing Socialist MEPs.

European Parliament Standing Committees

The European Parliament has twenty-three standing (or permanent) committees. Their task is to consider proposals for new legislation put forward by the Commission. Each committee appoints one of its members to write a report on the findings of the committee. (This person is known as the rapporteur.) A committee consists of between 37 and 171 MEPs (March 2007), and has a chair, a bureau and a secretariat. The political make-up of the committees reflects that of the plenary assembly.

The permanent committees are: Foreign Affairs, Development, International Trade, Budgets, Budgetary Control, Economic and Monetary Affairs, Employment and Social Affairs, Environment, Public Health and Food Safety, Industry, Research and Energy, Internal Market and Consumer Protection, Transport and Tourism, Regional Development, Agriculture and Rural Development, Fisheries, Culture and Education, Legal Affairs, Civil Liberties, Justice and Home Affairs, Constitutional Affairs, Women's Rights and Gender Equality, Petitions, Human Rights, and Security and Defence.

Other committees are set up to deal with special topics as they arise. For example, the collapse of the Equitable Life Assurance Society, and the alleged use of European countries by the CIA for the transport and illegal detention of prisoners.

These committees are subjected to lobbying and they carry out consultations. They decide on amendments which they consider are necessary in proposed legislation. Finally their reports are submitted to the European Parliament for consideration and voting. They hold their meetings in public.

European Security and Intelligence Force

This was planned at the European Council held in Feira, Portugal, in June 2000. The force was to consist of five thousand well-armed police, able to carry out actions in support of global peacekeeping missions as well as intelligence gathering and enforcing public order within the EU - capable of carrying out "preventative and repressive actions." It would be under the control of the Political and Security Committee, while effective operational control will be in the hands of the High Representative. It was considered that it would require a pool of more than 15,000 men committed and trained for service with the force. It saw action in Bosnia and Herzegovina starting January 2003. There is no public access to documents relating to the functioning of this force.

European Space Agency

The European Space agency is nominally an independent organisation but its links with the EU are very strong.

It is funded by seventeen states - two of which are not members of the EU - Norway and Switzerland. The other members are Austria, Belgium, Denmark, Finland, France, Germany, Greece, Ireland, Italy, Luxembourg, the Netherlands, Portugal, Spain, Sweden, and the United Kingdom. In addition, Canada, Hungary and the Czech republic are involved in some space projects.

The financial contributions of member states are assessed as a percentage of gross national product. The budget for 2005 was 2,977 million euros (approximately £2084 million). The space agency tries to invest in work in each of its member states, spending an amount similar to each state's financial contribution. The agency has a staff of approximately 1,900 people and has its headquarters in Paris.

Its purpose is to develop knowledge of space, the earth and its environment, and develop rocketry (the Ariane system), satellite based technology - including satellites for security, surveillance, telecommunications, broadcasting, navigation, meteorology, and military surveillance and control. The European Space Agency developed the Giotto space laboratory which studied Halley's Comet, and (with NASA) the Hubble Space Telescope.

In Kazakhstan, on 28 December, 2005, the European Space Agency launched the first satellite in the Galileo programme. This satellite was designed and built by Surrey Satellite Technology Limited in the UK in just three years. There will be 30 Galileo satellites in orbit within a few years. They will create a global positioning system of greater accuracy than the American GPS which is freely available to the world, courtesy of the Pentagon, and currently provides satellite navigation. In time, the Galileo system will be able to pinpoint objects to within a few centimetres and, for example, monitor the location of every car and mobile phone in the UK. The entire Galileo project is anticipated to cost £2.52 billion.

The work of the space agency is dependant on its backers who are almost entirely EU states who doubtless work with the approval of their electorates and parliaments. In addition the space agency works out its programme in conjunction with the EU. The European Space Agency and the European Union have together worked out a joint European strategy which was initiated on 2 December 1999 by a resolution of the Council of Ministers. This was followed up with the adoption of a "common strategy for space" document on 16 November 2000. The Commission has drawn up an action programme for "global monitoring for environment and security."

The European Space agency now operates under a framework agreement for joint co-operation which was endorsed by the Council of Ministers on 2 October 2003.

Whether funding comes through the EU, or from European states directly, almost all funding for the European Space programme comes from European tax payers.

European Union

The European Union is an association of 27 European states (2007). Bulgaria and Romania joined on 1 January 2007. The applications of Croatia, FYR Macedonia, and Turkey are under consideration. Switzerland and Norway, and other states created by the break-up of Yugoslavia may well join in due course.

The European Union is a partly-evolved supranational state which passes laws and controls the operation of businesses, institutions and citizens in many areas of economic activity and daily life.

It began with 6 member countries in 1952 who, after the horrors of the Second World War, wanted to work together in peace to develop their mutual prosperity through practical co-operation. They set up a supranational organisation to run their steel and coal production. At that time the organisation was known as the European Coal and Steel Community. In 1958 it became the European Economic Community, also known as the Common Market. At the same time the European Atomic Energy Community was also established. In 1967 the three founding organisations were merged to form the European Community. In 1994 the European Community was renamed the European Union.

It operates according to rules set out in treaties which have been agreed over a period of over half a century. These treaties were due to be replaced by a Constitution which was signed by heads of member states in Rome in October 2004. Almost all the provisions of the Constitution are a restatement of the provisions of the treaties but there are a number of significant developments too. The ratification process of the Constitution has come to a halt.

European Union Military Committee

This high level committee advises and makes recommendations to the Political and Security Committee. It is composed of the Chiefs of Defence of member states represented by their military delegates.

European Union Military Staff

Military experts seconded to the Council Secretariat by member states.

Europol

European law enforcement agency. See articles 275-277 and *Major Issues – Europol.*

Eurostat

Eurostat is the European Union's statistical office, based in Luxembourg, which compiles statistics on trade, employment, agriculture, energy etc. The statistics are mainly supplied by member states. Eurostat's statistics are available on the internet and in an annual *Yearbook.*

Foreign Affairs Council

In EU documents this is usually called the General Affairs Council (see below) or the Council.

The General Affairs Council - also known as the Foreign Affairs Council or the General Affairs and External Relations Council (GAEC)

Three names for this "Council" may lead to confusion. The names used for it in the Constitution are The General Affairs Council, the Foreign Affairs Council or (frequently) just the Council.

This is the senior Council of the European Union. Since June 2002 it has met once a month in either of two configurations to deal with two major policy areas. It is, therefore, two Councils and it would be helpful if EU documents would consistently use the names which seem to be in use by these Councils themselves.

1 The General Affairs Council and
2 The External Relations Council.

The two Councils work closely with the Commission. Their work is prepared by COREPER (see above). The personnel attending vary according to the purpose of the Council. However, they would both include the Foreign Secretary who was currently the President of the Council of Ministers, the President of the Commission, and the High Representative for the Common Foreign and Security Policy. Other members of these Councils are indicated below.

The General Affairs Council

This Council (attended primarily by Foreign Ministers of EU states) deals with matters that affect more than one of the Union's policies, especially when urgent problems arise, and it co-ordinates the work of all other Councils of Ministers. It would deal with matters such as negotiations on EU enlargement, preparation of the Union's multi-annual budget or institutional and administrative issues. It prepares work for meetings of the European Council, follows up on decisions of the European Council and deals with any matter that the European Council may delegate to it.

The External Action Council (or Foreign Affairs Council)

For Foreign Affairs/External Relations the Foreign Ministers of the member states of the EU plus the External Affairs Commissioner attend. If the agenda requires it Defence Ministers or ministers responsible for Development or Trade will also attend. The names of the Council are changed to suit the emphasis of the work in hand. These Councils operate with a core of Foreign Ministers.

This Council deals with the European Union's relationships with other countries: Foreign Policy, Security/Defence policy, Military Action, Foreign Trade and Development issues. A key figure in this Council and the General affairs Council is the Secretary General of the Council/the High Representative for the Common Foreign and Security Policy. He plays a lead role in formulating policy and seeing it through. This Council decides on joint action and agrees policies ("common positions"). It normally takes decisions by unanimity but see *Euro-terminology - Unanimity*. The Political and Security Committee makes policy proposals to this council. It would be this obscure committee which would take charge in what is termed crisis management situations including a war involving the European Union. See *Political and Security Committee.*

The Foreign Affairs Council directs the Commission in trade negotiations in consultation with Article 133 Committee. In some trade areas, such as investments and the provision of services, member states and the Union have responsibility in trade negotiations. (The Commission represents the EU in trade dispute negotiations at the WTO.)

The Foreign Affairs/External Action Council is involved in development co-operation. In this area its work is aimed at "complementing the development policies pursued by the Member States. Its main objectives are the sustainable economic and social development of developing countries, in particular that of the most disadvantaged amongst them, as well as the smooth and gradual integration of developing countries into the world economy and the eradication of poverty in those countries. At the same time, Community policy on development co-operation is aimed at reinforcing democracy and the rule of law, and promoting respect for human rights and fundamental freedoms." It is particularly involved with African, Caribbean and Pacific (ACP) States.

If the Constitution is ratified a new role would be created, that of Union Minister for Foreign Affairs. The Minister for Foreign Affairs would represent the European Union in most international negotiations where the European Council had agreed on a common foreign policy. He/she would be elected by a qualified majority vote of the European Council with the agreement of the President of the Commission (article 28). He or she would also be a Vice-President of the Commission. The Minister for Foreign Affairs would replace the previous roles of High Representative for the Common Foreign and Security Policy and the Commissioner for External Relations.

Government of the European Union

Officially, there is no European government. But the EU has power. It collects taxes, distributes funds, passes laws, takes decisions about economic and social policies directly affecting almost half a billion people, enters into international agreements, has eurocitizens, a europassport, a euroflag, a europolice-force, a euroarmy, a euroforeignpolicy, a eurocurrency, a central bank, a supreme court, and a euroanthem, but the power that controls all this is, dispersed, obscured amongst a variety of institutions and bodies according to complex rules.

Power is shared in varying ways by different elements within the EU: the Commission, the European Council, the various permutations of the Council of Ministers, the European Parliament, COREPER, the European Central Bank, and the European Court of Justice. For the EU citizen his or her attempt to know what is going on or who to hold responsible for anything the EU does is soundly frustrated. The EU government is invisible and elusive rather than transparent and accountable.

Eventually, if powers are not returned to member states, a visible and democratic EU government may be formed from members of the winning Europarty in a euroelection – if europarties ever become established (as envisaged in the *Nice Treaty*). Some say the real government of Europe is already the Commission others point to the Council or the European Council.

See *Democratic Deficit*, *European Union by stealth*, *Transparency*, and *Clear use of language* in *Major Issues* chapter and *Brussels* in *Euroterminology* chapter.

Justice and Home Affairs Council

This Council's task is the implementation of co-operation and common policies in justice and home affairs. Its concerns include border controls, asylum, immigration, the free movement of people within the EU, visas, international crime including trafficking, police co-operation, Europol, the *Schengen Agreement*, and data gathering on EU citizens.

Britain and Ireland do not subscribe to the Schengen rules on free movement of persons, external border controls and visa policy. As a result their representatives do not vote on matters related to Schengen in the Council.

Most matters in this field are decided by unanimity after consultation with the European Parliament. Others are decided by qualified majority voting in consultation or in co-decision with the European Parliament.

National parliaments/governments

Under the Constitution, if it is ratified, national parliaments will hand over more of their decision-making power to the EU, chiefly the European Council, the many variations of the Council, the Commission, the European Central Bank, the European court of Justice and COREPER.

In the areas of exclusive competencies only the European Union may pass laws and the role of member states is either to accept directly the EU legislation or, under the direction of the EU, to enact laws to achieve exactly the EU requirement.

In the open ended list of shared competences member state governments may only pass laws where the EU has decided not to take action.

Decisions within the EU are supposed to be taken at the lowest possible level, but under the subsidiarity regulation set out in Protocol 2 of the Constitution the EU starts with the assumption that the highest level is the right one. The Commission remains the principle originator of legislation and other institutions within the EU have the right to initiate action. Article 3 of the Protocol permits initiatives from a group of member states.

National parliaments have the right to argue that they, rather than the EU, should act when a piece of legislation in an area of "shared competence" is put forward. They are allowed six weeks following the presentation of a law or ruling by the Commission (even if they are absent on ten weeks' summer holiday) to present their case. The final decision on such a matter rests with the EU not the elected national parliaments.

Member states are required by the European Union to consult the European Central Bank before enacting any regulation connected with monetary policy. (Article 30/5.)

Parliaments have a formal role in looking at EU regulation and activity and evaluating the work of Europol and Eurojust. See articles 42, 260, and 259.

See *Major Issues – Subsidiarity,* and *Democratic deficit.*

OLAF – The European Anti-Fraud Office

A European Anti-Fraud Office was set up in June 1999, "to protect the interests of the European Union, to fight fraud, corruption and any other irregular activity, including misconduct within the European Institutions." Fraud is a big problem in the EU. You are encouraged to report anything you know about the mis-use of EU funds.

A free phone provides the opportunity for getting in touch free of charge with OLAF via all the Member States, in order to give information of interest to the Office.

Freephone numbers to report EU fraud

Austria: 0800 295 845

Belgium: 0800 1 24 26

Cyprus: 00800 01 05 20 04

Czech Republic: 00800 01 05 20 04

Denmark: 800 18 495

Estonia: 00800 01 05 20 04

Finland: 0800 112 595

France: 0800 917 295

Germany: 0800 182 0595

Greece: 00800 321 2595

Hungary : 00800 01 05 20 04

Ireland: 1 800 553 295

Italy: 800 878 495

Latvia: 00800 01 05 20 04

Lithuania: 00800 01 05 20 04

Luxembourg: 0800 35 95

Malta: 00800 01 05 20 04

Netherlands: 0800 02 245 95

Poland: 00800 01 05 20 04

Portugal: 0800 832 595

Romania: 0800 895 133

Slovakia: 00800 01 05 20 04

Slovenia: 9900 800 01 05 20 04

Spain: 900 993 295

Sweden: 02 079 1695

United Kingdom: 0800 963 595

(Numbers are from European Commission Anti-Fraud Office, 1 November 2006)

Ombudsman - The European Ombudsman - Head of EU Complaints Department

The Ombudsman is elected by the European Parliament. He or she is responsible for receiving, investigating and reporting on complaints from citizens and organisations about maladministration of all EU bodies. The present holder of the office, Jacob Soderman, has dealt with over 11,000 complaints. By 2002 complaints were arriving at the rate of over 2000 per year. He has published an account of the results he has achieved. See articles 49 and 335.

It is the task of the EU Parliament to investigate allegations of fraud (article 193 of the *Treaty Establishing the European Community* – as consolidated by the *Nice Treaty* – also the proposed Constitution, article 333). The Commission also has an office to deal with problems of fraud. See *OLAF* above.

Parliament

See European Parliament.

Political and Security Committee

This powerful committee is referred to in article 307. It does not appear in the Constitution's list of European institutions, yet in certain circumstances this committee could play a major role in European affairs. It could be in charge of a European war if Europe goes to war. It controls the Euroarmy and is assisted by a military committee with 140 members. In a war situation or at times when Europe's civilian or military forces are in operation in third countries this committee will exercise "political control and the strategic direction of the crisis management, operations." (Articles 307 and 309.) In the meantime its task, in addition to supervising the Rapid Reaction Force, is to keep a watch on international developments and offer advice, especially to the Foreign Affairs Council.

The committee was introduced by the *Maastricht Treaty* (article J8 which was later renumbered 25) and made its appearance in 2000. It meets as part of COREPER a minimum of twice weekly and consists of unelected permanent representatives of member states at the senior/ambassadorial level. It will be answerable to the EU Minister for Foreign Affairs (currently the High Representative for Common Foreign and Security Policy) and the Council. The Commission is involved in its work and is represented at its meetings.

Political parties (groupings) in the European Parliament

See Decision Makers – European Parliament

Rapid Reaction Force

Originally set up with 60,000 troops from EU nations that can be deployed at short notice.

See Euro army.

Special Committee on Agriculture

This was established at the beginning of the 1960s to deal with the highly technical nature of questions concerning agricultural markets and rural development. It prepares proposals for the Agriculture and Fisheries Council and works as part of COREPER.

Transport, Telecommunications and Energy Council

This so-called single Council is, in reality, three since it meets with three distinct sets of ministers depending on the topic. In one form or another the "Council" meets about every two months.

The overall policy of the three councils is "to establish modern and efficient systems that are viable in economic, social and environmental terms. The harmonious and sustainable development of infrastructures is crucial to the smooth functioning of the internal market and to the Union's economic and social cohesion."

In some matters these Councils operate by QMV, in others they act unanimously.

Transport Council

In transport there have been massive road building programmes (trans-European networks) where environmental impacts may have been under-considered. This Council developed common rules applicable to international transport affecting the Member States, decided the conditions under which transport firms may operate across the European Union, and is concerned to improve transport safety. Its current aim is to optimise energy consumption, transport time, routes and conditions.

Telecommunications Council

This Council has promoted a satellite global positioning system called Galileo which "is designed for civilian purposes, is open to international cooperation and will be exploited commercially."

The Council is working on the establishment of a Europe-wide integrated telecommunications network, the introduction of the information society, the opening up of national markets, the elimination of the regulatory disparities between Member States with regard to prices, standards, market-access conditions, public procurement, etc. It is keen to develop the use of broadband internet access.

The Union has launched several measures to open up its markets more widely to competition, particularly in certain key sectors, and to promote investment in research.

The Energy Council

The Council of Ministers' web site gives the impression that this Council has little idea what it is doing and is neither joined up with the activities of EURATOM nor environmental concerns. It tells us "Energy policy is essentially the remit of the Member States." However, the Council is considering proposals on the trans-European energy network in the electricity and gas sectors in order to make it more efficient. Meanwhile, considerable funds are expended on a seemingly independent and self-perpetuating European Atomic Energy Community (EURATOM) which was established in 1957 to develop nuclear energy.

The Energy Council is concerned about security of energy supply and is looking at renewable energy. The Energy Council is "working towards the establishment of a legislative framework for ensuring the smooth functioning of a competitive internal market."

The Energy Council seems to lack environmental awareness, commitment, any sense of its important remit, any sense of urgency and, dare one say, energy.

Western European Union (WEU)

This is a military alliance with similar aims to Nato. Original members were Belgium, Luxembourg, Holland, West Germany, France and Britain. They were later joined by Portugal, Spain and Greece. Later other states had observer status: Denmark, Ireland, Austria, Finland and Sweden. States with associate status are: Iceland, Norway, Turkey, the Czech Republic, Hungary and Poland. Other eastern European states are "associate partners." A declaration attached to the *Maastricht Treaty* said that the WEU was "an integral part of the development of the Union." In the *Treaty of Amsterdam* the WEU was described as supporting EU defence policy. The WEU draws on basically the same forces as the EU and is, in effect, the EU defence force. In spite of this the European Constitution refers to NATO as the foundation of the collective defence of those States which are members of it and the forum for its implementation.

In November 1999 the WEU appointed Javier Solana as its Secretary General.

The WEU has a satellite centre in Torrejon in Spain and an institute for security studies in Paris. These were taken over by the EU in January 2002.

The WEU had an armaments group whose work would now appear to have been taken over by the new EU Defence Agency.

See also, *Euro Army*.

Notes

1 www.consilium.europa.eu/cms3_fo/
2 See *Major Issues* chapter: *Clear use of language* and *Transparency*.
3 See *Euroterminology* chapter.
4 Sir John Weston, former British Ambassador to NATO quoted in News dot telegraph 11 January 2001
5 Centre for European Reform web site.
6 See the chapter devoted to web sites.
7 See *Major Issues* - *Transparancy*
8 Email to author, 20 June 2006.

European Union Decision-makers

The people who run Europe are largely uknown to the citizens of Europe. This chapter lists the chief sources of power within the European Union and names some of the key players. The chapter on Institutions is relevant to this topic.

1. The European Council

The strategic direction, the big policy decisions of the EU, are decided by the political heads of the member states assisted by their ministers for foreign affairs. They proposed and agreed the treaties which shape EU policies and control the EU. They accepted and signed the European Constitution. The current members of the European Council are:

Austria:
Alfred Gusenbauer, Federal Chancellor. Ds Ursula Plassnik, Federal Minister for Foreign Affairs.

Belgium:
Guy Verhofstadt, Prime Minister. Karel De Gucht, Minister for Foreign Affairs.

Bulgaria:
Georgi Parvanov, President. Sergey Stanishev, Prime Minister. Ivailo Georgiev Kalfin, Minister for Foreign Affairs.

Cyprus:
Tassos Papadopoulos, President. Erato Kozakou-Marcoullis, Minister for Foreign Affairs.

Czech Republic:
Mirek Topolanek, Prime Minister. Karel Schwarzenberg, Minister for Foreign Affairs.

Denmark:
Anders Fogh Rasmussen, Prime Minister. Per Stig Møller, Minister for Foreign Affairs.

Estonia:
Andrus Ansip, Prime Minister. Urmas Paet, Minister for Foreign Affairs.

Finland:
Matti Vanhanen, Prime Minister. Ilka Kanerva, Minister for Foreign Affairs.

France:
Nicolas Sarkozy, President. François Fillon, Prime Minister. Bernard Kouchner, Minister for Foreign Affairs.

Germany:
Angela Merkal, Federal Chancellor. Frank-Walter Steinmeier, Federal Minister for Foreign Affairs.

Hellenic Republic: (Greece)
Kostas Karamanlis, Prime Minister. Theodora Bakoyianni, Minister for Foreign Affairs.

Hungary:
Ferenc Gyurcsány, Prime Minister.
Kinga Goncz, Minister for Foreign Affairs.

Ireland:
Bertie Ahern, Prime Minister
Dermot Ahern, Minister for Foreign Affairs.

Italy:
Romano Prodi, Prime Minister.
Massimo D'Alema, Minister for Foreign Affairs.

Latvia:
Valdis Zatlers, President.
Algars Kalvitis, Prime Minister.
Artis Pabriks, Minister for Foreign Affairs.

Lithuania:
Valdas Adamkus, President.
Gedimina Kirkilas, Prime Minister.
Petras Vaitiekunas, Minister for Foreign Affairs.

Luxembourg:
Jean Claude Juncker, Prime Minister.
Jean Asselborn, Deputy Prime Minister and Minister for Foreign Affairs and Immigration.

Malta:
The Hon Lawrence Gonzi, Prime Minister. The Hon Michael Frendo, Minister for Foreign Affairs.

Netherlands:
Dr Jan Peter Balkenende, Prime Minister. Maxime Verhagen, Minister for Foreign Affairs.

Poland:
Donald Tusk, Prime Minister. Anna Fortyga, Minister for Foreign Affairs.

Portugal:
Jose Socrates, Prime Minister.
Luis Amado, Minister for Foreign Affairs and the Portuguese Communities.

Romania:
Traian Băsescu, President.
Cãlin Popescu Tariceanu, Prime Minister. Adrian Cioroianu, Minister for Foreign Affairs.

Slovakia:
Roberto Fico, Prime Minister.
Jan Kubis, Minister for Foreign Affairs.

Slovenia:
Janez Drnovsek, President of the Government. Dmitri Rupel, Minister for Foreign Affairs.

Spain:
Jose Luis Rodriguez Zapatero
President of the Government
Miguel Angel Moratinos Cuyabé
Minister for external Affairs
and Co-operation;

Sweden:
Fredrik Reinfeldt, Prime Minister
Carl Bildt, Minister for Foreign Affairs.

U.K.:
Gordon Brown, Prime Minister.
David Miliband, Secretary of State for Foreign and Commonwealth Affairs.

(Updated 31 October 2007)

2. The High Representative for Common Foreign and Security Policy

This person is the EU's chief international negotiator in security matters and is responsible for the control of the Euro Army, the Security Defence Agency, and the European Security Investigation Force. He is Secretary General of the Council of Ministers. The Present High Representative is Javier Solana, former Secretary General of NATO.

3. The Commission

Almost all EU laws originate with the Commission. The Commission proposes (and plans in detail) EU legislation and enforces compliance with it (supported by the European Court of Justice). The Commission prepares the EU budget and allocates and distributes huge sums of money to support farmers and "develop" regions. Each member state currently appoints one Commissioner. They each take charge of an area of responsibility.

The Commissioners, their approximate political positions and their roles

José Manuel Barroso (Centre-Right) Commission president, Portugal.
Jacques Barrot (Centre-Right) Vice president: transport, France.
Siim Kallas (Liberal) Vice president: administrative affairs, audit and anti-fraud, Estonia.
Franco Frattini (Centre-Right) Vice president: justice, freedom and security, Italy.
Günter Verheugen (Socialist) Vice president: enterprise and industry, Germany.
Margot Wallström (Socialist) Vice president: institutional relations and communication strategy, Sweden.
Joaquín Almunia (Socialist) Economic and monetary affairs, Spain.
Joe Borg (Centre-Right) Fisheries and maritime affairs, Malta.
Stavros Dimas (Centre-Right) Environment, Greece.
Benita Ferrero Waldner (Centre-Right) External relations and the European Neighbourhood Policy, Austria.
Ján Figel (Centre-Right) Education, training, culture and multilinguism, Slovakia.
Mariann Fischer Boel (Liberal) Agriculture and rural development, Denmark.
Dalia Grybauskaité (Independent) Financial programming and budget, Lithuania.
Danuta Hübner (Socialist) Regional policy, Poland.
László Kovács (Socialist) Taxation and customs union, Hungary.
Neelie Kroes (Liberal) Competition, Netherlands.
Markos Kyprianou (Liberal) Health and consumer protection, Cyprus.
Peter Mandelson (Socialist) Trade, UK.
Charlie McCreevy (Centre-Right) Internal market and services, Ireland.
Louis Michel (Liberal) Development and humanitarian affairs, Belgium.
Andris Piebalgs (Liberal) Energy, Latvia.
Janez Potocnik (Socialist) Science and research, Slovenia.
Viviane Reding (Centre-Right) Information society and media, Luxembourg.
Olli Rehn (Liberal) Enlargement, Finland.
Vladimir Špidla (Socialist) Employment, social affairs and equal opportunities, Czech Republic.

Meglena Kuneva, Consumer protection, Bulgaria.
Leonard Orban, Multilingualism, Romania.

(Updated 29 September 2007)

4. The Council

This, as explained in detail in the Institutions chapter, is actually fourteen sets of Ministers from the twenty-seven member states. In all some three hundred and seventy five ministers are involved. They are too many to be known widely amongst the people of Europe or to list here. The most important are the Ministers for Foreign Affairs. Their names appear above in the European Council section.

5. COREPER

This is the permanent body of representatives of EU member states. The lead members are each state's ambassador to the EU. These key people are supported by numerous committees of experts.

See *Institutions* chapter for more details about COREPER and its work.

6. The European Parliament

There are seven hundred and thirty six directly elected Members of the European Parliament.

Their names, with details of how to contact them by email, fax, phone and post can be found at:

www.europarl.europa.eu/members/public.do

You can also write to MEPs at one of the two European parliaments, European Parliament, Bât. Altiero Spinelli, 08G103, 60, rue Wiertz / Wiertzstraat 60, B-1047 Bruxelles/Brussel, Belgium OR European Parliament, Bât. Louise Weiss, T05089, Allée du Printemps, BP 10024/F, F-67070 Strasbourg Cedex, France.

The political groups within the European Parliament are also very important centres of power and influence.

See *European Parliament political groups* in the *Institutions* chapter.

7. The European Central Bank

This takes the key decisions on monetary policy and is independent of all other officials and institutions of the EU.

See *EU Institutions*.

8. The European Court of Justice

This court is the final arbiter in disputes between EU member states in any matter controlled by EU law.

See *EU Institutions*.

9. The Lobbyists

There are 15,000 professional lobbyists and 2,600 lobbying organisations based in Brussels[1] whose main purpose is to influence the decision-making of the EU. Although in theory the lobbyists can decide nothing, in practice some of them have been very influential.

See *Major Issues – Lobbying* and *Transparency.*

10. The Media

Again, although having no direct power the media and their very few owners do have considerable influence. They themselves come under the influence of lobbyists.

See *Major Issues – Media.*

11. Political parties

See *European Parliament political groups* in the *Institutions* chapter.

Notes

1 Europa press release of speech by Siim Kallas, Vice President of the European Commission.. Reference: SPEECH/05/628. Date: 20/10/2005.

Euroterminology and Important Concepts

This section consists of basic explanations of words and special concepts in common usage within the European Union (including types of rules, laws and voting systems), plus other concepts which are essential to an understanding of the European Union.

References to articles throughout this book are articles in the European Constitution (2004) unless otherwise stated.

About euroterminology

When a newcomer begins to read European Union documents he or she soon becomes aware of encountering a strange new language. It takes four main forms

- a large number of acronyms (dealt with in a separate chapter of this book)
- the use of a single word to cover several meanings - for example, the Council, Maastricht
- ordinary words which have been given new meanings - such as Petersberg tasks, *competence,* and *unanimity*
- new or foreign words - such as *eurobarometer, acquis, and eurojust*

See *Clear use of language* in *Major Issues* chapter.

Accountability

This is a key concept in the running of the European Union. The first aspect of accountability is the ability of citizens of the European Union to know who is responsible for decisions, policies and actions carried out for or in the name of the EU. Just as important are the abilities a) to honour or re-elect or promote wise, honest, courageous and successful politicians and administrators and b) to fire, vote-out, bring to court and punish politicians or administrators who are corrupt, negligent, incompetent or criminal. There is a degree of accountability within the EU but there are serious weaknesses. Those who direct policy and those who take the major decisions have no direct relationship with the European electorate as a whole. Policies have not been endorsed by the European electorate as a whole. A large proportion of decision makers have not been elected. Many that are elected have been elected by fragments of the European electorate. In the handling of the billions of euros of EU funds the eurocitizen cannot discover who receives this money. The EU's auditors report fraud on a massive scale which, they say, has continued for over a decade. Some senior politicians break international law with impunity.

See *Major Issues – Transparency, Democratic deficit, Finances of the EU, and Free trade wars*.

Acquis or acquis communautaire

This is the collection of laws and decisions of European institutions (the accepted agreements of the community of European states) which direct personal, institutional and commercial actions within EU states. It amounts to some 97,000 pages of documentation consisting of all the EU's treaties and laws, declarations and resolutions, international agreements on EU affairs and the judgments given by the Court of Justice. It also includes action that EU governments take together in the area of Justice and Home Affairs and on the Common Foreign and Security Policy. When a state joins the EU it has to accept the acquis communautaire and make it part of its own law. It is sometimes called the "community acquis".

Agriculture

This, of course, means farming, but in the EU it also includes "first stage processing" and fisheries.

See article 225.

Agrimonetary

Agrimonetary describes something such as a discussion document or policy which is to do with financial support for and control of agriculture by a state or superstate (such as the EU).

Advisory bodies

See EU institutions.

Brussels

As well as being the capital of Belgium this word is commonly used as a shorthand term to mean the central power of the European Union. The implication is that all EU decisions are taken in Brussels. In fact the EU has been constructed to share power around various groupings of people, institutions and venues so that power is not totally unified in any one city. The dispersal of power and institutions makes it hard to know who is responsible for what and where you might find anyone responsible for anything. Nevertheless, Brussels provides the home for the Commission, the Council of Ministers, the European Council, and is one of the two homes of the European Parliament (the other is in Strasbourg - the parliament has administrative offices in Luxembourg). The army of lobbying organisations seeking to influence EU decisions is based in Brussels and this clearly indicates the amount of power that is concentrated here.

Huge public notices in Brussels carry the message, "Brussels, capital of Europe." Europe has no capital, yet, but the city fathers have ambitions.

See *Strasbourg, Frankfurt* and *Luxembourg* below and *Government* in the *Institutions* chapter.

Budget

Long-term (multi-annual) budget: These are agreed for seven-year periods. The most recent was agreed in December 2005 to cover the years 2007-2013.[1] This long-term budget is necessary in order to carry out long-term planning.

The long-term budget does the following things:

- Sets overall limits on EU expenditure for the period
- Sets limits on expenditure under the various headings - for example, agriculture and fisheries, and regional policy
- Sets spending limits for each year
- Agrees contributions from each member state.

Annual budget: This is planned by the Commission. It then has to be agreed by both the Council and the European Parliament. The maximum expenditure allowed has been decided in the long term budget. The annual budget shares out funding under various headings.

Where the money comes from

- Direct contributions from member states, currently set at 1.24% of EU combined gross national incomes (GNI). In 2005 this amounted to £163 per EU citizen or 45 pence per day. This is a small proportion of national income as public expenditure in member states is 40% to 50% of GNI.
- A proportion of the VAT set at 1% of the price of a common base of goods.
- Money charged as a duty on agricultural imports to discourage the import of foreign produce.
- Customs duties levied on imported goods – with similar effects to those on agricultural imports.

Customs duties have produced decreasing amounts of money over the years as levels of tariffs have been reduced.

Where the money goes - EU budget 2006 - € 121.2 billion

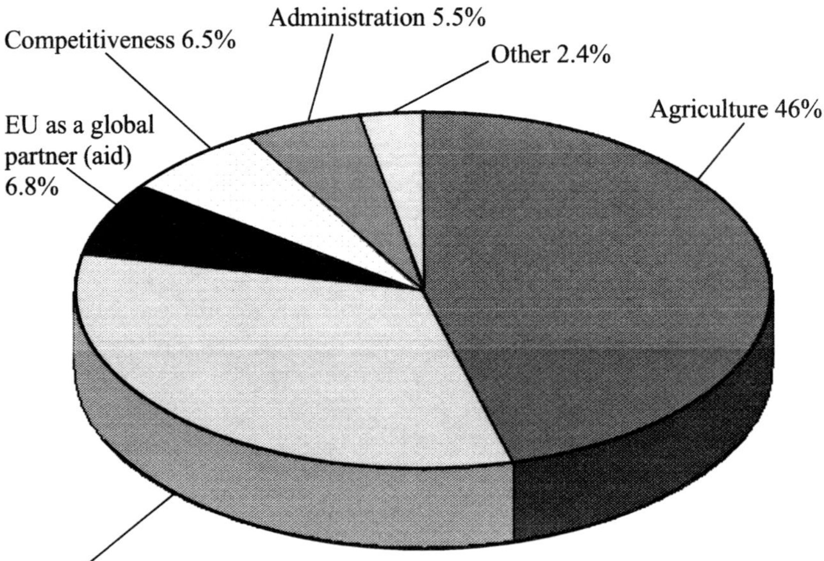

Planned expenditure (in € billion) 2006

Agriculture	56	46%
Cohesion – Prosperity (aid)	39.8	32.8%
EU as a global partner (aid)	8.3	6.8%
Competitiveness	7.9	6.5%
Administration	6.7	5.5%
Other	2.9	2.4%

TOTAL 121.2 billion euros

Details of 121.2 billion euros spending plan for 2006

- Agriculture: (46 per cent of the budget) includes direct aid and market measures 42.9 billion euros, rural development 11.8 billion euros, health & consumer protection (animal welfare & plant health) 0.3 billion euros, fisheries 1.0 billion euros.
- Cohesion and prosperity: (financial aid) (32.8 per cent of the budget) includes regional development 21.9 billion euros, cohesion fund (investment for environment and transport) 6.0 billion euros, and employment and social affairs 11 billion euros.
- EU as a global partner: (foreign aid) (6.8 per cent of the budget) includes external relations (excluding co-operation with Asia, Latin America, the Mediterranean, aid to victims of human rights violations) 3.2 billion euros, co-operation with African, Caribbean and Pacific (ACP) countries1.0 billion euros, enlargement 2.1 billion euros, humanitarian aid 0.5 billion euros.
- Competitiveness: (6.5 per cent of the budget) includes education and training 0.7 billion euros, research 4.2 billion euros, information society 1.2 billion euros, and energy and transport 1.1 billion euros.
- Administration: (5.5 per cent of the budget) includes the European Commission 3.1billion euros, other institutions 2.5 billion euros.
- Other: (2.4 per cent of the budget) includes environment 0.24 billion euros, (0.16% of total budget), freedom, security and justice 0.5 billion euros, citizenship (culture, health and consumer protection, employment and social affairs) 0.5 billion euros, aid to new EU countries 1.1 billion euros, reserves 0.48 billion euros. These figures do not take into account certain transition funds for the new EU countries, which are fixed by the accession treaties at €77 million for 2006.

Bycatch

When fishing is carried out with the nets or long lines (up to 40 miles long) many fish and other creatures (such as turtles and birds) are caught which are not the prime target of the fishermen. The non-target catch is the bycatch. The EU Fisheries Council of Ministers has tried to safeguard EU fish stocks and in particular species which it believes are endangered. Catching certain species at certain times and in certain areas has been banned. When fishermen set out to catch one or more particular species but accidentally catch other banned species, the bycatch (or discards), those accidentally caught are required by the EU to be discarded. That means they have to be thrown, dead or dying, back into the sea.

CAP - Common Agricultural Policy

The system set up in times of scarcity to guarantee food for all citizens at low prices and support the farming community. It developed into a system for giving tax money from European citizens mostly to Europe's richest land owners and has resulted in the overproduction of many food products which have been dumped in many countries ruining the livelihoods of hundreds of thousands of farmers around the world. It also encouraged intensive farming methods which have had adverse environmental effects. Thousands of farmers have been forced to give up farming. Food prices have been higher than they might have been. Recent reforms should do much to correct these problems. For a discussion of the successes, failures and problems of the Common Agricultural Policy see this topic in *Major issues,* and articles 225-232. For other acronyms see the *Acronyms* pages.

Changes in names for EU laws, decisions, directives, and regulations

See *Laws/rulings/decisions/acts of the European Union.*

Charter of Fundamental Rights of the Union

This is part of the European Constitution and is a relatively late addition to European Union thinking. It is a bringing together of the ideas contained in the recent European Community Treaties, international conventions such as the 1950 European Convention on Human Rights and the 1989 European Social Charter, constitutional traditions common to the Member States and various European Parliament declarations. The European Council, meeting in Cologne in June 1999, first proposed that there should be a Charter of Fundamental Rights of the Union. The Charter defines fundamental rights relating to dignity, liberty, equality, solidarity, citizenship and justice. It includes civil and political rights, workers' rights, data protection, bioethics and the right to good administration. It recognizes each citizen's responsibilities "to the human community and future generations." It provides no safeguards which do not already exist in member states. If it has any value at all then this is weakened or negated by a variety of contradictions, restrictions and get-out clauses. It bans discussion of limiting any of the Charter's "rights".

See *Major Issues*, articles 9, 10, 61 - 114 and the preamble that precedes article 61.

Co-decision procedure

Under the co-decision procedure legislation cannot be passed without the consent of both the European Parliament and the Council. Its introduction in 1992, by the *Treaty on European Union - Maastricht*, marked the beginning of real power for the European Parliament. The procedure was simplified by the *Treaty of Amsterdam*. Whilst the procedure now covers most topics there is still considerable scope for independent decision making by the Commission and the Commission retains the very important right to be the institution that initiates any new EU law or framework law.

Under the Constitution co-decision procedure will be known as "the ordinary legislative procedure." (Article 34/1 and 396.)

See, also, *Law-making* and *Laws/rulings/decisions/acts of the European Union*).

Cohesion Fund

Funds first set up under the *Maastricht Treaty* and distributed to member states whose GDP is less than 90% of the average of EU member states. One of the aims is to even out the regional wealth imbalances with the EU. The Cohesion Fund finances projects in two main areas - transport and the environment. Projects in the area of transport cover such items as road, port, airport and rail projects. Environmental projects have included improving water supply, waste water treatment, and solid waste projects.

The first recipients of money from the fund were Spain, Greece, Portugal and Ireland. In the period 1993-1999 they received €16,700 million - Spain received 55%, Greece and Portugal 18% each and Ireland 9%. The Spanish people voted in favour of the European Constitution. The 2000 to 2006 budget is €18 billion. It might be a factor which attracts applications from poorer countries for membership of the EU.

The Commission

See EU Institutions chapter.

Committee of the Regions

See EU Institutions chapter.

Competence

In the EU Competence is eurospeak for a power or right to decide something including the making of a variety of kinds of laws and the "co-ordination" of significant areas of human activity. (See articles 11 to 18.) The EU states have agreed to give to the EU institutions much of the power to take decisions which individual states used to hold. In the EU Constitution there are "exclusive competences" and "shared competences" plus a right of co-ordination of policy (including the economic policies of states, employment policies and social policies) which is a power to take decisions, but in this instance is not described as a competence.

See article 15.

Exclusive competences refer to the exclusive right of EU institutions to take decisions on a number of important matters. Europe decides. The member states comply. The exclusive competence areas are listed in the Constitution as: customs union, competition rules, conservation of marine and biological resources under the common fisheries policy, common commercial policy, concluding international agreements in certain circumstances, and (in the case of eurozone countries) competence to decide monetary policy. See article 13. In addition, "The Union's competence in matters of common foreign and security policy shall cover all areas of foreign policy and all questions relating to the Union's security." (Article 16.)

In the EU "shared" does not have its normal meaning. It equates roughly with the idea of "the right to start to take control." Once the EU has taken action in an area of "shared competence" then its regulations overrule the regulations of individual states and states may take no further independent action in these areas. Shared competences exist in many areas. The EU already dominates agriculture and trade. See article 14. In addition, if the EU Constitution is adopted, the EU institutions "shall have competence to carry out supporting, coordinating or complementary action . . . at the European level" in the following areas: human health, industry, culture, tourism, education, youth, sport, vocational training, civil protection, and administrative co-operation. See article 17. There is little that Europeans can do that the EU does not presume the right to control.

See *Major issues - Subsidiarity* and articles 11-18.

Competition

The rules on competition are intended to ensure that a European economic area based on market forces can function freely and fairly. The European Union's competition policy (Articles 81 to 89 of the *European Community Treaty* – articles 161-169 of the Constitution) is based on five main principles:

- the prohibition of concerted practices, agreements and associations between undertakings which may affect trade between Member States and prevent, restrict or distort competition within the internal market;
- the prohibition of abuse of a dominant position within the internal market, in so far as it may affect trade between Member States;
- prohibition of aid granted by the Member States, or through State resources in any form whatsoever, which threatens to distort competition by favouring certain undertakings or the production of certain goods;
- preventive supervision of mergers with a European dimension, by approving or prohibiting the envisaged alliances;
- liberalisation [privatisation] of certain sectors where public or private enterprises have hitherto evolved monopolistically, such as telecommunications, transport or energy.

The first two principles may, however, be subject to derogations [exceptions], particularly when an agreement between undertakings improves the production or distribution of products or promotes technical progress. In the case of state aid schemes, social subsidies, or subsidies to promote culture and conservation of heritage, are also examples of possible exceptions to the strict application of competition rules.

The Constitution would explicitly give the Commission, following authorisation by the Council, the possibility of adopting regulations granting exemption from competition rules which apply to undertakings and rules on state aid.

See articles 161-169, and *Major Issues – Free Trade (Competition)*

Conferral

Conferral is the conscious and deliberate passing of power from EU member states to EU institutions. The Constitution explains that the European Union may only take action on matters which member states have authorised in ratifying the Constitution. It gives the impression of a clear cut demarcation of powers between what member states may do and what the EU may do. This is not the case because substantial areas of policy come under the heading of "shared competences". The EU may act in these areas subject to certain procedures and tests which have to be applied on each occasion an idea for legislation within these areas is presented. The shared competence concept blurs the distinctions and the subsidiarity rules operate (against the claimed purpose) to make it highly likely that more and more direction will come from the EU with corresponding losses of power by individual states. This is because once the EU has legislated in a given area then member states are prevented from legislating themselves.

See *Competences* (above), *Major Issues – Subsidiarity*, articles 11 to 18, 115 and Protocol 2.

Constitution

See *European Constitution* below.

Constructive abstention

Decisions that require unanimity under EU treaties or the Constitution may be said to be unanimous even when some countries abstain. The procedure, introduced by the *Amsterdam Treaty*, is known as "constructive abstention." It means that "a Member State can choose not to apply a particular decision even though it agrees that it commits the Union as a whole." See *Unanimity*.

Copenhagen criteria

In June 1993, EU leaders meeting in Copenhagen set three criteria that any country wishing to become a member of the European Union must meet before it can join the European Union. First, it must have stable institutions guaranteeing democracy, the rule of law, human rights and respect for minorities. Second, it must have a functioning market economy. Third, it must take on board all the acquis (see above) and support the various aims of the European Union. In addition, it must have a public administration capable of applying and managing EU laws in practice. The EU reserves the right to decide when a candidate country has met these criteria and when the EU is ready to accept the new member.

COREPER

See EU Institutions chapter.

The Council and the Council of Ministers

See EU Institutions chapter.

The Council of Europe

See EU Institutions chapter.

Court of Auditors

See EU Institutions chapter.

The Council of Europe

This is not an EU institution. It is an intergovernmental organisation of forty-six European member states. It is based in Strasbourg and it aims (amongst other things) to protect human rights, to promote Europe's cultural diversity and to combat social problems such as xenophobia and intolerance. The Council of Europe was set up in 1949 and one of its early achievements was to draw up the *European Convention for the Protection of Human Rights and Fundamental Freedoms*. To enable citizens to exercise their rights under that Convention, it set up the European Court of Human Rights. The European Union's Constitution (article 9) commits the EU to this European convention insofar as it does not "affect the Union's competences as defined in the Constitution." This suggests that there may be an intention to apply limitations. It is difficult to identify what these may be.

Customs Union

See *Free trade.*

Decision-making procedures within the EU

The European Union has a number of procedures for creating laws.

- **Co-decision:** Under the co-decision procedure legislation cannot be passed without the consent of both the European Parliament and the Council. Co-decision procedure currently (2006) covers most topics. The Constitution calls this the "ordinary legislative procedure."
- **Consultation procedure:** Under the consultation procedure the Council of Ministers has the final say. This procedure covers the highly important issues of agriculture, home affairs, justice, harmonisation of fiscal control and administration and European monetary union. The Council sometimes completely ignores the advice of the democratically elected members of parliament. (See also *Other Procedures*.)
- **Other procedures:** Other less common procedures are the assent procedure and the co-operation procedure. Draft directives and draft regulations are published and interested parties can lobby the Commission and Member States before they are adopted. Nevertheless, European decisions, which are, in effect, laws may be made with discussions and decisions by the European Council, or the Council, or the Commission or the European Central Bank taking place behind closed doors.

Articles 20, 27, 325, 330–340, 396, and 397 refer to the European Parliament.

See also *Major Issues – Law making,* and *Democratic deficit,* and *Democratic deficit* below.

Defence Agency

See EU *Institutions* chapter.

Defence spending

Setting aside any idea of making any assessment of the threats faced by the European Union the Constitution commits member states to year on year increases in defence spending. Article 41/3 states, "Member States shall undertake progressively to improve their military capabilities."

Development

See *European Development Fund.*

Development aid

This is the transfer of resources to assist economic development in poorer regions. The European Union is the world's largest provider of development aid. Aid is administered by the Commission. Funds come from the community budget or from the European Development Fund which is dedicated to the development of the seventy seven African Caribbean and Pacific states.

Democratic deficit

The European Union is not a truly democratic institution. It has a parliament which can discuss EU activities and in a number of important matters it can propose amendments to proposed laws and vote against some sorts of laws to stop laws put forward by the Council on proposals from the Commission, but the law proposers, law writers and the most powerful and influential of the law makers of the European Union are not elected by the electorate of the European Union as a whole.

Much of the EU's decision making takes place behind closed doors. The role of individuals in decision making, their speeches and their votes are not recorded for public access. Serious obstacles are placed in the way of access to minutes of meetings. The principle decision making bodies are the European Council, the many permutations of "the Council", the Commission, and COREPER. With few exceptions their members are unknown to the 480 million people of the European Union. This is the opposite of open government.

European decision makers are unaccountable. They have passed laws to place themselves above the law and the proposed Constitution (article 11 of Protocol 7) would repeat immunities granted to all EU officials by the *Merger Treaty* of 1967.

The gap between what a true European Union democracy could be and the limited version that operates within the EU is known as the democratic deficit.

For a fuller discussion of this topic see the *Major Issues* chapter, and *Governance* below.

Derogation

Derogation means the making of exceptions in the application of EU laws. Officially "Derogations from the acquis are granted only in exceptional circumstances and are limited in scope." There are quite a lot of exceptional circumstances and also instances where whole areas of EU action operate in complete opposition to EU declared policies. See discussion on conflicts within the European Constitution. Opt-out is a form of derogation.

Directives

See *Major Issues - Law-making.*

Discards

See "bycatch".

Economic and Financial Committee

See EU Institutions chapter.

The Economic and Social Committee

See EU Institutions chapter.

Economic unification, economic integration

Achieving economic unification is a major step towards unifying separate states into a superstate. Countries become economically unified when they set up a controlling authority or authorities, whose decisions are binding on member states, to direct their monetary, fiscal, trade, employment and educational policies. This means a single currency, unified interest rates, unified external tariffs, harmonised (unified) tax system, unified qualifications, unified unemployment benefits and pension rights.

Members of the eurozone are furthest along this route. All signatories of the Constitution are committed to economic integration except Britain which has the right to join if and when it wishes. It is not required to do so. Some areas of economic life are controlled by Brussels and are therefore fully integrated into the European Union, including trade, agriculture and fisheries.

See *Euro* and *Eurozone*, plus *Major Issues – European Union by stealth.*

Enhanced co-operation

This is an arrangement whereby a group of EU countries (there must be at least eight of them) can work together in a particular field even if the other EU countries are unable or unwilling to join in at this stage. The outsiders must, however, be free to join in later if they wish. In this way Foreign and Defence Policy, for example, can be developed even when the understanding is that these policy areas will be decided by unanimous decision. It is not clear whether member countries in an "enhanced co-operation" group would be operating under their own policies or those agreed unanimously by all EU members.

See articles 416 – 423.

Enlargement

Enlargement is the adding of more states to the association of states which constitute the European Union. This topic is one of the most controversial developments of the European Union.

See *Major Issues - Enlargement* and articles 2 and 58.

Establishment

In the Constitution this means the right to set up a business or open a branch of an existing business in any state within the European Union.

See *Major Issues – Free trade.*

EU government

See *EU Institutions* chapter.

EURATOM

See *EU Institutions* chapter.

The euro

The currency used in the 12 eurozone countries. The currency came into use on 1 January 2002.

The existence of the euro is not simply a matter of coins and bank notes to be used in the EU but who controls monetary policy in every EU state. Where the euro is the currency decisions on interest rates are taken by the European Central Bank which, by EU Constitution rules, may not be criticised even if its policies lead, for example, to high unemployment.

The issue of currency is authorised by the European Central Bank. EU member countries not within the eurozone are expected to make serious efforts to adjust their economies to enable them to join the eurozone. The European Constitution commits countries which ratify it to adopt the euro as their currency.

In addition to the EU 12 eurozone members the euro is used in thirty-one other states and territories including Andorra, Kosovo, Monaco, Montenegro, San Marino, and Vatican City. Iraq switched its currency reserves from US dollars to euros in 2000 and traded its oil in euros from 2000 to 2003. This angered the US.

See *Institutions – European Central Bank, Major Issues – Charter of Fundamental Rights (Free speech), Eurozone* below, and articles 186,191, 192–202.

Euro Army

See *EU Institutions* chapter.

Eurobarometer

See *EU Institutions* chapter.

Eurojust

See *EU Institutions* chapter.

Euroland

The territory of the 27 EU member states.

Europa

The name of the EU's main official web site. http://europa.eu.int/

See *Web Sites Relating to the European Union,* for other EU web addresses.

European Arrest Warrants

These came into operation in eight European countries (Belgium, Denmark, Finland, Ireland, Portugal, Spain, Sweden, and UK) on 1 January 2003 as a replacement for previous extradition procedures. See *Major Issues*.

European Central Bank

See *EU Institutions* chapter.

European Community

See *EU Institutions* chapter.

European Community Treaty

The European Community Treaty, 1 July 1967, is the popular name for the treaty amalgamating the three European Community organisations: the European Coal and Steel Community, the European Economic Community and the European Atomic Energy Community. It is also known as the *Merger Treaty* and *The Treaty establishing a Single Council and a Single Commission of the European Communities*.

European Constitution

The term "European Constitution" is sometimes used somewhat loosely and means different things to different people. For example, when French voters were given the text of the Constitution they were given articles 1 - 448.

The Constitution may be taken to be the first "Constitution" document that was signed in Rome on 29 October 2004. This bears the official title *The Treaty establishing a Constitution for Europe*. The document is divided into major sections: a preamble and four parts. Part I may be regarded as the basic "Constitution". The other parts are:

- Part II – The Charter of Fundamental Rights of the Union

- Part III – The Policies and Functioning of the Union.
- Part IV – General and Final Provisions.

After article 448 the heads of the 25 EU states signed the document. This point is less than four pages into the *General and Final provisions* and much less than half the entire document. Most of what follows the signing is integral to the understanding and functioning of the provisions contained in articles 1- 448. Article 448 is followed by two short annexes. After this is "The Final Act". This is dated at the start, 30 September 2003 and at the end 29 October 2004. It lists all the documents which follow it and is signed by the heads of the 25 EU states plus Bulgaria, Romania and Turkey to indicate that that they are "adopting" them.

This remaining part of the "final provisions" contains 36 protocols, with their own preambles and separate numbered sequences of articles and 50 declarations. (This construction of the document with this baggage wagon of additional but vital material continues the tradition established by the writing of the *Treaty of Rome*, 1957.)

Normally a protocol will be written years after a convention or treaty has come into effect and their purpose is usually to amend or add extra provisions in the light of subsequent experience (as, for example, the various protocols to the Geneva Conventions).

The protocols of the European Constitution might have been integrated into the main text because they were prepared at the same time as the main text and without them this text cannot be properly interpreted. For ease of reference their articles might helpfully be numbered consecutively starting at 449. The content of their many preambles might have been consolidated in some way, or even vital ideas from them incorporated into the preamble of the entire Constitution.

At 465 A4 pages (as downloaded in English in pdf format from the internet) the European Constitution is probably the longest the world has ever known. One reason for this is that it is really two types of document in one: a constitution, and also a set of treaties and policy documents which includes procedures for amalgamating the countries of Europe into a single state.

The entire Constitution, with all its annexes, declarations and protocols, may be downloaded from the official EU source.[2] However, the Constitution (including some supplementary parts) included in this volume covers more than most people will need.

European convention for the protection of human rights and fundamental freedoms (1950)

This is a product of the Council of Europe, and for over 40 years was nothing to do with the EU. (See *Council of Europe* above.) It stated the civil and political rights of the citizens of Europe and led to the establishment of the European Court of Human Rights in 1959 to which citizens of Europe could take their cases if they believed that their governments or parts of their administration had abused their human rights. The *Maastricht Treaty* (1992), article F/2 (later numbered 6/2), stated that the Union would respect the rights guaranteed by the European Convention of 1950 "as general principles of Community law."

See *Major Issues - Charter of Fundamental Rights* and article 9/2.

The European Council

See *EU Institutions* chapter.

European Court of Justice

See EU Institutions chapter.

European Development Fund

This was set up by the 1957 *Treaty of Rome* to promote development in 77 African, Caribbean and the Pacific states by providing technical and financial assistance. Contributions to the EDF budgets which are set for five-year periods are ratified by EU member states. The Commission and other institutions manage the fund on a day-to-day basis.

The fund provides grants, risk capital and loans to the private sector. These may include European companies. The five-year programme to 2005 was allocated €13.5 billion which was added to the unexpended balances from previous budgets of €9.9 billion. The European Investment Bank contributed €1.7 billion for this period. (Source: Europa Web.)

European Parliament

See *EU Institutions* chapter.

European project

This is a term sometimes used in discussions about the development of the European Union. Most use it as a neutral term to denote the development of the European Union over half a century in the direction of the "ever closer union" of member states.

Others see the European Project in a more sinister light. In this interpretation the European Project is the idea that an international political elite class has planned to create a huge unified country out of the many states of Europe and they or their friends will take the leading roles in association with experts they have appointed. This development was planned to be brought about by slowly accruing powers to a centralised institution with power passing to it so gradually that the development would progress without challenge. Democratic approval for this unification plan was not a feature of Monnet's original ideas. (See the chapter on the development of the European Union.)

In recent years elements of democracy have been established within the European Union but the basic development plan, as advanced by the proposed Constitution, pays only token regard to the idea of advancing democracy.

The critics of the Convention which drafted the Constitution (whose observations appear in Part One) and the statement by Giuliano Amato, Vice President of the Convention which wrote the Constitution quoted in *Major Issues: European Union by stealth are* relevant to this view. The attitude of certain European leaders to a No vote on the Constitution shows some opposition to decisions democratically taken.

The European Project is sometimes called the integrationist project.

See also *Intergovernmentalism* and *Integration* below, the *Early Plans* chapter, and in *Major Issues: European Union by stealth, Integration, Democratic deficit, Transparency* and *United States of Europe.*

European Prosecutor

The establishment of a role of European Prosecutor is proposed by article 274.

European Union

See *EU Institutions* chapter.

Europol

See *EU Institutions* chapter.

Eurostat

See *EU Institutions* chapter.

Eurozone

The EU member states which have adopted the euro as their currency and who share a common monetary policy under the direction of the European Central Bank. The countries are: Austria, Belgium, Finland, France, Germany, Greece, Ireland, Italy, Luxembourg, the Netherlands, Portugal and Spain. The ten states which joined the European Union in 2004 will join the eurozone within about five years as their economies converge on the eurozone standard. In addition to the ten new member states there are three other EU states (the UK, Sweden and Denmark) which remain outside the eurozone.

For economic and monetary policy see articles 177-180 and 185-187.

Exclusive Economic Zones

These are the territorial waters belonging to states which extend certain distances from their shores. Within these waters they have exclusive rights to fishing and geological survey and mineral extraction. Over the latter part of the 20th century these areas were extended from 3 miles to six miles, from 6 miles to 12 miles, and then many states (starting with Iceland) extended their territorial waters to 200 miles from their coasts. Within the EU, member states have exclusive rights to the waters up to 12 miles from their shores and the European Union as a whole has access between 12 miles and 200 miles from the coastline of the European Union.

See the *Fisheries* section in the *Major Issues* chapter.

Federalism

Along with "integration," "intergovernmentalism," and "sovereignty" this is a key concept in the debates about the future of the European Union. Federalism is a political system in which partially independent states are united under a central government which is independently able to take decisions and direct the behaviour of these states in agreed areas without reference to the states. Examples of federal states are Germany, Switzerland, Canada, India, USA and the EU - although some member states of the EU attempt to maintain the belief that their sovereignty is undiminished by membership of the EU. (Examples of EU independent power include agriculture and fisheries, social policy, the environment and trade - where policies are directed by the EU from Brussels. The EU decides trading policy within the EU area and has the power to negotiate trading arrangements with non-EU states.) European law supersedes national laws in these areas. The EU has an independent budget. It is developing military and police powers. It has its own supreme court which has authority throughout the member states. It has leaders including a president. It has some EU foreign policies.

The EU is different from explicitly federal states in that its powers are continually expanding: it has convoluted and undemocratic decision making processes, and it lacks clear demarcation of powers between it and member states.

Federalism may also be seen as the *sharing* of power between the central government and states of a federation. The difference is a subtle one. The matter comes down to whether the central power is dominating the federal states or whether it is acting in friendly co-operation and harmony with the federal states. Germans tend to see federation as a system of power sharing whereas it is common in Britain to regard a federation as a system which subjects the federal states to the domination of a central authority.

See also *Functionalism and Neo-functionalism* and the chapters *Early Plans For European Co-operation and Unity,* and *Major Issues – Biggest Problems One to Five, Democratic Deficit, European Union by stealth* and *United States of Europe.*

Flexible labour practices

Flexible labour practices are such things as unilaterally re-writing contracts of employees, reducing job security guaranteed by contract, lowering wages, reducing rest periods and holidays, changing working hours, lowering safety standards and reducing pension rights. These may enable cost cutting and increasing competitiveness. For a business this may increase customers. For workers it may increase the numbers in work and job security (at a price). In state run services costs may be cut. For individual employeees and society as a whole there is a price to pay in terms of stress, morale and quality of life.

Foreign Affairs Council

See the *Institutions* chapter.

Foreign Policy

This is, of course, the policies of a state with regard to other states. The proposed Constitution sets out the final steps that may be taken to enable the EU to act as a single state in matters of foreign policy. This journey towards acting as a single state in foreign policy began in 1969 when the Hague European

Community summit commissioned a report on the possibilities of co-operating in foreign affairs. A committee, chaired by Etienne Davignon of Belgium, recommended a system to "harmonise points of view, concert attitudes, and, where possible, lead to common decisions." The committee proposed that foreign ministers of member states should meet twice a year. Nowadays they usually meet monthly.

Communiques announced talks, not on a Common Foreign Policy, but on "political co-operation".

It seems that the co-ordination of foreign policy began rather shyly because the work was not described by its most transparent name. Rather than saying they were discussing foreign policy co-operation they announced that they were discussing "political co-operation." Currently the meeting of EU Foreign Ministers is sometimes described as the Foreign Affairs Council, at other times it is called the General Affairs Council. Another name used is External Relations Council, and most recently, The General Affairs and External Relations Council.

See *Institutions,* and *Major Issues – Clear use of language,* and *Defence.*

The Four Freedoms of the EU

The EU web site proudly proclaims the four freedoms of the EU. "One of the great achievements of the EU has been to create a frontier-free area within which (1) people, (2) goods, (3) services and (4) money can all move around freely. This four-fold freedom of movement is sometimes called 'the four freedoms'." These freedoms are established primarily to facilitate trade and are at the heart of the European Union. The free movement of people has not been fully implemented. It carries concerns in connection with sovereignty, issues of citizenship and immigration control.

Frankfurt

Home of the European Central Bank.

Fraud

The scale of the misuse of EU funds and the failure of the accounting system to show satisfactorily (in the estimation of the Court of Auditors) how EU funds have been spent and distributed has led to the task of dealing with fraud in the EU being placed in the hands of one of its most senior officials, Vice President of the Commission, Siim Kallas.

See *OLAF* and *Court of Auditors* in the *Institutions* chapter, and *Accountability, Finances of the EU* and *Transparency* in the *Major Issues* chapter.

Free trade

The meaning of free trade has expanded in recent years. Free trade is normally understood to be international trade in goods and services free from import or export duties, quota restrictions (or other conditions, such as unnecessary technical specifications or professional qualifications, which might inhibit trade), or government payments or subsidies to its own exporters. The opposite of this definition of free trade is *protectionism.* Free trade can have both positive and negative results.

The European Union is based on free trade amongst its member states but goes further than being just a free trade area. It is based on the free movement of persons, services, goods and capital and where it operates tariffs or quota restrictions with third countries (ie outside the EU) the levels are fixed to be identical for all member states. It is, therefore, a customs union (which is more than a free trade area).

The European Union is developing the scope of free trade by introducing private ownership into public services (the operation of public services by commercial organisations). Article 147 states, "European framework laws shall establish measures to achieve the liberalisation [privatisation] of a specific service." Article 148 adds, "Member States shall endeavour to undertake liberalisation of services beyond the extent required by the European framework laws adopted pursuant to article 147 . . . To this end, the Commission shall make recommendations to the Member States concerned." This liberalisation opens the way for commercial organisations in any member state (and from anywhere in the world to run, either partially or completely, such services as prisons, health-care, and schools. In this way liberalisation/privatisation may extend the scope of free trade. Trade liberalisation is an important concern of the World Trade Organisation.

See *Major Issues - Free Trade.*

Functionalism and neo-functionalism

Functionalism and neo-functionalism are processes of transferring power. States begin by co-operating on a process or function of mutual benefit, for example the production of steel or satellite communications or combating disease. These acts of co-operation require international agreement and, because of the complexity of most issues require experts and specialised international bodies to decide what should be done and to make the rules. By ceding power to enable the functions to be carried out state sovereignty is eroded and passed to international or supranational bodies, or possibly to many international bodies. In a sense functionalism or functional transfer takes issues out of politics, the control of politicians and the influence of electorates.

Functionalism can perform great services for the world. For example, the world's postal services have been substantially managed by an international committee since 1874. Now with a membership of 190 countries it sets the rules for international mail exchanges, as well as having an advisory, mediating and liaison role.

Functionalism within the European Union is somewhat different. Functional co-operation is not aimed at taking issues out of political control in the normal sense, but of transferring political control of policy areas traditionally the preserve of the state to a new authority or state that is being created step by step with minimal publicity. Some call the European version of functionalism neo-functionalism. In both functionalism and neo-functionalism the democratic element that is present in democratic politics disappears unless special steps are taken to transfer full democratic powers to an electorate. The mere tacking on of a parliament as an adjunct of decision making done elsewhere is not democracy as we know it. This important topic is discussed more fully elsewhere.

See *Major Issues – Clear use of language, democratic deficit,* and *EU by stealth.*

General Affairs Council

See *EU Institutions chapter - Council.*

Globalisation – General

Globalisation means different things to different people and discussion of the topic may be frustrated by lack of agreed definitions. Globalisation in general terms can be said to be the dramatically increased interrelatedness of the people of the world – the way that news, sports, films, personalities, music, ideas, fashions, manufactured goods appear, almost simultaneously around the world.

Globalisation – Economic

Economic globalisation is the increasing dispersal around the world of economic activity which traditionally has been based in individual states and under the control of their governments. Such dispersal has happened on a small scale for centuries, but developments in transport, communications, and the removal of trade restrictions and exchange controls, especially since the mid twentieth century, has led to an acceleration of this trend.

International companies (trans-national corporations, TNCs) have been both promoters of "freeing trade" and prime beneficiaries of globalisation. The top 500 of these are estimated to account for 70% of global trade. In general they operate to maximise profits by manufacturing goods in countries where production costs are lowest. This may often mean that wages are lowest, worker protection is weakest, environmental standards are poorest. They are the force behind the World Trade Organisation, the World Bank and the IMF where they promote policies which will remove barriers to trade – such as ending the state ownership of industries or services (by privatisation), delaying or weakening regulations to protect people and the environment and ending trade discrimination by governments in favour of their own national manufactures, services or agricultural produce. Such policies have sometimes been imposed on developing countries as conditions for the receipt of aid and access to world markets. The policy is described as "free trade" but it is not free trade as understood by the founding fathers of economic thought.

Globalisation is associated with an increase in global wealth. It has implication for the distribution of employment and wealth, and for the power and influence of states (and therefore voters).

Whilst many trans-national corporations operate responsibly many do not. Globalisation is driven by the profit motive and a sense of social responsibilty or any permanent connection to any one state or people or humanity in general are not prime concerns. The corporations, by their ability to move at will from one country to another, may have an undemocratic influence on governments who may be pressured into maximising their appeal of usefulness of their countries to companies – at the expense of human and environmental needs.

(See *Major Issues – Free trade,* especially *Free trade fundamentalism*).

Governance

Some leading thinkers within the European Union are concerned about the gap between the governing, decision-making and administrative system and ordinary people who tend to view the whole system with indifference, hostility or cynicism. The Commission launched a White Paper on the topic of governance in July 2001 concerning all the rules, procedures and practices affecting how powers are exercised within the European Union. The stated aim was to adopt new forms of governance that would bring the Union closer to European citizens, make it more effective, reinforce democracy in Europe and consolidate the legitimacy of the institutions. It was accepted that the Union must reform itself in order to fill the democratic deficit of its institutions. It considered that this governance should lie in the framing and implementation of better and more consistent policies associating civil society organisations and the European institutions making European legislation clearer and more effective.

See *Democratic deficit* above and in *Major issues*, and the chapters in *Crisis of Confidence in the EU.*

Government of the European Union

See *Institutions* chapter.

Gymnich meetings

Informal meetings of the various groupings of the ministers of the various councils of Ministers, typically held in a country house, at the times of meetings of European leaders' meetings in the European Council. The first of these took place at Schloss Gymnich, near Bonn in April 1974.

High Representative

The role of High Representative for the Common Foreign and Security Policy was introduced in 1997 by the *Treaty of Amsterdam.* If the Constitution comes into force the role will be replaced by that of Minister for Foreign Affairs. The role of this unelected official is to act as Council Secretary General, represent the EU (on behalf of the Council) in discussions with third countries, and help formulate foreign policy ideas and carry them through. Javier Solana was appointed to this post in June 1999 by the European Council.

See *Western European Union.*

Integration

The integration of states is the process of co-operation between states which sees some of their functions - for example, running a tax system, healthcare, agriculture or defence - amalgamated into a combined authority or government. If a policy of ever closer integration is pursued the ultimate destination of an integration process would be that two (or more) states become one. One of the aims of the European Union seems to be to move from being a federal state to becoming a unified state. Present states would retain their cultural identities and power to act in purely local/regional matters. What else can be the ultimate destination of "ever closer union"?

See also *Federalism, Sovereignty, Economic unification, Functionalism and neo-functionalism*, and the chapter, *How plans for European co-operation and unity developed.*

Intellectual property rights

Intellectual property rights are primarily the rights of writers, composers, film makers, singers, artists, program writers and other creative people to receive financial reward when others use the fruit of their creative work. Such rights have existed for much of the world since the Berne Convention of 1886. Most states have their own laws on this topic and most are signatories to international agreements (the Berne Convention and the Universal Copyright Convention - both revised in 1971). The 1993 EU directive required member states of that time to bring their copyright law into a degree of uniformity. In Britain this resulted in a new copyright act in 1996.

The EU is concerned with the protection of creators' rights in databases, material broadcast by satellite and cable, rental and lending right, protection of computer programs, music, films, print media, software, performances, and broadcasts.

See article 176 and *Major issues - Intellectual property rights.*

Intergovernmentalism

This is an alternative to the European Union as we know it. It is the idea that rather than the governments of Europe giving away their powers and control to a central European power (or government or administration) - to create a "union" or a "United States of Europe" - they could work together intergovernmentally. That is to say that the governments of Europe could work together as a co-operative team to reach agreed solutions to common problems, thus retaining their sovereignty or right to independent action in all matters.

See also *European project.*

Inter-group

An inter-group is a cross-party, informal group of MEPs set up to consider or promote an idea.

Internal Market

The internal market is the name given to the trading relationships between member countries of the European Union. Barriers (controls of almost all types, import and export duties, quotas – limits on quantities of goods that may be exported or imported) are removed between member countries allowing free movement of persons, services, goods and capital. The Constitution establishes that the Council sets the guidelines and makes the rules to control the market with the proposals for these coming from the Commission.

See articles 130-132.

Internal Security

This is defined in an EU document as follows: “Internal security should at least include: the prevention and combating of crime, the prevention of the terrorist threat, intelligence exchange, public order management, the prevention and combating of criminal offences such as illegal immigration and trafficking in persons, the provision of an integrated management system for external borders as a major factor for preventing (certain) forms of crime within the EU and management with cross-border effects within the EU." (EU doc no: 6626/05)

Laeken Declaration

The *Laeken Declaration*, (also known as the Declaration on the Future of the European Union) of 15 December 2001, committed the Union to becoming more democratic, transparent and effective.

This Declaration posed 60 targeted questions on the future of the Union and set up a convention to find solutions to the problems identified. These were grouped into four main themes: the division and definition of powers, the simplification of the treaties, the institutional set-up, and moving towards a Constitution for European citizens.

The convention concluded its work on 10 July 2003 after reaching agreement on the proposed *Constitutional Treaty*. The convention failed to deal properly with the task it was set.

See the chapter, *About the Laeken Declaration*, and the *Laeken Declaration* itself.

Languages

At meetings of senior national officials discussions are simultaneously translated into the twenty official languages of the European Union. Day to day business is often conducted in French or English.

Law-making

Law-making in the European Union is not based on the policies put forward by a political party and approved by an electorate. Laws may be introduced only on the authority of the treaties which established the Union. Theses do however offer enormous scope for law-making. Statements within the treaties form what is called “the legal basis” of any proposed law.

The Commission is said to have the sole authority to propose laws. The Constitution would have allowed European laws and framework laws to “be adopted at the initiative of a group of member states, or of the European Parliament *on a recommendation from* the European Central Bank, or at the request of the European Court of Justice, or the European Investment Bank” (article 34/3).

There are four main procedures for passing laws: consultation, assent, co-decision, and a particular kind of law making which is described as “adopting a European decision”.

Under the consultation procedure the Council produces a text based on the Commission’s proposal and consults the European Economic and Social Committee, the Committee of the Regions, and the European Parliament. Parliament may approve the proposal or reject it or suggest amendments. When the council considers the amendments it may only approve them by a unanimous decision. The Council is free to ignore the views of the elected MEPs and often does.

Under the assent procedure a proposal from the Council may be approved or rejected by the European Parliament, but Parliament has no powers in this case to propose amendments.

In the co-decision procedure the Council puts forward a proposed law. The European Parliament may propose amendments and only when both Council and Parliament are in agreement may the proposal pass into law. If Council and Parliament cannot reach agreement a Conciliation Committee consisting of Members of Parliament and the Council meet to try to resolve disagreements. If they cannot reach agreement then the proposal is scrapped. If they do reach agreement then both Parliament and the Council must approve its terms in order for the proposal to become law.

European decisions (laws) may be adopted by the European Council, the Commission, the European Central Bank, and the Council meeting out of public gaze and without any democratic involvement or accountability.

The Constitution, if adopted, would have allowed citizens to propose legislation if a million signatures can be collected in support. (See article 47/4.) This does not guarantee that the Commission would act on such a proposal. In certain circumstances a group of member states or the European Central Bank or the Court of Justice may propose laws.

See *Laws/rulings* etc below, and *Major Issues – Law making*.

Laws/rulings/decisions/acts of the European Union

For an outsider or newcomer it is very difficult to grasp the legal status of the considerable number of types of EU regulations. The EU Constitution would have made matters clearer, but in an attempt to avoid the EU appearing to be a state EU leaders decided in June 2007 to abandon the use of the words "law" and "framework law." In European treaties prior to the European Constitution the following terms are used:

- European regulations and decisions. Under the Constitution these would both be called European laws.
- European directives and framework decisions would become European framework laws.
- Conventions would become either European laws or European framework laws.
- Common positions would be called decisions.
- The term "directive" was to be discontinued.

Under the Constitution the European Union would have made ten kinds of laws/rulings/decisions etc. Their names and purposes are as follows:

- European laws. These are laws which apply to every member state of the EU. They are binding in their entirety. (Articles 33 and 34.)
- European framework laws. These are laws which require member states to achieve certain results. It is left to national governments to frame

their laws and regulations to achieve the required results. (Articles 33 and 34.)

- European regulations. The European regulation is, "a non-legislative act of General application for the implementation of legislative acts and of certain provisions of the Constitution. It may either be binding in its entirety and directly applicable in all member states, or be binding as to the result to be achieved, upon each member state to which it is addressed, but shall leave to the national authorities the choice of form and methods." The Commission, the European Central Bank, and the Council may issue European regulations. (Articles 33 and 35.)
- European decisions. A European decision is "a non-legislative act, binding in its entirety" - a sort of law which has the effect of a law but is not a law. These may be adopted by the European Council, the Commission, the European Central Bank, and the Council. They may take the form of policy decisions which direct national governments to enact legislation to implement a binding Union act. (Articles 33, 35, and 37.)
- Delegated European regulations. In certain circumstances the Commission may make laws to supplement or amend existing laws. These laws only come into effect if the European Parliament fails to notice and take action to quash the Commissions laws. "European laws and framework laws may delegate to the Commission the power to adopt delegated European regulations to supplement or amend certain essential elements of the law or framework law." These delegated European regulations may enter into force by an inertia procedure. The regulations are approved if the European Parliament fails to disapprove of them within a stated time. However, in some cases the European Parliament or the Council will have the power to revoke the delegated regulations. (Article 36.)
- Implementing acts. These are acts passed by member states in order to implement legally binding acts of the European Union. These in turn may be required to confer further implementing powers on the Commission or the Council. (Article 37.)
- European implementing regulations and European implementing decisions. "Union implementing acts shall take the form of European implementing regulations or European implementing decisions." (Article 37.)
- International Agreements with non-EU States. "Agreements concluded by the Union are binding on the institutions of the Union and on its Member States." (Article 323.)
- Recommendations. These have no binding force. (Article 33.)
- Opinions. These, too, have no binding force. (Article 33.)

Binding laws, decisions, regulations take precedence over laws passed by member governments. This is an important fact to be borne in mind when considering issues of the sovereignty of member states. In June 2007 EU leaders decided to drop the term "law" and "framework law". Their statement in the Draft Inter-Governmental Conference Mandate reads as follows: (The references to "as agreed in the 2004 IGC" are to the Constitution.)

"u) In Article 249 (definition of EU acts: regulation, directive and decision), in a new Section 1 on the Union's legal acts, the definition of a decision will be aligned with the one agreed in the 2004 IGC.

v) As a consequence of dropping the denominations "law" and "framework law", the innovations agreed in the 2004 IGC will be adapted, while maintaining the distinction between what is legislative and what is not and its consequences. Accordingly, after Article 249, three Articles will be introduced on, respectively, acts which are adopted in accordance with a legislative procedure, delegated acts and implementing acts. The Article on legislative acts will state that acts (regulations, directives or decisions) adopted under a legislative procedure (ordinary or special) will be legislative acts. The terminology in the Articles on delegated and implementing acts, as agreed in the 2004 IGC, will be adapted accordingly."

See, *Major issues – Democratic deficit* and *Law making.*

Liberalisation

Another name for changing an economy to operate on free trade principles and, in particular, bring in privatisation.

See *Privatisation.*

Lisbon Strategy

A meeting of the European Council in March 2000 in Lisbon decided that Europe should have "the most dynamic knowledge-based economy in the world" by 2010. To achieve this the EU will spend billions of euros on research and development and encouraging high-tech industries. By February 2005 it had been decided to spend 3% of EU GDP on this plan.

See *Major Issues – Democratic deficit*

Lobbying

The art of influencing those who take decisions about our work, our lives our country and our world. It is a legal and necessary activity. For democracy to function those who are controlled by laws must have access to those who take decisions so that decision-makers are in touch with the real world. Three main types of lobbying occur. Lobbying by individuals, by businesses, and by NGOs and other organisations.

Members of the European Parliament may be lobbied by email or letter and a personal meeting is on rare occasions arranged. See *Decision-makers – European Parliament* for details of how to contact MEPs.

The Commission is constantly lobbied, especially by corporate lobbyists. (See discussion on lobbying in the *Major Issues* chapter.) The Commission is keen to know what public opinion is saying. It seeks the opinions of the advisory committees it has set up and carries out opinion research. See *Eurobarometer* above. The advisory committees are a route to influence.

Members of the European Council and the Council of Ministers may be reached in their capacity as members of individual parliaments. Many corporate lobbyists manage to get through to these bodies, but the chance of success for individuals are minimal.

Big corporations employ permanent lobbyists and spend significant sums of money to promote their ideas. An army of lobbyists with permanent offices resides in Brussels. The Commission estimates there are in the region of 15,000 lobbyists there.

See *European Decision Makers – The Lobbyists* and *Major Issues - Lobbying*.

Localism

localism is about thinking in terms of prioritising local action and the local community. It is allied to subsidiarity and tends to conflict with free trade.

See *Major Issues – Localism, Subsidiarity* and *Free trade.*

Luxembourg

This is the home of the European Court of Justice, the European Investment Bank, the European Court of Auditors and the bulk of the administrative offices of the European Parliament.

Maastricht Treaty

The *Maastricht Treaty* is the popular name of the *Treaty on European Union*. It came into effect in 1993 establishing the European Union. Previously it had been known as the European Community or the European Economic Community or the EEC or the EC (and unofficially as the Common Market).

See the *Treaties* chapter.

Majority voting

This is used most notably in the European Parliament and the Commission. The procedure for passing legislation through the European Parliament is explained in article 396.

Merger Treaty

Also known as the *European Community Treaty* or *The Treaty Establishing a Single Council and a Single Commission of the European Communities*. Signed 1965.

See *Treaties* chapter.

Militarism

The placing of great importance on military power and preparations out of proportion to actual defensive needs. The belief that, for a state, military power equates with security, influence and success. Most states achieve security through agreement, trade, and friendly co-operation with other states.

Minister for Foreign Affairs

See *Union Minister for Foreign Affairs.*

Multi-annual

An expression applied to the long-term budget of the EU which is planned to cover a seven year period.

See *Budget*.

National parliaments

See *EU Institutions* chapter.

Ombudsman - The European Ombudsman - Head of EU Complaints Department

See *EU Institutions* chapter.

Operational action

This is the Constitution's term for peace-keeping activities, military activities, military attack or war.

See article 297.

Petersberg tasks - Joint military action

These tasks were established in June 1992 at the Ministerial Council of the Western European Union (WEU) held at the Petersberg Hotel, not far from Bonn. On this occasion, the WEU Member States declared their readiness to make available military units from the whole spectrum of their conventional armed forces for military tasks conducted under the authority of the WEU. The different types of military tasks which the WEU can undertake were defined: apart from contributing to the collective defence in accordance with Article 5 of the *Washington Treaty* and Article V of the modified *Brussels Treaty*, military units of WEU Member States may be employed for:

- humanitarian and rescue tasks;
- peace-keeping tasks;
- tasks of combat forces in crisis management, including peacemaking.

These tasks are included in article 17 of the *Treaty on European Union (Maastricht)* and form an integral part of the European Security and Defence Policy (ESDP). (Article 309 of Constitution.)

Political co-operation

Eurospeak for co-operation between member states in matters of foreign policy – Common Foreign Policy.

Political and Security Committee

See *EU Institutions* chapter.

Precautionary Principle

The Precautionary Principle is about not taking unnecessary risks in matters which could affect the lives of millions of people. The concept of the precautionary principle was first set out for the European Union in a Commission communication adopted in February 2000 on "Recourse to the precautionary principle," in which it defined this concept and envisaged how it would be applied.

In this document, the Commission sets out the specific cases where this principle is applicable:

- where the scientific data are insufficient, inconclusive or uncertain;
- where a preliminary scientific evaluation shows that potentially dangerous effects for the environment and human, animal or plant health can reasonably be feared.

In both cases, the risks are incompatible with the high level of protection sought by the European Union.

The Communication also sets out the three rules which need to be followed for the precautionary principle to be observed:

- a complete scientific evaluation carried out by an independent authority in order to determine the degree of scientific uncertainty;
- an assessment of the potential risks and the consequences of inaction;
- the participation, under conditions of maximum transparency, of all the interested parties in the study of possible measures.

The Commission points out that the measures resulting from recourse to the precautionary principle may take the form of a decision to act or not to act, depending on the level of risk considered "acceptable". The Union applied this precautionary principle in the area of genetically modified organisms (GMOs) between 1999 and 2004, with the adoption of a moratorium on their commercialisation. This has now expired and an EU state seeking to ban GM foods would be breaking EU free trade rules.

Presidency

When a country "holds the presidency" of the EU it means that its senior politician chairs the meetings of the European Council and that ministers from that country chair all the meetings of the various Councils of Ministers for the period of the presidency (currently six months).

During this time the country holding the presidency organises the agenda of the European Council and the Council of Ministers to promote ideas it wishes to see adopted and to solve problems and reach agreements on other issues that have arisen or may arise in the running of the European Union. The President of the Council of Ministers is the Foreign Secretary of the country holding the presidency.

The General Affairs Council, acting under the presidency of the President of the Council of Ministers, prepares the work of the summit meetings of the EU's most senior politicians in the European Council where the strategic decisions of the EU are taken.

If the Constitution is ratified the post of President of the Council of Ministers will be held for two and a half years rather than six months with the aim of bringing greater continuity and stability to the work of the Council.

See *Council* in the *Institutions* chapter.

Privatisation

Also called liberalisation, is the taking into commercial ownership of public services such as the provision of water, prisons, social services, education and healthcare. The first aim of privatised services is to make a good profit and pay shareholders well. Public services, when run by state or other governmental authority, are run purely to provide the most effective public service. European Union policy is to privatise public services. The Constitution authorises this in articles 147 and 148. The Commission will make recommendations as to what shall be privatised. There is no right for an EU state to resist privatisation.

Behind this policy is the belief that competition in the provision of services may provide more efficient and cost-effective provision whilst, at the same time, opening up business opportunities. These latter may benefit national, or European companies or companies from anywhere in the world. There are serious risks with this policy of wholesale privatisation.

See *Major Issues – Free trade.*

Proportionality

This idea arrived in the *Maastricht Treaty*. The Constitution repeats it. The principle requires that any EU laws or regulations must be proportional in the sense that they must be required action appropriate to the task of achieving a specific EU objective and be no more far-reaching and no more expensive than is necessary. Articles 11/3 and 11/4.

Qualified majority voting - QMV

The various permutations of the Council take decisions by unanimous agreement, by a majority, or by a qualified majority. The Constitution adopts a "simplified" version of the QMV rules.

At present the voting procedure is governed by the *Treaty of Nice*, article 205. This states:

> "1. Save as otherwise provided in this Treaty, the Council shall act by a majority of its Members."

Where the Council is required to act by a qualified majority, the votes of its member states are weighted as shown in the table. This change was brought in by a protocol to the *Treaty of Nice*[3]

Germany 29	Bulgaria 10
United Kingdom 29	Austria 10
France 29	Slovakia 7
Italy 29	Denmark 7
Spain 27	Finland 7
Poland 27	Ireland 7
Romania 14	Lithuania 4
Netherlands 13	Luxembourg 4
Greece 12	Latvia 4
Belgium 12	Slovenia 4
Czech Republic 12	Estonia 4
Hungary 12	Cyprus 4
Portugal 12	Malta 3
Sweden 10	
	Total 344

Acts of the Council shall require for their adoption at least 258 votes[4] in favour, cast by a majority of members, where this treaty requires them to be adopted on a proposal from the Commission.

In other cases, for their adoption acts of the Council shall require at least 258 votes[4] in favour cast by at least two-thirds of the members.

When a decision is to be adopted by the Council by a qualified majority, a member of the Council may request verification that the Member States constituting the qualified majority represent at least 62% of the total population of the Union. If that condition is shown not to have been met, the decision in question shall not be adopted.[3]

Article 205 of the *Treaty of Nice* also stated, "Abstentions by Members present in person or represented shall not prevent the adoption by the Council of acts which require unanimity."

The Constitution required that one of two forms of QMV would operate in relation to the European Council and the Council.

According to article 25:

> 1. A qualified majority shall be defined as at least 55 % of the members of the Council, comprising at least fifteen of them and representing Member States comprising at least 65 % of the population of the Union. A blocking minority must include at least four Council members, failing which the qualified majority shall be deemed attained.
>
> 2. By way of derogation from paragraph 1, when the Council does not act on a proposal from the Commission or from the Union Minister for Foreign Affairs, the qualified majority shall be defined as at least 72% of the members of the Council, representing Member States comprising at least 65% of the population of the Union.
>
> 3. Paragraphs 1 and 2 shall apply to the European Council when it is acting by a qualified majority.
>
> 4. Within the European Council, its President and the President of the Commission shall not take part in the vote.

QM voting (QMV) has replaced unanimous voting in many areas because the need for all states to agree something slows the process of change as some states may not be convinced of the need for change or may not agree that a particular law is right for their citizens and therefore might use their veto. This leads to a feeling among many members that prospects for change, reform, development or improvement of the European Union are being or may be frustrated by a reluctant minority. From the point of view of a minority that may oppose change QMV means that policy decisions will be made and laws will come into effect in some countries when their governments do not agree with the new laws. Their sovereignty will be overruled.

The European Constitution provides for 45 new QMV situations. Protocol 34, article 2 states that paragraph 2 and 3 of article 25 of the Constitution was to have taken effect from 1 November 2009. The *Draft Reform Treaty* of 2007 proposed delays. See *Part Five The Reform Treaty - The Constitution Repackaged* for details.

See also *Euroterminology - Unanimity, Voting - The Commission and the European Parliament* and *Majority voting, Major Issues - Complication, Voting, Institutions - Agriculture and Fisheries*, article 25 and *Part Five The Reform Treaty - The Constitution Repackaged*.

Quota hopping

Under the Common Fisheries Policy member states are allocated quotas - set quantities - of fish they may catch from the EU waters.

Spanish fishermen increased their quotas by buying British boats and registering their boats in Britain, flying the British flag and claiming part of the UK fish quota. A 1988 UK Act of Parliament banned this practice, quota-hopping, but this law was overruled by the European Court.

See *Major Issues - Fisheries*

Rapporteur

The person appointed by a standing committee of the European Parliament to write a report on the findings of the committee.

See Institutions - *European Parliament Standing Committee.*

Reform Treaty

The *Reform Treaty* is a treaty to explain how to amend two other treaties.

The meeting of EU leaders in Brussels 21 to 23 June 2007 ordered the setting up of a conference (IGC) to draw up this new treaty. Their statement reads, "The *Reform Treaty* will introduce into the existing treaties, which remain in force, the innovations resulting from the 2004 IGC, [ie, the European Constitution] as set out below in a detailed fashion." They then set out in a "draft mandate" (a detailed and precise set of instructions) what was to go into the *Reform Treaty.*

The changes the *Reform Treaty* will bring in may be summarised as follows:

- The "abandoned" 2004 European Constitution will be taken to pieces and re-assembled keeping all key elements.
- The changes to existing EU treaties which the Constitution brought in will now be integrated into the *Treaty on European Union (Maastricht) and the Treaty Establishing the European Community (The Treaty of Rome, Nice Version).*
- The word "Constitution" will not be used. The result of this, together with the re-assembly of the elements of the Constitution is that it will seem as if the Constitution has dissappeared.
- There will be a few quite small changes to the provisions of the Constitution which will generally add a little more clarity and flexibility - including some opportunities for countries to opt out of some arrangements.

See *Part Five The Reform Treaty - EU Constitution Repackaged* which discusses the *Reform Treaty* in detail, and *Major Issues, Reform Treaty.*

Restrictive measures

This is the EU's euphemism for sanctions. (Article 322.)
See *Major Issues – Sanctions* (in the *Free trade* section).

Schengen (Agreement , Convention and Acquis)

The agreement signed at Schengen in Luxembourg on 14 June 1985, set out how Belgium, France, Germany, Luxembourg and the Netherlands would gradually remove their common border controls and introduce freedom of movement within their combined territory for all nationals of the signatory Member States, other Member States or third countries.

The Schengen Convention entered into force in 1995. It lays down the arrangements and guarantees for implementing freedom of movement. The *Schengen Agreement* and the Schengen Convention, and related agreements together form the "Schengen acquis" - the rules which any new member of the European Union must accept.

The Schengen area has gradually expanded: Italy signed up in 1990, Spain and Portugal in 1991, Greece in 1992, Austria in 1995 and Denmark, Finland and Sweden in 1996. Iceland and Norway, though not EU members, are also parties to the Convention.

Ireland and the United Kingdom are not parties to the agreements, but, under the protocol to the *Treaty of Amsterdam*, they may take part in some or all of the provisions of this acquis.

Moreover, although already a signatory to the Schengen Convention, Denmark may choose in the context of the European Union whether to apply any new decision taken on the basis of the Schengen acquis.

In the European Constitution the provisions relating to the area of freedom, security and justice are amplified by a series of protocols, relating in particular to the Schengen acquis and the special positions of certain Member States (United Kingdom, Ireland and Denmark).

Among other innovations in the Constitution:

- the scope of the Protocol on the position of the United Kingdom and Ireland is extended to include police co-operation;
- the opt-out in the Protocol on the position of Denmark is maintained. To encourage Denmark to waive its opt-out, there is an Annex with an intermediate scheme between the opt-out and full application of Union law.

See the *Treaties* chapter, and Protocol 17 of the Constitution.

Shared competence

See *Competence* (above).

Single market

A single market is an area which includes two or more states in which many actions are taken to maximise trade. As a first step customs duties on goods passing between states and quota restrictions are first reduced and then abolished. Agreement is then reached on a common external tariff, the abolition or harmonisation of state subsidies, legal harmonisation of matters relevant to the easy and equitable operation of trade, and agreement on the free movement between member states of goods, services, capital and people.

This may be taken further by having a single currency with a single monetary and fiscal authority.

See also *Sovereignty*.

Social dumping

States offer varying degrees of rights to workers. Some offer high levels of job security and redundancy pay, sickness benefits, maternity and paternity leave, guaranteed holidays with pay, safety at work, rights to form unions, strike, limited working hours and working week, and vocational training and education. Within the EU there are considerable variations. Obviously these rights are costly to provide. Some states have kept benefits at a low level to attract businesses to set up. When businesses, often multinational companies, shift production to states with lower tax rates and limited workers' rights they are said to be engaged in "social dumping". This is sometimes described as "exporting unemployment".

Social model (European Social Model)

This term is used to describe the high standards of state-provided welfare within the EU - protection of workers' rights, education, healthcare etc. Unfortunately the term may often lead to misunderstanding because it over-simplifies a complex picture. In fact there is not a single level of social protection and provision within the EU. There are wide variations across the EU and the picture is changing. For example, in the late 20th century and at the start of the 21st century UK governments took steps to curtail workers' rights and have started to take state provided welfare services to pieces by converting state provision of services into marketable units which may later be removed from state provision. As this book goes to press in early 2007 the state provision of free dentistry for all has undergone serious cutbacks. In contrast, for example, the state provision of support for free services remains very high in Denmark.

The pressures of the EU's free-trade policies to make their economies "competitive" discourage the provision of high standards of comprehensive free services provided by states, and encourage the erosion of workers' rights. In spite of these conflicting pressures the EU maintains commitments to keep up efforts to enhance social provision and harmonise it across the EU.

See the Social Policy section of the Constitution, articles 209-219 which basically reiterate the *Treaty Establishing the European Community* (articles 136- 148).

Solidarity

This is a commitment by EU states to assist each other in the event of terrorist attacks or other man-made or natural emergency or disaster. In addition, it is a vigorous demand for loyalty in foreign policy. Article 294 demands that "Member States shall support the common foreign and security policy actively and unreservedly in a spirit of loyalty and mutual solidarity. The Member States shall work together to enhance and develop their mutual political solidarity. They shall refrain from any action which is contrary to the interests of the Union or likely to impair its effectiveness as a cohesive force in international relations."

Article 41 states that if a member state is attacked "other member states shall have towards it an obligation of aid and assistance by all the means in their power". See also articles 16 and 43.

Sovereignty

Sovereignty is the ability of states to act independently and take decisions for themselves. Sovereignty is not absolute. No matter how powerful or independent a state may be it is constrained by the realities of its need to trade, communicate, and work with other states. In a federal system states possess reduced degrees of sovereignty dependent on how much power is given to or taken by the central government.

State sovereignty includes a state's power to decide its own relationships with other countries, the power to set its own interest rates to stimulate trade or reduce inflation, set its own tax levels, the power to establish its own laws and provisions regarding employment, pensions, healthcare, education, agriculture, law and order, environmental protection etc.

See also *Federalism, Integration, Intergovernmentalism* and the chapter, *Early plans for European co-operation and unity.*

Standing Committees

The European Parliament has twenty-five standing (or permanent) committees. See *European Union Institutions*.

Strasbourg

One of the homes of the European Parliament.
See also, *Brussels.*

Subsidiarity

The subsidiarity principle is intended to ensure that decisions are taken as closely as possible to the citizen. True (grass-roots) subsidiarity would consist of the lower levels of government making decisions until such time as it became apparent that decisions on a particular topic would need to be taken at a higher level. A kind of subsidiarity can exist where decisions are taken at the highest possible level until such time as the highest authority feels a matter is of too little importance to concern it and then allows a lower authority to take decisions. This latter (top-down) subsidiarity is, more or less, the version of subsidiarity operated by the EU.

Internationally states tend to operate on a "bottom up" approach. They handled their own pollution until it became apparent that states operating alone could not solve the problem. States then met together to try to achieve effective international controls. States in their quests for peace and security made many agreements but in the twentieth century they came to believe that a far wider range of participants in peace agreements were required and as a result set up the League of Nations, and when this failed they set up the United Nations. Sometimes international agreements arrive by the "top down" approach. For example , the World Bank and IMF, established by richer states, seek to influence all states.

In theory constant checks are made as to whether action at EU level is justified in the light of the possibilities available at national, regional or local level. For example, it makes sense for decisions about street parking, names of streets, the building of a community hall etc to be taken by a council which is in close touch with a local community. A decision to increase tax on petrol might be best taken at a national level, and a decision to put tax on aviation fuel could only be effective with international agreement. Specifically, the EU idea of subsidiarity is the principle whereby the Union does not, or is not supposed, to take action (except in the areas which fall within its exclusive competence) unless it is more effective than action taken at national, regional or local level. It is closely bound up with the principles of proportionality and necessity, which require that any action by the Union should not go beyond what is necessary to achieve the objectives of the *Treaty on European Union.*

The Edinburgh European Council of December 1992 set out subsidiarity rules in a declaration that serves as the basic explanation of the subsidiarity principle.

The European Constitution takes a step towards ensuring that the subsidiarity principle is applied by means of an obligation for the Union institutions to inform national parliaments at all stages of the legislative procedure. The Europa web site explains, "The establishment of an early-warning system regarding respect for the subsidiarity principle will enable national parliaments to ask the Commission to review a legislative proposal if they consider that it violates the principle." What limited powers state parliaments have is explained more fully elsewhere.

Since decision making within the EU starts from one of the central bodies (mainly the Commission, the Council or the European Council) and a central body (the European Court of Justice) adjudicates on whether decisions may be allowed to take place at a lower level, the control of subsidiarity remains firmly under the control of the highest level of decision making.

The Constitution does not set out clearly what matters will be decided by the EU and what matters will be decided by national or regional governments. Instead it sets up areas of doubt and dispute called "shared competences".

See *Major Issues - Subsidiarity*, articles 11-18 and Protocol 2.

Third countries

The European Union is seen as consisting of two (and more) states. Any state or country outside the European Union is referred to as a third country.

Trade agreements

The EU needs to trade. The EU is the world's largest importer of food, mainly tropical foods and animal feed. Almost 45% of its energy requirements are imported. Three quarters of its raw materials are imported. The European Union accounts for one fifth of total world trade. It operates within the rules of the WTO which is a force behind EU trade policy, and with the IMF and World Bank is the driving force for free trade around the world.

Trade agreements have been signed between the EU and other states and trading blocs. These include:

1976 Tunisia, Algeria and Morocco.
1997 Egypt, Syria, Jordan and Lebanon.
1975 Israel, Sri Lanka.
1975 Mexico.
1973 Uruguay.
1976 Bangladesh and the Pakistan.
1980 Brazil.
1981 India (plus a co-operation agreement with the ASEAN countries).
1983 Co-operation agreement with the five Andean pact states.
1984 The third Lomé Convention, agreement with 66 African, Caribbean and Pacific countries.
After 1991 Bulgaria, Romania, Albania, China, (temporarily) the Soviet Union, the Ukraine, Belarus, Kazakhstan, Kyrgistan, Georgia, Armenia, Azerbaijan, Moldova, and Uzbekistan.
1994 A partnership and co-operation agreement with Russia. (Russia supplies large amounts of energy to the EU.)
2000 Cotonou agreement replaced Lomé Convention, agreement. Arrangements with 78 African, Caribbean and Pacific countries.

Transparency

Transparency is sometimes called "open government" and is a key aspect of democratic government. It basically means that citizens of a state know what their government is doing and why. They are able to do such things as follow the making of state laws, observe parliamentary debates, read verbatim records of these debates and minutes or records of other important meetings relating to the functioning of the state. It also means they have access to reports brought before government and reports commissioned by government.

The EU, in its earlier forms, conducted its business in secret. In 1991 the *Maastricht Treaty*, article 191 (which became article 255 in the Amsterdam/Nice Treaties) first required some degree of transparency in the functioning of the European Community/European Union. As updated, this article set out citizens' rights to access to the documents of the European Parliament, the Council and the Commission, with a number of exceptions.

The Constitution, articles 50 and 399, would extend the right of access to include some documents for other institutions, and require the European Parliament to meet in public, and the Council "when considering and voting on a draft legislative act." Reports by Statewatch and others show that the open access to documents which has so long been a requirement has not been fully honoured. (See *Transparency* in *Major Issues.*)

Much of the operation of the European Union takes place in secret and information is often difficult or impossible to obtain.

There are plans to open up more of the EU's decision-making to the public.

See articles 50 and 399, and *Major Issues (Biggest Issue, Number Four,* and *Transparency).*

Unanimity

Unanimity has one clear meaning outside the EU. Decision-making by unanimity means that all present agree to a decision. In the EU the term "unanimity" usually has the conventional meaning, but there are exceptions outlined below.

In general the following areas require that decisions are arrived at unanimously: taxation, harmonisation in the field of social security and social protection, certain provisions in the field of justice and home affairs (the European Prosecutor, family law, operational police co-operation, etc), the flexibility clause (article 18) which allows action outside specific permission within the Constitution if it fulfils an EU objective (permitting effective re-writing of the Constitution by very few people), the Common Foreign and Security Policy (article 300, but see the discussion of complex exceptions under this heading), the finances of the Union, membership of the Union, citizenship including the granting of new rights and anti-discrimination measures, certain institutional issues including the electoral system and composition of the Parliament, certain appointments, composition of the Committee of the Regions and the European Economic and Social Committee, revision of the Constitution, etc.

The *Amsterdam* and *Nice Treaties* removed 90 areas previously protected by vetoes ie where decision was by unanimous agreement. The Constitution removes a further 60.

Unanimity EU style

Unanimity in the EU may take one of two unconventional forms:

1 It may mean that when matters are put to a vote there are abstentions but is no outright opposition. The EU calls this "constructive abstention"! It allows, for example, neutral countries which do not wish to be associated with military action to register their disagreement whilst not preventing others from taking military action. In plain language this is a kind of majority decision. Perhaps it should be called "special majority " decision-making or "unopposed majority" decision-making.

2 Another bending of the majority idea occurs when a group of member states, acting in an area of decision making which requires decision by unanimity (such as the Common foreign and security Policy), form an independent group taking independent action. This is called "enhanced co-operation". (Article 44.) They may take unanimous decisions *of this splinter group*. (Article 44/3.) The remaining member states have no veto over the action of this group. The Constitution envisages, in the realm of

defence, groups of states working in "permanent structured co-operation". (Articles 41, 310 and 312.) Therefore an area of EU policy which is often described as proceeding only with the full support of all member states (unanimity) may proceed without unanimous support.

In addition to these variations on unanimity, some areas of action which normally require unanimity allow exceptions. In the area of Common Foreign and Security policy the Constitution would allow four exceptions to the rule of unanimous decision-making. See articles 300/2/3/4 and 343.

See articles on matters which become "shared competences", articles 12-18. *Competences* above and especially *Major Issues – Defence and Foreign Policy* and *Clear use of language.*

Union Minister for Foreign Affairs

The Constitution described one of the most powerful roles in the European Union, the Union Minister for Foreign Affairs. In June 2007 EU leaders decided to change job title to "High Representative of the Union for Foreign Affairs and Security Policy". The Minister will be appointed by the European Council by QMV. He or she will conduct the Union's foreign policy and defence policy (described in the prolix terminology of EU documents as the two areas "Common Foreign and Security Policy" and "Common Security and Defence Policy"). This minister will be Secretary General of the Council of Ministers, preside over the Foreign Affairs Council and be a Vice-President of the Commission where he will co-ordinate the Commission's work in foreign and defence policy. He is responsible for the Defence Agency.

This role is currently filled by the European Union High Representative for Foreign Affairs and the External Affairs Commissioner.

See article 28, *Western European Union* below, *Major Issues - Union Minister for Foreign Affairs, Defence, Democratic deficit, Free trade wars, Decision-makers - High Representative for Common Foreign and Security Policy,* and *Part Five The Reform Treaty - The Constitution Repackaged.*

Voting - The Commission and the European Parliament

The Commissioners, at their regular Wednesday meetings or other special meetings, take decisions by a simple majority and then accept collective responsibility for them.

The European Parliament takes decisions by a simple majority of the votes cast. The exception is when passing a motion of censure on the European Commission (which would dismiss all the Commissioners). For such a censure motion to be carried two thirds of the votes cast, representing a majority of the members of parliament, must support it.

See also *Euroterminology - Qualified majority voting, Unanimity,* and *Majority voting, Major Issues - Complication, Voting, Institutions - Agriculture and Fisheries*, and article 25.

War – Going to war or being invaded

The EU tends to avoid using the word "war". It uses the term "operational action." See article 297. In its defence policy it does not usually talk of invasion or a military attack on member states although it does talk of "terrorist attack." Military invasion seems to be covered by the words "man-made disaster." See articles 43 and 329. Article 41/7 is more realistic and talks of a member state being "the victim of armed aggression on its territory".

Working time directive and UK working hours

The Working Time Directive (93/104/EC) of 1993 required all sectors of industry, commerce and public service throughout the European Union to limit the hours worked by employees to 48 per week, including overtime, rest periods and breaks. Employees were required to be given a minimum of four weeks paid leave per year. There are a few exemptions including: "managing executives or other persons with autonomous decision-making powers; family workers; workers officiating at religious ceremonies in churches and religious communities."

Originally the UK negotiated an opt-out for the directive, but now complies. According to the Commission (2004) "Latest figures show that about 16% of the workforce currently works more than 48 hours per week, compared with a figure of 15% at the beginning of the 1990s. About 8% of the workforce say they work over 55 hours per week, 3.2% over 60 hours per week and 1% over 70 hours per week. The UK is the only Member State where weekly working time has increased over the last decade."[5]

Notes

1 See 2007-2013 budget info at: http://ec.europa.eu/budget/prior_future/next_fin_framework_en.htm
2 (The Official Journal of the European Union, 16 December 2004/C310/01): http://europa.eu.int/eur/lex/JOHtml.
3 Protocol on the enlargement of the European Union 10 March 2001. Official Journal of the European Union, reference 80/80. With twenty-seven members the qualified majority is 73.4% of the votes. A blocking minority is 91 votes. Declaration 21 "on the qualified majority threshold and the number of votes for a blocking minority in an enlarged Union." 10 March 2001. Official Journal of the European Communities, reference C80/85.
4 The figure from 1 January 2007 is 255. Source Council web site 25 April 2007.
5 Europa press release reference MEMO/04/1 5 January 2004.

Part Four

The Constitution's Ideas

Many people worked long and hard at drafting the European Constitution. Valery Giscard d'Estaing, who was in charge of the whole process, said to them, "This is what you have to do if you want the people to build statues of you on horseback in the villages you all come from." - reported in the *Financial Times*, 21 June 2004.

"The unification of Europe is near." - European Union leaders, Laeken, December 2001.

The Constitution - a comprehensive guide to the EU

The European Constitution - dead or alive?

The European Constitution provides the best account of the aims, rules of operation, institutions and policies of the present European Union (2007) and the European Union of the future. It is the European Union's own account of its activities. It sets out details of some new procedures and the taking of more powers from member countries with the consequent increase in power of the euroauthorities. The system of "shared competences" enables a continuing shift of powers from national and regional authorities within the EU and into the hands of the central EU authority.

The heads of state of 25 European Union countries agreed the Constitution by signing it at a meeting in Rome on 29 October 2004. Bulgaria and Romania ratified the Constitution as part of the membership process prior to joining the EU on the 1 January 2007. To come into effect the Constitution needed to be ratified by the parliaments and people of all 27 EU member states. Its rejection by two states means that it could not come into operation in its current form.

The European Constitution lives on

By August 2007 eighteen EU member states had ratified the Constitution - showing that the majority of parliaments in the EU supported the provisions of the Constitution. Seven states decided to postpone their decision. The full provisions of the Constitution could not be put into operation. However, almost all of the elements of the European Constitution were already in force before it was signed because most of the Constitution consists of the provisions of five principle previous treaties: the *Treaty of Rome* 1957, the *EURATOM Treaty* of 1957, the *Maastricht Treaty* of 1991, the *Amsterdam Treaty* of 1997, and the *Nice Treaty* of 2001.

The Constitution also contains new elements which were being brought into operation without waiting for consent by the ratification process. These include plans to set up a new Euro Civil Service department - the External Action Service, the Defence Agency - to develop European arms industries, and the development of databases, in connection with the *Schengen Agreement*, holding personal information on every European citizen.

Furthermore, EU leaders were clearly not going to give up ideas they had committed themselves to. The June 2007 summit of EU leaders proved the truth of this. As discussed in Part Five, the Constitution's new ideas were transferred to existing treaties.

The result of this move was that the innovations of the 2004 Constitution became even harder to identify and therefore correspondingly difficult to assess.

The EU Constitution currently remains the most complete and intelligible guide to the rules and operation of the European Union. The Constitution lives on.

Reform of the EU or expansion of EU powers

The Constitution was clearly not designed to address the fundamental problems identified in the *Laeken Declaration.* EU leaders since 2001 have had other concerns which they consider far more pressing. In particular they wanted to devise a system which would allow the ten new member states of 2004 and two of 2007 to participate "effectively" in decision-making. What they mean by this is not having decisions held up because a few states disagree. (See the discussion on unanimity and voting in *Major Issues.*) In many instances under the existing treaties decisions could only be taken if there was unanimity amongst states. They quickly decided that the system they agreed at Nice was too complicated. The Constitution set out how most decisions would be taken by a "simplified" form of majority decision. Other changes planned to be brought about by the Constitution included:

- establishing the role of a European Foreign Minister ("the Union Minister of Foreign Affairs"
- extending the period of office of the President of the European Council from six months to two and a half years
- establishing the Defence Agency to promote EU arms spending
- establishing a new EU civil service – The External Action Service
- permitting the extension of EU data gathering on all EU citizens to facilitate Schengen border control effectiveness See *Major Issues - Data harvesting*
- extending the number of spheres in which the EU may take action thereby reducing the powers of member states to take independent action
- extending the range of laws that will be passed by the joint decision of the European Parliament and the Council
- increasing the maximum number of seats in the European Parliament.

These innovations, and many more (indicated in the following pages) have been preserved in the *Reform Treaty* (2007) and will be integrated into existing treaties.

Does the EU need a Constitution?

There is a special value in having a constitution. Every state should have one so that everyone can relate to the grand scheme that will create the best of all possible states. Perhaps for the first time, if the European Union had a constitution, it would establish in the minds of all Europeans that the EU really is a state in its own right with the power of independent action, with its own citizens and their distinctive European fundamental rights, and that it is the top tier of government of the member states. It would bring together the key ideas for the running of the European Union. Commercial, economic, social and other policy decisions could be removed and set out in separate documents to cover existing or changing arrangements. This would also have the effect of reducing its size considerably.

The EU Constitution has been made to seem as if it has disappeared. But it would seem like a failure of nerve if a new version, acceptable to all, were never produced. Writing a new constitution is not primarily a matter of finding the right form of expression but of first establishing the main line of development of the

European Union and finding practical answers to fundamental failings. Some EU leaders are in ignorance or denial about many matters and cannot believe that some of their deeply held convictions are not widely shared by the citizens of Europe. And they seek to gloss over grave institutional failings which, in their own right, create hostility to the European Project and detract from its merits. These matters are explored in the *Major Issues* chapter.

Key features of the European Constitution

"The illegal we do immediately, the unconstitutional takes a little longer." – Henry Kissinger, former American Secretary of State.

Valery Giscard d'Estaing, Former President of France and President of the Convention which wrote the Constitution, phoned M. Chirac, President of France, in March 2005 to warn him that it was a mistake to send out the entire three-part, 448-article Constitution to every French voter. 'I said, "Don't do it, don't do it. It is not possible for anyone to understand the full text."' - Interview in *The New York Times*, quoted in *euObserver*, 15 June 2005.

As already mentioned the "full text" which was sent to every French voter in the referendum on the proposed Constitution was in fact only the first 448 articles. Some one hundred and forty pages of protocols and declarations were not included. Giscard d' Estaing was half right, though, for most people the Constitution, like the EU itself, is incomprehensible. But this book should help.

Examining the Constitution little by little is rather like examining a forest tree by tree. We shall be in danger of entirely losing sight of the shape and nature of the forest as a whole. In addition, the EU Constitution has a number of false trails. This account of the Constitution is primarily of the surface meaning of the text with just a few pointers to possible difficulties. The reader is directed to the *Major Issues* chapter and especially *The Ten Biggest Problems* for an introduction to the big picture and for further exploration of points raised here. Important protocols and declarations are discussed in relevant sections of *Major Issues.*

Main provisions of the 2004 European Constitution

Note:

- See Part Five - *The Reform Treaty - The Constitution Repackaged* for an account of details of the limited changes to the Constitution brought in by the *Reform Treaty* 2007.
- "New" means that a commitment or provision in the Constitution has not previously appeared in any of the earlier treaties up to and including the *Nice Treaty* (2001).
- Special terms. Many of the special terms used throughout this book are explained in the chapter devoted to definitions - *Euroterminology*.
- The 2004 European Constitution is more correctly known as the *Treaty Establishing a Constitution for Europe.*

- The numbering and organisation of the Constitution is not designed to make it easy to use. It consists of: a preamble, four parts (each part being divided into sections which are called titles which are further divided into chapters). These four parts are divided into 448 articles. In addition there are two annexes, a Final Act, 36 protocols (many with preambles and each with its own numbered sequence of articles), plus 50 declarations. The parts are numbered with Roman numerals. In official documents the numbers of articles are preceded by the Roman numeral indicating which part an article comes from. This seems cumbersome and unhelpful so in this book articles are simply referred to by their numbers, or in the case of protocols by the protocol number followed by the article number. However, the reader who wishes to be able to refer to the original numbering system with the Roman numerals will find it is retained in the included text of the Constitution.
- All references in this book to specific "articles" are articles in the 2004 European Constitution (articles 1 to 448) unless otherwise stated.

The Preamble

The preamble begins by paying tribute to "the inviolable and inalienable rights of the human person, freedom, democracy, equality and the rule of law." It says that the EU wishes "to deepen the democratic and transparent nature of its public life and to strive for peace, justice and solidarity throughout the world."

After this commitment to principles of civilised life the preamble becomes controversial and talks of the peoples of Europe being determined to become "united ever more closely." This refers to the transfer of powers from national governments to the centralising power in Brussels – taking steps towards making Europe into a single country – the prime policy of the EU and one that has never been placed specifically before the citizens of Europe for democratic approval. If this policy does command wide support in Europe then the trend in some of the developments put forward in the Constitution are also likely to meet with approval. If not, the opposite applies. Opinion surveys suggest that public opinion is moving against "ever closer union". This is a fundamental policy issue on which the direction of the development of the European Union depends. Perhaps it should be put to the citizens of Europe in a referendum.

The preamble goes on to express a determination to develop the work of existing EU treaties and the 97,000 pages of existing EU regulations referred to here simply as the "Community Acquis".

The Preamble gives a fair flavour of the mode of thinking and presentation of its authors.

Part 1 - Constitution

Title 1 - Definitions and objectives of the Union - Articles 1 - 8

New:

- By accepting this Constitution the citizens and states of the European Union confer powers on the Union. The European Union directs the states and citizens of Europe within the spheres of power granted to it.

- Any law passed by the EU takes precedence over any laws of member states. - A statement of what the ECJ has long established.
- The Union adopts a legal personality with the right to conclude treaties in its own name on behalf of its member states. - A major transfer of power.
- The Union adopts certain "symbols" including an anthem and the euro.

Article 1 makes it very clear that the Constitution, if accepted, establishes that member governments give to EU institutions the power to direct and control the way Europe is run. "Member states confer competences . . . The Union shall coordinate the policies . . ."

Article 2 expresses the human values to which the constitution aspires.

Article 3 details the objectives of the EU, most of which are likely to be seen as highly desirable such as full employment and improvement of the quality of the environment.

Article 3 states, "the Union shall offer its citizens . . . an internal market where competition is free and undistorted." Nevertheless, "free" and "undistorted" are elastic concepts which may be difficult to operate effectively. Within the EU companies have grown up which have huge market power which inhibit the start-up of competitors and may be guilty of using powers in ways feared by Adam Smith – freedom leading to market distortion which limits freedom.

A policy of supporting free trade is one which would perhaps be best left to separate treaty arrangements or for the consideration of governments of the day, partly because it can never be implemented in its pure form and views as to its desirability change. In fact much of the EU's own current trading arrangements are far from free. The American Constitution gives Congress the power "to regulate commerce" but leaves it to Congress to adopt and change trade policies as it sees fit. See *Major Issues - Free trade* and *Common Agricultural Policy*.

Article 4 is concerned with the free movement of persons, services, goods and capital. Comments on services appear elsewhere in this introduction. Currently the commitment to the free movement of persons at borders is not fully implemented. There are prohibitions of citizens of the twelve newest member states working in most of the older member states and there are checks at many borders. These checks are due to be linked to a vast computer network and database which will record information on every EU citizen. The operation of these freedoms is expressed in articles 130-176.

Article 5 makes an unnecessary commitment which is also palpably false. "The Union shall respect the equality of Member States." Perhaps the authors were trying to be as impressive as the United Nations where the rule of the UN General Assembly is one country, one vote. But the authors cannot be unaware of their own rules on voting in the Council where each state has votes agreed according to a scale which gives them greatly varying power. For example, Germany, with a population of 82.5 million has 29 votes in meetings of the Council; Malta, with a population of 0.4 million has 3 votes in the Council. In the European Parliament Germany has 99 seats; Malta has 5. Payments to the EU by member states vary greatly. Receipts, in the form of financial help from EU coffers, also vary greatly from one member state to another and one region to another.

Amongst other things, the Union commits itself to respect certain rights of states. It shall respect their essential state functions, including, "maintaining law and order and safeguarding national security." But the EU has plans to be active in these spheres and the independence of member states in these matters is certainly eroded by this Constitution. A non-democratic harmonisation of laws is envisaged. Legal procedures envisaged in the Constitution do not match British legal procedures.

Article 6 states that the laws of the EU take precedence over the laws of its member states. This is new in a treaty/constitution but is not a new idea within the Union. It was established by the European Court of Justice in its ruling on a case in 1963 (Case 26/62 - Van Gend en Loos). The ruling stated, "The Community constitutes a new legal order of international law for the benefit of which the States have limited their Sovereign rights . . . Community law therefore . . . imposes obligations on individuals . . ." In many other cases the European Court of Justice has confirmed this. One further example, (Case 106/77 Italian Finance Administration v Simenthal (No2) [1978]), referred to "the principle of the precedence of Community law. . ." which rendered "automatically inapplicable any conflicting provision of current national law . . ." This was such as to, "preclude the valid adoption of new national legislative measures to the extent to which they would be incompatible with Community provisions."

Article 7 establishes the EU as a "legal personality" able to act as a state and make treaties on behalf of all member states. (Article 437 is relevant here as it abolishes the existing EU treaties to make way for the new arrangements.) The Union will have the right to make treaties independently of the member states and will have its own budget. Member states will be required to abide by terms negotiated by the EU on their behalf.

Article 8, which is headed "The symbols of the Union", should not be overlooked. Amongst the minor details of the Constitution is a major commitment. "The currency of the Union shall be the euro." By agreeing to the Constitution the governments and people of Europe agree to the euro as their currency and all that implies in terms of direction of their economies. (Britain has been allowed to opt out under the provisions of Protocol 13.)

See *Major Issues* - including *the Euro,* and *Free speech* (in *the Charter of Fundamental Rights* section), and later discussion on the Central Bank.

Title 2 - Fundamental Rights and Citizenship of the Union - Articles 9 and 10

Articles 9 and 10 deal with rights and citizenship. See also Charter of Fundamental Rights, a later section of the Constitution, articles 61-114, and articles 115-129.

Title 3 - Union Competences - Articles 11 - 18

New:

- Article 12. Categories of competence. For an explanation of "competence" see *Euroterminology*.
- Where the Union has "exclusive competence" to pass laws then member states may take no action.
- "Shared competence" allows member states to pass laws only when the Union does not. See *Euroterminology*.

- The Union will "define and implement a common foreign and security policy."
- Article 13 lists exclusive competences.
- Article 14. Areas of shared competence: energy is added to the list.
- Article 15. Member states must "co-ordinate their economic and employment policies" as directed by the Union.
- Article 17. The Union adds to the list of activities which it has powers to "carry out supporting, co-ordinating, or complementary action. . . at European level." The new areas are tourism, sport, civil protection, and administrative co-operation.
- Articles 13 – 17 list all the areas of human activity in which the EU may take action. See *Major Issues – Biggest problems 5 and 6 (Top down decision-making* and *Creeping centralisation)* plus *Subsidiarity* and *Euroterminology – Competences.*

Article 18. The powers adopted by the European Union as a consequence of the Constitution may be indefinitely extended without a rewriting of the Constitution or the approval of member states' parliaments or peoples. See also articles 44, 416, and 423.

Title 4 - The Union's Institutions and Bodies - Articles 19 - 32

New:

- Article 20. Normal law making process will be by joint decision of the European Parliament and the Council. These two bodies will agree the budget. European Parliament maximum membership now 750. Minimum seats for any member state will be 6 and maximum 96.
- Article 22 President of the European Council shall be elected by members to serve for two and a half years.
- Article 25. New complex QMV procedures to come into effect in 2009. The date is not explained here, but in Protocol 34.
- Article 26 sets out the duties and powers of the Commission including (26/2) "Union legislative acts may be adopted only on the basis of a Commission proposal, except where the Constitution provides otherwise." Article 26/7 stresses the complete independence of the Commission. See *Major Issues – Lobbying.*
- Article 27. The European Council will propose a candidate for President of the Commission subject to the approval of the European Parliament. See *Major Issues – President of the Commission.*
- Article 28. Subject to the approval of the President of the Commission, the European Council will appoint a Union Minister for Foreign Affairs. Democratic legitimacy could be improved here. See *Major Issues - Union Minister of Foreign Affairs* and *Euroterminology - Union Minister of Foreign Affairs.*

Articles 19 - 32 also describe the functions and duties of other EU institutions including advisory bodies.

Title 5 - Exercise of Union competence - Articles 33 - 43

New:

- Articles 34 and 35 describe "legislative acts" and "non-legislative acts".
- Article 40. "The European Union shall conduct a common foreign and security policy." Independent action by member states in matters of foreign affairs will not be allowed.
- Article 41/1. Euro army. It is sometimes asserted that the European Union does not have an army. In a sense this is true, and it is not mentioned by name here but it does have military forces at its command which are described here in somewhat evasive terms. (There is a central command. See *Major Issues – Euro army*.) "The common security and defence policy. . . shall provide the Union with an operational capacity drawing on civil and military assets. The Union may use them on missions outside the Union. . . the performance of these tasks shall be undertaken using capabilities provided by the Member States."
- Article 41/2. There will be a common defence policy. . . "when the European Council, acting unanimously, so decides." See *Euroterminology* and *Major Issues* chapter on the topic of *Defence and Foreign Policy* and *Unanimity*.
- Article 41/3. Euro army again. "Member States shall make civilian and military capabilities available to the Union for the implementation of the common security and defence policy."
- Article 41/3. Promoting arms sales and militarism. "Member States shall undertake progressively to improve their military capabilities. An agency in the field of defence capabilities development, research acquisition and armaments (European Defence Agency) shall be established . . . " The European Defence Agency was actually set up on 12 July 2004 with a first year budget of € 20,000,000. See also *Major issues – Security and defence policy*.
- Article 41/6. A group of member states may band together to form a military alliance within the Union.
- Article 43. In the event of man-made or natural disaster the Union and its member states shall act jointly in the spirit of solidarity.

Articles 33 to 43 describe other legal acts of the Union and give further details of foreign, security and defence policies and details of enhanced co-operation. Foreign security and defence are also the topics of articles 294 –312 and article 310.

Title 6 - The democratic life of the Union - Articles 45 - 52

New:

- Article 45. Citizens shall be treated equally by EU institutions.
- Article 46. "The functioning of the Union shall be founded on representative democracy." It does not appear to be true that the functioning of the Union is actually "founded on representative democracy." It was founded by representative democracies and was run, in its early years, by committees which were appointed by democratically elected leaders. The

significant point is that the appointed committees were given independent powers not subject to democratic control. Also, "founded on" is not the same as "operating on the basis of direct representative democracy". The convoluted, complex and patchy nature of EU democracy is discussed in *Major Issues – Democratic deficit* and *Subsidiarity*. Article 46 also states, "Decisions shall be taken as openly and as closely as possible to the citizen." See *Major Issues – Transparency* and *Subsidiarity*.
- Article 47. This explains the Union's principle of participatory democracy in which citizens will be able to make their views known to the Union which in turn will work in an open, coherent and transparent manner. Citizens may propose their own law if not less than 1,000,000 of them come together to invite the Commission to take action on a topic.
- Article 52 deals with the status of churches and non-confessional organisations.

Other articles within this section deal with the issues of consultation, the European Ombudsman, transparency, and data protection.

Title 7 - The Union's finances - Articles 53 - 55

New:

- Article 55 describes the multi-annual financial framework.

This section describes the budgetary and financial principles and how the Union shall provide itself with the means necessary to attain its objectives. See also articles 55, 94, 104, 402,412, and 415.

Title 8 - The Union and its neighbours - Article 57

The Union will attempt to live in peaceful co-operation with neighbouring states. This seems unduly restrictive. The word "neighbouring" might well be replaced with the word "all".

Title 9 - Union membership - Articles 58 - 60

New:

- Any member state may decide to withdraw from the Union.

Membership of the Union shall be open to all European states which respect the values referred to in article 2 and are committed to promoting them together. In the event of a serious breach of Union values by a state certain of its rights may be suspended. The "open-door" policy has points in its favour but also raises major concerns. See *Major Issues – Enlargement*.

Part 2 - The Charter of Fundamental Rights of the Union

Preamble

This charter has its own preamble which proclaims that, "the peoples of Europe, in creating an ever closer union among them, are resolved to share a peaceful future based on common values." The crucial matter of "ever closer union" has already been discussed in relation to the preamble of the Constitution itself.

The preamble states that the Union is based on the principles of democracy and the rule of law and "places the individual at the heart of its activities". These matters are discussed in the *Major Issues* chapter. See *Charter of Fundamantal Rights, Democratic deficit* and *Free trade wars* and *Rule of law?*

An important provision of the preamble states "The Charter will be interpreted by the courts of the Union and the Member States with due regard to the explanations prepared under the authority of the Praesidium of the Convention which drafted the Charter." What and where these explanations may be is not indicated. These "explanations" are, in fact, to be found in the 19 pages of *Declaration 12* which is not always attached to the Constitution. The commitment to the guiding power, in the courts, of "the explanations" appears to be contradicted in the opening remarks of the *Explanations*. "They do not, as such, have the status of law."

Title 1 - Dignity - Articles 61-65

These articles promise truly fundamental rights - rights to dignity, life, integrity of the person, freedom from inhuman and degrading treatment, forced labour and slavery. But all is not as it seems. See *Major Issues - Charter of Fundamental Rights* for a discussion of these topics.

Title 2 - Freedoms - Articles 66-79

These articles promise rights to such things as liberty and security, protection of personal data, freedom of thought, conscience and religion, freedom of expression and information, freedom of assembly and association etc.

Title 3 - Equality - Articles 80-86

Title 4 - Solidarity - Articles 87-98

This section covers workers' rights, social security, healthcare, environmental and consumer protection. These are subject to the laws and practices of member states and are therefore not actually guaranteed by the Constitution.

Title 5 - Citizens' Rights Articles 99-106

These cover voting, rights to stand in elections, rights to good administration, access to documents, right to petition etc. It is surprising that anyone has ever thought of not having a right to petition! See *Major Issues – Transparency* which discusses the difficulty of obtaining access to EU documents.

Title 6 - Justice - Articles 107-110

Such matters as right to an effective remedy and a fair trial, a right to "a fair and public hearing within a reasonable time." It does not include jury trials. There is no right to habeas corpus as such. See *Major Issues – Criminal justice.*

Title 7 - General provisions governing the interpretation and application of the charter - Article 111-114

This charter is aimed at EU institutions and only indirectly and to a limited extent at individual citizens. All EU institutions, bodies, offices, and agencies are expected to respect the rights and principles expressed in this charter. The charter does not extend Union law. All promised rights may be limited: "full account shall be taken of national laws and practises as specified in this charter." (Article 112/6). Since there are a number of areas in which the laws of member states conflict with EU law there are causes for doubt and conflict. For example, the right to strike (article 88) may conflict with UK industrial law. The statement just quoted suggests that national laws will prevail, but the Constitution has also confirmed that the final arbiter in disputes about EU law is the EU's own court, the European Court of Justice.

Article 114 makes it an offence to aim to limit the rights expressed in the Charter. Key rights include "free movement of . . . services, goods and capital, and the freedom of establishment". Therefore, it is against Union law to criticise Free Trade thereby suggesting a limitation (as this book has done). Also, "everyone has the right to freedom of expression." This freedom is guaranteed without limitation. Therefore to suggest that freedom of speech should be limited by laws against slander or libel or incitement to violence would be an offence under the Charter. The Charter also guarantees the "free movement of persons". Therefore to suggest that immigration within the EU should be controlled (thereby limiting the "free movement of persons") would also be an offence.

EU fundamental rights – conclusion/key issue

Promises set out in the Charter, when considered alongside qualifications and limitations, cannot give citizens many reasons for confidence that the rights have been properly considered or are guaranteed to be upheld. See *Major issues – Charter of Fundamental Rights.*

Part 3 - The policies and functioning of the Union

This large section of the Constitution, some 321 articles, is basically a consolidation of articles from two treaties: *The Treaty on European Union* (*the Maastricht Treaty*, 1992), and *The Treaty Establishing the European Community* (one of the *Treaties of Rome*, 1957, as updated by subsequent treaties, most recently the *Treaty of Nice*, 2001 and *The Accession Treaty, 2003*). There are only twenty or so new provisions:

New elements

- Consistency. Article 115. "The Union shall ensure consistency between the policies and activities . . ." See *Major Issues* and comments elsewhere which suggest a wide-scale failure to achieve actions which comply with many EU headline commitments.
- Employment standards. Article 117. Union action must take into account "requirements linked to the promotion of a high level of employment, the guarantee of adequate social protection, the fight against social exclusion, and a high level of education, training, and protection of human health." - These are clearly desirable aims, but freetraders will point out that such policies may make European goods uncompetitive in the world market. The need is for world standards in the treatment of workers to be raised to proposed or actual European levels.
- Anti-discrimination. Article 118. "In defining and implementing the policies and activities in this Part, the Union shall aim to combat discrimination based on sex, racial or ethnic origin, religion or belief, disability, age or sexual orientation."
- Animal welfare. Article 121. In formulating and implementing relevant policies, the Union and Member States shall "pay full regard to the requirements of animal welfare," while respecting various traditions etc.
- Terrorism. Article 160. To deal with non-state terrorism, "European laws shall define a framework for administrative measures with regard to capital movements and payments, such as freezing funds, financial assets or economic gains belonging to, or owned or held by, natural or legal persons, groups or non-state entities."
- Intellectual property rights. Article 176. (See *Euroterminology*.) By this article the Union first restates its claim to have the power to make intellectual rights uniform throughout the EU. It then states that it will set up "centralised Union-wide authorisation, co-ordination and supervision arrangements." See *Major Issues – Intellectual property rights*.
- Eurozone. Articles 194, 195 and 196. Provisions specific to states whose currency is the euro: mainly relating to measures to ensure budgetary discipline, set economic policy guidelines, and agree common positions, on matters relating to economic and monetary union, within "international financial institutions and conferences." - Joining the euro is both a marriage to many partners and a discipline.
- Agriculture and fisheries. Article 225. "Agricultural products" and "agricultural" are defined and refer not only to farming but also to fisheries.
- Promoting free trade world-wide. Article 292/e. A new mission for the EU which may not be wise and could prove costly. See *Major Issues, Free trade wars*.
- Space programme. Article 254. The EU will develop a space policy and take "necessary measures which may take the form of a European space programme."
- Energy. Article 256. Energy policy aims to have a functioning energy market, ensure security of supply, promote renewables, energy saving and efficiency. States will remain free to choose their own energy sources. See *Major Issues – Energy and the environment*.

- Freedom, security and justice. Articles 258, 259, and 260. The Area of freedom, security and justice is the EU. In the main the EU sets itself up as the central guiding or controlling authority in this area. Subsidiarity rules are extremely weak - as discussed elsewhere. "The European Council shall define the strategic guidelines . . ." "National Parliaments shall ensure that the proposals . . . comply with the principle of subsidiarity . . . and proportionality." "The Council may . . . with the Commission, conduct objective and impartial evaluation of the implementation of the Union policies referred to in this chapter by member states' authorities . . ." See *Major Issues – Area of Freedom, Security and Justice* and *Criminal Justice*.
- Immigration and asylum. Article 268. EU policies in this area will be governed by the principle of solidarity and fair sharing of responsibility, including its financial implications.
- Cross-border crime. Article 271. "European framework laws may establish minimum rules concerning the definition of criminal offences and sanctions in the area of particularly serious crime. A procedure is set out for dealing with situations in which EU proposals in this area conflict with individual states' laws.
- Tourism. Article 281. "The Union shall complement the action of member states in the tourism sector . . ."
- Civil protection. Article 284. "The Union shall encourage co-operation between member states . . ."
- Administrative co-operation. Article 285. The Union seeks to improve the capacity of member states to implement Union law.
- Minister for Foreign Affairs. This major new role would be created by article 296. There would be no accountability to the euroelectorate. See *Major Issues - Union Minister for Foreign Affairs.*
- Military development. Article 311. Tasks of the new European Defence Agency are defined here. They are basically to run the arms industries of Europe. "The agency shall carry out its task in liaison with the Commission where necessary." As the Defence Agency is responsible to the Minister for Foreign Affairs what precisely is the role of the Commission? This and related topics are discussed in the *Major Issues* chapter.
- Enhanced military co-operation. Article 312. Those states wishing to participate in this shall notify the Council and the Union Minister for Foreign Affairs. A group of states may act outside the practice of unanimity which is supposed to unite the EU in its Foreign Policy.
- Humanitarian aid. Article 321 sets out how this will be administered.
- Solidarity. Article 329. In the event of terrorist attack or natural or man-made disaster other member states will offer assistance.
- Legal appointments. Article 357. About the panel that shall be set up to give an opinion on the suitability of candidates for the roles of judges or Advocate General of the Court of Justice or the General Court.
- Multi-annual financial framework. Article 402. The framework will be set up for a period of at least five years. The procedures to be adopted are set out.

- Common provisions. Articles 413 and 414. "The European Parliament. The Council and the Commission shall ensure that the financial means are made available to allow the Union to fulfil its legal obligations in respect of third parties." The Commission has the duty to organise regular meetings between the Presidents of the European Parliament, the Council and the Commission.

Other important topics in this policy section

Non-discrimination and citizenship - articles 123 - 129.

The internal market - articles 130 -176

This is divided into 7 sections.

1 Establishment and functioning of the internal market, articles 130-132.
2 Free movement of persons and services, articles 133-150. This is divided into three subsections: 1, on workers (article 133-136), 2, on freedom of establishment (articles 137-143), 3, on freedom to provide services (articles 144-150).
3 Free movement of goods, articles 151-155. This is divided into three sub-sections: 1, customs union, article 151, 2, customs co-operation, article 152, and 3, the prohibition of quantitative restrictions articles 153-155.
4 Capital and payments, articles 156-160.
5 Rules on competition, articles 161-169. There are two subsections. 1, rules applying to undertakings, articles 161-166, and 2, aids granted by member states, articles 167-169.
6 Fiscal provisions, articles 170 and 171.
7 Common provisions, articles 172-176.

Free movement of workers. Articles 133-136. This may have both good and bad effects. It is therefore questionable whether it should be part of a constitution making it a policy to be followed for ever regardless of consequences. See *Major Issues – Enlargement*.

Freedom of establishment

Articles 137-143. Article 137 prohibits member states from making special restrictions applicable to citizens of other member states on the setting up of businesses. It also provides a loophole. States are finding ways to limit this freedom. See *Major Issues – Free Trade.*

Freedom to provide services

Articles 144-150. This section outlaws restrictions on freedom to provide services within the Union. Services are defined as services "where they are normally provided for remuneration" and include activities of an industrial character, commercial character, activities of craftsmen and the professions. See *Major Issues – Free Trade.*

Article 147 appears to open the way for teams of professionals from one or more EU states to set up private enterprises in competition with state enterprises such as hospitals, prisons, schools, the fire service and postal services. See *Major Issues – Free Trade.*

Free movement of goods

Articles 151-155. These set out the details of a tariff-free area comprising the member states of the European Union, with common tariffs on goods imported from third countries. Quantitative restrictions on the import and export of goods between member states are prohibited. However, restrictions on grounds of public morality and a number of other grounds are permitted, but these may not be used arbitrarily. State monopolies of a commercial character must ensure that no discrimination regarding the conditions under which goods are procured and marketed exist.

Free movement of capital

Articles 156-160. Restrictions on the free movement of capital and payments between member countries and third countries are prohibited. Member states retain their rights to impose taxes so long as these are not applied as a means of "arbitrary discrimination or a disguised restriction on the free movement of capital and payments."

Rules on competition

Article 3 of the Constitution says, "the Union shall contribute to . . . free and fair trade". Articles 161-169 set out these rules to make trade fair from a trader's point of view and do not constitute "Fair Trade" as is popularly understood. Unfair trading practices between member states are prohibited. These include such things as price fixing, and limiting or controlling production, markets, technical development, or investment, and the abuse of dominant market positions. The Commission has the power to levy fines on those who break the rules.

States may not grant aid to industries with the effect of distorting free trade. There are ways round this including giving "regional aid" and "research grants".

Fiscal provisions

Articles 170 and 171. Taxation may not be used to put the products of any EU member state at a disadvantage. The harmonisation of taxes throughout the EU to avoid market distortion will be proposed.

Common provisions

Articles 172-176. These include such matters as the need within the EU to achieve a high level of protection in matters such as health, safety, environmental and consumer protection, and establish EU-wide intellectual property rights. Economic and monetary policy - Articles 177 - 202.

Single currency of the European Union

The European Union shall have a single currency, the euro, a single monetary policy, a single exchange rate and the prime objective is price stability. Member states shall aim to achieve: "stable prices, sound public finances and monetary conditions and a stable balance of payments."

The above requirements are intended to apply to all member states in due course. The UK has an indefinite opt out which is covered in Protocol 13. See also Protocol 11 on the convergence criteria and Protocol 12 on the Euro Group.

Economic policy

Articles 178-184. Because Britain is not in the Eurozone a number of articles in this section do not apply to it. These are articles 1 and 84, paragraphs 6-11, article 185 paragraphs 1,2,3, and 5, and articles 190 and 191.

The main idea is that Member States "shall act in accordance with the principle of and an open market economy, with free competition" and that Member States "shall regard their economic policies as a matter of common concern and shall co-ordinate them within the Council, in accordance with article 178". Provisions are made for the monitoring of the economies of individual states and for taking corrective action when failures or difficulties arise.

Monetary policy

Articles 185-191. Because Britain is outside the Eurozone the following articles do not apply to Britain: article 185 paragraphs 1,2,3, and 5, articles 186, 190 and 191.

The primary objective is to maintain price stability. The tasks of the European Central Bank and the central banks of other states are set out. Low levels of unemployment is not an aim and the policy of the Central Bank may not be criticised by any EU official or elected person. See *Major Issues – Rigidity* and *Charter of Fundamental Rights (Free Speech)*

Articles 192-202.These articles deal with institutional provisions, provisions specific to Member States whose currency is the Euro, and transitional provisions.

Policies in other areas - articles 203 - 256

Employment

Articles 203-208. EU policy is to work towards developing a co-ordinated strategy for employment and particularly for promoting a skilled, trained and adaptable work force and labour markets responsive to economic change. Union policies are required to take into account the objective of a high level of employment.

Social policy

Articles 209-219. Objectives include the promotion of employment, improved living and working conditions, proper social protection, dialogue between management and labour, the development of human resources with a view to lasting high employment and the combating of exclusion. The Union promises to support and complement the activities of member states in a number of fields including improvement in particular, of the working environment to protect workers' health and safety, social security and social protection of workers, equality between women and men with regard to labour market opportunities and treatment and work, and the combating of social exclusion.

Economic, social and territorial cohesion

Articles 220-224. The Union aims at reducing disparities between the levels of development of the various regions and the backwardness of the least favoured regions. A large proportion of the EU's budget is spent on pursuing this policy.

Agriculture and Fisheries

Articles 225-232. Agricultural products are defined. The objectives of the common agricultural policy include increasing agricultural productivity by promoting technical progress and the optimum utilisation of labour, a fair standard of living for the agricultural community, stable markets, assured supplies of food, and reasonable prices for the consumer.

It is intended to establish a common organisation of agricultural markets. "The Council, on a proposal from the Commission may adopt a European regulation or decision authorising the granting of aid a) for the protection of enterprises handicapped by structural or natural conditions, and b) within the framework of economic development programmes."

With regards to fisheries the council has power to fix prices, levies, aid and quantitative limitations and to fix and allocate fishing opportunities.

There is no hint in this section that Agriculture and Fisheries consume the greater proportion of the EU budget which in 2004 amounted to € 100,000,000,000. Agricultural spending amounted to € 43,600,000,000, with most of the money going to the richest farmers.

See *Major Issues – Agriculture* and *Fisheries*.

Environment

Articles 233-234. The Union's policy objectives in this area are:

- Preserving, protecting and improving the quality of the environment
- Protecting human health
- Prudent and rational utilisation of natural resources
- Promoting measures at international level to deal with regional or worldwide environmental problems.

The EU plans to take measures affecting town and country planning, management of water resources, land use, and the energy choices made by member states. European laws will establish general action programmes.

Consumer protection

Article 235. The EU plans to contribute to the attainment of a high level of consumer protection.

Transport

Articles 236-245. This section particularly lacks vision and is possibly even more vague than most. The EU will establish "common rules applicable to international transport" and "measures to improve transport safety." There is no recognition of a connection between transport and its effects on the environment.

See *Major issues* and *The Constitution considered as a Document*.

Trans-European networks

Articles 246 and 247. The EU promises money for the building of major transport networks, and telecommunications and energy infrastructures. Interoperability is recognised as an important feature. The environment is not mentioned as a concern in this connection.

Research and technological development and space

Articles 248-255. The EU aims to promote scientific knowledge, develop technology and assist research activities to improve EU competitiveness. It aims to promote co-operation across the borders of member states. The EU will have a space policy and may spend money on a European space programme.

Energy

Article 256. As already noted the EU aims to have a functioning energy market, ensure security of supply, promote renewables, energy saving and efficiency. States will remain free to choose their own energy sources.

See *Major Issues - Energy and the environment.*

Area of freedom, security and justice

Articles 257-285.

General provisions

Articles 257-264. The aim is "a high level of security through measures to prevent and combat crime, racism and xenophobia and through measures for co-ordination and co-operation between police and judicial authorities and other competent authorities as well as through the mutual recognition of judgements in criminal matters and, if necessary by the approximation of criminal laws. The Union shall facilitate access to justice, in particular to the principle of mutual recognition of judicial and extra judicial decisions in civil matters."

See *Major Issues – Law making.*

It is the task of the European Council "to define the strategic guidelines for legislative and operational planning."

"A standing committee shall be set up within the Council in order to ensure that operational co-operation on internal security is promoted and strengthened within the Union."

Policies on border checks, asylum and immigration

Articles 265-268. There are three key aims with regard to borders.

- The removal of all controls whatsoever on people crossing borders within the European Union,

- The careful control and monitoring of everyone crossing external borders of the European Union,
- The introduction of an integrated management system for external borders (a shared database).

See *Major Issues – Data Harvesting.*

A common asylum policy will be developed in accordance with the Geneva Convention of July 1951, and the protocol of January 1967, relating to the status of refugees, and other relevant treaties. A common immigration policy will be aimed at ensuring the efficient management of migration flows, fair treatment of third country nationals and the prevention of, and enhanced measures to combat, illegal immigration and trafficking in human beings. The EU will establish common conditions of entry and residence and approaches to illegal immigration and unauthorised residence. Member states will remain free to determine the volume of admissions to their countries of third country nationals seeking work.

Judicial co-operation in civil matters

Article 269. The EU will develop judicial co-operation in civil matters which have cross-border implications.

Judicial co-operation in criminal matters

Articles 270-274. The EU will attempt to achieve mutual recognition of judgements and judicial decisions and the approximation or harmonisation of some laws. Particular concerns are cross-border crimes: terrorism, trafficking in human beings and sexual exploitation of women and children, illicit drug trafficking, illicit arms trafficking, money laundering, corruption, counterfeiting of means of payment, computer crime and organised crime.

The European prosecution agency, Eurojust, will be concerned with cross-border crime and co-operation between member states.

See *Major Issues – Area of Freedom, Security and Justice.*

Police co-operation

Articles 275-277. This describes the embryonic European police force, Europol. This section may present civil liberties concerns. "The Council may establish measures concerning operational co-operation between the authorities referred to in this article." An alternative to the centralised direction by the Council would be for individual states to retain the initiative to call on Europol for assistance, for example, in tackling cross border crime. In relation to the prevention, detection and investigation of criminal offences (not just cross-border crime, article 275) there will be co-operation between the police, customs and other specialised law enforcement services of all member states. They "may" establish "the collection, storage, processing, analysis and exchange of relevant information." In fact work on a major database is well under way (2005).

See *Major Issues - Area of freedom, security and justice*, *Law-making*, *Europol* and *Data Harvesting.*

Areas where the Union may take co-ordinating, complementary or supporting action

Articles 278-285. The European Union claims to wish to take decision-making as close to the people concerned as possible. That is the spirit of subsidiarity. In contradiction to these declared aims the European Union assumes the right to take action in many areas which seem ideally and rightfully the concern of state governments. These include public health (article 278), industry (article 279), culture (article 280), tourism (article 281), education, youth, sport and vocational training (articles 282 and 283), civil protection (article 284), and assisting with administrative co-operation (article 285).

See *Major Issues - Subsidiarity.*

Association of the overseas countries and territories

Articles 286-291. These articles set out details of the special relationship between the EU and territories associated with Denmark, France, the Netherlands and the United Kingdom.

The Union's external action

Articles 292-329. The European Union declares that it seeks to work with other states to advance democracy, the rule of law, human rights and fundamental freedoms, respect for human dignity, the principles of equality and solidarity, and respect for the principles of the *United Nations Charter* and international law. "It shall promote multilateral solutions to common problems, in particular in the framework of the United Nations."

See *Major Issues - Free Trade Wars.*

Common foreign and security policy

Articles 294-308. Member states are required to "support the common foreign and security policy actively and unreservedly in a spirit of loyalty and mutual solidarity." It is the task of the European Council to "define the general guidelines for the common foreign and security policy, including for matters with defence implications." It appears that "the Council" may declare war. The relevant Council would be the General Affairs Council. Article 297 is about operational action (which means military action). Decisions on these matters are binding on all member states according to article 297 paragraph 2.

According to article 300 decisions on these matters will be "adopted by the Council acting unanimously." Unanimous has a special meaning in this paragraph. Up to a third of member states may abstain and the decision will still be counted as unanimous. A state which abstains is not obliged to participate in military action. See *Unanimity* in *Euroterminology.*

The EU may conclude international agreements which commit member states. (Article 303.)

See *Major Issues - Defence and Foreign Policy.*

The common security and defence policy

Articles 309-312. Article 309 lists the kinds of tasks in which "the Union may use civilian and military means." "Civilian and military means" include "conflict prevention and peacekeeping tasks, tasks of combat forces in crisis management, including peacemaking and post-conflict stabilisation." See *Common Foreign and Security policy* above.

Article 310 describes how a group of member states may take independent action in the areas set out in article 309 at the request of the Council, which would presumably act by unanimous decision - though not as we understand unanimity. See *Euroterminology* and *Major Issues - Unanimity.*

Article 311 describes the work of the new European Defence Agency which will hope to ensure the technological modernisation of the defence forces of member states and advise states what to buy. This organisation will ensure year on year increases in defence spending. Although merely envisaged in the Constitution the Defence Agency has already been set up.

See *Major Issues - Defence*

Financial provisions

Article 313 describes how activities in the field of external action will be funded.

Common commercial policy

Article 314 explains how EU states will be good freetraders.

Article 315 details the solidarity expected of member states in trade matters and the procedures for negotiating with third countries.

Co-operation with third countries and humanitarian aid

Articles 316-318. The primary objective is the reduction and, in the long term, the eradication of poverty. The European Investment Bank should play a part. Member states of the EU will co-ordinate their overseas development work.

Economic and financial co-operation with third countries

Articles 319 and 320. The EU will work with countries other than developing countries to offer assistance.

Humanitarian aid

Article 321 is about offering help in disaster situations.

Restrictive measures

Article 322. This is about sanctions. These can be initiated at the suggestion of the Union Minister for Foreign Affairs and the Commission.

See *Major Issues - Sanctions.*

International agreements

Articles 323- 326. International agreements entered into by the European Union are binding on the institutions of the Union and on its member states. These articles set out the circumstances and procedures for the making of such agreements.

The Union's relations with international organisations and third countries and Union delegations

Article 327. The EU's Minister for Foreign Affairs and the Commission will be responsible for relations with the United Nations, the Council of Europe, the Organisation for Security and Co-operation in Europe, the organisation for Economic Co-operation and Development and other international organisations.

EU delegations to third countries act under the authority of the Union Minister for Foreign Affairs and are expected to work in close co-operation with the diplomatic and consular missions of member states.

Implementation of the solidarity clause

Article 329. EU member states are committed to come to the aid of any other member state in the event of a natural or man-made disaster. Help will be administered by the Council if the Minister of Foreign Affairs and the Commission so direct. The European Parliament will be kept informed.

The functioning of the Union

Institutions

The rules governing the Union's institutions are set out in articles 330 to 400.

Article 390 states that "the institutions, bodies, offices, and agencies of the Union shall ensure transparency in their work" and provide "public access to their documents."

See *European Union Institutions* chapter in *Nuts and bolts of the EU system*. See also *Major Issues - Accountability* and *Transparency*

Financial provisions including the annual budget and dealing with fraud are dealt with in articles 402 to 436.

Part 4 General and Final Provisions

Articles 437-448.

Article 437 explains that "This treaty establishing a constitution for Europe" replaces the previous treaties governing the operation of the European Union. Article 438 explains that a new European Union is created by this treaty.

Article 442 clarifies the status of the annexes and protocols in relation to the constitution. They "form an integral part thereof." If the proposed Constitution is rewritten most might beneficially be integrated rather than appearing as a succession of addendums. The legal status of the fifty declarations is not clear. See *Final act* below.

Article 443 paragraph 4 explains what may be done if there are problems with the ratification of the treaty.

Article 444. WARNING! This allows major changes in the constitution with minimal consultation or scrutiny. Whilst national parliaments must be notified of changes they do not have to positively agree changes. Silence will be interpreted as consent!

There is also a simplified revision procedure concerning internal Union policies and action. (Article 445.)

Final act

This lists not only the thirty six protocols but also the two annexes and fifty declarations which are added to the constitution as part of it and which were signed as such on 29 October 2004 by leaders of the member states.

Protocols

The titles of the protocols may be read in the Contents of this book. The texts of those protocols most relevant to people in the UK are printed in this book following the main text of the Constitution.

Declarations

These are a collection of fifty comments and understandings of what is expressed in the Constitution. Perhaps the most important are the "explanations" relating to the Charter of Fundamental Rights which are set out in Declaration 12. The "explanations" from this declaration are included in this book and discussed in the *Charter of Fundamental Rights* section in the *Major Issues* chapter.

Part Five

The Reform Treaty * - The Constitution Repackaged

"The paper [the *Reform Treaty*] is incomprehensible. Good! We need incomprehensible papers if we are to make progress . . . We have to be realistic." - Jean-Luc Dehaene, MEP, Former Prime Minister of Belgium, Vice President of the Convention which wrote the EU Constitution, quoted in *European Voice*, 17 October 2007.

"The Lisbon Treaty* itself cannot be understood by ordinary citizens since it can be understood only by also reading the treaties which it amends. . . The institutional proposals of the constitutional treaty – the only things which mattered for the members of the European Convention – are in the Lisbon treaty in their entirety but in a different order and inserted into previous treaties. - What is the purpose of this subtle manoeuvre? First and above all to escape from the constraint of having to hold a referendum by dispersing the articles and by renouncing the constitutional vocabulary." - Giscard d'Estaing, President of the Convention which wrote the EU Constitution, writing in *Le Monde*, 26 October 2007.

"The return to the traditional technique of amending existing Treaties is not the most user friendly approach, far from this. . . The *Reform Treaty* will be full of cross-references to the present treaties. It will not be easy to read and understand." - Margot Wallström, Vice-President of the European Commission, in charge of Institutional Relations and Communication. Speech at the European Economic and Social Committee Conference, 27 September, 2007.

---

* The *Reform Treaty* is also being called, *The Treaty of Lisbon* and, as a further alternative, *Treaty Amending the Treaty on European Union and the Treaty Establishing the European Community.*

"We welcome the emphasis placed by the European Council on providing EU citizens with "full and comprehensive information" and involving them in "permanent dialogue" which is said to be "particularly important" during the IGC [Intergovernmental Conference of leading ministers of EU states, 19 October 2007, meeting to agree the *Reform Treaty*]. However, the evidence until now has not been consistent with these ideals, with an essentially secret drafting process conducted by the Presidency, with texts produced at the last moment before pressing for agreement. The compressed timetable now proposed, having regard to the sitting terms of national parliaments, could not have been better designed to marginalise their role." - House of Commons, European Scrutiny Committee, 9 October 2007.

The Reform Treaty - The Constitution Repackaged

A new period of uncertanty

It had been announced that the the "Period of Reflection" (about what to do with the rejected Constitution) would end in the summer of 2008. But it came to an abrupt end at 5 am on Saturday 23 June 2007 when EU leaders, under EU President, Angela Merkel, announced that they had agreed a "draft mandate" for a *Reform Treaty*. (Printed later in this book.) So began the Period of Uncertainty.

When the European Parliament met on Wednesday 27 June the air was loud with praise for Angela Merkel in achieving an agreement. The EU, it appeared, could now "move forwards" again. But what had been achieved? Only an agreement among EU leaders on sixteen pages of notes setting out how a new "*Reform Treaty*" would amend two existing EU treaties. Some of the leaders might have been able to remember a similar agreement in 2004 when all the EU leaders of the time signed the Constitution - an earlier answer to all the EU's problems - only to find within a year that this answer was not acceptable to the people of Europe.

This time it may be different, not because Europeans will be won over by the amendments made to the Constitution, but because the Constitution will seem to have disappeared. It will be re-packaged and hidden in changes to existing treaties and so, EU leaders claim, will not need to be submitted to the people of Europe in referendums. The *Reform Treaty* is a ploy - not to win acceptance of the Constitution, but to avoid the possibility of its rejection.

Final texts were approved at the October summit of EU leaders in Lisbon. Formal signing is expected to take place on 13 December 2007. In the course of time citizens of Europe may become increasingly aware that the new plans are, with some minor modifications, the Constitution of 2004. Even if all EU governments ratify the *Reform Treaty* it will not answer the deep-seated problems of the EU, and the approach adopted by EU leaders to achieve agreement is shockingly underhand. It will not bring about a firm basis for progress and it will weaken the already shaky confidence of Europeans in the EU Project.

The *Reform Treaty* plan - Don't mention the Constitution

The plan for bringing back the Constitution is set out in the *Draft IGC Mandate* dated 22 June 2007.[1] There are fifty-one references to the Constitution in these sixteen pages but in forty-nine instances the reference is coded. The word Constitution is replaced by the expression "as agreed in the 2004 IGC" or a similar expression (that inter-governmental conference being the one that finalised the Constitution) or, in some places, this expression is replaced by an asterisk. The two direct references to the Constitution read as follows: "A single text called 'Constitution' is abandoned," and "The term 'Constitution' will not be used."

The *Reform Treaty* will be the elaborated plan, based on the mandate agreed in June 2007, setting out how the two basic treaties which currently direct the EU (the Treaty on the European Union, and the Treaty establishing the European Community) will stay in force but with virtually all of the elements of the Constitution that brought in new ideas inserted into these two treaties. (The Constitution of 2004 adopted the opposite approach of writing a new document into which the other two treaties were inserted.) The Mandate is explicit. "The *Reform Treaty* will introduce into the existing treaties, which remain in force, the innovations resulting from the 2004 IGC." Thus whole sections will be taken taken, with some minor changes, from the Constitution, plus, in their entirety and with additions, the protocols and declarations of the Constitution. The Charter of Fundamental Rights, which was part of the Constitution, will be published, and approved by the governments of the member states, as a separate document.

It can be seen already that the principle guiding the *Reform Treaty* is not that objections to the Constitution raised by European citizens must be addressed, but that the terminology and appearance of the content of the Constitution must be changed, disguised and dispersed so that citizens find it difficult to understand what is being agreed and so that they may be led to believe that the Constitution has been abandoned. This is not open, democratic government, and it is dishonest.

The so-called "*Reform Treaty*" is not a treaty to reform, but a treaty to deceive. Such changes in arrangements from those that appear in the Constitution, in almost all cases, address none of the major issues facing the EU - including those identified by EU leaders themselves in 2001. There are instances of minor tweaking of arrangements, but there is nothing that could justify the use of the word "Reform". The game EU leaders are attempting to play with the perceptions of EU citizens is plain enough, but, if anyone is in doubt, the architect of the Constitution has spelled out how the scheme is intended to work. Valery Giscard d'Estaing, wrote in *Le Monde* on 14 June, a few days before the form of the "reform" proposals had been settled:

> A last good idea consists of wanting to preserve part of the Constitution and camouflaging this by distributing it among several texts. The more innovative provisions [of the Constitution] would be simple amendments to the Nice and Maastricht treaties. The technical improvements would be gathered together in a bland and uncontroversial treaty. These texts would be put to Parliaments to vote on them one at a time. Thus public opinion would be led to accept, without knowing it, the proposals that we dare not present to them directly.

The *Economist* of 9 August 2007 quoted the former Belgian prime minister, Jean-Luc Dehaene who, in an interview in *Le Soir*, said it was "dangerous talk" to want "too much transparency and clarity" in the EU.

This policy of non-engagement with the European people was taken even further by the man in charge of drafting the *Reform Treaty*, Giuliano Amato, former Italian Prime Minister. His remarks on the writing of the *Reform Treaty* show arrogance and contempt for eurocitizens, yet he is a man who cannot be voted out of holding powerful EU positions and will not be brought before any Standards in EU Public Life committee. He said, at a meeting of the Centre for European Reform on 12 July 2007 that EU leaders "decided that the document should be unreadable. . . In order to make our citizens happy, to produce a document that they will never understand!"[2] - This is not an approach which will gain the support of the people of Europe.

How EU leaders responded to objections and demands

What issues did EU leaders address in drafting the mandate for the *Reform Treaty*? The most important was a demand from many EU leaders to keep the Constitution. The report from the Presidency to the Council and the European Council dated 14 June[3] referred to "the demand from those [eighteen] Member States which have already ratified that as much of the substance of the Constitutional Treaty as possible should be preserved." This demand was met. Speaking to the European Parliament, on 27 June, Angela Merkel was keen to point out, "The agreement reached in Brussels enables us to retain the substance of the Constitutional Treaty." And she was equally clear on the purpose. "European integration has to be striven for and consolidated time and again."

Superstatehood - changing the appearance, but forging ahead

Contrasting with these demands was the popular opposition to creating an EU superstate with a government that takes most of the decisions on behalf of member states. The approach of EU leaders to these demands has been to retain the reality they wanted whilst dropping words which might imply that the EU is any kind of state. Angela Merkel has explained, "We have renounced everything that makes people think of a state."[4] Gone are the words, Constitution, flag, anthem and motto. The Constitution would have introduced the terms "law" and "framework law" which was a sound move properly recognising their legal force. However, as states pass laws these terms must be dropped and the EU will continue using the terms "regulations", "directives" and "decisions".

The term, "President", with possible connotations of statehood, cannot be avoided. The EU's Foreign Minister, whose title is another sign of EU statehood, is to be work under another title whilst the role remains as described in the Constitution. He or she will be known as "the High Representative of the Union for Foreign Affairs and Security Policy."

Foreign and security policy

Foreign and Security Policy will follow the prescription of the Constitution with only minor changes. As in the Constitution the EU will have "a single legal personality" thereby being able to act as a superstate and enter into international agreements on behalf of member states and without the consent of their parliaments. Such international agreements would have to be within the bounds of the powers conferred by states on the EU but these limits offer enormous scope. Groups of nine or more member states will have the right to carry out military operations without the agreement of other member states. Majority rather than unanimous voting will be used to decide many issues. The new EU "Foreign Office" (the External Action service, mentioned in the Constitution) continues to be established and will inevitably take initiative and influence away from individual member states. "The European Action Service and permanent structured co-operation in the field of defence" will continue as stated in the Constitution. Member states will be committed to increase defence spending; and the EU's drive to take total EU control of all defence and security matters is asserted. The Mandate quotes the Constitution, "The Union's competence in matters of common foreign and security policy shall cover all areas of foreign policy and all questions relating to the Union's security, including the progressive framing of a common defence policy which might lead to a common defence."

The expression "might lead" suggests there is a vague and distant possibility of this occurrence. The Constitution sets out a simple and quick procedure whereby this could easily come about without reference to national parliaments (article 41/2) and this is repeated in the Draft *Reform Treaty*, article 48b. See *Major Issues* on this topic.

However, in contrast to all this, the Draft Mandate states, "national security remains the sole responsibility of each member state".[5] This may be the sentence that allows the UK government and others to assert that they keep their "independent foreign policy". It is as if the EU, in pursing policies and relationships with the other states of the world, and conducting operations with military forces will in no way affect the national security of member states and will, in some way, be operating independently from them. The Constitution and the Draft *Reform Treaty* state, "The Union's competence . . . shall cover . . . all questions relating to the Union's security." The *Reform Treaty* will guarantee mutually exclusive modes of behaviour: EU control of "all areas of foreign and security policy" whilst member states remain solely responsible for their national security. In practice, the eurocitizen does not know what the EU is doing in the sphere of foreign policy. The EU will be authorised to do as it pleases: either allow member states to do their own thing or tell them to do what the EU decides.

With its own new Foreign Service, its Defence Agency, its Foreign Minister (under his/her new title), its ability to call up military forces, and existing policies we can be sure that the EU will forge ahead with foreign policy initiatives and there may be little the UK, or any other member state, can do to stop it.

See *Major Issues* on this topic.

Subsidiarity

One of the most fervent demands of citizens has been that laws should, whenever possible, be passed at regional or state level, rather than EU level. All the opportunities the Constitution would have opened up for the EU to take over control and take decisions at a higher level will be there in the new documents. As an ineffectual and derisory gesture towards the demand for greater subsidiarity national parliaments will be granted eight weeks rather than six to make the case for states rather than the EU to pass a law on a given topic. It will remain with the EU to decide whether to agree with such a demand or not. The superstate rules.

See *Major Issues* on this topic.

Other changes the Reform Treaty will bring about.

Free trade

As this book has made clear, the EU has always had an ambivalent attitude towards free trade whilst always expressing wholehearted commitment to it. Although the EU is likely to continue to trade in whatever way suits it there are signs that attitudes may be softening slightly. France has been concerned to protect some of its own industries and companies. At the request of France, in what will become article 3 of the *Treaty on European Union*, the text taken from article 3 of the Constitution will drop the words "an internal market where competition is free and undistorted". This suggests that here may be an abandonment of the EU's less than wholehearted commitment to free trade. This may make some people happy, but the concept is reintroduced in a protocol. Now you don't have it, now you do. It's a game of words.

The Charter of Fundamental Rights

The *Charter of Fundamental Rights* was a contentious issue. The Presidency report said that there were demands from members both to include it and exclude it from whatever replaced the Constitution. The proposed solution is to exclude the text from forthcoming documents, but, nevertheless to state that it has legally binding force. This is slightly stronger wording than the Constitution which states, "The Charter will be interpreted by the Courts of the Union and the Member states." The Charter is meant to exist, but not be too visible or meaningful. Citizens obtaining the texts of the treaties will not see the Charter. The UK's objection to the legal nature of the Charter which might have affected UK employment law, has been met by allowing a British opt-out. It has been agreed that the Charter will not affect Poland's right to legislate in the matter of public morality and family law. Readers who have missed the chapter in this book on the Charter might like to read it to see how, in any case, the legal force of the Charter appears to be insignificant since it creates no requirement that does not already exist elsewhere. The mandate for the *Reform Treaty* confirms this. The Charter "does not create new rights or principles".[6]

Some people have questioned the effectiveness of the UK's opt-out from the Charter of Fundamental Rights. Judges from the European Court of Justice have suggested that the UK will not be able to avoid its requirements. However, the UK opt-out is unequivocally expressed in the Mandate's footnote 19.

> "Article 1
>
> 1. The Charter does not extend the ability of the Court of Justice, or any court or tribunal of the United Kingdom, to find that the laws, regulations or administrative provisions, practices or action of the United Kingdom are inconsistent with the fundamental rights, freedoms and principles that it reaffirms. 2. In particular, and for the avoidance of doubt, nothing in (Title IV) of the Charter creates justiciable rights applicable to the United Kingdom except in so far as the United Kingdom has provided for such rights in its national law.
>
> Article 2
>
> To the extent that a provision of the Charter refers to national laws and practices, it shall only apply in the United Kingdom to the extent that the rights or principles that it contains are recognised in the law or practices of the United Kingdom."

See *Major Issues* on this topic.

Voting in meetings of the Council

The highly complex voting system set out in the Constitution will be adopted

(See *Major Issues* for a discussion on this topic), but in response to Polish objections there will be a delay before the system comes into operation, and there will be transitional arrangements. The new arrangements do not make it easy for anyone to understand how the voting will work. They are a masterpiece of EU gobbledygook. They read as follows:

> "The double majority voting system, as agreed in the 2004 IGC, will take effect on 1 November 2014, until which date the present qualified majority system (Article 205 (2) TEC) will continue to apply. After that, during a transitional period until 31 March 2017, when a decision is to be adopted by qualified majority, a member of the Council may request that the decision be taken in accordance with the qualified majority as defined in Article 205 (2) of the present TEC.
>
> In addition, until 31 March 2017, if members of the Council representing at least 75% of the population or at least 75% of the number of Member States necessary to constitute a blocking minority as provided in Article (I-25(2)) indicate their opposition to the Council adopting an act by a qualified majority, the mechanism provided for in the draft Decision contained in Declaration Number 5 annexed to the Final Act of the 2004 IGC [sic]. As from 1 April 2017, the same mechanism will apply, the relevant percentages being, respectively, at least 55% of the population or at least 55% of the number of Member States necessary to constitute a blocking minority as provided in Article (I-25(2))."

See *Major Issues* on this topic.

Enlargement - admitting new member states

In recent years EU leaders have become sensitive to the fact that the rapid expansion of the number of member states has led to social tensions and other potential problems. The Draft Mandate for the *Reform Treaty* accordingly makes small changes to the admission procedures for candidate states. The effect of these changes is difficult to assess.

In both the *Treaty on European Union* and the Constitution membership was subject to the assent of the European Parliament by a majority vote. In the TEU and the proposed new version the word "absolute" is added before the word "majority". The Constitution and the Draft mandate require that national parliaments be notified of membership applications. The Draft Mandate adds a sentence which is in neither the TEU nor the Constitution. "The conditions of eligibility agreed upon by the European Council shall be taken into account." This gives the European Council scope to make the admission of new member states more difficult or easier should they so choose.

Police, Law, Justice, Home Affairs

The topic of the "Area of Freedom, Security and Justice" includes "general provisions, policies on border checks, asylum and immigration, judicial cooperation in civil matters, judicial co-operation in criminal matters and police cooperation." The Mandate takes six pages of the Constitution, articles 257 to 277 and adds them to the *Treaty Establishing the European Union* (after article 42) but makes a few changes.

The first states a way the member states of the EU might work together. Whilst this is a new statement it has surely always been open to them (and indeed all states) to work in this way, on any topic, without the permission of the EU. It is an alternative to all the treaties of the EU. "It shall be open to Member States to organize between themselves and under their responsibility forms of co-operation and co-ordination as they deem appropriate between the competent departments of their administrations responsible for safeguarding national security."

Constitution article 269 relates to family law with cross-border implications. This might be such things as laws prohibiting the families of migrant workers joining them in their host state. This article is modified with the addition of a new right of veto over family laws enacted by the EU. "The proposal referred to in the second subparagraph [family law with cross-border implication] shall be notified to the national parliaments. If a national Parliament makes known its opposition within six months of the date of such notification, the decision referred to in the second subparagraph shall not be adopted. In the absence of opposition, the Council may adopt the decision."

In the case of the Council discussing a draft directive on judicial co-operation on criminal matters or police co-operation which any minister of a member state believes may affect "fundamental aspects of its criminal justice system" that minister may have the draft directive referred to the European Council and temporarily suspend discussion on the topic. If the European Council achieves consensus the legislative procedure may be reinstated. In the meantime one third or more of the members of the Council may embark on "enhanced co-operation" to adopt the proposed directive.

The power to trigger a pause for thought, (sometimes misleadingly called the "emergency brake procedure") which creates a possibility to cancel a proposed action is a long way short of a veto and guarantees nothing to a state with fundamental concerns about a proposed law, harmonisation or EU police activities across borders.

A protocol will state that the UK will be able to opt out of requirements in this area. However, it is likely to be swept along to some extent by the tide of EU action in this policy area. For example, it is complying with EU pressure to introduce identity cards and contribute information to enable the setting up of an EU-wide database which will include personal information on every EU citizen. This database will be available to thousands of people at thousands of access points throughout the EU.

See *Major Issues* on this topic.

Services of general interest

Article 122 of the Constitution seemed to imply that such services should operate on free trade principles. The *Draft Mandate for the Reform Treaty* suggests otherwise. The Mandate requires the writing of a Protocol which will include the following words:

> "Article 1
>
> The shared values of the Union in respect of services of general economic interest within the meaning of Article 16 EC Treaty include in particular:

- the essential role and the wide discretion of national, regional and local authorities in providing, commissioning and organizing services of general economic interest as closely as possible to the needs of the users;

- the diversity between various services of general economic interest and the differences in the needs and preferences of users that may result from different geographical, social or cultural situations;

- a high level of quality, safety and affordability, equal treatment and the promotion of universal access and of user rights;

Article 2

The provisions of the Treaties do not affect in any way the competence of Member States to provide, commission and organise non-economic services of general interest."

Since all services may be charged for it is not clear what is meant by non-economic services or even if there are such things.

Real Reform

Integration and superstate versus limited EU powers

The key issue which is not addressed by the *Reform Treaty* goes back half a century to the opening concept of the Treaty of Rome, "Determined to lay the foundations of an ever-closer union among the peoples of Europe . . ."

It appears that the people of Europe are not convinced that their countries should for ever move closer and closer to other European countries until they merge into a single state. (This was recognised by EU leaders at Laeken in 2001.) Perhaps the majority want their own states to retain considerable and specific powers rather than allow all power to pass from the parliaments of their nation states to a central authority in Brussels, the European Union where their own country has just one voice among twenty-seven. Treaties since the Treaty of Rome, the Constitution, and now the repackaged Constitution all have passed, or were designed to pass, more power to Brussels. Both the Constitution and the *Reform Treaty* are designed to be the final positioning in this process. If citizens and state governments accept the *Reform Treaty*, and its underhand method of developing EU power, they will have no realistic hope of halting the process of political unification, and not just unification, but unification in the hands of a small power elite that cannot be removed as it cannot be voted out at the next election. A better EU is possible.

The EU needs some basic obvious reforms

The *Major Issues* section of this book reviews the topics which might be considered for reform, but for the sake of rounding off this chapter here are a few proposals:

- Taking decisions at the lowest possible level (subsidiarity) must become a genuine EU approach to handling political decision-making. The power to be reserved to member states needs to be specified and the open-ended "shared competences" and clauses which would allow a quick transfer of power to the EU without public debate (as in foreign and security policy) need to be removed from the *Reform Treaty*.

- Democracy must become a genuine feature of the EU. The EU should take steps to function as a democracy and support democracy as a desirable approach to government wherever the EU has influence.
- There needs to be a radical improvement in personal, institutional and political accountability within EU institutions.
- Corruption must be dealt with.
- Institutions must work transparently.
- Most importantly the EU could helpfully abandon its commitment to create a unified state ("ever closer union") and replace this commitment with a commitment of member states to trade and work together in peaceful co-operation to enhance the well-being, prosperity, peace and sustainability of Europe and the world.

Citizens' criticisms crushed for the present

Most of the time eurocitizens and their national parliaments are simply unaware of what the EU is doing. Few national politicians have a firm grasp of how the EU works and what its long-term policies are. Unable to read or understand the *Reform Treaty* documents in their worked-out final form (the revised treaties amended according to the prescriptions of the *Reform Treaty*), or to grasp their implication, the approval of national parliaments may go ahead without a hitch. They will toe the line.

The EU policy of ruling by means of secrecy, issuing inadequate, confusing, impenetrable or incomprehensible information is demonstrated by the way the proposed *Reform Treaty* is being handled. Because not one in a million Europeans can understand what EU leaders are doing they cannot object to the *Reform Treaty*. The end result will be that EU leaders will give themselves the opportunity to do just whatever they like and with the full authority of their own agreement unhindered by the direct democratic involvement of their peoples (unless Denmark and Ireland may upset the the plan). However, a fair number of eurocitizens will have a shrewd suspicion that something is sick in the heart of European government. Sooner or later EU citizens will revolt against this.

Radical reform is needed. The future of the European Union remains uncertain.

Notes

1 The Draft Inter-governmental Conference Mandate forms the last sixteen pages of *Presidency Conclusions, 21/22 June 2007*, EU Document 11177/07.

2 Quoted in the *Economist,* 9 August 2007.

3 Pursuing the treaty reform process, a report to the Council and European Council, 14 June 2007, reference 10659/07 POLGEN 67.

4 Quoted in El Pais, 25 June 2007.

5 Draft Mandate, Annexe 1, paragraph 4 (2).

6 Draft IGC Mandate, footnote 19.

Part six

Major Issues

"What the Union lacks and what the nation states have built up over centuries is - habitual trust." Dr. Marlene Wind, Associate Professor, University of Copenhagen. *A Critical Appraisal of the Commission White Paper on Governance*, 2001[1]

"People increasingly distrust institutions and politics . . . The problem . . . is particularly acute at the level of the European Union. Many people are losing confidence in a poorly understood and complex system." - *European Governance - a White Paper* prepared by the Commission, Brussels, 25 July 2001[2]

"What makes people unsatisfied
is that they accept lies."

D H Lawrence in *Courage*.

"Truth is the fundamental basis of democracy. MPs are elected to lead the country, not mislead it." - Adam Price MP in BBC2 programme, *The Ministry of Truth*, 11 October 2007.

What has gone wrong with the great European political experiment?

As mentioned elsewhere, the Constitution was officially abandoned in June 2007. The new ideas it contained are to be retained and added to existing treaties (with just a few very slight modifications). Comments in this chapter on "the Constitution" and its provisions therefore remain completely relevant.

As discussed in *Part One*, leaders of the European Union recognised some of the major failings of the EU in their *Laeken Declaration* of December 2001. When the 2004 Constitution, which they accepted as "the answer" to the EU's problems, was rejected by the people of France and Holland in 2005 these leaders were uncharacteristically stunned into silence. They seemed at a loss to understand what may be wrong with the political system which they are trying to direct. The best they could do was give themselves three more years to "reflect" and come up with convincing solutions.

What they are faced with is a crisis in public confidence which is shared by some politicians, including leaders of EU states. This is caused by:

- institutional defectiveness - including democratic weaknesses and a baffling complexity of organisational arrangements
- doubts about the unification of the states of Europe into a single superstate
- doubts about or rejection of key policies
- a sense that decision-makers are unknown, remote, unreachable and out-of-touch
- lack of integrity and accountability of politicians and bureaucrats
- endemic corruption
- the complexity, incomprehensibility and unacceptability of the Constitution.

EU leaders must properly understand the nature of the problems in order to resolve them if the EU is to regain direction, credibility and support from the citizens of Europe.

There are at least a dozen vital issues which EU leaders must address. The move by EU leaders in January 2007 to hide the Constitution's innovations by dispersing them among the articles of existing treaties was a seriously misjudged move - audacious, foolhardy and dishonest. If this re-assembly of the Constitution is introduced without eurocitizens having a chance to vote on it then antagonism to the EU project will escalate.

Major reform is needed to rescue the EU project. Without it the citizens' revolt will grow in strength and leaders of member states themselves will take unilateral action to backtrack on commitments - as they already have over free trade and immigration. (See *Tide turns against free trade* in *Free trade* and *Enlargement* below.)

Reforms may come in piecemeal actions by individual states, by the agreement of new treaties or through a radically re-written constitution. Whatever happens, the

European Union is likely to undergo significant change in the next few years. But what changes should be made? What should be the priorities?

The *At a glance* section looks at the biggest problems briefly. These are then explored in more detail in this chapter together with other major issues.

At a glance - The 12 biggest problems faced by the EU

One - the crux of the EU crisis: democratic deficit

There is a great deal of confusion about how democratic the European Union really is. Many think that because the European Parliament is elected then the EU must be democratic. They ignore the fact that the European parliament is significantly different from European state parliaments. It has few powers. The government of the EU is not formed from its members. It is not elected to carry through policies or initiate law-making. There is no opposition. It rubber stamps the EU. It can approve, or not, laws in certain categories which have been proposed and drafted by the unelected Commission, and it can comment and suggest. This power to approve laws is shared with the Council of Ministers. Laws in some areas, for example, agriculture, fisheries and home affairs, do not come to the European Parliament for approval.

Many think that because EU leaders (the Ministers of or Presidents of Member States) who meet as the European Council or the Council of Ministers were elected in their own countries then perhaps this makes the EU democratic. But these leaders were not elected by the EU electorate as members of an EU-wide political party with a European political programme of action. They were elected by widely dispersed electorates on mainly national issues. The programme of action that brought a leader to power in Malta is likely to be quite different from that of the leader of Finland or Poland or Britain. These leaders usually meet behind closed doors with the effect that eurocitizens cannot know what policy any minister is following or how he or she votes. If EU leaders adopt policies unpopular with the EU electorate as a whole, or with their own state electorates, no-one will even know what they have done or said. They cannot be seen to have any personal responsibility for their EU decisions. They cannot be voted out for the policies they pursue - either individually or as a group. They operate at one remove from the voters. These EU councils are really only sub-committees of twenty-seven European governments, but wield enormous power as if they have a direct mandate from the euroelectorate.

Then there is the "completely independent"[3] Commission with the authority to plan in detail, write and enforce EU laws, plan budgets, manage EU programmes, negotiate trade deals on behalf of all EU states and spend EU funds. This is the most clearly non-democratic element in the whole EU and run by twenty seven appointed leaders - one from each member state. At least at present (2007) each member state has an appointed representative, but as of November 2009 nine countries at any one time will not be represented by their own Commissioner, thereby reducing the participation of member states in an important area of EU decision-making.

There is no possibility for the eurovoter to vote for an alternative party or alternative policies. Top-level discussions, carried out in private, effectively exclude media interest and marginalise the euroelectorate.

In essence the EU's policymaking has gone on for half a century without the challenge of a political opposition, without critical media scrutiny of every new proposal and law and the feedback this may engender, and without the reality checks occasioned by politicians submitting themselves, their record and their proposals for the approval of the electorate in periodic elections. EU leaders have assumed that because they have been elected to do a job in their own separate 27 countries that this has entitled a few dozen of them to get together and run all 27 European Union countries as the United States of Europe. It is as if the leaders of parish councils had got together to run an entire country claiming that they were entitled to do so because they had been democratically elected.

See *Democratic deficit, Union Minister for Foreign Affairs, Patriotism - Political patriotism, Transparency, Accountability, Biggest problem number two - Integration, Biggest problem number three - Institutional defectivenes,* and *Lobbying.*

Two - Creeping integration, unification - Making the states of Europe into a single state

The architects of the EU planned, from the start, that sovereign member states would progressively, and almost imperceptibly, give up sovereign powers to central authorities. The plan excluded the idea of democratic consent. In spite of all the talk of democratic foundations the citizens of Europe have never agreed to any power being transferred to Brussels.

The Constitution, and earlier treaties, confirm this direction of travel. The Constitution talks of "the peoples of Europe . . . united ever more closely" (Preamble), "the peoples of Europe ... creating an ever closer union" (*Charter of Fundamental Rights*), and "the achievement of an ever-increasing degree of convergence of Member States' action" in foreign and security policy (article 40). A commitment to a direction (rather than a goal or a specific division of powers) means that there is no limit to the degree of integration or unification of the once independent states - or rather, that the end result will be complete unification.

Do eurocitizens realise that the Constitution in its original and re-assembled form, if ratified, would give them the United States of the European Union? If the entire euroelectorate were given the chance to vote on this matter would we vote to pass most of the power of our own elected governments to this new superstate?

See *Integration - the number one question, European Union by stealth - Pickpocketing democracy and sovereignty, Subsidiarity,* and *Integration - to integrate or not to integrate.*

Three - Institutional defectiveness

The European Union is a state that does not acknowledge that it is a state. When its leaders can dare to say to its citizens that that is what has been created then it will begin to be possible to understand what needs to be done to create a democratic and properly functioning organisation.

The EU has powers; it makes laws (which actually over-rule state laws); it exercises control; it collects and spends revenue; it runs a judiciary and a police force and has control of armies; it forms relationships and makes treaties with other states. Yet it has no identifiable government. No EU institution has overall responsibility for what the EU does. The EU's nonexistent government was not elected. It has no mandate. It cannot be voted out. There is a complex mix of shared powers which vary from situation to situation, and a merry go round of changing leadership, so that ultimately no one can be seen to be responsible for anything. - Yet this confused, centralised agglomeration of power (without defined limits) controls most of the major decision-making in Europe.

The organisational structure is excessively complex.

It lacks the functioning elements of a democracy.

Laws are made according to a variety of procedures by varying groups of people. Nothing has been specified as being exclusively the concern of individual member states. There is no provision for dealing with leaders who take action contrary to EU treaties or policies, or who act against the interests of eurocitizens, or who lie, or who break international or national law. Because so little decision-making is done openly it is unlikely that eurocitizens will ever know who is really responsible for a given policy and they cannot participate through the media in consideration of proposed or existing policies.

The EU has designed, and fallen into, an organisational black hole. It needs to come up with a simple, clear, transparent, effective and democratic structure if its leaders wish it to become an integrated European Union (as planned in the Constitution). Alternatively, EU leaders need to take a different course and allow the EU to become simply a free association of democratic sovereign states.

See also *Democratic deficit, European Union by stealth - pickpocketing democracy and sovereignty, Subsidiarity, The Commission, Transparency, Accountability, Defence and foreign policy, a key area of European integration* and *Integration - the number one question.*

Four - Lack of transparency

In 2001 European leaders called for more transparency in the EU.[4] In spite of an official policy of transparency (See *Euroterminology*) much of the EU documentation that should be available to the public remains unavailable.

Secrecy about who receives EU funding adds to this distrust and makes it possible for mismanagement and fraud to flourish.

Virtually all EU institutions operate behind closed doors leaving the electorate with a sense of exclusion, distrust and a sense of being dictated to. (However, on the positive side, the European Parliament debates may be followed live on the internet and in 2007, at last, some meetings of the Councils of Ministers will be viewable on the internet.)

Without open government there can be no public debate, no public confidence and no democracy. There is a danger that without popular support the state will founder. Transparency offers the hope of public confidence in the EU.

See *Transparency* below.

Five - Top-down decision making v subsidiarity

The European Union developed from trading agreements between a few European States and evolved into a centralised administration run by the Commission. The Commission has considerable independent powers to operate and control the functioning of the European Union - including the almost exclusive right to take the initiative to introduce and frame new laws. (In the European Coal and steel Community, which came into operation in 1952, it was the "High authority" - the forerunner of the European Commission which was able to override the authority of the member states in relevant areas.)

Despite its best efforts the Commission is out of sight and out of contact with the mass of the European electorate. Its policies are not tested in the furnace of democratic elections. The same problem, despite the best of intentions, considerable success and enormous effort, exists for other EU decision-makers in the COREPER, The Council and the European Council.

Strategic planning for the EU, the agreeing of European Union Treaties and the agreeing of the European Constitution was done by leaders of the EU states meeting as the European Council. Their decisions have been based on their personal beliefs and preferences - not on political programmes submitted to the electorate. No one knows, for example, if the citizens of Europe really approve of decisions in more policy areas coming under the control of Brussels via the "shared competences" procedures, if they approve of EU foreign policy and defence being controlled from Brussels, or if they approve of the commitment to increase privatisation, or if they approve of the aim of "ever closer union." Only rarely, and usually informally, does the euroelectorate have a voice in eurodecision-making.

Above the EU are other decision-makers. Major influences on the European Union include the World Bank, the World Trade Organisation and the International Monetary Fund, with their free trade rules and liberalisation policies. They seek to promote their policies throughout the world. The EU is both subject to their influence and also an important player in directing their policies. Power at these levels of influence is beyond the reaches of mere voters.

The principle of subsidiarity, introduced into the EU in article 5 of the *Treaty Establishing the European Community*, is that decisions are taken at the lowest practical level. The TEC and the EU Constitution (unlike, for example, the American Constitution) do not name any areas of political decision making that are to be reserved to state parliaments. The Constitution introduces the concept of "shared competences" for education and many other areas where decisions about who will take decisions will have to be agreed on an item by item basis. See article 14. Then there are "Areas of supporting, co-ordinating and complementary action" set out in article 17. These shared areas of activity create uncertainty, opportunities for disputes, confusion, delay, controversial decision-making and a sense that our own state governments have no control over almost all issues of vital concern to fellow countrymen. EU rules require that once the EU has made decisions in a certain policy topic then individual states may never take decisions in that area again.

The subsidiarity principle conflicts with the principle of ever closer union. Where decisions fail to be taken at the lowest possible level there is a reduction of democratic control. The EU preaches subsidiarity but has not organised itself to practise it. Actually it has organised itself to take more and more power to Brussels.

See *Subsidiarity, Localism* and *Free Trade (below) COREPER,* and *Commission (in Euroterminology),* and the sections in Part One: *European Leaders at the crossroads, 2001-2008,* and the text of *The Future of the European Union (The Laeken Declaration).*

Six - Lack of accountability

Lack of accountability is one of the greatest defects of the European Union. Accountability is of great concern in the EU in three areas:

1 financial accountability,
2 democratic accountability
3 accountability before the law.

If the EU can address these problems it could do much to bring about public confidence in the EU, its institutions and policies.

- Financial accountability is considered below in the *Finances of the EU - unsolved problems of European Union financial control - Fraud* and *Transparency* sections.
- Democratic accountability is considered in *Biggest Problems, Numbers One, Two, Four, Five*, and *Six*, and *Patriotism – Political patriotism, European Union by stealth - Pickpocketing democracy and sovereignty, Accountability, Defence and foreign Policy*, and *Democratic Deficit* (below). See also *COSI* in the *Institutions* chapter.
- Accountability before the law is considered in *Rule of law, Defence and Foreign policy* and *Biggest problem number ten.*

Seven - Problems with the Constitution and its replacements: size, complexity and purpose

A normal constitution of a state may describe the principles on which it is based and how the state will be organised. The European Constitution is three things

1 A constitution
2 A set of policies
3 A plan for integrating separate states into a single state.

It is an amalgamation of trade treaties, recipes for the blending of formerly independent functions of member states (for example, legal systems, some police functions, some defence functions, employment, social policy, health, education and culture), plus elements of a conventional constitution – a set of constitutional arrangements.

The part of the Constitution which actually deals with constitutional issues consists of articles 1 to 60 (some seventeen pages). The remainder of the Constitution (varying according to layout and page size) consists of a further two hundred and fifty very complex pages of policies, plans, principles and procedures. This is followed by a further one hundred and forty pages of additional material to supplement, modify or explain the preceding pages. Its replacement promises to be every bit as long and confusing (August 2007).

A constitution is a very long-term proposal which should give any citizen a quick and clear guide to the way his or her state is run. It should not be concerned with policies. Policies should be matters open to pragmatic change and subject to frequent testing and review by democratic processes (something which is generally not available within the EU, the exceptions being several referendums when approval of the EU and its policies has sometimes been negative, and usually less than enthusiastic). The combining of policy with constitution is a fundamental error which has made the Constitution very long, complex and (except for those with an exceptional degree of patience and many days of time to devote to its study) incomprehensible.

Sooner or later reality will impinge on fixed policies and leaders will realise the need for flexibility. This is happening with regard to the policy of free trade (the cornerstone of EU policy) which is being challenged by a growing desire for protectionism and economic patriotism. See *Free Trade* and *Patriotism - economic* below.

The Constitution lacks clarity, being overloaded with detail and avoidable complications and variations of procedures.

The commitment to "ever closer union" authorises the unification of the separate member states into a single state. Sometime soon voters may be faced with a state accompli.

See, *Constitution - does Europe need a constitution?* and *Constitution - preparing to re-write it or rescue the EU from crisis*, also *Part Four - The Constitution's Ideas*

Eight - EU enlargement

The EU has a virtually open-door policy towards new member states joining the EU. Certain basic conditions have to be met and the state has to be in or very close to Europe. (Article 58). This policy, combined with a policy of free movement of persons, capital and establishment, carries concern for job security, wage levels, social cohesion, house prices and shifting pressures on public services and utilities in existing member states. Substantial migrations across Europe since the great expansion of EU membership in 2004 has caused many people to question the wisdom of the EU's free-movement-of-persons-policy.

See *Free movement of persons* (in *Free trade and other EU trade policies*), *Enlargement,* and *House prices* (below).

Nine - Privatisation

This WTO policy appears in the Constitution under the name of "liberalisation". Though capable of bringing benefits in certain circumstances it is a policy which has met with disastrous consequences and massive opposition around the world. It is clearly driven by dogma and is applied regardless of particular circumstances, not analysis of the needs of most actual situations. States, might, with benefit, have the right to apply liberalisation when, how and if they see fit. The demand to liberalise public services under the direction of the Commission may not be in the best interests of individual states and may not have popular support. In fact, plans for privatisation have aroused considerable protests.

See *Free Trade* below, especially the section: *Free trade for companies providing services - 2006 EU Directive.*

Ten - Developing military force

The EU seems to be increasingly concerned with military action. Defence forces are planned to be used for activities which go far beyond defence and far beyond Europe. Defence spending is to be increased year after year.

There is an understandable concern with combating terrorism but solutions do not envisage attempting to understand what enrages terrorists or avoiding provocation to terrorism - which might usefully be one of the aims of the EU defence policy.

See *Defence and foreign policy* below, and *Euro army* in the *Institututions* chapter.

Eleven - powers to be taken by the replacements of the Constitution

The *Reform Treaty* 2007, following the plans set out in the Constitution, will:

- take more decision-making from the governments of member states, and make it possible for more policy areas to be directed centrally by the EU from Brussels including, eventually, the control of all defence, foreign policy and security
- allow virtually limitless addition of new member states
- open the door for the unification of all EU states into a single state
- grant new powers to collect data on eurocitizens
- allow the EU to expand its own police force (Europol) under its centralised control and not accountable to state, regional or local government
- set up a new "Defence Agency" to develop European arms industries and increase military spending by member states
- set up a new European Union Foreign Office - the External Action Service
- permit various other developments.

These policies may not enjoy much support from eurocitizens and may be part of the reason two member states rejected the Constitution.

Twelve - The EU's lack of consistency

The EU has striking failures to comply with its own principles and policies, and has inconsistencies and incompatibilities within or between policies. Here are a few examples of problem areas: commitments to free trade, democracy, peace, the rule of law including international law, subsidiarity, transparency, accountability, the protection of the environment, the free movement of people, the desire for full employment. All these fail to be observed or delivered to the extent that might reasonably be expected.

There is a lack of co-ordinated thinking on policy issues and sometimes a serious lack of commitment.

See *Double standards - Loss of credibility, Democratic deficit, Transparency, Subsidiarity, Free trade, Enlargement, Defence and foreign policy, Finances of the EU - unsolved problems of European Union financial control - Fraud, Transport, Energy and the environment.*

Major Issues in More Detail

Accessibility/openness/transparency

See *Transparency, European Union by stealth, Lobbying,* and *Clear use of language.*

Accountability

Financial accountability

In the EU the spending of over a hundred billion euros each year is still not properly accounted for. It is known that billions of euros go astray. The Commission is unable to say even who the ten biggest recipients of EU funds are. The Court of Auditors has found itself unable to approve the accounts for eleven years in a row. In the agricultural sector alone it is known and admitted that £2.2 billion have been handed out on the basis of fraudulent applications. Effective financial accounting is vital for confidence in the EU.

See *Finances of the EU*, below.

Democratic accountability

In the EU there is lack of accountability to the electorate. Most of those who take decisions have no direct mandate from the citizens of Europe. When they displease there is no procedure which can remove them. The body which initiates laws, the Commission, has no democratic legitimacy as it is elected by no-one and as far as its policies are concerned it is accountable to no body (except in the case of extreme malpractice when it can be dismissed as a whole by the European Parliament). EU treaties guarantee it complete independence. In contrast, within democratic state parliamentary systems the civil service is under the control of the elected party in power. It is therefore very clear who to hold responsible for the failures of any department. The party in power may deal with any problem itself or eventually the electorate may vote out the party it deems to have failed. In the EU system the Commission works with complete independence. No-one accepts responsibility for the work of any individual department. If a department makes bad or seriously unpopular decisions the Commissioner will be free to continue his/her work till the end of the five year term. No-one and no party can be voted out as a result of failures.

The Council, the European Council, and the Commission – the executive are not directly accountable to the European electorate as a whole. In their own countries EU leaders can always deny responsibility for any bad or unpopular EU decision on sound grounds. Each minister can honestly say, "It was an EU decision, not mine. I did not take the decision." Each of them has only one vote out of twenty seven on any decision and therefore they cannot be held personally responsible. With present arrangements their contribution to a decision can never be known. There are never any published records of how EU ministers have voted on any issue. The Commission believes that sometimes ministers misrepresent what they have done. "Member States do not communicate well about what the Union is doing and what they are doing in the Union. 'Brussels' is too easily blamed by Member States for difficult decisions that they themselves have agreed or even requested."[5] Decision making is collective, yet the group that makes decisions can never be voted out as a group.

See *Democratic deficit*, below.

Accountability before the law

In the EU there is no body to hold politicians responsible for incompetence or misbehaviour, however serious. Within the first page of the American Constitution we know who will have power to deal with political wrongdoing. The EU treaties and the Constitution do not envisage the possibility of political wrongdoing occurring. Functionaries of the EU have been placed above the law in certain circumstances. See Protocol 7, article 11. See also, *Rule of law* below.

Lack of accountability makes the functioning of democracy impossible and can give no eurocitizen any confidence in the European Union as an institution. This issue is of the utmost importance. The positive achievements of the European Union are lost sight of in the glare of this burning problem.

The EU needs to establish a body to ensure proper standards of behaviour in the higher echelons of the EU.

Agriculture - Unsolved problems of the Common Agricultural Policy

It has already been suggested that policies of the EU should be separate from a constitution. Setting this idea aside for this topic (and other policies that arise later), this item considers a few aspects of this important area.

Half a century ago agriculture employed 20 per cent of the work force of the original six member states producing 12 per cent of GNP. Now (December 2006) it employs just 7 per cent of the EU work force and accounts for only 3 per cent of total EU GDP. However, it remains the most costly sector of the EU budget, accounting for 46 per cent of spending in 2004; it has generated more EU legislation than any other area, and has the second largest department at the Commission. Throughout its history its work has been contentious.

Agriculture operates in the EU on principles completely at odds with EU philosophy. Rather than operating on free trade principles it operates as a controlled market with controlled prices and subsidies. Many complaints are brought against the agricultural policies.

- Prices to consumers have been kept artificially high, a shocking matter when there has been overproduction.
- The cost to EU tax payers of running the policy has been very high.
- Much of EU agricultural funding has gone to dealing with surpluses, for example by paying money to reduce the price of farm exports – thereby

encouraging the continuation of overproduction and the selling of foodstuffs at prices below cost. A great quantity of EU surplus food production has been given away to third world countries. As a result farmers in third world recipient countries have suffered because they could not sell their own produce at a profit and therefore could not make a living. Once they had gone out of business the countries' abilitity to sustain themselves began to disappear. Often the EU paid farmers for surplus production and then destroyed the unwanted food.

- EU states, self-sufficient in certain food products, have been forced to cut back production and admit imports (for example, UK milk producers).
- For years farmers have been well paid *not* to produce food (an EU system of payments to farmers called "set-aside").
- EU policies have encouraged the cutting down of hedges and trees, the use of chemical fertilizers and herbicides with some harmful effects including the production of high levels of CO2 in the manufacturing process.
- The payment of subsidies on the basis of land area has artificially increased the value of land and increased rental costs for tenant farmers so that the viability of their farming businesses have been threatened or destroyed.
- The EU has paid large sums of money to help its richest farmers.
- There has been a large amount of fraud in the administration of the Common Agriculture policy (revealed by the Court of Auditors). See *Finances of the EU*, below.
- Till quite recent times the EU agriculture sector did not concern itself with environmental issues or food quality.

When ten more states joined the EU in 2004 the farming scene changed radically adding to the problems of EU centralised planning and control. Four million more farmers joined the EU's existing seven million farmers. Thirty per cent more land was added to EU farmlands.

Yet in spite of severe problems European agriculture is in many ways a success story. The EU accounts for 20 per cent of world food exports. The EU is self sufficient in many key products, including vegetables, meat, dairy products, barley, wheat and wine.

In the Constitution agriculture is covered by articles 225 to 232 - just two pages. The aims of the policy are set out in article 227.

"1. The objectives of the common agricultural policy shall be:

(a) to increase agricultural productivity by promoting technical progress and by ensuring the rational development of agricultural production and the optimum utilisation of the factors of production, in particular labour;

(b) thus to ensure a fair standard of living for the agricultural community, in particular by increasing the individual earnings of persons engaged in agriculture;

(c) to stabilise markets;

(d) to assure the availability of supplies;

(e) to ensure that supplies reach consumers at reasonable prices.

2. In working out the common agricultural policy and the special methods for its application, account shall be taken of:

(a) the particular nature of agricultural activity, which results from the social structure of agriculture and from structural and natural disparities between the various agricultural regions;

(b) the need to effect the appropriate adjustments by degrees;

(c) the fact that in the Member States agriculture constitutes a sector closely linked with the economy as a whole."

Aims might have included:

- to produce sufficient quality food (GM free) for Europe's people
- to produce food as locally as possible to minimise transportation
- to encourage sustainable agriculture whilst reducing reliance on risky anti- environment and climate-changing chemicals.

Europe's farmers received £69.2 billion in 2005. This cost represents a charge of approximately £12 per week for a European family of four. Article 227 (which repeats article 33 of the *Treaty Establishing the European Community*) states that one of the aims is, "to ensure a fair standard of living for the agricultural community, in particular by increasing the individual earnings of persons engaged in agriculture". In actual fact three quarters of Europe's farmers survive on less than £5,000 per year, yet 70% per cent of the money paid out by the European Union to farmers goes to the 20% richest. For example, in France most money goes to huge agribusinesses such as Beghin-Say which receives £155, 000,000 per year.

In Britain an Oxfam report of 2004, *Spotlight On Subsidies - Cereal Injustice Under the CAP in Britain* - showed in detail how the common agricultural policy was paying huge benefits to some of the most wealthy men in the UK. It was also damaging small farmers, consumers, tax payers and the environment. (The sums quoted here are estimates calculated on the EU payment system which was based on the payment of a given sum for each hectare of land farmed. The UK and EU do not publish details of money paid to the farming community.)

> "The largest 2% of land holding in the UK account for around one fifth of total subsidies. . .
>
> Eastern England and Lincolnshire, two of the wealthiest agricultural regions in the UK, receive the bulk of CAP support. The poorest regions get the least support. We have identified 75 Farms in Lincolnshire that share around £16,000,000 in CAP subsidies. The 'Lincolnshire eight' - farms with more than 1,000 hectares - receive an average payment of more than £337,000. . .
>
> The Duke of Westminster, Britain's richest man . . .receives £326,000 CAP subsidies.
>
> The Duke of Marlborough. . . attracts around £369,000 cereal payments.
>
> Sir Adrian Swire. . . owns farms in Oxfordshire that are eligible for CAP payments of just under £200,000.

> Lord de Ramsey, the former head of the UK environment agency. . . receives CAP payments on cereals estimated at around £377,104. . .
>
> The sheer scale of the transfers involved raises fundamental questions about social justice and equity in the use of public finance. . .
>
> The UK government has prioritised increases in public spending aimed at overcoming poverty. The public subsidies to the country's richest farmers outstrip payments to its poorest people by a very wide margin. . .
>
> Because subsidies are based on land area, they artificially inflate the value of land and the price of rents. This is bad for tenants that include some of the poorest farmers in the UK; but it is a financial boon for landowners. We estimate that the rent inflation caused by CAP subsidies adds £64,000 to the rental income of the Duke of Marlborough's tenanted land, rising to more than £100,000 for the Duke of Grafton's estate in Eastern England.
>
> Losers from the CAP represent a far bigger constituency than the winners. Millions of farmers in developing countries lose because CAP sponsored export dumping destroys the markets in which they operate. Under the reformed CAP the EU will continue to export larger volumes of sugar, cereals, dairy and livestock at prices that do not reflect production costs. This will lower the international and domestic market prices for the agricultural goods produced by developing countries."
>
> - Oxfam 2004.

Reforms to the policy which came into operation in 2005/6 cut the direct link in payments to farmers between the amount of food produced and the amount paid in subsidy. Instead farmers are now being paid a single payment which is being progressively reduced and is linked to environmental conditions. The amount paid to support prices on some farm products has been reduced. Payments to the largest farms have been cut. These reforms have been possible, in part, because of the reduction in veto powers.

It is quite possible that if free trade principles had been allowed to operate in agriculture, and there had been no agriculture policy, that Europe's farmers would have risen to the challenge and produced the food that Europe needed. It is unlikely that they would have produced huge surpluses. It is likely that food prices would be lower. Eurocitizens would have been saved the vast tax revenues that have been paid to farmers.

Agriculture policy issues

Do Eurocitizens support the aims and costs of the common Agriculture Policy? If the aims of the EU Agriculture policy (article 227) are ones that eurocitizens do support can we have confidence that the EU is efficiently and effectively administering it?

Would the aims of the policy be more effectively achieved if each state looked after its own farmers, funding them with their own revenues? Perhaps member states would administer funds in a more open, honest and effective way, and give a better account to their electorates of what they are doing and why. It may be fair to point out, however, that fraud in the distribution of EU funds happens to a substantial extent in the administrations of member states.

Area of Freedom Security and Justice (Law and order) - Legal unification of Member States

Co-operation and bureaucratisation - Who rules - member states or the EU?

Whilst co-operation in matters which may enhance "freedom, security and justice" is self-evidently a good thing (article 257), actual decisions as to procedures, laws and control of the police within each EU state surely ought to be taken by directly elected governments. A new, independent EU police force, Europol, not accountable to member states undermines this situation. Article 258, in an extension of EU power, states, "The European Council shall define the strategic guidelines for legislative and operational planning within the area of freedom, security and justice". Should not member states retain responsibility for strategic planning for law and order matters within their own states? The EU principle of subsidiarity should ensure this, but the Constitution suggests otherwise.

Co-operation between states to catch criminals (including terrorists) who commit crimes in one country but reside or hide in another is a necessity (see article 271). Such co-operation neither needs an EU Constitution nor should it be confined to the EU. A case has not been made for making legal systems in EU states more or less the same. The wisdom or otherwise of "judicial co-operation in civil and criminal matters"(articles 269 and 270) with its consequent "approximation of laws and regulations of member states," sounds like an enormous bureaucratic task. Article 257 suggests no limitation on the number or categories of laws that may be unified (approximated) across EU states. Since the unification of laws across twenty-seven states would be done by bureaucrats rather than elected politicians there would be a loss of democracy here. The harmonisation of criminal laws might be a legal minefield which might be better not entered (articles 257 and 269).

Article 260 announces another big bureaucratic task - that of assessing what has been achieved in the application of mutual recognition of the laws of member states.

Issues here are: should criminal law, police and justice be directed by the EU's European Council and EU bureaucrats or by individual states? Is the task of making laws approximately the same throughout the EU necessary, democratic, desirable, practicable or likely to be cost effective?

See other *Major issues - Data Harvesting, Europol, European Arrest Warrant,* and *Criminal Justice.* See also *European Security and Intelligence Force* in the *Institutions* chapter.

Charter of Fundamental Rights of the European Union is of doubtful value

"Let's put people first. We were not made to serve the economy. The economy was made to serve us." - Jonathan Sacks, Chief Rabbi, UK.[118]

This charter, appears to be designed to make a single "document" which encompasses all the rights of EU citizens. These are the rights set out in the *Treaty on European Union* (guaranteed under TEU article 6/2) and the rights set out in the *Treaty Establishing the European Community* (TEC articles 17-21).

The *Treaty on European Union* commits EU states to "respect fundamental rights, as guaranteed by the *European Convention for the Protection of Human Rights and Fundamental Freedoms*". The Charter, which was included in the Constitution, is now planned to be attached to existing treaties. It effectively exists under current treaties. It was signed and "proclaimed" by the European Council, the Commission and the European Parliament in December 2000.[117]

The Preamble to this charter repeats the EU commitment to an "ever closer union" of member states, a key topic which has been discussed in relation to the preamble of the Constitution itself, in *Integration - the number one question* (below) and in *Biggest problem, number two.*

The rights already acknowledged by the Constitution in articles 2, 9 and 10 are elaborated in the *Charter of Fundamental Rights of the Union* (*Charter Preamble*, articles 61-114, plus Declaration 12, articles 1-54). This preamble proclaims, "The Union is founded on the indivisible, universal values of human dignity, freedom, equality and solidarity; it is based on the principles of democracy and the rule of law." The democratic credentials of the European Union are a major weakness which is discussed in this chapter under *Biggest problems* (one to four), *Defence and foreign policy* and *Democratic deficit.* The rule of law is a major feature of the EU, but there are some weaknesses. These are discussed in this chapter under *Rule of law* and *Defence and Foreign policy.*

Perhaps the greatest claim of the Preamble is that the Union "places the individual at the heart of its activities." This idea is a late and unconvincing addition to what is really at the heart of the European Union, international trading arrangements. "In the beginning," said European leaders in 2001, "it was more of an economic and technical collaboration."[6] In December 1989 (thirty seven years after the founding of the embryonic EU) eleven of the twelve EU leaders signed a *Charter of Social Rights of Workers*, but this obviously relates to people purely as necessary elements of the economic process. The idea of EU citizenship (and the concept of the individual citizen) first appeared in an EU agreement in the *Maastricht Treaty* which was signed in February 1992. This may have been an attempt to answer the complaint that the EU was about commerce, rather than about people. It may also be seen as a belated recognition of the importance of the individual citizen or as a step towards statehood for the EU. Economic Communities have traders and workers, but states have citizens.

With citizenship comes rights, admittedly somewhat limited in the case of the rebranded European Union:

- the right to move, reside and work anywhere in any member state
- the right to use the consular services of any member state when outside the EU
- the right of a citizen, when living within the EU but not in his/her home state, to vote in both municipal and European Parliamentary elections
- the right to petition the (virtually powerless) European Parliament
- the right to bring a complaint to the European Ombudsman.

The idea of a charter of fundamental rights appears not to have been discussed by European leaders until June 1999 (at the Cologne summit), over forty years after the beginning of the EU as "an economic and technical collaboration". In fact, the EU remains primarily concerned with economic relationships: trade, prosperity, competitiveness, agriculture, technology, space, nuclear power, energy, transport infrastructure, etc. Nevertheless, human rights now appear to be acknowledged in a detailed and serious way in the *Charter of Fundamental Rights.*

The four freedoms of the European Union particularly pointed out by the Preamble are the freedoms of "movement of persons, services, goods and capital." A further freedom has been added here, the "freedom of establishment," which means the freedom to set up a business. These are essentially freedoms which are designed to facilitate trade rather than fundamental human rights.

The American President, Franklin Roosevelt, had a view of fundamental rights which makes an interesting contrast with those especially promoted by the European Union. He said there were four essential human freedoms: freedom of speech and worship, and freedom from want and fear. These freedoms are at the heart of the human condition, and whilst these rights or freedoms appear in the *Charter*, they are not the ones that the EU chooses to stress.

No new rights, limited application, and existing rights curtailed

One would naturally expect that the rights accorded by this *Charter of Fundamental Rights* would apply directly to EU citizens. For example, "equality between women and men" (article 83). This "must be ensured in all areas, including employment, work and pay." This suggests that a complaint of sexual discrimination against an employer or any organisation might be taken to the European Court of Justice of the European Union in Luxembourg. But this is not the case. Article 111 on the subject of "field of operation" states "The provisions of this Charter are addressed to the institutions, bodies, offices and agencies of the Union with due regard to the principle of subsidiarity and to the Members States *only when they are implementing Union law.*" (Emphasis added.) This suggests that the Charter's status is that of a request to institutions and member states within the EU to make their own regulations compliant with the Charter and only "when implementing Union law." This is an extremely narrow field of application compared with rights which are guaranteed directly to all citizens at all times. It appears to demolish the broad value of the rights guaranteed by the charter.

Article 111 explains how the *Charter of Fundamental Rights* will make no difference to Union law. It adds nothing new. "The Charter does not extend the field of application of Union law . . ." This suggests that it has no intrinsic meaning. It is simply a repetition of what exists elsewhere in the Constitution and current European case law. However, in order to consider other issues relating to this charter we must set aside the apparent meaninglessness of it. After all, the limitations of application currently stipulated in the Constitution may one day be set aside and we would still have a charter with many unsatisfactory provisions.

There are interesting but unconvincing reassurances in this Charter and a few unexpected and serious curtailments of liberty.

The rights

What does this charter offer? The statements of rights seem clear, solid, unequivocal and, in most cases, highly desirable. They appear to have the legal force of the Union behind them. (The Preamble tells us "the Charter will be interpreted by the courts of the Union.") But commitments actually come with qualifications and get-out clauses and member states can ignore the EU's "fundamental rights" at will. (See below.) Some commitments appear to have unintended consequences.

The following are some of the main rights. Article 62 states "Everyone has the right to life. No one shall be condemned to the death penalty, or executed." Other articles deal with the following topics; article 64, the prohibition of torture, protection of personal data (article 68), freedom of expression - "Everyone has the right to freedom of expression. This right shall include freedom to hold opinions and to receive and impart information and ideas without interference by public authority and regardless of frontiers" (article 71), freedom of assembly and association including the right to join a trade union, equality before the law (article 80), the right of collective bargaining and action "including strike action" (article 88), social security and social assistance (article 94), health care, "Everyone has the right of access to preventive health care and the right to benefit from medical treatment under the conditions established by national laws and practices" (article 95), environmental protection (article 97), consumer protection (article 98), right of access to documents (article 102), right to an effective remedy and to a fair trial (article 107) and presumption of innocence. "Everyone who has been charged shall be presumed innocent until proved guilty according to law" (article 108).

Lack of commitment

We have seen that in matters of trade and control within the EU then EU law and rulings override national laws. In the matter of human rights the opposite is the case. Everything guaranteed in the *Charter of Fundamental Rights* may be overruled by national parliaments. "Full account shall be taken of national laws and practices." (Article 112/6.) Nations can do what they like in this area. The Charter guarantees no rights.

The unequivocal statement that everyone has the right to life is meaningless unless it is backed up by a power to discipline member states who violate it. For example, when, in 2005, a London policeman shot and killed an innocent man he suspected of terrorist intentions the UK Government might have been brought to account for an offence against the fundamental right to life but was not, presumably because British police, when killing terrorist suspects are not implementing Union law. Even after the tragic killing in 2005 Britain maintains its shoot-to-kill policy for police action when they are dealing with people they suspect of terrorist intentions. (An important rule for police action must always be that they use minimum force, but the present policy seems to go beyond this. Police need to have exceptionally good grounds for believing that an imminent threat to human life can only be averted by a lethal shot before this extreme action is taken.) The EU doesn't criticise or attempt to overturn this policy. The EU's *Charter of Fundamental Rights* doesn't reach this far.

The right of citizens to a fair trial is set out in article 107. It is currently guaranteed by the EU through its treaty commitment to the European Convention on Human Rights and Fundamental Freedoms.[7] Again, the EU does not take upon itself to monitor or criticise member states which fail to give its citizens fair trials. It has not condemned member states' use of detention/house arrest without due process of law policy. (For example,terrorist suspects in the UK.) In contrast, the non-EU body the European Court of Human Rights constantly criticises member states. For example, in 2006 it made many complaints against two EU members: 190 against Slovenia and 115 against Poland.

If the EU *Charter of Fundamental Rights* is to be credible it needs to monitor compliance with this charter and take action when there are problems.

One has to allow that some rights must admit exceptions (so that, for example, the right to free speech does not go so far as to allow incitement to racial hatred). But at least one right must be considered absolute and that is the right not to be tortured. This is set out in article 64. It must therefore be a concern that member states appear to have colluded with the American CIA in illegally detaining their own citizens for the purpose of questioning under duress and for indefinite detention without charge. Also, they appear to have allowed their air space and airports to be used for the purpose of moving these kidnap victims across and within Europe and to states outside Europe. A report by a committee of the European Parliament which was approved by the EP in February 2007[8] condemned the behaviour of many member states for their participation in such activities and for their unwillingness to answer questions about these activities.

The EU's website account of this report[9] made the following points:

- European countries have been "turning a blind eye" to flights operated by the CIA which, "on some occasions, were being used for extraordinary rendition or the illegal transportation of detainees."
- "At least 1245 flights operated by the CIA flew into European airspace or stopped over at European airports between the end of 2001 and the end of 2005", although, as MEPs emphasise, "not all those flights have been used for extraordinary rendition".
- MEPs mention up to 21 well-documented cases of extraordinary rendition in which rendition victims were transferred through a European country or were residents in a European state at the time of their kidnapping.
- Committee members deplore these renditions "as an illegal instrument used by the USA in the fight against terrorism" and condemn the "acceptance and concealing of the practice, on several occasions, by the secret services and governmental authorities of certain European countries".
- The report notes that the renditions investigated by the committee "in the majority of cases involved incommunicado detention and torture".
- MEPs also deplored "the lack of co-operation of many Member States and of the Council of the EU. . ." The Council, they said, initially withheld - and then provided only partial fragments of information pertaining to regular discussions with high-level US officials. The report calls this

behaviour "totally unacceptable". Such "shortcomings" of the Council, reads the report, "implicate all Member State governments, since they have collective responsibility as members of the Council".

- The national governments specifically criticised for their unwillingness to co-operate with Parliament's investigations were those of Austria, Italy, Poland, Portugal and the UK. The report also gives detailed evidence of investigations of illegal rendition or CIA flight cases involving Bosnia, Cyprus, Denmark, Former Yugoslav Republic of Macedonia (FYROM), Germany, Greece, Ireland, Romania, Spain, Sweden and Turkey.
- MEPs complained about "omissions" in statements by Javier Solana, the Council's High Representative for the Common Foreign and Security Policy and EU Counter-terrorism Co-ordinator Gijs de Vries.

EU member states are apparently operating with a mindset which suggests that current leaders have little or no real commitment to fundamental human rights.

Sometimes, even in the initial statements in this charter it can be seen that a claimed right is qualified, limited and may well not exist at all. For example, the right to healthcare, article 95. This, because if it is not guaranteed to be free it cannot be a right available to all citizens. It therefore becomes wishful thinking, an aspiration, not a right. Also, it is offered "under the conditions established by national laws and practices." These national laws and practices may offer comprehensive healthcare of the highest quality free for all citizens, but may offer inadequate healthcare and only to those who can pay for it.

Article 112 sets out details of how all the rights may be undermined. It immediately admits there may be limitations of rights. "Limitation on the exercise of the rights and freedoms recognised by this Charter must be provided for by law and respect the essence of those rights and freedoms." If you limit the right to life how do you "respect the essence of that right"? Surely it ceases to be a fundamental right. Similarly with the prohibition of torture and other rights. We must understand that the rights and the essence of the rights may be withheld.

Article 112 further states that, "limitations may be made only if they are necessary and genuinely meet objectives of general interest recognised by the Union or the need to protect the rights and freedoms of others." Free trade is a prime objective, freedom and interest of the EU. This is stressed in the Preamble of the *Charter of Fundamental Rights* and appears as a right in article 4 which guarantees within and by the Union "the free movement of persons, services, goods and capital and freedom of establishment". Details of this core concern are set out in articles 130-176 and repeat commitments of existing EU treaties. As written it therefore appears that freedoms may be curtailed in order to protect the free trade principle. This is reinforced by article 114 which prohibits "*any act* aimed at the destruction of any of the rights and freedoms recognised in this Charter *or at their limitation*." (Emphasis added.) People who support state run education and healthcare are seeking to limit free trade and are therefore guilty, under the EU *Charter of Fundamental Rights*, of trying to limit the "fundamental right" to free trade. If someone wrote "Down with Free Trade" on a wall then the EU, according to its own rules, should clamp down on such an attempt to destroy a freedom protected by the *Charter of Fundamental Rights*. Of course, it is not credible at the present time that free trade is intended to be protected from criticism in this way, but this is what the Charter says. A *Charter of Fundamental*

Rights should be written with the utmost care to avoid misinterpretation. Revised wording could aid clarity here.

There are pointers to immediately apparent erosions of EU fundamental rights.

The section authorising the limitation of rights ends with a cryptic statement. "The explanations drawn up as a way of providing guidance in the interpretation of the *Charter of Fundamental Rights* shall be given due regard by the courts of the Union and of the Member States." What this means is less than transparent. There is no pointer to what these "explanations" might be or where they may be found.

In fact, the "explanations" are to be found in *Declaration 12*, one of 50 declarations that are sometimes attached to the Constitution. The *Reform Treaty* will require that these Declarations will be attached to the revised treaties.

Explanation 3a quotes the European Convention for the Protection of Human Rights which would allow other occasions for lethal shooting by the police including rowdy demonstrations. (It should be noted that a violent response by police to a peaceful demonstration can quickly lead to general violence which might be described as a "riot". For example, the Peterloo Massacre.)

> Deprivation of life shall not be regarded as inflicted in contravention of this article when it results from the use of force which is no more than absolutely necessary:
>
> (a) in defence of any person from unlawful violence;
>
> (b) in order to effect a lawful arrest or to prevent the escape of a person lawfully detained;
>
> (c) in action lawfully taken for the purpose of quelling a riot or insurrection.

Explanation 3b relating to article 62 of the *Charter of Fundamental Rights* states, "A State may make provision in its law for the death penalty in respect of acts committed in time of war or of imminent threat of war . . ." Thus this important fundamental right, to be protected from execution by an EU state, is qualified rather than absolute. The term "war" used to be an unambiguous term, but with the "war on terrorism" new possibilities for the use of the death penalty appear to present themselves.

In 2002 the Council of Europe, the non-EU body, adopted *Protocol No. 13 to the Convention for the Protection of Human Rights and Fundamental Freedoms [European Convention on Human Rights]* which abolished the death penalty in all circumstances. By 1 February 2005 the following EU states had not ratified the agreement: France, Italy, Latvia, Luxembourg, Netherlands, Norway, Poland, Slovakia and Spain. At this time they retained the right to execution in times of war or imminent threat of war.

Rights removed by the *EU Charter of Fundamental Rights*

Free expression, which is a fundamental prerequisite of democratic societies, is not fully guaranteed. In fact, it is curtailed in certain circumstances. Whilst some very sensible limitations should be made, for example prohibiting slander and libel, incitement to racial hatred and incitement to violence (including wars of aggression) quite different reasons may be allowed for limiting free speech according to the "explanations" relating to article 71. These allow a state a number of justifications for limiting free speech and imposing "restrictions or penalties as are prescribed by law." This might well prove only too tempting to a state grown authoritarian if it feels the need to quell criticism. It can do so:

- "in the interest of national security, territorial integrity or public safety"
- "for the prevention of disorder or crime"
- "for the protection of health, or morals"
- "for maintaining the authority or impartiality of the judiciary".

The word "disorder" might be interpreted to mean merely a demonstration or a noisy crowd. Promoting a sporting event or protest which merely *might* lead to disorder may very easily become an illegal activity. As discussed elsewhere, that is the way Europol is thinking in connection with some forms of protest and it has plans to prevent protesters from travelling to express their views. The idea of "maintaining the authority of the judiciary" puts the judiciary above criticism, which is surely wrong.

There is a further problem with the guarantee of free expression. The Charter itself, if the words mean what they say, prohibits free expression in two important areas. First, the European Central Bank and the central banks of the non-eurozone states take decisions which directly affect the lives of 480 million Europeans, yet the representatives of these Europeans are forbidden by the Charter from voicing any criticism of the work of the banks. See *European Central Bank.*

Second, the *Charter of Fundamental Rights* itself may not be criticised for the reasons referred to above and set out in article 114. Whilst most people would wish to support most of the Charter insofar as it is meaningful there are surely areas that ought to be open for criticism.

For example, the suggestion above that there should be slander and libel laws, and laws against incitement to violence would limit free speech and therefore offend against article 114. Article 110 grants the right not to be tried twice for an offence for which a person has once been acquitted. It is a very long-standing right in British law. However, law in Britain has been changing in contravention of this fundamental EU right. For the first time in British legal history, as this is being written (November 2005), a man is about to be tried for a murder for which he was tried and acquitted some twenty years ago. Fresh evidence has been uncovered. The evidence may be overwhelming. If this is the case a retrial would seem only just. But the author of the last few sentences and the people who planned and changed British law to make a retrial possible are all guilty of the offence of aiming at the limitation of a right recognised in the Charter.

Article 88 gives a right to strike. Were it not for the fact that member states are free to ignore the EU's "fundamental" rights the British government, by seeking to limit this right to strike, is offending against the EU *Charter of Fundamental Rights.*

Another example is article 105. This states that "Every citizen of the Union has the right to move and reside freely within the territory of member states." What does "reside freely" mean in this context? Might it mean a guarantee of free housing - since there can be little freedom of movement for anyone who cannot afford the price of accommodation in a new host country? (Article 94 states, "The

Union recognizes and respects the right to social and housing assistance so as to ensure a decent existence for all those who lack sufficient resources." In the case of the mass movement of citizens of one Member State into another the new host state would presumably be expected to pay the costs.)

People in rich regions might want to consider restricting the rights of poor unemployed people to move into their area for this reason. At some time in the future freedom of residence might be criticised because millions of people are fleeing from one member state into another state where serious social difficulties may arise as a consequence of mass migration. Has a state no right to deny access to its territory in extreme situations? Must the right of free movement into one EU country from another be guaranteed to known major criminals or criminal gangs? To raise these issues is not yet illegal in the European Union, but the Charter would make it so. Currently many of the first fifteen member states restrict immigration from newer member states. (See *Enlargement*.)

As article 114 forbids any talking or writing about limiting the freedoms guaranteed in the Charter. Might the EU make good its promise to take legal action against people who want to discuss this issue? "The charter will be interpreted by the courts of the Union . . ." (Charter Preamble.)

What is the EU doing about the curtailing of rights to free speech and other human rights in Poland? Currently there are reports from Poland that the government, under the right wing Kaczynski brothers, is purging the administration of people with "incorrect political views". There are political attacks on the Constitutional Tribunal. Some politicians are openly homophobic and anti-Semitic. The Office of the Government Plenipotentiary for Equality of Men and Women has been closed.

Should the EU *Charter of Fundamental Rights* be scrapped?

Virtually all the freedoms and rights this charter might seem to guarantee are already guaranteed by the *European Convention for the Protection of Human Rights*, Conventions of the International Labour Organisation, other international laws or national laws. Not one of the rights set out here is actually guaranteed by the EU because all exist only so far as individual state laws permit. The Charter itself admits that it gives nothing new to anyone (article 111/2). The European *Charter of Fundamental Rights* is an empty shop. We have the *European Charter of Fundamental Window Dressing*. European Fundamental Rights are a mirage, but might the machine gunner on the roof one day turn out to be real?

Real EU Human Rights?

In contrast with the restrictions of the EU *Charter of Fundamental Rights* and Freedoms there is an apparent commitment to the *European Convention for the Protection of Human Rights and Fundamental Freedoms* in article 9. This commitment exists so long as it "shall not affect the Union's competences as defined in the Constitution". The commitment to the European Convention is limited with more conditions in the Preamble to The Charter. Here it reaffirms its commitment to *The European Convention*, "with due regard for the powers and tasks of the Union and the principle of subsidiarity . . ." This seems to mean that the European Union and member states can overrule anything in *The European*

Convention. The restrictions applied are vague and open-ended. Or are they? The rights guaranteed by the European convention and other international law are back again, in article 113, fully guaranteed.

So eurocitizens do have/may have human rights after all. Now you see them: now you don't. We are in the hall of mirrors of human rights. What are we to believe? The EU is fundamentally confused and confusing, and such confusion inspires no confidence.

Should the EU citizens rely on the *European Convention for the Protection of Human Rights and Fundamental Freedoms* instead of the *Charter of Fundamental Rights of the European Union*?

See also, *Criminal Justice, Europol, Enlargement,* and *Data Harvesting.*

Balance of power

Goran Persson, Swedish Prime Minister, speaking in Gothenburg on 15 June 2001 said, "It [the EU] is one of the few institutions we can develop as a balance to US world domination."

"Are we all clear that we want to build something that can aspire to be a world power?" - European Commission President, Romano Prodi, European Parliament, 13 February 2001.

Some people see the development of the European Union as a good thing because it may become a balance of power to the power of the United States. Some think in terms of economic power: others think in terms of military power. To this end the latter are keen to see the military development of the European Union.

It is strange that the idea of a military balance of power should have any following in Europe. Apart from the immorality and suicidal madness of contemplating armed conflict with America (or any other major power) Europeans have learned that old ideas of balance of power lead to insecurity and that there are better alternatives.

European states have balanced power between themselves and fought wars, mainly with quite primitive weapons, for centuries. Suffering has been immense, especially in two world wars. For half a century, with just a few setbacks, an alternative policy has been pursued: co-operation, mutual help and working together to solve common problems. As a consequence Europeans have enjoyed peace and prosperity. Would anyone suggest that we Europeans would now be more secure or better off if European states abandoned this policy of mutual support and co-operation and instead each member state armed and over-armed itself to balance or out-balance the other states in a bid for security or supremacy? How would these balances of power work out? From time to time one or another state, as in past dark ages, might attack a "rival" state with horrible and long-lasting consequences.

Europe knows from experience that international friendship, co-operation, trade and mutually assured assistance not only offer the prospect of better lives, but also the only prospect of security. Is it remotely possible that eurocitizens aspire to be part of a great military power in order, one day, to fight America (or perhaps China or Russia)?

See *The euro, Defence and foreign policy - successful foreign policy* and *Unite and be strong.*

Clear use of language, and transparency

Respect for one's readers dictates that a writer should strive for clarity of expression. The EU, in its official documentation, often seems to go out of its way to mystify and confuse its readers. Here are a few sample problems:

Opaque names

An example of this is the EU's naming of the Council of Ministers. This body has two other names which are frequently used - "the Council" and "Council of the European Union". But, in fact, this Council of Ministers is not, as its name implies, a single EU body. Officially there are nine bodies, all of which are "the Council of Ministers" (or one of its other two names). The explanation of this unsatisfactory use of language is that "the Council" began as a concept of a single decision-making body, but as more areas of responsibility/ control were added more people were brought in to take decisions and euro-thinkers saw the development as "the Council meeting in different configurations." But these separate councils have long been established and there can be no excuse for this continuing confusing use of language.

Some of these nine bodies have a single name. Others have two or three. Several of these nine bodies acknowledged on the Council of Ministers web site do not meet as a single body but as two or three. In total we have fourteen distinct bodies or councils any one of which is referred to in official EU publications as "The Council of Ministers" or "The Council" or "The Council of the European Union." Only by knowing the names and functions of the other councils and the context in which one of the three main names is used can anyone know which body (and therefore which ministers) will be involved. Accountability is hard to pin down when some three hundred and eighty people hide behind a term for a body which is officially explained as consisting of twenty-seven members.

As a further complication it should be noted that the Councils have equal power and equal rights to take decisions in any policy area. This can sometimes be turned to advantage when there is an urgent need to adopt a new law (or regulation) which is not controversial. In this situation any Council that happens to be meeting may take action in any area of Council business.

Article 166 refers to "services of general economic interest". The term is not defined. The reader is left in doubt. Legally the provision is open to dispute.

Treaties exist with varying names and in varying forms. For example, the *Nice Treaty*. This sounds like a unique treaty. In fact it is a variation on two treaties: the *Treaty on European Union* also known as the *Maastricht Treaty* and the *Treaty Establishing the European Economic Community* which is also known as the *Treaty of Rome* . When people refer to *The Treaty on European Union* do they mean the original treaty, or the treaty as it was amended by "the *Amsterdam Treaty*, or as it was amended by the *Nice Treaty*? The *Maastricht Treaty* itself, in addition to breaking new ground, also amended the *Treaty of Rome*. Sometimes the original *Maastricht Treaty*, as amended by both Amsterdam and Nice, is referred to as "the Consolidated Version of the Treaty on European Union". One can read the "Consolidated Version" and find that an article referred to by another writer writing about the *Maastricht Treaty* does not agree with the "Consolidated Version". This can be because, in the process of amendment, articles have had their numbers revised. Furthermore, when reading "the Consolidated Version" one may be unsure at what date a given article entered into the governance of the European Union. All this can be very confusing. A state committed to clear communication with its citizens would take greater care with its organisation and naming of key documents and its use of language. The Constitution had the merit of repealing existing treaties and replacing them, a fresh start. See the Treaties chapter for help on the topic of treaty names and contents. The *Reform Treaty* of 2007, scattering the innovations amongst the articles of existing treaties adds to the confusion and keeps the average eurocitizen from grasping what is going on.

Euphemism

Instead of war and peace-keeping the Constitution talks of "operational action." Instead of attack or military invasion the Constitution talks of "man-made disaster." See articles 297 and 329.

Empty or disconnected references

Within the Constitution there are many allusions to provisions elsewhere in the Constitution. However, when these occur the reader is left to search nearly 500 pages for the information. Even if references are found the reader is left in doubt because it is difficult to be sure all relevant or necessary references have been found.

For example:

"In the *specific cases provided for in the Constitution*, European laws and framework laws shall be adopted by the European Parliament with the participation of the Council, or by the latter with the participation of the European Parliament, in accordance with *special legislative procedures*." (Article 34/2.) What are the specific cases that are not specified? What are the unspecified special legislative procedures?

"Union legislative acts may be adopted only on the basis of a Commission proposal, *except where the Constitution provides otherwise*. Other acts shall be adopted on the basis of a Commission proposal *where the Constitution so provides.*" Where does the constitution provide otherwise? And where does it so provide?

"The European Council shall adopt European decisions *in the cases provided for in the Constitution*." (Article 35/1.) What are the "cases provided for in the Constitution"?

The authors of the Constitution could so easily have been precise and given the reference details. This is an abuse of the long-suffering Constitution reader. It leads to doubt and confusion and shows an indifference to the reasonable expectations and needs of the reader. Perhaps the re-packaged Constitution will avoid these faults.

Too much of the EU's key documents are unnecessarily difficult to follow and this hinders citizens in their appreciation of the EU and in participating as citizens in what might become a democracy.

For the full list of councils see "the Council" in the *Institutions* chapter, and for further discussion of this topic see the chapter entitled *The Constitution considered as a Document*, *European Union by stealth*, *Integration - the number one question*, *Complication* and *Transparency* below. See also the chapter on the early development of the European Union, *Institutions – Article 36 Committee* and *Article 133 Committee* and *Euroterminology* in the *Euroterminology* chapter.

Climate change

See *Energy and the environment* and *Free trade.*

The Commission

The Commission, with its 27 Commisioners and 21,000 or so staff, is much more than, and quite different from, a civil service operating under the direction of an elected government. It is an appointed administrative organisation officially independent of all other EU bodies (Constitution article 26/7, and *Treaty of Rome*, article 213, formerly 157). It has considerable independent powers of initiative and control, including:

- the right to decide upon new European Union laws and to draft them, (laws which supersede laws passed by member states).
- planning the budget and administering the spending of it.
- It exercises "co-ordinating, executive and management functions" (article 26/1).
- It interprets and administers the policies outlined in the treaties (or the Constitution or its replacement). Many of these allow great scope for developing programmes of action.
- Except for foreign and security matters it represents the EU in contacts and negotiations with other countries including all trade negotiations.

Concerns include:

- lack of democratic legitimacy. Eurocitizens did not vote for it or its policies. It cannot be voted out by the people it controls. It is above democracy.
- It directs policy. If it strays from the limitations imposed by EU treaties there is no procedure for holding those responsible to account or to direct them on agreed paths. (See *Defence and foreign policy* for an example of the Commission acting out of step wtih EU fundamental policies.)
- Although it consults its own appointed committees and closely watches opinion surveys it appears to control rather than serve the people of Europe.
- It works in secret in the sense that its discussions and debates are behind closed doors and the membership of its hundreds of committees, the names and organisation that lobby it, and records of the votes it takes are not a matter of public record.
- As it is required to act completely independently it may be somewhat resistant to criticism, but it is certainly not above being influenced since it is subject to intense lobbying. Observers of this legitimate process see a bias towards big business in its contacts and this presents a danger of acting undemocratically since many would argue that the EU should have an open-door policy for all EU citizens and seek to further the wellbeing of all citizens, not just those with the biggest budgets.

- The Commission is mandated to take instructions from no "institution, body, office or entity" (article 26/7). But this is not how the Commission works. It cannot take decisions at odds with the European Council or the Council. The Constitution, or treaties, need to clarify the relationship of the Commission with the rest of the EU power structure and reflect the actual arrangements that operate. The words used to express the nature of the independence of Commissioners might draw on the ideas set out in the oath taken by members of the British House of Lords if this is the sort of independence that is intended.[10]
- It can be very difficult to obtain information from the Commission about its activities and where it is spending billions of euros.
- Fraud has been a problem at the highest level and in the last eleven years the Court of Auditors has been unable to accept the accounts as evidence of proper administration of the EU's funds. Matters became so bad in 1999 that the European Parliament got to the verge of dismissing the Commission. This was avoided by the mass resignation of the Commissioners.

These are matters of immense importance. The Commission lacks democratic legitimacy, transparency and financial probity. The Court of Auditors needs to be adequately funded to fully investigate the failures in accounting, institute proper accounting procedures within the Commission and bring to trial those considered to be guilty of fraudulent behaviour. The credibility of the European Project is at stake.

There is a case for removing the right to initiate law making in the EU from the Commission and passing it to the European Parliament. The Commission's task would then be to administer the work of the EU. There would be more purpose to electing people to the European Parliament and the EU would become more democratic. Another alternative is that the principle of subsidiarity should apply here. The right to initiate legislation might be devolved to regional or national governments which would then need to gain general support amongst other EU states before bringing a proposal for legislation forward.

It would seem that to bring about a more democratic European Union the Commission should be directed by a democratically elected EU body with individual departments (directorates) specifically accountable for their work in the way that civil service departments are accountable in the governments of member states. The European Parliament might provide the necessary elected "Ministers in charge".

The present system of making the entire Commission (but not individuals) liable to dismissal by a two thirds majority vote of censure of the European Parliament does not offer the detailed day to day working supervision that is required.

See articles 26 and 27, *Finances of the EU, Lobbying, Transparency, Democratic deficit, Biggest problems* (*two, three, four, five, six*).

Complication

In EU treaties, the Constitution and its replacements there are many avoidable complicated rules of procedure and exceptions and variations. Why do this when it is so much easier to understand, remember and operate simple rules?

The example of voting

Some EU voting procedures (even the proposed "simplified" procedures that appear in the Constitution) are so complex that a mathematician is needed to work out if a vote has been carried. What is needed is to ensure that decisions are taken with the complete agreement or very substantial agreement of member states. This could be achieved by:

- the use of a requirement for true unanimity for the most important level of decisions, (such as changes to the Constitution, the accession of new members, decisions to send military forces into action, major changes of any kind)
- the use of the EU's special kind of "unanimity" with "constructive abstention" for a level of decision making just below the highest level,[11] and for the rest:
- a single requirement that for a vote to be carried there has to be an overwhelming majority vote in favour (OMV). At least 80% of states need to be in favour (or whatever percentage seems adequate to ensure acceptable EU-wide assent, but whatever figure is decided it should be fixed for all non-unanimity decisions). This is more or less how the EU currently interprets unanimity and is close to the effect of current QMV voting. Fixing the size of the overwhelming majority which member states would find acceptable is the critical issue, but whatever is decided it can only be better than the variety of permutations of rules currently in use.

The minority report of the Convention which wrote the Constitution proposed that for decisions requiring a majority, that majority should be a 75 per cent majority.

For a fuller discussion of voting problems in the EU see *Voting* below and *Qualified majority voting* in the Euroterminology chapter.

Constitution - Its purposes

The Constitution of 2004 sought to do four things:

1. Solve the problems identified by the Laeken conference of EU leaders in December 2001.
2. Bring the arrangements and policy commitments of the various treaties into a simplified single document.
3. Make it possible to transfer power from member states, in certain policy areas, to the European Union and thereby bring about the unification of member states.
4. Make a small number of administrative changes aimed at enabling the European Union, with its enlarged membership, to function more effectively.

A further aim was added in nine countries where real democratic involvement was permitted. This was the aim of seeking, through referendums, the approval of their populations for the policies, and political and administrative arrangements of the EU. Voting, in part, would be a judgement by the people on their satisfaction with the institutional arrangements, policies and performance of the EU so far.

The Issues here are:

- Why did EU leaders accept the Constitution as the "answer" to the problems they had identified at Laeken? It was obvious that the problems had been ignored.
- Why did they accept the Constitution which made significant steps towards making the EU into a superstate, when they had identified this as something EU citizens particularly did not want?
- Why were so many leaders who claim a commitment to involving their people in decision-making (democracy) unwilling to allow their people to vote on the Constitution?

Constitution – preparing to write an acceptable Constitution and rescue the EU from crisis

The rejection of the Constitution by the people of France and the Netherlands meant they did not consider that the problems identified by the Laeken conference had been solved and that there might be other issues which the Laeken conference had overlooked. It became clear to some that a substantial rethink is needed on EU policies, the way the EU operates and therefore on the Constitution and the re-packaged Constitution.

The problems identified in the *Laeken Declaration* and many more remain to be addressed. Before a revised constitution can be written, or the EU revitalised and gain the respect of eurocitizens, fundamental constitutional and other practical issues need to be resolved. These include:

1. **A unified state of Europe or an association of free states?** Ever closer union, has been the goal of European political development, assumed by European leaders, since the *Schumann Declaration* of May 1950. The 480 million citizens of the EU have not agreed to this. What should be done? See *Integration - the number one question.*

2. **Institutional confusion and democratic deficit.** The European Union needs to be transformed into a democracy with a simplified and clear structure.

3. **Accountability lacks credibility.** Rather than mere talk of accountability there should be specific measures defined to deal with politicians and officials who are fraudulent or commit other criminal offences or bring the Union into disrepute, or act outside treaty or constitutional agreements, or offend against international law and national law, including such matters as initiating wars of aggression. There should be watchdog committees to publicly examine politicians and officials on their decisions, policies and behaviour. The continuing failures in the financial accounting of the Commission and acknowledged fraud requires immediate and determined attention.

4. **Transparency.** There should be a great opening up of decision-making occasions to public view. Citizens should be able to access verbatim records in all official EU languages of speeches made at key institutions and be able to see records of votes cast, documents considered and, in good time, those to be considered, submissions from lobbyists, records of participation of lobbyists in EU working parties and on committees, sums of money granted to lobbyists or the companies they represent, etc.

5. **Subsidiarity**. A true basis for taking decisions at the lowest possible level of government needs to be established. The areas in which the EU may not take action should be clearly specified - for example, education, healthcare, law and order, culture, sport, tourism, agriculture, fisheries, etc. Consideration might be given to removing the right of initiative to create laws from the Commission and placing it with the member states or the European Parliament. A new ethos of subsidiarity and localism should permeate the thinking of the European Union rather than the ethos of centralised control which permeates EU thinking and planning at present.

6. **Maintaining state sovereignty**. Opt-outs are already used in the European Union. Might it be a good idea to allow state parliaments the right to accept or reject all EU laws and decisions or EU laws and decisions in certain policy areas (such as home affairs and foreign policy)?

7. **Clear commitment to human rights**. Human rights could be dealt with by means of a clear, unqualified statement of intention to abide by the *United Nations' Universal Declaration of Human Rights* and the European Convention for the Protection of Human Rights. The EU's own *Charter of Fundamental Rights* creates confusion and has too many qualifications and exceptions to be helpful. In particular the possibly unintended restrictions on freedom of speech should be reviewed. Should the EU's European Court of Justice take on matters of human rights when the Council of Europe's European Court of Human Rights already appears to be fulfilling this role with success?

8. **Consistent principles**. The currently declared principles of the European Union show inconsistencies. Further thought is needed to define principles with greater care and avoid making commitments which may not be achieved. It may be that some principles should be replaced with pragmatic aspirations.

The revised constitution

When the above matters, and the problems identified elsewhere in this Major Issues section, have been resolved it may be possible to write a new, short, simple constitution that will enjoy such wide support across the EU that it may be submitted with confidence to a referendum in every member state.

Important policy issues

It is suggested elsewhere that a constitution should not be concerned with specific policies. Outside of a constitution the EU has a pressing need to think through contentious policies in some areas. They are tests of the EU decision-making process by which eurocitizens may well judge the EU. These include:

- **Policy rigidity.** Should key policies be fixed by treaty or be subject to looser arrangements and pragmatic change?
- **Enlargement and immigration**. Should the open programme of EU enlargement, which has caused practical problems and aroused considerable fear, continue at its present pace? Associated with this policy, should the free movement of people (currently restricted by twelve EU states, October 2006) be formally limited?
- **Environment, climate change, transport, energy**. Should financial support for road building programmes and nuclear energy be reduced or

discontinued in order to switch funds to the EU's concern with environmental issues including developing rail transport, canals and airships, energy conservation measures and alternative energy sources?

- **Employment, housing, social well-being.** How much priority should the EU give to these topics? What should it do about them?
- **Free trade, protectionism, privatisation, moderated trade.** The EU is founded on free trade between members and it is not only its official policy for itself but it aims to promote free trade world wide. At the same time it practises protectionism with regard to agricultural products and textiles, a policy which is still contentious. Since the *Nice Treaty* the EU has been committed to privatisation (service liberalisation). The last of these is often associated with considerable problems and unpopularity. Perhaps the EU should declare a cautious and pragmatic approach to all these trade issues to allow itself the opportunity to adapt to varying needs. (See *Free trade*, below.)
- **Militarisation or defence.** Most EU countries have long been members of the United Nations and as such have professed a commitment to military action only in self defence or in peace-keeping under the specific direction of the United Nations. This is the declared policy, but practice, military preparations and policy statements show that EU leaders, acting without a democratic mandate, are seeking to increase EU military activity. Military expansion and interventionism as a policy appears to have little popular support within the EU. (See *Defence and foreign policy*, below.)
- **Europol and personal data.** The accountability of this force needs reviewing. Safeguards as to accuracy and limitations on the gathering, distribution and use of personal data need to be established and meet with general approval within the EU.
- **Agriculture.** Should the Common Agricultural Policy be ended and replaced by member states operating their own financial support programmes for farmers?
- **Fisheries.** Should the Common Fisheries Policy be ended, the territorial waters contained within the 200-mile-limit be returned to maritime states, and EU marine conservation measures replaced by member states operating their own conservation programmes in co-operation with other states under international agreements? (See *Fisheries* below.)

Constitution – re-writing it

What can a constitution do?

No constitution is a guarantee. At best it is a statement of aspirations, intentions, organisational arrangements and formal safeguards. In the hands of good politicians states will blossom, but no constitution can save states from violence and abuse when they are led by unprincipled leaders. Hitler came to power in a democracy. Contemporary politicians in states which regard themselves as democratic and civilised have backed brutal dictators. Some have even started wars of aggression in defiance of international law and the United Nations.

Citizens nevertheless look to constitutions for reassurance that the state is at least set up on the right lines, aiming for peace and security, for equality and justice, for the good and betterment of all, for democracy and sustainability, for peaceful co-operation with all nations in accordance with the *Charter of the United Nations* and other international law. In outline a constitution should show what institutions and power structures have been established to achieve the aims of the state, the limitation, separation and control of powers, the assignment of powers to different levels of government, and how these may ensure effective fulfilment of the aims of the constitution. It should show how the power of government as a whole is to be limited, made accountable and controlled by the citizens who entrust their well-being to their leaders. A constitution should be a beacon of effective organisation, principle, coherence and clarity.

What makes a good Constitution?

Citizens might reasonably expect the following to be included in a good Constitution for any state:

- Clear, consistent, brief statements of aims and guiding principles
- description of main institutions including the law making bodies
- description of the power structure - the responsibilities, powers and relationships of institutions and key officials, including how the government is elected
- clear, simple voting systems
- avoidance of avoidable complications, variations, exceptions
- the roles and rights of the citizen, including how he may make his voice heard through democratic processes (i.e. voting directly for those who take the decisions and make the laws, and promoting the policies he favours)
- how the workings of the government may be transparent so that the citizen may know exactly what is going on and who is responsible for decisions
- how the powers exercised by the government (the central decision-making authority) are to be shared between different levels of government by, for example, passing full control of healthcare or education to state or regional governments (the allocation of subsidiary powers)
- how the leaders, servants and institutions of the government may be questioned and give an account of themselves
- how they may be held responsible for their actions and removed or punished if found unsatisfactory or guilty of wrong-doing
- The whole document must be easy to refer to. Special arrangements, and explanations might helpfully be incorporated in the body of the treaty text and not in a multiplicity of additional documents.

For some other considerations regarding the re-writing of the Constitution please see *Biggest Problem, Number seven.*

Constitution and EU treaties – Official method for revision, normal procedure

The Constitution provides for its own revision by means of a procedure set out in article 443 for the ordinary revision of the Constitution. It is a thoughtful procedure well suited to the truly constitutional part of the Constitution. Changes would require ratification by the governments of all member states. For matters of policy that would be fixed by the Constitution this procedure is entirely unsuitable. See *Biggest Problem, Number seven, problems with the Constitution.*

Constitution and EU treaties – Official method for revision, quick route

A so-called "simplified" procedure is set out in article 444. This surprisingly avoids a proper ratification process. It is limited to certain matters. These include the important issue of allowing a reduction in the sovereignty of member states.

Effectively the European Council may take decisions to make amendments. There are only flimsy safeguards - a majority vote in the European Parliament and the receipt of no objections from national parliaments over a six month period. This seems almost equivalent to inertia selling. Is it possible that a state parliament might not get to hear of a decision? Is it possible that a state might be in crisis (over a war or economic collapse, for example) or in the process of changing governments and the details of EU rule changes get overlooked? Silence is taken as consent. Surely a positive agreement is essential in such serious matters.

Article 445 deals with a variation on the "simplified" procedure. This concerns the vast subject of the internal policies of the Union. These may be amended in part or completely on a recommendation of the European Parliament, any member state, or the Commission if the European Council, meeting in private, so decides. (It would first have to consult the European Parliament, the Commission and the European Bank.) Such changes would have to be specifically agreed by the member states. The changes might be of great importance, yet the participation of eurocitizens in discussing the issues might be nil. Is this a satisfactory arrangement?

The momentous decision to pass all defence and foreign policy decision-making to the EU, could be agreed upon at any time under the 2004 Constitution, in a few minutes, and in private by the twenty-seven ministers of the European Council. Eurocitizens and state parliaments would not have to be consulted. See *Defence and foreign policy.*

Criminal Justice

Habeas corpus and trial by jury - non EU concepts

The right of habeas corpus (the right of a person arrested to be brought publicly before a court to hear what crime he is accused of) does not appear in the EU Constitution or EU treaties. This right is regarded in Britain, America and a number of other countries as a fundamental protection of personal liberty. In Britain the right of habeas corpus was established by the Habeas Corpus Act of

1679. In the US the right of habeas corpus is declared in the American Constitution.

However, article 9/2 of the European Constitution states, "The Union shall accede to the *European Convention for the Protection of Human Rights and Fundamental Freedoms.*" Article 5 of this convention states, "Everyone who is deprived of his liberty by arrest or detention shall be entitled to take proceeding by which the lawfulness of his detention shall be decided speedily by a court and his release ordered if the detention is not lawful." This article echoes article 6/2 of the Treaty on European Union. The difference is that in the Constitution provision is made for not following the Convention: "Such accession shall not affect the Union's competences as defined in the Constitution". A public hearing is not part of the deal. There may be occasions when the right is suspended. The reform treaty will follow the wording of the Constitution.

The Constitution and the Reform Treaty will make the area of freedom, security and justice one in which shared competence operates. This might amount to a claimed right to overrule the *European Convention for the Protection of Human Rights and Fundamental Freedoms* when other EU needs are deemed to exist. The fact that a clear and unequivocal statement does not appear here is a concern.

Politicians who regard themselves as above the law themselves and who are allowed by their peers and people to go unpunished for their crimes may feel free to take away any right and overrule any law they choose. No constitution can prevent this: only the vigilance and prompt action of responsible leaders and citizens. In this very field of human rights this wiping away of fundamental rights has already happened. In 2001 the British government announced that the country was in "a state of emergency" and therefore it would not be bound by article 5 of the European Convention for the Protection of Human rights and Fundamental Freedoms. It then went ahead with arrests without charges being brought or trials held. Those arrested have been imprisoned and then placed under a kind of house arrest with severely curtailed liberties for years. This matter causes widespread outrage in Britain. Clearly the EU either has no power or no wish to safeguard article 5 of the European Convention. The EU is silent.

Trial by jury, a vital element in the British system of justice, is not envisaged in the EU Constitution or the *Reform Treaty* . Though not outlawed either what are its chances of survival in an EU keen on "harmonising" or "approximating" laws to make an equivalence of law operating throughout the EU? Trials procedures are actively being considered for regulation by the Commission.

EU treaties and the Constitution have given very little attention to the matter of arrest and trials procedures. These vary widely across the EU being disturbingly bad in some countries. The Netherlands has been condemned three times by the European Court of Human Rights for use of anonymous-witness statements. France has a high condemnation rate by the ECHR in cases relating to police brutality, excessive pre-trial detention periods and non-respect of defence rights. Portugal offers virtually no legal aid and has a poor record for supplying translators in trials of non-Portuguese-speaking defendants.[12]

The aim should surely be to bring arrest, detention and trials procedures in all EU member states up to at least an adequate standard. The Commission and NGOs such as Fair Trials Abroad are conscious of the problems and the Commission has produced a green paper on this topic (2003).[13] The paper proposes some essential features to be "harmonised" by raising the standards of states where trials may be less than fair. Defendants should have "the right to legal advice and assistance (representation) provided by a lawyer; the right to an interpreter and to translation of essential documents; the right for persons accused of an offence to obtain written information about their fundamental rights in a language they understand, which may take the form of a 'Letter of Right'; the right of vulnerable persons to proper protection; the right to consular assistance." Each of these rights is the subject of a chapter in the Green Paper.

In essence the issues here are the adequacy of EU trials procedures to safeguard the rights of those accused of misdemeanours and, for the UK at least, the potential reduction of rights in this area with loss of public hearings and trials by juries.

See also, *Area of freedom, security and justice*, *Data Harvesting, Europol,* and *European Arrest Warrant.*

Culture

If any area of life should remain under the sole control of the citizens of individual states and their own governments it is surely their culture. If subsidiarity is a meaningful concept in the Constitution and EU Treaties then culture should remain absolutely beyond the reach of the controlling fingers of the European Union. But article 280 says otherwise: "the Union shall contribute to the flowering of the cultures of the member states, while respecting their national and regional diversity and at the same time bringing the common cultural heritage to the fore."

The EU may put some money into cultural activities. That is to say, having taken money from member states it may return some of this money to them for projects an EU central authority deems desirable.

Data harvesting - EU's wide-access, all-encompassing identity database

Article 275 suggests that Europol, "may" collect, store and exchange information for the purpose of criminal investigation. Europol's officers will work with customs and member states' "competent authorities". No data protection, no limit to what may be recorded, no method for individual citizens to check the accuracy of recorded information, no limit to purposes, no limit to who may have access to data are indicated in this statement. EU citizens need to be protected by safeguards against the collection of unnecessary, out-of-date, inaccurate data, against mistakes in identification and the abuse of any data held on them. Access to data should be strictly and securely limited.

Europol did not wait for the ratification of the Constitution before going ahead with the development of this database. It already has a database called TECS and this will soon be linked to another database system storing a wide range of information on EU citizens. This is the SIS (Schengen Information System) which is itself in the course of rapid expansion. The prime purpose of SIS is to hold immigration records to support the *Schengen Agreement* on border controls. It holds 15,000,000 records under six headings:

- people wanted for arrest and extradition (Article 95 of the Schengen Agreement)
- people to be refused entry to the Schengen area (Article 96)
- missing and dangerous persons (Article 97)
- people wanted to appear in court (Article 98)
- people to be placed under surveillance (Article 99)
- lost and stolen objects (Article 100)

Most records concern lost or stolen identity documents. At the moment data held on people is strictly limited to name, distinguishing features, initial of second forename, date and place of birth, sex and nationality, plus information for police officers - whether the person is armed, or violent, the reason for the report and the action to be taken.

Every EU citizen to be recorded

In September 2004 the Justice and Home Affairs Council (one of the permutations of the Council of Ministers) commissioned a massive IT project to develop the capability of the SIS (Schengen Information System). The enhanced system will hold a greatly increased range of recorded information and will cover every EU citizen, yet the Council has done this without consulting the public, or EU and national parliaments. This is undemocratic and is, at least in part, illegal under EU law. Unfortunately it illustrates how remote and faceless groups within the EU system, unaccountable to EU citizens, may take action of major concern to every EU citizen regardless of their clear duties.

The development cost will be € 40,000,000, (approximately £26,000,000). The new system is called SIS II (the second generation Schengen Information System).

The development and the use of the current (2005/6) Schengen data base system is or should be controlled by the *Schengen Convention.* However, the legal requirement of this document, which set strict limits on what information may be stored and who may have access (*Schengen Convention* article 101), have been cast aside to allow a greatly increased range of data about citizens to be stored, including biometric data - digitised photographs and fingerprints. (It has already been decided to use biometric data in all EU travel documents: visas, passports and residence permits.) The information is "confidential". Access points in 2005 amounted to 125,000 among the fifteen participating states. There are plans to extend access to more agencies across the EU with its now twenty-seven member states.

New data will include all the data contained on European Arrest Warrants. (See below.) There is also a new category of "violent trouble maker." Subject to national legislation on travel bans this information will be used to prevent football hooligans and protesters travelling to countries where there is a "risk" that they may cause disorder. The natural place to protest about EU policies is Brussels since most decisions are taken here. It would be possible, using this database to exclude leaders of protests travelling from outside Belgium on the grounds that protests have the potential to lead to disorder.

Biometric data such as DNA information may be included. It would be an easy step to include all of member states' criminal records. "Suspected criminals" and people "suspected" of terrorism may be added and people linked with them such as family members. Combine all this with the use of informers and dishonest informers then the nightmare of the police state begins to emerge.

The *Schengen Convention*, an international agreement, set out the limits on access and data that may be recorded. Stepping outside the limits of the *Schengen Convention* the Council has, without legal authority, without a new international agreement, decided to open up the greatly extended database not only to the Europol but also to vehicle registration authorities, national and judicial prosecuting authorities and Eurojust. Without legislation the security and intelligence services have already been given access to SIS data. Will private security firms or banks be given access? Will educational establishments or taxation authorities or social services be given access? Will access pass to more and more organisations? Is anyone trying to protect the rights of citizens in this matter?

The new system is being designed so that it can be linked with another database, the Visa information system (VIS) which the EU Parliament voted against but which is implemented anyway. Another design feature is a capacity to easily add new categories of users. Data control and safeguards appear to be lost.

Further questions include: Who has authority to input data on individual citizens? What opportunity is there for citizens to check or challenge stored information?

All the new arrangements were agreed by the Justice and Home Affairs Council in 2003. The Commission was expected to propose legislation to authorise the new SIS II system by the end of 2004, but did not do so. Is there no body within the EU that may draw the attention of the Justice and Home Affairs Council to its duties and require it to conform with EU law and the *Schengen Convention*?

Without transparency

The source of most of the information in this account is *Statewatch Bulletin*, volume 15, number 1, January/February 2005. The information will not be widely known, for reasons given in Statewatch's conclusion which explains that their analysis required painstaking research into the activities of the Council and the Commission, but that their task was difficult because so little information had been made public by these institutions. "The deliberate shielding of this information has prevented parliamentary scrutiny and public debate around the development of SIS II and flies in the face of the EU's commitment to openness, democracy and human rights. Instead, the equally deliberate circumvention of the democratic process now threatens the human rights of those individuals who will be registered in SIS/VIS." The full bulletin may be read on the Statewatch web site at www.statewatch.org

Increasing numbers of British citizens will experience the new database in action from 2007. As a result of a Commission directive of 7 January 2005 those British citizens holding biometric passports will be required to undergo fingerprint checks when they enter France and several other European countries. This suggests that the EU commitment to open borders is not a genuine commitment.

See *Major issues – Identity cards*, *Europol, Habeas corpus* and *Area of Freedom, Security and Justice*.

Defence and foreign policy - Independence or integration?

"Defence is the hard core of sovereignty. Now we have a single currency, then why should we not have a common defence one day?" - Spanish Defence Minister Federico Trillo, European Parliament Committee on Foreign Affairs, 19 February 2002.

A state's ability to defend its citizens is one of its chief justifications, a mark of its effectiveness and power. The issues include:

- Who should defend each member state?
- Should the means of defending member states be pooled and be developed under a single command structure or is an agreement to come to each other's aid, as in NATO, the answer?
- Should agreements with regard to defence and foreign policy made in Brussels be subject to approval by member states' parliaments?
- Should the Constitution (as presently written), or a future treaty, allow a quick, short-cut procedure to allow all foreign policy decisions for all member states to be passed to Brussels?

Moving towards unification

The issues at stake here have immense significance for the future of Europe and it is not just the defence and foreign policies themselves which are important. The plan is explicitly for Europe to act increasingly as a single country in its relationships with the rest of the world. It already does this in, for example, the matter of trade negotiations which are in the hands of the European Union Trade Commissioner. Plans are well advanced for the integration of foreign policy and military forces across the European Union.

The Constitution and its replacements do more than make a few specific arrangements in this area. They requires a commitment of member states to move continuously towards unification with corresponding loss of rights to independent action by sovereign states. This commitment comes in article 40. "The European Union shall conduct a common foreign and security policy based on the . . . achievement of an ever-increasing degree of convergence of Member States' actions." It is not simply a commitment to a specified degree of convergence. The commitment is to move continuously towards full convergence/integration/ unification. Article 12 tells us that "The Union shall have the competence to define and implement a common foreign and security policy." Article 16 states "the Union's competence in matters of common foreign and security policy shall cover *all areas of foreign policy and all questions relating to the Union's security*, including the progressive framing of a common defence policy that might lead to a common defence. Member States shall . . . comply with the Union's action in this area. They shall refrain from any action contrary to the Union's interests or likely to impair its effectiveness." (Emphasis added.) Do citizens of each European country wish to have just one member of their own elected government have only fractional power to make decisions about all aspects of the foreign policy pursued by their country and matters of their national security? Their influence would amount to just one vote out of twenty seven. This is the situation that the Constitution's replacements will bring about. Some member states are likely to want to retain the possibility of independent action. Currently this is still possible.

Undiminished sovereignty - the misleading public image of the CFSP

The way foreign policy and defence policy are presented as working in the EU is that all states have a veto and therefore, at the present, there is no loss of sovereignty. They act unanimously. This is clearly agreed in article 300. "The European decisions referred to in this chapter [Foreign and Security Policy] shall be adopted by the Council acting unanimously." Unfortunately, there are occasions on which this rule does not apply. To begin with (as explained in *Voting* below), in the EU unanimity does not mean that everyone agrees. According to the EU's special definition of unanimity almost a third of member states, or states with almost a third of the population of Europe, may abstain and the decision will still be classed as unanimous (article 300, paragraph 1).

There are occasions when the unanimity rule is abandoned altogether. "By way or derogation from paragraph 1, the Council shall act by qualified majority: (a) when adopting European decisions defining a Union action or position on the basis of a European decision of the European Council relating to the Union's strategic interests and objectives as referred to in article 293." (Article 300, paragraph 2.) This paragraph lists three other instances when qualified majority voting may take the place of unanimity.

In addition, EU military action can already proceed without the veto being able to stop it. The Constitution and previous treaties allow for an inner club of EU states to frame policy and take action without the approval of the rest. "Those Member States whose military capabilities fulfil higher criteria . . . shall establish permanent structured co-operation within the Union framework." (Articles 41/6, 44 and 312.) "Only members of the Council representing the member states participating in enhanced co-operation shall take part in the vote. Unanimity shall be constituted by the votes of the representatives of the participating Member States only." (Article 44/3.)

The EU makes strident demands for loyalty from member countries. "The Member States shall support the common foreign and security policy actively and unreservedly in a spirit of loyalty and mutual solidarity," (Constitution articles 294/2 and 16/2 and article 11/2 TEU). It is therefore difficult to see how, if the inner club is engaged in "enhanced co-operation", it might not, sooner or later, draw the rest of Europe along with its policies. For example, an attack by a group of EU countries on Iran in pursuit of preventing nuclear weapons proliferation might draw retaliation against any EU country if the attack is perceived as "an EU attack". If Iran's response were to be an all out assault on one of the members of the special group of EU member states would not all other EU countries, because of their commitment to fellow members, be obliged to come to their assistance? The "inner club" will act in the name of the EU. Yet members who are not in the "inner club" will have no power of veto over its actions.

The new Euro army - the "European Defence Force"

Individual European states are currently being moved from the independent use and control of their own armed forces to one of commitment to and involvement in European Union decisions. The ultimate goal is a unified European Army.

Germany's Foreign Minister, Joschka Fischer, referring to the European Defence Force, said "This is a part of the European integration process."[120]

This process of unifying European defence policies and military activities is well advanced with 100,000 troops at the disposal of the EU and with a well staffed and developed EU command and control centre, operational since June 2001. Four EU military missions have already been undertaken. (For details see *Euro Army* in the *Institutions* chapter.) Under the Constitution and the *Reform Treaty* member states will be required to supply the necessary "civilian and military capabilities" for "the implementation of the common security and defence policy." (Article 41/3.) The Euro army would appear to operate in an information vacuum and be surrendered to the EU by member states with little or no control over it by elected representatives.

Permanent commitment to ever increasing defence spending - developing European arms industries

The prime role of any country's military forces should be defence, and its military preparedness should relate to estimated levels and types of threat. With regard to military spending there is no suggestion in the European Constitution or its replacements that it should relate to perceived threats. The prime concern of defence is set to one side. Instead the Constitution shows a keenness to have a constantly escalating military budget. "Member states shall undertake progressively to improve their military capabilities." The hand of the arms industry lobby seems evident. (See articles 41/3 and 311.) Do we not need a commitment that defence spending will be commensurate with calculated defence needs?

Arms procurement by individual states, which is a significant expression of a state's independence, will be directed by non-elected EU body, the European Defence Agency (article 311). (See the *Institutions* chapter for background information on this.) It will tell EU member states what they must buy (41/3). It is also required to develop the European arms industry (article 311). How the agency members are to be appointed is not explained in the Constitution. No democratic accountability is guaranteed by the Constitution and no transparency in their working. The risk of arms spending escaping the scrutiny and control of state parliaments seems likely.

The assumption of a need for ever-increasing improvements (ever-increasing arms expenditure), a key concern of the Defence Agency, should be challenged. The basis for arms spending needs defining. Is it to relate to the policy which guided NATO in its first fifty years, that of defence? Or is it to relate to a revised programme of taking military action anywhere in the world to further commercial aims and "principles"? If it relates purely to defence where is the analysis of potential threats that the member states' defence must be ready to deal with?

Defence spending inevitably has implications for social spending. The experience of Poland, under NATO direction, suggests the sort of modernising effect the Defence Agency might have. In that country, where 17% of the population lives below the poverty line, the government has spent $3,500,000,000 on new fighter planes and $250,000,000 on anti-tank missiles in response to NATO's modernisation demands.[14] When, in the last half century has Poland experienced a need for such weaponry? Who are Poland's potential enemies? Who carried out their threat assessment? Did the Polish people vote for this priority in their spending?

Whilst this huge expenditure is taking place can the Polish people not expect strict limits or even cutbacks on, for example, health and education spending?

The annual arms budget of Europe stands at approximately 160 billion euros. Defence spending has to be balanced with spending on other services. These issues require open public scrutiny and debate. The existence of the Defence Agency and its own appointed committees add further non-democratic layers of control or influence beyond the reach and scrutiny of the eurocitizen or the European Parliament or national parliaments. Should there be a Defence Agency? If so, how can its workings be publicly examined? Will the Defence Agency publish details of its contacts and dealings with employees and representatives of arms manufacturers?

The new EU Foreign Office

The signing of the Constitution in 2004 authorised the setting up of a new EU civil service, The External Action Service. Therefore this step does not require ratification. (Article 296/3 and *Declaration 24*.) Its role will be to facilitate and foster the relationships of the EU with foreign powers, formulate plans and advise EU leaders.

Independence in Defence and Foreign Policy V One Simple Step to Complete Integration

Like a chess player, EU leaders are making a number of moves in preparation for a single final move that will complete the game - the game of making EU states into a single state as far as the rest of the world is concerned. There is effectively an embryonic EU army with an EU military command centre, an EU military spending committee (the Defence Agency), an EU Foreign Office (the External Action Service), a high level planning and liaison committee (the Political and Security Committee), top decision-making bodies (the Foreign Affairs Council and the European Council) and a head of EU Foreign Affairs and Defence, the High Representative for the Common Foreign and Security Policy. Centralised decision-making is at present hampered (protected) by the unanimity rule in many instances. But it seems likely that sooner or later the commitment to "forge ever closer integration" will be honoured and there will be a simple move to dispense with the veto in this area. Such a move could be quickly decided upon with instant loss of sovereignty in foreign affairs and military matters and supported by a fully functioning system ready for action. Foreign affairs and military action would then be initiated and operated by the EU. In their relations with the rest of the world the states of the European Union would have converged.

Article 41, paragraph 2 explains how this will happen. "The common security and defence policy shall include the progressive framing of a common Union defence policy. This will lead to a common defence, when the European Council, acting unanimously, so decides." Just twenty-seven people could take this one simple decision. The British leader, under the British Constitution is empowered to enter into treaties without consulting anyone. Voters on a referendum on the replacements of the EU Constitution need to be aware of what they might be supporting in matters of foreign affairs and defence. In any case, top level EU thinking is planning this move so eurocitizens need to consider this issue and decide if it is what they want.

Defence and foreign policy - the uncontrolled use of power

The ordinary eurocitizen in the street, whose life and well-being may depend on wise decisions on EU defence and foreign policy, can have little knowledge about what policies EU leaders have adopted, who takes these decisions or how such decisions are taken. His opportunities to influence these decisions are therefore negligible.

In fact it is difficult to trace who really has the power to make decisions in this area.. The EU has an array of defence and foreign policy committees and councils. All of them operate behind closed doors, out of public view and knowledge. The result is that decision-makers are free to pursue policies without regard to public opinion or even treaty commitments and agreed (publicly stated) EU policies. There have been some tragic consequences.

Issues include:

- Is foreign policy something that should happen outside of democracy?
- Does it matter if the citizens of Europe have no knowledge of foreign policy discussions? Should there be a role for citizens in the momentous decisions of defence and foreign policy?
- Does it matter if EU leaders are free to adopt any foreign policy they fancy?

Present decision-making arrangements - Who decides foreign and military policy and action?

Within the guidelines set by the Constitution, and the *Reform Treaty* (which are wide and open to almost any interpretation) "the European Council shall identify the strategic interests and objectives of the Union." The lower ranking Council has a role in initiating action or decisions. This would be the General Affairs Council (also known as the General Affairs and External Relations Council or GAEC, alternatively known as the Foreign Affairs Council). "The European Council shall act unanimously on a recommendation from the Council." (Article 293.)

The Commission and the proposed Union Minister for Foreign Affairs may have some influence in military matters, but the official relationship of the Commission and this officer in matters of decision-making in foreign and defence matters is expressed in terms of great vagueness. "The Union Minister for Foreign Affairs may propose the use of both national resources and Union Instruments, together with the Commission where appropriate." (See article 41/4.) Also, "The Union Minister for Foreign Affairs, for the common foreign and security policy, and the Commission, for other areas of external action, may submit joint proposals to the Council." (Article 293.) At present, under article 27 of the *Treaty on European Union* (as consolidated at Nice, formerly article J-17), "The Commission shall be fully associated with the work carried out in the common foreign and security committee." What does this mean? Arrangements need to be clearer.

The European Parliament has no direct power in this area but may have some influence. "The European Parliament shall be regularly consulted on the main aspects and basic choices of the common foreign and security policy. It shall be kept informed of how it evolves." (Article 40/8.) "The European Parliament may ask questions of the Council and the Union Minister for Foreign Affairs or make recommendations to them" (article 304). The Union Minister for Foreign Affairs is obliged to "consult and inform the European Parliament and take Parliament's views into consideration. (Article 304.) The opening up of policy and actions to European Parliament scrutiny offers some transparency and is to be welcomed. However, it would be easy for decision-makers to neglect their relationship with the European Parliament and they remain free to act in complete opposition to its views. As in other areas of policy there is no democratic control in this arrangement and virtually no connection with the citizens of Europe.

A further EU body is involved in this policy area - the unelected Political and Security Committee. (See the *Institutions* chapter.) Its role is "to contribute to the definition of policies by delivering opinions to the Council . . . or the Union Minister for Foreign Affairs." In the event of a war this committee will exercise "the political control and strategic direction of the crisis management operations." It will run the war. If its members do a bad job they cannot be voted out.

However, an exception occurs when "the Council may entrust the implementation of a task to a group of Member States." When this occurs "Those member states, in association with the Union Minister for Foreign Affairs, shall agree among themselves on the management of the task." (Article 310.) Again, those who may manage a task (for example, military action which they decide to take on behalf of the EU) are not answerable to the electorate of the EU.

Expenditure in this area will normally come from the funds raised for the European Union primarily by taxation. In the case of military or defence expenditures these will be charged to each member state "in accordance with the gross national product scale," and thereby come as an extra expenditure taken directly out of the taxation of individual states (article 313), not out of the agreed EU budget.

Do these arrangements offer sufficient safeguards and control for member states or to satisfy eurocitizens?

Going to war

Going to war is described in the Constitution as "operational action." The decision to go to war or take any form of military action may be taken by the Council (meaning the General Affairs Council - also known as the Foreign Affairs Council, etc.). The decision has to be unanimous, but as already explained, according to the EU's special definition of unanimity almost a third of member states, or states with almost a third of the population of Europe, may abstain and the decision will still be classed as unanimous. (Article 300. See also 297, 299/2 and 307). And we have already seen how a small number of EU states may embark on independent action.

Dangerous independence of EU Foreign Policy Decision-makers

EU foreign policy decision-makers work at a distance from the EU electorates. Surely, at the very least, such serious matters as the commitment of a state's military forces to action ought not to be in the hands of an international committee in which each member state has very little power. Should not state parliaments have the right to be consulted and to veto plans when the EU decides to use a state's forces for military action? Support for decisions taken by the Council on any matter of military action could be made dependent on the agreement of state parliaments.

Lack of democracy in CFSP

Can there be democratic involvement in and democratic influence on EU foreign and security policy? The answer is "very little under present arrangements, and less than in member states." If the situation in the European Union is compared with that in member states we see that state parliaments often take a very active part in considering and monitoring developments in this area. Issues are explored in the media of each state and public awareness and debate is possible. Those responsible for the big decisions are directly responsible to their electorates. In certain circumstances elected members of parliament may block action by governments. This is not to say that member states are perfectly responsive to popular, or informed or principled opinion. Unprecedented, round-the-world anti-war protests preceded the attack on Iraq by the UK and America.The marching millions were proved to have better intelligence and to be wiser than the leaders insisting war was the only option. Public opinion was simply brushed aside.

But the situation is less democratic at the EU level. Links between EU politicians with their foreign and defence policies and the vast European electorate hardly exist. Whilst most citizens in any individual state will know who their own Prime Minister is, few will know even the names of many of their counterparts in the rest of the EU. They are the twenty-seven big decision-makers of the European Council. No-one in Europe could give an account of the position of each of them on any foreign policy issue. The situation is similar for the other main decision-making body in EU common foreign and security matters. Hardly anyone would even know that "the Council" would have a major role here or who the members of it might be. The decision-makers are out of touch with the people of Europe and the people of Europe are out of touch with them. They meet in secret. Transcripts of their meetings are not available. Information emerging after meetings is minimal. Decisions are taken over the heads of the people who will be affected by their plans. Democracy cannot work in an information vacuum. (See *Transparency*.)

If the EU is to enjoy the support of its citizens in matters of foreign policy it might help if the EU made greater efforts to explain its thinking, discuss issues openly and speak more to the media. The educated citizens of modern Europe might appreciate being presented with information and foreign policy choices and know what is being said and agreed in their name. Information in the public domain may be discussed. Politicians can receive feedback. It is likely that some EU foreign policies would incur massive opposition across Europe if eurocitizens knew how far the EU had strayed from its principles and what was being done in their name. For example, whilst the EU has been giving real support to the Palestinian people it has, at the same time and for many years been developing collaboration with the oppressors of the Palestinians, and in 2006 colluded in a plan to undermine democracy in Palestine. These important issues are explored in greater detail below in *EU foreign policy in action - aberrations.*

Here, again, transparency and accountability are important issues. When the fate of Europe and our relations with other states are under discussion should not the people of Europe have the right to see and hear the debates? Silence and ignorance breed apathy or hostility.

Defence and foreign policy - defence only, or worldwide military action?

"War is always the worst option." Jacques Chirac, former soldier.

Before the middle of the twentieth century Europe had a tragic record for military conflict. There are signs that the EU continues to think in terms of "military solutions" and has not really abandoned its old violent ways. In fact, it is developing its military capability.

- Its arms industries remain amongst the world's largest.
- The EU is committed to year on year increases in military spending.[15]
- And the twenty-one current EU countries that are members of Nato belong to an organisation that radically changed its fundamental policy in 1999 from a policy of using military force only in self defence or the defence of their alliance partners to a policy of military action anywhere in the world for a whole range of purposes.

A careful reading of the *Maastricht Treaty*, signed 1992, (article 11, previously J1) can be seen to be committing the EU to something beyond the policy of geographically limited territorial defence that was Nato's policy for fifty years.

Article 11 of the *Maastricht Treaty* makes commitments to advancing "in the wider world: democracy, the rule of law . . ." etc, "and respect for the principles of the *United Nations Charter* and international law." Article 309 - repeating article 17, previously J7 - of the *Maastricht Treaty*, spells out a range of tasks for which it might use military force - various kinds of "crisis management". The Constitution and the *Reform Treaty* include the encouragement of "the integration of all countries into the world economy, including through the progressive abolition of restrictions on international trade" - the promotion of free trade (article 292/e). Some EU countries have already used military force to further this aim. See below, *Defence and foreign policy - the EU's record.*

Compare these commitments with Nato Treaty commitments. The former Nato Treaty commitment (article 5), to which fourteen EU countries used to be committed (before April 1999) stated: "The parties agree that an armed attack against one or more of them in Europe or North America shall be considered an attack against them all." The military commitment of Nato members was, therefore, geographically limited, purely defensive in scope and, as a consequence, legal under the terms of the *Charter of the United Nations.*

At Nato's Fiftieth Anniversary Celebrations in Washington on 24 April 1999, Nato's leaders signed a new agreement which changed the nature of Nato and effectively changed its treaty. It was called, *The Alliances' Strategic Concept*. This stated, "The Strategic Concept will govern the Alliance's security and defence policy, its operational concepts, its conventional and nuclear force posture, and its collective defence arrangements."

It also stated, "The Alliance is based on common values of democracy, human rights and the rule of law. The Alliance will continue to respect the legitimate security interests of others, and seek the peaceful resolution of disputes as set out in the *Charter of the United Nations*." While Nato leaders were signing their new agreement Nato bombs rained down on a virtually defenceless Yugoslavia in an unprovoked attack, illegal under the Nuremberg Principles, under the *Charter of the United Nations* and in violation of the Nato treaty and the new *Strategic Concept.*

The document confirmed signatories' commitment to "the peaceful resolution of disputes, in which no country would be able to intimidate or coerce any other through the threat or use of force."

It announced it would take military action for new purposes which it termed "non article 5 crisis response operations" i.e. this would be military action which was not in defence of a member's territory. It would be active, and not necessarily invited, military action. The document gave an indication of where Nato might take action. "Alliance security must take account of the global context. . . the disruption of the flow of vital resources. . . the uncontrolled movement of large numbers of people, humanitarian emergencies. . . terrorism, sabotage, organised crime. . . Tasks will include controlling, protecting, and defending territory." The scope is very wide and it covers events everywhere in the world. It does not explain how, under international law, it might be controlling territory that does not belong to a member state. Nato envisages getting involved militarily in circumstances which are not in defence of the territories of its members. Article 309 of the EU's Constitution echoes these Nato commitments.

Why is this policy so disturbing when it is expressed with commitments to international law? Because we have seen that, in the case of Yugoslavia, the words were not honoured, nor were the attacks by Britain, an EU member, on Afghanistan and Iraq. It will be remembered that one of the seventeen reasons given for the attack on Iraq was to bring peace and democracy. Noble intentions: unacceptable means.

What is the connection with EU defence policy?

- Twenty-one EU member states have now signed up to the Nato agreement.
- Both Nato and the EU claim a commitment to democracy, human rights and to abide by international law and the *Charter of the United Nations.*
- Neither now thinks of military action as being confined to defence purposes only.
- Both are prepared to take action to support trade.
- Since 1999 we have seen Nato members collectively or individually in action as described in the above statements, committing acts of aggression in contravention of international law.

The issues here include:

- Do eurocitizens think that EU claims to support international law should be backed by a commitment to bring to justice any of their leaders who break international law?
- Do eurocitizens support the EU policy of active military engagement around the world? - Alternatively, would eurocitizens wish to have military power for defence purposes and in support of the only peace-keeping that could be legal under international law: peace-keeping under United Nations direction?
- Do eurocitizens support, contrary to the *Charter of the United Nations*, other forms of interference in the internal workings of other countries such as "destroying the heroin trade in Afghanistan" (an unsuccessful NATO mission in 2006). See *Charter of the United Nations*, article 2 (7).

The EU is increasingly active in preparing for military action whilst making few plans for studying or developing diplomacy, conflict resolution, humanitarian assistance or peace-building. Could there be a greater emphasis on developing peace-building task-forces with trained teams of doctors, house-builders, civil engineers, experts in conflict resolution and specialists in dealing with psychological trauma?

Defence and foreign policy - the EU's record

Kinds of foreign policy

First, some elementary observations: as we all know, foreign policies of governments are often not what they are claimed to be. There are three main types of foreign policy. First, "stated foreign policy". This consists of the official pronouncements of a government. Second, there is "actual foreign policy". This is how a government actually behaves in its relationships with other countries. Third, there is "Genuine (or whole or integrated) foreign policy". This occurs when a government's claimed and actual policies are the same. The ideas expressed in the stated policy are integrated into the enactment of policy and the policy possesses integrity.

Governments may choose to misrepresent their policies for two main reasons. They may be trying to convince the world and their own citizens that their policies are morally and legally sound when they are not. Alternatively they may try to present "a tough line" and appear to be strong, fixed, closed, determined and unyielding in their defence of their position. In considering international relations we need to be careful not to take every statement made by a state at face value. We need to be aware of "posturing" and the adoption of negotiating positions. Of course, in practice, all foreign policies are liable to change.

Two other kinds of foreign policy may be termed "selective" and "unstable". Unstable policies occur when governments are in a period of transition or are subject to internal power struggles. Selective policies occur when governments mark out certain countries for strikingly different treatment from their norm. This particularly occurs when a state or some states are (or - more likely - are alleged to be) a threat or hostile or "an enemy".

Successful foreign and defence policy

Friendship, trust and co-operation (mutually assured assistance) is the most powerful and effective of all defence policies and operates between almost all states almost all of the time. The phenomenal daily quantity of international communication, travel and trade is testament to this. International trade and the survival of life on earth depend on it.

States which operate through peaceful co-operation have little need of arms spending. Countries which stir up hostility tend to suffer from paranoia, need huge military budgets and still end up on a high state of alert with less security than law-abiding, friendly co-operative countries.

The EU's declared foreign policies are based on this understanding.

The centrality of the EU's commitment to peace

Nothing is more fundamental to the inspiration and purpose of the European Union than its commitment to the development of peace.

The most powerful and important motivation for the European unification process was the desire to end the violent conflicts that had ravaged Europe for centuries culminating in two world wars. The hostility of France and Germany towards each other had been a particular problem. The *Schuman Declaration* of 9 May 1950, introducing the first step in unification, the establishment of the Coal and Steel Community, stressed that it would "change the destiny of those regions which have long been devoted to the manufacture of the munitions of war, of which they have been the most constant victims. The solidarity and production thus established will make it plain that any war between France and Germany becomes not merely unthinkable, but materially impossible." He suggested that the Coal and Steel Community would "lead to the realisation of the first concrete foundation of a European federation indispensable to the preservation of peace."

When the Coal and Steel Community developed into the European Community, the *Treaty of Rome* (1957), which established it, included in its aims for its members "to preserve and strengthen peace and liberty," and "to ensure the development of their prosperity in accordance with the principles of the *Charter of the United Nations*". This commitment to the *United Nations' Charter* was equally a commitment to international law and the prevention of war since the United Nations is founded on a determination to abolish war and develop respect for international law.[16]

France and Germany agreed to work together on foreign policy in 1963 when they signed the *Treaty of the Elysée*.

European co-operation in matters of international affairs took a significant step forwards on 27 October 1970 with the establishment of "European Political Co-operation". (This would be more accurately/transparently described as "foreign policy co-operation".) This was an agreement for foreign ministers of the member countries to meet every six months to discuss and where possible reach agreement on matters of foreign policy. In 1972 they increased the frequency of their meetings to four times a year. In 1987 The Single European Act laid down procedures for foreign policy co-operation.

The *Treaty on European Union* (1992) developed an emphasis on a common foreign and security policy and developed the means to articulate it, plan joint action and monitor the process. Strategies were to be developed by the European Council. EU foreign policy was to be represented to the outside world by the President of the European Council assisted by the Secretary General of the Council acting as a new "High Representative for the common foreign and security policy" (TEU article 18). Member states were required to "inform and consult one another within the Council on any matter of foreign and security policy of general interest to ensure that the Union's influence is exerted as effectively as possible by means of concerted and convergent action" (TEU article 16). The Council was given the task of ensuring that EU foreign policy principles were complied with (TEU article 11).

The *Treaty on European Union* committed the EU to a policy of peace, friendship and co-operation with all nations and to acting, at all times, within international law including the *Charter of the United Nations* (TEU article 11). It made further commitments to such desirable things as seeking to advance democracy, the rule of law, and human rights. The *Reform Treaty* will give similar commitments. How do these commitments work out in practice?

EU foreign policy in action - positive achievements

For most of the time the EU operates a genuine foreign policy.[17] With virtually all neighbouring countries the EU has advanced programmes designed to improve trade, co-operation, security and mutual benefit. For example, there are agreed EU policies (or "strategies") on Russia, the Ukraine, the Mediterranean and the Middle East. The EU operates a "European Neighbourhood policy" and is developing this through a series of "Action Plans". Plans have been concluded since 2004 or are under negotiation with Morocco, Jordan, Tunisia, Egypt, Lebanon and Syria. There are existing co-operation agreements with Tunisia, Turkey and the Palestinian Authority (although Israel has blocked the implementation of this last agreement). There are very advanced arrangements with Israel, but these have mixed consequences and present serious problems which are discussed below.[18]

In a sense part of EU foreign policy is also its internal policy - in that member states each once regarded the others as foreign powers. Member states used to be competitors striving for independence from, or dominance over the others, seeking economic, military and political "balance" or advantage, and, over many centuries, often using appalling violence against each. As far as the current member states are concerned there can be no doubt that there has been a transformation of relationships which, whilst they cannot be described as always harmonious are nevertheless based on absolute commitments to co-operation, negotiation and mutual help. Peace has been achieved in the 27 EU states. Morally and practically the policy has brought enormous benefits - especially prosperity and security. This is the EU's most important achievement.

EU foreign policy in action - aberrations

With such benefits accruing from the EU policy of peace and co-operation it is hard to understand why the EU has not consistently followed this policy. Yet the violence unleashed against Yugoslavia in 1999, which has simply been glossed over by the European Union, and support for aggression in the Middle

East, which has largely been kept from public view, are extraordinary affairs that point to major weaknesses in the institutions of the EU. These matters of momentous international importance deserve examination in some detail.

Yugoslavia

In the spring of 1999 eleven of the fifteen member states of the EU (as members of NATO) supported or participated in a 79 day round-the-clock, relentless bombing campaign against Yugoslavia.[19] They were led into this venture by the US and UK and were joined by other members of NATO including three who are now EU members: the Czech Republic, Hungary and Poland. They were not acting "as the EU" but were the majority of EU states deliberately acting in breach of their word as partners in the promotion of peace, and their treaty and legal obligations.

Since Yugoslavia had not attacked another state, nor even threatened one, the NATO assault was a clear case of aggression - an act described in international law as "the supreme international crime".[19]

What were the causes and effects of this action? What needs to be done to prevent a similar aberration from EU principles in future? The bombing of Yugoslavia in 1999 was presented by politicians, with the uncritical support of the media, as justifiable on grounds of humanitarian concern for the Kosovo Albanians. Morally and legally such sentiments cannot justify such aggression.

Before the war there had been a serious dispute between the Kosovo's Serbs and Kosovo Albanians in Kosovo (a province of Yugoslavia). The Albanians had pursued a pacifist line under their venerated leader Ibrahim Rugova. The Yugoslav government had made concessions to the Kosovo Albanians. For example, their wish for an Albanian language university in Kosovo was granted. But then terrorists arrived on the scene and rejected the peaceful approach. With the arrival of the KLA, the Kosovo Liberation Army, violence erupted. The KLA provoked the Serb community by attacking it and the Yugoslav/Serb army responded. The violence escalated. The Serbs were fearful of being ethnically cleansed from their historic homeland. In January 1999 the British Foreign Secretary, Robin Cook, reported to parliament that the KLA were responsible for more deaths than the Serbs.

A conflict such as this may be resolved by capturing terrorists and criminals, cutting off arms supplies, diplomacy, patient mediation and economic assistance. The UK and US leaders, for reasons not immediately obvious, decided to adopt the lynch-mob approach to international diplomacy. They decided that it was their responsibility to solve the problem by assuming that the terrorist KLA were wholly justified in their violence and that the Serbs were wholly unjustified in theirs.

But take any problem and exercise extreme violence against one or both sides and the problem becomes a major intractable crisis. NATO nations (including many current EU members) effectively prejudged the rights and wrongs of the dispute and attacked the Serbs. They used the media to promote a black and white picture of the situation in which all Serbs were bad and all Kosovo Albanians (and the many Albanians who had joined them from outside Kosovo) were good. Soon after the bombing started, half the Kosovo Albanian population headed south into Albania (graphically recorded by the European media), and half of the Kosovo Serbian population headed north out of the Kosovo province. When the bombing stopped, 1400 Serbs in Kosovo were killed by Albanians, and Serbs, gypsies and Jews were ethnically cleansed from Kosovo by Kosovo Albanians whilst NATO (including EU) troops failed to take effective action to halt the process. European media missed this calamitous event. The NATO intervention, by driving the Serb army out of Kosovo had made the massacres and ethnic cleansing possible and probable. Serb forces had, in fact, been protecting their people from ethnic cleansers.

War for free trade

The immediate excuse for the start of NATO's bombing campaign was that the Yugoslav leader, Slobodan Milosevic (a Serb) would not sign a "peace agreement", the *Rambouillet Accord.* Politicians and the media emphasised Mr Milosevic's intransigence. They did not reveal the details of the agreement that he refused to sign. No doubt there were a number of reasons why Mr Milosevic would not sign - including the demand for NATO forces to occupy the whole of Yugoslavia. But amongst the reasons was the fact that the document attempted to impose free trade principles on a largely state-run Yugoslavia. Spreading "free trade" was a significant motivation for the aggression.

Article 1 of chapter 4a of the *Rambouillet Accord* stated: "the economy of Kosovo shall function in accordance with free market principles."

Paragraph 6 of this article stated "Federal and other authorities shall . . . ensure the free movement of persons, goods, services and capital to Kosovo, including from international sources."

Article 2 spelled out some of the details of the privatisation that the Americans and British were demanding. "The parties agree to re-allocate ownership and resources . . . in the following areas:

- Government-owned assets (including educational institutions, hospitals, and natural resources and production facilities);
- Pension and social insurance contributions;
- Revenues to be distributed under article 1.5;
- Any other matters relating to economic relations between the parties not covered by this agreement."

The peace agreement was in fact a demand for the commercial transformation of Kosovo.[20]

It was explained that the purpose of the bombing was to get the Serb/Yugoslav army out of Kosovo. Yet the targets selected in the bombing campaign hardly support this claim. Just fourteen tanks were hit whilst the score for industrial facilities was 372. Every single one of these targets was a state owned enterprise. Not one was a private undertaking. Targets included the Zastava state-owned car factory and the state-owned oil refinery and chemical works at Pancevo. Their destruction caused appalling and long-lasting pollution.[21]

After the war was officially over NATO troops were used to seize the Trepca mining complex, one of the richest sources of minerals in Europe. It was put into commercial ownership. The wholesale privatisation of Kosovo state enterprises was launched.

Eight years after the bombing is Kosovo a free trade utopia proving the effectiveness of European and American reform theories and methods? Two hundred thousand people (mainly Serbs) have been ethnically cleansed from Kosovo by the Kosovo Albanian extremists. Half the population lives in poverty. Unemployment stands at 65%. Crime and corruption are rife. The province is the major corridor for drug and human trafficking into Europe. Tensions remain high and large numbers of NATO troops remain in occupation, including 4000 Americans in their massive permanent base, Camp Bondsteel.

The idea of state ownership of any enterprise or service is anathema to the invisible mandarins of the WTO and the IMF. Transnational corporations and western finance must have access to every enterprise, service and resource in the world. Many members of the EU, on the evidence of 1999, share this philosophy and are prepared to go to extreme lengths in support of it.

One might expect that from the EU there would have been an official expression of outrage at such non-EU behaviour, and that a state committed to upholding international law would wish to bring to trial those leaders who were so clearly at fault. The EU was silent.

Foreign policy implications

The key issue here is should the unstated policy of the EU to use war to promote commercial opportunities be abandoned?

As things stand EU and NATO leaders appear to have got away with their crime and aberration from EU commitments to policies and principles. But a price has been paid. Confidence in EU commitments and politicians has been damaged.

The Israel/Palestine conflict

The conflict between Israel and Palestine provides another disturbing example of EU action straying from its principles. The EU's behaviour has helped to prolong for decades an appalling human tragedy that could have been resolved. This case illustrates how the EU's secretiveness can make it possible for EU decision-makers to pursue alien policies without challenge.

Stated EU policies towards Israel and Palestine almost always comply with EU principles including support for international law, but in important ways actual policies contradict the fine words.

The Israel/Palestine conflict is a battle between unequals. The Israelis are one of the most heavily armed nations on earth. The Palestinians are a virtually defenceless civilian population. The Israeli side is supported by powerful friends (the US and EU) and uses massive fire-power (tanks, helicopter gunships, missiles and F16 fighter/bombers) often against civilian institutions, homes and unarmed civilians. Israeli governments have inflicted a reign of terror on generations of Palestinians. The UN has identified Israel as the world's worst violator of human rights.[22]

Israel's behaviour is a daily violation of international law including, for 40 years, defiance of UN resolution 242. This calls for “the withdrawal of Israeli armed forces from territories occupied in the recent conflict”. This refers to the territories generally referred to as the West Bank, Gaza Strip and East Jerusalem occupied in the Six Day War, 5-10 June 1967. Many people assume that these territories would form a future Palestinian state.[23] Numerous subsequent resolutions re-affirm this demand. The Israeli occupation of these territories is illegal under international law.[24] The Israelis did withdraw settlements from the Gaza Strip in 2005 but have moved back with tanks and have continued to bomb and shell the area since their withdrawal causing many deaths.

Many religious, charitable and human rights organisations have commented on the situation in Palestine. The charity, Christian Aid, may be taken as an impartial and typical commentator. These brief extracts from their report, published in 2003, give an assessment of the situation at that time.[25]

> "Almost three quarters of Palestinians live on less than $2 a day - below the official UN poverty line. . . Responsibility for the current humanitarian crisis rests principally with Israel's military occupation of the Palestinian territories. . . Actions taken by the Israeli Government, for security or other reasons, have created a situation of de-development - of systematically stripping away the ingredients of a viable economy and society. . .
>
> After the Oslo Accords, agreement on Israeli military control meant that Israel controlled 82.8% of Palestinian territory. . . Israeli control over access to water limits Palestinian irrigation for agriculture, the drilling of water holes and personal consumption. Israeli allocation of water is five times that of Palestinians. . . Placing 3,000,000 people under what is effectively a siege inevitably has consequences for their health. . .
>
> Israeli government actions that impoverish Palestinians violate international humanitarian law, specifically the Fourth Geneva Convention and the Hague Regulations. Both regulate behaviour in war and in occupied territories. Collective punishment, for instance, as imposed by curfew and by closure, violates the Fourth Geneva Convention. Seizure or destruction of municipal property – the destruction of Palestinian authority buildings, for instance – is illegal under the Hague Regulations. Many Israeli actions violate UN Security Council resolution 242 and 338 that call for Israel to withdraw from territories occupied in 1967 and later resolutions calling for an end to violence.
>
> Had the other 160 signatories of the Geneva Conventions and the Hague Regulations taken their obligations seriously, the key issues in the conflict – the annexation of land settlements, closure and control of water – would have been confronted. The major powers – the US, UK and the rest of the EU – have the authority to make international law meaningful. . . They have not done so."

A letter to EU Foreign Ministers in October 2002 written on behalf of the Euro-Mediterranean Human Rights Network (EMHRN), the International Federation for Human Rights (FIDH) and the World Organisation Against Torture (OMCT) made many specific accusations. For example, human rights violations include "Wilful killings, arbitrary executions and targeted assassinations. More than 1400 Palestinians have been killed since the outbreak of the Second Intifada, [28 September 2000 - October 2002] whereof at least 79 were extra-judicially executed." And there have been "Massive arbitrary arrests of Palestinians. . . As of September 30, it is estimated that about 2,765 people have been detained in various facilities in Israel and the Occupied Territories . . . Many sources indicate inhuman conditions of detention, including torture." The Israeli government, in plain language, is a terrorist organisation.[26]

Since these reports were written the lives of Palestinians have become even more difficult. There has been the building of a huge wall across Palestinian territory. It has been declared illegal by the United Nations' own court, the International Court of Justice, but the Israelis continue constructing it regardless.

The EU and others against democracy

On 25 January 2006 there were Palestinian Authority parliamentary elections which were contested mainly by the ruling Fatah party and Hamas. Led by American former President, Jimmy Carter, international monitors, including EU representatives, declared the elections free and fair. This was in spite of the fact that two US organisations had interfered with the elections by funding their favoured Fatah candidates and providing them with training.[27]

Hamas gained 74 seats to Fatah's 45. The will of the people was clear. They rejected Fatah candidates, the Fatah record of corruption, Fatah policies of agreements and concessions to the Israelis which have brought not peace but hell on earth. The Palestinian people were asking for something better. The Hamas they were voting for had not campaigned on the basis of non-recognition of Israel, nor on the basis that Israel should be destroyed, and they were undoubtedly impressed by the rarely reported social work of Hamas in organising the provision of free food aid, medical assistance and education. Hamas election publicity contained these words, "Yes to a free, independent, and sovereign Palestinian state on every portion of the West Bank, Gaza Strip and Jerusalem without conceding on any part of historic Palestine".

Israel has never accepted the right of the Palestinians to live in peace anywhere. Their actual policy has been to crush all life and resistance out of them. They have been supported in this policy by American governments who give the largest share of their foreign aid to the Israeli government (currently about $2 billion every year) which is spent largely on US aircraft and weapons used against the Palestinians. The Israeli government does not want to negotiate with Palestinians who are asking for international law to be enforced on their behalf.

World opinion, as shown by many votes of the United Nations General Assembly and the insistent voices of international aid, human rights organisations and many churches support the claims of Palestinians. However, all this counts for little. The key decision makers are known as the Middle East Quartet. These are representatives of the UN, the EU, Russia and America. These were, in 2006, Kofi Annan, Secretary General of the United Nations, Russian Foreign Minister, Sergei Lavrov, High Representative for European Common Foreign and Security Policy, Javier Solana and U.S. Secretary of State, Condoleeza Rice.[28]

On 26 January 2006 Kofi Annan issued a statement on behalf of the Quartet saying, in effect, the Palestinian people had voted for change but they really still want the same things and have voted for the wrong people. They have to agree that the old agreements (which neither side has, in reality, accepted) were the right ones and there can be no weapons on the Palestinian side of the dispute. They must abandon their negotiating positions and their last means of exerting any influence against the Israeli onslaught.[29]

On 14 February the New York Times reported a meeting which had taken place in Jerusalem the day before. "The United States and Israel are discussing ways to destabilize the Palestinian government so that newly elected Hamas officials will fail and elections will be called again, according to Israeli officials and Western diplomats. The intention is to starve the Palestinian Authority of money and international connections to the point where, some months from now, its president, Mahmoud Abbas, is compelled to call a new election."

In support of the Israeli policy of bringing down a democratically elected government the EU joined in by cutting off vital financial support to the Hamas led government. The EU web site reports "Following the formation of the Hamas-led PA government in March 2006, the Commission has stopped political contacts and has temporarily put on hold its direct assistance to that government." It went on to say that it would increase direct humanitarian assistance to the population. Thus public services would cease to be funded, but the ensuing crisis would be alleviated by those who had helped to cause it. "The Commission stands ready to re-engage with a government that would reflect the Quartet principles." In other words the EU rejected the democratic decision of the Palestinian people and would only talk to an elected government that (a) would set aside the wishes expressed by voters and (b) agreed with EU views and the views of other members of the Quartet instead.

Money passing to the Palestinian Authority, including donations, passes through the Israeli banking system. The Israelis stopped this flow of money. The Israelis, on behalf of Palestinians, collect taxes including VAT on Palestinian products. The Israelis decided not to hand over this money. The result of cutting all funding to the Palestinian Authority and in effect stealing (temporarily) Palestinian money, has been that it was unable to pay full salaries to its 165,000 workers. On 9 May 2006 the Quartet's response to this imposed distress was, "The Quartet reiterates that the Palestinian Authority government must fulfil its responsibilities with respect to basic human needs, including health services, as well as for proper fiscal management and provision of services."

To undermine the democratic decision of the Palestinian people and make effective government in Palestine even more difficult the Israelis kidnapped members of the Palestinian Parliament. By 21 August 2006 the Israelis had captured and held in detention five cabinet ministers and more than twenty-four MPs, claiming that they were members of a terrorist organisation.

The role of violence

It is true that Hamas leaders have not renounced violence. How could they renounce violence in the face of continuing gross violence against them, gross harassment, land seizures, the confiscation of their tax revenues, the seizure of their incoming aid, destruction of their infrastructure, the kidnapping of democratically elected MPs, the assassination of Palestinian leaders?

In 2006 the Israelis continued their campaign of assassination by helicopter gunships, inevitably resulting in the deaths of many civilians and the destruction of many homes. In the Gaza Strip they destroyed bridges, shelled civilian areas and put out of action the only power station. "During the week of April 12 [2006], the Israeli Army fired more than 950 artillery tank shells and 46 F16 missiles in this densely populated, supposedly free Gaza strip. Overall 19 Palestinians were killed by the Army, including 3 children, during that week."[30] The feelings of Palestinians and the responses of their leaders receive little or no coverage in the British media.

Some Palestinians in the Gaza Strip continued to fire somewhat ineffective shells into Israel. In a raid two Israeli soldiers were killed and another captured, causing Israeli outrage which was widely and repeatedly reported by the British media.

EU responses to Palestinian and Israeli aggression

The EU has two kinds of response to this tragedy: stated responses and actual ones. The first consists of public pronouncements supporting international law, calling for an end to violence on both sides and respect for human rights. The tangible responses have been to give substantial actual aid to Palestinians, but at the same time offering every encouragement and support to the principle aggressors, welcoming Israel into the EU family and providing Israel with weapons.

The stated EU policy of supporting international law does not go as far as to support the most fundamental issue of demanding that Israelis respond to United Nations resolution 242.

An EU web site[31] tells us, "The European Union attaches great importance to the finding of a just and final settlement to the Arab Israeli conflict." It also tells us that the EU condemns the building of the separation barrier on Palestinian territory; the EU condemns the frequent demolition of Palestinian homes by the Israeli army; and it condemns planning laws operated by the Israelis to prevent Palestinians building homes.

The EU states, "The EU firmly believes that there can be no justification for military actions directed indiscriminately against civilian neighbourhoods. Collective penalties and all measures of intimidation, reprisals against protected persons and their property contravene the Fourth Geneva Convention. Such actions fuel mistrust and hatred and further hamper efforts to seek a political solution. The Israeli authorities should cease house demolitions and instead facilitate construction of legal Palestinian housing . . . The EU is seriously concerned at the destruction of Palestinian infrastructure and other facilities financed by the Union (damage to EU-funded projects either destroyed or damaged by Israeli military forces since 2002 is estimated to exceed €25 million). It urges Israel to put an end to this practice."[32]

In practical terms the EU offers financial help to Palestinians which is doubtlessly of great importance being life-saving on a big scale - vital wound dressing on a body that continues to suffer major injuries on an almost daily basis. "The European Commission allocates between 5-10 million Euros per annum, principally through the EU Partnership for Peace Programme. This provides support to local and international civil society initiatives which promote peace, tolerance and non-violence. The objective of this support is to contribute to the rebuilding of confidence within each society and between societies."[31]

Also, "the Commission has agreed to provide over €120 million to help the caretaker Palestinian government stabilise Palestinian Authority finances and meet the needs of the population. This includes a €40 million facility to cover energy bills (electricity, oil etc), an accelerated payment of €64 million to

UNRWA, to help meet the humanitarian needs of Palestinian refugees, and partial disbursement of budget support for the PA from the World Bank Trust Fund, amounting to €17.5 million."[31]

This is what the EU says about the violence in this region. "The EU position on violence and terrorism: the EU unreservedly condemns all acts of violence and terrorism and will continue its efforts to seek a peaceful resolution to the Israeli-Palestinian conflict based on the objectives laid out in the Quartet Roadmap. Terrorist attacks against Israel have no justification whatsoever and the EU has included Hamas, Islamic Jihad, and other armed Palestinian groups in its list of terrorist organisations."[32]

Will the EU end all relationships with all governments that have failed to renounce violence? This move is one sided and gives support and encouragement to the aggression of Israel. Why has Israel not been identified as a terrorist organisation[26] and more than that, identified as the state that has invaded, robbed, murdered and persecuted the Palestinian people for over half a century?

The statement goes on to give Israel a partial excuse for its violence. "The EU recognises Israel's right to protect its citizens from terrorist attacks." The contrast is striking. On one side violence is justified as "a right to protect". On the other, there is "no justification whatsoever." The right to protect its citizens sounds very reasonable, but should these citizens have a right to protection when they have taken up residence in lands from which their armies brutally drove Palestinians, acts illegal under international law?

The EU formally rebukes Israel. "However, it also emphasizes that the Israeli Government, in exercising this right, has to respect international law and human rights, avoid civilian casualties and take no action that aggravates the humanitarian and economic plight of the Palestinian people. It calls on Israel to abstain from punitive measures which are not in accordance with international law, including extra-judicial killings." Looking at the range of EU pronouncements we can see that EU stated policy towards Israel mostly supports international law but that, even at the level of stated policy, the EU fails to support UN resolutions, opposes democracy and delivers mixed messages.

The policies of Hamas and Israel compared - Hamas

The stated policy of Hamas in their founding charter of 1987 is one of uncompromising militancy in the fight against Israel. It called for the destruction of Israel and the return of the whole territory to Palestinian control.

Hamas has condemned the 1993 Oslo Peace Accords and rejected the political process within Palestine (until 2005). These are the stated policies.

In practice it can be seen that Hamas's policies are not so extreme. Hamas has now joined the political process and subjected its policies and candidates to a democratic election which was judged by EU monitors to be fair.

In numerous communications to the press (which have almost never been reported) their stated policies are changing.[33]

Hamas leaders have suggested that they might recognise Israel if it complied with UN resolution 242 and withdrew its illegal settlers now occupying Palestinian land. For example, Mahmoud Zahar, a leading Hamas hardliner, told *Ha'aretz*, "No one is thinking now about changing the charter, but in principle it is not impossible." (26 October 2005.) A moderate Hamas candidate in the election, standing in Nablus, Mohammed Ghazal, told Reuters (21 September 2005) that the group could change its 1988 charter calling for Israel's destruction and that it was open to negotiating with Israel. "The charter is not the Koran," Ghazal said. "Historically, we believe all Palestine belongs to Palestinians, but we're talking now about reality, about political solutions. . . . The realities are different." If Israel reached a stage where it felt able to talk to Hamas, Ghazal said, "I don't think there will be a problem of negotiating with the Israelis."[34]

In March 2006, the Hamas Palestinian government released its official legislative program. Under the heading "Recognition of Israel," it stated: "The question of recognizing Israel is not the jurisdiction of one faction, nor the government, but a decision for the Palestinian people." In other words Hamas was content to allow the democratic decision of the Palestinian people to prevail in a referendum. They would insist on nothing! This is official Hamas policy: a willingness to allow the recognition of the state of Israel.[35] However, Hamas has sound reasons to be cautious about "recognising Israel": (a) because it is not clear what would be recognised as Israel because Israel has no agreed borders, (b) Israel (the land within the pre-1967 borders) is an apartheid state in which Palestinians are not entitled to equal treatment under the law. In particular they are prohibited by law from living in 93% of the country as this land is reserved for Jews, (c) Israel shows no sign of recognising a viable Palestinian state, (d) Israel does not recognise the democratically elected Hamas led Palestinian government as a legitimate government, and (e) when the Palestinian Fatah group agreed to renounce violence and recognise Israel in 1989 the Palestinians significantly failed to gain control of their territorial entitlement under Resolution 242 and continued to suffer under Israeli oppression. It did not buy territory, peace or security: only further losses, more suffering and oppression.

In practice Hamas has encouraged and enabled suicide bombings and other acts of violence which killed four to five hundred Israelis between September 2000 and March 2006.[36]

After August 2004 suicide bombings were suspended and the level of violence was substantially decreased till well after the elections when Israeli violence escalated early in 2006. Hamas has not renounced violence, but seems, given the right circumstances, willing and able to control it.

The policies of Hamas and Israel compared - Israel

On the Israeli side we find assertions that the whole of what was known as Palestine should be known as Israel and that the only possibility of achieving this was and is through the use of force. A pioneer theorist who devised ideas for the establishment of the State of Israel in the land then known as Palestine was Ze'ev Jabotinski who promoted these views. Here are two of his statements.

"A voluntary agreement between us and the Arabs of Palestine is inconceivable now or in the foreseeable future... Every indigenous people will resist alien settlers as long as they see any hope of ridding themselves of the danger of foreign settlement."

"We must either suspend our settlement efforts or continue them without paying attention to the natives. Settlement can thus develop under the protection of force that is not dependent on the local population, behind an iron wall which they will be powerless to break down."[37]

David Ben-Gurion, the founding leader of Israel said in 1936, "We and they want the same thing: we both want Palestine, and that is the fundamental conflict."[38]

In 1937 he wrote, "I support compulsory transfer. I do not see in it anything immoral . . . The Arabs will have to go, but one needs an opportune moment for making it happen, such as a war." Eleven years later, when the British abandoned Palestine, he read the *Declaration of Independence*, founding the State of Israel in Palestine and led the Israeli army in the brutal seizure of Palestinian lands, the total destruction of many Palestinian villages, the killing of 13,000 Palestinians and the driving out of 700,000 more.

From 2001 the ruling Israeli Likud party had as its policy the absolute denial of the possibility of an independent Palestinian state. "The right of the Jewish people to the Land of Israel is an eternal right, not subject to dispute. . . The government will oppose the establishment of an independent Palestinian state."[39]

In January 2006 Ehud Olmert, then acting Israeli Prime Minister (and actual Prime Minister from 30 March 2006), said, "We firmly stand by the historic right of the people of Israel to the entire Land of Israel. Every hill in Samaria and every valley in Judea is part of our historic homeland."(Such a policy violates the Oslo Accords of 1993 and the "Roadmap".)[40]

On 24 January 2006, Olmert, retreating slightly from his firm stand said that he would proceed as soon as possible to the unilateral determination of permanent borders of the State of Israel. Israel would permanently "maintain control over the security zones, the Jewish settlement blocs, and those places which have supreme national importance to the Jewish people, first and foremost a united Jerusalem under Israeli sovereignty".[41] This is far short of what UN resolution 242 requires.

Actual policies - violence

The above are stated policies. Israeli reliance on force has always been an absolute commitment, an unwavering feature of their relationship with Palestinians. The Israelis have never renounced violence, using it for sixty years to seize more and more Palestinian land and to terrorise and oppress the Palestinian people. Almost all their victims have been civilians. Israel has never been asked to renounce violence and disband its forces.

In October 2006 the Israeli government, the Kadima coalition under Ehud Olmert, was joined by the Ysrael Beytenu party led by Avigdor Lieberman who was appointed Deputy Prime Minister. He has a hardline policy towards Palestinians. For example, he has said that Israeli Arab parliamentarians who went to Damascus and met with Hamas should be shot.[42] He has stated that the thousands of Palestinian prisoners held by Israel should be taken to the Dead Sea and drowned.[43]

According to polls this man is the second most popular politician in Israel.[44]

Israel does not show signs of wishing to moderate its violent, illegal and immoral treatment of Palestinians.

Palestinians have consistently lost ground to the Israelis for almost 60 years. They have hit back at Israelis time and time again in vain efforts to stem the tide of Israeli aggression, to reverse or slow down the loss of land and control to the Israelis, to give the Israelis some incentive to reach an agreement acceptable to Palestinians which one day might deliver peace. Palestinians have halted their violence for periods of time but these gestures have not resulted in reciprocation by the Israelis. Palestinian violence is typically recorded as terrorism whilst Israeli violence is typically excused as self-defence. Between 29 September 2000 and 26 October 2006 the Israelis killed 4,398 Palestinians and caused major damage to Palestinian homes and infrastructure.[45] The EU does not ban arms sales to Israel. Member states make their own decisions. In 2002 Germany temporarily banned arms sales to Israel in protest against the Israeli treatment of Palestinians. During 2005 the UK government licensed the sale of £22,500,000 worth of arms to Israel, doubling its previous year's sales. In 2006 it was supplying arms to Israel whilst Israel was ruthlessly bombing the infrastructure and people of Lebanon, creating another appalling disaster area.

Actual policy - claims to territory

Both sides claim a right to the entirety of Palestine as it existed in 1946. Leaders on both sides concede that the claims are not realistic.

The Israelis have rarely expected to drive out the last Palestinian. Even Ben-Gurion accepted that Israel could only exist in part of Palestine. Ehud Olmert quotes this fact on his own web site. "For true peace, Israel must relinquish a vast majority of the territories occupied in the Six Day War."[46]

However, Israeli policy is not the acceptance of UN resolutions, nor the acceptance of the Oslo Accords, nor acceptance of the "Road Map". They have decided to "create facts on the ground". This means building settlements and related infrastructure in the occupied territories and building a permanent barrier to annexe the territory they have decided to take. The aim is to pre-empt further negotiations; prevent the start of negotiations for as long as possible by extreme provocation of the Palestinian side and by insisting that the other side is not morally fit to negotiate; and insist on negotiating only with Palestinians who are subservient towards Israel and oppose the democratically expressed, popular will of the Palestinian people. In this policy they have been aided by the Quartet with the EU being fully active on behalf of the Israelis.

If, with the support or connivance of the European Union and the rest of the world, they bring off this plan it would leave the Palestinians with an unviable state and far short of their entitlement under international law.

International law, as expressed in United Nations resolution 242, sets the borders in the position they were before the Six Day War in 1967 when Israel took control of what then remained of Palestine. The Palestinians appear to be willing to accept the pre-1967 borders - something far less than they feel they are entitled to.

There is another possible solution which has worked for some nations long involved in bloody conflict: and that is to dissolve borders, barriers and discrimination. This was effectively done between England and Scotland. After centuries of terrible conflict citizens of both nations come and go freely across the disputed territories; they mingle, inter-marry hold, office in each other's administrations. The border is hardly more than a line on the map. This is the single state solution. A single state with equal rights for Palestinian and Israeli citizens could give them all the dignity and peace they desire. In view of the failure of past proposals almost nothing should be ruled out for consideration.

What cannot be acceptable, however, is the insistence that there is only one solution. The failed agreements of the past (the Oslo Accords and the Road Map) have brought an escalation of misery, anger and despair. They cannot be the answer to the ongoing Israeli/Palestinian crisis. The EU and the Quartet must engage in some fresh thinking here.

The "Peace Process"

"He who is convinced against his will, is of the same opinion still." - A traditional saying.

There are two views of the "Peace Process". From the Israeli side it is something they like to claim to be involved in and support even though they flagrantly fail to comply with agreements. It sounds acceptable in presenting their aims to the world's media. Under the guise of pursuing the "Peace Process" they can pursue their aim of destroying the viability of Palestinian society and play for time while they establish their own "solution". From the Palestinian point of view the peace process has been misnamed. All they have seen is a "Persecution Process", the infliction on the Palestinian people of a nightmare world that is driving them to despair, and all aided by Israel's international backers. When the "peace process" has been correctly identified as a "persecution process" it is easy to see why Palestinians are unenthusiastic about meeting their oppressors to engage in a process which holds out the probable prospect of continuing suffering and the imposition of profoundly unsatisfactory terms in an "agreement".

The call to the two sides to negotiate

Negotiation can work in the case of disputes between two peoples when there is an approximate equivalence of power between the parties. This has not existed and does not exist in the Israel/Palestine dispute. The situation has similarity with the situation of a householder who finds himself the victim of an armed gang that has taken over his house, taken his sons hostage, murdered his wife and is demanding everything he owns in order to get his sons back. At this point officers of the law come on the scene and say to the victim and the armed gang, "You must negotiate and come to a genuine agreement." What is actually needed is not negotiation but the enforcement of law.

With grossly unequal power the two sides have negotiated with the unsurprising result that Israel has negotiated the control of almost all the territory that was left to the Palestinians after earlier violent seizures of territory.

The role of the EU

We have seen how, when the Palestinian people clearly stated, in the January 2006 elections, their desire for new leaders with a new agenda in negotiation, the EU rejected the democratic will of the people and joined the cause of others who were insisting that the failed agreements and policies of the past are the only ones that can succeed. The EU brazenly set out to undermine a democratically elected government. The EU by withdrawing funding for the elected Palestinian government assisted in its overthrow. On 16 December 2006 Mahmoud Abbas, the Palestinian President responded to Israeli and Quartet pressure and called for new elections. The Israelis demanded that he "crack down" on Hamas terrorists. This was, in effect, a demand to start a civil war and weaken still further the devastated Palestinian people.

Yet the failures of Israel to renounce violence, cease violations of human rights, accept they are not entitled to the entire land of Palestine, abide by the principles of international law – all this brings no sanctions from the EU, no practical steps to bring about reformation of a country guilty of very long term violations of international law and human rights. The EU takes no steps to halt the British Government supply of weapons to Israel.

But the EU has not simply ignored Israeli behaviour. It has gone to great lengths to support, encourage and welcome Israel into a close association with the EU. For many years the EU has been developing trade with Israel with the objective of making Israel a virtual member of the EU.

Free trade arrangements began in 1975. An "Association Agreement" between Israel and the European Union was signed November 20, 1995. The preamble to the Agreement includes a declaration that the European Union, the member states and Israel are interested in promoting the integration of Israel's economy into the European economy. A new element in the Agreement was the section dealing with liberalization of the services and capital market and the right of establishment of firms. The section on co-operation dealt with a wide range of fields, including law, internal security, environment, education and infrastructure. Most of the areas of co-operation were new and reflected the mutual aspiration to expand the application of the primarily trade-related agreement of 1975 to economic and other areas as well. The Agreement created formal structures such as the Association Council, headed on the Israeli side by the Foreign Minister. The Agreement entered into force on June 1, 2000.[47]

The EU's European Investment Bank provides credits and guarantees for the funding of up to fifty percent of investment in projects which the EU seeks to promote in domains such as infrastructures, energy, industry, services and agriculture. For example, on 13 June 2000, Israel and the European Investment Bank signed a Framework Agreement enabling the European Investment Bank to grant loans for Israeli projects. At that time the Israel Electric Company expressed interest in receiving loans from the EIB for a project involving the conversion of utilities to gas. A loan totalling EUR 22 million for the Israel Airport Authority was in the pipeline.[48]

EU/Israel policy has developed under the Euro-Mediterranean Agreement. EU Member States and Israel have free trade in industrial products. The two sides have granted each other significant trade concessions for certain agricultural products, in the form of tariff reduction or elimination, either within quotas or for unlimited quantities. The agreement also calls for progressive and reciprocal liberalisation of trade for agricultural products. A new protocol to this effect entered force in February 2005.[48]

Israel has been developing a partnership with the EU on research and technical development. This began with a programme in August 1996. The (6th Framework) Programme for 2003-2006 was described by the EU as, "a key part of the EU's strategy to create a true European Research Area, an Internal Market for science and knowledge in which Israel will play a full role."[48]

These programmes permit Israeli universities, research institutes and companies to participate in hundreds of research projects with their European counterparts. The European Commission signed an agreement with Israel in July 2004 allowing Israel to participate in the EU's Galileo project for a Global Navigation Satellite System.

Another agreement is one which is specifically designed to further integrate Israel into the EU. This is the EU/Israel Action Plan which was adopted by the Commission in December 2004. The purpose of the agreement is described as follows: "The EU/Israel Action Plan allows for the possibility for Israel to participate progressively in key aspects of EU policies and programmes, to upgrade the scope and intensity of political co-operation, to encourage the approximation of Israeli legislation as a means to opening the EU internal market to Israel, and for the pursuit of greater liberalisation of trade, services and agriculture."[48]

Foreign policy issues raised by the EU's relationships with Yugoslavia, Israel and Palestine

General failures

- Lack of transparency. EU states keeps important information and knowledge of developments from the EU electorate thereby excluding democratic involvement and monitoring of the EU's relationships with other states.
- Lack of integrity. A failure to match actions with declared policies. How can the eurocitizen be expected to trust the policies stated in EU treaties when policies are not followed?
- Lack of accountability. A failure to have any body or procedure to monitor failings to comply with EU policies, principles and law, and take action to deal with the people guilty of failures and crimes.
- Arrogance and indifference. Ministers appear unconcerned by their foreign policy failures and the damage these have caused to their reputations and the name of the EU. Do EU ministers, MEPs and Commissioners appreciate the damage done to the EU's credibility with their citizens and the wider world caused by acquiescing in important breaches of key commitments?
- Trade has been treated as a higher priority than peace, international law, democracy and human rights - even to the point of using war in an attempt to develop commercial opportunities.[49]

Events in Israel and Palestine raise major issues not just for the EU but for the entire world. Key questions include:

Why has the Secretary General of the United Nations been allowed by UN member states (including EU members) to be a part of decisions relating to Palestine and Israel which run contrary to General Assembly resolutions?

Why has the EU colluded with other members of the Quartet in supporting "negotiations" between Israel and Palestine in which the Israelis, by creating a climate of extreme stress, deprivation and fear for the entire Palestinian people, have effectively applied extreme violence to exact terms favourable to themselves in "peace agreements" and palpably unfair to the Palestinian people?[50] (These terms stand in contrast with what the UN General Assembly has repeatedly decided.)

Knowing full well the oppression of the Palestinians by the Israelis, how has it been possible for EU officials and ministers[51], over several decades, to give the EU's wholehearted support to Israel, welcoming it into closer and closer integration into the EU, without there being public awareness and debate?

In the specific case of the EU's relationship with Israel and Palestine in 2006 how will the EU hold to account those who have acted against official policy by undermining democracy after the Palestinian elections?

How will the EU change its behaviour with regard to Israel and Palestine to support its declared policy of promoting peace, democracy and international law?

Has the EU the will or the strength to stand up to Israeli and American pressure and work for a just and speedy resolution to the Israeli/Palestinian conflict?

Foreign policy credibility gap - Regaining credibility

Eurocitizens can only view with dismay the EU's gross deviations from its foreign policy commitments. How can the EU restore faith in its politicians and policies, especially its defence and foreign policy? The answer must surely be genuine accountability. There must be a public body, itself accountable to elected politicians, responsible for ensuring honourable behaviour in public life. This must deal with more than relatively minor misdemeanours. It needs to be a real deterrent to gross misconduct. This public body should liaise with a prosecution service when criminal wrong-doing is suspected. As a sign that it is serious about standards in public life such a body needs to be set up and put into action immediately to deal with known outstanding breaches of international law. It needs to be visible and visibly active.

Credibility is a core issue. No one can be happy about the European Union or approve the Constitution or the *Reform Treaty* if he or she believes the EU's commitments are worthless, and nothing does more throughout the European Union to destroy respect for politicians than the silence of almost all politicians with regard to illegal military attacks and acquiescence in, or support for, violence and oppression and the flagrant undermining of democracy.

Defence and foreign policy - conclusions

Defence and foreign policy - key decisions

- Integration or independence
  Within the EU both defence and foreign policy are on a course which could lead to complete integration, the loss of each individual states' ability to make independent decisions. The *Reform Treaty* will ensure that this happens. Are the peoples of the EU truly decided that this is what they want?
- Armies for defence or to police the world?
  Do the people of the EU support increased military spending and an open commitment to take military action anywhere in the world or do they think military ambitions should be limited to defence and UN-authorised peace-keeping only?
- Achieving open and democratic decisions.
  How will the leaders of the EU open up debates to the public on key matters of foreign policy and so involve the people of Europe in these momentous

decisions? How will the people of Europe be able to vote out those who take decisions with which they disagree?

- **Integrity and accountability**
  How will the EU ensure its declared policies are followed and that leaders are held to account for their decisions?

See *Democratic deficit, Accountability, Transparency, Balance of power, Unite and be strong.* See also, in the *Institutions* chapter*: Euro Army, European Defence Agency, European External Action Service, European Union Military Committee, Political and Security Committee, European Military Staff.*

Democratic deficit

"I have never understood why public opinion about European ideas should be taken into account." Raymond Barre, French Prime Minister, 1976-1981.[52]

In state democracies the populations as a whole exercise limited but direct control on politicians by their ability in periodic elections to reject one set of politicians operating a certain bundle of policies with certain leaders and vote in an alternative party with different policies and different leaders. In effect, they elect a team with stated policies to make decisions about the way their country should be run. In addition, the politicians who are elected but who do not form the winning party form an opposition who meet with members of the ruling party in a parliament open to public attendance, even television coverage, to debate, question and analyse proposals for action and to question leading politicians on their handling of government affairs. The speeches are widely reported by the media and a word for word record is made of speeches and published on a daily basis so that the electorate may know what is going on in their name. The media coverage engenders public debate and possibly influential feedback to decision-makers. A great deal of decision-making is transparent and there are opportunities for the involvement of the electorate in the process.

Individual members of parliament must work openly and truthfully. If they are found guilty of trying to mislead parliament they are punished (except in the UK in recent years when a few senior ministers have assumed a right to be above the law in the matter of making the case for an illegal war, a scandal condoned by most members of parliament and the British electorate).

The democratic deficit within the European Union occurs:

- because those who take the decisions in the European Union have not been elected as a team with an agreed set of policies which they are committed to implementing and cannot be voted out as a team by the people of Europe. (See *Institutions, MEPs* for an account of their limited powers.)
- because the EU offers no policy alternatives and no possible changes of direction.
- because there is no identifiable government - only an exceedingly complex and largely incomprehensible method of sharing power amongst various EU bodies.
- because it is impossible for the eurocitizen to identify which elected leader carries responsibility for decisions in any area of policy.

- because there is no opposition within the decision making bodies to publicly scrutinise proposals (even though the European Parliament can nowadays discuss legislation and even block much of it).
- because there are important policy areas where the EU parliament has no power to block legislation or policy developments - areas include agriculture, fisheries, home affairs, foreign policy, justice and harmonisation of fiscal control and administration. (What can justify such restriction?)
- because some laws can be decided completely in secret by unelected bodies (The Commission, the Council when not legislating in co-operation with the European Parliament, the European Council and the European Central Bank can all create such laws. See *Euroterminology, Laws/rulings/ decisions/ acts of the European Union.*)
- because much of the power is centralised and key decision-makers are either unelected appointees (the Commissioners) or appointed from MPs elected on a domestic programme not a programme for Europe. The constitution is designed to transfer more decision-making to the EU and away from directly elected state governments.
- because of lack of transparency -
    1. Most EU institutions meet behind closed doors and it is not possible for EU citizens to know what line of argument politicians or Commissioners are pursuing.
    2. Eurocitizens cannot see the voting records of ministers, Commissioners, or members of EU committees. Verbatim records of the considerations of most decision making bodies are not available.
    3. Media coverage is minimal.
    4. Although the European Parliament is exceptional as its debates may be listened to with simultaneous translation into EU languages or even watched on the internet transcripts of debates are not properly available. *See Transparency - European Parliament.*
- because of legal immunities - see accountability above.
- because hardly any eurocitizen knows when or how decisions may be taken and by whom and according to which rules or procedures or system of voting.
- because large numbers of professional lobbyists, mainly for business interests (unrecorded, unreported and unbalanced by citizens' representatives) have obtained influential access to EU decision makers whose independence may be compromised.
- because no eurocitizen can know which party or politicians to vote for to bring about a change of direction or to repeal existing legislation.
- because the EU is run mostly by unknown politicians and unknown bureaucrats who are answerable only to their colleagues and their own consciences in their interpretation of EU treaties. These were, in any case, almost never matters approved by the populations of the EU.
- because the European Parliament, the Council and the European Council cannot be dissolved by a vote of no confidence or popular demand for an immediate election, and the Commission requires an almost prohibitively large qualified majority censure vote by the European Parliament to dissolve it.

- because eighteen of the EU's member states will not, or did not, submit the 2004 Constitution, which effectively would unite the states of Europe into a single state, to the judgement of their people.
- because the *Charter of Fundamental Rights,* according to the present text, would disallow criticism and change in important areas.
- because the EU and member states have allowed newspapers, magazines, television and radio to be controlled by a very tiny number of owners who may have enormous influence. Whether by accident or design, relatively little space is given to EU issues. Real democracy depends on healthy, diverse media, run by a wide range of diverse owners and organisations.
- because the larger the European Union becomes the less influence any individual or member state can have on its policies and government,
- because money spent by the EU is not accounted for to ordinary euro-citizens.
- because some EU policies have been fixed by treaties and therefore rule out change and alternative courses of action.
- because the EU, with its present institutions lacks the broad support of the people of Europe. This is shown by poor voter turn-out in euroelections, the resounding No votes to the Constitution in two founding member states and opinion polls on integration.

The Constitution and the *Reform Treaty* claim that the EU is founded on the values of democracy. In fact it was founded by representative democracies whose plans for the development of European co-operation excluded democratic representation. Lack of proper democratic representation is arguably the biggest flaw in the planning of the EU. The founding institution, the European Coal and Steel Community, was set up to be run by appointed officials with independent powers of decision making over its members, powers to actually overrule governments. The EU now performs many functions of a state, but it is not run as a democratic state. The restrictions of freedoms discernible in the *Charter of Fundamental Rights of the Union* and the extension of so-called "shared competences", which can only take more and more power away from sovereign governments, reduce the democratic validity and democratic control of the European Union.

In member states there are small but significant roles for citizens in making democratic systems work. Political parties usually develop policies through periods of discussion with their active members and their own politicians who have considerable face to face contact with electors and therefore know their concerns. They present the broad outlines of their policies to the public, and on the basis of these, the party's record and the reputations of individual politicians a party is elected to power. It's a crude and not entirely satisfactory system but it enjoys considerable support. In the European Union plans evolve differently and less democratically.

A typical example of eurodecision-making was the formulation of the "Lisbon Strategy".

This plan was decided upon by the European Council, meeting in private, in March 2000 in Lisbon. EU heads of state decided that Europe should have "the most dynamic knowledge-based economy in the world" by 2010. To achieve this the EU will spend billions of euros on research and development and encouraging high-tech industries. By February 2005 it had been decided to spend 3% of EU GDP on this plan. This may well be sound policy, but it would be interesting to know which lobbying organisations on behalf of which businesses lobbied these decision-makers and who received the grants. (See *Lobbying* below.) It would also be interesting to know how prominently this expensive programme featured in the election literature of those who took the decision.

It means huge hand-outs for certain institutions and industries and an increase in employment in certain areas as a result. Should not other areas of human activity have a share (or a larger share) of this funding and push for development? Renewable energy, energy conservation, low cost housing, healthcare, the arts, sport and leisure might produce more benefits for society as a whole, yet the decision was taken over the heads of euro-citizens. The democratic input was approximately nil.

Better forms of democracy are common. Within the EU system the best democracies are those run by the individual state or regional governments or local councils. These are better democracies because they derive power directly from their people, have best local knowledge, are best motivated and are directly accountable to their people.

Euroelite[53] – does it understand or care about democracy?

In Britain the Tony Blair government seems concerned to reduce democracy. County and District Council decision-making is now basically done by "cabinets" whilst the role of the majority of elected councillors has been reduced from being actively involved at the decision making stage to being simply a "rubber stamping" group. In 2006 came "the bill to abolish parliament" - The Legislative and Regulatory Reform Bill. This would have given ministers power to create laws without bringing them before parliament for approval. Faced with hostility from the Lords the government amended its proposals.

Those most responsible for the European Constitution display a similar hostility towards democracy. The man in charge of writing the Constitution, former French President, Valery Giscard d'Estaing believes that allowing the Constitution to be put to the French people to decide for or against was a misuse of democracy. In his view the Constitution was the only answer for Europe and if people reject it then they must have misunderstood it. For him democracy is not a matter of people deciding their own fate but of people having their fate decided for them by experts (like him) and then finding some means to convince the people that the policy has been democratically decided. Democracy, in his view, is a matter of finding the right means to endorse the decisions the elite has made. In an interview on 23 May 2006 he is reported as making the following remarks. "It is not France that has said No. It is 55 percent of the French people - 45 percent of the French people said Yes. . . If we had chosen to have a parliamentary vote last year the Constitution would have been easily adopted. It is the method that has provoked the rejection." He wanted the Constitution to be put before the French people again in a second referendum or simply be ratified by the French parliament. "People have the right to change their opinion. The people might consider they made a mistake."

Giscard d'Estaing also seems confused about the difference between democracy and international law. He considered that, apart from ensuring that the French people change their mind and approve the Constitution, the only problem remaining would be to find a way (suitable "modalities") of pushing it onto unwilling states. He appears to believe this can be done because of "a democratic decision." He seems not to know that when states make treaties they do this by a process of agreement between states. It is not possible for a majority of neighbouring states to take a vote and declare that the majority of them are in favour and therefore a treaty between all of them must be deemed to exist. Yet this is what Giscard d'Estaing is proposing.

"There are 16 out of 25 countries that have ratified the European Constitution. That's to say there's a qualified majority. There is an agreed text. The concern now is the modalities of adopting it."[54]

Jean-Luc Dehaene, Former Belgian Prime Minister and Vice-President of the EU Convention which wrote the Constitution, seems to see democracy as a matter of voting again and again until the decision he and other EU leaders have made gains approval. "If the answer is No, the vote will probably have to be done again, because it absolutely has to be Yes." (Quoted in the Irish Times, 2 June 2004)

The other Vice-President of the Convention that prepared the Constitution, former Italian Prime Minister, Giuliano Amato, also seems hostile to democratic accountability and the democratic process. Please see the remarks he made which are quoted in *European Union by stealth*, below. They include, "The Union is the vanguard of this changing world . . . The new entity is faceless and those who are in command can neither be pinned down nor elected."

We have the three leading players in the production of the European Constitution blatantly expressing a disregard for democratic processes. Should the euro-citizen not be suspicious and cautious about both the Constitution, the repackaged version and the European Project as a whole?

See also, *Divide and rule*, *The Commission*, *Charter of Fundamental Rights; Independence in Defence and Foreign Policy V One Simple Step to Complete Integration* in the *Defence and foreign policy* section; *Union Minister for Foreign Affairs, Law making, Lobbying, Subsidiarity, Rigidity, Voting* and *Transparency*, articles 45-52, Protocol 7 articles 9 and 11 and *Euroterminology - European government.*

Dictatorship?

The European Union is a very strange kind of political organisation. The European Union may be a democracy, but not as we know it. (No party with a political programme is elected to power.) It may be a dictatorship, but not as we know them.(Key policies have been set permanently by treaties, often years or decades earlier, a kind of dictatorship by treaty.) It is a state that is governed without a government. (Power is spread around various groups and individuals, but there is no identifiable government that can be held responsible for what happens.) Someone, we might expect, is leading it, but there is no visible leader. (Officially the leadership still changes every six months. Yet there is continuity. Who are the leaders making this happen?) There is a parliament, but members do not have direct power to bring in any change of policy.[55] In a democracy people have a say. In a democracy there are alternatives: alternative policies and alternative parties with alternative politicians and alternative leaders. But in the EU there is no alternative. Eurocitizens are voters but they cannot vote in a new party or vote for change. So what sort of political system is it? Is it a political system at all? Is it perhaps just a bureaucracy? Or is it a runaway horse which people are desperately trying to catch and bring under control? - Actually, it is something quite new: a eurocracy.

See various discussions on democracy, plus *Accountability, Data harvesting, Lobbying, Transparency, Propaganda, European Central Bank* and *Area of Freedom Security and Justice.*

Divide and rule

From the point of view of controlling countries or transforming their economies from one that is Communist or Socialist or just partly state run to one that is run entirely by private enterprise it is easiest to work with small states that are economically unviable. They will need economic support and all the help they can get. Arming secessionists in Yugoslavia assisted the break-up of Yugoslavia and made it easier to convert the resulting statelets to EU-friendly/dependent economies with greatly reduced state control of industries and services.

Quite what is behind the encouragement of regional governments as opposed to national governments within EU states is not clear. In the UK, Blair governments have been enthusiastic advocates of regional government. This has not been in response to public demand. On 4 November 2004 a referendum was held in the North East of England. In a 47.7 per cent turnout the vote was 22.1 per cent in favour and 77.9 per cent against. Four days later the Deputy Prime Minister announced that the referendum about a regional assembly for the North West had been postponed and the one planned for Yorkshire and Humberside had been cancelled.

The demand for a London Regional Assembly was stronger. In 1998 the turnout was 34.1 per cent. Votes against were 28 per cent. Votes in favour were 72 per cent – equivalent to 22 per cent of voters supporting the idea. The EU sees the UK as twelve regions including Scotland, Wales, London and Gibraltar. Some of the other regional governments may not exist but the regions are there on EU records and in EU plans. Non-democratic Regional Assemblies have been set up, for example, there is the South East Regional Assembly with 112 appointed members. Few citizens of the region know of its existence.[56]

The EU delivers substantial funds as regional aid to 254 European Union regions. The loyalty of regional leaders may therefore swing towards the new paymasters. Democracy may be melting away.

Double standards - Loss of credibility

The following ideas are explored more fully elsewhere, but it seems worth bringing together some of the matters which cause politicians and the EU to lose credibility. There appears to be a need for greater commitment to principles and policies and an awareness of how policies in one area may conflict with another. Examples:

- The EU is committed to promoting free trade throughout the world but practices protectionism iself.
- The EU is committed to free trade, yet has allowed the excessive growth of extremely large companies resulting in the inhibition of the start-up of competitors. For example, there is a concentration of media ownership into the hands of a few companies thereby weakening competition (and, incidentally, limiting the diversity of views that may be published).
- The EU is committed to aiming for full employment yet adopts policies that are likely to reduce employment within the Union by allowing work to pass to non-EU countries.
- The EU claims to be committed to democracy but in significant respects fails to operate as a democracy. It has even been known to deliberately undermine democracy.
- The EU is committed to transparency but operates for much of the time in secret.
- The EU is a highly centralised organisation, is accruing more and more powers, handing none back to member states and yet it claims to be committed to subsidiarity.
- The Constitution claims a commitment to the rule of law yet fails on an appropriate scale to bring functionaries of the EU associated with fraud before courts of law.
- The EU claims a commitment to strict adherence to international law (article 3), often criticises non-EU states for their behaviour but has a no-see policy with regard to the behaviour of EU member states when, for example, they indulged in illegal warfare. There is no system in place to hold any EU leader accountable for crimes under international law.
- The EU commits its member states to compliance with the European Convention on Human Rights and Fundamental Freedoms under article 6 of the *Maastricht Treaty*. It fails to take action when EU member states persist in flouting the rules.
- It claims concern for the environment yet supports, for example, massive road building programmes and nuclear energy and has presided over a big increase in air travel and severe damage to the marine ecosystem.
- The EU is in favour of peace and against violence, but allows its members to engage in military aggression, remains committed to military expansion and is a leading arms manufacturer.
- The EU condemns states outside the EU for their possession of nuclear weapons or aspirations to acquire them but does not criticise EU member states for the same behaviour.
- The EU condemns Iran for carrying out nuclear energy development which is legal under international law. The EU has been dedicated to the development of nuclear energy for half a century and continues this policy today.

This is not an exhaustive list but may suggest the enormous amount of reform and rethinking that is needed in the institutions and policies of the EU.

Employment

Full employment is one of the stated aims of the EU (article 3). A policy of free trade may be in conflict with this aim in certain circumstances. Free trade exposes all workers to competition from the entire world. Sales tend to go to the business offering quality at the lowest cost. Low cost comes from efficiency. Efficiency means making goods with fewest workers. Alternatively price advantage may be achieved by employing workers who are paid relatively little. Striving for competitive efficiency and putting well paid EU workers in competition with low paid third world countries is likely to mean job cuts within the EU. At the price of unhappy working conditions it is likely to be good for employment in poorer countries.

Because one of the claimed merits of the EU and its forerunners has always been that it is good for business and therefore also for employment it is interesting to look at the EU's record in unemployment which shows over twenty years of high unemployment and striking disparities between states.

EU unemployment rates

1973	2%
1983	10%
1994	11.4%
2006	8.2%

2006 figures come from the EU's Eurostat Department. This department gives a further breakdown which includes the following rates for individual countries. There are special factors which exacerbate some situations and assist others. See the statistics for corporation tax rates. Low rates may be a factor in attracting businesses to establish themselves in some countries.

Unemployment rates February 2006

Ireland	4.3%
Denmark	4.4%
Netherlands	4.4%
UK	4.9%
Poland	17%
Slovakia	15.8%
France	9.1%
Germany	8.9%

Employment is of immense importance to every society as an activity which gives the individual social meaning and purpose and because we are all dependent on employees to sustain life, maintain or advance prosperity and well-being and be the main customers for the goods and services that are are produced. Therefore, EU policies on employment or trade which either allow or encourage the drift of employment to other countries within or outside the EU or fail to care for the human and social needs of workers neglect the fundamental wellbeing of the state.

Is the EU genuinely pursuing a policy of full employment? If so, why is it not protecting jobs in the way that some US states are protecting jobs? (See *Tide turns against free trade* in the *Free trade* section.)

Working hours - working time directive

Now, at our advanced stage of technological development and civilisation, we should be living in a golden age of leisure. In fact most eurocitizens work as many hours as workers half a century ago. Something has failed in our organisation of society. The EU is trying to address this issue with its working time directive which seeks to limit working hours.

The aim is laudable but the directive is not well considered. The problem with it is that a worker whose hours of work are forcibly limited but who cannot meet his or her financial commitments in this reduced working time is forced to take a second job, possibly in the secret ("black") economy and may well end up working excessive hours which are personally damaging.

From the point of view of the state, it loses out on income tax when it forces workers into the secret economy. Businesses and state services may find the lack of "flexibility" in the labour force administratively problematic. For example, a business experiencing a sudden influx of orders may have to delay dealing with the welcome business, even if workers are willing or keen to work extra time. A hospital, faced with a major emergency may have to defy the law to cope with it. If organisations attempt to cope with the directive by taking on extra workers they are faced with additional, time-consuming and costly administrative overheads.

Some people suggest a link between levels of employment and the directive - those states that apply the directive tend to have higher levels of unemployment.

The UK has negotiated a partial opt-out from the regulation but this is under review and is expected to end in 2010. The arrangement limits the hours that a worker may be *required* to work to 48 in any one week, but a worker is currently free to work longer if he or she wishes. President Sarkozy, elected President of France in May 2007, plans to change the rules for French workers.

If housing costs could be controlled then it might be easier to reduce working hours. A solution to the competing needs and wishes of employers and employees is difficult to suggest.

See *Free Trade* especially *Tide turns against free trade* section, and *Free movement of persons* (in *Free trade and other EU trade policies*) below, *Enlargement* and *House prices* (below), *and Working time directive* in the *Nuts and Bolts* chapter.

Energy and the environment

The EU's basic environmental aims are set out in article 233 which repeats article 174 of the *Treaty Establishing the European Community* as updated by the *Treaty of Nice*.

> 1. Union policy on the environment shall contribute to the pursuit of the following objectives:
>
> (a) preserving, protecting and improving the quality of the environment;
>
> (b) protecting human health;
>
> (c) prudent and rational utilisation of natural resources;
>
> (d) promoting measures at international level to deal with regional or worldwide environmental problems.

> 2. Union policy on the environment shall aim at a high level of protection taking into account the diversity of situations in the various regions of the Union. It shall be based on the precautionary principle and on the principles that preventive action should be taken, that environmental damage should as a priority be rectified at source and that the polluter should pay.

EU energy objectives include this statement in article 256, "With regard for the need to preserve and improve the environment, Union policy on energy shall aim to . . . promote energy efficiency and energy saving and the development of new and renewable forms of energy."

These are sound objectives and the EU is very active in these areas. Unfortunately there is an area of its energy activities which has not been considered in the light of such modern objectives as protecting the environment and that is the EU's long-term commitment to nuclear energy. This may be seen in a late addition to the Constitution, Protocol 36 and hence the *Reform Treaty* where it will also be included. This amounts to a continuing commitment to the EURATOM project funded by EU tax payers. It is a support programme for the development and promotion of an energy source which carries high environmental and other risks and which is being discontinued by country after country.

Of all energy sources nuclear power poses one of the most persistent and immediately dangerous of environmental risks - radioactivity which will last for many thousands of years. After 50 years of using nuclear power there is still no safe solution to the problem of storing immensely hazardous waste for millennia. The decommissioning of Britain's small number of existing nuclear power stations is estimated to cost £70 billion and take 70 years to accomplish. Decisions taken to use nuclear energy commit future generations to work to clear up the mess over entire lifetimes and to pay for this work. Such a robbery of future generations is unprecedented in history.

Nuclear power is uniquely environmentally dangerous in the case of the storage of waste that will pose radiation threats for thousands of years, risk major accidents and be vulnerable to terrorist attack or theft of materials.

It is, incidentally, financially unviable when the expense of decommissioning obsolete reactors and storing waste are fully costed. The EU might go further to meet its environmental objectives if it ended funding for nuclear power and encouraged its phasing out. The money saved might be diverted to the development of sustainable energy and increased use of energy saving techniques. . This is the pressing need.

The EU has woken up late in its handling of energy. Failures, over decades, to conserve energy and minimise use has depleted the EU's own resources so that it is now dependent on suppliers, such as Russia, who may not be entirely dependable.

The EU's absolute commitment to free trade ignores the fact that free trade is a contributor to a phenomenal use of fossil fuels and climate change. EU agriculture policy has encouraged the use of chemical fertilisers which in their manufacture and use have adverse effects on the environment.

See also *Transport and the environment, Fisheries crisis* and *Constitution – preparing to write an acceptable constitution and rescue the EU from crisis.*

Enlargement of the EU - good for transnational corporations

The adding of more states to the 27 members and 480 million people that currently make up the European Union is one of the most controversial current issues in the EU.

Since membership is dependent on accepting a set of values including respect for human dignity, freedom, democracy, equality, the rule of law and respect for human rights (see articles 58 and 2) many see expansion as a moral mission to civilise EU neighbour countries. Corporate lobbyists would like to see the maximum enlargement, increasing the pool of cheap labour and simplifying lobbying, accounting and marketing and increasing the size of a tariff-free and quota-free market.

Some see potential problems: workers in the existing EU fear a depression of their wages and loss of employment as they compete with vast pools of unemployed or low-wage nationals of more states.

Other people fear:

- a loss of power to states whose values and political ideas they are unsure about
- an influx of people who practice a religion different from their own
- social unrest caused by social divisions and disparities of personal wealth
- an influx of foreign criminals. (Thirteen percent of Britain's jail population of 80,000 are foreigners, though by no means all from the EU. Of course, there are many British criminals operating abroad, too.)

There was a dramatic expansion of the EU in 2004 when ten new member states joined. (See *Key dates*.) Romania and Bulgaria joined on 1st January 2007. The Former Yugoslav Repbublic of Macedonia, Norway, Iceland and Switzerland are likely to join. (Norway has been accepted for membership twice and twice has turned down the offer as a result of referendums.) Morocco's application has been rejected. Negotiations are taking place with Turkey. Croatia applied to join in 2004. Albania, Bosnia-Herzegovina, Serbia, Montenegro, the Ukraine, Armenia, Azerbaijan, Georgia, Belarus, Moldova and Russia are all thought to be potential candidates. Is the open door policy wise? Should the pace be slowed down or the admission criteria changed?

Are fears of losing jobs and lower wages realistic? Here are some recent examples.

(a) The case of Irish Ferries and the Latvian sailors. Irish Ferries sail between Britain and Ireland and made a profit of 20 million euros in 2004. The chief executive is paid 687 thousand euros. In 2005 the company, facing this financial difficulty decided to register its boats in Cyprus and replace Irish sailors with Latvian sailors paying them 3.6 euros per hour, half the Irish minimum wage. The decision was taken to offer 543 existing staff dismissal or cuts of up to 50 per cent in their salaries. Three weeks of protests followed and a message of support was received from Peteris Krigers, President of LBAS, the Free Trade Union Confederation of Latvia (Latvijas Brîvo Arodbiedrîbu Savienîba). He said that the dispute was not unique and cited the Laval case in Sweden where it was proposed to bring in low wage Latvian labour. He said that as a result of the large numbers of Latvians working abroad there were difficulties filling vacancies in Latvia.[57] There was a Day of Action on 9 December 2005 around Ireland. It was joined by tens of thousands of workers. Around 40,000 demonstrated in Dublin alone. These included migrant workers who felt forced to work for desperately low wages. The dispute came to an end on 14 December with a concession to the strikers that the Latvians would be paid at least the full Irish minimum wage.[58]

(b) Net profits of the world's sixth-largest automotive group, PSA Peugeot Citroen, fell to just one billion euros in 2005 so it had become urgent for the company to save money.[59] On 18 April 2006 the closure of the Peugeot car plant at Ryton, Coventry was announced. The immediate loss of jobs was 2,300 workers, with two or three thousand other jobs lost in suppliers. Since 2003/4 Peugeot has been building new factories in Slovakia and the Czech Republic. Here wage levels are one third of those in the UK.[60] Peugeot had invested £450m in Ryton in the past 20 years and produced some 2.5 million cars at the plant.[61]

(c) New jobs may well be created to replace the old. They have experience of that in Coventry where the old Standard Motor works closed many years ago to be replaced with a business park. This now employs more workers than the old car manufacturer. A significant difference is that wage levels are approximately half those of present day local car factory workers.

(d) To be on the receiving end of new investment is a pleasant thing for states and workers. Even before it joined the EU this was happening in Hungary. But free trade and transnational corporations know no loyalty. As minimum wage rates rose in Hungary, so factories were moved to Romania, Baltic states and China.[62]

(e) Official figures suggest that from May 2004 to August 2006 between 400,000 and 600,000 eastern Europeans (members of the ten accession states of 2004) came to Britain. Non official sources suggest a much higher figure. The Guardian suggests that the movement of people from Poland is the biggest wave of migration into Britain for three centuries and quotes a "respected" Polish news magazine which estimated that a million Poles had moved to Britain in two years.[63] Several problems have arisen:

- There is anecdotal evidence that wage rates in, for example, the catering and building trades have dropped significantly – good for profit but bad for British workers and the Inland Revenue.
- Eastern European countries are experiencing a brain drain. For example, between May 2004, when Poland joined the EU, and July 2006 5000 Polish doctors left Poland for better paid jobs in the three EU countries which opened their borders - Sweden, Ireland and the UK. Fourteen per cent of Polish anaesthetists have applied for a certificate to leave Poland. The Polish health service is faced with serious problems.[63] Polish engineering firms, farmers and building trades are complaining of serious shortages of skilled workers.
- Based on anecdotal evidence, the potential exists for the new workers, here for "just two years", living in crowded temporary accommodation, to be able to afford to live on lower wages to take jobs from British workers who are living in more humanly acceptable accommodation.
- The flight of married Eastern European workers from their families to find work in the UK may have increased personal stress and family break-down.

- The problems are all avoidable, but at a price. Whatever view is taken there will be winners and losers. Where should the balance of loyalty lie with UK politicians - to UK workers, to UK business owners or to transnational corporations? Sometimes they have to choose between Britain and Europe.

As far as the ten accession states are concerned, many EU countries have held back from implementing the long-standing EU policy of free movement of persons within EU borders. EU leaders at the June summit in 2006 were talking of slowing the pace of enlargement. The policy of open borders, combined with increasing expansion, risks increasing eurocitizens' disaffection with the EU.

See *House prices*, and *Free movement of persons* in the section *Free trade and other EU trade policies.*

Equality

The EU is committed to equality in two areas: equality of member states and equality of citizens. Equality is stated as a founding value in article 2. Article 5 states, "The Union shall respect the equality of member states."

There is a problem with each of these claims. Member states are not actually treated equally within the European Union. In parliament, and where qualified majority voting operates in Council and European Council meetings, greater weight is given to countries with larger populations. Contributions to revenues are not equal, and receipts from EU funds by member states are not equal.

At the personal level EU citizens would expect to be equal before the law. As mentioned elsewhere, this is not the case. "Officials and other servants of the Union shall . . . be immune from legal proceedings in respect of acts performed by them in their official capacity, including their words spoken or written. They shall continue to enjoy this immunity after they have ceased to hold office." (Protocol 7, article 11.) Some EU leaders appear to be immune to prosecution under international law. See *Defence and foreign policy.*

The Euro

The Constitution committed member states to adopt the euro as its currency. (Articles 8 and 177.) The *Reform Treaty* will repeat this requirement. This is not simply a matter of coins and bank notes to be used in the EU but who controls monetary policy in every EU state.

Britain has been allowed an indefinite opt-out with the consequent curtailment of a few of its voting rights which concern the European Central Bank. (Protocol 13.) But should Britain join and become a full member of the European Union?

Adoption of the euro would give British traders dealing with EU countries, and travellers in the EU, the convenience of knowing precise values and costs and of avoiding currency conversion costs and losses. It might therefore help to increase trade and travel.

A less desirable effect is that adoption of the euro would lock Britain into an economic system over which it would have no control and little influence. It would commit Britain to a European Union single monetary policy and exchange rate policy and "entail compliance with the following guiding principles: stable prices, sound public finances and monetary conditions and a stable balance of payments." Britain's economic policy would be directed by the European Central Bank in Frankfurt.

There would be likely to be particular problems with the setting of interest rates which are controlled by the European Central Bank. The issue is especially sensitive for Britain where interest changes can have dramatic effects on mortgage holders who form a proportion of the population very much larger than in other EU states.

As Britain's economy appears to be performing better than that of the eurozone countries there does not seem to be a compelling case for joining the euro.

"It (the introduction of the euro) is not economic at all. It is a completely political step - The historical significance of the euro is to construct a bipolar economy in the world. The two poles are the dollar and the euro. This is the political meaning of the single European currency. It is a step beyond which there will be others. The euro is just an antipasto." - Commission President, Romano Prodi.[64]

"European monetary union has to be complemented by a political union - that was always the presumption of Europeans including those who made active politics before us. - What we need to Europeanise is everything to do with economic and financial policy. In this area we need much more, let's call it co-ordination and co-operation to suit British feelings, than we had before. That hangs together with the success of the euro." - German Chancellor Gerhard Schröder.[65]

European Arrest Warrants

European Arrest Warrants were initiated by ministers attending the Laeken European Council in December 2001 and are not mentioned in the Constitution. They are a replacement for previous extradition procedures. The warrants have to contain the following information: issuing judicial authority, statement of accusation and intention to prosecute, particulars of the person's identity, details of any other warrants issued, details of the alleged offences including time, place and the laws broken, possible sentence. An individual seized in one European country for deportation to another will be told his alleged crime but no evidence is required before an accused is sent to another country for trial.

To be removed possibly 1,000 miles or so to face charges presents huge problems for a defendant who may, after all, be mistakenly identified or innocent. It provides, through interstate co-operation in suppression or malpractice, an easy way of removing critics or other troublemakers if totalitarianism should develop in Europe.

The rights of the accused in such cases weighed against the powers of the state are substantially unbalanced. To reduce the risk of wrongful arrest ought there not to be procedures to minimise the risk? Ought there to be a compensation scheme in place for the occasions when injustice occurs through the use of this procedure?

See *Europol, Criminal Justice, Data Harvesting* and *Area of Freedom, Security and Justice.*

European Central Bank

"The primary objective of the European System of Central Banks shall be to maintain price stability." (Article 185.) This is an objective which few would challenge, but it is very narrow and it ought to be possible for there to be room for further thinking on this topic. What if someone should think it a good idea to make full employment an objective too?

If we take the words of the *Charter of Fundamental Rights* at face value the European Central Bank may not be urged to modify its policy which has been set by the terms of a treaty (*Treaty establishing the European Economic Community*, article 105). The bank and the central banks of member states have been placed above criticism from any person or body within the EU (article 188 - which repeats article 108 of the *Treaty Establishing the European Community*). No body, no MP or MEP may "seek to influence the members of the decision-making bodies of the European Central Bank or of the national central banks in the performance of their tasks" - even though their judgements may devastate economies.

The assumption that the Central Bank's policies are not only the best for today but for all time is surprising. It ought to be possible for MEPs and others to argue for changes of policy. Perhaps the rules governing the Bank need writing with more care. The grip of the treaty in directing policy for all time is unfortunate.

The comments of Joseph Stiglitz, former chief economist and senior vice president of the World Bank, may be worth considering.

"There is a widespread feeling that Europe's independent Central Bank exacerbated Europe's economic slowdown in 2001... The problems partly arose because the European Central Bank has a mandate to focus on inflation, a policy which the IMF has advocated around the world but one that can stifle growth or exacerbate an economic downturn. . . America's central bank (the US Federal Reserve Bank) has a mandate to focus not just on inflation, but also on employment and growth."[66]

How independent is the European Central Bank in reality and how much scope should it have for modifying policy? Of course, the intention of the Charter's wording may be to prohibit the use of financial inducements or personal attacks or threats or any other underhand or illegal form of persuasion, or to prohibit attempts to influence decision-makers to act in a way that does not keep in mind the general interest of the EU. If this is the case then the wording should be more precise and make the purpose clear.

See *Rights removed by the Constitution* in *Charter of Fundamental Rights, and Dictatorship.*

European Court of Justice

The Constitution proposes bringing criminal law relating to offences which may be carried out across borders under EU control (Articles 270 and 271). The ideas are carried forward in the *Reform Treaty*. In Britain a former chairman of the Bar, Lord Brennan QC, has expressed concern about this.

Three broad questions arise.

1. What is the jurisdiction of the ECJ?
2. Will there be effective judicial review over EU laws and institutions?

3. And will citizens have adequate access to challenge Community measures substantially affecting them?

See article 257 on "the approximation of criminal laws." The committee which will work on the approximation or harmonisation of EU criminal laws in order to standardise definitions of offences, penalties and rights of individuals effectively takes over from state legislatures in tuning state laws to EU standards. Through framework laws setting "minimum rules concerning the definition of criminal offences and sanctions in the areas of particularly serious crime" state governments may be required to modify their existing laws. This might encourage a simplistic approach to dealing with crime. Some states may have a purely punitive approach to dealing with crime whilst others may take an approach designed to rehabilitate criminals into society.

There may be great advantage in experts concerned with cross-border crime meeting to discuss effective approaches and make recommendations to EU and other governments, but is it wise to put the changing of legislation in the hands of an appointed EU committee?

The European Court of Justice makes the final judgement in disputes between member states and the Union. It interprets cases in the light of the treaties. As mentioned elsewhere, as these call for ever closer union, disputes about subsidiarity seem to be prejudged in favour of Union decision-making over state decision making.

At the EU summit in June 2007 the UK secured an opt-out in the field of Justice and Home Affairs.

See *Subsidiarity*, and *European Union by stealth* below.

European Union by stealth - Pickpocketing democracy and sovereignty

The 2004 Constitution and its replacement open the way to the complete unification of EU member states. This development is the continuation of the plan and methods devised by Jean Monnet in the 1950s which is being followed by EU leaders today. The idea was always to progress towards the end goal by small moves which in themselves arouse no opposition until at some point the grand design is completed. That is still the way the European Union is being developed. Proceeding by democratic decision-making is not part of the plan, in fact the planned final development of the European Union reduces democratic involvement and accountability.

One of the architects of the Constitution was former Italian Prime Minister Giuliano Amato, who was a Vice-President of the EU Convention which wrote it. In an interview with Barbara Spinelli, published in *La Stampa*, 13 July 2000, he explained how a new European state had been created and should be developed without arousing the knowledge or suspicions of the people and even the politicians of Europe.

> "One must act 'as if' in Europe: as if one wanted only very few things, in order to obtain a great deal, as if nations were to remain sovereign, in order to convince them to surrender their sovereignty. The Commission in Brussels, for example, must act as if it were a technical organism, in order to operate like a government ... and so on, camouflaging and toning down. The sovereignty lost at national level does not pass to any new subject. It is

entrusted to a faceless entity: NATO, the UN and eventually the EU. The Union is the vanguard of this changing world: it indicates a future of princes without sovereignty. The new entity is faceless and those who are in command can neither be pinned down nor elected . . . That is the way Europe was made too: by creating communitarian organisms without giving the organisms presided over by national governments the impression that they were being subjected to a higher power. That is how the Court of Justice as a supra-national organ was born. It was a sort of unseen atom bomb, which Schuman and Monnet slipped into the negotiations on the Coal and Steel Community. That was what the CSC itself was: a random mixture of national egotisms which became communitarian. I don't think it is a good idea to replace this slow and effective method - which keeps national states free from anxiety while they are being stripped of power - with great institutional leaps. Therefore I prefer to go slowly, to crumble pieces of sovereignty up little by little, avoiding brusque transitions from national to federal power. That is the way I think we will have to build Europe's common policies."

Is it acceptable to shift power from member states to the EU by subterfuge?

Europol, the EU's expanding police force

Europol, based in the Hague, is the European law enforcement organisation set up to work across the EU to handle information on criminals and criminal activities, including terrorism, and assist the police forces of EU member states (article 276, also *Treaty on European Union*, article 30). The intention is that Europol would not take action that could be taken by national or regional police forces, but it is not clear who will ensure that Europol sticks to its limited role or how it will be controlled on a day-to-day basis. Europol will have access to data on all EU citizens.

It appears that there is an intention to greatly increase the range of its tasks, power and influence as article 276 states, "European laws shall determine Europol's structure, operation, field of action and tasks." This seems to open the way for Europol to take over tasks from existing national or regional police forces. Directly elected national governments and local authorities surely need direct powers to control police activities within their countries. The *Reform Treaty* will not include the UK in these arrangements.

Police force accountability

Europol is funded by direct payments from member states. Its 2005 budget was €63,400,000, (approximately £44,000,000). Europol is accountable to the European Parliament and national parliaments (article 276). What can the European Parliament and national parliaments actually do to deal with the behaviour of Europol? And what does this accountability amount to in practice in the light of Protocol 7, article 11, which repeats earlier treaty arrangements.

> "Servants of the Union shall, subject to the provisions of the Constitution relating, on the one hand, to the rules on the liability of officials and other servants towards the Union and, on the other hand to the jurisdiction of the Court of Justice of the European Union in disputes between the Union and its officials and other servants, be immune from legal proceedings in

> respect of acts performed by them in their official capacity, including their words spoken or written. They shall continue to enjoy this immunity after they have ceased to hold office."

This Protocol is planned to be part of EU treaties by 2008. A virtually uncontrolled EU police force would seem to be potentially dangerous and anti-democratic.

See *Major issues - Habeas corpus, Data harvesting* and *Area of Freedom, Security and Justice* and articles 275 and 276.

Federalism

Europe is already a federal state. Do eurocitizens wish the European Union to go even further, achieving ever closer integration to become unified into one country with state parliaments demoted to the handling of minor matters? Or do they wish it to be a free association of independent sovereign states?

See *Integration - the number one question* in this chapter, and *Federalism* in the *Euroterminology* chapter.

Finances of the EU - unsolved problems of European Union financial control - Fraud

The existence of the Court of Auditors might suggest that excellent financial control will be exercised over the EU's vast spending of taxpayers' money. The *Treaty Establishing the European Economic Community* articles 246 and 247 reassuringly tells us that the Court of Auditors "shall examine the accounts of all the Union revenue and expenditure, and shall ensure good financial management."

There is an unfortunate discrepancy between the good intentions expressed in the Treaty and reality. For eleven years, 1995 to 2005, the Court of Auditors has been unable to offer assurances that EU budget was effectively, legally and properly implemented.

As mentioned in the section on the Commission, in 1999 the astonishing scandal of fraud, corruption and mismanagement at the highest level came to light. The Commission avoided ignominious mass dismissal by the European Parliament by an almost equally ignominious mass resignation.

In 2004 the auditor's reports said, "The Court's audit work has repeatedly shown that many irregularities occur." It indicated that 95% of the EU budget presented serious accounting problems.

In September 2004 the Court of Auditors' own report said that since 1971 £2.2 billion had been overpaid to Europe's farmers under the Common Agriculture Policy. This sum may be an underestimate because the extent of the loss was discovered as a result of spot checks not a total examination of the system. The court had been successful in reclaiming only 17 per cent of this sum. That meant a possible loss of £1.8 billion to European tax payers.

The following year the European Court of Auditors published its Annual Report on the implementation of the 2004 EU general budget (15 November 2005). Presenting the report the Court's President, Mr Weber, said at the plenary session of the European Parliament:

> The Court found that the vast majority of the payments' budget was again materially affected by errors of legality and regularity in the underlying transactions. . .
>
> In the case of Common Agricultural Policy expenditure (€43.6 billion euro) . . . the Court concluded that, viewed as a whole, the CAP expenditure was still materially affected by errors. . . For structural measures (€34.2 billion), the Court again found weaknesses in the Member States' management and control systems. . . For both the current (2000-2006) and previous (1994-1999) programming periods, a high incidence of errors of legality and regularity was detected in the Member States' declarations leading to payments by the Commission.

It was not until January 2001 that the EU first employed a qualified accountant as Chief Accountant. She was Marta Andreason who was horrified that there was not a system to record transactions properly. After she raised her concerns she was fired in May 2002.

This is an extract from her statements at an open meeting for MEPs and journalists in Strasbourg held on 13 November 2002:

> In summary my observations were as follows:
>
> The Commission does not have an accounting system that supports the accounts as presented each year. The balance sheet is built out of reports received from DGs [Director Generals] on spreadsheets.
>
> The Commission doesn´t have a secure, coherent and exhaustive system on which financial transactions are processed. Moreover the system does not allow traceability.
>
> There is a lack of compliance with basic accounting principles such as double-entry book keeping. In this sense the Commission has also breached its own existing Financial Regulation. Double-entry accounting is the most basic of systems, in use since the 13th century, which allows the control for each transaction of where the money is coming from and where it is going.
>
> The Commission does not have Official Accounting Books.
>
> There has not been a Treasury audit for the last ten years, whilst the same Treasurer has been in the post for more than twelve years.
>
> The Commission is unable to establish cash-flow statements, a basic element for the management of the € 98 billion funds entrusted to it.
>
> There are no basic internal controls established and respected within the Commission.
>
> I was asked to "certify" the accounts to be sent to the different Directorates for the purpose of establishing their Annual Declaration, in the knowledge - as repeatedly asserted by the Commission - that the accounting system on which the reports were based was not reliable. The Commission decided on a decentralized model to make each Director General fully accountable for the management of their budget. However the Commission has failed to provide them with the essential tool to manage the budget and give assurance on the quality of controls and reliability of the accounts. . .
>
> My communication to my hierarchy about the risks involved and proposals for urgent solution were disregarded. I then addressed my concerns to the President of the Commission, Mr. Prodi and the two vice-Presidents, Mr. Kinnock and Ms. De Palacio, on May 7th, 2002.

> I received no response from any of them, or any request for contact. I therefore wrote to the European Court of Auditors to inform them about the issues above, and ask them for their support to change.
>
> However, without having any contact with me to understand the issues I was raising, Mr Kinnock led the Commission to decide on May 22nd, about the withdrawal of my responsibility as Accounting Officer.

Financial mismanagement is a critical problem which must be resolved. A financially doubtful or fraudulent European Project cannot be worthy of the support of European citizens.

See *Transparency* (below) and *OLAF* in the *Institutions* chapter.

Fisheries Crisis

The Constitution gives few clues as to what the EU is trying to do here. Fisheries are mentioned in only two articles in the Constitution under the general heading *Agriculture and Fisheries*: articles 225 and 231. They simply assert that the EU will have a fisheries policy and will fix prices, share out the fishing and limit the catches.

The EU fisheries policy operates outside democracy. Remote bureaucrats control the fleets and oceans. EU political parties are not involved. They can offer no choices for the electorate. The bureaucrats cannot be voted out. Where are the equitable principles for the management of Europe's fishing industries? Where are the EU's published plans for the maintenance of the fish stocks and sustaining the viability of the marine ecosystem? National market organisations are replaced by common EU organisations with regulatory powers. Nothing the EU has done suggests that producers or their customers will be better served by EU involvement.

Yet fisheries policy in the EU is constantly in the news. Within the EU fish are a major food resource and the fishing industry provides the livelihood for about half a million EU workers, but what makes the topic such hot news is that European Union failures have brought upon us a major ecological crisis in the territorial waters of the EU and the developing nations of Africa with whom the EU has concluded agreements. Time and again the EU has made bad decisions in its attempts to control EU fisheries and safeguard marine ecology. Europeans need to decide whether centralised control of fisheries and marine ecology is safe in the hands of the centralised eurocracy in Brussels, and if not, what better arrangements might be made.

Technological "advances" in man's ability to scoop up millions of tons of fish from the seas and the rapid loss of fish stocks has alarmed millions of people across Europe who are concerned about the sustainable use of the earth's resources and fear the destruction of major parts of the marine ecosystem.

Conservationists' fears of wiping out fish stocks are justified. In the early 1990s scientists warned of the danger of destroying the entire cod fisheries in the great cod fishing area, the Grand Banks, off Newfoundland. Fishermen's experience and claims were that there were plenty of fish. Suddenly the cod disappeared and have not returned. Scientists have warned that the North Sea is in a perilous ecological state. EU management has failed to safeguard it.

Fisheries – background

After China and Peru the EU is the largest fish producer in the world, yet imports of fish far exceed exports. (1.6 million tonnes to 4.3 million tonnes in 1995.) Russia and Norway are major suppliers. Within the EU the average citizen is said to to consume 25 kilograms of fish per year.[67] The EU is the world's largest market for processed fish products and farmed fish such as sea bass, sea bream, salmon, trout and shellfish. EU fishing employs 260,000 fishermen plus a similar number in processing, marketing etc. Total value runs at approximately £14 billion per year.[121]

Britain exports 50 per cent of its catch to other EU countries - especially hake and sole to France and Spain. At the same time Britain imports approximately 75 per cent of the fish it consumes.

The EU's role in increasing problems in European waters

It was an early ambition of the founders of the EU to take charge of this primary food resource. It is referred to in article 32 of the *Treaty of Rome*, 1957. So contentious was the subject that it took a further 25 years of wrangling before the first common fisheries policy could be agreed.

In the meantime there were major developments. A policy was drawn up in 1970 which declared that member states should have free access to the territorial waters of other member states. Of the six members at the time France had the most to lose, but planners perhaps had in mind the four new applicant states: Denmark, Ireland, Norway and Britain - three of whom might vastly extend the fishing grounds of the original members. In the end, the Norwegian people thought what they would lose by joining the EU and opening up their fishing grounds would be too much so they rejected membership. The other applicants achieved a concession of an extension of their exclusive coastal fishing rights from six miles from shore to 12 miles (9.6 kilometres to 19.3 kilometres).

In 1975 Iceland declared that its territorial waters extended to 200 miles from its coastline in what was termed "an exclusive economic zone". Canada and Norway soon made similar declarations. These new limits received international endorsement in the Convention on the Law of the Sea, 1982. Two important effects have followed. First, fishermen who had traditionally fished in these waters were forced to concentrate their fishing in more restricted areas. Second, the door was opened for all states to declare similar extensions to their marine territories. This effectively and dramatically increased the loss of fishing opportunities experienced by member states with extensive coastlines as what might have been exclusively their own had, under EU rules, to be shared with other member states. Over-fishing became more likely.

In 1976 the British government passed an act extending its territorial waters out to a 200 mile limit. However, Community law overrules national laws and the European Court declared the British move illegal.

The next year the EU declared an EU 200 mile limit extending from the entire EU coastline - a fishing area open to all EU states.

Over these years awareness was growing that the seas supply of fish might one day be used up.

The first EU Common Fisheries Policy

In 1983 the EU at last agreed a common fisheries policy. It was to be revised at ten-year intervals. The basic elements were:

1. **Fishing zones.** The coastal waters belonging to the EU, extending to a 200 mile limit, were opened to all member states to fish throughout, except for a 12 mile limit from the coastline of member states which was reserved to these states.

2. **Conservation.** An attempt was made to conserve fish stocks by limiting the sizes of catches that were permitted to be landed - total allowable catches (TACs). The amounts were to be agreed by the Fisheries Council of Ministers before Christmas each year. There would be restrictions on fishing in certain areas, minimum mesh sizes for nets to allow young fish to escape, mature and breed, and in some cases minimum sizes of fish that might be landed. There were too many fishermen and too many boats. In an attempt to reduce fleets the EU introduced a compensation scheme for companies that scrapped boats, and funding for communities hit by the loss of jobs. Many fleets have been ordered to fish for no more than 15 days per month.

3. **Monitoring Systems** for aerial surveillance checks on fish landed and compulsory record-keeping were instituted.

4. **Marketing.** The EU set standards regarding packaging, quality, weight etc to apply across the EU. There were price guarantees funded by EU taxpayers and import duties levied on imported fish (lifted in times of scarcity).

5. **Extension of EU fishing territory.** Deals were done with many countries including developing nations in Africa on both the Atlantic and Indian Ocean seaboards to allow EU fishermen to fish their waters in exchange for financial and technical assistance. Reciprocal fishing deals were done with Norway, Canada, the USA and others. Currently about 20 per cent of EU fish is caught in these waters.

Increasing EU fleets, increasing problems

In 1986 two nations with very large fishing fleets joined the EU - Spain and Portugal. Overnight this doubled the number of fishermen in the EU and more than doubled the tonnage of the EU's fishing fleet. Spain and Portugal allowed free access to some of their fishing grounds in return for access to some EU areas. In 1995 full access was allowed for all.

There have been numerous complaints about EU fishermen, especially the Spanish, some of whom have been accused of not abiding by EU fishing rules. There have been many arrests and fines. Sometimes fines applied to the largest ships have been too small to be an effective deterrent to breaking the rules. But an important aspect of the problem has been inconsistency in the application of rules. *The Sunday Telegraph* of 23 March 2003 reported an unexpected glut of cod in waters off Cornwall that had resulted in Cornish fishing boats accidentally catching exceptional quantities of cod which EU regulations forbade them to land. They dumped hundreds of tons of dead or dying fish back into the sea because quotas were rigidly enforced by British officials. In fact twelve fishing boats had had their licenses suspended. The Cornish fishermen complained that French boats were fishing in the same waters, catching similar quantities of cod, but able to take them back to French ports and sell the fish openly because French enforcement was lax.

Quota hopping (see *Euroterminology*) has been another source of great bitterness in Britain. It was justified by the EU under the *Treaty of Rome*, article 32, which outlaws "discrimination on grounds of nationality." However, quotas are allocated by the Council of Ministers to *nations* (or more strictly speaking *states*). To allow a basic food resource of one nation to be transferred to another nation simply on the basis of the sale of vessels by individual owners shows the inadequacy of free trade deregulation. It could be argued that nations have fundamental rights to attempt to assure adequate food supplies for their citizens. EU policy here transferred food and jobs from one state to another merely by adherence to a doctrinaire technicality.

There is no doubt that fishermen everywhere are acutely aware of the growing crisis of dwindling fish stocks. The *New York Times* of 26 July 2003 quoted at length the remarks of a 53-year-old fisherman, Mr Christensen, Chairman of the Danish Society for a Living Sea. He claims the EU fishing fleet is far too large and is so partly because of grants of millions of pounds from the EU. He and his society are angry about trawlers which trawl the sea bed doing untold damage to the sea floor. They believe that such methods should be banned. He observes that fishing stocks are at an all-time low. In 1985, the Baltic yielded 800,000 tons of cod. In 2000, the catch was less than one-tenth of this. He says "There is a worldwide fishing crisis. New studies show that 90 percent of large predatory fish have disappeared in the past 50 years because of industrial-scale vessels that are chasing fish via satellites." They claim that ordinary, small-scale fishermen are not listened to by EU bureaucrats. The EU has failed to join with non-EU states in taking concerted action to solve the problem.

The EU seems incapable of even-handed administration of policies and all too ready to cave in to the demands of politicians who have no regard for the need for conservation. This complaint appeared in the *Stornaway Gazette* of 27 December 2002, just as the latest reforms were announced. It is quite typical of the anger expressed by fishing communities around Britain. "The Commission shows bias towards other member states: the French are allowed to fish for 25 days per month with no limitation on days when fishing cod or other species west of the Hebrides; hake conservation is now off the agenda to pacify the Spaniards; the ban on days at sea in the Irish box is cancelled to appease the Irish; the threatened 40 per cent reduction for plaice has been reduced to 10 per cent to satisfy the Dutch; and the Danes can continue industrial fishing - for fish meal - despite taking thousands of tons of cod, haddock and whiting as a bycatch (8lb of wild fish are required to produce 1lb.of farmed salmon)." It is possible that fishing communities in other member states may have a list of complaints about British fishermen.

Developments

In December 2002 reforms of the Common Fisheries Policy took place. It was agreed that a long-term approach to conservation was needed and scientific advice must be followed. Multi-annual plans for fish stock recovery would be adopted. Complaints about centralised decision-making would be answered by the setting up of regional advisory councils representing primarily fishermen and environmental groups. The granting of subsidies for the building of new vessels was ended. How genuine, realistic, enforceable, fair, acceptable and effective the latest policies may be remains to be seen.

Failures of a Common Fisheries Policy

The central task of a European fisheries policy is the safeguarding of sustainable fish stocks and the marine ecosystem. On 6th October, 2003 the BBC quoted a Royal Society's report claiming that "Europe's fish stocks are on the brink of collapse." Reports of serious fish stock decline are widespread. What mistakes have the EU planners made?

1. One of the greatest problems has been that whilst everyone in the fishing industry is aware of the need to conserve fish stocks and limit fishing they feel there is no point in personally exercising restraint if fishing vessels from other nations cannot be relied upon to show the same restraint. Why should one nation leave fish alone if others are going to sail in and take all they want? The first mistake of the Common Fisheries Policy was to remove national control of territorial waters opening them up to all EU fleets. At the outset, no-one could have foreseen how important this decision would prove to be, but it has become ever clearer as territorial limits have been extended and the need for conservation has become more desperate. Fishermen who stand to gain from conservation will be best motivated to operate proper conservation practices.

2. Another problem has been that too often fishermen have been able to escape detection when fishing illegally. Penalties for illegal fishing by the largest ships have been too small to deter.

3. Efforts to control quantities and kinds of fish caught have been largely impractical.

Impractical conservation efforts

(a) Limiting catches with quotas causes great bitterness between the fleets of competing nations. There is no truly fair system of sharing out the spoils of the sea. Exceeding quotas has been too easy for irresponsible or untrustworthy fishermen. With so many ports and so many landings of fish it has proved impossible to fully check on all the fish landed throughout the EU and some countries have taken little interest in enforcing quotas.

(b) Quotas for different species of fish which may be landed - whilst having a laudable aim - have proved disastrous. They have sometimes been allocated with clear injustice. Some states have been allowed to catch species which other states were not allowed to catch. This has not fostered respect for the quotas. Nets are largely unable to discriminate between species and it is inevitable that large numbers of non-target fish will be caught. As it is not permissible to land banned species, fishermen have been forced to throw back into the sea thousands of tons of fish, dead or dying - a total waste and a cause of pollution. According to *The Times* of 16 August 2003 "Fishermen claim that the build-up of dumped fish on the seabed is now so bad that they are being caught up in their nets." Not only have fish from the endangered species not been saved by this action, but the fish destroyed were not used to satisfy the demand for fish. This has resulted in the need for fishing actually to be increased to satisfy this demand when it might have been decreased by supplying fish that otherwise was totally lost.

(c) Scientific advice on suitable quotas is often not taken by the Fisheries Council of Ministers. Each of them is acutely conscious of the desperate demands of their fishermen to gain the largest possible share of the available overall quota for fish. For political reasons the quotas are set at levels which are far too high to meet the needs of conservation.

(d) Bycatches include more than fish. Turtles are often caught in large numbers and lost and many seabirds, including Albatross, too. Ecologically unsound fishing methods have been allowed to continue.

(e) Conservation measures adopted by EU vessels may not be as strict in the fishing areas of developing countries as they are in EU waters and fishing in these countries by local fishermen has been harmed by the fishing activities of EU vessels. Some conservationists and local fishing communities have accused the EU of plundering the fishing areas of developing nations.

(f) The policy of compensation for the destruction of fishing boats was logical but lacked common sense. Skippers compensated for destroying their fishing vessels were able to spend the money buying new ones. There are stories that some were able to claim for vessels sunk long ago. Simultaneous with the policy of reducing fishing fleets the EU gave millions of pound in grants to Spanish and Italian fishermen to build new boats with increased ability to catch fish.

(g) The practice of quota-hopping has embittered relationships between nations and their fishermen. The allocation each year of quotas of fish that each nation may catch was bound to be a contentious issue, but matters have been made a great deal worse by the system of quota-hopping. This allows fishermen of one nation to buy boats from another nation, fly the second nation's flag and acquire a proportion of that nation's fishing rights. The European Court has backed this practice. The situation has been made slightly more palatable by a requirement to land a proportion of catches at ports belonging to the original owners of fishing quotas.

(h) Sea-bed damage is being caused by nets dragged along the seabed. A Royal Commission report at of 2004 warned of "irreversible damage."

Micromanagement alienates the fishing community

Confidence in the EU as an authority capable of managing the EU's marine wealth and ecosystem is harmed by its ineptitude. Over-regulation created as a result of remote, centralised planning, out-of-touch with reality, has been astonishing in its lack of common sense and its ability to antagonise the fishing communities. For example, Directive 92/29 EEC of 31 March 1992 required even the smallest fishing boat of 12 feet in length to carry an emergency medical kit containing 620 items. These included insulin which is hardly a drug for a non-medical specialist to administer and urine testing papers for an emergency that is hard to imagine. A range of medical equipment has to be carried and medicines must include the following: cardio-circulatory analeptics, sympathomimetics, anti-angina preparations, diuretics, anti-haemorrhagics including uterotonics if there are women on board, medicines for gastric and duodenal disorders, anti-acid mucous dressings, anti-emetics, anti-diarrhoeals, intestinal antiseptics, haemorrhoid preparations, analgesics and anti-spasmodics, anti-pyretics and anti-inflammatory preparations, powerful analgesics, spasmolytics, anxiolytics, neuroleptics, anti-allergics and anti-anaphylactics, H1 anti-histaminics, injectable glucocorticoids, bronchiospasm preparations, anti-tussives, antibiotics (at least two families), anti-bacterial sulphamide, anti-parasitics, intestinal anti-infectives, anti-tetanus vaccines and immunoglobulins, plus compounds promoting rehydration, caloric intake and plasma expansion. Anything can happen at sea and it is best to be prepared. - Such kits can cost as much as £1800.

Another example is requirements regarding ladders on vessels. Commission Regulation (EEC) No 1382/87 of 20 May 1987on boarding ladders prescribes

1. that steps on ladders must be not less than 480mm long,
2. 115mm wide
3. and 23mm in thickness
4. equally spaced not less than 300mm or more than 380mm apart
5. and must be hardwood or other material of equivalent properties.
6. The side-ropes of the ladder must consist of two uncovered manila or equivalent ropes not less than 60mm in circumference.

In June 2002 Magnie Stewart, the owner of a Shetland fishing boat, *Defiant*, was accused of contravening this regulation because the Defiant's boarding ladder had synthetic ropes and had plastic rungs. The owner had noticed that manilla ropes became dangerous because they rotted and that wooden rungs could become very slippery. He had replaced the prescribed ladder with something he considered improved safety. As a result he was threatened with a £5,000 fine. Presumably the case against him was dropped as he appears to have complied with the regulation, but do central authorities have to direct the fishing industry down to specifying what constitutes a safe thickness of the steps of a ladder (23mm)? Surely international regulation should confine itself to bigger issues and assume a degree of intelligence, knowledge and responsibility exists in boat designers and fishermen. The EU is a state claiming to be committed to having decisions taken at the lowest possible level. Therefore this sort of micro-management by the EU central authority is as shocking as it is inappropriate.

Steps towards sustainable fishing

The depletion of fish stocks is a huge worldwide problem which must urgently be tackled. The EU alone cannot solve the problem. Fish are not confined to the waters of one nation. Over-fishing in one area can reduce fish in another area as fish migrate. International agreement is needed. Conferences of fishermen, addressed by leading conservationists, need to be organised at local, regional, national and international level. Fishermen faced with the collapse of their industry may come up with solutions or at least be more responsive to the conservation demands of others. Thousands of fishermen are already meeting but their voices seem not to be heard. There are international conferences on the topic, for example under UN auspices, sadly arriving at no effective conclusions.

As the world must catch less fish this must mean less or smaller fishing vessels and fewer fishermen. Fishing communities are going to need financial support to redirect their labour. However, if less fish are landed value will, to some extent, rise and potentially compensate fishermen.

Aquaculture, or fish farming, which already provides EU states with 20 per cent of their fish might be increased, but this system is not operating with complete success. Whereas marine fish were once considered natural and free from unnatural foods and chemicals this is now less true of farmed fish. Doubts have been cast on the quality of some fish food used and when disease has struck fish and have been treated with antibiotics which may have effects on human consumers, increasing their resistance to the drugs.

International agreement is needed to outlaw the most wasteful anti-conservation fishing practices, vessels and equipment. Such agreements probably need to be far more encompassing than the mere twenty-seven countries of the EU.

Nations might be better able to take effective control of their own fishermen if each state re-acquired responsibility for its own territorial waters, extending to 200 miles from their coasts. These might be increased beyond the present limits. States might conclude arrangements to allow some fishing by other states or negotiate rights to fish in waters of other states.

By international agreement substantial zones of the sea (20 to 50 per cent of the oceans) might be set aside as fish recovery areas or no-catch zones from which all fishing vessels would be banned. This is a simple, effective action which also has the merit of being relatively easy to enforce. Satellite monitoring of all fishing vessels is now practicable. Penalties for illegal fishing could be made sufficiently large to deter infringement.

The maximum size of fishing vessels might be drastically reduced. Some fishing methods might be outlawed.

As fishing for some species results in huge losses because of massive bycatches such species might be taxed worldwide to increase the price and so deter consumption and the wasteful and harmful fishing methods associated with the species.

To deter the deliberate fishing for endangered species taxes might be imposed on these too, ideally world-wide.

There is enormous wastage through the throwing back of unwanted or disallowed species. Usually the fish are already dead. Surely much of this might be used for either human or animal consumption.

European fisheries - Is there a role for the experts of the EU's centralised planning offices?

Is it appropriate for the management of the fisheries of twenty seven states to be in the control of the EU? Twenty-five years of preparing for the first Common Fisheries Policy and over 20 years of the Common Fisheries Policy in action seems to have exacerbated conflict between the fishermen of the European Union and brought EU fisheries to the brink of disaster.

So far, this centralised control of EU fisheries has failed in its most important task, that of ensuring sustainable fish stocks and a sustainable marine ecosystem. The precautionary principle has not been applied and the EU has shown determination to disallow another of its principles - subsidiarity. Democracy has not been one of its features. Administration has been inept and deaf to the voices of many of those it allegedly was attempting to help. The operation of the fisheries policy stands as a major argument against the existence of the European Union and its way of doing things.

Many individual nations outside the EU may have been equally ineffective, and no nation can offer a complete solution on its own, but Iceland took successful action to conserve cod stocks when it established the first 200 mile economic exclusion zone. A major problem actually created by EU policy was the EU insistence that a 200 mile economic exclusion zone could not be exclusively reserved to individual EU maritime states but must be open to the fishing fleets of all member states. This policy has been particularly disastrous for the UK fishing industry. It has massively increased the amount of fishing in what might have been exclusively British waters. Almost 80 per cent of the EU fishing zone would otherwise be open exclusively to British fishermen. The EU allows only 20 per cent of the EU catch quota to go to the UK.[68]

The seas of the European Union appear to be on the brink of an ecological disaster and the EU has abused the fishing territories of developing nations. A radical rethink is needed. Fisheries issues present a potential fracture point for the EU as states consider taking powers back into their own hands.

Foreign policy

See Defence and Foreign policy

Fraud

See Finances of the EU.

Free speech

See *Rights removed by the Constitution* in *Charter of Fundamental Rights* above.

Free trade, trade liberalisation and the European Union - the key issues

"If trade undermines life, narrows it or impoverishes it, then it can destroy the world. If it enhances life, then it can change the world." - Anita Roddick.

Trade is the very core of the European Union. The various treaties which have established the EU and which are consolidated and extended in the Constitution and the *Reform Treaty* have established the EU's trading and employment policies and their direction of development. These policies have been adopted in the context of the General Agreement on Tariffs and Trade organisation – GATT - (established in 1948) and, since 1995, in the context of the 26,000 page agreement which established the World Trade Organisation – the WTO – and subsequent negotiations and rulings of the WTO.

Free trade has been the policy of the EU, first between EU states within the borders of the EU, and then, progressively, with the rest of the world.

The nature of Free trade

Free trade is basically trade in goods and services which is maximised by the removal of tariffs/duties, quotas, bans, state imposed restrictions and subsidies. See also the *Euroterminology* chapter.

Free trade is often promoted as if it is the answer to all the world's problems. A more careful assessment might conclude that, like food, it is good for you, but that too much of it may slow you down, make you ill and even shorten your life. In theory free trade will have positive benefits:

- increase competition and efficiency and drive down prices giving the buyer a good deal,
- increase the volume of international trade thereby creating jobs, prosperity and profits,
- increase prosperity in countries which find themselves able to develop markets and sell at competitive prices,
- increase security as a result of economic interdependency between nations.

It is also likely to have negative effects:

- depressing the rights and benefits of workers by taking manufacturing and services to low wage countries, with low safety standards for workers, least healthcare, least job security, least holidays, longest working hours, least or non-existent pension rights, worst environmental standards;
- putting workers out of work in more prosperous economies where there is strong worker protection and social provision, thus decreasing levels of prosperity in these countries;
- taking administrative jobs such as call-centre work and arranging hospital appointments from high wage countries to low wage countries - for example from the UK to India and Africa;
- increasing the transport of goods and therefore carbon dioxide emissions;
- encouraging economic migration which often has the effect of breaking up families and communities and putting stress on recipient nations' social services;
- elevates the pursuit of money and profit to be the guiding principle of human existence;
- increases inequalities and, if pursued relentlessly, can lead to misery, violence and even war;
- siphoning skilled workers and service providers such as doctors into more highly paid economies leaving home states with a shortage of greatly needed people (free trade in services);
- increasing exploitative trade which feeds the growth of economic giants at the expense of what should be developing nations. For example, plantation economies may supply cheap raw materials (such as coffee) to the developed nations at the expense of food production and the environment at home.

The European Union has in mind to promote free trade and trade liberalisation throughout the world.[69]

But its own commitment to free trade is limited - as in most states that preach free trade as the ideal and necessary trading system. The EU controls and manipulates the activities and markets of European Agriculture and Fisheries. It subsidises agricultural exports. It imposes tariffs and quotas on imports of fish, agricultural products and clothing. It finds subtle ways of passing funding to help (subsidise?) European industries. The free functioning of international trade is also interfered with by the provision of export guarantees and government funded trade promotion - surprisingly, especially for the arms industry.

The promoters of free trade and trade liberalisation claim that it will create the greatest possible prosperity for all. An examination of levels of prosperity within the EU shows wide variations. The newest member states have not been involved long enough to test the system. However, there is clearly more to the creation of prosperity than adopting free-trade policies. For example, low levels of corporate taxation can attract business investment from one country into another, which has been part of the cause of Ireland's recent economic success.

The rules of the World Trade Organisation require EU states (and all WTO members) to ensure that there are absolutely no "unfair restrictions" on trade. Unfortunately one country's idea of what is a dangerous product, which they may want to ban from their country, may be another country's idea of an unjustified trade restriction. The WTO judges each case and is unsympathetic to countries which claim to fear the consequences of allowing certain products into their countries. (Some examples are given below.)

Removing all such restrictions on trade may be in the interest of the world's dominant economies and the largest transnational corporations, but in a great many countries the relentless imposition of total free trade and trade liberalisation has brought economic devastation, falling living standards to the point of increased impoverishment, rising crime rates, increased homelessness, reduced health care and education, high infant mortality and reduced life expectation. Examples include the former Soviet Union, Uganda and Argentina.[70]

Twelve issues present themselves to the people of the European Union in connection with free trade.

1 Should operation of free trade within the EU be expanded to include privatisation of all state-run industries and services?
2 Should it include unhindered freedom of movement of workers within the EU? If the free movement of workers is thought to be a good idea why not expand it to welcome into the EU workers from every country in the world?
3 Should it include allowing any company from a) any country within the EU to establish itself in any EU country without any conditions or restrictions, and b) any country outside the EU to establish itself in any EU country without any conditions or restrictions?
4 Should it allow the transfer of any and every EU industry a) to least-cost countries within the EU or b) to least-cost countries anywhere in the world?
5 Should the EU allow any service industry that can be conducted electronically by telephone or satellite link to be transferred a) to any country within the EU or b) to anywhere in the world?
6 Should the EU allow unlimited transfer of capital into and out of the EU?[71]
7 Should the EU restrict the movement of any goods or services into or out of the EU?
8 Should any or all of the above decisions be a matter for decision by the WTO or the EU or by individual states?
9 Should the EU take upon itself the "encouragement of free trade" (in its most elaborated, fundamentalist form) in every country around the world? (Article 292, 2 (e).) See *Defence and foreign policy*.
10 Should the EU be the servant of economic globalisation or the servant of the people of Europe in the context of the whole of humanity and a sustainable world?

11 How far the EU is a free agent in deciding EU trade policy is unclear. Much of its trade policy is driven by WTO agreements. The EU has a voice in the WTO. Should the EU support and encourage current WTO free trade policy or should it work to modify it in the direction of limiting liberalisation or increasing protectionism?

12 Should the extreme free-trade policies promoted by the WTO, the IMF and World Bank be subject to democratic process? No population anywhere in the world has voted for extreme free-trade WTO policies, yet those who resist its decision risk crippling sanctions being applied to them. Is there any role for democracy in trade policy decisions?

In order to answer these questions we need to look in some detail at trade policies of the EU, the beliefs and forces which lie behind some of these policies, and how policies translate into practice within the EU and in the rest of the world. Ultimately it should be possible to begin to form opinions about the kinds of trade policies which would be best for the citizens of the EU and the world and the environment.

Economic fundamentalism

Economic fundamentalism shares characteristics with other fundamentalisms. Fundamentalists seize on a small part of a doctrine, take it out of context, ignore essential other elements of the doctrine, and often ignore the general philosophy or core values of the doctrine they claim to be promoting. They elevate the chosen "revelation" to be the guiding principle of all action and then with zealous and even violent certainty set out to impose their misunderstanding on the rest of the world. Their zeal attracts many followers and these followers are vigorous in denouncing doubters.

Part of today's economic fundamentalism is the belief that all countries, by adopting free-trade fundamentalism (by removing all barriers to trade) will inevitably enjoy burgeoning prosperity. This theory is said to be one put forward by David Ricardo, who, in 1870, in *Principles of Political Economy and Taxation*, explained how countries which specialised in producing what they were best at could benefit by trading with other countries so that all were better off by the process. This can, and often does, happen. Ricardo, however, was aware that in some circumstances (overlooked by the promoters of free trade) this benign relationship could fail. He said that certain conditions were necessary for success including:

- That trade must be balanced between the trading partners, so that one did not become indebted or dependant on the other.
- Investment capital must stay in one country and not be allowed to flow from a high wage country to a low-wage country.
- Some countries in modern times have experienced economic meltdown when directed or persuaded by the IMF to abandon Ricardo's conditions.

The other key element of the free-trade faith is a belief in the self-correcting power of free trade. This belief is based on a partial reading of the theories expressed in *The Wealth of Nations* by Scottish economist, Adam Smith. He suggested that usually prices find a natural level because when vendors raise prices purchasers only continue to buy so long as they are satisfied with the price.

When purchasers stop buying then vendors lower prices to achieve sales. Adam Smith believed that in the right circumstances prices are always gravitating towards "the natural price".

The part of Adam Smith's theory which free-trade fundamentalists conveniently overlook is that Smith did not believe things would work out so well on all occasions. For example, he worried about cartels. "People of the same trade seldom meet together, even for merriment and diversion, but the conversation ends in a conspiracy against the public, or in some contrivance to raise prices." He was also deeply concerned that large corporations might use their power to dominate particular industries, influence politicians to achieve unfair advantages against their competitors and to suppress the wages of their workers. He was aware that politicians who supported market dominant corporations, which he termed "monopolists", would be described as having "a good understanding of trade" and those who were opposed to them would be abused, insulted, even threatened by the "furious and disappointed monopolists."

Referring to the combination of manufacturers in Britain in 1776 he complained that "like an overgrown standing army they have become formidable to the government and upon many occasions intimidate the Legislature." Today there is the formidable organised lobbying power of transnational corporations which operate through their associations such as the International Chamber of Commerce and European Round Table of Industrialists. These use their lobbying power to influence the World Trade Organisation and the European Union. In doing this they operate in the interest of their shareholders, mostly in private/secret, beyond proper scrutiny of the media, without democratic legitimacy, and possibly in some instances against the best interests of workers, some nations and the environment.

The World Trade Organisation guides the trade policies of the EU. How the WTO arrives at its decisions and who makes the decisions is important to the EU and EU citizens. The governmental delegations which negotiate rules at meetings of the WTO are not merely lobbied or influenced by trade organisations. Representatives of industry are part of negotiating teams. For example, in the discussions in the WTO Uruguay Round of trade talks on the subject of "intellectual property rights" the US Delegation consisted of 111 members. Of these, 96 were representatives of the private sector. How are governments going to be able to act on behalf of their people as a whole if they have been taken over by market traders?

Where should the EU place its weight in relation to the trade policies of the WTO? The world appears to be getting to a situation where it is controlled by a centralised power, and that power is the assembled might of transnational corporations, the unelected association of Mr Bigs, operating as a kind of world economic government through the WTO, IMF and World Bank.

Faith-based economics

It has been said that faith is believing something you know to be untrue. In the 21st century the world's most powerful economic enforcers work together to impose their economic faith in free market or free-trade policies on any and every country - even though they do not practice what they preach and they have found in many countries these policies bring untold human disaster. These are the doctrines of the World Bank, the World Trade Organisation and the International Monetary Fund. Their policies take the notion of free trade to the ultimate extreme in what is termed neo-liberal economics, or The Washington Consensus.

Although the EU has come into conflict with the WTO over the application of trade rules the EU is a committed supporter of the WTO. There is, therefore, a conflict of loyalties in EU leaders. Should their allegiance be to WTO rules or to the pragmatic service of its citizens?

Lack of faith in free trade

Those who have been the greatest promoters of free trade have been countries which have themselves already reached an advanced and advantageous level of development. What they have wanted has been to open up markets for their goods and services. Their aim has been to get other countries to remove tariff restrictions which were disincentives to their people buying the developed country's goods. And the same time they have typically not applied free-trade principles to themselves. Neither the EU nor the US actually practises free trade. They impose restrictions and duties on imports. They subsidise agricultural production.

If free trade is such a great idea why don't they act on it? If it is such a good idea why don't all countries practise it without being pressured into it? If the WTO, IMF and World Bank believe in democracy or the merits of their arguments, why do they impose it? Why should the EU decide it should tell others how to run their economies when it believes in democracy and subsidiarity? (Article 292/2e.)

Protectionism

Many economic commentators have noted how major economies, including the British and American, adopted for decades or even centuries, protectionist policies in order to favour and develop their own industries. Asian countries raised themselves from dire poverty after the Second World War to become the so-called Asian Economic Miracle by protecting their nascent industries.

Four of these stand out: South Korea, China, Taiwan and Japan. Their economic and social progress has been remarkable. Why? According to Joseph Stiglitz, former chief economic advisor to the World Bank and the winner of the Nobel Prize for economics "the countries have been successful not only in spite of the fact that they had not followed most of the dictates of of the Washington Consensus, but *because* they had not. . . the reductions in poverty in East Asia over the last three decades have been unprecedented."[72]

Unfortunately the economic progress has also been accompanied by a wide scale ecological pillage.

In the case of South Korea and Japan there was no foreign investment whatsoever. In other Asian countries foreign investment was kept under close control. Success was achieved by adopting policies opposite to those of the EU.

As already noted in the chart showing part of the history of free trade, the UK and US both established their economic power by the use of protectionism.

Protectionism itself is a risky economic policy and, like free trade, can never be the entire solution to economic problems. Protectionism can weaken the efficiency of an economy and keep prices higher than they might have been.

Wavering faith in free trade

<table>
<tr><th>UK</th><th>US</th></tr>
<tr><td>19th century: Britain dominated the world in manufactured goods. Promoted Free Trade.</td><td>1864 Protectionist. Abraham Lincoln raised import duties to record levels. (1870-1910 The US's period of fastest economic growth.)</td></tr>
<tr><td>1914 First World War. Strict quotas imposed on imports.</td><td>1913 Adopted free trade</td></tr>
<tr><td></td><td>1922 Applied 30% duty on imported manufactured goods.</td></tr>
<tr><td>1926 Resumed free trade then met new competition in textiles, coal and shipping.</td><td>1925 Tariffs raised to 37%.</td></tr>
<tr><td>1932 Abandoned free trade operated a system of favouring trade with British colonies.</td><td>1930 Tariffs raised to 48%.</td></tr>
<tr><td colspan="2">1929 -1933
Dramatic crash in world trade. Trading blocks developed.</td></tr>
<tr><td colspan="2">1944
Free Trade Redevelops</td></tr>
<tr><td></td><td>1945 US, economic winner (least destroyed country of WWII) Adopts free trade.</td></tr>
<tr><td colspan="2">1950's
Years of exceptional growth.</td></tr>
<tr><td colspan="2">1960's
Multiple Crises.</td></tr>
<tr><td></td><td>1971 President Nixon imposed trade quotas.</td></tr>
<tr><td colspan="2">1980's - 2007
US/UK/EU preach free trade to others. Retain significant restrictions and subsidies themselves.</td></tr>
</table>

Protectionism reduces the overall size of the market. The more protectionism becomes a policy of state after state the smaller the market for export becomes. Protectionism also carries a risk of very aggressive lobbying and even corruption from powerful industries pressing for protective tariffs and state subsidies.

Protectionism when?

There may be a case for nation states within Europe to take action at times to protect local producers, workers, industry, agriculture or fisheries. They may wish to impose a tariff barrier to protect nascent industry. There may be occasions when states believe it is desirable to ban certain imports. For example, a state may wish to ban meat produced by cruel farming methods or fireworks with an explosive power which they consider too dangerous or timber from endangered forests. They may wish to require government departments to source their requirements from local suppliers where possible, encourage everyone to reduce their purchases of imported goods by buying locally or nationally.

There is a special problem with the ownership of media. If any individual or company or state enterprise in the world may purchase news and publishing media within a state they place themselves in a powerful position to influence that society or even undermine society and the state. There would seem to be a case for keeping the ownership of media within a state at something close to one hundred per cent.

When the Welsh Assembly voted to ban GM crops it was told by the European Commission that it had no right to do so. The freedom of the exporter took precedence over the rights of citizens to be protected from something they considered harmful. This is free trade in action. It is European centralisation in action. It is a denial of local democracy and decision-making. The decision also appears to be in conflict with article 154 which allows the prohibition of goods "on grounds of public morality, public policy or public security; the protection of health and life of humans, animals or plants." This article was used by the French to ban British beef for many years on the reasonable grounds that it may have been a health risk.

Free flow of capital - Lessons from Asian crash?

The free flow of capital may be excellent for international speculators, but for many countries it is a high risk policy. In July 1997 came the Asian economic crisis. Asian countries had been urged to allow western investment in their economies. They did not need the money but were persuaded, in part to keep the goodwill of the countries where they sold so many of their products. Those countries which had allowed in foreign currency saw a panic outflow of capital. In Malaysia, South Korea, the Philippines and Indonesia the economies collapsed. As a "remedy" the IMF made loans of $95,000,000,000 coupled with its usual "conditionalities": high interest rates, government cutbacks, tax increases. Matters worsened. Unemployment soared. Poverty boomed. GDP sank. According to Joseph Stiglitz "the IMF itself had become a part of the countries' problem rather than part of the solution."[72]

Malaysia acting against all advice did not follow the IMF prescription and recovered quickly and more strongly. China and India maintain capital controls and whilst other economies in the region plummeted they prospered.

The economist, John Maynard Keynes, had a comment on international co-operation and international finance.

> "I sympathise with those who would minimise, rather than those who would maximise, economic entanglement between nations. Ideas, knowledge, art, hospitality, travel - these are the things which should of their nature be international. But let goods be homespun whenever it is reasonable and conveniently possible, and above all, let finance be primarily national."

Tide turns against free trade

There are conflicts within the EU over free trade, even though it is a key founding idea of the whole project. (See articles 3, 4 and 79.) A key conflict is between "market forces" with their in-built tendency to exploit workers, and "social protection". As the EU has evolved from the Common Market into the European Union it has attempted to accommodate the needs of ordinary citizens by bringing in measures for social protection. Hence commitments to full or high levels of employment (articles 3 and 205) and improved living and working conditions (articles 3, 209 and 210).

EU import tariffs, such as those on agriculture, fisheries and textiles, conflict with free-trade principles and are aimed at protecting EU industry and workers. However, the EU trade commissioner, Peter Mandelson, declares himself a "free trader" and as such is committed to the abolition of these protections. In this he is working in tune with the EU economic policy but in conflict with the EU social policy.

With 22,000,000 unemployed people within the EU isn't it time for an open discussion on this topic?

As transport and telecommunication have become cheaper and as free trade/globalisation has taken hold so the manufacture of goods has flown to low wage, low worker protection, and low environmental standards countries. The outsourcing of telephone call centre work to other countries has also had an impact. Is there a point at which protecting employment is more important than adherence to faith-based economic fundamentalism? What form of economic policy best serves the interests of the citizens of the European Union? Will the EU come clean on which policies it is actually intending to follow?

Moves to make the UK and France more competitive in 2006 by reducing workers' rights - cutting pension provision in the UK and making workers under 26 in France easy to fire - met with a huge wave of strikes in Britain and strikes and riots in France. Opposition to free trade policies is fiercer in the United States and now has substantial official backing. Should the EU take note of the shift towards anti-free-trade policies in the United States?

States and cities in the US have adopted "no outsourcing" policies and given preference in the award of contracts to local firms. There is a mass movement across the US against outsourcing. According to *Le Monde Diplomatique* (December 2005) "Between January 2003 and June 2005, local authorities in 46 of the 50 States considered at least one anti-outsourcing bill. Many states have rules requiring preference to be given to local or national firms for public contracts."

Within the EU there are calls for the boycott of the *General Agreement on Trade in Services* (GATS). In Liège, Belgium, at a European Convention of local government officers, 22-23 October 2005, a resolution was adopted calling for key service sectors to be excluded from GATS. The cities of Montreal, Turin, Vienna and Paris have declared themselves against GATS.

At the highest level within the EU, at the end of 2005 and in early 2006, national protectionism began to re-emerge. Spain was attempting to prevent the takeover of its energy company, Endesa, by German company, Eon. France announced in August 2005 a policy of "economic patriotism" by which it would take steps to stop the takeover of industries in strategic areas of the economy. In early 2006 it was attempting to prevent the Indian Steel Company, Mittal Steel, from taking over the French company, Arcelor. On 27 February 2006 the French government blocked the takeover of French energy company, Suez, by Italian energy company, ENEL.

These protectionist moves were condemned by Austrian Finance Minister, Karl Heinz-Grasser, as "unacceptable." However, Austria itself, in common with most other EU countries, has blocked the free movement of workers from the ten new EU states where wages are lower than in Austria. In March 2006 Luxembourg announced that it would take similar measures to France and Spain.

Of course, this protectionism contravenes EU trade laws.

A further move against free trade can be seen in the sustainability campaigns to protect energy resources and the environment. Foremost is the campaign to reduce food miles but the sustainability advantages of developing local economies and trading less widely are beginning to gain ground in a wider context as the consequences of future energy shortages emerge.

Trade ever more free

In the early days of trade, merchants or commercial companies traded in raw materials, manufactured goods, livestock and agricultural produce. Free trade was seen as the absence of restrictions or disincentives to trade caused by bans, quotas, subsidies and tariffs.

Nowadays the scope is widened to include the provision of services by individuals and companies operating across national boundaries without restrictions. This expansion of free trade into service industries, as an international expectation, began with the international trade negotiations which started in Uruguay in 1986 and concluded in 1994. These negotiations led to the setting up of the WTO in Geneva in 1995 with the task of reducing restrictions in trade further and policing and enforcing compliance with its trade rules.

The trend now is towards removing restrictions on any company setting up a business in any country in the world (and allowing it to close down at will, regardless of the social or political consequences), and the right to invest any amount of capital in any country and to remove it and any profit at any time.

The provision of cross border services can often be done by telephone and other electronic means - as in the movement of capital, and the operation of financial services, call centres and consultancies. All this without penalty or tariff - other than a payment of standard taxes on profit within state boundaries -

although there are ways transnational corporations normally and legally avoid or minimise such payments by the process of transfer pricing.

Public services and utilities

It used to be the case that governments in many countries provided a number of services and utilities which were considered to be vital to all or most citizens and which might otherwise have been monopolies. These include such things as the supply of water, electricity, railways, health care, education, ports and airports.

Transnational corporations, acting through the WTO, have for many years been demanding the opportunity for businesses to take over the running of state services in countries around the world. They want to "liberalise" services and trade liberalisation has entered into EU ideology as a fundamental economic principle. Hence the drive to liberalise (privatise) everything - not because local communities, acting pragmatically, have calculated that privatisation is in their best interest or will be the most effective way of delivering particular services, but because it has been centrally decided and decreed according to fundamentalist economic theory and without proper regard to human or even economic consequences. The EU embraces the idea that businesses from anywhere should be allowed to run and profit from services everywhere and has taken the first steps by promoting this within the EU itself.

Key provisions on privatisation - The EU is in charge

Article 15 of the 2004 Constitution confirmed the EU's powers to co-ordinate economic, employment and social policies of member states.

The key constitutional articles on privatisation are articles 147 and 148 which are a restatement of articles 52 and 53 of the *Treaty Establishing the European Community* (Consolidated version, Nice, 2002).[73] Article 147 states, "European framework laws shall establish measures to achieve the liberalisation of a specific service." The reference to "a specific service" (since it lacks the selection of any specific service) can only be understood as referring to all services. As each specific service is nominated by the Commission under the authority of a framework law then it becomes governed by EU competence.[74] The framework law will require member states to enact laws (implementation laws) to bring about the privatisation of the service. Member states will be prohibited from re-nationalising that service.

Article 148 states, "The Member States shall endeavour to undertake liberalisation of services beyond the extent required by the European framework laws adopted pursuant to Article 147, if their general economic situation and the situation of the economic sector concerned so permit. To this end, the Commission shall make recommendations to the Member States concerned." The Commission will, in effect, decide which services member states of the EU will privatise. It is not suggested that individual governments should take the initiative, still less local communities. There is no suggestion of a right to ignore the Commission's recommendations. No democracy and no subsidiarity here.

The expression "if their general economic situation . . . so permit" is open to interpretation. It may mean that if a service has been broken down into saleable parts, viable commercial units, then it should be sold to commercial enterprises. It may mean that if a service has run into serious financial difficulties then privatisation might present itself as the only solution to its problems. It is of concern that either interpretation might lead a government to manipulate the functioning of a service in order to make it look like a necessary or desirable candidate for privatisation. It might do this by breaking a service into small parts, managing it badly (by, for example, ceaseless re-organisation), or starving it of financial resources in order to present a service as "failing" and therefore ripe for privatisation. In situations like this privatisation can be presented to the public as "the only option left."

An alternative interpretation of the expression "if their general economic situation . . . so permit" is that it was inserted into the Constitution at the request of states (possibly reluctant to privatise) who wanted to be assured that they would not be pushed into privatisation at a time they considered inappropriate in view of their current economic situation. "Economic situation" would therefore relate to a state's economy rather than the economic situation within a service.

Services - free movement of

Existing arrangements to allow the free movement of provision of services across the EU are set out in articles 144-150. These repeat articles 49 -55 of the *Treaty Establishing the European Community*. Nationals of any member state may provide services in any other member state of the EU (article 144). This openness may be extended to any service provider from any country in the world if they are "established within the Union" (Constitution article 144 and *Treaty Establishing the European Community*, article 49). This effectively opens the way for companies from anywhere in the world to enter the EU and compete with EU businesses.

Consequences include:

- a more challenging business environment in each state since there is a potentially vast increase in competition.
- Highly skilled and trained people from the poorer regions may move to the richer regions with the likely consequence of depressing wages in the richer regions and the deprivation of poorer regions of much needed professionals. - See *Enlargement*.
- Another difficulty is that the training of professionals and technicians becomes more difficult for a state to plan because the number of such service providers who might arrive from other EU states or choose to move to other EU states will be difficult to predict.
- Although the EU has made great efforts to ensure that professional qualifications are brought into line with each other across the Union some doubts may arise in these areas. It might be difficult for employers in, say, Britain to check the qualifications and references of an architect, or electrician, or accountant or a surgeon trained in, say, Hungary who presents references and other documents in Hungarian. An English employer might have difficulty checking the authenticity of any translation offered. (At the same time, under EU laws which apply in some EU states, an employer would not be allowed to discriminate against a national of another member state.)

Free trade for companies providing services - Bolkestein Draft Directive

Some 70 per cent of EU trade and some 70 per cent of workers in the EU are in the services sector.[75]

The *Treaty of Rome* (1957) set out plans to achieve within the member states a free market in goods (which it has achieved) and also a free market in services (*Treaty of Rome*, article 3) which has not been completed. Article 48 of the *Treaty Establishing the European Community* (repeated as article 142 in the Constitution) requires companies from any EU state to be allowed to set up businesses in other EU states. Article 49 of the *Treaty Establishing the European Community* (Constitution article 144) requires the removal of restrictions on the provisions of services throughout the EU. Companies providing services long awaited an EU directive to make this a reality by requiring member states to enact the necessary enabling (framework) laws.

On 13 January 2004 the EU Commissioner, Fritz Bolkestein, submitted the Draft Directive on Services in the Internal Market for approval, under the co-decision procedure, by the Council and the European Parliament. If passed in its original form this directive would have allowed companies from any EU country to provide services including healthcare in any other EU country without the impediment of "red tape" such as licensing and vetting of standards, and would also allow these companies to operate under the laws of the country from which the company came (the "country of origin" principle). Under this proposal companies would have been allowed to set themselves up in EU countries where workers' rights and pay levels were the lowest and where standards for delivery of services (insurance cover, guarantees, health and safety standards, environmental requirements, etc) were most easily met. This would have enabled them to operate in other member countries with very competitive pricing whilst competing with local service providers, operating to possibly higher standards and experiencing much higher costs.

The companies would operate as independent states within other states as they would be operating in accordance with foreign laws. From the point of view of host countries the administrations would have to be knowledgeable about systems, laws, professional qualifications and standards in twenty-six other countries and whose documentation would exist in twenty-three different languages. This would have been likely to increase the difficulties of selecting service providers, administering standards and legal requirements, and increase the costs of bureaucracy. It would have been bound to lead to confusion and uncertainty. How standards might be guaranteed under such an open, diverse and multilingual system is hard to visualise.

There was to be no requirement to keep employment records in the host country. How might the French employee of a Latvian service provider pursue a complaint about a wages error in such circumstances? How could there be any protection of workers' rights in such a situation? The proposals precipitated massive protest within the EU. Approaching 100,000 trade unionists marched in Brussels against the proposed directive on 4 June 2004.

Services Directive, 2006 - Bolkestein modified

The final version of the directive (European Services Directive 2006/123/EC)[76] was passed on 12 December 2006 and came into effect on 28 December 2006. In its passage through the co-decision procedure some of the requirements of the directive were amended. Most importantly, a number of services were *excluded* from its scope including healthcare (both state run and private), financial services, electronic communications services and networks, services in the field of transport, including some port services; services of temporary work agencies; audiovisual services, including cinematographic services, whatever their mode of production, distribution and transmission and radio broadcasting; gambling activities which involve wagering a stake with pecuniary value in games of chance, including lotteries, gambling in casinos and betting transactions; some activities which are connected with the exercise of official authority; social services relating to social housing, childcare and support of families and persons provided by the state or by charities: private security services; and the field of taxation.

A vast number of services may now be provided by individuals and businesses from anywhere in the EU in any EU state, but before the new freedoms can apply member state parliaments are required to create laws to implement the directive - a process which may take two or three years.

Privatisation of public services - solution or delusion?

Those who supported the Bolkestein directive in its original form may still work for the full implementation of the original directive. The above services that are so far excluded from privatisation may one day be part of a full free market in services. Some states, most notably the UK, seem determined to press ahead with further privatisation without waiting to be told to do so by the EU. Apart from the Constitution itself possibly nothing the EU has done or has proposed has aroused so much opposition, resentment and distrust. The topic is of immense importance and a core issue of the EU. To what extent should service providers be allowed to operate in all EU states, and in particular, how much of services currently provided by states themselves should be handed over to commercial enterprises to provide? Experts are lined up in opposing camps. On one side there are those who believe that by privatising public services costs will be driven down, there will be better value for money, efficiency will improve. On the other side experts claim that privatisation is a recipe for chaos, loss of financial control, reduced efficiency and that some services may most economically and effectively be provided by states.

Should the EU have a precise policy commitment on privatisation (liberalisation) in either a treaty or a constitution?

At the heart of the issue is the simplistic theory that services provided by states are bad (inefficient). Services provided by businesses for profit are good. The EU takes the idea a step further by saying that not individual states should make the decisions about what should be privatised, but the EU Commission (article 148). They are complying with an agreement made at a meeting of the World Trade Organisation in 1994 - the *General Agreement on Trade in Services* (GATS). The aim of the agreement was to remove all restrictions that governments might put in place to prevent services, including public services, being sold off to and run by business organisations for profit.

EU countries have developed public services in many areas including health, social services, pension provision, education, transport, libraries, water, waste disposal, fire, police, prisons and postal services. In general the staff in these very large undertakings are dedicated to the provision of service and they have succeeded partly through individual ability and effort, but in large part to the extent that they have been adequately funded and well managed.

State-run and privatised services have to work with different aims. Because of a duty to pay shareholders an attractive return on their investments privatised public services have to demote the prime aim of service to the public and replace it with a prime duty to shareholders to maximise profits. This is likely to affect the quality of service.

The UK is ahead of other EU countries in developing privatisation and has some experience of this situation. In December 2003 the UK government introduced commercial "independent treatment centres" within the NHS to carry out some types of routine operations such as hip replacements and cataract surgery. There have been complaints that such services produce an exceptional number of post-operation complications which are then passed on to state providers of healthcare to sort out. A further problem is that such commercial providers are unable to treat patients as whole people since their philosophy is based on the specialisation of the car production line, not on a medical ethos of a commitment to the well-being of the whole person.

In any case, privatisation is not necessary to achieve the setting up of specialist units. Such units might be state run within a national health service and offer efficiency, the immediate possibility of comprehensive aftercare, economy and a better, more flexible use of highly skilled surgical staff.

When privatisation succeeds it is because of superior management or superior investment or both. Neither of these things are unique to privatised services. Public services too may be brilliantly managed and properly funded. For example, Spain's state run railways are low cost and more efficient than Britain's privatised railways. The Swiss Federal Railway, wholly owned by the Federal government and the cantons, also has an enviable reputation for efficiency. Where public services are failing the areas of management and funding need to be addressed.

Privatisation replaces the direct employment of individual people by the state with the employment of teams of people (businesses) organised to make a profit for team leaders (directors) dependent on their adroitness at "operating the system." Individual employees are thereby indirectly employed by the state. It is still actually state run but responsibility for success or failure (though resting with the ultimate organiser, the state) appears to be passed to the companies contracted to run sectors.

Both state-run and private enterprises need to control costs. This may be easier for state run organisations in full control of all physical and human resources than for a state to control the prices charged by a multiplicity of commercial service providers. The payment of salaries, for example, to National Health Service staff may be controlled with relative ease. When teams of people (private enterprises) take over the provision of services they will be paid by work done and targets met. It sounds like a recipe for improving services and avoiding waste and unnecessary costs. The idea is appealing but is fraught with difficulties which include the difficulty of setting appropriate targets, negotiating appropriate payments, monitoring the delivery of a service and enforcing proper compliance with the terms of contracts - all huge bureaucratic challenges. Splitting a state enterprise into a thousand privatised units may increase problems of ensuring proper provision of a service.

A small taste of the problems which may occur was experienced by the British National Health Service between 2004 and January 2007. The 2004 pay deal for doctors was based on a market philosophy of paying for services provided. The average pay for general practitioners for the year up to January 2007 was estimated to have risen by 30% to £106,000 - approximately ten times the rate of inflation. It is possible that a better service had been provided, but in an organisation trying to keep a tight control on its budgets such open-ended deals potentially open floodgates.[77]

Another problem is that actions may be taken by service providers to maximise profits to the detriment of the service which might otherwise have been appropriately provided, even when the target set is calculated to improve service. In 2004 the NHS set a target to encourage hospitals to see more patients more quickly. To encourage this the government decided to pay £1,200 to Primary Care Trusts for each patient admitted to hospital but released within 48 hours. In practice hospitals could rise to this challenge in one of three ways. They could do what the planners intended them to do and be more efficient in dealing with the patients they would normally admit; but they could maximise income in other ways: they could send some patients home early against their better judgement; or they could hospitalise more patients who come their way (even though they may not have needed to be admitted) in order to be able to send them home within 48 hours and so claim the bonus and the kudos of having "increased performance." The latter happened.

Accident and emergency cases at four UK foundation hospitals fell in the six months to October 2004, but admissions to hospital via A&E rose by at least 17 percent, according to a report in the *Health Service Journal*. The Department of Health described these figures as "exceptions". It considered, however, that the payments for results were a little high and decided to halve the £1,200 bonus from April 2005.

Privatisation - the employees' experience

The breaking up and privatisation of large state enterprises forces workers into smaller units thus reducing the collective bargaining power of trade unions. It therefore has great potential for reducing the pay levels and worsening the working conditions of workers. The process can also lead to reduced staffing levels with consequent increases of pressure on the staff retained. When financial difficulties occur in privatised enterprises if prices are not allowed to be increased there will be cuts: cuts in staff, cuts in safety standards, cuts in standards of provision.

The British National Health Service is increasingly being run on "business lines" with the result that even some of the best hospitals have been forced to make cuts in services. The Bradford Royal Infirmary, one of Britain's star hospitals in the new foundation hospitals programme found that it was spending beyond its allocated budget. The Royal College of Nursing reported that as a result many items became in short supply, including clean linen and tubing. There were cuts in the numbers of caterers and temporary nursing staff employed and car park security staff were dismissed. The hospital decided not to provide sandwiches or snack boxes for very ill patients.

In Germany, in preparation for the privatisation of German railways, EU directive 91/440/EEC increased working hours and cut thousands of jobs. The unspoken creed seems to be that efficient management equates with increased workload for fewer workers. Would it not be better to view management efficiency as achieving decreased workloads for increasing numbers of workers? Which is better for society? Which is appropriate in a constitution which claims to place people at the heart of its considerations?

Privatisation - unaccounted human costs

The EU is committing all member states to its "solution" to the "problem" of organising key services such as healthcare and education. Privatisation can never be a panacea for the problems of organising large enterprises. The basic challenges of organising financial resources, physical resources and people remain under all forms of organisation. The problem is the same size however you may rearrange the pieces. Organising state enterprises is much more than merely achieving economic efficiency. Low cost delivery of services, if achieved, is only the beginning. The question that needs answering is, taking into account *all* aspects of the issue - including the effects on people and society as a whole, will privatised provision of services lead to a happier outcome or will there be hidden costs to society?

Will children be better educated for the money invested? Will patient care and the health of nations be better for the money invested? Will bigger and more secure pensions be provided?[78] And so on. But we must look beyond the narrow focus of such appraisals because services and enterprises do not exist in a vacuum remote from society. The effect on society and the economy as a whole are of equal importance. Will there be a happier outcome for all those who worked and continue to work in the service sectors or will there be large unacknowledged costs in terms of increased unemployment and stress related illness? Might such human problems have an economic as well as a social cost to society as a whole? Will the potential increased stress have a knock on effect in destabilising families, inducing child neglect and family breakup? Will more children need to go into care or require financial help from the state? Will distressed children from distressed families find adjustment to education and to positive roles in society difficult or may they turn to harmful activities?

These are not theoretical remote possibilities. Depression, mental illness, family break-up, suicide, drug and alcohol abuse, violence are huge problems in European society and they have been increasing in recent years. The relationship of people to their work may well be an important factor. Obviously many other factors may also be related to the above problems.

Privatisation v democracy

The organisation of services is a momentous issue which is surely a matter for consideration by the people of Europe in the light of experience and current knowledge and circumstances. Or would eurocitizens prefer this matter to be centrally decided by the EU or the WTO regardless of experience and popular views? The drive to privatise state-run services is not a matter of moral principle which should guide the functioning of a state or superstate or even a group of countries determined to collaborate for their mutual benefit. On the other hand, taking decisions at the lowest practical level is a political principle which enjoys widespread support and is supposedly endorsed by the EU.

EU to free the world

Free trade is a core principle of the EU[79] but this objective was taken much further in the 2004 Constitution[80] and the Reform Treaty. It is proposed that the economic mission of the EU should now formally be extended to the whole world.

A great deal rests on the word "encourage." A friendly word of advice from an EU leader to a leader of another country can hardly be objected to. If it means destroying lives and livelihoods through sanctions and warfare, as in the case of Yugoslavia, that is another thing. (See *Defence and foreign Policy*.)

Since the EU is committed to the principle of democracy and subsidiarity a hands-off approach to other countries' trade policies might be more appropriate.

Free trade or free people?

When EU commitments conflict with one another citizens will wish to know which Constitutional commitment is to be the dominant one: the commitment to free trade or the commitment to public protection, free-trade or worker protection, free trade or concern for the environment, free trade or full employment, free trade or human rights, free trade or democracy.

Moderated trade

A commitment to "free-trade" by the EU can only be seen as a half-hearted, partial affair - apart from the untypical flurry of violent action against socialist Yugoslavia.

As indicated above, free trade is increasingly driven towards abandoning all controls, all social protection, under pressure from the unelected, undemocratic WTO and its *General Agreement on Trade in Services.* The EU is both a supporter and victim of the WTO. The nature of its commitment to free trade, trade liberalisation and the WTO needs clarifying.

Examples of the WTO policy of Profit Before People abound. Just four examples:

- the EU decided to ban imports of beef from the USA on health grounds in cases where the cattle had been treated with hormones. The USA challenged the ban and the WTO decided that Europe was attempting to impose an unfair impediment to free trade.
- When France (where 2000 workers a year die of asbestos poisoning) tried to protect its workers by banning the import of all forms of asbestos the WTO said that the ban violated WTO rules.
- The EU wanted to favour the import of bananas from former French and British African and Carribbean countries that rely on banana exports for survival. Three American fruit producing corporations, Chiqita, Dole and Del Monte objected, claiming that they would lose $520 million a year if

the EU plan were allowed. The small producers that the EU wished to support, however, stood to lose their means of existence. The WTO found in favour of the corporations.

- The EU itself has made use of the WTO to attempt to boost trade at the expense of people. Together with Japan the EU supported a US business lobbying group in challenging a law passed by Massachusetts which prohibited, on human rights grounds, government contracts with the military junta in Burma. They claimed that the law was a violation of the WTO's Agreement on Government Procurement.

There are people within the EU establishment committed to serving the needs of the people of Europe - hence the commitments within the EU treaties and the Constitution to social protection and care of all kinds. However, the dominant tendency within the EU is against this. We see this, for example, at a time when EU countries have never been so rich, in cut-backs in pension provision in Germany, Italy, Finland and Greece. In 2006 in the UK, too, the government also has plans to add years of work for millions of workers before their pensions will be paid. At the same time in the National Health Service - where UK spending has now risen to be at the European average there is an overspend of £800,000,000. The government has decided not to meet this bill and instead is requiring the trusts (the bodies given the responsibility for managing the National Health Service) to find their own solutions to their budget deficits. This application of "market economics" means the firing of workers. In one week in March 2006 redundancies for 2500 National Health Service workers were announced. Predictions of 25,000 job cuts in the National Health Service have been made.

Alternative solutions could have included more state funding (from a government which has spent £8,000,000,000 on unprovoked and illegal wars against Iraq and Afghanistan) or employing less management consultants whose fees are more than considerable or capping the prices pharmaceutical companies charge for drugs or putting overcharging pharmaceutical companies into state ownership. This last idea would not be rule-free trade, but it might be in the interests of the society the UK government is supposed to serve.

A tension will always remain between those advocating freedom from "market distortion" and those advocating protection and support for people, the environment, vital industries, and the state running of key services and monopolies. In spite of its free-trade posture, the EU will be slow to give up its subsidies to agriculture, fisheries, and research of all kinds, and various protectionist measures.

It is clear that what the EU has always favoured in practice, and will continue to favour, is a bias towards free trade ideas in a mix of trade freedoms and trade restrictions. Its real but unstated policy is a policy of moderated trade. If this could be openly stated it would then be possible to start a discussion on the kinds of moderations of trade practices which would be in the best interests of the citizens of the European Union.

Trade policy dictatorship

As a contributor to the World Trade Organisation policy it would then need to seek allies and argue for a humanising reform of WTO policies. No leading politician or official in the EU raises these issues as a matter for public discussion. Support is assumed. Policy is dictated.

EU trade policy needs to be debated within the EU and not imposed by a constitution or treaty. As the EU does not wholeheartedly operate the policy it claims to believe in it needs to clarify its thinking and then state plainly what its true trade policy is. As a suggestion, its purpose should be to benefit society as a whole and not just an elite minority, primarily the biggest corporations and their shareholders. Policies should be pragmatic and flexible to adapt to changing circumstances. Should not the policy be to moderate trade in the best interest of each EU state, the EU as a whole, and the world in general?

See *Localism*, below.

Free trade and other EU trade policies

Free movement of persons,employment

See articles 133-136 on the "free movement of persons". There are no easy judgements on this topic. From the point of view of an individual worker the idea that he or she may travel freely throughout the European Union and take up employment without discrimination and with full social benefit rights can only seem a positive and attractive proposition. The idea that wages for both immigrant and native employees should be equal seems just. From the point of view of employers the idea of extending the range of choice of candidates for employment may seem attractive. But this is not a situation in which everyone is guaranteed to win.

According to article 133 workers shall have the right to accept offers of employment. But there are limitations. One is a limitation "justified on grounds of public policy". This vague statement seems to open the door to a total negation of the "free movement of workers" policy. Also, the article does not apply to "employment in the public service".

The policy could run the risk of causing dramatic changes within states which may experience a large influx of immigrant workers. Already in some EU states unemployment is high. A substantial influx of immigrant workers could exacerbate this problem and give rise to social tensions within some member states. On several occasions in recent years the disaffected have rioted in the French banlieues. The potentially positive side of large movements of workers might be that they might lead to the equalisation of economies across Europe and thereby reduce tensions between member states. (See *Enlargement.*) A great increase in competition in richer countries for a limited number of jobs could have a significant effect which would be bad for workers but seen as good for employers, and that is that wage levels would be likely to be depressed. Higher paid workers might lose their jobs. (See *Losing jobs, lowering wages* in the *Enlargement of the EU* section above.)

A further problem is that allowing unrestricted movement of people across member state borders allows skilled workers who are much needed in their native country to move to a high wage areas, thus benefiting richer countries at the expense of poorer countries. This is happening. A significant part of the solution to this problem may be the continuation of EU policies for regional funding for development - though perhaps such a policy needs to be more in tune with local ideas than at present.

Free movement of persons has taken on a new form in the last decade. Immigrant workers no longer need to arrive in the EU to do some kinds of work formerly done by eurocitizens. A good deal of work is now electronically moved outside Europe. Jobs are off-shored. Perhaps good for business in the short term, but bad for EU employment and prosperity in the longer term.

Pragmatism rather than a simplistic ideological commitment to "free movement of persons" and "free trade" might be beneficial. Perhaps specific policies in this area should not be set out in a constitution.

See also the *Schengen Agreement* in the *Treaties* chapter, *Enlargement,* and *Charter of Fundamental Rights* above.

Freedom of establishment – Want to set up a business in another EU country?

In theory the EU's freedom of establishment regulations make it possible for any EU citizen to set up a business in any EU state without restriction (Constitution articles 133-143 which follow the *Treaty Establishing the European Community* articles 39 and 40). No EU state may place restrictions on the setting up of businesses by any EU citizens which do not equally apply to their own nationals. If operated according to plan this could set up a largely one-way flow of talent from poorer regions to more prosperous regions to the detriment of the poorer regions.

But this freedom is not absolute. Article 140 seems to allow any EU member state to restrict the open door policy at will. Article 140 allows for "special treatment for foreign nationals on grounds of public policy, public security or public health." The term "public policy" appears to cover anything a government might decide. Any restrictive action by a state would be open to challenge by the EU and a judgement by the European Court of Justice against a member state would be binding. Could not the terms of the open door policy be expressed more clearly at this stage?

An insight into the working of EU freedom of establishment rights is provided by the *Athens News* of 26 August 2005. This reported on a new law for immigrant entrepreneurs in Greece. The law was due to come into operation on 1 January 2006. It required that before any immigrant can set up a business in Greece he must have at least € 60,000 (£42,000) deposited in a Greek bank account. The report claims that similar conditions exist in other European Union countries. This law is clearly designed to severely restrict the number of immigrant entrepreneurs establishing businesses in Greece, but leaves wealthy people, bigger companies and rich multinationals an open door.

Competition and corporate giantism

> I see in the near future a crisis approaching that unnerves me and causes me to tremble for the safety of my country. . . corporations have been enthroned and an era of corruption in high places will follow, and the money power of the country will endeavour to prolong its reign by working upon the prejudices of the people until all wealth is aggregated in a few hands and the Republic is destroyed. - Abraham Lincoln, 21 Nov 1864.

Many see the US today as in just this situation with unbelievable wealth and power in the hands of the few, tax breaks for the rich, and a desperate, neglected and abused under class.

Adam Smith and a great many more economic and political observers have been acutely aware that companies which develop or merge to dominate a market by their sheer size pose a threat to society in many ways, including the ability to raise prices, unfairly depress the incomes of their suppliers, manipulate prices to crush or exclude smaller competitors and exploit workers. It is therefore a common feature of state laws to control trade by limiting the size of companies within their spheres of operation, breaking up cartels, and preventing the emergence of companies with dominating power within their business area.

The EU now controls the operation of trade within EU countries. It appears to have only the weakest of powers and the feeblest of intentions to deal with the growth of corporate power.

Repeating powers set out in the *Maastricht Treaty*, articles 161 and 162 are primarily concerned with keeping competition fair *between* EU states, not within individual states or the world as a whole (a matter the EU might have a policy on and take to the WTO).

A provision in the Constitution (Article 165) required any EU state that wishes to take action against undue accumulations of commercial power to apply to the Commission to take action. States cannot act in such matters without the permission of the Commission. It is for the Commission to take the initiative.

The EU has additional powers set out in the *EC Merger Regulation* of 20 January 2004. This concerns itself with mergers where "the combined aggregate worldwide turnover of all the undertakings concerned is more than 5,000 million euros," or where "the aggregate community wide turnover of each of at least two of the undertakings is more than 250,000,000 euros." Is this size set rather too high? It may be impossible for a layman to make out the case but it may seem to many that numerous companies in the world are simply too powerful, and their clustering round the WTO likes wasps on a honey pot has been bad for most smaller businesses and often for people in general.

How effective is the EU in dealing with monopolies and mergers?

What does it do about, for example, Rupert Murdoch and his News International and BskyB empire? - Effectively nothing. In one family we have the control of TV networks, satellite broadcasting, film studios, publishers, and 174 newspapers. Such is Murdoch's power that he was able to force the BBC out of China by denying access to his satellite. Whilst much of Murdoch's media empire operates outside Europe there is still a vast amount within it, and not just dominating certain aspects of the communications trade, but having the sinister overtones of having exceptional influence on the selection of "news" and immense opportunities to influence public opinion. It cannot have been coincidence that all of Murdoch's editors supported the war against Iraq in 2003. Can it be right that just one person or just one company with no particular connection or loyalty to any one country or any particular concern for the wellbeing of any one country, or even of humanity as a whole, can have such vast access to the public and power to shape public opinion? Surely, above all other companies, media companies need to be owned by residents of the states in which they operate and to be limited in size to encourage plurality of opinions.

Actually, the EU has made at least one move to limit Murdoch power. Murdoch's BskyB has dominated TV coverage of Premier League football since 1992. Starting from the 2007/8 season the Irish based broadcaster, Setanta, started to show many of the games. But this really is insignificant in terms of multiplying the number of media sources within the EU.

The EU seems sluggish at keeping company sizes down and competition at a healthy level. Or is it just not interested or capable? As a further example, the Italian company, Autostrade, owns about 60 per cent of Europe's toll roads. Really there is no other company to compare with it. Even so, in April 2006, it was planning to merge with Albertis, a Spanish company which owns three UK airports and controls 1500 kilometres of toll roads in Spain.[81]

Whilst Spanish companies may own British airports free trade rules have not been allowed to operate reciprocally. The Spanish government will not allow foreign ownership of its state owned airports. - It could be argued that airports are strategic assets that are too important for a state to allow into foreign or even private hands. Should EU free trade rules apply to strategic assets? Should the UK government be more robust in resisting the take-over of vital national concerns?

Italian politicians have been expressing doubts about the Autostrade/ Albertis merger which the companies have agreed - not because the new company would be too big, but because of a weakening of Italian control of Autostrade. Is the market dominance of Europe's toll roads conducive to best value for Europe's motorists?

Giantopolies

The problem faced by the EU and all countries is something perhaps fairly new in human history. It is not just a matter of market dominance or even monopoly power, but the problem of giantopoly - corporate power which is so great it can overwhelm and inhibit the start-up of competitors and dictate to states. The EU is not dealing with this problem. It is part of the problem. Only a combination of states, working on behalf of the citizens of the world, can begin to control these ultra-state forces.

There is no sign in any EU policy statement or in the Constitution that it is aware of the problem of global corporate giantism. Examples abound, but here is just one that has some relevance to the EU. Four companies dominate the global beef market, controlling 81 per cent of it. They are Cargill, Tyson, ConAgra, and Farmland National. Free trade in the presence of giants simply means freedom for the big to crush the weak. Freedom to wipe out the competition is not freedom as we know it, but tyranny.

There are some 60,000 transnational corporations in the world employing, at most, 180,000,000 people - less than 10% of the world's workforce. Most may well be working effectively in the interests of society as a whole, but it is amongst these companies that corporations with astounding wealth, power and influence are able to operate beyond the control of individual states, beyond democratic control and not necessarily in the best interests of people and the environment. Their methods are not only potentially harmful to workers, consumers and the planet, but also to the great majority of the world's small businesses.

Is it not high time at world level, EU level and state level that corporate giantism were tackled? Article 13 of the Constitution and now its replacements, will give the EU new powers including the exclusive power to establish "the competition rules necessary for the functioning of the internal market" and also to decide the "common commercial policy". The EU needs policies and these should be put up for public discussion. Where is democracy in all this? Do EU citizens really want to hand over all power in decision making in commercial policy to the unelected Commission which may be impervious to all influence except that of the most powerful corporate lobbyists? The eurocitizen needs to be able to see proposals for policy, debate them, and have the opportunity to elect people to represent their views. They would like to hear the arguments and see what is proposed and what is being done.

See also *Lobbying.*

Sanctions

Article 322 talks of "restrictive measures". This is code for economic sanctions. Imposing economic sanctions can have a devastating effect on the economy and living conditions within a country and sometimes be more vicious and deadly than overt war. The effect of sanctions against Yugoslavia and Iraq, countries where their economic policies were not approved of by the EU and the US, had dire human consequences. In Iraq over half a million children died as a direct result of sanctions. The UN sanctions regime, largely controlled by the USA and Britain, resulted in deaths and suffering on an enormous scale.

Article 322 should spell out

- on what grounds sanctions may be applied
- that the conditions for the lifting of sanctions must be publicly stated at the time of imposition - a time limit that will be reached or the fulfilment of a condition which will cause sanctions to be lifted
- who will be held accountable for their effects if they lead to economic ruin or loss of life
- how the humanitarian consequences will be monitored (a repeat of the malnutrition and deaths on a large scale caused by sanctions which occurred in Iraq in the 1990s must be avoided). For example, a group of monitors might be appointed with a requirement to report to the European Parliament and the Council at specified intervals.

Perhaps the European Parliament should be given the power to veto sanctions.

Subsidies

The EU has a "no subsidy" policy. Article 167 spells out how the granting of subsidies which may distort competition is prohibited. However, exceptions are allowed for such things as regional development. Farmers and fishermen also receive subsidies, and research grants totalling billions of euros are made in undisclosed amounts to un-named European industries. Clarity and transparency are needed on this topic.

It is the WTO which drives the no-subsidy policy. However, under Article XXI of the General Agreement on Tarriffs and Trade the WTO is happy to allow governments to award massive research and export subsidies to arms manufacturers. Does this happen in the EU? Should it happen?

There may well be many causes and organisations (including businesses) that the eurocitizen would be pleased to see supported with grants or subsidies. The need is for full reporting on where our money is being spent.

Eurozone, economic and monetary policy

The Constitution was written as if the adoption of the euro is the norm throughout the EU. Article 8 stated that "The currency of the Union (EU) shall be the euro." Article 177 confirmed this expectation. Currently (2007) it is contrary to the actual economic policies of 13 of the 27 EU member states. It would appear that the Constitution was demanding more than governments of the EU states are willing to give. If the euro is optional then this should be made clear that this is the case. The UK, as already mentioned, is allowed to stay outside the eurozone for as long as it wishes.

Article 13 gives the EU sole and exclusive legal power to decide policy as regards trade tariffs and quotas, monetary policy for the eurozone, competition rules for the internal market, fisheries conservation, commercial policy, and trade agreements with other countries. Are eurocitizens happy to pass all this responsibility over to the unknown bureaucrats of the EU?[82]

Freedom Security and Justice

See *Area of Freedom Security and Justice* above.

Giving our money away

Citizens of member states have a certain understanding of how their governments spend their taxes, but few eurocitizens will have much idea how much of their money goes to the EU and how the EU distributes that money. Yet every year the EU Commission gives away some 130 billion euros of eurocitizens' contributions made mainly through taxation (equivalent to about £200 from every man, woman and child in the EU). In addition sums of money that are difficult to quantify come from the taxation of each state, on an ability-to-pay basis, to fund various activities such as military operations and the Defence Agency. Is this money well spent? Should more of this money be retained within each country and allocated and administered by individual states, for example, payments to farmers, fishermen and regional aid?

It is difficult to know who the actual individual, institutional or corporate end recipients of the money are. The EU (Siim Kallas again) recognises this as a problem which must be corrected.

A third of the EU budget is spent on "cohesion". This is basically a way of investing money to help the poorer EU countries to develop their prosperity in order to be more equal partners in the European Union. It is a way of bolstering the unity of Europe. It encourages a sense of belonging and that the EU delivers positive benefits. Spain, as one of the chief beneficiaries of such funding was quite swift to ratify the Constitution. Cohesion funding can powerfully influence people to support the idea of the EU. Whilst the intention and effects of cohesion funding are positive, it may have the side effect of clouding people's judgement of the value of the European Union.

Approximately 46 per cent of the EU budget is spent on agriculture.

(See *Transparency*, below. See *Finances of the EU - unsolved problems of European Union financial control - Fraud*, above, and in *Part Three: Where the money goes - EU budget.*)

The average citizen needs to know more about what the EU is doing and how the Commission and other EU institutions spend our money.

See *Transparency,* below and *Finances of the EU,* above.

House prices - free movement of capital and people

Affordable homes

The price of houses used to reflect wage levels and people used to live relatively close to their work. The situation has changed. House prices in some areas are far outstripping wage increases. City dwellers, able to afford to commute long distances have moved to the countryside, wealthy people have bought second homes and holiday homes, speculators have bought property as investments, lending organisations have long included the income of two partners in estimating how large an offer of a loan may be, loans have become more generous relative to income, and rules regarding the movement of capital across borders have been relaxed or removed allowing a great increase in cross-border purchases of dwellings. Into this situation large influxes of migrant workers may exacerbate a shortage of affordable accommodation as they may, under the *Charter of Fundamental Rights* claim a right to "social housing".

Within the EU there has been a great increase in cross-border property-buying. Where buyers are moving into under-populated areas that benefit can be expected to be mutual. Similar benefits may occur when purchasers contribute to the development of tourism or other commercial activity. The establishment of foreign ghettos may not be quite so mutually beneficial. For example, in Spain where three quarters of a million Brits have bought homes[83] the Spanish seem to have grown tired of their new citizens. Thousands of Brits in Spain are complaining of legally backed harassment in the form of compulsory purchase orders on parts of their land or claims that their houses have been illegally constructed and must be demolished.[84]

For those rich enough to take advantage of the relaxation of rules regarding the residence of foreigners and the free movement of capital across borders, the new situation is very good news. For the less affluent, especially young people trying to buy their first home, the situation in many areas is becoming desperate. The UK housing charity, Shelter, reports that

- "Today [February 2007] nearly 100,000 households in England will have woken up in temporary accommodation - more than twice as many as in 1997.
- Nearly one in 10 children in England lives in overcrowded housing.[85]
- Black and minority ethnic households are six times more likely than white households to be overcrowded.

- Over 260,000 households in England are on waiting lists for properties with three or more bedrooms. Only about 5,000 social rented homes of this size are built each year."

EU policy

The EU operates conflicting policies in the matter of property. On the one hand is the freedom of the rich to purchase as many homes as they can afford in whichever country they choose. At the other end of the wealth spectrum millions are unable to afford a home. For them the EU policy is expressed in article 94/3. "In order to combat social exclusion and poverty, the Union recognises and respects the right to social and housing assistance so as to ensure a decent existence for all those who lack sufficient resources, in accordance with the rules laid down by Union law and national laws and practices." As is so often the case, the EU expression of good intentions amounts to no guarantee whatsoever because in the end it is up to the individual state to decide what it wants to do.

London's experience with housing

Perhaps the EU should learn from the experience of London which has long operated an open-door policy for foreign home-buyers.

With inflation at 2.4 per cent[86] house prices in London rose 7% in 2005 and almost 9% in 2006. In Kensington and Chelsea, the average price of a flat is now £590,000. The average price in that area has risen 11% per year since 2000.[87] Half of that borough's home-buyers are from overseas – some to live in the UK, some to have a holiday home, some to provide a home for a son or daughter studying at university, some for investment. They are attracted not simply by the ambience, culture, financial consultancies, and facilities of this great city, but also by tax incentives. The UK operates a "non-domiciled" tax rule which means that foreign nationals pay no tax on investments and income earned outside the UK.[87] On the sale of property foreign owners pay no capital gains tax.[88] Those buying the most expensive properties come from the Far East, the Middle East, other EU countries, and, increasingly, Russia.

The price of houses and flats in Central London has long been beyond the means of ordinary workers. The average price of a flat in Central London is now said to be between £500,000 and £1,000,000. The cost of a garage is in the region of £150,000, and a parking space may be bought for £100,000.[89] A semi-detached house in outer London costs around £350,000. Even Britain's wealthy are being pushed out of the London property market. In the twelve months to July 2006 of the properties sold for over £6M almost two thirds went to foreign buyers.[90]

Free-trade policies applied to the housing market in London (distorted by tax incentives) have caused serious difficulties for public authorities attempting to provide affordable homes for key workers and others. London's waiting list for council homes stands at 300,000. London councils built just 100 homes in 2006.[91] Should not London's homes be within the purchasing power of London's citizens?

Similar questions could be asked of other areas within the EU where local people find themselves squeezed down market, away from areas where they might find work, or away from their roots. Nationally, in the UK, one and a half million families are awaiting council homes. In many towns key public service workers cannot afford to buy homes. According to a 2007 Halifax report 70 per cent of UK towns fall into this category, and house purchase in 99 per cent of towns is impossible for a typical nurse.[92]

The EU's choice

The issue for the EU is this: should there be a totally free movement of people and capital or should markets be moderated or controlled in some way? To put it another way: have member states or the EU a duty to ensure affordable homes for their citizens or must priority be given to the "rights" of the rich?

See *Localism, Subsidiarity, Enlargement, Patriotism,* and *Employment.*

Identity cards, passports, residence permits

Under article 10 (2a) of the Constitution (repeating *Nice Treaty*, article 18) EU citizens shall have "the right to move and reside freely within the territory of the Member States." EU leaders have decided that this freedom must be carefully monitored and for this purpose the Constitution, in contrast with the *Nice Treaty*, would have given powers to an EU committee to record, supervise and monitor EU citizens. "A European law or framework law of the Council may establish measures concerning passports, identity cards, residence permits, or any other such document and measures concerning social security and social protection. The Council shall act unanimously after consulting the European Parliament." (Article 125.)

These proposals suggest that freedom of movement may be very closely controlled and not altogether free, that the EU will record and monitor every EU citizen and that it, rather than individual states, will control social security and social protection. Already, the EU is engaged in the collection of data on all EU citizens. Why should any eurocitizen need a residence permit if he or she may reside freely anywhere within the European Union? The term "establish measures" is so broad that it appears to offer permission to do almost anything. We need to know the EU's intentions. How much documentation, monitoring and control of citizens is it contemplating? What is meant by "social security" in this context? Is it a euphemism for "social control"? Is it a step towards severe restrictions on the movement of people? The concepts of "free movement" and "monitoring your every move" are contradictions. These are important questions for every eurocitizen.The UK government's decision to introduce identity cards appears not to have been entirely its own idea in response to "the terrorist threat", but a move to come into line with "EU thinking" on these matters. A rational assessment of the likelihood of terrorist threats that could be prevented with the use of identity cards suggests they would be of minimal use.[93]

Do European citizens consent to the giving of such significant powers to a committee of just twenty-seven appointees of EU governments? The eurovoter will not be aware of their discussions. A mere "consultation" with the European Parliament cannot be regarded as a democratic safeguard. The standard question must be applied. Is there a good reason why such matters should be decided centrally by the EU rather than by individual member states? Should member states, for example, take decisions regarding who should be granted permission to reside in their states or the nature of immigration controls and residence and travel documentation, or should these decisions be taken by the EU?

See *Data Harvesting*, and articles 275, 276, 10 and 125.

Integration – To integrate or not to integrate

"What they [citizens] expect is . . . not a European superstate" - EU leaders in the *Laeken Declaration*, 15 December 2001.

Twenty-seven European states are partially integrated. The process, which is at a very advanced stage, began because the founding states could see some immediate practical benefits in co-operation. They also had a vision of "a united Europe." Such an ideal may be interpreted in different ways. Many would say that all European countries (not just those in the EU) are already united in peaceful friendly relationships, and that is all the unity they desire. Others, the supporters of the European Project,[94] see unity as the joining together of the countries of Europe into one superstate, a federation of states, the United States of Europe.

Whilst a united Europe, in the second sense, may be a goal offering many benefits it surely cannot be a goal for which any price may be paid. Eurocitizens would be unhappy in a united Europe under a dictatorship and the current lack of democracy is a key reason for the low level of support.

Many of those who so strenuously work towards further integration in Europe appear to have accepted the aim of unity as a matter of blind faith, of almost religious dogma, which must be pursued at all cost, regardless of the nature of the state that is being created and oblivious to the shortcomings of the present organisation of the EU. Their uncritical zeal is an element in the problems currently faced by the EU.

On 8 August 2005, Hubert Vedrine, then French Foreign Minister, wrote in the *Irish Times*, that the European crisis might have been avoided.

"In saying this, I underestimate the religious fervour that has seized the European project. For all those who believed in the various ideologies of the second half of the 20th century, but survived their ruin, the rush into European integration became a substitute ideology.

They planned urgently to end the nation state. Everything outside this objective was heresy and had to be fought. This was in the spirit of Jean Monnet, the rejection of self and of history, of all common sense. European power was a variation, the code name for a counterweight to America . . . and towards which the Constitution was supposed to offer a magical shortcut."

Many senior EU politicians remain passionately committed to integration and even see it as the only road to salvation.

EU Commission Vice-President, Günter Verheugen, made the following statement:"I see a clear danger when people are saying less Europe is better. More integration is not the problem, it is the solution."[95]

Giscard d'Estaing, speaking at the London School of Economics, 28 February 2006, said, "Let's be clear about this: the rejection of the Constitutional Treaty in France was a mistake, which will have to be corrected."

Romano Prodi, President of the EU Commission, speaking in the European Parliament, 16 December 2003 expressed his belief that only by destroying the independence of the states of Europe could they be saved. "The integration of the whole continent is our nation-states' only chance of survival."

European integration should not be a matter of faith, but a matter for rational evaluation and democratic approval.

Integration – the number one question

Integration is the number one question for the citizens of Europe: should the states of Europe be integrated into a single European superstate, one country? Such a transformation is the greatest peaceful change that could happen to a group of states. The Constitution, if ratified by all member states, would have been the final step in realising this momentous shift of power and would have established this superstate in its final form. As Guy Verhofstadt, Belgian Prime Minister, said, "The Constitution is the capstone of a European Federal State."[96]

Another view on the significance of the Constitution has been spelled out by Vaclav Klaus, President of the Czech Republic.

"This is crossing the Rubicon, after which there will be no more sovereign states in Europe with fully-fledged governments and parliaments which represent legitimate interests of their citizens, but only one state will remain. Basic things will be decided by a remote federal government in Brussels and, for example, Czech citizens will be only a tiny particle whose voice and influence will be almost zero." He added, "We are against a European superstate." - Mlada Fronta Dnes, 29 September 2003.[97]

The draft *Reform Treaty* (August 2007) makes it clear that the Constitution's changes will simply be transferred to the revised treaties - the *Treaty on the European Union* and the *Treaty Establishing the European Community* (renamed *Treaty on the Functioning of the Union.*) The UK retains certain opt outs.

No democratic approval for the unification of Europe

The Constitution claimed that the EU is founded on values which include democracy (article 2). This suggests that the will of the people did or would authorise its establishment. This might have been achieved by referendums in all twenty-seven member states. Jacques Chirac seems to have envisaged the ratification process as one which would involve citizens who would give "their solemn approval".

"Let us act in such a way that it [an EU Constitution] becomes a reality in 2004 - Such a text would unite the Europeans by enabling them, through their solemn approval, to identify with a project. - What can we do so that Europe carries greater weight on the international stage? - Now we must define, without timidity, the areas where we want to go towards more Europe, within the framework desired by France, of a Federation of Nation States."[98]

Leaders of eighteen EU states did not agree that their people should be directly consulted on this subject, thereby revealing their lack of commitment to democratic principles. Their failure to consult their people directly also suggests that they believed that their people would not support them, that their people would reject the superstate idea. As we know, this was what EU leaders at Laeken believed was the popular view in 2001. Currently EU citizens show weakening support for this idea. According to Siim Kallas, Vice-President of the

European Commission, speaking in 2005, "Opinion polls show eroding support for European integration throughout the European Union."[119]

An imposed unification of Europe would not be a democratic unification. The way the Constitution may now be introduced by dispersal amongst existing treaties (August 2007) shows the hostility of EU leaders to the idea of submitting their plans for the approval of eurocitizens. It is an authoritarian, dictatorial move.

Making integration acceptable

Much of the current opposition to integration in Europe may spring from perceived failures of the present organisation of the European Union when compared with modern progressive and democratic states. The sense of being kept in the dark, of being powerless, of being ruled by arrogant, out-of-touch and sometimes violent leaders who meet in secret and place themselves above the law and who decide issues on doctrinaire rather than pragmatic grounds, who are inconsistent in their commitments to policies and principles, who preside over an administration where fraud and lack of accountability remain a serious problem, and where there seems to be no route to a democratic change of policy – all these perceptions – contribute to hostility to the integration project. A reformed EU might be more acceptable to the euroelectorate and confidence in full integration might, in the course of time, develop

Perhaps a partial dismantling of the Union might assist its reform.

It might be considered whether the EU should be abolished and replaced with a free association of independent European states.

Starting point for all europlanning

The stalled and incomplete ratification process leaves the question of unification unanswered. Yet it remains the starting point for all plans for development and change in the European Union. Totally different lines of development will follow from the Yes or No answer to this question.

If member states are to become a single state, then it will have to be reformed.

If the people of Europe reject the idea of complete integration and member states are to remain relatively independent then the demarcations of power (who controls education, farming, foreign policy etc) will need to be set out clearly. A precisely defined, limited integration of EU states, probably about the level of integration that exists at the moment or somewhat less, might well be far more acceptable to the people of Europe. The problems of dysfunctional organisation, lack of democracy, accountability, transparency etc would still need solving. Most significantly the expansion of eurocontrol would be halted or reversed.

This chapter, *Major Issues*, explores many of the above ideas, but see particularly *Biggest problem number two*, *European Union by stealth*, *Subsidiarity* and *Preparing to write an acceptable constitution and rescue the EU from crisis*. In the *Euroterminology* chapter see *European Project* and *Federalism*.

Intellectual property rights

The EU trade Commission is active in international negotiations on behalf of EU copyright holders. Perhaps it thought it had hit on a profitable idea when it decided to extend the period of copyright protection on creative work (books, music, plays etc). An EU directive of 29 October 1993 required the British government (along with all other EU state governments) to modify its copyright law in order to "harmonise" with EU standards. This meant, for example, that whereas copyright in the UK had normally lasted for 50 years after the death of an author the EU now required this period to be extended to 70 years - thus harmonising with German law. If the decision had been to harmonise with Spanish law the period would have been only 25 years.

It is questionable whether the extension of copyright period has been a good idea or any better than the ideas of individual states in this matter. The main beneficiaries have been the children (often very mature children) or grand children of authors and their lawyers. Whilst everyone would wish authors to be properly paid for their work and their immediate family not to be deprived of an income immediately on their death there seems a very poor case to be made for paying money to later generations and their lawyers. The losers may have been the general public as access to literary or other creative work which has survived the test of time may have been limited. For example, it is less likely that a great poem that is still protected by copyright will appear in an anthology than poems that are out of copyright and which may therefore be freely used without fees to the grandchildren of the author.

Since copyright also confers power to prohibit the use of copyright material or control the way in which it is used there is the risk that, for reasons good or bad, copyright-owning grandchildren or others may disallow the use of copyright material. In this way the public may be deprived of literature etc which otherwise it may have enjoyed or benefited from. Such problems have arisen with, for example, the writings of Samuel Beckett.

Article 176 of the Constitution states that the Union will set up "centralised Union-wide authorisation, co-ordination and supervision arrangements." Currently copyright owners or their agents authorise the use of their copyright material. How a centralised authority could handle such matters more efficiently is hard to imagine. It seems like more centralisation, more bureaucracy at tax payer's expense, more funds that might go astray, more cost to the consumer and the replacing of an effective working system with something more difficult to use.

Languages

The EU operates in twenty-three languages. Twenty-five to thirty percent of the administrators employed by the EU are involved in translation.

Might it be helpful, cheaper and more sensible to conduct all business in just a few languages? (The business of the European Central Bank is conducted in only one language, English.) Fewer official languages would ease co-operation and travel and help to unite Europe.

Law-making

Concerns are:

- Too many laws - 97,000 pages of acquis (translated into 23 languages) is beyond human comprehension.
- Too secret. Too much of the law-making process (all that undertaken by the Council, the European Council, the European Central Bank, and the

Commission) takes place in secret. The exception, very recently introduced, is that the Council, when considering laws under the co-decision procedure (with the European Parliament) will now (2007) be open to the public. Other Council business will not.

- Too lobbied. There is an impression that powerful groups have undue influence on EU law-makers. (See *Lobbying* below.)
- Too many types of laws. Eight binding types of regulation show a dispersal of governmental functions and cause confusion. (See *Euroterminology - Laws/Rulings* etc.)
- Some laws may be introduced by people working out of public view without due legislative process. "European decisions" are laws by another name. A "European decision" is defined in article 34 as "a non-legislative act, binding in its entirety." The Commission, the Council, the European Council and the European Central Bank can all create such laws in specific cases (which are not specified) according to article 35. This is rule by decree, not democracy.
- Tampering with laws. Plans to "harmonise" or "approximate" laws may take away democratic control, be an overwhelming and costly administrative task, and take away confidence in the existing bodies of state laws. (Article 257-3.) (See *Criminal justice* above.)
- The pace of regulation. Does the European Parliament have sufficient time for full consideration of proposals put before it?
- Why are so many categories of laws not brought to the European Parliament for approval? See (*Democratic deficit.*)

Localism

Localism is the idea that it is better, where possible, to "act locally". This means eating locally produced food, buying locally produced goods, working close to your home, using local support services such as schools, universities and hospitals, financing things locally, supporting local charities, supporting local artists, craftsmen, musicians, theatre, and sports. It does not exclude non-local action, but is an approach to making important choices and may have certain benefits – particularly mental, social and environmental. It develops communities and reduces transport and environmental costs. It emphasises human responsibility and connectedness.

It is in tune with subsidiarity and greater powers and independence for local government, but is in conflict with free trade principles (which emphasise the movement of goods, people, services and capital) and the centralising of political power.

Localism has the potential to be life enhancing. Over emphasised it has the potential to become narrow, parochial, unadventurous, bigoted, exclusive, selfish and self-defeating.

See *Free trade* above and *Subsidiarity* below.

Lobbying - The influencing of EU institutions

The proper government of any society depends, in large part, on healthy communication between government and citizens. Governments need to foster contacts with their citizens and citizens with concerns need ways of presenting their concerns to government. Lobbying is therefore both desirable and necessary. Concerns arise in the EU because

- there are special difficulties for ordinary citizens trying to influence the EU.
- some organisations may exercise undue influence. Some professional lobbying organisations have developed exceptional capacity to contact and influence decision-makers.
- A further concern is that of lack of transparency - the public being kept unaware of, for example, the extent and detail of corporate pressure applied to EU decision-makers.

EU officials are well aware of these problems and the dangers of the current defective system. Siim Kallas, Vice president of the Commission, responsible for Administrative Affairs and Anti-Fraud, writing in *The Wall Street Journal*, 6 February 2006 suggested the danger that the EU should try to avoid. He quoted the example of what appeared to be the pay-off for lobbying by one big American company operating in the United States. "The Center for Public Integrity in Washington estimates that the Lockheed Martin Corporation alone spent $55 million over five years in lobbying, and received, by the way, $94 billion in defense contracts. In Brussels, one estimate puts all lobbying budgets combined at 90 million euros each year. . . The danger in the European approach is, as is often the case, excessive naivety."

Lobbying as part of the democratic process

Citizens in any EU country who want to influence the government or political process in their own country have a number of opportunities to do so. These include voting for a party or candidate whose policies they support, writing or talking to their elected representatives, writing to government ministers, publicising an issue by writing in the media or just writing letters to the media, joining groups campaigning for causes they support, being active in political parties, standing for election and even forming a new political party to contest elections. When a government upsets a large proportion of the electors in a country they may vote the government out. This is how democracy in large countries falteringly works. Democracy is sketchy and weak in the EU. Most of the avenues of influence present in state democracies do not exist for EU citizens as far as the power exercised by EU governing institutions is concerned.

Most EU decision-making takes place beyond the reach of democratic awareness and direct democratic influence. The direction of the EU and key policies are fixed by treaties. This direction is developed by EU bodies but particularly by the European Council which is responsible for the strategic direction of the EU. The Commission interprets the treaties and has, with few exceptions, sole power to initiate law making in the EU (article 26/2). Members of the European Parliament together with members of the European Council have the power to pass (or reject) laws proposed by the Commission on many areas of activity. Some matters are decided by the unanimous decision of the Council. The monetary policy of the eurozone is decided by the European Central Bank. (Even outside the eurozone non-eurozone EU governments are committed to trying to bring their economies into line with the eurozone.) The European Court of Justice makes decisions which affect the lives of all European citizens.

Against this plethora of interrelated sources of power within the EU the poor citizen of the EU is understandably confused. The professional lobbyist has no such problems - as the case of the European Round Table of Industrialists illustrates. (See below.) To whom should the ordinary eurocitizen address his concerns? Virtually every avenue of influence to those who wield power in the EU is closed. Members of the European parliament are not elected on European party programmes and do not direct policy. Since they may have little knowledge of the forthcoming legislative programme at times of elections they may be unable to present a useful statement of the positions they may take on forthcoming legislation. EU citizens will have had no say whatsoever in the choice of 96% of the ministers in the European Council and the many Councils of Ministers (the proportion elected by citizens of other member states) and they will have no opportunity to vote any of the many permutations of these Councils out at the next election because that is not how they come to power. They will have had no input whatsoever in the appointment of the Commissioners. The citizens of Europe cannot vote out the "government" of the European Union. They cannot write to or for a European media which will be widely read across EU member states. In almost all cases they are unable to join EU-wide interest or pressure groups because very few exist. All these closed doors to the influence of citizens tend to keep EU decision-makers out of touch with grassroots concerns and help to make it the mere shadow of democracy that it is.

Who can influence the EU?

Any person or organisation that can present information or an argument for a particular course of action to an appropriate EU body has a chance of influencing decision-making in the EU. A large number of organisations congregate in Brussels for the purpose of influencing EU decision-makers. Fifteen thousand professional lobbyists work in Brussels according to the Commission. There are 2,600 special interest groups with permanent offices in Brussels. Siim Kallas tells us, "While lobbying is by no means a new phenomenon, every day new NGOs and lobby professionals from all over the world open "Representational" offices in Brussels."[99]

Some of them are backed by considerable wealth. One of the most significant lobbying organisations for over 20 years has been the European Round Table of Industrialists. The lobbying methods of this organisation could well serve as a model for others who wish to influence decision-makers. But few will match their financial resources. The combined turnover of the European Round Table of Industrialists' companies is 1,400 billion euros and they employ around four million people worldwide. Their forty-five members include Volvo, Phillips, Nestlé, Reed Elsevier, Thyssen Krupp, Nokia, Carlsberg, France Telecom, British Airways, Unilever, Total, MOL Hungarian Oil and Gas Company, Astra Zeneca, Volkswagen, Deutsche Telecom, Rolls Royce, Heineken, Bayer, BP, Royal Dutch Shell, Pirelli, and BT.

This is how the ERT describes its working methods:

> "ERT identifies the most important issues, analyses critical factors and makes its views known to policy-makers and political decision-takers at national and European level by means of reports, position papers and face-to-face discussion.
>
> At European level, the ERT has contact with the European Council, the European Commission, the Council of Ministers and the European Parliament.
>
> Every six months the ERT strives to meet the government that holds the EU presidency to discuss priorities.
>
> At national level, each member communicates ERT views to his own national government and Parliament, business colleagues and industrial federations, other opinion-formers and the press."

In 1989, according to its own account, "ERT strengthened its links with the European Commission, maintaining pressure for completion of the Single Market." In the following two years the ERT continued to lobby and produce reports arguing for the "Reshaping of Europe," work which bore fruit in the *Maastricht Treaty* of 1992.

> "The European Round Table of Industrialists sends messages to high level EU meetings. For example, in 2001 it sent a message to the European Council meeting in Gothenburg on the subject of "opening up the business opportunities of EU enlargement." This underlined the view that enlargement can contribute positively to business competitiveness for those in the existing EU and also countries at that time hoping to join the EU. Competitiveness may be a code word for reducing business costs by ditching western European workers in favour of lower paid workers in eastern Europe."

Of course, it is fair to argue that assisting poorer EU countries to achieve greater prosperity is a good thing both for their citizens and to achieve a fairer and more harmonious Europe. The loyalties of national politicians who are also Eurodecision-makers are torn on this issue. What would their electors wish?

> "ERT makes a great effort to involve leading EU figures in discussions. In October 2001 it wanted to promote its ideas on pension reform and organised a meeting with Commissioner Pedro Solbes, members of the European Parliament and pension experts from governments, business and academia. In December the same year the ERT lobbied the European Council in Laeken calling for "a stronger Europe."

One way to access European decision-makers is to invite them to lavish occasions. This is the ERT's account of its celebration of its 20th anniversary.

> "On 23 June 2003, ERT celebrated its 20th anniversary at a reception at the Palais d'Egmont in Brussels. The President of the European Commission, Romano Prodi, was guest of honour, joining members of the European Commission and European Parliament, ambassadors to the EU and ERT members, past and present, to mark 20 years of ERT activities."

ERT chairman, Gerhard Cromme, delivered the keynote speech in which he paid tribute to the work of the ERT in rescuing Europe from poor international competitiveness, entrenched national barriers and "a kind of eurosclerosis". He said that the EU had made enormous progress, not least through the internal market programme, EMU, and enlargement and that the ERT was proud at having been at the forefront of advocating those reforms, but the ERT would be working hard in the future to create an even more competitive and prosperous Europe.

In addition to the issues mentioned above the European Round Table of Industrialists has argued for the development of Europe's transport infrastructure, the reform of education and pension provision, greater investment in research and development, the control (limitation) of state spending and the strengthening of links with the US.

The way the EU has developed owes much to the input of the European Round Table of Industrialists.

Access for the privileged few

The EU claims to work transparently. Article 399 states, "The institutions, bodies, offices and agencies of the Union shall ensure transparency in their work." Yet the Commissioners work behind closed doors. The lobbying that goes on is unknown to most EU citizens. If transparency is to be anymore than a cynical and empty claim then full records of formal and informal contacts and correspondence with senior EU people should be maintained and the records should be accessible and searchable on the internet.

Access to EU decision-makers should be for all, not simply the most wealthy (and mostly big business). Balancing views should be sought from those who may be affected by policies, legislation and rulings. To ensure that Commissioners carry out proper consultation their activities should be subject to reporting and detailed public review and interrogation. Siim Kallas accepts this and things may change.

Of course the Commission would be right to argue that it does consult the public. It does this in two ways. The first is by conducting numerous opinion surveys and consultation with focus groups. The second is by consulting EU committees. See "eurobarometer" and "advisory bodies" in the sections *Euroterminology* and *Institutions*. This approach runs the risk of often measuring the effects on public opinion of a sometimes ill-informed or partisan media which is itself highly susceptible to the media lobbyists, the spinmasters of government, industry or other well-funded opinion-formers. Whilst this consultation is laudable it is not sufficient because it is likely to miss the detailed knowledge and experience of special interest or user groups and academia even though some of these are represented on the Economic and Social Committee.

The independence of these committees is open to question since their members are selected by the Commission. This may lead to the suspicion that members will be appointed on the basis that they may give the advice which Commissioners would like to hear. The committees might well be disbanded and replaced with other forms of consultation including public hearings on important topics under consideration.

In addition to straightforward lobbying carried out by individuals and organisations there are numerous "think tanks" - which may often appear to be independent organisations.

In America and now Europe organisations have sprung up with names which suggest independent academic foundations, socially or environmentally-minded research organisations or possibly government organisations. Many such organisations are lavishly funded and exist purely to promote the narrow interests of their sponsors by influencing, even shaping public debate and legislation.

Often these organisations have right-wing free-market agendas and push for a society ruled by market forces alone, with business operating without the restrictions of environmental concerns, regard for workers' welfare, or care for the sick, elderly or other disadvantaged people in society locally or in the world at large.

Exxon Mobil, which adamantly opposes the Kyoto Protocol has funded The International Policy Network, The Centre for the New Europe, Tech Central Station and the International Council for Capital Formation. The Centre for the New Europe also receives funding from US pharmaceuticals giants, Pfizer and Merck.

The Stockholm Network is an association of 120 think tanks. According to Corporate Europe Observatory, "the member groups are primarily dogmatic free-marketeers who want to introduce minimalist 'flat taxes' (thus ending redistribution via taxation), terminate social protection systems and privatise health care. They attack socially or environmentally progressive legislation, which is in place or under discussion, and that places restrictions on market activity."

The Stockholm Network and the Centre for the New Europe argue for free-market principles to be applied to the sale of medicines. This means allowing pharmaceutical companies to advertise medicines directly to the public, cutting out the interference of medical professionals who normally decide what the most appropriate or safe medication may be for particular people and their ailments.

The Centre for the New Europe, in line with a demand of Microsoft, argues for the patenting of software. It also argues for the patenting of ideas and knowledge. Corporations which hold the patents on ideas or knowledge would then control or licence the use of these ideas and knowledge, as a monopoly holder, for a period of 20 years. This proposal has, according to Corporate Europe Observatory, already found its way into a proposed EU directive (July 2005).

Open source software users (who may incidentally lack the financial resources of Microsoft and others) oppose this planned directive.

A final example of the attempts of big corporations to influence the EU in favour of their own profitability is British American Tobacco, the tobacco giant, which claims to practise corporate social responsibility. (They don't explain how tobacco can ever be sold responsibly.) The company offers funds to think tanks sympathetic to its trade.

Siim Kallas is well aware that lobbyists come in many guises and he wishes to include them all in his demands for openness, registration and adherence to a code of conduct. "There is an emerging European consensus that common rules should apply

- to all those who engage in lobbying, for profit or not. The register and code should apply
- to all public affairs consultants, accountants, lawyers, NGOs, think tanks, corporate lobbyists and trade associations."[99]

Against the public interest

According to Jorgo Riss of the Greenpeace European Unit:

> The public pays a heavy price for the big-money lobbying that goes on in Brussels, since legislation to improve health and the environment loses out every time. For example, eight years after the EU started addressing the environmental problems caused by 4.1 million tonnes of PVC plastic waste annually, the PVC industry has succeeded in preventing any real progress, and has recruited two senior Commission officials to a public relations exercise that recycles a mere 0.44% of this waste.

Joint task forces

These are committees set up by the Commission to explore issues and come up with solutions. It seems these do not begin with the eurocitizen at the heart of their deliberations but the corporate lobbyists. The Alliance for Lobbying Transparency and Ethics Regulation (ALTER-EU) makes this demand:

> The Commission must terminate cases of privileged access and undue influence granted to corporate lobbyists, for instance: joint task forces in which corporate interests are represented while public interest NGOs are not (such as Cars 21 which consists of Commission officials, CEOs and lobbyists from the automobile industry, but no environmental NGOs). And the privileged status accorded to business lobby groups like the European Services Forum and the Trans-Atlantic Business Dialogue.

Key issues relating to lobbying within the EU

- How can the unbalanced access of wealthy corporate lobbyists be balanced by the voices of the ordinary citizen, professionals, independent experts and organisations concerned about issues of human wellbeing and sustainability?
- Should there be a meaningful register, which is made public, of the number and nature of lobbyists' contacts with the EU decision makers and the level of the EU official contacted?
- Should there be a register of the basic lines of arguments of lobbyists, such as more spending on roads, more spending on sports facilities, cutbacks on health spending, increase spending on nuclear weapons?
- Should entertaining by lobbyists of EU personnel be allowed, and if so should it be a matter of public record?
- Can there be a requirement built into the presentation of any new law or regulation that the presenter indicates the extent of advice he or she has received from "interest groups" or individuals?
- Could a register be kept of recipients of EU grants which indicates the number and level of contacts the individual organisation has had with EU officials in relevant positions of influence?
- Can user interest groups be guaranteed access to balance the lobbying by corporate lobbyists?
- Should EU officials, on leaving office, be prohibited from joining lobbying organisations?

- Should there be a register of costs of gifts and "expenses" paid by lobbyists to EU officials and details of entertainment costs spent for the enjoyment of EU officials?

For an extensive account of the activities of corporate lobbyists, and the large number of companies involved, visit the web site of Corporate Europe Observatory and Alliance for Lobbying Transparency and Ethics Regulation (ALTER-EU). See also the Europa EU Commission web site.

The lobby for the control and accountability of lobbyists

This statement comes from a group of organisations concerned about the way lobbying is conducted within the EU.

"The undersigned organisations are deeply concerned about the growing influence of corporate lobby groups on European Union decision-making. Over 15,000 professional lobbyists now operate in Brussels, a large majority representing business interests. Yet, ethics and transparency rules around lobbying are virtually non-existent. Beyond the problem of business spending ever-increasing amounts to influence the political process, the European Commission has developed a tradition of awarding privileged access to corporate interests. The enormous influence of corporate lobbyists undermines democracy and all too frequently results in postponing, weakening or blocking urgently needed progress in EU social, environmental and consumer protections. As the first steps in addressing these problems, the Commission should take determined action to improve transparency around lobbying and ensure that no business groups are given privileged access and influence on EU policy-making.

We welcome the 'European Transparency Initiative' (ETI), launched in March 2005 by European Commissioner Siim Kallas, in particular, the objective to address the current lack of mandatory regulation and reporting of lobbying activities. A mandatory system for lobbying disclosure is urgently needed and must be shaped in a way that optimally enables democratic scrutiny of inputs into EU policy-making.

The undersigned organisations demand the following:

EU lobbying disclosure legislation which must include:

- A mandatory system of electronic registration and reporting for all lobbyists with a significant annual lobbying budget. The reports must be made available in a fully searchable, sortable and downloadable online database.
- Enforceable ethics rules for lobbyists (for instance prohibiting employment of officials or their relatives for lobbying purposes).
- An improved code of conduct for European Commission officials, including:
- Recording of formal and informal meetings between Commission officials and lobbyists and logging of correspondence (to be made available in a fully searchable online database).
- An extended 'cooling off' period before Commissioners and senior officials can start working for lobby groups or lobbying advisory firms.
- The European Commission should encourage the other EU institutions, particularly the European Parliament and the European Council, to develop similar rules.

- The Commission must terminate cases of privileged access and undue influence granted to corporate lobbyists, for instance:
    - joint taskforces in which corporate interests are represented while public interest NGOs are not (such as Cars 21 . . . [See above.]).
    - the privileged status accorded to business lobby groups like the European Services Forum and the Trans-Atlantic Business Dialogue.

These are minimum requirements if the 'European Transparency Initiative' is to achieve meaningful democratic progress. Vested interests are defending secrecy and privileged access by advocating "self-regulation", voluntary codes of conduct and other pseudo-solutions that do nothing to increase democratic scrutiny of the role of lobbyists in EU policy-making. If the EU institutions would endorse such proposals instead of introducing mandatory disclosure and ethics rules, it would fundamentally undermine the 'European Transparency Initiative'. We have formed the Alliance for Lobbying Transparency and Ethics Regulation (ALTER-EU) to prevent the failure of this important initiative."

For an extensive account of the activities of corporate lobbyists, and the large number of companies involved, visit the web site of Corporate Europe Observatory.

Media

"We know that nine out of 10 people will not have read the Constitution and will vote on the basis of what politicians and journalists say." - Jean-Luc Dehaene, Former Belgian Prime Minister and Vice-President of the EU Convention.[100]

For there to be a flourishing or even a functioning democracy in the European Union there needs to be wide, and critical examination of the decision making of the EU. Without it people are at the mercy of the politicians who interpret their own actions and decisions in a favourable light and a narrow range of media, many or most of which may have strong connections with the wealth and power elite. For example, in the lead up to the French referendum on the EU Constitution there was a massive media campaign with celebrities, politicians and the mainstream media pushing with all their strength for a Yes vote. If they had had even a moderately sound case they would have won easily. The media in France cannot be in a very healthy state to be so out of touch with its people and so uncritical of such an incompetent document of such immense importance.

Another important aspect of media in relation to democracy is that in a normal democratic state there are a variety of media operating across the entire country. In EU terms this would require there to be popular media widely followed across the twenty-seven member states. The EU, for reasons of history and language lacks this essential democratic element. This weakens EU democracy. To some extent the internet is beginning to fill this gap, but on an insignificant scale at the moment.

Part of the problem is the domination of media by huge commercial conglomerates. A competition policy which strives to keep media companies far smaller might lead to the emergence of more players and a greater divergence of views. The EU might usefully break up the present EU media corporations that currently dominate the field.

As for trans-europe media coverage, this has been achieved in coverage of the Eurovision Song Contest and football. At a cultural level surely there could be more variety. There is huge scope and need for the development of trans-Europe cultural and political coverage and programmes. If the UK is typical then it is likely that citizens of the European Union are almost entirely ignorant of the lives and culture of the people in the majority of EU states – fellow eurocitizens of the eurostate. There is a need for media entrepreneurs here to seize the opportunities and meet the needs of the citizens of Europe.

If you read, listen to and watch the British media you may gain the impression that Europe is another country worthy of the reporting of interesting snippets of news. Occasionally we learn of problems "between Britain and Europe" when, for example the UK is battling with "Europe" over its budget contribution. A separatist mindset persists. The fact that to a large degree the UK is a major part of the European Union and governed by (and part of) the bodies of the European Union seems not to have been understood yet. The European Union is grossly underreported in Britain with the result that few people in the UK are able to make informed judgements on EU issues. British media are failing in their duty to report and comment on the news that matters to its customers.

The EU itself makes a great effort to communicate what is going on. It spends considerable sums on presenting the EU to the media and the world. The budget in 2006 for staff alone was 121,976,317 euros (approximately £85,298,000).

See *Propaganda, Free trade – competition and corporate giantism,* and *Free trade – How effective is the EU in dealing with monopolies and mergers?* and *Democratic deficit.* For details of some web based media concerned with the European Union see the *Web sites and books relating to the EU* chapter.

Micromanagement

A matter which causes intense annoyance, has an adverse effect on the image of the EU, and can lead to the ridiculing of decision-makers is the management from Brussels of the minutiae of the activities of the eurocitizen. Sometimes, in attending to detail the remote administrators fail to handle the big decisions which really might benefit from some EU-wide planning. Examples include Brussels specifying the thickness of steps on fishing boats whilst managing the EU fishing industry so badly that the marine ecosystem of the North Sea is near collapse. See *Subsidiarity* and *Fisheries crisis*.

Militarisation

See *Defence and foreign policy* above.

Money given away by the EU

See *Giving our money away* above.

Nationalism

See *Patriotism – Political patriotism* below.

Neutrals De-neutralised

See *Unite and be strong* below.

Nuclear energy

See *Energy and the environment* above.

Nuclear weapons

EU states condemned Iraq for its alleged possession of nuclear weapons and Iran and North Korea for their nuclear weapons aspirations.[101] EU leaders do not turn their attention on their members' behaviour. Several EU states allow nuclear weapons to be stationed on their territories and others possess and are developing new nuclear weapons. They do not condemn India, Pakistan and Israel or other powers for their possession of nuclear weapons. Britain and France fail to honour their thirty-nine year old obligation under the *Nuclear Non Proliferation Treaty* (1968) to phase out all nuclear weapons. The EU has not suggested that the UN should send in inspectors to assess the extent of the failure of these two countries to divest themselves of WMD, nor that sanctions should be applied against them to encourage compliance.

Patriotism - Economic patriotism

Some EU states are taking decisions to keep control of major economic assets, such as airports, within their states and not allow them to be sold to foreign buyers. This is in contravention of EU free trade policy. France and Spain are preaching economic patriotism. The issue is: are they right to do so? If so a basic EU principle might usefully be formally modified. See *Free trade* above.

Patriotism - Political patriotism

When we eurocitizens vote in state elections we imagine that those we elect understand that we expect them to act primarily in the best interests of citizens of their own state. Two problems arise for eurocitizens. First, in contrast to pre-EU days, many of the decisions which affect our lives are taken beyond the reach of elected state parliaments. Decisions are taken by eurobureaucrats, Commissioners, and international committees, including COREPER, the Council and the European Council. (The Commision is appointed "to promote the general interest of the Union", not to look after the interests of communities that may find themselves in difficulty or consider they deserve special treatment.) Second, those elected politicians at the top of the winning national party in an election become, without any special mandate on euroaffairs, eurodecision-makers with loyalties to the the EU as a whole – the EU project, the EU acquis, and the EU treaties. Insofar as they move away from their home states to make decisions at a European level (behind closed doors) they move away from their own people and into the arms of the eurolobbyists with agendas that may conflict with the interests of their citizens. The power of the state representative on EU committees is typically one vote in twenty-seven. With so little power it is not surprising that the EU sometimes overrules the desires expressed by individual states - for example, in the extent of British territorial waters. It may be for better reasons than mere nostalgia that eurocitizens may wish to see more political patriotism in their own politicians and a better account of stances on EU issues in election manifestoes and public statements. Many would prefer to see more decisions taken at a local level.

Although the EU has its own elected Members of the European Parliament they are limited in what they may do for their electors because by EU rules they may not be given a binding mandate, and in any case, they have no powers to initiate any policy.

Who is to stand up for the local community or the citizens of a member state when they consider that EU policies are operating against their interest - for example, destroying their way of life or livelihood or allowing their homes to be sold to rich foreigners?

See *Localism, House prices, Agriculture and Fisheries, Subsidiarity*, and the chapter *Alternative Plans for EU Development.*

Politicians

See *Patriotism - political patriotism* above.

President of the Commission

This is one of the most powerful roles in the European Union. The Constitution would have had this person appointed by the European Council with the European Parliament having the power to veto the decision. This person could be appointed directly by the people of Europe or by the European Parliament. EU leaders, in the *Laeken Declaration*, thought all three alternatives should be considered and asked which would be more appropriate. Which would be most democratic or be most likely to engage the interest of eurovoters in EU affairs?

Propaganda

Propaganda is an organised attempt to persuade people to a point of view without permitting or encouraging the consideration of opposing views.

The EU is unique as a political organisation. It is a supranational organisation which in many respects acts like a state. At the present time the organisation is evolving and expanding, and the official policy of the organisation, passionately promoted by some leaders and enshrined in EU treaties, the Constitution and its replacements, is that of "ever closer union" - the total integration of its 27 member states into a United States of Europe. The aim may or may not be the best policy for Europeans. That is not the point. But this dismantling of the nation state is an idea which has never been debated and democratically accepted by the 480 million people of the EU.

Should the EU spend taxpayers' money on propaganda to promote the transfer of power from state governments to the central authority of the EU? This is what has been happening.

A good deal of money is spent on direct campaigns to persuade EU citizens to think of themselves as Europeans and to believe that government by the EU central authorities is preferable to government by their own elected parliaments. (See also *Giving our money away.*)

It is beyond the scope of this short item to identify, in EU budgets, those sums of money which may be truly described as for propaganda from those sums of money which are legitimate uses of money for the purposes of promoting education, dialogue, and information. But there can be no doubt that a good deal of money is spent with the direct aim of promoting the integrationist project. For example, in the section of the EU budget for 2006 for Education and Culture (Title 15) a sum of €3,120,000 (approximately £2,182,000) is allocated for "European integration in universities". The budget shows the total sum of €10.571,000 (£7,392,000 approximately) available for this purpose. The budget statement includes the following note. "This appropriation is intended to cover expenditure on European integration programmes in universities, such as the Jean Monnet chairs, which are designed to consolidate the European Union by encouraging universities, both inside and outside the Union, to create and develop courses and modules on European integration and to select them in line with the opinions of experts on the matter, and Jean Monnet centres." This is quite different from funding education aimed at encouraging and developing understanding based on an open-minded, unbiassed assessment of evidence.

Also in the Education and Culture section of the 2006 budget are sums given under the heading *Dialogue with Citizens* to "Support for activities and bodies active at European level in the field of active European citizenship". Spending includes €624,000 for "'Our Europe'Association", €2,960,000 for "Grants to organisations advancing the idea of Europe", €1,350,000 for "Associations and federations of European interest", €400,000 for "European think tanks".

The Europa (official EU) web site explains what the EU means by "Active European citizenship".[102] Under the heading "Active European citizenship - Council Decision 2004/100/EC of 26 January 2004 . . ." it states that "The European Union is keen to see its citizens play an active part in the implementation of Community policies." This is not what most people would understand by the word "dialogue".

It is not easy to discover what all these organisations actually do. For example, the "'Our Europe'Association" does not appear to have a web site and the best Google can do is find brief mentions of the organisation. The EU's own search engine is, for an organisation committed to transparency, quite unbelievable. It turns up 84 documents. The first and only relevant document is the "Active European Citizenship" page, just referred to which mentions the association only once - as an organisation it particularly wishes to support. No further information. The rest of the documents offered by the search engine had no titles and were all references to budgets. The description of the documents were incomprehensible and had a recognizable pattern which is nonsense in any language or perhaps it is in code.. A typical one read "No Title 3713Kb Budget Additional appropriations Total Heading Initial appropriations incl. changes Outturn % Appropriations Outturn % Appropriations Outturn % % n-1 1 AGRICULTURE 49.676,450 33.846,40 68,13 % 49,78 36,21 72,73 % 49.726,232 33.882,601 68,14 % 61,72 % 2 STRUCTURAL OPERATIONS 42.423,497 37.844,17 89,21 % 115,86 115,45 99,65 % 42.539,361 37.959,623 89,23 % 69,53 % 3 INTERNAL POLICIES 9.000,075 3.309,70 36,77 % 834,96 126,78 15,18 % 9.835,033 3.436,476 34,94 % 30,29 % 4 EXTERNAL ACTION 5.319,000 ..."

An attempt with the same search term on 17 May 2007 turned up equally unhelpful documents. Item 10, for example, was described as a Microsoft word document, but was in fact a pdf document. This was nothing about citizenship, but was a 636 page document, *PINE Prospects for Inland Navigation within the Enlarged Europe*. It was described as follows: "FFuullll FFiinnaall RReeppoor-rttPPIINNEEPPrroossppeeccttss ffoorrIInnllaanndd NNaavviiggaattiioonnwwi-itthhiinn tthheeEEnnllaarrggeedd Eeuurrooppee The outcomes and results of the PINE project are put down in three main deliverables: Full Final Report Final Concise Report Summary."

During the afternoon of the same day, using the same search term an entirely new list of offerings appeared, almost all not in English. This is something worse than incompetence, and cannot be caused by lack of funding for communication. The total sum allocated to "dialogue" was €37,134,000, (approximately £25,968,000). The website seems to work with a random confusion generator.

Sums allocated to "press and communication" may be for work of a purely non-propagandist nature. The sums expended are considerable. For staff the budget was €23,397,980, for buildings and related expenditure €40,264,500, and for other information activities €4,264,500. In total, €67,912,000 (approximately £47,491,000).

When the Constitution was coming up for consideration by various electorates the NO campaign complained of massive funding for a Yes vote, with an absence of funding for the No campaign.

In 2006/2007 the EU engaged in a dialogue on the future of Europe. The exercise may have been flawed (see *Part Seven - Alternative Plans for EU Development*) but it was a positive though insignificant move. Propaganda can mix with other forms of communication quite happily.

Are the budgets for the above activities being appropriately spent? Why is money not spent on open-minded intellectual exploration of ideas, rather than on the narrow promotion of EU orthodoxy? Who is questioning those who allocate and spend the money? What steps are they taking to report to the eurocitizen?

See *Integration - the number one question, Tolerance* and *Transparency.*

Public health - EU takeover V subsidiarity

Article 278/1 explains how the European Union will take a major role in directing the public health provision of EU member states. "Action by the Union . . . shall be directed towards improving public health, preventing human illness and disease, and obviating the sources of danger to physical and mental health." These may well be the right aims but should the EU or national governments be in control of policy and provision?

Establishing guidelines and monitoring

Article 278/2. "Member States shall, in liaison with the Commission, co-ordinate among themselves their policies and programmes in the areas referred to in paragraph 1. The Commission may . . . take any useful initiative to promote . . . the establishment of guidelines and indicators, the organisation of exchange of best practice, and the preparation of the necessary elements for periodic monitoring and evaluation." Do EU states need this degree of co-ordination, monitoring and direction in their health care provision?

Article 278/4 tells us that European laws or framework laws shall set standards regarding safety of organs and substances of human origin, blood and blood derivatives, and medicinal products. They will establish measures in the veterinary and phytosanitary fields which have as their direct objective the protection of public health, and measures concerning monitoring, early warning of, and combating serious cross-border threats to health.

Apart from the problem of cross border disease why should the EU be involved in directing major aspects of the health care of 27 states?

See also *Privatisation* above and *Services* below.

Reform Treaty, 2007

The *Reform Treaty* is extraordinary in the history of international agreements. What is actually new in this treaty in terms of arrangements between states is very little indeed - principally a delay in bringing in new voting plans which were previously agreed and opt-outs in some requirements for some states. These are the practical, tangible changes.

The remainder of the treaty consists of changing the names of things and re-arranging the elements of the *Treaty Establishing a Constitution for Europe* so it seems to have disappeared. It is an exercise in deception.

The EU needs real reform and a genuine willingness to address issues, not prevarication and the proliferation of confusion. The so-called *Reform Treaty* is, in reality, the Hide the Constitution Treaty.

Red tape

Businesses complain about a burden of regulation which they are supposed to know about, understand and act upon.

How can any business, any citizen or any lawyer cope with 97,000 pages of EU regulations? (See *Acquis* in *Euroterminology*.) How can anyone know for sure that this body of law has been correctly translated between the twenty-three official languages of the EU?

Deregulation and simplification are needed on a grand scale to make EU law humanly comprehensible and user-friendly. However, any process would need to be carried out with care. It would be disastrous if a slash and burn brigade rode in and destroyed vital regulation for the protection of the environment, workers' rights and human rights.

Restrictive measures

See *Sanctions* in *Free trade*, above.

Rigidity

Should actual policies be set down in a constitution (or the EU treaties), as if they can be decided and set for ever? This approach to policy effectively closes down policy debate. A commitment to policy inertia seems both unnecessary and potentially dangerous.

Rule of law

The European Union was founded, in part, on the rule of law. An important question is, who should be subject to the law?

It is often held that no-one is above the law. In England in 1215 King John signed the *Magna Carta*, an agreement which established that all were subject to the law, including the King himself and his officials.[103]

In the first article of the American Constitution the subject of impeachment is raised and specifies how the President of the United States may be tried and by whom. Article 2 states, "The President, Vice President and all civil officers of the United States, shall be removed from office on impeachment for, and on conviction of, treason, bribery, or other high crimes and misdemeanors."

The first article of The Fundamental Rights and Duties of Citizens in the Constitution of the People's Republic of China (article 33 of the Constitution) states, " All citizens of the People's Republic of China are equal before the law."

In the EU the breaking of international law, the Nuremberg Principles, and the violation of the *Charter of the United Nations*, by certain EU leaders not only passes without trials, but also without criticism. The Commitment of the EU to the rule of law is limited. See *Defence and Foreign policy* .

Sanctions

See *Sanctions* in *Free trade*, above.

Social security and social protection

The Constitution would have extended the powers of the Council set out in article 18 of the *Treaty Establishing the European Community*. Just twenty-seven members of the Council would be able to make laws concerning social security and social protection after consulting the European Parliament. "A European law or framework law of the Council may establish measures . . . concerning social security and social protection. The Council shall act unanimously after consulting the European Parliament." (Article 125.) Is this too much power in too few hands, too remote from the EU electorate?

In June 2007 the UK secured an opt out from these arrangements.

See *Identity cards*.

Society

> "There is no such thing as society. There are individual men and women, and there are families." - Margaret Thatcher.[104]

The European Union is a political organisation which, by implication, believes that it has constructed some kind of ideal social organisation. This is seen, for example, in the discourse of europhiles who talk warmly of "the European Social Model".[105] It is seen, too, in the treaties and in the proclamation of human rights in the 2004 Constitution, in commitments to the rule of law, democracy etc within the EU and the expressed intention to spread these principles. "The Union's action on the international scene shall be guided by the principles . . . which it seeks to advance in the wider world: democracy, the rule of law, universality and indivisibility of human rights and fundamental freedoms, respect for human dignity, the principles of equality and solidarity, and respect for the principles of the *United Nations Charter* and international law." Part of this advancement in the wider world is seen in the ambition of European leaders to expand the power base of the European Union, potentially doubling the population within two decades.

What sort of society have Europeans created? The people of the European Union have achieved a way of life which has a great deal to recommend it, particularly in that, for most citizens, the member states have provided within their borders a high degree of material comfort and security, enormous opportunities for personal development, freedom of expression, freedom from fear, the promotion of tolerance, respect for fellow human beings, and human dignity. (Such achievements can, of course, be seen in many other countries outside the European Union.)

But has the European Union really brought social organisation to a very high level? Are we now living in one of the most advanced civilisations the world has ever seen so that we are justified in wishing to spread the glories of our success to the rest of the world? Have EU leaders actually even given much thought to the kind of societies their policies are leading to? This is not a peripheral concern, but fundamental to the lives of every eurocitizen.

A founding principle and core belief of the EU is that free trade is the key to material and social progress. The Constitution and *Reform Treaty* would make it an objective of the EU to spread the practice of free trade around the world.[106] As an association of trading states the EU naturally wants to expand its markets. But perhaps before the EU seeks to expand its membership and influence we should reflect on the kind of society, or societies, that have developed across the EU.

Some would suggest that associated with its economic and social policies are some two-edged or less laudable human characteristics: materialism, permissiveness, acquisitiveness, greed, selfishness/individualism, competitiveness, exploitation, short-termism, workaholism, social problems (including stress and alcohol abuse) the down-grading of the role of parents and families, borrowing or stealing from the future to fund today, and aggression. And that as a result, families and social peace and social enrichment are at risk. Some suggest there is a growing divide between rich and poor with a growing underclass excluded from the well-being enjoyed by the majority. In addition, the sustainability of the economic theory is uncertain.

This doubt is increasing as change accelerates within the EU as a result of the 2004 and 2007 enlargements, with the development of free-trade/ liberalisation policies, and with the link between economic growth and environmental degradation and climate change becoming more widely recognised.

Are EU leaders conscious of all the important effects of their policies? The EU states that it "places the individual at the heart of its activities." Unstated contenders for prime focus might be international corporations or work. Perhaps it is all of these. We can see huge benefits from these interests, but it may be time to question whether the stress on freedoms of trade, free movement of goods, free movement of capital, free movement of services and free movement of people might lead to societies in turmoil.

Within the EU many aspects of social and economic organisation are in a state of change and uncertainty, with many apparent failures to effect policies, plus other problems and looming worries. This *Major Issues* chapter, often echoing observations of EU leaders, has noted many discrepancies between aims and achievements and many grave concerns. These include:

- The EU acknowledges major failings within its system including legislation overload, and lack of democracy, accountability, transparency, and subsidiarity
- The values claimed by the EU are not consistent or entirely credible.
- Connected with its free trade policy is a flight of manufacturing and jobs to countries outside the EU.
- Connected with a policy of free movement of capital is the cross-border buying of retirement homes, second homes and speculative investment in dwellings which, in some areas, is making homes unaffordable for local populations.
- Connected with its free movement of people policy are a sudden burgeoning of demands for homes in some areas, and depression of wage levels where there are influxes of workers from low wage economies. This mass movement of workers inevitably results in reduced employment opportunities for some local populations and a loss of key workers in the countries where qualified workers are abandoning low-wage work.
- Within the EU there are serious social problems which include, in some areas, high levels of unemployment and a widespread sense of job insecurity, increasing poverty, social unrest (for example, riots in France), high levels of crime, an influx of foreign criminals and a migration of some of our own; family breakdown,[107] increasing problems with drug abuse, gambling and alcoholism, increasing stress and mental illness, a sense of failure to achieve a work/life balance for many people, a failure to make homes affordable, insecurity of energy supplies, fears of long-term environmental damage and climate change, and on significant occasions an uncontrolled and un-criticised propensity to become involved in interstate aggression. In the case of the UK, in particular, there is a new fear of terrorism.
- Whilst the freedoms of free societies are greatly prized there is a sense that freedoms may now be giving way to greater surveillance, recording and supervision of citizens. With increasing power moved to the EU from member states there is a reduction of democratic involvement and power accompanied by growing alienation and cynicism between politicians and citizens.

Of course, most of these problems are not unique to the EU, but the problems are associated with and, at best, not assisted by EU policies.

Concepts lacking development in EU ideology include those of "human communities", society, the family, parenthood, localism, subsidiarity, work-life balance, equality, compassion, leisure, the arts, sports, public service, simplicity, sustainability, integrity, democracy, open government, accountability, commitments to peace and international law, and treaty commitments to nuclear disarmament.

Is it time for member states and the EU to re-appraise EU policies in the light of their effects on "wider society" and other societies within the EU? Is it time to reduce the pace of change and expansion? Is there a need to modify some policies in the light of experience?

See also *House prices, Free trade, Employment, Charter of Fundamental Rights, Enlargement, Democratic deficit, Biggest problem number 3 - Lack of accountability, Transparency, Subsidiarity, Data harvesting, European arrest warrants,* and *Criminal justice.*

Subsidiarity

Leaders of the European Union in their *Laeken Declaration*, 2001, stated, "Within the Union, the European institutions must be brought closer to its citizens." -.They also asked, "At what level is competence exercised in the most efficient way? How is the principle of subsidiarity to be applied here? And should we not make it clear that any powers not assigned by the Treaties to the Union fall within the exclusive sphere of competence of the Member States?" The Constitution, which was written in response to their criticisms and suggestions ignored what they said on this topic. Nothing in the Constitution (and the *Reform Treaty*) specify any area of human activity exclusively assigned to member states.

EU leaders have long been aware of one of the strongest criticisms of the EU: that it is a centralised power which takes decisions and passes laws far away from those affected; that it is remote, out-of-touch and therefore often inept in its decisions and actions. Their answer was "subsidiarity" - the taking of decisions as close to those affected by them as possible.

Back in 1992 The *Maastricht Treaty* stated, "This Treaty marks a new stage in the process of creating an ever closer union among the peoples of Europe, in which decisions are taken as closely as possible to the citizen."

The only problem with the second part of this statement is that policy and reality do not coincide.

In the Constitution the topic of subsidiarity is partly explained in article 11. "Under the principle of subsidiarity, in areas which do not fall within its exclusive competence, the Union shall act only if and insofar as the objectives of the proposed action cannot be sufficiently achieved by the Member States . . ." There appears to be no right for member states to challenge the alleged need to achieve any particular objective. Once the Union has passed laws in an area of activity that area may never again come under a state's jurisdiction. (Article 12 (2).) This is a recipe for states to lose control over area after area. Areas under threat include social policy and transport (article 14) and industry, culture, education and tourism (article 17). Surely these are areas self-evidently the right of states to deal with as they see fit.

Procedure - Sovereignty may slip away

Unfortunately the EU's whole mode of operation is based on centralised planning. It even reserves to itself the right to propose measures that it might accept should be dealt with at a lower level. In cases of dispute between Brussels and a member state government the matter will not be settled by national governments, but by the European Court. Since the task of the court is to "ensure that in the interpretation and application of this Treaty the law is observed" (*Treaty Establishing the European Union*, article 220.)[108] and since the *Treaty Establishing the European Union* commits members to "ever closer union" then in matters of dispute between member states and the EU the Court is set up to find in favour of ever closer union and against states doing their own thing (subsidiarity). The 2004 Constitution sets out the procedure for deciding if subsidiarity rules will apply.

The EU Commission takes the initiative and sends draft legislation to national parliaments. They have six weeks only to make their case for dealing with the matter themselves - article 6 of Protocol 2. (The *Reform Treaty* will extend the six week period to eight.) There is no indication of an extended period of time if parliaments are on holiday. They don't have a right to say that nothing should be done, only to try to prove that they can handle an action better than the EU. Having stated their case the EU "shall take account" of the views of national parliaments, but may still pass the laws unless one third of states have put in objections. If one third have claimed the matter should be dealt with by state parliaments then the draft legislation "must be reviewed." After this one of three things may happen. "The Commission or, where appropriate, the group of Member States, the European Parliament, the Court of Justice, the European Central Bank or the European Investment Bank, if the draft European legislative act originates from them, may decide to maintain, amend or withdraw the draft." But note: the EU Commission can ignore the wishes of state parliaments. The EU, not the elected state parliaments, takes the decision. In the case of serious disagreement the matter may be taken to the European Court of Justice - article 8. Still the EU decides.

The fact that the EU itself speaks of an "early warning system" (See *Euro terminology*) with regard to the imminent takeover of a power by the EU, suggests that the EU is not working in the spirit of subsidiarity. The essence of subsidiarity is that decisions are taken at the lowest possible level (closest to the people affected) until such time as a matter is seen to be part of a wider issue that can only be tackled at a higher level.

Subsidiarity and regional development

There is another area in which the EU is failing to follow the principle of subsidiarity, and that is in the spending of huge sums of money on regional development. How the money should be spent is decided centrally. It is not decided by the people of the regions meeting to decide for themselves how they feel their region could best be developed. The result may be that the corporate lobbyists for such things as road building win the handouts and the work whilst local ideas, local businesses and workers and local initiatives may be frustrated.

Subsidiarity v central planning

In spite of professions of a desire to take decisions as close to the people as possible the Constitution put forwards detailed plans for the remote, centralised, eurocontrol of most aspects of the eurocitizen's life.

But there is an exception to the general pattern. As a further twist to the doubt that exists over subsidiarity we have the *Charter of Fundamental Rights and Freedoms of the Union*. This, one might expect, would guarantee rights to all EU citizens at all times, but in fact subsidiarity *does* apply here. Member states may decide for themselves which rights, if any, they will grant to their citizens. Article 112 on the application of the *Charter of Fundamental Rights* states, "Full account shall be taken of national laws and practices as specified in this Charter."

Ensuring subsidiarity

The system of shared competences is a recipe for constant negotiation, constant disagreement. The only way of ensuring subsidiarity is by plainly specifying in a treaty or constitution those areas of policy which will be exclusively reserved to regional or state governments. This would not preclude the idea of reaching common agreements in such designated areas but it would take away the power of centralising EU authorities to take over policy making in areas that state government might wish to reserve to themselves. Such areas might well include education, healthcare, tourism, culture, sport, social policy, agriculture, fisheries, energy, and law and order.

The *Reform Treaty* (following the Constitution) will allow the possibility of EU control of the above areas by defining them as areas of "shared competence" or "areas of supporting, co-ordinating or complementary action". Constitutions and treaties should not deal in vague, drifting commitments. If divisions of power were clearly marked out it would set a lot of minds at rest. The precise limits of subsidiarity should be established.

Giving the Commission the principle right to initiate laws is the opposite of subsidiarity. (Article 26/2.) Why should it have any right in this area? Subsidiarity would be meaningful if member states ran their own affairs until the point where they realised that united action across the EU might be the only effective way to deal with an issue – such as tackling pollution or taxing aircraft fuel. At this point they might approach other EU states to work together to frame an EU law – no doubt employing the law-making skills of the Commission. This would be a true subsidiarity as opposed to centralised decision making controlled by the EU.

See *Biggest Problems 5 and 6 (Top Down Decision-making* and *Creeping Centralisation), Charter of Fundamental Rights and Freedoms of the Union, Defence and Foreign Policy, Euroterminology - Competences*, articles 11, 14, 17, 18, 111, 259, Protocol 2.

Tolerance

The EU's relations with countries outside the EU (see article 292) is almost entirely tolerant. However, events discussed in some detail above in the section, *Defence and Foreign policy* show the EU's failure to apply its commitment to tolerance consistently. The EU is opposed to Communism and Socialism and has taken violent action against states practising elements of these approaches to running an economy. (Article 292/e.)

The EU promotes policies of personal tolerance. Article 124, repeating measures of the *Nice Treaty* article 13, would confirm powers given to the Council to "combat discrimination based on sex, racial or ethnic origin, religion or belief, disability, age, or sexual orientation." Articles 80 to 86, part of the *Charter of Fundamental Rights of the Union,* take a similar line. Whilst the sentiments are wholly admirable, do such policies need to be supervised from Brussels? Is Brussels well placed and capable of protecting personal freedoms. The experience of countries outside the EU, such as New Zealand, Norway or Switzerland, show it is possible for individual states acting alone to promote and administer such policies satisfactorily.

See *Defence and Foreign policy, Propaganda,* and *Charter of Fundamental Rights.*

Transparency

"Secret government erodes the legitimacy of the European Union; the lack of information opens the dirty tricks department of 'make believe' spin. Lack of accountability results in a furious public opinion which feels deceived, and finally rejects the European project altogether. . . Transparency is needed to ensure a proper functioning of the decision making process. A closed system will always produce bad policies because it is deaf and disconnected. . . Transparency is needed to gain the trust of the public. Political institutions cannot perform without public confidence." - Siim Kallas, Vice-President of the European Commission and Commissioner for Administrative Affairs, Audit and Anti-Fraud.[111]

The *Treaty Establishing the European Community* (article 255) required EU documentation to be open to examination by EU citizens. Article 50 of the Constitution would have required Union bodies to work as openly as possible. But as things stand the EU can only be described as a closed and secretive organisation which stymies democracy, accountability and integrity.
Some of the main complaints are that

- the verbatim records of debates of key institutions are not available to the public.
- There is no public access to the deliberations of the European Council.
- The voting records of ministers and commissioners are not published.
- Access to the minutes of meetings of the many Councils of Ministers is very difficult: either a cumbersome written procedure, or, starting in 2007, difficult access via the internet.[109] Minutes, in any case, are a poor substitute for reading the arguments presented when the topics were discussed. They can be relied upon to keep the average eurocitizen firmly disinterested.
- Until 2007, all meetings of the Councils of Ministers were not open to public viewing. Now some meetings for legislation are supposed to be available to view live on the internet. But there are difficulties.[110] The most elementary steps towards being helpful and useful are not taken.
- The nature and numbers of ministers involved in "the Council" are deliberately obscured in official accounts, including the Constitution.
- Records of the numerous approaches and participation of big business, environmentalists and other lobbyists to Commissioners and ministers are not available.
- Proper records of who receives funding from the EU are not available.
- It is very difficult to get information out of the EU's institutions. EU web sites are not user friendly. Amongst other problems they often lack search boxes and are poor at responding to search criteria.
- The 2004 European Constitution is one of the world's most opaque, obscure, confused and confusing constitutional documents. The *Reform Treaty* is unlikely to improve matters.

Failures in transparency - the EU is aware

It is clear that right at the top of the Commission there is an acute awareness of the problem of lack of transparency and a determination to set matters right.

A green paper on the matter has been produced. (This may be viewed at http://ec.europa.eu/comm/eti/index_en.htm)

The European Union first made a commitment to transparency in 1992 in article 191 of the *Maastricht Treaty*. This commitment was repeated in the *Treaty of Amsterdam*, Article 255, giving all citizens of the Union, plus all natural or legal persons residing or having their registered offices in a Member State, the right of access to European Parliament, Council and Commission documents.

This article was implemented by a Regulation of 30 May 2001, but provides for two exceptions: cases in which access is automatically refused (for reasons of public security, defence, international relations) and cases in which access is refused except where there is an overriding public interest in disclosure (protection of commercial interests of a natural or legal person, for example). This means that decisions on defence spending, military activities of all kinds, suppression of dissent which might cause a public disturbance, and all international relations between the EU and the rest of the world are taken in secret and may never be open to public scrutiny and, therefore, informed comment. These matters are too important to be left to politicians acting in isolation and out of public view.

In 2007 the deliberations of institution and committees are beginning to be opened to the public. (The European Parliament has been open for some time.) But masses of documentation which should be available to the public remain hidden. What has been achieved in increasing transparency so far is very slight and will not meet the expectations of citizens who would like to be treated like the members of a democratic state.

Examples of blocked information

As Siim Kallas says, there are two ways of stopping people getting information. “A widely known method to prevent people from knowing, is either to say nothing or to drown them in puzzling documents.” These are the two methods used by the EU. Try looking for information on the EU official website, and you are likely to encounter either a nil response or a plethora of documents which do not get to the obvious point of your enquiry. A good test is to try to discover who receives EU funding. The European Union distributes about 120 billion euros each year of which 80 percent is spent in two policy areas: agriculture and structural funds. Two days of searching the EU web site in April 2006 to find out the names of some of the ultimate recipients of EU funding led to the names of just 12 fishermen’s associations that received funding in May 2003.

Who are the top ten recipients of EU funding?

As the EU's web sites did not reveal the answer, this question was presented directly to the office of Siim Kallas. The frank and helpful reply from his office contained the following information and the list of links mentioned here is included in the web references chapter.

> To be honest, I do not have the reply to this question. The EU budget is spent through hundreds of different programmes, and payments are made by Commission services, or through paying agencies located in the 27

> member states. In fact, almost 80% of the payments from the EU budget are made by the Member States, and the Commission does not know who the individual recipients are, except for specific expenditure subject to an audit. Some Member States make this information public for farm subsidies (to see which, you can visit www.farmsubisidy.org). In the Green paper mentioned above, the Commission proposes that Member States should accept, as a legal obligation, to publish their list of beneficiaries of EU funds in shared management. Hopefully, therefore, the situation will improve in the future.
>
> For the other 20% of the budget managed directly by the Commission, beneficiaries are published in the Official Journal. However, to make it easier for citizen to do the research you're interested in, the Commission has decided to create a central web portal. This work has started with the collection of a list of existing Commission web-sites. I attach a very preliminary list of relevant sites for major programmes managed by the Commission (in French, but once you're on the sites, you can switch to English). Again, thanks to the Transparency initiative, the user-friendliness of this should improve in the future. For the moment, it is not possible to look across the different programmes or, for that matter, identify all EU funding granted to a given region.
>
> In summary, the most encouraging reply I can give is that work has started to address this unsatisfactory situation.

Of all the EU states the UK has been one of the most secretive about the recipients of agricultural payments made from EU funds.

Other research experience.

A request to the Eurostat web site on 31 January 2006 for the populations of EU member states produced this message: "Dear User, The page you requested has been moved! Thank you for your understanding!" No further information was provided. Would it have been difficult to indicate the new location?

On 10 April 2006 the EU decided to withdraw aid to Palestinians. The Europa (web) official newspaper carried just seven short paragraphs on this very important item.

The decision was taken by the General Affairs and External Relations Council. The web site for this council has a home page. This gives a short description of the work of this Council. It does not have a search box. There are three links that may be clicked. The first is for the home page itself. The third is entitled *European Presidency Conclusions*, and the second is for "previous meetings". Clicking this last item takes you to their "archive". There is a clickable link for each month. On 2 May 2006 the last month listed was for a whole year earlier: April 2005. This is an organisation which is not interested in communicating with the public.

A search from the Europa home page on 2 May 2006 for "budget 2006" offered 12,454 documents. The first was a pdf document of 29 pages of tables of statistics with many technical terms. Clearly not intended for the man in the street. The second document was a clear, 11-page document which showed expenditure under broad headings - a good, user-friendly document.

The next was "Annual plan of work and budget breakdown". Details of how the budget broke down seemed like a welcome follow-on. However, this document had the wrong title as it related entirely to "Employment, social affairs, and equal opportunities." We might count this search as modestly successful, but it should be better.

The minutes of Council meetings are now available to the public on the internet. For half a century these innocuous documents have been shielded from public view. Although officially available to the public for many years the procedure for getting to see them until recent months could hardly be described as open access. The minutes could be obtained by applying in writing to the Secretary General of the Council. The official explanation of the procedure was provided by the EU web site.[112] "The Secretary General will reply within fifteen working days, although this can be extended by a further fifteen working days." If the application is refused the applicant may ask for a reconsideration of the request . If this is refused the applicant may complain to the Ombudsman "or bring an action before the Court of Justice." All this, just to have a bare outline of what had been decided!

After years of campaigning the Danish MEP, Jens-Peter Bonde, persuaded the Commission in February 2005 to state the number of working groups that were actively working for the Commission in 2004. The number was stated as a minimum of 1684. In addition there were non-active groups and management committees. The membership and details of remuneration and expenses (which are paid by the eurotaxpayer) were not revealed at the time. They work secretly and unknown to eurocitizens and are therefore unaccountable. He feels that as the people of Europe are paying for these committees this information should be readily available.

There are many complaints of difficulties in accessing EU documents:

- reports which should be freely accessible
- unwillingness to open documents to the public about issues the EU is about to take decisions on. (Sometimes these have later been made available - after decisions have been taken.)

Complaints have been made to the Ombudsman who has upheld the complaints. See the Statewatch web site for more details.

There are plans to open up more of the EU decision-making process to public view, but there is an immense distance to travel.

See *Reform may be at hand*, below. See also, *The Commission*, *Clear use of language*, *Biggest issue number four*, and *Data Harvesting* which describes the difficulty that Statewatch had tracking down information.

European parliament

The European Parliament has taken the lead in openness and has been ahead of other EU institutions. Here where some types of laws may be debated, and even rejected, there is almost satisfactory transparency. It is possible to follow debates in the European Parliament as they happen with simultaneous translation, using the internet.

However, the availability of transcripts of the deliberations of the European Parliament is unsatisfactory. The accounts of debates that may be read on the parliament's web site are available only in the original language in which they were delivered (May 2007). They should at least be available in the three or four most popular languages of the EU. Another serious problem is that their availability is not suitably signalled on the web site. A heading such as "Transcripts of debates", or "Verbatim records of debates" is essential if readers are to find them.

Elsewhere the Committee of the Regions, the Economic and Social Committee, the Commission, and the strategic planning group for the entire EU, the European Council - all meet with the public and media excluded, with no verbatim record, no record of votes taken and information about deliberations difficult to access. Whilst it is neither practical nor sensible to publish every word uttered in the discussions of the European Union the present situation is unsatisfactory.

Records of Lobbying contacts

In spite of being permanently assailed by thousands of lobbyists which influence the workings of the EU there are no publicly available records of these contacts. A major power acting on the EU ought to be a matter of public record. Such reforms may be on the way. (See below.)

Fraud

With so little information available to the public the scene is set for massive fraud. The danger is now clearly appreciated by the man responsible for developing transparency, Siim Kallas. He said, in his Nottingham speech in 2005, "Proper information and public awareness are needed to prevent the evil phenomenon of fraud or at least limit its scope." Dealing with EU fraud is a major part of his remit.

Reform may be at hand

Lack of transparency may have had a huge detrimental effect on the European Union both in terms of destroying confidence and in allowing politicians to plough ahead with developments that do not command public support. Many EU insiders are aware of what is at stake.

The "transparency initiative" launched by Siim Kallas is concentrating on three key areas: increasing the financial accountability of EU funding, strengthening personal integrity and independence of EU institutions, and imposing stricter controls on lobbying.

He appears to be getting some results. On 9 November 2005 his European Transparency Initiative was adopted by the Commission. It then decided to publish a Green Paper on the topic by the beginning of 2006 (details above) to launch a debate with all the stakeholders on how to improve transparency on the Community Funds, consultation with civil society and the role of the lobbies and NGOs in the European institutions' decision-making process. This is a promising start, but it still only amounts to a commitment to talk about the issue, not a commitment to do something. Eurocitizens will be watching for real action.

The Commission has undertaken to establish links on its web site to information on end beneficiaries of funds under centralised management. Links will also be established between the Commission's central portal on the web and the websites of the Member States, where data on end beneficiaries under shared management can be found. The coverage of the existing Commission register of documents will be improved, "in particular by creating synergies with SG Vista," with a view to making available the text of documents in full or in part in accordance with "access to documents" legislation. The Commission may soon be complying with EU regulations.

In the second half of 2006 Finland held the presidency of the EU. The Finns stated that they were determined to bring more transparency to the working of the EU. One of Finland's objectives during its Presidency was to develop European regulation on public access to documents. It also intended to increase the number of public sessions of the Council so that Council sessions on all matters of interest to citizens would be open to the public and broadcast on the internet. The Finns had some success.

Anti-transparency lobby

The Society of European Affairs Practitioners (SEAP) represents many lobbyists based in Brussels. It opposes the idea of a compulsory public register of clients and sources of income saying it would be an unnecessary step. It claimed that its self-regulatory ethics code is sufficient to ensure satisfactory ethical standards.[113]

See articles 50 and 399, and in this *Major Issues* chapter *Clear Use of Language*, *Propaganda*, *European Union by stealth*, *Data Harvesting*, *Giving away our money*, *Finances of the EU*, *Defence and foreign policy*; in *Eurotermi-nology* see *Transparency;* in the *Institutions* chapter see *European Security and Intelligence Force,* and *COSI.* The issue is explored in detail by *Statewatch.* See their website.

Transport and the environment

No meaningful and significant transport objectives were stated in the Constitution! The opening article of the transport section, (236) says, "The objectives of the Constitution shall, in matters governed by this Section, be pursued within the framework of a common transport policy." The objective of the policy is that it should be common to all member states. There should also be some common rules and a concern with transport safety. That basically is it.

The patient reader may glean by reading eleven inscrutable articles that transport is to assist in the working of the internal market and that there should be no subsidy to transport operators or discriminatory pricing against particular countries. The EU will encourage safety. Transport charges for crossing borders should be "fair". The EU will encourage the development of trans-European-networks.

In short there is a failure to recognise that transport policy has anything whatsoever to do with the environment and that this should be a major factor in establishing transport objectives. The development of major transport networks has been and is likely to be harmful to the environment. They will, of course, assist the free movement of goods and people and the movement of work into formerly inaccessible areas. Articles 236 to 247 refer.

Union Minister for Foreign Affairs

This major new role was to be established by article 28 of the Constitution, and potentially be one of the most powerful in the European Union. (See *Euroterminology - Union Minister for Foreign Affairs.*) The Constitution would have this person appointed by the European Council. It would be more democratic to have this person appointed by the people of Europe or the European Parliament. In the case of the President of the Commission (a similarly important role) EU leaders in their *Laeken Declaration* put forward these three alternatives and asked which would be more appropriate. Clearly they appreciate that people are rightly concerned about the democratic accountability of EU leaders. They were open to any of the alternative proposals. In a retrograde step the *Reform Treaty* keeps the job description for this minister intact whilst giving him/her a long eurocitizen-unfriendly title - "High Representative of the Union for Foreign Affairs and Security Policy".

New EU Foreign Office

The minister will be assisted by the European External Action Service (the new "Foreign Office" of the European Union, article 296) which the minister will "propose" after "consulting the European Parliament and after obtaining the consent of the Commission." - This raises the question of who is in control of EU foreign policy? Who is taking the decision? Why is the Commission to give permission to set up the European Action Service? Has it been instructed to do so? Who gave the Commission this authority to set up something which will cost a great deal to run? The unratified 2004 Constitution has already authorised the setting up of this new department, because it was agreed by the conference which proposed the Constitution that the signature of leaders on the Constitution would signal the start of preparations to establish it.[114] What would have happened if the Commission had opposed the setting up of this new bureaucracy? Should the setting up of a whole EU Foreign Office have been approved by member states?

EU foreign policy - who will direct it?

Will the Union Minister for Foreign Affairs run EU foreign policy? Article 295 says "The European Council shall define the general guidelines for the common foreign and security policy. . . The Council [that's the Foreign Affairs Council - or one of its other names] shall adopt the European decisions necessary for defining and implementing the common foreign and security policy on the basis of the general guidelines and strategic lines defined by the European Council." Once the European Council has set policy in motion, presumably along the lines of peaceful co-operation with all nations and compliance with the *Charter of the United Nations*, its work is finished in this area. Or will national leaders who make up the European Council or the Union Minister for Foreign Affairs come up from time to time with their own policy initiatives? Will the Union Minister for Foreign Affairs be able to take foreign policy decisions over the heads of member states? Will the eurovoter be able to vote the minister out of office?

Is there a role anywhere for the eurovoter to approve or disapprove policies adopted or to be adopted in our relationships with other countries? The record of the EU in sticking to the principles set out in EU treaties and other international agreements is unsatisfactory. See *Major Issues – Defence and foreign Policy*, and, in the *Euroterminology* chapter, *Union Minister for Foreign Affairs.*.

Unite and be strong

"Are we all clear that we want to build something that can aspire to be a world power? In other words, not just a trading bloc but a political entity. Do we realise that our nation states, taken individually, would find it far more difficult to assert their existence and their identity on the world stage." - Commission President Romano Prodi, European Parliament, 13 February 2001.[115]

It is sometimes argued that small countries, by joining the EU, can become "significant players on the world stage," that their voices can be heard in world affairs when otherwise they would have been swamped. This can only be true, however, in certain circumstances.

In the case of opposition to the Iraq war of 2003, for example, Ireland opposed the invasion. Most EU countries opposed the invasion, but their voices counted for nothing. They could not speak with an EU voice and act as a world power. The idea that by being part of the EU the relatively weak countries will speak with the strength of the many only applies when there is agreement among member states.

It is obvious that people or countries which band together with others who share their ideals and aims are likely to have more influence than if they remain isolated. Countries can and do combine around issues to promote their interests without becoming politically bound together or integrated, for example to organise the world telephone communication system, to establish the laws of the sea, and to combat climate change.

The EU failed with regard to the Iraq war because it did nothing as a body either to inhibit a member state's military aggression before the war, or to condemn it or suspend or expel it from membership afterwards for breach of its fundamental principles. (Articles 3, 292 and 294.)

Little Britain's voice in the EU counted for nothing in terms of EU support for its involvement in the Iraq war. It did not win the argument with fellow members of the EU.

In terms of defence, things may be rather different. Nato's core statement that an attack upon one member state will be considered as an attack upon all must act as a powerful deterrent to any would-be aggressor. The EU defence policy echoes this arrangement and in any case includes most Nato states. The EU Constitution is reluctant to use the words "war", "invasion" and "military attack." The Constitution implies the Nato defence policy without actually saying it. "The Union and its Member States shall act jointly in a spirit of solidarity if a Member State is the object of a terrorist attack or the victim of a natural or man-made disaster." (Article 41.) Presumably an invasion would be classed as a "man-made disaster." However, from the point of view of the non-militarist neutral members they may benefit from the protection without contributing much to actual defence if the alliance/union is ever put to the test. Their voices in favour of neutrality have not been heeded – although, as a balance to this, their separate, non-aggressive, defence policy certainly makes them less likely to be the victim of an attack.

United States of Europe

See *Integration - the number one question*, and *European Union by stealth – pickpocketing democracy and sovereignty*.

Violence, attitude to

The EU is committed to peace and the *Charter of the United Nations* which calls for an end to all war. (Constitution article 3, *Treaty Establishing the European Community* article 2, and Treaty Establishing the European Union article 2. *Charter of the United Nations*: Preamble and article 1.) The EU has demanded that the Palestinian Authority renounce violence.[116] Will the EU itself renounce violence? Will it call on Palestine's enemies to do the same? Will EU states scale back and ultimately abandon their role as some of the world's leading arms manufacturers?

Voting

Decision-making in committees, councils and parliaments is always done by seeking the broadest possible support. Informally a chairman may judge the general feeling of the meeting. For affairs of state and international relationships agreed voting procedures are needed. These need to be commensurate with the gravity of the matter under consideration, fair, easy to operate, understand and apply. In democracies voting needs to be open to public view.

The European Union has achieved all this only in relation to voting in the European Parliament. The Commission votes fairly and efficiently, but in secret. This will change in 2014 when one third of member states will not have a commissioner to represent them. (Article 26.) The Council and the European Council remain locked in complex confusion and cannot come to arrangements acceptable to all member states. In June 2007 the latest plan was grudgingly agreed by EU leaders by a means of a "compromise" arrangement which would see a seven year delay before the new voting system will come into operation.

If their plan is actually agreed to be a good one it should be put into operation at the earliest opportunity. If it is not satisfactory it should never be put into operation. How can any plan be satisfactory only if we wait seven years to get started? Are we waiting for EU leaders to grow up?

Unanimity

If any decision made by the Council has to be agreed by all member states before changes can be made or laws passed there are three consequences:

- all states are happy with the decisions taken
- it is very difficult to reach agreement, so very little change can be brought about
- even small countries have power over the others because they can use their power of veto as a bargaining chip to extract favours or concessions. (Of course, behaviour of this kind is dishonest, an abuse of negotiations which should settle matters solely on considerations relevant to the issue to be resolved. Such behaviour should be outlawed.)

Lack of unanimity is a very serious matter because the affect of less than full agreement is that some states can become subject to laws or arrangements which do not carry the consent (or may even carry the vehement opposition) of their elected governments. Some might argue that it is a benefit if any state may act as a brake on the taking of a particular decision because changes which even one state does not accept, may not be wise.

EU alternative voting systems

The EU has devised two solutions to the problem of states disagreeing.

First, to scrap true unanimity decision-making by adopting a modified unanimity system for some situations (*Treaty Establishing the European Community*, article 205);] second, to adopt a QMV (qualified majority voting) system with a range of complex variations. (See *Euroterminology, QMV* for the current basic rules and the *Nice Treaty* article 205. See *Defence and foreign policy* above for an exploration of some of the difficulties.)

The Constitution's attempt to come up with a "simplified" voting system that can be easily understood was not successful.

Article 25 of the Constitution defined the EU's new voting procedure. In itself it is complicated but it is surely unnecessary to have two versions of these cumbersome rules. The occasions for the use of QMV should be very clear and for the sake of simplicity and clarity there should be no further variations of QMV.

This is part of what the Constitution has to say about voting. The definition of qualified majority within the European Council and the Council can be found in article 25:

> "1. A qualified majority shall be defined as at least 55 % of the members of the Council, comprising at least fifteen of them and representing Member States comprising at least 65 % of the population of the Union. A blocking minority must include at least four Council members, failing which the qualified majority shall be deemed attained.
>
> 2. By way of derogation from paragraph 1, when the Council does not act on a proposal from the Commission or from the Union Minister for Foreign Affairs, the qualified majority shall be defined as at least 72 % of the members of the Council, representing Member States comprising at least 65 % of the population of the Union."

But here are some further regulations about voting, set out in article 300. Article 300, paragraph 1 explains that in the field of the Common Foreign and Security Policy "European decisions" are adopted by the Council acting unanimously. (It is explained that unanimously does not mean that everyone agrees to a decision.) Paragraphs 2 a, b, and c explain when the unanimity rule will not apply. It is difficult to see the principle at work here which causes so many eventualities to be considered of insufficient importance to require unanimity. Paragraph 2d introduces another procedure. Paragraph 3 introduces the opportunity for the European Council to make further changes to the voting system! Paragraph 4 explains that the procedures set out in paragraphs 2 and 3 will not be used on many occasions. This is the actual text:

> "2. By way of derogation from paragraph 1, the Council shall act by a qualified majority:

(a) when adopting European decisions defining a Union action or position on the basis of a European decision of the European Council relating to the Union's strategic interests and objectives, as referred to in Article III-293(1);

(b) when adopting a European decision defining a Union action or position, on a proposal which the Union Minister for Foreign Affairs has presented following a specific request to him or her from the European Council, made on its own initiative or that of the Minister;

(c) when adopting a European decision implementing a European decision defining a Union action or position;

(d) when adopting a European decision concerning the appointment of a special representative in accordance with Article III-302.

If a member of the Council declares that, for vital and stated reasons of national policy, it intends to oppose the adoption of a European decision to be adopted by a qualified majority, a vote shall not be taken. The Union Minister for Foreign Affairs will, in close consultation with the Member State involved, search for a solution acceptable to it. If he or she does not succeed, the Council may, acting by a qualified majority, request that the matter be referred to the European Council for a European decision by unanimity.

3. In accordance with Article I-40(7) the European Council may unanimously adopt a European decision stipulating that the Council shall act by a qualified majority in cases other than those referred to in paragraph 2 of this Article.

Paragraphs 2 and 3 shall not apply to decisions having military or defence implications."

This is the best voting procedure the EU can devise after fifty years of working on the problem. It is a remarkable failure.

Any voting system must be easy to understand and apply. See *Complication* above for a possible solution.

Transparency

The EU's commitment to transparency means that eurocitizens should see which countries are voting for which decisions.

Opt-outs

In highly contentious matters states that cannot go along with an idea might be allowed to opt out of an arrangement. This is not a new idea, but an extension of the way that this already happens with, for example, the euro and the Danish non-participation in the Defence Agency. It is happening with the UK in the sphere of justice and home affairs.

Removing anti-democratic restrictions in the European Parliament

In matters of law-making sometimes the European Parliament, in accordance with existing treaties, must vote its approval before a law can be passed. In other matters it does not have this power. It is difficult to see why this directly

elected body is excluded from some areas of law making. It is a deliberate limitation of democracy. The problem could easily be corrected.
See *Democratic Deficit, Defence and foreign policy* and *Complication* above, and *Euroterminology – Qualified majority voting* and *Unanimity.*

The way ahead

The rocky road to reform - the hole that has been dug

In 2001, with the *Laeken Declaration*, EU leaders showed an awareness of most of the serious problems facing the EU, and they appeared to have an open mind about how the problems might be solved. Giscard d'Estaing's Constitution, which was his Convention's response to the Laeken mandate, ignored the problems he had been invited to address.

In 2004 EU leaders, by signing the Constitution, embraced the abandonment of addressing the problems they had identified.

The two years' of "reflection" by EU leaders which followed the rejection of the Constitution by the people of the Netherlands and France in 2005 produced not a single idea to address the major problems.

On 15 May 2007, Angela Merkel, the German Chancellor and President of the EU, announced her proposal to integrate the EU Constitution into the two principle EU treaties. This would have the effect of subverting the agreement some member states had with their electorates to hold referendums. It was a policy with the potential to explode.

Power in their hands

No documents of the new proposals were available to eurocitizens, the media, or even the elected politicians of the EU before either the May or June meetings of EU leaders. Even the British negotiating team did not see the highly complex document until forty-eight hours before the crucial meeting which decided to accept the proposals for a "reform" treaty. Such documents that have emerged since (up to the time this book is going to press, October 2007) cannot possibly be understood without specialised knowledge and days of study.

By denying information to eurocitizens, the media and politicians at all levels across the EU, our EU leaders have effectively prevented democratic debate. There can be no such thing as an informed attitude of the European public to the *Reform Treaty*. Knowledge, and therefore power, has been retained by a small elite. This is not how democracies work.

Ending the crisis

What can be done to solve the EU crisis of lost confidence and lost sense of direction?

- Decide on the nature of the EU. Choose between ever closer union up to complete unification or everlasting friendship and co-operation? See *Constitution - preparing to write an acceptable constitution, Subsidiarity,* and *Integration - the number one question.*

- **Make the EU democratic, transparent, understandable and accountable.** Major institutional and attitude reform must take place to make the EU (its politicians, administrators and institutions) truly democratic, transparent, and accountable with a clearly defined power structure. It must simplify and clarify its workings and open itself up to public view. See *Democratic deficit, Accountability, Transparency, Defence and foreign policy*. Also *Part Five - The Reform Treaty*
- **New constitution writing time.** After the resolution of the above issues (and others) a short new Constitution, not a rehash of the 2004 Constitution, might be written in the confident expectation of public support. See *Addendum* below *.

Time for public policy debate

As a follow-on, wide-ranging debates across Europe need to be conducted on major policy issues:

- the pace of enlargement, immigration, the question of open borders
- free trade, protectionism, localism, privatisation, public sevices, employment, giantopolies, free movement of capital, attitudes to WTO policies, EU acceptance or qualification of WTO policies. Are too many policies fixed by treaty with the effect that they close down debate on alternative policies? (for example, the commitment to free trade which has never been fully implemented)
- environmental priorities, climate change, conservation, energy including nuclear power and renewables, transport
- agriculture and fisheries
- employment, housing, welfare, social well-being, health, education
- militarism, demilitarisation, eliminating nuclear weapons under the 1968 *Nuclear Non-proliferation Treaty*, commitment to the *United Nations Charter*, peaceful relations with all countries, and a common foreign policy openly discussed with public involvement in developing policies
- other issues.

Alternative proposals

For an entirely different judgement on what needs to be done see the ideas of the European Parliament and others in Part Seven- *Alternative Plans for EU Development* chapter.

Working time directive

See *Employment*.

Addendum*

Constitution or treaty?

Now that the "EU Constitution " has been dispersed into existing treaties it is claimed that there is no longer a constitution. This is just playing with words.

Whether we use the word "treaty" or "constitution" what is clear is that we are talking about is "an agreement about how the European Union is run, including agreements on how power is shared between it and its member states".

This leaves unanswered the question, Is the EU a state? If it is not a state then it should not be expected to have a dialogue with its citizens or even particularly consider their concerns or wishes. We can leave its leaders to do just what they like, meeting in private and telling us little or nothing about what they have decided. But if the EU is a not a state, under whose laws is this non-state that directs and controls the behaviour of its member states and their citizens operating?

Notes

1 The Jean Monnet Working Papers are published under the auspices of the Jean Monnet Program hosted at Harvard Law School from 1995 to 2001 and now based at New York University School of Law.

2 *European Governance - a White Paper* - Reference COM(2001) 428 final.

3 *Treaty Establishing the European Community*, article 213/2.

4 "The Union needs to become more democratic, more transparent and more efficient." – *Laeken Declaration*, 15 December 2001.

5 *European Governance - a White Paper* prepared by the Commission, Brussels, 25 July 2001. Reference COM(2001) 428 final.

6 *Laeken Declaration* 15 December 2001. See also, *The Treaty of Rome* in the Treaties chapter.

7 *European Convention on Human Rights and Fundamental Freedoms*, articles 5 and 6.

8 Refererence: 20070122IPR02273 23 1 07

9 www.europarl.europa.eu/news/expert/infopress_page/017-2287-023-01-04-902-20070122IPR02273-23-01-2007-2007-false/default_en.htm

10 Members of the House of Lords observe the 7 general principles of conduct identified by the Committee on Standards in Public Life. The 7 principles are: (a) Selflessness: Holders of public office should take decisions solely in terms of the public interest. They should not do so in order to gain financial or other material benefits for themselves, their family, or their friends. (b) Integrity: Holders of public office should not place themselves under any financial or other obligation to outside individuals or organisations that might influence them in the performance of their official duties. (c) Objectivity: In carrying out public business, including making public appointments, awarding contracts, or recommending individuals for rewards and benefits, holders of public office should make choices on merit. (d) Accountability: Holders of public office are accountable for their decisions and actions to the public and must submit themselves to whatever scrutiny is appropriate to their office. (e) Openness: Holders of public office should be as open as possible about all the decisions and actions that they take. They should give reasons for their decisions and restrict information only when the wider public interest clearly demands. (f) Honesty: Holders of public office have a duty to declare any private interests relating to their public duties and to take steps to resolve any conflicts arising in a way that protects the public interest.(g) Leadership: Holders of public office should promote and support these principles by leadership and example. Also: Primacy of the public interest. In the conduct of their parliamentary duties, Members of the House shall resolve any conflict between their personal interest and the public interest in favour of the public interest.

11 "Abstentions by members present in person or represented shall not prevent the adoption of such decisions." i.e. decisions to do with the common foreign and security policy. Also, "When abstaining in a vote, any member of the Council may qualify its abstention by making a formal declaration under the present sub-paragraph. In that case, it shall not be obliged to apply the decision . . . If the members of the Council qualifying their abstention in this way represent more than one third of the votes weighted in accordance with article 205 (2) of the *Treaty Establishing the European Community*, the decision shall not be adopted." *Treaty on European Union*, article 23. As things stand, there might be occasions when there is less support for a decision under the unanimity rule than under QMV.

12 *Monitoring the implementation of procedural safeguards in members states,* from Fair Trials abroad web site. www.fairtrialsabroad.org/

13 EU Green paper reference *COM/2003/0075 final.*

14 Neil Clark, The Guardian, 10 2 05.

15 See articles 41 and 311 and the discussion above on the work of a Defence Agency.

16 Preamble, *Treaty of Rome*, 1957, and *United Nations Charter* 1945 (Preamble and article 1.)

17 "Genuine" is used in the sense explained in the first paragraph of *Defence and foreign policy - the EU's record* above.

18 http://ec.europa.eu/comm/external_relations/israel/intro/index.htm and www.aprodev.net

19 "We will carry on pounding day after day until our objectives are secured." Tony Blair, 12 April 1999, quoted in *The Guardian*, 13 April 1999.

20 The proposed Constitution would make a new commitment to encouraging all countries to operate on free-trade principles (article 292/e).

21 Neil Clark, *The Guardian*, 21 September 2004.

22 The Jerusalem Post, 17 March 2006.

23 A note on names of territories: in 1918, when the British took control of what is now called Israel and the West Bank, Gaza Strip and East Jerusalem, the entire area was known as Palestine and the population of just over 550,000 people was 95 per cent Palestinian and 5 per cent Jewish. When David Ben Gurion declared the founding of the state of Israel in 1948 his wish was that the entire territory would be under Jewish control and be known as Israel. Palestine would no longer exist. Palestinians would be expelled. Many Palestinians believe that the whole of Israel should again be called Palestine.

24 UN Security Council Resolution 242, November 22, 1967 relating to the Six Day War contains the words, "Emphasizing the inadmissibility of the acquisition of territory by war . . ." UN General assembly Resolution 2625, 24 October 1970, elucidating existing UN principles, states, "The territory of a State shall not be the object of military occupation resulting from the use of force in contravention of the provisions of the Charter. The territory of a State shall not be the object of acquisition by another State resulting from the threat or use of force. No territorial acquisition resulting from the threat or use of force shall be recognized as legal."

25 *Losing Ground - Israel, poverty and the Palestinians* by David MacDowall and William Bell. Published by Christian Aid.

26 Terrorism may be defined as the the use or threatened use of violence to achieve political ends (war being an extreme variety of terrorism).

27 USAID and the National Democratic Institute.

28 At times these people may be joined by others; for example, on 9 May 2006, in New York they were joined by Austrian Foreign Minister Ursula Plassnik and European Commissioner for External Relations, Benita Ferrero-Waldner.

29 UN Department of Public Information statement SG/2103 PAL/2041 dated 26 January 2006. "The Palestinian people have voted for change, but it is the view of the Quartet that their aspirations for peace and statehood, as articulated by President Abbas [a member of the losing Fatah party] in his statement following the closing of polls yesterday, remain unchanged. The Quartet reiterates its view that there is a fundamental contradiction between armed group and militia activities and the building of a democratic state. A two-state solution to the conflict requires all participants in the democratic process to renounce violence and terror, accept Israel's right to exist, and disarm, as outlined in the Road Map."

30 *Israel's New Government, Old Policies,* Nick Dearden, *Z Magazine* June 2006.

31 http://ec.europa.eu/comm/external_relations/israel/intro/index.htm

32 http://ec.europa.eu/comm/external_relations/mepp/faq/index.htm

33 An exception was *The Times* which reported on 29 June 2006, "Largely obscured by the kidnap drama, Hamas made a potentially historic concession on Tuesday by implicitly recognising Israel in a deal with the mainstream Fatah movement that could lead to a government of national unity." *The Times* soon reverted to reporting on Hamas as "committed to Israel's destruction." Times 21 August 2006.

34 Reported by Seth Ackerman in *Mixed Signals - When Hamas hinted at peace, U.S. media wouldn't take the message.* http://www.fair.org/index.php?page=2974 September/October 2006.

35 Reported by AFP, 11 March 2006.

36 From 27 September 2000 to March 20, 2006, Hamas killed 430 Israelis. www.vitalperspective.typepad.com/vital_perspective_clarity/ files/Fatal_Hamas_Attacks_Since_9-00.pdf

37 Article, *The Iron Wall,* 1923, - Ze'ev Jabotinsky (1880-1940).

38 Ben-Gurion and the Palestinian Arabs: From Peace to War (Oxford, 1985) p 166.

39 Likud Party Platform, Jewish Virtual Library. http://www.jewishvirtuallibrary.org/jsource/Politics/likud.html

40 *Israel's New Government, Old Policies,* Nick Dearden, *Z Magazine* June 2006.

41 Federal News Service, 25 January 2006.

42 Reported in the New York Sun, 13 December 2006. www.nysun.com/article/45120?page_no=1

43 Johann Hari: *Ethnic cleansing returns to Israel's agenda* in the *Independent* 13 November 2006.

44 New York Sun 13 December 2006. www.nysun.com/article/45120?page_no=1

45 http://www.ifamericansknew.org/stats/deaths.html

46 www.pmo.gov.il/PMOEng/Communication/PMSpeaks/ speechdavid271106.htm

47 Web site of the Israeli Ministry of Foreign Affairs. http://www.mfa.gov.il/

48 Web site of the Israeli Ministry of Foreign Affairs. http://www.mfa.gov.il/

49 The only EU country to take part in the attack on Iraq in 2003 was the UK. Many reasons were put forward for the attack but a reason never stated was to open up Iraq's economy to the commercial participation of international companies, an aim which was achieved. An important early element of the takeover of Iraq was the selling off of state enterprises. On 19 September 2003 Paul Bremmer, the US Governor of Iraq, announced with order number 39 that 200 of Iraq's state industries and services would be privatised and available for purchase by any foreign investor. Iraq was to be made attractive for foreign investment by the reduction of corporation tax from 40% to 15%. All profits from this moment on could be removed from Iraq.

50 The Oslo Accords and the Road Map – negotiated under duress and therefore invalid under the Vienna Convention on the Law of Treaties.

51 For example, Javier Solana – High Representative for the Common Foreign and Security Policy, Benita Ferrero-Waldner – External Relations Commissioner, the Prime Ministers and Presidents of the EU member states (the European Council), and the members of the Council.
52 Quoted by John McCormick in *Understanding the European Union*, 2005.
53 Euroelite? A group of people, hard to identify, the EU's top decision-makers and planners.
54 Statements reported by EU Observer http://euobserver.com 23 May 2006.
55 It might be argued that there is a possibility for a kind of parliamentary initiative. Under article 192 of the *Treaty Establishing the European Community* MEPs are allowed to submit proposals only in the restricted area of implementing that treaty. In other words, proposals are only allowed if they help to put into effect policies already agreed by others. Furthermore, such a proposal must be backed by a majority of MEPs. The initiative must take the form of, "a request to the Commission to submit any appropriate proposal on matters which it considers that a Community act is required for the purpose of implementing this Treaty."
56 http://www.southeast-ra.gov.uk/our_work/index.html
57 From Press Release of TUC 9 December 2005.
58 BBC Radio 4 PM web 14 12 05
59 Fact from BBC Radio 4 PM programme web site 18 April 2006.
60 Economist 10 7 03.
61 Independent 19 4 06.
62 New Internationalist, April 2004.
63 The Guardian, 21 July 2006
64 Interview on CNN, 1 January 2002.
65 *The Times*, London, 22 February 2002.
66 *Globalization and its Discontents,* p45 – Joseph Stiglitz, 2002.
67 European Commission Fisheries Directorate General.
68 http://home.freeuk.net/nigelhadley/codwar.htm
69 The Constitution says that the EU will work "to encourage the integration of all countries into the world economy, including through the progressive abolition of restrictions on international trade." Article 292.
70 *Globalization and its discontents*, Joseph Stiglitz, Published by Allen Lane, 2002. Pages 133-165. *New Internationalist* magazines, March 2004, April 2004, April 2003.
71 Article 56 of the *Treaty establishing the European Community* (2002) states, "Within the framework of the provisions set out in this chapter, all restrictions on the movement of capital between member states and between member states and third countries shall be prohibited." This article is repeated in the Constitution, article 156. See *House prices*, below.
72 *Globalization and its discontents*, Joseph Stiglitz, Published by Allen Lane, 2002.
73 This gift of powers to corporations by way of privatisation pushed forward by the EU is not a new idea in Europe. Mrs Thatcher was active in privatisation in the UK in the 1980s. The idea has been taken up around the world. The EU embraced it as a policy under the *Nice Treaty* and it is going rapidly ahead.
74 Competence here means powers of regulation.
75 European Services Directive 2006/123/EC, 12 December 2006.
76 The 33 page text is available as a pdf file at http://eurlex.europa.eu/LexUriServ/LexUriServ.do?uri=CELEX:32006L0123:EN:NOT
77 The Guardian, 19 January 2007.

78 In the UK in recent years there has been a private-pensions disaster for tens of thousands of employees as businesses have gone bust or made drastic cut-backs on promised provision.
79 *Treaty Establishing the European Community*, articles 2 and 3, and 23-31. Constitution: articles 3 and 4, and 130-176.
80 Constitution article 292, paragraph 2 (e) states "The Union shall encourage the integration of all countries into the the world economy, including through the progressive abolition of restrictions on international trade." See also article 3 paragraph 4.
81 *Daily Telegraph*, 24 April 06
82 Economic and monetary policies are set out in articles 177 to 191.
83 Institute of Public Policy Research 2006
84 *Selling Houses Abroad*, Channel 4 TV programme, 24 April 2007.
85 Shelter explains that "The current overcrowding definition dates back to 1935, and requires kitchens to be counted as acceptable places to sleep. Under this outdated standard, children younger than 10 only count as half a person in the headcount, while babies don't count at all." http://england.shelter.org.uk
86 National Statistical Office. Consumer price indices for the twelve months to October 2006.
87 *The Economist*, 2 November 2006.
88 *South China Morning Post*, 22 November 2006.
89 Statistics attributed to Mira Bar-Hillel, Property Editor of London's *Evening Standard*, in article by Nick Cohen, *The Observer*, 19 November, 2006.
90 Penny Churchill, *Country Life*, 2 November 2006.
91 Reported by Jon Cruddas, Labour MP for Dagenham, on World at One programme, BBC Radio 4, 19 February 2007.
92 Halifax April 07 report quoted in The Independent, 16 April 2007.
93 Major terrorist outrages have been committed by terrorists with identity cards and the 2005 outrage in London could not have been prevented by any identity card law as the perpetrators were all legal British residents.
94 See Euroterminology
95 Reported in the *International Herald Tribune* of 8 June 2005.
96 Financial Times, 21 June 2004.
97 Quoted by www.free-europe.org
98 French President, Jacques Chirac, address to French Ambassadors, 27 August 2001 www.free-europe.org
99 Siim Kallas, article in *Wall Street Journal*, 6 February 2006.
100 Irish Times, 2 June 2004.
101 For example, Iran Focus, on 6 January 2006, quoted a statement released by the EU's Austrian presidency, "The EU views with serious concern the Government of Iran's intention to resume suspended nuclear activities". Xavier Solana, the EU's Foreign Policy spokesman, has condemned North Korea's nuclear tests.
102 http://europa.eu/scadplus/leg/en/lvb/l33218.htm
103 "If we, our chief justice, our officials, or any of our servants offend in any respect against any man, or transgress any of the articles of the peace or of this security, and the offence is made known to four of the said twenty-five barons, they shall come to us . . . to declare it and claim immediate redress." Magna Carta, signed by King John, 15 June 1215.
104 Interview in *Woman's Own*, 31 October, 1987.
105 See the report of the meeting of MPs and MEPs in the *Alternative Plans for EU Development* chapter. The social model relates primarily to the rights of workers, and the promotion of employment and worker mobility.
106 Constitution article 292 (e).

107 This century there are unprecedented levels of divorce and numbers of one-parent families; in the UK 100,000 children run away from home each year (according to the *Today* programme, BBC Radio 4, 18 May 2007).

108 This requirement is repeated in the Constitution, article 29/1.

109 When I tried to access Council minutes on 26 April 2007 I experienced the following difficulties. Around 9.30 am clicking on any year produced the message "An error occurred while processing this request!!!" Three hours later lists of meetings were produced. These gave the names of the committees and the dates and places of the meetings. Indications of the topics covered could easily have been provided and would have been helpful.

110 A visit to the Council web site on 26 April 2007 produced this result. "Open events live. No sessions available." "Forthcoming events. No sessions available." This fails to enable eurocitizens to plan to use the open service. Archive footage is almost entirely of press conferences. One actual archive Council session I attempted to play had such intermittent speech that it was unusable. The next worked very well, but the Windows Media Player had no forward button to move events along. For anyone trying to study what has been discussed this is very unhelpful. An archive video stream of a press conference under the banner of the German Presidency played on Real Player and was able to be advanced at will. Excellent. A live press conference the same day offering coverage only in English or German actually played only in German. The start was delayed but there was no information on screen to advise why the videostream had not started, nor none at the end to confirm that the event had taken place and was over.

111 Speech, Nottingham, 3 March 2005.

112 www.consilium.europa.eu/cm3_applications

113 *EurActiv* website, 18 Feb. 2005.

114 See *Declaration 24* at the end of the 2004 Constitution.

115 Quoted by www.free-europe.org

116 For example see EU Press Release reference 20060131IPR04891of 2 February 2006. MEPs, Commissioner Ferrero Waldner and EU presidency spokesman, Austrian Minister Winkler, all made this call.

117 http://europa.eu/scadplus/cig2004/debates2_en.htm#CHARTER

118 Jonathan Sacks, speaking on *Thought for the Day* on the *Today* programme, BBC Radio 4, 8 June 2007.

119 Europa press release. Reference: SPEECH/05/628. Date: 20/10/2005.

120 Daily Telegraph 18 November 2000.

121 OECD's figures 2003.

Part Seven

Alternative Plans for EU Development

This part consists mainly of the views of organisations and individuals who are proposing alternatives or amendments to the European Union Constitution, its replacements, or simply the way the European Union is run.

Did EU politicians understand the Constitution and the No vote?

A constitution no eurocitizen and no politician could understand?

As already noted, the ratification of the European Constitution ground to a halt with the French and Dutch rejection of it in referendums in the summer of 2005.

On taking over the presidency from the British Government on 1st January 2006 the Austrian Government announced that decisions must be taken on the Constitution and the whole matter resolved. But they were unable to resolve it.

There were no visible initiatives on this matter by the European Council during 2005, and what was said in private the eurocitizen cannot know. A speech made at St Antony's College, Oxford, by Tony Blair on 2 February 2006, suggests that EU leaders were having difficulty understanding the document they signed in October 2004. "The debate over Europe's Constitution. . . We spent two or three years in an intense institutional debate. . . There was only one drawback. Apart from better rules of internal governance, no-one in Europe knew what it was meant to solve. As the problems of the citizen grew ever more pressing, instead of bold policy reform and decisive change, we locked ourselves in a room at the top of the tower and debated things no ordinary citizen could understand. And yet I remind you the Constitution was launched under the title of Bringing Europe closer to its citizens."

The European Parliament's discussions have been in public and it is clear from these that most MEPs (who so recently approved the Constitution) found it difficult to believe that much rethinking needs to be done. In general they seem unaware of either the problems in the Constitution or the eurocitizens' concerns. They appear to have overlooked the fundamental and burning issues which have caused apathy or concern or anger and revolt against the EU and its Constitution. They feel that eurocitizens have basically not understood the European Union. They think it's not the text that needs changing but the context; or some of the details may need adjustment.

Have MEPs read the Constitution? If they have, do they understand it? What pro-Constitution MEPs see as "the answer," and their limited analysis of the Constitution, are summarised below.

On 18th January 2006 the European Parliament discussed a report about the Constitution and its rejection which was prepared by the European Parliament Committee on Constitutional Affairs - *European Parliament Report on the Period of Reflection*, 16 December 05. This report criticised the Council and Commission for lack of focus in "the period of reflection". The MEPs wanted to see a Europe-wide citizens' debate. To ensure "focus" the report proposed, in a process which looks like centralised direction, "guided" discussions which they have called "Parliamentary Forums" and "Citizens' Forums."

To help citizens to come to conclusions the European Parliament Constitutional Affairs Committee agreed to prepare "European papers" for guidance.

The committee would propose the topics to be discussed and the debates would have clear political goals.

The parliamentary forums were proposed for the spring of 2006, starting on 9th May, and the first would consist of conferences involving MPs from national parliaments and MEPs.

MEPs considered the key topics for consideration should be:

- the integration process
- the use of global role
- the European social and economic model
- security and justice
- and the financing of the Union.

They considered that a clear decision on the way forward should be taken before the end of 2007. The European Parliament would monitor the discussions and prepare their summaries of the ideas put forward during the debates.

The citizens' debates organised by the European Parliament

The European parliament's perfunctory report on the citizens' debates covers just two A4 sides[1] and does not add up to a basis on which one could rewrite the Constitution or make any amendments with confidence. Fortunately it is not the only report.

Discussions were organised in six member states: France, Germany, Greece, Sweden, Portugal and Poland - a total of sixteen events. The numbers involved were not great. For example in Greece 300. In Sweden 500. The events attracted considerable media coverage and generated demands for more effective communication from the EU and for more consultations of the EU with the ordinary citizens of Europe.

Extracts from the European Parliament's report

The very few conclusions set out in the report include:

- "The European social model and the EU's capacity to respond to globalisation were mentioned at all the meetings. Irrespective of the central topic of the forum, questions on the effects of economic liberalisation, fears about the impact and negative effects of globalisation - in particular the relocation of companies - were raised at all the forums. Safeguarding the social dimension of Europe, and maintaining a policy for employment, growth and competitiveness are all seen as challenges that must be met.
- Another across-the-board issue was the integration versus enlargement argument."

Why these two policies should be posed as opposites is a mystery, and the views of the majority of participants on the topic of integration was not made clear.

- "Public opinion varies considerably on the concept of enlargement. . . As an illustration, in Greece most participants said that they were in favour of enlargement, whereas in France there are still reservations about enlargement.
- The question of political integration also prompted participants to raise the issue of the constitutional treaty. Although the institutional question was not a priority in this action to tap into citizens views, [!] it did come up on several occasions. In Germany, it was linked to matters of political integration; the future of the Constitution was raised, as was the question of what prevented a referendum on the constitutional Treaty being held at European level. In Greece, participants supported a Yes to the European constitution if it was necessary to create a better Europe. In France, participants stressed that their No vote had been useful in calling for a better Europe. In Poland, the Constitution was declared dead."

Report on public debates on EU in Sweden

The report drawn up by Bjorn Kjellstrom of the European Parliament Information Office in Sweden gave many insights.

Seven events were organised in the form of after work debates. They were held in pubs or restaurants in seven small and medium-sized towns across Sweden. They were designed to attract citizens who usually do not participate in seminars on EU affairs. They were extremely successful in attracting media reporting of the events including the broadcasting of two events in full on national television. To make the events more appealing they were organised in the early evening and were chaired either by well-known journalists or stand-up comedians. The audiences were provided with a light meal for free!

Twelve out of Sweden's nineteen MEPs took part in at least one forum and eleven MPs from the Riksdag as well as local and regional politicians. Audiences were given green and red cards so that instant opinion polls could be taken on some topics.

The following are the main points made in his report:

Job security and salaries. Divisions of responsibilities

- "The one single issue that generated the most animated debates in all Swedish Fora concerned what the Union can do to create more jobs and how the labour market should be regulated. The question "How can we compete with Polish carpenters on a fair basis' surfaced in different forms in all debates. The discussions on these issues also mirrored a recurring theme in all Fora debates, namely what should be the responsibility of the Member State and what should be the responsibility of the Union."
- "The question about wage competition . . . Clearly, this was an issue of great concern but the common position of all the panels was that the Services Directive will outlaw wage dumping and that the Swedish system of collective bargaining will remain. And when doing a poll on 'Should there be equal pay for equal work?' in for example Karlstad, the result was almost a unanimous Yes."

- "In Karlstad and Skövde citizens in the audience asked what the European Union can do to prevent Europe from losing jobs in the manufacturing industry to low-salary countries."

Immigration

- "While many citizens were concerned about jobs moving abroad, the Skövde audience mentioned immigration as a means by which to solve the Swedish problem with an ageing population. And in Halmstad, 80 per cent of the young people in the audience said that they were willing to move abroad to get a job. Other opinions voiced in the debates include the argument that the small and medium sized companies must be better supported so that the educated Swedes can remain and work in Sweden (Halmstad) and that the Union makes a difference by supporting structural funds projects (Luleå)."

Sweden in the European Union

- "When for example the audience in Skövde was asked if they think that the EU is doing a good job, a majority responded positively. But if so, why are the Swedes so sceptical towards the EU? The predominant view on this issue was that most citizens consider the Swedish membership fee as too high. The notion that 'we give more than we get back' was shared by the audiences in most Fora.
- A more common view, as advocated by members of the audience in for example Skövde and Karlstad, was that the Union should concentrate its work on fewer areas and leave the rest to the Member States. The financing of the CAP was one area which for example the Luleå audience thought should be a candidate for financial cutbacks.
- In Karlstad a small majority voted No when asked if the EU has too much influence on national affairs and in Göteborg a clear majority declared that they want more decisions to be taken on a local level."

A Common European Defence and Europe in the World

- "In Skövde the audience was asked if they thought that the EU should develop a military defence capacity, and 70 per cent said that they thought so. But when responding to "Do you think that the EU should be mandated to deploy Swedish troops to fight abroad?" more than 90 per cent responded negatively. This line of reasoning was predominant in most Fora where this issue was debated. In Göteborg a majority of the audience declared itself in favour of an EU intervention in neighbouring nations - Belarus was cited as an example - in which human rights were grossly violated. But the use of armed forces should remain a strictly national prerogative. When asked about the general political influence of the EU today, half of the Göteborg audience considered the Union politically a weak global player while a clear majority considered it a strong economic actor."

Environment

- "When the audience in for example Karlstad was faced with the question if it is a good thing that the EU deals with environmental issues, more than 90 per cent voted Yes. This is clearly one of the Union's areas of competence which enjoys the greatest degree of support from the Swedes. . . an equally common position is that Sweden does not have very much to learn from the other Member States when it comes to protecting the environment."

The Common Agricultural Policy

- "The CAP is traditionally the EU policy area which the Swedish politicians love to hate, and this scepticism was clearly reflected in the Fora audiences' views. In Malmö and Skövde the citizens expressed strong concerns about the effects of the CAP on the developing world... When asked if Sweden needs a strong common agricultural policy in order for the Swedish agricultural sector to flourish, more than 75 per cent of the Skövde audience - most of whom lead their lives in an area dominated by agricultural industries - said that they do not think so. The general opinion at those Fora where the CAP was discussed was, however, that there is a need for an agricultural policy even though today's CAP is anything but optimal."

Consultation with European citizens - conclusions drawn from the above reports

Few but important conclusions may be drawn from Bjorn Kjellstrom's report on the Swedish consultation and other consultations carried out across Europe.

- Job insecurity, resulting from the movement of work to countries outside Europe is a major concern. This can be taken as a doubt about the free trade principles which are key elements of EU treaties and the proposed Constitution.
- Job insecurity and the depression of wage levels caused by migration within the EU is another concern and this may reflect a worry about the enlargement of the Union, though positive benefits were acknowledged.
- A further cause of concern about job security and wage levels results from privatisation/liberalisation policies.
- The EU is seen as important to the protection of the environment.
- Whilst a common defence policy is approved of, it is considered that the control of member state's military forces should remain in the hands of member states.There should be no integration of armed forces.
- The necessity of the Common Agricultural Policy is questioned.
- A reduced role for the European Union was advocated with more decisions being taken at a local level. Further integration was not favoured. Clarity was required on the division of responsibilities between the European Union and member states.

Conference on "The Future of Europe" MPs and MEPs debate the way forward

Two hundred and fifty MPs and MEPs met in Brussels on 8 and 9 May 2006. MEPs came from the 25 member countries, plus representatives of the Croatian, Romanian and Bulgarian parliaments. The meeting was chaired by the president of the European Parliament, Josep Borrell and Austrian Parliament President, Andreas Khol. Josep Borrell called for a "period of proposals" to follow the "period of reflection". He recognised that the citizens of Europe did not trust the EU and said they had perhaps "underestimated the unease of our fellow citizens. .. We are gathered here to debate how we can re-launch the dynamism of the European project and restore confidence among the people who have elected us."

It may have been unwise to move to the making of proposals without first analysing what the problems were. With so many people present at the conference it was perhaps inevitable that views would range so widely that little would be agreed. The following are selections from the comments as reported in press releases issued by the European Parliament.[2]

The meeting divided into four working groups. The first considered future enlargements.

Conference on "The Future of Europe" as reported in press releases of the European Parliament

Future enlargement

Enlargement was at the centre of the debate, as the present EU Treaty makes any further enlargements after the accession of Bulgaria and Romania impossible. Some parliamentarians therefore voiced grave doubts over future enlargement.

Hubert Haenel (French Senate) reminded the meeting that France has changed its Constitution so that after the accession of Croatia, any future enlargement will be submitted to a referendum. Greek MP Christos Papoutsis was all in favour of future enlargements, on condition that these would not weaken the European project or the institutions of the EU. Bronislaw Geremek (ALDE, Poland) said that the EU and its citizens had tired of enlargement. Austrian MP Werner Fasslabend said that the EU would increase in size by one third if Turkey and Ukraine joined and that this would drastically change the nature of the EU. He therefore favoured an intermediate status for such countries. Karin Thorborg of Sweden was happy with the present reflection period, which made it possible to review the EU's undemocratic decision-making processes and its policies, which are detrimental to poor countries and shape all countries in the same liberal market mould.

EU role in the world On EU foreign policy there was a large measure of consensus. Introducing the debate, German MP Michael Roth, said, "I don't want a renationalisation. Europe is the response to globalisation. No Member State can go it alone. Citizens expect more from the EU in terms of foreign policy". This view was echoed by Mr Carnero (PSE, Spain): "The Common Foreign and Security Policy is a factor of world stability. Therefore we want a Minister of Foreign Affairs and some sort of Energy Minister as well". Mr Brok (EPP-ED, Germany) added that "Member States cannot achieve much on their own: think of bodies like the WTO. In the future, the transatlantic community will continue to be a driving force in external affairs." Mr Kastens said that the draft constitutional treaty had contained all the answers: a common defence policy, security guarantees, a president, a foreign minister, common foreign representation and a legal personality. However, Belgian MP, Stef Goris, worried about the lack of parliamentary scrutiny in the EU foreign policy, in particular in the case of foreign missions such as to the Congo.

The European social model as a positive answer to globalisation

The need to find a positive answer to globalisation and a common approach to problems like high unemployment, low economic growth, a lack of trust in the European project and the existence and shape of the European social model were at the heart of the debate in this working group... A number of speakers said globalisation is Europe's major challenge at the moment, but noted that it also raises fear for many citizens.

Mr Othmar Karas (EPP-ED, Austria), who will present a report on the discussion, said it is essential to paint a positive picture of globalisation. "Nobody wants to create fear via globalisation. One has to accept that globalisation is taking place." Helga Machne (Member of the Austrian Parliament) said "globalisation is a good thing for Europe and should be used to solve the problem of unemployment and stagnation of economic growth". Mr Karas said globalisation should not imply social dumping and a loss of quality. Along with many speakers, he stressed that protectionism and nationalism are not the answer. Instead Europe needs to intensify collaboration and coordination and to enhance mutual understanding as well as the respect of differences.

Pierre Jonckheer (Greens/EFA, Belgium) referred to a recent Euro-barometer study showing that citizens want more decisions taken at European level.[3]

Eurobarometer's loaded questions

It should be noted that the questions were put in such a way that a pro EU answer was more likely. "For each of the following areas [thirteen were listed] please tell me if you believe that more decision-making should take place at a European level or on the contrary that less decision-making should take place at a European level."

The use of the words "at a European level" masked the words "by the European Union" (a more emotive but accurate term). The words "or on the contrary" deprived respondents of an alternative idea which might enable them to choose between tangible alternatives. The use of the words "or by national governments" would have been clearer. Even then, hostility to a party in power in their own country might suggest support for the EU as the lesser of two evils rather than whole-hearted support. The topics listed were identified in a far from neutral way. For example managing the economy was listed as "ensuring economic growth" as if decisions at a European level could be taken actually to achieve this. The control and administration of agriculture was listed as "the protection of agriculture." Planning and implementing employment policies were listed as "the fight against unemployment." Another section of the survey noted that there was very considerable dissatisfaction with the achievements of the European Union in handling various important matters especially unemployment, social rights, economic growth and agriculture.

It doesn't quite make sense that people would want much more of what they found very unsatisfactory. "European level" may not have been equated with the EU. It may well be that respondents were broadly in favour of international co-operation in tackling certain issues rather than believing that the EU would make better decisions than their own governments. How much do any of us understand about who is doing what to make things better or worse in any of the major areas of government? We are dealing here with perceptions, not understanding or reality. When people know so little about a topic how much are their opinions worth?

> The need to enhance the trust of citizens was emphasised by Outi Ojala (Member of the Finnish parliament), and echoed by many others. Opinions varied on the Lisbon strategy and the open method of coordination. Many agreed that the Lisbon process is not working properly, but, as Neven Mimica (Croatian parliament, president for the committee on European integration) said, it is part of the solution if implemented properly.

EU Funding

> There was broad agreement among participants of the working group on "future resources of the European Union" that the existing own-resources system should be replaced by a scheme more understandable to the public. Whether this system should be tax-based or built on existing instruments was the subject of a lively debate, as was the nature and the objectives of the Community's budget itself. Lord Grenfell from the UK House of Lords explained that a new form of own-resource would have to be "carefully scrutinised", and that differences on whether it should be tax-based or not "should be aired". Own-resources have been in the limelight since the start of the talks on the funding of the long-term spending plan of the European Union, the so-called "Financial Perspective". The own-resource system has not been reformed for almost 20 years, and many linked this with the difficulty in agreeing a new Financial Perspective for the 2007-13 period.
>
> '"EU tax and the public. An EU tax can hardly be justified to the citizens at this stage and would certainly not help the cause of the European Union," argued Christian Philip from the French National Assembly. "Any tax would have to be comprehensible by the public," Danish Folketinget Member Svend Auken said, "and thus everyone would understand it if we took it from a share of the benefits made by oil companies".
>
> "A tax-based system would have to be applied with a proper supra-national fiscal regime, which ensures that EU money is used transparently and managed appropriately," said Ilias Kallioras of the Greek Parliament. Participants were not short of imagination for new forms of funding: taxes on flights, company profits or even on short text messages sent by mobile phones.

The own-resources system was created in 1970 to finance the EU budget with four main instruments: funds from VAT, customs duties, agricultural levies, and contributions from Member States, the so-called "Gross National Income resource", calculated according to their wealth. Over time, the GNI resource has grown to represent the main source of funding of the EU, with a direct impact on deficit-threatened national budgets.

The Joint Parliamentary meeting came up with a concrete result as regards the debate on how the EU should be financed. Members of the European and national Parliaments agreed to set up a permanent working group to explore different options to finance EU policies.

Security and Justice

The need to improve the decision-making process in this area, while respecting national traditions, and the possibility of a common EU immigration policy were the main issues.

"Eurobarometer polls show people's concerns in this area and their expectations vis-à-vis Europe", said Jo Leinen (PES, Germany), in his opening statement. "We have the task of re-establishing confidence among citizens in Europe", added Mr Grosse-Brömer (EPP-ED, Germany). . . Elisabeth Arnold, President of the Danish Parliament Committee on European Affairs, stressed the need to proceed carefully in harmonising national criminal law as this issue affects national sovereignty. John Denham, Chairman of the UK House of Commons' Committee on Home Affairs, said, "We should focus on developing practical cooperation to solve practical problems". According to Mr Denham, because cultural differences among Member States are so wide the solution to improving the fight against crime cannot be to extend EU competence in this area."

On the issue of whether the EU should have a joint immigration policy, national and European parliamentarians had different ideas. For Michalis Chyssohoidis, a Socialist member of the Hellenic Parliament, the "time has come for a common immigration policy". Paulis Klavins, a member of the Latvian Parliament, raised the issue of countries with external European borders and said the EU should agree to some principles on a common answer to immigration related problems. According to Ryszard Legutko, Polish Senate Vice-President, a common immigration policy is the ultimate goal but cannot be achieved now. Lord Marlesford, a member of the House of Lords' committee for the European Union, said immigration policy must remain under national control and agreed with Mr Denham's comment that he didn't believe such a goal was "attainable".

Is the Constitution still alive? (2006)

Swedish MP Tuve Skanberg said that the Constitution is supported by a majority, but "there are criticisms and it is important to allow criticisms to be heard." A few voices, including Portuguese MP Honorio Novo, said that "the Constitution is dead". For Jens-Peter Bonde (IND/DEM, Denmark), "a new Constitution for Europe should be drawn up bottom up instead of top down. We should not vote any text which has not been approved by the majority of national parliaments."

According to the vice-President of the Polish Sejm, Jaroslaw Kalinowski, "the Treaty should be made simpler and more understandable for Europeans." Francis Wurtz (GUE/NGL, France) justified the rejection of the

Treaty by saying: "Citizens have the feeling that the EU is not a solution to globalisation, but part of the problem".

Austrian Chancellor Wolfgang Schüssel defended the Constitution: "The constitution treaty is the most successful attempt we've had so far to build on the achievements of the past 50 years," he said. "The way things stand, I don't see a better option."

José Manuel Barroso, President of the Commission, comments

President Barroso gave the closing address at the joint parliamentary meeting on the future of Europe. He suggested that the key issues were a need for consensus across Europe (currently absent), a need for positive achievements, the minimisation of bureaucracy and legislation, and institutions built on accountability, transparency, subsidiarity and trust. He said he would ensure that the Commission would increase democratic involvement in some of its decision making.

Here is a selection of his remarks:

"I would dearly have liked to have been able to stand here today and chart the next steps for the Constitution. But it is clear that there is as yet no consensus on the institutional settlement... Citizens want to see the European Union focusing on delivering its policies... The current Treaties set up an institutional system to deliver EU action...

But to fully achieve our goals, it needs to be based on two foundation stones. First, there has to be a broad political consensus about what Europe is trying to achieve - a consensus which must be in tune with citizens' key goals. Second, it needs the support of partners working at every level in every part of Europe...

EU institutions must continue to make the way the EU works more accessible and more effective... The work of the institutions must be based on key democratic principles - accountability, transparency, and trust. We must respect the principle of subsidiarity. We must minimise bureaucracy. We must take further steps to open up. The steps taken on better regulation have pushed this process further. . . Simplifying legislation and looking at alternatives, proper consultation and careful impact assessment is not a technical but political exercise, to respond to popular concerns about an excessively bureaucratic Europe. Further steps are needed. All the EU institutions have a responsibility to show that the European Union is here to serve its citizens, and to be accountable for the results... For too long national parliaments have been seen as semi-detached players on the European scene. This must change.

We do not need to wait for an institutional settlement to improve and facilitate the scrutiny by national parliaments of EU legislation. So, today, I announce to you that: First, the Commission wishes to transmit directly all new proposals and consultation papers to national parliaments, inviting them to react so as to improve the process of policy formulation. Second, that the Commission step up its political engagement with national parliaments.

The Amsterdam Treaty gave the European Union the power to bring police and judicial cooperation in criminal matters under Community rules. Similar steps could be taken for legal migration policies... This is an area where we must improve democratic accountability. We must ensure democratic control inside normal Community procedures, with European Parliament scrutiny. Equally, we must ensure national legislative control by national parliaments. We intend to look at this area, case by case, and make a proposal to use the powers we have to make these policies more effective and more democratic."

Conclusions based on reports of the two day conference of MPs and MEPs on "The Future of Europe"

A lack of confidence in eurocitizens with regard to the European Union was identified but there appears to have been little attempt to get to the heart of the problem of the rejection of the Constitution and widespread disaffection with the European Project - something which must be difficult in this sort of forum, though it should surely have been attempted. Nevertheless, numerous significant doubts were raised, and suggestions for modifications of the Constitution and endorsements of some policies were made. The assumption underlying virtually every contribution was that changes in the Constitution would have to take place. Blanket endorsements of the Constitution, such as that of the Austrian Chancellor, are not likely to lead to increased support for the European Union. The progress of the European Union, even its survival, depends on its ability to think its way through the present impasse.

Reactions of the European Parliamentary political groups to the Constitution - based on views expressed in English in the European Parliament on 18th January 2006.

(Note: A verbatim record in English of the speeches of those not addressing the parliament in English was not available when this account was prepared. Many points made by speakers are not developed. This is primarily because speakers had strict and often very brief allocations of time in which to make their points.)

Andrew Duff (ALDE), one of the co-authors of the European Parliament Report on the Period of Reflection, said that the way to resolve the crisis of the rejected Constitution could only be found with the "the close co-operation of national parliaments." He was surprised the presidents of the Austrian, Finnish, and German parliaments were reluctant to co-operate with the European Parliament on this matter. He wanted to see a debate about the reforms of:

- the common policies
- issues of competences
- instruments and
- procedures.

The resolution before Parliament stated that there were many possible solutions, but he believed that in practice there were only two. "The first is to supplement the present treaty with interpretative protocols or declarations. The second is to make rather more substantive changes to Part III so that we address the legitimate concerns and disquiet expressed by citizens in France and the Netherlands and in some other member states." (Part III deals with the Union's policies and the administrative organisation of each of its main institutions.)

Margot Wallstrom, Vice President of the Commission, said:

> "All wished to achieve a constitutional settlement to make Europe more transparent, more democratic and more effective. The question is how to achieve that settlement after the French and Dutch No votes. I was happy to see that all options regarding the Constitution remain open in your resolution. During the reflection period it is essential to listen to citizens, social partners, political parties, and national and regional parliaments without prejudging the result of the wider dialogue and debate. If we do not, this exercise will lose all its value. . . Recent Eurobarometer surveys have shown that European citizens' support for the concept of a Constitution for the European Union has increased by two percentage points over the past five months to 63 per cent. Therefore, as has been said many times in the Committee on Constitutional Affairs, it is important to change the context rather than the text. That is why the dialogue has to focus on the European project in connection with constitutional reform, and on the ultimate objective linked to the instruments to deliver it."

Alexander Stubb (PPE) believed that all options were open, but was confident a solution could be found by 2009.

Richard Corbett (PSE) said that the current treaties were not sufficient to enable the enlarged EU to function effectively so something had to change. There were many options: "supplementary interpretative declarations, extra protocols, rewriting part of the text, rewriting the whole text, starting a new text."

Jens-Peter Bonde (IND/DEM) was angry that the EU rule that treaty change must have unanimity amongst EU members was being ignored. "The proposed Constitution is dead! Still you urge national parliaments to break the law. You continue to propagate the text." He complained that EU taxpayers' money was being spent to promote the Yes campaign with nothing to the No campaign. "You finance further propaganda: €300,000 to the European Movement; €110,000 to the European Federalists; millions of Euros to those in favour of the Constitution. We demand a free, a fair and open debate with equal representation of the Yes and No sides. . . The SOS democracy inter-group has started a minority report. We reject the idea of a state constitution, ask for the existing treaties to be reviewed and for a co-operation agreement to be established instead."

Brian Crowley, on behalf of UEN, noted that many who voted for the Constitution may have irrational fears. "Until such time as we convince the citizens and allow them ownership of the European Union project, only then can we truly say that we have a citizens' Europe that rightfully belongs to them."

One of the Independent MEPs, James Hugh Allister (NI), said the report sought to "second-guess and repudiate the democratic verdict of the people of France and Holland by declaring that those results were not about rejecting the Constitution, but about dissent and other issues. Nonsense! The question on the ballot paper was about one thing only - the acceptability of the Constitution - and the answer was equally clear."

Roger Knapman (IDD/DEM) said that large proportions of a population of Europe do not want to continue pushing towards full political union.

Daniel Hannan (PPE) accused MEPs of seeking to implement the Constitution without popular consent. He claimed that part of it was already implemented.

"Look at the number of policies and institutions envisaged by the Constitution that have been or are being enacted regardless: the European External Action Service, the European Human Rights Agency, the European Defence Agency, the European Space Programme, the European External Borders Agency, a justiciable *Charter of Fundamental Rights*: none of these has any proper legal basis outside the Constitution. By adopting them anyway you demonstrate that you will allow no force - internal or external, neither your own rule book nor the expressed opposition of your peoples in the ballot box - to arrest the rush to political assimilation."

He considered that the Constitution had been rejected. "I know it is hard to accept rejection, but look at the figures: 55 per cent of French voters; 62 per cent of Dutch voters. . . current polls in the Netherlands show that 82 per cent of Dutch voters would now vote No."

Ian Hudghton (Verts/ALE) said "I cannot support this report. The text fails to recognise that the constitutional treaty has been rejected by electors in two member states. Undoubtedly if given the opportunity of a referendum, other rejections would also be delivered. The two rapporteurs want somehow to revive the core of the current, rejected, text. This does not seem to me to be credible. How can French and Dutch voters be expected to accept such arrogance. We are in a so-called period of reflection. Let us make it a period in which to rethink, replace, and not just regurgitate a document which has already been resoundingly rejected."

The report was approved by MEPs: 383 in favour, 125 against, with 51 abstentions.

The Europe of Democracies

An Alternative Constitution: Report by eight members of the Convention which drafted the European Constitution [full text]

We hereby submit the following 15 points for the consideration of our Prime ministers and fellow citizens.

The European Union (EU) shall not have a constitution. Instead, Europe should be organised on an interparliamentary basis by means of a Treaty on European Co-operation. This will create a Europe of Democracies (ED) in place of the existing EU. If the EU should have a new name it should be Europe of Democracies.

A slimline treaty

The present 97,000 pages of the acquis communautaire covering the EU and EEA must be radically simplified. Instead, focus shall be placed on cross-frontier issues where national parliaments cannot effectively act by themselves. Decisions on subsidiarity shall be resolved by the national parliaments.

Open to all democracies

Membership of the ED shall be open to any democratic European state which is a signatory of, and respects fully, the European Convention on Human Rights.

Simplified decision-making

The present 30 different ways of making decisions in the EU shall be reduced to two: laws and recommendations. Where qualified majority voting applies, the proposal in question shall require 75 % of the votes to be cast in favour, unless otherwise stated.

A veto on vital issues

Laws shall be valid only if they have been passed by national parliaments. A national parliament shall have a veto on an issue it deems important.

The common core issues

Laws shall deal with the rules for the Common Market and certain common minimum standards to protect employees, consumers, health, safety and the environment. In other areas the ED shall have the power to issue recommendations for Member States, which are always free to adopt higher standards.

Flexible co-operation

The ED may unanimously approve flexible cooperation for those nations that want to take part in closer co-operation. The ED shall also recognise and support other pan-European organisations, such as the Council of Europe.

Openness and transparancy

The decision-making process and relevant documents shall be open and accessible, unless a reasonable cause for exception is confirmed by qualified majority.

Straight forward council voting

A simplified voting system shall operate in the Council, which may comprise each Member State possessing one vote in the ED Council. A decision by qualified majority shall require the support of countries with more than half the total ED population.

National parliaments elect the commission

Every national parliament should elect its own member of the Commission. The Commissioner shall attend the European Scrutiny Committees of the national parliament concerned. National parliaments shall have the power to dismiss their Commissioner. The President of the Commission shall be elected by the national parliaments. National parliaments shall decide on the annual legislative programme and the Commission shall correspondingly act as a secretariat for the Council and the national parliaments.

No legislation by the court

Legal activism by the European Court in Luxembourg shall be curbed, and the Court shall respect the European Convention on Human Rights.

Partnership agreements

The Member States and the ED may enter into partnership agreements of mutual interest with states or groups of states. The ED shall respect the parliamentary democracy of its partners and may assist poorer ones with a financial aid, while fostering free trade agreements.

Better scrutiny

The European Ombudsman, the Court of Auditors and the Budget Control Committees of the European and national parliaments shall have access to all documents and all financial accounts.

Equality of languages

When legislating, all official ED languages shall be treated equally.

United Nations

The ED shall not have its own army. Peacekeeping and peacemaking should be mandated by the United Nations and the Organisation for Security and Cooperation in Europe. Member States shall decide themselves whether they opt for a common defence through NATO, independent defence, or follow a neutrality policy.

By Convention members:
William Abitbol (Alternate Member) European Parliament
Jens-Peter Bonde (Member) European Parliament
Per Dalgaard (Alternate Member) Denmark - Parliament
John Gormley (Alternate Member) Ireland - Parliament
David Heathcoat-Amory (Member) - UK - Parliament
Esko Seppanen (Alternate Member) European Parliament
Peter Skaarup (Member) Denmark - Parliament
Jan Zahradil (Member) Czech Republic - Parliament

This alternative report was attached to the Report from the Presidency of the Convention to the President of the European Council, 18 July 2003. Reference number: CONV 851/03 (ANNEX III)

Statement by Trade Unions Against the EU Constitution

Alternatives to the EU Constitution

"The contents of the proposed EU Constitution reveal that it is not "just another treaty" or a "tidying-up exercise" as government ministers have claimed. Supporters like to refer to the document as a "constitutional treaty" to downplay its significance. This description implies that this is comparable to previous EU treaties like Nice, Amsterdam, Maastricht and the Single European Act.

However, in international law, a treaty is a contract or agreement between independent states, as equal sovereign partners. A constitution is the fundamental law of a state, setting out its institutions of government, how it makes its laws, determines its policies and relates to other states.

This treaty will only be a treaty until the Constitution comes into effect. From then on it is the Constitution we will be bound by and will have to obey. It is likely that, if ratified, supporters will drop the word "treaty" and call it what it really is, a Constitution for a new state.

If the EU Constitution becomes part of our Constitution it will not be amendable except with the consent of other countries. Those pushing the Constitution are effectively asking us to abandon our right to determine the laws we agree to obey and to decide our own government, which is our most fundamental democratic right.

However, if the proposed Constitution is rejected the EU will continue on the basis of the Treaty of Nice, with the voting arrangements which that treaty laid down for an EU of 27 states. It would then be appropriate to revisit the 2001 *Laeken Declaration*, which launched the process of writing a constitution. The declaration talked of popular concerns about too many powers being exercised at EU rather than national level, and the need for a genuine debate on the kind of Europe people really want. Almost certainly that is not a Europe which is a state or superpower in its own right, run by a bureaucratic elite. It is more likely to be a Europe of co-operating independent democratic states, where powers are repatriated back to the EU member states from Brussels.

A new convention should be called for with peace and accountability as its goals. The EU needs to consider ways to bring about more democracy in Europe, not less. Such a Europe can only be one where national parliaments and voters have their rights restored and where democracy and representative government are re-established for the peoples and nations of our continent.

Opposing the EU Constitution does not mean leaving the EU. Now is the time to defend democracy across Europe and say no."

MEPs' alternative Constitution: "Europe Deserves Better"

[An alternative constitution proposed by dissenting members of the European Parliament.]

Committee on Constitutional Affairs - Report on the Treaty Establishing A Constitution For Europe. Minority opinion, pursuant to Rule 48 (3) of the Rules of Procedure.

More Democracy

Within all EU member states, laws are passed by elected representatives and consequently all laws can be democratically changed. These representatives are held responsible by the voters and they can be replaced in an election. This is the essence of representative democracy.

All EU Member States are democracies. At the heart of democracy lies the voter's right to choose his rulers.

The proposed EU constitution threatens the very idea of democracy. Certainly, we would still be able to vote, but in many areas, a majority vote in the EU would take precedence over our own national laws.

The EU Commission, where members are appointed rather than elected, has the sole and exclusive right to initiate legislation over which bureaucrats and the Council of Ministers, not the elected Parliament, have the final say. Why should we therefore vote "Yes" to an erosion of democracy?

Europe deserves better than the current draft proposal for a European constitution. Therefore we reject the constitution as it stands. We instead propose greater democracy in Europe:

Every country should appoint a commissioner over whom it has powers of scrutiny. Every country should have one vote in the Council of Ministers which is controlled by the national parliament. A 75% majority should be required to pass a bill within the EU representing at least 50% of the population. All EU laws must also be approved by national parliaments. Every national parliament should have the right of veto in vital areas.

The European Parliament must have the right of veto in all questions. If a bill is blocked, full decision-makings powers should revert to national parliaments.

All legislation should be public and possible to follow on the Internet. All preparation meetings and documents should be open - unless 75% have voted in favour of a derogation closing a meeting or a document which can be controlled by the Ombudsman and the court.

Less centralisation

The European Constitution introduces many new areas in which the EU can legislate in place of national parliaments. No vital area would be immune from EU interference. Majority voting is introduced in many new areas where the national parliaments would therefore be overruled. Furthermore, heads of government would be able to advance still further and change areas that today require unanimity, so that in the future such decisions would require only majority votes, where other countries could be overruled. Heads of government could also extend the power of the EU into new matters without referring it back to voters.

The EU must be much closer to its citizens. The European Constitution does the opposite - it centralises even more power in Brussels. This is why we recommend the rejection of the constitution. We propose more liberty in the member states, not more centralisation:

All laws should carry an integrated expiry date after which they would no longer apply unless specifically readopted. The 100,000 pages of existing EU legislation should be re-examined so that EU jurisdiction is confined to cross-border issues.

A real principle of subsidiarity should be introduced. The national parliaments should adopt the annual catalogue of laws and thereafter give the Commission the right to propose a bill.

All EU Decisions should be rationalised into two different types: laws and recommendations. Laws should apply only in cross-border areas where the member states cannot legislate effectively by themselves; recommendations could apply to matters of national interest.

The European Court of Justice should be confined to arbitrating cross-border disputes; it should be prevented from legislating beyond the text of the treaties.

No new superpower

The European Constitution gives the EU a “legal personality” to represent member states in relations with the rest of the world, and in doing so takes over the function of statehood under international law.

Any decision taken by the EU has priority over the democratically decided laws of member states. Even our national constitutions are ignored if they are in conflict with a decision coming from Brussels. This principle of federal state centralisation is now articulated in Article 6 of the new constitution and furthermorc it is the duty of member states to present any matter of dispute to the European Court of Justice.

The EU will get its own Ministry for Foreign Affairs and a joint military force. A President and a joint minister for Foreign Affairs will, together with a joint prime minister - the president of the Commission, represent EU in relations with other countries in the world.

The twenty-five member states will become constituent states akin to the US model, but with less freedom to legislate independently than American states enjoy. Therefore we recommend a rejection of the constitution.

Instead, we propose co-operation between free and independent nations. The world does not need a new superpower.

EU co-operation should not be based on a constitution but on an agreement between independent countries; a treaty that could be rescinded with two years notification.

The European Court of Justice and the EU authorities must respect the constitutions of the member states according to the way those constitutions are interpreted by their respective national Supreme Courts or Constitutional Courts.

A common European foreign policy must not prevent member states from acting independently at international level.

The military must be kept apart from civilian co-operation in the EU.

The President of the EU must be abolished in favour of a practical presidency where the duty is undertaken in rotation.

The EU must be cleaned up

We still have a budget where as much as 10 % of the money paid to Brussels is lost or stolen.

We still have an EU where, the Court of Auditors and the EU Parliamentary Committee on Budgetary Control are unable to effectively control the use of EU funds. The Ombudsman does not have access to all documents.

We have an EU fisheries policy which harms the interests of fishermen and an agricultural policy that is expensive for consumers and taxpayers alike that penalises farmers, harms the environment and impoverishes the Third World.

Money is frittered away in the structural and cohesion funds and in badly-run overseas aid projects.

For these reasons, too we recommend a rejection of the constitution.

We would concentrate on improving the EU's performance in exercising the powers it currently exercises, before bestowing any new ones on it.

Fair Referendum

Referenda concerning the draft proposal for the European Constitution must be held, where possible in all countries on the same day, so that European citizens get the final say in deciding the rules that govern our co-operation.

The referenda must be fair and free with equal resources allocated to both sides in all countries.

If a country rejects the constitution, a new and more representative convention must be appointed. This convention would prepare proposals for more democratic rules which can unite us instead of dividing Europeans as the current proposal does.

Respecting the result

If all 25 member states ratify the constitution according to their own democratic procedures, we will respect the people's verdict. But we are concerned that the other side displays no similar intention:

Several incoming Commissioners have indicated that they will implement parts of this Constitution with or without formal ratification.

MEPs have expressly demanded that they do so as a condition of their appointment.

Already, work has begun on establishing an EU foreign ministry and diplomatic service.

Even before the Constitution had been agreed, let alone ratified, the EU court had indicated that it would rule on the basis of the *Charter of Fundamental Rights*.

The Referendum Group calls on national governments to accept the verdict of their peoples. If one or more member states vote "No", the Constitution should be scrapped, and work should begin on a new intergovernmental treaty that would regulate a European Commonwealth of national democracies.

December 9th, 2004

Jens-Peter Bonde,
Wojciech Wierzejski,
James Hugh Allister
Mogens N.J. Camre

Rapporteurs: Richard Corbett and Íñigo Méndez de Vigo

Notes

1 European Parliament document reference PE 375.086/CPG, NT\618067EN.doc

2 Sources of conclusions and comments of MPs and MEPs are press releases of the European Parliament:

- http://www.europarl.europa.eu/news/expert/infopress_page/002-7839-128-05-19-901-
- 20060503IPR07838-08-05-2006-2006-false/default_en.htm
- http://www.europarl.europa.eu/news/expert/infopress_page/002-7841-128-05-19-901-
- 20060503IPR07840-08-05-2006-2006-false/default_en.htm
- http://www.europarl.europa.eu/news/expert/infopress_page/002-7843-128-05-19-901-
- 20060503IPR07842-08-05-2006-2006-false/default_en.htm http://www.europarl.europa.eu/news/expert/infopress_page/002-7845-128-05-19-901-
- 20060503IPR07844-08-05-2006-2006-false/default_en.htm

3 Eurobarometer Special Poll 251, published May 2006.

Part Eight

Mandate for the Reform Treaty

Text of EU document

Mandate for the Reform Treaty, EU text

[Instructions for "replacing" the EU Constitution, agreed 23 June by EU leaders, Brussels, under President Angela Merkel, Germany. Extract from EU text, *Presidency Conclusions - Brussels, 21/22 June 2007. Reference 11177/07*]

Draft IGC Mandate

The present mandate will provide the exclusive basis and framework for the work of the IGC that will be convened according to paragraph 10 of the European Council conclusions.

I. General Observations

1. The IGC is asked to draw up a Treaty (hereinafter called "Reform Treaty") amending the existing Treaties with a view to enhancing the efficiency and democratic legitimacy of the enlarged Union, as well as the coherence of its external action. The constitutional concept, which consisted in repealing all existing Treaties and replacing them by a single text called "Constitution", is abandoned. The Reform Treaty will introduce into the existing Treaties, which remain in force, the innovations resulting from the 2004 IGC, as set out below in a detailed fashion.

2. The Reform Treaty will contain two substantive clauses amending respectively the Treaty on the European Union (TEU) and the Treaty establishing the European Community. (TEC). The TEU will keep its present name and the TEC will be called Treaty on the Functioning of the Union, the Union having a single legal personality. The word "Community" will throughout be replaced by the word "Union"; it will be stated that the two Treaties constitute the Treaties on which the Union is founded and that the Union replaces and succeeds the Community. Further clauses will contain the usual provisions on ratification and entry into force as well as transitional arrangements. Technical amendments to the Euratom Treaty and to the existing Protocols, as agreed in the 2004 IGC, will be done via Protocols attached to the Reform Treaty.

3. The TEU and the Treaty on the Functioning of the Union will not have a constitutional character. The terminology used throughout the Treaties will reflect this change: the term "Constitution" will not be used, the "Union Minister for Foreign Affairs" will be called High Representative of the Union for Foreign Affairs and Security Policy and the denominations "law" and "framework law" will be abandoned, the existing denominations "regulations", "directives" and " decisions" being retained. Likewise, there will be no article in the amended Treaties mentioning the symbols of the EU such as the flag, the anthem or the motto. Concerning the primacy of EU law, the IGC will adopt a Declaration recalling the existing case law of the EU Court of Justice[1].

4. As far as the content of the amendments to the existing Treaties is concerned, the innovations resulting from the 2004 IGC will be integrated into the TEU and the Treaty on the Functioning of the Union, as specified in this mandate. Modifications to these innovations introduced as a result of the consultations held with the Member States over the past 6 months are clearly indicated

below. They concern in particular the respective competences of the EU and the Member States and their delimitation, the specific nature of the Common Foreign and Security Policy, the enhanced role of national parliaments, the treatment of the Charter of Fundamental Rights and a mechanism, in the area of police and judicial cooperation in criminal matters, enabling Member States to go forward on a given act while allowing others not to participate.

II. Amendments to the EU Treaty

5. Clause 1 of the Reform Treaty will contain the amendments to the present TEU.

In the absence of indications to the contrary in this mandate, the text of the existing Treaty remains unchanged.

6. The text of the first recital as agreed in the 2004 IGC will be inserted as a second recital into the Preamble.

7. The TEU will be divided into 6 Titles: Common Provisions (I), Provisions on democratic principles (II), Provisions on institutions (III), Provisions on enhanced cooperation (IV), General Provisions on the Union's External Action and specific Provisions on the Common Foreign and Security Policy (V), and Final Provisions (VI). Titles I, IV (present VII), V and VI (present VIII) follow the structure of the existing TEU, with amendments as agreed in the 2004 IGC.[2] The two other titles (II and III) are new and introduce innovations agreed in the 2004 IGC.

Common Provisions (I)

8. Title I of the existing TEU, containing inter alia Articles on the Union's values and objectives, on relations between the Union and the Member States, and on the suspension of rights of Member States,will be amended in line with the innovations agreed in the 2004 IGC (see Annex 1, Title I).

9. The Article on fundamental rights will contain a cross reference[3] to the Charter on fundamental rights, as agreed in the 2004 IGC, giving it legally binding value and setting out the scope of its application.

10. In the Article on fundamental principles concerning competences it will be specified that the Union shall act only within the limits of competences conferred upon it by the Member States in the Treaties.

Provisions on democratic principles (II)

11. This new Title II will contain the provisions agreed in the 2004 IGC on democratic equality, representative democracy, participatory democracy and the citizens' initiative. Concerning national parliaments, their role will be further enhanced compared to the provisions agreed in the 2004 IGC (see Annex 1, Title II):

- The period given to national parliaments to examine draft legislative texts and to give a reasoned opinion on subsidiarity will be extended from 6 to 8 weeks (the Protocols on national Parliaments and on subsidiarity and proportionality will be modified accordingly).
- There will be a reinforced control mechanism of subsidiarity in the sense that if a draft legislative act is contested by a simple majority of the votes

allocated to national parliaments, the Commission will re-examine the draft act, which it may decide to maintain, amend or withdraw. If it chooses to maintain the draft, the Commission will have, in a reasoned opinion, to justify why it considers that the draft complies with the principle of subsidiarity. This reasoned opinion, as well as the reasoned opinions of the national parliaments, will have to be transmitted to the EU legislator, for consideration in the legislative procedure. This will trigger a specific procedure:

- before concluding first reading under the ordinary legislative procedure, the legislator (Council and Parliament) shall consider the compatibility of the legislative proposal with the principle of subsidiarity, taking particular account of the reasons expressed and shared by the majority of national parliaments as well as the reasoned opinion of the Commission;
- If, by a majority of 55% of the members of the Council or a majority of the votes cast in the European Parliament, the legislator is of the opinion that the proposal is not compatible with the principle of subsidiarity, the legislative proposal shall not be given further consideration. (the Protocol on subsidiarity and proportionality will be modified accordingly).

A new general Article will reflect the role of the national parliaments.

Provisions on institutions (III)

12. The institutional changes agreed in the 2004 IGC will be integrated partly into the TEU and partly into the Treaty on the Functioning of the Union. The new Title III will give an overview of the institutional system and will set out the following institutional modifications to the existing system, i.e. the Articles on the Union's institutions, the European Parliament (new composition), the European Council (transformation into an institution and creation of the office of President), the Council (introduction of the double majority voting system and changes in the six-monthly Council presidency system, with the possibility of modifying it), the European Commission (new composition and strengthening of the role of its President), the Union Minister for Foreign Affairs (creation of the new office, its title being changed to High Representative of the Union for Foreign Affairs and Security Policy) and the Court of Justice of the European Union.[5]

13. The double majority voting system, as agreed in the 2004 IGC, will take effect on 1 November 2014, until which date the present qualified majority system (Article 205(2) TEC) will continue to apply. After that, during a transitional period until 31 March 2017, when a decision is to be adopted by qualified majority, a member of the Council may request that the decision be taken in accordance with the qualified majority as defined in Article 205(2) of the present TEC.

In addition, until 31 March 2017, if members of the Council representing at least 75% of the population or at least 75% of the number of Member States necessary to constitute a blocking minority as provided in Article [I-25(2)] indicate their opposition to the Council adopting an act by a qualified majority, the mechanism provided for in the draft Decision contained in Declaration n° 5 annexed to the Final Act of the 2004 IGC. As from 1 April 2017, the same mechanism will apply, the relevant percentages being, respectively, at least 55% of the population or at least 55% of the number of Member States necessary to constitute a blocking minority as provided in Article [I-25(2)].

Provisions on enhanced cooperation (IV)

14. Title IV (former Title VII of the existing TEU) will be amended as agreed in the 2004 IGC. The minimum number of Member States required for launching an enhanced cooperation will be nine. General Provisions on the Union's external action and specific Provisions on the Common Foreign and Security Policy (V)

General Provisions on the Union's external action and specific Provisions on the Common Foreign and Security Policy (V)

15. In Title V of the existing TEU, a first new Chapter on the general provisions on the Union's external action will be inserted containing two Articles, as agreed in the 2004 IGC, on the principles and objectives of the Union's external action and on the role of the European Council in setting the strategic interests and objectives of this action. The second Chapter contains the provisions of Title V[6] of the existing TEU, as amended in the 2004 IGC (including the European External Action Service and the permanent structured cooperation in the field of defence). In this Chapter, a new first Article will be inserted stating that the Union's action on the international scene will be guided by the principles, will pursue the objectives and will be conducted in accordance with the general provisions on the Union's external action which are laid down in Chapter 1. It will be clearly specified in this Chapter that the CFSP is subject to specific procedures and rules. There will also be a specific legal basis on personal data protection in the CFSP area[7].

Final Provisions (VI)

16. Title VI (former Title VIII of the existing TEU) will be amended as agreed in the 2004 IGC. There will in particular be an Article on the legal personality of the Union[8], an Article on voluntary withdrawal from the Union and Article 48 will be amended so as to bring together the procedures for revising the Treaties (the ordinary and the two simplified procedures). This Article, in its paragraph on the ordinary revision procedure, will make it clear that the Treaties can be revised to increase or reduce the competences conferred upon the Union. In Article 49, on conditions of eligibility and the procedure for accession to the Union, the reference to the principles will be replaced by a reference to the Union's values and the addition of a commitment to promoting such values, an obligation to notify the European Parliament and national parliaments of an application for accession to the Union and a reference to take into account the conditions of eligibility agreed upon by the European Council (see Annex 1, Title VI). The usual final provision will also be adapted (territorial scope, duration, ratification and authentic texts and translations).[9]

III. Amendments to the EC Treaty

17. Clause 2 of the Reform Treaty will contain the amendments to the present TEC, which will become the Treaty on the Functioning of the European Union.

18. The innovations as agreed in the 2004 IGC will be inserted into the Treaty by way of specific modifications in the usual manner. They concern the categories and areas of competences, the scope of qualified majority voting and of codecision, the distinction between legislative and non legislative acts, provisions inter alia on the Area of freedom, security and justice, the solidarity clause, the improvements to the governance of the euro, horizontal provisions such as the social clause, specific provisions such as public services, space, energy, civil protection, humanitarian aid, public health, sport, tourism, outermost regions, administrative cooperation, financial provisions (own resources, multiannual financial framework, new budgetary procedure).

19. The following modifications will be introduced compared to the results of the 2004 IGC (see Annex 2):

a) A new Article 1 will state the purpose of the Treaty on the functioning of the Union and its relation with the EU Treaty. It will state that the two Treaties have the same legal value.

b) In the Article on categories of competences, placed at the beginning of the TEC, it will be clearly specified that the Member States will exercise again their competence to the extent that the Union has decided to cease exercising its competence.[10]

c) In the Article on supporting, coordinating or complementary action, the introductory sentence will be amended so as to underline that the Union carries out actions to support, coordinate or supplement the actions of the Member States.

d) In Article 18(3), as amended in the 2004 IGC, the phrase on the adoption of measures on passports, identity cards, residence permits and similar documents will be removed and transferred to a similar legal basis on this issue to be placed in the Title on the Area of freedom, security and justice, in the Article on border checks.

e) In Article 20 (diplomatic and consular protection), as amended in the 2004 IGC, the legal basis will be amended so as to provide in this field for adoption of directives establishing coordination and cooperation measures.

f) In Article 286 (personal data protection), as amended in the 2004 IGC, a subparagraph will be inserted stating that the rules adopted on the basis of this Article will be without prejudice to those adopted under the specific legal basis on this subject which will be introduced in the CFSP Title (the IGC will also adopt a declaration on personal data protection in the areas of police and judicial cooperation in criminal matters, as well as, where appropriate, specific entries in the relevant Protocols on the position of individual Member States clarifying their applicability in this respect).

g) In Article 42 (aggregation of insurance periods and export of social security benefits), an addition will be made to stress that the procedure is halted in the brake system if the European Council does not take any action within 4 months (see point 1) of Annex 2).[11]

h) Article 60 (freezing of assets to combat terrorism), as amended in the 2004 IGC, will be transferred towards the end of the Chapter on general provisions in the Title on the Area of freedom, security and justice.

i) On the issue of services of general economic interest (cf. Article 16, as amended in the 2004 IGC) a Protocol will be annexed to the Treaties.[12].

j) In the Chapter on general provisions applying to the area of freedom, security and justice, insertion of a provision about cooperation and coordination by Member States in the field of national security (see point 2)(a) of Annex 2).

k) In the Chapter on judicial cooperation in civil matters, paragraph 3 of the Article on such cooperation, as agreed in the 2004 IGC, will be modified so as to give a role to national parliaments in the "passerelle" clause on family law (see point 2)(b) of Annex 2).

l) In the Chapters on judicial cooperation in criminal matters and on police cooperation, as amended in the 2004 IGC, in the Articles on mutual recognition of judgments, minimum rules on definition of criminal offences and sanctions, the European Public Prosecutor, and police cooperation, a new mechanism will be inserted enabling Member States to go forward with adopting measures in this field while allowing others not to participate (see point 2)(c) and (d) of Annex 2).Moreover, the scope of the Protocol on the position of the United Kingdom and Ireland (1997) will be extended so as to include, in relation to the UK, and on the same terms, the Chapters on judicial cooperation in criminal matters and on police cooperation. It may also address the application of the Protocol in relation to Schengen building measures and amendments to existing measures. This extension will take account of the UK's position under the previously existing Union acquis in these areas. Ireland will determine in due course its position with regard to that extension.

m) In Article 100 (measures in case of severe difficulties in the supply of certain products), a reference to the spirit of solidarity between Member States and to the particular case of energy as regards difficulties in the supply of certain product will be inserted (see point 3) of Annex 2).

n) In Article 152 (public health), as amended in the 2004 IGC, point (d) on measures concerning monitoring, early warning of and combating serious cross border threats to health will be transferred to the paragraph on adoption of incentive measures (the IGC will also adopt a declaration clarifying the internal market aspect of measures on the quality and safety standards for medicinal products and devices).

o) In the Article on European space policy, agreed in the 2004 IGC, it will be specified that measures adopted may not entail harmonisation of the laws and regulations of the Member States.

p) In Article 174 (environment), as amended in the 2004 IGC, the particular need to combat climate change in measures at international level will be specified (see point 4) of Annex 2).

q) In the Article on energy, agreed in the 2004 IGC, a reference to the spirit of solidarity between Member States will be inserted (see point 5) of Annex 2), as well as a new point (d) on the promotion of interconnection of energy networks.

r) At the beginning of the Part on the Union's external action, an Article will be inserted stating that the Union's action on the international scene will be guided by the principles, will pursue the objectives and will be conducted in accordance with the general provisions on the Union's external action which are laid down in Chapter 1 of Title V of the TEU.

s) In the Article on the procedure for concluding international agreements, it will be added that the agreement on the accession of the Union to the ECHR will be concluded by the Council, by unanimity and with ratification by Member States.

t) Article 229 A (extension of ECJ jurisdiction on disputes relating to European intellectual property rights) will remain unchanged.

u) In Article 249 (definition of EU acts: regulation, directive and decision), in a new Section 1 on the Union's legal acts, the definition of a decision will be aligned with the one agreed in the 2004 IGC.

v) As a consequence of dropping the denominations "law" and "framework law", the innovations agreed in the 2004 IGC will be adapted, while maintaining the distinction between what is legislative and what is not and its consequences. Accordingly, after Article 249, three Articles will be introduced on, respectively, acts which are adopted in accordance with a legislative procedure, delegated acts and implementing acts. The Article on legislative acts will state that acts (regulations, directives or decisions) adopted under a legislative procedure (ordinary or special) will be legislative acts. The terminology in the Articles on delegated and implementing acts, as agreed in the 2004 IGC, will be adapted accordingly.

w) In Article 308 (flexibility clause), as amended in the 2004 IGC, a paragraph will be added stating that this Article cannot serve as a basis for attaining objectives pertaining to the CFSP, and that any acts adopted pursuant to this Article will have to respect the limits set out in Article [III-308, second subparagraph].[13]

x) After Article 308, an Article will be inserted excluding from the coverage of the simplified revision procedure those legal bases which were not covered by this procedure in the texts as agreed in the 2004 IGC.

20. In addition, a number of provisions agreed in the 2004 IGC will be located in the Treaty on the Functioning of the Union (see list in Part B of Annex 2).

IV. Protocols and the Euratom Treaty

21. The new Protocols agreed in the 2004 IGC[14] will be annexed to the existing Treaties (i.e. Protocol on the role of national Parliaments in the European Union, Protocol on the application of the principles of subsidiarity and proportionality, Protocol on the Euro Group, Protocol on permanent structured cooperation in the field of defence and Protocol on the accession of the Union to the ECHR).

22. A Protocol annexed to the Reform Treaty will amend the existing Protocols, as agreed in the 2004 IGC (including the deletion of 10 of them).

23. A Protocol annexed to the Reform Treaty will make the necessary technical amendments, as agreed in the 2004 IGC, to the Euratom Treaty.

V. Declarations

24. In addition to the Declarations referred to in the present mandate, the Declarations as agreed by the 2004 IGC will be taken over by the present IGC, to the extent they relate to provisions or protocols examined during the present IGC.

Annex 1

Amendments to the EU Treaty

The purpose of this Annex is to clarify the exact drafting where necessary

Title I - Common provisions

*1)Insertion in the Preamble of the EU Treaty of the following second whereas clause**[15]*:*

"DRAWING INSPIRATION from the cultural, religious and humanist inheritance of Europe, from which have developed the universal values of the inviolable and inalienable rights of the human person, freedom, democracy, equality and the rule of law,"

2) *In Article 1, insertion of the following sentences:*

At the end of the first subparagraph: "... on which the Member States confer competences to attain objectives they have in common."

To replace the last subparagraph: "The Union shall be founded on the present Treaty and on the Treaty on the functioning of the European Union. It shall replace and succeed the European Community."

2bis *Insertion of an Article 2 on the values of the Union.**

3) Replacement of Article 2 on the Union's objectives, renumbered 3, with the following text:[16]

"1. The Union's aim is to promote peace, its values and the well-being of its peoples.

2. The Union shall offer its citizens an area of freedom, security and justice without internal frontiers, in which the free movement of persons is ensured in conjunction with appropriate measures with respect to external border controls, asylum, immigration and the prevention and combating of crime.

3. The Union shall establish an internal market. It shall work for the sustainable development of Europe based on balanced economic growth and price stability, a highly competitive social market economy, aiming at full employment and social progress, and a high level of protection and improvement of the quality of the environment.

It shall promote scientific and technological advance.

It shall combat social exclusion and discrimination, and shall promote social justice and protection, equality between women and men, solidarity between generations and protection of the rights of the child.

It shall promote economic, social and territorial cohesion, and solidarity among Member States.

It shall respect its rich cultural and linguistic diversity, and shall ensure that Europe's cultural heritage is safeguarded and enhanced.

3bis. The Union shall establish an economic and monetary union whose currency is the euro.

4. In its relations with the wider world, the Union shall uphold and promote its values and interests and contribute to the protection of its citizens. It shall contribute to peace, security, the sustainable development of the Earth, solidarity and mutual respect among peoples, free

and fair trade, eradication of poverty and the protection of human rights, in particular the rights of the child, as well as to the strict observance and the development of international law, including respect for the principles of the United Nations Charter.

5. The Union shall pursue its objectives by appropriate means commensurate with the competences which are conferred upon it in the Treaties."

4) *Replacement of Article 3 by an Article 4 on the relations between the Union and the Member States*, with the addition of the following at the beginning and of a sentence at the end of the present paragraph 1, renumbered 2:*

"1. In accordance with Article [I-11], competences not conferred upon the Union in the Treaties remain with the Member States.

2. The Union shall respect the equality of Member States before the Treaties as well as their national identities, inherent in their fundamental structures, political and constitutional, inclusive of regional and local self-government. It shall respect their essential State functions, including ensuring the territorial integrity of the State, maintaining law and order and safeguarding national security. In particular, national security remains the sole responsibility of each Member State.

(present paragraph 2 renumbered 3)."

5) *Replacement of Article 6 on fundamental rights with a text reading as follows:*[17-18-19-20]

"1. The Union recognises the rights, freedoms and principles set out in the Charter of Fundamental Rights of 7 December 2000, as adapted on [... 2007[21]], which shall have the same legal value as the Treaties.

The rights, freedoms and principles in the Charter shall be interpreted in accordance with the general provisions in Title VII of the Charter governing its interpretation and application and with due regard to the explanations referred to in the Charter, that set out the sources of those provisions.

2. The Union shall accede to the European Convention for the Protection of Human Rights and Fundamental Freedoms. Such accession shall not affect the Union's competences as defined in the Treaties.

3. Fundamental rights, as guaranteed by the European Convention for the Protection of Human Rights and Fundamental Freedoms and as they result from the constitutional traditions common to the Member States, shall constitute general principles of the Union's law."

6) *Insertion of an Article 7bis on the Union and its neighbours*.*

Title II - Provisions on democratic principles

7) *Insertion of a new Article on the role of national parliaments in the Union reading as follows:*

"National parliaments shall contribute actively to the good functioning of the Union:

a) through being informed by the institutions of the Union and having draft European legislative acts forwarded to them in accordance with the Protocol on the role of national parliaments in the European Union;

b) by seeing to it that the principle of subsidiarity is respected in accordance with the procedures provided for in the Protocol on the application of the principles of subsidiarity and proportionality;

c) by taking part, within the framework of the area of freedom, security and justice, in the evaluation mechanisms for the implementation of the Union policies in that area, in accordance with Article [III-260], and through being involved in the political monitoring of Europol and the evaluation of Eurojust's activities in accordance with Articles [III-276 and III-273];
d) by taking part in the revision procedures of the Treaties, in accordance with Article [IV-443 and IV-444]:
e) by being notified of applications for accession to the Union, in accordance with Article [49];
f) by taking part in the interparliamentary cooperation between national parliaments and with the European Parliament, in accordance with the Protocol on the role of national parliaments in the European Union."

Title V - General provisions on the Union's External Action and specific provisions on the Common Foreign and Security Policy

8) In Article 11, insertion of a paragraph 1 reading as follows (the current text of paragraph 1 being deleted):[22]

"1. The Union's competence in matters of common foreign and security policy shall cover all areas of foreign policy and all questions relating to the Union's security, including the progressive framing of a common defence policy that might lead to a common defence. The common foreign and security policy is subject to specific procedures. It shall be defined and implemented by the European Council and the Council acting unanimously, except where the Treaties provide otherwise. The adoption of legislative acts shall be excluded. The common foreign and security policy shall be put into effect by the High Representative of the Union for Foreign Affairs and Security Policy and by Member States, in accordance with the Treaties. The specific role of the European Parliament and of the Commission in this area is defined by the Treaties. The Court of Justice of the European Union shall not have jurisdiction with respect to these provisions, with the exception of its jurisdiction to monitor the compliance with Article [III-308] and to review the legality of certain decisions as provided for by Article [III-376, second subparagraph]."

Title VI - Final provisions

9) *In Article 49, first subparagraph, insertion of a new last sentence, the second subparagraph remaining unchanged:*

"Article 49 Conditions of eligibility and procedure for accession to the Union

Any European State which respects the values referred to in Article 2 and is committed to promoting them may apply to become a member of the Union. The European Parliament and national Parliaments shall be notified of this application. The applicant State shall address its application to the Council, which shall act unanimously after consulting the Commission and after receiving the assent of the European Parliament, which shall act by an absolute majority of its component members. The conditions of eligibility agreed upon by the European Council shall be taken into account."

Annex 2*[23]

Amendments to the EC Treaty

The purpose of this Annex is to clarify the exact drafting where necessary (A) and to clarify the location of certain provisions (B)

A. Modifications compared with the results as agreed in the 2004 IGC

1) In Article 42, insertion of amendments as agreed in the 2004 IGC, with addition of the following, at the end:

"Where a member of the Council declares that a draft legislative act referred to in the first subparagraph would affect important aspects of its social security system, including its scope, cost or financial structure, or would affect the financial balance of that system, it may request that the matter be referred to the European Council. In that case, the ordinary legislative procedure shall be suspended. After discussion, the European Council shall, within four months of this suspension, either:

(a) refer the draft back to the Council, which shall terminate the suspension of the ordinary legislative procedure,

or

(b) take no action or request the Commission to submit a new proposal; in that case, the act originally proposed shall be deemed not to have been adopted."

2) *Replacement, as agreed in the 2004 IGC, of Title IV with the provisions of a new Title on the area of freedom, security and justice*, which includes Chapter 1 (general provisions), Chapter 2 (policies on border checks, asylum and immigration), Chapter 3 (judicial cooperation in civil matters), Chapter 4 (judicial cooperation in criminal matters) and Chapter 5 (police cooperation).*

(a) In Chapter 1 (general provisions), insertion in [Article III-262] of the following new second subparagraph:

"It shall be open to Member States to organize between themselves and under their responsibility forms of cooperation and coordination as they deem appropriate between the competent departments of their administrations responsible for safeguarding national security."

(b) In Chapter 3 (judicial cooperation in civil matters), replacement of paragraph 3 of [Article III-269] as follows:

"3. Notwithstanding paragraph 2, measures concerning family law with cross-border implications shall be established by the Council, acting in accordance with a special legislative procedure. The Council shall act unanimously after consulting the European Parliament. The Council, on a proposal from the Commission, may adopt a decision determining those aspects of family law with cross-border implications which may be the subject of acts adopted by the ordinary legislative procedure. The Council shall act unanimously after consulting the European Parliament.

The proposal referred to in the second subparagraph shall be notified to the national Parliaments. If a national Parliament makes known its opposition within six months of the date of such notification, the decision referred to in the second subparagraph shall not be adopted. In the absence of opposition, the Council may adopt the decision."

(c) In Chapter 4 (judicial cooperation in criminal matters), replacement of, respectively, paragraphs 3 and 4 of [Article III-270] and of [Article III-271] by the following:

"3. Where a member of the Council considers that a draft directive as referred to in [paragraph 2 of III-270] [paragraphs 1 or 2 of III-271] would affect fundamental aspects of its criminal justice system, it may request that the draft directive be referred to the European Council. In that case, the ordinary legislative procedure shall be suspended. After discussion, and in case of a consensus, the European Council shall, within four months of this suspension, refer the draft back to the Council, which shall terminate the suspension of the ordinary legislative procedure.

Within the same timeframe, in case of disagreement, and if at least one third of the Member States wish to establish enhanced cooperation on the basis of the draft directive concerned, they shall notify the European Parliament, the Council and the Commission accordingly. In such a case, the authorisation to proceed with enhanced cooperation referred to in [Articles I-44(2)] and [III-419(1)] shall be deemed to be granted and the provisions on enhanced cooperation shall apply."

(d) In Chapter 4 (judicial cooperation in criminal matters) and in Chapter 5 (police cooperation) insertion of the following new last subparagraphs, respectively, in paragraph 1 of [III-274] and in paragraph 3 of [Article III-275]:

"In case of absence of unanimity in the Council, a group of at least one third of the Member States may request that the draft [regulation/measures] be referred to the European Council. In that case, the procedure in the Council shall be suspended. After discussion, and in case of a consensus, the European Council shall, within four months of this suspension, refer the draft back to the Council for adoption.

Within the same timeframe, in case of disagreement, and if at least one third of the Member States wish to establish enhanced cooperation on the basis of the draft [regulation/measures] concerned, they shall notify the European Parliament, the Council and the Commission accordingly. In such a case, the authorisation to proceed with enhanced cooperation referred to in [Articles I-44(2)] and [III-419(1)] shall be deemed to be granted and the provisions on enhanced cooperation shall apply."

[in III-275(3) only: "The specific procedure provided in the second and third subparagraphs shall not apply to acts which constitute a development of the Schengen acquis."].

3) In Article 100, replacement of paragraph 1 with the following:

"1. Without prejudice to any other procedures provided for in the Treaties, the Council, on a proposal from the Commission, may decide, in a spirit of solidarity between Member States, upon the measures appropriate to the economic situation, in particular if severe difficulties arise in the supply of certain products, notably in the area of energy."

4) *In Title XIX (environment), insertion of amendments as agreed in the 2004 IGC, with the replacement of the last indent in Article 174 by the following:*

"- promoting measures at international level to deal with regional or worldwide environmental problems, and in particular combating climate change."

5) *Insertion of a new Title on energy, as agreed in the 2004 IGC, with the replacement of the introductory sentence in paragraph 1 of the Article [III-256] by the following:*

"1. In the context of the establishment and functioning of the internal market and with regard for the need to preserve and improve the environment, Union policy on energy shall aim, in a spirit of solidarity between Member States, to: (...)."

B. Clarifications on the location of certain provisions*

6) Status of churches and non-confessional organisations (end of Title II on provisions of general application);

7) Citizenship of the Union (Part Two);

8) Legal basis for adopting the arrangements for the submission of a citizens' initiative [I-47(4)] (at the beginning of Article 27);

9) Transparency of the proceedings of the Union institutions, bodies, offices and agencies (Article 255, moved in Part Two);

10) Social partners and the social dialogue (beginning of the Chapter on social policy); 11) Solidarity clause (new Title VII in the Part on External Action);

12) European Ombudsman (in Article 195);

13) Provision under which the rules on QMV in the Council also apply to the European Council ([Article I- 25(3)] in the new Section 1bis on European Council);

14) Legal bases for adopting the list of Council configurations [Article I-24(4)] and the decision on the presidency of these configurations (Article I-24(7)] and replacement of Article 205(2) with the QMV rule applicable when the Council does not act on the basis of a Commission proposal [Article I-25(2)] (in Section 2 on Council);

15) Legal basis for the adoption of the rotation system for the composition of the Commission [Article I-26(6)(a) and (b)] (Section 3 on Commission);

16) European Central Bank (in Section 4bis in Part Five);

17) Court of Auditors (in Section 5 in Part Five);

18) The Union's Advisory Bodies (in Chapters 3 and 4 in Part Five);

19) Specific Title II on financial provisions (Chapters on the Union's own resources, the multiannual financial framework, the Union's annual budget, the implementation of the budget and discharge, common provisions and combating fraud);

20) A Title III and provisions on enhanced cooperation, including the transfer of Articles 27 A to 27 E and 40

to 40 B TEU and of the details on voting arrangements [Article I-44(3)];

21) Amendment of Article 309 with the details of voting rules in case of suspension of certain rights resulting from Union membership [Article I-59(5) and (6)];

22) Insertion in the General and Final Provisions of the details of territorial scope [Article IV-440(2) to (7)].

Notes

[1] Whilst the Article on primacy of Union law will not be reproduced in the TEU, the IGC will agree on the following Declaration: "The Conference recalls that, in accordance with well settled case-law of the EU Court of Justice, the Treaties and the law adopted by the Union on the basis of the Treaties have primacy over the law of Member States, under the conditions laid down by the said case-law." In addition, the opinion of the Legal Service of the Council (doc. 580/07) will be annexed to the Final Act of Conference.

[2] The content of Title VI on police and judicial cooperation in criminal matters will be put into the Title on the Area of freedom, security and justice in the Treaty on the Functioning of the Union (TFEU), see below under "Amendments to the EC Treaty".

[3] Therefore, the text of the Charter on fundamental rights will not be included in the Treaties.

[4] Including modalities of vote.

[5] There will be some drafting adaptations due to the merging of some provisions.

[6] The IGC will agree on the following Declaration: "The Conference underlines that the provisions in the Treaty on European Union covering the Common Foreign and Security Policy, including the creation of the office of High Representative of the Union for Foreign Affairs and Security Policy and the establishment of an External Action Service, do not affect the responsibilities of the Member States, as they currently exist, for the formulation and conduct of their foreign policy nor of their national representation in third countries and international organisations. The Conference also recalls that the provisions governing the Common Security and Defence Policy do not prejudice the specific character of the security and defence policy of the Member States. It stresses that the EU and its Member States will remain bound by the provisions of the Charter of the United Nations and, in particular, by the primary responsibility of the Security Council and of its Members for the maintenance of international peace and security.".

[7] With regard to the processing of such data by the Member States when carrying out activities which fall within the CFSP and ESDP and the movement of such data.

[8] The IGC will agree on the following Declaration: "The Conference confirms that the fact that the European Union has a legal personality will not in any way authorise the Union to legislate or to act beyond the competences conferred upon it by the Member States in the Treaties."

[9] Articles 41, 42, 46 and 50 of the TEU will be deleted, Article 47 being placed, as amended in the 2004 IGC, in the CFSP Chapter.

[10] (a) The IGC will also agree a Declaration in relation to the delimitation of competences: "The Conference underlines that, in accordance with the system of division of competences between the Union and the Member States as provided for in the Treaty on European Union, competences not conferred upon the Union in the Treaties remain with Member States. When the Treaties confer on the Union a competence shared with the Member States in a specific area, the Member States shall exercise their competence to the extent that the Union has not exercised, or has decided to cease exercising, its competence. The latter situation arises when the relevant EU institutions decide to repeal a legislative act, in particular to better ensure the constant respect for the principles of subsidiarity and proportionality. The Council may request, at the initiative of one or several of its Members (representatives of Member States) and in accordance with Article

208, the Commission to submit proposals for repealing a legislative act. Equally, the representatives of the governments of the Member States, meeting in an Intergovernmental Conference, in accordance with the ordinary revision procedure provided for in Article [IV-443] of the Treaty on European Union, may decide to amend the Treaties on which the Union is founded, including either to increase or to reduce the competences conferred on the Union in the said Treaties."

(b) The following Protocol will be annexed to the Treaties: "With reference to Article[I-12(2)] on shared competences, when the Union has taken action in a certain area, the scope of this exercise of competence only covers those elements governed by the Union act in question and therefore does not cover the whole area."

[11] The IGC will also agree a Declaration in relation to this Article: "The Conference recalls that in that case, in accordance with Article [I-21(4)], the European Council acts by consensus".

[12] The following Protocol will be annexed to the Treaties: "Protocol on services of general interest The High Contracting Parties, Wishing to emphasise the importance of services of general interest Have agreed upon the following interpretative provisions, which shall be annexed to the Treaty on European Union and to the Treaty on the Functioning of the Union:

Article 1 The shared values of the Union in respect of services of general economic interest within the meaning of Article 16 EC Treaty include in particular: - the essential role and the wide discretion of national, regional and local authorities in providing, commissioning and organizing services of general economic interest as closely as possible to the needs of the users; - the diversity between various services of general economic interest and the differences in the needs and preferences of users that may result from different geographical, social or cultural situations; - a high level of quality, safety and affordability, equal treatment and the promotion of universal access and of user rights;

Article 2 The provisions of the Treaties do not affect in any way the competence of Member States to provide, commission and organise non-economic services of general interest."

[13] The IGC will also agree two Declarations in relation to this Article:

1) "The Conference declares that the reference in Article 308 to objectives of the Union refers to the objectives as set out in Article [I-3(2) and (3)] and to the objectives of Articles [I-3(4)] with respect to external action under Part III, Title V of the Treaty. It is therefore excluded that an action based on Article 308 would only pursue objectives set out in Article[I-3(1)]. In this connection, the Conference notes that in accordance with Article [I-40(6)], legislative acts may not be adopted in the area of Common Foreign and Security Policy."

2) "The Conference underlines that, in accordance with the settled case-law of the Court of Justice of the European Union, Article 308, being an integral part of an institutional system based on the principle of conferred powers, cannot serve as a basis for widening the scope of Union powers beyond the general framework created by the provisions of the Treaties as a whole and, in particular, by those that define the tasks and the activities of the Union. In any event, Article 308 cannot be used as a basis for the adoption of provisions whose effect would, in substance, be to amend the Treaties without following the procedure which they provide for that purpose."

[14] Some of these Protocols are not necessary due to the fact that the existing Treaties are not repealed and are therefore not listed. It is underlined that all existing Treaties, including the Accession Acts, remain in force.

[15] Throughout this Annex, this sign (*) indicates that the innovations to be inserted are the same as those agreed by the 2004 IGC.

[16] The following Protocol will be annexed to the Treaties:

"Protocol on internal market and competition.

The High Contracting Parties, considering that the internal market as set out in Article 3 of the Treaty on European Union includes a system ensuring that competition is not distorted

Have agreed that, to this end, the Union shall, if necessary, take action under the provisions of the Treaties, including under Article 308 of the Treaty on the Functioning of the Union."

[17] The IGC will agree the following Declaration: "The Conference declares that:

1. The Charter of Fundamental Rights, which has legally binding force, confirms the fundamental rights guaranteed by the European Convention on Human Rights and Fundamental Freedoms and as they result from the constitutional traditions common to the Member States.

2. The Charter does not extend the field of application of Union law beyond the powers of the Union or establish any new power or task for the Union, or modify powers and tasks as defined by the Treaties." Two delegations reserved their right to consider whether they would join in this Protocol.

[18] Unilateral Declaration by Poland:

"The Charter does not affect in any way the right of Member States to legislate in the sphere of public morality, family law as well as the protection of human dignity and respect for human physical and moral integrity."

[19] The following Protocol will be annexed to the Treaties:

"The High Contracting Parties

Whereas in Article [xx] of the Treaty on European Union, the Union recognises the rights, freedoms and principles set out in the Charter of Fundamental Rights;

Whereas the Charter is to be applied in strict accordance with the provisions of the aforementioned Article [xx] and Title VII of the Charter itself;

Whereas the aforementioned Article [xx] requires the Charter to be applied and interpreted by the courts of the United Kingdom strictly in accordance with the Explanations referred to in that Article;

Whereas the Charter contains both rights and principles;

Whereas the Charter contains both provisions which are civil and political in character and those which are economic and social in character;

Whereas the Charter reaffirms the rights, freedoms and principles recognised in the Union and makes those rights more visible, but does not create new rights or principles;

Recalling the United Kingdom's obligations under the Treaty on European Union, the Treaty on the Functioning of the European Union, and Union law generally;

Noting the wish of the United Kingdom to clarify certain aspects of the application of the Charter;

Desirous therefore of clarifying the application of the Charter in relation to the laws and administrative action of the United Kingdom and of its justiciability within the United Kingdom;

Reaffirming that references in this Protocol to the operation of specific provisions of the Charter are strictly without prejudice to the operation of other provisions of the Charter;

Reaffirming that this Protocol is without prejudice to the application of the Charter to other Member States;

Reaffirming that this Protocol is without prejudice to other obligations of the United Kingdom under the Treaty on European Union, the Treaty on the Functioning of the European Union, and Union law generally;

Have agreed upon the following provisions which shall be annexed to the Treaty on European Union:

Article 1

1. The Charter does not extend the ability of the Court of Justice, or any court or tribunal of the United Kingdom, to find that the laws, regulations or administrative

provisions, practices or action of the United Kingdom are inconsistent with the fundamental rights, freedoms and principles that it reaffirms.

2. In particular, and for the avoidance of doubt, nothing in [Title IV] of the Charter creates justiciable rights applicable to the United Kingdom except in so far as the United Kingdom has provided for such rights in its national law.

Article 2

To the extent that a provision of the Charter refers to national laws and practices, it shall only apply in the United Kingdom to the extent that the rights or principles that it contains are recognised in the law or practices of the United Kingdom."

[20] Two delegations reserved their right to join in this Protocol.

[21] The version of the Charter as agreed in the 2004 IGC which will be re-enacted by the three Institutions in [2007]. It will be published in the Official Journal of the European Union.

[22] The IGC will agree the following Declaration: "In addition to the specific procedures referred to in [paragraph 1 of Article 11], the Conference underlines that the provisions covering CFSP including in relation to the High Representative of the Union for Foreign Affairs and Security Policy and External Action Service will not affect the existing legal basis, responsibilities, and powers of each Member State in relation to the formulation and conduct of its foreign policy, its national diplomatic service, relations with third countries and participation in international organisations, including a Member State's membership of the Security Council of the UN.

The Conference also notes that the provisions covering CFSP do not give new powers to the Commission to initiate decisions or increase the role of the European Parliament. The Conference also recalls that the provisions governing the Common Security and Defence Policy do not prejudice the specific character of the security and defence policy of the Member States."

[23] Throughout this Annex, this sign (*) indicates that the innovations to be inserted are the same as those agreed by the 2004 IGC.

[END OF OFFICIAL TEXT OF *DRAFT IGC MANDATE*]

Part Nine

Text of The EU Constitution

"With this Constitution, Europe is taking a decisive step towards political union." - Valery Giscard d'Estaing, on the occasion of presenting the text of the proposed Constitution to European leaders in Rome on 18 July 2003.

The EU Constitution is the popular name for *The Treaty Establishing a Constitution for Europe.*

Contents of the Treaty Establishing a Constitution for Europe

Part IV - General and Final Provisions

Protocols annexed to the Treaty Establishing a Constitution for Europe. There are 36 of these protocols. Those Included here are:

1. Protocol on the role of Member States' national parliaments in the European Union

2. Protocol on the application of the principles of subsidiarity and proportionality

7. Protocol on the privileges and immunities of the European Union

11. Protocol on the convergence criteria

12. Protocol on the Euro Group

13. Protocol on certain provisions relating to the United Kingdom of Great Britain and Northern Ireland as regards to Economic and Monetary Union

17. Protocol on the Schengen *acquis* integrated into the framework of the European Union

18. Protocol on the application of certain aspects of Article 130 of the Constitution to the United Kingdom and to Ireland *(border checks and travel arrangements)*

19. Protocol on the position of the United Kingdom and Ireland on policies in respect of border controls, asylum and immigration, judicial co-operation in civil matters and on police co-operation

21. Protocol on external relations of the Member States with regard to the crossing of external borders

22. Protocol on asylum for nationals of Member States

23. Protocol on permanent structured co-operation established by Article 41(6) and Article 312 of the Constitution

27. Protocol on the system of public broadcasting in the Member States

28. Protocol concerning Article 214 of the Constitution *(the 'Barber Protocol' on pension funds)*

29. Protocol on economic, social and territorial cohesion

31. Protocol on Article 40.3.3 of the Constitution of Ireland

32. Protocol relating to Article 9(2) of the Constitution on the accession of the Union to the European Convention on the

Declarations annexed to the Treaty Establishing a Constitution for Europe. There are 50 of these declarations. We include only one: Declaration 12. Explanations relating to the Charter of Fundamental Rights.

Treaty Establishing a Constitution for Europe

Preamble

HIS MAJESTY THE KING OF THE BELGIANS,
THE PRESIDENT OF THE CZECH REPUBLIC,
HER MAJESTY THE QUEEN OF DENMARK,
THE PRESIDENT OF THE FEDERAL REPUBLIC OF GERMANY,
THE PRESIDENT OF THE REPUBLIC OF ESTONIA,
THE PRESIDENT OF THE HELLENIC REPUBLIC,
HIS MAJESTY THE KING OF SPAIN,
THE PRESIDENT OF THE FRENCH REPUBLIC,
THE PRESIDENT OF IRELAND,
THE PRESIDENT OF THE ITALIAN REPUBLIC,
THE PRESIDENT OF THE REPUBLIC OF CYPRUS,
THE PRESIDENT OF THE REPUBLIC OF LATVIA,
THE PRESIDENT OF THE REPUBLIC OF LITHUANIA,
HIS ROYAL HIGHNESS THE GRAND DUKE OF LUXEMBOURG,
THE PRESIDENT OF THE REPUBLIC OF HUNGARY,
THE PRESIDENT OF MALTA,
HER MAJESTY THE QUEEN OF THE NETHERLANDS,
THE FEDERAL PRESIDENT OF THE REPUBLIC OF AUSTRIA,
THE PRESIDENT OF THE REPUBLIC OF POLAND,
THE PRESIDENT OF THE PORTUGUESE REPUBLIC,
THE PRESIDENT OF THE REPUBLIC OF SLOVENIA,
THE PRESIDENT OF THE SLOVAK REPUBLIC,
THE PRESIDENT OF THE REPUBLIC OF FINLAND,
THE GOVERNMENT OF THE KINGDOM OF SWEDEN,
HER MAJESTY THE QUEEN OF THE UNITED KINGDOM OF GREAT BRITAIN AND NORTHERN IRELAND.

Drawing Inspiration from the cultural, religious and humanist inheritance of Europe, from which have developed the universal values of the inviolable and inalienable rights of the human person, freedom, democracy, equality and the rule of law,

Believing that Europe, reunited after bitter experiences, intends to continue along the path of civilisation, progress and prosperity, for the good of all its inhabitants, including the weakest and most deprived; that it wishes to remain a continent open to culture, learning and social progress; and that it wishes to deepen the democratic and transparent nature of its public life, and to strive for peace, justice and solidarity throughout the world,

Convinced that, while remaining proud of their own national identities and history, the peoples of Europe are determined to transcend their former divisions and, united ever more closely, to forge a common destiny,

Convinced that, thus 'United in diversity', Europe offers them the best chance of pursuing, with due regard for the rights of each individual and in awareness of their responsibilities towards future generations and the Earth, the great venture which makes of it a special area of human hope,

Determined to continue the work accomplished within the framework of the Treaties establishing the European Communities and the Treaty on European Union, by ensuring the continuity of the Community acquis,

Grateful to the members of the European Convention for having prepared the draft of this Constitution on behalf of the citizens and States of Europe,

Have designated as their plenipotentiaries :

HIS MAJESTY
THE KING OF THE BELGIANS,
Guy Verhofstadt
Prime Minister;
Karel De Gucht
Minister for Foreign Affairs.

THE PRESIDENT
OF THE CZECH REPUBLIC,
Stanlislav Gross
Prime Minister;
Cyril Svoboda
Minister for Foreign Affairs.

HER MAJESTY
THE QUEEN OF DENMARK,
Anders Fogh Rasmussen
Prime Minister;
Per Stig Møller
Minister for Foreign Affairs.

THE PRESIDENT
OF THE FEDERAL REPUBLIC
OF GERMANY,
Gerhard Schröder
Federal Chancellor;
Joschka Fischer
Federal Minister for Foreign
Affairs.

THE PRESIDENT
OF THE REPUBLIC
OF ESTONIA,
Juhan Parts
Prime Minister;
Kristiina Ojuland
Minister for Foreign Affairs.

HIS MAJESTY
THE KING OF SPAIN,
Jose Luis Rodriguez Zapatero
President of the Government
Miguel Angel Moratinos Cuyabé
Minister for external Affairs and
Co-operation.

THE PRESIDENT
OF THE FRENCH REPUBLIC,
Jacques Chirac
President;
Jean Pierre Raffarin
Prime Minister;
Michel Barnier
Minister for Foreign Affairs.

THE PRESIDENT OF IRELAND,
Bertie Ahern
Prime Minister;
Dermot Ahern
Minister for Foreign Affairs.

THE PRESIDENT
OF THE ITALIAN REPUBLIC,
Silvio Berlusconi
Prime Minister;
Franco Frattini
Minister for Foreign Affairs.

THE PRESIDENT
OF THE REPUBLIC OF CYPRUS,
Tassos Papadopoulos
President;
George Iacovou
Minister for Foreign Affairs.

THE PRESIDENT
OF THE HELLENIC REPUBLIC,
Kostas Karamanlis
Prime Minister;
Petros G.Molyviatis
Minister for Foreign Affairs.

THE PRESIDENT
OF THE REPUBLIC OF LATVIA,
Varia Vike Freiberga
President;
Indulis Emsis
Prime Minister;
Artis Pabriks
Minister for Foreign Affairs.

THE PRESIDENT
OF THE REPUBLIC
OF LITHUANIA,
Valdas Adamkus
President;
Algirdas Mykolas Brazauskas
Prime Minister;
Antanas Valionis
Minister for Foreign Affairs.

HIS ROYAL HIGHNESS
THE GRAND DUKE
OF LUXEMBOURG,
Jean Claude Juncker
Prime Minister;
Jean Asselborn
Deputy Prime Minister, Minister
for Foreign Affairs and
Immigration.

THE PRESIDENT
OF THE REPUBLIC
OF HUNGARY,
Ferenc Gyurcsány
Prime Minister;
László Kovács
Minister for Foreign Affairs.

HER MAJESTY
THE QUEEN
OF THE NETHERLANDS,
Dr Jan Peter Balkenende
Prime Minister;
Dr Bernard R. Bot
Minister for Foreign Affairs.

THE FEDERAL PRESIDENT
OF THE REPUBLIC OF AUSTRIA,
Dr Wolfgang Schüssel
Federal Chancellor;
Ds Ursula Plassnik
Federal Minister for Foreign Affairs.

THE PRESIDENT
OF THE REPUBLIC OF POLAND,
Marek Belka
Primo Minicte;
Wlodzimierz Cimoszewicz
Minister for Foreign Affairs.

THE PRESIDENT
OF THE PORTUGUESE REPUBLIC,
Pedro Santana Lopes
Prime Minister;
Antonio Victor Martins Monteiro
Minister for Foreign Affairs
and the Portuguese Communities.

THE PRESIDENT
OF THE REPUBLIC OF SLOVENIA,
Anton Rop
President of the Government;
Ivo Vajgl
Minister for Foreign Affairs.

THE PRESIDENT
OF THE SLOVAK REPUBLIC,
Mikuláš Dzurinda
Prime Minister;
Eduard Kukan
Minister for Foreign Affairs.

THE PRESIDENT OF MALTA,
The Hon Lawrence Gonzi
Prime Minister;
The Hon Michael Frendo
Minister for Foreign Affairs.

THE PRESIDENT
OF THE REPUBLIC OF FINLAND,
Matti Vanhanen
Prime Minister;
Erkki Tuomioja
Minister for Foreign Affairs.

THE GOVERNMENT
OF THE KINGDOM OF SWEDEN,
Goran Persson
Prime Minister;
Laila Freivalds
Minister for Foreign Affairs.

HER MAJESTY THE QUEEN
OF THE UNITED KINGDOM
OF GREAT BRITAIN
AND NORTHERN IRELAND,
Tony Blair
Prime Minister;
The Rt. Hon Jack Straw
Secretary of State for Foreign
and Commonwealth Affairs.

Part I

Constitution

Title I
Definition and Objectives of the Union.

Article 1 Establishment of the Union

1. Reflecting the will of the citizens and States of Europe to build a common future, this Constitution establishes the European Union, on which the Member States confer competences to attain objectives they have in common. The Union shall coordinate the policies by which the Member States aim to achieve these objectives, and shall exercise on a Community basis the competences they confer on it.

2. The Union shall be open to all European States which respect its values and are committed to promoting them together.

Article 2 The Union's values

The Union is founded on the values of respect for human dignity, freedom, democracy, equality, the rule of law and respect for human rights, including the rights of persons belonging to minorities. These values are common to the Member States in a society in which pluralism, non-discrimination, tolerance, justice, solidarity and equality between women and men prevail.

Article 3 The Union's objectives

1. The Union's aim is to promote peace, its values and the well-being of its peoples.

2. The Union shall offer its citizens an area of freedom, security and justice without internal frontiers, and an internal market where competition is free and undistorted.

3. The Union shall work for the sustainable development of Europe based on balanced economic growth and price stability, a highly competitive social market economy, aiming at full employment and social progress, and a high level of protection and improvement of the quality of the environment. It shall promote scientific and technological advance.

It shall combat social exclusion and discrimination, and shall promote social justice and protection, equality between women and men, solidarity between generations and protection of the rights of the child. It shall promote economic, social and territorial cohesion, and solidarity among Member States. It shall respect its rich cultural and linguistic diversity, and shall ensure that Europe's cultural heritage is safeguarded and enhanced.

4. In its relations with the wider world, the Union shall uphold and promote its values and interests. It shall contribute to peace, security, the sustainable

development of the Earth, solidarity and mutual respect among peoples, free and fair trade, eradication of poverty and the protection of human rights, in particular the rights of the child, as well as to the strict observance and the development of international law, including respect for the principles of the United Nations Charter.

5. The Union shall pursue its objectives by appropriate means commensurate with the competences which are conferred upon it in the Constitution.

Article 4 Fundamental freedoms and non-discrimination

1. The free movement of persons, services, goods and capital, and freedom of establishment shall be guaranteed within and by the Union, in accordance with the Constitution.

2. Within the scope of the Constitution, and without prejudice to any of its specific provisions, any discrimination on grounds of nationality shall be prohibited.

Article 5 Relations between the Union and the Member States

1. The union shall respect the equality of Member States before the constitution as well as their national identities, inherent in their fundamental structures, political and constitutional, inclusive of regional and local self-government. it shall respect their essential State functions, including ensuring the territorial integrity of the State, maintaining law and order and safeguarding national security.

2. Pursuant to the principle of sincere cooperation, the Union and the Member States shall, in full mutual respect, assist each other in carrying out tasks which flow from the Constitution.

The Member States shall take any appropriate measure, general or particular, to ensure fulfilment of the obligations arising out of the Constitution or resulting from the acts of the institutions of the Union.

The Member States shall facilitate the achievement of the Union's tasks and refrain from any measure which could jeopardise the attainment of the Union's objectives.

Article 6 Union law

The Constitution and law adopted by the institutions of the Union in exercising competences conferred on it shall have primacy over the law of the Member States.

Article 7 Legal personality

The Union shall have legal personality.

Article 8 The symbols of the Union

The flag of the Union shall be a circle of twelve golden stars on a blue background.

The anthem of the Union shall be based on the 'Ode to Joy' from the Ninth Symphony by Ludwig van Beethoven.

The motto of the Union shall be: 'United in diversity'.
The currency of the Union shall be the euro.
Europe day shall be celebrated on 9 May throughout the Union.

Title II
Fundamental Rights and Citizenship of the Union.

Article 9 Fundamental rights

1. The Union shall recognise the rights, freedoms and principles set out in the Charter of Fundamental Rights which constitutes Part 2.

2. The Union shall accede to the European Convention for the Protection of Human Rights and Fundamental Freedoms. Such accession shall not affect the Union's competences as defined in the Constitution.

3. Fundamental rights, as guaranteed by the European Convention for the Protection of Human Rights and Fundamental Freedoms and as they result from the constitutional traditions common to the Member States, shall constitute general principles of the Union's law.

Article 10 Citizenship of the Union

1. Every national of a Member State shall be a citizen of the Union. Citizenship of the Union shall be additional to national citizenship and shall not replace it.

2. Citizens of the Union shall enjoy the rights and be subject to the duties provided for in the Constitution. They shall have:

(a) the right to move and reside freely within the territory of the Member States;

(b) the right to vote and to stand as candidates in elections to the European Parliament and in municipal elections in their Member State of residence, under the same conditions as nationals of that State;

(c) the right to enjoy, in the territory of a third country in which the Member State of which they are nationals is not represented, the protection of the diplomatic and consular authorities of any Member State on the same conditions as the nationals of that State;

(d) the right to petition the European Parliament, to apply to the European Ombudsman, and to address the institutions and advisory bodies of the Union in any of the Constitution's languages and to obtain a reply in the same language.

These rights shall be exercised in accordance with the conditions and limits defined by the Constitution and by the measures adopted there under.

Title III
Union Competences

Article 11 Fundamental principles

1. The limits of Union competences are governed by the principle of conferral. The use of Union competences is governed by the principles of subsidiarity and proportionality.

2. Under the principle of conferral, the Union shall act within the limits of the competences conferred upon it by the Member States in the Constitution to attain the objectives set out in the Constitution. competences not conferred upon the Union in the Constitution remain with the Member States.

3. Under the principle of subsidiarity, in areas which do not fall within its exclusive competence, the Union shall act only if and insofar as the objectives of the proposed action cannot be sufficiently achieved by the Member States, either at central level or at regional and local level, but can rather, by reason of the scale or effects of the proposed action, be better achieved at Union level.

The institutions of the Union shall apply the principle of subsidiarity as laid down in the Protocol on the application of the principles of subsidiarity and proportionality. National Parliaments shall ensure compliance with that principle in accordance with the procedure set out in that Protocol.

4. Under the principle of proportionality, the content and form of Union action shall not exceed what is necessary to achieve the objectives of the Constitution.

The institutions of the Union shall apply the principle of proportionality as laid down in the Protocol on the application of the principles of subsidiarity and proportionality.

Article 12 Categories of competence

1. When the Constitution confers on the Union exclusive competence in a specific area, only the Union may legislate and adopt legally binding acts, the Member States being able to do so themselves only if so empowered by the Union or for the implementation of Union acts.

2. When the Constitution confers on the Union a competence shared with the Member States in a specific area, the Union and the Member States may legislate and adopt legally binding acts in that area. The Member States shall exercise their competence to the extent that the Union has not exercised, or has decided to cease exercising, its competence.

3. The Member States shall coordinate their economic and employment policies within arrangements as determined by Part III, which the Union shall have competence to provide.

4. The Union shall have competence to define and implement a common foreign and security policy, including the progressive framing of a common defence policy.

5. In certain areas and under the conditions laid down in the Constitution, the Union shall have competence to carry out actions to support, coordinate or supplement the actions of the Member States, without thereby superseding their competence in these areas.

Legally binding acts of the Union adopted on the basis of the provisions in Part 3 relating to these areas shall not entail harmonisation of Member States' laws or regulations.

6. The scope of and arrangements for exercising the Union's competences shall be determined by the provisions relating to each area in Part 3.

Article 13 Areas of exclusive competence

1. The Union shall have exclusive competence in the following areas:

(a) customs union;

(b) the establishing of the competition rules necessary for the functioning of the internal market;

(c) monetary policy for the Member States whose currency is the euro;

(d) the conservation of marine biological resources under the common fisheries policy;

(e) common commercial policy.

2. The Union shall also have exclusive competence for the conclusion of an international agreement when its conclusion is provided for in a legislative act of the Union or is necessary to enable the Union to exercise its internal competence, or insofar as its conclusion may affect common rules or alter their scope.

Article 14 Areas of shared competence

1. The Union shall share competence with the Member States where the Constitution confers on it a competence which does not relate to the areas referred to in Articles 13 and 17.

2. Shared competence between the Union and the Member States applies in the following principal areas:

(a) internal market;

(b) social policy, for the aspects defined in Part III;

(c) economic, social and territorial cohesion;

(d) agriculture and fisheries, excluding the conservation of marine biological resources;

(e) environment;

(f) consumer protection;

(g) transport;

(h) trans-European networks;

(i) energy;

(j) area of freedom, security and justice;

(k) common safety concerns in public health matters, for the aspects defined in Part 3.

3. In the areas of research, technological development and space, the Union shall have competence to carry out activities, in particular to define and implement programmes; however, the exercise of that competence shall not result in Member States being prevented from exercising theirs.

4. In the areas of development cooperation and humanitarian aid, the Union shall have competence to carry out activities and conduct a common policy; however, the exercise of that competence shall not result in Member States being prevented from exercising theirs.

Article 15 The coordination of economic and employment policies

1. The Member States shall coordinate their economic policies within the Union. To this end, the Council of Ministers shall adopt measures, in particular broad guidelines for these policies.

Specific provisions shall apply to those Member States whose currency is the euro.

2. The Union shall take measures to ensure coordination of the employment policies of the Member States, in particular by defining guidelines for these policies.

3. The Union may take initiatives to ensure coordination of Member States' social policies.

Article 16 The common foreign and security policy

1. The Union's competence in matters of common foreign and security policy shall cover all areas of foreign policy and all questions relating to the Union's security, including the progressive framing of a common defence policy that might lead to a common defence.

2. Member States shall actively and unreservedly support the Union's common foreign and security policy in a spirit of loyalty and mutual solidarity and shall comply with the Union's action in this area. They shall refrain from action contrary to the Union's interests or likely to impair its effectiveness.

Article 17 Areas of supporting, coordinating or complementary action

The Union shall have competence to carry out supporting, coordinating or complementary action.

The areas of such action shall, at European level, be:

(a) protection and improvement of human health;
(b) industry;
(c) culture;
(d) tourism;
(e) education, youth, sport and vocational training;
(f) civil protection;
(g) administrative cooperation.

Article 18 Flexibility clause

1. If action by the Union should prove necessary, within the framework of the policies defined in Part 3, to attain one of the objectives set out in the Constitution, and the Constitution has not provided the necessary powers, the Council of Ministers, acting unanimously on a proposal from the European Commission and after obtaining the consent of the European Parliament, shall adopt the appropriate measures.

2. Using the procedure for monitoring the subsidiarity principle referred to in Article 11(3), the European Commission shall draw national Parliaments' attention to proposals based on this Article.

3. Measures based on this Article shall not entail harmonisation of Member States' laws or regulations in cases where the Constitution excludes such harmonisation.

Title IV
The Unions Institutions and Bodies

Chapter 1 - The Institutional Framework

Article 19 The Union's institutions

1. The Union shall have an institutional framework which shall aim to:

— promote its values,

— advance its objectives,

— serve its interests, those of its citizens and those of the Member States,

— ensure the consistency, effectiveness and continuity of its policies and actions.

This institutional framework comprises:

— The European Parliament,

— The European Council,

— The Council of Ministers (hereinafter referred to as the 'Council'),

— The European Commission (hereinafter referred to as the 'Commission'),

— The Court of Justice of the European Union.

2. Each institution shall act within the limits of the powers conferred on it in the Constitution, and in conformity with the procedures and conditions set out in it. The institutions shall practise mutual sincere cooperation.

Article 20 The European Parliament

1. The European Parliament shall, jointly with the Council, exercise legislative and budgetary functions. It shall exercise functions of political control and consultation as laid down in the Constitution. It shall elect the President of the Commission.

2. The European Parliament shall be composed of representatives of the Union's citizens. They shall not exceed seven hundred and fifty in number. Representation of citizens shall be degressively proportional, with a minimum threshold of six members per Member State. No Member State shall be allocated more than ninety-six seats.

The European Council shall adopt by unanimity, on the initiative of the European Parliament and with its consent, a European decision establishing the composition of the European Parliament, respecting the principles referred to in the first subparagraph.

3. The members of the European Parliament shall be elected for a term of five years by direct universal suffrage in a free and secret ballot.

4. The European Parliament shall elect its President and its officers from among its members.

Article 21 The European Council

1. The European Council shall provide the Union with the necessary impetus for its development and shall define the general political directions and priorities thereof. It shall not exercise legislative functions.

2. The European Council shall consist of the Heads of State or Government of the Member States, together with its President and the President of the Commission. The Union Minister for Foreign Affairs shall take part in its work.

3. The European Council shall meet quarterly, convened by its President. When the agenda so requires, the members of the European Council may decide each to be assisted by a minister and, in the case of the President of the Commission, by a member of the Commission. When the situation so requires, the President shall convene a special meeting of the European Council.

4. Except where the Constitution provides otherwise, decisions of the European Council shall be taken by consensus.

Article 22 The European Council President

1. The European Council shall elect its President, by a qualified majority, for a term of two and a half years, renewable once. In the event of an impediment or serious misconduct, the European Council can end his or her term of office in accordance with the same procedure.

2. The President of the European Council:

(a) shall chair it and drive forward its work;

(b) shall ensure the preparation and continuity of the work of the European Council in cooperation with the President of the Commission, and on the basis of the work of the General Affairs Council;

(c) shall endeavour to facilitate cohesion and consensus within the European Council;

(d) shall present a report to the European Parliament after each of the meetings of the European Council. The President of the European Council shall, at his or her level and in that capacity, ensure the external representation of the Union on issues concerning its common foreign and security policy, without prejudice to the powers of the Union Minister for Foreign Affairs.

3. The President of the European Council shall not hold a national office.

Article 23 The Council of Ministers

1. The Council shall, jointly with the European Parliament, exercise legislative and budgetary functions. It shall carry out policy-making and coordinating functions as laid down in the Constitution.

2. The Council shall consist of a representative of each Member State at ministerial level, who may commit the government of the Member State in question and cast its vote.

3. The Council shall act by a qualified majority except where the Constitution provides otherwise.

Article 24 Configurations of the Council of Ministers

1. The Council shall meet in different configurations.

2. The General Affairs Council shall ensure consistency in the work of the different Council configurations.

It shall prepare and ensure the follow-up to meetings of the European Council, in liaison with the President of the European Council and the Commission.

3. The Foreign Affairs Council shall elaborate the Union's external action on the basis of strategic guidelines laid down by the European Council and ensure that the Union's action is consistent.

4. The European Council shall adopt by a qualified majority a European decision establishing the list of other Council configurations.

5. A Committee of Permanent Representatives of the Governments of the Member States shall be responsible for preparing the work of the Council.

6. The Council shall meet in public when it deliberates and votes on a draft legislative act. To this end, each Council meeting shall be divided into two parts, dealing respectively with deliberations on Union legislative acts and non-legislative activities.

7. The Presidency of Council configurations, other than that of Foreign Affairs, shall be held by Member State representatives in the Council on the basis of equal rotation, in accordance with the conditions established by a European decision of the European Council. The European Council shall act by a qualified majority.

Article 25 Definition of qualified majority within the European Council and the Council

1. A qualified majority shall be defined as at least 55 % of the members of the Council, comprising at least fifteen of them and representing Member States comprising at least 65 % of the population of the Union.

A blocking minority must include at least four Council members, failing which the qualified majority shall be deemed attained.

2. By way of derogation from paragraph 1, when the Council does not act on a proposal from the Commission or from the Union Minister for Foreign Affairs, the qualified majority shall be defined as at least 72 % of the members of the Council, representing Member States comprising at least 65 % of the population of the Union.

3. Paragraphs 1 and 2 shall apply to the European Council when it is acting by a qualified majority.

4. Within the European Council, its President and the President of the Commission shall not take part in the vote.

Article 26 The European Commission

1. The Commission shall promote the general interest of the Union and take appropriate initiatives to that end. It shall ensure the application of the Constitution, and measures adopted by the institutions pursuant to the Constitution. It shall oversee the application of Union law under the control of the Court of Justice of the European Union. It shall execute the budget and manage programmes. It shall exercise coordinating, executive and management functions, as laid down in the Constitution. With the exception of the common foreign and security policy, and other cases provided for in the Constitution, it shall ensure the Union's external representation. It shall initiate the Union's annual and multiannual programming with a view to achieving inter-institutional agreements.

2. Union legislative acts may be adopted only on the basis of a Commission proposal, except where the Constitution provides otherwise. Other acts shall be

adopted on the basis of a Commission proposal where the Constitution so provides.

3. The Commission's term of office shall be five years.

4. The members of the Commission shall be chosen on the ground of their general competence and European commitment from persons whose independence is beyond doubt.

5. The first Commission appointed under the provisions of the Constitution shall consist of one national of each Member State, including its President and the Union Minister for Foreign Affairs who shall be one of its Vice-Presidents.

6. As from the end of the term of office of the Commission referred to in paragraph 5, the Commission shall consist of a number of members, including its President and the Union Minister for Foreign Affairs, corresponding to two thirds of the number of Member States, unless the European Council, acting unanimously, decides to alter this number.

The members of the Commission shall be selected from among the nationals of the Member States on the basis of a system of equal rotation between the Member States. This system shall be established by a European decision adopted unanimously by the European Council and on the basis of the following principles:

(a) Member states shall be treated on a strictly equal footing as regards determination of the sequence of, and the time spent by, their nationals as members of the commission; consequently, the difference between the total number of terms of office held by nationals of any given pair of Member States may never be more than one;

(b) subject to point (a), each successive Commission shall be so composed as to reflect satisfactorily the demographic and geographical range of all the Member States.

7. In carrying out its responsibilities, the Commission shall be completely independent. Without prejudice to Article I-28(2), the members of the Commission shall neither seek nor take instructions from any government or other institution, body, office or entity. They shall refrain from any action incompatible with their duties or the performance of their tasks.

8. The Commission, as a body, shall be responsible to the European Parliament. In accordance with Article 340, the European Parliament may vote on a censure motion on the Commission. If such a motion is carried, the members of the Commission shall resign as a body and the Union Minister for Foreign Affairs shall resign from the duties that he or she carries out in the Commission.

Article 27 The President of the European Commission

1. Taking into account the elections to the European Parliament and after having held the appropriate consultations, the European Council, acting by a qualified majority, shall propose to the European Parliament a candidate for President of the Commission. This candidate shall be elected by the European Parliament by a majority of its component members. If he or she does not obtain the required majority, the European Council, acting by a qualified majority, shall within one month propose a new candidate who shall be elected by the European Parliament following the same procedure.

2. The Council, by common accord with the President-elect, shall adopt the list of the other persons whom it proposes for appointment as members of the Commission. They shall be selected, on the basis of the suggestions made by Member States, in accordance with the criteria set out in Article 26 (4) and (6), second subparagraph.

The President, the Union Minister for Foreign Affairs and the other members of the Commission shall be subject as a body to a vote of consent by the European Parliament. On the basis of this consent the Commission shall be appointed by the European Council, acting by a qualified majority.

3. The President of the Commission shall:

(a) lay down guidelines within which the Commission is to work;

(b) decide on the internal organisation of the Commission, ensuring that it acts consistently, efficiently and as a collegiate body;

(c) appoint Vice-Presidents, other than the Union Minister for Foreign Affairs, from among the members of the Commission.

A member of the Commission shall resign if the President so requests. The Union Minister for Foreign Affairs shall resign, in accordance with the procedure set out in article 28(1), if the President so requests.

Article 28 The Union Minister for Foreign Affairs

1. The European Council, acting by a qualified majority, with the agreement of the President of the Commission, shall appoint the Union Minister for Foreign Affairs. The European Council may end his or her term of office by the same procedure.

2. The Union Minister for Foreign Affairs shall conduct the Union's common foreign and security policy. He or she shall contribute by his or her proposals to the development of that policy, which he or she shall carry out as mandated by the Council. The same shall apply to the common security and defence policy.

3. The Union Minister for Foreign Affairs shall preside over the Foreign Affairs Council.

4. The Union Minister for Foreign Affairs shall be one of the Vice-Presidents of the Commission. He or she shall ensure the consistency of the Union's external action. He or she shall be responsible within the Commission for responsibilities incumbent on it in external relations and for coordinating other aspects of the Union's external action. In exercising these responsibilities within the Commission, and only for these responsibilities, the Union Minister for Foreign Affairs shall be bound by Commission procedures to the extent that this is consistent with paragraphs 2 and 3.

Article 29 The Court of Justice of the European Union

1. The Court of Justice of the European Union shall include the Court of Justice, the General Court and specialised courts. It shall ensure that in the interpretation and application of the Constitution the law is observed.

Member States shall provide remedies sufficient to ensure effective legal protection in the fields covered by Union law.

2. The Court of Justice shall consist of one judge from each Member State. It shall be assisted by Advocates-General.

The General Court shall include at least one judge per Member State.

The Judges and the Advocates-General of the Court of Justice and the Judges of the General Court shall be chosen from persons whose independence is beyond doubt and who satisfy the conditions set out in Articles 355 and 356. They shall be appointed by common accord of the governments of the Member States for six years. Retiring Judges and Advocates-General may be reappointed.

3. The Court of Justice of the European Union shall in accordance with Part III:

(a) rule on actions brought by a Member State, an institution or a natural or legal person;

(b) give preliminary rulings, at the request of courts or tribunals of the Member States, on the interpretation of Union law or the validity of acts adopted by the institutions;

(c) rule in other cases provided for in the Constitution.

Chapter II - The Other Union Institutions and Advisory Bodies

Article 30 The European Central Bank

1. The European Central Bank, together with the national central banks, shall constitute the European System of Central Banks. The European Central Bank, together with the national central banks of the Member States whose currency is the euro, which constitute the Eurosystem, shall conduct the monetary policy of the Union.

2. The European System of Central Banks shall be governed by the decision-making bodies of the European Central Bank. The primary objective of the European System of Central Banks shall be to maintain price stability. Without prejudice to that objective, it shall support the general economic policies in the Union in order to contribute to the achievement of the latter's objectives. It shall conduct other Central Bank tasks in accordance with Part III and the Statute of the European System of Central Banks and of the European Central Bank.

3. The European Central Bank is an institution. It shall have legal personality. It alone may authorise the issue of the euro. It shall be independent in the exercise of its powers and in the management of its finances. Union institutions, bodies, offices and agencies and the governments of the Member States shall respect that independence.

4. The European Central Bank shall adopt such measures as are necessary to carry out its tasks in accordance with Articles 185 to 191 and Article 196, and with the conditions laid down in the Statute of the European System of Central Banks and of the European Central Bank. In accordance with these same Articles, those Member States whose currency is not the euro, and their central banks, shall retain their powers in monetary matters.

5. Within the areas falling within its responsibilities, the European Central Bank shall be consulted on all proposed Union acts, and all proposals for regulation at national level, and may give an opinion.

6. The decision-making organs of the European Central Bank, their composition and operating methods are set out in Articles 382 and 383, as well as in the Statute of the European System of Central Banks and of the European Central Bank.

Article 31 The Court of Auditors

1. The Court of Auditors is an institution. It shall carry out the Union's audit.

2. It shall examine the accounts of all Union revenue and expenditure, and shall ensure good financial management.

3. It shall consist of one national of each Member State. Its members shall be completely independent in the performance of their duties, in the Union's general interest.

Article 32 The Union's advisory bodies

1. The European Parliament, the Council and the Commission shall be assisted by a Committee of the Regions and an Economic and Social Committee, exercising advisory functions.

2. The Committee of the Regions shall consist of representatives of regional and local bodies who either hold a regional or local authority electoral mandate or are politically accountable to an elected assembly.

3. The Economic and Social Committee shall consist of representatives of organisations of employers, of the employed, and of other parties representative of civil society, notably in socioeconomic, civic, professional and cultural areas.

4. The members of the Committee of the Regions and the Economic and Social Committee shall not be bound by any mandatory instructions. They shall be completely independent in the performance of their duties, in the Union's general interest.

5. Rules governing the composition of these Committees, the designation of their members, their powers and their operations are set out in Articles 386 to 392.

The rules referred to in paragraphs 2 and 3 governing the nature of their composition shall be reviewed at regular intervals by the Council to take account of economic, social and demographic developments within the Union. The Council, on a proposal from the Commission, shall adopt European decisions to that end.

Title V
Exercise of Union Competence

Chapter 1 - Common Provisions

Article 33 The legal acts of the Union

1. To exercise the Union's competences the institutions shall use as legal instruments, in accordance with Part III, European laws, European framework laws, European regulations, European decisions, recommendations and opinions..

A European law shall be a legislative act of general application. It shall be binding in its entirety and directly applicable in all Member States.

A European framework law shall be a legislative act binding, as to the result to be achieved, upon each Member State to which it is addressed, but shall leave to the national authorities the choice of form and methods.

A European regulation shall be a non-legislative act of general application for the implementation of legislative acts and of certain provisions of the Constitution. It may either be binding in its entirety and directly applicable in all Member States, or be binding, as to the result to be achieved, upon each Member State to which it is addressed, but shall leave to the national authorities the choice of form and methods.

A European decision shall be a non-legislative act, binding in its entirety. A decision which specifies those to whom it is addressed shall be binding only on them. Recommendations and opinions shall have no binding force.

2. When considering draft legislative acts, the European Parliament and the Council shall refrain from adopting acts not provided for by the relevant legislative procedure in the area in question

Article 34 Legislative acts

1. European laws and framework laws shall be adopted, on the basis of proposals from the Commission, jointly by the European Parliament and the Council under the ordinary legislative procedure as set out in Article 396. If the two institutions cannot reach agreement on an act, it shall not be adopted.

2. In the specific cases provided for in the Constitution, European laws and framework laws shall be adopted by the European Parliament with the participation of the Council, or by the latter with the participation of the European Parliament, in accordance with special legislative procedures.

3. In the specific cases provided for in the Constitution, European laws and framework laws may be adopted at the initiative of a group of Member States or of the European Parliament, on a recommendation from the European Central Bank or at the request of the Court of Justice or the European Investment Bank.

Article 35 Non-legislative acts

1. The European Council shall adopt European decisions in the cases provided for in the Constitution.

2. The Council and the Commission, in particular in the cases referred to in Articles 36 and 37, and the European Central Bank in the specific cases provided for in the constitution, shall adopt European regulations and decisions.

3. The Council shall adopt recommendations. It shall act on a proposal from the Commission in all cases where the Constitution provides that it shall adopt acts on a proposal from the Commission. It shall act unanimously in those areas in which unanimity is required for the adoption of a Union act.

The Commission, and the European Central Bank in the specific cases provided for in the Constitution, shall adopt recommendations.

Article 36 Delegated European regulations

1. European laws and framework laws may delegate to the Commission the power to adopt delegated European regulations to supplement or amend certain non-essential elements of the law or framework law.

The objectives, content, scope and duration of the delegation of power shall be explicitly defined in the European laws and framework laws. The essential elements of an area shall be reserved for the European law or framework law and accordingly shall not be the subject of a delegation of power.

2. European laws and framework laws shall explicitly lay down the conditions to which the delegation is subject; these conditions may be as follows:

(a) the European Parliament or the Council may decide to revoke the delegation;

(b) the delegated European regulation may enter into force only if no objection has been expressed by the European Parliament or the Council within a period set by the European law or framework law.

For the purposes of (a) and (b), the European Parliament shall act by a majority of its component members, and the Council by a qualified majority.

Article 37 Implementing acts

1. Member States shall adopt all measures of national law necessary to implement legally binding Union acts.

2. Where uniform conditions for implementing legally binding Union acts are needed, those acts shall confer implementing powers on the Commission, or, in duly justified specific cases and in the cases provided for in Article I-40, on the Council.

3. For the purposes of paragraph 2, European laws shall lay down in advance the rules and general principles concerning mechanisms for control by Member States of the Commission's exercise of implementing powers.

4. Union implementing acts shall take the form of European implementing regulations or European implementing decisions.

Article 38 Principles common to the Union's legal acts

1. Where the Constitution does not specify the type of act to be adopted, the institutions shall select it on a case-by-case basis, in compliance with the applicable procedures and with the principle of proportionality referred to in Article 11.

2. Legal acts shall state the reasons on which they are based and shall refer to any proposals, initiatives, recommendations, requests or opinions required by the Constitution.

Article 39 Publication and entry into force

1. European laws and framework laws adopted under the ordinary legislative procedure shall be signed by the President of the European Parliament and by the President of the Council.

In other cases they shall be signed by the President of the institution which adopted them.

European laws and framework laws shall be published in the Official Journal of the European Union and shall enter into force on the date specified in them or, in the absence thereof, on the twentieth day following their publication.

2. European regulations, and European decisions which do not specify to whom they are addressed, shall be signed by the President of the institution which adopted them.

European regulations, and European decisions when the latter do not specify to whom they are addressed, shall be published in the Official Journal of the European Union and shall enter into force on the date specified in them or, in the absence thereof, on the twentieth day following that of their publication.

3. European decisions other than those referred to in paragraph 2 shall be notified to those to whom they are addressed and shall take effect upon such notification.

Chapter II - Specific Provisions

Article 40 Specific provisions relating to the common foreign and security policy

1. The European Union shall conduct a common foreign and security policy, based on the development of mutual political solidarity among Member States, the identification of questions of general interest and the achievement of an ever-increasing degree of convergence of Member States' actions.

2. The European Council shall identify the Union's strategic interests and determine the objectives of its common foreign and security policy. The Council shall frame this policy within the framework of the strategic guidelines established by the European Council and in accordance with Part III.

3. The European Council and the Council shall adopt the necessary European decisions.

4. The common foreign and security policy shall be put into effect by the Union Minister for Foreign Affairs and by the Member States, using national and Union resources.

5. Member States shall consult one another within the European Council and the Council on any foreign and security policy issue which is of general interest in order to determine a common approach. Before undertaking any action on the international scene or any commitment which could affect the Union's interests, each Member State shall consult the others within the European Council or the Council. Member States shall ensure, through the convergence of their actions, that the Union is able to assert its interests and values on the international scene. Member States shall show mutual solidarity.

6. European decisions relating to the common foreign and security policy shall be adopted by the European Council and the Council unanimously, except in the cases referred to in Part III. The European Council and the Council shall act on an initiative from a Member State, on a proposal from the Union Minister

for Foreign Affairs or on a proposal from that Minister with the Commission's support. European laws and framework laws shall be excluded.

7. The European Council may, unanimously, adopt a European decision authorising the Council to act by a qualified majority in cases other than those referred to in Part III.

8. The European Parliament shall be regularly consulted on the main aspects and basic choices of the common foreign and security policy. It shall be kept informed of how it evolves.

Article 41 Specific provisions relating to the common security and defence policy

1. The common security and defence policy shall be an integral part of the common foreign and security policy. It shall provide the Union with an operational capacity drawing on civil and military assets. The Union may use them on missions outside the Union for peace-keeping, conflict prevention and strengthening international security in accordance with the principles of the United Nations Charter. The performance of these tasks shall be undertaken using capabilities provided by the Member States.

2. The common security and defence policy shall include the progressive framing of a common Union defence policy. This will lead to a common defence, when the European Council, acting unanimously, so decides. It shall in that case recommend to the Member States the adoption of such a decision in accordance with their respective constitutional requirements.

The policy of the Union in accordance with this Article shall not prejudice the specific character of the security and defence policy of certain Member States, it shall respect the obligations of certain Member States, which see their common defence realised in the North Atlantic Treaty Organisation, under the North Atlantic Treaty, and be compatible with the common security and defence policy established within that framework.

3. Member States shall make civilian and military capabilities available to the Union for the implementation of the common security and defence policy, to contribute to the objectives defined by the Council. Those Member States which together establish multinational forces may also make them available to the common security and defence policy.

Member States shall undertake progressively to improve their military capabilities. An Agency in the field of defence capabilities development, research, acquisition and armaments (European Defence Agency) shall be established to identify operational requirements, to promote measures to satisfy those requirements, to contribute to identifying and, where appropriate, implementing any measure needed to strengthen the industrial and technological base of the defence sector, to participate in defining a European capabilities and armaments policy, and to assist the Council in evaluating the improvement of military capabilities.

4. European decisions relating to the common security and defence policy, including those initiating a mission as referred to in this Article, shall be adopted by the Council acting unanimously on a proposal from the Union Minister for Foreign Affairs or an initiative from a Member State. The Union Minister for

Foreign Affairs may propose the use of both national resources and Union instruments, together with the Commission where appropriate.

5. The Council may entrust the execution of a task, within the Union framework, to a group of Member States in order to protect the Union's values and serve its interests. The execution of such a task shall be governed by Article 310.

6. Those Member States whose military capabilities fulfil higher criteria and which have made more binding commitments to one another in this area with a view to the most demanding missions shall establish permanent structured cooperation within the Union framework. Such cooperation shall be governed by Article 312. It shall not affect the provisions of Article 309.

7. If a Member State is the victim of armed aggression on its territory, the other Member States shall have towards it an obligation of aid and assistance by all the means in their power, in accordance with Article 51 of the United Nations Charter. This shall not prejudice the specific character of the security and defence policy of certain Member States.

Commitments and cooperation in this area shall be consistent with commitments under the North Atlantic Treaty Organisation, which, for those States which are members of it, remains the foundation of their collective defence and the forum for its implementation.

8. The European Parliament shall be regularly consulted on the main aspects and basic choices of the common security and defence policy. It shall be kept informed of how it evolves.

Article 42 Specific provisions relating to the area of freedom, security and justice

1. The Union shall constitute an area of freedom, security and justice:

(a) by adopting European laws and framework laws intended, where necessary, to approximate laws and regulations of the Member States in the areas referred to in Part III;

(b) by promoting mutual confidence between the competent authorities of the Member States, in particular on the basis of mutual recognition of judicial and extrajudicial decisions;

(c) by operational cooperation between the competent authorities of the Member States, including the police, customs and other services specialising in the prevention and detection of criminal offences.

2. National Parliaments may, within the framework of the area of freedom, security and justice, participate in the evaluation mechanisms provided for in Article 260. They shall be involved in the political monitoring of Europol and the evaluation of Eurojust's activities in accordance with Articles 276 and 273.

3. Member States shall have a right of initiative in the field of police and judicial cooperation in criminal matters, in accordance with Article 264.

Article 43 Solidarity clause

1. The Union and its Member States shall act jointly in a spirit of solidarity if a Member State is the object of a terrorist attack or the victim of a natural or

man-made disaster. The Union shall mobilise all the instruments at its disposal, including the military resources made available by the Member States, to:

(a) prevent the terrorist threat in the territory of the Member States; protect democratic institutions and the civilian population from any terrorist attack; assist a Member State in its territory, at the request of its political authorities, in the event of a terrorist attack;

(b) assist a Member State in its territory, at the request of its political authorities, in the event of a natural or man-made disaster.

2. The detailed arrangements for implementing this Article are set out in Article 329.

Chapter III - Enhanced Co-operation

Article 44 Enhanced co-operation

1. Member States which wish to establish enhanced co-operation between themselves within the framework of the Union's non-exclusive competences may make use of its institutions and exercise those competences by applying the relevant provisions of the Constitution, subject to the limits and in accordance with the procedures laid down in this Article and in Articles 416 to 423.

Enhanced co-operation shall aim to further the objectives of the Union, protect its interests and reinforce its integration process. Such co-operation shall be open at any time to all Member States, in accordance with Article 418.

2. The European decision authorising enhanced co-operation shall be adopted by the Council as a last resort, when it has established that the objectives of such cooperation cannot be attained within a reasonable period by the Union as a whole, and provided that at least one third of the Member States participate in it. The Council shall act in accordance with the procedure laid down in Article 419.

3. All members of the Council may participate in its deliberations, but only members of the Council representing the Member States participating in enhanced cooperation shall take part in the vote.

Unanimity shall be constituted by the votes of the representatives of the participating Member States only.

A qualified majority shall be defined as at least 55 % of the members of the Council representing the participating Member States, comprising at least 65 % of the population of these States.

A blocking minority must include at least the minimum number of Council members representing more than 35 % of the population of the participating Member States, plus one member, failing which the qualified majority shall be deemed attained.

By way of derogation from the third and fourth subparagraphs, where the Council does not act on a proposal from the Commission or from the Union Minister for Foreign Affairs, the required qualified majority shall be defined as at least 72 % of the members of the Council representing the participating Member States, comprising at least 65 % of the population of these States.

4. Acts adopted in the framework of enhanced co-operation shall bind only participating Member States. They shall not be regarded as part of the acquis which has to be accepted by candidate States for accession to the Union.

Title VI
The Democratic Life of the Union

Article 45 The principle of democratic equality

In all its activities, the Union shall observe the principle of the equality of its citizens, who shall receive equal attention from its institutions, bodies, offices and agencies.

Article 46 The principle of representative democracy

1. The functioning of the Union shall be founded on representative democracy.

2. Citizens are directly represented at Union level in the European Parliament. Member States are represented in the European Council by their Heads of State or Government and in the Council by their governments, themselves democratically accountable either to their national Parliaments, or to their citizens.

3. Every citizen shall have the right to participate in the democratic life of the Union. Decisions shall be taken as openly and as closely as possible to the citizen.

4. Political parties at European level contribute to forming European political awareness and to expressing the will of citizens of the Union.

Article 47 The principle of participatory democracy

1. The institutions shall, by appropriate means, give citizens and representative associations the opportunity to make known and publicly exchange their views in all areas of Union action.

2. The institutions shall maintain an open, transparent and regular dialogue with representative associations and civil society.

3. The Commission shall carry out broad consultations with parties concerned in order to ensure that the Union's actions are coherent and transparent.

4. Not less than one million citizens who are nationals of a significant number of Member States may take the initiative of inviting the Commission, within the framework of its powers, to submit any appropriate proposal on matters where citizens consider that a legal act of the Union is required for the purpose of implementing the Constitution. European laws shall determine the provisions for the procedures and conditions required for such a citizens' initiative, including the minimum number of Member States from which such citizens must come.

Article 48 The social partners and autonomous social dialogue

The Union recognises and promotes the role of the social partners at its level, taking into account the diversity of national systems. It shall facilitate dialogue between the social partners, respecting their autonomy. The Tripartite Social Summit for Growth and Employment shall contribute to social dialogue.

Article 49 The European Ombudsman

A European Ombudsman elected by the European Parliament shall receive, examine and report on complaints about maladministration in the activities of the Union institutions, bodies, offices or agencies, under the conditions laid down in the Constitution. The European Ombudsman shall be completely independent in the performance of his or her duties.

Article 50 Transparency of the proceedings of Union institutions, bodies, offices and agencies

1. In order to promote good governance and ensure the participation of civil society, the Union institutions, bodics, offices and agencies shall conduct their work as openly as possible.

2. The European Parliament shall meet in public, as shall the Council when considering and voting on a draft legislative act.

3. Any citizen of the Union, and any natural or legal person residing or having its registered office in a Member State shall have, under the conditions laid down in Part III, a right of access to documents of the Union institutions, bodies, offices and agencies, whatever their medium.

European laws shall lay down the general principles and limits which, on grounds of public or private interest, govern the right of access to such documents.

4. Each institution, body, office or agency shall determine in its own rules of procedure specific provisions regarding access to its documents, in accordance with the European laws referred to in paragraph 3.

Article 51 Protection of personal data

1. Everyone has the right to the protection of personal data concerning him or her.

2. European laws or framework laws shall lay down the rules relating to the protection of individuals with regard to the processing of personal data by Union institutions, bodies, offices and agencies, and by the Member States when carrying out activities which fall within the scope of Union law, and the rules relating to the free movement of such data. Compliance with these rules shall be subject to the control of independent authorities.

Article 52 Status of churches and non-confessional organisations

1. The Union respects and does not prejudice the status under national law of churches and religious associations or communities in the Member States.

2. The Union equally respects the status under national law of philosophical and non-confessional organisations.

3. Recognising their identity and their specific contribution, the Union shall maintain an open, transparent and regular dialogue with these churches and organisations.

Title VII
The Unions Finances

Article 53 Budgetary and financial principles

1. All items of Union revenue and expenditure shall be included in estimates drawn up for each financial year and shall be shown in the Union's budget, in accordance with Part III.

2. The revenue and expenditure shown in the budget shall be in balance.

3. The expenditure shown in the budget shall be authorised for the annual budgetary period in accordance with the European law referred to in Article 412.

4. The implementation of expenditure shown in the budget shall require the prior adoption of a legally binding Union act providing a legal basis for its action and for the implementation of the corresponding expenditure in accordance with the European law referred to in Article 412, except in cases for which that law provides.

5. With a view to maintaining budgetary discipline, the Union shall not adopt any act which is likely to have appreciable implications for the budget without providing an assurance that the expenditure arising from such an act is capable of being financed within the limit of the Union's own resources and in compliance with the multiannual financial framework referred to in Article 55.

6. The budget shall be implemented in accordance with the principle of sound financial management. Member States shall cooperate with the Union to ensure that the appropriations entered in the budget are used in accordance with this principle.

7. The Union and the Member States, in accordance with Article III-415, shall counter fraud and any other illegal activities affecting the financial interests of the Union.

Article 54 The Union's own resources

1. The Union shall provide itself with the means necessary to attain its objectives and carry through its policies.

2. Without prejudice to other revenue, the Union's budget shall be financed wholly from its own resources.

3. A European law of the Council shall lay down the provisions relating to the system of own resources of the Union. In this context it may establish new categories of own resources or abolish an existing category. The Council shall act unanimously after consulting the European Parliament. That law shall not enter into force until it is approved by the Member States in accordance with their respective constitutional requirements.

4. A European law of the Council shall lay down implementing measures of the Union's own resources system insofar as this is provided for in the European law adopted on the basis of paragraph 3. The Council shall act after obtaining the consent of the European Parliament.

Article 55 The multiannual financial framework

1. The multiannual financial framework shall ensure that Union expenditure develops in an orderly manner and within the limits of its own resources. It shall

determine the amounts of the annual ceilings of appropriations for commitments by category of expenditure in accordance with Article 402.

2. A European law of the Council shall lay down the multiannual financial framework. The Council shall act unanimously after obtaining the consent of the European Parliament, which shall be given by a majority of its component members.

3. The annual budget of the Union shall comply with the multiannual financial framework.

4. The European Council may, unanimously, adopt a European decision authorising the Council to act by a qualified majority when adopting the European law of the Council referred to in paragraph 2.

Article 56 The Union's budget

A European law shall establish the Union's annual budget in accordance with Article 404.

Title VIII
The Union and its Neighbours

Article 57 The Union and its neighbours

1. The Union shall develop a special relationship with neighbouring countries, aiming to establish an area of prosperity and good neighbourliness, founded on the values of the Union and characterised by close and peaceful relations based on cooperation.

2. For the purposes of paragraph 1, the Union may conclude specific agreements with the countries concerned. These agreements may contain reciprocal rights and obligations as well as the possibility of undertaking activities jointly. Their implementation shall be the subject of periodic consultation.

Title IX
Union Membership

Article 58 Conditions of eligibility and procedure for accession to the Union

1. The Union shall be open to all European States which respect the values referred to in Article 2, and are committed to promoting them together.

2. Any European State which wishes to become a member of the Union shall address its application to the Council. The European Parliament and national Parliaments shall be notified of this application. The Council shall act unanimously after consulting the Commission and after obtaining the consent of the European Parliament, which shall act by a majority of its component members. The conditions and arrangements for admission shall be the subject of an agreement between the Member States and the candidate State. That agreement shall be subject to ratification by each contracting State, in accordance with its respective constitutional requirements.

Article 59 Suspension of certain rights resulting from Union membership

1. On the reasoned initiative of one third of the Member States or the reasoned initiative of the European Parliament or on a proposal from the Commission, the Council may adopt a European decision determining that there is a clear risk of a serious breach by a Member State of the values referred to in Article 2. The Council shall act by a majority of four fifths of its members after obtaining the consent of the European Parliament.

Before making such a determination, the Council shall hear the Member State in question and, acting in accordance with the same procedure, may address recommendations to that State. The Council shall regularly verify that the grounds on which such a determination was made continue to apply.

2. The European Council, on the initiative of one third of the Member States or on a proposal from the Commission, may adopt a European decision determining the existence of a serious and persistent breach by a Member State of the values mentioned in Article 2, after inviting the Member State in question to submit its observations. The European Council shall act unanimously after obtaining the consent of the European Parliament.

3. Where a determination under paragraph 2 has been made, the Council, acting by a qualified majority, may adopt a European decision suspending certain of the rights deriving from the application of the Constitution to the Member State in question, including the voting rights of the member of the Council representing that State. The Council shall take into account the possible consequences of such a suspension for the rights and obligations of natural and legal persons. In any case, that State shall continue to be bound by its obligations under the Constitution.

4. The Council, acting by a qualified majority, may adopt a European decision varying or revoking measures adopted under paragraph 3 in response to changes in the situation which led to their being imposed.

5. For the purposes of this Article, the member of the European Council or of the Council representing the Member State in question shall not take part in the vote and the Member State in question shall not be counted in the calculation of the one third or four fifths of Member States referred to in paragraphs 1 and 2. Abstentions by members present in person or represented shall not prevent the adoption of European decisions referred to in paragraph 2.

For the adoption of the European decisions referred to in paragraphs 3 and 4, a qualified majority shall be defined as at least 72 % of the members of the Council, representing the participating Member States, comprising at least 65 % of the population of these States.

Where, following a decision to suspend voting rights adopted pursuant to paragraph 3, the Council acts by a qualified majority on the basis of a provision of the Constitution, that qualified majority shall be defined as in the second subparagraph, or, where the Council acts on a proposal from the Commission or from the Union Minister for Foreign Affairs, as at least 55 % of the members of the Council representing the participating Member States, comprising at least 65 % of the population of these States. In the latter case, a blocking minority must include at least the minimum number of Council members representing more than 35 % of the population of the participating Member States, plus one member, failing which the qualified majority shall be deemed attained.

6. For the purposes of this Article, the European Parliament shall act by a two-thirds majority of the votes cast, representing the majority of its component members.

Article 60 Voluntary withdrawal from the Union

1. Any Member State may decide to withdraw from the Union in accordance with its own constitutional requirements.

2. A Member State which decides to withdraw shall notify the European Council of its intention. In the light of the guidelines provided by the European Council, the Union shall negotiate and conclude an agreement with that State, setting out the arrangements for its withdrawal, taking account of the framework for its future relationship with the Union. That agreement shall be negotiated in accordance with Article 325(3). It shall be concluded by the Council, acting by a qualified majority, after obtaining the consent of the European Parliament.

3. The Constitution shall cease to apply to the State in question from the date of entry into force of the withdrawal agreement or, failing that, two years after the notification referred to in paragraph 2, unless the European Council, in agreement with the Member State concerned, unanimously decides to extend this period.

4. For the purposes of paragraphs 2 and 3, the member of the European Council or of the Council representing the withdrawing Member State shall not participate in the discussions of the European Council or Council or in European decisions concerning it. A qualified majority shall be defined as at least 72 % of the members of the Council, representing the participating Member States, comprising at least 65 % of the population of these States.

5. If a State which has withdrawn from the Union asks to rejoin, its request shall be subject to the procedure referred to in Article 58.

Part II

The Charter of Fundamental Rights of the Union

Preamble

The peoples of Europe, in creating an ever closer union among them, are resolved to share a peaceful future based on common values.

Conscious of its spiritual and moral heritage, the Union is founded on the indivisible, universal values of human dignity, freedom, equality and solidarity; it is based on the principles of democracy and the rule of law. It places the individual at the heart of its activities, by establishing the citizenship of the Union and by creating an area of freedom, security and justice.

The Union contributes to the preservation and to the development of these common values while respecting the diversity of the cultures and traditions of the peoples of Europe as well as the national identities of the Member States and the organisation of their public authorities at national, regional and local levels; it seeks to promote balanced and sustainable development and ensures free movement of persons, services, goods and capital, and the freedom of establishment.

To this end, it is necessary to strengthen the protection of fundamental rights in the light of changes in society, social progress and scientific and technological developments by making those rights more visible in a Charter.

This Charter reaffirms, with due regard for the powers and tasks of the Union and the principle of subsidiarity, the rights as they result, in particular, from the constitutional traditions and international obligations common to the Member States, the European Convention for the Protection of Human Rights and Fundamental Freedoms, the Social Charters adopted by the Union and by the Council of Europe and the case-law of the Court of Justice of the European Union and of the European Court of Human Rights. In this context the Charter will be interpreted by the courts of the Union and the Member States with due regard to the explanations prepared under the authority of the Praesidium of the Convention which drafted the Charter and updated under the responsibility of the Praesidium of the European Convention.

Enjoyment of these rights entails responsibilities and duties with regard to other persons, to the human community and to future generations.

The Union therefore recognises the rights, freedoms and principles set out hereafter.

Title I
Dignity

Article 61 Human dignity

Human dignity is inviolable. It must be respected and protected.

Article 62 Right to life

1. Everyone has the right to life.
2. No one shall be condemned to the death penalty, or executed.

Article 63 Right to the integrity of the person

1. Everyone has the right to respect for his or her physical and mental integrity.

2. In the fields of medicine and biology, the following must be respected in particular:

(a) the free and informed consent of the person concerned, according to the procedures laid down by law;

(b) the prohibition of eugenic practices, in particular those aiming at the selection of persons;

(c) the prohibition on making the human body and its parts as such a source of financial gain;

(d) the prohibition of the reproductive cloning of human beings.

Article 64 Prohibition of torture and inhuman or degrading treatment or punishment

No one shall be subjected to torture or to inhuman or degrading treatment or punishment.

Article 65 Prohibition of slavery and forced labour

1. No one shall be held in slavery or servitude.
2. No one shall be required to perform forced or compulsory labour.
3. Trafficking in human beings is prohibited.

Title II
Freedoms

Article 66 Right to liberty and security

Everyone has the right to liberty and security of person.

Article 67 Respect for private and family life

Everyone has the right to respect for his or her private and family life, home and communications.

Article 68 Protection of personal data

1. Everyone has the right to the protection of personal data concerning him or her.

2. Such data must be processed fairly for specified purposes and on the basis of the consent of the person concerned or some other legitimate basis laid down by law. Everyone has the right of access to data which has been collected concerning him or her, and the right to have it rectified.

3. Compliance with these rules shall be subject to control by an independent authority.

Article 69 Right to marry and right to found a family

The right to marry and the right to found a family shall be guaranteed in accordance with the national laws governing the exercise of these rights.

Article 70 Freedom of thought, conscience and religion

1. Everyone has the right to freedom of thought, conscience and religion. This right includes freedom to change religion or belief and freedom, either alone or in community with others and in public or in private, to manifest religion or belief, in worship, teaching, practice and observance.

2. The right to conscientious objection is recognised, in accordance with the national laws governing the exercise of this right.

Article 71 Freedom of expression and information

1. Everyone has the right to freedom of expression. This right shall include freedom to hold opinions and to receive and impart information and ideas without interference by public authority and regardless of frontiers.

2. The freedom and pluralism of the media shall be respected.

Article 72 Freedom of assembly and of association

1. Everyone has the right to freedom of peaceful assembly and to freedom of association at all levels, in particular in political, trade union and civic matters, which implies the right of everyone to form and to join trade unions for the protection of his or her interests.

2. Political parties at Union level contribute to expressing the political will of the citizens of the Union.

Article 73 Freedom of the arts and sciences

The arts and scientific research shall be free of constraint. Academic freedom shall be respected.

Article 74 Right to education

1. Everyone has the right to education and to have access to vocational and continuing training.

2. This right includes the possibility to receive free compulsory education.

3. The freedom to found educational establishments with due respect for democratic principles and the right of parents to ensure the education and teaching of their children in conformity with their religious, philosophical and pedagogical convictions shall be respected, in accordance with the national laws governing the exercise of such freedom and right.

Article 75 Freedom to choose an occupation and right to engage in work

1. Everyone has the right to engage in work and to pursue a freely chosen or accepted occupation.

2. Every citizen of the Union has the freedom to seek employment, to work, to exercise the right of establishment and to provide services in any Member State.

3. Nationals of third countries who are authorised to work in the territories of the Member States are entitled to working conditions equivalent to those of citizens of the Union.

Article 76 Freedom to conduct a business

The freedom to conduct a business in accordance with Union law and national laws and practices is recognised.

Article 77 Right to property

1. Everyone has the right to own, use, dispose of and bequeath his or her lawfully acquired possessions. No one may be deprived of his or her possessions, except in the public interest and in the cases and under the conditions provided for by law, subject to fair compensation being paid in good time for their loss. The use of property may be regulated by law insofar as is necessary for the general interest.

2. Intellectual property shall be protected.

Article 78 Right to asylum

The right to asylum shall be guaranteed with due respect for the rules of the Geneva Convention of 28 July 1951 and the Protocol of 31 January 1967 relating to the status of refugees and in accordance with the Constitution.

Article 79 Protection in the event of removal, expulsion or extradition

1. Collective expulsions are prohibited.

2. No one may be removed, expelled or extradited to a State where there is a serious risk that he or she would be subjected to the death penalty, torture or other inhuman or degrading treatment or punishment.

Title III
Equality

Article 80 Equality before the law

Everyone is equal before the law.

Article 81 Non-discrimination

1. Any discrimination based on any ground such as sex, race, colour, ethnic or social origin, genetic features, language, religion or belief, political or any other opinion, membership of a national minority, property, birth, disability, age or sexual orientation shall be prohibited.

2. Within the scope of application of the Constitution and without prejudice to any of its specific provisions, any discrimination on grounds of nationality shall be prohibited.

Article 82 Cultural, religious and linguistic diversity

The Union shall respect cultural, religious and linguistic diversity.

Article 83 Equality between women and men

Equality between women and men must be ensured in all areas, including employment, work and pay.

The principle of equality shall not prevent the maintenance or adoption of measures providing for specific advantages in favour of the under-represented sex.

Article 84 The rights of the child

1. Children shall have the right to such protection and care as is necessary for their well-being. They may express their views freely. Such views shall be taken into consideration on matters which concern them in accordance with their age and maturity.

2. In all actions relating to children, whether taken by public authorities or private institutions, the child's best interests must be a primary consideration.

3. Every child shall have the right to maintain on a regular basis a personal relationship and direct contact with both his or her parents, unless that is contrary to his or her interests.

Article 85 The rights of the elderly

The Union recognises and respects the rights of the elderly to lead a life of dignity and independence and to participate in social and cultural life.

Article 86 Integration of persons with disabilities

The Union recognises and respects the right of persons with disabilities to benefit from measures designed to ensure their independence, social and occupational integration and participation in the life of the community.

Title IV
Solidarity

Article 87 Workers' right to information and consultation within the undertaking

Workers or their representatives must, at the appropriate levels, be guaranteed information and consultation in good time in the cases and under the conditions provided for by Union law and national laws and practices.

Article 88 Right of collective bargaining and action

Workers and employers, or their respective organisations, have, in accordance with Union law and national laws and practices, the right to negotiate and conclude collective agreements at the appropriate levels and, in cases of conflicts of interest, to take collective action to defend their interests, including strike action.

Article 89 Right of access to placement services

Everyone has the right of access to a free placement service.

Article 90 Protection in the event of unjustified dismissal

Every worker has the right to protection against unjustified dismissal, in accordance with Union law and national laws and practices.

Article 91 Fair and just working conditions

1. Every worker has the right to working conditions which respect his or her health, safety and dignity.
2. Every worker has the right to limitation of maximum working hours, to daily and weekly rest periods and to an annual period of paid leave.

Article 92 Prohibition of child labour and protection of young people at work

The employment of children is prohibited. The minimum age of admission to employment may not be lower than the minimum school-leaving age, without prejudice to such rules as may be more favourable to young people and except for limited derogations.

Young people admitted to work must have working conditions appropriate to their age and be protected against economic exploitation and any work likely to harm their safety, health or physical, mental, moral or social development or to interfere with their education.

Article 93 Family and professional life

1. The family shall enjoy legal, economic and social protection.

2. To reconcile family and professional life, everyone shall have the right to protection from dismissal for a reason connected with maternity and the right to paid maternity leave and to parental leave following the birth or adoption of a child.

Article 94 Social security and social assistance

1. The Union recognises and respects the entitlement to social security benefits and social services providing protection in cases such as maternity, illness, industrial accidents, dependency or old age, and in the case of loss of employment, in accordance with the rules laid down by Union law and national laws and practices.

2. Everyone residing and moving legally within the European Union is entitled to social security benefits and social advantages in accordance with Union law and national laws and practices.

3. In order to combat social exclusion and poverty, the Union recognises and respects the right to social and housing assistance so as to ensure a decent existence for all those who lack sufficient resources, in accordance with the rules laid down by Union law and national laws and practices.

Article 95 Health care

Everyone has the right of access to preventive health care and the right to benefit from medical treatment under the conditions established by national laws and practices. A high level of human health protection shall be ensured in the definition and implementation of all Union policies and activities.

Article 96 Access to services of general economic interest

The Union recognises and respects access to services of general economic interest as provided for in national laws and practices, in accordance with the Constitution, in order to promote the social and territorial cohesion of the Union.

Article 97 Environmental protection

A high level of environmental protection and the improvement of the quality of the environment must be integrated into the policies of the Union and ensured in accordance with the principle of sustainable development.

Article 98 Consumer protection

Union policies shall ensure a high level of consumer protection.

Title V
Citizens' Rights

Article 99 Right to vote and to stand as a candidate at elections to the European Parliament

1. Every citizen of the Union has the right to vote and to stand as a candidate at elections to the European Parliament in the Member State in which he or she resides, under the same conditions as nationals of that State.

2. Members of the European Parliament shall be elected by direct universal suffrage in a free and secret ballot.

Article 100 Right to vote and to stand as a candidate at municipal elections

Every citizen of the Union has the right to vote and to stand as a candidate at municipal elections in the Member State in which he or she resides under the same conditions as nationals of that State.

Article 101 Right to good administration

1. Every person has the right to have his or her affairs handled impartially, fairly and within a reasonable time by the institutions, bodies, offices and agencies of the Union.

2. This right includes:

(a) the right of every person to be heard, before any individual measure which would affect him or her adversely is taken;

(b) the right of every person to have access to his or her file, while respecting the legitimate interests of confidentiality and of professional and business secrecy;

(c) the obligation of the administration to give reasons for its decisions.

3. Every person has the right to have the Union make good any damage caused by its institutions or by its servants in the performance of their duties, in accordance with the general principles common to the laws of the Member States.

4. Every person may write to the institutions of the Union in one of the languages of the Constitution and must have an answer in the same language.

Article 102 Right of access to documents

Any citizen of the Union, and any natural or legal person residing or having its registered office in a Member State, has a right of access to documents of the institutions, bodies, offices and agencies of the Union, whatever their medium.

Article 103 European Ombudsman

Any citizen of the Union and any natural or legal person residing or having its registered office in a Member State has the right to refer to the European Ombudsman cases of maladministration in the activities of the institutions, bodies, offices or agencies of the Union, with the exception of the Court of Justice of the European Union acting in its judicial role.

Article 104 Right to petition

Any citizen of the Union and any natural or legal person residing or having its registered office in a Member State has the right to petition the European Parliament.

Article 105 Freedom of movement and of residence

1. Every citizen of the Union has the right to move and reside freely within the territory of the Member States.

2. Freedom of movement and residence may be granted, in accordance with the Constitution, to nationals of third countries legally resident in the territory of a Member State.

Article 106 Diplomatic and consular protection

Every citizen of the Union shall, in the territory of a third country in which the Member State of which he or she is a national is not represented, be entitled to protection by the diplomatic or consular authorities of any Member State, on the same conditions as the nationals of that Member State.

Title VI
Justice

Article 107 Right to an effective remedy and to a fair trial

Everyone whose rights and freedoms guaranteed by the law of the Union are violated has the right to an effective remedy before a tribunal in compliance with the conditions laid down in this Article.

Everyone is entitled to a fair and public hearing within a reasonable time by an independent and impartial tribunal previously established by law. Everyone shall have the possibility of being advised, defended and represented.

Legal aid shall be made available to those who lack sufficient resources insofar as such aid is necessary to ensure effective access to justice.

Article 108 Presumption of innocence and right of defence

1. Everyone who has been charged shall be presumed innocent until proved guilty according to law.

2. Respect for the rights of the defence of anyone who has been charged shall be guaranteed.

Article 109 Principles of legality and proportionality of criminal offences and penalties

1. No one shall be held guilty of any criminal offence on account of any act or omission which did not constitute a criminal offence under national law or international law at the time when it was committed. Nor shall a heavier penalty be imposed than that which was applicable at the time the criminal offence was committed. If, subsequent to the commission of a criminal offence, the law provides for a lighter penalty, that penalty shall be applicable.

2. This Article shall not prejudice the trial and punishment of any person for any act or omission which, at the time when it was committed, was criminal according to the general principles recognised by the community of nations.

3. The severity of penalties must not be disproportionate to the criminal offence.

Article 110 Right not to be tried or punished twice in criminal proceedings for the same criminal offence

No one shall be liable to be tried or punished again in criminal proceedings for an offence for which he or she has already been finally acquitted or convicted within the Union in accordance with the law.

Title VII

General Provisions Governing the Interpretation and Application of the Charter

Article 111 Field of application

1. The provisions of this Charter are addressed to the institutions, bodies, offices and agencies of the Union with due regard for the principle of subsidiarity and to the Member States only when they are implementing Union law. They shall therefore respect the rights, observe the principles and promote the application thereof in accordance with their respective powers and respecting the limits of the powers of the Union as conferred on it in the other Parts of the Constitution.

2. This Charter does not extend the field of application of Union law beyond the powers of the Union or establish any new power or task for the Union, or modify powers and tasks defined in the other Parts of the Constitution.

Article 112 Scope and interpretation of rights and principles

1. Any limitation on the exercise of the rights and freedoms recognised by this Charter must be provided for by law and respect the essence of those rights and freedoms. Subject to the principle of proportionality, limitations may be made only if they are necessary and genuinely meet objectives of general interest recognised by the Union or the need to protect the rights and freedoms of others.

2. Rights recognised by this Charter for which provision is made in other Parts of the Constitution shall be exercised under the conditions and within the limits defined by these relevant Parts.

3. Insofar as this Charter contains rights which correspond to rights guaranteed by the Convention for the Protection of Human Rights and Fundamental Freedoms, the meaning and scope of those rights shall be the same as those laid down by the said Convention. This provision shall not prevent Union law providing more extensive protection.

4. Insofar as this Charter recognises fundamental rights as they result from the constitutional traditions common to the Member States, those rights shall be interpreted in harmony with those traditions.

5. The provisions of this Charter which contain principles may be implemented by legislative and executive acts taken by institutions, bodies, offices and agencies of the Union, and by acts of Member States when they are implementing Union law, in the exercise of their respective powers. They shall be judicially cognisable only in the interpretation of such acts and in the ruling on their legality.

6. Full account shall be taken of national laws and practices as specified in this Charter.

7. The explanations drawn up as a way of providing guidance in the interpretation of the Charter of Fundamental Rights shall be given due regard by the courts of the Union and of the Member States.

Article 113 Level of protection

Nothing in this Charter shall be interpreted as restricting or adversely affecting human rights and fundamental freedoms as recognised, in their respective fields of application, by Union law and international law and by international agreements to which the Union or all the Member States are party, including the European Convention for the Protection of Human Rights and Fundamental Freedoms, and by the Member States' constitutions.

Article 114 Prohibition of abuse of rights

Nothing in this Charter shall be interpreted as implying any right to engage in any activity or to perform any act aimed at the destruction of any of the rights and freedoms recognised in this Charter or at their limitation to a greater extent than is provided for herein.

PART III

The Policies and Functioning of the Union

Title I
Provisions of General Application

Article 115

The Union shall ensure consistency between the policies and activities referred to in this Part, taking all of its objectives into account and in accordance with the principle of conferral of powers.

Article 116

In all the activities referred to in this Part, the Union shall aim to eliminate inequalities, and to promote equality, between women and men.

Article 117

In defining and implementing the policies and actions referred to in this Part, the Union shall take into account requirements linked to the promotion of a high level of employment, the guarantee of adequate social protection, the fight against social exclusion, and a high level of education, training and protection of human health.

Article 118

In defining and implementing the policies and activities referred to in this Part, the Union shall aim to combat discrimination based on sex, racial or ethnic origin, religion or belief, disability, age or sexual orientation.

Article 119

Environmental protection requirements must be integrated into the definition and implementation of the policies and activities referred to in this Part, in particular with a view to promoting sustainable development.

Article 120

Consumer protection requirements shall be taken into account in defining and implementing other Union policies and activities.

Article 121

In formulating and implementing the Union's agriculture, fisheries, transport, internal market, research and technological development and space policies, the Union and the Member States shall, since animals are sentient beings, pay full regard to the requirements of animal welfare, while respecting the legislative or administrative provisions and customs of Member States relating in particular to religious rites, cultural traditions and regional heritage.

Article 122

Without prejudice to Articles 5, 166, 167 and 238, and given the place occupied by services of general economic interest as services to which all in the Union attribute value as well as their role in promoting its social and territorial cohesion, the Union and the Member States, each within their respective competences and within the scope of application of the Constitution, shall take care that such services operate on the basis of principles and conditions, in particular economic and financial conditions, which enable them to fulfil their missions. European laws shall establish these principles and set these conditions without prejudice to the competence of Member States, in compliance with the Constitution, to provide, to commission and to fund such services.

Title II
Non-Discrimination and Citizenship

Article 123

European laws or framework laws may lay down rules to prohibit discrimination on grounds of nationality as referred to in Article 4(2).

Article 124

1. Without prejudice to the other provisions of the Constitution and within the limits of the powers assigned by it to the Union, a European law or framework law of the Council may establish the measures needed to combat discrimination based on sex, racial or ethnic origin, religion or belief, disability, age or sexual orientation. The Council shall act unanimously after obtaining the consent of the European Parliament.

2. By way of derogation from paragraph 1, European laws or framework laws may establish basic principles for Union incentive measures and define such measures, to support action taken by Member States in order to contribute to the achievement of the objectives referred to in paragraph 1, excluding any harmonisation of their laws and regulations.

Article 125

1. If action by the Union should prove necessary to facilitate the exercise of the right, referred to in

Article 10(2)(a), of every citizen of the Union to move and reside freely and the Constitution has not provided the necessary powers, European laws or framework laws may establish measures for that purpose.

2. For the same purposes as those referred to in paragraph 1 and if the Constitution has not provided the necessary powers, a European law or framework law of the Council may establish measures concerning passports, identity cards, residence permits or any other such document and measures concerning social security or social protection. The Council shall act unanimously after consulting the European Parliament.

Article 126

A European law or framework law of the Council shall determine the detailed arrangements for exercising the right, referred to in Article 10(2)(b), for every citizen of the Union to vote and to stand as a candidate in municipal elections and elections to the European Parliament in his or her Member State of residence without being a national of that State. The Council shall act unanimously after consulting the European Parliament. These arrangements may provide for derogations where warranted by problems specific to a Member State.

The right to vote and to stand as a candidate in elections to the European Parliament shall be exercised without prejudice to Article 330(1) and the measures adopted for its implementation.

Article 127

Member States shall adopt the necessary provisions to secure diplomatic and consular protection of citizens of the Union in third countries, as referred to in Article 10(2)(c).

Member States shall commence the international negotiations required to secure this protection.

A European law of the Council may establish the measures necessary to facilitate such protection. The Council shall act after consulting the European Parliament.

Article 128

The languages in which every citizen of the Union has the right to address the institutions or bodies under Article 10(2)(d), and to have an answer, are those listed in Article 448(1). The institutions and bodies referred to in Article 10(2)(d) are those listed in Articles 19(1), second subparagraph, 30, 31 and 32 and also the European Ombudsman.

Article 129

The Commission shall report to the European Parliament, to the Council and to the Economic and Social Committee every three years on the application of Article 10 and of this Title. This report shall take account of the development of the Union.

On the basis of this report, and without prejudice to the other provisions of the Constitution, a European law or framework law of the Council may add to the rights laid down in Article 10. The Council shall act unanimously after obtaining the consent of the European Parliament. The law or framework law concerned shall not enter into force until it is approved by the Member States in accordance with their respective constitutional requirements.

Title III
Internal Policies and Action

Chapter 1 - Internal Market

Section 1 - Establishment and Functioning of the Internal Market

Article 130

1. The Union shall adopt measures with the aim of establishing or ensuring the functioning of the internal market, in accordance with the relevant provisions of the Constitution.

2. The internal market shall comprise an area without internal frontiers in which the free movement of persons, services, goods and capital is ensured in accordance with the Constitution.

3. The Council, on a proposal from the Commission, shall adopt European regulations and decisions determining the guidelines and conditions necessary to ensure balanced progress in all the sectors concerned.

4. When drawing up its proposals for achieving the objectives set out in paragraphs 1 and 2, the Commission shall take into account the extent of the effort that certain economies showing differences in development will have to sustain for the establishment of the internal market and it may propose appropriate measures.

If these measures take the form of derogations, they must be of a temporary nature and must cause the least possible disturbance to the functioning of the internal market.

Article 131

Member States shall consult each other with a view to taking together the steps needed to prevent the functioning of the internal market being affected by measures which a Member State may be called upon to take in the event of serious internal disturbances affecting the maintenance of law and order, in the event of war, serious international tension constituting a threat of war, or in order to carry out obligations it has accepted for the purpose of maintaining peace and international security.

Article 132

If measures taken in the circumstances referred to in Articles 131 and 436 have the effect of distorting the conditions of competition in the internal market, the Commission shall, together with the Member State concerned, examine how these measures can be adjusted to the rules laid down in the Constitution.

By way of derogation from the procedure laid down in Articles 360 and 361, the Commission or any Member State may bring the matter directly before the Court of Justice if the Commission or Member State considers that another Member State is making improper use of the powers provided for in Articles 131 and 436. The Court of Justice shall give its ruling in camera.

Section 2 - Free movement of Persons and Services

Subsection 1 - Workers

Article 133

1. Workers shall have the right to move freely within the Union.

2. Any discrimination based on nationality between workers of the Member States as regards employment, remuneration and other conditions of work and employment shall be prohibited.

3. Workers shall have the right, subject to limitations justified on grounds of public policy, public security or public health:

(a) to accept offers of employment actually made;

(b) to move freely within the territory of Member States for this purpose;

(c) to stay in a Member State for the purpose of employment in accordance with the provisions governing the employment of nationals of that State laid down by law, regulation or administrative action;

(d) to remain in the territory of a Member State after having been employed in that State, subject to conditions which shall be embodied in European regulations adopted by the Commission.

4. This Article shall not apply to employment in the public service.

Article 134

European laws or framework laws shall establish the measures needed to bring about freedom of movement for workers, as defined in Article 133. They shall be adopted after consultation of the Economic and Social Committee.

Such European laws or framework laws shall aim, in particular, to:

(a) ensure close co-operation between national employment services;

(b) abolish those administrative procedures and practices and those qualifying periods in respect of eligibility for available employment, whether resulting from national legislation or from agreements previously concluded between Member States, the maintenance of which would form an obstacle to liberalisation of the movement of workers;

(c) abolish all such qualifying periods and other restrictions provided for either under national legislation or under agreements previously concluded between Member States as impose on workers of other Member States conditions regarding the free choice of employment other than those imposed on workers of the State concerned;

(d) set up appropriate machinery to bring offers of employment into touch with applications for employment and to facilitate the achievement of a balance between supply and demand in the employment market in such a way as to avoid serious threats to the standard of living and level of employment in the various regions and industries.

Article 135

Member States shall, within the framework of a joint programme, encourage the exchange of young workers.

Article 136

1. In the field of social security, European laws or framework laws shall establish such measures as are necessary to bring about freedom of movement for workers by making arrangements to secure for employed and self-employed migrant workers and their dependants:

(a) aggregation, for the purpose of acquiring and retaining the right to benefit and of calculating the amount of benefit, of all periods taken into account under the laws of the different countries;

(b) payment of benefits to persons resident in the territories of Member States.

2. Where a member of the Council considers that a draft European law or framework law referred to in paragraph 1 would affect fundamental aspects of its social security system, including its scope, cost or financial structure, or would affect the financial balance of that system, it may request that the matter be referred to the European Council. In that case, the procedure referred to in Article 396 shall be suspended. After discussion, the European Council shall, within four months of this suspension, either:

(a) refer the draft back to the Council, which shall terminate the suspension of the procedure referred to in Article 396, or

(b) request the Commission to submit a new proposal; in that case, the act originally proposed shall be deemed not to have been adopted.

Subsection 2 - Freedom of establishment

Article 137

Within the framework of this Subsection, restrictions on the freedom of establishment of nationals of a Member State in the territory of another Member State shall be prohibited. Such prohibition shall also apply to restrictions on the setting-up of agencies, branches or subsidiaries by nationals of any Member State established in the territory of any Member State.

Nationals of a Member State shall have the right, in the territory of another Member State, to take up and pursue activities as self-employed persons and to set up and manage undertakings, in particular companies or firms within the meaning of the second paragraph of Article 142, under the conditions laid down for its own nationals by the law of the Member State where such establishment is effected, subject to Section 4 relating to capital and payments.

Article 138

1. European framework laws shall establish measures to attain freedom of establishment as regards a particular activity. They shall be adopted after consultation of the Economic and Social Committee.

2. The European Parliament, the Council and the Commission shall carry out the duties devolving upon them under paragraph 1, in particular:

(a) by according, as a general rule, priority treatment to activities where freedom of establishment makes a particularly valuable contribution to the development of production and trade;

(b) by ensuring close co-operation between the competent authorities in the Member States in order to ascertain the particular situation within the Union of the various activities concerned;

(c) by abolishing those administrative procedures and practices, whether resulting from national legislation or from agreements previously concluded between Member States, the maintenance of which would form an obstacle to freedom of establishment;

(d) by ensuring that workers from one Member State employed in the territory of another Member State may remain in that territory for the purpose of taking up activities therein as self-employed persons, where they satisfy the conditions which they would be required to satisfy if they were entering that State at the time when they intended to take up such activities;

(e) by enabling a national of one Member State to acquire and use land and buildings situated in the territory of another Member State, insofar as this does not conflict with the principles laid down in Article 227(2);

(f) by effecting the progressive abolition of restrictions on freedom of establishment in every branch of activity under consideration, both as regards the conditions for setting up agencies, branches or subsidiaries in the territory of a Member State and as regards the conditions governing the entry of personnel belonging to the main establishment into managerial or supervisory posts in such agencies, branches or subsidiaries;

(g) by co-ordinating to the necessary extent the safeguards which, for the protection of the interests of members and others, are required by Member States of companies or firms within the meaning of the second paragraph of Article 142 with a view to making such safeguards equivalent throughout the Union;

(h) by satisfying themselves that the conditions of establishment are not distorted by aids granted by Member States.

Article 139

This Subsection shall not apply, so far as any given Member State is concerned, to activities which in that State are connected, even occasionally, with the exercise of official authority European laws or framework laws may exclude certain activities from application of this Subsection.

Article 140

1. This Subsection and measures adopted in pursuance thereof shall not prejudice the applicability of provisions laid down by law, regulation or administrative action in Member States providing for special treatment for foreign nationals on grounds of public policy, public security or public health.

2. European framework laws shall co-ordinate the national provisions referred to in paragraph 1.

Article 141

1. European framework laws shall make it easier for persons to take up and pursue activities as selfemployed persons. They shall cover:

(a) the mutual recognition of diplomas, certificates and other evidence of formal qualifications;

(b) the co-ordination of the provisions laid down by law, regulation or administrative action in Member States concerning the taking-up and pursuit of activities as self-employed persons.

2. In the case of the medical and allied and pharmaceutical professions, the progressive abolition of restrictions shall be dependent upon co-ordination of the conditions for the exercise of such professions in the various Member States.

Article 142

Companies or firms formed in accordance with the law of a Member State and having their registered office, central administration or principal place of business within the Union shall, for the purposes of this Subsection, be treated in the same way as natural persons who are nationals of Member States.

'Companies or firms' means companies or firms constituted under civil or commercial law, including co-operative societies, and other legal persons governed by public or private law, save for those which are non-profit-making.

Article 143

Member States shall accord nationals of the other Member States the same treatment as their own nationals as regards participation in the capital of companies or firms within the meaning of the second paragraph of Article 142, without prejudice to the application of the other provisions of the Constitution.

Subsection 3 - Freedom to provide services

Article 144

Within the framework of this Subsection, restrictions on freedom to provide services within the Union shall be prohibited in respect of nationals of Member States who are established in a Member State other than that of the person for whom the services are intended.

European laws or framework laws may extend this Subsection to service providers who are nationals of a third State and who are established within the Union.

Article 145

Services shall be considered to be 'services' for the purposes of the Constitution where they are normally provided for remuneration, insofar as they are not governed by the provisions relating to freedom of movement for persons, goods and capital. 'Services' shall in particular include:

(a) activities of an industrial character;

(b) activities of a commercial character;

(c) activities of craftsmen;

(d) activities of the professions.

Without prejudice to Subsection 2 relating to freedom of establishment, the person providing a service may, in order to do so, temporarily pursue his or her activity in the Member State where the service is provided, under the same conditions as are imposed by that State on its own nationals.

Article 146

1. Freedom to provide services in the field of transport shall be governed by Section 7 of Chapter III relating to transport.

2. The liberalisation of banking and insurance services connected with movements of capital shall be effected in step with the liberalisation of movement of capital.

Article 147

1. European framework laws shall establish measures to achieve the liberalisation of a specific service. They shall be adopted after consultation of the Economic and Social Committee.

2. European framework laws referred to in paragraph 1 shall as a general rule give priority to those services which directly affect production costs or the liberalisation of which helps to promote trade in goods.

Article 148

The Member States shall endeavour to undertake liberalisation of services beyond the extent required by the European framework laws adopted pursuant to Article 147(1), if their general economic situation and the situation of the economic sector concerned so permit. To this end, the Commission shall make recommendations to the Member States concerned.

Article 149

As long as restrictions on freedom to provide services have not been abolished, the Member States shall apply such restrictions without distinction on grounds of nationality or of residence to all persons providing services within the meaning of the first paragraph of Article 144.

Article 150

Articles 139 to 142 shall apply to the matters covered by this Subsection.

Section 3 - Free Movement of Goods

Subsection 1 Customs union

Article 151

1. The Union shall comprise a customs union which shall cover all trade in goods and which shall involve the prohibition between Member States of cus-

toms duties on imports and exports and of all charges having equivalent effect, and the adoption of a common customs tariff in their relations with third countries.

2. Paragraph 4 and Subsection 3 on the prohibition of quantitative restrictions shall apply to products originating in Member States and to products coming from third countries which are in free circulation in Member States.

3. Products coming from a third country shall be considered to be in free circulation in a Member State if the import formalities have been complied with and any customs duties or charges having equivalent effect which are payable have been levied in that Member State, and if they have not benefited from a total or partial drawback of such duties or charges.

4. Customs duties on imports and exports and charges having equivalent effect shall be prohibited between Member States. This prohibition shall also apply to customs duties of a fiscal nature.

5. The Council, on a proposal from the Commission, shall adopt the European regulations and decisions fixing Common Customs Tariff duties.

6. In carrying out the tasks entrusted to it under this Article the Commission shall be guided by:

(a) the need to promote trade between Member States and third countries;

(b) developments in conditions of competition within the Union insofar as they lead to an improvement in the competitive capacity of undertakings;

(c) the requirements of the Union as regards the supply of raw materials and semi-finished goods; in this connection the Commission shall take care to avoid distorting conditions of competition between Member States in respect of finished goods;

(d) the need to avoid serious disturbances in the economies of Member States and to ensure rational development of production and an expansion of consumption within the Union.

Subsection 2 - Customs co-operation

Article 152

Within the scope of application of the Constitution, European laws or framework laws shall establish measures in order to strengthen customs co-operation between Member States and between them and the Commission.

Subsection 3 - Prohibition of quantitative restrictions

Article 153

Quantitative restrictions on imports and exports and all measures having equivalent effect shall be prohibited between Member States.

Article 154

Article 153 shall not preclude prohibitions or restrictions on imports, exports or goods in transit justified on grounds of public morality, public policy or public security; the protection of health and life of humans, animals or plants; the protection of national treasures possessing artistic, historic or archaeological value; or the protection of industrial and commercial property. Such prohibitions or restrictions shall not, however, constitute a means of arbitrary discrimination or a disguised restriction on trade between Member States.

Article 155

1. Member States shall adjust any State monopolies of a commercial character so as to ensure that no discrimination regarding the conditions under which goods are procured and marketed exists between nationals of Member States.

This Article shall apply to any body through which a Member State, in law or in fact, either directly or indirectly supervises, determines or appreciably influences imports or exports between Member States. It shall likewise apply to monopolies delegated by the State to others.

2. Member States shall refrain from introducing any new measure which is contrary to the principles laid down in paragraph 1 or which restricts the scope of the Articles dealing with the prohibition of customs duties and quantitative restrictions between Member States.

3. If a State monopoly of a commercial character has rules which are designed to make it easier to dispose of agricultural products or obtain for them the best return, steps should be taken in applying this Article to ensure equivalent safeguards for the employment and standard of living of the producers concerned.

Section 4 - Capital and Payments

Article 156

Within the framework of this Section, restrictions both on the movement of capital and on payments between Member States and between Member States and third countries shall be prohibited.

Article 157

1. Article 156 shall be without prejudice to the application to third countries of any restrictions which existed on 31 December 1993 under national or Union law adopted in respect of the movement of capital to or from third countries involving direct investment — including investment in real estate, establishment, the provision of financial services or the admission of securities to capital markets. With regard to restrictions which exist under national law in Estonia and Hungary, the date in question shall be 31 December 1999.

2. European laws or framework laws shall enact measures on the movement of capital to or from third countries involving direct investment — including investment in real estate, establishment, the provision of financial services or the admission of securities to capital markets.

The European Parliament and the Council shall endeavour to achieve the objective of free movement of capital between Member States and third countries to the greatest extent possible and without prejudice to other provisions of the Constitution.

3. Notwithstanding paragraph 2, only a European law or framework law of the Council may enact measures which constitute a step backwards in Union law

as regards the liberalisation of the movement of capital to or from third countries. The Council shall act unanimously after consulting the European Parliament.

Article 158

1. Article 156 shall be without prejudice to the right of Member States:

(a) to apply the relevant provisions of their tax law which distinguish between taxpayers who are not in the same situation with regard to their place of residence or with regard to the place where their capital is invested;

(b) to take all requisite measures to prevent infringements of national provisions laid down by law or regulation, in particular in the field of taxation and the prudential supervision of financial institutions, or to lay down procedures for the declaration of capital movements for purposes of administrative or statistical information, or to take measures which are justified on grounds of public policy or public security.

2. This Section shall be without prejudice to the applicability of restrictions on the right of establishment which are compatible with the Constitution.

3. The measures and procedures referred to in paragraphs 1 and 2 shall not constitute a means of arbitrary discrimination or a disguised restriction on the free movement of capital and payments as defined in Article 156.

4. In the absence of a European law or framework law provided for in Article 157(3), the Commission or, in the absence of a European decision of the Commission within three months from the request of the Member State concerned, the Council, may adopt a European decision stating that restrictive tax measures adopted by a Member State concerning one or more third countries are to be considered compatible with the Constitution insofar as they are justified by one of the objectives of the Union and compatible with the proper functioning of the internal market. The Council shall act unanimously on application by a Member State.

Article 159

Where, in exceptional circumstances, movements of capital to or from third countries cause, or threaten to cause, serious difficulties for the functioning of economic and monetary union, the Council, on a proposal from the Commission, may adopt European regulations or decisions introducing safeguard measures with regard to third countries for a period not exceeding six months if such measures are strictly necessary. It shall act after consulting the European Central Bank.

Article 160

Where necessary to achieve the objectives set out in Article 257, as regards preventing and combating terrorism and related activities, European laws shall define a framework for administrative measures with regard to capital movements and payments, such as the freezing of funds, financial assets or economic gains belonging to, or owned or held by, natural or legal persons, groups or non-State entities.

The Council, on a proposal from the Commission, shall adopt European regulations or European decisions in order to implement the European laws referred to in the first paragraph. The acts referred to in this Article shall include necessary provisions on legal safeguards.

Section 5 - Rules on Competition

Subsection 1 - Rules applying to undertakings

Article 161

1. The following shall be prohibited as incompatible with the internal market: all agreements between undertakings, decisions by associations of undertakings and concerted practices which may affect trade between Member States and which have as their object or effect the prevention, restriction or distortion of competition within the internal market, and in particular those which:

(a) directly or indirectly fix purchase or selling prices or any other trading conditions;

(b) limit or control production, markets, technical development, or investment;

(c) share markets or sources of supply;

(d) apply dissimilar conditions to equivalent transactions with other trading parties, thereby placing them at a competitive disadvantage,

(e) make the conclusion of contracts subject to acceptance by the other parties of supplementary obligations which, by their nature or according to commercial usage, have no connection with the subject of such contracts.

2. Any agreements or decisions prohibited pursuant to this Article shall be automatically void.

3. Paragraph 1 may, however, be declared inapplicable in the case of:

— any agreement or category of agreements between undertakings,

— any decision or category of decisions by associations of undertakings,

— any concerted practice or category of concerted practices, which contributes to improving the production or distribution of goods or to promoting technical or economic progress, while allowing consumers a fair share of the resulting benefit, and which does not:

(a) impose on the undertakings concerned restrictions which are not indispensable to the attainment of these objectives;

(b) afford such undertakings the possibility of eliminating competition in respect of a substantial part of the products in question.

Article 162

Any abuse by one or more undertakings of a dominant position within the internal market or in a substantial part of it shall be prohibited as incompatible with the internal market insofar as it may affect trade between Member States.

Such abuse may, in particular, consist in:

(a) directly or indirectly imposing unfair purchase or selling prices or other unfair trading conditions;

(b) limiting production, markets or technical development to the prejudice of consumers;

(c) applying dissimilar conditions to equivalent transactions with other trading parties, thereby placing them at a competitive disadvantage;

(d) making the conclusion of contracts subject to acceptance by the other parties of supplementary obligations which, by their nature or according to commercial usage, have no connection with the subject of such contracts.

Article 163

The Council, on a proposal from the Commission, shall adopt the European regulations to give effect to the principles set out in Articles 161 and 162. It shall act after consulting the European Parliament.

Such regulations shall be designed in particular:

(a) to ensure compliance with the prohibitions laid down in Article 161(1) and in Article 162 by making provision for fines and periodic penalty payments;

(b) to lay down detailed rules for the application of Article 161(3), taking into account the need to ensure effective supervision on the one hand, and to simplify administration to the greatest possible extent on the other;

(c) to define, if need be, in the various branches of the economy, the scope of Articles 161 and 162;

(d) to define the respective functions of the Commission and of the Court of Justice of the European Union in applying the provisions laid down in this paragraph;

(e) to determine the relationship between Member States' laws and this Subsection as well as the European regulations adopted pursuant to this Article.

Article 164

Until the entry into force of the European regulations adopted pursuant to Article 163, the authorities in Member States shall rule on the admissibility of agreements, decisions and concerted practices and on abuse of a dominant position in the internal market in accordance with their national law and Article 161, in particular paragraph 3, and Article 162.

Article 165

1. Without prejudice to Article 164, the Commission shall ensure the application of the principles set out in Articles 161 and 162. On application by a Member State or on its own initiative, and in co-operation with the competent authorities in the Member States, which shall give it their assistance, the Commission shall investigate cases of suspected infringement of these principles.

If it finds that there has been an infringement, it shall propose appropriate measures to bring it to an end.

2. If the infringement referred to in paragraph 1 is not brought to an end, the Commission shall adopt a reasoned European decision recording the infringement of the principles. The Commission may publish its decision and authorise Member States to take the measures, the conditions and details of which it shall determine, needed to remedy the situation.

3. The Commission may adopt European regulations relating to the categories of agreement in respect of which the Council has adopted a European regulation pursuant to Article 163, second paragraph, (b).

Article 166

1. In the case of public undertakings and undertakings to which Member States grant special or exclusive rights, Member States shall neither enact nor maintain in force any measure contrary to the Constitution, in particular Article 4(2) and Articles 161 to 169.

2. Undertakings entrusted with the operation of services of general economic interest or having the character of an income-producing monopoly shall be subject to the provisions of the Constitution, in particular to the rules on competition, insofar as the application of such provisions does not obstruct the performance, in law or in fact, of the particular tasks assigned to them. The development of trade must not be affected to such an extent as would be contrary to the Union's interests.

3. The Commission shall ensure the application of this Article and shall, where necessary, adopt appropriate European regulations or decisions.

Subsection 2 - Aid granted by Member States

Article 167

1. Save as otherwise provided in the Constitution, any aid granted by a Member State or through State resources in any form whatsoever which distorts or threatens to distort competition by favouring certain undertakings or the production of certain goods shall, insofar as it affects trade between Member States, be incompatible with the internal market.

2. The following shall be compatible with the internal market:

(a) aid having a social character, granted to individual consumers, provided that such aid is granted without discrimination related to the origin of the products concerned;

(b) aid to make good the damage caused by natural disasters or exceptional occurrences;

(c) aid granted to the economy of certain areas of the Federal Republic of Germany affected by the division of Germany, insofar as such aid is required in order to compensate for the economic disadvantages caused by that division. Five years after the entry into force of the Treaty establishing a Constitution for Europe, the Council, acting on a proposal from the Commission, may adopt a European decision repealing this point.

3. The following may be considered to be compatible with the internal market:

(a) aid to promote the economic development of areas where the standard of living is abnormally low or where there is serious underemployment, and of the regions referred to in Article 424, in view of their structural, economic and social situation;

(b) aid to promote the execution of an important project of common European interest or to remedy a serious disturbance in the economy of a Member State;

(c) aid to facilitate the development of certain economic activities or of certain economic areas, where such aid does not adversely affect trading conditions to an extent contrary to the common interest;

(d) aid to promote culture and heritage conservation where such aid does not affect trading conditions and competition in the Union to an extent that is contrary to the common interest;

(e) such other categories of aid as may be specified by European regulations or decisions adopted by the Council on a proposal from the Commission.

Article 168

1. The Commission, in co-operation with Member States, shall keep under constant review all systems of aid existing in those States. It shall propose to the latter any appropriate measures required by the progressive development or by the functioning of the internal market.

2. If, after giving notice to the parties concerned to submit their comments, the Commission finds that aid granted by a Member State or through State resources is not compatible with the internal market having regard to Article 167, or that such aid is being misused, it shall adopt a European decision requiring the Member State concerned to abolish or alter such aid within a period of time to be determined by the Commission.

If the Member State concerned does not comply with this European decision within the prescribed time, the Commission or any other interested Member State may, in derogation from Articles 360 and 361, refer the matter to the Court of Justice of the European Union directly.

On application by a Member State, the Council may adopt unanimously a European decision that aid which that State is granting or intends to grant shall be considered to be compatible with the internal market, in derogation from Article 167 or from European regulations provided for in Article 169, if such a decision is justified by exceptional circumstances. If, as regards the aid in question, the Commission has already initiated the procedure provided for in the first subparagraph of this paragraph, the fact that the Member State concerned has made its application to the Council shall have the effect of suspending that procedure until the Council has made its attitude known. If, however, the Council has not made its attitude known within three months of the said application being made, the Commission shall act.

3. The Commission shall be informed by the Member States, in sufficient time to enable it to submit its comments, of any plans to grant or alter aid. If it considers that any such plan is not compatible with the internal market having regard to Article 167, it shall without delay initiate the procedure provided for in paragraph 2 of this Article. The Member State concerned shall not put its proposed measures into effect until this procedure has resulted in a final decision.

4. The Commission may adopt European regulations relating to the categories of State aid that the Council has, pursuant to Article 169, determined may be exempted from the procedure provided for by paragraph 3 of this Article.

Article 169

The Council, on a proposal from the Commission, may adopt European regulations for the application of Articles 167 and 168 and for determining in particular the conditions in which Article 168(3) shall apply and the categories of aid exempted from the procedure provided for in Article 168(3). It shall act after consulting the European Parliament.

Section 6 - Fiscal Provisions

Article 170

1. No Member State shall impose, directly or indirectly, on the products of other Member States any internal taxation of any kind in excess of that imposed directly or indirectly on similar domestic products. Furthermore, no Member State shall impose on the products of other Member States any internal taxation of such a nature as to afford indirect protection to other products.

2. Where products are exported by a Member State to the territory of another Member State, any repayment of internal taxation shall not exceed the internal taxation imposed on them whether directly or indirectly.

3. In the case of charges other than turnover taxes, excise duties and other forms of indirect taxation, remissions and repayments in respect of exports to other Member States may not be granted and countervailing charges in respect of imports from Member States may not be imposed unless the provisions contemplated have been previously approved for a limited period by a European decision adopted by the Council on a proposal from the Commission.

Article 171

A European law or framework law of the Council shall establish measures for the harmonisation of legislation concerning turnover taxes, excise duties and other forms of indirect taxation provided that such harmonisation is necessary to ensure the establishment and the functioning of the internal market and to avoid distortion of competition. The Council shall act unanimously after consulting the European Parliament and the Economic and Social Committee.

Section 7 - Common Provisions

Article 172

1. Save where otherwise provided in the Constitution, this Article shall apply for the achievement of the objectives set out in Article 130. European laws or framework laws shall establish measures for the approximation of the provisions laid down by law, regulation or administrative action in Member States which have as their object the establishment and functioning of the internal market. Such laws shall be adopted after consultation of the Economic and Social Committee.

2. Paragraph 1 shall not apply to fiscal provisions, to those relating to the free movement of persons or to those relating to the rights and interests of employed persons.

3. The Commission, in its proposals submitted under paragraph 1 concerning health, safety, environmental protection and consumer protection, shall take as a base a high level of protection, taking account in particular of any new development based on scientific facts. Within their respective powers, the European Parliament and the Council shall also seek to achieve this objective.

4. If, after the adoption of a harmonisation measure by means of a European law or framework law or by means of a European regulation of the Commission,

a Member State deems it necessary to maintain national provisions on grounds of major needs referred to in Article 154, or relating to the protection of the environment or the working environment, it shall notify the Commission of these provisions as well as the grounds for maintaining them.

5. Moreover, without prejudice to paragraph 4, if, after the adoption of a harmonisation measure by means of a European law or framework law or by means of a European regulation of the Commission, a Member State deems it necessary to introduce national provisions based on new scientific evidence relating to the protection of the environment or the working environment on grounds of a problem specific to that Member State arising after the adoption of the harmonisation measure, it shall notify the Commission of the envisaged provisions and the reasons for them.

6. The Commission shall, within six months of the notifications referred to in paragraphs 4 and 5, adopt a European decision approving or rejecting the national provisions involved after having verified whether or not they are a means of arbitrary discrimination or a disguised restriction on trade between Member States and whether or not they constitute an obstacle to the functioning of the internal market.

In the absence of a decision by the Commission within this period the national provisions referred to in paragraphs 4 and 5 shall be deemed to have been approved.

When justified by the complexity of the matter and in the absence of danger to human health, the Commission may notify the Member State concerned that the period referred to in this paragraph will be extended for a further period of up to six months.

7. When, pursuant to paragraph 6, a Member State is authorised to maintain or introduce national provisions derogating from a harmonisation measure, the Commission shall immediately examine whether to propose an adaptation to that measure.

8. When a Member State raises a specific problem on public health in a field which has been the subject of prior harmonisation measures, it shall bring it to the attention of the Commission which shall immediately examine whether to propose appropriate measures.

9. By way of derogation from the procedure laid down in Articles 360 and 361, the Commission and any Member State may bring the matter directly before the Court of Justice of the European Union if it considers that another Member State is making improper use of the powers provided for in this Article.

10. The harmonisation measures referred to in this Article shall, in appropriate cases, include a safeguard clause authorising the Member States to take, for one or more of the non-economic reasons referred to in Article 154, provisional measures subject to a Union control procedure.

Article 173

Without prejudice to Article 172, a European framework law of the Council shall establish measures for the approximation of such laws, regulations or administrative provisions of the Member States as directly affect the establishment or functioning of the internal market. The Council shall act unanimously after consulting the European Parliament and the Economic and Social Committee.

Article 174

Where the Commission finds that a difference between the provisions laid down by law, regulation or administrative action in Member States is distorting the conditions of competition in the internal market and that the resultant distortion needs to be eliminated, it shall consult the Member States concerned.

If such consultation does not result in agreement, European framework laws shall establish the measures necessary to eliminate the distortion in question. Any other appropriate measures provided for in the Constitution may be adopted.

Article 175

1. Where there is reason to fear that the adoption or amendment of a provision laid down by law, regulation or administrative action of a Member State may cause distortion within the meaning of Article 174, a Member State desiring to proceed therewith shall consult the Commission. After consulting the Member States, the Commission shall address to the Member States concerned a recommendation on such measures as may be appropriate to avoid the distortion in question.

2. If a Member State desiring to introduce or amend its own provisions does not comply with the recommendation addressed to it by the Commission, other Member States shall not be required, pursuant to Article 174, to amend their own provisions in order to eliminate such distortion. If the Member State which has ignored the recommendation of the Commission causes distortion detrimental only to itself, Article 174 shall not apply.

Article 176

In the context of the establishment and functioning of the internal market, European laws or framework laws shall establish measures for the creation of European intellectual property rights to provide uniform intellectual property rights protection throughout the Union and for the setting up of centralised Union-wide authorisation, co-ordination and supervision arrangements.

A European law of the Council shall establish language arrangements for the European intellectual property rights. The Council shall act unanimously after consulting the European Parliament.

Chapter II - Economic and Monetary Policy

Article 177

For the purposes set out in Article I-3, the activities of the Member States and the Union shall include, as provided in the Constitution, the adoption of an economic policy which is based on the close co-ordination of Member States' economic policies, on the internal market and on the definition of common objectives, and conducted in accordance with the principle of an open market economy with free competition.

Concurrently with the foregoing, and as provided in the Constitution and in accordance with the procedures set out therein, these activities shall include a single currency, the euro, and the definition and conduct of a single monetary policy and exchange-rate policy, the primary objective of both of which shall be to maintain price stability and, without prejudice to this objective, to support general economic policies in the Union, in accordance with the principle of an open market economy with free competition.

These activities of the Member States and the Union shall entail compliance with the following guiding principles: stable prices, sound public finances and monetary conditions and a stable balance of payments.

Section 1 - Economic Policy

Article 178

Member States shall conduct their economic policies in order to contribute to the achievement of the Union's objectives, as defined in Article I-3, and in the context of the broad guidelines referred to in Article 179(2). The Member States and the Union shall act in accordance with the principle of an open market economy with free competition, favouring an efficient allocation of resources, and in compliance with the principles set out in Article 177.

Article 179

1. Member States shall regard their economic policies as a matter of common concern and shall co-ordinate them within the Council, in accordance with Article 178.

2. The Council, on a recommendation from the Commission, shall formulate a draft for the broad guidelines of the economic policies of the Member States and of the Union, and shall report its findings to the European Council.

The European Council, on the basis of the report from the Council, shall discuss a conclusion on the broad guidelines of the economic policies of the Member States and of the Union. On the basis of this conclusion, the Council shall adopt a recommendation setting out these broad guidelines. It shall inform the European Parliament of its recommendation.

3. In order to ensure closer co-ordination of economic policies and sustained convergence of the economic performances of the Member States, the Council, on the basis of reports submitted by the Commission, shall monitor economic developments in each of the Member States and in the Union, as well as the consistency of economic policies with the broad guidelines referred to in paragraph 2, and shall regularly carry out an overall assessment.

For the purpose of this multilateral surveillance, Member States shall forward information to the Commission on important measures taken by them in the field of their economic policy and such other information as they deem necessary.

4. Where it is established, under the procedure referred to in paragraph 3, that the economic policies of a Member State are not consistent with the broad guidelines referred to in paragraph 2 or that they risk jeopardising the proper functioning of economic and monetary union, the Commission may address a warning to the Member State concerned. The Council, on a recommendation from the Commission, may address the necessary recommendations to the

Member State concerned. The Council, on a proposal from the Commission, may decide to make its recommendations public.

Within the scope of this paragraph, the Council shall act without taking into account the vote of the member of the Council representing the Member State concerned.

A qualified majority shall be defined as at least 55 % of the other members of the Council, representing Member States comprising at least 65 % of the population of the participating Member States.

A blocking minority must include at least the minimum number of these other Council members representing more than 35 % of the population of the participating Member States, plus one member, failing which the qualified majority shall be deemed attained.

5. The President of the Council and the Commission shall report to the European Parliament on the results of multilateral surveillance. The President of the Council may be invited to appear before the competent committee of the European Parliament if the Council has made its recommendations public.

6. European laws may lay down detailed rules for the multilateral surveillance procedure referred to in paragraphs 3 and 4.

Article 180

1. Without prejudice to any other procedures provided for in the Constitution, the Council, on a proposal from the Commission, may adopt a European decision laying down measures appropriate to the economic situation, in particular if severe difficulties arise in the supply of certain products.

2. Where a Member State is in difficulties or is seriously threatened with severe difficulties caused by natural disasters or exceptional occurrences beyond its control, the Council, on a proposal from the Commission, may adopt a European decision granting, under certain conditions, Union financial assistance to the Member State concerned. The President of the Council shall inform the European Parliament of the decision adopted.

Article 181

1. Overdraft facilities or any other type of credit facility with the European Central Bank or with the central banks of the Member States (hereinafter referred to as 'national central banks') in favour of Union institutions, bodies, offices or agencies, central governments, regional, local or other public authorities, other bodies governed by public law, or public undertakings of Member States shall be prohibited, as shall the purchase directly from them by the European Central Bank or national central banks of debt instruments.

2. Paragraph 1 shall not apply to publicly owned credit institutions which, in the context of the supply of reserves by central banks, shall be given the same treatment by national central banks and the European Central Bank as private credit institutions.

Article 182

Any measure or provision, not based on prudential considerations, establishing privileged access by Union institutions, bodies, offices or agencies, central governments, regional, local or other public authorities, other bodies governed by public law, or public undertakings of Member States to financial institutions shall be prohibited.

Article 183

1. The Union shall not be liable for or assume the commitments of central governments, regional, local or other public authorities, other bodies governed by public law, or public undertakings of any Member State, without prejudice to mutual financial guarantees for the joint execution of a specific project. A Member State shall not be liable for or assume the commitments of central governments, regional, local or other public authorities, other bodies governed by public law, or public undertakings of another Member State, without prejudice to mutual financial guarantees for the joint execution of a specific project.

2. The Council, on a proposal from the Commission, may adopt European regulations or decisions specifying definitions for the application of the prohibitions laid down in Articles 181 and 182 and in this Article. It shall act after consulting the European Parliament.

Article 184

1. Member States shall avoid excessive government deficits.

2. The Commission shall monitor the development of the budgetary situation and of the stock of government debt in the Member States in order to identify gross errors. In particular it shall examine compliance with budgetary discipline on the basis of the following two criteria:

(a) whether the ratio of the planned or actual government deficit to gross domestic product exceeds a reference value, unless:

(i) either the ratio has declined substantially and continuously and reached a level that comes close to the reference value, or

(ii) alternatively, the excess over the reference value is only exceptional and temporary and the ratio remains close to the reference value;

(b) whether the ratio of government debt to gross domestic product exceeds a reference value, unless the ratio is diminishing sufficiently and approaching the reference value at a satisfactory pace.

The reference values are specified in the Protocol on the excessive deficit procedure.

3. If a Member State does not fulfil the requirements under one or both of these criteria, the Commission shall prepare a report. The Commission's report shall also take into account whether the government deficit exceeds government investment expenditure and take into account all other relevant factors, including the medium-term economic and budgetary position of the Member State.

The Commission may also prepare a report if, notwithstanding the fulfillment of the requirements under the criteria, it is of the opinion that there is a risk of an excessive deficit in a Member State.

4. The Economic and Financial Committee set up under Article 192 shall formulate an opinion on the Commission's report.

5. If the Commission considers that an excessive deficit in a Member State exists or may occur, it shall address an opinion to the Member State concerned and shall inform the Council accordingly.

6. The Council shall, on a proposal from the Commission, having considered any observations which the Member State concerned may wish to make and after an overall assessment, decide whether an excessive deficit exists. In that case it shall adopt, without undue delay, on a recommendation from the Commission, recommendations addressed to the Member State concerned with a view to bringing that situation to an end within a given period. Subject to paragraph 8, those recommendations shall not be made public. Within the scope of this paragraph, the Council shall act without taking into account the vote of the member of the Council representing the Member State concerned.

A qualified majority shall be defined as at least 55 % of the other members of the Council, representing Member States comprising at least 65 % of the population of the participating Member States.

A blocking minority must include at least the minimum number of these other Council members representing more than 35 % of the population of the participating Member States, plus one member, failing which the qualified majority shall be deemed attained.

7. The Council, on a recommendation from the Commission, shall adopt the European decisions and recommendations referred to in paragraphs 8 to 11.

It shall act without taking into account the vote of the member of the Council representing the Member State concerned.

A qualified majority shall be defined as at least 55 % of the other members of the Council, representing Member States comprising at least 65 % of the population of the participating Member States.

A blocking minority must include at least the minimum number of these other Council members representing more than 35 % of the population of the participating Member States, plus one member, failing which the qualified majority shall be deemed attained.

8. Where it adopts a European decision establishing that there has been no effective action in response to its recommendations within the period laid down, the Council may make its recommendations public.

9. If a Member State persists in failing to put the Council's recommendations into practice, the Council may adopt a European decision giving notice to the Member State to take, within a specified time-limit, measures for the deficit reduction which the Council judges necessary to remedy the situation.

In such a case, the Council may request the Member State concerned to submit reports in accordance with a specific timetable in order to examine the adjustment efforts of that Member State.

10. As long as a Member State fails to comply with a European decision adopted in accordance with paragraph 9, the Council may decide to apply or, as the case may be, intensify one or more of the following measures:

(a) require the Member State concerned to publish additional information, to be specified by the Council, before issuing bonds and securities;

(b) invite the European Investment Bank to reconsider its lending policy towards the Member State concerned;

(c) require the Member State concerned to make a non-interest-bearing deposit of an appropriate size with the Union until the Council considers that the excessive deficit has been corrected;

(d) impose fines of an appropriate size.

The President of the Council shall inform the European Parliament of the measures adopted.

11. The Council shall repeal some or all of the measures referred to in paragraph 6 and paragraphs 8, 9 and 10 if it considers the excessive deficit in the Member State concerned to have been corrected. If the Council has previously made public recommendations, it shall state publicly, as soon as the European decision referred to in paragraph 8 has been repealed, that there is no longer an excessive deficit in the Member State concerned.

12. The rights to bring actions provided for in Articles 360 and 361 shall not be exercised within the framework of paragraphs 1 to 6 or paragraphs 8 and 9.

13. Further provisions relating to the implementation of the procedure laid down in this Article are set out in the Protocol on the excessive deficit procedure.

A European law of the Council shall lay down the appropriate measures to replace the said Protocol. The Council shall act unanimously after consulting the European Parliament and the European Central Bank.

Subject to the other provisions of this paragraph, the Council, on a proposal from the Commission, shall adopt European regulations or decisions laying down detailed rules and definitions for the application of the said Protocol. It shall act after consulting the European Parliament.

Section 2 - Monetary Policy

Article 185

1. The primary objective of the European System of Central Banks shall be to maintain price stability. Without prejudice to this objective, the European System of Central Banks shall support the general economic policies in the Union in order to contribute to the achievement of its objectives as laid down in Article 3. The European System of Central Banks shall act in accordance with the principle of an open market economy with free competition, favouring an efficient allocation of resources, and in compliance with the principles set out in Article 177.

2. The basic tasks to be carried out through the European System of Central Banks shall be:

(a) to define and implement the Union's monetary policy;

(b) to conduct foreign-exchange operations consistent with Article 326;

(c) to hold and manage the official foreign reserves of the Member States;

(d) to promote the smooth operation of payment systems.

3. Paragraph 2(c) shall be without prejudice to the holding and management by the governments of Member States of foreign-exchange working balances.

4. The European Central Bank shall be consulted:

(a) on any proposed Union act in areas within its powers;

(b) by national authorities regarding any draft legislative provision in areas within its powers, but within the limits and under the conditions set out by the Council in accordance with the procedure laid down in Article 187(4).

The European Central Bank may submit opinions to the Union institutions, bodies, offices or agencies or to national authorities on matters within its powers.

5. The European System of Central Banks shall contribute to the smooth conduct of policies pursued by the competent authorities relating to the prudential supervision of credit institutions and the stability of the financial system.

6. A European law of the Council may confer specific tasks upon the European Central Bank concerning policies relating to the prudential supervision of credit institutions and other financial institutions with the exception of insurance undertakings. The Council shall act unanimously after consulting the European Parliament and the European Central Bank.

Article 186

1. The European Central Bank shall have the exclusive right to authorise the issue of euro bank notes in the Union. The European Central Bank and the national central banks may issue such notes. Only the bank notes issued by the European Central Bank and the national central banks shall have the status of legal tender within the Union.

2. Member States may issue euro coins subject to approval by the European Central Bank of the volume of the issue.

The Council, on a proposal from the Commission, may adopt European regulations laying down measures to harmonise the denominations and technical specifications of coins intended for circulation to the extent necessary to permit their smooth circulation within the Union. The Council shall act after consulting the European Parliament and the European Central Bank.

Article 187

1. The European System of Central Banks shall be governed by the decision-making bodies of the European Central Bank, which shall be the Governing Council and the Executive Board.

2. The Statute of the European System of Central Banks is laid down in the Protocol on the Statute of the European System of Central Banks and of the European Central Bank.

3. Article 5(1), (2) and (3), Articles 17 and 18, Article 19(1), Articles 22, 23, 24 and 26, Article 32(2), (3), (4) and (6), Article 33(1)(a) and Article 36 of the Statute of the European System of Central Banks and of the European Central Bank may be amended by European laws:

(a) either on a proposal from the Commission and after consultation of the European Central Bank;

(b) or on a recommendation from the European Central Bank and after consultation of the Commission.

4. The Council shall adopt the European regulations and decisions laying down the measures referred to in Article 4, Article 5(4), Article 19(2), Article 20, Article 28(1), Article 29(2), Article 30(4) and Article 34(3) of the Statute of the European System of Central Banks and of the European Central Bank. It shall act after consulting the European Parliament:

(a) either on a proposal from the Commission and after consulting the European Central Bank;

(b) or on a recommendation from the European Central Bank and after consulting the Commission.

Article 188

When exercising the powers and carrying out the tasks and duties conferred upon them by the Constitution and the Statute of the European System of Central Banks and of the European Central Bank, neither the European Central Bank, nor a national central bank, nor any member of their decision-making bodies shall seek or take instructions from Union institutions, bodies, offices or agencies, from any government of a Member State or from any other body. The Union institutions, bodies, offices or agencies and the governments of the Member States undertake to respect this principle and not to seek to influence the members of the decision-making bodies of the European Central Bank or of the national central banks in the performance of their tasks.

Article 189

Each Member State shall ensure that its national legislation, including the statutes of its national central bank, is compatible with the Constitution and the Statute of the European System of Central Banks and of the European Central Bank.

Article 190

1. In order to carry out the tasks entrusted to the European System of Central Banks, the European Central Bank shall, in accordance with the Constitution and under the conditions laid down in the Statute of the European System of Central Banks and of the European Central Bank, adopt:

(a) European regulations to the extent necessary to implement the tasks defined in Article 3(1)(a), Article 19(1), Article 22 and Article 25(2) of the Statute of the European System of Central Banks and of the European Central Bank and in cases which shall be laid down in European regulations and decisions as referred to in Article 187(4);

(b) European decisions necessary for carrying out the tasks entrusted to the European System of Central Banks under the Constitution and the Statute of the European System of Central Banks and of the European Central Bank;

(c) recommendations and opinions.

2. The European Central Bank may decide to publish its European decisions, recommendations and opinions.

3. The Council shall, under the procedure laid down in Article 187(4), adopt the European regulations establishing the limits and conditions under which the European Central Bank shall be entitled to impose fines or periodic penalty payments on undertakings for failure to comply with obligations under its European regulations and decisions.

Article 191

Without prejudice to the powers of the European Central Bank, European laws or framework laws shall lay down the measures necessary for use of the euro as the single currency. Such laws or framework laws shall be adopted after consultation of the European Central Bank.

Section 3 - Institutional Provisions

Article 192

1. In order to promote co-ordination of the policies of Member States to the full extent needed for the functioning of the internal market, an Economic and Financial Committee is hereby set up.

2. The Committee shall have the following tasks:

(a) to deliver opinions at the request of the Council or of the Commission, or on its own initiative, for submission to those institutions;

(b) to keep under review the economic and financial situation of the Member States and of the Union and to report on it regularly to the Council and to the Commission, in particular with regard to financial relations with third countries and international institutions;

(c) without prejudice to Article 344, to contribute to the preparation of the work of the Council referred to in Article 159, Article 179(2), (3), (4) and (6), Articles 180, 183 and 184, Article 185(6), Article 186(2), Article 187(3) and (4), Articles 191 and 196, Article 198(2) and (3), Article 201, Article 202(2) and (3) and Articles 322 and 326, and to carry out other advisory and preparatory tasks assigned to it by the Council;

(d) to examine, at least once a year, the situation regarding the movement of capital and the freedom of payments, as they result from the application of the Constitution and of Union acts; the examination shall cover all measures relating to capital movements and payments; the Committee shall report to the Commission and to the Council on the outcome of this examination. The Member States, the Commission and the European Central Bank shall each appoint no more than two members of the Committee.

3. The Council, on a proposal from the Commission, shall adopt a European decision laying down detailed provisions concerning the composition of the Economic and Financial Committee. It shall act after consulting the European Central Bank and the Committee. The President of the Council shall inform the European Parliament of that decision.

4. In addition to the tasks referred to in paragraph 2, if and as long as there are Member States with a derogation as referred to in Article 197, the Committee shall keep under review the monetary and financial situation and the general payments system of those Member States and report regularly to the Council and to the Commission on the matter.

Article 193

For matters within the scope of Article 179(4), Article 184 with the exception of paragraph 13, Articles 191, 196, Article 198(3) and Article 326, the Council or a Member State may request the Commission to make a recommendation or a proposal, as appropriate. The Commission shall examine this request and submit its conclusions to the Council without delay.

Section 4 - Provisions Specific to Member States Whose Currency is the Euro

Article 194

1. In order to ensure the proper functioning of economic and monetary union, and in accordance with the relevant provisions of the Constitution, the Council shall, in accordance with the relevant procedure from among those referred to in Articles 179 and 184, with the exception of the procedure set out in Article 184(13), adopt measures specific to those Member States whose currency is the euro:

(a) to strengthen the co-ordination and surveillance of their budgetary discipline;

(b) to set out economic policy guidelines for them, while ensuring that they are compatible with those adopted for the whole of the Union and are kept under surveillance.

2. For those measures set out in paragraph 1, only members of the Council representing Member States whose currency is the euro shall take part in the vote.

A qualified majority shall be defined as at least 55 % of these members of the Council, representing Member States comprising at least 65 % of the population of the participating Member States.

A blocking minority must include at least the minimum number of these Council members representing more than 35 % of the population of the participating Member States, plus one member, failing which the qualified majority shall be deemed attained.

Article 195

Arrangements for meetings between ministers of those Member States whose currency is the euro are laid down by the Protocol on the Euro Group.

Article 196

1. In order to secure the euro's place in the international monetary system, the Council, on a proposal from the Commission, shall adopt a European decision establishing common positions on matters of particular interest for economic and monetary union within the competent international financial institutions and conferences. The Council shall act after consulting the European Central Bank.

2. The Council, on a proposal from the Commission, may adopt appropriate measures to ensure unified representation within the international financial institutions and conferences. The Council shall act after consulting the European Central Bank.

3. For the measures referred to in paragraphs 1 and 2, only members of the Council representing Member States whose currency is the euro shall take part in the vote.

A qualified majority shall be defined as at least 55 % of these members of the Council, representing Member States comprising at least 65 % of the population of the participating Member States.

A blocking minority must include at least the minimum number of these Council members representing more than 35 % of the population of the participating Member States, plus one member, failing which the qualified majority shall be deemed attained.

Section 5 Transitional Provisions

Article 197

1. Member States in respect of which the Council has not decided that they fulfil the necessary conditions for the adoption of the euro shall hereinafter be referred to as 'Member States with a derogation'.

2. The following provisions of the Constitution shall not apply to Member States with a derogation:

(a) adoption of the parts of the broad economic policy guidelines which concern the euro area generally (Article 179(2));

(b) coercive means of remedying excessive deficits (Article 184(9) and (10));

(c) the objectives and tasks of the European System of Central Banks (Article 185(1), (2), (3) and (5));

(d) issue of the euro (Article 186);

(e) acts of the European Central Bank (Article 190);

(f) measures governing the use of the euro (Article 191);

(g) monetary agreements and other measures relating to exchange-rate policy (Article 326);

(h) appointment of members of the Executive Board of the European Central Bank (Article 382 (2));

(i) European decisions establishing common positions on issues of particular relevance for economic and monetary union within the competent international financial institutions and conferences (Article 196(1));

(j) measures to ensure unified representation within the international financial institutions and conferences (Article 196(2)).

In the Articles referred to in points (a) to (j), 'Member States' shall therefore mean Member States whose currency is the euro.

3. Under Chapter IX of the Statute of the European System of Central Banks and of the European Central Bank, Member States with a derogation and their national central banks are excluded from rights and obligations within the European System of Central Banks.

4. The voting rights of members of the Council representing Member States with a derogation shall be suspended for the adoption by the Council of the measures referred to in the Articles listed in paragraph 2, and in the following instances:

(a) recommendations made to those Member States whose currency is the euro in the framework of multilateral surveillance, including on stability programmes and warnings (Article 179(4));

(b) measures relating to excessive deficits concerning those Member States whose currency is the euro (Article 184(6), (7), (8) and (11)).

A qualified majority shall be defined as at least 55 % of the other members of the Council, representing Member States comprising at least 65 % of the population of the participating Member States.

A blocking minority must include at least the minimum number of these other Council members representing more than 35 % of the population of the participating Member States, plus one member, failing which the qualified majority shall be deemed attained.

Article 198

1. At least once every two years, or at the request of a Member State with a derogation, the Commission and the European Central Bank shall report to the Council on the progress made by the Member States with a derogation in fulfilling their obligations regarding the achievement of economic and monetary union. These reports shall include an examination of the compatibility between the national legislation of each of these Member States, including the statutes of its national central bank, and Articles 188 and 189 and the Statute of the European System of Central Banks and of the European Central Bank. The reports shall also examine whether a high degree of sustainable convergence has been achieved, by analysing how far each of these Member States has fulfilled the following criteria:

(a) the achievement of a high degree of price stability; this is apparent from a rate of inflation which is close to that of, at most, the three best performing Member States in terms of price stability;

(b) the sustainability of the government financial position; this is apparent from having achieved a government budgetary position without a deficit that is excessive as determined in accordance with Article 184(6);

(c) the observance of the normal fluctuation margins provided for by the exchange-rate mechanism of the European monetary system, for at least two years, without devaluing against the euro;

(d) the durability of convergence achieved by the Member State with a derogation and of its participation in the exchange-rate mechanism, being reflected in the long-term interest-rate levels. The four criteria laid down in this paragraph and the relevant periods over which they are to be respected are developed further in the protocol on the convergence criteria. the reports from the commission and the european central bank shall also take account of the results of the integration of markets, the situation and development of the balances of payments on current account and an examination of the development of unit labour costs and other price indices.

2. After consulting the European Parliament and after discussion in the European Council, the Council, on a proposal from the Commission, shall adopt a European decision establishing which Member States with a derogation fulfil the necessary conditions on the basis of the criteria laid down in paragraph 1, and shall abrogate the derogations of the Member States concerned.

The Council shall act having received a recommendation of a qualified majority of those among its members representing Member States whose currency is the euro. These members shall act within six months of the Council receiving the Commission's proposal.

The qualified majority referred to in the second subparagraph shall be defined as at least 55 % of these members of the Council, representing Member States comprising at least 65 % of the population of the participating Member States. A blocking minority must include at least the minimum number of these

Council members representing more than 35 % of the population of the participating Member States, plus one member, failing which the qualified majority shall be deemed attained.

3. If it is decided, in accordance with the procedure set out in paragraph 2, to abrogate a derogation, the Council shall, on a proposal from the Commission, adopt the European regulations or decisions irrevocably fixing the rate at which the euro is to be substituted for the currency of the Member State concerned, and laying down the other measures necessary for the introduction of the euro as the single currency in that Member State. The Council shall act with the unanimous agreement of the members representing Member States whose currency is the euro and the Member State concerned, after consulting the European Central Bank.

Article 199

1. If and as long as there are Member States with a derogation, and without prejudice to Article 187(1), the General Council of the European Central Bank referred to in Article 45 of the Statute of the European System of Central Banks and of the European Central Bank shall be constituted as a third decision-making body of the European Central Bank.

2. If and as long as there are Member States with a derogation, the European Central Bank shall, as regards those Member States:

(a) strengthen co-operation between the national central banks;

(b) strengthen the co-ordination of the monetary policies of the Member States, with the aim of ensuring price stability;

(c) monitor the functioning of the exchange-rate mechanism;

(d) hold consultations concerning issues falling within the competence of the national central banks and affecting the stability of financial institutions and markets;

(e) carry out the former tasks of the European Monetary Co-operation Fund which had subsequently been taken over by the European Monetary Institute.

Article 200

Each Member State with a derogation shall treat its exchange-rate policy as a matter of common interest. In so doing, it shall take account of the experience acquired in co-operation within the framework of the exchange-rate mechanism.

Article 201

1. Where a Member State with a derogation is in difficulties or is seriously threatened with difficulties as regards its balance of payments either as a result of an overall disequilibrium in its balance of payments, or as a result of the type of currency at its disposal, and where such difficulties are liable in particular to jeopardise the functioning of the internal market or the implementation of the common commercial policy, the Commission shall immediately investigate the position of the State in question and the action which, making use of all the means at its disposal, that State has taken or may take in accordance with the Constitution. The Commission shall state what measures it recommends the Member State concerned to adopt.

If the action taken by a Member State with a derogation and the measures suggested by the Commission do not prove sufficient to overcome the difficulties which have arisen or which threaten, the Commission shall, after consulting the Economic and Financial Committee, recommend to the Council the granting of mutual assistance and appropriate methods.

The Commission shall keep the Council regularly informed of the situation and of how it evolves.

2. The Council shall adopt European regulations or decisions granting such mutual assistance and laying down the conditions and details of such assistance, which may take such forms as:

(a) a concerted approach to or within any other international organisations to which Member States with a derogation may have recourse;

(b) measures needed to avoid deflection of trade where the Member State with a derogation, which is in difficulties, maintains or reintroduces quantitative restrictions against third countries;

(c) the granting of limited credits by other Member States, subject to their agreement.

3. If the mutual assistance recommended by the Commission is not granted by the Council or if the mutual assistance granted and the measures taken are insufficient, the Commission shall authorise the Member State with a derogation, which is in difficulties, to take protective measures, the conditions and details of which the Commission shall determine. Such authorisation may be revoked and such conditions and details may be changed by the Council.

Article 202

1. Where a sudden crisis in the balance of payments occurs and a European decision as referred to in Article 201(2) is not immediately adopted, a Member State with a derogation may, as a precaution, take the necessary protective measures. Such measures must cause the least possible disturbance in the functioning of the internal market and must not be wider in scope than is strictly necessary to remedy the sudden difficulties which have arisen.

2. The Commission and the other Member States shall be informed of the protective measures referred to in paragraph 1 not later than when they enter into force. The Commission may recommend to the Council the granting of mutual assistance under Article 201.

3. The Council, acting on a recommendation from the Commission and after consulting the Economic and Financial Committee may adopt a European decision stipulating that the Member State concerned shall amend, suspend or abolish the protective measures referred to in paragraph 1.

Chapter III - Policies in Other Areas

Section 1 Employment

Article 203

The Union and the Member States shall, in accordance with this Section, work towards developing a co-ordinated strategy for employment and particularly for promoting a skilled, trained and adaptable workforce and labour markets responsive to economic change with a view to achieving the objectives referred to in Article 3.

Article 204

1. Member States, through their employment policies, shall contribute to the achievement of the objectives referred to in Article 203 in a way consistent with the broad guidelines of the economic policies of the Member States and of the Union adopted pursuant to Article 179(2).

2. Member States, having regard to national practices related to the responsibilities of management and labour, shall regard promoting employment as a matter of common concern and shall co-ordinate their action in this respect within the Council, in accordance with Article 206.

Article 205

1. The Union shall contribute to a high level of employment by encouraging co-operation between Member States and by supporting and, if necessary, complementing their action. In doing so, the competences of the Member States shall be respected.

2. The objective of a high level of employment shall be taken into consideration in the formulation and implementation of Union policies and activities.

Article 206

1. The European Council shall each year consider the employment situation in the Union and adopt conclusions thereon, on the basis of a joint annual report by the Council and the Commission.

2. On the basis of the conclusions of the European Council, the Council, on a proposal from the Commission, shall each year adopt guidelines which the Member States shall take into account in their employment policies. It shall act after consulting the European Parliament, the Committee of the Regions, the Economic and Social Committee and the Employment Committee.

These guidelines shall be consistent with the broad guidelines adopted pursuant to Article 179(2).

3. Each Member State shall provide the Council and the Commission with an annual report on the principal measures taken to implement its employment policy in the light of the guidelines for employment as referred to in paragraph 2.

4. The Council, on the basis of the reports referred to in paragraph 3 and having received the views of the Employment Committee, shall each year carry out an examination of the implementation of the employment policies of the

Member States in the light of the guidelines for employment. The Council, on a recommendation from the Commission, may adopt recommendations which it shall address to Member States.

5. On the basis of the results of that examination, the Council and the Commission shall make a joint annual report to the European Council on the employment situation in the Union and on the implementation of the guidelines for employment.

Article 207

European laws or framework laws may establish incentive measures designed to encourage co-operation between Member States and to support their action in the field of employment through initiatives aimed at developing exchanges of information and best practices, providing comparative analysis and advice as well as promoting innovative approaches and evaluating experiences, in particular by recourse to pilot projects. They shall be adopted after consultation of the Committee of the Regions and the Economic and Social Committee.

Such European laws or framework laws shall not include harmonisation of the laws and regulations of the Member States.

Article 208

The Council shall, by a simple majority, adopt a European decision establishing an Employment Committee with advisory status to promote co-ordination between Member States on employment and labour market policies. It shall act after consulting the European Parliament. The tasks of the Committee shall be:

(a) to monitor the employment situation and employment policies in the Union and the Member States;

(b) without prejudice to Article 344, to formulate opinions at the request of either the Council or the Commission or on its own initiative, and to contribute to the preparation of the Council proceedings referred to in Article 206.

In fulfilling its mandate, the Committee shall consult management and labour.

Each Member State and the Commission shall appoint two members of the Committee.

Section 2 - Social Policy

Article 209

The Union and the Member States, having in mind fundamental social rights such as those set out in the European Social Charter signed at Turin on 18 October 1961 and in the 1989 Community Charter of the Fundamental Social Rights of Workers, shall have as their objectives the promotion of employment, improved living and working conditions, so as to make possible their harmonisation while the improvement is being maintained, proper social protection, dialogue between management and labour, the development of human resources with a view to lasting high employment and the combating of exclusion.

To this end the Union and the Member States shall act taking account of the diverse forms of national practices, in particular in the field of contractual relations, and the need to maintain the competitiveness of the Union economy.

They believe that such a development will ensue not only from the functioning of the internal market, which will favour the harmonisation of social systems, but also from the procedures provided for in the Constitution and from the approximation of provisions laid down by law, regulation or administrative action of the Member States.

Article 210

1. With a view to achieving the objectives of Article 209, the Union shall support and complement the activities of the Member States in the following fields:

(a) improvement in particular of the working environment to protect workers' health and safety;

(b) working conditions;

(c) social security and social protection of workers;

(d) protection of workers where their employment contract is terminated;

(e) the information and consultation of workers;

(f) representation and collective defence of the interests of workers and employers, including codetermination, subject to paragraph 6;

(g) conditions of employment for third-country nationals legally residing in Union territory;

(h) the integration of persons excluded from the labour market, without prejudice to Article 283;

(i) equality between women and men with regard to labour market opportunities and treatment at work;

(j) the combating of social exclusion;

(k) the modernisation of social protection systems without prejudice to point (c).

2. For the purposes of paragraph 1:

(a) European laws or framework laws may establish measures designed to encourage co-operation between Member States through initiatives aimed at improving knowledge, developing exchanges of information and best practices, promoting innovative approaches and evaluating experiences, excluding any harmonisation of the laws and regulations of the Member States;

(b) in the fields referred to in paragraph 1(a) to (i), European framework laws may establish minimum requirements for gradual implementation, having regard to the conditions and technical rules obtaining in each of the Member States. Such European framework laws shall avoid imposing administrative, financial and legal constraints in a way which would hold back the creation and development of small and medium-sized undertakings.

In all cases, such European laws or framework laws shall be adopted after consultation of the Committee of the Regions and the Economic and Social Committee.

3. By way of derogation from paragraph 2, in the fields referred to in paragraph 1(c), (d), (f) and (g), European laws or framework laws shall be adopted by the Council acting unanimously after consulting the European Parliament, the Committee of the Regions and the Economic and Social Committee.

The Council may, on a proposal from the Commission, adopt a European decision making the ordinary legislative procedure applicable to paragraph 1(d), (f) and (g). It shall act unanimously after consulting the European Parliament.

4. A Member State may entrust management and labour, at their joint request, with the implementation of European framework laws adopted pursuant to paragraphs 2 and 3 or, where appropriate, with the implementation of European regulations or decisions adopted in accordance with Article 212.

In this case, it shall ensure that, no later than the date on which a European framework law must be transposed, or a European regulation or decision implemented, management and labour have introduced the necessary measures by agreement, the Member State concerned being required to take any necessary measure enabling it at any time to be in a position to guarantee the results imposed by that framework law, regulation or decision.

5. The European laws and framework laws adopted pursuant to this Article:

(a) shall not affect the right of Member States to define the fundamental principles of their social security systems and must not significantly affect the financial equilibrium of such systems;

(b) shall not prevent any Member State from maintaining or introducing more stringent protective measures compatible with the Constitution.

6. This Article shall not apply to pay, the right of association, the right to strike or the right to impose lockouts.

Article 211

1. The Commission shall promote the consultation of management and labour at Union level and shall adopt any relevant measure to facilitate their dialogue by ensuring balanced support for the parties.

2. For the purposes of paragraph 1, before submitting proposals in the social policy field, the Commission shall consult management and labour on the possible direction of Union action.

3. If, after the consultation referred to in paragraph 2, the Commission considers Union action desirable, it shall consult management and labour on the content of the envisaged proposal.

Management and labour shall forward to the Commission an opinion or, where appropriate, a recommendation.

4. On the occasion of the consultation referred to in paragraphs 2 and 3, management and labour may inform the Commission of their wish to initiate the process provided for in Article 212(1).

The duration of this process shall not exceed nine months, unless the management and labour concerned and the Commission decide jointly to extend it.

Article 212

1. Should management and labour so desire, the dialogue between them at Union level may lead to contractual relations, including agreements.

2. Agreements concluded at Union level shall be implemented either in accordance with the procedures and practices specific to management and labour and the Member States or, in matters covered by Article 210, at the joint request

of the signatory parties, by European regulations or decisions adopted by the Council on a proposal from the Commission. The European Parliament shall be informed. Where the agreement in question contains one or more provisions relating to one of the areas for which unanimity is required pursuant to Article 210(3), the Council shall act unanimously.

Article 213

With a view to achieving the objectives of Article 209 and without prejudice to the other provisions of the Constitution, the Commission shall encourage co-operation between the Member States and facilitate the co-ordination of their action in all social policy fields under this Section, particularly in matters relating to:

(a) employment;

(b) labour law and working conditions;

(c) basic and advanced vocational training;

(d) social security;

(e) prevention of occupational accidents and diseases;

(f) occupational hygiene;

(g) the right of association and collective bargaining between employers and workers. To this end, the Commission shall act in close contact with Member States by making studies, delivering opinions and arranging consultations both on problems arising at national level and on those of concern to international organisations, in particular initiatives aiming at the establishment of guidelines and indicators, the organisation of exchange of best practice, and the preparation of the necessary elements for periodic monitoring and evaluation. The European Parliament shall be kept fully informed.

Before delivering the opinions provided for in this Article, the Commission shall consult the Economic and Social Committee.

Article 214

1. Each Member State shall ensure that the principle of equal pay for female and male workers for equal work or work of equal value is applied.

2. For the purpose of this Article, 'pay' means the ordinary basic or minimum wage or salary and any other consideration, whether in cash or in kind, which the worker receives directly or indirectly, in respect of his employment, from his employer. Equal pay without discrimination based on sex means:

(a) that pay for the same work at piece rates shall be calculated on the basis of the same unit of measurement;

(b) that pay for work at time rates shall be the same for the same job.

3. European laws or framework laws shall establish measures to ensure the application of the principle of equal opportunities and equal treatment of women and men in matters of employment and occupation, including the principle of equal pay for equal work or work of equal value. They shall be adopted after consultation of the Economic and Social Committee.

4. With a view to ensuring full equality in practice between women and men in working life, the principle of equal treatment shall not prevent any Member State from maintaining or adopting measures providing for specific advantages

in order to make it easier for the under-represented sex to pursue a vocational activity, or to prevent or compensate for disadvantages in professional careers.

Article 215

Member States shall endeavour to maintain the existing equivalence between paid holiday schemes.

Article 216

The Commission shall draw up a report each year on progress in achieving the objectives of Article 209, including the demographic situation within the Union. It shall forward the report to the European Parliament, the Council and the Economic and Social Committee.

Article 217

The Council shall, by a simple majority, adopt a European decision establishing a Social Protection Committee with advisory status to promote co-operation on social protection policies between Member States and with the Commission. The Council shall act after consulting the European Parliament.

The tasks of the Committee shall be:

(a) to monitor the social situation and the development of social protection policies in the Member States and within the Union;

(b) to promote exchanges of information, experience and good practice between Member States and with the Commission;

(c) without prejudice to Article 344, to prepare reports, formulate opinions or undertake other work within the scope of its powers, at the request of either the Council or the Commission or on its own initiative.

In fulfilling its mandate, the Committee shall establish appropriate contacts with management and labour.

Each Member State and the Commission shall appoint two members of the Committee.

Article 218

The Commission shall include a separate chapter on social developments within the Union in its annual report to the European Parliament.

The European Parliament may invite the Commission to draw up reports on any particular problems concerning social conditions.

Article 219

1. In order to improve employment opportunities for workers in the internal market and to contribute thereby to raising the standard of living, a European Social Fund is hereby established; it shall aim to render the employment of workers easier and to increase their geographical and occupational mobility within the Union, and to facilitate their adaptation to industrial changes and to changes in production systems, in particular through vocational training and retraining.

2. The Commission shall administer the Fund. It shall be assisted in this task by a Committee presided over by a member of the Commission and composed of representatives of Member States, trade unions and employers' organisations.

3. European laws shall establish implementing measures relating to the Fund. Such laws shall be adopted after consultation of the Committee of the Regions and the Economic and Social Committee.

Section 3 - Economic, social and Territorial Cohesion

Article 220

In order to promote its overall harmonious development, the Union shall develop and pursue its action leading to the strengthening of its economic, social and territorial cohesion.

In particular, the Union shall aim at reducing disparities between the levels of development of the various regions and the backwardness of the least favoured regions.

Among the regions concerned, particular attention shall be paid to rural areas, areas affected by industrial transition, and regions which suffer from severe and permanent natural or demographic handicaps such as the northernmost regions with very low population density and island, cross-border and mountain regions.

Article 221

Member States shall conduct their economic policies and shall co-ordinate them in such a way as, in addition, to attain the objectives set out in Article 220. The formulation and implementation of the Union's policies and action and the implementation of the internal market shall take into account those objectives and shall contribute to their achievement. The Union shall also support the achievement of these objectives by the action it takes through the Structural Funds (European Agricultural Guidance and Guarantee Fund, Guidance Section; European Social Fund; European Regional Development Fund), the European Investment Bank and the other existing financial instruments.

The Commission shall submit a report to the European Parliament, the Council, the Committee of the Regions and the Economic and Social Committee every three years on the progress made towards achieving economic, social and territorial cohesion and on the manner in which the various means provided for in this Article have contributed to it. This report shall, if necessary, be accompanied by appropriate proposals.

European laws or framework laws may establish any specific measure outside the Funds, without prejudice to measures adopted within the framework of the Union's other policies. They shall be adopted after consultation of the Committee of the Regions and the Economic and Social Committee.

Article 222

The European Regional Development Fund is intended to help to redress the main regional imbalances in the Union through participation in the development and structural adjustment of regions whose development is lagging behind and in the conversion of declining industrial regions.

Article 223

1. Without prejudice to Article 224, European laws shall define the tasks, the priority objectives and the organisation of the structural funds, which may involve grouping the Funds, the general rules applicable to them and the provisions necessary to ensure their effectiveness and the co-ordination of the Funds with one another and with the other existing Financial Instruments.

A Cohesion Fund set up by a European law shall provide a financial contribution to projects in the fields of environment and trans-European networks in the area of transport infrastructure.

In all cases, such European laws shall be adopted after consultation of the Committee of the Regions and the Economic and Social Committee.

2. The first provisions on the Structural Funds and the Cohesion Fund to be adopted following those in force on the date on which the Treaty establishing a Constitution for Europe is signed shall be established by a European law of the Council. The Council shall act unanimously after obtaining the consent of the European Parliament.

Article 224

European laws shall establish implementing measures relating to the European Regional Development Fund. Such laws shall be adopted after consultation of the Committee of the Regions and the Economic and Social Committee.

With regard to the European Agricultural Guidance and Guarantee Fund, Guidance Section, and the European Social Fund, Articles 231 and 219(3) respectively shall apply.

Section 4 - Agriculture and Fisheries

Article 225

The Union shall define and implement a common agriculture and fisheries policy.

'Agricultural products' means the products of the soil, of stock-farming and of fisheries and products of first-stage processing directly related to these products. References to the common agricultural policy or to agriculture, and the use of the term 'agricultural', shall be understood as also referring to fisheries, having regard to the specific characteristics of this sector.

Article 226

1. The internal market shall extend to agriculture and trade in agricultural products.

2. Save as otherwise provided in Articles 227 to 232, the rules laid down for

the establishment and functioning of the internal market shall apply to agricultural products.

3. The products listed in Annex I shall be subject to Articles 227 to 232.

4. The operation and development of the internal market for agricultural products must be accompanied by a common agricultural policy.

Article 227

1. The objectives of the common agricultural policy shall be:

(a) to increase agricultural productivity by promoting technical progress and by ensuring the rational development of agricultural production and the optimum utilisation of the factors of production, in particular labour;

(b) thus to ensure a fair standard of living for the agricultural community, in particular by increasing the individual earnings of persons engaged in agriculture;

(c) to stabilise markets;

(d) to assure the availability of supplies;

(e) to ensure that supplies reach consumers at reasonable prices.

2. In working out the common agricultural policy and the special methods for its application, account shall be taken of:

(a) the particular nature of agricultural activity, which results from the social structure of agriculture and from structural and natural disparities between the various agricultural regions;

(b) the need to effect the appropriate adjustments by degrees;

(c) the fact that in the Member States agriculture constitutes a sector closely linked with the economy as a whole.

Article 228

1. In order to attain the objectives set out in Article 227, a common organisation of agricultural markets shall be established.

This organisation shall take one of the following forms, depending on the product concerned:

(a) common rules on competition;

(b) compulsory co-ordination of the various national market organisations;

(c) a European market organisation.

2. The common organisation established in accordance with paragraph 1 may include all measures required to attain the objectives set out in Article 227, in particular regulation of prices, aids for the production and marketing of the various products, storage and carryover arrangements and common machinery for stabilising imports or exports.

The common organisation shall be limited to pursuit of the objectives set out in Article 227 and

shall exclude any discrimination between producers or consumers within the Union.

Any common price policy shall be based on common criteria and uniform methods of calculation.

3. In order to enable the common organisation referred to in paragraph 1 to attain its objectives, one or more agricultural guidance and guarantee funds may be set up.

Article 229

To enable the objectives set out in Article 227 to be attained, provision may be made within the framework of the common agricultural policy for measures such as:

(a) an effective co-ordination of efforts in the spheres of vocational training, of research and of the dissemination of agricultural knowledge; this may include joint financing of projects or institutions;

(b) joint measures to promote consumption of certain products.

Article 230

1. The Section relating to rules on competition shall apply to production of and trade in agricultural products only to the extent determined by European laws or framework laws in accordance with Article 231(2), having regard to the objectives set out in Article 227.

2. The Council, on a proposal from the Commission, may adopt a European regulation or decision authorising the granting of aid:

(a) for the protection of enterprises handicapped by structural or natural conditions;

(b) within the framework of economic development programmes.

Article 231

1. The Commission shall submit proposals for working out and implementing the common agricultural policy, including the replacement of the national organisations by one of the forms of common organisation provided for in Article 228(1), and for implementing the measures referred to in this Section.

These proposals shall take account of the interdependence of the agricultural matters referred to in this Section.

2. European laws or framework laws shall establish the common organisation of the market provided for in Article 228(1) and the other provisions necessary for the pursuit of the objectives of the common agricultural policy and the common fisheries policy. They shall be adopted after consultation of the Economic and Social Committee.

3. The Council, on a proposal from the Commission, shall adopt the European regulations or decisions on fixing prices, levies, aid and quantitative limitations and on the fixing and allocation of fishing opportunities.

4. In accordance with paragraph 2, the national market organisations may be replaced by the common organisation provided for in Article 228(1) if:

(a) the common organisation offers Member States which are opposed to this measure and which have an organisation of their own for the production in question equivalent safeguards for the employment and standard of living of the producers concerned, account being taken of the adjustments that will be possible and the specialisation that will be needed with the passage of time, and

(b) such an organisation ensures conditions for trade within the Union similar to those existing in a national market.

5. If a common organisation for certain raw materials is established before a common organisation exists for the corresponding processed products, such raw

materials as are used for processed products intended for export to third countries may be imported from outside the Union.

Article 232

Where in a Member State a product is subject to a national market organisation or to internal rules having equivalent effect which affect the competitive position of similar production in another Member State, a countervailing charge shall be applied by Member States to imports of this product coming from the Member State where such organisation or rules exist, unless that State applies a countervailing charge on export.

The Commission shall adopt European regulations or decisions fixing the amount of these charges at the level required to redress the balance. It may also authorise other measures, the conditions and details of which it shall determine.

Section 5 - Environment

Article 233

1. Union policy on the environment shall contribute to the pursuit of the following objectives:

(a) preserving, protecting and improving the quality of the environment;

(b) protecting human health;

(c) prudent and rational utilisation of natural resources;

(d) promoting measures at international level to deal with regional or worldwide environmental problems.

2. Union policy on the environment shall aim at a high level of protection taking into account the diversity of situations in the various regions of the Union. It shall be based on the precautionary principle and on the principles that preventive action should be taken, that environmental damage should as a priority be rectified at source and that the polluter should pay.

In this context, harmonisation measures answering environmental protection requirements shall include, where appropriate, a safeguard clause allowing Member States to take provisional steps, for non-economic environmental reasons, subject to a procedure of inspection by the Union.

3. In preparing its policy on the environment, the Union shall take account of:

(a) available scientific and technical data;

(b) environmental conditions in the various regions of the Union;

(c) the potential benefits and costs of action or lack of action;

(d) the economic and social development of the Union as a whole and the balanced development of its regions.

4. Within their respective spheres of competence, the Union and the Member States shall co-operate with third countries and with the competent international organisations. The arrangements for the Union's co-operation may be the subject of agreements between the Union and the third parties concerned.

The first subparagraph shall be without prejudice to Member States' competence to negotiate in international bodies and to conclude international agreements.

Article 234

1. European laws or framework laws shall establish what action is to be taken in order to achieve the objectives referred to in Article 233. They shall be adopted after consultation of the Committee of the Regions and the Economic and Social Committee.

2. By way of derogation from paragraph 1 and without prejudice to Article 172, the Council shall unanimously adopt European laws or framework laws establishing:

(a) provisions primarily of a fiscal nature;

(b) measures affecting:

(i) town and country planning;

(ii) quantitative management of water resources or affecting, directly or indirectly, the availability of those resources;

(iii) land use, with the exception of waste management;

(c) measures significantly affecting a Member State's choice between different energy sources and the general structure of its energy supply. The Council, on a proposal from the Commission, may unanimously adopt a European decision making the ordinary legislative procedure applicable to the matters referred to in the first subparagraph. In all cases, the Council shall act after consulting the European Parliament, the Committee of the Regions and the Economic and Social Committee.

3. European laws shall establish general action programmes which set out priority objectives to be attained. Such laws shall be adopted after consultation of the Committee of the Regions and the Economic and Social Committee.

The measures necessary for the implementation of these programmes shall be adopted under the terms of paragraph 1 or 2, as the case may be.

4. Without prejudice to certain measures adopted by the Union, the Member States shall finance and implement the environment policy.

5. Without prejudice to the principle that the polluter should pay, if a measure based on paragraph 1 involves costs deemed disproportionate for the public authorities of a Member State, such measure shall provide in appropriate form for:

(a) temporary derogations, and/or

(b) financial support from the Cohesion Fund.

6. The protective measures adopted pursuant to this Article shall not prevent any Member State from maintaining or introducing more stringent protective measures. Such measures must be compatible with the Constitution. They shall be notified to the Commission.

Section 6 - Consumer Protection

Article 235

1. In order to promote the interests of consumers and to ensure a high level of consumer protection, the Union shall contribute to protecting the health, safety and economic interests of consumers, as well as to promoting their right to information, education and to organise themselves in order to safeguard their interests.

2. The Union shall contribute to the attainment of the objectives referred to in paragraph 1 through:

(a) measures adopted pursuant to Article 172 in the context of the establishment and functioning of the internal market;

(b) measures which support, supplement and monitor the policy pursued by the Member States.

3. European laws or framework laws shall establish the measures referred to in paragraph 2(b).

Such laws shall be adopted after consultation of the Economic and Social Committee.

4. Acts adopted pursuant to paragraph 3 shall not prevent any Member State from maintaining or introducing more stringent protective provisions. Such provisions must be compatible with the Constitution. They shall be notified to the Commission.

Section 7 - Transport

Article 236

1. The objectives of the Constitution shall, in matters governed by this Section, be pursued within the framework of a common transport policy.

2. European laws or framework laws shall implement paragraph 1, taking into account the distinctive features of transport. They shall be adopted after consultation of the Committee of the Regions and the Economic and Social Committee.

Such European laws or framework laws shall establish:

(a) common rules applicable to international transport to or from the territory of a Member State or passing across the territory of one or more Member States;

(b) the conditions under which non-resident carriers may operate transport services within a Member State;

(c) measures to improve transport safety;

(d) any other appropriate measure.

3. When the European laws or framework laws referred to in paragraph 2 are adopted, account shall be taken of cases where their application might seriously affect the standard of living and level of employment in certain regions, and the operation of transport facilities.

Article 237

Until the European laws or framework laws referred to in Article 236(2) have been adopted, no Member State may, unless the Council has unanimously adopted a European decision granting a derogation, make the various provisions governing the subject on 1 January 1958 or, for acceding

States, the date of their accession less favourable in their direct or indirect effect on carriers of other Member States as compared with carriers who are nationals of that State.

Article 238

Aids shall be compatible with the Constitution if they meet the needs of co-ordination of transport or if they represent reimbursement for the discharge of certain obligations inherent in the concept of a public service.

Article 239

Any measures adopted within the framework of the Constitution in respect of transport rates and conditions shall take account of the economic circumstances of carriers.

Article 240

1. In the case of transport within the Union, discrimination which takes the form of carriers charging different rates and imposing different conditions for the carriage of the same goods over the same transport links on grounds of the Member State of origin or of destination of the goods in question shall be prohibited.

2. Paragraph 1 shall not prevent the adoption of other European laws or framework laws pursuant to Article 236(2).

3. The Council, on a proposal from the Commission, shall adopt European regulations or decisions for implementing paragraph 1. It shall act after consulting the European Parliament and the Economic and Social Committee.

The Council may in particular adopt the European regulations and decisions needed to enable the institutions to secure compliance with the rule laid down in paragraph 1 and to ensure that users benefit from it to the full.

4. The Commission, acting on its own initiative or on application by a Member State, shall investigate any cases of discrimination falling within paragraph 1 and, after consulting any Member State concerned, adopt the necessary European decisions within the framework of the European regulations and decisions referred to in paragraph 3.

Article 241

1. The imposition by a Member State, in respect of transport operations carried out within the Union, of rates and conditions involving any element of support or protection in the interest of one or more particular undertakings or industries shall be prohibited, unless authorised by a European decision of the Commission.

2. The Commission, acting on its own initiative or on application by a Member State, shall examine the rates and conditions referred to in paragraph 1, taking account in particular of the requirements of an appropriate regional economic policy, the needs of underdeveloped areas and the problems of areas seriously affected by political circumstances on the one hand, and of the effects of such rates and conditions on competition between the different modes of transport on the other.

After consulting each Member State concerned, the Commission shall adopt the necessary European decisions.

3. The prohibition provided for in paragraph 1 shall not apply to tariffs fixed to meet competition.

Article 242

Charges or dues in respect of the crossing of frontiers which are charged by a carrier in addition to the transport rates shall not exceed a reasonable level after taking the costs actually incurred thereby into account.

Member States shall endeavour to reduce these costs.

The Commission may make recommendations to Member States for the application of this Article.

Article 243

The provisions of this Section shall not form an obstacle to the application of measures taken in the Federal Republic of Germany to the extent that such measures are required in order to compensate for the economic disadvantages caused by the division of Germany to the economy of certain areas of the Federal Republic affected by that division. Five years after the entry into force of the Treaty establishing a Constitution for Europe, the Council, acting on a proposal from the Commission, may adopt a European decision repealing this Article.

Article 244

An Advisory Committee consisting of experts designated by the governments of the Member States shall be attached to the Commission. The Commission, whenever it considers it desirable, shall consult the Committee on transport matters.

Article 245

1. This Section shall apply to transport by rail, road and inland waterway.

2. European laws or framework laws may lay down appropriate measures for sea and air transport.

They shall be adopted after consultation of the Committee of the Regions and the Economic and Social Committee.

Section 8 - Trans-European Networks

Article 246

1. To help achieve the objectives referred to in Articles 130 and 220 and to enable citizens of the Union, economic operators and regional and local communities to derive full benefit from the setting-up of an area without internal frontiers, the Union shall contribute to the establishment and development of trans-European networks in the areas of transport, telecommunications and energy infrastructures.

2. Within the framework of a system of open and competitive markets, action by the Union shall aim at promoting the interconnection and interoperability of national networks as well as access to such networks. It shall take account in particular of the need to link island, landlocked and peripheral regions with the central regions of the Union.

Article 247

1. In order to achieve the objectives referred to in Article 246, the Union:

(a) shall establish a series of guidelines covering the objectives, priorities and broad lines of measures envisaged in the sphere of trans-European networks; these guidelines shall identify projects of common interest;

(b) shall implement any measures that may prove necessary to ensure the interoperability of the networks, in particular in the field of technical standardisation;

(c) may support projects of common interest supported by Member States, which are identified in the framework of the guidelines referred to in point (a), particularly through feasibility studies, loan guarantees or interest-rate subsidies; the Union may also contribute, through the Cohesion Fund, to the financing of specific projects in Member States in the area of transport infrastructure.

The Union's activities shall take into account the potential economic viability of the projects.

2. European laws or framework laws shall establish the guidelines and other measures referred to in paragraph 1. Such laws shall be adopted after consultation of the Committee of the Regions and the Economic and Social Committee.

Guidelines and projects of common interest which relate to the territory of a Member State shall require the agreement of that Member State.

3. Member States shall, in liaison with the Commission, co-ordinate among themselves the policies pursued at national level which may have a significant impact on the achievement of the objectives referred to in Article 246. The Commission may, in close co-operation with the Member States, take any useful initiative to promote such co-ordination.

4. The Union may co-operate with third countries to promote projects of mutual interest and to ensure the interoperability of networks.

Section 9 - Research and Technological Development and Space

Article 248

1. The Union shall aim to strengthen its scientific and technological bases by achieving a European research area in which researchers, scientific knowledge and technology circulate freely, and encourage it to become more competitive, including in its industry, while promoting all the research activities deemed necessary by virtue of other Chapters of the Constitution.

2. For the purposes referred to in paragraph 1 the Union shall, throughout the Union, encourage undertakings, including small and medium-sized undertakings, research centres and universities in their research and technological development activities of high quality. It shall support their efforts to co-operate with one another, aiming, notably, at permitting researchers to co-operate freely across borders and at enabling undertakings to exploit the internal market potential, in particular through the opening-up of national public contracts, the defini-

tion of common standards and the removal of legal and fiscal obstacles to that co-operation.

3. All the Union's activities in the area of research and technological development, including demonstration projects, shall be decided on and implemented in accordance with this Section.

Article 249

In pursuing the objectives referred to in Article 248, the Union shall carry out the following activities, complementing the activities carried out in the Member States:

(a) implementation of research, technological development and demonstration programmes, by promoting co-operation with and between undertakings, research centres and universities;

(b) promotion of co-operation in the field of the Union's research, technological development and demonstration with third countries and international organisations;

(c) dissemination and optimisation of the results of activities in the Union's research, technological development and demonstration;

(d) stimulation of the training and mobility of researchers in the Union.

Article 250

1. The Union and the Member States shall co-ordinate their research and technological development activities so as to ensure that national policies and the Union's policy are mutually consistent.

2. In close co-operation with the Member States, the Commission may take any useful initiative to promote the co-ordination referred to in paragraph 1, in particular initiatives aiming at the establishment of guidelines and indicators, the organisation of exchange of best practice, and the preparation of the necessary elements for periodic monitoring and evaluation. The European Parliament shall be kept fully informed.

Article 251

1. European laws shall establish a multiannual framework programme, setting out all the activities financed by the Union. Such laws shall be adopted after consultation of the Economic and Social Committee.

The framework programme shall:

(a) establish the scientific and technological objectives to be achieved by the activities provided for in Article 249 and lay down the relevant priorities;

(b) indicate the broad lines of such activities;

(c) lay down the maximum overall amount and the detailed rules for the Union's financial participation in the framework programme and the respective shares in each of the activities provided for.

2. The multiannual framework programme shall be adapted or supplemented as the situation changes.

3. A European law of the Council shall establish specific programmes to implement the multiannual framework programme within each activity. Each specific programme shall define the detailed rules for implementing it, fix its

duration and provide for the means deemed necessary. The sum of the amounts deemed necessary, fixed in the specific programmes, shall not exceed the overall maximum amount fixed for the framework programme and each activity. Such a law shall be adopted after consulting the European Parliament and the Economic and Social Committee.

4. As a complement to the activities planned in the multiannual framework programme, European laws shall establish the measures necessary for the implementation of the European research area. Such laws shall be adopted after consulting the Economic and Social Committee.

Article 252

1. For the implementation of the multiannual framework programme, European laws or framework laws shall establish:

(a) the rules for the participation of undertakings, research centres and universities;

(b) the rules governing the dissemination of research results. Such European laws or framework laws shall be adopted after consultation of the Economic and Social Committee.

2. In implementing the multiannual framework programme, European laws may establish supplementary programmes involving the participation of certain Member States only, which shall finance them subject to possible participation by the Union.

Such European laws shall determine the rules applicable to supplementary programmes, particularly as regards the dissemination of knowledge as well as access by other Member States. They shall be adopted after consultation of the Economic and Social Committee and with the agreement of the Member States concerned.

3. In implementing the multiannual framework programme, European laws may make provision, in agreement with the Member States concerned, for participation in research and development programmes undertaken by several Member States, including participation in the structures created for the execution of those programmes. Such European laws shall be adopted after consultation of the Economic and Social Committee.

4. In implementing the multiannual framework programme the Union may make provision for co-operation in the Union's research, technological development and demonstration with third countries or international organisations. The detailed arrangements for such co-operation may be the subject of agreements between the Union and the third parties concerned.

Article 253

The Council, on a proposal from the Commission, may adopt European regulations or decisions to set up joint undertakings or any other structure necessary for the efficient execution of the Union's research, technological development and demonstration programmes. It shall act after consulting the European Parliament and the Economic and Social Committee.

Article 254

1. To promote scientific and technical progress, industrial competitiveness and the implementation of its policies, the Union shall draw up a European space policy. To this end, it may promote joint initiatives, support research and technological development and co-ordinate the efforts needed for the exploration and exploitation of space.

2. To contribute to attaining the objectives referred to in paragraph 1, European laws or framework laws shall establish the necessary measures, which may take the form of a European space programme.

3. The Union shall establish any appropriate relations with the European Space Agency.

Article 255

At the beginning of each year the Commission shall send a report to the European Parliament and the Council. The report shall include information on activities relating to research, technological development and the dissemination of results during the previous year, and the work programme for the current year.

Section 10 - Energy

Article 256

1. In the context of the establishment and functioning of the internal market and with regard for the need to preserve and improve the environment, Union policy on energy shall aim to:

(a) ensure the functioning of the energy market;

(b) ensure security of energy supply in the Union, and

(c) promote energy efficiency and energy saving and the development of new and renewable forms of energy.

2. Without prejudice to the application of other provisions of the Constitution, the objectives in paragraph 1 shall be achieved by measures enacted in European laws or framework laws. Such laws or framework laws shall be adopted after consultation of the Committee of the Regions and the Economic and Social Committee. Such European laws or framework laws shall not affect a Member State's right to determine the conditions for exploiting its energy resources, its choice between different energy sources and the general structure of its energy supply, without prejudice to Article 234(2)(c).

3. By way of derogation from paragraph 2, a European law or framework law of the Council shall establish the measures referred to therein when they are primarily of a fiscal nature. The Council shall act unanimously after consulting the European Parliament.

Chapter IV - Area of Freedom, Security and Justice

Section 1 - General Provisions

Article 257

1. The Union shall constitute an area of freedom, security and justice with respect for fundamental rights and the different legal systems and traditions of the Member States.

2. It shall ensure the absence of internal border controls for persons and shall frame a common policy on asylum, immigration and external border control, based on solidarity between Member States, which is fair towards third-country nationals. For the purpose of this Chapter, stateless persons shall be treated as third-country nationals.

3. The Union shall endeavour to ensure a high level of security through measures to prevent and combat crime, racism and xenophobia, and through measures for co-ordination and co-operation between police and judicial authorities and other competent authorities, as well as through the mutual recognition of judgments in criminal matters and, if necessary, through the approximation of criminal laws.

4. The Union shall facilitate access to justice, in particular through the principle of mutual recognition of judicial and extrajudicial decisions in civil matters.

Article 258

The European Council shall define the strategic guidelines for legislative and operational planning within the area of freedom, security and justice.

Article 259

National Parliaments shall ensure that the proposals and legislative initiatives submitted under Sections 4 and 5 of this Chapter comply with the principle of subsidiarity, in accordance with the arrangements laid down by the Protocol on the application of the principles of subsidiarity and proportionality.

Article 260

Without prejudice to Articles 360 to 362, the Council may, on a proposal from the Commission, adopt European regulations or decisions laying down the arrangements whereby Member States, in collaboration with the Commission, conduct objective and impartial evaluation of the implementation of the Union policies referred to in this Chapter by Member States' authorities, in particular in order to facilitate full application of the principle of mutual recognition. The European Parliament and national Parliaments shall be informed of the content and results of the evaluation.

Article 261

A standing committee shall be set up within the Council in order to ensure that operational co-operation on internal security is promoted and strengthened within the Union. Without prejudice to Article 344, it shall facilitate co-ordination of the action of Member States' competent authorities. Representatives of the Union bodies, offices and agencies concerned may be involved in the proceedings of this committee. The European Parliament and national Parliaments shall be kept informed of the proceedings.

Article 262

This Chapter shall not affect the exercise of the responsibilities incumbent upon Member States with regard to the maintenance of law and order and the safeguarding of internal security.

Article 263

The Council shall adopt European regulations to ensure administrative co-operation between the relevant departments of the Member States in the areas covered by this Chapter, as well as between those departments and the Commission. It shall act on a Commission proposal, subject to Article 264, and after consulting the European Parliament.

Article 264

The acts referred to in Sections 4 and 5, together with the European regulations referred to in Article 263 which ensure administrative co-operation in the areas covered by these Sections, shall be adopted:

(a) on a proposal from the Commission, or

(b) on the initiative of a quarter of the Member States.

Section 2 - Policies on Border Checks, Asylum and Immigration

Article 265

1. The Union shall develop a policy with a view to:

(a) ensuring the absence of any controls on persons, whatever their nationality, when crossing internal borders;

(b) carrying out checks on persons and efficient monitoring of the crossing of external borders;

(c) the gradual introduction of an integrated management system for external borders.

2. For the purposes of paragraph 1, European laws or framework laws shall establish measures concerning:

(a) the common policy on visas and other short-stay residence permits;

(b) the checks to which persons crossing external borders are subject;

(c) the conditions under which nationals of third countries shall have the freedom to travel within the Union for a short period;

(d) any measure necessary for the gradual establishment of an integrated management system for external borders;

(e) the absence of any controls on persons, whatever their nationality, when crossing internal borders.

3. This Article shall not affect the competence of the Member States concerning the geographical demarcation of their borders, in accordance with international law.

Article 266

1. The Union shall develop a common policy on asylum, subsidiary protection and temporary protection with a view to offering appropriate status to any third-country national requiring international protection and ensuring compliance with the principle of non-refoulement. This policy must be in accordance with the Geneva Convention of 28 July 1951 and the Protocol of 31 January 1967 relating to the status of refugees, and other relevant treaties.

2. For the purposes of paragraph 1, European laws or framework laws shall lay down measures for a common European asylum system comprising:

(a) a uniform status of asylum for nationals of third countries, valid throughout the Union;

(b) a uniform status of subsidiary protection for nationals of third countries who, without obtaining European asylum, are in need of international protection;

(c) a common system of temporary protection for displaced persons in the event of a massive inflow;

(d) common procedures for the granting and withdrawing of uniform asylum or subsidiary protection status;

(e) criteria and mechanisms for determining which Member State is responsible for considering an application for asylum or subsidiary protection;

(f) standards concerning the conditions for the reception of applicants for asylum or subsidiary protection;

(g) partnership and co-operation with third countries for the purpose of managing inflows of people applying for asylum or subsidiary or temporary protection.

3. In the event of one or more Member States being confronted by an emergency situation characterised by a sudden inflow of nationals of third countries, the Council, on a proposal from the Commission, may adopt European regulations or decisions comprising provisional measures for the benefit of the Member State(s) concerned. It shall act after consulting the European Parliament.

Article 267

1. The Union shall develop a common immigration policy aimed at ensuring, at all stages, the efficient management of migration flows, fair treatment of third-country nationals residing legally in Member States, and the prevention of, and enhanced measures to combat, illegal immigration and trafficking in human beings.

2. For the purposes of paragraph 1, European laws or framework laws shall establish measures in the following areas:

(a) the conditions of entry and residence, and standards on the issue by Member States of long-term visas and residence permits, including those for the purpose of family reunion;

(b) the definition of the rights of third-country nationals residing legally in a Member State, including the conditions governing freedom of movement and of residence in other Member States;

(c) illegal immigration and unauthorised residence, including removal and repatriation of persons residing without authorisation;

(d) combating trafficking in persons, in particular women and children.

3. The Union may conclude agreements with third countries for the readmission to their countries of origin or provenance of third-country nationals who do not or who no longer fulfil the conditions for entry, presence or residence in the territory of one of the Member States.

4. European laws or framework laws may establish measures to provide incentives and support for the action of Member States with a view to promoting the integration of third-country nationals residing legally in their territories, excluding any harmonisation of the laws and regulations of the Member States.

5. This Article shall not affect the right of Member States to determine volumes of admission of third-country nationals coming from third countries to their territory in order to seek work, whether employed or self-employed.

Article 268

The policies of the Union set out in this Section and their implementation shall be governed by the principle of solidarity and fair sharing of responsibility, including its financial implications, between the Member States. Whenever necessary, the Union acts adopted pursuant to this Section shall contain appropriate measures to give effect to this principle.

Section 3 - Judicial co-operation in Civil Matters

Article 269

1. The Union shall develop judicial co-operation in civil matters having cross-border implications, based on the principle of mutual recognition of judgments and decisions in extrajudicial cases. Such co-operation may include the adoption of measures for the approximation of the laws and regulations of the Member States.

2. For the purposes of paragraph 1, European laws or framework laws shall establish measures, particularly when necessary for the proper functioning of the internal market, aimed at ensuring:

(a) the mutual recognition and enforcement between Member States of judgments and decisions in extrajudicial cases;

(b) the cross-border service of judicial and extrajudicial documents;

(c) the compatibility of the rules applicable in the Member States concerning conflict of laws and of jurisdiction;

(d) co-operation in the taking of evidence;

(e) effective access to justice;

(f) the elimination of obstacles to the proper functioning of civil proceedings, if necessary by promoting the compatibility of the rules on civil procedure applicable in the Member States;

(g) the development of alternative methods of dispute settlement;

(h) support for the training of the judiciary and judicial staff.

3. Notwithstanding paragraph 2, a European law or framework law of the Council shall establish measures concerning family law with cross-border implications. The Council shall act unanimously after consulting the European Parliament. The Council, on a proposal from the Commission, may adopt a European decision determining those aspects of family law with cross-border implications which may be the subject of acts adopted by the ordinary legislative procedure. The Council shall act unanimously after consulting the European Parliament.

Section 4 - Judicial co-operation in Criminal Matters

Article 270

1. Judicial co-operation in criminal matters in the Union shall be based on the principle of mutual recognition of judgments and judicial decisions and shall include the approximation of the laws and regulations of the Member States in the areas referred to in paragraph 2 and in Article 271.

European laws or framework laws shall establish measures to:

(a) lay down rules and procedures for ensuring recognition throughout the Union of all forms of judgments and judicial decisions;

(b) prevent and settle conflicts of jurisdiction between Member States;

(c) support the training of the judiciary and judicial staff;

(d) facilitate co-operation between judicial or equivalent authorities of the Member States in relation to proceedings in criminal matters and the enforcement of decisions.

2. To the extent necessary to facilitate mutual recognition of judgments and judicial decisions and police and judicial co-operation in criminal matters having a cross-border dimension, European framework laws may establish minimum rules. Such rules shall take into account the differences between the legal traditions and systems of the Member States.

They shall concern:

(a) mutual admissibility of evidence between Member States;

(b) the rights of individuals in criminal procedure;

(c) the rights of victims of crime;

(d) any other specific aspects of criminal procedure which the Council has identified in advance by a European decision; for the adoption of such a decision, the Council shall act unanimously after obtaining the consent of the European Parliament.

Adoption of the minimum rules referred to in this paragraph shall not prevent Member States from maintaining or introducing a higher level of protection for individuals.

3. Where a member of the Council considers that a draft European framework law as referred to in paragraph 2 would affect fundamental aspects of its

criminal justice system, it may request that the draft framework law be referred to the European Council. In that case, the procedure referred to in Article 396 shall be suspended. After discussion, the European Council shall, within four months of this suspension, either:

(a) refer the draft back to the Council, which shall terminate the suspension of the procedure referred to in Article 396, or

(b) request the Commission or the group of Member States from which the draft originates to submit a new draft; in that case, the act originally proposed shall be deemed not to have been adopted.

4. If, by the end of the period referred to in paragraph 3, either no action has been taken by the European Council or if, within 12 months from the submission of a new draft under paragraph 3(b), the European framework law has not been adopted, and at least one third of the Member States wish to establish enhanced co-operation on the basis of the draft framework law concerned, they shall notify the European Parliament, the Council and the Commission accordingly.

In such a case, the authorisation to proceed with enhanced co-operation referred to in Articles 44(2) and 419(1) shall be deemed to be granted and the provisions on enhanced co-operation shall apply.

Article 271

1. European framework laws may establish minimum rules concerning the definition of criminal offences and sanctions in the areas of particularly serious crime with a cross-border dimension resulting from the nature or impact of such offences or from a special need to combat them on a common basis.

These areas of crime are the following: terrorism, trafficking in human beings and sexual exploitation of women and children, illicit drug trafficking, illicit arms trafficking, money laundering, corruption, counterfeiting of means of payment, computer crime and organised crime.

On the basis of developments in crime, the Council may adopt a European decision identifying other areas of crime that meet the criteria specified in this paragraph. It shall act unanimously after obtaining the consent of the European Parliament.

2. If the approximation of criminal laws and regulations of the Member States proves essential to ensure the effective implementation of a Union policy in an area which has been subject to harmonisation measures, European framework laws may establish minimum rules with regard to the definition of criminal offences and sanctions in the area concerned. Such framework laws shall be adopted by the same procedure as was followed for the adoption of the harmonisation measures in question, without prejudice to Article 264.

3. Where a member of the Council considers that a draft European framework law as referred to in paragraph 1 or 2 would affect fundamental aspects of its criminal justice system, it may request that the draft framework law be referred to the European Council. In that case, where the procedure referred to in Article 396 is applicable, it shall be suspended. After discussion, the European Council shall, within four months of this suspension, either:

(a) refer the draft back to the Council, which shall terminate the suspension of the procedure referred to in Article 396 where it is applicable, or

(b) request the Commission or the group of Member States from which the draft originates to submit a new draft; in that case, the act originally proposed shall be deemed not to have been adopted.

4. If, by the end of the period referred to in paragraph 3, either no action has been taken by the European Council or if, within 12 months from the submission of a new draft under paragraph 3(b), the European framework law has not been adopted, and at least one third of the Member States wish to establish enhanced co-operation on the basis of the draft framework law concerned, they shall notify the European Parliament, the Council and the Commission accordingly.

In such a case, the authorisation to proceed with enhanced co-operation referred to in Articles 44(2) and 419(1) shall be deemed to be granted and the provisions on enhanced co-operation shall apply.

Article 272

European laws or framework laws may establish measures to promote and support the action of Member States in the field of crime prevention, excluding any harmonisation of the laws and regulations of the Member States.

Article 273

1. Eurojust's mission shall be to support and strengthen co-ordination and co-operation between national investigating and prosecuting authorities in relation to serious crime affecting two or more Member States or requiring a prosecution on common bases, on the basis of operations conducted and information supplied by the Member States' authorities and by Europol.

In this context, European laws shall determine Eurojust's structure, operation, field of action and tasks. Those tasks may include:

(a) the initiation of criminal investigations, as well as proposing the initiation of prosecutions, conducted by competent national authorities, particularly those relating to offences against the financial interests of the Union;

(b) the co-ordination of investigations and prosecutions referred to in point (a);

(c) the strengthening of judicial co-operation, including by resolution of conflicts of jurisdiction and by close co-operation with the European Judicial Network. European laws shall also determine arrangements for involving the European Parliament and national Parliaments in the evaluation of Eurojust's activities.

2. In the prosecutions referred to in paragraph 1, and without prejudice to Article 274, formal acts of judicial procedure shall be carried out by the competent national officials.

Article 274

1. In order to combat crimes affecting the financial interests of the Union, a European law of the Council may establish a European Public Prosecutor's Office from Eurojust. The Council shall act unanimously after obtaining the consent of the European Parliament.

2. The European Public Prosecutor's Office shall be responsible for investigating, prosecuting and bringing to judgment, where appropriate in liaison with

Europol, the perpetrators of, and accomplices in, offences against the Union's financial interests, as determined by the European law provided for in paragraph 1. It shall exercise the functions of prosecutor in the competent courts of the Member States in relation to such offences.

3. The European law referred to in paragraph 1 shall determine the general rules applicable to the European Public Prosecutor's Office, the conditions governing the performance of its functions, the rules of procedure applicable to its activities, as well as those governing the admissibility of evidence, and the rules applicable to the judicial review of procedural measures taken by it in the performance of its functions.

4. The European Council may, at the same time or subsequently, adopt a European decision amending paragraph 1 in order to extend the powers of the European Public Prosecutor's Office to include serious crime having a cross-border dimension and amending accordingly paragraph 2 as regards the perpetrators of, and accomplices in, serious crimes affecting more than one Member State. The European Council shall act unanimously after obtaining the consent of the European Parliament and after consulting the Commission.

Section 5 - Police Co-operation

Article 275

1. The Union shall establish police co-operation involving all the Member States' competent authorities, including police, customs and other specialised law enforcement services in relation to the prevention, detection and investigation of criminal offences.

2. For the purposes of paragraph 1, European laws or framework laws may establish measures concerning:

(a) the collection, storage, processing, analysis and exchange of relevant information;

(b) support for the training of staff, and co-operation on the exchange of staff, on equipment and on research into crime-detection;

(c) common investigative techniques in relation to the detection of serious forms of organised crime.

3. A European law or framework law of the Council may establish measures concerning operational co-operation between the authorities referred to in this Article. The Council shall act unanimously after consulting the European Parliament.

Article 276

1. Europol's mission shall be to support and strengthen action by the Member States' police authorities and other law enforcement services and their mutual co-operation in preventing and combating serious crime affecting two or more Member States, terrorism and forms of crime which affect a common interest covered by a Union policy.

2. European laws shall determine Europol's structure, operation, field of action and tasks. These tasks may include:

(a) the collection, storage, processing, analysis and exchange of information forwarded particularly by the authorities of the Member States or third countries or bodies;

(b) the co-ordination, organisation and implementation of investigative and operational action carried out jointly with the Member States' competent authorities or in the context of joint investigative teams, where appropriate in liaison with Eurojust. European laws shall also lay down the procedures for scrutiny of Europol's activities by the European Parliament, together with national Parliaments.

3. Any operational action by Europol must be carried out in liaison and in agreement with the authorities of the Member State or States whose territory is concerned. The application of coercive measures shall be the exclusive responsibility of the competent national authorities.

Article 277

A European law or framework law of the Council shall lay down the conditions and limitations under which the competent authorities of the Member States referred to in Articles 270 and 275 may operate in the territory of another Member State in liaison and in agreement with the authorities of that State. The Council shall act unanimously after consulting the European Parliament.

Chapter V - Areas Where The Union May Take Co-ordinating, Complementary or Supporting Action

Section 1 - Public Health

Article 278

1. A high level of human health protection shall be ensured in the definition and implementation of all the Union's policies and activities.

Action by the Union, which shall complement national policies, shall be directed towards improving public health, preventing human illness and diseases, and obviating sources of danger to physical and mental health. Such action shall cover:

(a) the fight against the major health scourges, by promoting research into their causes, their transmission and their prevention, as well as health information and education;

(b) monitoring, early warning of and combating serious cross-border threats to health. The Union shall complement the Member States' action in reducing drug-related health damage, including information and prevention.

2. The Union shall encourage co-operation between the Member States in the areas referred to in this Article and, if necessary, lend support to their action. It shall in particular encourage co-operation between the Member States to improve the complementarity of their health services in cross-border areas.

Member States shall, in liaison with the Commission, co-ordinate among themselves their policies and programmes in the areas referred to in paragraph 1.

The Commission may, in close contact with the Member States, take any useful initiative to promote such co-ordination, in particular initiatives aiming at the establishment of guidelines and indicators, the organisation of exchange of best practice, and the preparation of the necessary elements for periodic monitoring and evaluation. The European Parliament shall be kept fully informed.

3. The Union and the Member States shall foster co-operation with third countries and the competent international organisations in the sphere of public health.

4. By way of derogation from Article 12(5) and Article 17(a) and in accordance with Article 14 (2)(k), European laws or framework laws shall contribute to the achievement of the objectives referred to in this Article by establishing the following measures in order to meet common safety concerns:

(a) measures setting high standards of quality and safety of organs and substances of human origin, blood and blood derivatives; these measures shall not prevent any Member State from maintaining or introducing more stringent protective measures;

(b) measures in the veterinary and phytosanitary fields which have as their direct objective the protection of public health;

(c) measures setting high standards of quality and safety for medicinal products and devices for medical use;

(d) measures concerning monitoring, early warning of and combating serious cross-border threats to health. Such European laws or framework laws shall be adopted after consultation of the Committee of the Regions and the Economic and Social Committee.

5. European laws or framework laws may also establish incentive measures designed to protect and improve human health and in particular to combat the major cross-border health scourges, as well as measures which have as their direct objective the protection of public health regarding tobacco and the abuse of alcohol, excluding any harmonisation of the laws and regulations of the Member States. They shall be adopted after consultation of the Committee of the Regions and the Economic and Social Committee.

6. For the purposes of this Article, the Council, on a proposal from the Commission, may also adopt recommendations.

7. Union action shall respect the responsibilities of the Member States for the definition of their health policy and for the organisation and delivery of health services and medical care. The responsibilities of the Member States shall include the management of health services and medical care and the allocation of the resources assigned to them. The measures referred to in paragraph 4(a) shall not affect national provisions on the donation or medical use of organs and blood.

Section 2 - Industry

Article 279

1. The Union and the Member States shall ensure that the conditions necessary for the competitiveness of the Union's industry exist. For that purpose, in

accordance with a system of open and competitive markets, their action shall be aimed at:

(a) speeding up the adjustment of industry to structural changes;

(b) encouraging an environment favourable to initiative and to the development of undertakings
throughout the Union, particularly small and medium-sized undertakings;

(c) encouraging an environment favourable to co-operation between undertakings;

(d) fostering better exploitation of the industrial potential of policies of innovation, research and technological development.

2. The Member States shall consult each other in liaison with the Commission and, where necessary, shall co-ordinate their action. The Commission may take any useful initiative to promote such co-ordination, in particular initiatives aiming at the establishment of guidelines and indicators, the organisation of exchange of best practice, and the preparation of the necessary elements for periodic monitoring and evaluation. The European Parliament shall be kept fully informed.

3. The Union shall contribute to the achievement of the objectives set out in paragraph 1 through the policies and activities it pursues under other provisions of the Constitution. European laws or framework laws may establish specific measures in support of action taken in the Member States to achieve the objectives set out in paragraph 1, excluding any harmonisation of the laws and regulations of the Member States. They shall be adopted after consultation of the Economic and Social Committee.

This Section shall not provide a basis for the introduction by the Union of any measure which could lead to distortion of competition or contains tax provisions or provisions relating to the rights and interests of employed persons.

Section 3 - Culture

Article 280

1. The Union shall contribute to the flowering of the cultures of the Member States, while respecting their national and regional diversity and at the same time bringing the common cultural heritage to the fore.

2. Action by the Union shall be aimed at encouraging co-operation between Member States and, if necessary, supporting and complementing their action in the following areas:

(a) improvement of the knowledge and dissemination of the culture and history of the European peoples;

(b) conservation and safeguarding of cultural heritage of European significance;

(c) non-commercial cultural exchanges;

(d) artistic and literary creation, including in the audiovisual sector.

3. The Union and the Member States shall foster co-operation with third countries and the competent international organisations in the sphere of culture, in particular the Council of Europe.

4. The Union shall take cultural aspects into account in its action under other provisions of the Constitution, in particular in order to respect and to promote the diversity of its cultures.

5. In order to contribute to the achievement of the objectives referred to in this Article:

(a) European laws or framework laws shall establish incentive measures, excluding any harmonisation of the laws and regulations of the Member States. They shall be adopted after consultation of the Committee of the Regions;

(b) the Council, on a proposal from the Commission, shall adopt recommendations.

Section 4 - Tourism

Article 281

1. The Union shall complement the action of the Member States in the tourism sector, in particular by promoting the competitiveness of Union undertakings in that sector. To that end, Union action shall be aimed at:

(a) encouraging the creation of a favourable environment for the development of undertakings in this sector;

(b) promoting co-operation between the Member States, particularly by the exchange of good practice;

2. European laws or framework laws shall establish specific measures to complement actions within the Member States to achieve the objectives referred to in this Article, excluding any harmonisation of the laws and regulations of the Member States.

Section 5 - Education, Youth, Sport and Vocational Training

Article 282

1. The Union shall contribute to the development of quality education by encouraging co-operation between Member States and, if necessary, by supporting and complementing their action. It shall fully respect the responsibility of the Member States for the content of teaching and the organisation of education systems and their cultural and linguistic diversity.

The Union shall contribute to the promotion of European sporting issues, while taking account of the specific nature of sport, its structures based on voluntary activity and its social and educational function. Union action shall be aimed at:

(a) developing the European dimension in education, particularly through the teaching and dissemination of the languages of the Member States;

(b) encouraging mobility of students and teachers, inter alia by encouraging the academic recognition of diplomas and periods of study;

(c) promoting co-operation between educational establishments;

(d) developing exchanges of information and experience on issues common to the education systems of the Member States;

(e) encouraging the development of youth exchanges and of exchanges of socio-educational instructors and encouraging the participation of young people in democratic life in Europe;

(f) encouraging the development of distance education;

(g) developing the European dimension in sport, by promoting fairness and openness in sporting competitions and co-operation between bodies responsible for sports, and by protecting the physical and moral integrity of sportsmen and sportswomen, especially young sportsmen and sportswomen.

2. The Union and the Member States shall foster co-operation with third countries and the competent international organisations in the field of education and sport, in particular the Council of Europe.

3. In order to contribute to the achievement of the objectives referred to in this Article:

(a) European laws or framework laws shall establish incentive measures, excluding any harmonisation of the laws and regulations of the Member States. They shall be adopted after consultation of the Committee of the Regions and the Economic and Social Committee;

(b) the Council, on a proposal from the Commission, shall adopt recommendations.

Article 283

1. The Union shall implement a vocational training policy which shall support and complement the action of the Member States, while fully respecting the responsibility of the Member States for the content and organisation of vocational training.

Union action shall aim to:

(a) facilitate adaptation to industrial change, in particular through vocational training and retraining;

(b) improve initial and continuing vocational training in order to facilitate vocational integration and reintegration into the labour market;

(c) facilitate access to vocational training and encourage mobility of instructors and trainees and particularly young people;

(d) stimulate co-operation on training between educational or training establishments and firms;

(e) develop exchanges of information and experience on issues common to the training systems of the Member States.

2. The Union and the Member States shall foster co-operation with third countries and the competent international organisations in the sphere of vocational training.

3. In order to contribute to the achievement of the objectives referred to in this Article:

(a) European laws or framework laws shall establish the necessary measures, excluding any harmonisation of the laws and regulations of the Member States. They shall be adopted after consultation of the Committee of the Regions and the Economic and Social Committee;

(b) the Council, on a proposal from the Commission, shall adopt recommendations.

Section 6 - Civil Protection

Article 284

1. The Union shall encourage co-operation between Member States in order to improve the effectiveness of systems for preventing and protecting against natural or man-made disasters. Union action shall aim to:

(a) support and complement Member States' action at national, regional and local level in risk prevention, in preparing their civil-protection personnel and in responding to natural or man-made disasters within the Union;

(b) promote swift, effective operational co-operation within the Union between national civil-protection services;

(c) promote consistency in international civil-protection work.

2. European laws or framework laws shall establish the measures necessary to help achieve the objectives referred to in paragraph 1, excluding any harmonisation of the laws and regulations of the Member States.

Section 7 - Administrative co-operation

Article 285

1. Effective implementation of Union law by the Member States, which is essential for the proper functioning of the Union, shall be regarded as a matter of common interest.

2. The Union may support the efforts of Member States to improve their administrative capacity to implement Union law. Such action may include facilitating the exchange of information and of civil servants as well as supporting training schemes. No Member State shall be obliged to avail itself of such support. European laws shall establish the necessary measures to this end, excluding any harmonisation of the laws and regulations of the Member States.

3. This Article shall be without prejudice to the obligations of the Member States to implement Union law or to the prerogatives and duties of the Commission. It shall also be without prejudice to other provisions of the Constitution providing for administrative co-operation among the Member States and between them and the Union.

Title IV
Association of the Overseas Countries and Territories

Article 286

1. The non-European countries and territories which have special relations with Denmark, France, the Netherlands and the United Kingdom shall be associated with the Union. These countries and territories, hereinafter called the 'countries and territories', are listed in Annex II. This title shall apply to Green-

land, subject to the specific provisions of the Protocol on special arrangements for Greenland.

2. The purpose of association shall be to promote the economic and social development of the countries and territories and to establish close economic relations between them and the Union. Association shall serve primarily to further the interests and prosperity of the inhabitants of these countries and territories in order to lead them to the economic, social and cultural development to which they aspire.

Article 287

Association shall have the following objectives:

(a) Member States shall apply to their trade with the countries and territories the same treatment as they accord each other pursuant to the Constitution;

(b) each country or territory shall apply to its trade with Member States and with the other countries and territories the same treatment as that which it applies to the European State with which it has special relations;

(c) Member States shall contribute to the investments required for the progressive development of these countries and territories;

(d) for investments financed by the Union, participation in tenders and supplies shall be open on equal terms to all natural and legal persons who are nationals of a Member State or of one of the countries and territories;

(e) in relations between Member States and the countries and territories, the right of establishment of nationals and companies or firms shall be regulated in accordance with the provisions of Subsection 2 of Section 2 of Chapter I of Title III relating to the freedom of establishment and under the procedures laid down in that Subsection, and on a non-discriminatory basis, subject to any acts adopted pursuant to Article 291.

Article 288

1. Customs duties on imports into the Member States of goods originating in the countries and territories shall be prohibited in conformity with the prohibition of customs duties between Member States provided for in the Constitution.

2. Customs duties on imports into each country or territory from Member States or from the other countries or territories shall be prohibited in accordance with Article 151(4).

3. The countries and territories may, however, levy customs duties which meet the needs of their development and industrialisation or produce revenue for their budgets.

The duties referred to in the first subparagraph shall not exceed the level of those imposed on imports of products from the Member State with which each country or territory has special relations.

4. Paragraph 2 shall not apply to countries and territories which, by reason of the particular international obligations by which they are bound, already apply a non-discriminatory customs tariff.

5. The introduction of or any change in customs duties imposed on goods imported into the countries and territories shall not, either in law or in fact, give rise to any direct or indirect discrimination between imports from the various Member States.

Article 289

If the level of the duties applicable to goods from a third country on entry into a country or territory is liable, when Article 288(1) has been applied, to cause deflections of trade to the detriment of any Member State, the latter may request the Commission to propose to the other Member States that they take the necessary measures to remedy the situation.

Article 290

Subject to the provisions relating to public health, public security or public policy, freedom of movement within Member States for workers from the countries and territories, and within the countries and territories for workers from Member States, shall be regulated by acts adopted in accordance with Article 291.

Article 291

The Council, on a proposal from the Commission, shall adopt unanimously, on the basis of the experience acquired under the association of the countries and territories with the Union, European laws, framework laws, regulations and decisions as regards the detailed rules and the procedure for the association of the countries and territories with the Union. These laws and framework laws shall be adopted after consultation of the European Parliament.

Title V
The Unions External Action

Chapter 1 - Provisions Having General Application

Article 292

1. The Union's action on the international scene shall be guided by the principles which have inspired its own creation, development and enlargement, and which it seeks to advance in the wider world: democracy, the rule of law, the universality and indivisibility of human rights and fundamental freedoms, respect for human dignity, the principles of equality and solidarity, and respect for the principles of the United Nations Charter and international law.

The Union shall seek to develop relations and build partnerships with third countries, and international, regional or global organisations which share the principles referred to in the first subparagraph. It shall promote multilateral solutions to common problems, in particular in the framework of the United Nations.

2. The Union shall define and pursue common policies and actions, and shall work for a high degree of co-operation in all fields of international relations, in order to:

(a) safeguard its values, fundamental interests, security, independence and integrity;

(b) consolidate and support democracy, the rule of law, human rights and the principles of international law;

(c) preserve peace, prevent conflicts and strengthen international security, in accordance with the purposes and principles of the United Nations Charter, with the principles of the Helsinki Final Act and with the aims of the Charter of Paris, including those relating to external borders;

(d) foster the sustainable economic, social and environmental development of developing countries, with the primary aim of eradicating poverty;

(e) encourage the integration of all countries into the world economy, including through the progressive abolition of restrictions on international trade;

(f) help develop international measures to preserve and improve the quality of the environment and the sustainable management of global natural resources, in order to ensure sustainable development;

(g) assist populations, countries and regions confronting natural or man-made disasters;

(h) promote an international system based on stronger multilateral co-operation and good global governance.

3. The Union shall respect the principles and pursue the objectives set out in paragraphs 1 and 2 in the development and implementation of the different areas of the Union's external action covered by this Title and the external aspects of its other policies. The Union shall ensure consistency between the different areas of its external action and between these and its other policies. The Council and the Commission, assisted by the Union Minister for Foreign Affairs, shall ensure that consistency and shall co-operate to that effect.

Article 293

1. On the basis of the principles and objectives set out in Article 292, the European Council shall identify the strategic interests and objectives of the Union.

European decisions of the European Council on the strategic interests and objectives of the Union shall relate to the common foreign and security policy and to other areas of the external action of the Union. Such decisions may concern the relations of the Union with a specific country or region or may be thematic in approach. They shall define their duration, and the means to be made available by the Union and the Member States.

The European Council shall act unanimously on a recommendation from the Council, adopted by the latter under the arrangements laid down for each area. European decisions of the European Council shall be implemented in accordance with the procedures provided for in the Constitution.

2. The Union Minister for Foreign Affairs, for the area of common foreign and security policy, and the Commission, for other areas of external action, may submit joint proposals to the Council.

Chapter II - Common Foreign and Security Policy

Section 1 - Common Provisions

Article 294

1. In the context of the principles and objectives of its external action, the Union shall define and implement a common foreign and security policy covering all areas of foreign and security policy.

2. The Member States shall support the common foreign and security policy actively and unreservedly in a spirit of loyalty and mutual solidarity.

The Member States shall work together to enhance and develop their mutual political solidarity. They shall refrain from any action which is contrary to the interests of the Union or likely to impair its effectiveness as a cohesive force in international relations.

The Council and the Union Minister for Foreign Affairs shall ensure that these principles are complied with.

3. The Union shall conduct the common foreign and security policy by:

(a) defining the general guidelines;

(b) adopting European decisions defining:

(i) actions to be undertaken by the Union;

(ii) positions to be taken by the Union;

(iii) arrangements for the implementation of the European decisions referred to in points (i) and (ii);

(c) strengthening systematic co-operation between Member States in the conduct of policy.

Article 295

1. The European Council shall define the general guidelines for the common foreign and security policy, including for matters with defence implications.

If international developments so require, the President of the European Council shall convene an extraordinary meeting of the European Council in order to define the strategic lines of the Union's policy in the face of such developments.

2. The Council shall adopt the European decisions necessary for defining and implementing the common foreign and security policy on the basis of the general guidelines and strategic lines defined by the European Council.

Article 296

1. The Union Minister for Foreign Affairs, who shall chair the Foreign Affairs Council, shall contribute through his or her proposals towards the preparation of the common foreign and security policy and shall ensure implementation of the European decisions adopted by the European Council and the Council.

2. The Minister for Foreign Affairs shall represent the Union for matters relating to the common foreign and security policy. He or she shall conduct political dialogue with third parties on the Union's behalf and shall express the Union's position in international organisations and at international conferences.

3. In fulfilling his or her mandate, the Union Minister for Foreign Affairs shall be assisted by a European External Action Service. This service shall work in co-operation with the diplomatic services of the Member States and shall comprise officials from relevant departments of the General Secretariat of the Council and of the Commission as well as staff seconded from national diplomatic services of the Member States. The organisation and functioning of the European External Action Service shall be established by a European decision of the Council. The Council shall act on a proposal from the Union Minister for Foreign Affairs after consulting the European Parliament and after obtaining the consent of the Commission.

Article 297

1. Where the international situation requires operational action by the Union, the Council shall adopt the necessary European decisions. Such decisions shall lay down the objectives, the scope, the means to be made available to the Union, if necessary the duration, and the conditions for implementation of the action.

If there is a change in circumstances having a substantial effect on a question subject to such a European decision, the Council shall review the principles and objectives of that decision and adopt the necessary European decisions.

2. The European decisions referred to in paragraph 1 shall commit the Member States in the positions they adopt and in the conduct of their activity.

3. Whenever there is any plan to adopt a national position or take national action pursuant to a European decision as referred to in paragraph 1, information shall be provided by the Member State concerned in time to allow, if necessary, for prior consultations within the Council. The obligation to provide prior information shall not apply to measures which are merely a national transposition of such a decision.

4. In cases of imperative need arising from changes in the situation and failing a review of the European decision pursuant to the second subparagraph of paragraph 1, Member States may take the necessary measures as a matter of urgency, having regard to the general objectives of that decision.

The Member State concerned shall inform the Council immediately of any such measures.

5. Should there be any major difficulties in implementing a European decision as referred to in this Article, a Member State shall refer them to the Council which shall discuss them and seek appropriate solutions. Such solutions shall not run counter to the objectives of the action or impair its effectiveness.

Article 298

The Council shall adopt European decisions which shall define the approach of the Union to a particular matter of a geographical or thematic nature. Member States shall ensure that their national policies conform to the positions of the Union.

Article 299

1. Any Member State, the Union Minister for Foreign Affairs, or that Minister with the Commission's support, may refer any question relating to the

common foreign and security policy to the Council and may submit to it initiatives or proposals as appropriate.

2. In cases requiring a rapid decision, the Union Minister for Foreign Affairs, of the Minister's own motion or at the request of a Member State, shall convene an extraordinary meeting of the Council within forty-eight hours or, in an emergency, within a shorter period.

Article 300

1. The European decisions referred to in this Chapter shall be adopted by the Council acting unanimously.

When abstaining in a vote, any member of the Council may qualify its abstention by making a formal declaration. In that case, it shall not be obliged to apply the European decision, but shall accept that the latter commits the Union. In a spirit of mutual solidarity, the Member State concerned shall refrain from any action likely to conflict with or impede Union action based on that decision and the other Member States shall respect its position. If the members of the Council qualifying their abstention in this way represent at least one third of the Member States comprising at least one third of the population of the Union, the decision shall not be adopted.

2. By way of derogation from paragraph 1, the Council shall act by a qualified majority:

(a) when adopting European decisions defining a Union action or position on the basis of a European decision of the European Council relating to the Union's strategic interests and objectives, as referred to in Article 293(1);

(b) when adopting a European decision defining a Union action or position, on a proposal which the Union Minister for Foreign Affairs has presented following a specific request to him or her from the European Council, made on its own initiative or that of the Minister;

(c) when adopting a European decision implementing a European decision defining a Union action or position;

(d) when adopting a European decision concerning the appointment of a special representative in accordance with Article 302. If a member of the Council declares that, for vital and stated reasons of national policy, it intends to oppose the adoption of a European decision to be adopted by a qualified majority, a vote shall not be taken. The Union Minister for Foreign Affairs will, in close consultation with the Member State involved, search for a solution acceptable to it. If he or she does not succeed, the Council may, acting by a qualified majority, request that the matter be referred to the European Council for a European decision by unanimity.

3. In accordance with Article 40(7) the European Council may unanimously adopt a European decision stipulating that the Council shall act by a qualified majority in cases other than those referred to in paragraph 2 of this Article.

4. Paragraphs 2 and 3 shall not apply to decisions having military or defence implications.

Article 301

1. When the European Council or the Council has defined a common approach of the Union within the meaning of Article I-40(5), the Union Minister

for Foreign Affairs and the Ministers for Foreign Affairs of the Member States shall co-ordinate their activities within the Council.

2. The diplomatic missions of the Member States and the Union delegations in third countries and at international organisations shall co-operate and shall contribute to formulating and implementing the common approach referred to in paragraph 1.

Article 302

The Council may appoint, on a proposal from the Union Minister for Foreign Affairs, a special representative with a mandate in relation to particular policy issues. The special representative shall carry out his or her mandate under the Minister's authority.

Article 303

The Union may conclude agreements with one or more States or international organisations in areas covered by this Chapter.

Article 304

1. The Union Minister for Foreign Affairs shall consult and inform the European Parliament in accordance with Article I-40(8) and Article I-41(8). He or she shall ensure that the views of the European Parliament are duly taken into consideration. Special representatives may be involved in briefing the European Parliament.

2. The European Parliament may ask questions of the Council and of the Union Minister for Foreign Affairs or make recommendations to them. Twice a year it shall hold a debate on progress in implementing the common foreign and security policy, including the common security and defence policy.

Article 305

1. Member States shall co-ordinate their action in international organisations and at international conferences. They shall uphold the Union's positions in such fora. The Union Minister for Foreign Affairs shall organise this co-ordination.

In international organisations and at international conferences where not all the Member States participate, those which do take part shall uphold the Union's positions.

2. In accordance with Article 16(2), Member States represented in international organisations or international conferences where not all the Member States participate shall keep the latter, as well as the Union Minister for Foreign Affairs, informed of any matter of common interest.

Member States which are also members of the United Nations Security Council shall concert and keep the other Member States and the Union Minister for Foreign Affairs fully informed.

Member States which are members of the Security Council will, in the execution of their functions, defend the positions and the interests of the Union, without prejudice to their responsibilities under the United Nations Charter.

When the Union has defined a position on a subject which is on the United Nations Security Council agenda, those Member States which sit on the Security

Council shall request that the Union Minister for Foreign Affairs be asked to present the Union's position.

Article 306

The diplomatic and consular missions of the Member States and the Union delegations in third countries and international conferences, and their representations to international organisations, shall co-operate in ensuring that the European decisions defining Union positions and actions adopted pursuant to this Chapter are complied with and implemented. They shall step up co-operation by exchanging information and carrying out joint assessments.

They shall contribute to the implementation of the right of European citizens to protection in the territory of third countries as referred to in Article 10(2)(c) and the measures adopted pursuant to Article 127.

Article 307

1. Without prejudice to Article 344, a Political and Security Committee shall monitor the international situation in the areas covered by the common foreign and security policy and contribute to the definition of policies by delivering opinions to the Council at the request of the latter, or of the Union Minister for Foreign Affairs, or on its own initiative. It shall also monitor the implementation of agreed policies, without prejudice to the powers of the Union Minister for Foreign Affairs.

2. Within the scope of this Chapter, the Political and Security Committee shall exercise, under the responsibility of the Council and of the Union Minister for Foreign Affairs, the political control and strategic direction of the crisis management operations referred to in Article 309.

The Council may authorise the Committee, for the purpose and for the duration of a crisis management operation, as determined by the Council, to take the relevant measures concerning the political control and strategic direction of the operation.

Article 308

The implementation of the common foreign and security policy shall not affect the application of the procedures and the extent of the powers of the institutions laid down by the Constitution for the exercise of the Union competences referred to in Articles 13 to 15 and 17.

Similarly, the implementation of the policies listed in those Articles shall not affect the application of the procedures and the extent of the powers of the institutions laid down by the Constitution for the exercise of the Union competences under this Chapter.

Section 2 - The Common Security and Defence Policy

Article 309

1. The tasks referred to in Article 41(1), in the course of which the Union

may use civilian and military means, shall include joint disarmament operations, humanitarian and rescue tasks, military advice and assistance tasks, conflict prevention and peace-keeping tasks, tasks of combat forces in crisis management , including peace-making and post-conflict stabilisation. All these tasks may contribute to the fight against terrorism, including by supporting third countries in combating terrorism in their territories.

2. The Council shall adopt European decisions relating to the tasks referred to in paragraph 1, defining their objectives and scope and the general conditions for their implementation. The Union Minister for Foreign Affairs, acting under the authority of the Council and in close and constant contact with the Political and Security Committee, shall ensure co-ordination of the civilian and military aspects of such tasks.

Article 310

1. Within the framework of the European decisions adopted in accordance with Article 309, the Council may entrust the implementation of a task to a group of Member States which are willing and have the necessary capability for such a task. Those Member States, in association with the Union Minister for Foreign Affairs, shall agree among themselves on the management of the task.

2. Member States participating in the task shall keep the Council regularly informed of its progress on their own initiative or at the request of another Member State. Those States shall inform the Council immediately should the completion of the task entail major consequences or require amendment of the objective, scope and conditions determined for the task in the European decisions referred to in paragraph 1. In such cases, the Council shall adopt the necessary European decisions.

Article 311

1. The Agency in the field of defence capabilities development, research, acquisition and armaments (European Defence Agency), established by Article 41(3) and subject to the authority of the Council, shall have as its task to:

(a) contribute to identifying the Member States' military capability objectives and evaluating observance of the capability commitments given by the Member States;

(b) promote harmonisation of operational needs and adoption of effective, compatible procurement methods;

(c) propose multilateral projects to fulfil the objectives in terms of military capabilities, ensure co-ordination of the programmes implemented by the Member States and management of specific co-operation programmes;

(d) support defence technology research, and co-ordinate and plan joint research activities and the study of technical solutions meeting future operational needs;

(e) contribute to identifying and, if necessary, implementing any useful measure for strengthening the industrial and technological base of the defence sector and for improving the effectiveness of military expenditure.

2. The European Defence Agency shall be open to all Member States wishing to be part of it. The Council, acting by a qualified majority, shall adopt

a European decision defining the Agency's statute, seat and operational rules. That decision should take account of the level of effective participation in the Agency's activities. Specific groups shall be set up within the Agency bringing together Member States engaged in joint projects. The Agency shall carry out its tasks in liaison with the Commission where necessary.

Article 312

1. Those Member States which wish to participate in the permanent structured co-operation referred to in Article 41(6), which fulfil the criteria and have made the commitments on military capabilities set out in the Protocol on permanent structured co-operation shall notify their intention to the Council and to the Union Minister for Foreign Affairs.

2. Within three months following the notification referred to in paragraph 1 the Council shall adopt a European decision establishing permanent structured co-operation and determining the list of participating Member States. The Council shall act by a qualified majority after consulting the Union Minister for Foreign Affairs.

3. Any Member State which, at a later stage, wishes to participate in the permanent structured co-operation shall notify its intention to the Council and to the Union Minister for Foreign Affairs.

The Council shall adopt a European decision confirming the participation of the Member State concerned which fulfils the criteria and makes the commitments referred to in Articles 1 and 2 of the Protocol on permanent structured co-operation. The Council shall act by a qualified majority after consulting the Union Minister for Foreign Affairs. Only members of the Council representing the participating Member States shall take part in the vote.

A qualified majority shall be defined as at least 55 % of the members of the Council representing the participating Member States, comprising at least 65 % of the population of these States.

A blocking minority must include at least the minimum number of Council members representing more than 35 % of the population of the participating Member States, plus one member, failing which the qualified majority shall be deemed attained.

4. If a participating Member State no longer fulfils the criteria or is no longer able to meet the commitments referred to in Articles 1 and 2 of the Protocol on permanent structured co-operation, the Council may adopt a European decision suspending the participation of the Member State concerned.

The Council shall act by a qualified majority. Only members of the Council representing the participating Member States, with the exception of the Member State in question, shall take part in the vote.

A qualified majority shall be defined as at least 55 % of the members of the Council representing the participating Member States, comprising at least 65 % of the population of these States.

A blocking minority must include at least the minimum number of Council members representing more than 35 % of the population of the participating Member States, plus one member, failing which the qualified majority shall be deemed attained.

5. Any participating Member State which wishes to withdraw from perma-

nent structured co-operation shall notify its intention to the Council, which shall take note that the Member State in question has ceased to participate.

6. The European decisions and recommendations of the Council within the framework of permanent structured co-operation, other than those provided for in paragraphs 2 to 5, shall be adopted by unanimity. For the purposes of this paragraph, unanimity shall be constituted by the votes of the representatives of the participating Member States only.

Section 3 - Financial Provisions

Article 313

1. Administrative expenditure which the implementation of this Chapter entails for the institutions shall be charged to the Union budget.

2. Operating expenditure to which the implementation of this Chapter gives rise shall also be charged to the Union budget, except for such expenditure arising from operations having military or defence implications and cases where the Council decides otherwise. In cases where expenditure is not charged to the Union budget it shall be charged to the Member States in accordance with the gross national product scale, unless the Council decides otherwise. As for expenditure arising from operations having military or defence implications, Member States whose representatives in the Council have made a formal declaration under Article 300(1), second subparagraph, shall not be obliged to contribute to the financing thereof.

3. The Council shall adopt a European decision establishing the specific procedures for guaranteeing rapid access to appropriations in the Union budget for urgent financing of initiatives in the framework of the common foreign and security policy, and in particular for preparatory activities for the tasks referred to in Article 41(1) and Article 309. It shall act after consulting the European Parliament. Preparatory activities for the tasks referred to in Article 41(1) and Article 309 which are not charged to the Union budget shall be financed by a start-up fund made up of Member States contributions.

The Council shall adopt by a qualified majority, on a proposal from the Union Minister for Foreign Affairs, European decisions establishing:

(a) the procedures for setting up and financing the start-up fund, in particular the amounts allocated to the fund;

(b) the procedures for administering the start-up fund;

(c) the financial control procedures.

When the task planned in accordance with Article I-41(1) and Article 309 cannot be charged to the Union budget, the Council shall authorise the Union Minister for Foreign Affairs to use the fund. The Union Minister for Foreign Affairs shall report to the Council on the implementation of this remit.

Chapter III - Common Commercial Policy

Article 314

By establishing a customs union in accordance with Article 151, the Union shall contribute, in the common interest, to the harmonious development of world trade, the progressive abolition of restrictions on international trade and on foreign direct investment, and the lowering of customs and other barriers.

Article 315

1. The common commercial policy shall be based on uniform principles, particularly with regard to changes in tariff rates, the conclusion of tariff and trade agreements relating to trade in goods and services, and the commercial aspects of intellectual property, foreign direct investment, the achievement of uniformity in measures of liberalisation, export policy and measures to protect trade such as those to be taken in the event of dumping or subsidies. The common commercial policy shall be conducted in the context of the principles and objectives of the Union's external action.

2. European laws shall establish the measures defining the framework for implementing the common commercial policy.

3. Where agreements with one or more third countries or international organisations need to be negotiated and concluded, Article 325 shall apply, subject to the special provisions of this Article.

The Commission shall make recommendations to the Council, which shall authorise it to open the necessary negotiations. The Council and the Commission shall be responsible for ensuring that the agreements negotiated are compatible with internal Union policies and rules.

The Commission shall conduct these negotiations in consultation with a special committee appointed by the Council to assist the Commission in this task and within the framework of such directives as the Council may issue to it. The Commission shall report regularly to the special committee and to the European Parliament on the progress of negotiations.

4. For the negotiation and conclusion of the agreements referred to in paragraph 3, the Council shall act by a qualified majority. For the negotiation and conclusion of agreements in the fields of trade in services and the commercial aspects of intellectual property, as well as foreign direct investment, the Council shall act unanimously where such agreements include provisions for which unanimity is required for the adoption of internal rules. The Council shall also act unanimously for the negotiation and conclusion of agreements:

(a) in the field of trade in cultural and audiovisual services, where these agreements risk prejudicing the Union's cultural and linguistic diversity;

(b) in the field of trade in social, education and health services, where these agreements risk seriously disturbing the national organisation of such services and prejudicing the responsibility of Member States to deliver them.

5. The negotiation and conclusion of international agreements in the field of transport shall be subject to Section 7 of Chapter III of Title III and to Article 325.

6. The exercise of the competences conferred by this Article in the field of the common commercial policy shall not affect the delimitation of competences between the Union and the Member States, and shall not lead to harmonisation of legislative or regulatory provisions of the Member States insofar as the Constitution excludes such harmonisation.

Chapter IV - co-operation With Third Countries and Humanitarian Aid

Section 1 - Development Co-operation

Article 316

1. Union policy in the field of development co-operation shall be conducted within the framework of the principles and objectives of the Union's external action. The Union's development co-operation policy and that of the Member States shall complement and reinforce each other.

Union development co-operation policy shall have as its primary objective the reduction and, in the long term, the eradication of poverty. The Union shall take account of the objectives of development co-operation in the policies that it implements which are likely to affect developing countries.

2. The Union and the Member States shall comply with the commitments and take account of the objectives they have approved in the context of the United Nations and other competent international organisations.

Article 317

1. European laws or framework laws shall establish the measures necessary for the implementation of development co-operation policy, which may relate to multiannual co-operation programmes with developing countries or programmes with a thematic approach.

2. The Union may conclude with third countries and competent international organisations any agreement helping to achieve the objectives referred to in Articles 292 and 316.

The first subparagraph shall be without prejudice to Member States' competence to negotiate in international bodies and to conclude agreements.

3. The European Investment Bank shall contribute, under the terms laid down in its Statute, to the implementation of the measures referred to in paragraph 1.

Article 318

1. In order to promote the complementarity and efficiency of their action, the Union and the Member States shall co-ordinate their policies on development co-operation and shall consult each other on their aid programmes, including in international organisations and during international conferences. They may undertake joint action. Member States shall contribute if necessary to the implementation of Union aid programmes.

2. The Commission may take any useful initiative to promote the co-ordination referred to in paragraph 1.

3. Within their respective spheres of competence, the Union and the Member States shall co-operate with third countries and the competent international organisations.

Section 2 - Economic, Financial and Technical co-operation with Third Countries

Article 319

1. Without prejudice to the other provisions of the Constitution, and in particular Articles 316 to 318, the Union shall carry out economic, financial and technical co-operation measures, including assistance, in particular financial assistance, with third countries other than developing countries. Such measures shall be consistent with the development policy of the Union and shall be carried out within the framework of the principles and objectives of its external action. The Union's measures and those of the Member States shall complement and reinforce each other.

2. European laws or framework laws shall establish the measures necessary for the implementation of paragraph 1.

3. Within their respective spheres of competence, the Union and the Member States shall co-operate with third countries and the competent international organisations. The arrangements for Union co-operation may be the subject of agreements between the Union and the third parties concerned. The first subparagraph shall be without prejudice to Member States' competence to negotiate in international bodies and to conclude agreements.

Article 320

When the situation in a third country requires urgent financial assistance from the Union, the Council shall adopt the necessary European decisions on a proposal from the Commission.

Section 3 Humanitarian Aid

Article 321

1. The Union's operations in the field of humanitarian aid shall be conducted within the framework of the principles and objectives of the external action of the Union. Such operations shall be intended to provide ad hoc assistance and relief and protection for people in third countries who are victims of natural or man-made disasters, in order to meet the humanitarian needs resulting from these different situations. The Union's operations and those of the Member States shall complement and reinforce each other.

2. Humanitarian aid operations shall be conducted in compliance with the principles of international law and with the principles of impartiality, neutrality and non-discrimination.

3. European laws or framework laws shall establish the measures defining the framework within which the Union's humanitarian aid operations shall be implemented.

4. The Union may conclude with third countries and competent international organisations any agreement helping to achieve the objectives referred to in paragraph 1 and in Article 292. The first subparagraph shall be without prejudice to Member States' competence to negotiate in international bodies and to conclude agreements.

5. In order to establish a framework for joint contributions from young Europeans to the humanitarian aid operations of the Union, a European Voluntary Humanitarian Aid Corps shall be set up. European laws shall determine the rules and procedures for the operation of the Corps.

6. The Commission may take any useful initiative to promote co-ordination between actions of the Union and those of the Member States, in order to enhance the efficiency and complementarity of Union and national humanitarian aid measures.

7. The Union shall ensure that its humanitarian aid operations are co-ordinated and consistent with those of international organisations and bodies, in particular those forming part of the United Nations system.

Chapter V - Restrictive Measures

Article 322

1. Where a European decision, adopted in accordance with Chapter II, provides for the interruption or reduction, in part or completely, of economic and financial relations with one or more third countries, the Council, acting by a qualified majority on a joint proposal from the Union Minister for Foreign Affairs and the Commission, shall adopt the necessary European regulations or decisions. It shall inform the European Parliament thereof.

2. Where a European decision adopted in accordance with Chapter II so provides, the Council may adopt restrictive measures under the procedure referred to in paragraph 1 against natural or legal persons and groups or non-State entities.

3. The acts referred to in this Article shall include necessary provisions on legal safeguards.

Chapter VI - International Agreements

Article 323

1. The Union may conclude an agreement with one or more third countries or international organisations where the Constitution so provides or where the conclusion of an agreement is necessary in order to achieve, within the framework of the Union's policies, one of the objectives referred to in the Constitution, or is provided for in a legally binding Union act or is likely to affect common rules or alter their scope.

2. Agreements concluded by the Union are binding on the institutions of the Union and on its Member States.

Article 324

The Union may conclude an association agreement with one or more third countries or international organisations in order to establish an association involving reciprocal rights and obligations, common actions and special procedures.

Article 325

1. Without prejudice to the specific provisions laid down in Article 315, agreements between the Union and third countries or international organisations shall be negotiated and concluded in accordance with the following procedure.

2. The Council shall authorise the opening of negotiations, adopt negotiating directives, authorise the signing of agreements and conclude them.

3. The Commission, or the Union Minister for Foreign Affairs where the agreement envisaged relates exclusively or principally to the common foreign and security policy, shall submit recommendations to the Council, which shall adopt a European decision authorising the opening of negotiations and, depending on the subject of the agreement envisaged, nominating the Union negotiator or head of the Union's negotiating team.

4. The Council may address directives to the negotiator and designate a special committee in consultation with which the negotiations must be conducted.

5. The Council, on a proposal by the negotiator, shall adopt a European decision authorising the signing of the agreement and, if necessary, its provisional application before entry into force.

6. The Council, on a proposal by the negotiator, shall adopt a European decision concluding the agreement. Except where agreements relate exclusively to the common foreign and security policy, the Council shall adopt the European decision concluding the agreement:

(a) after obtaining the consent of the European Parliament in the following cases:

(i) association agreements;

(ii) Union accession to the European Convention for the Protection of Human Rights and Fundamental Freedoms;

(iii) agreements establishing a specific institutional framework by organising co-operation procedures;

(iv) agreements with important budgetary implications for the Union;

(v) agreements covering fields to which either the ordinary legislative procedure applies, or the special legislative procedure where consent by the European Parliament is required. The European Parliament and the Council may, in an urgent situation, agree upon a time-limit for consent.

(b) after consulting the European Parliament in other cases. The European Parliament shall deliver its opinion within a time-limit which the Council may set depending on the urgency of the matter. In the absence of an opinion within that time-limit, the Council may act.

7. When concluding an agreement, the Council may, by way of derogation from paragraphs 5, 6 and 9, authorise the negotiator to approve on the Union's behalf modifications to the agreement where it provides for them to be adopted by a simplified procedure or by a body set up by the agreement. The Council may attach specific conditions to such authorisation.

8. The Council shall act by a qualified majority throughout the procedure. However, it shall act unanimously when the agreement covers a field for which unanimity is required for the adoption of a Union act as well as for association agreements and the agreements referred to in Article 319 with the States which are candidates for accession.

9. The Council, on a proposal from the Commission or the Union Minister for Foreign Affairs, shall adopt a European decision suspending application of an agreement and establishing the positions to be adopted on the Union's behalf in a body set up by an agreement, when that body is called upon to adopt acts having legal effects, with the exception of acts supplementing or amending the institutional framework of the agreement.

10. The European Parliament shall be immediately and fully informed at all stages of the procedure.

11. A Member State, the European Parliament, the Council or the Commission may obtain the opinion of the Court of Justice as to whether an agreement envisaged is compatible with the Constitution. Where the opinion of the Court of Justice is adverse, the agreement envisaged may not enter into force unless it is amended or the Constitution is revised.

Article 326

1. By way of derogation from Article 325, the Council, either on a recommendation from the European Central Bank or on a recommendation from the Commission and after consulting the European Central Bank, in an endeavour to reach a consensus consistent with the objective of price stability, may conclude formal agreements on an exchange-rate system for the euro in relation to the currencies of third States. The Council shall act unanimously after consulting the European Parliament and in accordance with the procedure provided for in paragraph 3.

The Council, either on a recommendation from the European Central Bank or on a recommendation from the Commission and after consulting the European Central Bank, in an endeavour to reach a consensus consistent with the objective of price stability, may adopt, adjust or abandon the central rates of the euro within the exchange-rate system. The President of the Council shall inform the European Parliament of the adoption, adjustment or abandonment of the central rates of the euro.

2. In the absence of an exchange-rate system in relation to one or more currencies of third States as referred to in paragraph 1, the Council, acting either on a recommendation from the European Central Bank or on a recommendation from the Commission and after consulting the European Central Bank, may formulate general orientations for exchange-rate policy in relation to these currencies. These general orientations shall be without prejudice to the primary objective of the European System of Central Banks, to maintain price stability.

3. By way of derogation from Article 325, where agreements on matters relating to the monetary or exchange-rate system are to be the subject of negotiations between the Union and one or more third States or international organisations, the Council, acting on a recommendation from the Commission and after consulting the European Central Bank, shall decide the arrangements for the negotiation and for the conclusion of such agreements. These arrangements shall ensure that the Union expresses a single position. The Commission shall be fully associated with the negotiations.

4. Without prejudice to Union competence and Union agreements as regards economic and monetary union, Member States may negotiate in international bodies and conclude agreements.

Chapter VII - The Union's Relations with International Organisations and Third Countries and Union Delegations

Article 327

1. The Union shall establish all appropriate forms of co-operation with the organs of the United Nations and its specialised agencies, the Council of Europe, the Organisation for Security and co-operation in Europe and the Organisation for Economic co-operation and Development.

The Union shall also maintain such relations as are appropriate with other international organisations.

2. The Union Minister for Foreign Affairs and the Commission shall be instructed to implement this Article.

Article 328

1. Union delegations in third countries and at international organisations shall represent the Union.

2. Union delegations shall be placed under the authority of the Union Minister for Foreign Affairs.

They shall act in close co-operation with Member States' diplomatic and consular missions.

Chapter VIII - Implementation of the Solidarity Clause

Article 329

1. Should a Member State be the object of a terrorist attack or the victim of a natural or man-made disaster, the other Member States shall assist it at the request of its political authorities. To that end, the Member States shall co-ordinate between themselves in the Council.

2. The arrangements for the implementation by the Union of the solidarity clause referred to in Article 43 shall be defined by a European decision adopted by the Council acting on a joint proposal by the Commission and the Union Minister for Foreign Affairs. The Council shall act in accordance with Article 300(1) where this decision has defence implications. The European Parliament shall be informed.

For the purposes of this paragraph and without prejudice to Article 344, the Council shall be assisted by the Political and Security Committee with the support of the structures developed in the context of the common security and defence policy and by the Committee referred to in Article 261; the two committees shall, if necessary, submit joint opinions.

3. The European Council shall regularly assess the threats facing the Union in order to enable the Union and its Member States to take effective action.

Title VI
The Functioning of the Union

Chapter I - Provisions Governing the Institutions

Section 1 - The Institutions

Subsection 1 - The European Parliament

Article 330

1. A European law or framework law of the Council shall establish the necessary measures for the election of the Members of the European Parliament by direct universal suffrage in accordance with a uniform procedure in all Member States or in accordance with principles common to all Member States. The Council shall act unanimously on initiative from, and after obtaining the consent of, the European Parliament, which shall act by a majority of its component members. This law or framework law shall enter into force after it has been approved by the Member States in accordance with their respective constitutional requirements.

2. A European law of the European Parliament shall lay down the regulations and general conditions governing the performance of the duties of its Members. The European Parliament shall act on its own initiative after seeking an opinion from the Commission and after obtaining the consent of the Council. The Council shall act unanimously on all rules or conditions relating to the taxation of Members or former Members.

Article 331

European laws shall lay down the regulations governing the political parties at European level referred to in Article 46(4), and in particular the rules regarding their funding.

Article 332

The European Parliament may, by a majority of its component Members, request the Commission to submit any appropriate proposal on matters on which it considers that a Union act is required for the purpose of implementing the Constitution. If the Commission does not submit a proposal, it shall inform the European Parliament of the reasons.

Article 333

In the course of its duties, the European Parliament may, at the request of a quarter of its component Members, set up a temporary Committee of Inquiry to investigate, without prejudice to the powers conferred by the Constitution on other institutions or bodies, alleged contraventions or maladministration in the implementation of Union law, except where the alleged facts are being examined before a court and while the case is still subject to legal proceedings.

The temporary Committee of Inquiry shall cease to exist on submission of its report. A European law of the European Parliament shall lay down the detailed provisions governing the exercise of the right of inquiry. The European Parliament shall act on its own initiative after obtaining the consent of the Council and of the Commission.

Article 334

In accordance with Article 10(2)(d), any citizen of the Union, and any natural or legal person residing or having its registered office in a Member State, shall have the right to address, individually or in association with other persons, a petition to the European Parliament on a matter which comes within the Union's fields of activity and which affects him, her or it directly.

Article 335

1. The European Parliament shall elect a European Ombudsman. In accordance with Articles 10(2)(d) and 49, he or she shall be empowered to receive complaints from any citizen of the Union or any natural or legal person residing or having its registered office in a Member State concerning instances of maladministration in the activities of the Union's institutions, bodies, offices or agencies, with the exception of the Court of Justice of the European Union acting in its judicial role.

In accordance with his or her duties, the Ombudsman shall conduct inquiries for which he or she finds grounds, either on his or her own initiative or on the basis of complaints submitted to him or her direct or through a member of the European Parliament, except where the alleged facts are or have been the subject of legal proceedings. Where the Ombudsman establishes an instance of maladministration, he or she shall refer the matter to the institution, body, office or agency concerned, which shall have a period of three months in which to inform him or her of its views. The European Ombudsman shall then forward a report to the European Parliament and the institution, body, office or agency concerned. The person lodging the complaint shall be informed of the outcome of such inquiries.

The Ombudsman shall submit an annual report to the European Parliament on the outcome of his or her inquiries.

2. The Ombudsman shall be elected after each election of the European Parliament for the duration of its term of office. The Ombudsman shall be eligible for reappointment.

The Ombudsman may be dismissed by the Court of Justice at the request of the European Parliament if he or she no longer fulfils the conditions required for the performance of his or her duties or if he or she is guilty of serious misconduct.

3. The Ombudsman shall be completely independent in the performance of his or her duties. In the performance of those duties he or she shall neither seek nor take instructions from any institution, body, office or agency. The Ombudsman shall not, during his or her term of office, engage in any other occupation, whether gainful or not.

4. A European law of the European Parliament shall lay down the regulations and general conditions governing the performance of the Ombudsman's duties. The European Parliament shall act on its own initiative after seeking an opinion from the Commission and after obtaining the consent of the Council.

Article 336

The European Parliament shall hold an annual session. It shall meet, without requiring to be convened, on the second Tuesday in March. The European Parliament may meet in extraordinary part-session at the request of a majority of its component members or at the request of the Council or of the Commission.

Article 337

1. The European Council and the Council shall be heard by the European Parliament in accordance with the conditions laid down in the Rules of Procedure of the European Council and those of the Council.

2. The Commission may attend all the meetings of the European Parliament and shall, at its request, be heard. It shall reply orally or in writing to questions put to it by the European Parliament or by its members.

3. The European Parliament shall discuss in open session the annual general report submitted to it by the Commission.

Article 338

Save as otherwise provided in the Constitution, the European Parliament shall act by a majority of the votes cast. Its Rules of Procedure shall determine the quorum.

Article 339

The European Parliament shall adopt its Rules of Procedure, by a majority of its component members. The proceedings of the European Parliament shall be published in the manner laid down in the Constitution and the Rules of Procedure of the European Parliament.

Article 340

If a motion of censure on the activities of the Commission is tabled before it, the European Parliament shall not vote thereon until at least three days after the motion has been tabled and shall do so only by open vote.

If the motion of censure is carried by a two-thirds majority of the votes cast, representing a majority of the component members of the European Parliament, the members of the Commission shall resign as a body and the Union Minister for Foreign Affairs shall resign from duties that he or she carries out in the Commission. They shall remain in office and continue to deal with current business until they are replaced in accordance with Articles 26 and 27. In this case, the term of office of the members of the Commission appointed to replace them shall expire on the date on which the term of office of the members of the Commission obliged to resign as a body would have expired.

Subsection 2 - The European Council

Article 341

1. Where a vote is taken, any member of the European Council may also act on behalf of not more than one other member. Abstentions by members present in person or represented shall not prevent the adoption by the European Council of acts which require unanimity.

2. The President of the European Parliament may be invited to be heard by the European Council.

3. The European Council shall act by a simple majority for procedural questions and for the adoption of its Rules of Procedure.

4. The European Council shall be assisted by the General Secretariat of the Council.

Subsection 3 - The Council of Ministers

Article 342

The Council shall meet when convened by its President on his or her own initiative, or at the request of one of its members or of the Commission.

Article 343

1. Where a vote is taken, any member of the Council may act on behalf of not more than one other member.

2. Where it is required to act by a simple majority, the Council shall act by a majority of its component members.

3. Abstentions by members present in person or represented shall not prevent the adoption by the Council of acts which require unanimity.

Article 344

1. A committee consisting of the Permanent Representatives of the Governments of the Member States shall be responsible for preparing the work of the Council and for carrying out the tasks assigned to it by the latter. The Committee may adopt procedural decisions in cases provided for in the Council's Rules of Procedure.

2. The Council shall be assisted by a General Secretariat, under the responsibility of a Secretary- General appointed by the Council . The Council shall decide on the organisation of the General Secretariat by a simple majority.

3. The Council shall act by a simple majority regarding procedural matters and for the adoption of its Rules of Procedure.

Article 345

The Council, by a simple majority, may request the Commission to undertake any studies the Council considers desirable for the attainment of the common objectives, and to submit any appropriate proposals to it. If the Commission does not submit a proposal, it shall inform the Council of the reasons.

Article 346

The Council shall adopt European decisions laying down the rules governing the committees provided for in the Constitution. It shall act by a simple majority after consulting the Commission.

Subsection 4 - The European Commission

Article 347

The members of the Commission shall refrain from any action incompatible with their duties. Member States shall respect their independence and shall not seek to influence them in the performance of their tasks.

The members of the Commission shall not, during their term of office, engage in any other occupation, whether gainful or not. When entering upon their duties they shall give a solemn undertaking that, both during and after their term of office, they will respect the obligations arising therefrom and in particular their duty to behave with integrity and discretion as regards the acceptance, after they have ceased to hold office, of certain appointments or benefits. In the event of any breach of these obligations, the Court of Justice may, on application by the Council, acting by a simple majority, or the Commission, rule that the person concerned be, according to the circumstances, either compulsorily retired in accordance with Article 349 or deprived of his or her right to a pension or other benefits in its stead.

Article 348

1. Apart from normal replacement, or death, the duties of a member of the Commission shall end when he or she resigns or is compulsorily retired.

2. A vacancy caused by resignation, compulsory retirement or death shall be filled for the remainder of the member's term of office by a new member of the same nationality appointed by the Council, by common accord with the President of the Commission, after consulting the European Parliament and in accordance with the criteria set out in Article 26(4).The Council may, acting unanimously on a proposal from the President of the Commission, decide that such a vacancy need not be filled, in particular when the remainder of the member's term of office is short.

3. In the event of resignation, compulsory retirement or death, the President shall be replaced for the remainder of his or her term of office in accordance with Article 27(1).

4. In the event of resignation, compulsory retirement or death, the Union Minister for Foreign Affairs shall be replaced, for the remainder of his or her term of office, in accordance with Article 28(1).

5. In the case of the resignation of all the members of the Commission, they shall remain in office and continue to deal with current business until they have been replaced, for the remainder of their term of office, in accordance with Articles 26 and 27.

Article 349

If any member of the Commission no longer fulfils the conditions required for the performance of his or her duties or if he or she has been guilty of serious misconduct, the Court of Justice may, on application by the Council, acting by a simple majority, or by the Commission, compulsorily retire him or her.

Article 350

Without prejudice to Article 28(4), the responsibilities incumbent upon the Commission shall be structured and allocated among its members by its President, in accordance with Article 27(3). The President may reshuffle the allocation of those responsibilities during the Commission's term of office. The members of the Commission shall carry out the duties devolved upon them by the President under his or her authority.

Article 351

The Commission shall act by a majority of its members. Its Rules of Procedure shall determine the quorum.

Article 352

1. The Commission shall adopt its Rules of Procedure so as to ensure both its own operation and that of its departments. It shall ensure that these rules are published.

2. The Commission shall publish annually, not later than one month before the opening of the session of the European Parliament, a general report on the activities of the Union.

Subsection 5 - The Court of Justice of the European Union

Article 353

The Court of Justice shall sit in chambers, as a Grand Chamber or as a full Court, in accordance with the Statute of the Court of Justice of the European Union.

Article 354

The Court of Justice shall be assisted by eight Advocates-General. Should the Court of Justice so request, the Council may, acting unanimously, adopt a European decision to increase the number of Advocates-General. It shall be the duty of the Advocate-General, acting with complete impartiality and independence, to make, in open court, reasoned submissions on cases which, in accordance with the Statute of the Court of Justice of the European Union, require his or her involvement.

Article 355

The Judges and Advocates-General of the Court of Justice shall be chosen from persons whose independence is beyond doubt and who possess the qualifications required for appointment to the highest judicial offices in their respective countries or who are jurisconsults of recognised competence; they shall be appointed by common accord of the governments of the Member States after consultation of the panel provided for in Article 357.

Every three years there shall be a partial replacement of the Judges and Advocates-General, in accordance with the conditions laid down in the Statute of the Court of Justice of the European Union.

The Judges shall elect the President of the Court of Justice from among their number for a term of three years.

He or she may be re-elected.

The Court of Justice shall adopt its Rules of Procedure. Those Rules shall require the consent of the Council.

Article 356

The number of Judges of the General Court shall be determined by the Statute of the Court of Justice of the European Union. The Statute may provide for the General Court to be assisted by Advocates- General.

The members of the General Court shall be chosen from persons whose independence is beyond doubt and who possess the ability required for appointment to high judicial office. They shall be appointed by common accord of the governments of the Member States after consultation of the panel provided for in Article 357.

The membership of the General Court shall be partially renewed every three years.

The Judges shall elect the President of the General Court from among their number for a term of three years.

He or she may be re-elected.

The General Court shall establish its Rules of Procedure in agreement with the Court of Justice.

The Rules shall be subject to the consent of the Council.

Unless the Statute provides otherwise, the provisions of the Constitution relating to the Court of Justice shall apply to the General Court.

Article 357

A panel shall be set up in order to give an opinion on candidates' suitability to perform the duties of Judge and Advocate-General of the Court of Justice and the General Court before the governments of the Member States make the appointments referred to in Articles 355 and 356.

The panel shall comprise seven persons chosen from among former members of the Court of Justice and the General Court, members of national supreme courts and lawyers of recognised competence, one of whom shall be proposed by the European Parliament. The Council shall adopt a European decision establishing the panel's operating rules and a European decision appointing its members. It shall act on the initiative of the President of the Court of Justice.

Article 358

1. The General Court shall have jurisdiction to hear and determine at first instance actions or proceedings referred to in Articles 365, 367, 370, 372 and

374, with the exception of those assigned to a specialised court set up under Article 359 and those reserved in the Statute of the Court of Justice of the European Union for the Court of Justice. The Statute may provide for the General Court to have jurisdiction for other classes of action or proceeding.

Decisions given by the General Court under this paragraph may be subject to a right of appeal to the Court of Justice on points of law only, under the conditions and within the limits laid down by the Statute.

2. The General Court shall have jurisdiction to hear and determine actions or proceedings brought against decisions of the specialised courts.

Decisions given by the General Court under this paragraph may exceptionally be subject to review by the Court of Justice, under the conditions and within the limits laid down by the Statute of the Court of Justice of the European Union, where there is a serious risk of the unity or consistency of Union law being affected.

3. The General Court shall have jurisdiction to hear and determine questions referred for a preliminary ruling under Article 369, in specific areas laid down by the Statute of the Court of Justice of the European Union.

Where the General Court considers that the case requires a decision of principle likely to affect the unity or consistency of Union law, it may refer the case to the Court of Justice for a ruling.

Decisions given by the General Court on questions referred for a preliminary ruling may exceptionally be subject to review by the Court of Justice, under the conditions and within the limits laid down by the Statute, where there is a serious risk of the unity or consistency of Union law being affected.

Article 359

1. European laws may establish specialised courts attached to the General Court to hear and determine at first instance certain classes of action or proceeding brought in specific areas. They shall be adopted either on a proposal from the Commission after consultation of the Court of Justice or at the request of the Court of Justice after consultation of the Commission.

2. The European law establishing a specialised court shall lay down the rules on the organisation of the court and the extent of the jurisdiction conferred upon it.

3. Decisions given by specialised courts may be subject to a right of appeal on points of law only or, when provided for in the European law establishing the specialised court, a right of appeal also on matters of fact, before the General Court.

4. The members of the specialised courts shall be chosen from persons whose independence is beyond doubt and who possess the ability required for appointment to judicial office. They shall be appointed by the Council, acting unanimously.

5. The specialised courts shall establish their Rules of Procedure in agreement with the Court of Justice. Those Rules shall require the consent of the Council.

6. Unless the European law establishing the specialised court provides otherwise, the provisions of the Constitution relating to the Court of Justice of the European Union and the provisions of the Statute of the Court of Justice of

the European Union shall apply to the specialised courts. Title I of the Statute and Article 64 thereof shall in any case apply to the specialised courts.

Article 360

If the Commission considers that a Member State has failed to fulfil an obligation under the Constitution, it shall deliver a reasoned opinion on the matter after giving the State concerned the opportunity to submit its observations.

If the State concerned does not comply with the opinion within the period laid down by the Commission, the latter may bring the matter before the Court of Justice of the European Union.

Article 361

A Member State which considers that another Member State has failed to fulfil an obligation under the Constitution may bring the matter before the Court of Justice of the European Union.

Before a Member State brings an action against another Member State for an alleged infringement of an obligation under the Constitution, it shall bring the matter before the Commission.

The Commission shall deliver a reasoned opinion after each of the States concerned has been given the opportunity to submit its own case and its observations on the other party's case both orally and in writing. If the Commission has not delivered an opinion within three months of the date on which the matter was brought before it, the absence of such opinion shall not prevent the matter from being brought before the Court.

Article 362

1. If the Court of Justice of the European Union finds that a Member State has failed to fulfil an obligation under the Constitution, that State shall be required to take the necessary measures to comply with the judgment of the Court.

2. If the Commission considers that the Member State concerned has not taken the necessary measures to comply with the judgment referred to in paragraph 1, it may bring the case before the Court of Justice of the European Union after giving that State the opportunity to submit its observations. It shall specify the amount of the lump sum or penalty payment to be paid by the Member State concerned which it considers appropriate in the circumstances.

If the Court finds that the Member State concerned has not complied with its judgment it may impose a lump sum or penalty payment on it.

This procedure shall be without prejudice to Article 361.

3. When the Commission brings a case before the Court of Justice of the European Union pursuant to Article 360 on the grounds that the Member State concerned has failed to fulfil its obligation to notify measures transposing a European framework law, it may, when it deems appropriate, specify the amount of the lump sum or penalty payment to be paid by the Member State concerned which it considers appropriate in the circumstances.

If the Court finds that there is an infringement it may impose a lump sum or penalty payment on the Member State concerned not exceeding the amount specified by the Commission. The payment obligation shall take effect on the date set by the Court in its judgment.

Article 363

European laws and regulations of the Council may give the Court of Justice of the European Union unlimited jurisdiction with regard to the penalties provided for in them.

Article 364

Without prejudice to the other provisions of the Constitution, a European law may confer on the Court of Justice of the European Union, to the extent that it shall determine, jurisdiction in disputes relating to the application of acts adopted on the basis of the Constitution which create European intellectual property rights.

Article 365

1. The Court of Justice of the European Union shall review the legality of European laws and framework laws, of acts of the Council, of the Commission and of the European Central Bank, other than recommendations and opinions, and of acts of the European Parliament and of the European Council intended to produce legal effects vis-à-vis third parties. It shall also review the legality of acts of bodies, offices or agencies of the Union intended to produce legal effects vis-à-vis third parties.

2. For the purposes of paragraph 1, the Court of Justice of the European Union shall have jurisdiction in actions brought by a Member State, the European Parliament, the Council or the Commission on grounds of lack of competence, infringement of an essential procedural requirement, infringement of the Constitution or of any rule of law relating to its application, or misuse of powers.

3. The Court of Justice of the European Union shall have jurisdiction under the conditions laid down in paragraphs 1 and 2 in actions brought by the Court of Auditors, by the European Central Bank and by the Committee of the Regions for the purpose of protecting their prerogatives.

4. Any natural or legal person may, under the conditions laid down in paragraphs 1 and 2, institute proceedings against an act addressed to that person or which is of direct and individual concern to him or her, and against a regulatory act which is of direct concern to him or her and does not entail implementing measures.

5. Acts setting up bodies, offices and agencies of the Union may lay down specific conditions and arrangements concerning actions brought by natural or legal persons against acts of these bodies, offices or agencies intended to produce legal effects in relation to them.

6. The proceedings provided for in this Article shall be instituted within two months of the publication of the act, or of its notification to the plaintiff, or, in the absence thereof, of the day on which it came to the plaintiff's knowledge, as the case may be.

Article 366

If the action is well founded, the Court of Justice of the European Union shall declare the act concerned to be void.

However, the Court shall, if it considers this necessary, state which of the effects of the act which it has declared void shall be considered as definitive.

Article 367

Should the European Parliament, the European Council, the Council, the Commission or the European Central Bank, in infringement of the Constitution, fail to act, the Member States and the other institutions of the Union may bring an action before the Court of Justice of the European Union to have the infringement established. This Article shall apply, under the same conditions, to bodies, offices and agencies of the Union which fail to act.

The action shall be admissible only if the institution, body, office or agency concerned has first been called upon to act. If, within two months of being so called upon, the institution, body, office or agency concerned has not defined its position, the action may be brought within a further period of two months. Any natural or legal person may, under the conditions laid down in the first and second paragraphs, complain to the Court that an institution, body, office or agency of the Union has failed to address to that person any act other than a recommendation or an opinion.

Article 368

The institution, body, office or agency whose act has been declared void, or whose failure to act has been declared contrary to the Constitution, shall be required to take the necessary measures to comply with the judgment of the Court of Justice of the European Union.

This obligation shall not affect any obligation which may result from the application of the second paragraph of Article 431.

Article 369

The Court of Justice of the European Union shall have jurisdiction to give preliminary rulings concerning:

a) the interpretation of the Constitution;

b) the validity and interpretation of acts of the institutions, bodies, offices and agencies of the Union. Where such a question is raised before any court or tribunal of a Member State, that court or tribunal may, if it considers that a decision on the question is necessary to enable it to give judgment, request the Court to give a ruling thereon.

Where any such question is raised in a case pending before a court or tribunal of a Member State against whose decisions there is no judicial remedy under national law, that court or tribunal shall bring the matter before the Court.

If such a question is raised in a case pending before a court or tribunal of a Member State with regard to a person in custody, the Court shall act with the minimum of delay.

Article 370

The Court of Justice of the European Union shall have jurisdiction in disputes relating to compensation for damage provided for in the second and third paragraphs of Article 431.

Article 371

The Court of Justice shall have jurisdiction to decide on the legality of an act adopted by the European Council or by the Council pursuant to Article I-59 solely at the request of the Member State concerned by a determination of the European Council or of the Council and in respect solely of the procedural stipulations contained in that Article.

Such a request must be made within one month from the date of such determination. The Court shall rule within one month from the date of the request.

Article 372

The Court of Justice of the European Union shall have jurisdiction in any dispute between the Union and its servants within the limits and under the conditions laid down in the Staff Regulations of Officials and the Conditions of Employment of other servants of the Union.

Article 373

The Court of Justice of the European Union shall, within the limits hereinafter laid down, have jurisdiction in disputes concerning:

(a) the fulfilment by Member States of obligations under the Statute of the European Investment Bank. In this connection, the Board of Directors of the Bank shall enjoy the powers conferred upon the Commission by Article 360;

(b) measures adopted by the Board of Governors of the European Investment Bank. In this connection, any Member State, the Commission or the Board of Directors of the Bank may institute proceedings under the conditions laid down in Article 365;

(c) measures adopted by the Board of Directors of the European Investment Bank. Proceedings against such measures may be instituted only by Member States or by the Commission, under the conditions laid down in Article 365, and solely on the grounds of non-compliance with the procedure provided for in Article 19(2), (5), (6) and (7) of the Statute of the Bank;

(d) the fulfilment by national central banks of obligations under the Constitution and the Statute of the European System of Central Banks and of the European Central Bank. In this connection, the powers of the Governing Council of the European Central Bank in respect of national central banks shall be the same as those conferred upon the Commission in respect of Member States by Article 360. If the Court of Justice of the European Union finds that a national central bank has failed to fulfil an obligation under the Constitution, that bank shall be required to take the necessary measures to comply with the judgment of the Court.

Article 374

The Court of Justice of the European Union shall have jurisdiction to give judgment pursuant to any arbitration clause contained in a contract concluded by or on behalf of the Union, whether that contract be governed by public or private law.

Article 375

1. Save where jurisdiction is conferred on the Court of Justice of the European Union by the Constitution, disputes to which the Union is a party shall not on that ground be excluded from the jurisdiction of the courts or tribunals of the Member States.

2. Member States undertake not to submit a dispute concerning the interpretation or application of the Constitution to any method of settlement other than those provided for therein.

3. The Court of Justice shall have jurisdiction in any dispute between Member States which relates to the subject-matter of the Constitution if the dispute is submitted to it under a special agreement between the parties.

Article 376

The Court of Justice of the European Union shall not have jurisdiction with respect to Articles 40 and 41 and the provisions of Chapter II of Title V concerning the common foreign and security policy and Article 293 insofar as it concerns the common foreign and security policy.

However, the Court shall have jurisdiction to monitor compliance with Article 308 and to rule on proceedings, brought in accordance with the conditions laid down in Article 365(4), reviewing the legality of European decisions providing for restrictive measures against natural or legal persons adopted by the Council on the basis of Chapter II of Title V.

Article 377

In exercising its powers regarding the provisions of Sections 4 and 5 of Chapter IV of Title III relating to the area of freedom, security and justice, the Court of Justice of the European Union shall have no jurisdiction to review the validity or proportionality of operations carried out by the police or other law-enforcement services of a Member State or the exercise of the responsibilities incumbent upon Member States with regard to the maintenance of law and order and the safeguarding of internal security.

Article 378

Notwithstanding the expiry of the period laid down in Article 365(6), any party may, in proceedings in which an act of general application adopted by an institution, body, office or agency of the Union is at issue, plead the grounds specified in Article 365(2) in order to invoke before the Court of Justice of the European Union the inapplicability of that act.

Article 379

1. Actions brought before the Court of Justice of the European Union shall not have suspensory effect. The Court may, however, if it considers that circumstances so require, order that application of the contested act be suspended.

2. The Court of Justice of the European Union may in any cases before it prescribe any necessary interim measures.

Article 380

The judgments of the Court of Justice of the European Union shall be enforceable under the conditions laid down in Article 401.

Article 381

The Statute of the Court of Justice of the European Union shall be laid down in a Protocol. A European law may amend the provisions of the Statute, with the exception of Title I and Article 64. It shall be adopted either at the request of the Court of Justice and after consultation of the Commission, or on a proposal from the Commission and after consultation of the Court of Justice.

Subsection 6 - The European Central Bank

Article 382

1. The Governing Council of the European Central Bank shall comprise the members of the Executive Board of the European Central Bank and the Governors of the national central banks of the Member States without a derogation as referred to in Article 197.

2. The Executive Board shall comprise the President, the Vice-President and four other members.

The President, the Vice-President and the other members of the Executive Board shall be appointed by the European Council, acting by a qualified majority, from among persons of recognised standing and professional experience in monetary or banking matters, on a recommendation from the Council and after consulting the European Parliament and the Governing Council of the European Central Bank.

Their term of office shall be eight years and shall not be renewable.

Only nationals of Member States may be members of the Executive Board.

Article 383

1. The President of the Council and a member of the Commission may participate, without having the right to vote, in meetings of the Governing Council of the European Central Bank. The President of the Council may submit a motion for deliberation to the Governing Council of the European Central Bank.

2. The President of the European Central Bank shall be invited to participate in meetings of the Council when it is discussing matters relating to the objectives and tasks of the European System of Central Banks.

3. The European Central Bank shall address an annual report on the activities of the European System of Central Banks and on the monetary policy of both the previous and the current year to the European Parliament, the European Council, the Council and the Commission. The President of the European Central Bank shall present this report to the European Parliament, which may hold a general debate on that basis, and to the Council. The President of the European Central Bank and the other members of the Executive Board may, at the request of the European Parliament or on their own initiative, be heard by the competent bodies of the European Parliament.

Subsection 7 - The Court of Auditors

Article 384

1. The Court of Auditors shall examine the accounts of all revenue and expenditure of the Union. It shall also examine the accounts of all revenue and expenditure of any body, office or agency set up by the Union insofar as the instrument establishing that body, office or agency does not preclude such examination.

The Court of Auditors shall provide the European Parliament and the Council with a statement of assurance as to the reliability of the accounts and the legality and regularity of the underlying transactions which shall be published in the *Official Journal of the European Union*. This statement may be supplemented by specific assessments for each major area of Union activity.

2. The Court of Auditors shall examine whether all revenue has been received and all expenditure incurred in a lawful and regular manner and whether the financial management has been sound. In doing so, it shall report in particular on any cases of irregularity.

The audit of revenue shall be carried out on the basis of the amounts established as due and the amounts actually paid to the Union.

The audit of expenditure shall be carried out on the basis both of commitments undertaken and payments made.

These audits may be carried out before the closure of accounts for the financial year in question.

3. The audit shall be based on records and, if necessary, performed on the spot in the other institutions, or on the premises of any body, office or agency which manages revenue or expenditure on behalf of the Union and in the Member States, including on the premises of any natural or legal person in receipt of payments from the budget. In the Member States the audit shall be carried out in liaison with national audit bodies or, if these do not have the necessary powers, with the competent national departments. The Court of Auditors and the national audit bodies of the Member States shall co-operate in a spirit of trust while maintaining their independence. These bodies or departments shall inform the Court of Auditors whether they intend to take part in the audit.

The other institutions, any bodies, offices or agencies managing revenue or expenditure on behalf of the Union, any natural or legal person in receipt of payments from the budget, and the national audit bodies or, if these do not have the necessary powers, the competent national departments, shall forward to the Court of Auditors, at its request, any document or information necessary to carry out its task.

In respect of the European Investment Bank's activity in managing Union revenue and expenditure, rights of access by the Court of Auditors to information held by the Bank shall be governed by an agreement between the Court of Auditors, the Bank and the Commission. In the absence of an agreement, the Court of Auditors shall nevertheless have access to information necessary for the audit of Union expenditure and revenue managed by the Bank.

4. The Court of Auditors shall draw up an annual report after the close of each financial year. It shall be forwarded to the other institutions and shall be

published, together with the replies of these institutions to the observations of the Court of Auditors, in the *Official Journal of the European Union.*

The Court of Auditors may also, at any time, submit observations, particularly in the form of special reports, on specific questions and deliver opinions at the request of one of the other institutions.

It shall adopt its annual reports, special reports or opinions by a majority of its component members. However, it may establish internal chambers in order to adopt certain categories of reports or opinions under the conditions laid down by its Rules of Procedure.

It shall assist the European Parliament and the Council in exercising their powers of control over the implementation of the budget.

It shall adopt its Rules of Procedure. Those rules shall require the consent of the Council.

Article 385

1. The members of the Court of Auditors shall be chosen from among persons who belong or have belonged in their respective States to external audit bodies or who are especially qualified for this office. Their independence must be beyond doubt.

2. The members of the Court of Auditors shall be appointed for a term of six years. Their term of office shall be renewable. The Council shall adopt a European decision establishing the list of members drawn up in accordance with the proposals made by each Member State. It shall act after consulting the European Parliament.

The members of the Court of Auditors shall elect their President from among their number for a term of three years. He or she may be re-elected.

3. In the performance of their duties, members of the Court of Auditors shall neither seek nor take instructions from any government or from any other body. They shall refrain from any action incompatible with their duties.

4. Members of the Court of Auditors shall not, during their term of office, engage in any other occupation, whether gainful or not. When entering upon their duties they shall give a solemn undertaking that, both during and after their term of office, they will respect the obligations arising therefrom and in particular their duty to behave with integrity and discretion as regards the acceptance, after they have ceased to hold office, of certain appointments or benefits.

5. Apart from normal replacement, or death, the duties of a member of the Court of Auditors shall end when he or she resigns, or is compulsorily retired by a ruling of the Court of Justice pursuant to paragraph 6. The vacancy thus caused shall be filled for the remainder of the member's term of office.

Save in the case of compulsory retirement, members of the Court of Auditors shall remain in office until they have been replaced.

6. A member of the Court of Auditors may be deprived of his or her office or of his or her right to a pension or other benefits in its stead only if the Court of Justice, at the request of the Court of Auditors, finds that he or she no longer fulfils the requisite conditions or meets the obligations arising from his or her office.

Section 2 - The Unions Advisory Bodies

Subsection 1 - The Committee of the Regions

Article 386

The number of members of the Committee of the Regions shall not exceed 350. The Council, acting unanimously on a proposal from the Commission, shall adopt a European decision determining the Committee's composition.

The members of the Committee and an equal number of alternate members shall be appointed for five years. Their term of office shall be renewable. No member of the Committee shall at the same time be a member of the European Parliament.

The Council shall adopt the European decision establishing the list of members and alternate members drawn up in accordance with the proposals made by each Member State.

When the mandate referred to in Article I-32(2) on the basis of which they were proposed comes to an end, the term of office of members of the Committee shall terminate automatically and they shall then be replaced for the remainder of the said term of office in accordance with the same procedure.

Article 387

The Committee of the Regions shall elect its chairman and officers from among its members for a term of two and a half years.

It shall be convened by its chairman at the request of the European Parliament, of the Council or of the Commission. It may also meet on its own initiative.

It shall adopt its Rules of Procedure.

Article 388

The Committee of the Regions shall be consulted by the European Parliament, by the Council or by the Commission where the Constitution so provides and in all other cases in which one of these institutions considers it appropriate, in particular those which concern cross-border co-operation.

The European Parliament, the Council or the Commission shall, if it considers it necessary, set the Committee, for the submission of its opinion, a time-limit which shall not be less than one month from the date on which the chairman receives notification to this effect. Upon expiry of the timelimit, the absence of an opinion shall not prevent further action.

Where the Economic and Social Committee is consulted, the Committee of the Regions shall be informed by the European Parliament, the Council or the Commission of the request for an opinion. Where it considers that specific regional interests are involved, the Committee of the Regions may issue an opinion on the matter. It may also issue an opinion on its own initiative.

The opinion of the Committee, together with a record of its proceedings, shall be forwarded to the European Parliament, to the Council and to the Commission.

Subsection 2 - The Economic and Social Committee

Article 389

The number of members of the Economic and Social Committee shall not exceed 350.

The Council, acting unanimously on a proposal from the Commission, shall adopt a European decision determining the Committee's composition.

Article 390

The members of the Economic and Social Committee shall be appointed for five years. Their term of office shall be renewable.

The Council shall adopt the European decision establishing the list of members drawn up in accordance with the proposals made by each Member State.

The Council shall act after consulting the Commission. It may obtain the opinion of European bodies which are representative of the various economic and social sectors and of civil society to which the Union's activities are of concern.

Article 391

The Economic and Social Committee shall elect its chairman and officers from among its members for a term of two and a half years.

It shall be convened by its chairman at the request of the European Parliament, of the Council or of the Commission. It may also meet on its own initiative.

It shall adopt its Rules of Procedure.

Article 392

The Economic and Social Committee shall be consulted by the European Parliament, by the Council or by the Commission where the Constitution so provides. It may be consulted by these institutions in all cases in which they consider it appropriate. It may also issue an opinion on its own initiative.

The European Parliament, the Council or the Commission shall, if it considers it necessary, set the Committee, for the submission of its opinion, a time-limit which shall not be less than one month from the date on which the chairman receives notification to this effect. Upon expiry of the time limit, the absence of an opinion shall not prevent further action.

The opinion of the Committee, together with a record of its proceedings, shall be forwarded to the European Parliament, to the Council and to the Commission.

Section 3 - The European Investment Bank

Article 393

The European Investment Bank shall have legal personality.

Its members shall be the Member States.

The Statute of the European Investment Bank is laid down in a Protocol.

A European law of the Council may amend the Statute of the European Investment Bank. The Council shall act unanimously, either at the request of the European Investment Bank and after consulting the European Parliament and the Commission, or on a proposal from the Commission and after consulting the European Parliament and the European Investment Bank.

Article 394

The task of the European Investment Bank shall be to contribute, by having recourse to the capital markets and utilising its own resources, to the balanced and steady development of the internal market in the Union's interest. For this purpose the European Investment Bank shall, operating on a non-profit-making basis, in particular grant loans and give guarantees which facilitate the financing of the following projects in all sectors of the economy:

(a) projects for developing less-developed regions

(b) projects for modernising or converting undertakings or for developing fresh activities called for by the establishment or functioning of the internal market, where these projects are of such a size or nature that they cannot be entirely financed by the various means available in the individual Member States;

(c) projects of common interest to several Member States which are of such a size or nature that they cannot be entirely financed by the various means available in the individual Member States. In carrying out its task, the European Investment Bank shall facilitate the financing of investment programmes in conjunction with assistance from the Structural Funds and other Union financial instruments.

Section 4 - Provisions Common to Union Institutions, Bodies, Offices and Agencies

Article 395

1. Where, pursuant to the Constitution, the Council acts on a proposal from the Commission, it may amend that proposal only by acting unanimously, except in the cases referred to in Articles 55, 56, 396(10) and (13), 404 and 405(2).

2. As long as the Council has not acted, the Commission may alter its proposal at any time during the procedures leading to the adoption of a Union act.

Article 396

1. Where, pursuant to the Constitution, European laws or framework laws are adopted under the ordinary legislative procedure, the following provisions shall apply.

2. The Commission shall submit a proposal to the European Parliament and the Council.

First reading

3. The European Parliament shall adopt its position at first reading and communicate it to the Council.

4. If the Council approves the European Parliament's position, the act concerned shall be adopted in the wording which corresponds to the position of the European Parliament.

5. If the Council does not approve the European Parliament's position, it shall adopt its position at first reading and communicate it to the European Parliament.

6. The Council shall inform the European Parliament fully of the reasons which led it to adopt its position at first reading. The Commission shall inform the European Parliament fully of its position.

Second reading

7. If, within three months of such communication, the European Parliament:

(a) approves the Council's position at first reading or has not taken a decision, the act concerned shall be deemed to have been adopted in the wording which corresponds to the position of the Council;

(b) rejects, by a majority of its component members, the Council's position at first reading, the proposed act shall be deemed not to have been adopted;

(c) proposes, by a majority of its component members, amendments to the Council's position at first reading, the text thus amended shall be forwarded to the Council and to the Commission, which shall deliver an opinion on those amendments.

8. If, within three months of receiving the European Parliament's amendments, the Council, acting by a qualified majority:

(a) approves all those amendments, the act in question shall be deemed to have been adopted;

(b) does not approve all the amendments, the President of the Council, in agreement with the President of the European Parliament, shall within six weeks convene a meeting of the Conciliation Committee.

9. The Council shall act unanimously on the amendments on which the Commission has delivered a negative opinion.

Conciliation

10. The Conciliation Committee, which shall be composed of the members of the Council or their representatives and an equal number of members representing the European Parliament, shall have the task of reaching agreement on a joint text, by a qualified majority of the members of the Council or their representatives and by a majority of the members representing the European Parliament within six weeks of its being convened, on the basis of the positions of the European Parliament and the Council at second reading.

11. The Commission shall take part in the Conciliation Committee's proceedings and shall take all necessary initiatives with a view to reconciling the positions of the European Parliament and the Council.

12. If, within six weeks of its being convened, the Conciliation Committee does not approve the joint text, the proposed act shall be deemed not to have been adopted.

Third reading

13. If, within that period, the Conciliation Committee approves a joint text, the European Parliament, acting by a majority of the votes cast, and the Council, acting by a qualified majority, shall each have a period of six weeks from that approval in which to adopt the act in question in accordance with the joint text. If they fail to do so, the proposed act shall be deemed not to have been adopted.

14. The periods of three months and six weeks referred to in this Article shall be extended by a maximum of one month and two weeks respectively at the initiative of the European Parliament or the Council.

Special provisions

15. Where, in the cases provided for in the Constitution, a law or framework law is submitted to the ordinary legislative procedure on the initiative of a group of Member States, on a recommendation by the European Central Bank, or at the request of the Court of Justice, paragraph 2, the second sentence of paragraph 6, and paragraph 9 shall not apply. In such cases, the European Parliament and the Council shall communicate the proposed act to the Commission with their positions at first and second readings. The European Parliament or the Council may request the opinion of the Commission throughout the procedure, which the Commission may also deliver on its own initiative. It may also, if it deems it necessary, take part in the Conciliation Committee in accordance with paragraph 11.

Article 397

The European Parliament, the Council and the Commission shall consult each other and by common agreement make arrangements for their co-operation. To that end, they may, in compliance with the Constitution, conclude interinstitutional agreements which may be of a binding nature.

Article 398

1. In carrying out their missions, the institutions, bodies, offices and agencies of the Union shall have the support of an open, efficient and independent European administration. 2. In compliance with the Staff Regulations and the Conditions of employment adopted on the basis of Article 427, European laws shall establish provisions to that end.

Article 399

1. The institutions, bodies, offices and agencies of the Union shall ensure transparency in their work and shall, pursuant to Article I-50, determine in their rules of procedure specific provisions for public access to their documents. The Court of Justice of the European Union, the European Central Bank and the European Investment Bank shall be subject to the provisions of Article 50(3) and to this Article only when exercising their administrative tasks.

2. The European Parliament and the Council shall ensure publication of the documents relating to the legislative procedures under the terms laid down by the European law referred to in Article 50(3).

Article 400

1. The Council shall adopt European regulations and decisions determining:

(a) the salaries, allowances and pensions of the President of the European Council, the President of the Commission, the Union Minister for Foreign Affairs, the members of the Commission, the Presidents, members and Registrars of the Court of Justice of the European Union, and the Secretary-General of the Council;

(b) the conditions of employment, in particular the salaries, allowances and pensions, of the President and members of the Court of Auditors;

(c) any payment to be made instead of remuneration to the persons referred to in points (a) and (b).

2. The Council shall adopt European regulations and decisions determining the allowances of the members of the Economic and Social Committee.

Article 401

Acts of the Council, of the Commission or of the European Central Bank which impose a pecuniary obligation on persons other than Member States shall be enforceable.

Enforcement shall be governed by the rules of civil procedure in force in the Member State in the territory of which it is carried out. The order for its enforcement shall be appended to the decision, without other formality than verification of the authenticity of the decision, by the national authority which the government of each Member State shall designate for this purpose and shall make known to the Commission and the Court of Justice of the European Union

When these formalities have been completed on application by the party concerned, the latter may proceed to enforcement by bringing the matter directly before the competent authority, in accordance with the national law.

Enforcement may be suspended only by a decision of the Court of Justice of the European Union. However, the courts of the country concerned shall have jurisdiction over complaints that enforcement is being carried out in an irregular manner.

Chapter II - Financial Provisions

Section 1 - The Multiannual Financial Framework

Article 402

1. The multiannual financial framework shall be established for a period of at least five years in accordance with Article 55.

2. The financial framework shall determine the amounts of the annual ceilings on commitment appropriations by category of expenditure and of the annual ceiling on payment appropriations. The categories of expenditure, limited in number, shall correspond to the Union's major sectors of activity.

3. The financial framework shall lay down any other provisions required for the annual budgetary procedure to run smoothly.

4. Where no European law of the Council determining a new financial framework has been adopted by the end of the previous financial framework, the ceilings and other provisions corresponding to the last year of that framework shall be extended until such time as that law is adopted.

5. Throughout the procedure leading to the adoption of the financial framework, the European Parliament, the Council and the Commission shall take any measure necessary to facilitate the successful completion of the procedure.

Section 2 - The Unions Annual Budget

Article 403

The financial year shall run from 1 January to 31 December.

Article 404

European laws shall establish the Union's annual budget in accordance with the following provisions:

1. Each institution shall, before 1 July, draw up estimates of its expenditure for the following financial year. The Commission shall consolidate these estimates in a draft budget which may contain different estimates.

The draft budget shall contain an estimate of revenue and an estimate of expenditure.

2. The Commission shall submit a proposal containing the draft budget to the European Parliament and to the Council not later than 1 September of the year preceding that in which the budget is to be implemented. The Commission may amend the draft budget during the procedure until such time as the Conciliation Committee, referred to in paragraph 5, is convened.

3. The Council shall adopt its position on the draft budget and forward it to the European Parliament not later than 1 October of the year preceding that in which the budget is to be implemented. The Council shall inform the European Parliament in full of the reasons which led it to adopt its position.

4. If, within forty-two days of such communication, the European Parliament:

(a) approves the position of the Council, the European law establishing the budget shall be adopted;

(b) has not taken a decision, the European law establishing the budget shall be deemed to have been adopted;

(c) adopts amendments by a majority of its component members, the amended draft shall be forwarded to the Council and to the Commission. The President of the European Parliament, in agreement with the President of the Council, shall immediately convene a meeting of the Conciliation Committee. However, if within ten days of the draft being forwarded the Council informs the European Parliament that it has approved all its amendments, the Conciliation Committee shall not meet.

5. The Conciliation Committee, which shall be composed of the members of the Council or their representatives and an equal number of members representing the European Parliament, shall have the task of reaching agreement on a joint text, by a qualified majority of the members of the Council or their representa-

tives and by a majority of the representatives of the European Parliament within twenty-one days of its being convened, on the basis of the positions of the European Parliament and the Council.

The Commission shall take part in the Conciliation Committee's proceedings and shall take all the necessary initiatives with a view to reconciling the positions of the European Parliament and the Council.

6. If, within the twenty-one days referred to in paragraph 5, the Conciliation Committee agrees on a joint text, the European Parliament and the Council shall each have a period of fourteen days from the date of that agreement in which to approve the joint text.

7. If, within the period of fourteen days referred to in paragraph 6:

(a) the European Parliament and the Council both approve the joint text or fail to take a decision, or if one of these institutions approves the joint text while the other one fails to take a decision, the European law establishing the budget shall be deemed to be definitively adopted in accordance with the joint text, or

(b) the European Parliament, acting by a majority of its component members, and the Council both reject the joint text, or if one of these institutions rejects the joint text while the other one fails to take a decision, a new draft budget shall be submitted by the Commission, or

(c) the European Parliament, acting by a majority of its component members, rejects the joint text while the Council approves it, a new draft budget shall be submitted by the Commission, or

(d) the European Parliament approves the joint text whilst the Council rejects it, the European Parliament may, within fourteen days from the date of the rejection by the Council and acting by a majority of its component members and three-fifths of the votes cast, decide to confirm all or some of the amendments referred to in paragraph 4(c). Where a European Parliament amendment is not confirmed, the position agreed in the Conciliation committee on the budget heading which is the subject of the amendment shall be retained. The European law establishing the budget shall be deemed to be definitively adopted on this basis.

8. If, within the twenty-one days referred to in paragraph 5, the Conciliation Committee does not agree on a joint text, a new draft budget shall be submitted by the Commission.

9. When the procedure provided for in this Article has been completed, the President of the European Parliament shall declare that the European law establishing the budget has been definitively adopted.

10. Each institution shall exercise the powers conferred upon it under this Article in compliance with the Constitution and the acts adopted thereunder, with particular regard to the Union's own resources and the balance between revenue and expenditure.

Article 405

1. If at the beginning of a financial year no European law establishing the budget has been definitively adopted, a sum equivalent to not more than one twelfth of the budget appropriations entered in the chapter in question of the budget for the preceding financial year may be spent each month in respect of

any chapter in accordance with the European law referred to in Article 412; that sum shall not, however, exceed one twelfth of the appropriations provided for in the same chapter of the draft budget.

2. The Council, on a proposal by the Commission and in compliance with the other conditions laid down in paragraph 1, may adopt a European decision authorising expenditure in excess of one twelfth, in accordance with the European law referred to in Article 412. The Council shall forward the decision immediately to the European Parliament.

The European decision shall lay down the necessary measures relating to resources to ensure application of this Article, in accordance with the European laws referred to in Article 54(3) and (4).

It shall enter into force thirty days following its adoption if the European Parliament, acting by a majority of its component members, has not decided to reduce this expenditure within that time limit.

Article 406

In accordance with the conditions laid down by the European law referred to in Article 412, any appropriations, other than those relating to staff expenditure, that are unexpended at the end of the financial year may be carried forward to the next financial year only.

Appropriations shall be classified under different chapters grouping items of expenditure according to their nature or purpose and subdivided in accordance with the European law referred to in Article 412.

The expenditure of:

— the European Parliament,

— the European Council and the Council,

— the Commission, and

— the Court of Justice of the European Union shall be set out in separate sections of the budget, without prejudice to special arrangements for certain common items of expenditure.

Section 3 - Implementation of the Budget and Discharge

Article 407

The Commission shall implement the budget in co-operation with the Member States, in accordance with the European law referred to in Article 412, on its own responsibility and within the limits of the appropriations allocated, having regard to the principles of sound financial management. Member States shall co-operate with the Commission to ensure that the appropriations are used in accordance with those principles.

The European law referred to in Article 412 shall establish the control and audit obligations of the Member States in the implementation of the budget and the resulting responsibilities. It shall establish the responsibilities and detailed rules for each institution concerning its part in effecting its own expenditure.

Within the budget the Commission may, subject to the limits and conditions laid down by the European law referred to in Article 412, transfer appropriations from one chapter to another or from one subdivision to another.

Article 408

The Commission shall submit annually to the European Parliament and to the Council the accounts of the preceding financial year relating to the implementation of the budget. The Commission shall also forward to them a financial statement of the Union's assets and liabilities.

The Commission shall also submit to the European Parliament and to the Council an evaluation report on the Union's finances based on the results achieved, in particular in relation to the indications given by the European Parliament and the Council pursuant to Article 409.

Article 409

1. The European Parliament, on a recommendation from the Council, shall give a discharge to the Commission in respect of the implementation of the budget. To this end, the Council and the European Parliament in turn shall examine the accounts, the financial statement and the evaluation report referred to in Article 408, the annual report by the Court of Auditors together with the replies of the institutions under audit to the observations of the Court of Auditors, the statement of assurance referred to in the second subparagraph of Article 384(1) and any relevant special reports by the Court of Auditors.

2. Before giving a discharge to the Commission, or for any other purpose in connection with the exercise of its powers over the implementation of the budget, the European Parliament may ask to hear the Commission give evidence with regard to the execution of expenditure or the operation of financial control systems. The Commission shall submit any necessary information to the European Parliament at the latter's request.

3. The Commission shall take all appropriate steps to act on the observations in the decisions giving discharge and on other observations by the European Parliament relating to the execution of expenditure, as well as on comments accompanying the recommendations on discharge adopted by the Council.

4. At the request of the European Parliament or the Council, the Commission shall report on the measures taken in the light of these observations and comments and in particular on the instructions given to the departments which are responsible for the implementation of the budget. These reports shall also be forwarded to the Court of Auditors.

Section 4 - Common Provisions

Article 410

The multiannual financial framework and the annual budget shall be drawn up in euro.

Article 411

The Commission may, provided it notifies the competent authorities of the Member States concerned, transfer into the currency of one of the Member States its holdings in the currency of another Member State, to the extent necessary to enable them to be used for purposes which come within the scope of the Constitution. The Commission shall as far as possible avoid making such transfers if it possesses cash or liquid assets in the currencies which it needs.

The Commission shall deal with each Member State concerned through the authority designated by that State. In carrying out financial operations the Commission shall employ the services of the bank of issue of the Member State concerned or of any other financial institution approved by that State.

Article 412

1. European laws shall establish:

(a) the financial rules which determine in particular the procedure to be adopted for establishing and implementing the budget and for presenting and auditing accounts;

(b) rules providing for checks on the responsibility of financial actors, in particular authorising officers and accounting officers. Such European laws shall be adopted after consultation of the Court of Auditors.

2. The Council shall, on a proposal from the Commission, adopt a European regulation laying down the methods and procedure whereby the budget revenue provided under the arrangements relating to the Union's own resources shall be made available to the Commission, and the measures to be applied, if need be, to meet cash requirements. The Council shall act after consulting the European Parliament and the Court of Auditors.

3. The Council shall act unanimously until 31 December 2006 in all the cases referred to by this Article.

Article 413

The European Parliament, the Council and the Commission shall ensure that the financial means are made available to allow the Union to fulfil its legal obligations in respect of third parties.

Article 414

Regular meetings between the Presidents of the European Parliament, the Council and the Commission shall be convened, on the initiative of the Commission, under the budgetary procedures referred to in this Chapter. The Presidents shall take all the necessary steps to promote consultation and the reconciliation of the positions of the institutions over which they preside in order to facilitate the implementation of this Chapter.

Section 5 - Combating Fraud

Article 415

1. The Union and the Member States shall counter fraud and any other illegal activities affecting the Union's financial interests through measures taken in accordance with this Article. These measures shall act as a deterrent and be such as to afford effective protection in the Member States and in all the Union's institutions, bodies, offices and agencies.

2. Member States shall take the same measures to counter fraud affecting the Union's financial interests as they take to counter fraud affecting their own financial interests.

3. Without prejudice to other provisions of the Constitution, the Member States shall co-ordinate their action aimed at protecting the Union's financial interests against fraud. To this end they shall organise, together with the Commission, close and regular co-operation between the competent authorities.

4. European laws or framework laws shall lay down the necessary measures in the fields of the prevention of and fight against fraud affecting the Union's financial interests with a view to affording effective and equivalent protection in the Member States and in all the Union's institutions, bodies, offices and agencies. They shall be adopted after consultation of the Court of Auditors.

5. The Commission, in co-operation with Member States, shall each year submit to the European Parliament and to the Council a report on the measures taken for the implementation of this Article.

Chapter III - Enhanced co-operation

Article 416

Any enhanced co-operation shall comply with the Constitution and the law of the Union. Such co-operation shall not undermine the internal market or economic, social and territorial cohesion. It shall not constitute a barrier to or discrimination in trade between Member States, nor shall it distort competition between them.

Article 417

Any enhanced co-operation shall respect the competences, rights and obligations of those Member States which do not participate in it. Those Member States shall not impede its implementation by the participating Member States.

Article 418

1. When enhanced co-operation is being established, it shall be open to all Member States, subject to compliance with any conditions of participation laid down by the European authorising decision. It shall also be open to them at any other time, subject to compliance with the acts already adopted within that framework, in addition to any such conditions.

The Commission and the Member States participating in enhanced co-operation shall ensure that they promote participation by as many Member States as possible.

2. The Commission and, where appropriate, the Union Minister for Foreign Affairs shall keep the European Parliament and the Council regularly informed regarding developments in enhanced co-operation.

Article 419

1. Member States which wish to establish enhanced co-operation between themselves in one of the areas covered by the Constitution, with the exception of

fields of exclusive competence and the common foreign and security policy, shall address a request to the Commission, specifying the scope and objectives of the enhanced co-operation proposed. The Commission may submit a proposal to the Council to that effect. In the event of the Commission not submitting a proposal, it shall inform the Member States concerned of the reasons for not doing so.

Authorisation to proceed with enhanced co-operation shall be granted by a European decision of the Council, which shall act on a proposal from the Commission and after obtaining the consent of the European Parliament.

2. The request of the Member States which wish to establish enhanced co-operation between themselves within the framework of the common foreign and security policy shall be addressed to the Council. It shall be forwarded to the Union Minister for Foreign Affairs, who shall give an opinion on whether the enhanced co-operation proposed is consistent with the Union's common foreign and security policy, and to the Commission, which shall give its opinion in particular on whether the enhanced co-operation proposed is consistent with other Union policies. It shall also be forwarded to the European Parliament for information. Authorisation to proceed with enhanced co-operation shall be granted by a European decision of the Council acting unanimously.

Article 420

1. Any Member State which wishes to participate in enhanced co-operation in progress in one of the areas referred to in Article 419(1) shall notify its intention to the Council and the Commission.

The Commission shall, within four months of the date of receipt of the notification, confirm the participation of the Member State concerned. It shall note where necessary that the conditions of participation have been fulfilled and shall adopt any transitional measures necessary with regard to the application of the acts already adopted within the framework of enhanced co-operation.

However, if the Commission considers that the conditions of participation have not been fulfilled, it shall indicate the arrangements to be adopted to fulfil those conditions and shall set a deadline for reexamining the request. On the expiry of that deadline, it shall re-examine the request, in accordance with the procedure set out in the second subparagraph. If the Commission considers that the conditions of participation have still not been met, the Member State concerned may refer the matter to the Council, which shall decide on the request. The Council shall act in accordance with Article 44(3). It may also adopt the transitional measures referred to in the second subparagraph on a proposal from the Commission.

2. Any Member State which wishes to participate in enhanced co-operation in progress in the framework of the common foreign and security policy shall notify its intention to the Council, the Union Minister for Foreign Affairs and the Commission.

The Council shall confirm the participation of the Member State concerned, after consulting the Union Minister for Foreign Affairs and after noting, where necessary, that the conditions of participation have been fulfilled. The Council, on a proposal from the Union Minister for Foreign Affairs, may also adopt any transitional measures necessary with regard to the application of the acts already adopted within the framework of enhanced co-operation. However, if the Council considers that the conditions of participation have not been fulfilled, it shall indicate the arrangements to be adopted to fulfil those conditions and shall set a deadline for re-examining the request for participation. For the purposes of this paragraph, the Council shall act unanimously and in accordance with Article 44(3).

Article 421

Expenditure resulting from implementation of enhanced co-operation, other than administrative costs entailed for the institutions, shall be borne by the participating Member States, unless all members of the Council, acting unanimously after consulting the European Parliament, decide otherwise.

Article 422

1. Where a provision of the Constitution which may be applied in the context of enhanced co-operation stipulates that the Council shall act unanimously, the Council, acting unanimously in accordance with the arrangements laid down in Article 44(3), may adopt a European decision stipulating that it will act by a qualified majority.

2. Where a provision of the Constitution which may be applied in the context of enhanced co-operation stipulates that the Council shall adopt European laws or framework laws under a special legislative procedure, the Council, acting unanimously in accordance with the arrangements laid down in Article 44(3), may adopt a European decision stipulating that it will act under the ordinary legislative procedure. The Council shall act after consulting the European Parliament.

3. Paragraphs 1 and 2 shall not apply to decisions having military or defence implications.

Article 423

The Council and the Commission shall ensure the consistency of activities undertaken in the context of enhanced co-operation and the consistency of such activities with the policies of the Union, and shall co-operate to that end.

Title VII
Common Provisions

Article 424

Taking account of the structural economic and social situation of Guadeloupe, French Guiana, Martinique, Réunion, the Azores, Madeira and the Canary Islands, which is compounded by their remoteness, insularity, small size, difficult topography and climate, economic dependence on a few products, the permanence and combination of which severely restrain their development, the Council, on a proposal from the Commission, shall adopt European laws, framework laws, regulations and decisions aimed, in particular, at laying down the conditions of application of the Constitution to those regions, including common policies. It shall act after consulting the European Parliament.

The acts referred to in the first paragraph concern in particular areas such as customs and trade policies, fiscal policy, free zones, agriculture and fisheries policies, conditions for supply of raw materials and essential consumer goods, State aids and conditions of access to structural funds and to horizontal Union programmes.

The Council shall adopt the acts referred to in the first paragraph taking into account the special characteristics and constraints of the outermost regions without undermining the integrity and the coherence of the Union legal order, including the internal market and common policies.

Article 425

The Constitution shall in no way prejudice the rules in Member States governing the system of property ownership.

Article 426

In each of the Member States, the Union shall enjoy the most extensive legal capacity accorded to legal persons under their laws; it may, in particular, acquire or dispose of movable and immovable property and may be a party to legal proceedings. To this end, the Union shall be represented by the Commission. However, the Union shall be represented by each of the institutions, by virtue of their administrative autonomy, in matters relating to their respective operation.

Article 427

The Staff Regulations of officials and the Conditions of employment of other servants of the Union shall be laid down by a European law. It shall be adopted after consultation of the institutions concerned.

Article 428

The Commission may, within the limits and under conditions laid down by a European regulation or decision adopted by a simple majority by the Council, collect any information and carry out any checks required for the performance of the tasks entrusted to it.

Article 429

1. Without prejudice to Article 5 of the Protocol on the Statute of the European System of Central Banks and of the European Central Bank, measures for the production of statistics shall be laid down by a European law or framework law where necessary for the performance of the Union's activities.

2. The production of statistics shall conform to impartiality, reliability, objectivity, scientific independence, cost-effectiveness and statistical confidentiality. It shall not entail excessive burdens on economic operators.

Article 430

The members of the Union's institutions, the members of committees, and the officials and other servants of the Union shall be required, even after their duties have ceased, not to disclose information of the kind covered by the obligation of professional secrecy, in particular information about undertakings, their business relations or their cost components.

Article 431

The Union's contractual liability shall be governed by the law applicable to the contract in question.

In the case of non-contractual liability, the Union shall, in accordance with the general principles common to the laws of the Member States, make good any damage caused by its institutions or by its servants in the performance of their duties.

Notwithstanding the second paragraph, the European Central Bank shall, in accordance with the general principles common to the laws of the Member States, make good any damage caused by it or by its servants in the performance of their duties.

The personal liability of its servants towards the Union shall be governed by the provisions laid down in their Staff Regulations or in the Conditions of Employment applicable to them.

Article 432

The seat of the Union's institutions shall be determined by common accord of the governments of the Member States.

Article 433

The Council shall adopt unanimously a European regulation laying down the rules governing the languages of the Union's institutions, without prejudice to the Statute of the Court of Justice of the European Union.

Article 434

The Union shall enjoy in the territories of the Member States such privileges and immunities as are necessary for the performance of its tasks, under the conditions laid down in the Protocol on the privileges and immunities of the European Union.

Article 435

The rights and obligations arising from agreements concluded before 1 January 1958 or, for acceding States, before the date of their accession, between one or more Member States on the one hand, and one or more third countries on the other, shall not be affected by the Constitution.

To the extent that such agreements are not compatible with the Constitution, the Member State or States concerned shall take all appropriate steps to eliminate the incompatibilities established. Member States shall, where necessary, assist each other to this end and shall, where appropriate, adopt a common attitude.

In applying the agreements referred to in the first paragraph, Member States shall take into account the fact that the advantages accorded under the Constitution by each Member State form an integral part of the Union and are thereby inseparably linked with the creation of institutions on which powers have been conferred by the Constitution and the granting of identical advantages by all the other Member States.

Article 436

1. The Constitution shall not preclude the application of the following rules:

(a) no Member State shall be obliged to supply information the disclosure of which it considers contrary to the essential interests of its security;

(b) any Member State may take such measures as it considers necessary for the protection of the essential interests of its security which are connected with the production of or trade in arms, munitions and war material; such measures shall not adversely affect the conditions of competition in the internal market regarding products which are not intended for specifically military purposes.

2. The Council, on a proposal from the Commission, may unanimously adopt a European decision making changes to the list of 15 April 1958 of the products to which the provisions of paragraph 1 (b) apply.

Part IV

General and Final Provisions

Article 437 - Repeal of earlier Treaties

1. This Treaty establishing a Constitution for Europe shall repeal the Treaty establishing the European Community, the Treaty on European Union and, under the conditions laid down in the Protocol on the acts and treaties having supplemented or amended the Treaty establishing the European Community and the Treaty on European Union, the acts and treaties which have supplemented or amended them, subject to paragraph 2 of this Article.

2. The Treaties on the Accession:

(a) of the Kingdom of Denmark, Ireland and the United Kingdom of Great Britain and Northern Ireland;

(b) of the Hellenic Republic;

(c) of the Kingdom of Spain and the Portuguese Republic;

(d) of the Republic of Austria, the Republic of Finland and the Kingdom of Sweden, and

(e) of the Czech Republic, the Republic of Estonia, the Republic of Cyprus, the Republic of Latvia, the Republic of Lithuania, the Republic of Hungary, the Republic of Malta, the Republic of Poland, the Republic of Slovenia and the Slovak Republic, shall be repealed.

Nevertheless:

— the provisions of the Treaties referred to in points (a) to (d) and set out or referred to in the Protocol on the Treaties and Acts of Accession of the Kingdom of Denmark, Ireland and the United Kingdom of Great Britain and Northern Ireland, of the Hellenic Republic, of the Kingdom of Spain and the Portuguese Republic, and of the Republic of Austria, the Republic of Finland and the Kingdom of Sweden shall remain in force and their legal effects shall be preserved in accordance with that Protocol,

— the provisions of the Treaty referred to in point (e) and which are set out or referred to in the Protocol on the Treaty and Act of Accession of the Czech Republic, the Republic of Estonia, the Republic of Cyprus, the Republic of Latvia, the Republic of Lithuania, the Republic of Hungary, the Republic of Malta, the Republic of Poland, the Republic of Slovenia and the Slovak Republic shall remain in force and their legal effects shall be preserved in accordance with that Protocol.

Article 438 - Succession and legal continuity

1. The European Union established by this Treaty shall be the successor to the European Union established by the Treaty on European Union and to the European Community.

2. Until new provisions have been adopted in implementation of this Treaty or until the end of their term of office, the institutions, bodies, offices and agencies existing on the date of the entry into force of this Treaty shall, subject to Article 439, exercise their powers within the meaning of this Treaty in their composition on that date.

3. The acts of the institutions, bodies, offices and agencies adopted on the basis of the treaties and acts repealed by Article 437 shall remain in force. Their legal effects shall be preserved until those acts are repealed, annulled or amended in implementation of this Treaty. The same shall apply to agreements concluded between Member States on the basis of the treaties and acts repealed by Article 437.

The other components of the acquis of the Community and of the Union existing at the time of the entry into force of this Treaty, in particular the inter-institutional agreements, decisions and agreements arrived at by the Representatives of the Governments of the Member States, meeting within the Council, the agreements concluded by the Member States on the functioning of the Union or of the Community or linked to action by the Union or by the Community, the declarations, including those made in the context of intergovernmental conferences, as well as the resolutions or other positions adopted by the European Council or the Council and those relating to the Union or to the Community adopted by common accord by the Member States, shall also be preserved until they have been deleted or amended.

4. The case-law of the Court of Justice of the European Communities and of the Court of First Instance on the interpretation and application of the treaties and acts repealed by Article 437, as well as of the acts and conventions adopted for their application, shall remain, mutatis mutandis, the source of interpretation of Union law and in particular of the comparable provisions of the Constitution.

5. Continuity in administrative and legal procedures commenced prior to the date of entry into force of this Treaty shall be ensured in compliance with the Constitution. The institutions, bodies, offices and agencies responsible for those procedures shall take all appropriate measures to that effect.

Article 439 - Transitional provisions relating to certain institutions

The transitional provisions relating to the composition of the European Parliament, to the definition of a qualified majority in the European Council and in the Council, including those cases where not all members of the European Council or Council vote, and to the composition of the Commission, including the Union Minister for Foreign Affairs, shall be laid down in the Protocol on the transitional provisions relating to the institutions and bodies of the Union.

Article 440 - Scope

1. This Treaty shall apply to the Kingdom of Belgium, the Czech Republic, the Kingdom of Denmark, the Federal Republic of Germany, the Republic of Estonia, the Hellenic Republic, the Kingdom of Spain, the French Republic, Ireland, the Italian Republic, the Republic of Cyprus, the Republic of Latvia, the Republic of Lithuania, the Grand Duchy of Luxembourg, the Republic of Hungary, the Republic of Malta, the Kingdom of the Netherlands, the Republic of Austria, the Republic of Poland, the Portuguese Republic, the Republic of Slovenia, the Slovak Republic, the Republic of Finland, the Kingdom of Sweden and the United Kingdom of Great Britain and Northern Ireland.

2. This Treaty shall apply to Guadeloupe, French Guiana, Martinique, Réunion, the Azores, Madeira and the Canary Islands in accordance with Article 424.

3. The special arrangements for association set out in Title IV of Part III shall apply to the overseas countries and territories listed in Annex II.

This Treaty shall not apply to overseas countries and territories having special relations with the United Kingdom of Great Britain and Northern Ireland which are not included in that list.

4. This Treaty shall apply to the European territories for whose external relations a Member State is responsible.

5. This Treaty shall apply to the Åland Islands with the derogations which originally appeared in the Treaty referred to in Article 437(2)(d) and which have been incorporated in Section 5 of Title V of the Protocol on the Treaties and Acts of Accession of the Kingdom of Denmark, Ireland and the United Kingdom of Great Britain and Northern Ireland, of the Hellenic Republic, of the Kingdom of Spain and the Portuguese Republic, and of the Republic of Austria, the Republic of Finland and the Kingdom of Sweden.

6. Notwithstanding paragraphs 1 to 5:

(a) this Treaty shall not apply to the Faeroe Islands;

(b) this Treaty shall apply to Akrotiri and Dhekelia, the sovereign base areas of the United Kingdom of Great Britain and Northern Ireland in Cyprus, only to the extent necessary to ensure the implementation of the arrangements originally provided for in the Protocol on the Sovereign Base Areas of the United Kingdom of Great Britain and Northern Ireland in Cyprus, annexed to the Act of Accession which is an integral part of the Treaty referred to in Article 437(2)(e), and which have been incorporated in Title III of Part II of the Protocol on the Treaty and Act of Accession of the Czech Republic, the Republic of Estonia, the Republic of Cyprus, the Republic of Latvia, the Republic of Lithuania, the Republic of Hungary, the Republic of Malta, the Republic of Poland, the Republic of Slovenia and the Slovak Republic;

(c) this Treaty shall apply to the Channel Islands and the Isle of Man only to the extent necessary to ensure the implementation of the arrangements for those islands originally set out in the Treaty referred to in Article 437(2)(a), and which have been incorporated in Section 3 of Title II of the Protocol on the Treaties and Acts of Accession of the Kingdom of Denmark, Ireland and the United Kingdom of Great Britain and Northern Ireland, of the Hellenic Republic, of the Kingdom of Spain and the Portuguese Republic, and of the Republic of Austria, the Republic of Finland and the Kingdom of Sweden.

7. The European Council may, on the initiative of the Member State concerned, adopt a European decision amending the status, with regard to the Union, of a Danish, French or Netherlands country or territory referred to in paragraphs 2 and 3. The European Council shall act unanimously after consulting the Commission.

Article 441 - Regional unions

This Treaty shall not preclude the existence or completion of regional unions between Belgium and Luxembourg, or between Belgium, Luxembourg and the Netherlands, to the extent that the objectives of these regional unions are not attained by application of the said Treaty.

Article 442 - Protocols and Annexes

The Protocols and Annexes to this Treaty shall form an integral part thereof.

Article 443 - Ordinary revision procedure

1. The government of any Member State, the European Parliament or the Commission may submit to the Council proposals for the amendment of this Treaty. These proposals shall be submitted to the European Council by the Council and the national Parliaments shall be notified.

2. If the European Council, after consulting the European Parliament and the Commission, adopts by a simple majority a decision in favour of examining the proposed amendments, the President of the European Council shall convene a Convention composed of representatives of the national Parliaments, of the Heads of State or Government of the Member States, of the European Parliament and of the Commission. The European Central Bank shall also be consulted in the case of institutional changes in the monetary area. The Convention shall examine the proposals for amendments and shall adopt by consensus a recommendation to a conference of representatives of the governments of the Member States as provided for in paragraph 3.

The European Council may decide by a simple majority, after obtaining the consent of the European Parliament, not to convene a Convention should this not be justified by the extent of the proposed amendments. In the latter case, the European Council shall define the terms of reference for a conference of representatives of the governments of the Member States.

3. A conference of representatives of the governments of the Member States shall be convened by the President of the Council for the purpose of determining by common accord the amendments to be made to this Treaty.

The amendments shall enter into force after being ratified by all the Member States in accordance with their respective constitutional requirements.

4. If, two years after the signature of the treaty amending this Treaty, four fifths of the Member States have ratified it and one or more Member States have encountered difficulties in proceeding with ratification, the matter shall be referred to the European Council.

Article 444 - Simplified revision procedure

1. Where Part III provides for the Council to act by unanimity in a given area or case, the European Council may adopt a European decision authorising the Council to act by a qualified majority in that area or in that case.

This paragraph shall not apply to decisions with military implications or those in the area of defence.

2. Where Part III provides for European laws and framework laws to be adopted by the Council in accordance with a special legislative procedure, the European Council may adopt a European decision allowing for the adoption of such European laws or framework laws in accordance with the ordinary legislative procedure.

3. Any initiative taken by the European Council on the basis of paragraphs 1 or 2 shall be notified to the national Parliaments. If a national Parliament makes known its opposition within six months of the date of such notification, the European decision referred to in paragraphs 1 or 2 shall not be adopted. In the absence of opposition, the European Council may adopt the decision.

For the adoption of the European decisions referred to in paragraphs 1 and 2, the European Council shall act by unanimity after obtaining the consent of the European Parliament, which shall be given by a majority of its component members.

Article 445 - Simplified revision procedure concerning internal Union policies and action

1. The Government of any Member State, the European Parliament or the Commission may submit to the European Council proposals for revising all or part of the provisions of Title III of Part III on the internal policies and action of the Union.

2. The European Council may adopt a European decision amending all or part of the provisions of Title III of Part III. The European Council shall act by unanimity after consulting the European Parliament and the Commission, and the European Central Bank in the case of institutional changes in the monetary area.

Such a European decision shall not come into force until it has been approved by the Member States in accordance with their respective constitutional requirements.

3. The European decision referred to in paragraph 2 shall not increase the competences conferred on the Union in this Treaty.

Article 446 - Duration

This Treaty is concluded for an unlimited period.

Article 447 - Ratification and entry into force

1. This Treaty shall be ratified by the High Contracting Parties in accordance with their respective constitutional requirements. The instruments of ratification shall be deposited with the Government of the Italian Republic.

2. This Treaty shall enter into force on 1 November 2006, provided that all the instruments of ratification have been deposited, or, failing that, on the first day of the second month following the deposit of the instrument of ratification by the last signatory State to take this step.

Article 448 - Authentic texts and translations

1. This Treaty, drawn up in a single original in the Czech, Danish, Dutch, English, Estonian, Finnish, French, German, Greek, Hungarian, Irish, Italian, Latvian, Lithuanian, Maltese, Polish, Portuguese, Slovak, Slovenian, Spanish and Swedish languages, the texts in each of these languages being equally authentic, shall be deposited in the archives of the Government of the Italian Republic, which will transmit a certified copy to each of the governments of the other signatory States.

2. This Treaty may also be translated into any other languages as determined by Member States among those which, in accordance with their constitutional order, enjoy official status in all or part of their territory. A certified copy of such translations shall be provided by the Member States concerned to be deposited in the archives of the Council.

IN WITNESS WHEREOF, the undersigned plenipotentiaries have signed this Treaty

List of Protocols annexed to the Treaty Establishing a Constitution for Europe

1 Protocol on the role of national Parliaments in the European Union
2 Protocol on the application of the principles of subsidiarity and proportionality
3 Protocol on the Statute of the Court of Justice of the European Union
4 Protocol on the Statute of the European System of Central Banks and of the European Central Bank
5 Protocol on the Statute of the European Investment Bank
6 Protocol on the location of the seats of the institutions and of certain bodies, offices, agencies and departments of the European Union
7 Protocol on the privileges and immunities of the European Union
8 Protocol on the Treaties and Acts of Accession of the Kingdom of Denmark, Ireland and the United Kingdom of Great Britain and Northern Ireland, of the Hellenic Republic, of the Kingdom of Spain and the Portuguese Republic, and of the Republic of Austria, the Republic of Finland and the Kingdom of Sweden Constitution/L/en 2
9 Protocol on the Treaty and the Act of Accession of the Czech Republic, the Republic of Estonia, the Republic of Cyprus, the Republic of Latvia, the Republic of Lithuania, the Republic of Hungary, the Republic of Malta, the Republic of Poland, the Republic of Slovenia and the Slovak Republic
10 Protocol on the excessive deficit procedure
11 Protocol on the convergence criteria
12 Protocol on the Euro Group
13 Protocol on certain provisions relating to the United Kingdom of Great Britain and Northern Ireland as regards economic and monetary union
14 Protocol on certain provisions relating to Denmark as regards economic and monetary union
15 Protocol on certain tasks of the National Bank of Denmark
16 Protocol on the Pacific Financial Community franc system
17 Protocol on the Schengen acquis integrated into the framework of the European Union
18 Protocol on the application of certain aspects of Article 130 of the Constitution to the United Kingdom and to Ireland Constitution/L/en 3
19 Protocol on the position of the United Kingdom and Ireland on policies in respect of border controls, asylum and immigration, judicial cooperation in civil matters and on police cooperation
20 Protocol on the position of Denmark
21 Protocol on external relations of the Member States with regard to the crossing of external borders
22 Protocol on asylum for nationals of Member States
23 Protocol on permanent structured cooperation established by Article 41(6) and Article 312 of the Constitution
24 Protocol on Article 41(2) of the Constitution

Selected protocols annexed to the Treaty establishing a Constitution for Europe

The protocols included here are numbers 1,2,7,13,17,18,19,21,22,23, 27,28 and 29

1. Protocol on the role of national parliaments in the European Union

THE HIGH CONTRACTING PARTIES,

RECALLING that the way in which national Parliaments scrutinise their governments in relation to the activities of the Union is a matter for the particular constitutional organisation and practice of each Member State;

DESIRING to encourage greater involvement of national Parliaments in the activities of the European Union and to enhance their ability to express their views on draft European legislative acts as well as on other matters which may be of particular interest to them,

HAVE AGREED UPON the following provisions, which shall be annexed to the Treaty establishing a Constitution for Europe and to the Treaty establishing the European Atomic Energy Community:

TITLE I

INFORMATION FOR NATIONAL PARLIAMENTS

Article 1

Commission consultation documents (green and white papers and communications) shall be forwarded directly by the Commission to national Parliaments upon publication. The Commission shall also forward the annual legislative programme as well as any other instrument of legislative planning or policy to national Parliaments, at the same time as to the European Parliament and the Council.

Article 2

Draft European legislative acts sent to the European Parliament and to the Council shall be forwarded to national Parliaments.

For the purposes of this Protocol, "draft European legislative acts" shall mean proposals from the Commission, initiatives from a group of Member States, initiatives from the European Parliament, requests from the Court of Justice, recommendations from the European Central Bank and requests from the European Investment Bank for the adoption of a European legislative act.

Draft European legislative acts originating from the Commission shall be forwarded to national Parliaments directly by the Commission, at the same time as to the European Parliament and the Council.

Draft European legislative acts originating from the European Parliament shall be forwarded to national Parliaments directly by the European Parliament.

Draft European legislative acts originating from a group of Member States, the Court of Justice, the European Central Bank or the European Investment Bank shall be forwarded to national Parliaments by the Council.

Article 3

National Parliaments may send to the Presidents of the European Parliament, the Council and the Commission a reasoned opinion on whether a draft European legislative act complies with the principle of subsidiarity, in accordance with the procedure laid down in the Protocol on the application of the principles of subsidiarity and proportionality.

If the draft European legislative act originates from a group of Member States, the President of the Council shall forward the reasoned opinion or opinions to the governments of those Member States.

If the draft European legislative act originates from the Court of Justice, the European Central Bank or the European Investment Bank, the President of the Council shall forward the reasoned opinion or opinions to the institution or body concerned.

Article 4

A six-week period shall elapse between a draft European legislative act being made available to national Parliaments in the official languages of the

Union and the date when it is placed on a provisional agenda for the Council for its adoption or for adoption of a position under a legislative procedure. Exceptions shall be possible in cases of urgency, the reasons for which shall be stated in the act or position of the Council. Save in urgent cases for which due reasons have been given, no agreement may be reached on a draft European legislative act during those six weeks. Save in urgent cases for which due reasons have been given, a ten-day period shall elapse between the placing of a draft European legislative act on the provisional agenda for the Council and the adoption of a position.

Article 5

The agendas for and the outcome of meetings of the Council, including the minutes of meetings where the Council is deliberating on draft European legislative acts, shall be forwarded directly to national Parliaments, at the same time as to Member States' governments.

Article 6

When the European Council intends to make use of Article IV-444(1) or (2) of the Constitution, national Parliaments shall be informed of the initiative of the European Council at least six months before any European decision is adopted.

Article 7

The Court of Auditors shall forward its annual report to national Parliaments, for information, at the same time as to the European Parliament and to the Council.

Article 8

Where the national Parliamentary system is not unicameral, Articles 1 to 7 shall apply to the component chambers.

TITLE II

INTER-PARLIAMENTARY CO-OPERATION

Article 9

The European Parliament and national Parliaments shall together determine the organisation and promotion of effective and regular interparliamentary cooperation within the Union.

Article 10

A conference of Parliamentary Committees for Union Affairs may submit any contribution it deems appropriate for the attention of the European Parliament, the Council and the Commission. That conference shall in addition promote the exchange of information and best practice between national Parliaments and the European Parliament, including their special committees. It may also organise interparliamentary conferences on specific topics, in particular to debate matters of common foreign and security policy, including common security and defence policy. Contributions from the conference shall not bind national Parliaments and shall not prejudge their positions.

2. Protocol on the application of the principles of subsidiarity and proportionality

THE HIGH CONTRACTING PARTIES,

WISHING to ensure that decisions are taken as closely as possible to the citizens of the Union;

RESOLVED to establish the conditions for the application of the principles of subsidiarity and proportionality, as laid down in Article 11 of the Constitution, and to establish a system for monitoring the application of those principles,

HAVE AGREED UPON the following provisions, which shall be annexed to the Treaty establishing a Constitution for Europe:

Article 1

Each institution shall ensure constant respect for the principles of subsidiarity and proportionality, as laid down in Article 11 of the Constitution.

Article 2

Before proposing European legislative acts, the Commission shall consult widely. Such consultations shall, where appropriate, take into account the regional and local dimension of the action envisaged. In cases of exceptional urgency, the Commission shall not conduct such consultations. It shall give reasons for its decision in its proposal.

Article 3

For the purposes of this Protocol, "draft European legislative acts" shall mean proposals from the Commission, initiatives from a group of Member States, initiatives from the European Parliament, requests from the Court of Justice, recommendations from the European Central Bank and requests from the European Investment Bank for the adoption of a European legislative act.

Article 4

The Commission shall forward its draft European legislative acts and its amended drafts to national Parliaments at the same time as to the Union legislator.

The European Parliament shall forward its draft European legislative acts and its amended drafts to national Parliaments.

The Council shall forward draft European legislative acts originating from a group of Member States, the Court of Justice, the European Central Bank or the European Investment Bank and amended drafts to national Parliaments.

Upon adoption, legislative resolutions of the European Parliament and positions of the Council shall be forwarded by them to national Parliaments.

Article 5

Draft European legislative acts shall be justified with regard to the principles of subsidiarity and proportionality. Any draft European legislative act should contain a detailed statement making it possible to appraise compliance with the principles of subsidiarity and proportionality.

This statement should contain some assessment of the proposal's financial impact and, in the case of a European framework law, of its implications for the rules to be put in place by Member States, including, where necessary, the regional legislation. The reasons for concluding that a Union objective can be better achieved at Union level shall be substantiated by qualitative and, wherever possible, quantitative indicators. Draft European legislative acts shall take account of the need for any burden, whether financial or administrative, falling upon the Union, national governments, regional or local authorities, economic operators and citizens, to be minimised and commensurate with the objective to be achieved.

Article 6

Any national Parliament or any chamber of a national Parliament may, within six weeks from the date of transmission of a draft European legislative act, send to the Presidents of the European Parliament, the Council and the Commission a reasoned opinion stating why it considers that the draft in question does not comply with the principle of subsidiarity. It will be for each national Parliament or each chamber of a national Parliament to consult, where appropriate, regional parliaments with legislative powers.

If the draft European legislative act originates from a group of Member States, the President of the Council shall forward the opinion to the governments of those Member States.

If the draft European legislative act originates from the Court of Justice, the European Central Bank or the European Investment Bank, the President of the Council shall forward the opinion to the institution or body concerned.

Article 7

The European Parliament, the Council and the Commission, and, where appropriate, the group of Member States, the Court of Justice, the European Central Bank or the European Investment Bank, if the draft legislative act originates from them, shall take account of the reasoned opinions issued by national Parliaments or by a chamber of a national Parliament.

Each national Parliament shall have two votes, shared out on the basis of the national Parliamentary system. In the case of a bicameral Parliamentary system, each of the two chambers shall have one vote.

Where reasoned opinions on a draft European legislative act's non-compliance with the principle of subsidiarity represent at least one third of all the votes allocated to the national Parliaments in accordance with the second paragraph, the draft must be reviewed. This threshold shall be a quarter in the case of a draft European legislative act submitted on the basis of Article 264 of the Constitution on the area of freedom, security and justice.

After such review, the Commission or, where appropriate, the group of Member States, the European Parliament, the Court of Justice, the European Central Bank or the European Investment Bank, if the draft European legislative act originates from them, may decide to maintain, amend or withdraw the draft. Reasons must be given for this decision.

Article 8

The Court of Justice of the European Union shall have jurisdiction in actions on grounds of infringement of the principle of subsidiarity by a European legislative act, brought in accordance with the rules laid down in Article 365 of the Constitution by Member States, or notified by them in accordance with their legal order on behalf of their national Parliament or a chamber of it.

In accordance with the rules laid down in the said Article, the Committee of the Regions may also bring such actions against European legislative acts for the adoption of which the Constitution provides that it be consulted.

Article 9

The Commission shall submit each year to the European Council, the European Parliament, the Council and national Parliaments a report on the application of Article 11 of the Constitution.

This annual report shall also be forwarded to the Committee of the Regions and to the Economic and Social Committee.

7. Protocol on the privileges and immunities of the European Union

THE HIGH CONTRACTING PARTIES,

CONSIDERING that, in accordance with Article 434 of the Constitution, the Union shall enjoy in the territories of the Member States such privileges and immunities as are necessary for the performance of its tasks,

HAVE AGREED upon the following provisions, which shall be annexed to the Treaty establishing a Constitution for Europe and to the Treaty establishing the European Atomic Energy Community:

CHAPTER I
PROPERTY, FUNDS, ASSETS AND OPERATIONS OF THE UNION

Article 1

The premises and buildings of the Union shall be inviolable. They shall be exempt from search, requisition, confiscation or expropriation. The property and assets of the Union shall not be the subject of any administrative or legal measure of constraint without the authorisation of the Court of Justice.

Article 2

The archives of the Union shall be inviolable.

Article 3

The Union, its assets, revenues and other property shall be exempt from all direct taxes.

The governments of the Member States shall, wherever possible, take the appropriate measures to remit or refund the amount of indirect taxes or sales taxes included in the price of movable or immovable property, where the Union makes, for its official use, substantial purchases the price of which includes taxes of this kind. These provisions shall not be applied, however, so as to have the effect of distorting competition within the Union.

No exemption shall be granted in respect of taxes and dues which amount merely to charges for public utility services.

Article 4

The Union shall be exempt from all customs duties, prohibitions and restrictions on imports and exports in respect of articles intended for its official use. Articles so imported shall not be disposed of, whether or not in return for payment, in the territory of the State into which they have been imported, except under conditions approved by the government of that State.

The Union shall also be exempt from any customs duties and any prohibitions and restrictions on import and exports in respect of its publications.

CHAPTER II COMMUNICATIONS AND LAISSEZ-PASSER

Article 5

For their official communications and the transmission of all their documents, the institutions of the Union shall enjoy in the territory of each Member State the treatment accorded by that State to diplomatic missions.

Official correspondence and other official communications of the institutions of the Union shall not be subject to censorship.

Article 6

1. Laissez-passer in a form to be prescribed by a European regulation of the Council acting by a simple majority, which shall be recognised as valid travel documents by the authorities of the Member States, may be issued to members and servants of the institutions of the Union by the Presidents of these institutions. These laissez-passer shall be issued to officials and other servants under conditions laid down in the Staff Regulations of officials and the Conditions of Employment of other servants of the Union.

The Commission may conclude agreements for these laissez-passer to be recognised as valid travel documents within the territory of third States.

CHAPTER III MEMBERS OF THE EUROPEAN PARLIAMENT

Article 7

No administrative or other restriction shall be imposed on the free movement of members of the European Parliament travelling to or from the place of meeting of the European Parliament.

Members of the European Parliament shall, in respect of customs and exchange control, be accorded:

(a) by their own governments, the same facilities as those accorded to senior officials travelling abroad on temporary official missions;

(b) by the governments of other Member States, the same facilities as those accorded to representatives of foreign governments on temporary official missions.

Article 8

Members of the European Parliament shall not be subject to any form of inquiry, detention or legal proceedings in respect of opinions expressed or votes cast by them in the performance of their duties.

Article 9

During the sessions of the European Parliament, its members shall enjoy:

(a) in the territory of their own State, the immunities accorded to members of their Parliament;

(b) in the territory of any other Member State, immunity from any measure of detention and from legal proceedings.

Immunity shall likewise apply to members while they are travelling to and from the place of meeting of the European Parliament.

Immunity cannot be claimed when a member is found in the act of committing an offence and shall not prevent the European Parliament from exercising its right to waive the immunity of one of its members.

CHAPTER IV REPRESENTATIVES OF MEMBER STATES TAKING PART IN THE WORK OF THE INSTITUTIONS OF THE UNION

Article 10

Representatives of Member States taking part in the work of the institutions of the Union, their advisers and technical experts shall, in the performance of their duties and during their travel to and from the place of meeting, enjoy the customary privileges, immunities and facilities.

This Article shall also apply to members of the advisory bodies of the Union.

CHAPTER V OFFICIALS AND OTHER SERVANTS OF THE UNION

Article 11

In the territory of each Member State and whatever their nationality, officials and other servants of the Union shall:

(a) subject to the provisions of the Constitution relating, on the one hand, to the rules on the liability of officials and other servants towards the Union and, on the other hand, to the jurisdiction of the Court of Justice of the European Union in disputes between the Union and its officials and other servants, be immune from legal proceedings in respect of acts performed by them in their official capacity, including their words spoken or written. They shall continue to enjoy this immunity after they have ceased to hold office;

(b) together with their spouses and dependent members of their families, not be subject to immigration restrictions or to formalities for the registration of aliens;

(c) in respect of currency or exchange regulations, be accorded the same facilities as are customarily accorded to officials of international organisations;

(d) enjoy the right to import free of duty their furniture and effects at the time of first taking up their post in the State concerned, and the right to re-export free of duty their furniture and effects, on termination of their duties in that State, subject in either case to the conditions considered to be necessary by the government of the State in which this right is exercised;

(e) have the right to import free of duty a motor car for their personal use, acquired either in the State of their last residence or in the State of which they are nationals on the terms ruling in the home market in that State, and to re-export it free of duty, subject in either case to the conditions considered to be necessary by the government of the State concerned.

Article 12

Officials and other servants of the Union shall be liable to a tax, for the benefit of the Union, on salaries, wages and emoluments paid to them by the Union, in accordance with the conditions and procedure laid down by a European law. That law shall be adopted after consultation of the institutions concerned.

Officials and other servants of the Union shall be exempt from national taxes on salaries, wages and emoluments paid by the Union.

Article 13

In the application of income tax, wealth tax and death duties and in the application of conventions on the avoidance of double taxation concluded between Member States of the Union, officials and other servants of the Union who, solely by reason of the performance of their duties in the service of the Union, establish their residence in the territory of a Member State other than their State of domicile for tax purposes at the time of entering the service of the Union, shall be considered, both in the State of their actual residence and in the State of domicile for tax purposes, as having maintained their domicile in the latter State provided that it is a member of the Union. This provision shall also apply to a spouse, to the extent that the latter is not separately engaged in a gainful occupation, and to children dependent on and in the care of the persons referred to in this Article.

Movable property belonging to persons referred to in the first paragraph and situated in the territory of the State where they are staying shall be exempt from death duties in that State. Such property shall, for the assessment of such duty, be considered as being in the State of domicile for tax purposes, subject to the rights of third States and to the possible application of provisions of international conventions on double taxation.

Any domicile acquired solely by reason of the performance of duties in the service of other international organisations shall not be taken into consideration in applying the provisions of this Article.

Article 14

The scheme of social security benefits for officials and other servants of the Union shall be laid down by a European law. That law shall be adopted after consultation of the institutions concerned.

Article 15

The categories of officials and other servants of the Union to whom Article 11, the second paragraph of Article 12, and Article 13 shall apply, in whole or in part, shall be determined by a European law. That law shall be adopted after consultation of the institutions concerned.

The names, grades and addresses of officials and other servants included in such categories shall be communicated periodically to the governments of the Member States.

CHAPTER VI PRIVILEGES AND IMMUNITIES OF MISSIONS OF THIRD STATES ACCREDITED TO THE UNION

Article 16

The Member State in whose territory the Union has its seat shall accord the customary diplomatic privileges and immunities to missions of third States accredited to the Union.

CHAPTER VII GENERAL PROVISIONS

Article 17

Privileges, immunities and facilities shall be accorded to officials and other servants of the Union solely in the interests of the Union.

Each institution of the Union shall be required to waive the immunity accorded to an official or other servant wherever that institution considers that the waiver of such immunity is not contrary to the interests of the Union.

Article 18

The institutions of the Union shall, for the purpose of applying this Protocol, cooperate with the responsible authorities of the Member States concerned.

Article 19

Articles 11 to 14 and Article 17 shall apply to members of the Commission.

Article 20

Articles 11 to 14 and Article 17 shall apply to the Judges, the Advocates-General, the Registrars and the Assistant Rapporteurs of the Court of Justice of the European Union, without prejudice to the provisions of Article 3 of the Protocol on the Statute of the Court of Justice of the European Union concerning immunity from legal proceedings of Judges and Advocates-General.

Articles 11 to 14 and Article 17 shall also apply to the members of the Court of Auditors.

Article 21

This Protocol shall also apply to the European Central Bank, to the members of its organs and to its staff, without prejudice to the Protocol on the Statute of the European System of Central Banks and of the European Central Bank.

The European Central Bank shall, in addition, be exempt from any form of taxation or imposition of a like nature on the occasion of any increase in its capital and from the various formalities which may be connected therewith in the State where the Bank has its seat. The activities of the Bank and of its organs carried on in accordance with the Statute of the European System of Central Banks and of the European Central Bank shall not be subject to any turnover tax.

Article 22

This Protocol shall also apply to the European Investment Bank, to the members of its organs, to its staff and to the representatives of the Member States taking part in its activities, without prejudice to the Protocol on the Statute of the Bank.

The European Investment Bank shall in addition be exempt from any form of taxation or imposition of a like nature on the occasion of any increase in its capital and from the various formalities which may be connected therewith in the State where the Bank has its seat. Similarly, its dissolution or liquidation shall not give rise to any imposition. Finally, the activities of the Bank and of its organs carried on in accordance with its Statute shall not be subject to any turnover tax.

13. Protocol on certain provisions Relating to the United Kingdom of Great Britian and Northern Ireland as regards economic and monetary union

THE HIGH CONTRACTING PARTIES,

RECOGNISING that the United Kingdom shall not be obliged or committed to adopt the euro without a separate decision to do so by its government and Parliament;

GIVEN that on 16 October 1996 and 30 October 1997 the United Kingdom government notified the Council of its intention not to participate in the third stage of economic and monetary union, under the terms of paragraph 1 of the Protocol on certain provisions relating to the United Kingdom of Great Britain and Northern Ireland, annexed to the Treaty establishing the European Community;

NOTING the practice of the government of the United Kingdom to fund its borrowing requirement by the sale of debt to the private sector,

HAVE AGREED upon the following provisions, which shall be annexed to the Treaty establishing a Constitution for Europe:

Article 1

Unless the United Kingdom notifies the Council that it intends to adopt the euro, it shall be under no obligation to do so.

Article 2

In view of the notice given to the Council by the United Kingdom government on 16 October 1996 and 30 October 1997, Articles 3 to 8 and 10 shall apply to the United Kingdom.

Article 3

The United Kingdom shall retain its powers in the field of monetary policy according to national law.

Article 4

Articles 30(2), with the exception of the first and last sentences thereof, 30(5), 177, second paragraph, 184(1), (9) and (10), 185(1) to (5), 186, 188, 189, 190, 191, 196, 198(3), 326 and 382 of the Constitution shall not apply to the United Kingdom. The same applies to Article 179(2) of the Constitution as regards the adoption of the parts of the broad economic policy guidelines which concern the euro area generally.

In the provisions referred to in the first paragraph, references to the Union or the Member States shall not include the United Kingdom and references to national central banks shall not include the Bank of England.

Article 5

The United Kingdom shall endeavour to avoid an excessive government deficit.

Articles 192(4) and 200 of the Constitution shall apply to the United Kingdom as if it had a derogation.

Articles 201 and 202 of the Constitution shall continue to apply to the United Kingdom.

Article 6

The voting rights of the United Kingdom shall be suspended for the adoption by the Council of the measures referred to in the Articles listed in Article 4 and in the instances referred to in the first subparagraph of Article 197(4) of the Constitution. For this purpose the second and third subparagraphs of Article 197(4) of the Constitution shall apply.

The United Kingdom shall also have no right to participate in the appointment of the President, the Vice-President and the other members of the Executive Board of the European Central Bank under the second, third and fourth subparagraphs of Article 382(2) of the Constitution.

Article 7

Articles 3, 4, 6, 7, 9(2), 10(1), (2) and (3), 11(2), 12(1), 14, 16, 18, 19, 20, 22, 23, 26, 27, 30, 31, 32, 33, 34 and 50 of the Protocol on the Statute of the European System of Central Banks and of the European Central Bank (the "Statute") shall not apply to the United Kingdom.

In those Articles, references to the Union or the Member States shall not include the United Kingdom and references to national central banks or shareholders shall not include the Bank of England.

References in Articles 10(3) and 30(2) of the Statute to "subscribed capital of the European Central Bank" shall not include capital subscribed by the Bank of England.

Article 8

Article 199 of the Constitution and Articles 43 to 47 of the Statute shall have effect, whether or not there is any Member State with a derogation, subject to the following amendments:

(a) References in Article 43 of the Statute to the tasks of the European Central Bank and the European Monetary Institute shall include those tasks that still need to be performed after the introduction of the euro owing to the decision of the United Kingdom not to adopt the euro.

(b) In addition to the tasks referred to in Article 46 of the Statute, the European Central Bank shall also give advice in relation to and contribute to the preparation of any European regulation or any European decision of the Council with regard to the United Kingdom taken in accordance with Article 9(a) and (c) of this Protocol.

(c) The Bank of England shall pay up its subscription to the capital of the European Central Bank as a contribution to its operational costs on the same basis as national central banks of Member States with a derogation.

Article 9

The United Kingdom may notify the Council at any time of its intention to adopt the euro. In that event:

(a) The United Kingdom shall have the right to adopt the euro provided only that it satisfies the necessary conditions. The Council, acting at the request of the United Kingdom and under the conditions and in accordance with the procedure laid down in Article 198(1) and (2) of the Constitution, shall decide whether it fulfils the necessary conditions.

(b) The Bank of England shall pay up its subscribed capital, transfer to the European Central Bank foreign reserve assets and contribute to its reserves on the same basis as the national central bank of a Member State whose derogation has been abrogated.

(c) The Council, acting under the conditions and in accordance with the procedure laid down in Article 198(3) of the Constitution, shall take all other necessary decisions to enable the United Kingdom to adopt the euro.

If the United Kingdom adopts the euro pursuant to the provisions of this Article, Articles 3 to 8 shall cease to have effect.

Article 10

Notwithstanding Article 181 of the Constitution and Article 21(1) of the Statute, the Government of the United Kingdom may maintain its "ways and means" facility with the Bank of England if and so long as the United Kingdom does not adopt the euro.

17. Protocol on the Shengen Acquis integrated into the framework of the European Union

THE HIGH CONTRACTING PARTIES,

RECALLING that the provisions of the Schengen acquis consisting of the Agreements on the gradual abolition of checks at common borders, signed by some Member States of the European Union in Schengen on 14 June 1985 and on 19 June 1990, as well as related agreements and rules adopted on the basis of these agreements, have been integrated into the framework of the European Union by a Protocol annexed to the Treaty on European Union and to the Treaty establishing the European Community;

DESIRING to preserve the Schengen acquis, as developed since the entry into force of the abovementioned Protocol, within the framework of the Constitution, and to develop this acquis in order to contribute towards achieving the objective of offering citizens of the Union an area of freedom, security and justice without internal borders;

TAKING INTO ACCOUNT the special position of Denmark;

TAKING INTO ACCOUNT the fact that Ireland and the United Kingdom of Great Britain and Northern Ireland do not participate in all the provisions of the Schengen acquis; provision should, however, be made to allow those Member States to accept other provisions of this acquis in full or in part;

RECOGNISING that, as a consequence, it is necessary to make use of the provisions of the Constitution concerning closer cooperation between some Member States;

TAKING INTO ACCOUNT the need to maintain a special relationship with the Republic of Iceland and the Kingdom of Norway, both States being bound by the provisions of the Nordic passport union, together with the Nordic States which are members of the European Union;

HAVE AGREED UPON the following provisions, which shall be annexed to the Treaty establishing a Constitution for Europe,

Article 1

The Kingdom of Belgium, the Czech Republic, the Kingdom of Denmark, the Federal Republic of Germany, the Republic of Estonia, the Hellenic Republic, the Kingdom of Spain, the French Republic, the Italian Republic, the Republic of Cyprus, the Republic of Latvia, the Republic of Lithuania, the Grand Duchy of Luxembourg, the Republic of Hungary, the Republic of Malta, the Kingdom of the Netherlands, the Republic of Austria, the Republic of Poland, the Portuguese Republic, the Republic of Slovenia, the Slovak Republic, the Republic of Finland and the Kingdom of Sweden shall be authorised to implement closer cooperation among themselves in areas covered by provisions defined by the Council which constitute the Schengen acquis. This cooperation shall be conducted within the institutional and legal framework of the Union and with respect for the relevant provisions of the Constitution.

Article 2

The Schengen acquis shall apply to the Member States referred to in Article 1, without prejudice to Article 3 of the Protocol on the Treaty and the Act of Accession of the Czech Republic, the Republic of Estonia, the Republic of Cyprus, the Republic of Latvia, the Republic of Lithuania, the Republic of Hungary, the Republic of Malta, the Republic of Poland, the Republic of Slovenia and the Slovak Republic. The Council will substitute itself for the Executive Committee established by the Schengen agreements.

Article 3

The participation of Denmark in the adoption of measures constituting a development of the Schengen acquis, as well as the implementation of these measures and their application to Denmark, shall be governed by the relevant provisions of the Protocol on the position of Denmark.

Article 4

Ireland and the United Kingdom of Great Britain and Northern Ireland, may at any time request to take part in some or all of the provisions of the Schengen acquis.

The Council shall adopt a European decision on this request. It shall act by a unanimous decision of the members referred to in Article 1 and of the member representing the government of the Member State concerned.

Article 5

Proposals and initiatives to build upon the Schengen acquis shall be subject to the relevant provisions of the Constitution.

In this context, where either Ireland or the United Kingdom or both have not notified the President of the Council in writing within a reasonable period that they wish to take part, the authorisation referred to in Article 419(1) of the Constitution shall be deemed to have been granted to the Member States referred to in Article 1 and to Ireland or the United Kingdom where either of them wishes to take part in the areas of cooperation in question.

Article 6

The Republic of Iceland and the Kingdom of Norway shall be associated with the implementation of the Schengen acquis and its further development. Appropriate procedures shall be agreed to that effect in an Agreement to be concluded with those States by the Council, acting by the unanimity of its members mentioned in Article 1. That Agreement shall include provisions on the contribution of Iceland and Norway to any financial consequences resulting from the implementation of this Protocol.

A separate Agreement shall be concluded by the Council, acting unanimously, with Iceland and Norway for the establishment of rights and obligations between Ireland and the United Kingdom of Great Britain and Northern Ireland on the one hand, and Iceland and Norway on the other, in domains of the Schengen acquis which apply to these States.

Article 7

For the purposes of the negotiations for the admission of new Member States into the European Union, the Schengen acquis and further measures adopted by the institutions within its scope shall be regarded as an acquis which must be accepted in full by all States candidates for admission.

18. Protocol on the application of certain aspects of article 130 of the Constitution to the United Kingdom and to Ireland

THE HIGH CONTRACTING PARTIES,

DESIRING to settle certain questions relating to the United Kingdom and Ireland;

HAVING REGARD to the existence for many years of special travel arrangements between the United Kingdom and Ireland,

HAVE AGREED UPON the following provisions, which shall be annexed to the Treaty establishing a Constitution for Europe:

Article 1

The United Kingdom shall be entitled, notwithstanding Articles 130 and 265 of the Constitution, any other provision of the Constitution, any measure adopted under the Constitution, or any international agreement concluded by the Union or by the Union and its Member States with one or more third States, to exercise at its frontiers with other Member States such controls on persons seeking to enter the United Kingdom as it may consider necessary for the purpose:

(a) of verifying the right to enter the United Kingdom of citizens of Member States and of their dependants exercising rights conferred by Union law, as well as citizens of other States on whom such rights have been conferred by an agreement by which the United Kingdom is bound; and

(b) of determining whether or not to grant other persons permission to enter the United Kingdom.

Nothing in Articles 130 and 265 of the Constitution or in any other provision of the Constitution or in any measure adopted under it shall prejudice the right of the United Kingdom to adopt or exercise any such controls. References to the United Kingdom in this Article shall include territories for whose external relations the United Kingdom is responsible.

Article 2

The United Kingdom and Ireland may continue to make arrangements between themselves relating to the movement of persons between their territories ("the Common Travel Area"), while fully respecting the rights of persons referred to in Article 1, first paragraph, point (a), of this Protocol. Accordingly, as long as they maintain such arrangements, the provisions of Article 1 of this Protocol shall apply to Ireland under the same terms and conditions as for the United Kingdom.

Nothing in Articles 130 and 265 of the Constitution, in any other provision of the Constitution or in any measure adopted under it shall affect any such arrangements.

Article 3

The other Member States shall be entitled to exercise at their frontiers or at any point of entry into their territory such controls on persons seeking to enter their territory from the United Kingdom or any territories whose external relations are under its responsibility for the same purposes stated in Article 1 of this

Protocol, or from Ireland as long as the provisions of Article 1 of this Protocol apply to Ireland.

Nothing in Articles 130 and 265 of the Constitution or in any other provision of the Constitution or in any measure adopted under it shall prejudice the right of the other Member States to adopt or exercise any such controls.

Article 4

This Protocol shall also apply to acts which remain in force by virtue of Article IV-438 of the Constitution.

19. Protocol on the position of the United Kingdom and Ireland on policies in respect of border controls, asylum and immigration, judicial cooperation in civil matters and on police cooperation

THE HIGH CONTRACTING PARTIES,

DESIRING to settle certain questions relating to the United Kingdom and Ireland;

HAVING REGARD to the Protocol on the application of certain aspects of Article 130 of the Constitution to the United Kingdom and Ireland,

HAVE AGREED UPON the following provisions which shall be annexed to the Treaty establishing a Constitution for Europe:

Article 1

Subject to Article 3, the United Kingdom and Ireland shall not take part in the adoption by the Council of proposed measures pursuant to Section 2 or Section 3 of Chapter IV of Title III of Part III of the Constitution or to Article 260 thereof, insofar as that Article relates to the areas covered by those Sections, to Article263 or to Article 275(2)(a) of the Constitution. The unanimity of the members of the Council, with the exception of the representatives of the governments of the United Kingdom and Ireland, shall be necessary for acts of the Council which must be adopted unanimously.

For the purposes of this Article, a qualified majority shall be defined as at least 55% of the members of the Council representing the participating Member States, comprising at least 65% of the population of these States.

A blocking minority must include at least the minimum number of Council members representing more than 35% of the population of the participating Member States, plus one member, failing which the qualified majority shall be deemed attained.

By way of derogation from the second and third paragraphs, where the Council does not act on a proposal from the Commission or from the Union Minister for Foreign Affairs, the required qualified majority shall be defined as at least 72% of the members of the Council representing the participating Member States, comprising at least 65% of the population of these States.

Article 2

In consequence of Article 1 and subject to Articles 3, 4 and 6, none of the provisions of Section 2 or Section 3 of Chapter IV of Title III of Part III of the Constitution or of Article 260 of the Constitution, insofar as that Article relates to the areas covered by those Sections, or of Article 263 or Article 275(2)(a) of the Constitution, no measure adopted pursuant to those Sections or Articles, no provision of any international agreement concluded by the Union pursuant to those Sections or Articles, and no decision of the Court of Justice of the European Union interpreting any such provision or measure shall be binding upon or applicable in the United Kingdom or Ireland; and no such provision, measure or decision shall in any way affect the competences, rights and obligations of those States; and no such provision, measure or decision shall in any way affect the Community or Union acquis nor form part of Union law as they apply to the United Kingdom or Ireland.

Article 3

1. The United Kingdom or Ireland may notify the Council in writing, within three months after a proposal has been presented to the Council pursuant to Section 2 or Section 3 of Chapter IV of Title III of Part III of the Constitution or after a proposal or initiative has been presented to the Council pursuant to Article 263 or to Article 275(2)(a) of the Constitution, that it wishes to take part in the adoption and application of any such proposed measure, whereupon that State shall be entitled to do so. The unanimity of the members of the Council, with the exception of a member which has not made such a notification, shall be necessary for acts of the Council which must be adopted unanimously. A measure adopted under this paragraph shall be binding upon all Member States which took part in its adoption. The European regulations or decisions adopted pursuant to Article 260 of the Constitution shall lay down the conditions for the participation of the United Kingdom and Ireland in the evaluations concerning the areas covered by Section 2 or Section 3 of Chapter IV of Title III of Part III of the Constitution.

For the purposes of this Article, a qualified majority shall be defined as at least 55% of the members of the Council representing the participating Member States, comprising at least 65% of the population of these States. A blocking minority must include at least the minimum number of Council members representing more than 35% of the population of the participating Member States, plus one member, failing which the qualified majority shall be deemed attained. By way of derogation from the second and third subparagraphs, where the Council does not act on a proposal from the Commission or from the Union Minister for Foreign Affairs, the required qualified majority shall be defined as at least 72% of the members of the Council representing the participating Member States, comprising at least 65% of the population of these States.

2. If after a reasonable period of time a measure referred to in paragraph 1 cannot be adopted with the United Kingdom or Ireland taking part, the Council may adopt such measure in accordance with Article 1 without the participation of the United Kingdom or Ireland. In that case Article 2 applies.

Article 4

The United Kingdom or Ireland may, at any time after the adoption of a measure pursuant to Section 2 or Section 3 of Chapter IV of Title III of Part III of the Constitution or to Article 263 or to Article 275(2)(a) of the Constitution, notify its intention to the Council and to the Commission that it wishes to accept that measure. In that case, the procedure provided for in Article 420(1) of the Constitution shall apply mutatis mutandis.

Article 5

A Member State which is not bound by a measure adopted pursuant to Section 2 or Section 3 of Chapter IV of Title III of Part III of the Constitution, to Article 263 or to Article 275(2)(a) of the Constitution, shall bear no financial consequences of that measure other than administrative costs entailed for the institutions, unless all members of the Council, acting unanimously after consulting the European Parliament, decide otherwise.

Article 6

Where, in cases referred to in this Protocol, the United Kingdom or Ireland is bound by a measure adopted pursuant to Section 2 or Section 3 of Chapter IV of Title III of Part III of the Constitution, to Article 260 of the Constitution, insofar as that Article relates to the areas covered by those Sections, to Article 263 or to Article 275(2)(a) of the Constitution, the relevant provisions of the Constitution shall apply to that State in relation to that measure.

Article 7

Articles 3 and 4 shall be without prejudice to the Protocol on the Schengen acquis integrated into the framework of the European Union.

Article 8

Ireland may notify the Council in writing that it no longer wishes to be covered by the terms of this Protocol. In that case, this Protocol shall no longer apply to Ireland.

21. Protocol on external relations of the member states with regard to the crossing of external borders

THE HIGH CONTRACTING PARTIES,

TAKING INTO ACCOUNT the need of the Member States to ensure effective controls at their external borders, in cooperation with third countries where appropriate,

HAVE AGREED UPON the following provision, which shall be annexed to the Treaty establishing a Constitution for Europe:

Sole Article

The provisions on the measures on the crossing of external borders included in Article 265(2)(b) of the Constitution shall be without prejudice to the competence of Member States to negotiate or conclude agreements with third countries as long as they respect Union law and other relevant international agreements.

22. Protocol on asylum for nationals of member states

THE HIGH CONTRACTING PARTIES,

WHEREAS, in accordance with Article 9(1) of the Constitution, the Union recognises the rights, freedoms and principles set out in the Charter of Fundamental Rights;

WHEREAS pursuant to Article 9(3) of the Constitution, fundamental rights, as guaranteed by the European Convention for the Protection of Human Rights and Fundamental Freedoms, constitute part of the Union's law as general principles;

WHEREAS the Court of Justice of the European Union has jurisdiction to ensure that in the interpretation and application of Article 9(1) and (3) of the Constitution the law is observed by the Union;

WHEREAS pursuant to Article 58 of the Constitution, any European State, when applying to become a member of the Union, must respect the values set out in Article 2 of the Constitution;

BEARING IN MIND that Article 59 of the Constitution establishes a mechanism for the suspension of certain rights in the event of a serious and persistent breach by a Member State of those values;

RECALLING that each national of a Member State, as a citizen of the Union, enjoys a special status and protection which shall be guaranteed by the Member States in accordance with the provisions of Title II of Part I and Title II of Part III of the Constitution;

BEARING IN MIND that the Constitution establishes an area without internal frontiers and grants every citizen of the Union the right to move and reside freely within the territory of the Member States;

WISHING to prevent the institution of asylum being resorted to for purposes alien to those for which it is intended;

WHEREAS this Protocol respects the finality and the objectives of the Geneva Convention of 28 July 1951 relating to the status of refugees,

HAVE AGREED UPON the following provisions which shall be annexed to the Treaty establishing a Constitution for Europe:

Sole Article

Given the level of protection of fundamental rights and freedoms by the Member States of the European Union, Member States shall be regarded as constituting safe countries of origin in respect of each other for all legal and practical purposes in relation to asylum matters. Accordingly, any application for asylum made by a national of a Member State may be taken into consideration or declared admissible for processing by another Member State only in the following cases:

(a) if the Member State of which the applicant is a national proceeds, availing itself of the provisions of Article 15 of the European Convention for the Protection of Human Rights and Fundamental Freedoms, to take measures derogating in its territory from its obligations under that Convention;

(b) if the procedure referred to in Article 59(1) or (2) of the Constitution has been initiated and until the Council, or, where appropriate, the European Council, adopts a European decision in respect thereof with regard to the Member State of which the applicant is a national;

(c) if the Council has adopted a European decision in accordance with Article 59(1) of the Constitution in respect of the Member State of which the applicant is a national or if the European Council has adopted a European decision in accordance with Article 59(2) of the Constitution in respect of the Member State of which the applicant is a national;

(d) if a Member State should so decide unilaterally in respect of the application of a national of another Member State; in that case the Council shall be immediately informed; the application shall be dealt with on the basis of the presumption that it is manifestly unfounded without affecting in any way, whatever the case may be, the decision-making power of the Member State.

23. Protocol on permanent structured cooperation established by article 41(6) and article 312 of the Constitution

THE HIGH CONTRACTING PARTIES,

HAVING REGARD TO Article 41(6) and Article 312 of the Constitution,

RECALLING that the Union is pursuing a common foreign and security policy based on the achievement of growing convergence of action by Member States;

RECALLING that the common security and defence policy is an integral part of the common foreign and security policy; that it provides the Union with operational capacity drawing on civil and military assets; that the Union may use such assets in the tasks referred to in Article 309 of the Constitution outside the Union for peace-keeping, conflict prevention and strengthening international security in accordance with the principles of the United Nations Charter; that the performance of these tasks is to be undertaken using capabilities provided by the Member States in accordance with the principle of a single set of forces;

RECALLING that the common security and defence policy of the Union does not prejudice the specific character of the security and defence policy of certain Member States;

RECALLING that the common security and defence policy of the Union respects the obligations under the North Atlantic Treaty of those Member States, which see their common defence realised in the North Atlantic Treaty Organisation, which remains the foundation of the collective defence of its members, and is compatible with the common security and defence policy established within that framework;

CONVINCED that a more assertive Union role in security and defence matters will contribute to the vitality of a renewed Atlantic Alliance, in accordance with the Berlin Plus arrangements;

DETERMINED to ensure that the Union is capable of fully assuming its responsibilities within the international community;

RECOGNISING that the United Nations Organisation may request the Union's assistance for the urgent implementation of missions undertaken under Chapters VI and VII of the United Nations Charter;

RECOGNISING that the strengthening of the security and defence policy will require efforts by Member States in the area of capabilities;

CONSCIOUS that embarking on a new stage in the development of the European security and defence policy involves a determined effort by the Member States concerned;

RECALLING the importance of the Minister for Foreign Affairs being fully involved in proceedings relating to permanent structured cooperation,

HAVE AGREED UPON the following provisions, which shall be annexed to the Constitution:

Article 1

The permanent structured cooperation referred to in Article 41(6) of the Constitution shall be open to any Member State which undertakes, from the date of entry into force of the Treaty establishing a Constitution for Europe, to:

(a) proceed more intensively to develop its defence capacities through the development of its national contributions and participation, where appropriate, in multinational forces, in the main European equipment programmes, and in the activity of the Agency in the field of defence capabilities development, research, acquisition and armaments (European Defence Agency), and

(b) have the capacity to supply by 2007 at the latest, either at national level or as a component of multinational force groups, targeted combat units for the missions planned, structured at a tactical level as a battle group, with support elements including transport and logistics, capable of carrying out the tasks referred to in Article 309, within a period of 5 to 30 days, in particular in response to requests from the United Nations Organisation, and which can be sustained for an initial period of 30 days and be extended up to at least 120 days.

Article 2

To achieve the objectives laid down in Article 1, Member States participating in permanent structured cooperation shall undertake to:

(a) cooperate, as from the entry into force of the Treaty establishing a Constitution for Europe, with a view to achieving approved objectives concerning the level of investment expenditure on defence equipment, and regularly review these objectives, in the light of the security environment and of the Union's international responsibilities;

(b) bring their defence apparatus into line with each other as far as possible, particularly by harmonising the identification of their military needs, by pooling and, where appropriate, specialising their defence means and capabilities, and by encouraging cooperation in the fields of training and logistics;

(c) take concrete measures to enhance the availability, interoperability, flexibility and deployability of their forces, in particular by identifying common objectives regarding the commitment of forces, including possibly reviewing their national decision-making procedures;

(d) work together to ensure that they take the necessary measures to make good, including through multinational approaches, and without prejudice to undertakings in this regard within the North Atlantic Treaty Organisation, the shortfalls perceived in the framework of the "Capability Development Mechanism";

(e) take part, where appropriate, in the development of major joint or European equipment programmes in the framework of the European Defence Agency.

Article 3

The European Defence Agency shall contribute to the regular assessment of participating Member States' contributions with regard to capabilities, in particular contributions made in accordance with the criteria to be established inter alia on the basis of Article 2, and shall report thereon at least once a year. The assessment may serve as a basis for Council recommendations and European decisions adopted in accordance with Article 312 of the Constitution.

27. Protocol on the system of public broadcasting in the member states

THE HIGH CONTRACTING PARTIES,

CONSIDERING that the system of public broadcasting in the Member States is directly related to the democratic, social and cultural needs of each society and to the need to preserve media pluralism,

HAVE AGREED UPON the following interpretative provisions, which shall be annexed to the Treaty establishing a Constitution for Europe:

Sole Article

The provisions of the Constitution shall be without prejudice to the competence of Member States to provide for the funding of public service broadcasting insofar as such funding is granted to broadcasting organisations for the fulfilment of the public service remit as conferred, defined and organised by each Member State, and insofar as such funding does not affect trading conditions and competition in the Union to an extent which would be contrary to the common interest, while the realisation of the remit of that public service shall be taken into account.

28. Protocol concerning article 214 of the Constitution

THE HIGH CONTRACTING PARTIES,

HAVE AGREED upon the following provision, which shall be annexed to the Treaty establishing a Constitution for Europe:

Sole Article

For the purposes of Article 214 of the Constitution, benefits under occupational social security schemes shall not be considered as remuneration if and insofar as they are attributable to periods of employment prior to 17 May 1990, except in the case of workers or those claiming under them who have before that date initiated legal proceedings or introduced an equivalent claim under the applicable national law.

29. Protocol on economic, social and territorial cohesion

THE HIGH CONTRACTING PARTIES,

RECALLING that Article 3 of the Constitution includes the objective of promoting economic, social and territorial cohesion and solidarity between Member States and that the said cohesion figures among the areas of shared competence of the Union listed in Article 14(2)(c) of the Constitution;

RECALLING that the provisions of Section 3 of Chapter III of Title III of Part III of the Constitution, on economic, social and territorial cohesion as a whole provide the legal basis for consolidating and further developing the Union's action in this field, including the creation of a fund;

RECALLING that Article 223 of the Constitution envisages setting up a Cohesion Fund;

NOTING that the European Investment Bank is lending large and increasing amounts for the benefit of the poorer regions;

NOTING the desire for greater flexibility in the arrangements for allocations from the Structural Funds;

NOTING the desire for modulation of the levels of Union participation in programmes and projects in certain Member States;

NOTING the proposal to take greater account of the relative prosperity of Member States in the system of own resources,

HAVE AGREED upon the following provisions, which shall be annexed to the Treaty establishing a Constitution for Europe:

Sole Article

1. The Member States reaffirm that the promotion of economic, social and territorial cohesion is vital to the full development and enduring success of the Union.

2. The Member States reaffirm their conviction that the Structural Funds should continue to play a considerable part in the achievement of Union objectives in the field of cohesion.

3. The Member States reaffirm their conviction that the European Investment Bank should continue to devote the majority of its resources to the promotion of economic, social and territorial cohesion, and declare their willingness to review the capital needs of the European Investment Bank as soon as this is necessary for that purpose.

4. The Member States agree that the Cohesion Fund shall provide Union financial contributions to projects in the fields of environment and trans-European networks in Member States with a per capita GNP of less than 90% of the Union average which have a programme leading to the fulfilment of the conditions of economic convergence as set out in Article 184 of the Constitution.

5. The Member States declare their intention of allowing a greater margin of flexibility in allocating financing from the Structural Funds to specific needs not covered under the present Structural Funds regulations.

6. The Member States declare their willingness to modulate the levels of Union participation in the context of programmes and projects of the Structural

Funds, with a view to avoiding excessive increases in budgetary expenditure in the less prosperous Member States.

7. The Member States recognise the need to monitor regularly the progress made towards achieving economic, social and territorial cohesion, and state their willingness to study all necessary measures in this respect.

8. The Member States declare their intention of taking greater account of the contributive capacity of individual Member States in the system of own resources, and of examining means of correcting, for the less prosperous Member States, regressive elements existing in the present own resources system.

Declaration 12

Concerning the explantions relating to the Charter of Fundamental Rights

The Conference takes note of the explanations relating to the Charter of Fundamental Rights prepared under the authority of the Praesidium of the Convention which drafted the Charter and updated under the responsibility of the Praesidium of the European Convention, as set out below.

EXPLANATIONS RELATING TO THE CHARTER OF FUNDAMENTAL RIGHTS

These explanations were originally prepared under the authority of the Praesidium of the Convention which drafted the Charter of Fundamental Rights of the European Union. They have been updated under the responsibility of the Praesidium of the European Convention, in the light of the drafting adjustments made to the text of the Charter by that Convention (notably to Articles 51 and 52 1) and of further developments of Union law. Although they do not as such have the status of law, they are a valuable tool of interpretation intended to clarify the provisions of the Charter.

PREAMBLE

The peoples of Europe, in creating an ever closer union among them, are resolved to share a peaceful future based on common values.

Conscious of its spiritual and moral heritage, the Union is founded on the indivisible, universal values of human dignity, freedom, equality and solidarity; it is based on the principles of democracy and the rule of law. It places the individual at the heart of its activities, by establishing the citizenship of the Union and by creating an area of freedom, security and justice.

The Union contributes to the preservation and to the development of these common values while respecting the diversity of the cultures and traditions of the peoples of Europe as well as the national identities of the Member States and the organisation of their public authorities at national, regional and local levels; it seeks to promote balanced and sustainable development and ensures free movement of persons, services, goods and capital, and the freedom of establishment. To this end, it is necessary to strengthen the protection of fundamental rights in the light of changes in society, social progress and scientific and technological developments by making those rights more visible in a Charter.

This Charter reaffirms, with due regard for the powers and tasks of the Union and the principle of subsidiarity, the rights as they result, in particular, from the constitutional traditions and international obligations common to the Member States, the European Convention for the Protection of Human Rights and Fundamental Freedoms, the Social Charters adopted by the Union and by the

Council of Europe and the case law of the Court of Justice of the European Union and of the European Court of Human Rights. In this context the Charter will be inter-preted by the courts of the Union and the Member States with due regard to the explanations prepared under the authority of the Praesidium of the Convention which drafted the Charter and updated under the responsibility of the Praesidium of the European Convention. Enjoyment of these rights entails responsibilities and duties with regard to other persons, to the human community and to future generations.

The Union therefore recognises the rights, freedoms and principles set out hereafter.

TITLE I

DIGNITY

Article 1

Relating to article 61 of the Constitution *Human dignity*

Explanation

The dignity of the human person is not only a fundamental right in itself but constitutes the real basis of fundamental rights. The 1948 Universal Declaration of Human Rights enshrined human dignity in its preamble: "Whereas recognition of the inherent dignity and of the equal and inalienable rights of all members of the human family is the foundation of freedom, justice and peace in the world." In its judgment of 9 October 2001 in case C-377/98 Netherlands v. European Parliament and Council, 2001 ECR 7079, at grounds No 70 - 77, the Court of Justice confirmed that a fundamental right to human dignity is part of Union law.

It results that none of the rights laid down in this Charter may be used to harm the dignity of another person, and that the dignity of the human person is part of the substance of the rights laid down in this Charter. It must therefore be respected, even where a right is restricted.

Article 2

Relating to article 62 of the Constitution *Right to life*

Explanation

1. Paragraph 1 of this Article is based on the first sentence of Article 2(1) of the ECHR, which reads as follows:

"1. Everyone's right to life shall be protected by law..."

2. The second sentence of the provision, which referred to the death penalty, was superseded by the entry into force of Article 1 of Protocol No 6 to the ECHR, which reads as follows: "The death penalty shall be abolished. No-one shall be condemned to such penalty or executed." Article 2(2) of the Charter [Article 112(3) of the Constitution] is based on that provision.

3. The provisions of Article 2 of the Charter [Article 112 of the Constitution] correspond to those of the above Articles of the ECHR and its Protocol. They have the same meaning and the same scope, in accordance with Article 52(3) of the Charter [Article 112(3) of the Constitution] . Therefore, the "negative" definitions appearing in the ECHR must be regarded as also forming part of the Charter:

(a) Article 2(2) of the ECHR:

"Deprivation of life shall not be regarded as inflicted in contravention of this article when it results from the use of force which is no more than absolutely necessary:

(a) in defence of any person from unlawful violence;

(b) in order to effect a lawful arrest or to prevent the escape of a person lawfully detained;

(c) in action lawfully taken for the purpose of quelling a riot or insurrection."

(b) Article 2 of Protocol No 6 to the ECHR:

"A State may make provision in its law for the death penalty in respect of acts committed in time of war or of imminent threat of war; such penalty shall be applied only in the instances laid down in the law and in accordance with its provisions..."

Article 3

Relating to article 63 of the Constitution *Right to the integrity of the person*

Explanation

1. In its judgment of 9 October 2001 in case C-377/98 Netherlands v. European Parliament and Council, 2001 ECR 7079, at grounds No 70, 78 - 80, the Court of Justice confirmed that a fundamental right to human integrity is part of Union law and encompasses, in the context of medicine and biology, the free and informed consent of the donor and recipient.

2. The principles of Article 3 of the Charter [Article 63 of the Constitution] are already included in the Convention on Human Rights and Biomedicine, adopted by the Council of Europe (ETS 164 and additional protocol ETS 168). The Charter does not set out to depart from those principles, and therefore prohibits only reproductive cloning. It neither authorises nor prohibits other forms of cloning. Thus it does not in any way prevent the legislature from prohibiting other forms of cloning.

3. The reference to eugenic practices, in particular those aiming at the selection of persons, relates to possible situations in which selection programmes are organised and implemented, involving campaigns for sterilisation, forced pregnancy, compulsory ethnic marriage among others, all acts deemed to be international crimes in the Statute of the International Criminal Court adopted in Rome on 17 July 1998 (see its Article 7(1)(g)).

Article 4

Relating to article 64 *Prohibition of torture and inhuman or degrading treatment or punishment*

Explanation

The right in Article 4 [Article 64 of the Constitution] is the right guaranteed by Article 3 of the ECHR, which has the same wording: "No one shall be subjected to torture or to inhuman or degrading treatment or punishment". By virtue of Article 52(3) of the Charter [Article112(3) of the Constitution], it therefore has the same meaning and the same scope as the ECHR Article.

Article 5

Relating to article 65 *Prohibition of slavery and forced labour*

Explanation

1. The right in Article 5(1) and (2)[Article 65 of the Constitution] corresponds to Article 4(1) and (2) of the ECHR, which has the same wording. It therefore has the same meaning and scope as the ECHR Article, by virtue of Article 52(3) of the Charter [Article 112(3) of the Constitution]. Consequently:

– no limitation may legitimately affect the right provided for in paragraph 1;

– in paragraph 2, "forced or compulsory labour" must be understood in the light of the "negative" definitions contained in Article 4(3) of the ECHR:

"For the purpose of this article the term "forced or compulsory labour" shall not include:

(a) any work required to be done in the ordinary course of detention imposed according to the provisions of Article 5 of this Convention or during conditional release from such detention;

(b) any service of a military character or, in case of conscientious objectors in countries where they are recognised, service exacted instead of compulsory military service;

(c) any service exacted in case of an emergency or calamity threatening the life or well-being of the community;

(d) any work or service which forms part of normal civic obligations."

2. Paragraph 3 stems directly from human dignity and takes account of recent developments in organised crime, such as the organisation of lucrative illegal immigration or sexual exploitation networks. The annex to the Europol Convention contains the following definition which refers to trafficking for the purpose of sexual exploitation: "traffic in human beings: means subjection of a person to the real and illegal sway of other persons by using violence or menaces or by abuse of authority or intrigue with a view to the exploitation of prostitution, forms of sexual exploitation and assault of minors or trade in abandoned children". Chapter VI of the Convention implementing the Schengen Agreement, which has been integrated into the Union's acquis, in which the United Kingdom and Ireland participate,contains the following wording in Article 27(1) which refers to illegal immigration networks:

" The Contracting Parties undertake to impose appropriate penalties on any person who, for financial gain, assists or tries to assist an alien to enter or reside within the territory of one of the Contracting Parties in breach of that Contracting Party's laws on the entry and residence of aliens." On 19 July 2002, the Council adopted a framework decision on combating trafficking in human beings (OJ L

203/1) whose Article 1 defines in detail the offences concerning trafficking in human beings for the purposes of labour exploitation or sexual exploitation, which the Member States must make punishable by virtue of that framework decision.

TITLE II

FREEDOMS

Article 6

Relating to Article 66 *Right to liberty and security*

Explanation

The rights in Article 6 [Article 66 of the Constitution] are the rights guaranteed by Article 5 of the ECHR, and in accordance with Article 52(3) of the Charter [Article 112(3) of the Constitution], they have the same meaning and scope. Consequently, the limitations which may legitimately be imposed on them may not exceed those permitted by the ECHR, in the wording of Article 5:

"1. Everyone has the right to liberty and security of person. No one shall be deprived of his liberty save in the following cases and in accordance with a procedure prescribed by law:

(a) the lawful detention of a person after conviction by a competent court;

(b) the lawful arrest or detention of a person for non-compliance with the lawful order of a court or in order to secure the fulfilment of any obligation prescribed by law;

(c) the lawful arrest or detention of a person effected for the purpose of bringing him before the competent legal authority on reasonable suspicion of having committed an offence or when it is reasonably considered necessary to prevent his committing an offence or fleeing after having done so;

(d) the detention of a minor by lawful order for the purpose of educational supervision or his lawful detention for the purpose of bringing him before the competent legal authority;

(e) the lawful detention of persons for the prevention of the spreading of infectious diseases, of persons of unsound mind, alcoholics or drug addicts or vagrants;

(f) the lawful arrest or detention of a person to prevent his effecting an unauthorised entry into the country or of a person against whom action is being taken with a view to deportation or extradition.

2. Everyone who is arrested shall be informed promptly, in a language which he understands, of the reasons for his arrest and of any charge against him.

3. Everyone arrested or detained in accordance with the provisions of paragraph 1.c of this article shall be brought promptly before a judge or other officer authorised by law to exercise judicial power and shall be entitled to trial within a reasonable time or to release pending trial. Release may be conditioned by guarantees to appear for trial.

4. Everyone who is deprived of his liberty by arrest or detention shall be entitled to take proceedings by which the lawfulness of his detention shall be decided speedily by a court and his release ordered if the detention is not lawful.

5. Everyone who has been the victim of arrest or detention in contravention of the provisions of this Article shall have an enforceable right to compensation."

The rights enshrined in Article 6[Article 66 of the Constitution] must be respected particularly when the European Parliament and the Council adopt laws and framework laws in the area of judicial cooperation in criminal matters, on the basis of Articles 270, 271 and 273 of the Constitution, notably to define common minimum provisions as regards the categorisation of offences and punishments and certain aspects of procedural law.

Article 7

Relating to Article 68 *Respect for private and family life*

Everyone has the right to respect for his or her private and family life, home and communications.

Explanation

The rights guaranteed in Article 7 [Article 67 of the Constitution] correspond to those guaranteed by Article 8 of the ECHR. To take account of developments in technology the word "correspondence" has been replaced by "communications".

In accordance with Article 52(3) [Article 112(3) of the Constitution], the meaning and scope of this right are the same as those of the corresponding article of the ECHR. Consequently, the limitations which may legitimately be imposed on this right are the same as those allowed by Article 8 of the ECHR:

"1. Everyone has the right to respect for his private and family life, his home and his correspondence.

2. There shall be no interference by a public authority with the exercise of this right except such as is in accordance with the law and is necessary in a democratic society in the interests of national security, public safety or the economic well-being of the country, for the prevention of disorder or crime, for the protection of health or morals, or for the protection of the rights and freedoms of others."

Article 8

Relating to Article 68 *Protection of personal data*

Explanation

This Article has been based on Article 286 of the Treaty establishing the European Community and Directive 95/46/EC of the European Parliament and of the Council on the protection of individuals with regard to the processing of personal data and on the free movement of such data (OJ L 281, 23.11.1995) as well as on Article 8 of the ECHR and on the Council of Europe Convention of 28 January 1981 for the Protection of Individuals with regard to Automatic Processing of Personal Data, which has been ratified by all the Member States. Article 286 EC Treaty is now replaced by Article 51 of the Constitution. Reference is also made to Regulation No 45/2001 of the European Parliament and of the Council on the protection of individuals with regard to the processing of personal data by the Community institutions and bodies and on the free movement of such data (OJ L 8, 12.1.2001). The abovementioned Directive and Regulation contain conditions and limitations for the exercise of the right to the protection of personal data.

Article 9

Relating to Article 69 *Right to marry and right to found a family*

Explanation

This Article is based on Article 12 of the ECHR, which reads as follows: "Men and women of marriageable age have the right to marry and to found a family according to the national laws governing the exercising of this right." The wording of the Article has been modernised to cover cases in which national legislation recognises arrangements other than marriage for founding a family. This Article neither prohibits nor imposes the granting of the status of marriage to unions between people of the same sex. This right is thus similar to that afforded by the ECHR, but its scope may be wider when national legislation so provides.

Article10

Relating to Article 70 *Freedom of thought, conscience and religion*

Explanation

The right guaranteed in paragraph 1 corresponds to the right guaranteed in Article 9 of the ECHR and, in accordance with Article 52(3) of the Charter [Article 112(3) of the Constitution], has the same meaning and scope. Limitations must therefore respect Article 9(2) of the Convention, which reads as follows: "Freedom to manifest one's religion or beliefs shall be subject only to such limitations as are prescribed by law and are necessary in a democratic society in the interests of public safety, for the protection of public order, health or morals, or for the protection of the rights and freedoms of others."

The right guaranteed in paragraph 2 corresponds to national constitutional traditions and to the development of national legislation on this issue.

Article11

Relating to Article 71 *Freedom of expression and information*

1. Everyone has the right to freedom of expression. This right shall include freedom to hold opinions and to receive and impart information and ideas without interference by public authority and regardless of frontiers.

2. The freedom and pluralism of the media shall be respected.

Explanation

1. Article 11 [Article 71 of the Constitution] corresponds to Article 10 of the European Convention on Human Rights, which reads as follows:

"1. Everyone has the right to freedom of expression. This right shall include freedom to hold opinions and to receive and impart information and ideas without interference by public authority and regardless of frontiers. This Article shall not prevent States from requiring the licensing of broadcasting, television or cinema enterprises.

2. The exercise of these freedoms, since it carries with it duties and responsibilities, may be subject to such formalities, conditions, restrictions or penalties as are prescribed by law and are necessary in a democratic society, in the interests of national security, territorial integrity or public safety, for the prevention of disorder or crime, for the protection of health or morals, for the protection of the reputation or rights of others, for preventing the disclosure of information received in confidence, or for maintaining the authority and impartiality of the judiciary."

Pursuant to Article 52(3) of the Charter [Article 112(3) of the Constitution], the meaning and scope of this right are the same as those guaranteed by the ECHR. The limitations which may be imposed on it may therefore not exceed those provided for in Article 10(2) of the Convention, without prejudice to any restrictions which competition law of the Union may impose on Member States' right to introduce the licensing arrangements referred to in the third sentence of Article 10(1) of the ECHR.

2. Paragraph 2 of this Article spells out the consequences of paragraph 1 regarding freedom of the media. It is based in particular on Court of Justice case law regarding television, particularly in case C-288/89 (judgment of 25 July 1991, Stichting Collectieve Antennevoorziening Gouda and others [1991] ECR 4007), and on the Protocol on the system of public broadcasting in the Member States annexed to the EC Treaty and now to the Constitution, and on Council Directive 89/552/EC (particularly its seventeenth recital).

Article 12

Relating to Article 72 *Freedom of assembly and of association*

Explanation

Paragraph 1 of this Article corresponds to Article 11 of the ECHR, which reads as follows: "1. Everyone has the right to freedom of peaceful assembly and to freedom of association with others, including the right to form and to join trade unions for the protection of his interests.

2. No restrictions shall be placed on the exercise of these rights other than such as are prescribed by law and are necessary in a democratic society in the interests of national security or public safety, for the prevention of disorder or crime, for the protection of health or morals or for the protection of the rights and freedoms of others. This article shall not prevent the imposition of lawful restrictions on the exercise of these rights by members of the armed forces, of the police or of the administration of the State."

The meaning of the provisions of paragraph 1 is the same as that of the ECHR, but their scope is wider since they apply at all levels including European level. In accordance with Article 52(3) of the Charter [Article 112(3) of the Constitution], limitations on that right may not exceed those considered legitimate by virtue of Article 11(2) of the ECHR.

2. This right is also based on Article 11 of the Community Charter of the Fundamental Social Rights of Workers.

3. Paragraph 2 of this Article corresponds to Article 46(4) of the Constitution.

Article 13

Relating to Article 73 *Freedom of the arts and sciences*

Explanation

This right is deduced primarily from the right to freedom of thought and expression. It is to be exercised having regard to Article 1 [Article 61 of the Constitution] and may be subject to the limitations authorised by Article 10 of the ECHR.

Article 14

Relating to Article 74 *Right to education*

Explanation

1. This Article is based on the common constitutional traditions of Member States and on Article 2 of the Protocol to the ECHR, which reads as follows: "No person shall be denied the right to education. In the exercise of any functions which it assumes in relation to education and to teaching, the State shall respect the right of parents to ensure such education and teaching in conformity with their own religious and philosophical convictions."

It was considered useful to extend this article to access to vocational and continuing training (see point 15 of the Community Charter of the Fundamental Social Rights of Workers and Article 10 of the Social Charter) and to add the principle of free compulsory education. As it is worded, the latter principle merely implies that as regards compulsory education, each child has the possibility of attending an establishment which offers free education. It does not require all establishments which provide education or vocational and continuing training, in particular private ones, to be free of charge. Nor does it exclude certain specific forms of education having to be paid for, if the State takes measures to grant financial compensation. Insofar as the Charter applies to the Union, this means that in its training policies the Union must respect free compulsory education, but this does not, of course, create new powers. Regarding the right of parents, it must be interpreted in conjunction with the provisions of Article 24. [Article 84 of the Constitution.]

2. Freedom to found public or private educational establishments is guaranteed as one of the aspects of freedom to conduct a business but it is limited by respect for democratic principles and is exercised in accordance with the arrangements defined by national legislation.

Article 15

Relating to Article 75 *Freedom to choose an occupation and right to engage in work*

Explanation

Freedom to choose an occupation, as enshrined in Article 15(1) 1, is recognised in Court of Justice case law (see inter alia judgment of 14 May 1974, Case 4/73 Nold [1974] ECR 491, paragraphs 12 to 14 of the grounds; judgment of 13 December 1979, Case 44/79 Hauer [1979] ECR 3727; judgment of 8 October 1986, Case 234/85 Keller [1986] ECR 2897, paragraph 8 of the grounds).

This paragraph also draws upon Article 1(2) of the European Social Charter, which was signed on 18 October 1961 and has been ratified by all the Member States, and on point 4 of the Community Charter of the Fundamental Social Rights of Workers of 9 December 1989. The expression "working conditions" is to be understood in the sense of Article 213 of the Constitution.

Paragraph 2 deals with the three freedoms guaranteed by Articles 4 and 133, 137 and 144 of the Constitution, namely freedom of movement for workers, freedom of establishment and freedom to provide services.

Paragraph 3 has been based on TEC Article 137(3), fourth indent, now replaced by Article 210(1)(g) of the Constitution, and on Article 19(4) of the European Social Charter signed on 18 October 1961 and ratified by all the Member States. Article 52(2) of the Charter [Article 112(2) of the Constitution] is therefore applicable. The question of recruitment of seamen having the nationality of third States for the crews of vessels flying the flag of a Member State of the Union is governed by Union law and national legislation and practice.

Article 16

Relating to Article 76 *Freedom to conduct a business*

Explanation

This Article is based on Court of Justice case law which has recognised freedom to exercise an economic or commercial activity (see judgments of 14 May 1974, Case 4/73 Nold [1974] ECR 491, paragraph 14 of the grounds, and of 27 September 1979, Case 230-78 SPA Eridiana and others [1979] ECR 2749, paragraphs 20 and 31 of the grounds) and freedom of contract (see inter alia Sukkerfabriken Nykøbing judgment, Case 151/78 [1979] ECR 1, paragraph 19 of the grounds, and judgment of 5 October 1999, C-240/97 Spain v. Commission, [1999] ECR 6571, paragraph 99 of the grounds) and Article 3(2) of the Constitution, which recognises free competition. Of course, this right is to be exercised with respect for Union law and national legislation. It may be subject to the limitations provided for in Article 52(1) of the Charter [Article 112(1) of the Constitution].

Article 17

Relating to Article 77 *Right to property*

Explanation

This Article is based on Article 1 of the Protocol to the ECHR:

"Every natural or legal person is entitled to the peaceful enjoyment of his possessions. No one shall be deprived of his possessions except in the public interest and subject to the conditions provided for by law and by the general principles of international law.

The preceding provisions shall not, however, in any way impair the right of a State to enforce such laws as it deems necessary to control the use of property in accordance with the general interest or to secure the payment of taxes or other contributions or penalties."

This is a fundamental right common to all national constitutions. It has been recognised on numerous occasions by the case law of the Court of Justice, initially in the Hauer judgment (13 December 1979, ECR [1979] 3727). The wording has been updated but, in accordance with Article 52(3) [Article 112(3) of the Constitution], the meaning and scope of the right are the same as those of the right guaranteed by the ECHR and the limitations may not exceed those provided for there.

Protection of intellectual property, one aspect of the right of property, is explicitly mentioned in paragraph 2 because of its growing importance and Community secondary legislation. Intellectual property covers not only literary and artistic property but also inter alia patent and trademark rights and associated rights. The guarantees laid down in paragraph 1 shall apply as appropriate to intellectual property.

Article 18

Relating to Article 78 *Right to asylum*

The right to asylum shall be guaranteed with due respect for the rules of the Geneva Convention of 28 July 1951 and the Protocol of 31 January 1967 relating to the status of refugees and in accordance with the Constitution.

Explanation

The text of the Article has been based on TEC Article 63, now replaced by Article 266 of the Constitution, which requires the Union to respect the Geneva Convention on refugees. Reference should be made to the Protocols relating to the United Kingdom and Ireland annexed to the [Treaty of Amsterdam] Constitution and to Denmark to determine the extent to which those Member States implement Union law in this area and the extent to which this Article is applicable to them. This Article is in line with the Protocol on Asylum annexed to the Constitution.

Article 19

Relating to Article 79 *Protection in the event of removal, expulsion or extradition*

Explanation

Paragraph 1 of this Article has the same meaning and scope as Article 4 of Protocol No 4 to the ECHR concerning collective expulsion. Its purpose is to guarantee that every decision is based on a specific examination and that no single measure can be taken to expel all persons having the nationality of a particular State (see also Article 13 of the Covenant on Civil and Political Rights).

Paragraph 2 incorporates the relevant case law from the European Court of Human Rights regarding Article 3 of the ECHR (see Ahmed v. Austria, judgment of 17 December 1996, [1996] ECR VI-2206 and Soering, judgment of 7 July 1989).

TITLE III

EQUALITY

Article 20

Relating to Article 80 *Equality before the law*

Explanation

This Article corresponds to a general principle of law which is included in all European constitutions and has also been recognised by the Court of Justice as a basic principle of Community law (judgment of 13 November 1984, Case 283/83 Racke [1984] ECR 3791, judgment of 17 April 1997, Case 15/95 EARL [1997] ECR I–1961, and judgment of 13 April 2000, Case 292/97 Karlsson [2000] ECR 2737).

Article 21

Relating to Article 21 *Non-discrimination*

1. Any discrimination based on any ground such as sex, race, colour, ethnic or social origin, genetic features, language, religion or belief, political or any other opinion, membership of a national minority, property, birth, disability, age or sexual orientation shall be prohibited.

2. Within the scope of application of the Constitution and without prejudice to any of its specific provisions, any discrimination on grounds of nationality shall be prohibited.

Explanation

Paragraph 1 draws on Article 13 of the EC Treaty, now replaced by Article 124 of the Constitution, Article 14 of the ECHR and Article 11 of the Convention on Human Rights and Biomedicine as regards genetic heritage. Insofar as this corresponds to Article 14 of the ECHR, it applies in compliance with it.

There is no contradiction or incompatibility between paragraph 1 and Article 124 of the Constitution which has a different scope and purpose: Article 124 confers power on the Union to adopt legislative acts, including harmonisation of the Member States' laws and regulations, to combat certain forms of discrimination, listed exhaustively in that Article. Such legislation may cover action of Member State authorities (as well as relations between private individuals) in any area within the limits of the Union's powers. In contrast, the provision in paragraph 1 does not create any power to enact anti-discrimination laws in these areas of Member State or private action, nor does it lay down a sweeping ban of discrimination in such wide-ranging areas. Instead, it only addresses discriminations by the institutions and bodies of the Union themselves, when exercising powers conferred under other articles of Parts I and III of the Constitution, and by Member States only when they are implementing Union law. Paragraph 1 therefore does not alter the extent of powers granted under Article 124 nor the interpretation given to that Article.

Paragraph 2 corresponds to Article 4(2) of the Constitution and must be applied in compliance with that Article.

Article 22

Relating to Article 82 *Cultural, religious and linguistic diversity*

Explanation

This Article has been based on Article 6 of the Treaty on European Union and on Article 151(1) and (4) of the EC Treaty, now replaced by Article 280(1) and (4) of the Constitution, concerning culture. Respect for cultural and linguistic diversity is now also laid down in Article 3(3) of the Constitution. The Article is also inspired by Declaration No 11 to the Final Act of the Amsterdam Treaty on the status of churches and non-confessional organisations, now taken over in Article 52 of the Constitution.

Article 23

Relating to Article 83 *Equality between women and men*

Explanation

The first paragraph has been based on Articles 2 and 3(2) of the EC Treaty, now replaced by Articles 3 and 116 of the Constitution which impose the objective of promoting equality between men and women on the Union, and on Article 141(1) of the EC Treaty, now replaced by Article 214(1) of the Constitution. It draws on Article 20 of the revised European Social Charter of 3 May 1996 and on point 16 of the Community Charter on the rights of workers.

It is also based on Article 141(3) of the EC Treaty, now replaced by Article 214(3) of the Constitution, and Article 2(4) of Council Directive 76/207/EEC on the implementation of the principle of equal treatment for men and women as regards access to employment, vocational training and promotion, and working conditions.

The second paragraph takes over in shorter form Article 214(4) of the Constitution which provides that the principle of equal treatment does not prevent the maintenance or adoption of measures providing for specific advantages in order to make it easier for the under-represented sex to pursue a vocational activity or to prevent or compensate for disadvantages in professional careers. In accordance with Article 52(2) [Article 112(2) of the Constitution], the present paragraph does not amend

Article 24

Relating to Article 84 *The rights of the child*

Explanation

This Article is based on the New York Convention on the Rights of the Child signed on 20 November 1989 and ratified by all the Member States, particularly Articles 3, 9, 12 and 13 thereof.

Paragraph 3 takes account of the fact that, as part of the establishment of an area of freedom, security and justice, Union legislation on civil matters having cross-border implications, for which Article 269 of the Constitution confers power, may include notably visiting rights ensuring that children can maintain on a regular basis a personal and direct contact with both his or her parents.

Article 25

Relating to Article 85 *The rights of the elderly*

Explanation

This Article draws on Article 23 of the revised European Social Charter and Articles 24 and 25 of the Community Charter of the Fundamental Social Rights of Workers. Of course, participation in social and cultural life also covers participation in political life.

Article 26

Relating to Article 86 *Integration of persons with disabilities*

Explanation

The principle set out in this Article is based on Article 15 of the European Social Charter and also draws on point 26 of the Community Charter of the Fundamental Social Rights of Workers.

TITLE IV
SOLIDARITY

Article 27

Relating to Article 87 *Workers' right to information and consultation within the undertaking*

Explanation

This Article appears in the revised European Social Charter (Article 21) and in the Community Charter on the rights of workers (points 17 and 18). It applies under the conditions laid down by Union law and by national laws. The reference to appropriate levels refers to the levels laid down by Union law or by national laws and practices, which might include the European level when Union legislation so provides. There is a considerable Union acquis in this field: Articles 211 and 212 of the Constitution, and Directives 2002/14/EC (general framework for informing and consulting employees in the European Community), 98/59/EC (collective redundancies), 2001/23/EC (transfers of undertakings) and 94/45/EC (European works councils).

Article 28

Relating to Article 88 *Right of collective bargaining and action*

Explanation

This Article is based on Article 6 of the European Social Charter and on the Community Charter of the Fundamental Social Rights of Workers (points 12 to 14). The right of collective action was recognised by the European Court of Human Rights as one of the elements of trade union rights laid down by Article 11 of the ECHR. As regards the appropriate levels at which collective negotiation might take place, see the explanation given for the above Article. The modalities and limits for the exercise of collective action, including strike action, come under national laws and practices, including the question of whether it may be carried out in parallel in several Member States.

Article 29

Relating to Article 89 *Right of access to placement services*

Explanation

This Article is based on Article 1(3) of the European Social Charter and point 13 of the Community Charter of the Fundamental Social Rights of Workers.

Article 30

Relating to Article 90 *Protection in the event of unjustified dismissal*

Explanation

This Article draws on Article 24 of the revised Social Charter. See also Directive 2001/23/EC on the safeguarding of employees' rights in the event of transfers of undertakings, and Directive 80/987/EEC on the protection of employees in the event of the insolvency of their employer, as amended by Directive 2002/74/EC.

Article 31

Relating to Article 91 *Fair and just working conditions*

Explanation

1. Paragraph 1 of this Article is based on Directive 89/391/EEC on the introduction of measures to encourage improvements in the safety and health of workers at work. It also draws on Article 3 of the Social Charter and point 19 of the Community Charter on the rights of workers, and, as regards dignity at work,

on Article 26 of the revised Social Charter. The expression "working conditions" must be understood in the sense of Article 213 of the Constitution.

2. Paragraph 2 is based on Directive 93/104/EC concerning certain aspects of the organisation of working time, Article 2 of the European Social Charter and point 8 of the Community Charter on the rights of workers.

Article 32

Relating to Article 92 *Prohibition of child labour and protection of young people at work*

Explanation

This Article is based on Directive 94/33/EC on the protection of young people at work, Article 7 of the European Social Charter and points 20 to 23 of the Community Charter of the Fundamental Social Rights of Workers.

Article 33

Relating to Article 93 *Family and professional life*

Explanation

Article 33(1) [Article 93 of the Constitution] is based on Article 16 of the European Social Charter. The second paragraph draws on Council Directive 92/85/EEC on the introduction of measures to encourage improvements in the safety and health at work of pregnant workers and workers who have recently given birth or are breastfeeding and Directive 96/34/EC on the framework agreement on parental leave concluded by UNICE, CEEP and the ETUC. It is also based on Article 8 (protection of maternity) of the European Social Charter and draws on Article 27 (right of workers with family responsibilities to equal opportunities and equal treatment) of the revised Social Charter. "Maternity" covers the period from conception to weaning.

Article 34

Relating to Article 94 *Social security and social assistance*

Explanation

The principle set out in Article 34(1) [Article 94 of the Constitution] is based on Articles 137 and 140 of the EC Treaty, now replaced by Articles 210 and 213 and on Article 12 of the European Social Charter and point 10 of the Community Charter on the rights of workers. The Union must respect it when exercising the powers conferred on it by Articles 210 and 213 of the Constitution. The reference to social services relates to cases in which such services have been introduced to provide certain advantages but does not imply that such services must be created where they do not exist. "Maternity" must be understood in the same sense as in the preceding Article.

Paragraph 2 is based on Articles 12(4) and 13(4) of the European Social Charter and point 2 of the Community Charter of the Fundamental Social Rights of Workers and reflects the rules arising from Regulation No 1408/71 and Regulation No 1612/68.

Paragraph 3 draws on Article 13 of the European Social Charter and Articles 30 and 31 of the revised Social Charter and point 10 of the Community Charter. The Union must respect it in the context of policies based on Article 210 of the Constitution.

Article 35

Relating to Article 95 *Health care*

Explanation

The principles set out in this Article are based on Article 152 of the EC Treaty, now replaced by Article 278 of the Constitution, and on Articles 11 and 13 of the European Social Charter. The second sentence of the Article takes over Article 278(1).

Article 36

Relating to Article 96 *Access to services of general economic interest*

Explanation

This Article is fully in line with Article 122 of the Constitution and does not create any new right. It merely sets out the principle of respect by the Union for the access to services of general economic interest as provided for by national provisions, when those provisions are compatible with Union law.

Article 37

Relating to Article 97 *Environmental protection*

Explanation

The principles set out in this Article have been based on Articles 2, 6 and 174 of the EC Treaty, which have now been replaced by Articles 3(3), 119 and 233 of the Constitution. It also draws on the provisions of some national constitutions.

Article 38

Relating to Article 98 *Consumer protection*

Explanation

The principles set out in this Article have been based on Article 153 of the EC Treaty, now replaced by Article 235 of the Constitution.

TITLE V
CITIZENS' RIGHTS

Article 39

Relating to Article 99 *Right to vote and to stand as a candidate at elections to the European Parliament*

Explanation

Article 39 [Article 99 of the Constitution] applies under the conditions laid down in Parts I and III of the Constitution, in accordance with Article 52(2) of the Charter [Article 112(2) of the Constitution]. Article 39(1) [Article 99 of the Constitution] corresponds to the right guaranteed in Article 10(2) of the Constitution (cf. also the legal base in Article 126 for the adoption of detailed arrangements for the exercise of that right) and Article 39(2) [Article 99 of the Constitution] corresponds to Article 20(2) of the Constitution. Article 39(2) [Article 99 of the Constitution] takes over the basic principles of the electoral system in a democratic State.

Article 40

Relating to Article 100 *Right to vote and to stand as a candidate at municipal elections*

Explanation

This Article corresponds to the right guaranteed by Article 10(2) of the Constitution (cf. also the legal base in Article 126 for the adoption of detailed arrangements for the exercise of that right).In accordance with Article 52(2) of the Charter [Article 112(2) of the Constitution], it applies under the conditions set out in these Articles of Parts I and III of the Constitution.

Article 41

Relating to Article 101 *Right to good administration*

Explanation

Article 41 [Article 101 of the Constitution] is based on the existence of the Union as subject to the rule of law whose characteristics were developed in the case law which enshrined inter alia good administration as a general principle of law (see inter alia Court of Justice judgment of 31 March 1992 in Case C-255/90 P, Burban [1992] ECR 2253, and Court of First Instance judgments of 18 September 1995 in Case T-167/94 Nölle [1995] ECR II-2589, and 9 July 1999 in Case T-231/97 New Europe Consulting and others [1999] ECR II-2403). The wording for that right in the first two paragraphs results from the case law (Court of Justice judgment of 15 October 1987 in Case 222/86 Heylens [1987] ECR

4097, paragraph 15 of the grounds, judgment of 18 October 1989 in Case 374/87 Orkem [1989] ECR 3283, judgment of 21 November 1991 in Case C-269/90 TU München [1991] ECR I-5469, and Court of First Instance judgments of 6 December 1994 in Case T-450/93 Lisrestal [1994] ECR II-1177, 18 September 1995 in Case T-167/94 Nölle [1995] ECR II-258) and the wording regarding the obligation to give reasons comes from Article 253 of the EC Treaty, now replaced by Article 38(2) of the Constitution (cf. also the legal base in Article 398 of the Constitution for the adoption of legislation in the interest of an open, efficient and independent European administration). Paragraph 3 reproduces the right now guaranteed by Article 431 of the Constitution. Paragraph 4 reproduces the right now guaranteed by Articles 10(2)(d) and 129 of the Constitution. In accordance with Article 52(2) of the Charter [Article 112(2) of the Constitution], those rights are to be applied under the conditions and within the limits defined by Part III of the Constitution.

The right to an effective remedy, which is an important aspect of this question, is guaranteed in Article 47 of this Charter [Article 107 of the Constitution].

Article 42

Relating to Article 102 *Right of access to documents*

Explanation

The right guaranteed in this Article has been taken over from Article 255 of the EC Treaty, on the basis of which Regulation 1049/2001 has subsequently been adopted. The European Convention has extended this right to documents of institutions, bodies and agencies generally, regardless of their form, see Article 50(3) of the Constitution. In accordance with Article 52(2) of the Charter [Article 112(2) of the Constitution], the right of access to documents is exercised under the conditions and within the limits for which provision is made in Articles 50(3) and 399.

Article 43

Relating to Article 103 *European Ombudsman*

Explanation

The right guaranteed in this Article is the right guaranteed by Articles 10 and 335 of the Constitution. In accordance with Article 52(2) of the Charter 1, it applies under the conditions defined in these two Articles.

Article 44

Relating to Article 104 Right to petition

Explanation

The right guaranteed in this Article is the right guaranteed by Articles 10 and 334 of the Constitution. In accordance with Article 52(2) of the Charter [Article

112(2) of the Constitution], it applies under the conditions defined in these two Articles.

Article 45

Relating to Article 105 *Freedom of movement and of residence*

Explanation

The right guaranteed by paragraph 1 is the right guaranteed by Article 10(2)(a) of the Constitution (cf. also the legal base in Article 125; and the judgement of the Court of Justice of 17 September 2002, C-413/99 Baumbast, [2002] ECR 709). In accordance with Article 52(2) of the Charter [Article 112(2) of the Constitution], it applies under the conditions and within the limits defined for which provision is made in Part III of the Constitution. Paragraph 2 refers to the power granted to the Union by Articles 265 to 267 of the Constitution. Consequently, the granting of this right depends on the institutions exercising that power.

Article 46

Relating to Article 106 *Diplomatic and consular protection*

Explanation

The right guaranteed by this Article is the right guaranteed by Article 10 of the Constitution; cf. also the legal base in Article 127. In accordance with Article 52(2) of the Charter [Article 112(2) of the Constitution], it applies under the conditions defined in these Articles.

TITLE VI

JUSTICE

Article 47

Relating to Article 107 *Right to an effective remedy and to a fair trial*

Explanation

The first paragraph is based on Article 13 of the ECHR:

"Everyone whose rights and freedoms as set forth in this Convention are violated shall have an effective remedy before a national authority notwithstanding that the violation has been committed by persons acting in an official capacity." However, in Union law the protection is more extensive since it guarantees the right to an effective remedy before a court. The Court of Justice enshrined that right in its judgment of 15 May 1986 as a general principle of Union law (Case 222/84 Johnston [1986] ECR 1651; see also judgment of 15 October 1987, Case 222/86 Heylens [1987] ECR 4097 and judgment of 3 December 1992, Case C-97/91 Borelli [1992] ECR 6313). According to the

Court, that general principle of Union law also applies to the Member States when they are implementing Union law. The inclusion of this precedent in the Charter has not been intended to change the system of judicial review laid down by the Treaties, and particularly the rules relating to admissibility for direct actions before the Court of Justice of the European Union. The European Convention has considered the Union's system of judicial review including the rules on admissibility, and confirmed them while amending them as to certain aspects, as reflected in Articles 353 to 381 of the Constitution, and in particular in Article 365(4). Article 47 [Article 107 of the Constitution] applies to the institutions of the Union and of Member States when they are implementing Union law and does so for all rights guaranteed by Union law.

The second paragraph corresponds to Article 6(1) of the ECHR which reads as follows:

"In the determination of his civil rights and obligations or of any criminal charge against him, everyone is entitled to a fair and public hearing within a reasonable time by an independent and impartial tribunal established by law. Judgment shall be pronounced publicly but the press and public may be excluded from all or part of the trial in the interests of morals, public order or national security in a democratic society, where the interests of juveniles or the protection of the private life of the parties so require, or to the extent strictly necessary in the opinion of the court in special circumstances where publicity would prejudice the interests of justice."

In Union law, the right to a fair hearing is not confined to disputes relating to civil law rights and obligations. That is one of the consequences of the fact that the Union is a community based on the rule of law as stated by the Court in Case 294/83, "Les Verts" v. European Parliament (judgment of 23 April 1986, [1988] ECR 1339). Nevertheless, in all respects other than their scope, the guarantees afforded by the ECHR apply in a similar way to the Union. With regard to the third paragraph, it should be noted that in accordance with the case law of the European Court of Human Rights, provision should be made for legal aid where the absence of such aid would make it impossible to ensure an effective remedy (ECHR Judgment of 9.10.1979, Airey, Series A, Volume 32, 11). There is also a system of legal assistance for cases before the Court of Justice of the European Union.

Article 48

Relating to Article 108 *Presumption of innocence and right of defence*

Explanation

Article 48 [Article 108 of the Constitution] is the same as Article 6(2) and (3) of the ECHR, which reads as follows:

"2. Everyone charged with a criminal offence shall be presumed innocent until proved guilty according to law.

3. Everyone charged with a criminal offence has the following minimum rights:

(a) to be informed promptly, in a language which he understands and in detail, of the nature and cause of the accusation against him;

(b) to have adequate time and facilities for the preparation of his defence;

(c) to defend himself in person or through legal assistance of his own choosing or, if he has not sufficient means to pay for legal assistance, to be given it free when the interests of justice so require;

(d) to examine or have examined witnesses against him and to obtain the attendance and examination of witnesses on his behalf under the same conditions as witnesses against him;

(e) to have the free assistance of an interpreter if he cannot understand or speak the language used in court."

In accordance with Article 52(3) [Article 112(3) of the Constitution], this right has the same meaning and scope as the right guaranteed by the ECHR.

Article 49

Relating to Article 109 *Principles of legality and proportionality of criminal offences and penalties*

Explanation

This Article follows the traditional rule of the non-retroactivity of laws and criminal sanctions. There has been added the rule of the retroactivity of a more lenient penal law, which exists in a number of Member States and which features in Article 15 of the Covenant on Civil and Political Rights.

Article 7 of the ECHR is worded as follows:

"1. No one shall be held guilty of any criminal offence on account of any act or omission which did not constitute a criminal offence under national or international law at the time when it was committed. Nor shall a heavier penalty be imposed than the one that was applicable at the time the criminal offence was committed.

2. This Article shall not prejudice the trial and punishment of any person for any act or omission which, at the time when it was committed, was criminal according to the general principles of law recognised by civilised nations."

In paragraph 2, the reference to "civilised" nations has been deleted; this does not change the meaning of this paragraph, which refers to crimes against humanity in particular. In accordance with Article 52(3) [Article 112(3) of the Constitution], the right guaranteed here therefore has the same meaning and scope as the right guaranteed by the ECHR.

Paragraph 3 states the general principle of proportionality between penalties and criminal offences which is enshrined in the common constitutional traditions of the Member States and in the case law of the Court of Justice of the Communities.

Article 50

Relating to Article 110 *Right not to be tried or punished twice in criminal proceedings for the same criminal offence*

Explanation

Article 4 of Protocol No 7 to the ECHR reads as follows:

"1. No one shall be liable to be tried or punished again in criminal proceedings under the jurisdiction of the same State for an offence for which he has already been finally acquitted or convicted in accordance with the law and penal procedure of that State.

2. The provisions of the preceding paragraph shall not prevent the reopening of the case in accordance with the law and the penal procedure of the State concerned, if there is evidence of new or newly discovered facts, or if there has been a fundamental defect in the previous proceedings, which could affect the outcome of the case.

3. No derogation from this Article shall be made under Article 15 of the Convention." The "non bis in idem" rule applies in Union law (see, among the many precedents, the judgment of 5 May 1966, Cases 18/65 and 35/65, Gutmann v. Commission [1966] ECR 103 and a recent case, the decision of the Court of First Instance of 20 April 1999, Joined Cases T-305/94 and others, Limburgse Vinyl Maatschappij NV v. Commission [1999] ECR 931). The rule prohibiting cumulation refers to cumulation of two penalties of the same kind, that is to say criminal law penalties.

In accordance with Article 50 1, the "non bis in idem" rule applies not only within the jurisdiction of one State but also between the jurisdictions of several Member States. That corresponds to the acquis in Union law; see Articles 54 to 58 of the Schengen Convention and the judgment of the Court of Justice of 11 February 2003, C-187/01 Gözütok (not yet published), Article 7 of the Convention on the Protection of the European Communities' Financial Interests and Article 10 of the Convention on the fight against corruption. The very limited exceptions in those Conventions permitting the Member States to derogate from the "non bis in idem" rule are covered by the horizontal clause in Article 52(1) of the Charter [Article 112(1) of the Constitution] concerning limitations. As regards the situations referred to by Article 4 of Protocol No 7, namely the application of the principle within the same Member State, the guaranteed right has the same meaning and the same scope as the corresponding right in the ECHR.

TITLE VII

GENERAL PROVISIONS GOVERNING THE INTERPRETATION AND APPLICATION OF THE CHARTER

Article 51

Relating to Article 111 *Field of application*

Explanation

The aim of Article 51 1 is to determine the scope of the Charter. It seeks to establish clearly that the Charter applies primarily to the institutions and bodies of the Union, in compliance with the principle of subsidiarity. This provision was drafted in keeping with Article 6(2) of the Treaty on European Union, which required the Union to respect fundamental rights, and with the mandate issued by Cologne European Council. The term "institutions" is enshrined in Part I of the Constitution. The expression "bodies, offices and agencies" is commonly used in the Constitution to refer to all the authorities set up by the Constitution or by secondary legislation (see, e.g., Articles 50 or 51 of the Constitution).

As regards the Member States, it follows unambiguously from the case law of the Court of Justice that the requirement to respect fundamental rights defined in a Union context is only binding on the Member States when they act in the scope of Union law (judgment of 13 July 1989, Case 5/88 Wachauf [1989] ECR 2609; judgment of 18 June 1991, ERT [1991] ECR 2925); judgment of 18 December 1997 (C-309/96 Annibaldi [1997] ECR 7493). The Court of Justice confirmed this case law in the following terms: "In addition, it should be remembered that the requirements flowing from the protection of fundamental rights in the Community legal order are also binding on Member States when they implement Community rules ..." (judgment of 13 April 2000, Case C-292/97, [2000] ECR 2737, paragraph 37 of the grounds). Of course this rule, as enshrined in this Charter, applies to the central authorities as well as to regional or local bodies, and to public organisations, when they are implementing Union law.

Paragraph 2, together with the second sentence of paragraph 1, confirms that the Charter may not have the effect of extending the competences and tasks which the other Parts of the Constitution confer on the Union. Explicit mention is made here of the logical consequences of the principle of subsidiarity and of the fact that the Union only has those powers which have been conferred upon it. The fundamental rights as guaranteed in the Union do not have any effect other than in the context of the powers determined by Parts I and III of the Constitution. Consequently, an obligation, pursuant to the second sentence of paragraph 1, for the Union's institutions to promote principles laid down in the Charter, may arise only within the limits of these same powers.

Paragraph 2 also confirms that the Charter may not have the effect of extending the field of application of Union law beyond the powers of the Union as established in the other Parts of the Constitution. The Court of Justice has already established this rule with respect to the fundamental rights recognised as part of Union law (judgment of 17 February 1998, C-249/96 Grant, 1998 ECR 621, paragraph 45 of the grounds). In accordance with this rule, it goes without saying that the incorporation of the Charter into the Constitution cannot be understood as extending by itself the range of Member State action considered to be "implementation of Union law" (within the meaning of paragraph 1 and the above-mentioned case law).

Article 52

Relating to Article 112 *Scope and interpretation of rights and principles*

Explanation

The purpose of Article 52 1 is to set the scope of the rights and principles of the Charter, and to lay down rules for their interpretation. Paragraph 1 deals with the arrangements for the limitation of rights. The wording is based on the case law of the Court of Justice: "... it is well established in the case law of the Court that restrictions may be imposed on the exercise of fundamental rights, in particular in the context of a common organisation of the market, provided that those restrictions in fact correspond to objectives of general interest pursued by the Community and do not constitute, with regard to the aim pursued, disproportionate and unreasonable interference undermining the very substance of those rights" (judgment of 13 April 2000, Case C-292/97, paragraph 45 of the grounds). The reference to general interests recognised by the Union covers both the objectives mentioned in Article 2 of the Constitution and other interests protected by specific provisions of the Constitution such as Articles 5(1), 133(3), 154 and 436.

Paragraph 2 refers to rights which were already expressly guaranteed in the Treaty establishing the European Community and have been recognised in the Charter, and which are now found in other Parts of the Constitution (notably the rights derived from Union citizenship). It clarifies that such rights remain subject to the conditions and limits applicable to the Union law on which they are based, and for which provision is now made in Parts I and III of the Constitution. The Charter does not alter the system of rights conferred by the EC Treaty and now taken over by Parts I and III of the Constitution.

Paragraph 3 is intended to ensure the necessary consistency between the Charter and the ECHR by establishing the rule that, insofar as the rights in the present Charter also correspond to rights guaranteed by the ECHR, the meaning and scope of those rights, including authorised limitations, are the same as those laid down by the ECHR. This means in particular that the legislator, in laying down limitations to those rights, must comply with the same standards as are fixed by the detailed limitation arrangements laid down in the ECHR, which are thus made applicable for the rights covered by this paragraph, without thereby adversely affecting the autonomy of Union law and of that of the Court of Justice of the European Union.

The reference to the ECHR covers both the Convention and the Protocols to it. The meaning and the scope of the guaranteed rights are determined not only by the text of those instruments, but also by the case law of the European Court of Human Rights and by the Court of Justice of the European Union. The last sentence of the paragraph is designed to allow the Union to guarantee more extensive protection. In any event, the level of protection afforded by the Charter may never be lower than that guaranteed by the ECHR.

The Charter does not affect the possibilities of Member States to avail themselves of Article 15 ECHR, allowing derogations from ECHR rights in the event of war or of other public dangers threatening the life of the nation, when they take action in the areas of national defence in the event of war and of the maintenance of law and order, in accordance with their responsibilities recognised in Articles 5 (1), 131, 262 of the Constitution.

The list of rights which may at the present stage, without precluding developments in the law, legislation and the Treaties, be regarded as corresponding to rights in the ECHR within the meaning of the present paragraph is given hereafter. It does not include rights additional to those in the ECHR.

1. Articles of the Charter where both the meaning and the scope are the same as the corresponding Articles of the ECHR:

– Article 2 [Article 62of the Constitution] corresponds to Article 2 of the ECHR – Article 4 [Article 64 of the Constitution] corresponds to Article 3 of the ECHR – Article 5(1) and (2) [Article 65 of the Constitution]correspond to Article 4 of the ECHR – Article 6 [Article 66 of the Constitution] corresponds to Article 5 of the ECHR – Article 7 [Article 67 of the Constitution] corresponds to Article 8 of the ECHR – Article 10(1) [Article 70 of the Constitution] corresponds to Article 9 of the ECHR – Article 11 [Article 71 of the Constitution] corresponds to Article 10 of the ECHR without prejudice to any restrictions which Union law may impose on Member States' right to introduce the licensing arrangements referred to in the third sentence of Article 10(1) of the ECHR – Article 17 [Article 77 of the Constitution]corresponds to Article 1 of the Protocol to the ECHR – Article 19(1) [Article 79 of the Constitution] corresponds to Article 4 of Protocol No 4 – Article 19(2) [Article 79 of the Constitution] corresponds to Article 3 of the ECHR as interpreted by the European Court of Human Rights – Article 48 [Article 108 of the Constitution] corresponds to Article 6(2) and(3) of the ECHR – Article 49(1) (with the exception of the last sentence) and (2) [Article 109 of the Constitution] correspond to Article 7 of the ECHR

2. Articles where the meaning is the same as the corresponding Articles of the ECHR, but where the scope is wider:

– Article 9 [Article 69 of the Constitution] covers the same field as Article 12 of the ECHR, but its scope may be extended to other forms of marriage if these are established by national legislation – Article 12(1) [Article 72 of the Constitution] corresponds to Article 11 of the ECHR, but its scope is extended to European Union level – Article 14(1) [Article 74 of the Constitution] corresponds to Article 2 of the Protocol to the ECHR, but its scope is extended to cover access to vocational and continuing training – Article 14(3) [Article 74 of the Constitution] corresponds to Article 2 of the Protocol to the ECHR as regards the rights of parents – Article 47(2) and (3) [Article 107 of the Constitution] correspond to Article 6(1) of the ECHR, but the limitation to the determination of civil rights and obligations or criminal charges does not apply as regards Union law and its implementation – Article 50 [Article 110 of the Constitution] corresponds to Article 4 of Protocol No 7 to the ECHR, but its scope is extended to European Union level between the Courts of the Member States.

– Finally, citizens of the European Union may not be considered as aliens in the scope of the application of Union law, because of the prohibition of any discrimination on grounds of nationality. The limitations provided for by Article 16 of the ECHR as regards the rights of aliens therefore do not apply to them in this context.

The rule of interpretation contained in paragraph 4 has been based on the wording of Article 6(2) of the Treaty on European Union (cf. now the wording of Article 9(3) of the Constitution) and takes due account of the approach to common constitutional traditions followed by the Court of Justice (e.g., judgment of 13 December 1979, Case 44/79 Hauer [1979] ECR 3727; judgment of 18 May 1982, Case 155/79, AM&S, [1982] ECR 1575). Under that rule, rather than following a rigid approach of "a lowest common denominator", the Charter rights concerned should be interpreted in a way offering a high standard of protection which is adequate for the law of the Union and in harmony with the common constitutional traditions.

Paragraph 5 clarifies the distinction between "rights" and "principles" set out in the Charter. According to that distinction, subjective rights shall be respected, whereas principles shall be observed (Article 51 (1)) [Article 111 of the Constitution]. Principles may be implemented through legislative or executive acts (adopted by the Union in accordance with its powers, and by the Member States only when they implement Union law); accordingly, they become significant for the Courts only when such acts are interpreted or reviewed. They do not however give rise to direct claims for positive action by the Union's institutions or Member States authorities. This is consistent both with case law of the Court of Justice (Cf. notably case law on the "precautionary principle" in Article 174 (2) TEC (replaced by Article 233 of the Constitution): judgment of the CFI of 11 September 2002, T-13/99, Pfizer vs. Council, with numerous references to earlier case law; and a series of judgments on Article 33 (ex-39) on the principles of agricultural law, e.g. judgment of the Court of Justice C- 265/85, Van den Berg, 1987 ECR 1155: scrutiny of the principle of market stabilisation and of reasonable expectations) and with the approach of the Member States' constitutional systems to "principles" particularly in the field of social law. For illustration, examples for principles recognised in the Charter include e.g. Articles 25, 26 and 37 [Articles 85, 86 and 97 of the Constitution]. In some cases, an Article of the Charter may contain both elements of a right and of a principle, e.g. Articles 23, 33 and 34 [Articles 83, 93 and 94 of the Constitution].

Paragraph 6 refers to the various Articles in the Charter which, in the spirit of subsidiarity, make reference to national laws and practices.

Article 53

Relating to Article 113 Level of protection

Explanation

This provision is intended to maintain the level of protection currently afforded within their

respective scope by Union law, national law and international law. Owing to its importance,

mention is made of the ECHR.

Article 54

Relating to Article 114 *Prohibition of abuse of rights*

Explanation

This Article corresponds to Article 17 of the ECHR:

"Nothing in this Convention may be interpreted as implying for any State, group or person any right to engage in any activity or perform any act aimed at the destruction of any of the rights and freedoms set forth herein or at their limitation to a greater extent than is provided for in the Convention." [END]

Sources of Information

Web sites Relating to the European Union

These web addresses worked when we used them, but web addresses are notorious for changing frequently. We are sorry if a few of these no longer function.

General

A to Z index of European Union websites: www.eurunion.org/infores/eu index.htm
Your MP. You can find your MP at: www.theyworkforyou.com
www.euro-know.org
www.wikipedia.org
Action Committee for the United States of Europe : www.ena.lu/europe/formation-community/action-committee-united-states-EuropePathe-1956.htm
Action Committee for the United States of Europe: www.namebase.org/xaaa/ Action-Committee-United-states-europe.html
European Round Table of Industrialists: www.ert.be/
States which reveal farm subsidy payments: www.farmsubsidy.org

European Union official web sites

Main web site: http://europa.eu.int/
The Commission: http://ec.europa.eu/
The Commission in the UK: www.cec.org.uk/
The Council (The Council of Ministers): http://ue.eu.int/en/summ.htm
European Court of Auditors: www.eca.eu.int
Court of Justice: http://curia.eu.int
European Court of Justice: http://europa.eu.int/cj/en/index.htm
European Central Bank: www.ecb.int
European Ombudsman: www.euro-ombudsman.eu.int
European Parliament. Transcripts, live debates, archives, etc: www.europarl.europa.eu/
Statistical office (Eurostat): www.europa.eu.int/comm/eurostat
Legislation (CELEX database): www.europa.eu.int/celex
Legislation (EUR-Lex database): www.europa.eu.int/eur-lex
Contact details for Members of the European Parliament: www.europarl.europa.eu/members/public.do
Directory of current European laws: http://europa.eu.int/
Active European citizenship promotion: http://europa.eu/scadplus/leg/en/lvb/133218.htm

EU Budget

EU Budget: http://europa.eu.int/comm/budget/budget_detail/index_en.htm
Budget In detail 2006: http://ec.europa.eu/budget/budget_detail/current_year_en.htm
Document we used: http://ec.europa.eu/budget/publications/budget_in_fig_en.htm
Budget official journal. Source of real detail: http://eurlex.europa.eu/JOHtml.do?uri=OJ:L:2006:078:SOM:EN:HTML

Parties in the European Parliament

Party of European Socialists: http://www.socialistgroup.org/
European People's Party/European Democrats: http://www.epp-ed.eu/
Alliance of Liberals and Democrats for Europe: http://alde.europarl.eu.int/
Greens/ European Free Alliance: http://www.greens-efa.org/
European United Left/ Nordic Green Left Group: http://www.guengl.org/
Independence/ Democracy Group: http://indemgroup.org/
Union for a Europe of Nations: http://www.uengroup.org/

Constitution and Treaties

The text of the Constitution, as printed in this book, contains all the sections that most readers will find important and useful. However, the total text of the *The Treaty Establishing a Constitution for Europe* (2004) includes not only the text of the Constitution (Preamble and articles 1- 448) but also two short annexes, *The Final Act*, 36 protocols, and 50 declarations - a total of 465 A4 pages in pdf format. This may be downloaded from the official EU source (The Official Journal of the European Union, 16 December 2004/C310/01).

Full text of EU Constitution, annexes, the final act, protocols, and declarations: http://europa.eu.int/constitution/index_en.htm
www.europa.eu.int/abc/treaties_en.htm
www.europa.eu.int-lex/en/search_treaties.html

Website for the EU constitution text also has the texts of *The Nice Treaty, Amsterdam Treaty, Maastricht Treaty, Single European Act, Treaty of Rome* and *Treaty of Paris:* http://www.unizar.es/euroconstitucion/Treaties/Treaty_Const.htm
www.eurotreaties.com/eurotexts.html

Legal Issues

NGO Fair Trials Abroad: www.fairtrialsabroad.org/

European Monitoring system. Recording violations of principles and values in all member states of the European Union. www.euromos.org

European Criminal Bar Association. The ECBA aims to promote the fundamental rights of persons under investigation, suspects, accused and convicted persons. The ECBA consists of specialist defence lawyers in the member countries of the Council of Europe. Membership is open to all lawyers, whether practicing or in academic life, who support those aims. Has a turgid newsletter with no sense that it has anything of interest to communicate to the wider world.

http://www.ecba.org

Organisations critical of the EU

New Internationalist. Magazine concerned with international issues and global justice. www.newint.org
Yes to the European Constitution: http://www.yes-campaign.net/
European Constitution no campaign: http://www.europeannocampaign.com/
Centre for European Reform: www.cer.org.uk
Reform think tank. www.openeurope.org.uk
Fair Trials: www.fairtrialsabroad.org
Corporate Responsibility: www.corporate-responsibility.org/
Shelter. Homelessness charity: http://england.shelter.org.uk
Amnesty International: www.amnesty.org
Corporate Europe Observatory: www.corporateeurope.org
www.free-europe.org

Democracy

www.democracy-movement.org.uk
www.democraticdeficit.org.uk

Environment

Environmental Justice Foundation: www.ejfoundation.org

Transparancy

Alliance for Lobbying Transparency and Ethics Regulation: http://www.alter-eu.org/statement
Statewatch. Concerned with civil liberties issues: www.statewatch.org
European Court of Auditors: www.eca.eu.int
*Green paper on the Commission's Transparency Initiative (2006):*http://ec.europa.eu/comm/eti/index_en.htm
Corporate Europe Observatory: www.corportateeurope.org

Defence

European Military Press Association: http://www.empa.hu/cikk/c33.html
EU defence information: http://www.consilium.europa.eu/cms3_fo/showPage.asp?id=1065&lang=en
European Defence Agency: www.eda.europa.eu/
Military expenditure: http://www.fas.org/man/crs/

Media

The European Union's own news services include the following but the web sites of the main bodies all carry news. Once sites have been accessed, English versions may be selected.

http://europa.eu/geninfo/whatsnew.htm
http://europa.eu/press_room/index_en.htm
Produced for US readers: http://www.eurunion.org/news/home.htm

Free Europe. Quotations from EU senior politicians: www.free-europe.org
The EU's own daily paper, *Europa.* www.europa.eu
Media. EU Media site http://europa.eu.int/comm/avpolicy/ media/forma_fr.html
Youth. Lists of granted projects: http://europa.eu.int/comm/youth/program /examples_en.html
EU culture pages: http://europa.eu.int/comm/culture/eac/other_actions/ support_eur_org/memorial_fr.html
Culture 2000. Projets annuels soutenus : http://europa.eu.int/comm/culture /eac/culture2000/project_annuel/projects1_fr.html
Culture 2000 . Projets pluriannuels soutenus : http://europa.eu.int/comm /culture/eac/culture2000/pluriannuel/projects2_fr.html
Culture 2000. Actions expérimentales soutenues : http://europa.eu.int/ comm/culture/eac/other_actions/exp_act/exp_act_fr.html
Education. Co-opération UE-Canada, projets soutenus : http://europa.eu. int/comm/education/programmes/eu-canada/projects_en.html
Education. Co-opération UE-USA, projets soutenus : http://europa.eu. int/comm/education/programmes/eu-usa/projects_en.html
Erasmus Mundus. Liste des projets sélectionnés : http://europa.eu.int /comm/education/programmes/mundus/index_fr.html

Other EU web news sources

Eu Observer. As a not-for-profit organisation, the EUobserver is a rarity in the news business. It appeals for donations but warns that these will not influence the content. http://euobserver.com

Euractive. EurActive describes itself as follows: "EurActiv.com is the independent media portal fully dedicated to EU affairs. EurActiv has an original business model, based on five elements (corporate sponsoring, EurActor membership, advertising, EU projects, and content syndication). It is well funded and the content usage is free. Slogan "Efficacité et transparence des acteurs européens". www.euractiv.com

Euronews. Euronews appears in seven languages and includes video footage. www.euronews.net

European Voice. Access to the Front page is free but for full usage readers need to subscribe to the paper edition. Owned by the Economist Newspaper Limited: www.europeanvoice.com

EU Business. EU business news. www.eubusiness.com
Indymedia. Independent media organisation. www.indymedia.org/en/
BBC - Where member states stand: http://news.bbc.co.uk/2/hi/europe /3954327.stm
BBC – EU - myths and realities: http://news.bbc.co.uk/1/hi/world/europe /3825521.stm
EUABC – Reader's Guide to the EU Constitution: http://www.euabc.com/ ?page_id=207&s=04e646c43d22fc06342fa5c04849d50b

Ratification of the Constitution

Details on the progress of ratification of the Constitution:
http://europa.eu.int/constitution/ratification_en.htm

Background and history to the European Union

http://www.jean-monnet.ch/en/
http://www.ena.lu/europe/formation-community/indexEN.html
http://www.historiasiglo20.org/europe/
http://www.opendemocracy.net/

International Organisations

World Bank: www.worldbank.org/
International Monetary Fund (IMF): www.imf.org
World Trade Organization (WTO): www.wto.org
United Nations: www.un.org
European Round Table of Industrialists: www.ert.be/
Federation of American Scientists: www.fas.org/man/crs/
World Resources Institute: www.wri.org/
International Energy Agency: www.iea.org/
Council of Europe: www.coe.fr
North Atlantic Treaty Organisation (NATO): www.nato.int
Organization for Economic Cooperation and Development (OECD): www.oecd.org
Organization for Security and Cooperation in Europe (OSCE): www.osce.org

Statistics

See International Organisations, above and, for national incomes: www.nationmaster.com and www.worldwide-tax.com

EU and Israel

EU websites

http://ec.europa.eu/comm/external_relations/israel/intro/index.htm
http://ec.europa.eu/comm/external_relations/mepp/faq/index.htm#6.

Israeli websites

Israeli Prime Minister's Office: www.pmo.gov.il/PMOEng/
Israeli Ministry of Foreign Affairs: http://www.mfa.gov.il/
Jewish Virtual Library: http://www.jewishvirtuallibrary.org

Palestinian websites

www.palestinecampaign.org
www.electronicintifada.net
www.palestinemonitor.org

Other websites on Israel/Palestine

United Nations account of the history of the Palestine problem: www.un.org/depts/dpa/ngo/history.html
Christian Aid: www.christian-aid.org.uk
MidEast Web. Middle East Conflict and Peace Process Source Documents. Includes UNSCOP Report - *Report of the UN Special Committee on Palestine:*
www.mideastweb.org/history.htm
Association for One Democratic State in Palestine/Israel with a discussion forum: www.one-democratic-state.org/
Fairness and Accuracy in Reporting: www.fair.org/index.
Hamas killings: www.vitalperspective.typepad.com/vital_perspective_clarity/files/Fatal_Hamas_Attacks_Since_9-00.pdf
A website on the Israel/Palestine conflict: www.ifamericansknew.org/stats/deaths.html
APRODEV. This is an association of the major development and humanitarian aid organisations in Europe which work closely together with the World Council of Churches: www.aprodev.net
World Council of Churches. 2006 Statement on the conflict in Israel/Palestine: www.oikoumene.org/index

Further reading on the EU and related topics

Guide to the European Union
Dick Leonard
Profile Books
2005

The Penguin Companion to the European Union
Timothy Bainbridge
Penguin Books
2003

Understanding the European Union
John McCormick
Palgrave Macmillan
2005

Globalization and its Discontents
Joseph Stiglitz
Penguin Books
2002

For an analysis of problems associated with privatisation:
New Labour's Attack on Public Services
Dexter Whitfield
Spokesman
www.spokesmanbooks.com

Losing Ground - Israel, poverty and the Palestinians
David McDowall
Christian Aid
2003

Periodicals

The Economist
Journal of Common Market Studies
West European Politics
Journal of European Public Policy
Comparative European Politics
Official Journal of the European Communities
General Report on the Activities of the European Union. Annual report with information on key policy developments and statistics.
Bulletin of the European Union. Published ten times per year. Official record of events and policies, and further reading on the EU and related topics.

Main EU institutions and agencies

European Parliament
Secretariat
Centre Européen, Plateau du Kirchberg
L-2929 Luxembourg
Tel. +352 43001
www.europarl.eu.int

European Parliament
Bat. Altiero Spinelli
60 Rue Wiertz
B-1047 Brussels
Belgium

European Parliament
Allée du Printemps, B.P. 1024
F67070 Strasbourg
France

European Ombudsman
1 avenue du Président-Robert-Schuman
BP 403 FR
F-67001 Strasbourg Cedex
France
Tel. 33 3 8817 2313

European Central Bank (formerly European Monetary Institute)
Kaiserstrasse 29
D-60311 Frankfurt am Main
Germany
Tel. +49 69 13440
www.ecb.int

European agency for the evaluation of medicinal products (EMEA)
7 Westferry Circus
Canary Wharf
London E1 4HB
UK
Tel. +44 20 7418 8400
www.emea.eu.int

European agency for the evaluation of medicinal products (EMEA)
7 Westferry Circus
Canary Wharf
London E1 4HB
UK
Tel. +44 20 7418 8400
www.emea.eu.int

European Data Protection Supervisor
Rue Wiertz 60
B-1047 Brussels
Belgium
Tel. +32 2 2831900
www.edps.eu.int

European centre for the development of vocational training
123 Europe
GR-55001 Thessaloniki
Greece
Tel. +30 2310 490111
www.cedefop.eu.int

European foundation for the improvement of living and working conditions (Eurofound)
Wyattwille Road
Loughlinstown
Dublin 18
Ireland
Tel. +353 1 2043100
www.eurofound.eu.int

Community plant variety office (CPVO)
3 boulevard Maréchal-Foch
F-49100 Angers Cedex 02
France
Tel. +33 2 4125 6400
www.cdt.eu.int

Translation centre for the bodies of the European Union (CDT)
Bátiment Nouvel Hémicycle
1 rue du Fort Thungen
L-1499 Luxembourg
Tel. +352 42 17111
www.cdt.eu.int

European monitoring centre on racism and xenophobia (EUMC)
Rahlgasse 3
A-1060 Vienna
Austria
Tel. +43 1 580300
www.eumc.eu.int

European environment agency (EEA)
Kongens Nytorv 6
DK-1050 Copenhagen K
Denmark
Tel. +45 33 367100
www.eea.eu.int

European training foundation (ETF)
Villa Gualino
Viale Settimo Severo 65
I-10133 Turin
Italy
Tel. +39 011 6302222
www.etf.eu.int

European monitoring centre for drugs and drug addiction (EMCDDA)
Rua da Cruz de Santa Apolónia 23-25
P-1149-045 Lisbon
Portugal
Tel. +351 218 113000
www.emcdda.eu.int

Office for Harmonisation in the internal market (OHMI)
Apartado de Correos 77
E-03080 Alicante
Spain
Tel. +34 96 5139100
www.oami.eu.int

European agency for safety and health at work (EU-OSHA)
Gran Via 33
E-48009 Bilbao
Spain
Tel. +34 94 4794360
www.agency.osha.eu.int

Committee of the Regions
Rue Belliard 79
B-1040 Brussels
Belgium
Tel +32 2 2822211
www.cor.eu.int

European agency for reconstruction (EAR)
Egnatia 4
GR-54626 Thessaloniki
Greece
Tel. +30 2310 505100
www.ear.eu.int

European food safety authority (EFSA)
Rue de Genéve 10
B-1140 Brussels
Belgium
Tel. +32 2 3372111
www.efsa.eu.int

European maritime safety agency (AESM)
Rue de Genéve 12
B-1049 Brussels
Belgium
Tel. +32 2 7020200
www.emsa.eu.int

Economic and Social Committee
Rue Belliard 99
B-1040 Brussels
Belgium
Tel. +32 2 5469011
www.esc.eu.int

European Investment Bank
100 Boulevard Konrad Adenauer
L-2950 Luxembourg
Tel. +352 43791
www.eib.org

Council of the European Union
General Secretariat
Rue de la Loi 175
B-1048 Brussels
Belgium

European Network and information security agency (ENISA)
Rue Belliard 7,B-7 02/56
Tel. +32 2 2856111
www.ue.eu.int

European Commission
Rue de la Loi 200
B-1049 Brussels
Belgium
Tel. +32 2 2991111
www.europa.eu.int/comm

Court of Justice of the European Communities
Boulevard Konrad Adenauer
L-2925 Luxembourg
Tel. +352 43031
www.curia.eu.int

European Court of Auditors
12 rue Alcide de Gasperi
L-1615 Luxembourg
Tel. +352 43981
www.eca.eu.int

Index

Q

R

U

V

W

Minds at War

The Poetry and Experience of the First World War

Edited by David Roberts

The Classic poems (Wilfred Owen, Siegfried Sassoon, Isaac Rosenberg, and others), plus women poets and popular verse. The largest anthology of poetry of the First World War. This encyclopaedic volume also includes extracts from poets' letters and diaries, and comments of pundits, politicians and other contemporaries.

400 pages. 9"x6" Paperback. Illustrated.
Sixth printing. ISBN 978-0-9528969-0-6
£14-99 UK

Out in the Dark

Poetry of the First World War

in context and with basic notes

Edited by David Roberts

This anthology contains the most important poems and poets of the First World War, with many other poets of special interest.

Comments of past and present day critics, and basic explanatory notes on unusual expressions and vocabulary make this poignant anthology especially valuable for students.

190 pages 9"x6" Paperback. Illustrated.
Seventh printing. ISBN 0 9528969 1 5 £8-99 UK

Lessons from Iraq - the UN must be reformed

By David Roberts

A pamphlet examining the astonishing failures of the UN Security Council in its dealings with Iraq and proposes practical reforms. 24 pages. Published by, and available from, *Action for UN Renewal*, 3 Whitehall Court, London SW1A 2EL £1-50, post free.

Kosovo War Poetry

by David Roberts

Poetry and verse exploring the tragedy of the Kosovo war. It includes the widely studied *Pilot's Testament* which may be seen on our website.

60 pages Paperback ISBN 0 9528969 2 3 £4-99

For more information about our war poetry books and many contemporary war poems please see our website: www.warpoetry.co.uk

Connie Clarkson's

Asian Flavours

For two of the most magnificent women I am proud to know –
Ruth and Elizabeth, with all my love

First published in 2002 by New Holland Publishers (NZ) Ltd
Auckland • Sydney • London • Cape Town

218 Lake Road, Northcote, Auckland, New Zealand
14 Aquatic Drive, Frenchs Forest, NSW 2086, Australia
86–88 Edgware Road, London W2 2EA, United Kingdom
80 McKenzie Street, Cape Town 8001, South Africa
www.newhollandpublishers.com

ISBN: 1 877246 84 0

Publishing manager: Renée Lang **Design:** Gina Hochstein **Editor:** Alison Mudford

10 9 8 7 6 5 4 3 2 1

Colour reproduction by Pica Digital, Singapore
Printed by Craft Print pte Ltd, Singapore

Connie Clarkson's

Asian Flavours

An album of memories and recipes

photographed by Kieran Scott

contents

below left: *My mother and her parents*
below right: *My paternal grandmother*
opposite page: *At the age of 10 months with my maternal great-grandmother*
opposite page below: *Even at the tender age of three, I was taking charge*

My maternal great-grandmother always said that there were two types of people in the world – those who live to eat and those who eat to live. Singaporeans are definitely the former. She was a wise woman. This is the story of the fabulous cuisine I live to eat and the extraordinary women who helped me to create Asia in my kitchen.

My culinary journey really began in my grandmothers' kitchens in Singapore in the early 1960s. It was – and still is – an extraordinary country of countless religions, feasts and celebrations, a cacophony of languages and, best of all, a mecca for fine food. I learnt about Nonya food and culture from my mother's family and about patience and devotion from my father's mother.

My fondest memory of my paternal grandmother's kitchen was the skimming of the soup. The stock was always sparkling clear as all she did was skim. All day. Just before lunch a million bones went into the cavernous pot on the slowest of heats. It was always pork or chicken, never fish or beef. Then the skimming began. Any blemish that had the temerity to float to the top was removed with infinite care, leaving only the clearest, most flavoursome stock which she flavoured lightly with salt, light soy sauce and, at the very last minute before serving, various combinations of Chinese spinach, watercress, fishballs, julienne belly pork, deep fried shallots, finely sliced spring onions, fresh prawns or hand-shelled fresh crabmeat. Soup was always a highlight and no cook could ever reproduce it to equivalent standard. Good soup cannot be hurried. When it comes to patience, Dad's mother is my role model. Her name was Koh Swee Neo but I called her Ah Ma.

A story of fabulous cuisine and extraordinary women

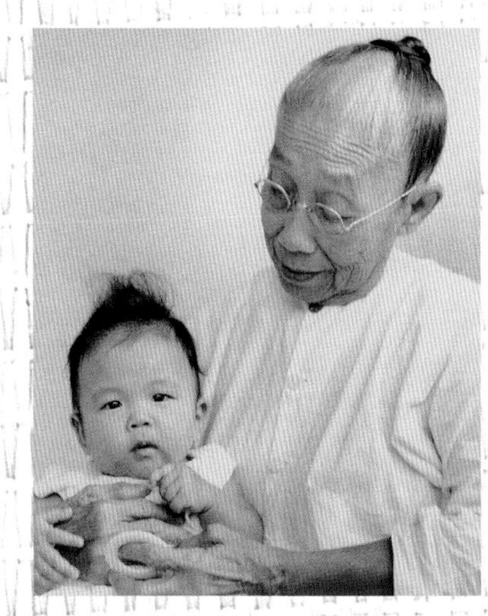

Ah Ma lived with me and my parents, accompanied by a maid, a cook and my nanny. She was small, immaculately groomed and dressed in the flappy black trousers and butterfly-buttoned tunics of the Mainland Chinese. Her hair was smoothed into a knot at the base of her neck and secured by a black lacquer clip. She had little broken feet that had been bound as a tiny child but released before the bones could totally set in the lotus shape so revered by our ancestors as erotic. I never knew why her feet were released but have a fantasy that as a girl she was rescued by my grandfather who had fallen in love with her and took her away with him to the far off island of Singapore. She never really spoke of him.

Our little apartment in Emerald Hill Road, where we lived until I was six, was a stone's throw from Orchard Road, the hub of shopping, hotels and some of the best food in my memory. We lived according to the silent rules of the privileged middle class. My parents were 'in business' as they put it. Mum was one of Singapore's foremost hair stylists from the 1950s until the late 1970s. Dad ran the business which, at its height, consisted of three salons, 30 employees and clientele that included most of the local glitterati and the cream of the expat British and New Zealand Army and Navy wives. I was mothered by my nanny and our home was managed by my grandmother, assisted by the maid and the cook. It was perfectly acceptable to have 'servants' and one knew that the privacy of home was shared by non-family members who would eventually know almost everything about everyone. In this environment, my paternal grandmother ruled supreme.

Ah Ma prepared all our meals with the help of the cook. We went through a stream of cooks, as it was impossible to find one who could please both my parents and my grandmother. I recall the demise of one cook because she sauced everything with Heinz Tomato Ketchup. Until the day he died in 1990, my father could not face Heinz Tomato Ketchup without mentioning that cook. There were standards to uphold, even at home.

Ah Ma fed and looked after me, but my mother's mother, Maude Tan, taught me to love cooking, about Nonya cuisine and about looking after those you love.

My mother's family were Peranakan or Straits Chinese. The womenfolk were called Nonya and the men Baba, although all four terms have been used interchangeably over the years. The early 1800s saw the Mainland Chinese traders travelling to Penang, Malacca and Singapore to trade, spending about five months of the year away from home. These traders eventually made second homes in Malacca with Malay 'wives' who would look after the business while they went 'home' to their Chinese wives. These Chinese wives were never brought to Malacca.

The children of these second marriages, in those days, often married among themselves and, over time, most of the

opposite page top: *My maternal grandmother, Maude Tan*
opposite page below: *The marriage of my maternal grandparents, Maude Tan and Tan Cheng Tee*
left: *My maternal great-grandmother*
below: *My mother as a young woman (before she married my father)*

members of these communities settled in Malacca and in Singapore, which was home to my family.

The Peranakan women or Nonya had privileged upbringings. The families were invariably wealthy, as only the thrifty Chinese businessmen knew the benefits of shrewd trading and saving. Servants looked after the mundane household tasks and the ladies spent their days being taught by British tutors, embroidering fine linen and, best of all, planning and preparing exquisite meals for the men.

Consequently, the dishes were tasty but preparation was time-consuming. Ingredients were sliced finely, cubed minutely, marinated over long periods of time and everything was beautifully garnished. This is where I learned that if you loved them, you fed them. I must have been totally adored, for I cannot remember a day in my childhood that I was wanting for the best.

I grew up in Maude Tan's Peranakan kitchen, wreathed in the aromas of pandan leaves, fresh baked bread and steaming vanilla custard. She cooked and sold 'kuey' for a living. 'Kuey' is Malay for cake. Mama, as I called her, made three items regularly: Bak Chang, or sweet pork dumplings wrapped in glutinous rice and pandan leaves; Bun Su Si, or minced pork buns both curried or plain; and Kuey Salaad, or egg custard flavoured with pandan leaves and steamed over a layer of sweet glutinous rice.

As these three typical Peranakan desserts were becoming increasingly hard to find, Mama was a legend in her own time. Her customers came from all corners of Singapore and her phone rang hot each day with orders. Each dessert was a labour of love.

Each day began with a trip to the wet market. Mama or Kong Kong (Grandfather) would walk to market to buy all essentials for the day and ride the trishaw home. I remembered thinking that the small trishaw riders, with their sinewy calves and forearms, would never be able to pedal the laden trishaw to the top of Emerald Hill Road, where number 166 was, without taking a break or the trishaw falling apart. This was where my grandparents lived all their married lives, where my mother and her only brother were born and where I lived from the age of six until I left for New Zealand.

It was my great-grandmother's job to separate the glutinous rice from the normal rice. Glutinous rice is never pure – there is always a percentage of plain rice in the mix. Only pure glutinous rice would do for Mama's kuey. My great-grandmother, or Cho Cho, was a tiny stooped lady, crippled with Parkinson's disease. She had no short-term memory but her long-term recall would make an elephant weep and her wisdom was infallible. I will never forget her rationale about evading capture. She believed that if you are running away from an elephant, you should run in zigzags as an elephant is big and cumbersome and would have difficulty darting from

opposite page top: *Centrepoint market and hawker centre in Singapore*
opposite page below: *Great-granny and me in 1962*
below: *Mum in 1963*

side to side. If you are running away from a snake, you should run in a straight line because snakes move in zigzags and your chances of escape are better if you cover less ground. Lao Tsu in *The Art of War* said that in order to win a war you must know how your enemy thinks and act accordingly. But my great-grandmother could not read, she was just wise. She walked with the aid of a small cane chair which she sat in when not using it as a walking frame. Cho Cho sat all day in her little chair with a tray on her knee, separating the rice grain by grain. We would use at least four kilos of rice a day.

Life in Mama's kitchen was perfectly orderly. The bread dough was always first on the agenda. While it was proving, fillings for both the buns and the Bak Chang were made. The maid would be cleaning and stripping the pandan leaves ready for wrapping the Bak Chang. Once all the ingredients were ready, we assembled the buns first, then the Bak Chang. It was not unusual for us to make 500 buns, 400 Bak Chang and seven trays of Kuey Salaad in a day. The steamed custard was the last to be assembled, once the glutinous rice was picked over, washed and cooked.

It was a ritual without variation. I understood that if I arrived in the kitchen at 10am, I would be given the task of glazing the first batch of buns with beaten egg using a soft rabbit's fur brush. I knew that at 11am we would be lowering the first batch of dumplings into the pot, and that at 3pm I would be counting and packaging the orders for collection. When I was three, my assistance was indulged fondly, with the maid hovering to ensure I did little damage to the finished product or myself. As I grew older, I was instructed in the art of painting beaten egg on bread dough so soft that even the slightest

below: *My great-grandfather's grave*
opposite page top: *My great-grandfather's funeral*
opposite page below: *My father as a boy*

pressure would leave a blemish. It then became expected that I would perform impeccably. Never a cross word, never any pressure, just a natural assumption that if one wanted to play, one played with total dedication, or not at all. I felt so secure with the confidence that only totally beloved children can feel. It was so seductive.

The women spent all day together, talked together and worked together. When I eventually left for New Zealand, I understood the value of the support they gave to each other and also what an extraordinary businesswoman my grandmother was. In a little house in the middle of Singapore, she ran a profitable catering business with word of mouth her only marketing tool. She had all the business she wanted. She managed a small team of women who not only respected and obeyed her every instruction unquestioningly, but also remained loyal to her for over three decades – she had no staff turnover. It has always been a matter of great pride for me to have grown up at the feet of, and been a part of, the lives of three generations of such strong and wonderful women.

Nonya cuisine is a synthesis of the many tastes from both the Chinese and Malay cultures. There is always curry, coconut cream, tamarind, lime, lemon grass, chilli, ginger and garlic. These ingredients are supplemented by three very distinctive herbs – screw pine or pandan leaves, leper limes or limau purut and coriander.

Nonya dishes are labour intensive but well worth the effort. My most treasured eating experience is Poh Piah or fresh spring rolls. This was indeed a labour of love. A tradition that came first from Mama, and was then carried on by my mother, Poh Piah was an event that was prepared for days in advance and consumed with appropriate reverence and appreciation.

The spring rolls were wrapped in paper-thin fresh crêpes made from chicken and duck eggs. Each crêpe was reinforced by a rice flour crêpe and filled with finely shredded bamboo shoots braised with pork, prawns, garlic and soy sauce. This was garnished with crunchy cos lettuce, hand-shelled fresh crabmeat, extra cooked shrimp, coriander leaves, crispy fried garlic, blanched beansprouts and a sweet soy sauce and chilli if desired. Mama would begin the bamboo shoot mixture at least four days in advance, as the longer it stood, the tastier it became. The bamboo shoots and pork were finely shredded. All ingredients were made the same shape and size. I remember the day we bought a food processor with a shredder attachment. My father, who was into high-tech labour-saving devices, blithely suggested that it might save a lot of time. It was to be the first and last time that he made the suggestion. While the time saving was fully acknowledged, it was also dismissed as rendering the food 'not authentic'. Authenticity is of prime consideration with Nonya food. My mother would travel miles for the 'authentic' frypan used for the crêpes, or the 'authentic' rice crêpe, or chilli sauce, or serving plate.

The consuming of spring rolls is just as important and steeped in tradition as the making. One rolls one's own. Always. And there is an 'authentic' procedure to follow, too. Demonstrations for the uninitiated began each meal. First the egg crêpe, then the rice crêpe, then the lettuce, then the beansprouts. Then as much bamboo shoot mixture as was possible to fit on the crêpe. Then the garnishes. Finally, the sauces and the rolling. This was the ultimate challenge – who could roll and eat the largest spring roll without splitting the crêpe. My father held the record with great pride for many years, only to be toppled by my first boyfriend. Needless to say, ours was not a long-term relationship – I think he learned that you never outdo your girlfriend's father in spring roll rolling and get to keep the girl as well. Making spring rolls – or rice paper rolls – takes a lot less time these days, but I must admit to pangs of guilt if I take any short cuts. The roots of tradition run deep.

The Nonya understood the art of hospitality and the value of feeding their men. I was brought up with the notion that cooking is a worthy accomplishment, an art form and a gift to your family. Mum always said, 'If you want to show them you love them, cook for them.' When I was little, 'them' referred to friends and family. As I grew older, it became, 'If you want them to fall in love with you, cook for them.' 'Them' had become the boyfriends and suitors she imagined would swarm around her precious only daughter, ready to bestow on her fine gold, jewels and all the adoration in the world. Although the gold and jewels eluded me, it is from this that I began to understand what good hospitality meant.

opposite page: *Mum's granddad, my great-granddad*
below: *Me in front of Columba College*

In January 1976 I said goodbye to my father at the solid green front door of the Columba College boarding house in Dunedin. It dawned on me for the first time in my life that I was now very much on my own. I recall thinking that the only way the pain was going to go away was if I made it go away. No one was going to take it away for me.

My first meal at Columba College (where I spent 1976 and 1977) was grey silverside with white mustard sauce, grey peas, white mashed potatoes, and lifeless cabbage, all clinging to a solid white plate that would have bounced when dropped on marble. For a Singaporean, who had until then had the opportunity to eat out every meal for a year without going to the same restaurant twice, this was pure torture. I realized very quickly that the only way I was going to survive this culinary desert of the late seventies in New Zealand was to create my own oasis. This was when necessity created Asia in my kitchen.

The only supplier of Asian ingredients in Dunedin was a Chinese fruiterer in George Street called Wing On. The only curry powder was Vencat and the best soy sauce, in fact the only soy sauce available, was Superior Soy. Fish was still frozen the moment it was caught, prawns did not really make it to the fish shop. We had a house mistress at Columba College called Miss Naidu (I don't know where she came from, but she was Indian) who would cook curries and make purris in her flat each weekend. The aroma of garlic and curry drove me to distraction and Miss Naidu's flat on the top floor became a little oasis.

I began to experiment with the limited resources available to me from Wing On and, even if I say so myself, it was not bad at all. So, at the same time that I was learning to cut my toast into four and only buttering each quarter as I ate it, I was also experimenting with rehydrating desiccated coconut with warm milk for curries and substituting gin for Chinese wine in Soy Sauce Chicken.

I have always maintained that running a restaurant is like having a dinner party at home – just bigger. We prepare the best food from the best ingredients possible. We make sure that the house is clean and beautiful, the flowers lovely, the table perfect. We chill the wine correctly and dress appropriately. When our guests are with us, we make sure they are happy and want for nothing. We entertain, we want them to feel at home, to feel special. When they leave, they thank us and we hope they will come again. Then we clear up and go to bed. The only difference with a restaurant is the bill at the end!

It was no surprise, therefore, to all those who knew and loved me that in 1995, together with two business partners, I fulfilled my lifelong dream to became a restaurateur. I bought an icon of the Auckland hospitality scene, The French Café. After four months, my partners and I parted company and I became sole owner. Perhaps being an only child, I had never learned to share. I had eaten at The French Café many times before purchasing it and had always felt that it had a quality, an intimacy, a welcome that was not particularly evident in many eating establishments in Auckland. It was to become home for four amazing years and I can still recall the little thrill of delight I always felt when I turned the key in the front door each day and took that first step into the Chilcott Room. It was to become the second all-consuming passion of my life, the first being my now erstwhile 17-year marriage to the inimitable Hugh and our two stunning daughters Ruth and Elizabeth. In fact, my preoccupation with the business was the reason I survived the insanity of divorce with grace. A restaurant is like an insatiable and jealous lover who demands total devotion, attention and absolute fidelity. There was no time for pain. By the time I had sold the restaurant and was able to surface and face the world, the pain had passed.

opposite top: *A publicity shot at The French Café*
opposite bottom: *Sampling The French Café's cuisine*
left: *Myself, Ray McVinne and my mother in Singapore several years ago*
below: *Overseeing the lunch menu at The French Café*

Our food was cutting-edge stuff in those days. I took Kate Fay, my ingenious chef, to Singapore on an eating spree. Her instructions were to eat, eat and eat. It was such fun. We ate everything, all day and everywhere. We were joined by our friend and foodie extraordinaire Ray McVinnie for some of the time. Both Kate and Ray made acquaintance (while I renewed mine) with as many of the exquisite taste sensations as possible. The results were gratifying. Kate was able to introduce some great tastes to our menu and the response was encouraging. She deconstructed Peking Duck, Hokkien Mee and Poh Piah. While my grandmothers might have turned in their graves, I was so proud.

There are a few regrets in my life – but spending four years in The French Café is definitely not one of them. I had never been so challenged, humbled, engrossed or invigorated. I made great friends, drank stunning wine and learned much about human nature. The hospitality business is extremely hard and relentless and to get it all right is nigh on impossible. I like to think we had a damn good run at it and acquitted ourselves with a certain amount of merit.

In this book, I have put together not only the Peranakan recipes that translate well into our New Zealand environment, but also many of the childhood recipes that I love and that my children ask for when they come home. Hainanese Chicken Rice, Mr De Cruz's Chicken Curry, Wonton Soup, Soy Sauce Chicken and of course Poh Piah are our family favourites.

below: *Elizabeth (left) and Ruth, my two daughters*
opposite: *My maternal grandmother at a picnic*

Creating an entire meal from the recipes in the book is quite simple. I approach it just as I would a western meal. For meat eaters, we look at a cross-section of dishes to include a main meat, vegetables and a starch or carbohydrate. Rice is a staple ingredient but not always mandatory. In fact, there are no rules. Desire is, as always, a purely subjective notion. The meals in my parents' home always comprised a green vegetable dish such as pan fried choy sum (Chinese spinach), a lovely clear soup, rice, either a fish, chicken or meat dish and perhaps some Ma Po Tau Fu or Braised Soy Bean Cake. All dishes are served family style. This means that all the dishes are put in the middle of the table at the same time, each with a serving spoon, and we help ourselves. You might have seen the 'lazy Susans' used in Chinese restaurants – these are round, revolving extensions in the middle of a table that bring the many dishes closer to each diner in turn.

While family-style dining is the norm in most Asian households, the 'fine dining' Chinese banquet dishes are brought to the table individually. Diners sample each dish before the next is produced. I recall the experience of sitting through a 10-course Chinese wedding banquet. One must always have a survival strategy in mind or end up being caught out before the tenth course with no room to eat another mouthful and insulting the host. So, the rule is a little at a time because there is always more to come! (Besides, they always put the most exotic and expensive dishes at the end.)

When serving Asian food, chopsticks are the most obvious implements to use. However, this is not the case all the time. In Singapore, we eat

rice on a flat plate. Chopsticks would be hopeless for picking up Chinese rice, which should be loose and fluffy, unless the rice is served in a bowl. (Japanese rice is short-grained and sticks together so chopsticks aren't a problem.) So, we usually use a fork in the left hand and a spoon in the right.

After 26 years, New Zealand is definitely home, but we still eat with a fork and spoon at home and I am unable to go for long without rice and chilli and soy sauce. They say you can take the girl out of Asia, but you cannot take Asia out of the girl. I pay tribute to my matrilineal heritage and salute the three generations of fabulous women who taught me that to live to eat is a wonderfully hedonistic pleasure that I am proud to continue to pursue.

Connie Clarkson 2002

The wet markets of Singapore in the 1960s were a symphony of noise, sights and smells. People conversed in what seemed like a million different languages with little difficulty. Indian vendors sold mountains of red, green and yellow ready-ground spice pastes alongside the market gardeners with their baskets of vegetables, pineapples, mangoes, coconuts and tomatoes. Customers came to the market in shorts, sarongs or brilliantly coloured saris. The smells that greeted customers at the door were just as varied. The delicious smells of cooked food from the hawker stalls made it very difficult to concentrate on shopping. It was not unusual to follow a path of ever-changing smells of spices, then meat, then fish.

I loved shopping for dry goods, fruit and vegetables. The smells were beautiful, the stalls were dry, clean and orderly. I hated going into the meat and seafood section where vendors scaled and gutted fish, skinned pork and dressed chickens. Going to market with my grand-

chicken
texture & taste

mother was an adventure, particularly when it came to buying chicken. The live birds were kept in cane cages. My grandmother would choose her birds and money changed hands. We then left to complete our shopping. On our return, we collected the dressed birds sealed tightly in individual plastic bags. It took me many years to realise that the fluffy brooding birds and the dressed and bagged chickens were one and the same.

Supermarkets have replaced all the drama of the wet markets with air conditioning, lots of polystyrene packaging and cling film. Now the drama of buying chicken is only in deciding which cut to purchase and how much.

I am convinced that chicken dishes are successful in Asia because the light texture of the meat and the simple clean richness of the flavour is well suited to the more subtle Asian tastes. I have included in this collection of chicken recipes some comfort dishes from my childhood, some more elegant and adventurous items as well as the family favourites that have survived my transition from Singapore to New Zealand.

Barbecued Spicy Chicken

This is one of our favourite Malay chicken dishes. In the old days, we would barbecue the chicken over charcoal ovens in the open kitchen at the back of my grandmother's house. This was the signature dish of a Malay lady who helped her in the kitchen for many years. In the old days, maids were 'taken into service' and lived in the household they served. Kakak ('Big Sister' in Malay) began working as a maid for my grandmother when in her teens and stayed with our family until she retired in her 60s.

Serves 4

2 cloves garlic (or 1 teaspoon crushed garlic)
thumb-sized piece fresh ginger
1 tablespoon freshly squeezed lime juice
1/2 teaspoon salt
500g (1 lb) chicken drumsticks
1 recipe spice paste (see below)

spice paste

4 small red chillies (for a milder dish remove seeds or decrease number of chillies)
15 small red onions or shallots
10 cloves garlic (or 3 teaspoons crushed)
2 tomatoes
2 tablespoons vegetable oil
1/4 cup freshly squeezed lime juice
1 tablespoon sugar
salt and pepper to taste

Combine the garlic, ginger, lime juice and salt and season the chicken pieces. Cover and set aside.

To prepare the spice paste, put the chillies, onions or shallots, garlic and tomatoes into a blender and blend to a fine paste.

Heat the oil in a pan and stirfry the paste over a low heat for 5 minutes or until fragrant.

Add the lime juice, sugar, salt and pepper and stir until combined. Cool.

Rub the cool paste over the seasoned drumsticks and marinate for at least 30 minutes (preferably overnight) to allow the flavours to penetrate.

Cook on a barbecue or in a moderate oven preheated to 180°C (350°F) for about 20 minutes or until golden brown and tender.

Serve hot or cold with steamed white rice and a green salad.

Chicken and Cabbage Salad

I love the fresh clean taste of Vietnamese food. This coleslaw-style salad, with a Vietnamese dressing, is brilliant for a summer barbecue. With the assistance of a food processor or a grater, the whole salad is simple to rustle up. I usually prepare four times the amount of dressing, which keeps well in the fridge.

Serves 4

dressing

1 fresh red chilli, seeded and minced

2 small cloves garlic, minced

1 1/2 tablespoons sugar

2 tablespoons fish sauce

3 tablespoons freshly squeezed lime juice

2 tablespoons water

salad

1 small onion, thinly sliced

2 tablespoons white vinegar

1 whole chicken breast, steamed or poached

4 cups finely shredded cabbage

1 cup finely shredded carrot

3 tablespoons finely shredded mint leaves

large handful coriander sprigs to garnish

Combine all the dressing ingredients and stir until the sugar has dissolved. Set aside.

To make the salad, toss the onion and vinegar in a small bowl and stand for 10 minutes. Drain and set aside.

Skin and bone the chicken breast and shred the meat into thin strips.

In a large bowl, toss the chicken, cabbage, carrot, onion, mint and dressing.

Arrange on individual plates or a large platter.

Garnish with coriander leaves.

Peranakan Chicken Curry

This is a simple curry that my grandmother used to cook for lunch. I use the curry powders available in supermarkets but find that the ones made in Singapore or Malaysia give the best result. A good yellow potato works well with this recipe, as the rich flavour withstands the spices in the curry.

Serves 6

7 cloves garlic, peeled and crushed, or 2 teaspoons crushed garlic
1/2 thumb-sized piece fresh ginger, peeled
10 shallots or small red onions
2 tablespoons curry powder (or to taste)
2 tablespoons water
1.5kg (3lb) chicken pieces
1/3 cup vegetable oil
2 cups coconut milk
salt to taste
600g (1lb 5oz) potatoes, peeled and cut into 3cm (1 1/4 in) cubes

Put the garlic, ginger and shallots in a food processor and process until they form a fine paste.

Mix the curry powder and water into a thick paste.

Mix half of the curry paste with the processed ingredients. Reserve the rest of the curry paste.

Rub the curry paste and garlic mixture over the chicken pieces and marinate for 30 minutes.

Heat a wok or saucepan and add the oil. Add remaining curry paste to the hot oil, stirring constantly to prevent sticking, and fry until fragrant.

Add the marinated chicken and reduce the heat to medium.

Stir continuously until the chicken is browned and half cooked.

Add the coconut milk and salt to taste. Simmer for 30 minutes.

Add the potatoes and simmer until potatoes and chicken are cooked.

Serve with white rice or crusty French bread.

Chicken and Mushroom Casserole

This typical Cantonese dish has a delicious savoury flavour, so it's great with a plain green vegetable such as gai lan (Chinese broccoli), and noodles or rice. It's the perfect recipe to resort to when you are at a loss for inspiration and the supermarket checkout looms near, especially if you already have the basic sauces in your cupboard.

Serves 4

150g (5oz) mushrooms (use a selection of button, oyster, abalone, shiitake or straw mushrooms if available)
1 tablespoon sesame oil
1 thumb-sized piece fresh ginger, peeled and sliced thinly
500g (1lb) boneless chicken breast, cut into strips
2 tablespoons light soy sauce
1 tablespoon dark soy sauce
1 tablespoon oyster sauce
2 cups water
2 teaspoons sugar
salt to taste
1 tablespoon cornflour mixed with 1/4 cup water
pepper to taste

Prepare the mushrooms by trimming the stems and peeling if required. Heat the sesame oil until hot, then fry the ginger for a minute.

Add the chicken pieces and brown.

Add the mushrooms, the soy sauces, oyster sauce, water, sugar and salt and simmer for about 20 minutes till the chicken is cooked.

Just before serving, adjust the seasoning and thicken with the cornflour paste.

Mr De Cruz's Favourite Satay Chicken

Mr De Cruz was a boarder in my maternal grandmother's home in Emerald Hill Road in the 1940s. He ate with the family and this satay recipe was one of his favourites from my grandmother's repertoire. I never really knew what he did for a living, but he stayed with my grandparents for many years and was considered part of our family until he moved away in the early 1960s.

Serves 4

1 cup chopped shallots or red onions
2 fresh red chillies (or to taste)
1 teaspoon prepared shrimp paste (Thai or Asian, available in most Asian food stores)
4–5 candlenuts (or use macadamia nuts or almonds)
1 teaspoon sugar
salt and pepper to taste
1.5kg (3lb) chicken pieces

Blend the shallots, chillies, shrimp paste, candlenuts, sugar, salt and pepper in a food processor or blender until they form a fine paste.

Rub the paste over the chicken pieces and stand for a minimum of 3 hours or preferably overnight in the fridge. To cook, either bake in a moderate oven preheated to 190°C (375°F) for 20 minutes or barbecue until cooked through.

Serve with plain rice and a green salad.

Mango Chicken

In this recipe the sharp taste of the fish sauce brings out the sweetness of the mango. Fresh mango gives the best flavour but well-drained tinned mango is a good substitute. This makes a good summer dinner served with a glass of riesling or pinot gris.

Serves 4

oil for frying chicken
4 skinned and boned chicken breasts, cut into 1cm (3/8 in) cubes
3 tablespoons vegetable oil
1 tablespoon crushed garlic
1 red chilli, seeded and finely sliced
1/2 cup snow peas, blanched
3 tablespoons fish sauce
1 teaspoon lime juice
sugar and salt to taste
1/2 cup mango, sliced
1/2 cup peeled and diced tomatoes
1/2 cup cashew nuts

Heat oil in a frypan or wok.

Brown the chicken, drain and put aside.

Heat the vegetable oil in a separate pan and sauté the garlic and chilli until fragrant. Add the browned chicken, snow peas, fish sauce, lime juice, sugar and salt. Stirfry until the chicken is tender.

Just before serving, add the mango, tomato and nuts. Stir through until warm.

Serve with a crisp salad and rice.

Crispy Fried Chicken

Memories of hot, tasty, mouth-watering crispy chicken wings dipped in a mixture of cut chillies and soy sauce inspired this recent development. I suspect it had its origins in the Malay culture as my earliest memory of this taste came from my pre-teen years, from the food that our Malay housekeepers gave us at Hari Raya (the end of the fasting time for Muslims).

Serves 4

juice of 2 limes
1/2 cup light soy sauce
1/4 cup rice wine (gin may be used as a substitute)
2 tablespoons white sugar
freshly ground black pepper
1 teaspoon crushed garlic
1/2 teaspoon salt
1 tablespoon finely chopped coriander
1kg (2lb) chicken wings (about 12 pieces)
oil for deep frying

wedges of fresh lime to garnish

Combine the first 8 ingredients and marinate the chicken wings in the mixture for at least 2 hours or preferably overnight.

Heat the oil until very hot, reduce the heat and immediately deep fry the chicken wings until golden brown and cooked. This should take about 10 minutes. Drain and serve immediately with wedges of fresh lime.

Soy Sauce Chicken

This recipe takes me back to my childhood when I had my own 'amah' or nanny to look after me until I was 10. Her job was to take me to school, tidy up after me, feed me and amuse me. She would even bone the chicken after cooking so I did not have to dirty my little hands. This dish truly appeals to young children as it is tasty and comforting, especially in winter when accompanied by steaming fragrant jasmine rice.

Serves 6

marinade

1 tablespoon rice wine
1 teaspoon crushed fresh ginger
1 teaspoon light soy sauce
pepper to taste

2kg (4lb) chicken pieces, bone in
2 tablespoons vegetable oil
1 spring onion, thinly sliced
1 thumb-sized piece fresh ginger
1 teaspoon crushed garlic
1 tablespoon rice wine
1/2 cup light soy sauce
1/4 cup dark soy sauce
1/4 teaspoon five-spice powder
200ml (7fl oz) water
1 teaspoon sugar

Combine all the marinade ingredients and marinate the chicken pieces for 30 minutes.

Heat the oil in a saucepan and stirfry the spring onion, ginger and garlic until fragrant. Add the remaining ingredients and bring to the boil. Add the chicken pieces and bring back to the boil.

Turn the heat down very low and simmer until chicken is tender and the gravy reduced by a quarter.

Serve with plain white rice.

Kung Pao Chicken Dice

This is the quintessential Szechuan dish. Legend has it that a new governor or 'Kung Pao' was assigned to the Szechuan province at the end of the Ching dynasty. To welcome him, the noblemen held a special banquet and instructed the chefs to prepare some new dishes. This dish was his favourite and was duly named Kung Pao Chicken Dice in his honour.

Serves 4

500g (1lb) boneless chicken cut into 1cm (3/8in) cubes
oil for frying
1 tablespoon fried peanuts

seasoning 1
1 egg white
1 teaspoon salt
1 tablespoon cornflour

seasoning 2
25g (1oz) dried chillies cut into 2cm (3/4in) lengths (remove seeds for a milder dish)
1 teaspoon crushed garlic

seasoning 3
1 tablespoon light soy sauce
1 tablespoon rice wine
1 teaspoon sugar
1 teaspoon white vinegar
1 tablespoon cornflour
1 teaspoon sesame oil

Marinate the chicken in seasoning 1 for 30 minutes. Heat the oil in a wok or frypan and fry the chicken until cooked. This should take only a few minutes.

Drain the chicken and set aside, retaining the hot oil.

Use a little of this oil to stirfry seasoning 2 ingredients for a while, taking care not to burn the chillies. Add seasoning 3 and mix well. Add the cooked chicken and fried peanuts and stirfry for a few more seconds.

Serve with white rice.

Hainanese Chicken Rice

One of the highlights of growing up in Singapore was the 'takeaway' culture. It was far more convenient and cheaper to 'buy home' (as my family referred to sending out for take-aways) than cook from scratch.

My favourite takeaway was (and still is) Hainanese Chicken Rice. Two dollars bought a boned and sliced braised chicken leg, a large cup of steaming fragrant jasmine rice cooked with chicken stock, and sliced raw cucumber and pineapple. The sauces make the dish. Traditional sauces are chilli vinegar sauce, finely grated salted ginger and oil, and dark soy sauce. Nothing is wasted in the preparation of Hainanese Chicken Rice. The stock that the chicken is cooked in is used for the rice and soup if there is any remaining. There is no added fat so the condiments are what make the dish come alive.

Serves 4

enough chicken stock to cover a 1.5kg (3lb) chicken
1 teaspoon light soy sauce
1 teaspoon crushed garlic
1 teaspoon crushed fresh ginger
1 spring onion, chopped into quarters
1 tablespoon coriander, chopped
1 tablespoon rice wine (gin may be used as a substitute)
1.5kg (3lb) chicken
glaze for the cooked chicken made of 1 teaspoon each of dark soy sauce, oyster sauce and sesame oil

garnish

1 cucumber, seeded, skinned and sliced
½ small pineapple, skinned and sliced
fresh coriander
Flavoured Rice (see page 108)
Chilli Ginger Sauce (see page 122)

In a large stockpot, bring the stock, soy sauce, garlic, ginger, spring onion, coriander and rice wine to the boil. Carefully immerse the whole chicken in the stock. Turn off the heat, cover the pot and let the chicken stand for 15 minutes. Remove the chicken from the pot, plunge into a sink of cold water and drain. Bring the stock back to the boil, add the chicken and repeat the steeping process two or three times until the chicken is cooked (about 45 minutes steeping time in total).

Reserve the stock for cooking the rice and the soup course.

Cut the chicken into bite-sized pieces and brush with prepared glaze. Bone the chicken if desired.

Garnish with cucumber and pineapple and serve with flavoured rice, chilli ginger sauce and dark soy sauce.

Serve the remaining stock as accompanying soup.

Paper Wrapped Chicken

My best memory of this dish is the fragrance of the sesame oil when the packages are fried. If done well, the chicken is hot, tender and juicy. The novelty of having to undo a package to reach your food makes a great dinner party talking point. In the old days this was a very popular Yum Cha dish.

Serves 4

1.5kg (3lb) chicken pieces

seasoning

2 sprigs coriander, finely chopped

2 spring onions, finely chopped

5 cloves garlic (or 2 teaspoons crushed garlic)

5cm (2in) piece fresh ginger, finely grated and juiced

1/2 tablespoon rice wine

1 teaspoon five-spice powder

3 tablespoons oyster sauce

2 tablespoons light soy sauce

1 teaspoon sesame oil

1 teaspoon dark soy sauce

1 teaspoon salt

1/2 teaspoon sugar

1/2 teaspoon pepper

2 teaspoons cornflour

greaseproof paper made into 10cm x 15cm (4in x 6in) bags (use a stapler or secure with toothpicks)

1 tablespoon vegetable oil mixed with 1 teaspoon sesame oil

2 cups vegetable oil for deep frying

cucumber and tomato slices to garnish

Put the chicken into a large bowl.

Add the seasoning ingredients and marinate for at least 3 hours.

Lightly brush the inside of the bags with the combined oils.

Put a piece of chicken in each bag (or 2 pieces if they are small) and secure the open end with a toothpick.

Heat the oil for deep frying in a wok or saucepan and, when hot, deep fry the packages until the chicken is cooked – about 15 minutes. If necessary reduce the heat so as not to scorch the paper bags.

Drain the packages on kitchen paper and serve hot, garnished with cucumber and tomato slices.

Have finger bowls available if required.

Sesame Chicken Cakes

When time is of the essence, these chicken cakes make a great entrée or finger food. When I do have the time, I make double or triple the recipe, freezing the pre-shaped cakes and keeping a quantity of the dipping sauce in the fridge for emergencies. (If you are going to freeze a batch, make sure that you are using fresh, not thawed, chicken.)

Serves 4 as an entrée

dipping sauce

1 teaspoon crushed garlic
1 teaspoon sugar
1 tablespoon sesame oil
2 tablespoons white vinegar
4 tablespoons light soy sauce
1 teaspoon toasted sesame seeds
1 spring onion, thinly sliced

chicken cakes

500g (1lb) skinned and boned chicken meat, minced
1 1/2 teaspoons sesame seeds, toasted
1 tablespoon grated fresh ginger
pinch ground black pepper
1/4 teaspoon cayenne
1 tablespoon light soy sauce
1 teaspoon sesame oil
3 tablespoons oil for frying

1 bunch mesclun greens to garnish

Blend all the dipping sauce ingredients and set aside.

In a mixing bowl, combine all the chicken cake ingredients. Form mixture into twelve 5cm (2in) flat cakes.

Preheat a skillet over a medium–high heat and add the oil. When hot, fry the chicken cakes in a single layer until cooked and golden brown on both sides.

Serve garnished with mesclun greens and the dipping sauce on the side.

Fragrant Soy Roasted Duck Breast

Many years ago there was a goose and duck man who parked his hawker cart by the Singapore River and from it sold the best-tasting and most succulent soy-braised goose and duck I have ever eaten.

My favourite cuts were goose wings and duck drumsticks. You could buy any amount of any combination you chose. Mr Goose and Duck man would chop the braised meat up into bite-sized pieces if required, using his enormous cleaver on a mammoth round chopping block. I recall having to leap aside on many occasions to avoid the small fragments of flying sauce and bone.

This is my attempt at braised duck. These days, supermarkets have duck available on request, in any cut required. I have used breasts but experiment with variations if you wish.

Serves 2 for a main or 4 for an entrée

2 duck breasts (about 500–600g/1lb), skin on
1/2 teaspoon five-spice powder
1 cinnamon stick (about 8cm/3in long)
6 star anise pods
10 cloves
2 teaspoons crushed garlic
1/2 cup light soy sauce
1 tablespoon dark soy sauce
1 tablespoon white sugar
1 stalk lemon grass, bruised
1 teaspoon ground turmeric
1 cup water

Place the duck breasts in a small roasting pan and marinate in the rest of the ingredients for at least 2 hours, but preferably overnight.

When ready to cook, preheat the oven to 200°C (400°F). Remove the duck from the pan, and place the roasting pan with the marinade on the element and bring to the boil. Turn the heat to low, put the duck breasts in again and simmer for about 5 minutes.

Then put the pan in the oven and roast until the duck is cooked but still pink. This should take 15–20 minutes. Remove the duck and keep it warm while you reduce the pan drippings to make a sauce. To do this, place the roasting dish back on the element and bring to the boil. Boil gently until the juices are reduced a little – about 5 minutes.

To serve, slice the breasts into thin slices, arrange attractively on individual plates or a platter and drizzle with the sauce. Garnish with the used cinnamon stick and star anise pods if still intact.

Serve with steaming jasmine rice.

In the introduction to his most recent book *A Cook's Tour*, the inimitable Anthony Bourdain asks, 'You're getting the electric chair tomorrow morning. They're gonna strap you down, turn up the juice, and fry your ass until your eyes sizzle and pop like McNuggets. You've got one meal left. What are you having for dinner?' My answer would have to be steamed blue swimmer crab with cut chilli and soy sauce. I'd also need chicken congee (rice porridge), Hainanese Chicken Rice and Bluff oysters too.

I love crab. In this chapter, I am shamelessly making a bid for people to eat more crab. I know that you will get your hands dirty. I know that it takes much determination, skill and bloody-mindedness to extract the meat. But it's worth it! There is nothing more delicate yet flavoursome than freshly cooked crab. I do think that our convenience-foods generation has almost lost the ability to enjoy the tactile experience and satisfaction of preparing a meal from scratch and eating with our fingers.

seafood
sweet & delicate

My fondest memory of Sundays in Emerald Hill Road with my parents is of lunch after church. Dad went to the wet market and brought home leaping shrimp and fresh crab with each little claw individually bound to prevent nipped fingers. My grandmother would have the steamer and boiling pot ready and in minutes we would be feasting on the best food in town. The sublime flavour of the fresh seafood needed no adornment.These meals lasted ages and there was much conversation to be had as well. Magic.

I grew up with the truth that all seafood must be fresh or even alive just before cooking. The eyes of fish must be bright and the smell fresh, clean and not 'fishy'. Twenty years ago, I mourned the total lack of fresh fish and shellfish. These days, we have the luxury of being able to be insistent about the quality and freshness of most seafood and I look forward to the day when live prawns become available as well.

Fresh seafood needs little intervention to bring out the sweet, delicate tastes. In fact, a case has to be made here for 'less is more'.

Shrimp and Scallops in Coconut Lime Sauce

I began a love affair with ceviche in Fiji. The taste of limes and coconut is so compelling that once the thought occurs, gratification must be immediate. This Thai version can be served with drinks. Use little forks or toothpicks.

Serves 4

250g (8oz) large shrimp
2 teaspoons salt
250g (8oz) scallops
2 1/4 teaspoons sugar
1/3 cup fresh lime juice
1/2 cup coconut cream
garnish
2 shallots, thinly sliced
1 red chilli, coarsely chopped
1 green chilli, coarsely chopped
1 tablespoon chopped fresh coriander leaves

Shell and devein the shrimp. Toss with 1 teaspoon of the salt and stand for 10 minutes. Rinse with cold water, drain and pat dry.

Toss the shrimps and scallops with the sugar, lime juice and remaining salt in a bowl.

Set aside for 10 minutes.

Arrange the seafood and marinade in a single layer on a heatproof microwave dish and pour the coconut cream over it.

Microwave on high for 5 minutes until the shrimp are bright orange and firm. Garnish with shallots, chillies and coriander.

Serve warm or chilled.

Coconut Chilli Prawns

The sweetness of the coconut brings out the sweetness in the prawns in this recipe – it's fabulous with a glass of pinot noir.

Serves 4

1kg (2lb) large prawns
2 tablespoons grated coconut
1 teaspoon aniseed powder
1 teaspoon white pepper
1/4 cup water
6 tablespoons vegetable oil
3 onions, 1 sliced and 2 coarsely chopped
sprig of curry leaves
4 tomatoes, peeled and chopped
1 red chilli, cut lengthwise and seeded
1 teaspoon chilli powder
1 level teaspoon ground turmeric
salt to taste

Trim off the prawn beards and tails, leaving the shell on. Carefully slit the prawn backs and remove the cord. Set aside.

Blend the coconut, aniseed powder and pepper with the water.

Heat the oil and fry the coconut mixture until it is fragrant, then add the sliced onion.

Continue frying until the onion becomes translucent.

Add the curry leaves and tomatoes and fry until the tomatoes are soft. Add all the other ingredients.

Cook covered until the prawns are bright red and cooked and the gravy is thick.

Serve hot with rice.

Prawn Toasts

White rice is, and always will be, a staple ingredient in the Asian diet. But we also do great things with bread and this recipe is one example. Asian bread recipes usually involve covering a slice of bread with a tasty spread of minced meat or seafood, frying until crisp and serving in bite-sized pieces. This is a very simple and effective recipe that is ideal with drinks or in a lunch box.

Serves 6 as an entrée

500g (1lb) uncooked prawns, shelled and deveined
1 teaspoon salt
1 spring onion, minced
½ teaspoon grated fresh ginger
1 teaspoon rice wine or dry sherry
½ teaspoon cornflour
1 Chinese sausage, coarsely chopped
6 slices thick white bread

Put all the ingredients except the bread in a food processor and process until combined. Divide into 6 portions and spread each portion evenly over a slice of bread.

Grill or deep fry until golden brown.

Cut into small triangles and serve hot with a sweet chilli sauce.

Broiled Prawns with Tomato and Hot Bean Sauce

Sunday lunches at Emerald Hill Road were legendary. Accompanying my father home from the market were crawling crab, leaping shrimp and fresh green prawns destined to be steamed with chilli and soy sauce. Perfect.

Serves 4

8 king prawns
oil for frying
1 tablespoon minced fresh ginger
1 tablespoon minced spring onion
2 tablespoons minced garlic
1/4 cup tomato sauce
1 tablespoon hot bean sauce
1 tablespoon cornflour mixed with 3 tablespoons water

seasoning

1 tablespoon rice wine
1 teaspoon salt
1 tablespoon light soy sauce
1 teaspoon sugar
1 tablespoon chicken stock powder

Trim off the prawn beards and tails, leaving the shell on. Carefully slit the prawn backs and remove the cord.

Heat the oil in a frypan and cook the prawns over a low heat until they are bright red and well done. Remove and set aside.

Add a little more oil to the frypan if it is dry, then stir in everything except the prawns and cornflour paste. Add the prawns and bring to the boil.

Lower the heat and simmer until there is almost no juice left. Add the cornflour paste. Thicken, then serve immediately.

Otak Otak (Grilled Fish Cakes with Nonya Spices)

Hawkers were mobile in the mid 1960s in Singapore. The Otak Otak man would call his presence in our street, a long pole balanced across his shoulders with a clay barbecue strung to each end. His fish cakes were wrapped in banana leaves and barbecued to order. These days, the cakes are ideal as a spicy summer main course or as a nibble with drinks.

Serves 6

750g (1lb 8oz) white fish fillets
2 teaspoons salt
1 tablespoon sugar
½ teaspoon pepper
1 large egg, beaten
1 recipe spice paste (see below)
4 fresh or frozen kaffir lime leaves
24 medium shrimp, deveined and shelled

spice paste

8 dried red chillies (seeded)
2 stalks lemon grass or 1 tablespoon lemon grass powder
2 slices fresh ginger
2 candlenuts or macadamia nuts
2 spring onions
3 cloves garlic
½ teaspoon turmeric
¾ teaspoon ground coriander
½ teaspoon shrimp paste or anchovy paste
1 cup coconut cream

Put the fish into a food processor and process to a fine paste. Add the salt, sugar, pepper and egg and process until combined.

Transfer the mixture to a bowl and fold in the spice paste until well combined. With wet hands, shape into 24 patties.

Place the patties on a baking tray and grill under a medium heat until golden on one side. Turn and cook the other side.

Serve warm with a salad. Alternatively, the mixture may be spread on toast points, then grilled and served as finger food.

For the spice paste, soak the chillies in hot water for 15 minutes.

Add all the ingredients (except coconut cream) to a food processor and process until fine.

Heat ¼ cup of the coconut cream in a saucepan over a medium heat, stirring until it becomes thick and oily. Add the contents of the food processor and cook until the mixture is fragrant and oily – about 5 minutes.

Add the remaining coconut cream. Bring to the boil, stirring constantly. Cook until incorporated. Cool before adding to the fish mixture.

Spice paste can be made a few hours ahead or frozen until required.

Drunken Fish

This recipe comes from my father's ancestors, the Teochew people who originated from Swatow, a city at the mouth of the Han River in the Guangdong (or Canton) province of China. I love the simplicity of the flavours. In Singapore, we would use a fish called pomfret, and its closest substitute is flounder or sole. You will need a steamer big enough to hold a whole flounder weighing about 1kg (2lb). Fillets may be used, but as Dad's mum would say, 'If you use the whole fish, the bones will make the dish sweeter.'

Serves 2

1 whole flounder weighing about 1kg (2lb), gutted and scaled with the skin on
60g (2oz) pickled mustard greens (choy sum), finely sliced
1 tomato, cut in wedges
3 tablespoons shredded fresh ginger
2 spring onions, sliced diagonally into 4cm (1 1/2 in) lengths
2 red chillies, seeded and finely sliced
4 dried Chinese mushrooms, soaked in hot water until soft, stems removed and sliced finely
1/4 cup oyster sauce
1 teaspoon sesame oil
2 tablespoons light soy sauce
1 tablespoon sugar
2 tablespoons rice wine
1/2 cup chicken stock

Find a moderately deep heatproof dish (a pie dish is ideal) that will fit in the steamer and also hold the flounder.

Place the flounder in the dish and spread all the other ingredients evenly over it.

Put the dish into the steamer and cover tightly.

Steam for 15–20 minutes or until the fish is just cooked.

Serve immediately.

Pickled mustard greens are available fresh or in tins from most Asian food stores. Shredded cabbage with a teaspoon of white vinegar may be substituted.

If a large steamer is not available, wrap the dressed flounder in aluminium foil and bake in a 180°C (350°F) preheated oven.

Tamarind Fish

My great friend Margaret and I were in Wellington recently and happened upon a tiny Asian noodle house in Lambton Quay where we had a delicious Tamarind Fish Curry with steaming white rice. It reminded me of this most beloved Nonya recipe, which is so easy to cook and looks great on the plate. Here is my version.

Serves 2

1 teaspoon ground turmeric or a thumb-size piece of turmeric, finely grated
1 1/2 tablespoons shrimp paste (or sambal blachan)
1/4 cup vegetable oil
12 small red onions, finely sliced
2 teaspoons crushed garlic
1 stalk lemon grass, sliced
4 fresh chillies, seeded and finely sliced
6 tablespoons tamarind pulp soaked in 3 cups water, strained, use only the liquid for the recipe
500g (1lb) firm white fish fillets cut into 4cm (1 1/2in) strips (snapper or hapuku)
6 tablespoons sugar
1 teaspoon salt

Process the turmeric and shrimp paste and set aside.

In a hot pan, add the oil and stirfry the onions, garlic, lemon grass and chillies. Remove the mixture and set aside, keeping the leftover oil in the pan.

In the same pan, stirfry the turmeric and shrimp paste with a little water to prevent catching on the bottom of the pan. When fragrant, add the tamarind juice, stir and bring to the boil. Add the fried ingredients, fish, sugar and salt.

Simmer for 10 minutes or until the fish is just cooked.

Serve immediately with plenty of white rice to mop up the gravy.

Bakwan Kepiting (Crab and Pork Ball Soup)

The key to this delicious Nonya soup is good chicken stock. I make my stock from either chicken frames or necks available from all supermarkets. For seasoning I use garlic, fresh coriander, a dash of soy sauce, salt and pepper to taste.

This soup was part of my maternal grandmother's Chinese New Year menu and evokes happy memories of fire crackers, late nights for a small girl, presents of little red envelopes of crisp new money and pretty new dresses.

Serves 6

meatballs

250g (8oz) lean pork
125g (4oz) raw prawns, shelled
125g (4oz) fresh or canned crabmeat
2 dried black Chinese mushrooms, soaked and finely sliced
1 tablespoon grated carrot, boiled for 1 minute
1 spring onion, finely sliced
1 egg
1 teaspoon cornflour
½ teaspoon salt
white pepper to taste

soup

1 tablespoon vegetable oil
2 cloves garlic, finely sliced
5 cups chicken stock
1 cup finely shredded bamboo shoots
salt to taste

garnish

fresh coriander leaves
fried onion flakes
fried sliced garlic

Combine all the meatball ingredients in a food processor and blend until fine. Any white fish may be used instead of the prawns. Put aside.

Heat the oil in a heavy-bottomed saucepan and quickly fry the garlic until golden brown. This should take a few seconds. Add the chicken stock and bamboo shoots and simmer for 15 minutes.

Shape the pork mixture into 2½cm (1in) balls and drop into the simmering stock. Cook for 10–15 minutes.

Serve piping hot, garnished with fresh coriander and onion and garlic flakes.

Both onion and garlic flakes are available from most Asian food stores. If unavailable, thinly slice 100g (3½oz) each of small red onions and garlic and fry in hot oil until golden brown. This should only take a minute. Drain on paper towels and store in airtight jars. Makes enough for 2 recipes.

Curry Leaves Crab Marsala

Eating at The Banana Leaf in Singapore is extraordinary: seated at long communal tables – no reservations or private tables, and ordering from a buffet of mouthwatering Southern Indian curries. A waiter spoons steaming basmati rice onto your very own banana leaf. Another waiter offers jugs of ice-cold freshly squeezed sweetened lime juice. The food is superb. I have, in the face of the amusement of Banana Leaf staff, NZ Agriculture and Fisheries and the distress of flight attendants, accompanied 12 cooked Banana Leaf Blue Swimmer Curry Crabs back to Auckland just to prolong the experience. This recipe is close. Even without blue swimmer crab the taste is sensational, just use equivalent amounts of prawns or crayfish (rock lobster). Forget the table cloths, roll out the bibs, kitchen paper and finger bowls.

Serves 4

3/4 cup water
50g (2oz) curry leaves
30g (1oz) coriander leaves
15 blanched almonds
10 cloves garlic
3cm (1 1/4in) piece fresh ginger
4 green chillies
10 shallots
1/2 cup vegetable oil
1 onion, sliced
a few sprigs curry leaves
1 1/2 teaspoons aniseed, coarsely pounded
1 teaspoon dhal
5 tomatoes, peeled and chopped
6–7 crabs, cleaned, shelled and cut in half
1 teaspoon ground turmeric
2 teaspoons ground cumin
1 tablespoon ground coriander
2 teaspoons ground chilli
salt to taste
1/4–1/2 cup water

Blend the first eight seasoning ingredients in a food processor until they form a fine paste of seasoning.

Heat the oil and fry the onion, curry leaves, aniseed and dhal, until fragrant. Add the tomatoes and seasoning paste and stirfry until fragrant and well mixed, approximately 10 minutes, making sure the paste does not burn.

Add remaining ingredients (including crabs) and heat, stirring occasionally, until thoroughly cooked.

Serve hot with crusty French bread.

Dhal (Indian lentils) is available in most supermarkets and health food stores.

Crab Summer Salad

My father's measure of true love was whether or not someone would hand-shell a crab for you. He really loved me. I guess you could view this recipe as a test of true love, based on Dad's definition, as it calls for cooked fresh crabmeat. For the unromantic among us, crabmeat is readily available in cans or on request at fish markets. Crabmeat is used in this recipe to create a delicately flavoured, fresh summer salad that can be served as a first course or a light lunch with a crisp pinot gris.

Serves 4

1/3 cup plus 1 teaspoon rice vinegar
1 tablespoon sugar
1/2 teaspoon soy sauce
1/4 teaspoon salt
1/4 teaspoon wasabi paste
250g (8oz) cooked crabmeat, well drained
1 small, thin cucumber
4 leaves green or red-leaf lettuce
garnish
1 sheet of nori (seaweed sheets used for sushi), cut into 3cm x 1cm (1 1/4in x 3/8in) strips (use scissors)

Mix the 1/3 cup rice vinegar, sugar, soy sauce, salt and wasabi in a small bowl. Stir to dissolve the sugar then put aside.

Place the crabmeat in a bowl; break into coarse shreds, removing any bits of shell or cartilage. Sprinkle with the remaining 1 teaspoon rice vinegar and toss lightly.

Cut the cucumber crosswise into very thin slices.

Add the cucumber to the crab meat, add the dressing and toss lightly until thoroughly mixed. Line a serving bowl or 4 individual bowls with lettuce. Spoon the crabmeat mixture over the lettuce.

Garnish with nori strips.

Deep Fried Squid

My paternal grandmother came from Southern China. She had the '101-wonderful-ways-with-squid' prize. Here is her Squid Wisdom – baby squid must be crisp, large squid must be tender and all squid must be very fresh. This recipe can be served with a fresh green salad or with steamed white rice.

Serves 4

1kg (2lb) baby squid 4–5cm (1 1/2–2in) long
oil for deep frying

marinade

3 tablespoons fish curry powder
2 tablespoons light soy sauce
1 tablespoon sugar
1 teaspoon sesame oil
2 tablespoons cornflour
1 egg, lightly beaten

sauce

1 tablespoon vegetable oil
2 tablespoons honey
1 tablespoon tomato sauce
1 tablespoon Worcestershire sauce
1 tablespoon fresh lime juice
1 tablespoon chilli sauce
1 tablespoon light soy sauce
1 teaspoon sesame oil
1 teaspoon dark soy sauce
1 cup chicken stock
2 tablespoons cornflour mixed with 1/4 cup water

Wash and dry the squid thoroughly. Do not remove the tentacles or skin.

Mix all the marinade ingredients and combine with the squid.

Meanwhile, make the sauce. Heat the vegetable oil in a wok and add all the ingredients except the blended cornflour.

Bring to the boil, then add the cornflour and cook over a low heat until thickened and clear.

Heat the oil for deep frying in another wok or frypan and deep fry the squid until crisp and brown, then drain.

Stir into the sauce and serve immediately.

Salmon Teriyaki

My introduction to this salmon dish was in Fukuoka, in the early 1970s. I was at a ryokan (Japanese inn) and we were served tiny baby salmon, delicately flavoured and perfectly grilled, as part of a glorious banquet. This dish is based on that memory and is fabulous on a bed of udon noodles and served with a fresh green salad.

Serves 4

500g (1lb) salmon steaks or fillets
2 tablespoons soy sauce
1 tablespoon mirin
2 teaspoons sake
1 teaspoon sugar
75g (3oz) daikon, peeled
1 tablespoon vegetable oil

Cut the salmon into 4 equal pieces and place in a shallow glass bowl.

Mix the soy sauce, mirin, sake and sugar in a small bowl and stir to dissolve the sugar. Pour the marinade over the salmon and stand for 10 minutes. Drain and set aside, reserving the marinade.

Grate the daikon, then drain but do not squeeze. Set aside.

Heat the oil in a medium skillet over a medium heat. Fry the salmon for 2–3 minutes or until light brown. Turn and cook about 2 minutes more or until the fish flakes easily with fork. Reduce heat to low and add the marinade. Cook just until the salmon pieces are well-coated and the sauce is hot – about 1 minute.

Serve immediately with grated daikon and pan juices from the skillet if desired.

My earliest memory of beef is Sizzling Shashlick Steak at The Emerald Steak House on the ground floor of Emerald Mansions, the apartment block where my parents and I lived from the time I was six until I was 12 years old. It was my father's favourite meal at our 'local' restaurant and it was an event each time the very large piece of sirloin was brought sizzling on a red-hot cow-shaped cast-iron steak plate nestled in its own wooden tray. It must have been a popular dish as I recall being lulled to sleep most nights by the delicious smell of sizzling Shashlick Steak floating through my bedroom window, which was just a few feet away from the restaurant kitchen.

In my experience in Asia, the Malay people eat beef, the Chinese favour pork and the Malay and Indian Muslims have wonderful lamb and mutton recipes. However, not as much meat is consumed as chicken, fish or vegetables. My paternal grandmother took much care in preparing any meat, making sure that the cooking smells were either heavily disguised or

meat
succulent morsels

eliminated in the cooking. I have always wondered if this is why most Asian meat dishes tend to be highly seasoned or spiced.

Until I came to New Zealand in 1976, I didn't eat much lamb. The smell of lamb cooking was something that my family found intolerable and the myth that strong body odour was the result of too much lamb was common among the Chinese friends I grew up with. This all changed, though, and I recall the days when we would put a leg of lamb or mutton in the oven before church and come home several hours later to the mouthwatering smells of a roast in progress. Our juicy Sunday roasts with pumpkin, kumara, minted baby peas, crispy roasted armadillo potatoes and gravy were a far cry from the grey silverside and lifeless cabbage of my boarding school days.

The selection of recipes in this chapter mostly use common cuts of meat available in supermarkets or butchers, although some cuts may have to be requested. The recipes are also easy to prepare, taste great and look spectacular.

Barbecued Beef Salad Wrapped in Rice Paper

I love the freshness of Vietnamese food. The mint, lime and garlic create a riot of tastes on the palate and set the juices running. This dish is perfect for a summer lunch with a chilled beaujolais or as an entrée. It is excellent for a group of people who don't know each other as it provides a talking point at the beginning of the meal.

Serves 6

500g (1lb) boneless beef round (2½cm/1in thick)
2 stalks fresh lemon grass, white part only (or 2 tablespoons dried lemon grass soaked in warm water for 1 hour)
2 shallots
3 cloves garlic
1 fresh serrano chilli
1 tablespoon sugar
1 tablespoon Vietnamese fish sauce (nuoc nam)
1 tablespoon sesame oil
1 tablespoon sesame seeds
50g (2oz) dried rice stick noodles
boiling water
12 large red lettuce leaves
1 small English cucumber, peeled and cut in thin matchsticks
24 fresh mint leaves
36 fresh coriander leaves, each with a little stem

Nuoc Cham Dipping Sauce (see page 123)
12 x 30cm (12in) dried rice paper circles

Cut the beef into 8cm x 2cm (3in x ¾in) pieces. Slice each piece across the grain into 5mm (¼in) thick strips.

Slice lemon grass into 2cm (¾in) lengths and put them into a food processor with the shallots, garlic, chilli and sugar and process to a paste. Transfer to a bowl and mix in the fish sauce, sesame oil and sesame seeds. Add the beef slices, and marinate for at least 3 hours or overnight.

In a bowl cover the rice stick noodles with boiling water, stand 1 minute, then drain. Arrange the noodles, lettuce, cucumber strips, mint and coriander in separate piles on a platter, leaving space for the beef. Refrigerate. Just before serving, barbecue the beef strips for 30 seconds on each side until nicely seared. Arrange the beef on the platter.

Have a dish of dipping sauce and one or more wide bowls of warm water on the table. Each guest dips a rice paper circle into a water bowl and immediately spreads it flat on a dinner plate or a damp towel. The circle will rehydrate and become pliable in a few seconds.

To make a rice paper roll, lay a lettuce leaf in the middle of the moistened circle. Top it with 2 or 3 slices of beef, a tablespoon of noodles, several strips of cucumber and a few leaves of mint and coriander. Fold the near edge of the paper over the filling, then roll up the paper around the filling, keeping it taut. Halfway through, fold over one end to enclose the filling, then continue rolling. Dip the open end of the roll into the dipping sauce and eat with your fingers.

Beef with Oyster Sauce

In this very traditional Chinese recipe oyster sauce adds a rich flavour to the beef.

Serves 4

marinade

1/2 teaspoon baking soda
1 teaspoon sugar
1 tablespoon cornflour
1 tablespoon soy sauce
3 tablespoons water
2 tablespoons vegetable oil

500g (1lb) lean beef (scotch or fillet)
8 tablespoons oil
500g (1lb) broccoli, cut into small pieces
2 teaspoons rice wine
1/2 teaspoon salt
1 teaspoon sugar
3 spring onions, cut into 2cm (3/4in) lengths
15 slices fresh ginger
2 tablespoons oyster sauce
1 tablespoon water
1 teaspoon sugar
1/2 teaspoon cornflour
1/2 teaspoon sesame oil

Slice the beef very thinly into 2.5cm (1in)-long strips, then put in a bowl with the marinade ingredients.

Marinate for at least 30 minutes (this can be done the day before and kept covered in the fridge). Just before cooking, add 2 tablespoons cooking oil and mix well.

Cook the broccoli in boiling water for about 2 minutes. Drain.

Heat a frypan with 2 tablespoons of the oil and quickly stirfry the broccoli for 1 minute, seasoning with the wine, salt and sugar. Remove to a plate.

Heat the remaining 6 tablespoons oil in a frypan until hot. Add the beef and fry until it is cooked – this should take about 10 seconds.

Remove the beef and drain the oil from the frypan, retaining 2 tablespoons. If there is no remaining oil, add another 2 tablespoons to the pan.

Fry the spring onions and ginger in the remaining oil. Return the beef to the frypan and stir quickly over high heat before adding the remaining ingredients. Stir until thickened and heated through.

Pour over green vegetables and serve with plain white rice.

Peking Braised Lamb

Back in the days when I had access to lamb from my parents'-in-law Hawke's Bay farm, I would bone it myself. But these days cubed and packaged supermarket lamb definitely suffices!

Serves 4

2 tablespoons vegetable oil
4 spring onions, cut into 2 1/2cm (1in) lengths
4 slices fresh ginger
1 large onion, finely sliced
1kg boned lamb shoulder (weight excludes bones), cut into smallish cubes
4 aniseed pods
4 teaspoons smooth peanut butter
1 cinnamon stick
3 tablespoons dark soy sauce
2 tablespoons rice wine
2 tablespoons hoisin sauce
60g (2oz) rock sugar (or white sugar)
2 cups stock

Preheat the oven to 180°C (350°F).

Heat the oil in a cast-iron casserole (if not using cast iron, perform all pre-cooking steps in a wok or frypan and transfer to an ovenproof casserole for the oven).

Sauté the spring onions, ginger slices and onion until fragrant. Add the lamb cubes and brown.

Add the remaining ingredients. Bring to the boil then remove from the heat.

Place the casserole in the oven and bake for 1 hour or until the lamb is tender and the sauce is reduced by half.

Serve with white rice.

Beef Rendang

Rendang is a traditional Malay dish with a distinctive rich coconut taste. My mother always says that to rush a rendang is to spoil it, so leave plenty of time to cook this popular Malay dish. In fact, it is best to prepare it one or two days ahead of time to allow the flavour to soak into the beef.

Serves 4

1 x 400ml can coconut cream
2 teaspoons sugar
1/2 teaspoon salt
750g (1lb 8oz) beef, rump or fillet, cut into 3cm (1 1/4in) cubes
1 onion, sliced

seasoning

1 tablespoon ground coriander
1/2 teaspoon ground cumin
1/2 thumb-sized piece fresh ginger, pounded or minced
1 1/2 tablespoons chilli powder (or less if preferred), blended to a paste with a little water
1 stalk lemon grass, bruised or peel of 1/2 lemon

Place the coconut cream, sugar and salt in a saucepan. Add the seasoning ingredients, mix well, then add the meat and onion. Bring to the boil over a high heat, then simmer gently until the meat is cooked and tender – add more water if necessary. Stir occasionally to prevent the spices from settling on the bottom of the saucepan.

Serve with fragrant turmeric rice or plain rice and a salad.

Chinese Fillet Beef Steak

In many Chinese restaurants, the sizzling steak is brought to the table on a preheated cast-iron hotplate. This is an adaptation of that popular dish. It is important to marinate the meat for as long as you can as this tenderises the meat and gives it the distinctive crunchy texture for which this dish is well known.

Serves 4

500g (1lb) fillet steak, sliced 1cm (1/2in) thick

marinade

3/4 cup water
1 1/2 teaspoons baking soda
1 teaspoon sugar
3/4 teaspoon salt
2 1/2 teaspoons light soy sauce
1 teaspoon Worcestershire sauce
2 tablespoons cornflour
2 tablespoons vegetable oil
1/2 egg, beaten
1/4 cup oil for frying

gravy

3/4 teaspoon sugar
1/4 teaspoon salt
1/2 teaspoon sesame oil
1 1/2 tablespoons tomato sauce
1 1/2 tablespoons Worcestershire sauce
1/2 cup water

Allow as much time as possible to prepare the meat – up to 9 hours.

Soak the sliced meat in water for 1 hour. Drain the meat and discard the water. Flatten and dry the meat between clean tea towels or paper towels.

Mix together all the marinade ingredients and marinate the meat strips for up to 8 hours, refrigerated.

To serve, mix the gravy ingredients in a small saucepan and bring to the boil. Take off the heat and set aside.

When ready to serve, heat a frypan until very hot, add about 1/4 cup oil and heat until it smokes.

With the frypan over a very high heat, place the pieces of meat in it one at a time.

Turn the meat over and fry for 2 minutes.

Remove the cooked meat to a serving platter and cover it with gravy.

Serve immediately with fried or white rice, or stirfried rice noodles and a plain green vegetable.

Sautéed Lamb with Spring Onions

This dish comes from the north of China, also home to its famous cousin Peking Duck. The secret is to use the highest heat and cook quickly, as this seals the juices for a tender result.

Serves 4

500g (1lb) lean lamb (use lamb loin preferably), sliced very thinly
2 tablespoons light soy sauce
salt to taste
2 tablespoons Chinese rice wine
1/2 teaspoon ground white pepper
2 tablespoons vegetable oil (to marinate lamb)
1 tablespoon dark soy sauce
2 tablespoons brown vinegar
2 tablespoons sesame oil
500g (1lb) spring onions (trim the tops and slice diagonally into 4cm (1 3/4in) lengths)
3 tablespoons oil for frying
6 large cloves garlic, thinly sliced

Marinate the lamb in a bowl with the light soy sauce, salt, wine, pepper and oil for at least 15 minutes. This can be done well in advance if time permits.

In a small bowl, combine the dark soy sauce, vinegar and sesame oil. Set aside.

Assemble the marinated lamb, spring onions and small bowl of seasoning sauce close by your cooking surface, as the next step needs to be done quickly.

In a frypan preheat the remaining oil until very hot.
Add the garlic and lamb pieces and stirfry quickly for about 10 seconds. Add the spring onions and seasoning sauce and toss through until thoroughly heated and the lamb is just cooked.

Serve immediately.

Beef or Mutton Satay

One of my fondest memories of Singapore is the smell of cooking satay floating through the neighbourhood and the sweet anticipation of biting into a small, perfectly formed stick of satay beef. The satay man was one of the regular hawkers on Emerald Hill Road where I lived for most of my childhood. We would signal him to stop, place an order and he would barbecue the sticks of delicious satay in his charcoal burner on our front porch.

Serves 4

500g (1lb) mutton, veal, rump or fillet ends, cut into small pieces
oil for grilling

marinade

2 candlenuts or hazelnuts
1 clove garlic
2 slices fresh ginger
4 shallots
2 teaspoons ground coriander
1 teaspoon ground turmeric
1 teaspoon ground cumin
1 teaspoon salt
2 tablespoons sugar
2 tablespoons oil
3 tablespoons peanuts, roasted and ground

Soak 20 satay sticks or skewers in water for 30 minutes to prevent burning.

Put all the marinade ingredients in a food processor or blender and process until it forms a fine paste.

Rub the marinade into the meat and leave for 1 hour. Thread a few pieces of meat on the top half of each satay stick. Grill the meat, brushing with additional oil to prevent burning. This can also be done on the barbecue.

Serve with a peanut sauce (see page 86).

Hainanese Oxtail Stew

My mother has been cooking oxtail stews since I was about five years old. Her recipe is the classic red wine-based oxtail stew from her many contacts with expat British and New Zealanders living in Singapore in the late 1960s and early 1970s. I discovered that the Hainanese had their own recipe and, after many attempts at reproducing the flavours, I arrived at this version that has become an instant hit at dinner parties.

Tamarind, as the key flavour, lifts the taste to another dimension. The key to using tamarind well is to include a little sugar, as this takes the edge off the fruit's acidity.

Serves 4

2kg (4lb) oxtail pieces
6 tablespoons oil
10 little red onions
2 teaspoons crushed garlic
2 tablespoons chilli paste (or reduce to suit taste)
1 teaspoon ground turmeric
3 tablespoons tomato paste
2 cups tamarind juice (available from most Asian food stores. Alternatively soak 200g (7oz) tamarind pulp in 2 cups water, strain and squeeze for the juice)
2 tablespoons sugar
5 kaffir lime leaves (if unavailable, substitute the thinly sliced rind of 2 green limes)
2 stalks lemon grass (cut off tops and bash the ends with a rolling pin to release the flavour)
5 slices fresh ginger (or 1 teaspoon ground ginger)
12 cups water
salt and pepper to taste

Preheat the oven to 180˚C (350˚F).

Trim as much fat off the oxtail pieces as possible. Heat 2 tablespoons of the oil in a cast-iron casserole that has a tight-fitting lid and brown the oxtail pieces. (Use a wok or frypan if a cast-iron casserole is not available and transfer to an ovenproof casserole when ready.) Remove the oxtail pieces and drain on kitchen paper.

Put the onions, garlic, chilli paste and turmeric in a blender or food processor and blend until it forms a fine paste. Heat the remainder of the oil in the casserole and add the prepared spice paste, stirring constantly to prevent burning. Continue frying until fragrant. This should take about 5–7 minutes. Add the tomato paste, tamarind juice, sugar, lime leaves, lemon grass, ginger, water and oxtail.

Cover the casserole and bake in the oven for 3 hours or until the oxtail is tender, stirring occasionally to prevent sticking.

Before serving, carefully skim off as much of the oil that has floated to the top of the cooking liquid as possible.

Serve with steaming hot fragrant jasmine rice.

Babi Assam (Tamarind Pork)

My grandmother always said that cooking was about balance. Consequently, whenever tamarind is used, a bit of sugar is required to balance the sourness and bring out the full flavour. A simple and delicious treatment of pork, this is one of the well remembered tastes of my childhood. The sour tamarind taste cuts through the richness of pork.

Serves 4

spice paste

4 candlenuts

20 shallots

1 tablespoon shrimp paste

1/3 cup vegetable oil

1 1/2 tablespoons salted soybeans, pounded

600g (1lb 5oz) belly pork, cut into cubes

1 teaspoon salt

2 1/2–3 tablespoons sugar (adjust to taste)

1 tablespoon tamarind paste, mixed with 2 1/4 cups water and drained; discard tamarind pulp and reserve liquid

10 green chillies, slit lengthwise

5 red chillies, slit lengthwise

Put all the spice paste ingredients in a food processor and process until they form a fine paste. Set aside.

Heat a frypan until hot and add the oil. Reduce the heat to low. Stirfry the spice paste until fragrant and light brown, stirring constantly so as to prevent sticking.

Adjust to a medium heat, sprinkle in a little water, then add the soybeans and pork. After a few minutes, sprinkle with water again to prevent burning, then add the salt, sugar and tamarind water.

Bring to the boil and cook until the liquid has reduced by half.

Add the chillies and simmer until the pork is tender.

Serve with plain white rice.

Babi Tempra (Braised Pork in a Thick Sweet and Sour Lime Sauce)

The mark of a great Peranakan cook is the perfection of the Babi Tempra – to quote one of the best, my mother, 'Not too sweet, not too sour, just right.' This brings to mind the feature common to all my culinary mentors – constant tasting. I have been taught that one must always taste the food one cooks, and taste several times, not just once. My maternal grandmother would taste once for sweetness, once for saltiness, once for hotness and so on.

Here the richness of the pork is well balanced by the limes. For best results, keep overnight. Chicken or fish may be used instead of pork.

Serves 4

1/3 cup vegetable oil
4 onions, sliced thinly
4 fresh chillies, sliced crosswise
600g (1lb 5oz) lean pork, sliced
4 tablespoons sugar
4 tablespoons dark soy sauce
4 tablespoons lime juice
1/2 teaspoon salt

Heat a frypan until very hot, add the oil and when hot stirfry the onions. Add the chillies then the pork.

When the pork is half cooked, add the sugar, lower heat to medium, and add the soy sauce, lime juice and salt. Simmer for 2 minutes.

Variations

Chicken Tempra

Cut half a small chicken into small pieces. Prepare in exactly the same manner, but add 1/4 cup water before simmering.

Fish Tempra

Fry 300g (10oz) fish (any firm white fish, in small steaks) in some oil. Remove the fish and discard the oil. In the same frypan, add the 1/3 cup oil and fry the other ingredients. Once the sauce is ready, add the fried fish, coat it well with sauce, and serve immediately.

Bak Kuk The (Singapore Pork Rib Tea Soup)

This can be served as a main course with a side of white rice, or as a starter. The flavouring can sometimes be bought as a prepared spice bag (resembling bouquet garni) from Asian food shops, but skimming the broth is still the most important step for a nicely flavoured but clear soup.

Serves 4 to 6

500g (1lb) pork back ribs, chopped into 5cm (2in) lengths
1 large clove garlic, crushed
6 cups water
1 cinnamon stick
3 whole star anise
1 teaspoon white peppercorns
1 1/2 teaspoons sugar
1 level teaspoon salt
3 tablespoons dark soy sauce, or to taste

garnishes

2 tablespoons crisp fried small red onion flakes (may be bought ready fried, or deep fry finely sliced red onions until brown then drain)

soy sauce and thinly sliced red chillies, for dipping

Combine the pork, garlic and water in a large saucepan and bring to the boil. Cook for 5 minutes. Skim and discard the scum from the surface.

Add the cinnamon, star anise, peppercorns, sugar, salt and soy sauce. Reduce the heat to low and simmer until the pork is tender, about 45 minutes.

Discard the excess fat from the soup before serving. Serve the soup in deep bowls with 3–4 pieces of pork per serving and onion flakes scattered over the top.

Combine the soy sauce and chillies to taste in small bowls as a dipping sauce.

Serve with a bowl of white rice on the side.

Tau Yu Bak (Soy Sauce Pork)

This dish is a taste of my childhood that my daughters also know well. I can recall, at the age of three or four, my nanny running after me with a bowl of Tau Yu Bak and rice, hoping to make me stand still long enough to sneak a spoonful into my unsuspecting mouth. I was much more intent on playing in the garden of our Katoug home than on dinner. While I never succumbed to chasing after my daughters to get them to eat, I introduced them to this dish at a very young age and it continues to be a favourite. This dish can be prepared in advance and improves with standing in the refrigerator overnight. A leaner cut of pork may be used if preferred.

Serves 4 to 6

1 tablespoon vegetable oil
600g (1lb 5oz) belly pork, skin on and cut into cubes
6 cloves garlic, pounded or mashed
1/3 cup sugar (or less to taste)
3/4 cup dark soy sauce (or less to taste)
1 1/4 cups water

Heat a frypan until hot, add the oil, then the pork and fry until brown. Lower the heat. Add the garlic and sugar and fry until the sugar glazes the meat.

Add the soy sauce, mixing well. After a few minutes, add enough water to cover the meat and simmer until the meat is tender – about 30 minutes.

Serve with white or fried rice and a green vegetable.

I grew up knowing vegetables were never 'just' vegetables. I have clear memories of 'temple food' as my granny called it. Temple food was vegetarian food made in the Buddhist temples and sold by the monks and nuns in the markets. The most remarkable thing about this food was that the predominantly soy bean-based product it contained was moulded and coloured to resemble meat. From soy bean sausages and drumsticks to steak and lamb chops made from vegetables, the sheer artistry was undeniable. The only problem was it all tasted the same!

The vegetable stalls in the Singapore wet markets were visually stunning. I could never forget the abundance of iridescent green leaves nestled close to deep purple eggplant, piled high beside dazzling orange carrots, or the piles of earthy yams and potatoes invaded by coiling snake beans and pyramids of snowy white beansprouts. After inspecting them all closely we would make our choice and return home, suitably laden.

vegetables
essential sides

Cleaning and preparing vegetables ready for cooking is something I associate with my great-grandmother. It was one of the meticulous processes that belonged to her alone, in the semi open-air kitchen of the house in which my mother was born. I recall my great-grandmother sitting in her little cane chair with a tray on her knee that held at least a kilo of beansprouts. She would methodically tail each one until every sprout was 'cleaned'. Phenomenal.

Vegetables are an essential accompaniment to all Asian meals. Often the simplest green vegetable such as bok choy is steamed and served with a dash of oyster sauce – a perfect companion to a spicy main course.

The rule for vegetables is not to overcook them. The best flavours are obtained by blanching or stirfrying until crisp then enhancing the natural taste with a little sauce.

The selection of dishes I have chosen for this chapter are all perfect as side dishes, with Gado Gado especially good as a vegetarian main course.

Stuffed Dried Mushrooms with Broccoli

Dried Chinese mushrooms have an intense and delicious flavour similar to porcini mushrooms. This dish is mostly seen as part of Yum Cha selections, but can be served on a Chinese spoon to have with drinks or as a side for dinner. Mushrooms can be prepared beforehand and stored in the refrigerator for several hours before steaming.

Serves 6

12 large dried black Chinese mushrooms
2 cups warm water
1 tablespoon vegetable oil
2 cloves garlic, smashed and chopped
1 chicken stock cube
2 teaspoons cornflour mixed with 1 tablespoon cold water
250g (8oz) broccoli, broken into florets, cooked until tender just before serving

filling

250g (8oz) raw prawn meat
100g (3 1/2 oz) fresh or canned crabmeat
3 water chestnuts
1/2 teaspoon salt
white pepper

Rinse the mushrooms then leave to soak in the warm water for about 2 hours. Drain, reserving the liquid. Discard stems and squeeze the mushrooms dry.

Heat the oil in a saucepan and gently fry the garlic for about 15 seconds. Raise the heat and add the mushrooms. Stirfry for 1 minute, then add the mushroom soaking liquid and stock cube. Simmer very gently for about 1 hour or until the mushrooms are tender.

While mushrooms are simmering, prepare the filling. Combine the ingredients in a food processor or chop all the ingredients with a cleaver to get a paste.

Remove the mushrooms from the cooking liquid, drain and cool. Thicken the cooking liquid with the cornflour paste and set the sauce aside. When cooled, sprinkle the inside of each cap with a little cornflour. Press on some of the filling, mounding it slightly.

Steaming: Use a regular steamer or fill the bottom of a wok with about 2 1/2 cm (1in) of water, and balance 2 chopsticks 7 1/2 cm (3in) apart in the bottom. Place the mushrooms in a single layer on a heatproof plate and balance on top of the chopsticks. Cover with the wok lid and steam for 20 minutes.

Arrange the mushrooms in the centre of a serving platter. Combine any liquid in the steaming plate with the prepared sauce. Reheat the sauce and pour over the mushrooms. Arrange broccoli around the edge of the platter and serve.

Gado Gado

An Indonesian vegetarian dish, this is wonderful for a summer barbecue or as a substantial main course. The peanut sauce can also be used to accompany mutton or beef satay (page 74) and in fact both satay and Gado Gado are often served together.

Serves 4

500g (1lb) beansprouts
1kg (2lb) cabbage, shredded
6 small bean curd cakes, deep fried and cut into strips
500g (1lb) long beans or green beans, cut into 4cm (1 1/2 in) lengths and parboiled
500g (1lb) potatoes, boiled until cooked, then sliced
1 large cucumber, skin left on, sliced diagonally
10 hard-boiled eggs, sliced
200g (7oz) lettuce
fried prawn crackers to garnish

Peanut Sauce

2/3 cup vegetable oil
6 cloves garlic, pounded
10 shallots
2 tablespoons pounded chillies or 1 tablespoon chilli powder
2 stalks lemon grass, bruised, or peel of 1/2 lemon
1 tablespoon tamarind paste
1/2 cup water
500g (1lb) peanuts, roasted and ground (or 350g [11 1/2 oz] jar of crunchy peanut butter)
450ml (16fl oz) water
1/2 cup sugar
salt to taste

Blanch the beansprouts and cabbage. Prepare the remaining vegetables and then arrange them all on a large platter. Just before serving, pour over the peanut sauce (which should be at room temperature) and garnish with prawn crackers.

For the peanut sauce: Heat a frypan until very hot. Add the oil and stirfry the garlic, shallots, chillies and lemon grass or peel until fragrant. Remove the lemon grass. Prepare the tamarind juice by mixing the tamarind paste with the water. Strain and add the liquid only. (As an alternative, use 1 tablespoon of lemon juice.) Simmer for 1 minute.

Add the ground peanuts and water. Bring to the boil then add the sugar and salt.

Boil until the mixture is thick – this should take about 15 minutes.

Eggplant Curry

I used this recipe when making one of my first attempts at cooking Indian food and it was an immediate hit. It can be served with steak or as a vegetarian main course with a green salad and rice or as a side dish with steak.

Serves 6

375g (13oz) eggplant
1 1/2 teaspoons salt
1/4 teaspoon ground turmeric
1/2 cup vegetable oil
1 teaspoon coriander seeds
1/2 teaspoon cumin seeds
1/4 teaspoon fennel seeds
1/4 teaspoon brown mustard seeds
pinch fenugreek
1/2 teaspoon chilli powder
2 tablespoons vegetable oil
1 medium onion, sliced
1 clove garlic, finely chopped
1 cup coconut milk
2 teaspoons vinegar

Cut the eggplant across in slices. Sprinkle with 1 teaspoon salt and the turmeric. Heat oil in a frypan and fry the eggplant for 2 minutes on each side. Set aside.

Roast the coriander, cumin, fennel, mustard seeds and fenugreek in a dry pan until dark brown, then grind finely. Add the chilli powder and enough cold water to make a stiff paste.

Heat the second measure of oil and fry the onion and garlic until soft. Add the spice paste and fry for 2–3 minutes, adding a little more oil if the mixture threatens to stick to the pan. Pour in the coconut milk and bring to the boil, stirring constantly. Add the fried eggplant and 1/2 teaspoon salt and simmer for 3–5 minutes.

Add the vinegar, cook a moment longer, then serve either hot or cold.

Fried Beansprouts

Beansprouts are an underrated vegetable. The Chinese use beansprouts in many noodle dishes to add a crisp, fresh consistency. It is very important not to overcook beansprouts as they go mushy very quickly. This recipe is a simple side dish for most meat dishes.

Serves 2
250g (8oz) beansprouts
2 tablespoons vegetable oil
1 clove garlic, lightly crushed
4 slices fresh ginger
1 teaspoon light soy sauce
1/4 teaspoon salt
2 spring onions, cut in 2 1/2 cm (1in) lengths

Wash the beansprouts, drain thoroughly and pinch off any brown straggly tails.

Heat the oil in a wok and fry the garlic until golden, then discard, retaining the flavoured oil. Fry the beansprouts and ginger in the garlic-flavoured oil over a high heat, tossing constantly, for 1 minute. Add the soy sauce, salt and spring onion and continue to stirfry for another minute. The beansprouts should be slightly crisp.

Sambal Timun

Serves 6
sambal
3 tablespoons dried prawns
1 teaspoon dried shrimp paste
2 fresh red chillies
2 tablespoons Chinese lime juice or juice from half-ripe kumquat or lemon
1–2 teaspoons sugar
1/2 teaspoon salt

2 medium cucumbers
150g (5oz) belly pork, boiled in one piece and sliced, or 1 chicken liver and 1 chicken gizzard, boiled and sliced

Prepare the sambal mixture first. Soak the dried prawns in hot water for 10 minutes, drain, then pound coarsely and set aside. Thoroughly grill the dried shrimp paste on both sides then pound together with the chillies. Add the prawns, then pound a little, then mix in all the other sambal ingredients. Add more sugar and lime juice to taste.

To remove any bitterness from the cucumber, cut 1cm (3/8in) off the top. Rub the cut portion in a circular motion for 30 seconds over the cut surface. A white 'scum' will accumulate on both surfaces. Discard the cut top portion. Repeat with the second cucumber, then cut in half lengthwise and cut diagonally into pieces about 2 1/2 cm (1in) wide.

Combine cucumber, sliced meat and sambal. Serve immediately to prevent softening.

Spinach with Sesame Seed Dressing

I have always loved Japanese food for its simplicity, elegance, healthiness and purity of flavours. Malaysian and Indian curries create delightful mayhem with the tastebuds and addiction to the chilli taste is a very real phenomenon, but the minimalistic elegance of the Japanese taste is equally seductive, leaving us with a feeling of wellbeing and wanting more.

For this reason, I frequently rely on Japanese vegetables to complement the spicier treatments of the food from the rest of Asia. The nuttiness of the sesame seeds is perfect with the spinach in this recipe.

Serves 4

2 1/2 tablespoons white sesame seeds
1/2 teaspoon sugar
2 teaspoons Japanese soy sauce
1 1/2 tablespoons dashi
4 cups water
1/4 teaspoon salt
350g (12oz) spinach

Heat the sesame seeds in a small heavy-bottomed frypan over a medium heat until the seeds are golden, shaking the pan constantly. Put the toasted seeds, sugar, soy sauce and dashi in a food processor and process until smooth. Set aside.

Bring the water to the boil in a saucepan, add the salt and blanch the spinach until tender. This should take 2–3 minutes. Drain the spinach and rinse under cold running water to stop the cooking process. Drain and squeeze the spinach to remove excess water. Cut into bite-sized pieces.

Put spinach into a bowl, add the dressing and toss to mix. Serve with a main course and rice.

Taukwa Goreng (Spicy Bean Curd Salad)

Bean curd is versatile, nutritious and delicious. There are many types – the two most common are soft and hard bean curd. It is important to use the hard variety for this recipe as deep frying soft bean curd until golden brown is impossible. This recipe is great for lunch or to accompany a summer barbecue.

Serves 4

4–5 large pieces hard bean curd or tofu
oil for deep frying
1 small cucumber
150g (5oz) beansprouts

sauce

2–3 fresh red chillies, seeded (reduce number for a milder dish)
4 shallots or 1/2 medium red or brown onion
2 tablespoons palm sugar
4 heaped tablespoons crunchy peanut butter
1 tablespoon thick black soy sauce
1/3 cup tamarind water (1 tablespoon tamarind paste mixed with 1/2 cup water and strained, retaining the liquid and discarding the pulp)
salt to taste
1/4 cup water

Wipe the bean curd dry with a paper towel and deep fry in hot oil for 4–5 minutes until golden brown. Drain, then cut into thick slices. Leave to cool.

Prepare the sauce by processing chillies and shallots with just a little water until fine. Add the palm sugar and process to mix, then combine with all other ingredients. Put the sauce into a bowl.

Scrape the skin of the cucumber with a fork, rub with a little salt, rinse, then slice finely. Blanch the beansprouts in boiling water for 30 seconds, drain, run under cold water to refresh, then drain thoroughly.

To serve the salad, arrange cucumber slices on a large platter. Put the sliced bean curd on top and scatter with beansprouts. Pour over the sauce and serve immediately.

Chinese Mustard Greens and Oyster Sauce

This dish epitomises the phrases 'simple is best' and 'less is more' to perfection. A regular feature at Yum Cha, I always watch with fascination every time the vegetable trolley approaches our table. The waiter patiently blanches and cuts the vegetables with speed and precision. It's truly an art.

The crisp, fresh and uncluttered texture and taste of this dish is the perfect foil for most highly seasoned meals.

Serves 4

6 cups water
1 teaspoon salt
500g (1lb) Chinese mustard greens
6 tablespoons oyster sauce

Bring the water and salt to a rolling boil in a wok or large saucepan.

Quickly blanch the Chinese mustard greens in the boiling water until the stalks are just tender and the leaves are still bright green – this should only take 2–3 minutes.

Drain the vegetables and cut into 10cm (4in) lengths.

Arrange in a neat pile on a serving tray and drizzle with oyster sauce just before serving.

Japanese Pumpkin

Another great example of 'simple is best'. This recipe relies on a good, nutty, flavoursome pumpkin or squash. The sugar accentuates the nuttiness of the vegetable and the result is a mouth-filling accompaniment to any meat dish.

A family favourite, this dish was championed by Ruth and Elizabeth's dad, Hugh, who is a devotee of Japanese food.

Serves 4

500g (1lb) pumpkin or squash
1 1/2–2 cups dashi
2 1/2 tablespoons sugar
1 tablespoon mirin
1 1/2 tablespoons Japanese soy sauce

Cut the pumpkin in half and remove the seeds. Wash and cut into pieces about 5cm (2in) square. Remove the skin if desired.

Place the pumpkin, skin-side down, in a heavy saucepan. Add 1 1/2 cups dashi, the sugar and mirin.

Heat to boiling over a medium heat. Boil vigorously for 4 minutes then gently turn pieces over. Continue boiling, covered, for 4 more minutes.

Add the soy sauce and the remaining dashi, if needed.

Continue boiling, covered, for 7–8 minutes longer, just until tender. Serve hot or cool to room temperature.

Szechuan Eggplant

I grew up calling eggplant 'brinjal'. Dad's mum was fabulous with eggplant. She always salted eggplant pieces to remove the bitterness and frequently cooked it with salted fish pieces and minced pork. This was where I learned that you cannot hurry a good thing. Salting the eggplant pieces was relatively easy, it was the minced pork that took the time. My grandmother would hand mince the pork. After removing the thick skin, she would cut the slab of meat into smaller and smaller pieces. Then, using a large meat cleaver on a well pitted board, she would begin the mincing. The house would fill with the sound of the fast, rhythmic thumping of the cleaver on wood. This continued until she had the finest of smooth-textured mince.

This is a variation on my grandmother's recipe. I have left out the salted fish – it has an aroma that is an acquired taste and the addition of oyster sauce more than compensates for the slight salty seafood taste so essential to the dish. Firm purple eggplant works best.

Serves 6

1kg (2lb) eggplant (aubergine), cut into 3cm (1 1/4 in) cubes
1 tablespoon salt
1/2 cup vegetable oil
500g (1lb) finely minced pork
2 teaspoons chopped fresh ginger
1 teaspoon crushed garlic
1 tablespoon hot bean paste
2 tablespoons light soy sauce
3 tablespoons oyster sauce
1 teaspoon sugar
1 level teaspoon salt
3/4 cup stock (chicken or vegetable)
2 teaspoons brown vinegar
2 teaspoons sesame oil
2 tablespoons chopped spring onion

Sprinkle the eggplant with the salt and mix it through. Let the mixture stand in a colander over the sink or a plate (to catch any drips) for 15 minutes. Thoroughly rinse the eggplant with cold water to remove the salt.

Heat 6 tablespoons of the oil in a wok or deep frypan until hot. Add the rinsed eggplant pieces, turn the heat to low and stirfry for 3 minutes or until the pieces are soft. Drain the eggplant on paper towels, pressing slightly to remove excess oil, and set aside.

Heat the remaining oil in the same pan and brown the pork, breaking up the mince into fine pieces. Add the ginger, garlic and the hot bean paste and stirfry for a few seconds. Then add the soy sauce, oyster sauce, sugar, salt and stock and bring the mixture to the boil. Turn the heat to low and simmer for 5–7 minutes, until the minced pork is cooked.

Add the drained eggplant and cook for another minute or until the sauce has reduced slightly. Add the vinegar and sesame oil and stir well. Mix in the spring onion. Serve with white rice.

When I cast around for words to describe the place noodles and rice occupied in the world that I grew up in, 'essential', 'comfort', 'limitless', come to mind. I remember when I first had beef, but my memory does not stretch back far enough to the time I had my first grain of rice or string of noodles. I suspect that my children are the same.

I recall my parents' amazement when they heard that I was able to store 10kg bags of rice in non-airtight containers in Dunedin and not attract weevils. In humid Singapore, the bag would have been infested within days.

I had the honour of introducing a little girl to the joys of noodle eating (her parents have eclectic tastes and I have adopted them as honorary Singaporeans because they are my only non-Asian friends who request cut chilli and soy sauce when we eat at Asian restaurants). The Pink Princess, Lucy, was two at the time and reigning supreme from her high chair throne.

noodles & rice
staples of life

Realising that I was dealing with a virgin noodle eater, I picked up a single egg noodle in my chopsticks and placed the end gently into the tiny rosebud mouth, readying myself to rescue any rejected bits. The single noodle disappeared with the speed and appropriate sound effects of a true native noodle eater and the rosebud mouth was positioned to receive the next offering. Lucy has never looked back and perhaps the memory of our interaction may find its way to the surface when she is grown.

For perfect rice the first prerequisite is a rice cooker. No self-respecting Asian household is without one. My parents had several of varying sizes, the largest of which made rice for 50 people. In fact, they must have known about my future profession 20 years in advance, as I had it sent out to us for The French Café. Alas, it was to no avail. Our Kate insisted on the boiling and straining method (as for pasta). You can take a girl to the rice cooker but you can't make her turn it on!

This chapter contains a wide cross section of essential recipes from many countries.

Fried Hokkien Noodles

The hawkers in Singapore have had their nomadic existences curtailed and are mostly housed in food halls these days. At one time, though, our favourite afternoon sound was the 'klock klock' of bamboo stick on bamboo block to announce the approach of the Noodle Boy. Mr Noodle Boy was the runner for The Noodle Man who would park his cart at the bottom of our road. Mr Noodle Boy took the orders and our empty bowls and, after an efficient amount of time, returned to exchange our bowls of fragrant steaming noodles garnished with pink prawns, white beansprouts and green spring onions for the 50 cents or a dollar we had ready.

Thick fresh yellow noodles are best for this recipe, but dried noodles can be substituted.

Serves 6

500g (1lb) fresh yellow noodles
3 tablespoons vegetable oil
250g (8oz) raw prawns, peeled (reserve shells and heads)
1 cup water
8–10 cloves garlic, pounded finely
2 eggs, lightly beaten
250g (8oz) beansprouts
250g (8oz) boiled belly pork, finely sliced
salt and pepper to taste

garnish

1–2 fresh red chillies, finely sliced lengthwise
2 spring onions, cut in 2½cm (1in) lengths
few stalks or sprigs young celery, finely chopped

Put the fresh noodles in a bowl and cover with boiling water. Stand for 1 minute, then drain and set aside. If using dried noodles, cook as per instructions on packaging.

Heat 1 tablespoon of oil in a saucepan and fry the prawn shells and heads, stirring constantly, for 1 minute. Add the water and bring to the boil. Cover the saucepan and simmer for 5 minutes, then pour through a sieve and discard the shells. Simmer the prawns in this stock until cooked. Strain and reserve the stock.

Heat the remaining oil in a large wok or frypan and gently fry the garlic until golden, to flavour the oil. Discard the garlic, reserving the oil.

Raise the heat, and when the oil is really hot pour in the beaten eggs. Stir constantly for 1 minute, then add the noodles, beansprouts and ½ cup of the prawn stock. Cook over a high heat for 1 minute. Add the cooked prawns, the sliced pork, the remaining stock and salt and pepper to taste. Cook until most of the liquid is absorbed and the pork is cooked through.

Garnish with chilli, spring onion and celery and serve hot.

Simmered Noodle Casserole

This Japanese-inspired winter dish is perfect for lunch.

Serves 4

12 cups water
350g (12oz) dried udon noodles
200g (7oz) skinned and boned chicken, cut into 2cm (3/4in) cubes
1/3 cup plus 1 teaspoon soy sauce
1 tablespoon sake
3/4 teaspoon salt
100g (3 1/2oz) spinach
4 medium or 8–12 small fresh Chinese mushrooms, stems removed
1.3 litres (2 1/4 pints) dashi
1/2 teaspoon sugar
1 medium carrot, pared and thinly sliced (cut slices into halves or quarters if desired)
3 teaspoons mirin
4 eggs
4–6 large spring onions, cut in 4cm (1 1/2in) lengths
seven-spice powder to taste

Bring 8 cups of the water to the boil in a large saucepan. Add the noodles, a few at a time, stirring gently to separate. When the water returns to a full rolling boil, add 1 cup of the cold water. Repeat. When the water returns to the boil, check for doneness. Cook the noodles until firm–tender. Drain and set aside.

Place chicken in a small bowl and sprinkle with 1 tablespoon of soy sauce and all the sake. Let stand for 10 minutes.

Place the remaining 2 cups water, 1/4 teaspoon salt and the spinach in a large saucepan; bring to the boil. Reduce the heat to medium and simmer for 2 minutes. Rinse under cold running water and cut into 2cm lengths..

Place 150ml (5fl oz) dashi, 1 teaspoon soy sauce, the sugar and carrot in a saucepan; bring to the boil. Make shallow, V-shaped cuts on the cap of each mushroom and add them to the pan, after 2 minutes. Boil gently for another minute. Drain and set aside.

Place the chicken, the remaining dashi and soy sauce, salt and the mirin in a large saucepan; bring to the boil over a medium–high heat. Simmer for 5 minutes until chicken is cooked. Just before serving break the eggs into the stock and poach until soft. Reduce the heat to low to maintain a gentle simmer.

Place the noodles evenly in 4 individual (3–4 cup capacity) bowls; top with the vegetables. Pour in the broth to cover the noodles, distributing the chicken evenly. Add the spinach and spring onions. Serve immediately with the seven-spice powder on the side.

Pho Hanoi Beef Soup with Rice Noodles

Quintessentially Vietnamese, this soup is traditionally a breakfast offering but it seems a shame to be deprived of such a meal at any time of the day.

Serves 8

2 x 2 1/2 cm (1in) chunks fresh ginger
3 shallots, unpeeled
1 onion, unpeeled
10 cups water
750g (1 1/2 lb) oxtails, chopped into sections
500g (1lb) beef shanks
2 whole star anise
1 cinnamon stick
3 whole cloves
1/4 cup Vietnamese fish sauce (nuoc nam)
1 teaspoon salt, or to taste
250g (8oz) flat rice stick noodles, soaked in water for 20 minutes
180g (6oz) beef fillet steak, trimmed of fat and sliced paper-thin
2 spring onions, cut in 5cm (2in) lengths
1 onion, sliced very thinly
2 cups beansprouts
1/4 cup coarsely chopped fresh coriander leaves
1 lime, sliced into 8 wedges
2 red chillies, thinly sliced

Put the ginger, shallots and onion on a baking tray and set them under a hot grill until charred.

Combine the water, oxtails and beef shanks in a stockpot and bring to the boil. Thoroughly skim and discard the scum from the surface. Add the charred ingredients, star anise, cinnamon and cloves. Reduce the heat to low and simmer for 2 hours. Remove the oxtails and reserve for another use. Remove the meat from the shanks, shred the meat and reserve. Return the shank bones to the simmering stock. Simmer 1 hour longer.

Strain the stock, discard the bones, degrease the stock, and return it to the stockpot. Add the fish sauce and salt to taste and keep at a low simmer.

Bring 12 cups water to the boil in a separate pot. Drain the noodles, add them to the pot and boil until tender – about 1 minute. Drain the noodles in a colander and divide among 8 deep soup bowls. Top each bowl of noodles with shredded cooked beef, raw beef slices, onions and beansprouts. Ladle about 1 1/4 cups hot stock into each bowl; this will cook the beef. Top with fresh coriander.

Serve with a wedge of lime and chillies for seasoning.

Chilled Summer Noodles

An unusual but very effective dish that Ruth and Elizabeth's dad Hugh was champion of. It is perfect for long summer evenings. Serve with a crisp pinot gris or gewürztraminer.

Serves 4

dipping sauce

350ml (12fl oz) dashi

1/3 cup mirin

1/3 cup soy sauce

12 cups water

350g (12oz) dried somen noodles (soba noodles can be used as an alternative)

12 medium (or 8 large) shrimp, in shells

1/4 teaspoon salt

4 cups ice water

8 to 12 ice cubes

2 small tomatoes, cut into wedges

1 long, thin cucumber (preferably unwaxed), cut diagonally into thin slices

2 spring onions

2 tablespoons grated, peeled, fresh ginger

Boil the dashi, mirin and soy sauce in a large saucepan. Cover the dipping sauce, and refrigerate until cold.

Bring 8 cups water to the boil in a large saucepan. Add the noodles, a few at a time, stirring gently to separate. When the water returns to a full rolling boil, add 1 cup cold water; repeat, using another cup cold water. When the water returns to the boil, check for doneness. When noodles are firm–tender (do not overcook), drain in a colander and rinse well under cold running water. Drain; cover with damp kitchen towel. Cool completely.

Shell each shrimp, leaving the tail and section of shell nearest the tail attached. Remove the veins. Boil the remaining 2 cups water and the salt in a large saucepan over a high heat then add the shrimp. When the water returns to the boil, reduce the heat to medium and simmer until the shrimp are opaque and firm, 2–3 minutes. Drain and cool completely.

Divide the noodles between 4 medium bowls, and add ice water, even with the top of the noodles. Add 2 or 3 ice cubes to each bowl. Top each serving with shrimp, tomato and cucumber. Place dipping sauce in 4 small bowls.

To serve, give each person a bowl of noodles and a bowl of dipping sauce. To eat, dip noodles, vegetables and shrimp in sauce mixed with a choice of spring onion and/or ginger.

Laksa Lemak

Being 'banished' to the ends of the earth had its advantages in the form of regular care packages that arrived from Singapore. Among the goodies Mum would send me were individually portioned homemade vacuum-packed laksa spice paste ground to perfection and ready to go. It was the forerunner of the convenience kits available in supermakets these days. All I had to do was add coconut cream, noodles, garnishes and Singapore had arrived at my dinner table. Laksa is perfect as a winter one-pot meal.

Serves 6

12 dried red chillies, seeded
5 candlenuts or macadamia nuts
100g (3oz) fresh ginger, peeled
5 stalks lemon grass
1 thumb-length piece fresh turmeric or 1 teaspoon ground turmeric
200g (7oz) small red onions, sliced
3cm (1 1/4in)-square piece dried shrimp paste (sambal blachan)
2 cloves garlic, crushed
1 teaspoon peppercorns
1/2 cup oil
20g (3/4 oz) dried shrimp
1 tablespoon ground coriander
3 x 400ml (14fl oz) cans coconut milk
salt to taste
500g (1lb) thick rice noodles

garnishes

2 large fish cakes, sliced, or fish balls
300g (10oz) cooked prawns
1 handful Vietnamese mint
200g (7oz) beansprouts
1 medium cucumber
1 tablespoon chilli paste

Soak the seeded chillies in water for 5 minutes, then drain and slice roughly. Put in a food processor with the nuts, ginger and white part of the lemon grass stalks (discard the remainder). Add the turmeric, onions, shrimp paste, garlic and peppercorns and process to a fine paste. Set aside.

Heat the oil in a deep saucepan until it shimmers. When up to temperature, add the prepared spice paste and the dried prawns (processed or pounded finely) and fry, stirring constantly to prevent catching. Fry until fragrant and the spices are a little crispy and golden brown but not singed.

Add the coriander and continue stirring for 30 seconds. Pour in the coconut milk, reduce heat and simmer gently for 20 minutes. Add salt to taste. Turn off the heat and set aside until you are ready to serve.

While the gravy is boiling, prepare the garnishes. Slice the fish cakes (usually available in Asian food stores or some larger fish markets). Peel the cooked prawns, thinly shred the mint, scald beansprouts for 30 seconds and drain. Seed and peel the cucumber and shred into fine strips.

To serve, place equal amounts of noodles and garnishes into 4 bowls. (If using dried noodles, boil the noodles in water until cooked.) Pour over the hot gravy and serve with chilli paste on the side.

Flavoured Rice

It's best to cook rice by the absorption method or in the microwave if you haven't got a rice cooker. I like fragrant jasmine rice, but these methods also apply to ordinary white rice.

Absorption method

Wash enough rice for 4 people – about 1 cup – until the water runs clear.

Put the washed rice in a heavy-bottomed saucepan with a close-fitting lid, cover with enough hot stock to reach a depth of 1½ cm (¾ in) above the level of the rice. For plain rice, replace stock with hot water.

Cover tightly with the pot lid and bring stock and rice mixture to the boil.

Turn down the heat to the lowest possible setting and 'steam' the rice until all the stock is absorbed – this should take about 15–20 minutes.

Stir the rice to loosen the grains and serve.

Microwave

Place the same amount of washed rice and stock into a microwave-proof container large enough so that the stock will not boil over during cooking time. Cover the container with a lid and microwave on high for 15 minutes.

Stir to loosen and serve.

Easy Fried Rice

This typical easy recipe for fried rice is a great way of dealing with leftovers. The ingredients suggested below are very flexible so use your imagination. My father always said the secret to the best fried rice ever was to begin with cold cooked rice. And, of course, he was never wrong.

Serves 4 as a main or 6 as a side dish

2 tablespoons vegetable oil
1 stalk celery, finely chopped
1 medium red or brown onion, sliced
250g (8oz) of any or several of the following: prawns, raw or cooked; red barbecued pork (char siew); sliced Chinese sausage (lap cheong); lean ham, diced; cooked chicken
2 dried black mushrooms, soaked and shredded
2 eggs
1/4 teaspoon salt
2 teaspoons light soy sauce
4–5 cups cold cooked white rice
2 tablespoons cooked green peas
2 spring onions, finely chopped

sliced fresh red chilli and celery leaves to garnish

Heat the oil in a frypan and gently fry the celery and onion until soft. Add the prawns if using raw and cook until they turn pink. Add the remaining meats and dried mushrooms and cook gently for 3 minutes.

Beat the eggs with the salt and soy sauce and add to the frypan. Stir over a high heat until set. Add the rice and peas and cook, stirring constantly, for 2 minutes.

Mix in half the spring onion and serve garnished with the remaining spring onion, chilli and celery leaves.

Chow Fan (Cantonese Fried Rice)

This is a recipe for Chinese fried rice. 'Chow' means 'to fry', and 'Fan' means 'rice' in Cantonese. My father was the expert fried rice maker in our family. Apart from his golden rule of beginning with cold rice for the best loose, fluffy fried rice, his other pearl of wisdom was uniformity. All ingredients added to the cold rice must be of the same size and shape if possible. He was sure it made the dish look better. Being the precise man that he was, the ingredients were indeed perfectly uniform when Dad was on chopping duty.

Serves 4 as a main or 6 as a side dish

500g (1lb) uncooked rice, washed
3 1/3 cups water
1/2 cup oil
6 eggs
2 teaspoons salt
2 teaspoons light soy sauce
2 teaspoons water
sugar to taste
500g (1lb) prawns, peeled
200g (7oz) pork, cut into small cubes
6 stalks spring onions, finely sliced

Put the rice and water in a heavy-based saucepan with a tight-fitting lid. Cover tightly and bring to the boil over a high heat.

Reduce the heat to low, sit the lid ajar and 'steam' the rice until all the liquid is absorbed and the rice is cooked and fluffy. Pour the rice onto a platter and stand until cold. Rice can be cooked a day ahead, covered in plastic wrap and kept in the fridge.

Heat a frypan until very hot and add half the oil. Beat the eggs until combined and fry until just cooked. Remove from the pan, cut into strips and set aside.

Combine the salt, soy sauce, water and sugar to taste. Set aside. Add the remaining oil to the frypan, stirfry the prawns until half cooked, then add the pork and the soy sauce mix. Stirfry for a further 2–3 minutes until the pork is cooked through.

Add the rice, breaking up any lumps, and stirfry for a few minutes over a medium heat. Add the cooked egg and stirfry for a few minutes.

Serve on a large platter and garnish with sliced spring onions.

Nasi Goreng (Malay Fried Rice)

The difference between Malay fried rice and Chinese fried rice is in the spice paste. Only the Malay people use spice paste which gives the rice a very distinct 'curry' flavour. I have found this a good dish to make when one has to 'bring a plate', as it's economical, tastes great and can be prepared in advance.

Serves 4 as a main and 6 as a side dish

thumb-sized chunk tamarind pulp
1/2 cup boiling water
1 small red onion
1 1/2 tablespoons chopped garlic
2 red chillies, chopped, or 1 teaspoon Indonesian ground chilli paste (sambal ulek)
1 teaspoon shrimp paste
1/2 teaspoon ground turmeric
1 teaspoon salt, or to taste
3 tablespoons vegetable oil
150g (5oz) medium shrimp, shelled and deveined
1/2 cup diced red pepper (capsicum)
1/2 cup peas
1 cup shredded purple cabbage
6 cups cooked long grain white rice
2 tablespoons dark soy sauce
1 tablespoon light soy sauce
3 spring onions, thinly sliced
1/2 cup diced cooked chicken
1/2 cup barbecued pork or ham

garnishes
fresh coriander leaves
sliced cucumber
omelet shreds (fry beaten eggs into thin omelets and shred finely when cool)

Cover the tamarind pulp with the boiling water. Mash the fibres and seeds with the back of a fork. When the tamarind is dissolved, strain it, reserving 1/3 cup of the tamarind water. Discard the pulp. Set aside.

Put the onion, garlic, chillies, shrimp paste, turmeric and salt into a food processor and blend to a fine paste. Shrimp paste can be replaced with anchovy paste if preferred.

Heat a wok over a medium heat. Add the oil and paste of spices and fry gently until brown and fragrant.

Turn the heat to high and fry the shrimp until they turn bright orange.

Add the vegetables and stirfry until crisp.

Add the rice and stirfry until the grains are separated.

Add the rest of the ingredients, including the tamarind water, and cook until heated through.

Garnish with coriander leaves, sliced cucumber and omelet shreds.

Nasi Lemak (Delicious Coconut Rice)

The closest translation for the Malay word 'lemak' is 'rich' or 'delicious'. Cooking with coconut milk gives the rice a rich, creamy taste that is perfect with anything spicy and especially good with grilled or fried turmeric-flavoured fish. My grandmother advised that when cooking with coconut a pinch of salt would bring out the flavour, even in a dessert.

Serves 6 as a side dish

500g (1lb) long grain rice

2 1/2 cups coconut milk

1 teaspoon salt

1 screw pine leaf (optional)

Wash the rice thoroughly, drain and set aside.

Bring the coconut milk slowly to the boil, while stirring constantly. Add the rice, salt and screw pine leaf (if using) and stir. Simmer with the saucepan lid slightly ajar until all the liquid has evaporated. Cover the saucepan tightly, and turn the heat as low as possible and cook for about 20 minutes. Take great care during cooking or the bottom of the rice will burn.

Fluff up the rice with a fork, cover the saucepan, and leave to stand until needed.

Serve as accompaniment for fish or chicken dishes.

Clay Pot Rice

Clay pot cooking is a time-honoured tradition in China and translates beautifully into the Western kitchen. Clay pots withstand very high heats and can be used on the cooktop as well as in the oven. If you do not have a clay pot, a cast-iron casserole is a very good substitute. I have always thought of Clay Pot Rice as the Chinese cousin of Spanish paella. My grandmother's clay pot litany was 'Save time, only one pot to wash and keeps all the goodness in.' I like that a lot.

Serves 4

300g (10oz) boneless chicken, cut into bite-sized pieces
2 tablespoons oyster sauce
2 teaspoons dark soy sauce
1/2 teaspoon sesame oil
2 teaspoons cornflour
pepper to taste
1 Chinese sausage (available in most Asian food stores), cut into bite-sized pieces
1 1/2 cups uncooked jasmine rice
1 1/2 cups water
5 dried Chinese mushrooms, soaked in water for 1 hour, then squeezed dry and stalks removed
100g (3oz) mustard greens (choy sum) or any green leafy vegetable

Preheat the oven to 180°C (350°F).

Marinate the chicken pieces in the oyster sauce, soy sauce, sesame oil, cornflour and pepper. Stand for 10 minutes.

Put the marinated chicken and any residual marinade into a clay pot with the sausage, rice and water. Cover and bake in the oven for 1 hour or until all the water is absorbed and the rice is cooked.

Remove the lid, fluff up the rice with a fork and place the mushrooms and mustard greens on the top of the rice. Replace the lid and return the clay pot to the oven for a further 15 minutes.

Stand for 5 minutes before serving.

The place of soup in our family meals over the years is undisputed. Quite simply, a meal is not complete without a soup dish. Why is this? I suppose it's about tradition – if one does something often enough and for long enough it becomes tradition. This is certainly the case in my family.

As a child the clear soups I consumed at each meal had always been lovingly skimmed by my grandmother, as I have already described in the main introduction to this book. Regarding my own children, I fondly assume that should they ever recount their own 'soup story' at some future time they would most likely speak about the importance of chicken macaroni soup in their lives. This goes back to the days when they were both still tiny, and when I was preoccupied with trying to make the perfect Hainanese chicken rice dish. In the process I generated copious amounts of leftover cooked chicken and soup. Given that my two little princesses adored macaroni (as many small children are inclined to do), and wanted to eat

soups & sauces
warmth & flavour

it at every opportunity, I quickly saw the potential for making a soup with the leftovers. Before long chicken macaroni soup – with the addition of the basic but essential combination of cut chilli and soy sauce – had taken on major comfort food status for the whole family and remains so to this day.

It's time to talk about sauces – or more specifically one of the main ingredients of Asian sauces, chilli. On our table at home one could always find cut fresh chilli, pickled green chillies, chilli sauce, shrimp chilli paste, chilli oil and, of course, the mandatory bottle of soy sauce.

For years I have puzzled over the seductive nature of the taste of chilli, which to me is just not logical. It can bring tears to the eyes, a glow to the cheeks, it can even make the room swim. I recall my father's reaction to banana leaf prawn curry (a dish so hot it practically glows in the dark). He hissed through his teeth in pain, and the beads of perspiration on his fevered, albeit receding hairline proclaimed to all and sundry that this curry was the best in the world. Only chilli can cause such a juxtaposition of culinary pain and pleasure.

Chicken and Macaroni Soup

Both children and adults love this soup as a comfort dish that is perfect for lunches. It is a good idea to make this dish using the leftover stock from Hainanese Chicken Rice (see page 35).

Serves 4–6

4 litres (8 pints) water
1/2 teaspoon peppercorns
1 small chicken
300g (10oz) macaroni
1 chicken stock cube
salt to taste
1 teaspoon sugar
garnish
4 slices bread, cut into cubes and deep fried to make croutons
20 shallots, sliced and fried
4 stalks Chinese celery

Bring the water to the boil with the peppercorns. Submerge the whole chicken in the pot, bring back to the boil and simmer until the chicken juices run clear. Remove the chicken, cool and shred the meat off the carcass, putting the bones back into the stock. Reserve the meat and simmer the bones for another 30 minutes. Meanwhile cook the macaroni according to the maker's instructions. Add the stock cube, salt and sugar to the soup.

To serve, divide the macaroni between 4–6 bowls depending on the size of the meal. Arrange the chicken meat on top and pour hot soup over the cooked ingredients.

Garnish with the croutons, shallots and celery.

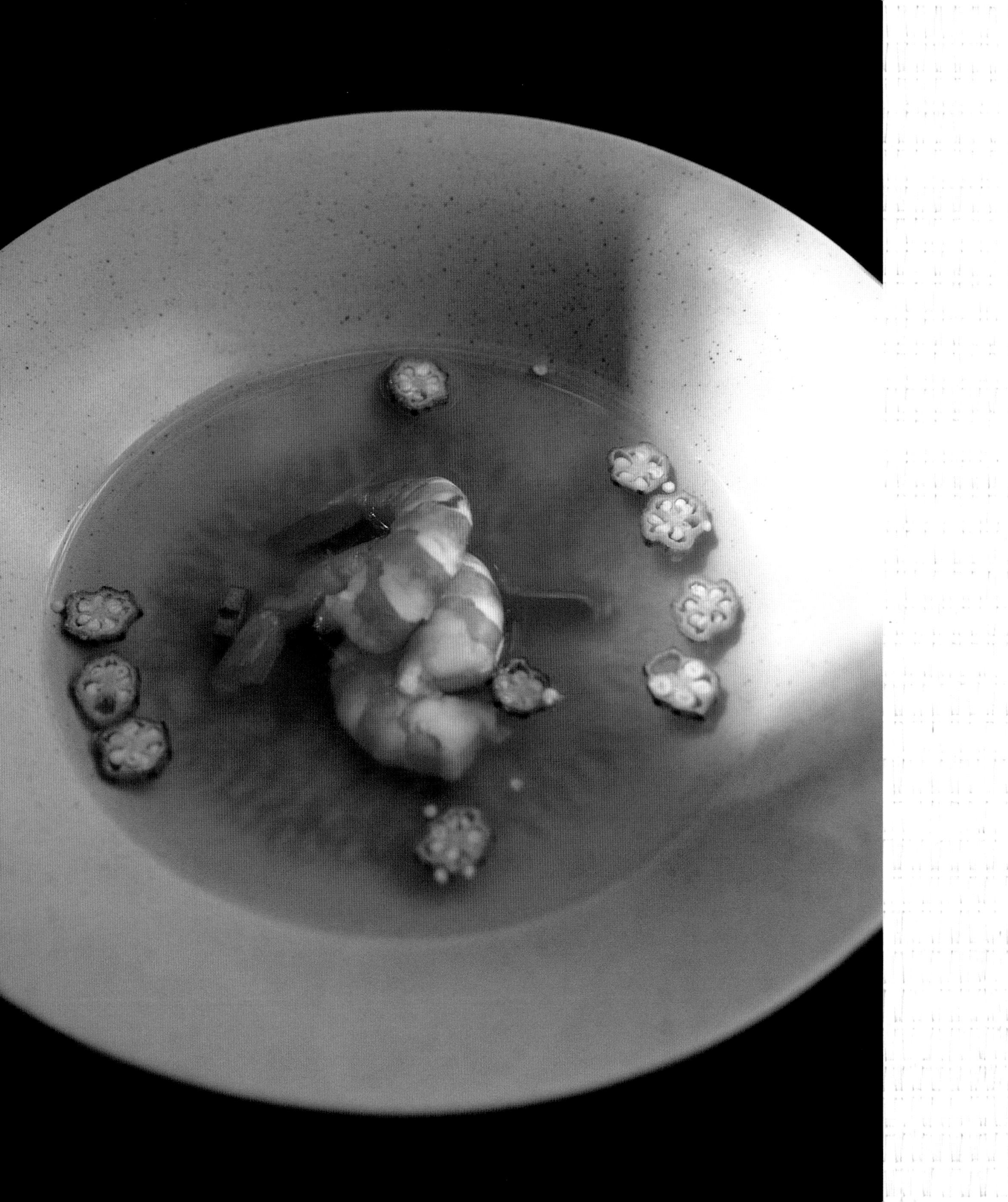

Clear Soup with Prawns

In my grandmother's kitchen, this soup would have been created from long-simmered stock, which she had hovered over, constantly skimming so that it was perfectly clear. These days few of us have that much time available, but this combination of ingredients still makes a flavoursome soup.

Serves 4

2 pods okra
2 cups water
1 teaspoon salt
8 medium prawns with shells and heads removed
4 cups dashi
1 teaspoon light soy sauce

Cut the okra crosswise into thin slices.

Put the water and salt into a saucepan and bring to the boil. Add the prawns and cook until they have turned red – about 3 minutes. Drain the prawns and set aside.

Combine the dashi, soy sauce and okra in a saucepan and bring to the boil. Remove from the heat.

To serve, place 1 or 2 prawns into each bowl, ladle the soup over and garnish with strips of lemon rind if desired.

Soto Ayam (Indonesian Chicken Soup)

Here's a clear chicken soup that is wholesome, substantial, tangy and spicy, ideal for a first course or as a side dish.

Serves 6 as a starter or 4 as a main

500g (1lb) chicken pieces (or 1/2 a small chicken)
4 cups water
1 teaspoon salt
1 teaspoon black peppercorns
1 teaspoon ground coriander
4 candlenuts or macadamia nuts
1–2 cloves garlic
4–6 shallots or 1 small red or brown onion
1 slice fresh ginger
1/4 teaspoon ground turmeric
2 tablespoons vegetable oil
1 cup coconut milk
1 fragrant lime leaf or young citrus leaf
100g (4oz) cellophane noodles or Chinese rice vermicelli
1–2 waxy potatoes, boiled and sliced
100g (4oz) beansprouts, scalded
few spinach or silver beet leaves, scalded
1–2 hard-boiled eggs, sliced

garnish
fried onion flakes (avaliable from Asian food stores)
fresh coriander leaves

Simmer the chicken in the water and salt until tender. Allow to cool in the liquid, then remove the chicken and dice, reserving the stock.

In a food processor, blend the peppercorns and ground coriander together. Then blend in the candlenuts, garlic, shallots and ginger until fine.

Combine both mixtures with the turmeric.

Heat the oil in a heavy saucepan and gently fry the spice mixture for 3–5 minutes. Add the reserved chicken stock, cover the pan and simmer for 5 minutes.

Pour in the coconut milk and add the lime leaf.

Simmer gently, uncovered, stirring frequently, for another 5 minutes.

To serve, put some noodles, potatoes, beansprouts, leafy vegetable, egg and chicken into the bottom of each bowl. Pour over the soup, and garnish.

Serve with cut chilli and soy sauce.

Wonton Soup

This recipe comes from Shanghai and was taught to our family by my maternal grandmother's neighbour, Aunty Mei Mei. We used to have competitions to see who could eat the most wontons and Dad always won.

Serves 6

250g (8oz) minced pork
250g (8oz) spinach (washed and blanched)
2 tablespoons light soy sauce
1 egg
1 teaspoon cornflour
pepper to taste
1 packet wonton wrappers (approx 50 sheets)
3 litres (6 pints) water plus an additional 6 cups
1/3 cup soy sauce
1 1/2 teaspoons sesame oil

garnish

fried onion flakes (available from Asian food stores)
fresh coriander leaves

Put the pork, spinach, soy sauce, egg, cornflour and pepper in a food processor and blend until just combined.

Make the wontons by placing a teaspoon of the pork mixture in the middle of each wrapper. Moisten the edges of the wrapper and fold over diagonally until the opposite corners meet. Press to seal. You should finish with a triangle of wonton pastry with a small lump of filling on the straight edge. This recipe should make about 50 wontons. Set aside.

Put the 3 litres of water in a saucepan and the additional 6 cups of water into another. Set out 6 deep soup bowls and put a tablespoon of soy sauce and 1/4 teaspoon of sesame oil into each bowl.

Bring both saucepans to the boil. Into the larger one, drop about 8–10 wontons and cook until they float to the top and the pork is cooked, keeping the water on a rolling boil. This should take about 3–4 minutes. When cooked, lift out the wonton with a slotted spoon, shake off excess water and place gently into a soup bowl. Repeat the process until all the wontons are cooked and shared amongst the soup bowls.

Ladle a cup of boiling water from the smaller saucepan over the wontons in each bowl, giving it a little stir to mix in the soy and sesame oil.

Garnish with onion flakes and fresh coriander. Serve immediately with a side dish of cut chilli and soy sauce.

Tofu Mushroom Soup

This simple soup has a dashi base. Dashi is a soup stock made from bonito fish and can either be made from scratch, or from powdered stock readily available from most Asian food stores.

Serves 4

170g (6oz) soft tofu (bean curd)

4 Chinese mushrooms (soaked in hot water until soft)

4 cups dashi

3 tablespoons miso

Cut the tofu into smallish cubes and set aside.

Remove and discard any stems from the mushrooms and slice thinly.

Place the dashi and mushrooms in a saucepan. Heat to boiling and boil for 1 minute. Add the tofu cubes.

Place the miso in a small bowl. Add a ladle of hot soup to the bowl, carefully stirring to dissolve the miso.

Add the contents of the small cup back to the soup and stir gently to mix, serving immediately.

Chilli Ginger Sauce

This can be served with Hainanese Chicken Rice (see page 35), or any chicken or meat dish.

100g (3 1/2oz) red chillies, chopped (discard seeds for a milder sauce)

30g (1oz) garlic cloves

30g (1oz) fresh ginger

1 tablespoon white vinegar

1–2 teaspoons sugar

1/2 teaspoon salt

Blend all ingredients until fine. This sauce keeps well in the fridge.

Nuoc Cham (Vietnamese Dipping Sauce)

This sauce can be used for cooking or with any red meat or chicken dishes.

4 cloves garlic
2 fresh chillies
2 teaspoons sugar
1/3 cup fish sauce
4 tablespoons fresh lime juice
1/3–1/2 cup water

Blend the garlic, chillies and sugar until fine. Add the other ingredients, adjusting amount of water to taste. Strain into a dipping bowl or jar if storing.

Sweet and Sour Plum Sauce

Great with spring rolls or fried wontons.

1/2 cup white vinegar
1/3 cup sugar
3 preserved plums in brine, pitted (these are available in most Asian food stores)

Bring the vinegar and sugar to the boil.

Mash the plums finely with a fork and stir into the syrup. Store in the fridge.

Seafood Dip

3 cloves garlic
3 medium tomatoes
1 tablespoon vegetable oil
1 cup chicken stock
pinch of salt
1 teaspoon sugar

Mince the garlic finely. Peel, seed and chop the tomatoes finely.

Heat the oil and sauté the garlic until golden. Add the tomatoes, stir for 5 minutes, then add stock.

Bring to the boil, season to taste with salt and sugar and reduce by a third.

aniseed similar to caraway seed, has a light licorice flavour, used in sweet or savoury cooking

bamboo shoots cream coloured spear-like shoots of the bamboo plant. Sold in cans as pieces or thin strips. Refrigerate for up to a week immersed in water

bean curd soft bean curd is made by setting soy bean liquid with gypsum. Hard bean curd is simply soft bean curd compressed to remove the water

beansprouts young shoots of the mung bean. Can be bought fresh (store for up to a week) or in cans (rinse before using)

bok choy a member of the cabbage family, ideal for stir-frying

candlenut white waxy nut used to add body and flavour. Can substitute macadamia nuts

cellophane noodles/vermicelli noodles starchy noodles good for salads and deep frying

char siew strips of pork that have been marinated and barbecued

Chinese celery similar to coriander. Young western celery shoots can be substituted if required

Chinese lime juice normally requires juice of the kaffir lime but ordinary green limes can be substituted

Chinese rice wine Shaoshing brand is best but dry sherry can be substituted

choy sum Chinese spinach available in most supermarkets or Chinese vegetable shops

coconut cream preferably use squeezed juice from fresh shredded coconut, but if unavailable, use canned coconut cream available from supermarkets

crab meat available either in cans or from wholesale fish suppliers. I find that if I ask at the supermarket fish counter they will put in a special order

cumin seeds from the same family as coriander, these seeds are available either whole or ground and are essential in most curries

curry leaves available dried or fresh and have a distinctive Indian curry aroma. Can be frozen until required although they then lose colour

daikon Japanese white radish, used in salads, soups or as a garnish

dashi made from the bonito fish, available as flakes or powdered stock, commonly used as a soup base or as a stock

dhal Indian lentils available from most health food shops and supermarkets

dried prawns generally used for flavour, but they need to be soaked prior to using

fennel seeds essential in most Indian curries, available ground or whole

fish curry powder curry powders vary in their composition according to the accompanying main ingredient. Fish curry powder has a more piquant flavour and may be bought in most Asian food stores. If unavailable, a generic curry powder can be substituted

fish sauce thin salty sauce made from fermented dried fish, used instead of soy sauce. Common in Vietnamese, Chinese, Indonesian and Thai cooking

five spice powder blend of star anise, fennel, cloves, aniseed, cassia. Available in most food stores or supermarkets

gai lan Chinese broccoli or kale

hoisin sauce sweet brownish-red sauce made from garlic, chilli, spices and soy beans. Store in fridge once opened. Great as a marinade for chicken or pork

hot bean sauce thick brown sauce made from soy beans, chilli and garlic. Excellent as a stir-fry base but as it is very salty, use sparingly

hot pepper oil oil flavoured with pepper and chilli. Use sparingly in marinades or as a frying agent

jasmine rice long grain rice with a lovely jasmine aroma once cooked

kaffir lime leaves the kaffir lime is a tiny green lime with an intense flavour and nose. Essential in Thai and Peranakan food. Leaves are used either dried or fresh

lap cheong Chinese pork sausages; as they are dried they will keep indefinitely in the fridge

lemon grass native Asian grass, sometimes known as Citronella grass. The white bulb is commonly bashed before using to release flavour. Can be bought dried or fresh

mirin sweet Japanese sake used for cooking; substitute sherry if preferred

miso thick salty paste made from fermented soy beans, can be red or brown

glossary

Bringing Asia to your kitchen is so simple these days. All you need are some basic ingredients in the cupboard and most dishes become possible. I suggest: • a good light soy sauce • a good dark soy sauce • fish sauce • garlic • ginger • sesame oil • oyster sauce • brown sugar • peanut oil • chicken stock • a basic curry powder • coconut milk • chilli paste or dried chillies

mushrooms, Chinese mainly sold dried, with a strong aroma. Must be soaked in hot water before using

mushrooms, shiitake the most commonly used Japanese mushroom, available either dried or fresh. Same treatment as Chinese mushrooms

nori Japanese seaweed, either dried or fresh, used as garnish, in sushi and as a flavouring for soups

nuoc nam Vietnamese fish sauce

okra slender green vegetable, commonly known as ladies' fingers. Can be steamed, but also good in stir-fries

onion flakes deep fried finely sliced small red onions, available ready fried; store indefinitely in an air-tight container

oyster sauce thick brown sauce made from oysters, soy sauce and salt. Available as 'flavoured' sauce – not as intense as 'pure' sauce. Great with vegetables or as a base for stir-fry dishes

palm sugar made from the sugar palm as well as the palmyra palm, rich brown sugar compressed into cakes, available from most Asian food stores. Substitute fine brown sugar

red onion flakes *see* onion flakes

rice stick noodles broad white ribbon-like noodles, excellent in soups. Need to be rehydrated in boiling water for 5 minutes before using

rice vinegar usually colourless but strong tasting. Used to tenderise meat or to add flavour to fish stews

rice wine *see* Chinese rice wine

rock sugar large crystals of white sugar; normal sugar can be substituted

sake Japanese rice wine, traditionally served warm in tiny ceramic cups

sambal ulek Indonesian chilli paste

screw pine leaf broad green leaf of the pandanas plant, has a fragrant aroma, used to flavour desserts and rice dishes

serrano chilli small red chilli

sesame oil extracted from toasted sesame seeds. Used sparingly as a flavouring for savoury dishes

sesame seeds tiny flat black or white seeds; used to flavour desserts and savoury dishes, can be roasted prior to using

shallot small reddish-brown onion, used more than any other kind in Asian cooking. Red onion can be substituted

shrimp paste/blachan made from dried shrimp, used sparingly to flavour meat or seafood. Has a very intense, pungent smell when fried

shrimp chilli paste made from shrimp paste, chillies and garlic. Commonly used as a condiment at the dinner table, can be bought ready-made from Asian food stores

snow pea flat green pea pod, used whole or shredded in soups or as part of vegetable stir-fry dishes

somen noodles fine round, white wheat flour noodles

soy sauce salty sauce made from soy beans, available in 'light', 'dark' and 'sweet' styles. 'Light' (most widely used) is thin and watery. 'Dark' is used when extra colour is required (in marinades). 'Sweet' is used for flavour and is slightly thick and viscous

star anise eight-pointed star-shaped spice with an aniseed flavour

tamarind paste from the fleshy pod of the tamarind tree. The paste is usually mixed with hot water and drained to obtain the juice commonly used in Malay cooking. Tamarind juice can be bought from some Asian food stores

tofu *see* bean curd

turmeric an orange-fleshed root, ground after drying to produce a bright yellow powder used in most curries

udon noodles these Japanese noodles made from wheat flour, salt and water may be round or flat and of varying length

vermicelli rice noodles extra-thin noodles used to add bulk to soups

Vietnamese mint/kesom a dark green herb with spear-shaped leaves; has a distinctive smell and is used most commonly in Vietnamese dishes

wasabi paste a Japanese delicacy, traditionally made from the wasabi root, but more commonly from horseradish. Essential for Japanese food, especially sushi and sashimi

water chestnut crisp snowy white nut, available fresh or canned

index

acknowledgements

Thank you Mum for teaching me about cooking for the masses. Thanks also to Ray McVinnie for getting me my first spot on radio which began my 'foodie' career. To Brian Edwards for making me talk on radio each month while he ate the subject matter on hand. Writing a cookbook was his idea. To the late Stanley Hams RSM who taught me patiently about wine conviviality. To my lifelines, Gillian Sanson, Margaret Casey, Ivan Connell, Shirley and Vic Williams, David Savage, Jane Osbourne, Cons and Doug Breen, Judith Baragwanath, Diane and Terry Snow, and JR. It's just not possible without you.
And to everyone at New Holland, especially Reneé, Belinda and Andrew for nurturing me through the publishing process.

GEOGRAPHY

FOR EDEXCEL

A LEVEL YEAR 2

Series editor Bob Digby

Catherine Hurst Lynn Adams Russell Chapman Dan Cowling

Endorsement statement

In order to ensure that this resource offers high-quality support for the associated Pearson qualification, it has been through a review process by the awarding body. This process confirms that this resource fully covers the teaching and learning content of the specification or part of a specification at which it is aimed. It also confirms that it demonstrates an appropriate balance between the development of subject skills, knowledge and understanding, in addition to preparation for assessment.

Endorsement does not cover any guidance on assessment activities or processes (e.g. practice questions or advice on how to answer assessment questions), included in the resource nor does it prescribe any particular approach to the teaching or delivery of a related course.

While the publishers have made every attempt to ensure that advice on the qualification and its assessment is accurate, the official specification and associated assessment guidance materials are the only authoritative source of information and should always be referred to for definitive guidance.

Pearson examiners have not contributed to any sections in this resource relevant to examination papers for which they have responsibility.

Examiners will not use endorsed resources as a source of material for any assessment set by Pearson.

Endorsement of a resource does not mean that the resource is required to achieve this Pearson qualification, nor does it mean that it is the only suitable material available to support the qualification, and any resource lists produced by the awarding body shall include this and other appropriate resources.

OXFORD
UNIVERSITY PRESS

Great Clarendon Street, Oxford, OX2 6DP, United Kingdom

Oxford University Press is a department of the University of Oxford. It furthers the University's objective of excellence in research, scholarship, and education by publishing worldwide. Oxford is a registered trade mark of Oxford University Press in the UK and in certain other countries

Series editor: Bob Digby

Authors: Catherine Hurst, Lynn Adams, Russell Chapman, Dan Cowling

The moral rights of the authors have been asserted

Database right of Oxford University Press (maker) 2017

First published in 2017

British Library Cataloguing in Publication Data
Data available

ISBN 978-0-19-836648-5

10 9 8 7 6 5 4 3

Paper used in the production of this book is a natural, recyclable product made from wood grown in sustainable forests. The manufacturing process conforms to the environmental regulations of the country of origin.

Printed in Great Britain by Bell and Bain Ltd., Glasgow

Acknowledgements
The publisher and authors would like to thank the following for permission to use photographs and other copyright material:

Cover: reptiles4all/Shutterstock; **p6(t):** Ross Parry/SWNS Group; **p6(b):** Andrew Findlay/Alamy Stock Photo; **p9(l):** Steve Hillebrand/US Fisheries and Wildlife Service ; **p9(r):** Shutterstock; **p10:** NASA/JPL; **p17(t):** Trevor Chriss/Alamy Stock Photo; **p17(b):** Shutterstock; **p21:** Julia Gavin/Alamy Stock Photo; **p25:** iStockphoto; **p26:** © Crown Copyright 2016, Met Office.; **p27:** Ross Parry/SWNS; **p31(t):** Citizen of the Planet/ Alamy Stock Photo; **p31(b):** NASA Earth Observatory images by Jesse Allen, using data from the Level 1 and Atmospheres Active Distribution System (LAADS).; **p31(b):** NASA Earth Observatory images by Jesse Allen, using data from the Level 1 and Atmospheres Active Distribution System (LAADS).; **p34:** BLM Collection/Alamy Stock Photo; **p40:** ZUMA Press, Inc./Alamy Stock Photo; **p45:** Tal-Ya Water Technolgies Ltd. www.tal-ya.com; **p47:** Paul Glendell/Alamy Stock Photo; **p51:** Joerg Boethling/Alamy Stock Photo; **p53:** iStockphoto; **p58:** Bob Digby; **p59:** Alexander Lutsenko/Alamy Stock Photo; **p62:** Jason Edwards/National Geographic/Getty Images; **p66:** NASA Earth Observatory/NOAA NGDC; **p71(t):** Courtesy of EDF Energy; **p71(b):** Paul Glendell/Alamy Stock Photo; **p77:** Milesy/Alamy Stock Photo; **p79:** Courtesy of Eco Sustainable Solutions Ltd http://www.thisiseco.co.uk/; **p83:** Image courtesy Jacques Descloitres, MODIS Rapid Response Team at NASA GSFC; **p84:** Emily Guerin; **p85(l):** iStockphoto; **p85(r):** Shutterstock; **p88(t):** Ulet Ifansasti/Greenpeace; **p88(b):** iStockphoto; **p90:** Jon Bower Canada/Alamy Stock Photo; **p91:** Thomas Cockrem/Alamy Stock Photo; **p94:** imageBROKER/Alamy Stock Photo; **p95:** Bill Barksdale/Design Pics Inc/Alamy Stock Photo; **p96(t):** Johner Images/ Alamy Stock Photo; **p96(b):** Courtesy of SaskPower; **p100:** IBL/REX/Shutterstock; **p101:** iStockphoto; p108, 109: Bob Digby; p113, 114(t): iStockphoto; **p114(b):** AsianDream/ iStockphoto; p116, 118(t): iStockphoto; **p118(b):** epa european pressphoto agency b.v./ Alamy Stock Photo; **p119:** Sue Cunningham Photographic/Alamy Stock Photo; **p121:** Martin Charles Hatch/Shutterstock; **p122:** Lyroky/Alamy Stock Photo; **p123:** Paul Vidler/Alamy Stock Photo; **p124(t):** US Air Force Photo/Alamy Stock Photo; **p124(b):** dbimages/Alamy Stock Photo; **p126:** iStockphoto; **p127:** Shutterstock; **p128:** REUTERS/ Alamy Stock Photo; **p130:** iStockphoto; **p132:** Europena Environment Agency/ Joint Research Centre (JRC) http://www.eea.europa.eu/data-and-maps/figures/global-greenhouse-gas-emissions-2005; **p135(t):** Bob Digby; **p135(b):** Neil Setchfield/Alamy Stock Photo; **p139:** fuyi/Fotolia; **p142:** REUTERS/Alamy Stock Photo; **p143:** Geoffrey Robinson/Alamy Stock Photo; **p144(t):** epa european pressphoto agency b.v./Alamy Stock Photo; **p144(b):** JohnFScott/iStockphoto; **p145:** PurpleImages/iStockphoto; **p146:** Purestock/Alamy Stock Photo; **p150:** Dan Tucker/Alamy Stock Photo; **p153(t):** Bob Digby; **p153(b):** SHAUN CURRY/Getty Images; **p154:** REUTERS/Alamy Stock Photo; **p157(t):** JOSE CENDON/AFP/Getty Images; **p157(b):** Aldo Pavan/Horizons WWP/ TRVL; **p159(t):** Aerial Archives/Alamy Stock Photo; **p159(b):** David J. Green - business themes/Alamy Stock Photo; **p161:** AAP Image/Mick Tsikas; **p162:** Li Tao/Xinhua/ Alamy Stock Photo; **p163:** Tom Hanley/Alamy Stock Photo; **p164(t):** REUTERS/ Alamy Stock Photo; **p164(b):** Joerg Boethling/Alamy Stock Photo; **p165(t):** Logan Abassi/UN/MINUSTAH/Xinhua/Alamy Stock Photo; **p165(b):** Claudiad/iStockphoto; **p166:** Luiz Rampelotto/Pacific Press/LightRocket via Getty Images; **p168(t):** Graeme Robertson/Getty Images; **p168(b):** Johnny Saunderson/Alamy Stock Photo; **p169(t):** National Geographic Creative/Alamy Stock Photo; **p169(m):** Barry Lewis/Alamy Stock Photo; **p169(b):** FAYEZ NURELDINE/AFP/Getty Images; **p171:** Ahmed Deeb/ NurPhoto/ZUMA Wire/Alamy Stock Photo; **p172:** U.S. Air Force photo by Tech. Sgt. Michael R. Holzworth/US Navy ; **p173:** Roger Bacon/REUTERS/Alamy Stock Photo; **p174:** Sovannara/Xinhua/Alamy Stock Photo; **p178:** Alan Moir, Sydney Morning Herald; **p179:** Bob Digby; **p180:** Penny Tweedie/Alamy Stock Photo; **p181:** Hemis/ Alamy Stock Photo; **p182:** FEISAL OMAR/REUTERS/Alamy Stock Photo; **p185(t):** PASCAL GUYOT/AFP/Getty Images; **p185(b):** JACKY NAEGELEN/REUTERS/Alamy Stock Photo; **p186:** iStockphoto; **p187:** InsectWorld/Shutterstock; **p189(t):** Olivier Asselin/ Alamy Stock Photo; **p189(m):** James Gathany/CDC; **p189(b):** punghi/Shutterstock; **p190:** Jake Lyell/Alamy Stock Photo; **p191(t):** jbdodane/Alamy Stock Photo; **p191(b):** Pacific Press/Getty Images; **p192:** Akintunde Akinleye/REUTERS/Alamy Stock Photo; **p193:** REUTERS/Alamy Stock Photo; **p194(t):** Chris Hondros/Getty Images; **p194(b):** Haider Al-assadee/EPA/REX/Shutterstock; **p197:** T. McCoy/U.S. Navy via Getty Images; **p198:** John Moore/Getty Images; **p199:** Simon Lim ABACA/PA Images; **p200:** Florian Kopp/imageBROKER/Alamy Stock Photo; **p204:** Carlos Mora/Alamy Stock Photo; **p205:** Stocktrek Images, Inc./Alamy Stock Photo; **p206(t):** Trinity Mirror/Mirrorpix/ Alamy Stock Photo; **p206(b):** DIMITAR DILKOFF/AFP/Getty Images; **p207:** UN Photo; **p208(t):** Xinhua/Alamy Stock Photo; **p208(b):** Agencja Fotograficzna Caro/Alamy Stock Photo; **p209:** Christopher Scott/Alamy Stock Photo; **p213:** Ian G Dagnall/ Alamy Stock Photo; **p216:** iStockphoto, **p218:** Ashley Cooper/Corbis News/Getty Images; **p220:** Istvan Csak/Shutterstock; **p225:** iStockphoto; **p226(t):** Shutterstock; **p226(b):** Bob Krist/Getty Images; **p227(t):** Luriya Chinwan/Shutterstock; **p227(b):** Bob Digby; **p228:** Adalbert von Rößler/Wikimedia Commons/Public Domain; **p233:** Bettman/Getty Images; **p234(t):** Planet News Archive/SSPL/Getty Images; **p234(b):** Vickie Flores/REX/Shutterstock; **p235(t):** Shutterstock; **p235(b):** The WebGL Globe is an open platform for visualizing geographic data. By The Google Data Arts Team; **p236:** David Doubilet/National Geographic/Getty Images; **p240(t):** vintageusa1/Alamy Stock Photo; **p241(b):** PhotoStock-Israel/Alamy Stock Photo; **p242:** ZUMA Press, Inc./ Alamy Stock Photo; **p244(t):** iStockphoto; **p244(b):** Wim Wiskerke/Alamy Stock Photo; **p248:** Shutterstock; **p249:** NASA; **p250:** Nature and Science/Alamy Stock Photo; **p252:** Pascal Guyot/AFP/Getty Images; **p253:** Steve Wood/REX/Shutterstock; **p254(t):** Cameron Spencer/Getty Images; **p254(m):** Anthony Devlin PA Archive/PA Images; **p254(b):** Kyodo News/Getty Images; **p256:** Christopher Furlong/Getty Images; **p257:** anthony asael/Alamy Stock Photo; **p258(t):** REUTERS/Alamy Stock Photo; **p258(b):** Reproduced by kind permission of PRIVATE EYE magazine. Map created by suemarcar © OpenStreetMap contributors © CARTO © Crown copyright Ordnance Survey; **p259:** iStockphoto; **p260:** Oso Media/Alamy Stock Photo; **p261:** Newzulu/ Alamy Stock Photo; **p263:** REUTERS/Alamy Stock Photo; **p284(t):** REUTERS/Alamy Stock Photo; **p284(b):** DOD/S.Dupuis/Alamy Stock Photo; **p286:** KeystoneUSA-ZUMA/ REX/Shutterstock; **p290(t):** Bob Digby; **p290(b):** Photofusion/Getty Images; p292, 294: Bob Digby; **p298:** amc/Alamy Stock Photo; **p300:** Bob Digby; **p302:** mattphoto/Alamy Stock Photo; **p312:** Ulrich Doering/Alamy Stock Photo;

Design/page layout and artwork: Kamae Design

Bob Digby would like to thank Adam Jameson for helping with research, particularly 'Books to read', 'Music to listen to', and 'Films to see' for each chapter, and David Holmes for help and advice in the preparation of chapter 8 Fieldwork and the Independent Investigation.

Russell Chapman would like to thank Min Kyoo-Kim, Will Silver, and UCS Library staff for helping with research for chapter 2 The carbon cycle and energy security, Jack Drew for helping with research for chapter 5 Migration, identity and sovereignty, and Faven and Sheila for their personal migration stories.

GEOGRAPHY

FOR EDEXCEL

A LEVEL YEAR 2

Series editor Bob Digby

Catherine Hurst Lynn Adams Russell Chapman
Dan Cowling

Endorsement statement

In order to ensure that this resource offers high-quality support for the associated Pearson qualification, it has been through a review process by the awarding body. This process confirms that this resource fully covers the teaching and learning content of the specification or part of a specification at which it is aimed. It also confirms that it demonstrates an appropriate balance between the development of subject skills, knowledge and understanding, in addition to preparation for assessment.

Endorsement does not cover any guidance on assessment activities or processes (e.g. practice questions or advice on how to answer assessment questions), included in the resource nor does it prescribe any particular approach to the teaching or delivery of a related course.

While the publishers have made every attempt to ensure that advice on the qualification and its assessment is accurate, the official specification and associated assessment guidance materials are the only authoritative source of information and should always be referred to for definitive guidance.

Pearson examiners have not contributed to any sections in this resource relevant to examination papers for which they have responsibility.

Examiners will not use endorsed resources as a source of material for any assessment set by Pearson.

Endorsement of a resource does not mean that the resource is required to achieve this Pearson qualification, nor does it mean that it is the only suitable material available to support the qualification, and any resource lists produced by the awarding body shall include this and other appropriate resources.

OXFORD
UNIVERSITY PRESS

Great Clarendon Street, Oxford, OX2 6DP, United Kingdom

Oxford University Press is a department of the University of Oxford. It furthers the University's objective of excellence in research, scholarship, and education by publishing worldwide. Oxford is a registered trade mark of Oxford University Press in the UK and in certain other countries

Series editor: Bob Digby

Authors: Catherine Hurst, Lynn Adams, Russell Chapman, Dan Cowling

The moral rights of the authors have been asserted

Database right of Oxford University Press (maker) 2017

First published in 2017

British Library Cataloguing in Publication Data
Data available

ISBN 978-0-19-836648-5

10 9 8 7 6 5 4 3

Paper used in the production of this book is a natural, recyclable product made from wood grown in sustainable forests. The manufacturing process conforms to the environmental regulations of the country of origin.

Printed in Great Britain by Bell and Bain Ltd., Glasgow

Acknowledgements
The publisher and authors would like to thank the following for permission to use photographs and other copyright material:

Cover: reptiles4all/Shutterstock; **p6(t):** Ross Parry/SWNS Group; **p6(b):** Andrew Findlay/Alamy Stock Photo; **p9(l):** Steve Hillebrand/US Fisheries and Wildlife Service ; **p9(r):** Shutterstock; **p10:** NASA/JPL; **p17(t):** Trevor Chriss/Alamy Stock Photo; **p17(b):** Shutterstock; **p21:** Julia Gavin/Alamy Stock Photo; **p25:** iStockphoto; **p26:** © Crown Copyright 2016, Met Office.; **p27:** Ross Parry/SWNS; **p31(t):** Citizen of the Planet/ Alamy Stock Photo; **p31(b):** NASA Earth Observatory images by Jesse Allen, using data from the Level 1 and Atmospheres Active Distribution System (LAADS).; **p31(b):** NASA Earth Observatory images by Jesse Allen, using data from the Level 1 and Atmospheres Active Distribution System (LAADS).; **p34:** BLM Collection/Alamy Stock Photo; **p40:** ZUMA Press, Inc./Alamy Stock Photo; **p45:** Tal-Ya Water Technolgies Ltd. www.tal-ya.com; **p47:** Paul Glendell/Alamy Stock Photo; **p51:** Joerg Boethling/Alamy Stock Photo; **p53:** iStockphoto; **p58:** Bob Digby; **p59:** Alexander Lutsenko/Alamy Stock Photo; **p62:** Jason Edwards/National Geographic/Getty Images; **p66:** NASA Earth Observatory/NOAA NGDC; **p71(t):** Courtesy of EDF Energy; **p71(b):** Paul Glendell/Alamy Stock Photo; **p77:** Milesy/Alamy Stock Photo; **p79:** Courtesy of Eco Sustainable Solutions Ltd http://www.thisiseco.co.uk/; **p83:** Image courtesy Jacques Descloitres, MODIS Rapid Response Team at NASA GSFC; **p84:** Emily Guerin; **p85(l):** iStockphoto; **p85(r):** Shutterstock; **p88(t):** Ulet Ifansasti/Greenpeace; **p88(b):** iStockphoto; **p90:** Jon Bower Canada/Alamy Stock Photo; **p91:** Thomas Cockrem/Alamy Stock Photo; **p94:** imageBROKER/Alamy Stock Photo; **p95:** Bill Barksdale/Design Pics Inc/Alamy Stock Photo; **p96(t):** Johner Images/ Alamy Stock Photo; **p96(b):** Courtesy of SaskPower; **p100:** IBL/REX/Shutterstock; **p101:** iStockphoto; p108, 109: Bob Digby; p113, 114(t): iStockphoto; **p114(b):** AsianDream/ iStockphoto; p116, 118(t): iStockphoto; **p118(b):** epa european pressphoto agency b.v./ Alamy Stock Photo; **p119:** Sue Cunningham Photographic/Alamy Stock Photo; **p121:** Martin Charles Hatch/Shutterstock; **p122:** Lyroky/Alamy Stock Photo; **p123:** Paul Vidler/Alamy Stock Photo; **p124(t):** US Air Force Photo/Alamy Stock Photo; **p124(b):** dbimages/Alamy Stock Photo; **p126:** iStockphoto; **p127:** Shutterstock; **p128:** REUTERS/ Alamy Stock Photo; **p130:** iStockphoto; **p132:** Europena Environment Agency/ Joint Research Centre (JRC) http://www.eea.europa.eu/data-and-maps/figures/global-greenhouse-gas-emissions-2005; **p135(t):** Bob Digby; **p135(b):** Neil Setchfield/Alamy Stock Photo; **p139:** fuyi/Fotolia; **p142:** REUTERS/Alamy Stock Photo; **p143:** Geoffrey Robinson/Alamy Stock Photo; **p144(t):** epa european pressphoto agency b.v./Alamy Stock Photo; **p144(b):** JohnFScott/iStockphoto; **p145:** PurpleImages/iStockphoto; **p146:** Purestock/Alamy Stock Photo; **p150:** Dan Tucker/Alamy Stock Photo; **p153(t):** Bob Digby; **p153(b):** SHAUN CURRY/Getty Images; **p154:** REUTERS/Alamy Stock Photo; **p157(t):** JOSE CENDON/AFP/Getty Images; **p157(b):** Aldo Pavan/Horizons WWP/ TRVL; **p159(t):** Aerial Archives/Alamy Stock Photo; **p159(b):** David J. Green - business themes/Alamy Stock Photo; **p161:** AAP Image/Mick Tsikas; **p162:** Li Tao/Xinhua/ Alamy Stock Photo; **p163:** Tom Hanley/Alamy Stock Photo; **p164(t):** REUTERS/ Alamy Stock Photo; **p164(b):** Joerg Boethling/Alamy Stock Photo; **p165(t):** Logan Abassi/UN/MINUSTAH/Xinhua/Alamy Stock Photo; **p165(b):** Claudiad/iStockphoto; **p166:** Luiz Rampelotto/Pacific Press/LightRocket via Getty Images; **p168(t):** Graeme Robertson/Getty Images; **p168(b):** Johnny Saunderson/Alamy Stock Photo; **p169(t):** National Geographic Creative/Alamy Stock Photo; **p169(m):** Barry Lewis/Alamy Stock Photo; **p169(b):** FAYEZ NURELDINE/AFP/Getty Images; **p171:** Ahmed Deeb/ NurPhoto/ZUMA Wire/Alamy Stock Photo; **p172:** U.S. Air Force photo by Tech. Sgt. Michael R. Holzworth/US Navy ; **p173:** Roger Bacon/REUTERS/Alamy Stock Photo; **p174:** Sovannara/Xinhua/Alamy Stock Photo; **p178:** Alan Moir, Sydney Morning Herald; **p179:** Bob Digby; **p180:** Penny Tweedie/Alamy Stock Photo; **p181:** Hemis/ Alamy Stock Photo; **p182:** FEISAL OMAR/REUTERS/Alamy Stock Photo; **p185(t):** PASCAL GUYOT/AFP/Getty Images; **p185(b):** JACKY NAEGELEN/REUTERS/Alamy Stock Photo; **p186:** iStockphoto; **p187:** InsectWorld/Shutterstock; **p189(t):** Olivier Asselin/ Alamy Stock Photo; **p189(m):** James Gathany/CDC; **p189(b):** punghi/Shutterstock; **p190:** Jake Lyell/Alamy Stock Photo; **p191(t):** jbdodane/Alamy Stock Photo; **p191(b):** Pacific Press/Getty Images; **p192:** Akintunde Akinleye/REUTERS/Alamy Stock Photo; **p193:** REUTERS/Alamy Stock Photo; **p194(t):** Chris Hondros/Getty Images; **p194(b):** Haider Al-assadee/EPA/REX/Shutterstock; **p197:** T. McCoy/U.S. Navy via Getty Images; **p198:** John Moore/Getty Images; **p199:** Simon Lim ABACA/PA Images; **p200:** Florian Kopp/imageBROKER/Alamy Stock Photo; **p204:** Carlos Mora/Alamy Stock Photo; **p205:** Stocktrek Images, Inc./Alamy Stock Photo; **p206(t):** Trinity Mirror/Mirrorpix/ Alamy Stock Photo; **p206(b):** DIMITAR DILKOFF/AFP/Getty Images; **p207:** UN Photo; **p208(t):** Xinhua/Alamy Stock Photo; **p208(b):** Agencja Fotograficzna Caro/Alamy Stock Photo; **p209:** Christopher Scott/Alamy Stock Photo; **p213:** Ian G Dagnall/ Alamy Stock Photo; **p216:** iStockphoto; **p218:** Ashley Cooper/Corbis News/Getty Images; **p220:** Istvan Csak/Shutterstock; **p225:** iStockphoto; **p226(t):** Shutterstock; **p226(b):** Bob Krist/Getty Images; **p227(t):** Luriya Chinwan/Shutterstock; **p227(b):** Bob Digby; **p228:** Adalbert von Rößler/Wikimedia Commons/Public Domain; **p233:** Bettman/Getty Images; **p234(t):** Planet News Archive/SSPL/Getty Images; **p234(b):** Vickie Flores/REX/Shutterstock; **p235(t):** Shutterstock; **p235(b):** The WebGL Globe is an open platform for visualizing geographic data. By The Google Data Arts Team; **p236:** David Doubilet/National Geographic/Getty Images; **p240(t):** vintageusa1/Alamy Stock Photo; **p241(b):** PhotoStock-Israel/Alamy Stock Photo; **p242:** ZUMA Press, Inc./ Alamy Stock Photo; **p244(t):** iStockphoto; **p244(b):** Wim Wiskerke/Alamy Stock Photo; **p248:** Shutterstock; **p249:** NASA; **p250:** Nature and Science/Alamy Stock Photo; **p252:** Pascal Guyot/AFP/Getty Images; **p253:** Steve Wood/REX/Shutterstock; **p254(t):** Cameron Spencer/Getty Images; **p254(m):** Anthony Devlin PA Archive/PA Images; **p254(b):** Kyodo News/Getty Images; **p256:** Christopher Furlong/Getty Images; **p257:** anthony asael/Alamy Stock Photo; **p258(t):** REUTERS/Alamy Stock Photo; **p258(b):** Reproduced by kind permission of PRIVATE EYE magazine. Map created by suemarcar © OpenStreetMap contributors © CARTO © Crown copyright Ordnance Survey; **p259:** iStockphoto; **p260:** Oso Media/Alamy Stock Photo; **p261:** Newzulu/ Alamy Stock Photo; **p263:** REUTERS/Alamy Stock Photo; **p284(t):** REUTERS/Alamy Stock Photo; **p284(b):** DOD/S.Dupuis/Alamy Stock Photo; **p286:** KeystoneUSA-ZUMA/ REX/Shutterstock; **p290(t):** Bob Digby; **p290(b):** Photofusion/Getty Images; p292, 294: Bob Digby; **p298:** amc/Alamy Stock Photo; **p300:** Bob Digby; **p302:** mattphoto/Alamy Stock Photo; **p312:** Ulrich Doering/Alamy Stock Photo;

Design/page layout and artwork: Kamae Design

Bob Digby would like to thank Adam Jameson for helping with research, particularly 'Books to read', 'Music to listen to', and 'Films to see' for each chapter, and David Holmes for help and advice in the preparation of chapter 8 Fieldwork and the Independent Investigation.

Russell Chapman would like to thank Min Kyoo-Kim, Will Silver, and UCS LIbrary staff for helping with research for chapter 2 The carbon cycle and energy security, Jack Drew for helping with research for chapter 5 Migration, identity and sovereignty, and Faven and Sheila for their personal migration stories.

Contents

Contents

How to use this book

This is the second of two books in this series, written for the Edexcel GCE in Geography. This particular book (Book 2) has been written to meet the content requirements of Topics 5, 6, 7 and 8 in the A level course. Each chapter has been clearly arranged in terms of the enquiry questions in the specification, and each section begins with the key ideas as well as the synoptic themes and/or key concepts covered in that section.

About the questions in this book:

- 'Over to you' questions are designed for collaborative work in class, generally in pairs or larger groups.
- 'On your own' questions provide opportunities for independent, private study.
- Skills questions (indicated by the icon) are aimed at meeting the geographical and statistical skills requirements for A level.
- Exam-style questions are included for A level, with marks allocated. These reflect the same command words and mark allocations that you will meet in the A level examinations for these topics.
- At appropriate points, chapters focus on the synoptic themes – Players, Attitudes, and Futures. These, plus associated questions, will help to prepare you for Paper Three in the A level examination.

The water cycle and water insecurity

Chapter overview – introducing the topic

This chapter studies the water cycle and the ways in which water has become a major issue in terms of both quantity and quality in different parts of the world.

In the specification, this topic has been framed around three Enquiry Questions:

1. What are the processes operating within the hydrological cycle from global to local scale?
2. What factors influence the hydrological system over short- and long-term timescales?
3. How does water insecurity occur and why is it becoming such a global issue for the twenty-first century?

The sections in this chapter provide the content and concepts needed to help you answer these questions.

Synoptic themes

Underlying the content of every topic are three synoptic themes that 'bind' or glue the whole specification together:

1. Players
2. Attitudes and Actions
3. Futures and Uncertainties

1 Players

Players are individuals, groups and organisations involved in making decisions that affect people and places, collectively known as **stakeholders**. Players can be national or international individuals and organisations (e.g. IGOs like the UN), national and local governments, businesses (from small operations to the largest TNCs), as well as pressure groups and NGOs, together with others.

Players that you'll study in this topic include:

- Section 1.4 – The role played by **planners** in managing water use.
- Section 1.9 – How different **users** play a role in national and international conflicts over water.
- Section 1.10 – The role of **a range of different players** in reducing the risk of water conflict, particularly in large river basins.

2 Attitudes and Actions

People's attitudes to water supply and water quality issues vary, which influences the actions taken to deal with them, e.g. policies in managing water. People's values and attitudes depend on several factors:

- Their political views (left- or right-wing, for example), and/or their religious beliefs.
- The priorities given to people versus profit.
- The importance of social justice and equality.
- Attitudes towards water (e.g. whether to conserve or exploit).

Attitudes and Actions that you'll study in this topic include:

- Section 1.10 – How and why different people have contrasting attitudes to water supply.

3 Futures and Uncertainties

Decisions and actions taken by players today will affect people in the future. Faced with water management issues now, for example, will similar problems occur in the future, or have lessons been learned? Do those who are most vulnerable in terms of supply today face a bleak or a better future?

Futures and Uncertainties that you'll study in this topic include:

- Section 1.7 – Variations in future projections about drought and flood risk, depending on climate change.
- Section 1.8 – Variations in future predictions of water scarcity and stress, depending on factors such as supply and climate change.

1.1 A world of extremes

In this section, you'll learn how the hydrological cycle responds to weather conditions.

EQ1 Sections 1.1 to 1.4 in this book ask what processes operate within the hydrological cycle from global to local scales.

Not in living memory...

On 6 December 2015, Malham Cove in the Pennines of North Yorkshire became Britain's highest waterfall. Surface runoff poured over the edge of its 80-metre-high cliff face (see Figure 1). It's hard to know when this event last happened, because Malham is in limestone country – and limestone is a permeable rock – so normally there is no surface water. As Figure 2 shows, in limestone areas such as Malham surface water goes underground and percolates through underground bedding planes and joints. It then runs along the impermeable rocks underneath before re-emerging as a stream such as the one at the foot of Malham Cove. However, by 6 December, heavy rain from Storm Desmond had saturated the limestone, causing a surface stream and waterfall to form.

Figure 1 *Storm Desmond caused Malham Cove to become a stunning waterfall for the first time in centuries*

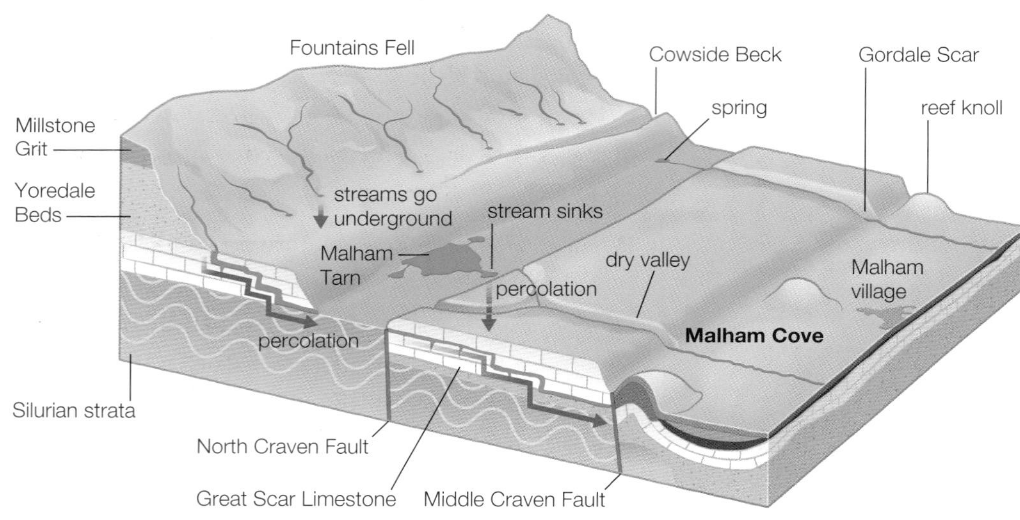

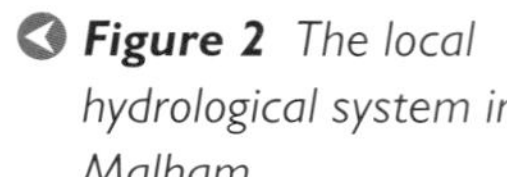
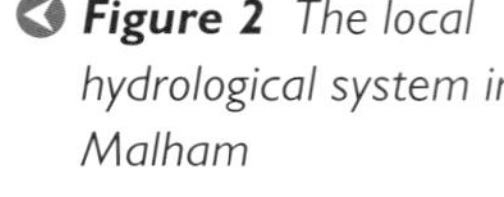

Figure 2 *The local hydrological system in Malham*

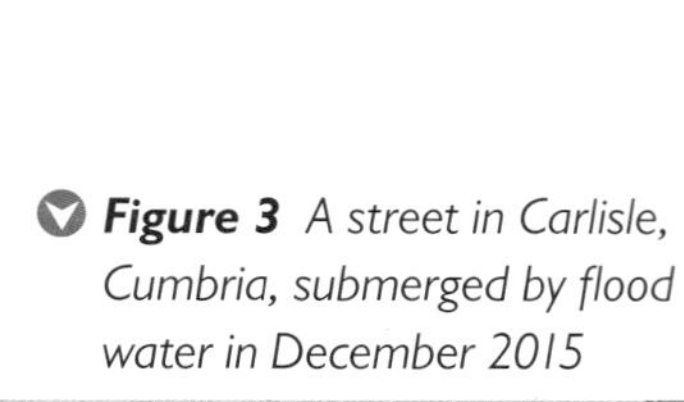

Figure 3 *A street in Carlisle, Cumbria, submerged by flood water in December 2015*

The dry valley leading to Malham Cove was formed by meltwater at the end of the last Ice Age, when the limestone joints and bedding planes were filled with ice – making the limestone impermeable. This landscape is a relic of past climatic conditions! But after days of heavy rain brought to Malham and the Lake District by Storm Desmond, the local hydrological systems were saturated. In the Lake District, in Cumbria, a month's worth of rain (in places over 350 mm) fell in a single day! As Figure 3 shows, major floods occurred in Cumbria as a result of the heavy December rainfall (see Figure 4), which saturated surface soils and reduced the ability of the landscape to absorb the excess water.

Figure 4 *The distribution and relative amounts of rainfall across the UK in December 2015, compared to the December averages for 1981 to 2010*

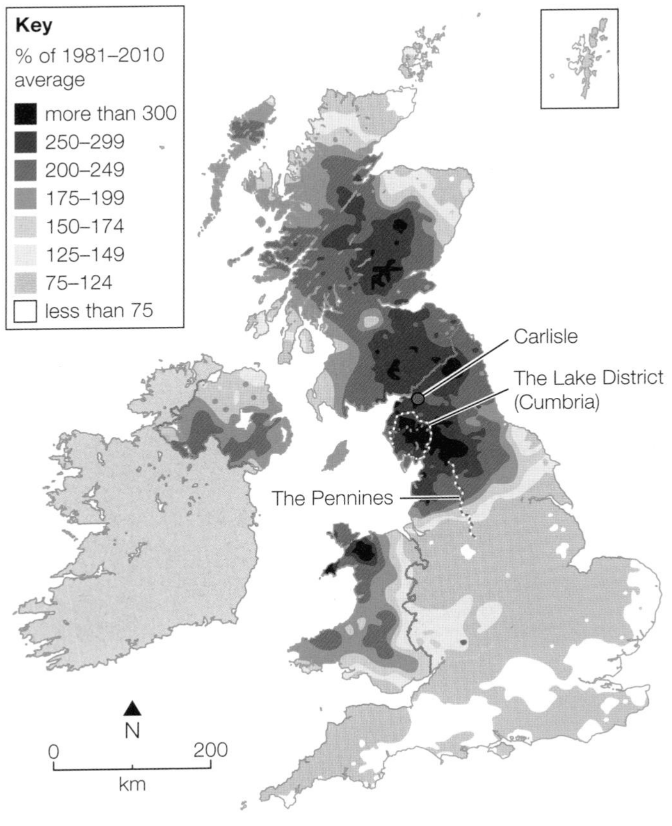

Figure 5 *The drainage basin seen as a simple system. The basin itself can appear to be a 'black box' until its local characteristics are revealed.*

Saturated systems

Cumbria is the wettest county in England; its annual rainfall is over 2000 mm. The region's average monthly rainfall varies from 200 mm in the winter months to 85 mm in summer. However, within that, places such as Borrowdale receive up to 3300 mm a year. In three years in which severe flooding took place:

- December 2005 – 200 mm of rain fell in 36 hours
- November 2009 – 316 mm fell in 24 hours
- December 2015 – 341 mm fell in 24 hours

The short-lived waterfall at Malham and the three major flood events across Cumbria were extreme – but they were simply responses to local hydrological conditions. Sections 1.2 to 1.4 of this chapter examine the processes at work within defined geographical areas, known as **drainage basins**, in which hydrological processes operate as a **system**. Figure 5 shows a simple system with the drainage basin as a 'black box' store where 'local' factors and processes are hidden.

- Precipitation is the **input** of water into a local system; the land surface characteristics determine what happens next.
- Local rock types, the quantity of water and the available energy, control the **throughput** of water through a local **store**.
- Evaporation, transpiration and stream flow are the **outputs** of this system.

Whenever inputs change, there is a knock-on effect throughout the system – upsetting natural balances.

Over to you

1 **a** In pairs, list the factors which explain why the waterfall at Malham appeared in December 2015.
b Assemble the factors into a system diagram like that in Figure 5.
c Identify those factors in the 'black box' that caused the waterfall.

2 Explain, with examples, how the following determine the quantity of surface water within a drainage basin: (**a**) precipitation, (**b**) rock type, (**c**) land use.

3 Use an atlas to suggest the factors inside the 'black box' that caused the flooding in Cumbria in 2015.

On your own

4 Distinguish between the following:
a input, output, throughput
b a drainage basin, a 'system', and a 'black box'

5 Refer to Figures 3 and 4 and write a synopsis of the impacts of heavy rainfall on the Pennines and Cumbria in December 2015.

6 The flooding in 2005 was the kind that could be expected once in 200 years (called the return period). Find out, and explain, why return periods between flood events are decreasing.

1.2 The global hydrological cycle

In this section, you'll learn about the importance of the global hydrological cycle to life on Earth.

KEY CONCEPTS

- **Causality** – the causes of the global hydrological cycle
- **Systems** – how the global hydrological cycle functions

Where is all the water?

The amount of water available worldwide is finite. If a 4.5-litre jug represents all of the water on Earth, a single tablespoonful represents the available freshwater.

- As Figure 1 shows, freshwater makes up just 2.5% of the water on Earth.
- NASA estimates that every drop of freshwater has been consumed at least once before, because water flows through a closed hydrological cycle (see Figure 2).
- Solar energy causes water to evaporate from both sea and land, which then returns as precipitation.

However, as Figure 3 shows, most freshwater is locked up as either ice or groundwater for anything from 1000 to 10 000 years.

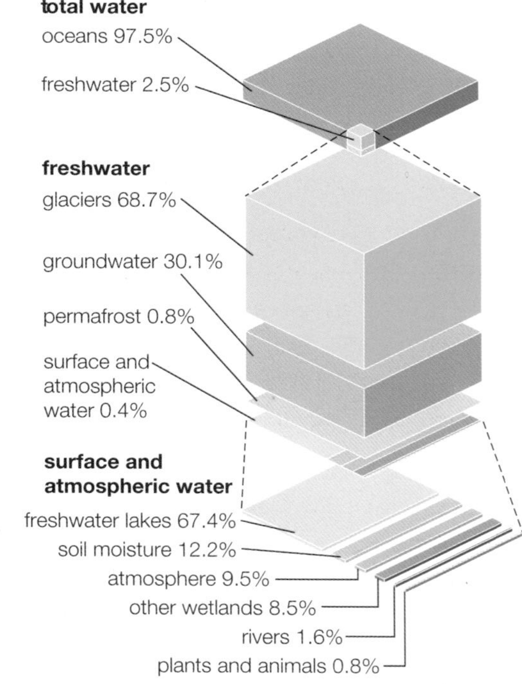

Figure 1 *The size and distribution of global water stores*

The global hydrological cycle – a closed system

The total amount of water in the world does not change; the hydrological cycle is a **closed system**. No inputs occur from outside and nothing is lost. However, as Figure 2 shows, water's nature and form changes all the time. Two processes – **solar energy** and **gravitational potential energy** – drive the global hydrological cycle. More evaporation occurs as the global climate warms, which increases moisture levels in the atmosphere. This in turn can lead to increased condensation as air cools, and therefore greater precipitation. This explains why some places may experience increased cloud cover and precipitation as climate changes.

Gravitational potential energy keeps water moving through the system in a sequence of inputs, outputs, stores and flows.

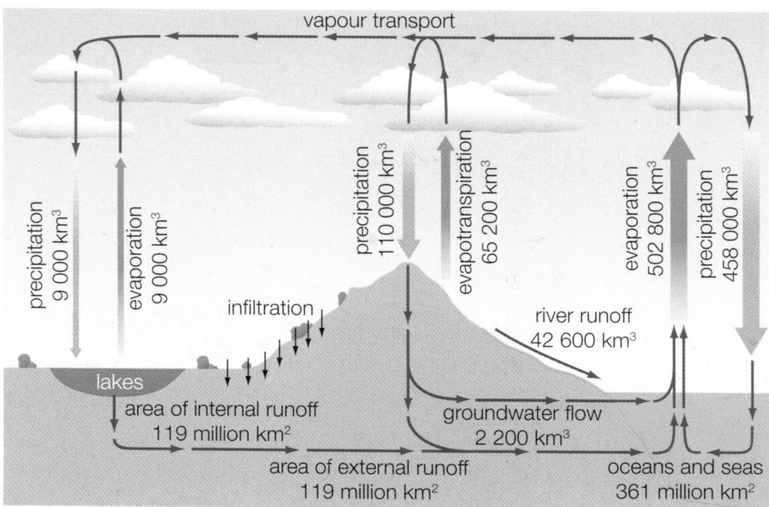

Figure 2 *The global hydrological cycle. Note how nothing is lost or gained – it operates as a closed system.*

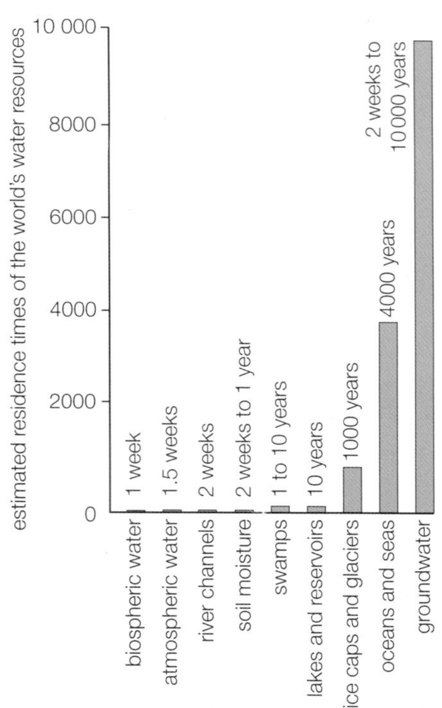

Figure 3 *The estimated storage times of the world's water resources. Some groundwater has been stored undisturbed for thousands of years and is referred to as fossil or paleo water.*

- At a global scale the system is continuous, with **outputs** governing **inputs** because nothing is lost or gained.
- However, shifts in the world's climatic zones mean that some **stores** are depleting, e.g. the ice in the Polar regions and in mountain glaciers is melting without being replenished.
- In areas that are warming, ground surfaces dry out as evaporation increases. Global air circulation then takes this extra vapour to cooler areas, where it condenses into clouds and precipitation.

Key words

Closed system – Where inputs and outputs are balanced. As shown in Section 1.1, a system has **inputs** and **outputs**, linked by **stores** and **flows**.

Solar energy – Energy from the sun, heating water and causing evaporation/transpiration.

Gravitational potential energy – Ways in which water accelerates under gravity, thus transporting it to rivers and eventually to the sea.

Global extremes

Solar energy is concentrated in the Tropics, where much is absorbed by the sea. Evaporation from the sea produces high rainfall; 74% of the world's rainfall occurs at sea (most within the Tropics). The rest is distributed unevenly, both spatially and in time. The seasonal monsoons and droughts of Asia and Africa contrast with the temperate climates of North West Europe.

Different climatic regions vary in the nature and size of their inputs, transfers and flows of water. The polar and tropical rainforest regions described in Figure 4 provide clear examples of how different hydrological processes compare.

Figure 4 *Comparing the hydrology of polar and tropical rainforest regions*

Polar hydrology

- There are freeze/thaw seasonal differences.
- Winter snow insulates the ground and 85% of solar radiation is reflected.
- Permafrost creates impermeable surfaces.
- Lakes and rivers are frozen.
- Limited vegetation cover reduces heat absorption.
- The spring thaw causes rapid runoff.
- The summer thaw produces surface runoff, increasing evaporation tenfold.
- The freeze-thaw cycle causes the seasonal release of biogenic gases (caused by plant decomposition) into the atmosphere, as well as carbon and nutrients into rivers and seas.
- It is characterised by orographic or frontal precipitation (see Section 1.3) and low humidity.
- Annual precipitation is less than 200 mm.

The cryosphere. *Here, seasonal thaws bring increased surface saturation and thinning permafrost. If this thaw becomes continuous, water flows away and is lost – known as* **cryosphere loss**.

Tropical rainforest hydrology

- Few seasonal differences.
- Dense vegetation intercepts and consumes up to 75% of precipitation.
- 50-75% of precipitation then returns by evapotranspiration.
- Evapotranspiration cools the air as energy is used during the process.
- Rainforests generate their own rain; most is recycled within the Tropics.
- Less than 25% of rainfall reaches rivers or other surface water.
- There is limited surface infiltration or groundwater.
- Rainforests are 'cloud factories'.
- Deforestation reduces evaporation, in turn reducing vapour and local rainfall.
- There are constant high temperatures.
- It is characterised by convectional rainfall (see Section 1.3) and high humidity.
- Annual precipitation is over 2000 mm.

Tropical rainforests. *Here, permanently dense forest produces high rates of evapotranspiration, with water returning to the surface as precipitation that feeds large rivers such as the Amazon.*

Global stores and flows

Life depends on freshwater. Most of it is locked up in the **cryosphere** (glaciers and ice sheets), or below the surface as groundwater. Less than 0.4% of freshwater is contained within surface lakes, rivers, the biosphere and atmosphere at any one time, and much of that is transferred globally by flows known as fluxes. These fluxes vary with the season and the temperature, and the variation is known as **annual fluxes**. Figure 5 lists the quantities of water involved.

Store to store	Process	Flux/flow amount of water (in km^3 per year)
Oceans and atmosphere	Evaporation Precipitation	400 000 370 000
Landmasses and atmosphere	Evaporation Precipitation	60 000 90 000
Landmasses and oceans	Surface runoff	30 000

Figure 5 *Annual fluxes (or flows) of water between global stores*

The global water budget

As Figure 5 shows, oceans lose more water through evaporation than they gain through precipitation, whereas the opposite is true for landmasses. Surface runoff makes up the difference – known as the **balance**. If this balance were disturbed, the oceans would receive more water and the continents would dry. The balance is known as the global **water budget** and it ensures that this does not happen.

Water does not stay in the atmosphere for long. Its **residence time** is short because the yearly flux of 460 000 km^3 (i.e. oceans to atmosphere plus land to atmosphere in Figure 5) is almost 35 times greater than the amount of water the atmosphere can hold at any one time. Water resides in oceans for longer periods; the oceans are 3000 times bigger than either the annual flux to or from the atmosphere, or from the land.

The importance of the Tropics

The steep angle of the sun over tropical oceans allows intense solar radiation, causing high evaporation. Trade winds transfer water vapour towards the Inter-Tropical Convergence Zone (**ITCZ**). There, strong **convectional** currents lift the air so that it cools and condenses into clouds, causing heavy rainstorms. Most of the world's rainfall is created in the ITCZ, so this is the biggest flux (see Figure 5) transferring water from oceans to land. Figure 6 shows the ITCZ – a wide belt of clouds within the Tropics. These huge atmospheric flows of moisture are called **tropospheric rivers**.

Figure 6 *Water vapour and the ITCZ. The ITCZ is confined to the Tropics throughout the year – moving with the sun into the northern hemisphere in May-August, and into the southern hemisphere during October-February*

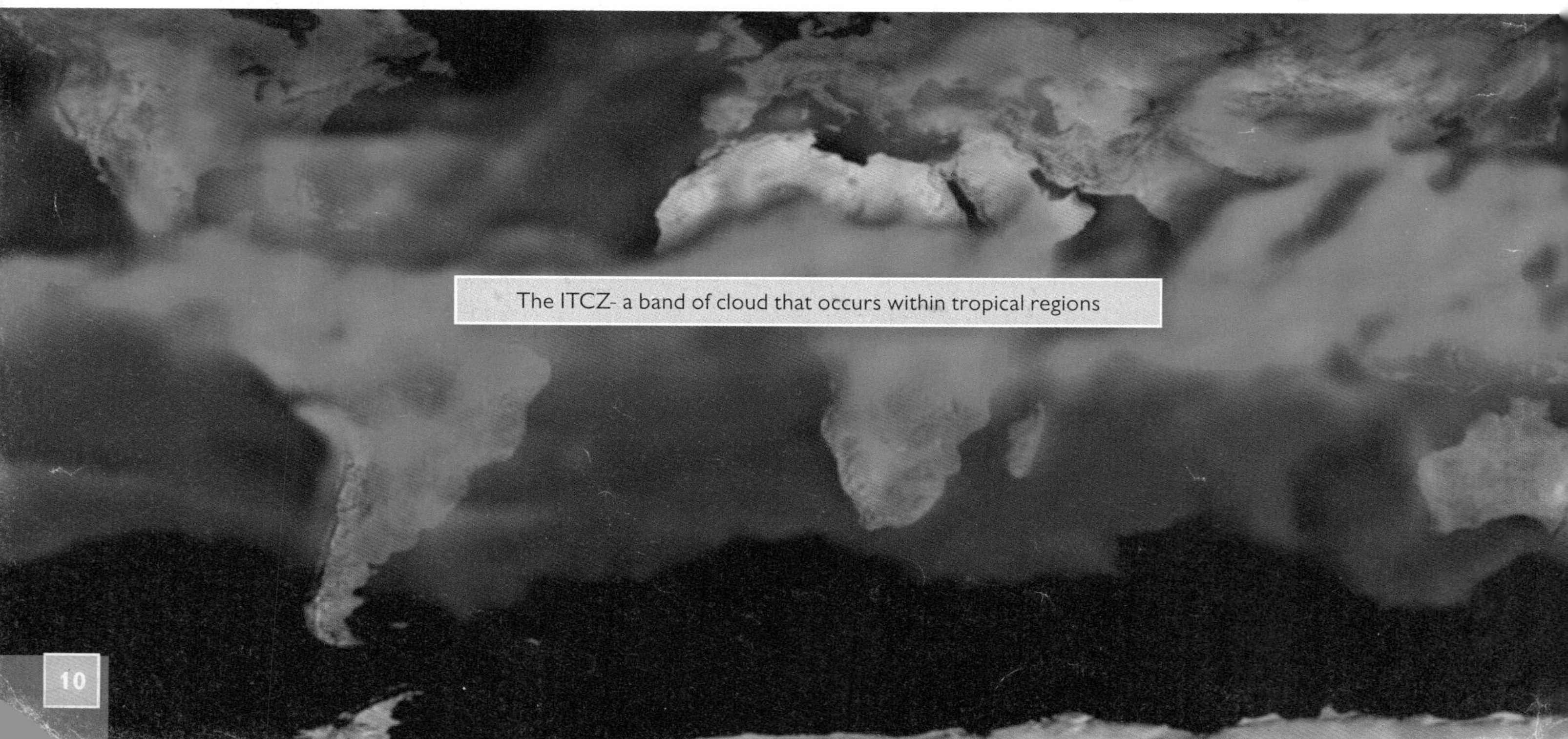

The importance of the polar regions

About two-thirds of the Earth's freshwater is locked up in the cryosphere – places where the temperature remains below freezing for much of the year, such as ice sheets and glaciers. However, as the global climate continues to warm, some of the frozen cryosphere water is released by melting to flow into the sea – adding to the closed hydrological cycle.

The polar regions contribute to the circulation of water and the transfer of heat around the world, which drive the global hydrological cycle. An ocean circulation occurs, known as the **thermohaline circulation** – sometimes called the global conveyor belt – which is explained in Figure 7.

How the thermohaline circulation works:

1. Ocean water in the polar regions is colder, more saline (salty) and denser than in the Tropics, so it sinks.
2. The cold sinking water draws in warmer water from the ocean surface above, which in turn draws water across the surface from the Tropics.
3. The movement of water from the Tropics draws cold water up from the ocean bottom, to be warmed again.

Fossil water

Untapped ancient stores of freshwater exist in the polar regions and beneath many deserts. New technologies now make it possible to access the water stores, known as **aquifers**, beneath Greenland's ice sheet and under the Kenyan desert. For example, Kenya's Lotikipi aquifer contains an estimated 200 billion cubic metres of freshwater – that's 70 years' supply at Kenya's current rates of use, even without the natural replenishment that it receives from mountain streams.

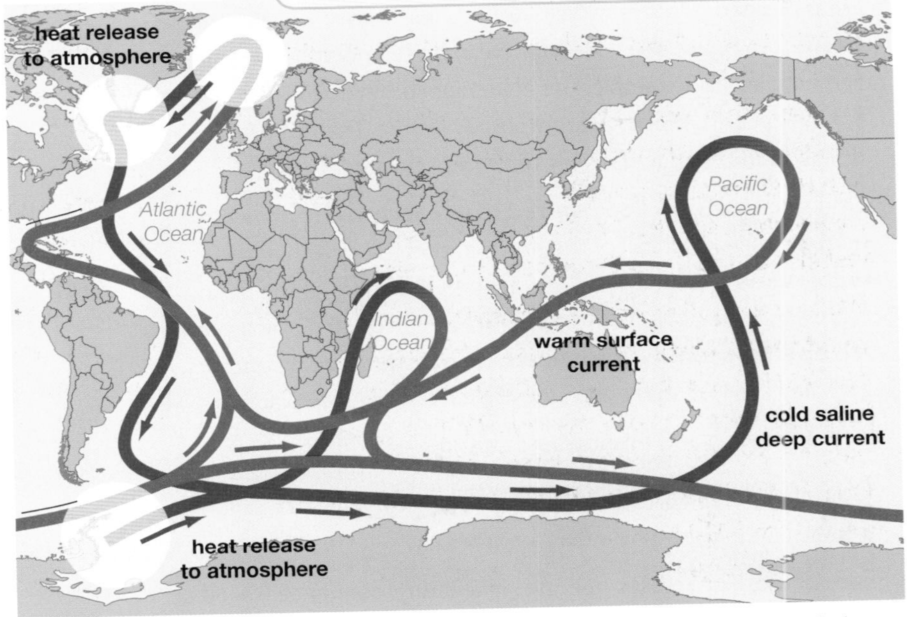

Figure 7 *The thermohaline circulation – also known as the global conveyor belt – a flow of warm and cold water that circulates around the world's oceans*

Over to you

1. Use the data in Figure 2 to construct a system diagram, with inputs, black box, and outputs. It should contain (**a**) proportional flow lines representing the amounts of water involved in each case, (**b**) proportional flow lines which show processes within the 'black box'.
2. In pairs, draw a mind map to show how climate change could alter residence times, storage capacities and global fluxes.
3. In pairs, identify the key differences between:
   - **a** tropical and polar region stores/fluxes.
   - **b** the influences of tropical and polar regions on the global hydrological system.

On your own

4. Distinguish between the following groups of terms: (**a**) global water budget, global water balance, and water residence times, (**b**) stores and fluxes, (**c**) groundwater and fossil/ancient water.
5. Why are the cryosphere and fossil groundwater stores under threat?
6. Research new technologies that make fossil water accessible. Use the *National Geographic* website to search for 'fossil water and world freshwater'. Write a brief report entitled 'Accessing Fossil Water'.

Exam-style question

Explain how the global hydrological cycle operates as a closed system. *(6 marks)*

1.3 Local hydrological cycles – drainage basins

In this section, you'll learn that the drainage basin is an open system within the global hydrological cycle.

KEY CONCEPTS

- **Causality** – the causes of processes within drainage basins
- **Systems** – how the drainage basin functions as an open system

Open systems

The *global* hydrological cycle is a closed system – it is a continuous cycle and, over the longer term, nothing is gained or lost. But at a local scale, hydrological processes operate within areas drained by a river and its tributaries, known as a **drainage basin** (see Figure 1A). Drainage basins vary enormously in size and nature – for example, the Mississippi basin drains nearly 3.3 million km^2, much of it remote, whilst the Thames basin drains 16 000 km^2 and is very densely populated.

Drainage basins are also referred to as **catchment areas**, because they 'catch' all of the precipitation falling within the **watershed** – an imaginary line around the edges of the basin, separating one basin from another (see Figure 1A). Drainage basins are **open systems** – their inputs are not governed by outputs, and they can lose more than they receive. They lose water by:

- evaporation and evapotranspiration to the atmosphere
- surface runoff, also known as overland flow, to the sea
- percolation into groundwater stores.

Each of these processes operates in a natural sequence (called a sequential system), i.e. where one step follows another. The sequences are shown in Figure 1B.

Hydrological processes

When precipitation occurs, the water can only follow three pathways. It can:

- reach the land surface and then **infiltrate** (soak into) the topsoil
- run off the surface as **overland flow** (also known as **surface runoff**)
- be **evaporated** back into the atmosphere.

Any pathway taken may be delayed by the following:

- The water could be **intercepted** by plants or buildings, before either evaporating or infiltrating into the surface.
- Some surface water infiltrates through the surface and eventually **percolates** through the rocks underneath to become **groundwater**, where it may be stored in **aquifers** for some time.

Surface runoff occurs over impermeable, saturated or baked surfaces – eventually reaching river channels as **streamflow**.

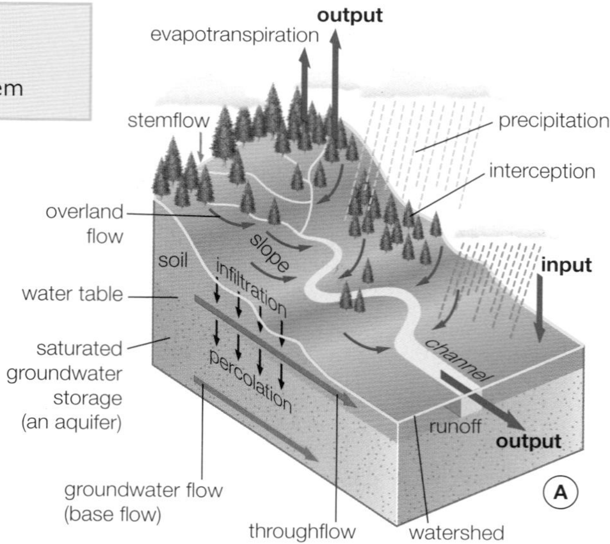

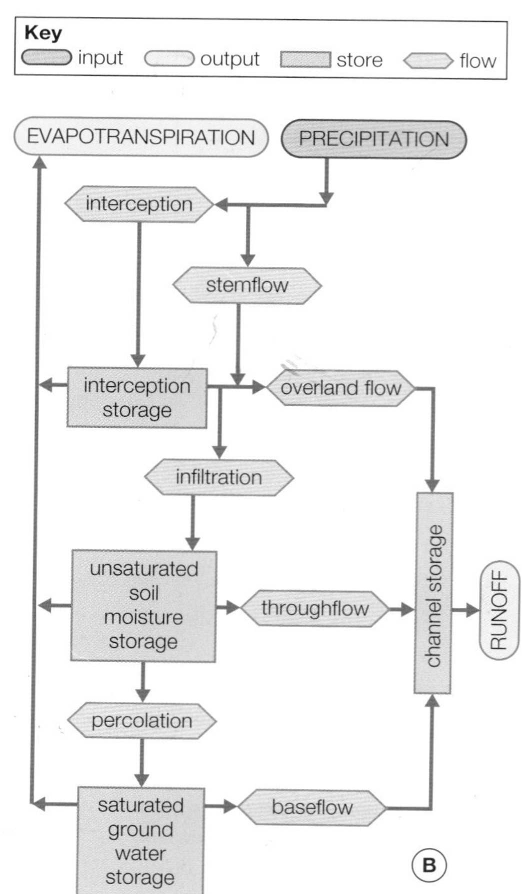

Figure 1 Two systems: (**A**) the drainage basin system, and (**B**) how the drainage basin operates in a series of sequential events (a sequential system)

The hydrological cycle – know your terms!

Inputs

- **Precipitation** – Moisture in any form.

Storage

- **Interception** – Temporary storage, as water is captured by plants, buildings and hard surfaces before reaching the soil.
- **Vegetation storage** – Any moisture taken up by vegetation and held within plants.
- **Surface storage** – Any surface water in lakes, ponds, puddles.
- **Soil moisture** – Water held within the soil.
- **Groundwater storage** – Water held within permeable rocks (also known as an aquifer).
- **Channel storage** – Water held in rivers and streams.

Flows and processes

- **Infiltration** – Water entering the topsoil. Most common during slow or steady rainfall.
- **Throughflow** – Also known as inter-flow; water seeping laterally through soil below the surface, but above the water table.
- **Percolation** – The downward seepage of water through rock under gravity, especially on permeable rocks e.g. sandstone and chalk.
- **Stem flow** – Water flowing down plant stems or drainpipes.
- **Base flow** – Also known as **groundwater flow**. Slow-moving water that seeps into a river channel.
- **Channel flow** – The volume of water flowing within a river channel (also called discharge, and runoff).
- **Surface runoff** – Also called overland flow. Flow over the surface during an intense storm, or when the ground is frozen, saturated or on impermeable clay.

Outputs

- **Evaporation** – The conversion of water to vapour.
- **Transpiration** – Water taken up by plants and transpired onto the leaf surface.
- **Evapotranspiration** – The combined effect of evaporation and transpiration.
- **River discharge** – The volume of water passing a certain point in the channel over a certain amount of time.

Drainage basin factors

Solar energy and gravity control the natural movements of water within a drainage basin. However, the shape, relief, geology, vegetation, climate and land uses of each basin determine what happens to the precipitation when it falls – known as the **basin-wide** factors. These are illustrated in Figure 2.

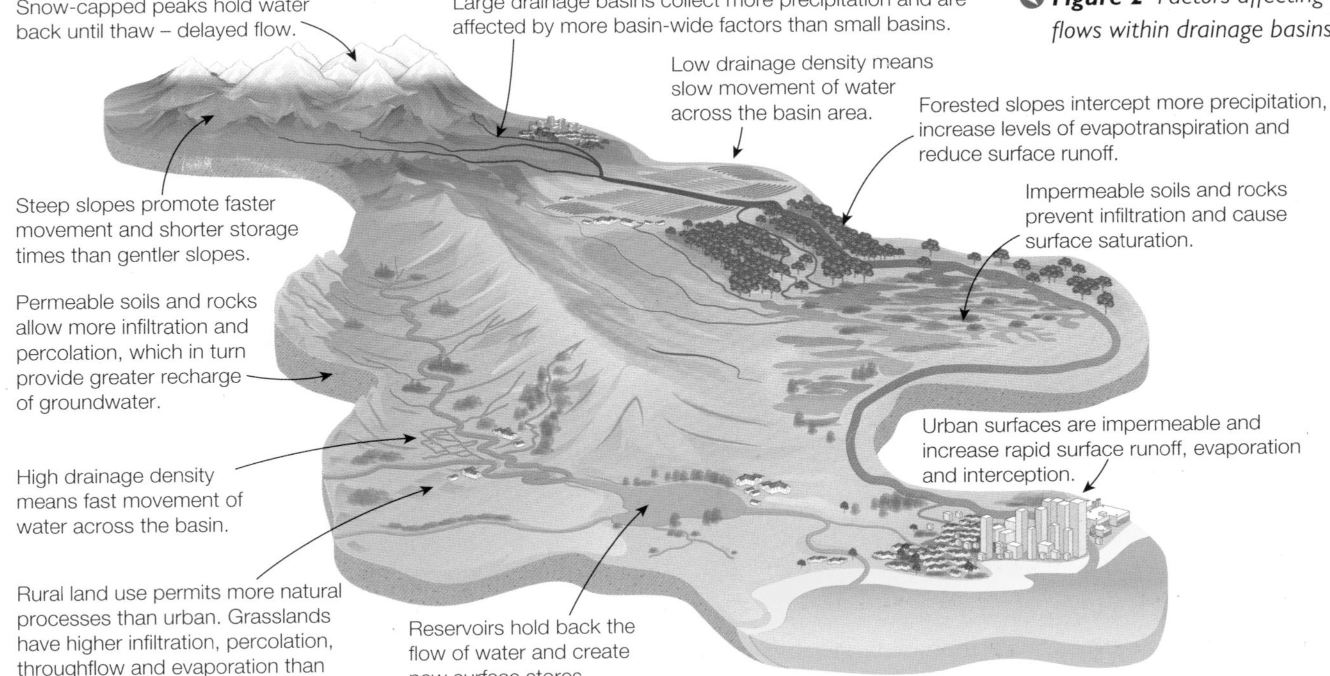

***Figure 2** Factors affecting flows within drainage basins*

The precipitation input

When warm moist air rises, it cools – causing water vapour to condense, clouds to form and eventually rain or snow to fall. Figure 3 explains how air can be forced to rise in three ways.

- Drainage basins located on the western side of the UK – and exposed to air masses approaching from the Atlantic – are particularly prone to **orographic** and **frontal** rainfall. North-western counties, such as Cumbria, can receive over 2000 mm of rainfall a year, and are prone to saturated surfaces, high **water tables** and **antecedent** moisture (water from one storm that has not had time to drain away before more rain arrives) – all of which make flooding more likely.
- Drainage basins in East Anglia are much drier, but in the summer months can experience heavy bursts of rain due to **convectional** air instability. In these months the ground warms up, evaporation takes place and the air above is heated and rises. Summer thunderstorms produce short bursts of heavy rain, which can lead to **flash flooding** when dry soil surfaces become waterlogged very quickly, causing rapid surface runoff.

Figure 3 *Different types of rainfall affecting the UK*

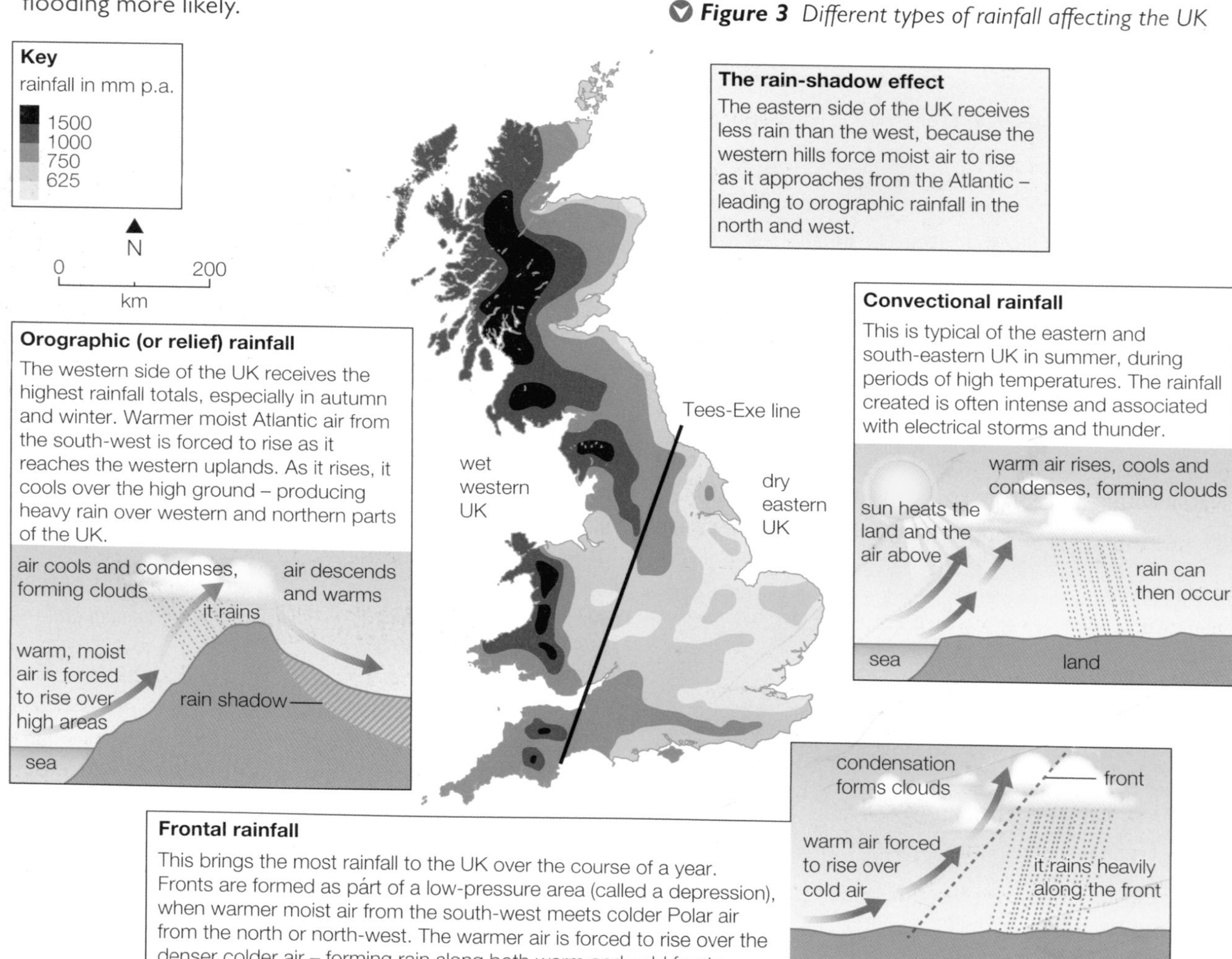

Human impacts on drainage basins

Overabstraction

The Thames basin is home to 13 million people. It is also one of the driest areas in the UK, averaging just 690 mm of rainfall a year. It's a basin under pressure from growing water demands and greater abstraction. Over 40% of London's water comes from chalk aquifers. These are replenished by rain falling on the Marlborough Downs to the west of London, the Chilterns to the north, and the North Downs to the south. Abstracting too much water from groundwater reserves leads to rivers drying up in times of low rainfall.

Deforestation

The Tropics have a key role in the global hydrological system (see Section 1.2). However, they are also fragile natural environments, and the complex biodiversity of their forests flourishes on relatively thin soils. The removal of the dense forest canopy protecting the vital topsoil can have devastating consequences. Human activities such as the clearing of forests for new roads and palm oil plantations, and modern agribusinesses, disrupt the drainage basin cycle by accelerating natural processes. Figure 4 shows how deforestation can change natural hydrological processes.

Figure 4 *The hydrological system before and after deforestation*

Changing land use – urbanisation

Building new storage reservoirs, or abstracting more water from rivers and groundwater reserves, helps to satisfy the increasing water demands of expanding cities at the expense of natural water flows. The physical character of urban areas can also affect the local hydrological cycle. Figure 5 shows how the impermeable surfaces of built-up areas can alter the natural flow of water.

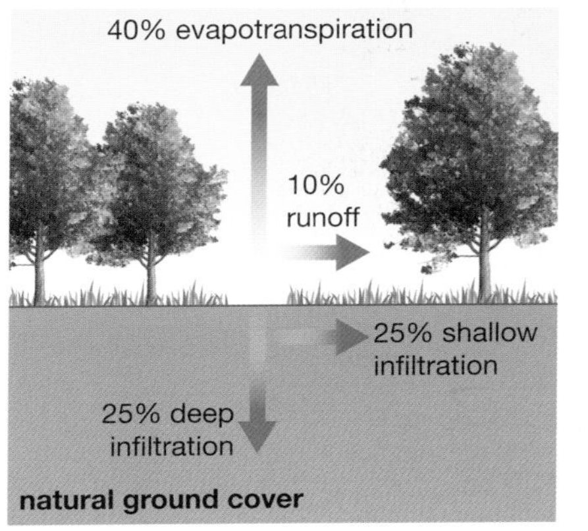

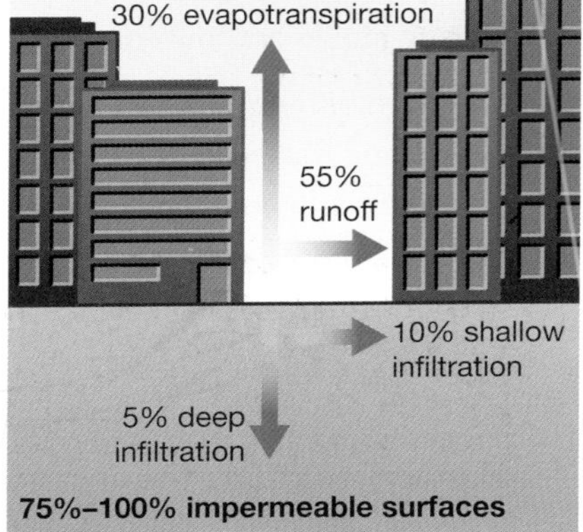

Figure 5 *How urbanisation affects the hydrological cycle*

Reservoirs

Man-made storage reservoirs interrupt the natural flows of water, by delaying the flows through a drainage basin and adding to the amounts lost through evaporation. It is estimated that 7% more water is evaporated from the world's reservoirs than is actually used by people. Man-made reservoirs have other impacts too:

- In the Tropics, mats of floating plants on the reservoir's surface make evapotranspiration rates six times higher than in open water.
- Salinity levels within the reservoir can also rise as its water evaporates.
- Dams reduce the river flow below them, leading to the loss of vegetation. For example, Kenya's Tana River floodplain forest is dying because dams built upstream have now eliminated floods there.
- Reservoirs abstract water from the drainage basin.

Exam-style question

Explain why a drainage basin can be regarded as an open system. *(6 marks)*

Over to you

1. Make a copy of Figure 1B. Using Figures 2 to 4, annotate your copy to show how (**a**) physical, and (**b**) human activity can alter natural inputs, stores, flows and outputs of a drainage basin.
2. In pairs, draw flow diagrams to show a sequence of events to illustrate how (**a**) deforestation and (**b**) urbanisation can contribute to:
   - **i** downstream flooding
   - **ii** potential water shortages.

On your own

3. Write a report analysing the impacts of changing land uses caused by human activities within a drainage basin.

1.4 The water balance and river regimes

In this section, you'll learn how the hydrological cycle influences water budgets and river systems at a local scale.

SYNOPTIC THEME AND KEY CONCEPTS

- **Players** – the role of planners in managing water use
- **Causality** – how the hydrological cycle influences water budgets and river systems; how and why storm hydrographs vary
- **Systems** – how river systems are influenced by local factors and those elsewhere

Key word

Potential evapotranspiration (PE) – An estimate of the amount of water lost through evaporation and transpiration in any given period, depending on temperature and air humidity.

Water budgets

In the short term, water availability varies from day to day; month to month and year to year. But over a longer period, there is usually a natural rhythm that balances out times of surplus with times of deficit. This balance is called the **water budget** and reflects the differences between inputs and outputs in any given area.

A drainage basin provides the best geographical unit to observe and measure these rhythms, because factors within the basin control how much water is available at any given time. Figure 1 shows the key components of a water budget, including natural and human factors that affect hydrological processes.

This budget can also be expressed as the **water balance equation**. It balances precipitation (**P**), runoff/river discharge (**Q**), potential evapotranspiration (**E**) and soil moisture and groundwater storage (**S**). Each year, whatever falls as precipitation should be balanced by the other components – written as the equation: **P = Q + E +/– S**. These factors can also be shown on an annual budget graph, such as Figure 2.

Inputs	Outputs
• Precipitation • Water diversion into the area • Groundwater flow into the area • Surface water flow into the area • Surface runoff into the area	• Evapotranspiration • Water diversion out of the area • Groundwater flow out of the area • Surface water flow out of the area • Surface runoff out of the area • Industrial or residential uses within the area

Figure 1 *The components of the water budget of any given place*

A Precipitation exceeds potential evapotranspiration (PE). Soil water is full with a soil moisture surplus for plants, runoff and groundwater recharge.

B Potential evapotranspiration exceeds precipitation. Soil moisture is used up by plants, or lost by evaporation (called soil moisture utilisation).

C Soil moisture store is now used up. Precipitation is likely to be absorbed by soil, rather than produce runoff. River levels will fall or dry up completely.

D Deficiency of soil moisture, as the store is used up. PE exceeds precipitation. Plants must adapt to survive and crops need irrigation.

E Precipitation exceeds PE. Soil moisture is recharged.

F Soil moisture is now full. Field capacity is reached. Additional rainfall will percolate to the water table, and groundwater stores will be recharged.

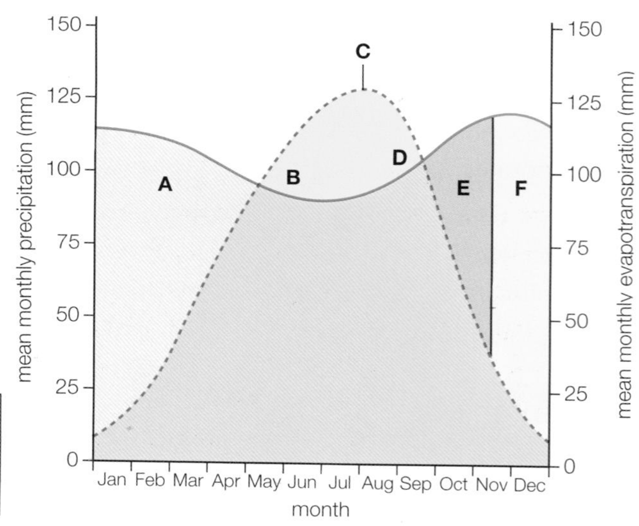

Key
precipitation
potential evapotranspiration

Figure 2 *The components of a water budget – the annual budget graph for a temperate climate like that of the UK*

	Jan	Feb	Mar	Apr	May	June	July	Aug	Sept	Oct	Nov	Dec
Rainfall (mm)	78	59	48	49	54	48	58	60	63	70	75	77
Potential evapotranspiration (mm)	5	11	31	50	82	95	97	88	60	33	12	5

Figure 3 *Water budget data for south Hampshire*

Rainfall effectiveness and water availability

Land use changes in river basins affect water availability and quality. Figures 2 and 3 show that PE exceeds precipitation in the summer – leading to lower water levels in rivers, lakes and ponds. The **soil moisture** content also declines, and vegetation may wilt. However, there is a delay between the onset of dry weather and reduced soil moisture, just as there is between rainfall and runoff.

The UK's 'water year' begins in October, when rainfall exceeds evaporation. Storage areas are **recharged** from that point, and are usually full by January. Overland flow increases until there is a water **surplus**, which then raises the flood risk. As temperatures rise and rainfall decreases in spring, soils lose moisture and, by late summer, a **deficit** exists.

Effective rainfall is the amount of precipitation remaining after evaporation. This means that places with similar annual rainfall can experience very different water issues. For example, as Figure 4 shows, parts of East Anglia in the UK receive similar annual rainfall to arid Arizona in the USA, but the rainfall effectiveness of both places is very different.

Soil moisture in the hydrological cycle

The capacity of soil to retain moisture is vital to the hydrological cycle. The maximum capacity that a soil can hold is known as its **field** (or **infiltration**) **capacity**. This is reduced whenever evapotranspiration exceeds precipitation, causing a **water deficit**.

In south Essex (Figure 4A), irrigation is needed for farming. Without it, a dry landscape would exist like that in Figure 4B. Rainfall in Essex is spread fairly evenly throughout the year, whereas Coronado in Arizona has short intensive bursts separated by periods of drought. Precipitation following a dry period is known as **recharge**, when soil moisture levels increase. If soils saturate above field capacity, a **water surplus** occurs, generating surface runoff. **Flash flooding** is common in dry lands, where sun-baked soils cannot absorb intensive storm rains fast enough. The surface soil becomes saturated, causing rapid surface runoff.

Figure 4 *Similar amounts of rainfall but different landscapes:*

A *Great Wakering in Essex receives an average of 548 mm annually*

B *Coronado Memorial Park in Arizona, USA, receives an average of 517 mm annually*

A altitude 5 metres average temperature 10.1°C
average rainfall 548 mm

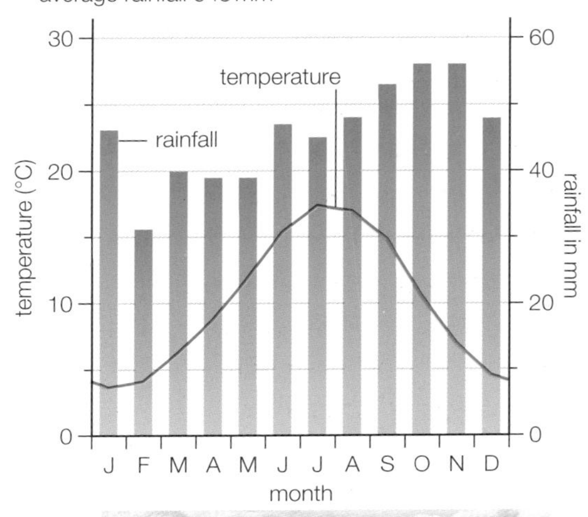

B altitude 464 metres average temperature 11.5°C
average rainfall 517 mm

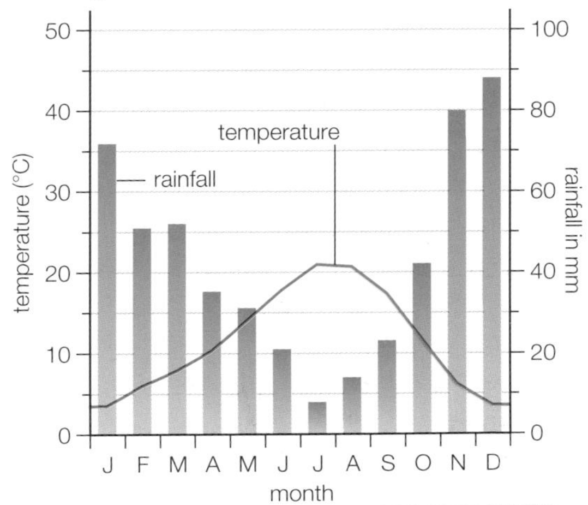

Patterns of flow – regimes and hydrographs

So far it's clear that the amount of precipitation reaching a river depends on both local and drainage basin-wide factors, as well as climatic controls.

- The pattern of a river's flow (or **discharge**) throughout the year reflects all of these factors. The annual pattern of flow is known as a river's **regime**.
- At a local level, the effects of an individual storm can be shown on a **storm hydrograph**.

River regimes

Tropical rivers generally have fairly uniform flow patterns, especially in areas where rain falls every month. However, worldwide, river regimes tend to have a seasonal pattern whereby they respond directly to the amount of precipitation. There are two main types of river regimes:

- **Simple regimes** – These are where the river experiences a period of seasonally high discharge, followed by low discharge. They are typical of rivers where the inputs depend on glacial meltwater, snowmelt or seasonal storms (e.g. monsoons). Rivers within temperate climates, which rise in mountainous regions where summer snowmelt occurs, tend to be like this (e.g. the Rhône in Figure 5).
- **Complex regimes** – These are where larger rivers cross several different relief and climatic zones, and therefore experience the effects of different seasonal climatic events. This is true of rivers like the Mississippi or Ganges (and the three rivers described in Figure 6). Human factors can also contribute to their complexity, such as damming rivers for energy or irrigation.

A river's regime reflects differences in precipitation, temperature, evapotranspiration and land use throughout the river's catchment during the year. Characteristics of the drainage basin itself (shape, geology, soil type, land cover), as well as human intervention, influence a river's regime. Some of the world's longest rivers are several thousand kilometres in length, so they may cross several climatic zones and encounter very different land uses and population densities along their length. The longer the river, the more complex the variables tend to be – making the regime more complex. Figure 6 provides examples of three complex river regimes.

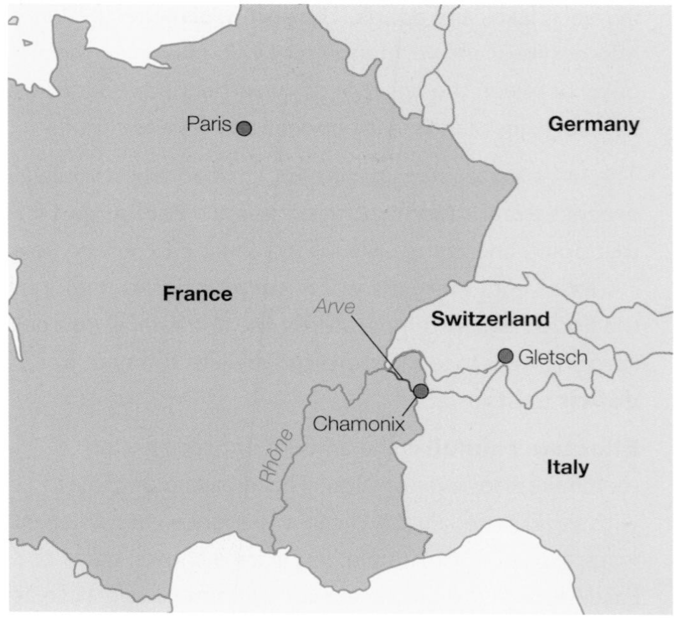

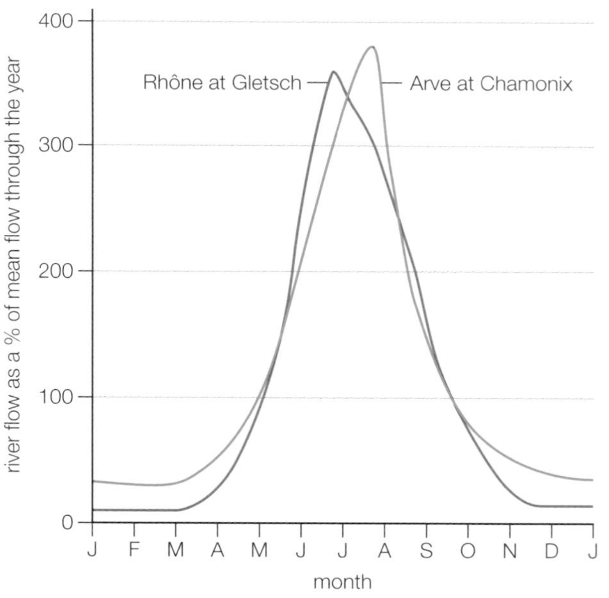

Figure 5 *A simple river regime for the rivers Rhône and Arve, where the rivers respond to localised factors within southern France and Switzerland*

River	Flow patterns	Major influences
Yukon, Alaska, USA	**High flow:** Spring and summer (caused by snowmelt) **Low/no flow:** Winter (when precipitation is frozen) **Seasonable variability:** Very large **Human influences:** Relatively few – most of its landscape is wilderness. Some HEP use for mining industries	Tundra, taiga, and mountain climates Higher summer temperatures, rainfall and snowmelt coincide
Amazon, Brazil	**High flow:** Wetter season **Low/no flow:** Drier season **Seasonable variability:** Moderate variability – fed by Andean rivers outside rainforest region **Human influences:** Increasing (although a low percentage of its flow at present); large dams used by Brazil's major cities for irrigation and HEP	Rainforest climate Seasonal precipitation – rainfall in every month but divided into higher and lower rainfall seasons Evapotranspiration levels very high
Murray-Darling, Australia (also see pages 42–3)	**High flow:** Wet season **Low/no flow:** Dry season **Seasonable variability:** High **Human influences:** Its waters are drawn by: • Australia's major cities • farms for irrigation	Seasonal sub-tropical climate – monsoon climate in northern tributaries of Queensland, which feeds the Darling; temperate climate in the south, which feeds the Murray Most of the basin lies in a rain shadow and undergoes long periods of drought

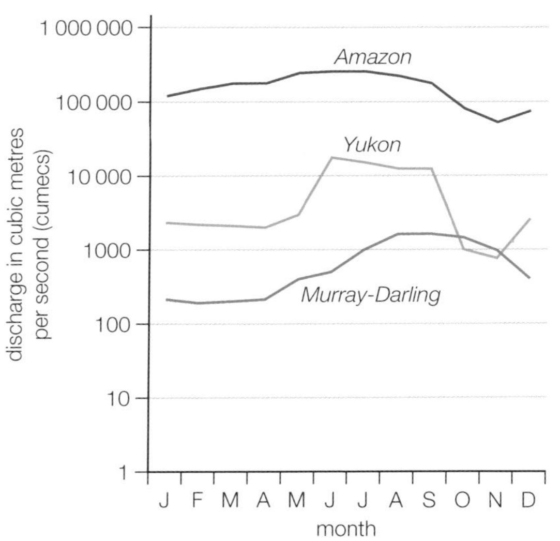

Figure 6 *Discharge patterns in three complex river regimes measured at the mouth of each river. Note the logarithmic y-axis on the graph (see Section 6.2). Consider to what extent latitude plays a part in the patterns shown (e.g. of the Yukon).*

Storm hydrographs

A **hydrograph** is a graph showing the **discharge** (volume of water) of a river at a given point over a period of time. A storm hydrograph – like that in Figure 7 – shows how a river responds to a particular storm, and displays both rainfall and discharge. When rain starts to fall, only a fraction of it will fall directly into the actual river channel, so the discharge does not increase immediately. Most rain falls onto the valley sides and takes time to reach the river. As the water makes its way into the river, the discharge increases – as shown by the **rising limb** on the graph. The gap between the peak (maximum) rainfall and peak discharge (highest river level) is known as the **lag time**.

Figure 7 *Characteristic features of a storm hydrograph. Each one tends to be slightly different, because it reflects the characteristics of the storm and of the river basin.*

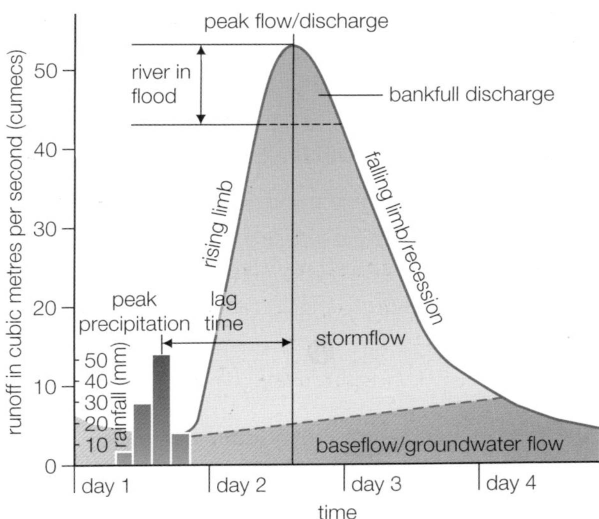

BACKGROUND

How and why storm hydrographs vary

Each storm hydrograph reflects the localised and contemporary characteristics of the drainage basin. Every change in land use and each previous period of weather will determine the timing and height of the peak. How quickly a river's flow will respond, depends on the factors listed in Figure 8.

How physical factors affect hydrographs

- **Size.** Larger catchments typically have higher flows, but take longer for peak flow to occur.
- **Shape.** Circular catchments concentrate water more quickly; in long narrow catchments, water takes time to reach a point downstream.
- **Drainage density (i.e. many or few tributaries).** Dense drainage networks carry water more efficiently, which increases the concentration of flows and in turn increases peak flow.
- **Rock permeability.** Permeable rocks allow increased infiltration, percolation and groundwater flow, which reduce surface runoff.
- **Soil characteristics.** Permeable and dry soils increase infiltration; deep soils can store more water before reduced rates of infiltration occur. Infiltration reduces surface runoff and evaporation.
- **Relief.** Steep catchments transfer water quickly, increasing peak flow and reducing lag time.
- **Vegetation type and characteristics.** Vegetation increases interception and evapotranspiration, plus infiltration through the presence of roots in the soil, thus reducing runoff and river flow.

How human factors affect hydrographs

- **Land use (e.g. naturally vegetated vs. agriculture).** Deforestation reduces vegetation cover. Ploughing furrows up/downslope increases runoff.
- **Urbanisation.** Concreted areas, roads and buildings have low permeability and increase overland flow via drains, thus reducing lag times and increasing peak flows.
- **Water management (e.g. dams/reservoirs, abstraction).** Dams/reservoirs regulate flows downstream by storing water. Abstraction lowers groundwater levels and increases percolation and infiltration when rain falls.

change in hydrograph shape A
higher peak flow
shorter time lag to peak flow
circular catchment shape
dense drainage network
impermeable geology
impermeable, waterlogged or shallow soils
steep terrain
sparse vegetation
land used for human activity
heavily urbanised
no water management intervention

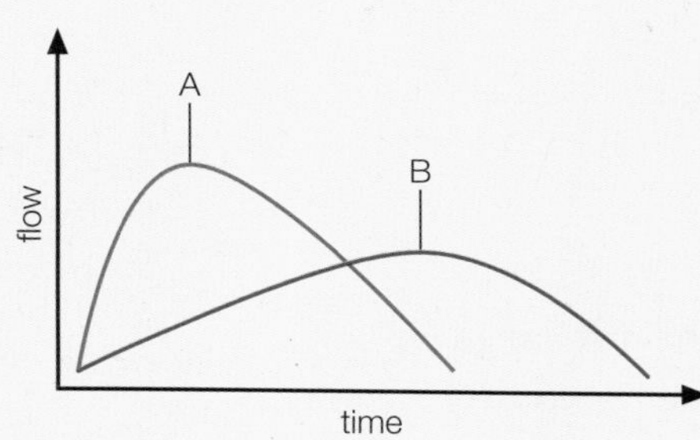

change in hydrograph shape B
lower peak flow
longer time lag to peak flow
linear catchment shape
sparse drainage network
permeable geology
permeable, dry or deep soils
flat terrain
dense vegetation
natural land uses
low or no urbanisation
water management intervention

Figure 8 *Factors that determine response times and peak flow*

Players in the hydrological cycle: planners

Within the UK, planners are required to determine whether any proposed development (e.g. a new housing estate or industrial use) will influence flood risk with the change in land use. Within England, the National Planning Policy Framework (NPPF) sets out strict guidelines.

Figure 9 shows that decisions vary depending on how much weight is given to environmental factors (which maintain river flow unaltered) versus those favouring economic development (which alter river flow). Economic development increases the likelihood of higher flow and a faster response time. Developers have to show that land use changes will not increase runoff beyond that estimated for a 'greenfield' site.

Figure 9 How key changes to land use can influence decisions made by planners

Figure 10 A green (planted) roof on Adnam's Brewery distribution centre in Southwold, Suffolk

SuDS systems

Recently, **Sustainable Drainage Systems (SuDS)** have been introduced to reduce runoff produced from rainfall. Examples of these include:

- green roofs (see Figure 10) – vegetation cover planted over a waterproof membrane
- infiltration basins – shallow depressions dug out to delay runoff and increase infiltration
- permeable pavements – to delay runoff by using gaps between pavement slabs
- rainwater harvesting – collecting rainwater from roofs to be recycled, e.g. for irrigating gardens
- soak-away – a channel dug out to disperse surface water into the ground
- filter drains – trenches filled with gravel to take runoff away
- detention basins – to delay storm runoff for a few hours.
- wetlands – retention areas with marsh/wetland vegetation.

Over to you

1 **a** Using the data in Figure 3, draw a water budget graph, and complete it so that it resembles Figure 2.

b Does south Hampshire have an annual water surplus or deficit?

c Using the data, outline the duration and characteristics of the periods of (**i**) recharge, (**ii**) surplus, (**iii**) utilisation, and (**iv**) deficit in south Hampshire.

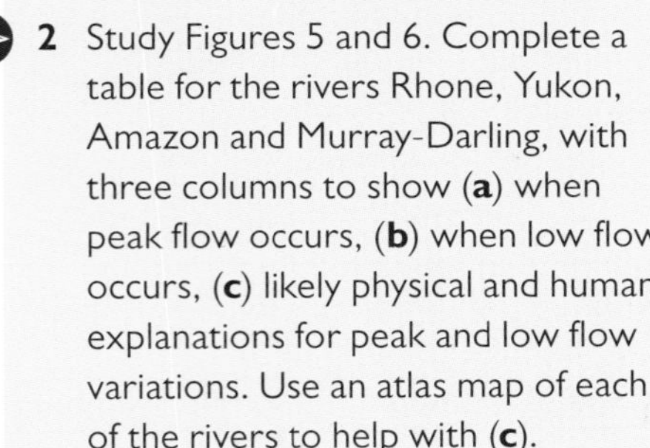

2 Study Figures 5 and 6. Complete a table for the rivers Rhone, Yukon, Amazon and Murray-Darling, with three columns to show (**a**) when peak flow occurs, (**b**) when low flow occurs, (**c**) likely physical and human explanations for peak and low flow variations. Use an atlas map of each of the rivers to help with (**c**).

On your own

3 Distinguish between the following groups of terms: (**a**) water budget and water balance equation, (**b**) soil moisture, infiltration capacity, and field capacity; (**c**) water deficit, water recharge and water surplus; (**d**) surface runoff and flash flood; (**e**) river regime and storm hydrograph.

4 Using Figures 7 and 8, draw, annotate and explain how storm hydrographs might behave in these circumstances:

a A rapid downpour on an urban area in winter after a prolonged wet period.

b A gentle summer fall of rain on an area of chalk or limestone geology.

c Prolonged heavy winter rain over a circular river basin.

5 **a** Using Figure 9, contrast natural and urban water balances.

b Outline ways in which planners can influence a river's response to storm events.

c In pairs, discuss how far planners should insist on the universal use of SuDS measures like that illustrated in Figure 10.

Exam-style question

Using examples, assess the extent to which the hydrological cycle can influence river systems at a local scale. (*12 marks*)

Deficits within the hydrological system

In this section, you'll learn that deficits within the hydrological system result from physical processes and have significant impacts.

EQ2 Sections 1.5 to 1.7 ask what factors influence the hydrological system over short- and long-term timescales.

KEY CONCEPTS

- **Causality** – the varying causes of drought
- **Systems** – how weather systems and ecosystems are irretrievably linked
- **Feedback** – how one event leads to another within a climatic system
- **Resilience** – the ability of rainforests and wetlands to sustain themselves

Tropical droughts – Rio's taps run dry!

It is difficult to believe that countries in wet tropical climates can suffer drought. Yet the period 2014-15 witnessed the worst drought in Brazil for 80 years. Water levels in some of the world's largest HEP schemes were so low that power supplies were suspended, agriculture was in crisis, and urban taps ran dry.

Causes of the 2014–15 drought

Rainfall in Brazil is normally predictable:

- Moist air moves in a westerly direction from the South Atlantic across the Amazon Basin.
- When the moist air encounters the high Andes mountain range to the west of the continent, it is forced to turn southwards – maintaining the flow of moisture around the Basin.

However, Figure 1 shows what happened in 2014-15:

- A series of high-pressure systems diverted rain-bearing winds further north, away from the Amazon, and also prevented them from diverting southwards from the Andes.
- Heavy rains then occurred in Bolivia and Paraguay, whilst dry air remained over Brazil.

Impacts of the 2014–15 drought

Both *The Guardian* and *The Economist* described the drought as Brazil's worst. Its impacts led to street protests in São Paulo, Brazil's largest city, and included:

- water rationing for 4 million people; water supplies were cut off for three days a week in some towns
- the halting of HEP production, which led to power cuts
- the depletion of Brazil's 17 largest reservoirs to dangerously low levels (see Figure 2) – some down to just 1% of capacity
- increased groundwater abstraction, which led aquifers to become dangerously low
- a reduced crop of Arabica coffee beans (Brazil is the world's largest producer of these), which pushed up global coffee prices by 50%.

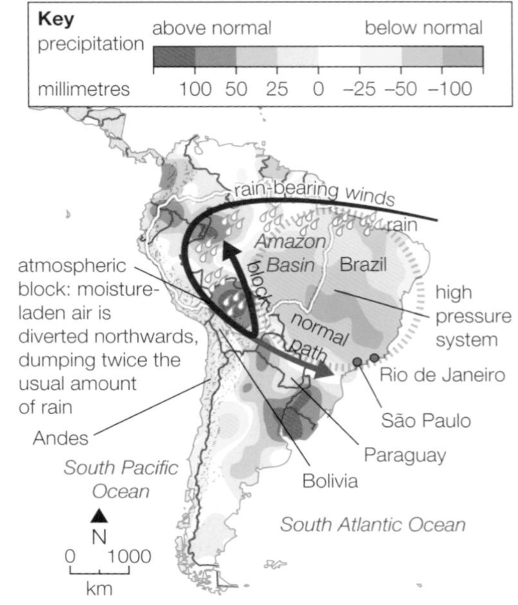

Figure 1 *The weather systems that brought drought to Brazil in 2014-15*

Figure 2 *Drought impacts on Brazil: flows into the Cantareira reservoir system, 1930–2014*

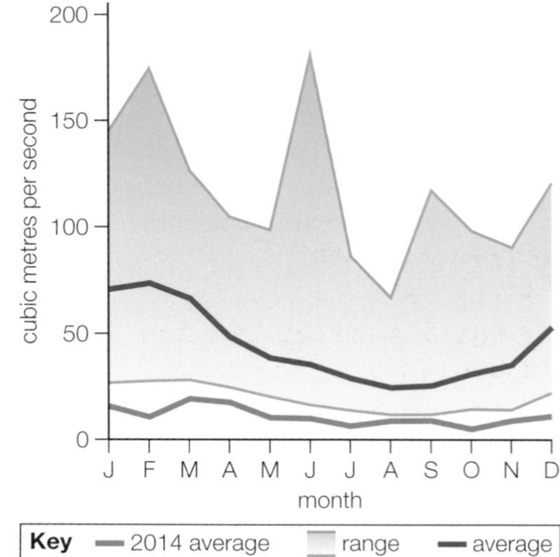

Deforestation, droughts and feedback

There have been three droughts in Brazil since 2000, and links between these more frequent periods of drought are becoming clearer. In 2014, climate scientists reported that deforestation in the Amazon may now have passed a **tipping point** – in other words, changing hydrological and climatic cycles permanently.

Rainforests recycle half of their rainfall, but the **positive feedback loop** of deforestation and less rainfall is reducing the ability of the rainforest to regenerate. As a result of this, fragile rainforest ecosystems are less **resilient**. Thinning forests have reduced soil water storage and evapotranspiration. In turn, these lead to changing weather patterns – with lower precipitation. Figure 4 shows a 'domino effect' of feedback loops that reinforce the drying of the Tropics.

Section 1.2 discussed the importance of tropical stores and **flux** – forests regulate regional climate and generate flows of moisture across the continent. Now, the combined risk of global climate change, ENSO cycles (see Section 1.7) and deforestation will probably alter this so that extreme weather will become more frequent. Drought could mean that:

- the Amazon rainforest's capacity to absorb carbon will decline
- regional water cycles will change and soil temperatures will increase
- the Amazon rainforest will be replaced with savannah-like grasslands
- more wildfires will increase the level of carbon in the atmosphere
- reduced rainfall will threaten Brazil's dependency on HEP (which generates 70% of its electricity)
- the world will lose a major carbon sink and source of moisture.

BACKGROUND

What is a drought?

Droughts exist when there is a **water deficit** in a particular place over a period of time, compared to the average rainfall for that same period. In the UK, that's 15 consecutive days with less than 0.2 mm rainfall (so most droughts are short-term); in Libya it's 2 years (much longer term)!

As Figure 3 shows, there are three types of drought:

- **Meteorological** – the degree of dryness compared to 'normal' precipitation
- **Agricultural** – insufficient water for crops, so that they wilt without irrigation
- **Hydrological** – where drainage basins suffer shortfalls.

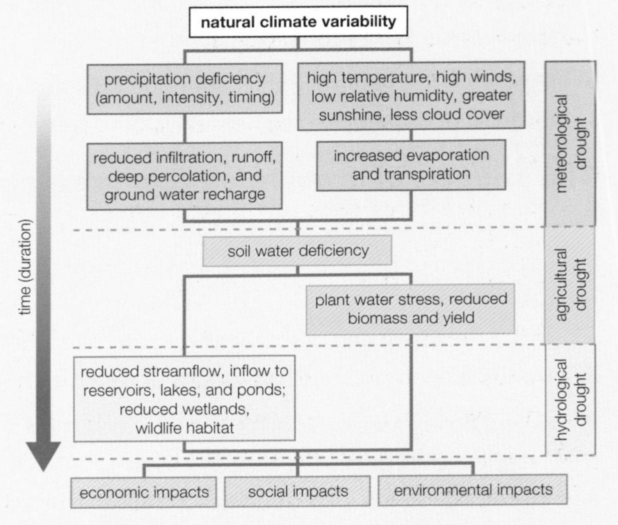

Figure 3 *Three types of drought, based on their causes*

Key words

Positive feedback – A cyclical sequence of events that amplifies or increases change.

Negative feedback – A cyclical sequence of events that damps down or neutralises the effects of a system.

Tipping point – When a system changes from one state to another.

Resilience – The ability of a system to 'bounce back' and survive.

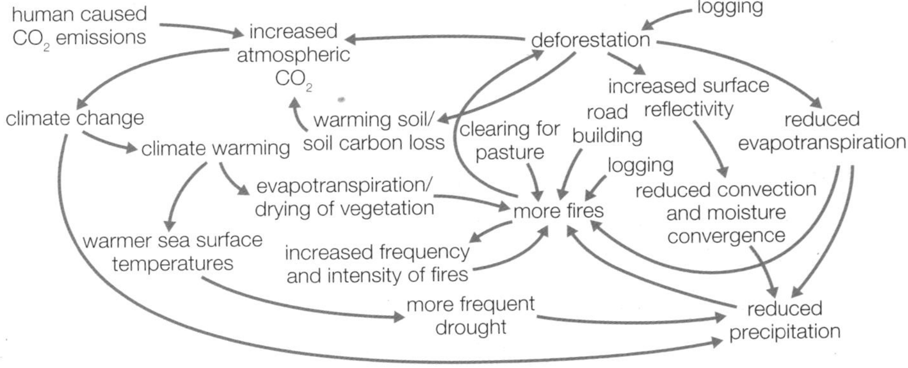

Figure 4 *Complex feedback loops show what is happening in rainforests*

Human activity and drought

Brazil's 2014–15 drought was not simply meteorological, as described in Figure 3. Human activity also contributed, due to over-abstraction of surface-water resources and groundwater aquifers, as water companies tried to maintain the water supply for factories and services, and residents tried to avoid cuts in supply.

Drought particularly affected the south-east of Brazil. In São Paulo state, industries, domestic users and farming increasingly used groundwater as rivers ran low. Groundwater became the only water source for the urban poor and for remote rural areas.

- The problem was caused by the high fees (US$3000) charged by Brazil's government for granting a license to drill a well. In addition, drilling a single well can cost between US$35 000 and US$100 000.
- This cost meant that many people avoided payment and instead drilled illegal wells, which were not monitored for water safety.
- Between January and October 2014, 25 000 licenses to allow drilling were made by São Paulo's state government. However, hydrologists believe that this was only 30% of the real number (i.e. that 70% of all new wells in the state were illegal!) and they raised concerns at shrinking groundwater levels.
- Illegal wells are generally shallower and less filtered by bedrock, so they contain industrial pollutants and higher levels of bacteria.

The impacts of drought on rainforest ecosystems

The Amazon rainforest is referred to as 'the Earth's lungs', because it absorbs CO_2 and returns oxygen to the atmosphere. Its 400 billion trees also transport humidity inland from the Atlantic Ocean. This 'flying river in the sky' takes up to 20 billion tonnes of water vapour daily from the forest and dumps it as rain on central and southern Brazil. By contrast, the Amazon River carries 17 million tonnes of water back to the Atlantic each day.

Prolonged drought causes forest stress, and sets up a series of chain reactions. Younger trees die, which reduces the canopy cover – this, in turn, reduces humidity, water vapour and therefore rainfall. Exposed to tropical sunlight, dying vegetation and surface tree litter create a potential tinderbox that can easily catch fire. Lightning storms and high winds frequently turn a small fire into a wildfire. Long-term drought means shorter trees and thinner canopies. Figure 5 shows the hydrological impacts of drought on forests.

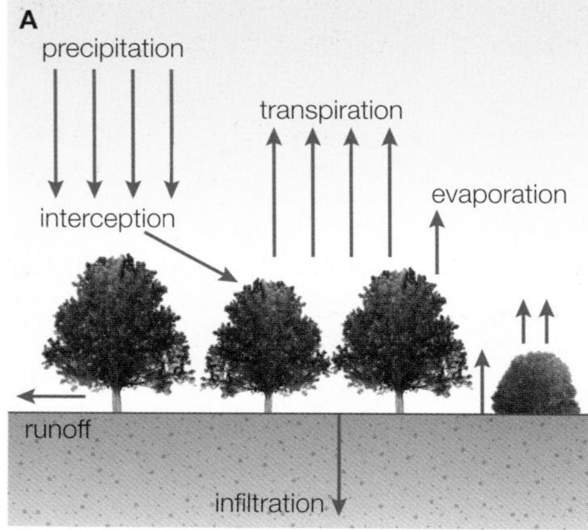

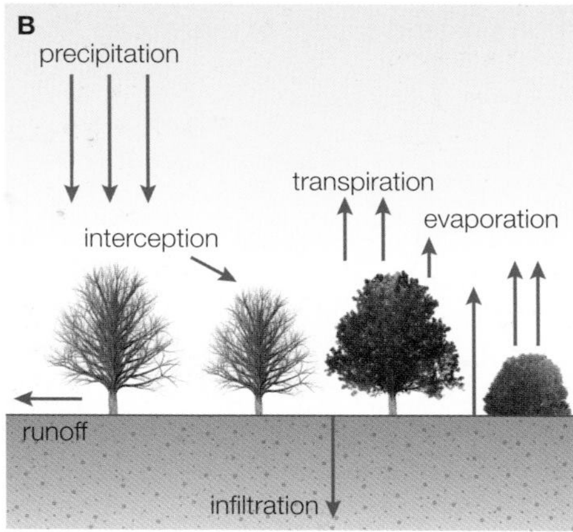

Figure 5 Changes in water fluxes as forests die off. The number and length of arrows in diagram **A** (the native forest) changes to the expected and/or observed increases or decreases in those fluxes in diagram **B**, following forest die-off.

The impacts of drought on wetland ecosystems

The Pantanal is a large wetland area in central South America, 140 000 km² of which lie within Brazil. It lies in the Upper Paraguay River Basin (see Figure 6), and its aquatic and bird wildlife make it among the world's most significant freshwater ecosystems. The river's floodplain is vital – it's surrounded by areas with seasonal rainfall, which means that the aquatic and bird life there depends on the permanent wetland for survival.

As Figure 7 shows, seasonal rainfall floods the Pantanal between November and April. At this time, the Pantanal changes from terrestrial into aquatic habitats. Flooding generally covers 80% of the Pantanal, but even in dry years the river is permanent – and wetlands near the river retain up to 60% of floodwater throughout the year.

Areas of land near the river are filled with forest, which gradually changes to savanna grassland as the distance from the river increases. It is here that the 2014-15 drought affected the Pantanal the most, testing its resilience and long-term survival:

- The drought increased tree mortality, which in turn reduced habitats for wild animals – as well as for cattle ranching and ecotourism.
- Wildfires became a major threat, caused by cattle ranchers deliberately setting old grass on fire during the dry season to clear vegetation left ungrazed by their cattle (their normal method of land management). However, during the drought, those deliberate fires easily spread out of control into the wetlands and forest.

Figure 6 *An aerial view of the Pantanal wetland near the border where Brazil, Bolivia and Paraguay meet*

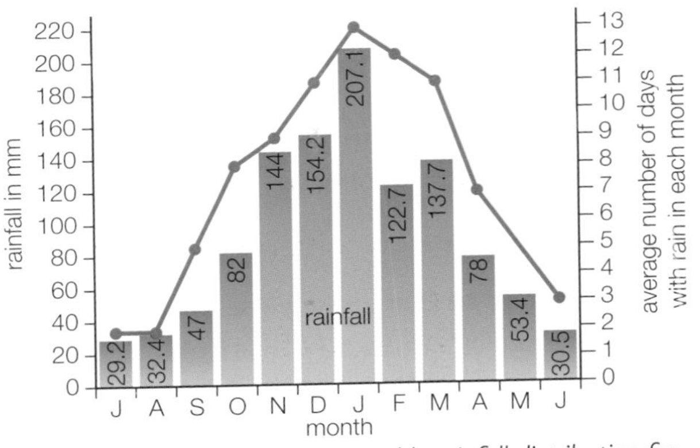

Figure 7 *The average monthly rainfall distribution for Corumba, Brazil, in the Upper Paraguay River Basin*

Over to you

1. Use Figure 1 to summarise the weather patterns over South America that led to (**a**) normal rainfall over the Amazon, and (**b**) the 2014-15 drought.
2. Use Figure 2 to outline (**a**) the progress of the drought during 2014, (**b**) its impacts.
3. Using Figure 3, identify – using the material in this section – areas of Brazil where meteorological, agricultural and hydrological drought occurred in 2014-15. Annotate these on a sketch copy of Figure 1.
4. In pairs, copy Figure 4 and annotate it with (**a**) causes of drought in the Pantanal, (**b**) its impacts, using Figure 5.

On your own

5. Distinguish between the following pairs of terms: (**a**) high-pressure and low-pressure weather systems, (**b**) water deficit and drought, (**c**) positive and negative feedback loops, (**d**) meteorological, agricultural and hydrological drought.

6. **a** Google the phrase 'global trends in floods and droughts'. Create a spreadsheet of major droughts over the previous five years.
   b Create a 750-word summary of your findings about the (**i**) location, (**ii**) duration, (**iii**) trends, and (**iv**) severity of droughts.
7. Using the information in this section, justify recommendations to (**a**) reduce the number of illegal wells drilled for groundwater, (**b**) alter the grass-burning practices of cattle herders in the Pantanal.

Exam-style question

Using examples, assess ways in which deficits within the hydrological system can have significant impacts. (*12 marks*)

1.6 Surpluses within the hydrological system

In this section, you'll learn that surpluses within the hydrological system can lead to flooding, with significant impacts for people.

KEY CONCEPTS

- **Causality** – the varying causes of flooding
- **Systems** – how weather systems are linked to the causes of flooding
- **Resilience** – the ability of places to respond to floods and their impacts

A recurring deluge

The northwest of the UK is familiar with heavy rain. The combination of warm wet westerly winds – plus uplands such as the Cumbrian fells – creates orographic rainfall (see Section 1.3). As a result, places in Cumbria are the wettest in England, e.g. Seathwaite averages over 2 metres of rainfall a year. Places such as this should be prepared for flooding. Nevertheless, it was still surprising when it occurred twice in a decade (2005 and 2009). However when it occurred for a third time in 2015, that suggested that something unusual was happening within the local hydrological system.

Figure 1 Cumbria and Storm Desmond

Storm Desmond

Storm Desmond hit Cumbria in December 2015 (see Figure 1). It was caused by the deep Atlantic **low-pressure** system (depression) shown in Figure 2A. Associated fronts stretched across northern Britain, bringing prolonged and heavy rainfall through a mechanism known as a 'warm conveyor' (see Figure 3). Figure 2B shows the intensity of the rainfall on a radar map.

In December 2015, Storm Desmond brought record-breaking rainfall to Cumbria:

- On 5 December, Honister Pass recorded 341.4 mm of rain in just 24 hours.
- 405 mm of rain fell at Thirlmere in 38 hours.
- 5200 homes were flooded.
- Major roads and rail services were disrupted for several days.
- A landslide closed a section of the West Coast Mainline between Preston and Carlisle.
- 61 000 homes lost power when an electrical substation was flooded.

Key
cold fronts
warm fronts
occluded fronts

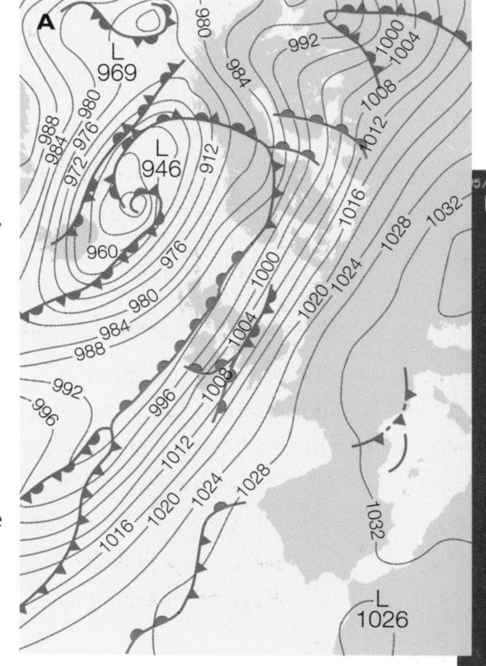

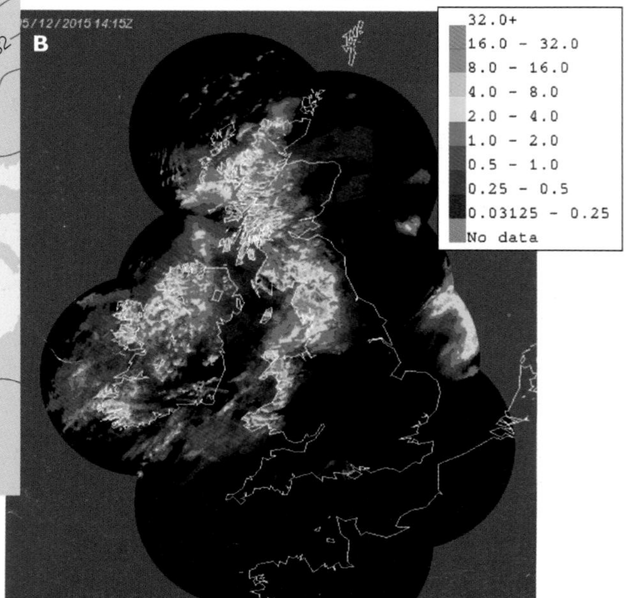

Figure 2 *(**A**) Storm Desmond synoptic chart, (**B**) Storm Desmond rainfall radar map. Note that the numbers in the key are not related to amounts of rain – just the intensity of rainfall as shown on a satellite photo. The higher the number on the scale, the greater the intensity of rain.*

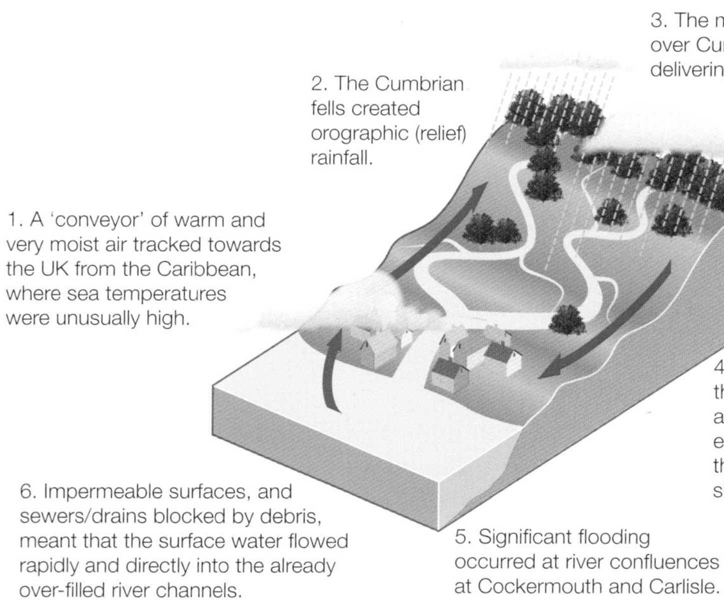

Figure 3 *The warm conveyor belt and Storm Desmond*

What caused the flooding?

Storm Desmond caused major disruption, with the greatest impacts due to flooding; Carlisle was worst hit by severe flooding from the River Eden (see Figure 4). The December flooding was worsened by the already saturated ground conditions – across northwest England and north Wales, November 2015 had been the second wettest November since 1910 (only November 2009 was wetter).

One theory that helps to explain the long periods of wet weather in 2005, 2009 and 2015, all of which caused flooding in Cumbria, is the position of the **jet stream**. Jet streams are the driving force which determine the direction of depressions and their speed of movement. This band of fast-moving air moves north and south, but it remained over the northwest longer than usual, bringing in rain-laden depressions from across the Atlantic.

Figure 4 *Flooding in Carlisle as a result of Storm Desmond*

BACKGROUND

Other causes of flooding

- **Storms and flash flooding.** Occasionally, dramatic floods occur following intense torrential storms. These are called **flash floods** and are often associated in the UK with extreme rainfall events in the summer months. The intensity of the rainfall exceeds the capacity of the river to cope with the amount of water – and flooding results. In September 2016, flash flooding caused travel chaos in parts of England as thunderstorms deposited almost half a month's worth of rain in some places within hours.
- **Monsoon rainfall.** This occurs across South and Southeast Asia between May and September. In July 2016, heavy **monsoon rains** in the Philippines led to flooding, landslides and evacuations in villages just to the northwest of the capital Manila. Monsoon rains are often heavy, but in this case a larger-than-normal low-pressure system brought heavier rain than usual.
- **Snowmelt.** Flooding can occur when snow melts and the resulting water cannot infiltrate into the soil or ground surface. In the winter of 2013, Norfolk Police reported flooding caused by melting snow and ice, after very mild, wet and windy weather caused rapid thawing. The combination of heavy rain and the thaw brought flooding in some places.

Exacerbating the flood risk

Changing land use

Farmers not only produce food, they also manage and maintain the landscape. However, some people argue that not all farmers' actions are positive. For example, the environmentalist George Monbiot refers to the Cumbrian landscape as 'sheep-wrecked uplands', and he suggests that farmers often make matters worse – overgrazing by sheep means that bare slopes now replace forests.

- Previously, trees absorbed and slowly released water; meandering channels slowed the flow, and bogs held water back.
- Now we have bare and drier soils; straightened and dredged channels; faster runoff; reduced stream lag times, and higher discharge peaks. Rainwater now reaches floodplains quicker – and it's on many floodplains that we find increasingly impermeable surfaces, as urban areas expand. If you add in unusually high levels of rainfall, flooding may now be inevitable.

Mismanaging rivers

Before 2005, a combination of raised riverbanks, pumping stations and diversion channels carried surplus water away from built-up areas in Cumbria. These **hard-engineering** schemes are common in Cumbria, and were reinforced after the 2005 floods. The design of these schemes is based on the **flood-return period** – a statistical estimate of how often a flood of a certain magnitude is likely to occur, based on past flood levels (e.g. a 1-in-50-year or a 1-in-100-year flood). However, as Figure 5 shows, we don't always get it right. It is now reasonable to expect that – given climate change and further changes in land use – we will face more extreme storms and flooding, so many smaller-scale flood protection schemes may be overwhelmed.

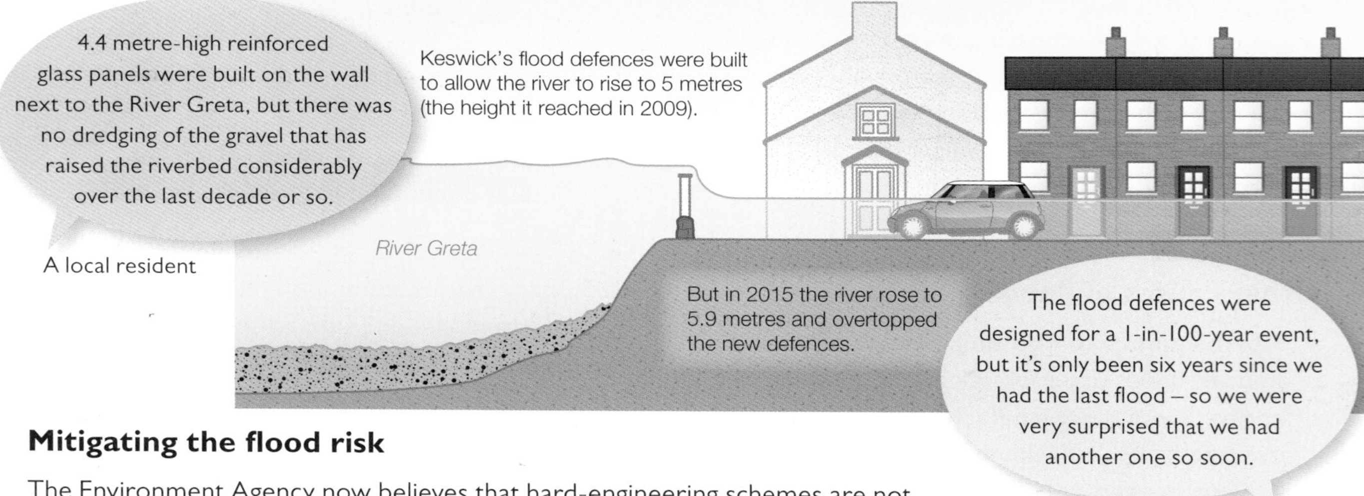

Figure 5 *Keswick's flood defences*

Mitigating the flood risk

The Environment Agency now believes that hard-engineering schemes are not the solution to flooding. They are very expensive and – as in Cumbria – often can't cope with the most extreme flooding. Instead, The Environment Agency thinks that **soft-engineering** solutions are the way forward, including the:

- reafforestation of upland areas to reduce rapid surface runoff
- restoration of river channels to their natural meandering states
- restoration of floodplains to their natural absorbent states, to store floodwater
- refusal of planning permission to build or expand developments near rivers.

The longer-term impacts of flooding

Despite flooding in 2005 and 2009, the scale of the 2015 Cumbrian floods caught people unawares, and the economic disruption – although short-lived – was significant (see Figure 6). In Carlisle, the United Biscuits factory (the city's biggest employer) closed for weeks before eventually reopening with a smaller workforce. By 2015, the new Turkish owners were forced to reconsider the factory's future in this high-risk area.

When floods – such as those of 2005, 2009 and 2015 – hit three times in such a short period, it becomes inevitable that investors, residents and businesses will re-evaluate their longer-term plans. Increased flooding in the UK is forcing key **players** to weigh up the costs and benefits of staying where they are, and is also challenging communities to re-assess the flood threat in their surroundings.

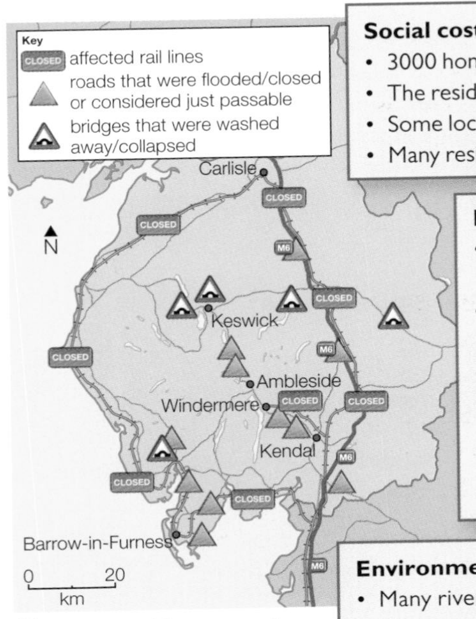

Figure 6 *The costs of Cumbria's flooding*

Social costs

- 3000 homes were flooded in 2005, and over 5200 in 2015.
- The residents of those properties had to live in temporary accommodation.
- Some local services, such as schools, healthcare, shops and offices were forced to close temporarily.
- Many residents suffered anxiety, stress and psychological trauma.

Economic costs

- Many businesses closed, and transport and infrastructure (bridges, roads, sewers) were damaged.
- The cost of the flooding in Cumbria was £100 million in 2005, £270m in 2009 and £400–500m in 2015.
- Insurance claims caused by flooding across the UK in 2015 exceeded £6 billion.
- Farmers lost hedgerows and expensive dry-stone walls were washed away; many sheep also drowned.
- House prices fell in flood-risk areas.
- The risk of repeated flooding deterred tourists from visiting.

Environmental costs

- Many river banks were eroded, which added to future flood risks.
- Rivers were choked with debris and contaminated with sewage and effluents/pollutants.
- Soils were eroded, habitats destroyed and ecosystems affected.
- The saturated ground led to the decomposition of dead plants and animals – giving off noxious gases such as hydrogen sulphide. Other poisons contaminated the food chain and threatened wildlife.
- The saturated ground also led to landslides.

Over to you

1 **a** Using the National River Flow Archive website, download flow data for the Cocker River floods of 2015.
  b Plot the storm hydrograph for the duration of the flood period and describe the nature of the event.

2 **a** Research online the phrase 'Dartmouth Flood Observatory Global Active Archive of Large Flood Events', to find their table of recent flood events.
  b Download the data for the most recent flood events, and sort it into the largest floods, by (for example) the numbers who died.
  c Record the location and severity of the ten largest events.
  d What trends do you notice? What are the likely consequences of these trends?

3 Study the synoptic chart in Figure 2A and (**a**) outline the causes of the heavy rain shown in Figure 2B, (**b**) explain the pattern of weather that led to the flooding in northwest England.

4 In pairs, research one flood event outside the UK caused by **either** a flash downpour **or** heavy monsoon rainfall. Produce a six-slide PowerPoint presentation to show (**a**) the weather processes leading to the flood, (**b**) its impacts, (**c**) the extent to which human causes can be identified as well as physical.

On your own

5 Distinguish between the following pairs of terms: (**a**) a low-pressure system and fronts, (**b**) frontal and orographic rainfall (see Section 1.3).

6 Using the information in this section, prepare a 5-minute contribution to a debate on the motion that 'The 2015 flooding in Cumbria was both predictable and preventable'.

Exam-style question

Using examples, assess the extent to which human actions can exacerbate flood risk. (*12 marks*)

1.7 Climate change

In this section, you'll learn how climate change may have significant impacts on the hydrological cycle, both globally and locally.

Good, bad and unpredictable

The climate is changing. For example, unless greenhouse gas emissions are significantly reduced, the risk of winter flooding in the UK is predicted to increase by four and a half times by 2100, and the risk of summer drought by three times.

Globally, more rain in some places might reduce current water scarcity, but a deficit could result in other areas. Some places are already benefiting from these changes, while others face problems.

Climate change affects the inputs, stores and outputs within the hydrological cycle. So, climate change leading to droughts will:

- mean a reduction in inputs
- reduce the level of water stored in soil, rivers and lakes
- increase the importance of groundwater flow
- cause initial high rates of evaporation.

1 The good – the Sahel

Rainfall is variable in the Sahel region, which – as Figure 1 shows – forms the southern fringe of the Sahara Desert. The amount of rainfall there varies from 100 mm to 600 mm per year, and Figure 2 shows the annual variations in rainfall from the average since 1900.

The 1970s and 1980s were tough for the Sahel region. Up to 90% of its annual rainfall falls between July and September, as part of the West African Monsoon. However, in the 1970s and 1980s, the rains failed – with a decline in rainfall of up to 40% between the 1950s and 1980s. Drought, poverty and civil war, especially in Eritrea and Ethiopia, drove people out of the Sahel and onto marginal land. Many died, particularly in the famine made famous by Bob Geldof's 'Band Aid' in 1984–5.

Re-greening the desert

The Sahel's climate appears to be changing, although it may just be part of a climate cycle. As Figure 2 shows, since 1996 there have been several wet years in between the droughts. Although the evidence is small at present, it does point to an opportunity for '**re-greening**' – the conversion of dry landscapes to productive farmland.

SYNOPTIC THEME AND KEY CONCEPTS

- **Futures** – projections of future drought and flood risk
- **Causality** – how climate change may impact upon the hydrological cycle
- **Systems** – how climate change affects inputs and outputs within the hydrological cycle
- **Inequality** – how inequalities may result between areas of water surplus and water scarcity
- **Threshold** – the point in the hydrological cycle at which sudden or rapid change occurs

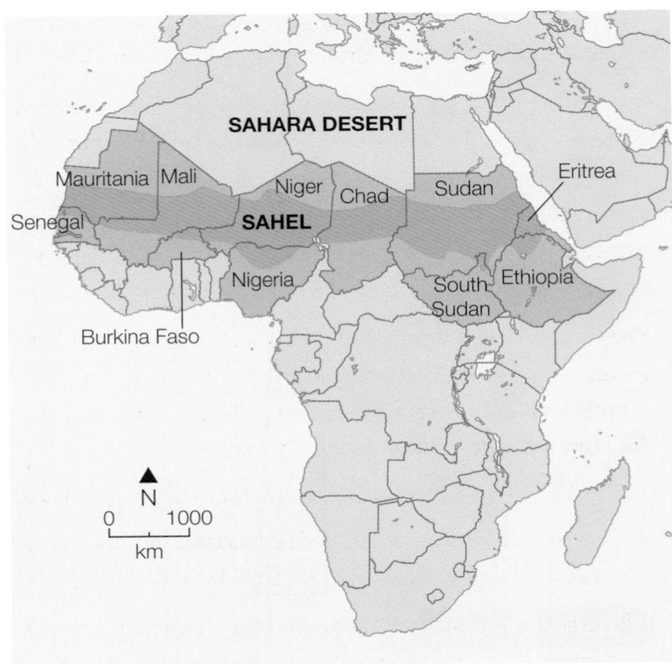

Figure 1 *The Sahel region and the countries through which it runs*

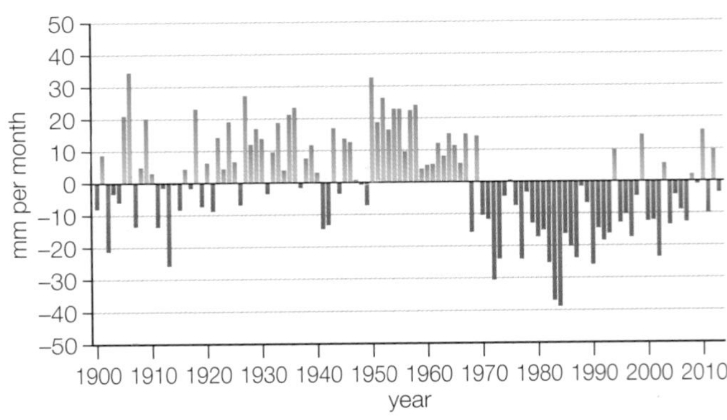

Figure 2 *Variations in the amount of rainfall during the Sahel's rainy season each year, in comparison with the average amount of rainfall for 1900–2013 (shown as '0' on the scale)*

Re-greening is a restoration technique that involves planting trees and bushes alongside other sustainable land management schemes. It is popular in Malawi, Burkina Faso, Ethiopia and Niger, where hundreds of thousands of farmers benefit from increasing yields. Re-greening is also referred to as a 'farmer-managed natural regeneration' (FMNR). Its benefits include:

- natural regeneration of water-retaining shrubs and trees
- low cost reforesting
- the use of water-harvesting techniques. For example, Burkina Faso's farmers build stone lines or dig improved planting pits to trap the limited rainfall on fields and increase yields.

Figure 3 *Castaic Lake, California, was at half its usual capacity in 2014*

2 The bad – California

Almost 40 million Californians are facing increasing problems due to recent variations in rainfall in the state, which evidence suggests result from climate change. Droughts are normal features of the Californian climate, but in 2014 the Sierra Nevada region experienced three times the normal number of wildfires, because the ground was so dry.

Climate scientists at Cornell University are forecasting intense **mega-droughts** lasting 30 years, as well as decade-long dry periods. Climate change is cited as the reason, and already farmers are abandoning their fields. 2015 marked the fourth year of continuous drought in California – the worst in 1200 years – and water rationing was imposed on cities. Forecasts now suggest a 50% chance of mega-droughts hitting southwest California, and a 90% chance of a decade-long drought.

Eleven of the years between 2000 and 2015 were drought years for the states of Arizona, California, Nevada, New Mexico, Oklahoma and Texas. Combined, these states have a population equal to that of the UK. The drought in these states has two causes:

- Firstly, rising temperatures have led to **increased evaporation rates**.
- Secondly, there has been **a fall in precipitation** – a trend expected to continue during the next decades of the twenty-first century.

If forecasts of mega-droughts are true, 'business as usual' will simply not be possible in terms of meeting future water demands. Already there is evidence of problems:

- Surface runoff and soil moisture levels have declined.
- Forested areas have reverted to scrub and grassland.
- Although groundwater – often used to make up the shortfall in supply – has kept up with the demand from cities such as Los Angeles and Las Vegas, levels fell by 30 metres between 2011 and 2015.
- Reservoir levels have also fallen (see Figure 3). In October 2016, water storage was 77% of the average for the time of year – but levels varied. Lake Shasta had 102% of averaged historical levels, but Lake Cachuma (which supplies urban southern California) was down to 9%.
- Snowpack (or permanent snow) levels in California in 2015 were at record lows due to high temperatures and a lack of winter storms (see Figure 4). Snowpack is crucial, because its meltwater provides one third of the water used by California's cities and farms.

Figure 4 *Snowpack in California in (**A**) 2010 and (**B**) 2015. 2015 was the fourth consecutive year in which the snowpack level was below normal.*

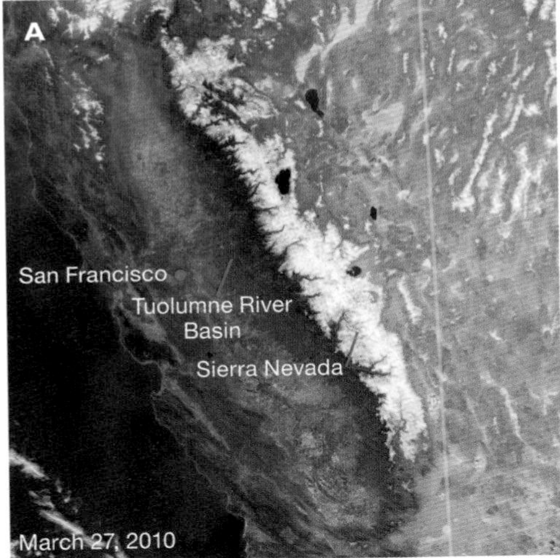

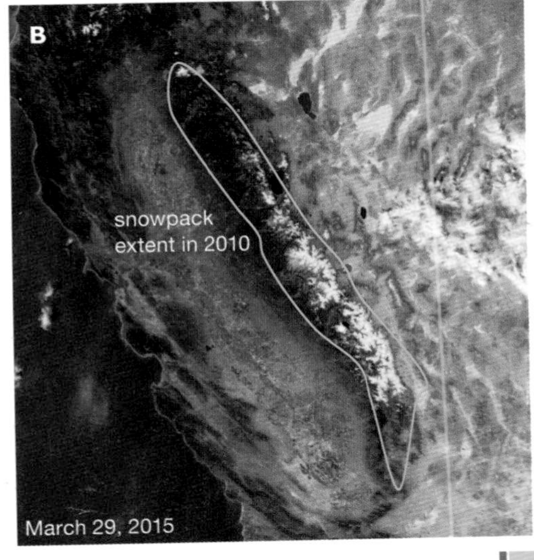

Predicting future climate change

Global climate patterns are mainly caused by atmospheric circulation, but ocean currents also play a part. This is shown in the Pacific Ocean, where climatic fluctuations and extremes can be intense.

Normal years

In 'normal' years, Pacific winds circulate around the **Walker Cell** (see Figure 5). Winds travel westwards along the surface of the Pacific, taking warm surface water with them. The cold Peruvian current that flows northwards along the west coast of South America is drawn into the circulation and flows westwards. As it flows west, it is heated by the sun. Warm, moist air rises over Indonesia, creating a low-pressure area and heavy rain. The air then circulates east in the upper atmosphere, sinking into the cooler high-pressure area over western South America, giving dry conditions that create Peru's Atacama Desert.

La Niña

At times, the 'normal' situation intensifies and is known as **La Niña**. During La Niña, low pressure over the western Pacific becomes lower, and high pressure over the eastern Pacific higher. As a result, rainfall increases over Southeast Asia, and South America suffers drought. Trade winds strengthen due to the increased pressure difference between the two areas. La Niña can occur just before or after El Niño.

El Niño

During **El Niño** years, pressure systems and weather patterns reverse (see Figure 6). Warmer waters develop in the eastern Pacific, with temperatures rising by up to 8°C. Low pressure forms, drawing in westerly winds from the Pacific. Warm, moist air rises, creating heavy rainfall over the eastern Pacific. The air then circulates west in the upper atmosphere. The descending air then creates drier conditions which lead to drought in Northern Australia and Indonesia.

Key words

The Walker Cell – The circulation of air whereby upper atmospheric air moves eastwards, and surface air moves west across the Pacific, causing trade **winds**. It is named after Sir Gilbert Walker, who first identified it in the 1920s.

El Niño – This is the Spanish phrase for 'boy child'. It occurs every 3-8 years around Christmas (hence the name) and can last for 14-22 months.

Figure 5 *Atmospheric circulation in the Walker circulation cell*

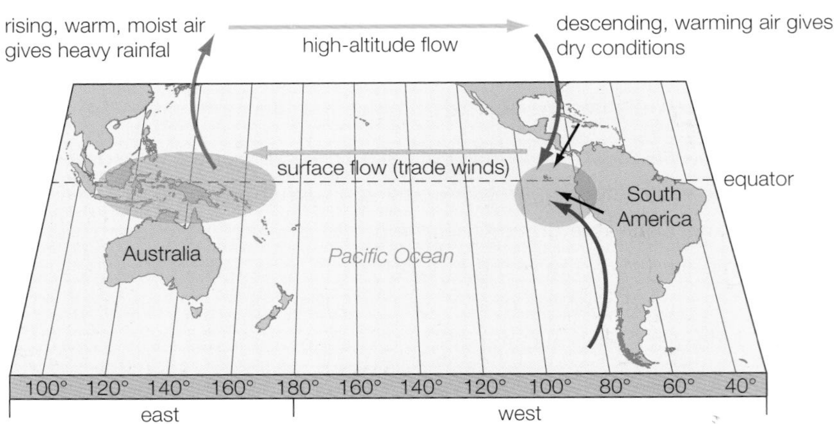

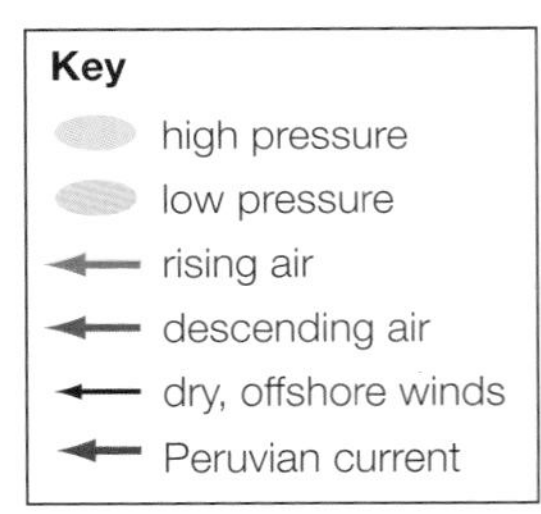

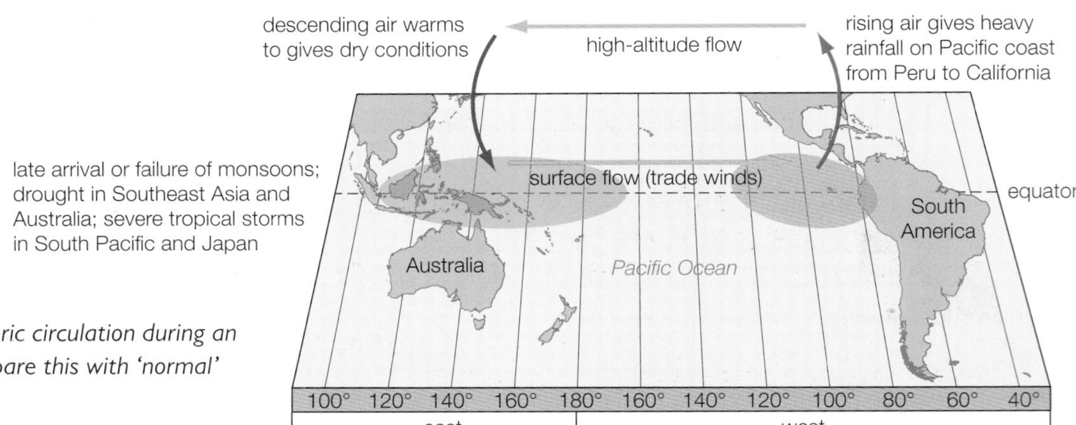

Figure 6 *Atmospheric circulation during an El Niño event. Compare this with 'normal' years in Figure 5.*

The Southern Oscillation Index

The change in air pressure between 'normal' years and El Niño is called the El Niño Southern Oscillation (**ENSO**). Its strength, direction and speed is called the Southern Oscillation Index (SOI). Meteorologists record air pressure at Easter Island (west of South America) and subtract it from that at Darwin in northern Australia to calculate the SOI. A sharp drop indicates that El Niño is imminent. Most droughts affecting eastern and northern Australia result from ENSO and El Niño.

Futures and uncertainties

Although El Niño events have been occurring for at least 15 000 years, it is possible that climate change is increasing their duration and intensity. Computer modelling shows that as greenhouse gases warm the planet:

- different regions of the world will warm at different rates
- La Niña and El Niño events will become more extreme
- regions bordering the Pacific will see flood seasons following drought, and vice versa.

A *Royal Society* report used climate models to estimate flood and drought frequencies by 2100 (see Figures 7A and 7B). These assume a 'business-as-usual' approach to climate change and a global population of 9 billion. However, predictions are uncertain. El Niño rarely arrives when expected; typically it lasts 14-22 months, but it can be longer or shorter. Further research could improve our understanding of the impact of climate change on La Niña and El Niño events, but there is little doubt that ENSO cycles and climate change could significantly impact on future water security (see Section 1.8).

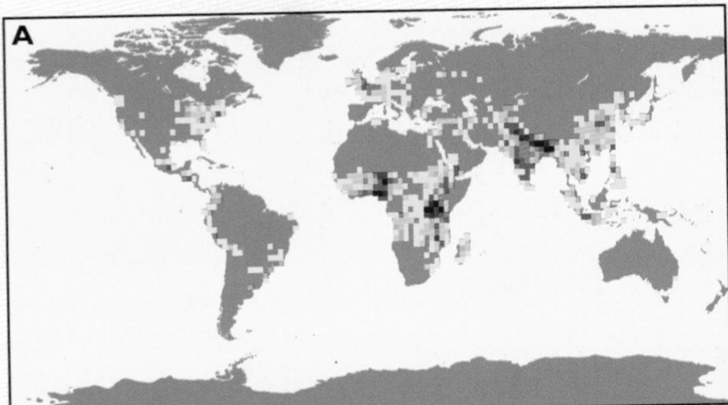

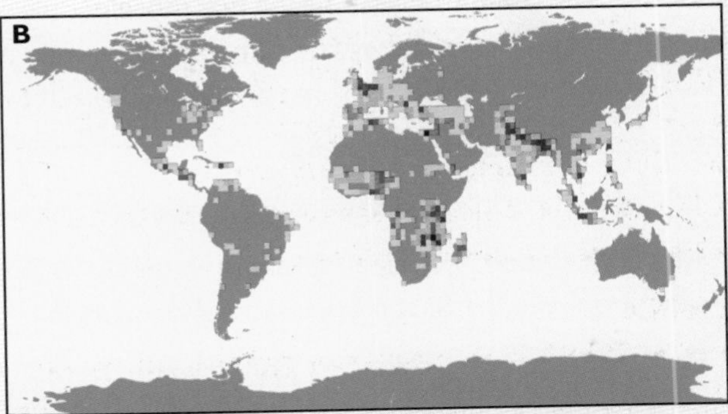

Figure 7 *Projected changes in people's exposure to floods (**A**), and drought (**B**) by 2100. The darkest colours show the greatest projected increases in exposure to these hazards.*

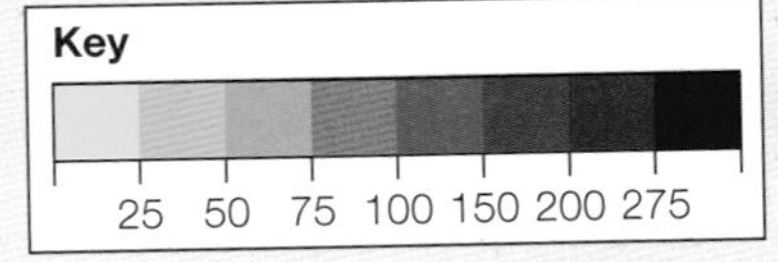

Over to you

1. In pairs, study Figure 2 and (**a**) describe the rainfall patterns between 1900 and 2013, (**b**) assess the idea that climate change may be 're-greening the Sahel'.
2. In pairs, draw a system diagram to show how climate change affects the hydrological cycle in California. Show impacts on stores, flows, snowpack, reservoirs, lakes, soil moisture, runoff, and stream flow.
3. **a** Search online for 'impacts of El Niño on California'. In pairs, produce a six-slide presentation to outline its effects.
   b Carry out similar research for Australia.
   c Compare the impacts.

On your own

4. Distinguish between the following terms: (**a**) drought and mega-drought, (**b**) El Niño and La Niña, (**c**) ENSO and SOI.
5. How far might it be possible to predict future water surpluses and deficits based on greater understanding of ENSO cycles?

Exam-style question

Using examples, assess the impacts that climate change may have on the hydrological cycle. (*12 marks*)

1.8 Water insecurity – the causes

In this section, you'll learn about the physical and human causes of water insecurity.

EQ3 Sections 1.8 to 1.10 examine why water insecurity occurs and why it is becoming a global issue for the twenty-first century.

A global water crisis?

The UN's annual World Water Development Reports repeatedly warn that the balance between human demand and the availability of water is at a precarious point: '*the lack of freshwater is emerging as the biggest challenge of the twenty-first century*'. Access to safe water for people is seen as both a fundamental need and a basic human right, but for too many people it still represents part of their daily struggle. Water shortages (i.e. quantity) and a lack of access to safe water (i.e. quality) cause serious problems for a third of the world's population.

SYNOPTIC THEME AND KEY CONCEPTS

- **Futures** – predictions of future water scarcity and stress
- **Causality** – the causes of water insecurity
- **Inequality** – how inequalities may result between areas of water surplus and water scarcity
- **Risk** – how climate change increases the risk of water scarcity for people and the environment

A growing mismatch: is there enough water for everyone?

In theory, there is no global water shortage; only 50% of available water is actually used. However, rapid population growth in areas where supplies are limited, together with an uneven distribution of global supply and a deterioration in water quality, means that more people are facing severe water shortages. A **world water gap** exists between the 'haves' and 'have-nots' – as wealthy nations consume greater and greater quantities of water.

The supporting data are alarming:

- 12% of the world's population consumes 85% of its water.
- 1.8 billion people lack clean drinking water, 2.4 billion lack adequate sanitation, and 0.7 billion face water shortages.
- Every 90 seconds, a child dies from a water-borne disease. 0.8 million people die from diarrhoea as a result of dirty water each year; 25% of people drink water contaminated with faeces.
- Half of the world's rivers and lakes are badly polluted (see Figure 1), and half of the rivers no longer flow all year.
- Food supplies are also threatened as water shortages increase.

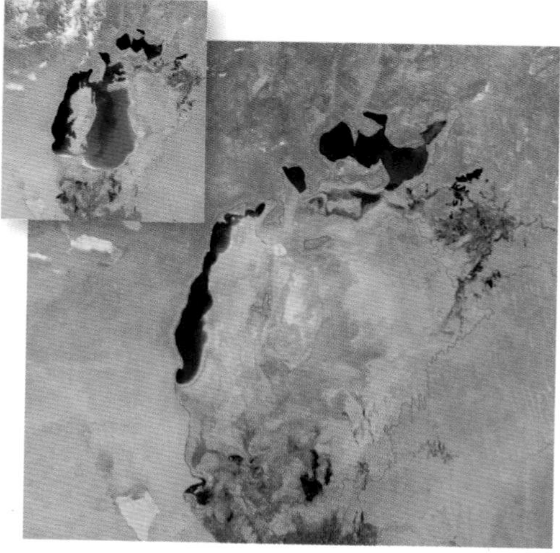

Figure 1 *The decreasing size of Kazakhstan's Aral Sea between 2000 (inset) and 2014 (main). The source rivers of this inland sea are used to supply large-scale agricultural irrigation – preventing its natural replenishment. Evaporation is increasing the sea's salinity, and pollution levels are so high that most fish have died.*

In water-impoverished areas, women and children spend many hours each day collecting water. Expressed in terms of how much they could earn in that same time, this translates into US$24 billion in lost economic benefits each year, and denies girls a good education.

Stress and scarcity

As the global population increases, the numbers affected by **water stress** and **water scarcity** are expected to rise sharply. By 2025, the combination of population growth and economic growth is expected to have created a 20% increase in demand for water supplies – but by then half the world's population will be living in water-deficit areas.

Key words

Water scarcity – An imbalance between demand and supply, classified as: **physical scarcity** (insufficient water to meet demand; also the definition for **water deficit**) or **economic scarcity** (people can't afford water, even when it's available).

Water stress – If a country's water consumption exceeds 10% of its renewable freshwater supply, including difficulties in obtaining new *quantities* of water (e.g. from aquifers, lakes or rivers), as well as poor water *quality* restricting usage.

Together, these terms add up to **water insecurity** (where present and future supplies cannot be guaranteed), leading to a need for physical (e.g. dam building) or political and economic solutions (e.g. supply agreements between countries).

When a country's water consumption exceeds 10% of its renewable freshwater supply, it is said to be **water stressed**. This means that it has less than 1700 m^3 (or 1700 tonnes) of water available per person per year, which can cause temporary shortages. When the amount available falls below 1000 m^3 per person per year, a country experiences **water scarcity** (see Figure 2). This can threaten food supplies, reduce economic development and cause environmental damage.

Figure 2 *Global water scarcity, by type*

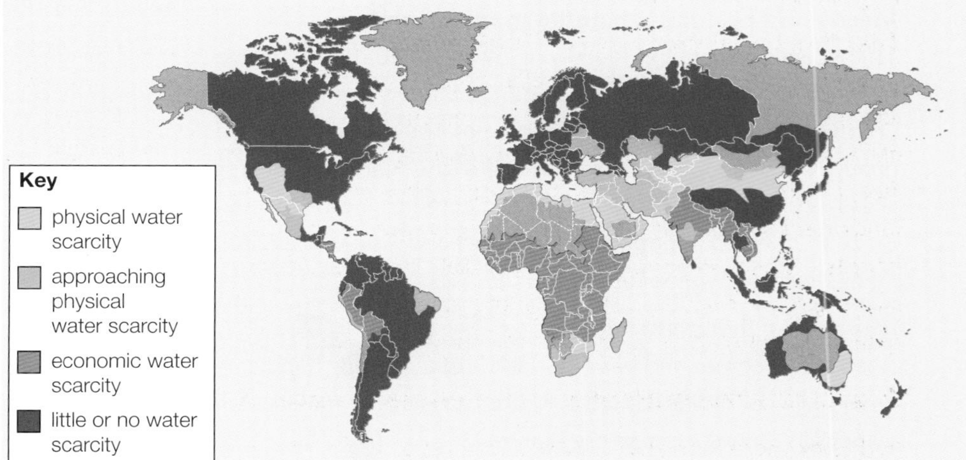

Causes of water insecurity

People's health, welfare and livelihoods depend on secure supplies of freshwater, but high demand and the misuse of water resources put these at risk. Regional insecurities vary, but some of the most significant problems are shown in Figure 3.

Asia and the Pacific

Critical health problems – a third of the population lacks access to safe drinking water; there are 500 000 diarrhoea-related infant deaths each year in Asia.

Water pollution – the level of bacterial waste from human sources is ten times greater than recommended levels.

Overuse:

- Agriculture uses 90% of freshwater withdrawals in South Asia.
- Salinity and arsenic (from industrial pollution) affect 60% of the groundwater supplies across the Indo-Gangetic Basin – 750 million people cannot drink or use groundwater for irrigation.
- Aquifer depletion in Asia led to a drop in water availability from 10 000 m^3 per capita in the 1950s, to less than 3700 m^3 in 2010.
- Withdrawals in West Asia exceed natural replacement.
- A billion gallons of raw sewage is dumped into the Ganges each day.
- 42% of China's sewage and 45% of its industrial waste is dumped into the Yangtze River each year.
- China has only 6% of the world's freshwater.

Europe/Central Asia

- A lack of access to clean drinking water in Eastern Europe and Central Asia.
- Increasing water consumption, with half of Europe's cities over-exploiting their groundwater reserves.
- Declining water quality in countries with groundwater pollution (from nitrates, pesticides, heavy metals and hydrocarbons), e.g. the Aral Sea, the Mediterranean, Scandinavian lakes.

North America

- Aquifer depletion is increasing, due to both population and urban growth, and the expansion of irrigation and industry (e.g. cotton farming in Texas).
- Changes to rainfall in California (blamed on El Niño and climate change) have led to drought, declining groundwater supplies and falling reservoirs.
- Water pollution from agricultural runoff has contaminated many ground and surface waters.

Africa

- It is predicted that 25 African countries will face either water stress or water scarcity by 2025.
- 19 of the 25 countries in the world with the lowest access to clean water are in Africa – and all have the highest child mortality rates.
- There is a lack of groundwater protection from agricultural uses (which make up 80% of total water use).
- There is a lack of risk preparedness and mitigation – flooding, droughts and storms displace people and cause chronic health issues.

Latin America and the Caribbean

- Groundwater contamination and depletion from the increasing release of hazardous wastes from mining, agriculture and industry.
- Poor sanitation – only 2% of the sewage in Latin America is treated.
- Economic scarcity, with conflict over access to – and use of – water.

Figure 3 *Regional issues related to global water insecurity*

Under pressure

During the twentieth century, the global population increased by four times – but water consumption increased by six times. This gap was caused by improved living standards, resulting from economic development. Increased access to water, flush toilets, baths and showers has created a demand for water that shows no sign of slowing.

Increasing population and urbanisation

The world's population is growing by about 80 million per year, and is predicted to reach 9.1 billion by 2050. But demand for water is rising twice as fast. Increasing urbanisation is causing local pressure on the availability of freshwater, especially in drought-prone areas. More than half of the world's population now lives in urban areas, and urban populations are projected to increase to 6.3 billion by 2050. By 2030, the urban population in Africa and Asia is predicted to double – putting further pressure on water resources.

Improving living standards

The rising incomes and living standards of a growing middle class in developing and emerging economies has led to sharp increases in water use, which can be unsustainable (especially where supplies are scarce).

Changing consumption patterns, such as increasing meat consumption, building larger homes and increased use of cars, appliances and energy-consuming devices, involves increased water consumption in both their production and use.

Figure 4 *The wells supplying public water, together with the soil and groundwater stores, were all contaminated with toxic compounds as a result of seepage from a leaking industrial tank at the Retiro Industrial Park in San German, Puerto Rico.*

Industrialisation

The OECD report *Environmental Outlook to 2050* predicted that global water demand for manufacturing would increase by 400% from 2000 to 2050 – far more than any other sector. Most of the increase will be in emerging economies and developing countries, with implications for both water supply and quality. Where water use is not well regulated, pollution could increase dramatically – with industrial spillage and poor waste management leading to contaminated groundwater and rivers, like the example in Figure 4.

Agriculture

Agriculture is by far the largest user of water (consuming 70%, and occasionally 90%, in some developing countries). By 2050, global agriculture will need to produce 60% more food to meet the demands of the growing population. But current increases in agricultural demands for freshwater are unsustainable. The inefficient use of water for crop production is:

- depleting aquifers and reducing river flow
- degrading wildlife habitats
- increasing pesticide and fertilizer pollution as they seep into groundwater
- causing waterlogging and increased salinity (20% of the world's irrigated land now suffers from salinity).

For example, as Figure 5 shows, groundwater supplies in Israel and Gaza are being contaminated by salt, as salt water is drawn into aquifers when freshwater is pumped out.

Figure 5 *Encroachment by salt water into Israel and Gaza's coastal aquifer*

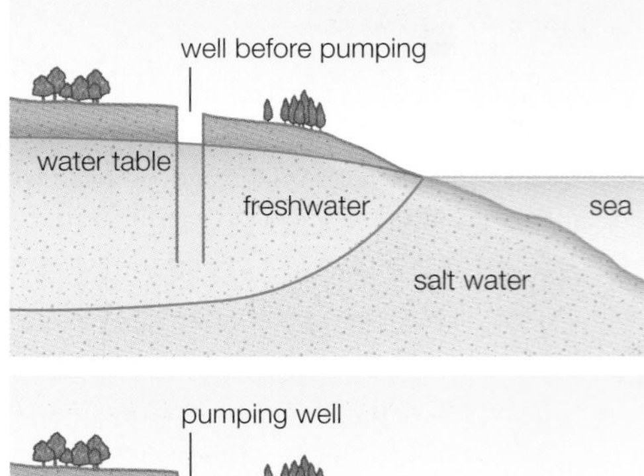

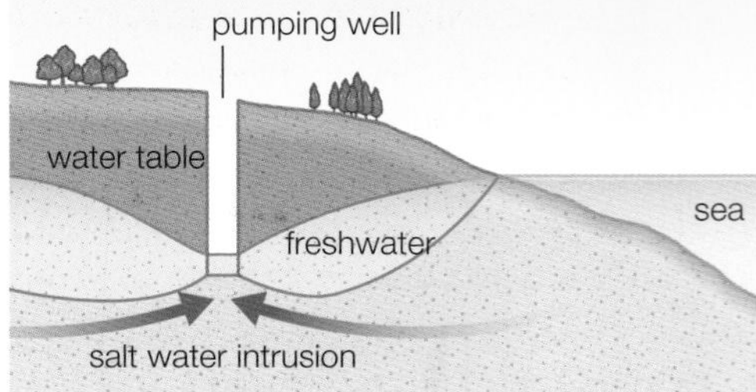

Futures and uncertainties about water stress

Demand for water is rising – but where will it all come from? As Section 1.7 showed, climate change will make some areas drier and others wetter – creating drought in some places and floods in others. Using a range of computer models and socio-economic scenarios, the World Resources Institute scored and ranked the likelihood of future water stress, shown in Figure 6. Their map shows that 33 countries are predicted to be facing extremely high levels of water stress by 2040.

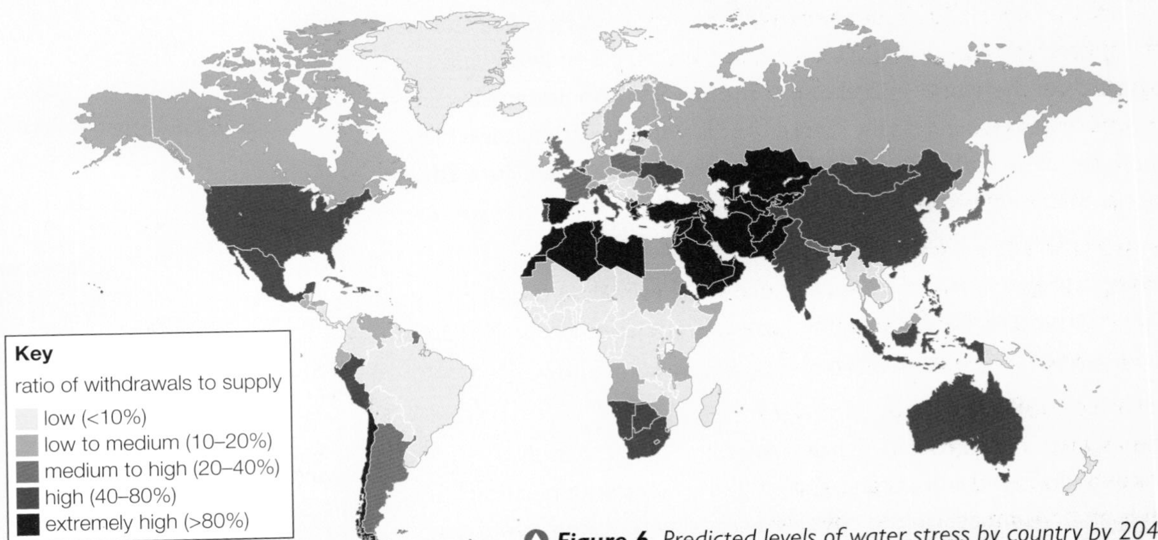

Figure 6 *Predicted levels of water stress by country by 2040*

Figure 6 shows that: 14 of the most highly stressed countries are in the Middle East. This is one of the world's most water-insecure regions. Countries there make heavy use of groundwater and desalinated seawater, but face major challenges. Countries such as the USA, China and India also face insecurities. High water stress is expected to remain constant, but specific areas such as the southwest USA (see Section 1.7) could see water stress increase by 40–70%. Chile is also expected to become highly water stressed by 2040; it is likely to face a decrease in water supply due to rising temperatures and shifting rainfall patterns.

Whatever the cause, extremely high water stress means that countries are dependent on limited amounts of water, and are vulnerable to changes in supply, which threatens both water security and economic growth.

Over to you

1 Draw a table with the following causes of water insecurity in one column:
- Physical – climate variability; salt water encroachment at the coast
- Human – overabstraction from rivers, lakes and aquifers; water contamination from agriculture; industrial water pollution.

Add examples for each cause in a second column.

 2 **a** In pairs, use an atlas to identify (**i**) the world's major climate zones where water is scarce at some time, (**ii**) areas of high population density.

b Search online to find the world's (**i**) ten largest populations and (**ii**) ten largest economies.

c Analyse the information obtained from (**a**) and (**b**) to predict areas of potential water stress and scarcity.

d Compare your analysis with the maps in Figures 2 and 6. How well do your findings match?

On your own

3 Distinguish between the following sets of terms: (**a**) water gap, water insecurity, water stress and water scarcity; (**b**) salt water encroachment and salinity.

4 Explain why women stand to gain most from improved water supplies globally.

5 Debate the motion that 'Projections of future water insecurity are simply alarmist'.

Exam-style question

Evaluate the extent to which water insecurity is the result of physical or human causes. (*20 marks*)

1.9 Water insecurity – the consequences

In this section, you'll learn that there are consequences and risks associated with water insecurity.

SYNOPTIC THEME AND KEY CONCEPTS

- **Players** – the role of different users in national and international conflicts over water
- **Causality** – the varying causes of physical water scarcity, and of conflicts between water users

Water scarcity

Almost 20% of the world's population (about 1.2 billion people) live in areas where water is physically scarce. Areas with low rainfall and high temperatures can suffer from **physical** water scarcity (see Figure 2 in Section 1.8). In the future, climate change will affect the natural water balance and the availability of water even more:

- Changes in patterns and frequency of rainfall will affect the recharging of water stores.
- Increases in temperature will increase evaporation and transpiration rates.

Human activities, including: land use changes; soil degradation; withdrawals for agriculture and industry; and water contamination will also have an impact on the physical availability of water resources.

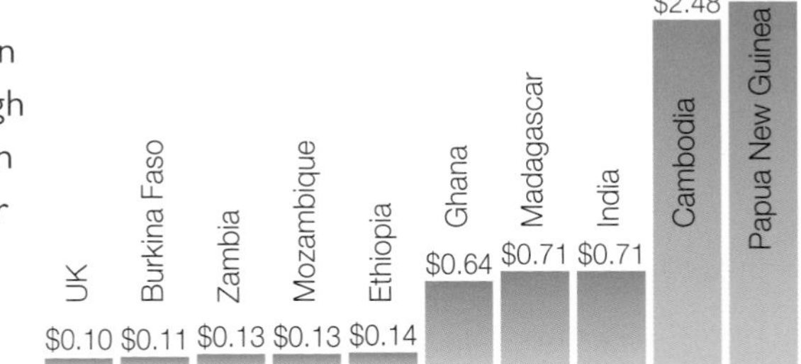

Figure 1 How the price of water varies in different Low Income Countries, in comparison with the UK

While water falls freely as rain, collecting, storing, purifying and distributing it is expensive. Often people cannot afford 'processed' water, and in many parts of the world (predominantly in Africa, parts of Southeast Asia, South and Central America) **economic** water scarcity exists (see Figure 2 in Section 1.8). Figure 1 shows how much the cost of obtaining water can impact on the incomes of those in Low Income Countries.

Water privatisation in Bolivia

In 1999, Agua del Tunari took over the Bolivian city of Cochabamba's water system. The company immediately raised the price of water supplies so that they cost 20% of the average income of Cochabamba's urban poor. People protested for 4 days, and the Bolivian government cancelled the contract.

Why the price of water varies

Traditionally, governments or local authorities provided water as a service, charging for it at cost price. Often, colonial governments installed limited infrastructure to cover what were at the time small cities.

However, massive urban growth has now outgrown that limited infrastructure, and the IMF restricts government spending on services such as water (see Section 3.5). So, in many countries, responsibility for water provision is now controlled by the private sector. To governments, passing the responsibility for modernising the ageing water infrastructure over to private companies seemed like a good idea in the late twentieth century. However, as a result, consumers have had to pay significantly higher charges for their water supplies (to provide profits for the private companies and also to cover their extra investment costs). This has created conflicts, as the Bolivia box shows.

Even in High Income Countries, water charges vary:

- In Canada, where supplying water still lies within the public sector, charges to consumers are 80% less than in Germany.
- Ireland only began charging for water in 2012! In 2016, water bills there were 75% less than in the UK.
- Denmark has the world's most expensive water. Its government aims to cut water consumption through high pricing – based on passing on all costs to the consumer.

All change

The Pacific Institute (a US think-tank) states that 'water is far too important to human health and the health of our environment to be placed entirely in private hands'. By 2015, many of the world's major cities were taking back control of their water supplies.

BACKGROUND

The Water Poverty Index

The Water Poverty Index (WPI) was developed in 2002 as a means of monitoring progress and prioritising water needs in response to UN Millennium Development Goals that address poverty and water access. It was developed mainly for use at a community scale, although it can also be applied nationally.

The WPI is based on five components:

1. **Water resources** – the physical availability, quality and total amount available.
2. **Access to water** – the distance from safe water for drinking, cooking, irrigation and industrial uses.
3. **Handling capacity** – effective management, infrastructure and income.
4. **Use of water** – for domestic, agricultural and industrial uses.
5. **Environmental indicators** – the ability to sustain nature and ecosystems.

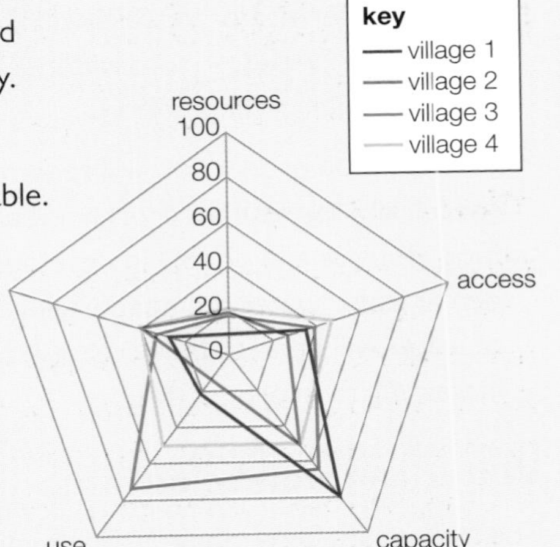

Figure 2 *A Water Poverty Index pentagram for four villages in Sri Lanka*

Each component is given a value up to a maximum of 20. A community or country that meets all of the criteria for all five components would score 100. Figure 2 shows a WPI diagram for four different village (community) locations in Sri Lanka, and Figure 3 shows the individual component scores, as well as the total WPI scores, for four different countries in the Americas.

Country	1 Water resources	2 Access to water	3 Handling capacity	4 Use of water	5 Environmental indicators	Water Poverty Index
Argentina	12.4	9.7	15.3	12.8	12.6	**62.8**
Chile	13.1	16.2	13.8	14.9	12.5	**70.5**
El Salvador	7.6	11.4	12.6	12.9	8.7	**53.2**
Haiti	6.1	4.8	10.5	4.3	7.0	**32.7**

Figure 3 *Water Poverty Index (WPI) scores for four countries in the Caribbean and the Americas. The five indicators are scored out of 20 (where 20 is best). The WPI then combines all five scores to reach an index out of 100.*

Water and economic development

Water is essential for producing many goods and services – including food, energy and manufacturing. Industrialisation drives economic development by increasing output, jobs and incomes. As a population grows, and an economy develops, demands for water increase rapidly. In 2015, the UN's *World Water Development Report* predicted a 55% increase in the demand for water, based on existing trends. It stated that a **water gap** – a 40% shortfall in supply – could exist by 2030. Figure 4 shows that most growth in demand is coming from the BRICs (Brazil, Russia, India and China), where rapid economic development has been occurring.

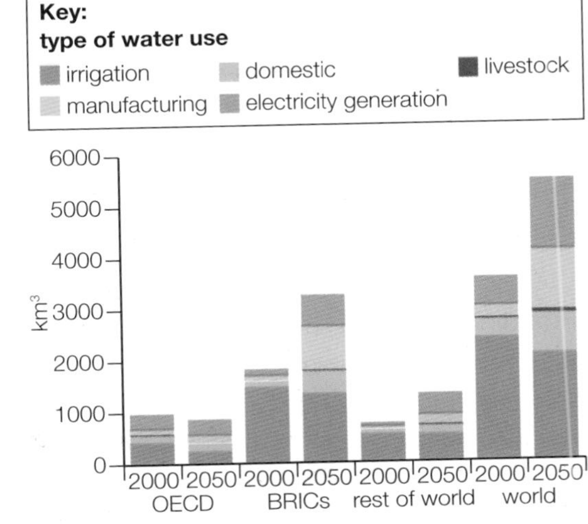

Figure 4 *Expected increases in overall demands for water between 2000 and 2050*

Overall global demand is increasing because:

- nearly all forms of **energy generation** need water as part of the production process. Thermal power generation and hydropower (which account for 80% and 15% of global electricity generation respectively) both require large quantities of water. 75% of water consumption in the UK is linked to energy generation.
- by 2050 food production will require 140% more water; specifically, **agriculture** will need to produce 60% more food globally, and double in developing countries. These demands for water are not sustainable, so the efficient use of water will need to be increased by reducing losses and increasing crop productivity.

Water and well-being

The Millennium Development Goals adopted in 2000 aimed to halve the number of people without access to safe drinking water and sanitation by 2015. This target was vital for tackling the global issues of human health and well-being. However, by 2016, almost 800 million people across the world still lacked access to improved (i.e. treated) water supplies.

There is a strong link between poverty and a lack of safe water, or – to put it another way – there is a definite positive correlation between wealth (measured by GDP per capita) and access to safe water and sanitation. The World Health Organisation states that 'every dollar spent on improving sanitation generates an average economic benefit of US$7', thus reducing poverty and increasing economic development. A lack of investment in basic water infrastructure across the developing world means that, as the box on the right shows, children die every day.

As Figure 6 shows, improving safe water supplies not only improves health but also eases time pressures on girls and promotes social inclusion. Girls often miss school during menstruation as there is nowhere for them to clean themselves. In addition, water is essential for food preparation especially when it's eaten uncooked, e.g. most fruit.

Water – potential for conflict

As the risks of physical water shortages grow, so does the potential for conflict. 263 rivers, along with many aquifers, cross or form political boundaries around the world – and 90% of all countries share water basins with at least one of their neighbours. In order to meet the increasing demand, the flow of many major rivers has been affected by the construction of dams, reservoirs and diversion schemes.

Water availability in Nigeria

Water-related diseases cost Adana Haruna, a 30-year-old mother of six in Nigeria, dearly. As well as losing a son, her family was plunged into debt by medical bills:

> I had to go to the river for water. I lost a boy from cholera. Each month one of my children would get sick. I would spend a day taking them to the clinic 14 km away. Medicine was very expensive, so I would have to take a loan or buy on credit and it would be a month before I could pay it back. By then another child was sick. We were always in debt from illnesses.

In Nigeria, 335 000 children die each year from water-borne diseases.

Figure 5 *People in Kano, northern Nigeria, collecting water from a tap which is next to an open sewage drain*

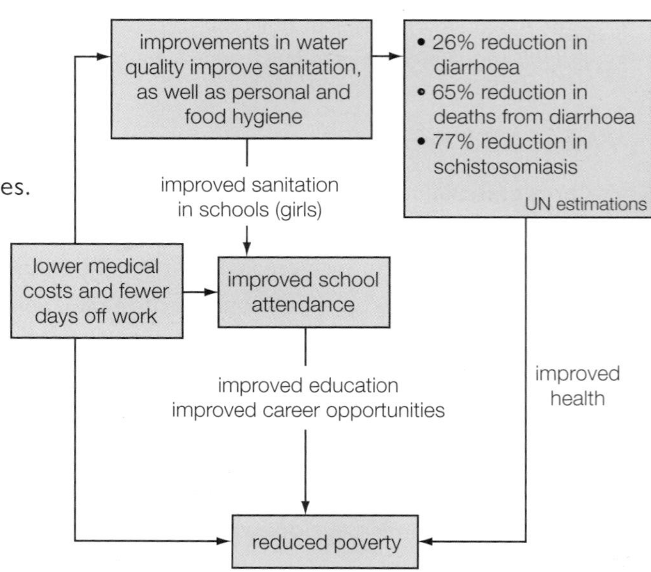

Figure 6 *The spiral of well-being – sanitation works!*

Conflicts can arise when patterns of economic development on either side of a political boundary are uneven. Borders can become zones of tension as scarcity, stress and quality issues begin to build up. As the box on the right shows, 'hotspots' can then emerge where water is contested – with the biggest risks arising when one country actually threatens its neighbours' water supplies.

Turkey, Syria and Iraq

Turkey is a large country; at 780 000 km², it's three times the size of the UK. Although rainfall there is abundant, regional variations and summer droughts in Anatolia (in southeast Turkey) – plus shortages in the capital, Ankara, and in Istanbul – forced the government to embark on the US$32 billion Southeastern Anatolia Project (also known as GAP from its name in Turkish).

GAP is also an attempt to improve incomes in Anatolia – the least developed part of Turkey – by developing an integrated water and energy supply system. But the scale of the GAP project (as shown by the fact file) has the potential for conflict with its neighbours, Syria and Iraq, because it involves damming the Euphrates and Tigris Rivers, which provide both countries with much of their water.

Fact file

Turkey's water budget:

- Total input is an average of 643 mm of rainfall per year.
- 55% is lost as evaporation and transpiration, 14% goes into groundwater, and 15% is unusable – leaving only 16% for use.

The aims of the GAP project are to:

- construct 22 dams, 19 hydroelectric power plants and two water transfer tunnels
- provide irrigation for 1.7 million hectares (20% of Turkey's cultivable land)
- diversify agriculture into cash crops (nuts, fruit, vegetables)
- stop the migration of young people from the region (by increasing jobs and improving education and health facilities)
- help the southeast Anatolian economy to grow by 400%
- help the Turkish economy as a whole to grow by 12%.

Contested water resources

China v India – The Brahmaputra River could be diverted to ease scarcity problems in southern China, but this would then reduce supplies to India.

China v Myanmar, Cambodia, Laos, Thailand and Vietnam – Chinese dams along the headwaters of the Mekong River threaten downstream nations, but some of these have also been damming or taking more water from the river.

Egypt v Ethiopia, Sudan, South Sudan and Uganda – The Blue and White Nile Basins supply Egypt with vital water, but 85% of it comes from the countries further upstream, where population growth and increasing demands could threaten Egypt's supplies.

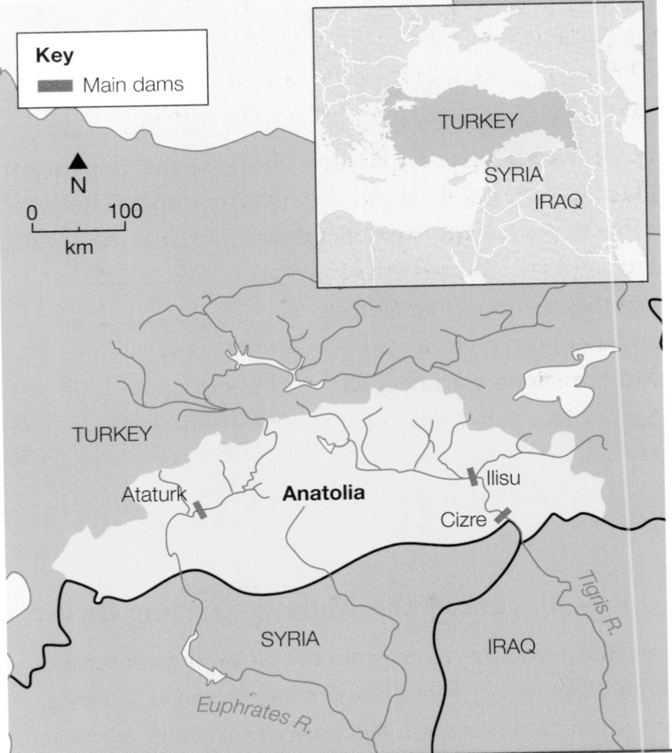

Turkey agreed to release water from the Ilisu Dam for Syria – but not Iraq – at a rate agreed by international law. However just downstream from Ilisu, and north of the border, Turkey intends to build the Cizre Dam to collect additional water for irrigation before the Tigris crosses the border. Some projections claim that by 2040 the Tigris and Euphrates Rivers will no longer reach the sea, due to a combination of dam activity and climate change.

Figure 7 *The Southeastern Anatolia Project (GAP)*

The Murray-Darling Basin

As Figure 8 shows, the Murray-Darling Basin (MDB) covers 1 million km² of southeast Australia (about four times the size of the UK), and it's home to more than 2 million people. Its basin:

- contains two rivers, the Murray and the Darling (see Figure 8)
- covers 14% of the Australian land mass
- provides 75% of Australia's water (85% of the country's irrigation water)
- provides 40% of the nation's farm produce.

However, the MDB is under threat from increasing and competing demands. There has been a five-fold increase in water extraction since the 1920s, which has not always been well managed or co-ordinated. Difficulties arise because the MDB is so large that it comprises different natural environments, ranging from rainforests in sub-tropical Queensland to hot semi-desert areas in South Australia.

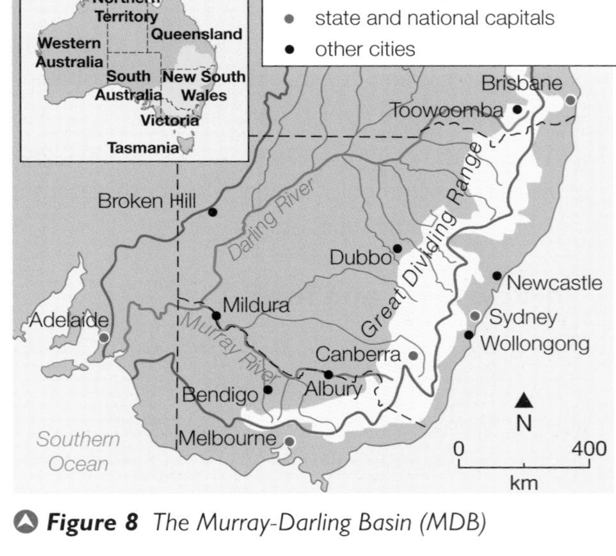

Figure 8 *The Murray-Darling Basin (MDB)*

Because of Australia's size, together with variations in ENSO cycles (see Section 1.7), annual, seasonal and local variations in rainfall occur – even between different parts of the Basin at the same time! Some areas can experience surpluses while others are in deficit (see Figure 9). Figure 6 in Section 1.4 (page 19) shows the flow pattern of the Murray-Darling (compared with the Amazon and Yukon), along with some of the factors that affect their flow patterns. Regulation and entitlements to water are needed to ensure that all cities and users can receive water when and where it's needed.

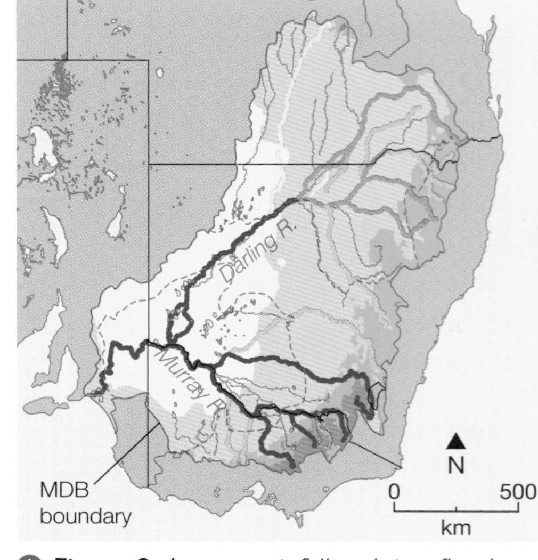

Figure 9 *Average rainfall and river flow/discharge in the MDB*

Key players in the Murray-Darling Basin

Those who use water from the MDB, and consume food grown there, have an interest in the way the resource is managed. **Agriculture** is the major player – taking the most water and increasingly demanding more. **Irrigation** boosts profits, and crops that yield the best returns (like cut flowers, vegetables, grapes and nuts) have been replacing beef and sheep.

Others with a stake in the MDB include:

- **urban** residents in the major cities of southeast Australia, its most populated region (both inside and outside the MDB)
- **industrial** users, e.g. Queensland's mining industry
- **aquaculture**, freshwater fishing
- **leisure** interests and those offering recreational activities
- the **local** and **state governments** of Victoria, New South Wales and Queensland
- **environmental groups** e.g. Environment Victoria
- international **heritage** and **conservation** agencies
- indigenous people's groups, where traditional water rights for aboriginal groups are threatened.

A plan for the MDB

The MDB includes 23 major river systems. Since 1901, there have been agreements, policies and plans in place to use the MDB's waters fairly and responsibly. In 2012, a new Basin Plan came into effect, which aimed to strike a balance between access to water for communities in the Basin and the provision of adequate water for the environment.

The Basin Plan determines the amount of water that can be extracted for consumption – both by the user (urban, industrial and agriculture) and by state and federal governments – so that there isn't a negative impact on the natural environment and functions of the rivers, groundwater and wetlands of the Basin.

But not everyone is happy about the plan, as Figure 10 shows.

> Farmers and rural communities in the MDB claim that too much water has been taken back from irrigated farmland for the river and its environment, to the point where whole districts have now lost much of their irrigation water, farmers can no longer grow food – and communities are dying. In one area, irrigated farming has shrunk so much that 500 farm jobs disappeared between 2012 and 2014 and the population fell by 18%. As predictions of another El Niño event loomed, farmers complained about 'environmental' water flowing freely down the rivers.

Adapted from *The Australian*, July 2015

Figure 10 *Reactions by farmers to 'environmental water' – kept in the river to maintain water quality and wetlands – which they cannot extract for irrigation*

Over to you

1. In pairs, design and draw a labelled mind map or spider diagram outlining environmental and economic problems resulting from inadequate water.
2. **a** Copy the pentagram diagram below and use the data in Figure 3 to plot the five WPI indicators for Argentina, Chile, El Salvador and Haiti.
   b Compare the four countries and identify their two greatest future needs.

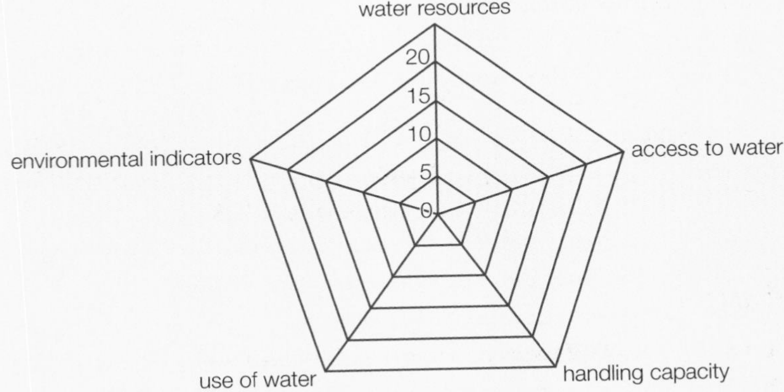

3. **a** Using Figure 6 in Section 1.4, compare the seasonal variations in the three rivers (Murray-Darling, Amazon, Yukon).
   b In pairs, suggest and explain what the impact might be on river flow of present and potential future dams along each river.
4. **a** Begin by making a copy of the blank conflict matrix in Section 1.10 (page 47). Then, in pairs, identify six players and users from this section and complete your matrix to show the degree of agreement and conflict between those players.
   b Explain the conflicts that you have identified.

On your own

5. Define the following terms: **(a)** economic water scarcity, **(b)** water privatisation, **(c)** Water Poverty Index.
6. Explain how and why water varies so much in **(a)** demand between different countries, **(b)** cost between different countries.
7. Research 'water provision in ...' for three countries (Ireland, Denmark and the UK). Write a brief report of 400 words on why the price of water varies so much in these three countries.

Exam-style question

Assess the risks associated with water insecurity. (*12 marks*)

1.10 Water insecurity – managing supplies

In this section, you'll learn that there are different approaches to managing water supplies, and that some are more sustainable than others.

SYNOPTIC THEMES AND KEY CONCEPTS

- **Players** – the role of different players in reducing the risk of water conflict
- **Actions** – how and why people have contrasting attitudes to water supply
- **Interdependence** – the extent to which water supplies can be secured through international agreements
- **Sustainability** – the effectiveness of hard versus more-sustainable methods of restoring water supplies and water conservation

Managing water supplies – hard engineering

Managing water supplies using **hard engineering** (a technological fix) has long been common. The use of dams to provide controllable supplies of water for domestic, industrial and agricultural uses, as well as to regulate river flows and prevent flooding, has been adopted throughout the world for many years. Other schemes – including water transfer projects and desalination plants – are also used to manage water supplies, but such schemes have pros and cons as Figure 1 shows.

***Figure 1** Managing water supplies using hard engineering: China's Three Gorges Dam and South-North Water Transfer Project (see map), together with Israel's Desalination Project*

Key facts	Pros and cons
The Three Gorges Dam • Designed to control flooding on the Yangtze, improve water supply by regulating river flow, generate HEP and make the river navigable. • Controversial and very expensive. • Enables surplus water to build up and be diverted to northern China via the South-North Water Transfer Project. • Electricity generated is vital for China's growth.	**The Three Gorges Dam** • 632 km² of land has been flooded to form the reservoir. • 1.3 million people have been relocated from 1500 villages and towns. • The reservoir's water quality is low, because waste from industry, sewage and farms enters from upstream. • Decomposing vegetation in the reservoir produces methane, which is released when water passes through the HEP turbines.
The South-North Water Transfer Project • The Beijing region has 35% of China's population, and 40% of its arable land – but only 7% of its water. • Three routes will take water from the Yangtze to northern China: (a) a Western route to the Yellow River, (b) an Eastern route via a series of lakes, and (c) a Central route. • The cost is US$70 billion. Due for completion by 2050.	**The South-North Water Transfer Project** • It will submerge 370 km² of land. • 345 000 people will have to relocate. • It risks draining too much water from southern China. • The Eastern route is industrial and risks further pollution. • Will reduce the risk of water shortages in Beijing and boost economic development. • Will reduce the abstraction of groundwater.
Israel's Desalinisation Project • Desalinisation plants provide a reliable and predictable supply of water. • Five plants were opened by 2013, taking water directly from the Mediterranean Sea. • Aims to provide 70% of Israel's domestic water supplies by 2020.	**Israel's Desalinisation Project** • Each plant requires its own power station and adds to CO_2 emissions, but much of the energy used is solar. • Produces vast amounts of salt/brine, containing anti-scaling agents that harm ecosystems. • Produces up to 600 tonnes of potable water per hour.

Managing water supplies sustainably

Water management in Israel

Israel's climate, natural geography and politics has forced it to manage its limited water supplies efficiently. The National Water Carrier was developed to transfer water from the Sea of Galilee in northern Israel to the highly populated centre of the country and the dry south. Israel's current water-management strategies include managing **limited supplies** through:

- using **smart irrigation**, where drip systems allow water to drip slowly to plants' roots through a system of valves and pipes – reducing wastage and evaporation
- **recycling** sewage water for agricultural use (65% of crops are produced in this way)
- reducing agricultural consumption (see Figure 2), and importing water in food as **virtual water**
- adopting stringent **conservation** techniques
- managing demand by charging **'real value' prices** for water to reflect supply costs which include ecosystem management.

Israel also acquires **new supplies** by:

- importing 50 million tonnes of water per year by ship from Turkey (known as the Manavgat Project, agreed in 2004).
- piping seawater from the Red Sea and Mediterranean to new inland desalination plants.

Key word

Virtual water – Water transferred by trading in crops and services that require large amounts of water for their production. By importing a tonne of wheat from a water-rich area, a water-stressed area can save 1000 cubic metres of water.

Figure 2 *Using plastic trays to collect dew and condensation which is then funnelled straight to the plant's roots, reducing the amount of water needed by crops or trees by up to 50%*

Restoring aquifers in Saudi Arabia

In the 1980s, Saudi Arabia pioneered the use of circular irrigation systems to grow enough wheat to feed itself and its neighbours, using water from its own aquifers. Water levels within its aquifers fell sharply. Now, the government imports grain (see Figure 3) and wheat farms have been abandoned to reduce demands upon aquifers supplying irrigation water.

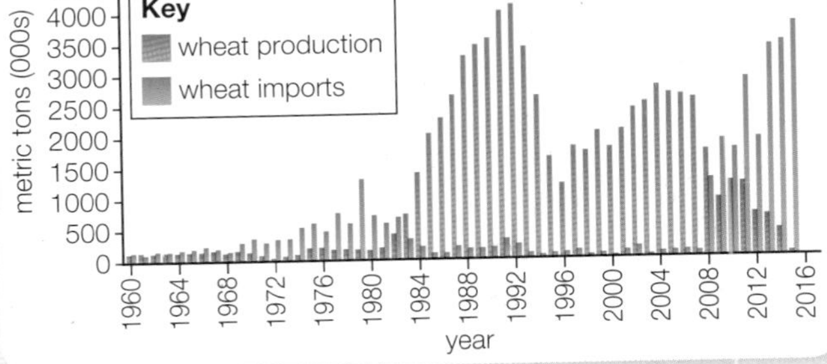

Figure 3 *Changes to wheat production in Saudi Arabia, which now relies on wheat imports*

Holistic management in Singapore

Singapore is a small country and its 5.4 million people are urban. Singapore's neighbour, Malaysia, has traditionally supplied 80% of its water, but by 2010 this volume had halved.

- Per capita water consumption fell from 165 litres per day in 2000 to 150 in 2015, through metering the water supply and educating the public.
- Leakages have been cut to 5% (the UK's figure is 20%).
- Water prices are scaled – the price rises if water usage goes above a certain level.
- Subsidies protect the poorest citizens from expensive water.
- The whole of Singapore is a water harvesting catchment. Diversified supplies include local catchment water, recycled water and desalinated water.

Sharing the Colorado River

For most of the twentieth century, Californians depended on water from the Colorado River. Throughout the century, numerous treaties and agreements were needed to allocate 'fair shares' of the Colorado's water to the surrounding seven US states and Mexico (see Figure 4). An agreement originally made in 1922 (the Colorado Compact), when the population was lower – and the average rainfall 10% higher – is now out-of-date, so pressures on the Colorado River are now building:

- Mexico takes 10% of the total flow.
- The states in the Lower Basin take 50% and the Upper Basin falls short by 10%.
- California takes 20% more than its allocation, which had been agreed separately in 1963.
- Native Americans are owed 5%, but they could claim more because their reservations extend along the river and two of its tributaries.

Figure 4 *The Colorado River Basin*

BACKGROUND

The Colorado

- The Colorado River drains 7% of the USA and covers an area 1.1 times the size of France.
- It supplies water to eight states, contains 11 major dams and reservoirs, irrigates 1.4 million hectares of farmland and provides drinking water for 50 million Americans.
- It also controls flooding and produces HEP.
- Water storage in Lake Powell and Lake Mead was at 43% of capacity in 2016.
- Demand and climate change have depleted storage to 48%.
- Since the 1990s, the average annual Colorado flow has decreased by 15%.
- The 11-year average temperature has increased by 2°C since 1970.
- The Colorado River Basin has been in a persistent drought since 2000.

New agreements

A combination of climate change, population growth, economic development and lifestyle changes has made the old Colorado agreements obsolete, so:

- in 2007, a new agreement was reached. Instead of sharing the Colorado's water, the seven US states divide up the shortages. The amount of water available determines supplies to each state. As a result, California has reduced the amount it extracts by 20%.
- in 2012 an agreement called Minute 139 was signed between the USA and Mexico. It gives Mexico the right to store some of its Colorado River water in Lake Mead. In return, water providers in the Colorado River Basin will be able to purchase water conserved through improving Mexico's canals and storage infrastructure.

Understanding attitudes and actions towards water supply

Water is seen as an entitlement in the USA – part of high living standards. However, increasingly, water restrictions are now occurring, which can create conflicts between water providers and users. The following actions and policies are now being considered or adopted:

- **Domestic conservation.** 30% of water could be saved by repairing leaks or metering supplies. Planting drought-tolerant plants in gardens, and using smart irrigation systems, could save even more.
- **Re-using wastewater** from sewage treatment for landscape irrigation and industry, or to recharge aquifers, is also an option.

- Concrete storm-drains could redirect and **save storm water** into urban parks for irrigation.
- Farms use 80% of California's water. **Reducing irrigation** by 10% would actually double the amount of water available for urban areas.
- If **smart planning** were introduced, new housing would be permitted only where water supplies are adequate.

Players in reducing water conflict

Across the world, efforts are being made to manage water resources more effectively and reduce the risks of conflict. The key players include:

- **The United Nations.** Its Economic Commission for Europe **(UNECE)** Water Convention aims to protect and ensure the quantity, quality and sustainable use of trans-boundary water resources by helping with co-operation and resolving issues. It was established in Helsinki (1992-96) to resolve water issues, and adopted the **Integrated Water Resource Management** (IWRM) at basin scale. IWRM is a policy setting out that water resources are an integral component of ecosystems, a natural resource and a socio-economic good. It promotes co-ordinated management of water, land and related resources in a sustainable way.
- **The EU.** Its Water Framework Directive (WFD) and Hydropower, agreed in Berlin in 2000, set targets to restore rivers, lakes, canals and coastal waters to 'good condition'. The framework was a policy requiring basin-wide assessments of all risks to natural environments posed by new developments.
- **National government agencies** e.g. the UK's Environment Agency, which checks compliance with EU Frameworks, although this may change post-Brexit.

Figure 5 *The UK faced EU fines In January 2016, because the River Teign (in Devon) turned red due to pollution from a nearby quarry*

Exam-style question

Assess the effectiveness of strategies designed to make water use more sustainable. *(12 marks)*

Over to you

1 **a** In pairs, draw a table to compare the costs and benefits of the Three Gorges Dam, the South-North Water Transfer Project, and Israel's desalination project.

b Highlight them in three colours for economic, social and environmental.

c Score each cost and benefit using a 1–5 scoring system (where 1 is poor).

d Compare the points for each project and decide which you think is (**i**) the most effective project, (**ii**) the most sustainable project.

2 **a** In pairs, use this section to list the key players, users and actions across the world in supplying, using and making policies about water use.

b Copy and complete the conflict matrix to show the degree of agreement and conflict between these players.

c Explain the conflicts that you have identified.

	Player A	Player B	Player C	Player D	Player E
Player A					
Player B					
Player C					
Player D					
Player E					
Player F					

Key

++ Strong agreement
+ Some agreement
-- Strong disagreement
- Some disagreement

On your own

3 Compare one researched example of an Integrated Water Resource Management scheme with one where the Water Framework Directive was used. How effective are these in terms of managing water quality or quantity?

4 Compare the costs and benefits of different methods being used in California and Israel to manage water shortages.

Conclusion – revisiting the Enquiry Questions

These are the key questions that drive the whole topic:

1 What are the processes operating within the hydrological cycle from global to local scale?

2 What factors influence the hydrological system over short- and long-term timescales?

3 How does water insecurity occur and why is it becoming such a global issue for the twenty-first century?

Having studied this topic, you can now consider some answers to these questions, using the synoptic themes to frame your ideas.

Players – discussion point 1

Working in groups, consider two instances from this chapter where the actions taken by governments at different levels, or planners or users, were found to be in conflict over issues to do with water quantity and quality. Explain your views.

Attitudes and Actions – discussion point 2

Working in groups, discuss and draw a diagram which shows how and why people have different attitudes towards water supply.

Futures and Uncertainties – discussion point 3

Working in groups, consider the different scenarios concerning (a) climate change and (b) increased demand, caused by economic growth, rising living standards and increased population. Use instances from this chapter to identify the actions that should be taken to manage future water demands. Explain your views.

Books, music, and films on this topic

Books to read

1. *Flood* by Richard Doyle (2002)

   A novel based on a flood scenario when the Thames Barrier in London failed due to a huge storm surge combining with a high tide.

2. *The Grapes of Wrath* by John Steinbeck (1939)

   A novel about a family of farmers who are forced to leave their homes due to drought, as well as a description of the devastating impact that this can have on the agricultural industry.

3. *The Water Wars* by Cameron Stracher (2011)

   A story about a boy's struggle in a world in which water is even more scarce and valuable than ever; a possible Dystopian future if water insecurities continue to worsen.

Music to listen to

1. 'When the levee breaks' By Led Zeppelin (1971)

   A song originally written in 1929, based on the great Mississippi Flood of 1927 and the effect that this had on the people and economy of the area.

2. 'The Flood' by Take That (2010)

   This song was written about a flood, a natural disaster that can take place as a result of the water cycle getting out of balance.

Films to see

1. *Flood* (2007)

   A disaster film portraying the implications of a flood sweeping through London, when the Thames Barrier fails.

2. *More Than A River – The Murray-Darling system and its people* (2005)

   A documentary about the social and economic importance the system plays, and the need to protect its future.

3. *Blue Gold: World Water Wars* (2008)

   A documentary assessing the impact on politics and the environment of a dwindling water supply, and the potential for 'water wars'.

The carbon cycle and energy security

Chapter overview – introducing the topic

This chapter studies the carbon cycle and ways in which energy is a major global issue – not just in terms of security of supply, but also because of its impact on the carbon cycle.

In the specification, this topic has been framed around three Enquiry Questions:

1. How does the carbon cycle operate to maintain planetary health?
2. What are the consequences for people and the environment of our increasing demand for energy?
3. How are the carbon and water cycles linked to the global climate system?

The sections in this chapter provide the content and concepts needed to help you answer these questions.

Synoptic themes

Underlying the content of every topic are three synoptic themes that 'bind' or glue the whole specification together:

1. Players
2. Attitudes and Actions
3. Futures and Uncertainties

1 Players

Players are individuals, groups and organisations involved in making decisions that affect people and places, collectively known as **stakeholders**. Players can be national or international individuals and organisations (e.g. IGOs like the UN), national and local governments, businesses (from small operations to the largest TNCs), as well as pressure groups and NGOs, together with others.

Players that you'll study in this topic include:

- Section 2.5 – The role of TNCs, the Organisation of the Petroleum Exporting Countries (OPEC), consumers, and governments in securing energy pathways and supplies.
- Section 2.6 – The role of business in developing reserves, versus environmental groups and affected communities.

2 Attitudes and Actions

People's attitudes to energy supply and climate change vary, which influences the actions taken to deal with them, e.g. policies in managing greenhouse gas emissions. People's values and attitudes depend on several factors:

- Their political views (left- or right-wing, for example), and/or their religious beliefs.
- The priorities given to people versus profit.
- The importance of social justice and equality.
- Attitudes towards climate change (e.g. whether to reduce carbon emissions or maintain 'business as usual').

Attitudes and Actions that you'll study in this topic include:

- Section 2.5 – Those of different players towards nuclear power.
- Section 2.9 – Those of global consumers to environmental issues.
- Section 2.10 – Those of different countries, TNCs and people towards climate change.

3 Futures and Uncertainties

Decisions and actions taken by players today will affect people in the future. Faced with evidence about rising greenhouse gas emissions, for example, will climate change worsen or have lessons been learned? How far do those who are most vulnerable in terms of the impacts of climate change face a bleak future?

Futures and Uncertainties that you'll study in this topic include:

- Section 2.9 – The uncertainty of global projections about the changing water cycle.
- Section 2.10 – The uncertainty of global projections about climate change.

2.1 2015 – The year it all changed?

In this section, you'll learn about the conflict between increasing energy use and maintaining the global climate.

The essence of conflict

During 2007–8, the world was in the grip of a global financial crisis. The banking crisis led to a drop in consumer demand, which, in the short term, caused sharp falls in energy prices, and therefore lower costs for industry. For a brief time before instability due to the Arab Spring and the Libyan Crisis brought shortages and price rises, consumer spending increased and energy consumption rose. The world had been saved.

Or had it? In December 2015, in response to concerns expressed in news headlines such as those in Figure 1, 195 countries adopted the first legally binding global climate deal at the Paris Climate Conference (COP21). Governments agreed to a long-term goal of keeping the increase in global temperature to well below 2°C above pre-industrial levels.

This goal will require serious reductions in global greenhouse gas emissions – no small aim, given the world's reliance on fossil fuels. Figure 2 shows no slow-down in overall fossil fuel consumption – in 2015, the world consumed over 11 billion tonnes. The carbon found in fossil fuels comes from organic matter. Although they took millions of years to form, burning them takes just seconds. In doing so, carbon is released as carbon dioxide (CO_2), which is the main driver of obvious climate change:

- 2015 began a year of record global average temperatures.
- By 2016, the longest hot spell in 137 years had occurred – 0.9°C hotter than the average for the twentieth-century.

Figure 3 shows CO_2 emissions from energy use. Every major climate scientist connects the rise in global temperatures to CO_2 emissions. How can they be stopped from rising further?

Cheap coal fuels India's economic progress

The Paris Climate Conference calls for a limit on greenhouse gas emissions

2015 – the hottest year on record so far...

Global average ocean surface temperatures reach 1°C above pre-industrial levels

The global average concentration of carbon dioxide exceeds 400 parts per million for the first time in the Northern Hemisphere

Fossil fuel consumption grows 0.6% in 2014–15

Fossil fuel production is at all-time high in the USA

Figure 1 *Fuel's Paradise: Winter 2015*

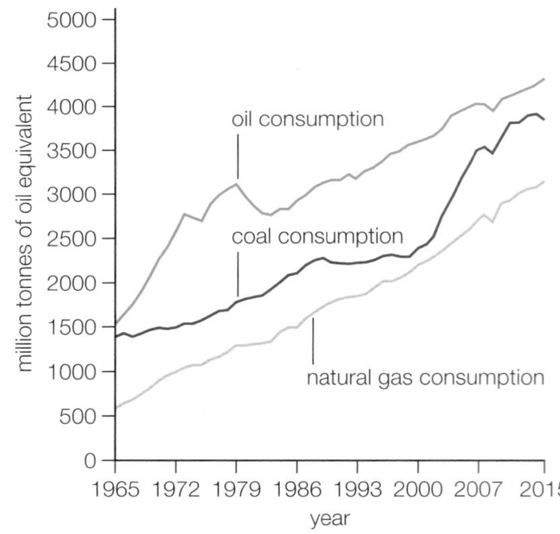

Figure 2 *Global fossil fuel consumption, 1965–2015*

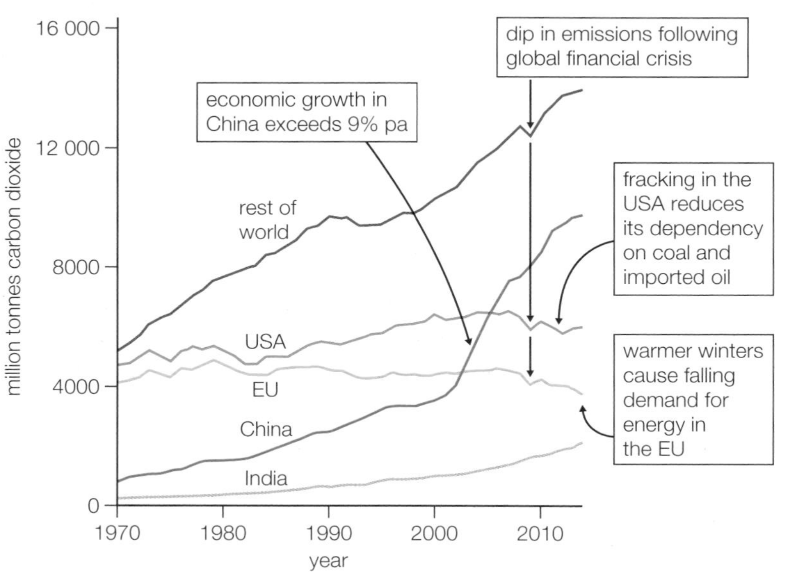

Figure 3 *Carbon dioxide emissions from energy use, 1970–2015*

Giving up fossil fuels? The case of India

For some countries, abandoning fossil fuels could threaten their economic development. India, for example:

- depends on coal for 66% of its energy needs. Just one day after the 2015 Paris Climate Conference agreed to reduce global CO_2 emissions, India declared that it intended to double its coal output by 2020!
- accounts for 6% of global CO_2 emissions. It's the third largest emitter after China and the USA, and it wants to reduce its dependence on imported fuel, such as oil and gas, which means more use of domestic coal.

New infrastructure, an expanding middle class, and 600 million new users of electricity are driving India's development and demand for coal. But it comes at a cost. Child labour in India's coalmines, as shown in Figure 4, helps to keep the cost of coal low and promote economic growth, but it also causes suffering and takes children out of education.

Figure 4 *Exploiting India's abundant coal supplies is helping to drive its economic growth, but it has also resulted in the exploitation of child labour in opencast coalmines like the one pictured. Up to 10 000 children work in the mines of Kuju District alone.*

Why do oil prices fluctuate?

The fluctuating price of oil tends to reflect political and economic factors, but particularly market demand. In the past, if demand suddenly rose, the OPEC producers (see page 70) tended to increase oil production in order to prevent a sharp rise in price, or reduce production to maintain the price if demand fell. However, fracking has changed the picture. The world's largest oil market is the USA, which drives much of what happens to the oil price. US oil prices have fallen sharply since 2012 (see Figure 5), as a result of large new supplies of oil and shale gas from the USA and Canada. OPEC producers have often cut prices to compete and maintain market share, and also for geopolitical motives.

The USA became energy secure in oil and gas in 2015, a marked change from its dependence on imported oil and gas in 2000. New Canadian sources come from tar sands and fracking. Fracked gas emits less CO_2 than coal when used to generate electricity. As a result, between 2008 and 2015, the USA's CO_2 emissions fell by 7.7%, even though its economy and its oil consumption grew by 9%.

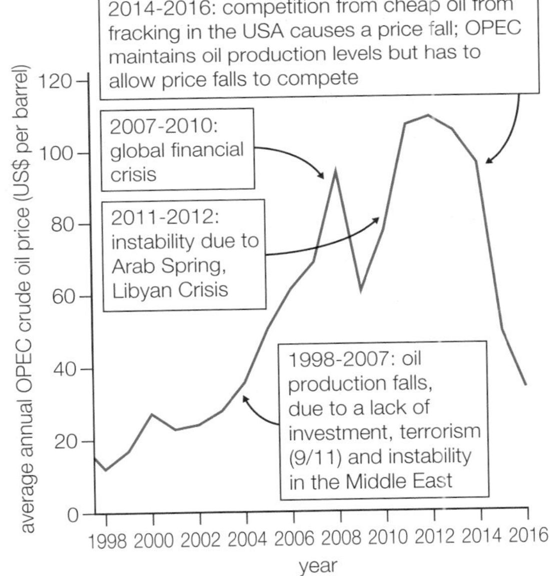

Figure 5 *Changes in the OPEC crude oil price, 1998–2016*

Over to you

1. In pairs, use Figures 2 and 5 to draw a spider diagram which shows how national, international and global factors can affect oil production and consumption.
2. Use Figure 3 to assess (**a**) the links between consumption of oil and its impacts on the atmosphere, (**b**) why the Paris COP21 conference agreement was needed.
3. Discuss in pairs and feed back your ideas to the question 'Can child labour ever be justified?'

On your own

4. Explain how far the following factors could affect the Paris COP21 conference agreement:
   - **a** Increased demand for fossil fuels in India and China.
   - **b** A refusal by future governments to accept the link between CO_2 emissions and climate change.

2.2 The carbon cycle

In this section, you'll learn that most global carbon is locked up in terrestrial stores as part of the long-term geological cycle.

EQ1 Sections 2.2 to 2.4 investigate how the carbon cycle operates to maintain planetary health.

Understanding carbon

Carbon provides the major building blocks for all life on Earth. It regulates our climate, making it warm enough to survive, and is **stored** within rocks, plants and the oceans.

- **Stores** of carbon are also referred to as **pools, stocks** and **reservoirs**.
- There are **terrestrial, oceanic** and **atmospheric** stores.
- **Flux** refers to the **movement** or **transfer** of carbon between stores. Fluxes create cycles and feedbacks.

Human activity is part of the carbon cycle, and planetary health is placed at risk as more carbon enters the atmosphere. However, the amounts added by human activity are tiny compared with the flows that are exchanged naturally between oceans, land and atmosphere every day.

KEY CONCEPTS

- **Systems** – how the carbon cycle operates with inputs, stores, flows and outputs
- **Equilibrium** – how the carbon cycle is maintained in a balance

The geological carbon cycle

The geological carbon cycle (see Figure 1) is a natural cycle that moves carbon between land, oceans and atmosphere. This movement involves a number of chemical reactions that create new stores which trap carbon for significant periods of time. There tends to be a natural balance between carbon production and absorption within this cycle. However, there can be occasional disruptions and short periods before the equilibrium is restored, such as when major volcanic eruptions emit large quantities of carbon into the atmosphere, or when natural climate changes occur.

Figure 1 shows six important natural stores and fluxes:

1. Terrestrial carbon, held within the mantle, is released into the atmosphere as carbon dioxide (CO_2) when volcanoes erupt (see Figure 2). This is known as '**out-gassing**'.
2. CO_2 within the atmosphere combines with rainfall to produce a weak acid (carbonic acid; also known as acid rain) that dissolves carbon-rich rocks, releasing bicarbonates. This is **chemical weathering**.
3. Rivers transport weathered carbon and calcium sediments to the oceans, where they are deposited.
4. Carbon in **organic matter** from plants and from animal **shells and skeletons** sinks to the ocean bed when they die, building up strata of coal, chalk and limestone.
5. Carbon-rich rocks are subducted along plate boundaries and eventually emerge again when volcanoes erupt.
6. The presence of intense heating along subduction plate boundaries metamorphoses (or alters) sedimentary rocks by baking, creating **metamorphic** rocks. CO_2 is released by the metamorphism of rocks rich in carbonates during this process.

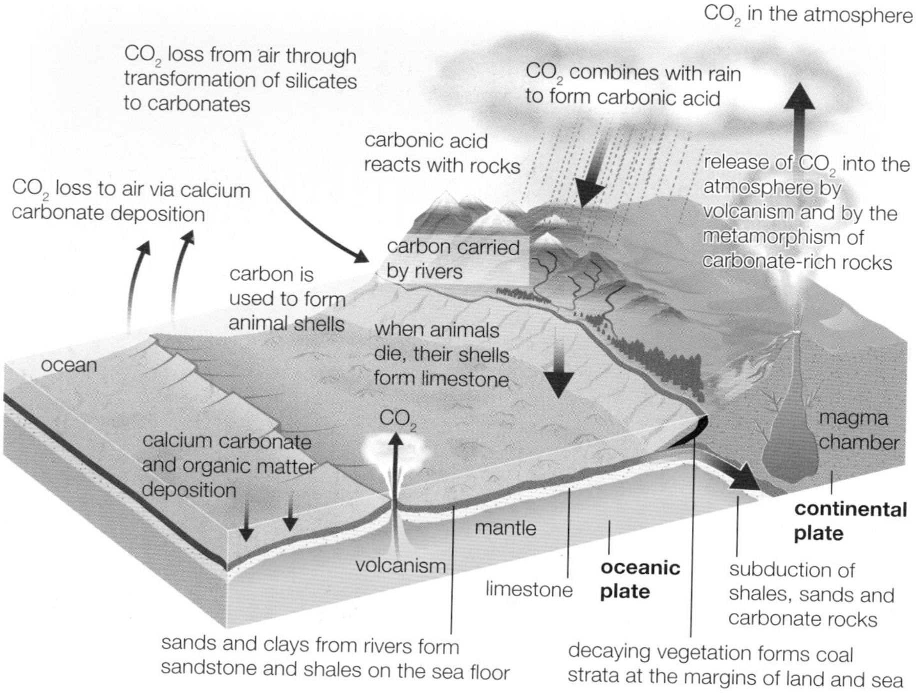

Figure 1 *The geological carbon cycle*

The carbon cycle illustrated in Figure 1 contains two types of carbon: geological and biologically derived. **Geological carbon** results from the formation of sedimentary carbonate rocks – limestone and chalk – in the oceans, and **biologically derived carbon** is stored in shale, coal and other sedimentary rocks.

Maintaining an equilibrium

The impact of emissions from volcanic eruptions is to send extra CO_2 into the atmosphere, which leads to rising temperatures, increased evaporation and higher levels of atmospheric moisture. This, in turn, leads to increased acid rain, which weathers rocks and creates biocarbonates that will eventually be deposited as carbon on the ocean floor. The process is slow – perhaps a few hundred thousand years – but this **chemical weathering** process slowly rebalances the carbon cycle.

The bio-geochemical carbon cycle

Biological and chemical processes determine just how much of the carbon available on the Earth's surface is stored or released at any one time. That's why it's often referred to as the **bio-geochemical carbon cycle**. The role of living organisms is critical in maintaining the efficient running of this system, because they control the overall balance between storage, release, transfer and absorption.

As Figure 3 shows, the four key processes in the cycle are:

- **photosynthesis** – removing CO_2 from the atmosphere to promote plant growth
- **respiration** – releasing CO_2 into the atmosphere as animals consume plant growth and breathe
- **decomposition** – breaking down organic matter and releasing CO_2 into soils
- **combustion** of biomass and fossil fuels – releasing CO_2 and other greenhouse gases into the atmosphere.

Together, these four processes continuously transfer carbon from one store to another. The time period over which the carbon stays in any one store is important, and – since the Industrial Revolution – deeply buried stores of carbon have been exploited and burnt, releasing CO_2 into the atmosphere. Figure 3 shows the bio-geochemical cycle and the enhanced flow of CO_2 from the geosphere (i.e. the Earth) to the atmosphere as a result of combustion caused by human activities.

In 2010, the Eyjafjallajökull volcano in Iceland erupted – emitting CO_2 into the atmosphere, plus extensive ash clouds that spread across Europe. The eruption emitted between 150 000 and 300 000 tonnes of CO_2 per day – placing it in the same emissions league as small-to-medium-sized European countries such as Portugal or Ireland. But it contributed less than 0.3% of global emissions of greenhouse gases in 2010.

Figure 2 *Eyjafjallajökull in Iceland erupting in April 2010, sending ash and carbon dioxide high into the atmosphere*

Figure 3 *The bio-geochemical carbon cycle*

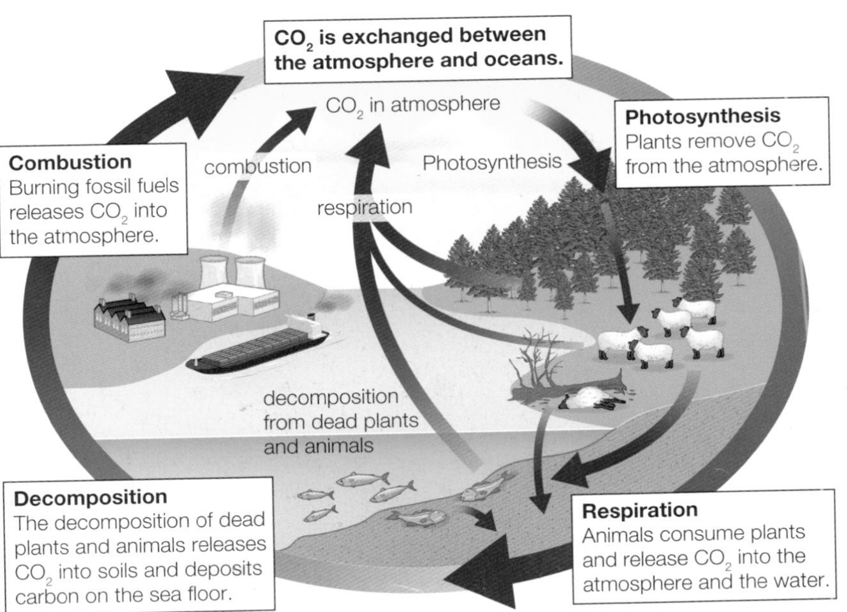

How much carbon is there?

The Earth's total carbon store is very large (see the blue numbers in Figure 4), but it's the rate of exchange (**flux**) between the individual stores that matters most. Scientists measure the amount of carbon on Earth in **gigatonnes (Gt)** or **petagrams (Pg)**. Each Gt or Pg of carbon equals one billion tonnes. It's estimated that 180 Gt of carbon has been added to the atmosphere as a result of burning fossil fuels. Whilst this is tiny in comparison to the amounts transferred naturally, it is enough to alter the concentration of greenhouse gases in the atmosphere, and to trigger climate change. Figure 4 shows the relative sizes of the different stores and fluxes.

Types of carbon

Carbon comes in several forms, and we need to know where these occur within the carbon cycle, because – as they flow between stores – the balances can be altered and the knock-on effects can impact on the cycle. Carbon cycling is simply the movement from one form to another over time.

The three forms of carbon are:

- **inorganic** – found in rocks as bicarbonates and carbonate (the Earth's largest carbon store)
- **organic** – found in plant material
- **gaseous** – found as CO_2, CH_4 (methane) and CO (carbon monoxide).

Fluxes and balances

Figure 4 shows the significance of natural carbon exchanges, as well as the results of human activities such as energy generation. Every year, vast quantities of carbon are exchanged between stores (shown in blue in Figure 4). These exchanges are called **fluxes** (shown in red in Figure 4). Inorganic carbon is released by chemical weathering very slowly, over decades or hundreds of years, but fluxes between the Earth's surface, plants and atmosphere are much faster – a matter of months or seasons. Fluxes within the carbon cycle can be shown using proportional arrows. The width of each arrow is drawn in proportion to the amount of carbon transferred.

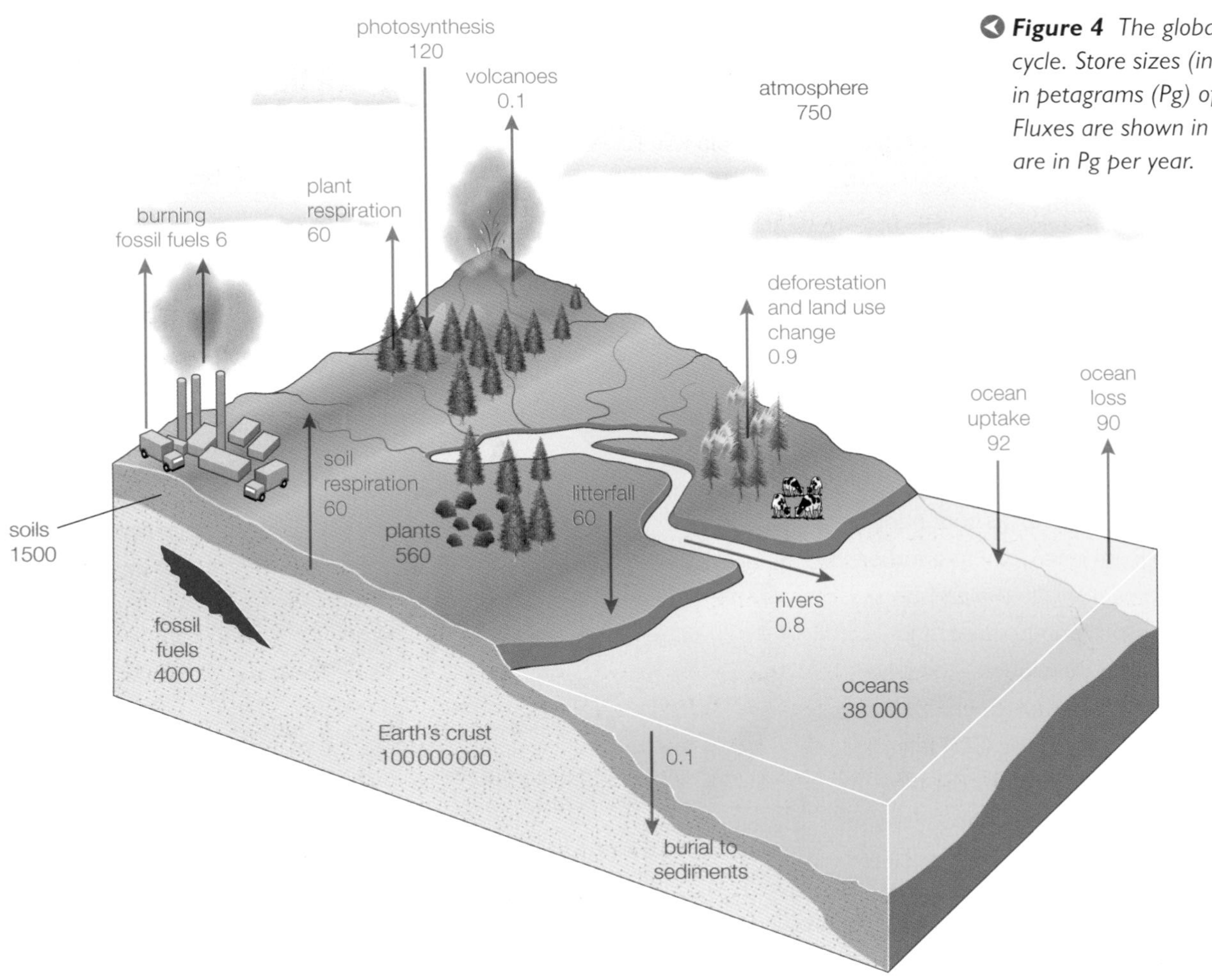

Figure 4 *The global carbon cycle. Store sizes (in blue) are in petagrams (Pg) of carbon. Fluxes are shown in red, and are in Pg per year.*

Variations in carbon fluxes

As well as adding carbon to the atmosphere, the Earth's carbon reservoirs also remove it into carbon sinks in a series of fluxes. These are shown in Figure 5. The speed of fluxes between these sinks varies, both globally and over time.

Fast and slow

The quickest cycle is completed in seconds, as plants take carbon from the atmosphere through photosynthesis. They then release it by respiration. Sunlight, temperature and moisture all control the speed of these processes. If it's too dark, hot or cold they decrease. Low levels of CO_2 in the atmosphere also reduce the speed of the cycle.

Dead organic material in soils may retain carbon for years – or even centuries – waiting to be broken down. Note that the tree on the left in Figure 5 is alive and therefore is taking in CO_2 from the atmosphere, and the one on the right is dead, so the CO_2 it holds eventually makes its way to the sea via the soil and decomposition. Some organic materials may become buried so deeply that they don't decay at all – instead transforming into sedimentary rocks, such as limestone, or coal, or alternatively into hydrocarbons (commonly referred to as oil and natural gas). CO_2 is then only released when these are burned, or when limestone is used industrially, e.g. when making cement.

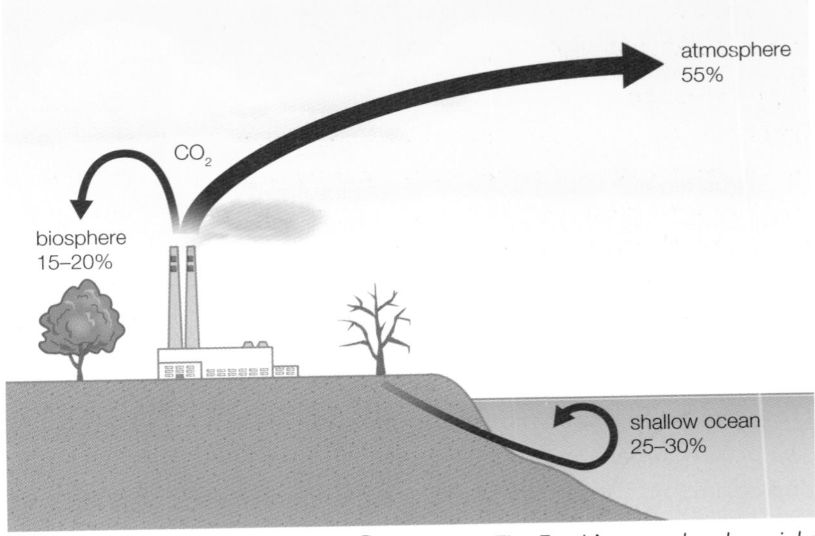

Figure 5 *The Earth's natural carbon sinks*

Geographical patterns

Since regional climates influence rates of photosynthesis and respiration, it's not surprising to see that CO_2 fluxes vary with latitude. Levels are always higher in the Northern Hemisphere, because it contains greater landmasses and greater temperature variations than in the Southern Hemisphere.

Exam-style question

Explain the importance of fluxes to the carbon cycle. *(6 marks)*

Over to you

1 In pairs, draw a spider diagram to show the importance of the following to the carbon cycle: (**a**) volcanic eruptions, (**b**) chemical weathering, (**c**) respiration, (**d**) decomposition, (**e**) photosynthesis, (**f**) the combustion of fossil fuels.

2 **a** Re-draw Figure 4 as a flow diagram with flow arrows in proportion to the fluxes shown in the diagram. Use a scale of 100 petagrams = 10 mm; for small amounts, simply use a pencil line.

b Using Figure 4 and your flow diagram, explain the extent to which the elements of the carbon cycle are in equilibrium.

3 Why is it significant that some fluxes are fast and others are slow?

4 In pairs, discuss and explain why there is increasing concern about carbon emissions being added to the atmosphere by human activities, when the amounts concerned are small compared to those of natural emissions.

On your own

5 Distinguish between the following pairs of terms: (**a**) store and flux, (**b**) out-gassing and absorption of carbon, (**c**) bio-geochemical and geologically derived carbon cycles.

6 Explain why the geological carbon cycle is so-called.

7 Explain why it's important that the carbon cycle maintains an equilibrium.

2.3 Carbon sequestration

In this section, you'll learn that biological processes sequester (take up) carbon on land and in the oceans on shorter timescales.

KEY CONCEPTS

- **Systems** – how the carbon cycle operates in ocean waters and on land
- **Equilibrium** – how the carbon cycle is maintained in a balance on the land and in the sea

The biological carbon pump

It can take millions of years for carbon to move through the carbon cycle between rocks, soil, rivers, oceans and the atmosphere. Each year no more than 100 million tonnes move through this slow cycle. However, one part of the cycle moves faster – at the surface of the ocean, there's always an exchange of carbon dioxide (CO_2); some dissolves into the water as some is vented out to the air above. This is known as the **biological carbon pump** – the processes shown in Figure 1 transfer between 5 and 15 gigatonnes of carbon from the atmosphere to the deep ocean each year via the processes shown.

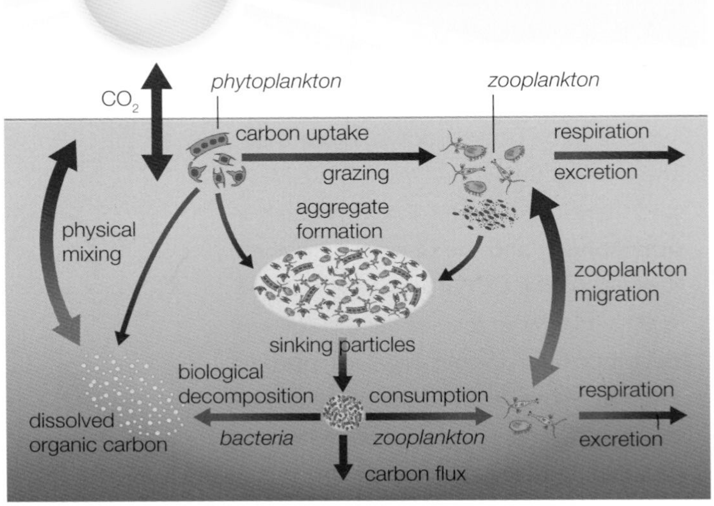

Figure 1 *The biological carbon pump. In the diagram, zooplankton are animal plankton, and phytoplankton are plankton capable of carrying out photosynthesis.*

How the biological carbon pump works

The ocean's surface layer contains tiny phytoplankton, also known as micro-algae. In some ways, they are similar to terrestrial plants; they contain chlorophyll and need sunlight to live. They also have shells, and **sequester** (take up) CO_2 through photosynthesis – creating calcium carbonate as their shells develop. Then, when they die, these carbon-rich micro-organisms sink to the ocean floor and remain there, accumulating as sediment.

This particular process is known as the **carbonate pump**, and is a part of the biological carbon pump. It is crucial, because it pumps CO_2 out of the atmosphere and into the ocean store. Without the contributions of phytoplankton, the CO_2 concentration in the atmosphere would be far higher than it already is.

This is a naturally efficient system, but it's also fragile. Phytoplankton require nutrients in vast quantities, and existing ocean temperatures and currents maintain a constant supply. The recycling of particles that sink in deep waters by upwelling currents is critical. The global movement of water through the **thermohaline circulation** (explained briefly on the right and in more detail with a diagram on page 11) maintains the pump. However, slight changes in water temperature can alter the flow. Pollution and turbulence also reduce light penetration and slow the pump down. Each of these factors is vulnerable to climate change – making the risk of the pump breaking down a real one.

How the thermohaline circulation works

- The water in the far North Atlantic is cold and very **saline** (salty), which makes it denser and heavier – causing it to sink.
- By sinking, it draws warmer water in from the ocean surface above. This, in turn, draws water across the ocean surface from the Tropics/equatorial region.
- Eventually, this movement from the Tropics draws cold water up from the ocean bottom, ready to be warmed again.

Is the Gulf Stream failing?

During 2004, there was some alarm amongst ocean and climate scientists when the northeasterly Atlantic current, known as the Gulf Stream, appeared to stall for ten days. Those monitoring ocean temperatures became concerned that the current was slowing, and indeed data seemed to show that the speed of ocean circulation between the Gulf of Mexico and Europe had slowed by 30% since 2000.

The scientists' hypothesis for the cause was as follows:

- Melting Arctic ice was increasing the amount of freshwater entering the North Atlantic.
- The ocean's salinity was declining as a result, preventing cold water from sinking there.
- This meant that there was nowhere for the warm waters of the Gulf Stream to go – the North Atlantic was losing its pulling effect.

By investigating this hypothesis, research since 2004 has suggested that the Gulf Stream has slowed by 6 million tonnes of water per second over 12 years.

Key words

Carbon sequestration – The removal and storage of carbon from the atmosphere. Usually occurs in oceans, forests and soils through photosynthesis.

Photosynthesis – The use of energy from sunlight to produce nutrients from carbon dioxide and water.

Thermohaline circulation – An ocean current that produces both vertical and horizontal circulations of warm and cold water around the world's oceans.

Terrestrial stores

Terrestrial (land-based) **primary producers** sequester carbon through the process of photosynthesis, just as phytoplankton does in the ocean. Figure 2 shows just how much carbon is stored in the world's biomes.

Primary producers and consumers

In terrestrial ecosystems, carbon is found in plants, animals, soils and micro-organisms such as bacteria and fungi. Leaves, roots, dead material, decaying litter and brown organic residues in soil all contain carbon. The exchange of carbon between plants and the atmosphere is rapid. Green plants are **primary producers** that use solar energy to produce biomass – plant growth on land and algae and phytoplankton in water. CO_2 is absorbed and converted into new plant growth during **photosynthesis**. As plants grow, they release CO_2 into the atmosphere through **respiration**.

Organisms known as **primary consumers** – bugs, beetles, larvae and herbivores – depend and feed on producers, and return carbon to the atmosphere during respiration. In turn, organisms such as insects, worms and bacteria feed on dead plants, animals and waste, and are therefore known as **biological decomposers**.

Biome	Area	Global carbon stocks		
		Vegetation	Soil	Total
Tropical forests	1.76	212	216	**428**
Temperate forests	1.04	59	100	**159**
Boreal forests	1.37	88	471	**559**
Tropical savannas	2.25	66	264	**330**
Temperate grasslands	1.25	9	295	**304**
Deserts & semi-deserts	4.55	8	191	**199**
Tundra	0.95	6	121	**127**
Wetlands	0.35	15	225	**240**
Croplands	1.60	3	128	**131**
Total	**15.12**	**466**	**2011**	**2477**

Figure 2 *The estimated size of terrestrial carbon stores; the areas are in billions of hectares, and global carbon stocks in gigatonnes (see Section 2.2).*

The role of trees

The growth of vegetation depends on water, nutrients and sunlight. 95% of a tree's biomass (the leaves, branches, trunk and roots) is made up from the CO_2 that it sequesters and converts into cellulose (a carbon compound). **Carbon fixation** turns gaseous carbon – CO_2 – into living organic compounds that grow. The amount of carbon stored within a tree, woodland or forest depends on the balance between photosynthesis and respiration. Figure 3 shows this simple cycle.

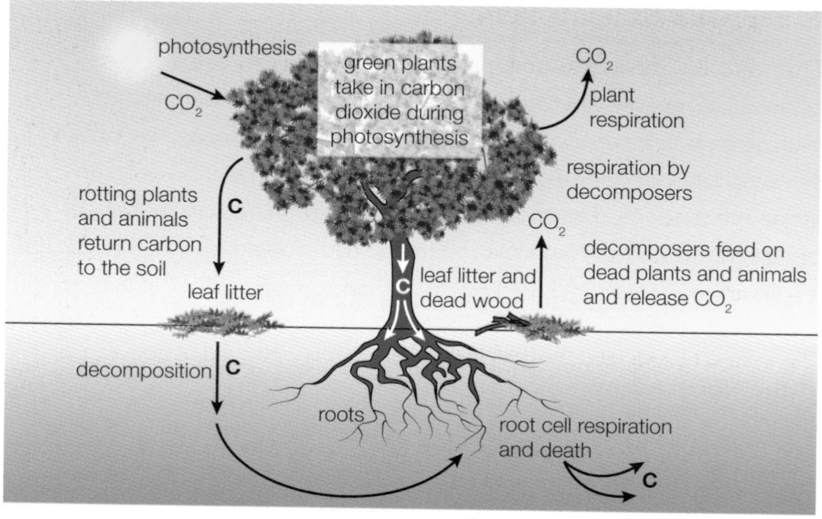

Figure 3 *The tree carbon cycle*

Mangroves and the role of soil

Biological carbon can be stored in soils in the form of dead organic matter, or returned back to the atmosphere as a result of decomposition. Depending on the nature of the soil this process can be relatively quick (e.g. a few years) or, as in tundra soils, very slow. But deforestation and land use change can release carbon stores very rapidly, as mangroves show.

Mangrove forests are found along tropical and sub-tropical tidal coasts in Africa, Australia, Asia and the Americas. They are vital processors, sequestering almost 1.5 metric tonnes of carbon per hectare every year. Figure 4a shows the carbon cycle in mangrove forests. Mangrove soils consist of thick organic layers of litter, humus and peat, which contain high levels of carbon – over 10%. Undisturbed mangroves grow quickly and absorb large amounts of carbon. Submerged below high tides twice a day, their soils are **anaerobic** – that is, without oxygen. Bacteria and microbes cannot survive without oxygen, so the decomposition of plant matter is slow. As a result, little of the carbon can be respired back to the atmosphere, and the store remains intact. Any plant matter trapped by tree roots (see Figure 4B) tends to stay as it decomposes slowly, and may remain stored for thousands of years.

However, if mangroves are drained or cleared, carbon is released back to the atmosphere. Throughout the tropical world, mangroves are being cleared for tourism, shrimp farms and aquaculture. According to Malaysian researchers, if just 2% of the world's mangroves are lost, the amount of carbon released will be 50 times the natural sequestration rate.

A

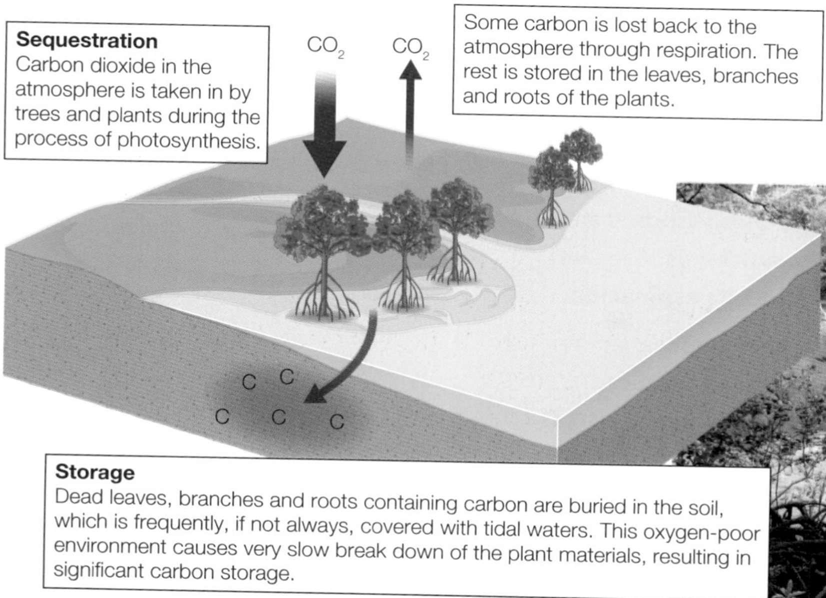

Sequestration
Carbon dioxide in the atmosphere is taken in by trees and plants during the process of photosynthesis.

Some carbon is lost back to the atmosphere through respiration. The rest is stored in the leaves, branches and roots of the plants.

Storage
Dead leaves, branches and roots containing carbon are buried in the soil, which is frequently, if not always, covered with tidal waters. This oxygen-poor environment causes very slow break down of the plant materials, resulting in significant carbon storage.

B

Figure 4 *Mangroves – a vital store of carbon. (**A**) shows the carbon cycle within mangroves, and (**B**) shows the complexity of mangroves in the Daintree rainforest of northern Queensland in Australia*

Tundra soils

Much of the soil in the tundra region is permanently frozen and contains ancient carbon. Microbe activity is only active in the surface layer of the soil when it thaws. The rest of the time the roots and dead and decayed organic matter are frozen, locking any carbon into an icy store. Tundra soils contain carbon that has been trapped for hundreds of thousands of years.

Figure 5 Permafrost in tundra areas – it's the permanently frozen layer exposed in this soil at about 1-2 metres depth. The top layer thaws out in summer.

Tropical forests as carbon stores

Tropical rainforests are huge carbon sinks, but they are fragile and can quickly disappear. Carbon within rainforests is mainly stored in trees, plant litter and dead wood. Soils are relatively thin and lacking in nutrients, because litter layers that cover them, though very deep, decompose rapidly and the nutrients released are rapidly consumed by vegetation.

As the litter and dead wood decay, they are recycled so quickly that a soil store does not develop. Even carbon given off by decomposers is rapidly recycled. Tropical rainforests absorb more atmospheric CO_2 than any other terrestrial biome, accounting for 30% of global net primary production, although they cover just 17% of the Earth's surface. If they all died off the world would lose a massive carbon sink, as shown in Figure 6.

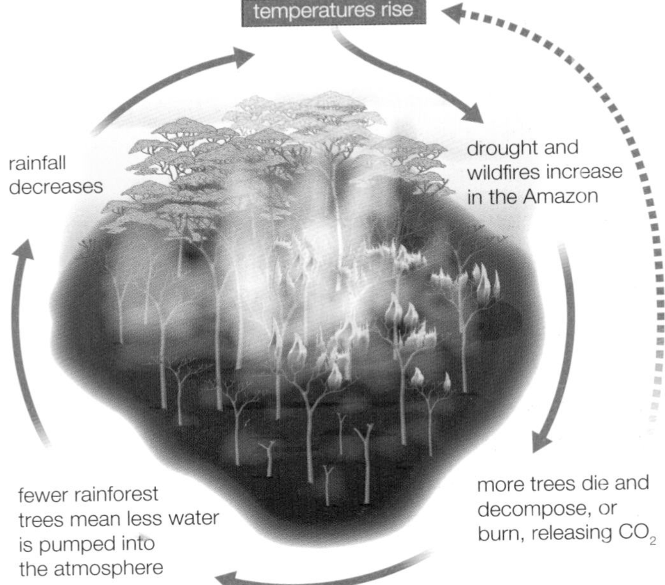

Figure 6 If the rainforests die off …

Exam-style question

Explain the significance of carbon sequestration. (6 marks)

Over to you

1. Working in pairs, use Figure 7 on page 11, together with Figure 1 in this section, to draw a systems diagram (with inputs, flows, stores and outputs) showing how the biological pump works in oceans.
2. Explain the varying proportions of vegetation and soil as carbon stores in each of the biomes shown in Figure 2.
3. Using Figure 7 on page 11 to help you, design a mind map to show possible outcomes if the Gulf Stream were to continue slowing or even stop.
4. In pairs, design an information leaflet explaining the global and local significance of mangroves.

On your own

5. Distinguish between the following pairs of terms: (**a**) carbon sequestration and photosynthesis; (**b**) biological carbon pump and thermohaline circulation; (**c**) primary producers and consumers.
6. Explain the significance of soil in the carbon cycle.
7. Explain the potential interruptions to the carbon cycle caused by the destruction of rainforests.

2.4 A balanced carbon cycle

In this section, you'll learn that a balanced carbon cycle is important for sustaining other Earth systems, but also that human activities are increasingly altering the carbon cycle.

KEY CONCEPTS

- **Systems** – how the carbon cycle sustains other Earth systems
- **Equilibrium** – how the carbon cycle is balanced, and how that balance is disturbed by human activities
- **Feedback** – the impacts of change on the carbon cycle as carbon stores are released

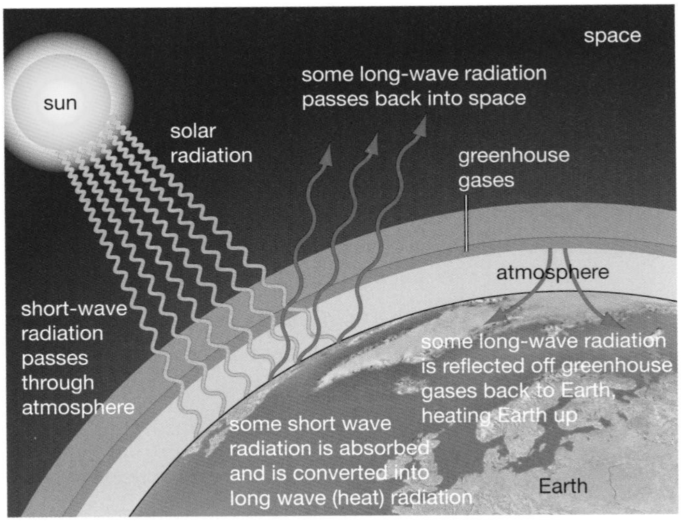

The natural greenhouse effect

The sun is the natural driver of almost all of the Earth's atmospheric energy. Energy is received as incoming solar radiation (light) from the sun. Dark surfaces on the Earth absorb this solar radiation and then radiate it back as heat. However, that warmth alone is insufficient to permit life on Earth, because it would simply be radiated into the atmosphere and lost into space unless something prevented it from escaping. One of the most vital roles of the carbon cycle is the release of carbon dioxide (CO_2), and other gases such as methane (CH_4) into the atmosphere. These, together with nitrous oxide, halocarbons, ozone and water vapour are all known as **greenhouse gases**. They absorb and reflect back some of the radiated heat from the Earth's surface. By retaining this heat, they keep the Earth's surface 16°C warmer than it would otherwise be – warm enough to sustain life on Earth.

The processes controlling the amounts and concentrations of these greenhouse gases in the Earth's atmosphere affect the global climate, so CO_2 and CH_4 (both carbon-based gases) each contribute to the **natural greenhouse effect** shown in Figure 1.

Figure 1 The natural greenhouse effect

Key word

Greenhouse effect – The warming of the atmosphere as gases such as CO_2, CH_4 and water vapour absorb heat energy radiated from the Earth.

Greenhouse gases

CO_2 is the most common greenhouse gas (89% of the total), but Figure 2 lists others. Together they act as a blanket, retaining heat, but CO_2 has the highest **radiative forcing effect (RFE)** of all gases emitted by human activities – it holds on to more heat for longer.

Figure 2 Greenhouse gases – their sources and effects

Greenhouse gas	% of greenhouse gases produced	Sources	Warming power compared to CO_2	% increase since 1850
Carbon dioxide (CO_2) • Makes up only 0.04% of the Earth's atmosphere • 20% will stay in the atmosphere for 800 years	89%	burning fossil fuels; deforestation	1	+30%
Methane (CH_4) Stays in the atmosphere for 10 years	7%	gas pipeline leaks; rice farming; cattle farming	21 times more powerful	+250%
Nitrous oxide (N_2O) • Stays in the atmosphere for 100 years • Traps infrared radiation changing to nitric oxide that destroys ozone – allowing harmful ultraviolet rays into the atmosphere	3%	jet aircraft engines, cars and lorries; fertilisers; sewage farms; production of synthetic chemicals	250 times more powerful	+16%
Halocarbons	1%	used in industry, solvents and cooling equipment	3000 times more powerful	not natural

The enhanced greenhouse effect

The concentrations of several greenhouse gases (including atmospheric carbon: CO_2 and CH_4) in the atmosphere have increased by 25% since 1750, when industrialisation began in the UK, and are now increasing faster than ever. Since the 1980s, 75% of CO_2 emissions have come from burning fossil fuels. Most climate researchers believe that this is the cause of increased global temperatures – and is leading to an **enhanced greenhouse effect**.

Human activities, such as burning fossil fuels and deforestation, release natural stores of carbon and nitrogen, which then combine with oxygen to form greenhouse gases:

- Carbon combines with oxygen to form CO_2.
- Nitrogen combines with oxygen to form N_2O (nitrous oxide).

Also as global temperatures increase, so too does the level of water vapour in the atmosphere. Increasing global temperatures leads to greater evaporation of water, leading to greater condensation. This causes increased cloud cover, trapping heat in the atmosphere.

Climate patterns – temperature and precipitation

Given that CO_2 and other greenhouse gases naturally help to maintain the Earth's temperature – and also determine the distribution of temperature and precipitation – then changing their concentrations is likely to alter these distribution patterns.

Key word

Enhanced greenhouse effect – The increase in the natural greenhouse effect, said to be caused by human activities that increase the quantity of greenhouse gases in the Earth's atmosphere.

Temperature

The amount of solar energy (solar insolation) reaching the Earth's surface varies at different locations, which in turn influences temperature. The angle of the sun's rays makes solar insolation intense at the Equator, but dispersed over a wider area at the Poles. Different characteristics of the Earth's surface (e.g. how light or dark it is) also affect how much heat is absorbed or reflected (known as the **albedo**) – snow reflects heat and dark forests absorb it. Figure 3 shows average annual global temperatures. Heat is redistributed around the globe by air movement (wind), caused by both pressure differences and ocean currents.

Precipitation

The heating of the Earth's atmosphere and surface controls the temperature, pressure, movement and moisture content of the air. Warm air rises and cools, leading water vapour to condense and clouds to form.

- Because solar radiation (insolation) is most intense over the Equator, convection and low-pressure systems dominate there. Rainfall is high all year.
- As the air pressure rises around 30° north and south of the Equator, precipitation decreases. Clouds rarely form there.
- In the mid latitudes, air masses of different characteristics meet, and low-pressure systems bring rainfall.
- Nearer the Poles, precipitation falls as the air cools further and is dense and dry – creating polar deserts.

Regional and seasonal variations also occur, because of the effects of relief and the migration of global pressure patterns and wind systems as the sun moves north and south.

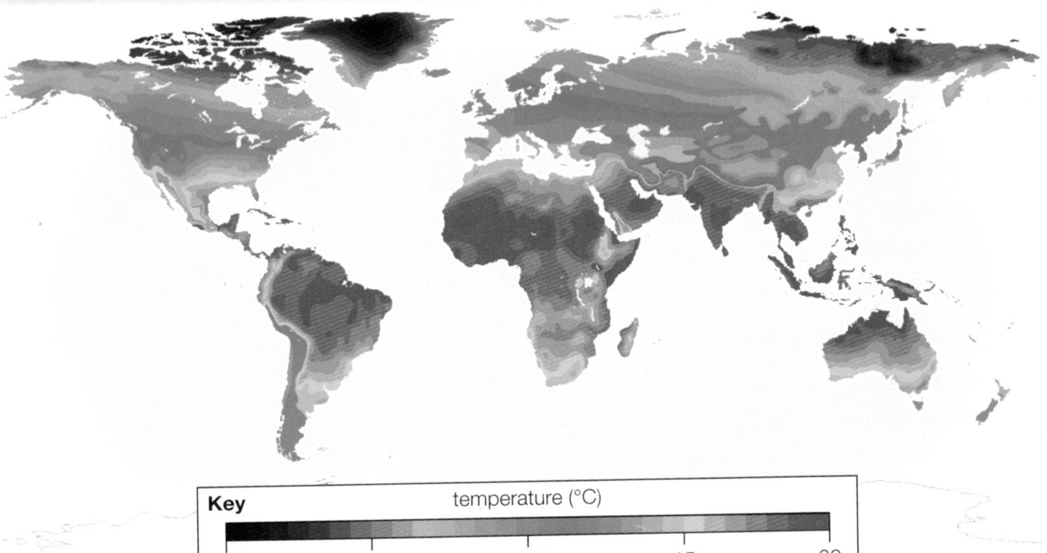

Figure 3 *The average annual global temperatures of mainland areas, excluding Antarctica. Without winds, these temperatures would be much more extreme towards both the Equator and the Poles.*

Regulating the composition of the atmosphere

Photosynthesis is a vital process in regulating the composition of the atmosphere:

- Phytoplankton in the oceans sequester CO_2 through the process of photosynthesis – pumping it out of the atmosphere and into the ocean store. This action is known as the biological carbon pump (see Section 2.3), and the processes transfer 5-15 Gt of carbon from the atmosphere to the ocean each year.
- Terrestrial photosynthesis (i.e. land-based) enables plants to sequester 100-120 Gt of CO_2 a year. This is then released back into the atmosphere through respiration and decomposition.

Figure 4 shows how different ecosystems absorb CO_2 as a result of photosynthesis:

- Anything that affects the level of phytoplankton in the world's oceans (in either a positive or a negative way), or the area of land covered by forest (e.g. through deforestation, changes in land use), will have an impact on the level of carbon sequestration. This in turn will affect the composition of the atmosphere.
- Tropical rainforest climates are ideal for plant growth, which promotes photosynthesis.
- The marine equivalents of rainforests in terms of plant growth are coral reefs and mangroves (see Section 2.3). Warm tropical shallow waters are ideal for both.
- Deserts, meanwhile, are areas of sparse vegetation – hence relatively little CO_2 is absorbed there.

The increased melting of Arctic sea ice means that greater expanses of ocean are now exposed to direct sunlight, because seasonal thaws there last longer. Increasing photosynthesis by phytoplankton, referred to above, is now resulting in algal blooms in Arctic waters (see Figure 5). As a result, more CO_2 is being absorbed there.

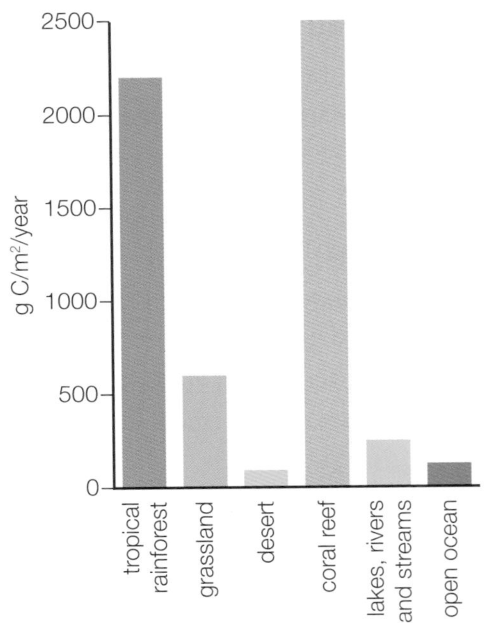

Figure 4 *Carbon absorption resulting from photosynthesis in different ecosystems*

Figure 5 *Increased algal blooms in the Arctic*

Soil and carbon

Carbon is vital in soils. Figure 6 shows that organic material is the medium by which carbon passes through the system, and it also supports micro-organisms that maintain the nutrient cycle, break down organic matter, provide pore spaces for infiltration and storage of water, and enhance plant growth. Without carbon, the nutrient and water cycles cannot operate properly.

The amount of stored carbon depends on the system:

- The amount of organic carbon stored within soil = inputs (plant litter and animal waste) minus outputs (decomposition, erosion and uptake in plant growth).
- The size of the store depends on different biomes (see Figure 3 in Section 2.3).

Figure 6 *The carbon balance within soils*

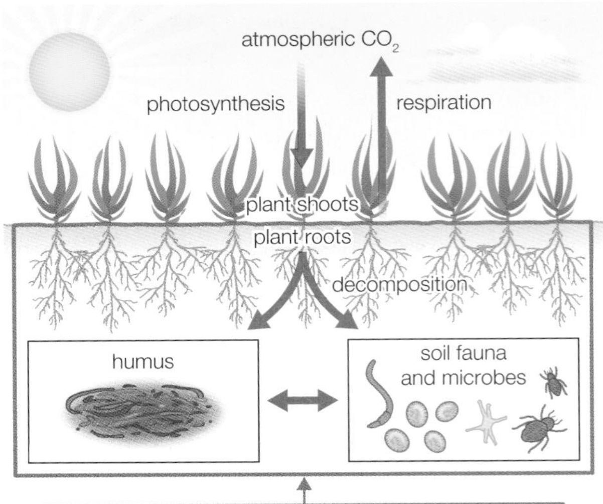

Healthy soils usually:

- are dark, crumbly and porous
- contain many worms and other organisms
- provide air, water and nutrients for micro-organisms and plants to thrive
- contain more carbon or organic matter
- sequester carbon
- improve resilience to wetter weather, because they enable infiltration and percolation of water (reducing soil erosion and flood risk)
- retain moisture, which regulates soil temperature during heatwaves and reduces the effects of droughts.

In the Northern Hemisphere, winter's organic decay increases the amount of CO_2, while spring's renewed plant growth causes a reduction (as new plant growth absorbs it). If winters become shorter, it's possible that less CO_2 will be released. It's possible, too, that climate change will create a natural response, and that more CO_2 will be absorbed, altering the balance.

Ecosystem productivity

About 1% of the solar insolation reaching Earth is captured by photosynthesis and used by plants to produce organic material or **biomass**. The rate at which plants produce biomass is called **primary productivity**. Figure 7 contrasts the **net** primary productivity (i.e. the amount of biomass produced by plants, minus the energy lost through respiration). Tropical rainforest climates (warm and humid, with a year-round growing season) allow for high primary productivity. In comparison, tundra ecosystems, with a cold and dry climate, grow more slowly and have a much lower level of productivity.

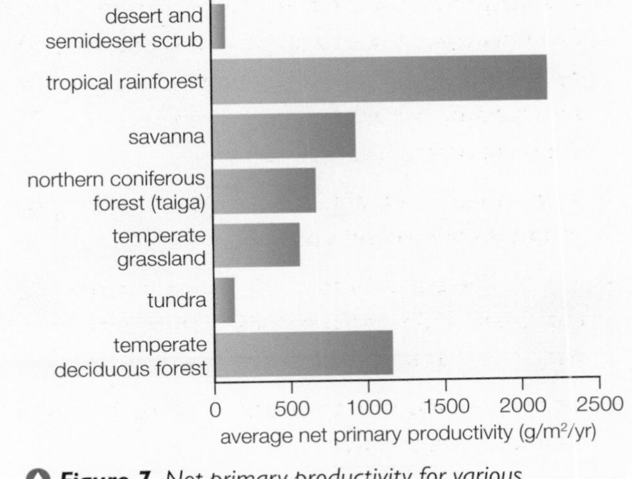

Figure 7 *Net primary productivity for various ecosystems*

Fossil fuel combustion

Fossil fuels are extremely important long-term carbon stores, comprising carbon locked away within the remains of organic matter. Today, most of the world's oil and gas is extracted from rocks that are 70–100 million years old; coal is even older. When burnt to generate energy, the stored carbon is released – primarily as CO_2 – into the atmosphere. It has several implications.

1 Balance

Earth's carbon reservoirs act as both sources (adding carbon to the atmosphere) and sinks (removing it from the atmosphere). If the sources and sinks are equal, the carbon cycle is said to be in **equilibrium** (or **balance**). Maintaining a steady amount of CO_2 in the atmosphere helps to stabilise global temperatures. However, human activities (e.g. fossil fuel combustion and deforestation) have increased CO_2 inputs into the atmosphere, without any corresponding increases in the natural sinks (such as oceans and forests). Hence atmospheric stores of carbon have increased, which is widely believed to be the main cause of rising global temperatures.

The process of fossil fuel combustion has altered the balance of carbon **pathways** (i.e. flows) and stores – with carbon being released in large amounts from stores, the flows have greatly increased. Since the late 1950s, the most abundant flow – inputs of atmospheric CO_2 – has been measured by the Hawaiian Volcanic Observatory. Their findings are given in Figure 8, and they show an alarming increase in levels of atmospheric CO_2.

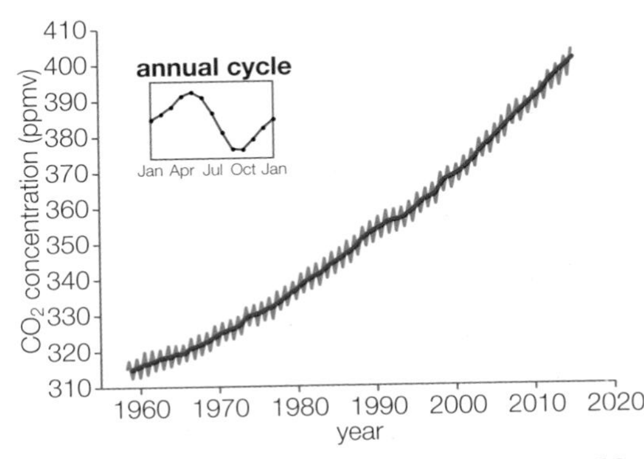

Figure 8 *Recent increases in atmospheric CO_2*

2 Implications for climate

Rising levels of atmospheric CO_2 are believed to be causing global temperatures to increase, causing climate to change. However, the increases will probably vary:

- Across Europe, annual average land temperatures are projected to increase by more than the global average (see Figure 9A). The largest increases are expected to be over Eastern and Northern Europe in winter, and over Southern Europe in summer.
- Annual precipitation (see Figure 9B) is projected to increase in Northern Europe and to decrease in Southern Europe – increasing the differences between regions that are currently wet, and those currently dry.
- Extreme weather events are also likely to increase in both intensity and frequency.

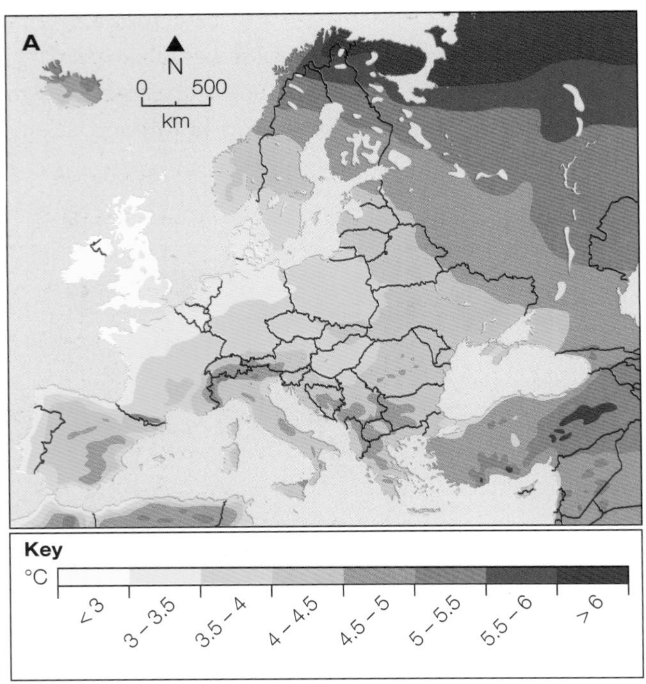

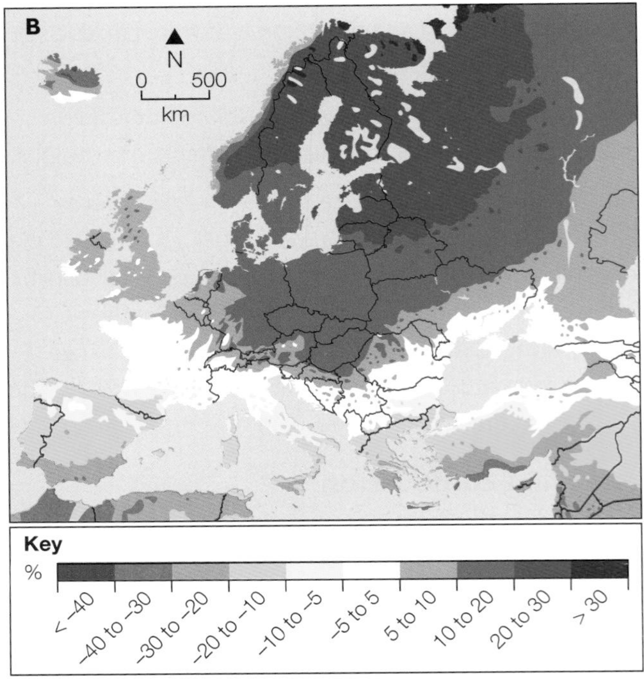

Figure 9 *Projected changes to European annual mean temperature (**A**) and annual precipitation (**B**) for 2071–2100, compared to 1971–2000*

3 Arctic amplification

The Arctic region is warming twice as fast as the global average. This phenomenon is known as **Arctic amplification**. Melting permafrost releases CO_2 and CH_4, increasing the concentration of these greenhouse gases in the atmosphere and leading to increased global temperatures and further melting (see Figure 10).

Climate change is altering the Arctic tundra ecosystem. Rapid warming has contributed to extensive melting of sea ice in the summer months, as well as greatly reduced snow cover and a reduction in permafrost. Shrubs and trees, previously unable to survive in the tundra, have started to establish themselves. The same is true of animals; in Alaska, the red fox has spread northwards, and now competes with the Arctic fox for food and territory.

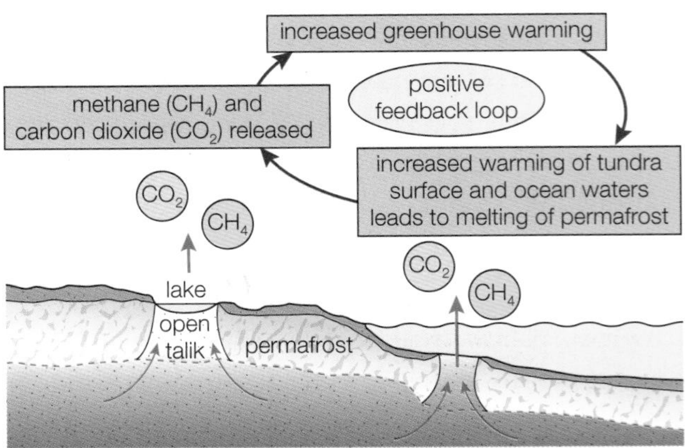

Figure 10 *Melting permafrost exacerbates global warming*

But not all scientists agree that melting permafrost will release stored carbon as carbon dioxide and methane:

- Some studies show that as permafrost thaws, the stored carbon remains in the soil and is used by new vegetation.
- Warmer temperatures accelerate decomposition, releasing carbon and nutrients.
- Nutrients encourage plant growth and the removal of carbon from the atmosphere through photosynthesis (decreasing the level of greenhouse gases in the atmosphere).

Implications for the hydrological cycle

Projected changes to temperature and precipitation patterns across Europe (see Figure 9) would also impact on the hydrological cycle. In the summer months, much of Europe's water comes from the melting of Alpine glaciers. But according to climate scientists, by 2100 the Eastern Alps will be completely ice-free, together with a large part of the Western Alps – affecting the hydrological cycle as follows:

- Precipitation in the form of snow could diminish and rainfall patterns change.
- River discharge patterns may also change, with greater flooding in winter and drought in summer.
- As Alpine glaciers melt, water flows lead to increased sediment yield. Once the glaciers have retreated, discharge and sediment yields fall and water quality declines.

BACKGROUND

The debate about carbon pathways

Previously, frozen stores of carbon meant slow pathways. Now increased thawing has accelerated the process of carbon release and a **faster pathway** is emerging. In theory, constant levels of CO_2 in the atmosphere are maintained if photosynthesis keeps pace with the release of greenhouse gases. However, increased thawing means that water and methane are also being released as ancient vegetation decomposes and trapped gases seep to the surface. Plants and micro-organisms grow faster than before and respire CO_2. Two possible pathways could unfold:

- **Pathway 1**. Shrubs and trees invade the Arctic landscape and store more carbon than is being released into the atmosphere. A short-term balance is reached – i.e. **negative feedback**.
- **Pathway 2**. The decomposition of plant material in wet soils reduces carbon stores by releasing more CO_2 and CH_4 into the atmosphere. Increased greenhouse gases reinforce global warming in the longer term – i.e. **positive feedback**. Scientists believe that this will add as much carbon to the atmosphere each year as all of the land use changes in the rest of the world combined.

Over to you

1 Make a copy of Figure 1 and, using the text in this section, annotate it to show the enhanced greenhouse effect.

2 a Study Figures 3 and 9. Research world maps online showing projected changes to global temperature and precipitation patterns, using the phrase 'changing temperature patterns caused by climate change', and then doing the same for rainfall or precipitation patterns.

b On a blank world map or maps, shade and annotate those areas with the greatest projected temperature and precipitation changes as a result of climate change.

c How far are the temperature and precipitation results similar in terms of the regions likely to be affected? In pairs, hypothesise the global implications of this.

3 Working in pairs, draw a mind map to show contrasts between Pathways 1 and 2 in the Arctic.

4 Still in pairs, draw a spider diagram to show the importance of the following to the carbon cycle: (**a**) seas, (**b**) soils.

On your own

5 Distinguish between the following pairs of terms: (**a**) natural and enhanced greenhouse effects, (**b**) positive and negative feedback, (**c**) climate change and Arctic amplification.

6 Explain the sentence: 'Without carbon, the nutrient and water cycles cannot operate properly'.

7 Copy Figure 6 and annotate it to show the significance of soil to the carbon cycle.

8 Use the NASA, NOAA and EarthLabs websites to research further the likely impacts of changing carbon cycles, disappearing permafrost, oceanic carbon and carbon in soils. Create a presentation entitled – 'Carbon – costs and benefits of having too much'.

Exam-style question

Explain why a balanced carbon cycle is important for sustaining other Earth systems. *(6 marks)*

2.5 Energy security

In this section, you'll learn that energy security is a key goal for countries, with most still relying on fossil fuels.

EQ2 Sections 2.5 to 2.7 investigate the consequences for people and the environment of our increasing demands for energy.

Keeping the lights on

As Figure 1 shows, the Earth when viewed at night from space is a wondrous sight! Some places are brightly lit, while others are in total darkness. The concentrations of light correspond roughly with the consumption of fossil fuels to produce electricity. However, brightness doesn't always correspond with population size. For example, Madagascar lies to the east of Mozambique, in the Indian Ocean. As a developing country, its population of some 23 million uses little energy. By contrast, Manhattan Island in New York City is home to 1.7 million people, each of whom consumes more energy in a year than an average Madagascan will in a lifetime. Therefore, the bright areas in Figure 1 tend to correlate with higher levels of economic development, and show where energy consumption is greatest.

SYNOPTIC THEME AND KEY CONCEPT

- **Players** – the roles played by TNCs, OPEC (the Organisation of the Petroleum Exporting Countries), governments and consumers in securing energy pathways and supplies
- **Globalisation** – the globalised nature of the energy industry and the players involved

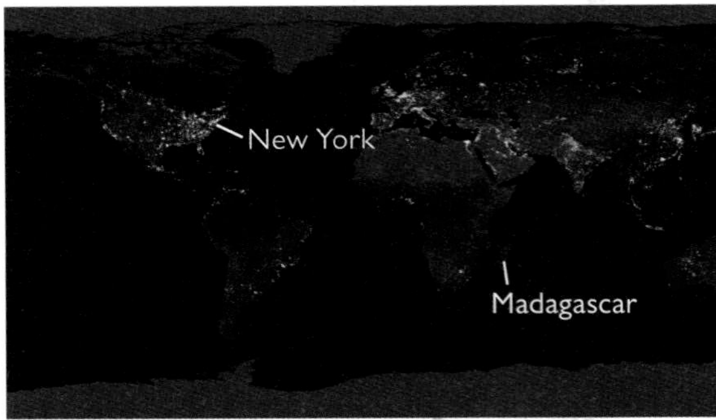

Figure 1 *The world at night when viewed from space*

Energy consumption

The amount of energy consumed depends on many things – lifestyle, climate, technology, availability and need. Global consumption continues to rise as countries develop economically. As Figure 2 shows, there is a close correlation between GDP per capita and energy consumption. Energy consumption is expressed as units of energy use in **tonnes of oil equivalent** per capita.

Urban consumption – London

Over half of the world's people now live in cities. Cities consume 75% of the world's energy and produce 80% of its greenhouse gas emissions. For example, the area comprising the City of London generates 1.7 million tonnes of carbon per year, with its resident population averaging 1.8 tonnes of carbon per capita. London's energy demands are met through a web of national and international supply lines, and involve several key players (see pages 70–71).

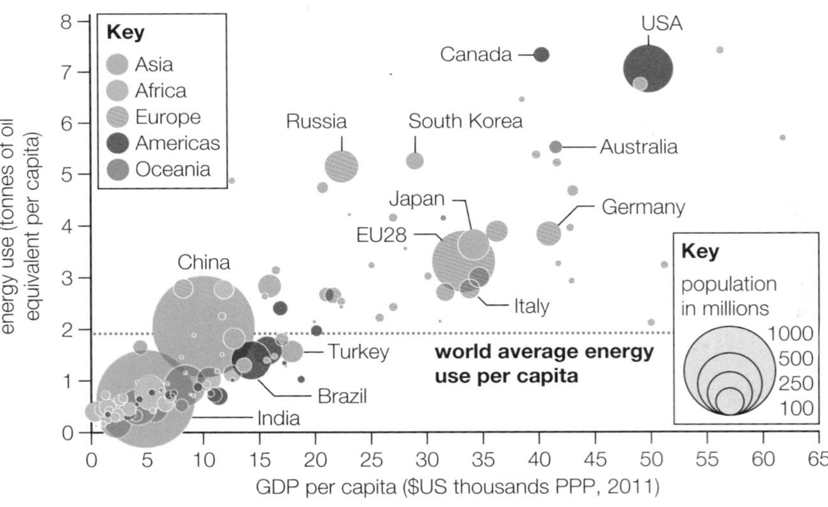

Figure 2 *The relationship between GDP per capita and energy use in 2011*

Rural consumption – Peru

By contrast, thanks to a national programme of solar-panel installation, electricity was made available to 500 000 people in remote villages across Peru between 2006 and 2015. The electricity now available in rural Peru charges phones, powers lights and TVs, and extends the working (and studying) day. The increased productivity it provides, allows extra processing of cereals, meat, cocoa and wood – helping to boost incomes and raise rural living standards. The increasing energy consumption – crucially, from a sustainable source – is helping to bring sustainable development and a brighter future for Peru's villagers.

The energy mix

No country on Earth depends on just a single source for its energy; an **energy mix** is required – depending on what is available most easily, or cheaply, or effectively, or securely.

Primary and secondary energy sources

Primary energy sources are those which are consumed in their raw form. They include burning fossil fuels (coal, oil and natural gas), nuclear energy (controlling uranium or plutonium to create heat via atomic reaction), and renewable sources (using solar, wind or wave energy). Primary sources can also be used to generate electricity, which is a **secondary energy source**. It flows through power lines and infrastructure to power homes and businesses.

Domestic and overseas sources

Despite economic and population growth in the UK, the adoption of energy-saving technologies in, for example, home heating and vehicle engines, resulted in the UK consuming less energy in 2015 than in 1998. More of its energy also came from renewable sources. However, at the same time, declining **domestic** North Sea oil and gas reserves have made the UK increasingly dependent on **imported** energy. Because the UK now imports more energy than it produces domestically, the country has an **energy deficit** and is **energy insecure**. By contrast, countries with surplus energy (e.g. Russia) are **energy secure**. Figure 3 shows the UK's growing reliance on imported energy; it has now returned to a level last seen in the mid-late 1970s.

Renewable and non-renewable sources

There are many different sources of energy, which can be classified as:

- **non-renewable** (or **finite**) e.g. coal, oil and gas. Exploitation and use of these stocks will eventually lead to their exhaustion. Traditionally, coal has been the major source for producing electricity.
- **renewable**, e.g. solar, wind and wave power. These are continuous flows of nature, which can be constantly reused.
- **recyclable**, e.g. reprocessed uranium and plutonium from nuclear power plants and heat recovery systems.

In 2015, renewable sources (including onshore and offshore wind farms, solar farms, hydroelectric dams and biomass) accounted for 25% of the UK's electricity generation. This was the first year in which renewable sources produced more UK electricity than coal did.

Key words

Tonnes of oil equivalent – This is a unit which is designed to include all forms of energy by comparing them with oil in terms of heat output. It measures each type of energy by calculating the amount of heat obtained by burning one tonne, and then converting it to however much oil would be required to produce an equivalent amount of energy.

Energy security – This means being able to access reliable and affordable sources of energy. These may be domestic, but could also include energy sources from 'friendly' countries.

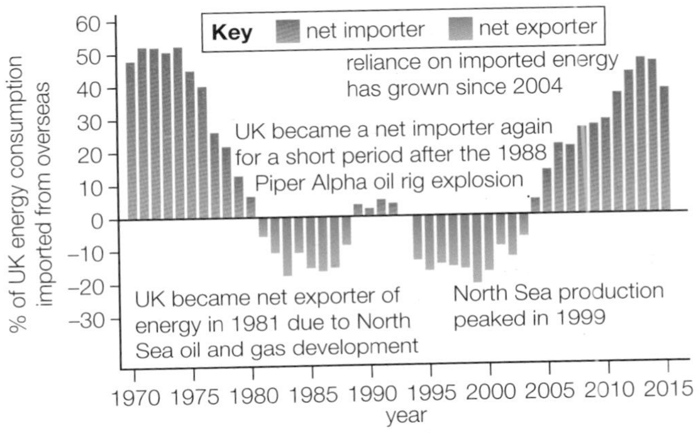

Figure 3 *The UK's changing energy security*

Figure 4 *The UK's energy imports in 2015 and where they came from*

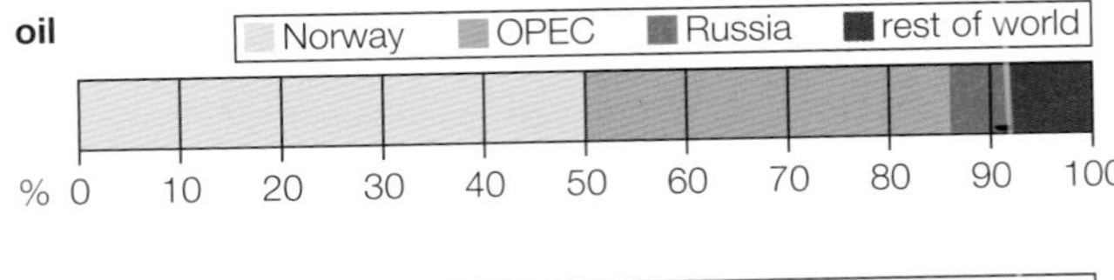

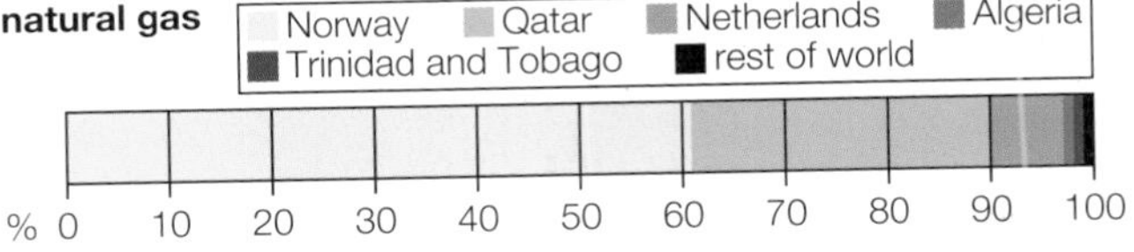

By 2015:

- a third of the UK's fuel imports consisted of crude oil – and 50% of that came from Norway. But Norway now provides less than it used to, and OPEC suppliers (see page 70) make up much of the shortfall.
- natural gas made up 29% of the UK's fuel imports. Again, Norway was the main provider (over 60%). Most gas comes through pipelines under the North Sea. The UK also imports liquid gas – 98% from Qatar, which arrives by supertanker.

Factors affecting energy consumption: the UK and Norway compared

A country's energy mix reflects a range of factors. In the past, energy consumption increased as economic development and the standard of living rose. Meeting the increasing demand often meant exploiting more resources – those most readily accessible were often the cheapest and therefore made up the biggest component of the energy mix. Figure 5 shows how different factors shaped energy decisions in the UK and Norway.

***Figure 5** Factors affecting energy use in the UK and Norway*

Factor	UK	Norway
Physical availability	Until the 1970s, the UK depended heavily on domestic coal from Yorkshire, Derbyshire, Nottinghamshire, South Wales and north-east England. It was also among global leaders in nuclear technology from the 1950s–70s, but lost momentum after the discovery of large reserves of North Sea oil and gas, whose increased use after the 1970s greatly altered the UK's energy mix.	Because Norway is mountainous, with steep valleys and plentiful rainfall, HEP is the natural energy choice. Much of the oil and natural gas in Norway's territorial waters is exported (e.g. to the UK, see Figure 4). Coal from Svalbard is also exported.
Cost	The North Sea reserves became a 'secure' alternative to dependency on Middle Eastern oil, after prices there rose in the early 1970s. However, North Sea oil is expensive to extract, so if global prices fall (as they did in 1997-98 and 2014-15), it becomes less viable. Stocks of North Sea oil and gas are also declining, which is forcing the UK to import more (see Figures 3 and 4).	Norsk Hydro runs over 600 HEP sites, which supply 97.5% of Norway's renewable electricity. HEP costs are low once capital investment is complete. However, the transfer of electricity from HEP production in remote regions to urban population centres and isolated settlements is expensive.
Technology	There are 150 years' worth of coal reserves left in the UK, but current technology and environmental policy make its extraction and use unrealistic and expensive. The UK's last deep coal mine closed in 2015, although 80% of the UK's primary energy still came from fossil fuels. The technology exists for 'clean coal' (that is, absorbing CO_2 emissions), but coal has lost its political support.	Deepwater drilling technology enabled both Norway and the UK to develop North Sea oil and gas extraction.
Political considerations	The increasing reliance on imported energy sources affects the UK's energy security, and this has become a political issue. However, public concern is also growing over new and proposed fracking and nuclear sites. The privatisation of the UK's energy supply industry in the 1980s now means that overseas companies (e.g. France's EDF and Germany's E-on) decide which energy sources are used to meet UK demand. They buy primary energy on international markets.	HEP has been used since 1907, and the Norwegian Water and Energy Directorate manages the nation's power supply. The Norwegian government has an interventionist approach, which prevents foreign companies from owning any primary energy source sites – waterfalls, mines, forests. Royalties and taxes paid into the government from the sale of fossil fuels boost the standard of living through government spending, but profits also go to a sovereign wealth fund to prepare for a future without fossil fuels and investment in environmentally sustainable projects.
Level of economic development	GDP per capita (PPP) = US$41 200 (2015) Energy use per capita = 2752 kg oil equivalent (2014) Average annual household energy costs = £1300 (2015)	GDP per capita (PPP) = US$61 500 (2015) Energy use per capita = 5854 kg oil equivalent (2014) Average annual household energy costs = £2400 (2015)
Environmental priorities	In 2015, the UK committed to a 40% reduction in domestic greenhouse gas emissions by 2030, compared to 1990 levels. It intends to broaden its energy mix with renewable sources (especially wind) and more nuclear power. However, the UK also abandoned its 'Green Deal' conservation and insulation schemes in 2015. In 2015, the UK's CO_2 emissions were 7.13 tonnes per capita (down from a peak of 11.5 in 1980).	In 2015, Norway committed to a 40% reduction in domestic greenhouse gas emissions by 2030, compared to 1990 levels. Norway is the third largest exporter of hydrocarbons, and is expanding its output. Norway's 'Policy for Change' was launched in 2016, with a domestic target of being carbon neutral by 2050. In 2015, Norway's CO_2 emissions were 11.74 tonnes per capita (up from 11.6 tonnes in 1989).

Changing consumption

Figure 6 shows how overall energy consumption has changed in Norway and the UK, plus changes in their fossil fuel consumption.

A
total energy use (kg of oil equivalent per capita)
6500
6000
5500
5000
4500
4000
3500
3000
2500
2000
Norway
UK
1960 1965 1970 1975 1980 1985 1990 1995 2000 2005 2010
year
B
fossil fuel use (% of total from Graph A)
100
95
90
85
80
75
70
65
60
55
50
UK
Norway
1960 1965 1970 1975 1980 1985 1990 1995 2000 2005 2010
year

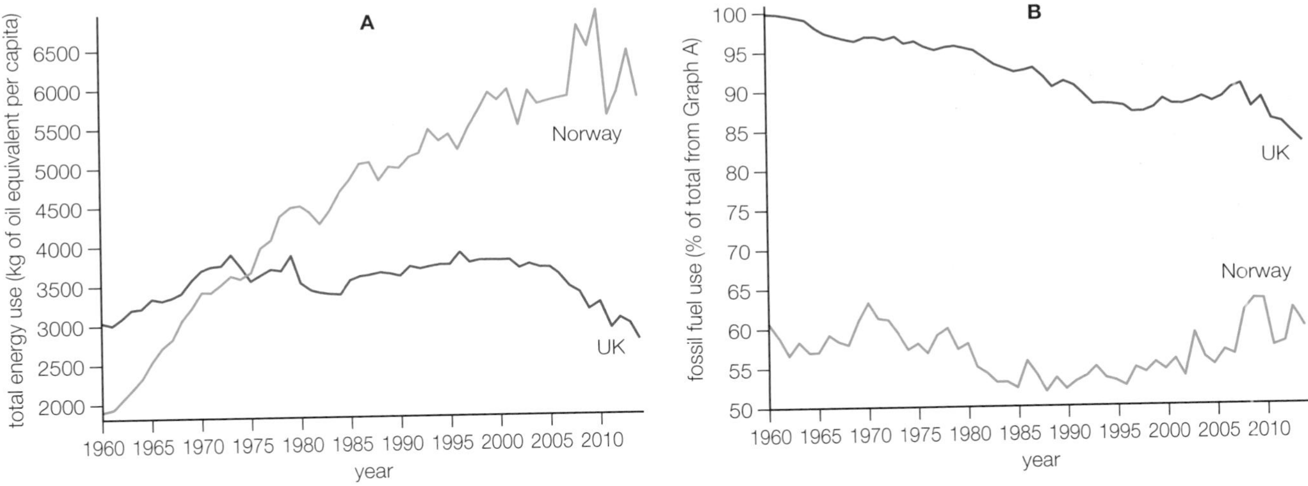

Figure 6 *Overall energy consumption per capita in the UK, compared with Norway (**A**), plus changing fossil fuel consumption as a percentage of the total (**B**)*

The changing energy mix

As Figure 5 shows, different factors cause the energy mix of a country to change over time. Figures 7 and 8 show the changing energy mixes of the UK and Norway over the last 40 or so years.

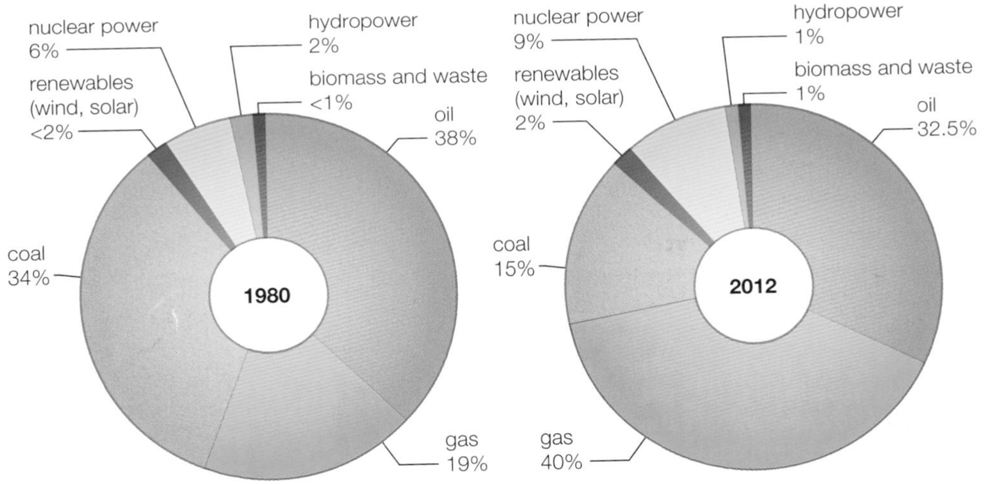

nuclear power
6%
hydropower
2%
renewables
(wind, solar)
<2%
biomass and waste
<1%
oil
38%
coal
34%
1980
gas
19%
nuclear power
9%
hydropower
1%
renewables
(wind, solar)
2%
biomass and waste
1%
oil
32.5%
coal
15%
2012
gas
40%

Figure 7 *The changing energy mix in the UK, 1980–2012*

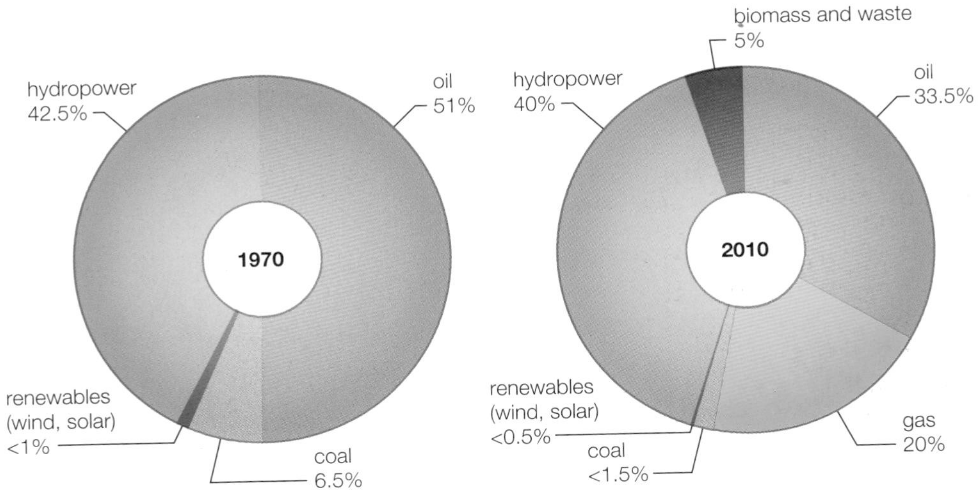

hydropower
42.5%
oil
51%
1970
renewables
(wind, solar)
<1%
coal
6.5%
biomass and waste
5%
hydropower
40%
oil
33.5%
2010
renewables
(wind, solar)
<0.5%
coal
<1.5%
gas
20%

Figure 8 *The changing energy mix in Norway, 1970–2010*

Energy players

Obtaining primary energy in the twenty-first century involves more than merely having abundant resources within easy reach. Some of the key players who have roles in securing **energy pathways** and supplies are discussed here. This section of text focuses on the geopolitical issues involved in obtaining energy, and problems related to energy pathways (discussed further in Section 2.6).

Key word

Energy pathway – This term describes the flow of energy between a producer and a consumer, and how it reaches the consumer, e.g. pipeline, transmission lines, ship, rail.

Energy player	Role	Examples
Energy TNCs TNCs operate across the world	• TNCs explore, exploit and distribute energy resources. • They own supply lines and invest in distribution and the processing of raw materials, as well as electricity production and transmission. • They respond to market conditions to secure profits for their shareholders.	• Old players: BP (UK) and Shell (UK-Netherlands); Exxon/Mobil (USA). • 'New' players: Petrobras (Brazil); PetroChina Corp (China); Reliance (India); Rosneft, Luckoil and Gazprom (Russia) All companies listed here are in the global top 20 energy companies.

Rank	Company	Country in which located	Output – million barrels of oil equivalent (BOE) per day	
			2004	2014–15
1	Aramco	Saudi Arabia	10.8	12.0
2	Gazprom	Russia	9.8	8.3
3	National Iranian Oil	Iran	5.1	6.0
4	Exxon/Mobil	USA	4.6	4.7
5	Rosneft	Russia	0.3	4.7

Figure 9 *The five largest energy TNCs*

Energy player	Role	Examples
OPEC The Organisation of Petroleum Exporting Countries is a permanent inter-governmental organisation (IGO). Its members are oil producing and exporting countries, like Saudi Arabia, where oil is their main – or only – export, and is therefore vital for their social and economic well-being. Between them, OPEC producers control 81% of proven world oil reserves (see Figure 10).	OPEC's mission is to co-ordinate and unify the petroleum policies of its members, to ensure the stabilisation of oil markets in order to secure: • an efficient, economic and regular supply of petroleum to consumers • a steady income for producers • a fair return for those investing in the industry.	In the past, OPEC set oil production quotas to respond to economic conditions – boosting supplies when demand rose and reducing them when demand fell. However, from 2012-16, maintaining output at high levels kept oil prices low – possibly to compete with the USA's increased oil production from fracking, which caused a collapse in global oil prices.

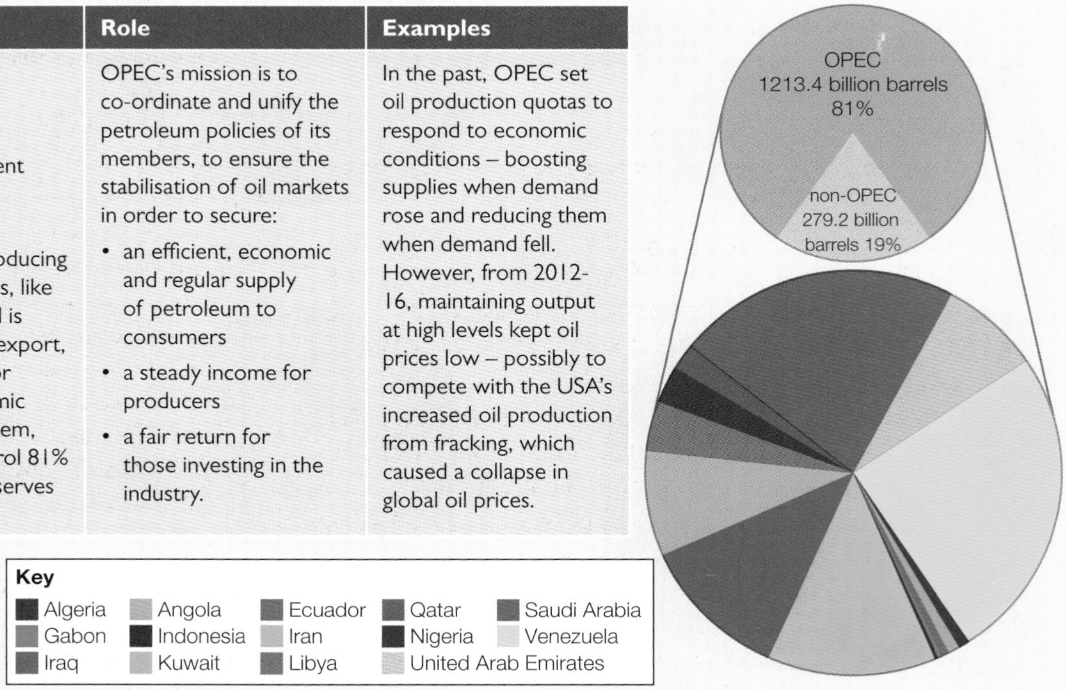

Figure 10 *OPEC's share of global crude oil reserves, 2015*

Energy player	Role	Examples
National governments	• To meet international obligations, whilst securing energy supplies for the nation's present and future, as well as supporting the country's economic growth. • Regulating the role of private companies and setting environmental priorities.	• EDF (France) and China General Nuclear are two government-backed energy TNCs involved in developing new nuclear power plants in the UK, e.g. Hinkley Point C (see Figure 11). • EU governments aim to fulfil CO_2 emissions targets and reduce fossil fuel dependency.

Energy player	Role and factors affecting consumer attitudes
Consumers	Create demand. Purchasing choices are often based on price/cost issues, e.g. petrol prices can be keenly competitive between supermarkets. Consumers have some power over oil companies, e.g. by purchasing electric cars, or installing solar panels to cut home energy costs. But until 2015, most solar panels and wind farms in the EU and the UK were only installed because of the large government subsidies on offer. The expansion of nuclear energy (see Figure 11), as well as the extraction of oil and gas by fracking, are both controversial in the UK and across the EU. There have been widespread protests against both (see Figure 12).

Figure 11 *The proposed new nuclear power station at Hinkley Point, Somerset*

Figure 12 *The UK government gave the go-ahead to a new generation of nuclear power stations, but people protested.*

Over to you

1 In pairs, suggest reasons for the differences in energy consumption between New York and Madagascar outlined at the start of this section.

2 Use Figure 2 to (**a**) describe, and (**b**) explain the relationships between economic development and energy consumption per capita.

3 Using Figures 7 and 8, (**a**) compare changes in the energy mixes of the UK and Norway in the past four decades (**b**) compare the energy mix of the two countries in the twenty-first century, (**c**) suggest reasons for the changes, using material in this section.

4 In pairs, draw a mind map to show how the following can influence a country's energy mix: resource availability; accessibility and affordability; government policies; technology; development levels; environmental concerns; and public perceptions.

5 Make a copy of the conflict matrix in Section 2.6 (page 77), replacing the six players there with four key players (TNCs, OPEC, National governments, Consumers) in securing pathways and energy supplies. Complete the matrix and explain (**a**) the levels of agreement and (**b**) the levels of disagreement that you identify.

On your own

6 Distinguish between the following pairs of terms: (**a**) non-renewable and renewable resources; (**b**) primary and secondary sources of energy; (**c**) energy mix and energy security.

7 **a** Select one of the top five energy companies in Figure 9, and refer to their own websites to develop a profile for the company. Show where they operate, their future plans, and how the company relates to governments and consumers.

b Now develop a similar profile for an environmental pressure group (e.g. Greenpeace), and how and why they offer a different viewpoint.

Exam-style question

Assess the extent to which one or more countries that you have studied is energy secure. (*12 marks*)

Fossil fuels – still the norm

In this section, you'll learn that a reliance on fossil fuels to drive economic development is still the global norm.

The location of fossil fuels

Fossil fuels are not distributed evenly across the world; their location is determined by underlying geology. The three tables in Figure 1 show the top ten countries in 2014-15 in terms of their reserves of coal, oil and natural gas.

SYNOPTIC THEME AND KEY CONCEPT

- **Players** – the role of business in developing reserves, versus environmental groups and affected communities
- **Resilience** – the threats posed to native plant communities in Canada as a result of tar sands mining

	Coal	Million tonnes
1	USA	237 295
2	Russia	157 010
3	China	114 500
4	Australia	76 400
5	India	60 600
6	Germany	40 548
7	Ukraine	33 873
8	Kazakhstan	33 600
9	South Africa	30 156
10	Colombia	6746

	Oil	Billion barrels*
1	Venezuela	297.6
2	Saudi Arabia	267.9
3	Canada	173.1
4	Iran	154.6
5	Iraq	141.4
6	Kuwait	104.0
7	UAE	97.8
8	Russia	80.0
9	Libya	48.0
10	Nigeria	37.2

*1 barrel = 35 UK gallons or 158 litres

	Natural gas	Billion m^3
1	Russia	47 800
2	Iran	33 610
3	Qatar	25 200
4	Turkmenistan	17 500
5	USA	9459
6	Saudi Arabia	8150
7	UAE	6089
8	Venezuela	5524
9	Nigeria	5153
10	Algeria	4504

Figure 1 The top ten countries for coal (2015), oil (2014), and natural gas (2014) reserves

BACKGROUND

Geology

Coal, oil and natural gas all formed under past geological conditions, which determine where in the world they are found.

Most coal in Western Europe and North America was formed during the Carboniferous period (between 300 and 360 million years ago), when the landmass of which these regions formed a part was located within the Tropics. Successive layers of rainforest-type trees within swamp forests accumulated as they fell, and were then transformed under the pressure of over-lying strata into seams of coal.

Oil and natural gas are generally younger than coal, and were formed during the Mesozoic era (between 250 and 260 million years ago). Like coal, they are organic in origin – forming from the fossil remains of plants and animals that died and were buried under alternate layers of mud (later becoming shale) and sand (becoming sandstone) on ocean floors. Heat and pressure then converted these fossil remains into oil and natural gas, which accumulated in the porous sandstone. Subsequent earth movements trapped 'pockets' of the oil and natural gas within the sandstone, capped by non-porous shale, where the rocks had folded or faulted (see Figure 2).

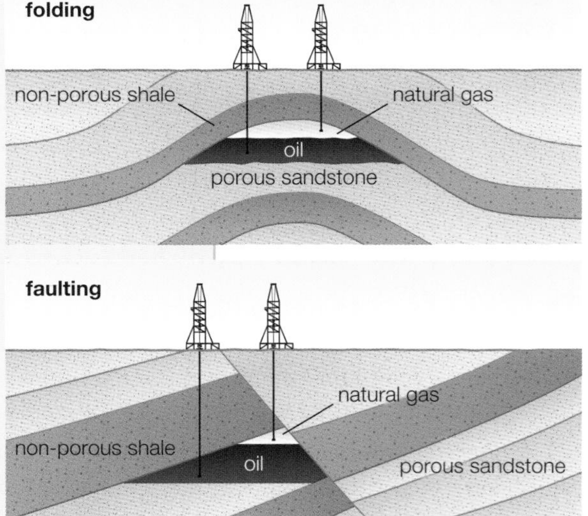

Figure 2 How oil and natural gas accumulate in alternate bands of non-porous shale and porous sandstone, where folding has formed anticlines or faulting has formed trapped 'reservoirs'

Fossil fuel demand

As more countries develop, the global demand for different sources of energy is increasing. The primary energy sources used by different countries change over time, but fossil fuels still make up 86% of the global energy mix. Figure 3 shows that the global consumption of different energy sources has increased by about 50% since the 1990s. As Figure 4 shows, it is China's rapid economic growth that has largely driven this increase, with, for example, Chinese oil consumption doubling between 2000 and 2010. It is expected that China's demand for oil will continue to increase at twice the global average, so that by 2035 China will be the world's largest energy importer.

The problem is the mismatch between where fossil fuels are found and where the demand for them is greatest. China has the world's fourteenth largest oil reserves, but that's only 10% of the size of Canada's, so it still needs to import huge quantities of oil. It is now the world's second largest oil importer (behind the USA).

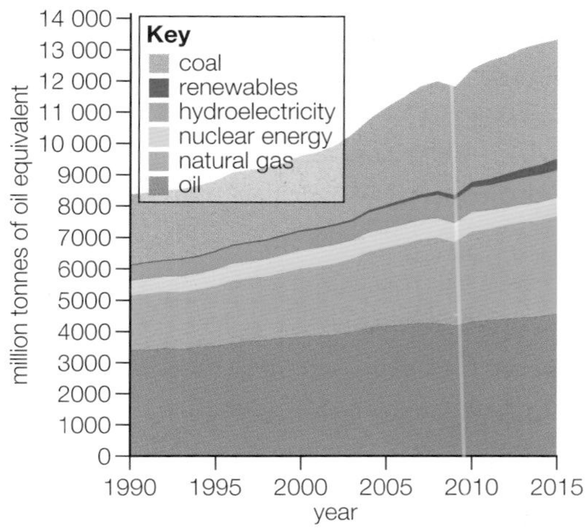

Figure 3 *Rising world energy consumption by type of energy, 1990-2015*

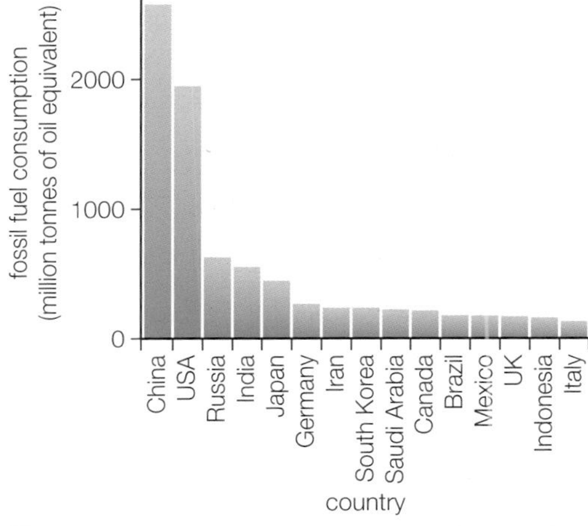

Figure 4 *The world's largest consumers of fossil fuels*

Energy pathways

The 4188 km-long ESPO (East Siberia Pacific Ocean) pipeline exports crude oil from Russia to China, South Korea and Japan. It was built by the Russian energy company Transneft, and was completed in 2012. Transneft also operates the pipeline. ESPO is an example of an energy **pathway** – the flow of energy between a producer and consumer. Other methods include transmission lines, shipping routes, road and rail.

Transporting natural gas by pipeline is efficient and increasingly international. Some of the world's largest pipelines carry billions of cubic metres of gas across thousands of kilometres. These pathways depend on **multilateral** (between many countries) and **bilateral** (between two countries) agreements. For security reasons, when companies like Russia's Gazprom export 80% of their gas to Europe, they try to avoid **transit states** whenever they can. For example, the Nord Stream pipeline runs 1200 km along the bed of the Baltic Sea, and the South Stream pipeline runs under the Black Sea to Bulgaria.

Key word

Transit state – A country or state through which energy flows on its way from producer to consumer.

Other major pipelines

- The Yamal-Europe pipeline – A 4107 km gas pipeline that runs from Russia through Belarus and Poland into Germany.
- Keystone XL oil and The Rockies Express – These are gas pipelines between western Canada and Nebraska and Ohio in the northern USA.
- The Trans-Mediterranean (Transmed) – A 2475 km gas pipeline from Algeria to Italy, via Tunisia and Sicily (with a branch into Slovenia).
- The West-East Gas Pipeline Project (WEPP) – This connects the natural gas reserves of the Tarim Basin in Xinjiang, western China (and in Turkmenistan) with the growing energy markets of the Yangtze and Pearl Delta regions.
- Kazakhstan-China – A 2800 km pipeline that transports crude oil from western Kazakhstan to Xinjiang, western China.

Trade flows and shipping routes

About half of the world's oil is moved by tankers travelling on fixed shipping routes. Figure 5 shows the major trade flows of oil in 2015 – from source to destination – together with the eight major **chokepoints**. Over half of the world's oil goes through these chokepoints – a narrow sea channel or convergence where key transport routes can easily be disrupted. For example, 20% of the world's oil passes through the Strait of Hormuz, a 39 km-wide stretch of water between the Gulf of Oman and the Persian Gulf. If chokepoints are blocked or threatened – even temporarily – energy prices can rise quickly. Oil transit chokepoints are a crucial element in global energy security.

Figure 6 shows global trade flows of gas in 2015 – via pipelines as natural gas and via tankers as liquid natural gas (LNG).

Figure 5 *Trade flows of oil in 2015, plus the eight major chokepoints*

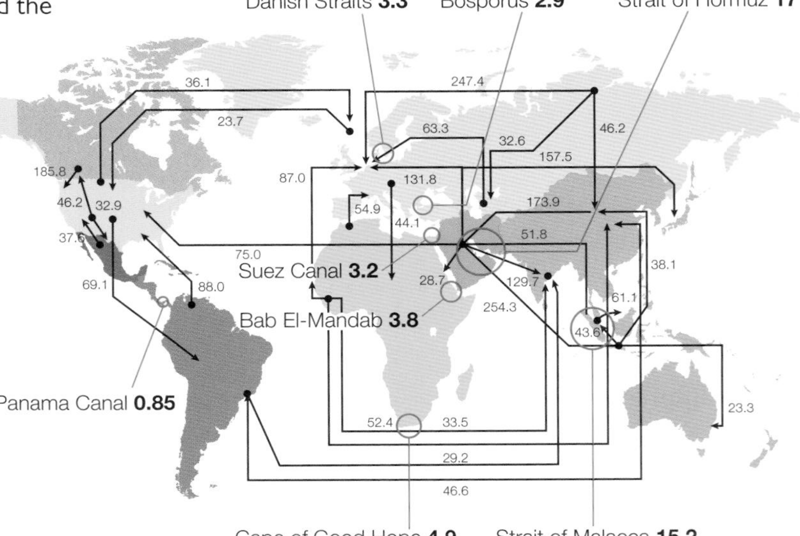

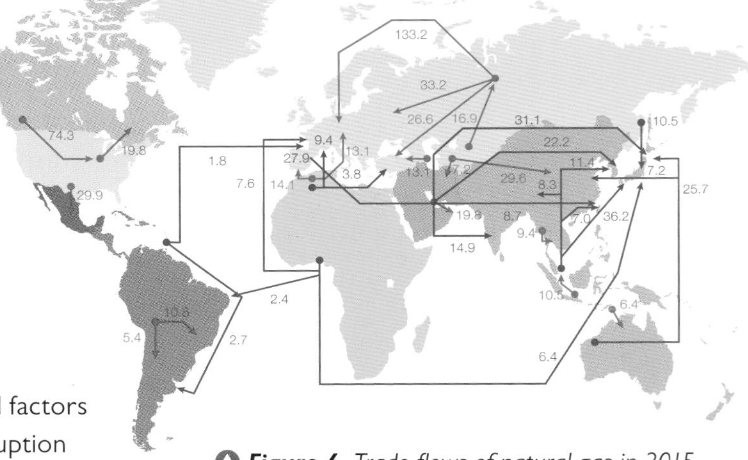

Figure 6 *Trade flows of natural gas in 2015*

Disrupting energy pathways

Securing energy resources involves **geopolitical** factors concerning ownership, use and control. Any disruption to pathways resulting from militant action (including **piracy**), natural hazards, and political conflict can undermine energy security.

- In December 2015, the International Maritime Bureau reported piracy attacks along the Strait of Malacca, between Malaysia, Indonesia and Singapore (see Figure 5). This is the world's second largest chokepoint for oil and gas transit by tanker. Criminal gangs frequently seized ships for hostage payments – over 500 attacks occurred from 2009–15.
- The Trans Forcados, Efurun-Otor and Escravos pipelines in Nigeria were bombed in 2016 by militants, resulting in a loss of 300 000 barrels of crude oil a day.
- During a stormy winter in 2013, UK gas reserves fell to 6 hours' worth, as storm damage paralysed an import pipeline.

Political conflict and energy pathways

The ongoing Syrian conflict has involved two superpowers and their allies during the 2010s:

- on one side, Russia and its Shia non-fundamentalist allies
- on the other, the USA and its fundamentalist Sunni allies.

These sides are involved in the battle for control over Syrian territory. Many argue that for the two superpowers the key reason is the proposed construction of oil and gas pipelines through Syria to supply fuel into Europe, the world's largest energy market. In recent decades, oil and gas have frequently been at the root of international tension, and **proxy wars** have been common.

- Currently, Russia is the world's biggest supplier of both oil and gas, but Shiite Iran (its ally) wants a share of the European market, which Russia supports. Having Iran onside gives Russia control over European energy, while strengthening a non-fundamentalist bloc between Asia and the Middle East. Iran wants to export its gas via pipelines through Syria, which explains why it defends the Syrian government against those trying to overthrow and replace President Assad.
- Meanwhile, Sunni Qatar and Saudi Arabia also seek to become Europe's main suppliers of gas and oil respectively. Each would *also* need to be pipelined through Syria! Qatar and Saudi Arabia are US allies, which explains why the USA and its allies are happy for Al Q'aeda and other jihadists to conquer a strip through Syria over which US companies would build pipelines, allowing other US companies such as Exxon to market Middle Eastern oil and gas in Europe.

Developing unconventional fossil fuels

Geologists have been predicting 'peak oil' for some years – i.e. that oil production will reach a global peak, before declining sharply. The argument is that the world has finite reserves of oil, coal and natural gas, so fossil fuels may be reaching an end. However, Canada now exploits tar sands to boost its energy security, and an abundance of shale gas in the USA (produced by fracking) has brought an energy boom. At the same time, geopolitics can make access to resources difficult, or cause the prices of oil and gas to increase, making unconventional fuels like shale gas more economically viable.

Unconventional fossil fuels

These are produced using different methods to those used for conventional fossil fuels.

- **Deep water oil** – as accessible reserves (e.g. North Sea oil) run out, prospecting companies have to look into deeper ocean waters with greater risks and costs, e.g. the Gulf of Mexico and Brazil's off-shore reserves.
- **Tar sands** – also known as oil sands, bituminous sands or extra heavy oil. These are naturally occurring mixtures of sand, clay, water and a dense viscous form of petroleum called **bitumen**. Canada has 73% of known global stocks.
- **Shale gas** – usually methane in coal seams, or natural gas trapped in fractures and pores of sandstones and shales.
- **Oil shale** – deposits of organic compounds called kerogen in sedimentary rocks that have not undergone sufficient pressure, heat or time to become conventional oil. The USA has 77% of known global reserves.

Figure 7 shows the growth of unconventional oil and gas production in the USA.

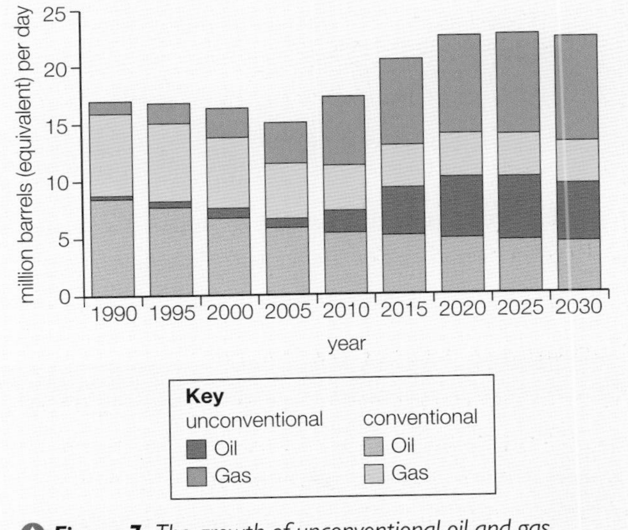

Figure 7 *The growth of unconventional oil and gas production in the USA*

Key word

Proxy war – A war instigated by a major power that is not always directly involved in the fighting.

Canadian tar sands

Canada has the world's largest reserves of tar sands, with three major deposits in Alberta – the Athabasca, Cold Lake and Peace River deposits shown in Figure 8. Together, they cover an area larger than England. Extracting the oil is expensive and difficult, but it helps to improve Canada's energy security.

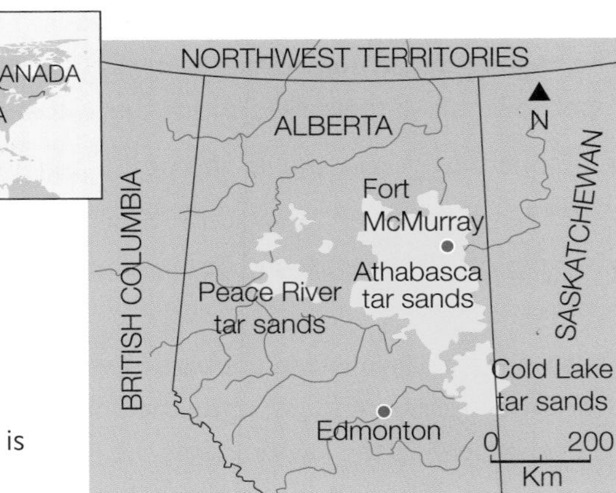

Figure 8 *The location of Canada's tar sands*

Tar sands are extracted by opencast mining. The extracted material is crushed and mixed with water, and the bitumen is separated before it can be used. Tar sands can also be pumped out – high-pressure steam is injected underground to separate the bitumen from the sand.

Exploiting tar sands involves several key players – shown in the panel – and brings various costs and benefits, outlined in Figure 9.

Tar sands – the players

- **Governments** – Alberta regional government and Canada's national government promote tar sands for energy security and economic development. Alberta's government says: 'Experts say the world will be dependent on fossil fuels for the foreseeable future. With the third largest proven reserves of oil in the world, Alberta must help to meet global demand, while ensuring sustainable and responsible extraction'.
- **Oil companies** – Local and international companies include Syncrude/Suncor, Shell, Exxon Mobil, and BP. Syncrude says that: 'As a large producer of crude oil from the oil sands, Syncrude has a tremendous and positive impact on the economies of Alberta and Canada.'
- **Environmental pressure groups** – Greenpeace called for an end to the 'industrialisation of indigenous territories, forests and wetlands in Northern Alberta'.
- **Local communities** experience costs and benefits:
  - New jobs (in an area where other employment is limited) and local businesses benefit from trade.
  - Fears over pollution in the Athabasca River, atmospheric toxins and an increased incidence of rare cancers and auto-immune diseases.
  - Disruption to traditional ways of life (the area is inhabited by many indigenous people).
  - Gambling, substance abuse, and crime have risen.
  - There is now a housing crisis, as thousands of workers have been shipped in.

The costs of exploiting tar sands	The benefits of exploiting tar sands
• It's only viable when the price of crude oil exceeds US$40 a barrel. It costs US$10-$20 a barrel to extract bitumen from tar sands, compared with US$2 for conventional oil (2015 prices). • It's very energy-intensive. It takes 1 barrel of conventional oil to produce 3 barrels of oil from tar sands. • It takes between 2 and 5 barrels of water to produce every barrel of oil. • About 1.8 million tonnes of toxic wastewater are produced every day. • It produces huge quantities of waste – it takes 2 tonnes of mined tar sands to produce one tonne of oil. • It adds to greenhouse gas emissions. • 470 km^2 of Alberta's woodlands taiga forest has been removed.	• It provides an alternative source of oil. • By 2030, it could meet 16% of North America's oil needs. • It offers energy security for Canada and the USA. 28% of Canada's oil is used in Canada; 70% is exported to the USA. • It can serve as a fuel stopgap, until more renewable and cleaner energy sources become viable. • Environmental protection is in place to ensure that mining companies are required to reclaim land disturbed by extraction. • It earns vital revenues for local and national economies.

Figure 9 *Tar sands – costs and benefits*

Implications for the carbon cycle

The extraction and use of tar sands have several impacts on the carbon cycle – all of them negative:

- Carbon emissions rise due to their extraction, production and use.
- Carbon absorption falls due to deforestation (removal of the taiga).

Consequences for the environment

Canada's tar sands are found in deposits in ecologically fragile and isolated areas, and in native taiga and peat bogs.

- Large-scale opencast mining destroys forest and peat bogs (see Figure 10), causing a loss of ecosystems and habitats. Although only about 0.2% of Alberta's forest has been destroyed, the sheer devastation caused by mining (shown in Figure 10) reduces the resilience of the native Taiga environment. Syncrude claims to have replanted 20% of its mined land, but environmentalists argue that the real figure is less than 1%.
- Extraction creates spoil heaps – dumps for waste soil and sand.
- Tailings (or waste material) ponds are created, which contain contaminated toxic wastewater caused by oil extraction and processing.
- Caribou populations have declined sharply in areas of oil extraction. They have become easy prey for wolves, which are now culled to preserve the caribou. Even so, the local caribou population is expected to be extinct by 2040.

Figure 10 *A Canadian tar sands mine operated by Suncor at Fort McMurray, Athabasca*

Exam-style question

Assess the geopolitical risks to the world of its reliance on fossil fuels. (*12 marks*)

Over to you

1 Using the data in Figure 1, combine the three rank orders by awarding points for each rank – 1 = 10 points, 2 = 9 points etc. In this way, identify the five most geopolitically significant countries in terms of energy sources.

2 In pairs, study the maps showing source producers and flows of oil (Figure 5) and gas (Figure 6).

a Using the sources (shown by dots) and flows (shown by arrows), calculate the inflow and outflow of oil to each continental region shown in the key, and show these in a table.

b What do your calculations show about the relative importance of the different regions as (**i**) producers, (**ii**) consumers?

c Identify the chokepoints in Figure 5. Using this information and the answers to Question 1 above, discuss and prepare a rank order of the significance of each of these chokepoints. Justify your order and compare it with that of others.

3 Draw a table to show the costs and benefits of tar sands in Canada. How far do benefits outweigh the costs?

4 Copy and complete the matrix to identify the conflicts between players in the tar sands industry.

	Player A	Player B	Player C	Player D	Player E
Player A National government					
Player B Regional/local government					
Player C Energy company					
Player D Local resident					
Player E Local business					
Player F Environmentalist					

Key

++ Strong agreement	-- Strong disagreement
+ Some agreement	- Some disagreement

On your own

5 Prepare for a class debate on the following motion: 'Energy sources are as effective as any military weaponry'.

6 Draw a new version of the carbon cycle, to show the impact of exploiting tar sands. Justify the changes you have identified.

Alternatives to fossil fuels

In this section, you'll learn that there are alternatives to fossil fuels – each with costs and benefits.

KEY CONCEPT

- **Sustainability** – the extent to which alternatives to fossil fuels can be regarded as 'sustainable'

The UK's changing energy mix

In October 2016, Hinkley Point C – the UK's newest nuclear power station – was given the go-ahead. The UK government believes that **low-carbon** energy supplies are the most effective way to fill a looming energy generation gap. In 2015, low-carbon generation (renewables and nuclear energy) supplied 47% of the UK's electricity; wind and solar farms, HEP and biomass between them supplied 24%, compared to coal's 22%.

The UK's use of fossil fuels is falling, and there are plans to close all traditional coal-fired power stations by 2025. Although the UK has 150 years' worth of coal reserves, it is energy insecure; 60% of its energy is imported. In order to reduce carbon emissions and create a more secure future, the UK is committed to decoupling the economy from fossil fuels by:

- increasing renewable energy – especially wind and solar. According to Friends of the Earth, wind energy could provide 25% of the UK's electricity needs by 2020. Solar power is also growing rapidly – up by 86% between 2014 and 2015 (see Figure 1). However, each energy source has only expanded through large government subsidies.
- developing a new generation of nuclear power stations, e.g. Hinkley Point C which alone will provide 7% of the UK's electricity.
- reducing energy use through technologies such as LED light bulbs.
- recycling energy which would normally be wasted.

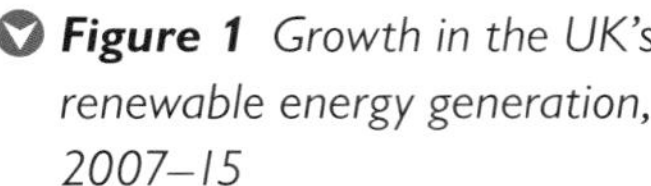

Figure 1 Growth in the UK's renewable energy generation, 2007–15

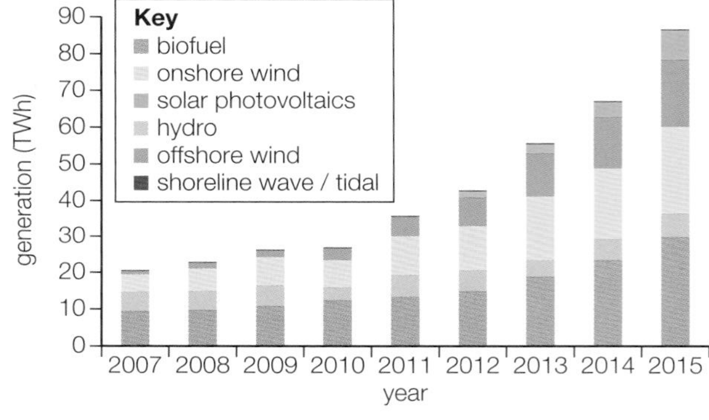

Renewable and recyclable energy sources

In a privatised energy market, energy companies prefer income to risk. New investment only comes when the government guarantees a minimum price per mega-watt hour (MwH), known as the **strike price**. Hinkley Point C was only agreed when the strike price was raised to £92.50/MwH. The costs will be passed on to customers' bills. A similar arrangement exists for renewables.

Renewable:

- Biomass – heat energy from wood, plants, animal and general waste. Strike price £80/MwH.
- Solar power – energy from the sun, generating electricity via photovoltaic cells. Strike price £50-80/MwH.
- Wind energy – moving air turns a propeller-driven generator. Strike price – onshore wind £80/MwH, offshore £115-120/MwH.
- Wave and tidal energy – moving water flows through a barrage, driving turbines. No strike price; technology is at the research stage.
- Hydroelectric power (HEP) – the vertical release of water turns a turbine to drive a generator. Strike price £100/MwH.

Recyclable:

- Nuclear power – the use of atomic reactions to obtain heat, in turn heating water and generating steam to drive a turbine. Strike price for Hinkley Point C £92.50/MwH.
- Heat recovery systems, or a ground source heat pump – where heat from air inside a building (or underground in a garden) is used to warm air drawn from outside. Installation is an individual decision – costs vary between £1200 and £3000 for a house, saving £200 on annual energy bills.

Alternatives to fossil fuels – costs and benefits

1 Nuclear power

- **Japan** – before the earthquake and tsunami of 2011, 27% of Japan's electricity came from nuclear power. The Fukushima nuclear plant was severely damaged in the earthquake and released dangerous levels of radiation. Japan then closed all of its nuclear reactors. However, nuclear energy has since been reintroduced as part of Japan's energy mix.
- In the UK, **Hinkley Point C** is an £18 billion project, which will provide energy for 60 years, and 25 000 jobs, involving French state-owned EDF and China General Nuclear.

2 Wind power

- **Hornsea Project 1** – 190-metre-high wind turbines (higher than London's Gherkin building) will eventually provide power for a million homes once completed in 2020. Located 121 km off the coast of Yorkshire, it will create 2000 construction jobs.
- **Quarrendon Fields, Aylesbury** – A wind turbine 25 metres taller than other onshore turbines will supply 2000 homes, but some local residents see it as a blot on the landscape, potentially harmful to birds, and the supply can be intermittent depending on when it's windy.

3 Solar power

Chapel Lane Solar Farm, Christchurch – It cost £50 million and covers an area the equivalent of 175 football pitches. It's the UK's largest solar farm, serving 60 000 households or 75% of the homes in Bournemouth. A supporter of the **Campaign to Protect Rural England (CPRE)** claims that these energy sources are expensive, because solar and wind energy still aren't viable without a high strike price. They also consume productive farmland, which some people argue should be producing food at a time when food costs are rising.

Figure 2 *The UK's largest solar farm – Chapel Lane, Christchurch*

The growth of biofuels

Brazil was the first country to produce biofuel from sugar cane in the 1970s. The bio-ethanol it produced was cheaper than petrol, and was used as a vehicle fuel. Brazil has since become the world's leading producer of bio-ethanol, and a leader in cutting carbon emissions. Cars running on bio-ethanol emit 80% less CO_2 than petrol-driven cars. Brazil aims to double bio-ethanol production by 2024.

Other countries have followed suit. Forests have been cleared in Malaysia to plant oil palms (used to produce bio-diesel). Oilseed rape in the EU, and maize in the USA, have been grown for the same reason. The motivation is to reduce carbon emissions, but the downside is deforestation – and, in Brazil, social unrest has also occurred; farm workers have lost land to grow sugar cane and cannot now grow food for themselves. Many farm workers end up moving to the cities.

This 'green fuel' has reinforced rural inequalities. Swiss, Swedish and American companies have been buying land to grow sugar and soy – inflating land prices. This boom has seen biofuel growth double in area since 2000, while rice and wheat have fallen by 10-20%. Figure 3 shows the global growth in biofuels.

BACKGROUND

Biofuels is the general name for fuels produced from organic matter (**biomass**), including plant material and animal waste. **Biofuel** is commonly used to refer to liquid fuels used in vehicles. These include: bio-ethanol – produced from sugar cane, sugar beet, maize and wheat; bio-diesel – produced from vegetable oil and animal fats; bio-methane – produced from sewage, domestic and animal waste, and organic waste.

Figure 3 *Growth in biofuel production in different global regions, 2004–2014*

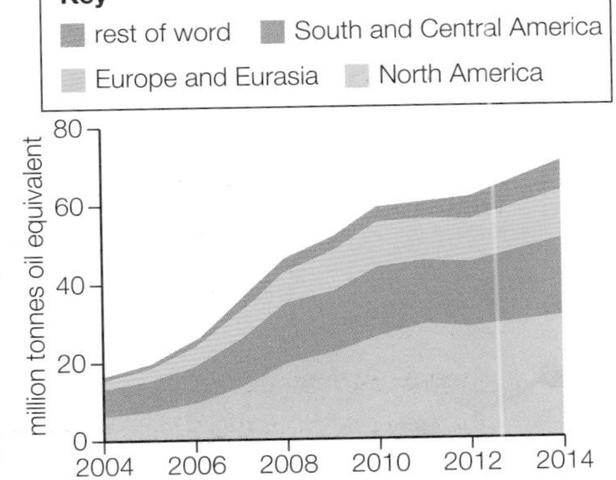

How 'carbon neutral' are biofuels?

On the face of it, producing biofuels seems like a good idea. Since 2003, Brazil's use of bio-ethanol has reduced the country's CO_2 emissions by more than 350 million tons. However, contrary to first impressions, some biofuels cannot be regarded as 'carbon neutral'. Figure 4 shows pros and cons in growing crops used for biofuel, such as *Jatropha Curcas*, a non-edible, oilseed-rich plant.

Figure 4 *A SWOT analysis of biofuels*

Strengths
- Renewable energy source
- Lower emissions than fossil fuels
- Bio-degradable
- Easily grown and does not need specialist machinery

Weaknesses
- Takes land from food production
- Needs pesticides and fertilisers, which use fossil fuels in their production, so they're not carbon neutral
- Requires large volumes of water
- Clearing forest to grow this crop means the loss of a carbon sink and increased CO_2 emissions from the deforestation (which are 35-60% higher than savings from using biofuels) – again throwing doubt on the crop's 'carbon neutrality'

Opportunities
- Provides rural inward investment and local development projects
- Positive multiplier effects in rural regions
- Fuel earns export income
- Infrastructure improvements (e.g. improved roads, piped water) often provided by growers

Threats
- Takes investment away from food production
- Contaminates water resources with pesticides or the overuse of fertilisers
- Food shortages occur, which lead to higher food prices

The move to alternatives to fossil fuels is not straightforward. The fact that biofuels generally produce lower emissions than fossil fuels (see Figure 5), doesn't make them 'carbon-neutral'.

- Biomass requires a fuel to 'kick-start' burning. Figure 5 shows some fuels labelled as 'CHP' – Combined Heat and Power – in which natural gas is used. Drax coal-fired power station in North Yorkshire occasionally burns wood pellets and biomass instead of coal. But coal is needed to 'fire up' the biomass, and some biomass fuels can therefore produce between 150% and 400% more CO_2 than coal!
- Most renewable installations, such as wind turbines, require industrial processes that use energy during their construction – indirectly adding to CO_2 emissions.
- Figure 5 shows the varied carbon footprints of biofuels, some of which (such as rapeseed) produce greater carbon emissions than crude oil. There are recent 'second generation' fuels, shown in Figure 5 as '2G', but their emissions vary. Figure 5 distinguishes between 'land-using' fuels (i.e. crops which are specifically grown to burn) and those which are 'non-land using' (i.e. only waste by-products are burned, such as straw).

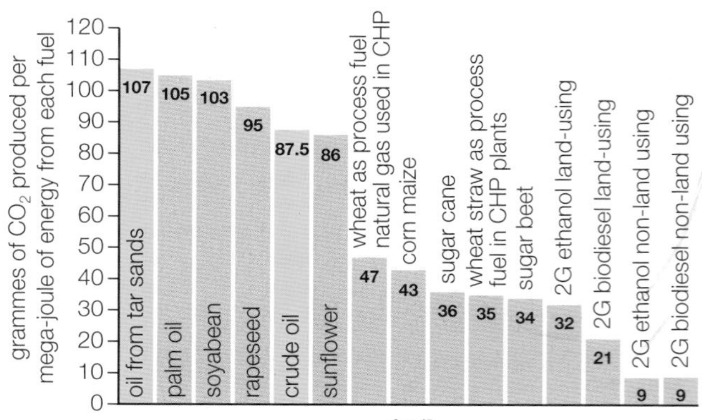

Figure 5 *Comparing emissions from different biofuel sources – units are amounts of CO_2 produced per mega-joule of energy from each fuel when burned*

Reducing carbon emissions: other approaches

While demand for energy is increasing, the need to drive down carbon emissions is greater. The use of radical alternatives could help to achieve that, although some uncertainty exists about how far this is possible:

1 **Carbon capture and storage (CCS)** – This uses technology to capture CO_2 emissions from coal-fired power stations. Figure 6 shows how carbon capture works. The gas is transported to a site where it's stored, compressed and transported by pipeline to an injection well, where it's injected in liquid form into suitable geological reservoirs, e.g. underground aquifers. Theoretically, CCS could cut global CO_2 emissions by up to 19%. However, it's not currently financially viable; in 2016, there was just one commercial CCS plant (see page 96). Like many coal-fired operations, E.ON's power station at Kingsnorth on the Thames estuary is ready to be adapted to CCS should it become viable, but until then that option lies unused.

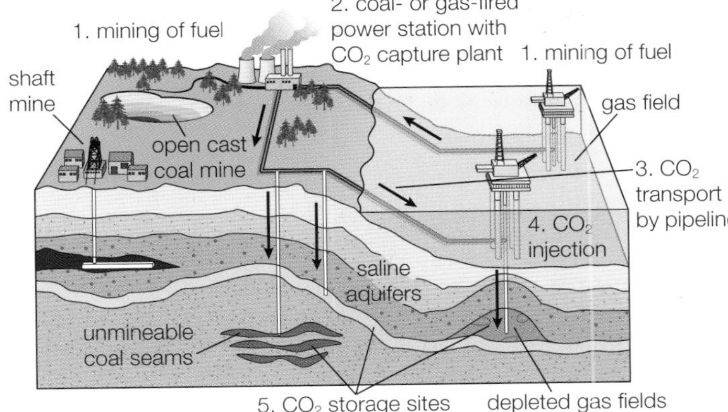

Figure 6 *Carbon capture and storage*

2 **Hydrogen fuel cells** – Hydrogen is the most abundant element in the universe, but it's usually combined with other elements such as carbon. Once separated, it provides an alternative to oil. Fuel cells convert chemical energy in hydrogen to electricity, with pure water as a by-product. Hydrogen fuel cells are far more energy efficient than petrol engines in vehicles. Separating hydrogen from other elements initially requires energy, but this can be provided by renewable sources such as solar or wind power.

3 **Electric vehicles** – Traditionally, problems with electric vehicles include their range, (i.e. distance travelled before recharging) and price. Cars were often limited to 80–90 miles between charges. Tesla's new electric cars extend over 200 miles, and are cheaper than many electric cars, although they still cost over £25 000.

Over to you

1 a In pairs, draw a table to show the advantages and disadvantages of the following energy types: biomass, solar power, wind energy, wave and tidal energy, HEP, nuclear power, and heat recovery systems. Add further details from research if needed.

b How far do you think strike price should be the most important factor in deciding energy sources?

2 a Using Figure 5, compare the emissions from the different energy sources shown.

b In pairs, decide on an energy mix for the UK which would **(i)** be affordable and **(ii)** create low CO_2 emissions.

On your own

3 Distinguish between renewable and recyclable energy sources.

4 Use material from this section and updated research (e.g. progress on Hinkley Point C, renewable alternatives) to write 1000 words evaluating three strategies:

a Business as usual,

b A fully green agenda of renewables and recyclables,

c An alternative strategy of your own.

Exam-style question

Evaluate the extent to which alternatives to fossil fuel energy sources provide an energy secure future. (*20 marks*)

2.8 Threats to the carbon and water cycles

In this section, you'll learn that biological carbon cycles and the water cycle are threatened by human activities.

EQ3 Sections 2.8 to 2.10 investigate how the carbon and water cycles are linked to the global climate system.

KEY CONCEPTS

- **Causality** – the causes of changes to the water and carbon cycles brought about by human activities
- **Systems** – the ways in which ecosystems respond to change
- **Resilience** – the impacts of human activities on the resilience of natural systems

Growing demands

Climate change is happening. The first two decades of the twenty-first century have brought extreme droughts in Brazil, Australia and the USA, and torrential rains and flooding in Europe, Japan and South Africa. At the same time, average global temperatures are the highest on record. In addition, growing global demands for fuel, food and other resources have led to land use changes, which are threatening both the carbon and water cycles.

Deforestation in Madagascar

Since the 1950s, Madagascar's tropical forests have been cleared at a rapid rate. Small-scale clearance by farmers had long been common in the country, but a growing international demand for tropical hardwood, an expanding population – and debt repayments – meant that the Madagascan government began to encourage farmers to clear more land in order to grow cash crops to earn foreign currency to help repay the country's debts. Before 1950, Madagascar had 11.6 million hectares of tropical forest, but by 1985 that had been reduced to 3.8 million hectares – a loss of two-thirds!

Figure 1A shows predicted levels of deforestation in Madagascar's Andapa forest by 2030. In both Figures 1A and 1B, deforestation and CO_2 emissions are represented in orange for the period 2010–20, and blue for the period 2020–30. Green on the map represents the remaining forest. As the rainforest disappears, so CO_2 emissions increase.

Deforestation has a major impact on the size of the terrestrial carbon store. Figure 2 shows the fluxes and size of carbon stores in an undisturbed tropical forest. Removing the forest has a colossal impact on both fluxes and stores.

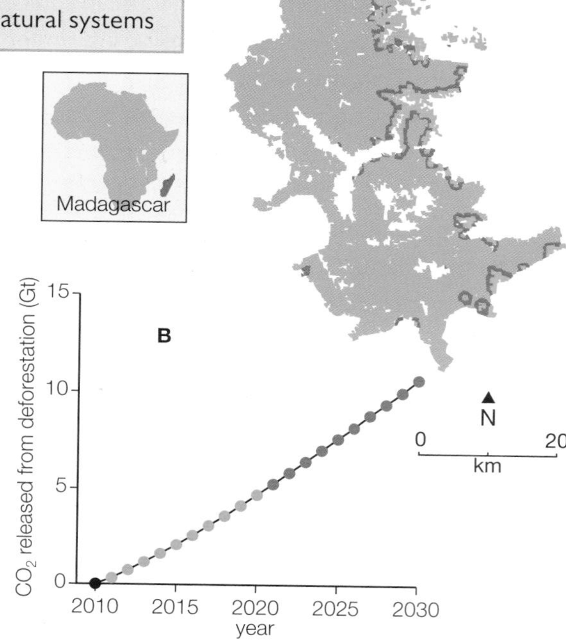

Figure 1 *Predicted levels of deforestation (**A**) and CO_2 emissions (**B**) in Andapa, Madagascar, by 2030 (using GIS)*

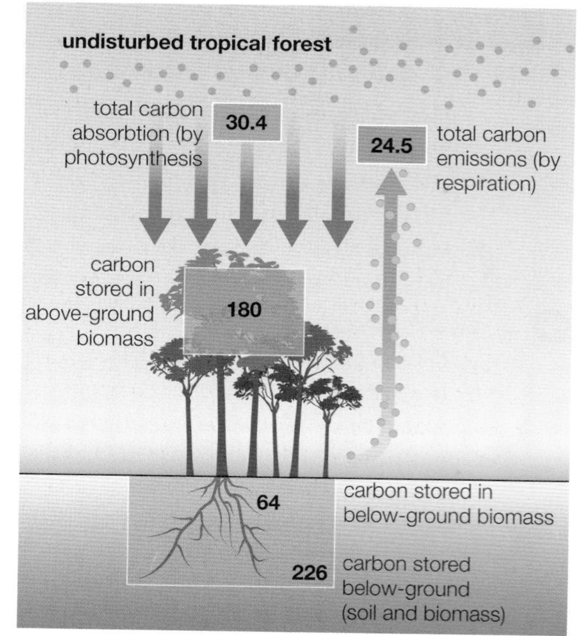

Figure 2 *Carbon stores (green/brown) and fluxes (blue/red) in an undisturbed tropical forest (the units used for stores are 'tonnes of carbon per hectare', and for fluxes are 'tonnes of carbon per hectare per year')*

Deforestation also affects rivers, landscapes and soil health. Figure 3 shows that the waters of the rivers Sofia (bottom) and Betsiboka (top) have turned red as a result of soil erosion caused by deforestation in Madagascar's Central Highlands. Soil erosion now exceeds 400 tonnes per hectare per year in some areas. Extensive logging of inland rainforests and coastal mangroves means that, after heavy rainfall, soil is washed from the hillsides into streams and rivers (such as those circled in Figure 3) – eventually clogging the coastal waterways with sediment. Figure 4 summarizes the impact of deforestation on the water cycle, soil health, the atmosphere and biosphere.

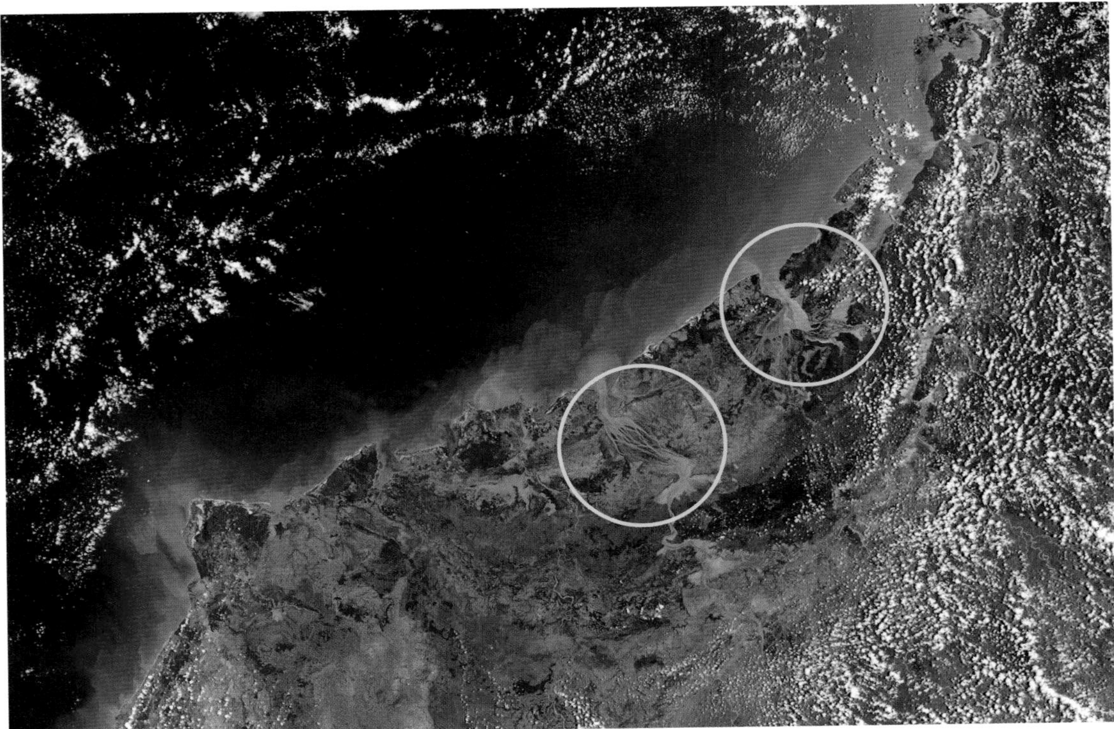

Figure 3 *Madagascar – eroded soil turns rivers red, and is also clearly visible in coastal estuaries and in the sediment plumes spreading out to sea*

Impacts on the water cycle	Impacts on soil health	Impacts on the atmosphere	Impacts on the biosphere
• Infiltration is decreased. • Runoff and erosion are increased. • Flood peaks are higher and the lag time is shorter. • Increased discharge leads to flooding. • More eroded material is carried in the river, both as bed load and as silt and clay in suspension. • Annual rainfall is reduced and the seasonality of rainfall increases.	• Raindrop impact washes finer particles of clay and humus away. • Coarser and heavier sands are left behind. • CO_2 is released from decaying woody material. • Biomass is lost, due to reduced plant growth / photosynthesis. • Rapid soil erosion leads to a loss of nutrients. • Increased **leaching** (the loss of nutrients from the soil by infiltration) means that minerals are lost.	• Turbulence is increased as the heated ground induces convectional air currents. • Oxygen content is reduced and transpiration rates are lower. • Reduced shading leads to more direct sunlight reaching the forest floor. • Reduced evapotranspiration makes it less humid. • The air is dryer (as above). • Evapotranspiration rates from the resultant grasslands are about one-third that of the tropical rainforest.	• Evaporation from vegetation is reduced. • Less absorption of CO_2 means a reduced carbon store. • Species diversity is reduced (e.g. less-resilient forest plants die off). • Ecosystem services are reduced (see page 86). • The decrease in habitats means that fewer animal species survive. • Biomass is lost, because of reduced plant growth / photosynthesis.

Figure 4 *The impacts of deforestation*

Converting grasslands to farming

Between 2007 and 2015, a biofuel 'rush' swept across the American Midwest – often referred to as the Prairies. Farmers were encouraged to grow corn, soya, canola (a type of rapeseed) and sugar cane as part of the US Environmental Protection Agency's Renewable Fuel Standard policy. This policy aimed to:

- increase the amount of ethanol being used in petrol
- boost the economies of rural US states
- reduce US dependence on overseas oil imports
- reduce CO_2 emissions from transport.

Figure 5 *The prairies of North Dakota are being ploughed up to grow corn for biofuel*

The growth in biofuel crop production reflected a growing global demand (see Section 2.7). By 2013 the price of corn had trebled, and a number of US states (such as North Dakota; see Figure 5) were cashing in. Grasslands – traditionally used for cattle ranching – were ploughed up, and in some states the area of corn being cultivated doubled. Over 5.5 million hectares of natural grassland disappeared across the American Midwest, which matches the rate of rainforest deforestation across Brazil, Malaysia and Indonesia.

The impacts of converting grasslands

When natural ecosystems – like grasslands – are destroyed, there can be serious consequences for the carbon and water cycles, as well as for soil health (see Figure 6). America's Midwest is prone to dry summers, and is at risk from wind-blown soil erosion, which would also have a detrimental effect on the soil carbon store (see Figure 7).

Figure 6 *The positives of grasslands, and the disadvantages of converting them to biofuel crops*

The benefits of natural grasslands	The disadvantages of converting grasslands to grow biofuel crops
Grasslands: • trap moisture and floodwater • absorb toxins from soils • maintain healthy soils • provide cover for dry soils • maintain natural habitats • act as a carbon sink – absorbing CO_2 and releasing O_2 all year round (a 'lung effect') • act as a terrestrial carbon store.	• The initial removal of grasslands releases CO_2 from soils into the atmosphere. • Annual ploughing enables soil bacteria to release CO_2. • Biofuel crops need carbon-based nitrogen fertiliser and chemical pesticides, so they produce a net increase in CO_2 emissions. • Biofuel crops are heavy consumers of water, so they need irrigation which has a significant impact on aquifers. • Cultivated soils are liable to erosion by runoff and wind. • Natural habitats are reduced. • The 'lung effect' is reduced.

Afforestation

Trees provide a vital carbon store – sequestering carbon during photosynthesis. Therefore, it makes sense to re-plant trees when deforestation has occurred, or better still to establish forests on land not previously forested. This is known as **afforestation**. Afforestation effectively counters all of the negative impacts of deforestation outlined in Figure 4.

The EU's Afforestation Grant Scheme encourages the planting of forests for their value as terrestrial carbon stores and for the ecosystem services that they provide (see page 86).

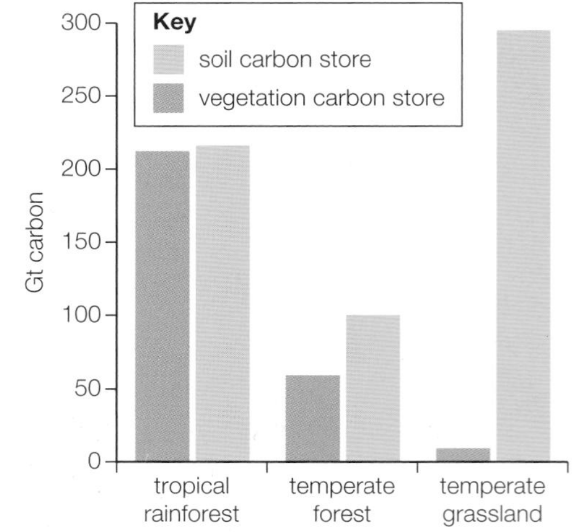

Figure 7 *Carbon stores for tropical rainforest, temperate forest and temperate grassland*

Ocean acidification

The world's oceans are a major carbon sink – they have absorbed about 30% of the CO_2 produced as a result of human activities since 1800, and about 50% of that produced by burning fossil fuels. Figure 8 shows that as CO_2 in the ocean increases, the ocean pH decreases – it becomes more acidic. This is known as **ocean acidification**.

As the ocean becomes more acidic, corals cannot absorb the alkaline calcium carbonate that they need to maintain their skeletons, and reefs begin to dissolve. Ocean acidification has lowered the pH of the ocean by about 0.1. That means that it's now about 30% more acidic than it was in 1750, in the early days of the Industrial Revolution.

late 1800s reduced acidity

seawater pH
9
8
7
lower concentration of atmospheric CO_2
CO_2 carbon dioxide
carbonate ions
H_2CO_3 carbonic acid
H^+ free hydrogen ions
HCO_3^- bicarbonate
abundant healthy corals molluscs and other marine calcifiers

2100 (projected) increased acidity

seawater pH
9
8
7
higher concentration of atmospheric CO_2
CO_2 carbon dioxide
fewer carbonate ions
H_2CO_3 carbonic acid
H^+ free hydrogen ions
HCO_3^- bicarbonate
fewer, smaller marine calcifiers

Figure 8 *Ocean acidification*

Corals matter

Corals – which are marine invertebrates – get their brilliant colour (see Figure 9A) from algae that live in their tissues. The most important role of the algae is to provide food to the coral through the carbohydrates produced during photosynthesis. Coral has a narrow temperature range within which it can live; never below 18°C, and ideally in the range of 23-29°C. If water becomes too warm, the algae are ejected and the coral turns white – known as **coral bleaching** (see Figure 9B).

The biggest cause of coral bleaching is climate change, which raises ocean temperatures. If CO_2 emissions continue at their current rate, the pH of the ocean surface could be lowered to 7.8 by 2100, which would dissolve coral skeletons and cause reefs to disintegrate.

Increased acidification risks crossing the **critical threshold** for the health of coral reefs and other marine ecosystems. If coral reefs are destroyed, we will lose the vital ecosystem services that they provide. They:

- shelter 25% of marine species
- protect shorelines
- support fishing industries
- provide income from tourism.

Figure 9 *Healthy coral (**A**) and bleached coral (**B**)*

BACKGROUND

Ecosystem services

The concept of ecosystem services helps us to understand the use and management of natural resources. Human health and well-being depends on services provided by ecosystems and their components – water, soil, nutrients and organisms.

Ecosystem services can be defined as:

- **supporting services** – These keep ecosystems healthy by providing other services, including soil formation, photosynthesis, nutrient cycling and water cycling.
- **provisioning services** – These are the products obtained from ecosystems, including food, fibre, fuel, genetic resources, natural medicines and pharmaceuticals.
- **regulating services** – These are the benefits obtained from the regulation of ecosystem processes, including regulating air quality, climate, water, erosion, disease and pollination.
- **cultural services** – These are the non-material benefits that people obtain from ecosystems, such as spiritual well-being, recreation, education and science.

Damage to any one of these four services can place an ecosystem at risk, and within each of them there are critical thresholds beyond which the damage becomes irreversible. As climate changes and temperatures rise, corals, forests and oceans are all threatened and carbon stores are being lost.

Increasing drought

The natural greenhouse effect (see Section 2.4) keeps the Earth warm enough to sustain life. But increased carbon emissions are enhancing the greenhouse effect so much that the global climate is changing. Climate change could have several impacts, including:

- an increase in the frequency and intensity of storms and hurricanes
- rising sea levels
- more-frequent floods, droughts and heat waves.

Any change in ocean currents and atmospheric circulation could also affect patterns of precipitation, evapotranspiration and temperature, as climate belts move in response to climate change.

As the planet warms, not only have the Earth's climate zones begun to shift, but – according to climate scientists at the University of Colorado – they are doing so at an accelerating rate. The scientists used climate-model simulations to investigate shifts in climate zones. They found that, for an initial 2°C warming, about 5% of the Earth's land area effectively shifts to a new climate zone. The pace of change then quickens for the next 2°C of warming, with an additional 10% of land area shifting to a new climate zone.

Certain regions – such as North America, Europe, and other mid- and high-latitude regions – will undergo more changes than tropical and sub-tropical regions. In addition, the coldest zones of the planet are decreasing in extent, and dry areas are increasing. It's likely that today's arid and semi-arid areas will expand into continental areas of Asia, as well as parts of northern and sub-Saharan Africa, as shown in Figure 10.

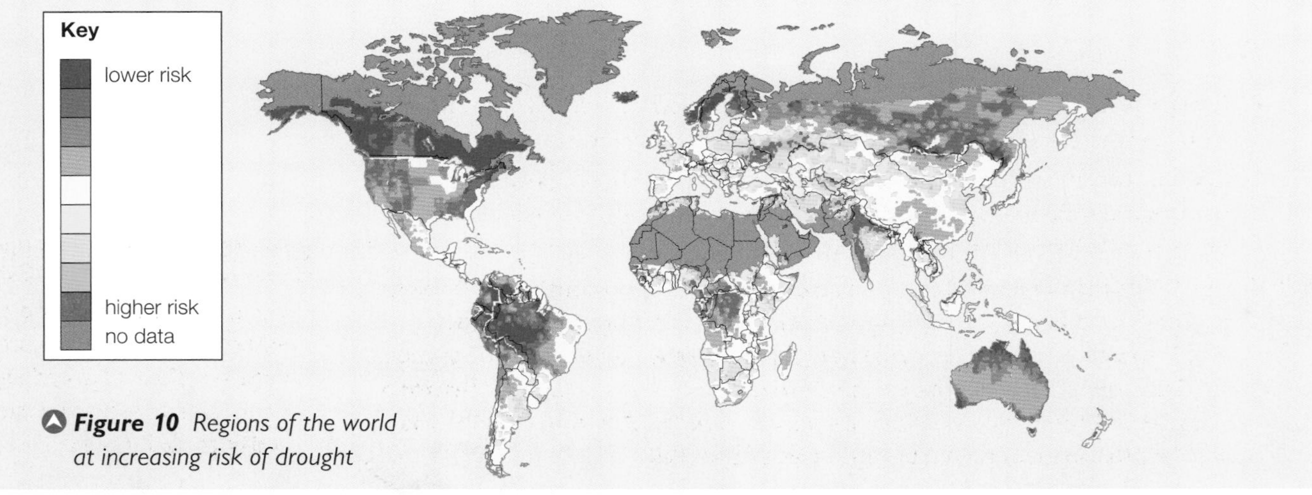

Figure 10 *Regions of the world at increasing risk of drought*

Drought in the Amazon

The Amazon Basin suffered severe droughts in 2005 and 2010, and the drought of 2014–15 was the worst to hit Brazil for 80 years. The Amazon Basin plays a key role in the Earth's carbon cycle, holding 17% of the terrestrial vegetation carbon store. Figure 11 shows the extent and scale of the Amazon drought of 2010.

A study of the 2010 Amazon drought showed that trees died and growth rates declined. The drought effectively shut down the Amazon's function as a carbon sink. Forest fires broke out – burning trees and litter and releasing CO_2. There are further concerns that, as climate change increases temperatures and alters rainfall patterns across South America, the Amazon rainforest will change from a carbon sink to a carbon source. This could accelerate global warming.

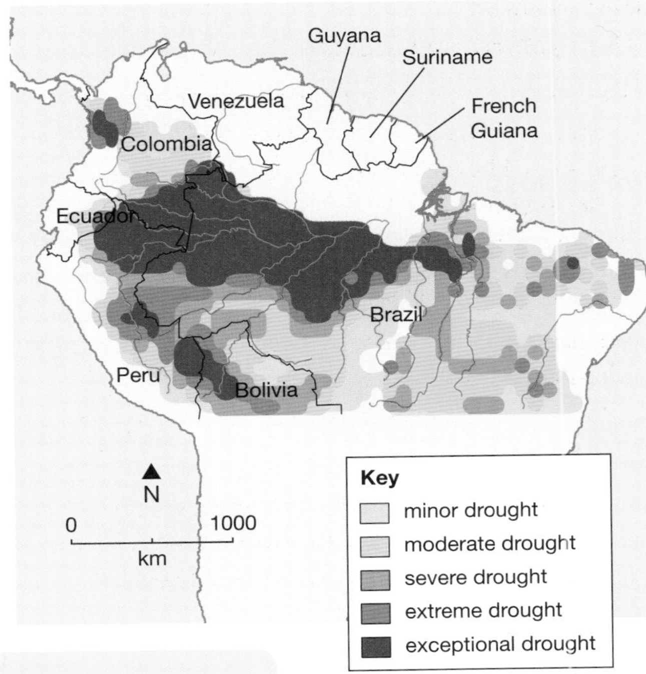

Figure 11 *The extent of drought in the Amazon Basin in 2010*

Over to you

1 **a** In pairs, list the ways in which climate change is affecting (**i**) the hydrological cycle, (**ii**) the carbon cycle and (**iii**) the health of soils in the three study areas covered in this unit.
b Redraw Figure 2 to show changes to fluxes and stores when tropical rainforests are disturbed by deforestation or drought.

2 Now design a similar diagram to show how converting grasslands to biofuels in the American Midwest affects (**a**) the water cycle and (**b**) the carbon cycle.

3 **a** In pairs, research the term 'Ecosystem services in …' for each of the four ecosystems listed in the table below. The University of Maryland Centre for Environmental Science website will help.
b Using your research, copy and complete the table.

Marine ecosystem	Ecosystem services	Threats to services and recorded losses
Mangroves		
Coral reefs		
Sea grass		
Coastal wetlands		

On your own

4 Explain (**a**) the evidence for, and (**b**) the likely impacts of shifting climatic belts and more-frequent droughts on the world's tropical rainforests.

5 Choose two contrasting areas to illustrate how increasing population, economic development and climate change put pressure on (**a**) human well-being and (**b**) the natural environment.

6 Use GIS to map land-use changes – such as deforestation – over time, as follows:
a Research the phrase 'changing land use on satellite images' in Google.
b Identify three countries where changing land use is showing visible impacts.
c Create your own presentation to show land-use changes, e.g. deforestation, grassland conversion or afforestation. Use Figures 1A and 1B to guide you.
d Describe and explain the trends in these countries.

Exam-style question

Using examples, evaluate the extent to which the carbon cycle and the water cycle are being threatened by human activities. (*20 marks*)

2.9 Degrading the water and carbon cycles

In this section, you'll learn that there are implications for human well-being from the degradation of the water and carbon cycles.

Forest loss

Palm oil is the most commonly produced vegetable oil – it's used in foods such as frozen pizzas and biscuits, and also in cosmetics and as biofuel. 66 million tonnes of it are produced every year, with half of the palm oil imported into the EU being used as biofuel.

The warm, humid climate of the Tropics provides perfect conditions for growing oil palms. Huge areas of rainforest in Southeast Asia, Latin America and Africa are being – or have been – bulldozed or burned (see Figure 1A) to create land for oil palm plantations like the one in Figure 1B. In the process, they release vast amounts of carbon into the atmosphere. Indonesia is the world's largest producer of palm oil, and in 2015 its greenhouse gas emissions temporarily overtook those of the USA – caused mostly by burning forests.

Impacts on well-being

The palm oil industry meets a growing demand for a much-desired raw material, but local communities can come off badly as a result. Many depend on rainforests for everything they need to survive, but smallholders and indigenous people who have inhabited the forest for generations are often driven away by the actions of the palm oil producers. In Indonesia, over 700 land conflicts in 2016 were linked to the palm oil industry.

Palm oil production is also tough on animals. The loss of biodiversity and habitat endangers species such as the orang-utan, Borneo elephant and Sumatran tiger, each of which is moving closer to extinction as its rainforest home is cleared for oil palms.

Protecting forest stores?

In May 2011, Indonesia's President declared a 'forest moratorium', aimed at reducing deforestation. With US$1 billion of funding from the UN and the Norwegian government, the moratorium stopped the issuing of permits for the clearance of primary forest or peatland for timber, wood pulp or palm oil. By 2013, emissions had fallen by between 1% and 2.5%, and in May 2015 the moratorium was extended to help Indonesia further reduce its CO_2 emissions by 26% by 2020. However, its effectiveness is limited. Clearance permits that had already been issued before 2011 went ahead, and illegal logging remains a problem – so the moratorium only reduced clearance by 15%.

SYNOPTIC THEMES AND KEY CONCEPTS

- **Actions** – attitudes and actions of global consumers to environmental issues
- **Futures** – the uncertainty of global projections about the changing water cycle
- **Systems** – the impact of climate change on the water cycle
- **Globalisation** – the impacts of global trade in palm oil
- **Threshold** – the point in the hydrological and carbon cycles when sudden or rapid change occurs

Figure 1 *Deforestation in Indonesia (**A**) to create huge oil palm plantations like the one shown in (**B**)*

BACKGROUND

Kuznet's Curve

Since the 1970s, environmental concerns have begun to take a higher place on the political agenda in developed countries. In those countries where human development, water and food supply are no longer seen as priorities (because they are taken for granted), many people realise that environmental care for the planet is important. This is a concept known as Kuznet's Curve (see Figure 2).

Figure 2 *Kuznet's Curve and Indonesia's position on the curve*

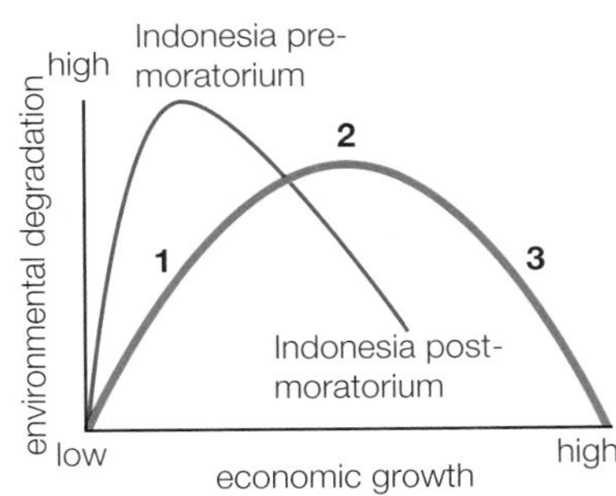

Key

Stage 1
Rapid economic development occurs when demand for products has impacts on the environment.

Stage 2
Concern at degradation leads to action to protect the environment.

Stage 3
Reinforcement of Stage 2 occurs with education programmes and funding for environmental protection.

Forest recovery

Indonesia's forest moratorium shows that forest stores can be protected. Data from the UN's FAO suggest that High Income Countries (HICs) are now the only country category with expanding forested areas (see Figure 3).

Although the global forested area fell by 3% between 1990 and 2015, this trend may be starting to change:

- Between 2010 and 2015, an average of 7.6 million hectares of forest were lost every year, but 4.3 million hectares were also gained – leaving a net annual loss of 3.3 million hectares. This net annual loss was half that of the 1990s.
- The temperate forest area (covering many HICs) has increased, although the tropical forest area (covering many LICs) has decreased. Rates of forest loss are highest in Low Income Countries (see Figure 3).
- China aims to increase its forested area by 23% between 2015 and 2020.
- Brazil has halved its rate of deforestation since 2000 – but that's still a loss.

Figure 3 *Global trends in forest cover 1990-2015 – using World Bank income categories, which are based on Gross National Income (GNI) per capita. Data are from the UN's FAO, 2015.*

GNI per capita 2015	Forested area (thousands of hectares)					Change %
	1990	2000	2005	2010	2015	
High (above US$12 746)	1 808 959	1 817 229	1 817 957	1 825 524	1 830 347	1.2%
Upper middle (US$4126–12 745)	1 254 645	1 237 046	1 231 708	1 228 041	1 228 186	−2.1%
Lower middle (US$1046–4125	591 378	557 059	550 997	542 767	533 344	−9.8%
Low ($1045 or less)	464 070	435 090	422 921	410 211	398 135	−14.2%
Unclassified	9218	9179	9161	9131	9121	−1.1%
Total	**4 128 269**	**4 055 602**	**4 032 743**	**4 015 673**	**3 999 134**	**−3.1%**

Attitudes and actions

Consumers often make their views felt about issues such as palm oil production by joining environmental **pressure groups**, such as WWF and Greenpeace, and supporting their campaigns. Joining is usually by subscription, and the money raised is used to fund campaigns that often involve direct action. For example, in 2016, Greenpeace activists blockaded a palm oil refinery in Rotterdam, owned by the IOI Group (a leading palm oil TNC and one of Malaysia's largest property development companies). A Greenpeace report linked the company's suppliers of palm oil to deforestation, forest fires and human rights abuses. A campaigner said 'Unilever and Nestlé have cancelled contracts with IOI, but it has not changed its practices. We hope that our action will give them the push to do what is necessary to protect rainforests and people'. IOI responded that 'whilst there have been fires in our Indonesian developments, these were not started by IOI'.

Climate change and Yukon

Yukon, shown in Figure 4A, is a territory in the far northwest of Canada, and a significant part of it lies within the Arctic Circle. Like most Arctic and sub-Arctic areas, it has seen temperatures rise sharply, and forecasts are for continued warming. The increasing temperature has implications for precipitation patterns, river regimes and water stores:

- Increasing temperatures lead to increased evaporation and atmospheric water vapour.
- Across Yukon, winter precipitation increased between 1950 and 1998. However, a greater proportion fell as rain in spring and less as snow than previously. Climate scientists agree that annual precipitation will increase by between 5% and 20% by 2100.
- Snowmelt now begins earlier in Yukon, and snow cover is decreasing. This alters **river regimes**, bringing earlier peak flows to most river basins.
- Between 1958 and 2008, the total ice area in Yukon shrank by 22% and, as glaciers recede, streamflow is decreasing – despite an initial increase in meltwater.
- Climate change is leading to thawing of the permafrost – so water penetrates deeper into the soil, instead of forming surface runoff.
- Since 2000, inflows to the Yukon River (see Figure 4B) have increased by 39% due to increasing temperature and precipitation.
- As the permafrost thaws, climate change could increase the amount of groundwater.

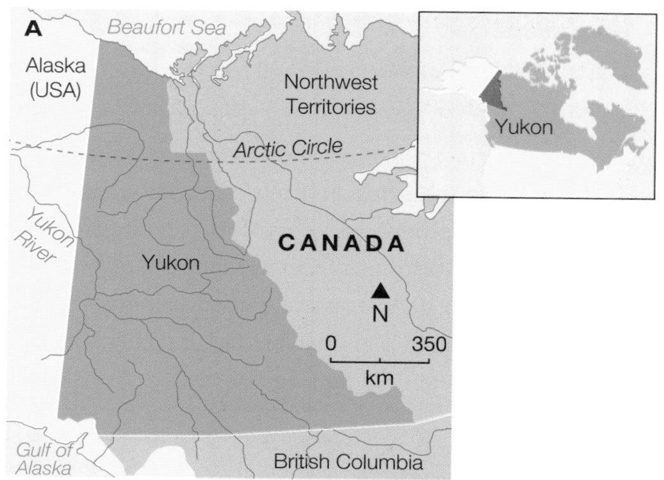

Figure 4 *Yukon (**A**) and the Yukon River (**B**)*

Changing precipitation patterns

Climate models predict that, as temperatures rise, precipitation patterns will change in two main ways:

- Firstly, existing patterns will strengthen. This is commonly called 'wet get wetter, dry get drier'. Warmer air traps more water vapour, and climate scientists expect more water to fall in those parts of the Earth that are already wet. But because the Earth is a closed system – and precipitation is balanced by evaporation – an increase in dry areas is also expected.
- Secondly, as atmospheric circulation changes, a shift in storm tracks will move storms further from the Equator towards the Poles.

Futures and uncertainties

A team of European climate scientists believes that the twentieth century was neither much drier nor wetter for half the globe than previously. Their research showed that temperature increases in the twentieth century may not have affected rainfall as much as had been thought.

The team used tree rings, lake sediment and historical data to produce a new picture of past climate. They found larger areas with relatively wetter conditions in the ninth to eleventh centuries, and in the twentieth century. But drier conditions than those recorded in the twentieth century had been widespread between the twelfth and nineteenth centuries. This study challenges some climate models, because it shows limitations in trying to predict which regions may become wetter or drier in a warmer world.

Threats to ocean health

The well-being and survival of many coastal communities depends on the health of the ocean and marine ecosystems, especially in developing countries.

Protecting mangroves

Mangrove forests (see Section 2.3) are found along the tropical and sub-tropical coasts of Africa, Australia, Asia and the Americas. They are one of the most complex ecosystems on the planet, and mangrove trees with their prop roots (shown in Figure 5) provide a wide range of benefits, such as:

- stabilising coastlines against erosion
- collecting nutrient-rich sediments trapped between the entangled prop roots
- providing protection and shelter against extreme weather (e.g. storm winds and floods) and tsunami, by absorbing and dispersing surges
- providing nurseries for coastal fish away from predators.

Figure 5 *Mangroves protect vulnerable coastlines. The tangle of prop roots slows down storm surge waves, and also helped to protect areas of tropical coastline against the 2004 Asian tsunami.*

However, globally, half of all mangrove forests have been lost since 1950, and clearing mangroves for tourist developments or shrimp and prawn aquaculture has accounted for over 25% of this loss.

Food

520 million of the poorest people on Earth depend on fisheries for their food and income. Climate change is altering the distribution and productivity of species, food webs and biological processes. It's not just tropical waters that are affected: warming waters in the North Atlantic are killing the cold-water plankton that North Atlantic cod eat; Arctic krill stocks (food for whales) are declining by up to 75% per decade in some parts of the Southern Ocean.

Coral reefs shelter 25% of marine species. But ocean acidification and warming oceans are leading to coral bleaching, which affects food sources and incomes for people living in coastal communities.

Tourism

Higher water temperatures in 2016 caused the worst coral bleaching ever recorded on Australia's Great Barrier Reef. Globally, coral reefs are tourist attractions, but damage to the coral can directly impact on the income that local people derive from tourism.

The main cause of the damage has been climate change, added to reefs being lost by coastal pollution caused by industrial and agricultural runoff, as well as oil spills. All of these problems directly affect coastal zones and reduce income from tourism.

Over to you

1 a In pairs, carry out a SWOT analysis (Strengths, Weaknesses, Opportunities and Threats) of the forest moratorium in Indonesia.

b How worthwhile do you consider the forest moratorium to be? Explain.

2 a In pairs, research climate maps which model future climate patterns. Google 'maps of future climate' to help you. Refer also to maps of water stress or scarcity (Section 1.8, Figures 2 and 6) and drought (Section 2.8, Figure 10).

b Select up to three world or regional maps to show areas most at risk from water shortages or floods in the future.

c Design a 6–10 slide presentation to show your findings.

3 Design a systems diagram of the water cycle to show the impact of rising temperatures on evaporation, water vapour, precipitation, river regimes, the cryosphere, and drainage basin stores in Yukon.

On your own

4 Assess the usefulness of Kuznet's Curve in (**a**) accounting for the past, (**b**) explaining the present, and (**c**) predicting the future relationship between people and the natural environment.

5 Explain how climate change could affect coastal communities who depend on fishing, coastal protection and tourism.

Exam-style question

Referring to examples, evaluate the implications for human well-being caused by the degradation of the water and carbon cycles. (*20 marks*)

2.10 Responding to climate change

In this section, you'll learn that further planetary warming risks a large-scale release of stored carbon, requiring responses from different players at different scales.

Future emissions

For three decades, climate scientists have warned that increasingly rapid melting of the Arctic ice cap could cause uncontrollable global climate change. 'The warning signs are getting louder,' said Marcus Carson of the Stockholm Environmental Institute. The problem is that much of what could happen is clouded by uncertainty. As energy consumption rises, global greenhouse gas emissions are expected to continue to increase. However, what is not certain is by how much they will increase, or where the greatest increases will be. Figure 1 shows emissions for the period 2001–12 – but what will future trends be?

SYNOPTIC THEMES AND KEY CONCEPTS

- **Attitudes and actions** – of different countries, TNCs and people towards climate change
- **Futures** – the uncertainty of global projections about climate change
- **Systems** – how greenhouse gases play a part in the carbon and water cycles
- **Feedback** – how different processes lead to feedback in the carbon cycle
- **Mitigation and adaptation** – ways in which such policies can be implemented

Region	2001	2002	2003	2004	2005	2006	2007	2008	2009	2010	2011	2012
Europe	6078	6057	6244	6248	6224	6319	6276	6192	5698	5937	5902	5856
Asia	9074	9521	10336	11309	12156	12998	13827	14206	14817	15725	16867	17489
USA	5728	5656	5734	5820	5830	5741	5818	5638	5224	5470	5334	5123
Canada	531	537	559	554	560	551	580	564	528	540	546	543
Latin America & Caribbean	1296	1293	1295	1353	1425	1457	1517	1601	1563	1655	1699	1765
Africa	796	827	868	911	952	973	1025	1078	1072	1118	1112	1135
Australia & Oceania	385	389	398	413	418	422	433	436	439	431	432	430

Figure 1 *Greenhouse gas emissions (in millions of tonnes) by country or region, 2001–12*

Atmospheric concentration levels

Greenhouse gas concentrations are likely to continue to increase, as emerging economies such as India industrialise further. The problem is that greenhouse gases remain in the atmosphere for a long time. Even if global emissions were to stabilise or decrease, surface air temperatures would continue to warm because greenhouse gases would still be added to the atmosphere faster than carbon sinks could re-absorb them.

Because of the difficulties involved in projecting future emission levels, and the capacity of carbon sinks to absorb them, climate scientists use a range of scenarios to show projected greenhouse gas concentrations. Figure 2 shows four different emissions scenarios. The highest emissions pathway assumes that emissions will continue to rise throughout the twenty-first century, as prosperity and demand rise. The lowest emissions pathway assumes that emissions will peak by 2020 and then decline as low-emissions technology develops further.

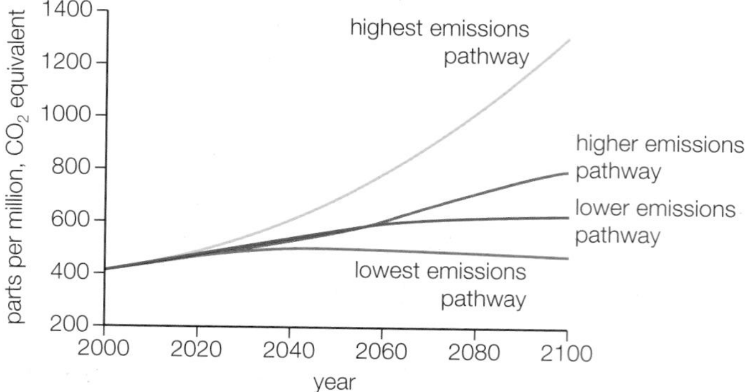

Figure 2 *Four projected scenarios for atmospheric greenhouse gas concentrations*

Climate warming

Climate models predict that surface temperatures will continue to rise, with increases between 2000 and 2100 in the range of 2-6°C. Temperatures are expected to warm more rapidly over the Northern Hemisphere (which has more land than ocean), and some regions (e.g. the Arctic) will see larger increases than the global average. Figure 3 shows a range of possible surface temperature increases, linked to different emissions scenarios.

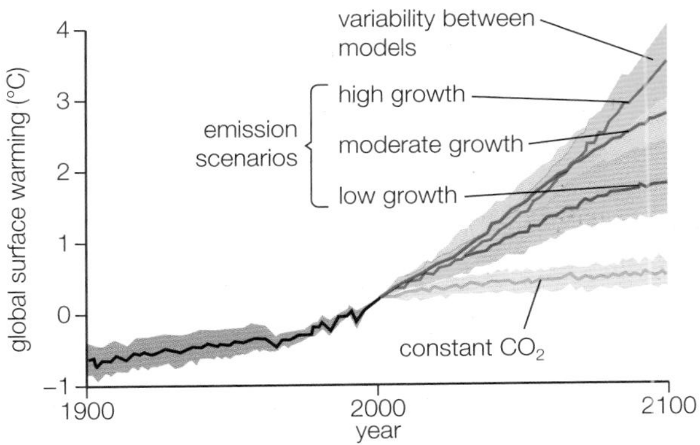

Figure 3 *Projected global surface warming (in °C) under different emissions scenarios*

Why is future climate change so uncertain?

A range of physical and human factors help to make future predictions about climate change uncertain.

Physical factors

- **Oceans** and forests act as carbon sinks and store heat. Oceans take decades to respond to changes in greenhouse gas concentrations. Their response to higher levels of greenhouse gases and higher temperatures will continue to affect the global climate for possibly hundreds of years.
- Human factors also play a role in forests. Section 2.9 showed that, although the amount of forested land is increasing in High Income Countries, the overall global total is falling – particularly in the Tropics.

Human factors

- **Economic growth.** After the financial crisis of 2007–8, there was a worry that rising CO_2 emissions would follow the recovery of global GDP. However, after rising by 4% per year since 2000, the rate of emissions growth fell to 1% by 2012–13, and 0.5% by 2014. Nevertheless, total carbon emissions still reached a new record.
- **Energy sources.** Energy consumption grew by 2% between 2008 and 2014. However, renewable sources made up two-thirds of the increase in electricity production in 2015.
- **Population change.** Increasing affluence in emerging economies means a potential extra billion consumers by 2050 – with spending power equal to the USA. Changing diets and increased mobility mean more emissions.

Feedback mechanisms

One of the uncertainties about climate change concerns **feedback mechanisms**, such as carbon release from peatlands and permafrost – and tipping points, including forest die back and alterations to the thermohaline circulation. Feedback in climate systems can either dampen or amplify responses to external factors that affect global climate; **negative feedback** dampens the original process, and **positive feedback** amplifies it.

Peatlands

Most of the world's wetlands are peat. Peat is the accumulation of partly decayed vegetation, and stores large amounts of carbon, because of the low rate of carbon breakdown (decomposition) in cold waterlogged soils.

Warming causes peat to dry out as water tables fall, as well as increasing the rate of decomposition.

A warming of 4°C causes a 40% loss of soil organic carbon from shallow peat, and 86% from deep peat. Peatlands tend to emit carbon in the form of methane, increasing the concentration of greenhouse gases.

Permafrost

When permafrost melts, it releases trapped carbon into the atmosphere as CO_2 and methane – increasing atmospheric greenhouse gas concentrations and leading to increased temperatures and melting.

Tipping points

A climate tipping point is a critical threshold. At a particular moment in time, a small change in the global climate system can transform a relatively stable system into a very different state. Two particular phenomena are capable of creating tipping points – forest die back and changes to the thermohaline circulation.

Forest die back

Rainfall in the Amazon Basin is largely recycled from moisture within the forest. If the rainforest is subject to drought (such as in Brazil in 2014–15; see Section 1.5), trees die back. A tipping point could be reached, where the level of die back actually stops the recycling of moisture within the rainforest – resulting in further die back.

In the boreal forest ecosystem – stretching across Europe and Siberia – hot, dry summers lead to water stress and cause trees to die. A tipping point could be reached where the trees will no longer absorb enough CO_2 from the atmosphere, leading to increased levels of greenhouse gases.

Figure 4 *Forest die back on Mt Lusen, Bavaria*

Changes to the thermohaline circulation

Cold, deep water in the North Atlantic forms part of the thermohaline circulation (see Section 1.2). To keep the 'conveyor belt' of warm water heading from the Tropics towards Britain, heavy, salty water must sink in the north. However, the melting of the northern ice sheets releases significant quantities of freshwater into the ocean, which is lighter and less salty – thus blocking and slowing the conveyor belt. As ice sheets melt, the ocean circulation is susceptible to a critical tipping point. Figure 5 shows how a collapse in the thermohaline circulation *might* affect global temperatures.

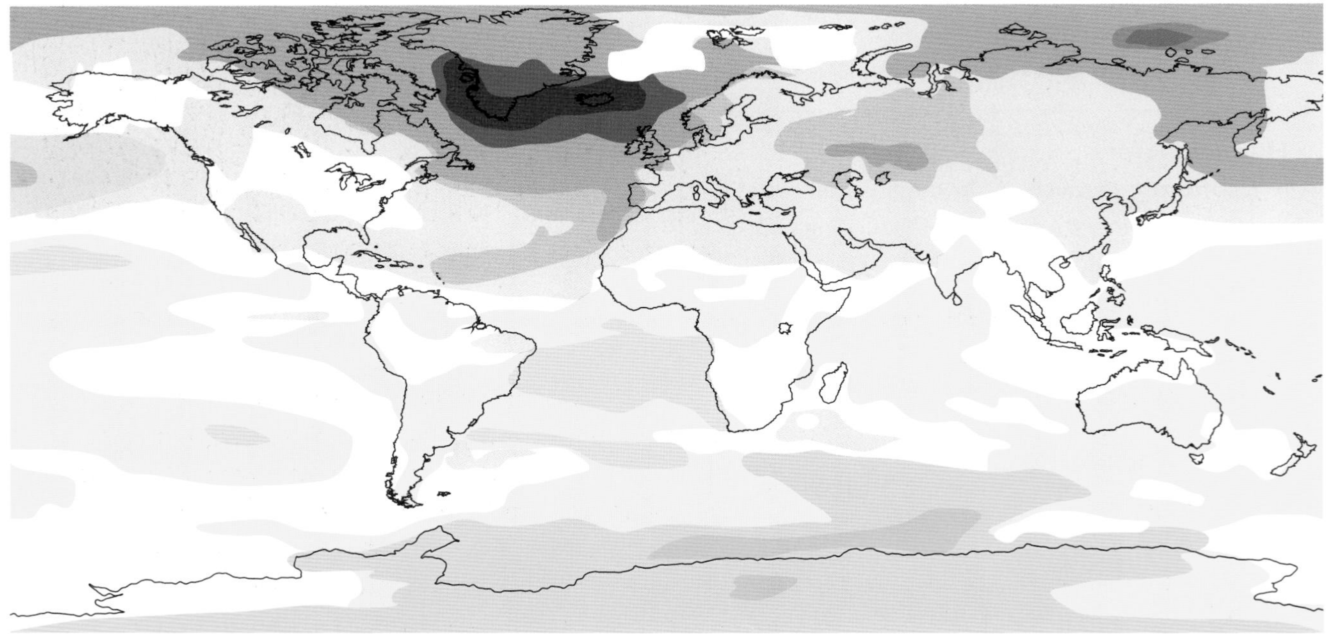

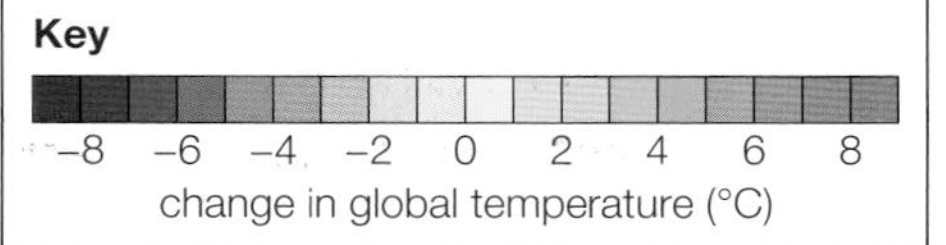

Figure 5 *Possible global changes to annual temperatures, 30 years after a collapse of the thermohaline circulation*

Facing the future

Even if greenhouse gas emissions were to stabilise or perhaps fall, the planet would continue to warm. It would be important to assess consequent changes, whilst trying to prevent them from worsening.

The IPCC outlined two approaches to the future:

- **Adaptation strategies** – adopt new ways of doing things in order to live with the likely outcomes of climate change.
- **Mitigation strategies** – re-balance the carbon cycle and reduce any impacts of climate change.

Each strategy challenges human behaviour and is costly; some are untested. Others require simple changes to the way people live, such as changing travel patterns (i.e. drive less), consuming locally produced food, or reducing waste. The IPCC states 'The scale of the challenge is daunting – these actions face barriers related to financing, public perception and a longstanding dependence of markets and institutions on fossil fuels'. Agreements at a global scale are needed, as well as national efforts which impact on people's everyday lives.

Adaptation strategies

1 Water conservation and management

Israel has a range of strategies to manage its limited supplies of freshwater:

- Smart irrigation (see Section 1.10).
- Recycling sewage water for agricultural use.
- Reducing agricultural consumption and importing water in food as virtual water.
- Adopting stringent conservation techniques.
- Managing demand by charging 'real value' prices for water to reflect the cost of supply and of ecosystem management.

2 Land-use planning and flood-risk management

Different strategies can be used to adapt to climate change. They include land-use zoning – a technique used for flood management, where development on floodplains is limited to low-impact things like playing fields and parks. This is a low-cost approach to flood management. Infiltration occurs naturally and surface runoff is reduced along with the risk of wider flooding.

3 Resilient agricultural systems

Conservation cropping is growing in use, from the USA to Syria and Iraq. It involves growing crops using a no-tilling (ploughing) approach. It uses fewer fertilisers, retains stubble and grows cover crops. The benefits include increased yields and incomes for farmers, plus improved soil structure, healthier soils, water conservation and erosion control.

Figure 6 *Maize grown using conservation cropping*

4 Solar radiation management

This is a form of **climate engineering**, which aims to reflect solar rays and so reduce global warming. Examples of techniques include pumping sulphur aerosols into the upper atmosphere, cloud brightening, and space-based reflectors. The advantages include the fact that these techniques could be deployed relatively quickly, and they offset some of the effects of greenhouse gases. The disadvantages include uncertainty about how effective they would be, together with ethical, social and political issues surrounding their use – plus they are potentially expensive.

Mitigation strategies

1 Carbon taxation

A carbon tax is a fee or cost paid by users of fossil fuels, which is directly linked to the level of CO_2 emissions that the fuel produces. It won't guarantee a reduction in the level of CO_2 emissions, but the idea is that it sends a message to change to a form of energy which produces fewer emissions. The UK's carbon price floor (CPF) is a tax on fossil fuels used to generate electricity, and came into effect in 2013.

2 Energy efficiency

A study in 2014 identified Germany as a world leader in energy efficiency. The study ranked the world's 16 major economies that had done most to increase energy efficiency. Germany's policies included:

- requiring residential and commercial buildings to reduce energy consumption by 25%
- loans to renovate older, energy-consuming properties
- subsidies to improve efficiencies in manufacturing.

Germany's economy has grown, while still increasing its efficiency and reducing the negative environmental impacts of energy use. The USA was ranked thirteenth, having made some progress – but was still wasting a lot of energy.

3 Afforestation and reforestation

This is discussed in Section 2.9. Canada and Sweden lead on afforestation and reforestation, but South Korea has had a remarkable turnaround. Forest degradation in South Korea accelerated during the Second World War and the Korean War (1950-53). Illegal logging, the use of firewood and the expansion of slash and burn agriculture added to its destruction. The government included forest rehabilitation projects as part of its economic development plans. Between 1961 and 1995, the area of forested land in South Korea rose from 4 to 6.3 million hectares, and by 2008 11 billion trees had been planted. About two-thirds of South Korea is now forested. The benefits include the restoration of degraded environments, the prevention of soil erosion, and the provision of forest sinks and stores of CO_2.

4 Renewable switching

Sweden leads the way in switching energy sources from fossil fuels to the use of renewables. Oil has fallen from providing 75% of Sweden's energy in 1970, to 20% today. The benefits of Sweden's move to clean and renewable energy are clear – although it consumes more energy per capita than many other countries, its carbon emissions are comparatively low. 83% of Sweden's electricity is produced by nuclear and hydroelectric power. Combined heat and power plants produce 10% (mainly powered by biofuels), and around 7% comes from wind power.

Figure 7 *A Swedish HEP station*

5 Carbon capture storage

In 2014, Boundary Dam in Canada's Saskatchewan Province became the world's first commercial carbon capture coal-fired power plant (see Figure 8). It aims to cut CO_2 emissions by 90% by trapping it underground before it can reach the atmosphere (see Section 2.7 on CCS). Saskatchewan's state-owned electricity provider expects to reduce greenhouse gas emissions by about 1 million tonnes a year, the equivalent of 250 000 cars.

Figure 8 *Boundary Dam CCS power station, Canada*

Global agreements and national actions

One of the main problems related to climate change is the uncertainty surrounding the rate and scale of the change. Rising global emissions affect all countries, but in different ways. Attempts to agree strategies to tackle climate change are notoriously difficult, because many countries try to protect their own interests. The most significant climate agreement to date has been the **2015 Paris Agreement**. At the UN's Paris Climate Conference (COP21) in December 2015, 195 countries adopted the first universally legally binding global climate deal. It set out an action plan to:

- limit the average global temperature increase to 1.5°C above pre-industrial levels
- report on the implementation of individual national plans to reduce emissions
- strengthen the ability to adapt to and be resilient in dealing with the impacts of climate change
- provide adaptation support for developing countries
- continue to support initiatives in developing countries aimed at reducing emissions.

The Paris Agreement came into force in November 2016 – 96 states, accounting jointly for 66% of global emissions, ratified the treaty.

Actions and attitudes

Achieving agreement about actions to deal with climate change depends on the co-operation of many groups:

- The **Governments** of countries at different levels of development may disagree about the best ways to achieve progress. Some fear that curbing emissions universally might hamper economic growth for developing countries, and also that they are being unfairly penalised now, given that the damage has already been done by existing industrialised nations. Governments are wary of losing votes by introducing energy levies or taxes to cut energy consumption.
- Globalisation has helped **TNCs** to develop trading advantages and access global markets. Reduced greenhouse gas emissions could increase their manufacturing costs. However, there are benefits in promoting 'green' consumer products.
- **People** in countries at risk from rising sea levels view climate change as more of an urgent problem than others. In Australia – one of the world's highest per capita energy consumers – there is growing resistance to policies that would put their coal miners out of work, or increase fuel costs.

Some claims about actions that are apparently achieving climate change goals can be deceptive. For example, a fall in CO_2 emissions across the EU in 2014–15 was less to do with changing attitudes and more to do with the fact that a warmer winter led to reduced energy consumption.

Over to you

1 **a** Using the data in Figure 1, plot a graph to show greenhouse gas emissions in the seven regions and countries shown.
b Calculate the means for each of the seven regions and countries and calculate the rates of change for 2001– 2012.
c In pairs, discuss the patterns shown by your data and the implications (**i**) globally, (**ii**) for the individual regions and countries.

2 Using your findings above, study Figures 2 and 3 and assess which of the projections is most likely. Justify your assessments.

3 In pairs, decide (**a**) whether changes to peatlands and permafrost represent positive or negative feedback mechanisms, and (**b**) how serious each of the tipping point scenarios might be.

4 **a** In pairs, complete a table to show the costs and benefits of each of the four adaptation and five mitigation strategies.
b Score each of the costs and benefits on a scale from 1 (weak) to 5 (strong). Add the scores.
c Which three strategies do you consider strongest? Justify your choices.

On your own

5 Write a 500-word analysis titled 'Is there a place for carbon pricing?'.

Exam-style question

Evaluate the responses from different players to the threat of a large-scale release of stored carbon caused by planetary warming. (*20 marks*)

Conclusion – revisiting the Enquiry Questions

These are the key questions that drive the whole topic:

1 How does the carbon cycle operate to maintain planetary health?

2 What are the consequences for people and the environment of our increasing demand for energy?

3 How are the carbon and water cycles linked to the global climate system?

Having studied this topic, you can now consider some answers to these questions, using the synoptic themes to frame your ideas.

Players – discussion point 1
Working in groups, consider two instances from this chapter where the actions taken by governments at different levels, or planners or users, were found to be in conflict over issues to do with energy supply and greenhouse gas emissions. Explain your views.

Attitudes and Actions – discussion point 2
Working in groups, discuss and draw a diagram which shows how and why people have different attitudes towards energy supply.

Futures and Uncertainties – discussion point 3
Working in groups, consider the different scenarios concerning (a) climate change, and (b) increased energy demand caused by economic growth, rising living standards and increased population. Use instances from this chapter to identify the actions that should be taken to manage greenhouse gas emissions. Explain your views.

Books, music, and films on this topic

Books to read

1. *The Quest: Energy, Security, and the Remaking of the Modern World* by Daniel Yergin (2011)

   This book looks at the pivotal role that energy plays in economic and political systems, together with the scope for change in future.

2. *Powerdown: Options and Actions for a Post-Carbon World* by Richard Heinberg (2004)

   This book assesses the implications of peak oil on the world's economy and different approaches to combat them.

3. *Energy Security: Economics, Politics, Strategies, and Implications* by Carlos Pascual and Jonathan Elkind (2009)

   This is an in-depth view into what energy security is and what it means for different countries.

Music to listen to

1. 'The Price of Oil' (2002) by Billy Bragg

   This is a protest song telling a story of global economics and society relying on oil prices and how these have led to wars.

2. 'Radioactive' (2013) by Imagine Dragons

   This song tells of a future with a possible energy revolution. It alludes to nuclear energy and its dangers.

3. 'Temper' (1996) by A System of a Down

   War and energy take centre stage in this protest song with an emphasis on the USA.

Films to see

1. *Switch* (2012)

   An insight into global energy use and what the future of energy may look like. It addresses the economics of future energy sources.

2. *Syriana* (2005)

   A geopolitical thriller in which a US energy firm loses control of Middle East oil fields, showing the impacts of energy insecurity.

3. *There Will Be Blood* (2007)

   A film about cashing in on the Californian oil boom in the late nineteenth and early twentieth centuries.

4. *Bitter Lake* (2015)

   A BBC documentary by British filmmaker Adam Curtis, which outlines the relationship between the USA and Saudi Arabia.

Superpowers

3

Chapter overview – introducing the topic

This chapter studies superpowers and shifting global influence in the modern world.

In the specification, this topic has been framed around three Enquiry Questions:

1 What are superpowers and how have they changed over time?

2 What are the impacts of superpowers on the global economy, political systems, and the physical environment?

3 What spheres of influence are contested by superpowers and what are the implications of this?

The sections in this chapter provide the content and concepts needed to help you answer these questions.

Synoptic themes

Underlying the content of every topic are three synoptic themes that 'bind' or glue the whole specification together:

1 Players

2 Attitudes and Actions

3 Futures and Uncertainties

1 Players

Players are individuals, groups and organisations involved in making decisions that affect people and places, collectively known as **stakeholders**. Players can be national or international individuals and organisations (e.g. IGOs like the UN), national and local governments, businesses (from small operations to the largest TNCs), as well as pressure groups and NGOs, together with others.

Players that you'll study in this topic include:

- Section 3.5 – The role of **TNCs** in maintaining power and wealth.
- Section 3.6 – The role of **powerful countries** as 'global police'.
- Section 3.9 – The role of **emerging powers** as potential superpowers.

2 Attitudes and Actions

The actions of superpowers and emerging superpowers have a very significant impact on the global economy, global politics and the environment. These depend on several factors:

- The political views of superpower governments (left- or right-wing, for example).
- Policies concerning people versus profit, and the importance of social justice and equality.
- Attitudes towards the environment.

Attitudes and Actions that you'll study in this topic include:

- Section 3.6 – Those of global IGOs in international decision-making.
- Section 3.7 – Those of different countries in reducing carbon emissions and reaching global agreements on environmental issues.
- Section 3.8 – Those of global players in relation to resources.
- Section 3.9 – Contrasting cultural ideologies between the USA and emerging powers.

3 Futures and Uncertainties

Decisions and actions taken by superpowers and key players today will affect people in the future. Faced with global economic or environmental issues now, for example, will similar problems occur in the future, or have lessons been learned? Do those who are most susceptible to the impacts of global decision-making today face a bleak or a better future?

Futures and Uncertainties that you'll study in this topic include:

- Section 3.10 – The uncertainty over future power structures in the changing balances of global power.

3.1 Making an impact

In this section, you'll learn how geopolitical power can be assessed in both 'hard' and 'soft' ways.

Strictly reaches 50!

In April 2014, there were big celebrations at the BBC in London. *Strictly Come Dancing*, one of the UK's most popular TV programmes, had added another overseas franchise to its list of countries producing their own versions of the programme – making 50 in all! Known as *Dancing with the Stars* beyond the UK, the *Strictly* format is produced elsewhere under licence, from which the BBC receives substantial royalties. From its first UK broadcast in 2004, the *Strictly* format has now spread to countries as diverse as Australia, Sweden (see Figure 1), Kazakhstan and India. Slovenia was the fiftieth overseas franchise to be sold.

Figure 1 *The 2015 winners of* Dancing with the Stars, *Sweden's version of the BBC's overseas brand for* Strictly Come Dancing

As well as successful formats, the BBC also sells its own programmes overseas. Even with a change of presenters in 2016, the UK version of *Top Gear* is shown in over 100 countries, and on most international airlines, and is the world's most popular TV series. Together with BBC News, it gives the Corporation huge global reach, and is a major part of the UK's continuing influence in the world. It's an example of the UK's '**soft power**', a term first used in 1990 by Joseph Nye, a political scientist at Harvard University. He used it to describe the power that arises from three of a country's resources:

- its **culture** (in places where that's attractive to others)
- its **political values** (e.g. its democracy or its overseas image)
- its **foreign policies** (where these have a widely supported moral authority).

Hard and soft power

If 'soft' power exists, then logically there must also be a thing called '**hard power**'. At its extreme, hard power is the expression of a country's will or influence through military force. However, few actions or policies actually result in military force, and there are many other ways of wielding power, as Figure 2 shows. The contrast between hard and soft power is therefore best seen as a spectrum, which consists of a range of actions that could be taken by countries to express their power or influence. Nye claimed that the world's most powerful and influential countries use a combination of hard and soft power to achieve what he called 'smart power'.

Figure 2 *The 'hard' and 'soft' power spectrum*

Hard power				**Soft power**
Military force or its threat	Economic sanctions and diplomatic actions	Coercive policy, e.g. tied aid or trade agreements	Political influence, moral authority, economic influence	Cultural attractiveness

Creating a soft-power index

In 2012, the UK-based magazine *Monocle*, together with the UK Institute for Government, produced a soft-power index. It used a range of data, such as: overseas aid contributions, the number of embassies operating overseas, income inequality, democracy and personal freedoms (e.g. the recognition of gay marriage). In the index, shown in Figure 3, some 'small' countries exert influence well above their size, e.g. Sweden (5th). Of the world's larger countries (both in size and population) Brazil scores highly (17th), but China (21st), Russia (28th), and India (36th) do not – mainly due to a lack of personal freedoms there. The UK topped the league, partly because 2012 was the year of the London Olympics, and also because of the high level of personal freedoms in the UK compared to many other countries.

Rank	Country	Score
1	UK	7.289
2	USA	6.989
3	Germany	6.484
4	France	6.472
5	Sweden	5.752
6	Japan	5.613
7	Denmark	5.598
8	Switzerland	5.553
9	Australia	5.534
10	Canada	5.417
11	South Korea	5.350
12	Norway	5.327
13	Finland	5.267
14	Italy	5.186
15	Netherlands	5.161
16	Spain	4.981
17	Brazil	4.675
18	Austria	4.650
19	Belgium	4.556
20	Turkey	4.263

Figure 3 *'Soft power' rankings produced by the magazine Monocle and the UK Institute for Government in 2012*

How effective is soft power?

China has recently expanded its military power and range of weapons in order to add to its position as an economic power. However, hard military power is not always successful, and it's also expensive, both in terms of money and lives. In recent years, China has sought to increase its geopolitical and economic influence through investment in Africa and Australia for mineral resources (see Sections 3.3 and 3.9). As Section 3.5 shows, the USA uses its influence in the WTO to promote 'free trade'.

Many countries rely on soft power for overseas influence, because it's both attractive and effective. For some decades, the Olympic and Paralympic Games have been used by host countries to improve their global 'brand'. Rio's Games in 2016 (see Figure 4) were part of Brazil's aspiration as an emerging economy to join global power rankings, following Tokyo, Japan (1964), Seoul, South Korea (1988) and Beijing, China (2008).

Figure 4 *The Maracana football stadium, site of the Rio Olympics opening ceremony in 2016 – it was hoped that the Games would raise Brazil's profile on the global rankings of influence and power*

Over to you

1. Copy Figure 2 and add rows for 'UK examples' and 'Examples from other countries'. In pairs, add examples to each type of hard and soft power.
2. In groups, select one each of China, Russia and India. Research examples which explain (**a**) its low position in 'soft power' rankings, (**b**) how it could improve its ranking. Your research could include human rights, democracy and personal freedoms. Present your findings.

On your own

3. Using examples, explain how culture and sport, political values and foreign policies can improve a country's soft-power ranking.
4. Select one country from Figure 3. Research how its characteristics have placed it in the top 20 rankings.

3.2 What is a superpower?

In this section, you'll learn how geopolitical power stems from a range of countries' human and physical characteristics.

EQ1 In Sections 3.2 to 3.4, you'll ask what superpowers are and how they've changed over time.

KEY CONCEPT

- **Causality** – exploring the causes that allow some countries to claim superpower status, but not others

What does 'superpower' mean?

Type 'superpower' into an Internet search engine and you'll find several definitions. One – by a writer, Alice Lyman Miller – defines a superpower as a country with 'the capacity to project dominating **power** and **influence** anywhere in the world, sometimes in more than one region of the globe at a time'. The word was first used at the end of the Second World War to describe the global influence held by the British Empire, the USA and the USSR (Soviet Union).

However, since 1945, the world has changed:

- The British Empire has disappeared, with its members gaining independence.
- The Soviet Union collapsed in 1991, breaking up into 15 independent states.
- Only the USA remains as a major power. Indeed, it has had so much power in recent decades that it has become a **hegemon**, or supreme power.

However, the twenty-first century has started to provide challenges to American power. For example, the BRICs – Brazil, Russia, India and China – all aim for superpower status in their own right, however ambitious that may be.

But how does a country gain power and influence? Seven factors that help to assess who might rival the USA now or in the future are:

1. physical size and geographical position
2. economic power and influence
3. demographic factors
4. political factors
5. military strength
6. cultural influence
7. access to natural resources.

1 Physical size and geographical position

Physical size and geographical position are important, because each one determines the area over which a country has potential influence. Larger countries usually have greater resources and influence.

For example, Russia is the world's largest country (see Figure 1); it covers a vast area from the Baltic to the Pacific, with feet in both Europe and Asia, and it controls significant resources as a result. One example is the Arctic region – and the vast untapped natural resources that lie beneath it – which is mainly under the influence of Russia and Canada, because they are the largest countries bordering the region.

However Russia's relations with its neighbours are complex because, as Figure 1 shows, there are 14 of them – varying from Norway (a democracy) to China (an authoritarian one-party state). Russia exerts its influence over each neighbour in different ways.

Figure 1 *The world's six largest countries*

Country	Approximate area (km^2)	Time zones	Land neighbours that it potentially influences
1 Russia	17 million	11	Azerbaijan, Belarus, China, Estonia, Finland, Georgia, Kazakhstan, North Korea, Latvia, Lithuania, Mongolia, Norway, Poland, Ukraine
2 Canada	10 million	6	USA
3 USA	9.8 million	4	Canada, Mexico (and it's also a mere 75 km from Russia across the frozen Bering Strait)
4 China	9.6 million	5	Afghanistan, Bhutan, Burma (Myanmar), India, Kazakhstan, North Korea, Kyrgyzstan, Laos, Mongolia, Nepal, Pakistan, Russia, Tajikistan, Vietnam, Hong Kong, Macau
5 Brazil	8.5 million	4	Argentina, Bolivia, Colombia, French Guiana, Guyana, Paraguay, Peru, Suriname, Uruguay, Venezuela
6 Australia	7.7 million	2-3	None

2 Economic power and influence

Has China's rapid industrialization been sufficient to challenge the USA as ***the*** economic superpower? Figure 2 shows the world's ten largest economies by percentage of global GDP. These countries influence much of the overall global economy. Between them, they:

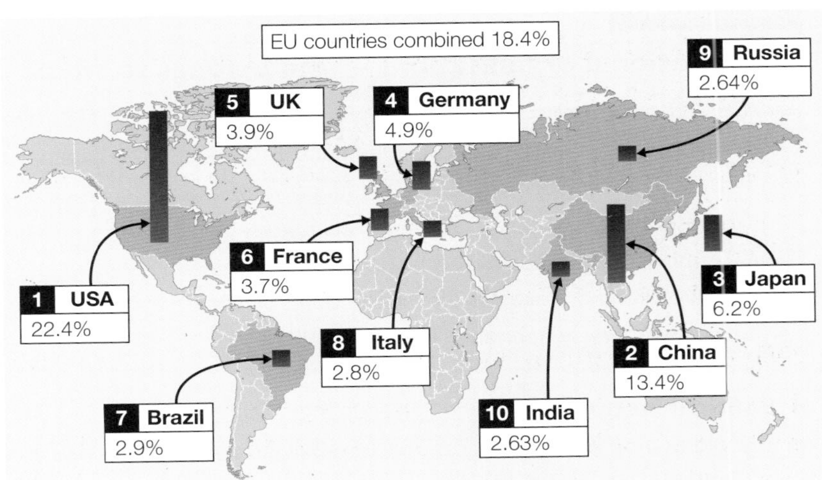

Figure 2 *The world's ten largest economies in 2015. The data show the percentage of global GDP produced by each country.*

- **earn 65% of global GDP**. They earn the greatest amounts and then they spend it! The world's five largest consumer markets are the USA, China, Japan, Germany and the UK.
- **control investment**. Most investment is targeted in these ten countries, because companies investing there are more likely to make bigger profits. In 2015, half of all global investment passed through London, creating jobs in London's financial sector (e.g. investment banks, insurance, legal services).
- have the world's most **powerful currencies**, e.g. the US dollar and – despite its weaknesses – the euro. The EU and the USA between them produce over 40% of global GDP. Their currencies are therefore seen as relatively 'safe', together with the UK pound, the Swiss franc and the Singapore dollar.
- determine global **economic policies**, by joining political and economic organisations such as the G20, or trading blocs (e.g. the EU). Their strength determines what happens to global trade or interest rates.

The world's 20 largest economies also give the most aid to the world's poor. They decide which countries receive aid, and the conditions under which that aid may be given. In some cases, aid is granted only to those agreeing to policies specified by the countries providing aid.

3 Demographic factors

Figure 3 shows the world's ten most populous countries. Population size can be a key to economic success, e.g. by providing a sufficient labour force to generate economic growth. The UK has used inward migration since the 1990s as a means of increasing its labour force in shortage areas. China and India each use their large populations as a source of cheap labour in manufacturing. A large population also spurs economic growth because it provides a market. For example, all EU member states have access to a single market of over 500 million people, made up of their combined domestic populations.

Yet a large population is not critical to power. Singapore's total population is about half that of London – yet it has a major influence on Southeast Asia's economy, through attracting investment, and it has also become a key player in the economy of the whole Asia region.

Figure 3 *The world's ten most populous countries in 2015*

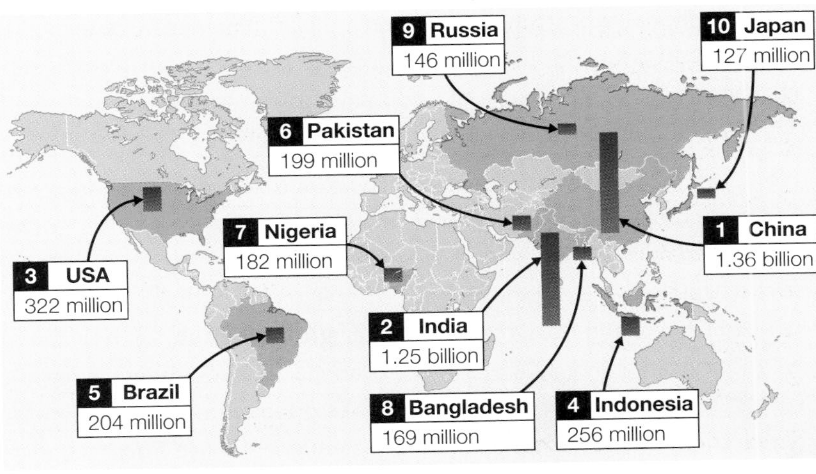

BACKGROUND

International organisations – who belongs to what?

- **OECD members:** Australia, Austria, Belgium, Canada, Chile, Czech Republic, Denmark, Estonia, Finland, France, Germany, Greece, Hungary, Iceland, Ireland, Israel, Italy, Japan, South Korea, Latvia, Luxembourg, Mexico, Netherlands, New Zealand, Norway, Poland, Portugal, Slovak Republic, Slovenia, Spain, Sweden, Switzerland, Turkey, UK, USA.
- **G8 members:** Canada, France, Germany, Italy, Japan, Russia, UK, USA.
- **G20 members:** The G8 members plus Argentina, Australia, Brazil, China, European Union (as a single member), India, Indonesia, Mexico, Saudi Arabia, South Africa, South Korea, Turkey.

4 Political factors

In a world of international migrations, extensive trade partnerships and capital transfers, few individual countries hold much influence in their own right. Most have decided that greater influence can be achieved by linking up with like-minded countries. In 1960, the Organisation for Economic Cooperation and Development (OECD) began with 20 of the world's most-developed economies as founder members, and it now has 35. Its aim is to promote global development by sharing common issues and policies.

However, other international organisations have now superceded the OECD in influence:

- Until recently, the most influential group was the G8 – a group of eight OECD members whose economies were amongst the world's largest.
- But as the global shift in economic power has moved towards Asia (see Figure 2), there has been a shift away from the established G8. A much broader group – the G20 – now includes the G8 members plus 12 others. It includes all of the BRICs (Brazil, Russia, India and China) and the EU (as a single entity). The G20 has become an increasingly significant decision-making forum, and between its members it now represents half of the world's population.

The role of these international organisations has become more significant as economic problems now assume a global dimension. For example, in 2008, the G20 collectively organised a recovery plan to tackle the global banking crisis.

5 Military strength

Historically, military strength has been a major influence in determining power. Most countries use military forces to protect themselves against challengers, so one measure of a country's power is the size of its military. The world's ten largest armies are shown in Figure 4.

However, military size is often less significant than national defence budgets and technology. As Figure 5 shows, the USA dominates all other countries in terms of military budget and capability, with 37% of all global military spending; China is a distant second. US military technology is also ahead of both China's and Russia's, with greater **global reach**, i.e. how far weaponry can travel. 12% of the USA's annual military budget is spent on research, development and testing – that's double the amount spent on research by China, and nearly as much as Russia's entire military budget.

Rank	Country	Size of army
1	China	2 333 000
2	USA	1 492 200
3	India	1 325 000
4	North Korea	1 190 000
5	Russia	845 000
6	Pakistan	643 800
7	South Korea	630 000
8	Iran	523 000
9	Turkey	510 600
10	Vietnam	482 000

Figure 4 *The world's ten largest armies in 2016*

Rank	Country	Military spending (US$ billion)
1	USA	597.5
2	China	145.8
3	Saudi Arabia	81.9
4	Russia	81.8
5	UK	56.2
6	India	48.0
7	France	46.8
8	Japan	41.0
9	Germany	36.7
10	South Korea	33.5

Figure 5 *The world's ten largest military budgets in 2016*

In recent years China has expanded its military but, as Figure 6 shows, its interests lie mainly in the Asia region. Its military interest beyond that is minor at present. China's focus is the security of the South China Sea – inside the two island chains shown in Figure 6 – of which many are disputed territories (see page 137). China aims to dominate the seas as far as the First Island Chain, which it sees as its sphere of influence.

Many countries regard membership of the UN Security Council as the ultimate status in military power. There are five permanent Security Council members (the USA, UK, Russia, China and France), and its job is mainly a balancing act to approve military intervention only when justified in particular conflicts. Its permanent membership is based on those countries that were considered victors of the Second World War in 1945. But as other countries have grown economically and in military status (e.g. India, Pakistan and Israel), permanent membership of the Security Council is contentious.

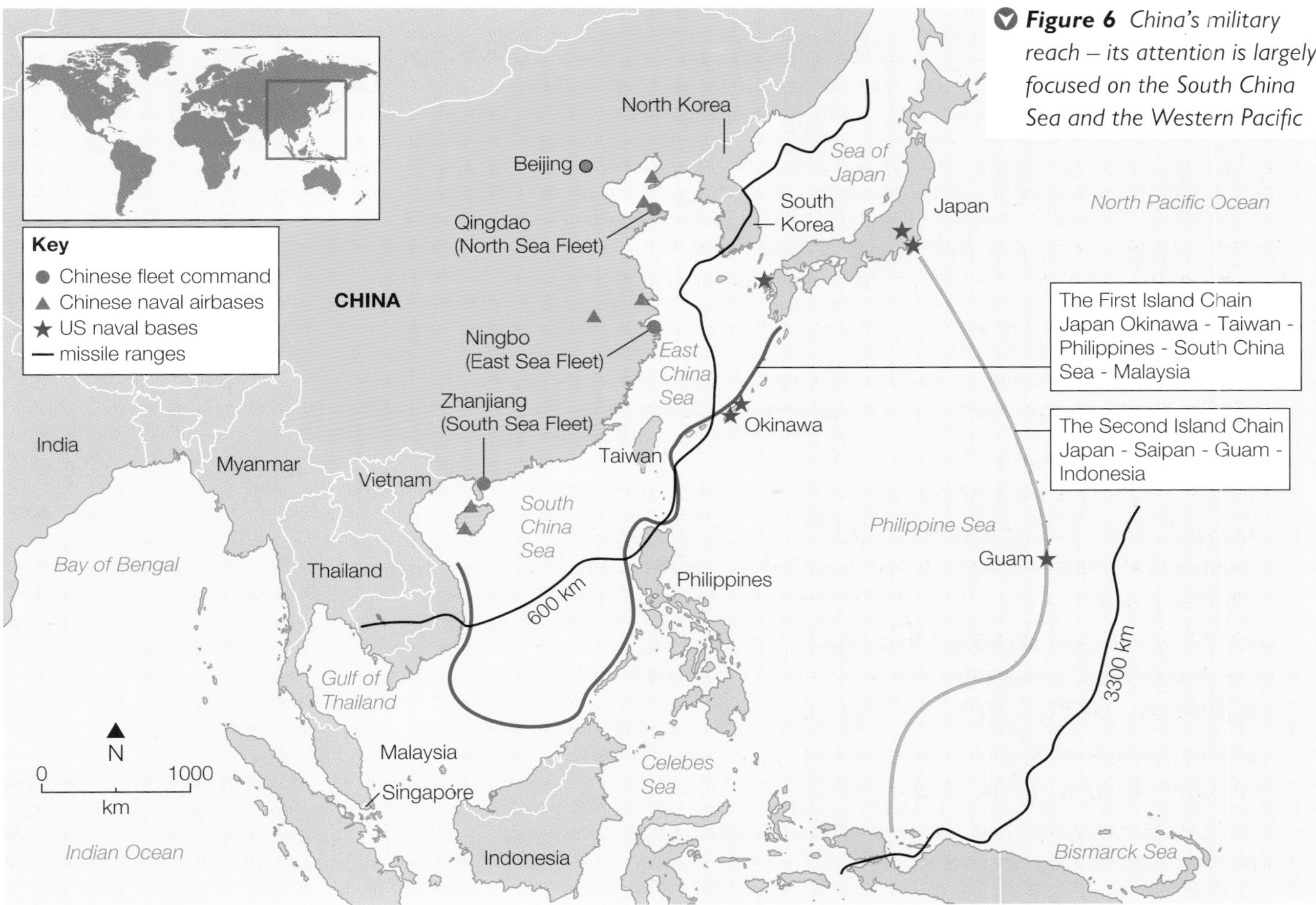

Figure 6 *China's military reach – its attention is largely focused on the South China Sea and the Western Pacific*

6 Cultural influence

If you read *The Times* or *The Sun* newspapers, or watch *The Simpsons*, you are providing income for News Corporation and its owner Rupert Murdoch. News Corporation is an American media company that began in Australia, and which has extensive interests including film production, newspapers, satellite TV and a strong influence on global affairs. Its newspapers carry particular political viewpoints with wide influence:

- Every winning political party in UK General Elections since 1979 has been promoted by *The Sun*. In the 2016 referendum campaign, it argued against Britain's EU membership.
- News Corporation actively promotes Christianity, and Fox News in the USA has been strongly in favour of the 'War on Terror'.

Increased globalisation has led to a global culture, spread via multimedia TNCs such as Time-Warner, Disney, News Corporation (all American), or Sony (Japanese). They dominate global culture by deciding which films people can watch, which radio stations they can listen to and what music is recorded and played. Similarly, most UK commercial radio stations are owned by a few large companies, and three record companies (Sony BMG, Universal and Warner) dominate UK music production.

7 Access to natural resources

Some resources are essential to economic development, e.g. oil or metals. Iron ore (see Figure 7) is the basis of a steel industry, while energy sources such as oil, gas and coal are used in electricity production or industrial processing. However, the possession of natural resources does not of itself guarantee development. Many countries' natural resources are actually managed by major TNCs, e.g. Shell and BP have developed many of Nigeria's oilfields. Australia has huge reserves of iron ore, but it exports most of it (to China) and gains little of the value added by manufacturing. Nonetheless, possession of key resources gives some leverage over others, e.g. the influence of OPEC countries in setting global oil prices.

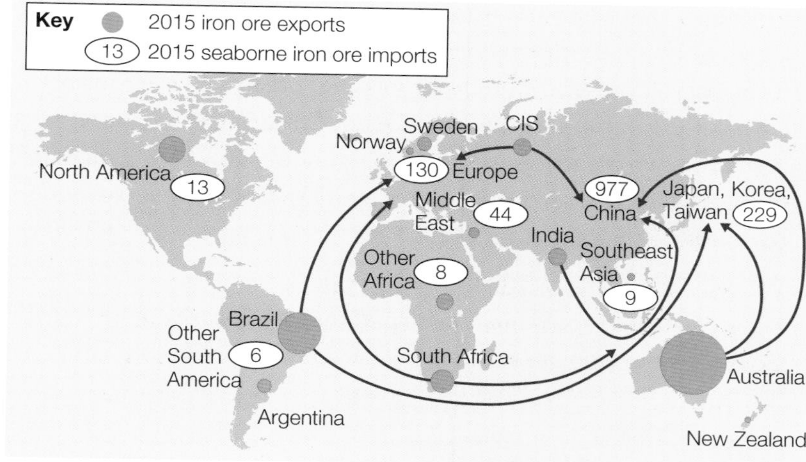

Figure 7 *Global trade flows between iron ore exporting countries and markets in 2015. The orange circles are proportional to the amounts of iron ore exported, and the import numbers are in million tonnes. The map therefore shows iron ore 'superpowers'*

The changing centre of power

Studying the geographical expression of power is a branch of Geography known as **geopolitics**. Geographers are interested in the changing shift of global power, and the mechanisms for maintaining it. The late twentieth and early twenty-first centuries have shown shifts in the balance of power between different countries.

Mackinder's 'heartland'

The geographical balance of power and how it has changed is illustrated by a theory developed in 1904 by Halford John Mackinder, an early-twentieth-century geographer. His theory, known as **geo-strategic location theory**, argued that whoever controlled Europe and Asia (the world's biggest landmass) would control the world. He identified a **heartland** called the 'world island', from Eastern Europe into Russia, at the centre of which was a 'pivot' (see Figure 8).

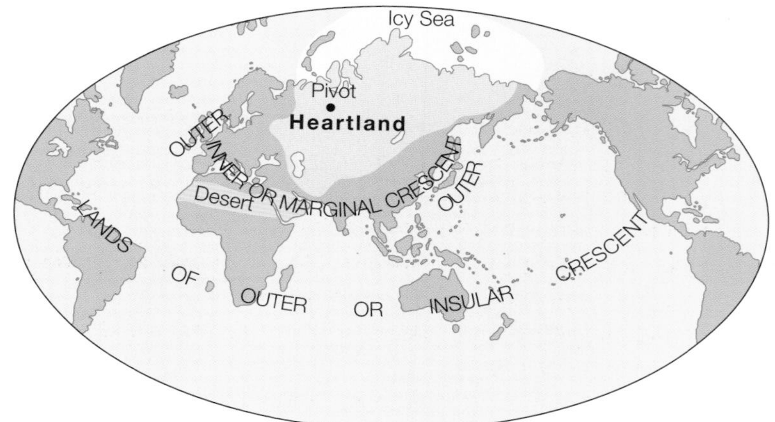

Figure 8 *Mackinder's 'heartland'*

Mackinder believed that three things determined power in this region:

- Whoever ruled the most strategic part of Europe would command the heartland.
- Whoever ruled the heartland would command the world island, i.e. Europe and Russia.
- Whoever controlled the world island ruled the world.

The further away from the heartland a country was, the less influence it would have – on the map these are shown as 'Inner or Marginal Crescent' and 'Outer or Insular Crescent'.

According to Mackinder's theory, Russia *should* be the world's global power; its location and resources give it many advantages. However, Mackinder also believed that Russia has two natural disadvantages:

- Its many borders (see Figure 1) mean that it can be attacked from many directions.
- Because much of its coast is frozen in winter, it has few year-round ports.

Mackinder thought that the 'heartland' could shift geographically – especially as a result of sea power. He also believed that Britain's nineteenth-century industrialisation had shifted the centre of power westwards. Using sea power, he believed that the UK could dominate everywhere from Western Europe to the Pacific, as well as the Eurasian land mass – and potentially the world.

The twenty-first century global shift

What Mackinder called the 'heartland' has certainly been the pivot of power over time, but it is changing. Figure 9 shows how the position of the global economic centre of gravity has changed since the year AD1.

- In Figure 9, the centre is 'pulled' towards the country/region with the largest GDP – so the map shows the importance of the British industrial revolution (1820-1913), and how it shifts with the industrial rise of the USA (1913-1960)
- The changing positions between 2000 and the predicted change by 2025 reflect the growing importance of China. The shift between 2000, 2010 and then to 2025 is the fastest in history.
- Asia's rise since 1960, and China's since 1990, helps to restore the pre-1800 situation (and is viewed that way in China).

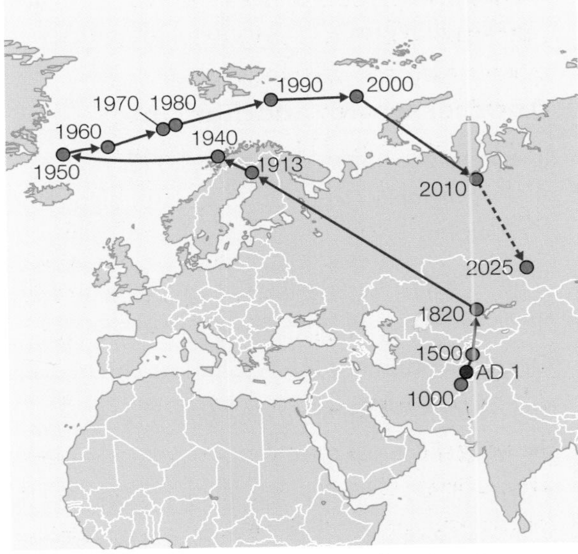

Figure 9 *The changing centre of gravity of power since AD1*

Over to you

1. In pairs, discuss and then rank which criteria are most important in creating the world's superpowers – physical size, economic power, demographic factors, political factors, military strength, cultural influence, and access to natural resources.
2. Refer to Figures 1 and 2 in Section 6.1. Using these two figures to guide you, design your own versions to create:
   - **a** a simple global power index, using the tables and maps of data in this section
   - **b** a weighted index, in which you decide which criteria are more important in creating a true index of global power.
3. Devise a short presentation to the class to explain your ranking of countries by their index of global power.
4. Using these criteria, use data in this section to decide which of the following countries or groups deserve the title of 'superpower', with your reasons: the USA, the EU, Russia, China, Brazil, the UK, France, Germany, Japan, plus one country or group not in this list but which you think should be considered.

On your own

5. Research the 'worldmapper' website (worldmapper.org). Select and justify three ***other*** criteria to help decide who are the world's superpowers.
6. Using the evidence in this section, decide on the strengths and weaknesses of Mackinder's geo-strategic location theory.
7. Write 600 words on 'To what extent has Mackinder's geo-strategic location theory stood the test of time?'

Exam-style question

Assess the extent to which geopolitical power stems from a range of countries' human and physical characteristics. (*12 marks*)

3.3 Changing patterns of power

In this section, you'll learn how patterns of power change over time and can be uni-, bi- or multi-polar.

KEY CONCEPTS

- **Causality** – the causes of geopolitical power, conflict and balance
- **Equilibrium** – the balance of power between nations of similar strengths

Another world, another time

Imagine a geography class in the 1890s reading the following excerpt from *A new geography comparative,* a textbook published in 1894 by Professor J. D. Meiklejohn:

'When the first European settlers visited [Australia], *they found … not the smallest trace … of what is called civilisation.'*

Or this, written in 1881 by Charlotte M. Mason:

'the aborigines, who are a miserable race of savages … do not seem able to learn the ways of civilised men.'

Today these comments would be regarded as racist, but this was how Victorian writers saw the world; and Victorian students learnt their geography by reading about it. The above writers made no mention of the highly developed skills used by Australia's aboriginal groups to enable them to live in the harsh desert environment (see Figure 1); nor that their beliefs about spirits, land and culture were as complex as Christianity.

Figure 1 *The Australian desert environment provided food, water and shelter to aboriginal peoples. These rock paintings are several hundred years old – dating from well before white colonists arrived in Australia in 1788.*

Key word

Colonialism – Where an external nation takes direct control of a territory, often by force.

Like all of the 'pink' parts of the world shown in Figure 2, Australia in the nineteenth century was under British **colonial** rule, as part of the British Empire. It was imperial power with the British monarch as Head of State. Other European countries, such as France and Spain, also had colonial empires – so there was no single superpower. This was a **multi-polar** world – with several poles or centres – although the British Empire was the largest.

British (and other European) people **believed** that it was right to colonise and rule over the world, both:

- **politically**, because land gave power, and
- **economically**, because colonies possessed raw materials and provided a market for European manufactured goods.

Although many colonies were taken without force, colonial power was maintained by populating them with British farmers, colonial administrators and military forces. The indigenous peoples were suppressed, their cultures were ignored, and their land was taken. Racist language was frequently used to describe them. Colonialism was supported by a belief in moral superiority – that God was on Britain's side. Colonialists argued that they brought stability and trade. However, there were frequent uprisings.

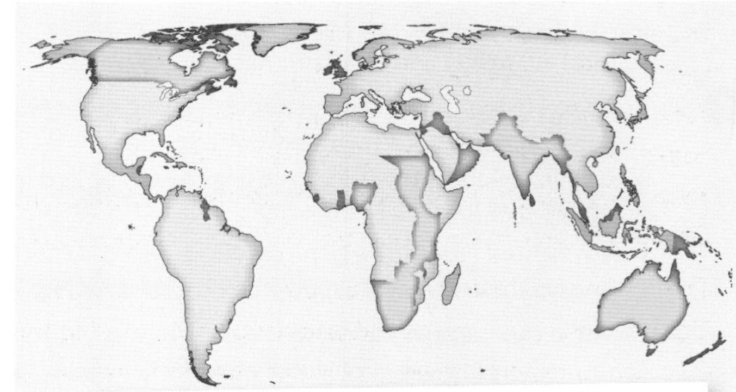

Rule Britannia!
When Britain first at Heav'n's command
Arose from out the azure main;
Arose, arose from out the azure main;
This was the charter, the charter of the land,
And guardian angels sang this strain:
Rule, Britannia! Britannia, rule the waves!
Britons never, never, never shall be slaves!

Figure 2 *The areas shaded pink on the map were those ruled over by Britain as part of the British Empire. The lyrics of 'Rule Britannia' show that Britain believed it was fulfilling 'Heav'n's command'.*

The emergence of a bi-polar world

Different patterns of power bring varying stability and risk. Colonialism gave the UK political and economic power, which lasted for decades, but there were underlying historical developments that would ultimately challenge this:

- Rapid American industrialisation after the 1860s challenged British economic power. Transcontinental rail links – and the exploitation of huge reserves of coal and metals (and later oil) – gave the USA an economic power base which allowed it to overtake the UK economically by the 1880s.
- The Russian Revolution of 1917 created a massive new federal state – the USSR or Soviet Union – and communist governments under Lenin (1917-24) and Stalin (1924-53) undertook massive and rapid industrialisation. By 1941, the USSR had overtaken the UK as the world's second largest economy, and as a result was able to resist the German onslaught in the Second World War.

Figure 3 European members of NATO, and the position of the Iron Curtain, during the Cold War (see page 110). The 'curtain' existed between 1945 and 1990, when former communist countries of Eastern Europe abandoned communism. Most former Warsaw Pact members are now part of NATO.

By 1945, a **bi-polar** – two-sided – world had emerged, with the USA and the USSR establishing themselves as global powers. Power was maintained militarily, politically, economically and culturally.

Military influence

The **military** basis of power between the USA and the USSR was significant. Russian political and military influence extended through Eastern and Central Europe after the end of the Second World War. In 1944–5, Russian tanks swept through Eastern Europe to the heart of Germany, to ensure a strong bargaining position in post-war peace negotiations – and also to reduce the power of Germany, which was split in 1945 into occupied military zones (the eastern zone occupied by the USSR). The occupied military zones became two separate countries – the Russian zone became East Germany, and the British/French/US zones became West Germany. Germany stayed as two countries until German reunification in 1990.

The USSR also deliberately created a buffer of 'friendly' countries in Eastern and Central Europe to shield it from possible future attacks from the West. In effect, it installed communist governments in satellite states, including Poland, Hungary and East Germany, under Moscow's influence. The border between Eastern and Western Europe became known as the 'Iron Curtain' (see Figure 3), and it was heavily defended. At its most extreme was the Berlin Wall, built in 1961 (see Figure 4), which divided the city between East and West Germany, even though geographically Berlin was located within East Germany.

Figure 4 The Berlin Wall, visible evidence of the Iron Curtain between Eastern and Western Europe.

The result was a balance of power between the West and the USSR. Both sides had nuclear weapons, and military alliances formed on either side of the 'curtain' (see Figure 3):

- Those countries supporting the USSR formed the Warsaw Pact (military) and the Council for Mutual Economic Assistance (for economic strength).
- Those countries supporting the USA formed the North Atlantic Treaty Organisation (NATO).

Political influence

The post-war period ushered in a time of post-colonial power, in which major powers used **political influence** rather than direct or military rule. The Eastern European countries were not *directly* ruled by Moscow – but its influence ranged from economic planning to military operations. Elections were held, but all candidates were Communist Party members approved by Moscow. Any deviation from Moscow's policies was dealt with harshly, even with military invasion, as was the case in Hungary in 1956 and Czechoslovakia in 1968.

The period of balanced power between the USA and the USSR became known as the 'Cold War', with an uneasy peace maintained by NATO. Some countries outside Europe were supported by one side or the other, such as Russia's support for Fidel Castro in Cuba. It is often argued that the balance between the two power blocs created global stability, but there were still serious clashes – such as the 1962 Cuban missile crisis. However, behind any political clash there always lay the nuclear threat to both sides, which prevented open conflict from breaking out.

Economic influence

As well as building stocks of nuclear weapons throughout NATO, the USA adopted a strategy of extending its economic influence. After 1945, it strengthened Western European countries through its Marshall Plan – a programme of financial aid shown in Figure 5A. The aim was to rebuild war damage, promote economic development and prevent the poverty that was believed to be the root cause of communist influence.

US influence also grew with inward investment into countries such as Japan, Singapore and the Philippines, to enable economic growth and prevent the further spread of communism. In the 1970s, the 'Asian Tiger' economies, such as Singapore, grew supported by American investment. This influence is known as **neo-colonialism** (new colonialism), and has greatly influenced global development. However, as Figure 5B shows, many of the current US aid programmes are focused on military, rather than development, aims.

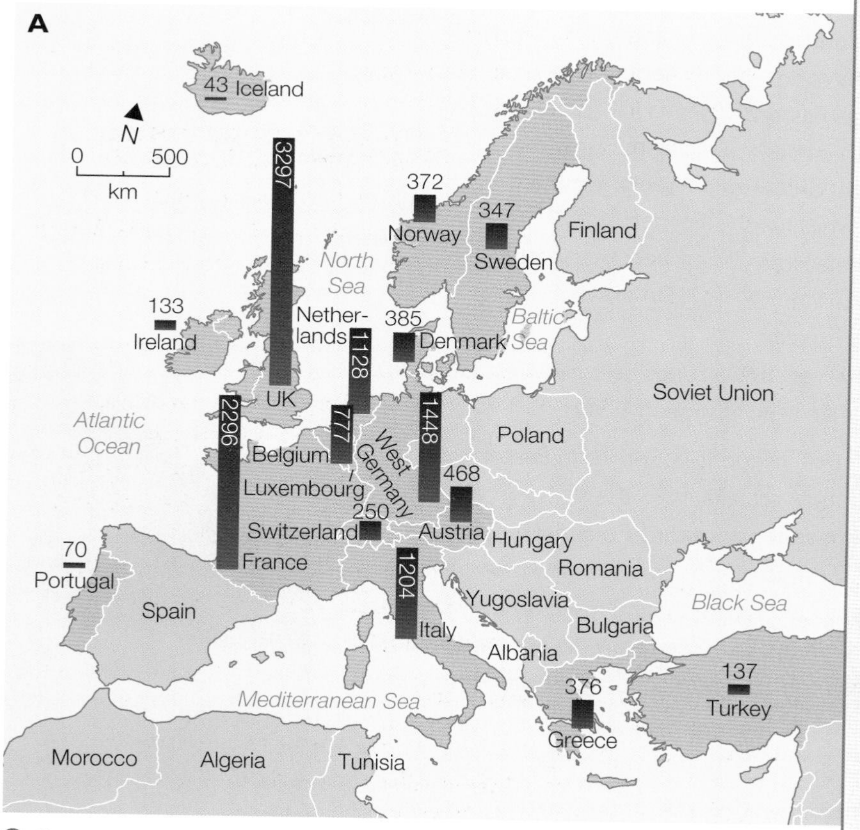

Factfile: US aid in 2014 **B**

Total aid granted: US$35 billion

Almost a quarter went to five countries:

- **Israel**: US$3.1 billion (about 9% of the total) – was used for military financing
- **Egypt**: US$1.5 billion – almost 90% was used for military activity
- **Afghanistan**: US$1.1 billion; **Jordan**: US$1.0 billion; and **Pakistan**: US$933 million – almost all was used for economic development

Of the US$35 billion spent:

- US$8.4 billion (24%) went towards global health programmes
- US$5.9 billion (17%) was used for foreign military financing
- US$4.6 billion (13%) provided economic support (e.g. debt cancellation)
- US$2.5 billion (7%) was used for development assistance.

Figure 5 *US aid: (**A**) to European countries as part of the Marshall Plan between 1948 and 1952 (in US$ millions), and (**B**) the top five recipients in 2014 and the main uses to which the aid money was put*

Cultural influence

The Cold War was based on propaganda rather than military conflict. Although the Korean and Vietnam Wars resulted in armed conflict against communist expansion, propaganda between the two sides was to last for several decades. In the USA, the McCarthy trials – led by Senator McCarthy in the early 1950s – were designed to expose to the American public any suspect with communist leanings. Accusations were reported daily on television and radio. Hollywood also produced films designed to generate suspicion of communists (e.g. 'The Red Menace'), portraying the US in a moral, freedom-fighting light. You can find out more by searching 'The Red Scare: A Filmography' online.

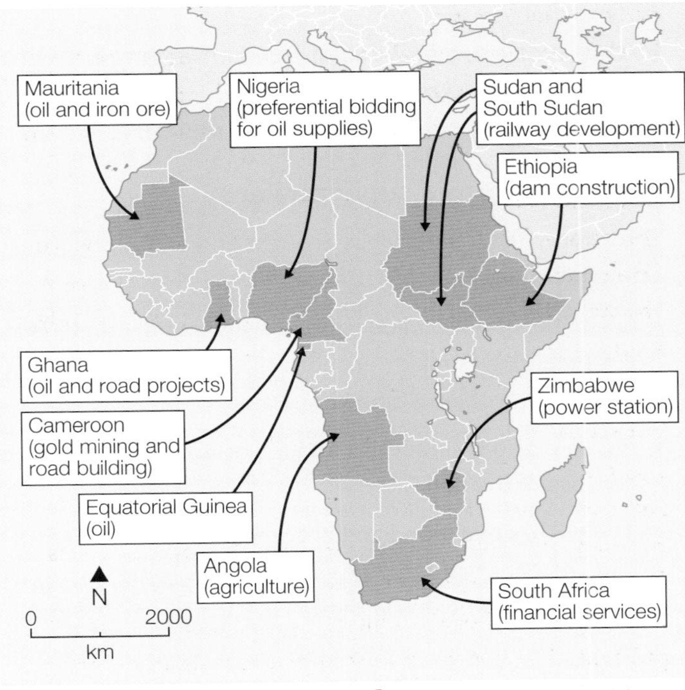

Figure 6 *The main African recipients of Chinese investment, 2004–2014*

The rise of China

In November 1989, the Berlin Wall fell – followed shortly by East Germany's communist government. Within months, other communist governments in Eastern Europe collapsed, followed in 1991 by the USSR itself. It left the USA as the sole superpower in a **uni-polar** world – i.e. without rivals. Since then, its economic, cultural, political and military strength has been virtually unrivalled.

However, in recent years, China's rapid economic growth – and the dependence of the USA on China for manufactured goods – has challenged America's power and influence. China is also seeking global influence through, for example, its investment in many African countries (see Figure 6). And it's also expanding militarily (see Section 3.2). However, China's economic progress also presents domestic risks. Its government, which censors the Internet and limits personal freedoms, is increasingly facing opposition as its population becomes better educated and financially better off. Section 3.4 explores this in detail.

Exam-style question

Explain two ways in which nations have maintained power and influence over other countries. *(6 marks)*

Over to you

1 In pairs, research a six-slide PowerPoint on one former British colony. Focus on (**a**) the reasons for the colonisation; (**b**) how local people were treated by the British; (**c**) how power was maintained; (**d**) challenges to the colonial authorities.

2 **a** In pairs, research world maps to show past, present and future influence and political alliances of the following:
- **i** a European country (not the UK) with a colonial Empire
- **ii** a non-European country which became very powerful in the twentieth century
- **iii** a non-European country which you think will become more powerful in the twenty-first century.

b Write a report of 750 words, including maps, on the changing influence of these countries.

3 **a** In pairs, draw four large overlapping circles (a Venn diagram), labelled political, military, economic, and cultural. In each, label ways in which the UK, USA, USSR and China maintained power. Use Figures 2, 3, 5 and 6 to help.

b Which of the four circles is (**i**) most and (**ii**) least important in giving countries power and influence? Suggest reasons.

On your own

4 Distinguish between the following groups of terms: (**a**) uni-, bi- and multi-polar power; (**b**) colonialism and neo-colonialism.

5 Explain how aid (Figure 5) and investment overseas (Figure 6) can extend a country's power and influence.

3.4 Emerging superpowers?

In this section, you'll learn how emerging powers vary in their influence, and that this can change rapidly over time.

Rising economic superpowers

The twenty-first century has brought enormous political and economic changes:

- China's economic influence is growing rapidly, and India and Brazil are emerging as major economies, although not without some economic problems along the way.
- Russia is also re-emerging as a major economic power, after the 1991 collapse of the USSR.
- The EU has expanded and become the world's largest economic trading bloc. Its expansion to 28 member states (prior to the UK leaving) means that it now competes with the USA for global economic dominance. In 2015, it actually exceeded the USA in terms of economic power (see Figure 1), although it still lags behind in terms of GDP per capita, productivity per employee, Internet usage and car ownership.
- The emerging economies of Asia, including India and Indonesia, are growing so rapidly that they are likely to be major global players by 2050, as Figure 2 shows. The predictions outlined in Figure 2 were made in 2015 by the consultancy company PwC (formerly known as PricewaterhouseCoopers), based on current GDP and growth rates and likely global shifts towards Asia.

KEY CONCEPTS

- **Causality** – the causes of economic and political emergence among some nations
- **Equilibrium** – how the balance of power can change as different nations emerge economically and politically

	USA	EU
GDP total in US$ PPP	17.5 trillion	18.3 trillion
% growth per year	2.4%	1.9%

Figure 1 *Comparing 2015 economic data between the USA and the EU. The data are in US$ PPP (Purchasing Power Parity) – a measure which allows currencies to be expressed in terms of what they will buy at local prices, making them comparable with others.*

Position in 2015	Predicted position by 2050
2	1 China
10	2 India
1	3 USA
20	4 Indonesia
21	5 Nigeria
7	6 Brazil
9	7 Russia
3	8 Japan
39	9 Philippines
6	10 UK

Figure 2 *Predictions about the world's ten biggest economies by 2050 (by GDP), in comparison with their actual positions in 2015*

Global governance

The USA has also been joined by other players in wider global matters too. At the annual UN Climate Change Conference, new key players have emerged in promoting an agenda for reduced greenhouse gas emissions. These contrast with earlier agreements (such as Kyoto, 1997) where the USA was accused of dragging its heels. Now, formal meetings of the UN's Conference of the Parties (COP) seek to establish legally binding obligations for countries to reduce their emissions. One measure of ongoing commitment to emissions reductions is the number of delegates a country sends to each meeting; the countries with the highest numbers of delegates at the 2015 meeting included China, France, Canada and Russia – but also Morocco, Peru and Guinea. However, some global economies did less well; Japan was 21st (168 delegates), the USA 35th (124), and Australia 93rd (46).

New BRICs on the block

The global economy is changing rapidly, and it's likely that a new economic order will have been created by 2050. A new era of potential superpowers is emerging to challenge the uni-polar world dominated by the USA (see Section 3.3). In 2000, writer Richard Scase predicted rapid economic growth in four countries that he collectively named the **BRICs** – Brazil, Russia, India and China – to which other people have since added South Africa (so, the BRICSs!). Key development indicators for these five countries are shown in Figure 3, in comparison with the USA. Scase predicted that India's economy would overtake that of the UK by 2022 and that of the USA by 2050.

However, at present the BRICSs don't yet rival the USA as economic superpowers. Their combined GDP in 2014 was US$16.4 trillion – about 8% less than the USA. But, as Figure 4 shows, China alone accounts for about 60% of the total GDP of all five BRICSs, so if China is excluded from the data in Figures 3 and 4, the BRICSs as a group suddenly seem much less powerful.

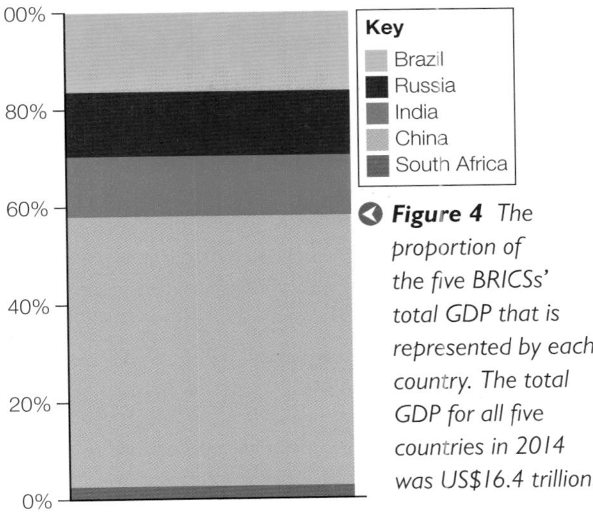

Figure 4 The proportion of the five BRICSs' total GDP that is represented by each country. The total GDP for all five countries in 2014 was US$16.4 trillion.

	USA	Brazil	Russia	India	China	South Africa
HDI	0.916	0.755	0.798	0.609	0.727	0.407
GDP per capita US$ PPP	55 837	15 359	24 451	6 089	14 239	13 165
Internet users (% pop)	88.2	60.1	71.3	34.8	52.2	48.9
GDP from agriculture (%)	1.6	5.8	4	17.9	9.7	2.5
Population growth rate (%)	0.77	0.8	0.19	1.25	0.44	-0.48

Figure 3 Key indicators in 2014 for the five BRICS countries, in comparison with the USA

Assessing the four BRICs

Which of the BRICs can claim superpower status? Each has evolving strengths and weaknesses. The following text panels compare the economic, political, military, cultural, demographic and environmental strengths and weaknesses of each BRICs country, which could help to inhibit or advance its economic and geopolitical role in the future. The small size of South Africa's economy compared to the others (see Figure 4) has led it to be omitted from this analysis.

Brazil

Economic

- Brazil is important regionally in South America, because it produces half of South America's GDP (in 2015), although it does rely on primary products for export, rather than manufacturing.
- It has huge natural resources and is self-sufficient in both food and energy. It's an agricultural superpower, the third largest producer of iron ore, the second largest of biofuel, the fifteenth largest of oil, and the third largest of HEP.

Political

- Brazil has been politically less stable in recent years, with accusations of corruption, as well as protests every year since 2013, caused by government spending cuts and perceived government corruption.

Military

- It spends over 60% of South America's total military budget, but Figure 8 on page 115 shows that militarily Brazil is the least significant of the BRICs.

Cultural

- Brazil has a global reputation as a footballing nation. It hosted the 2014 Football World Cup, as well as the 2016 Olympics/Paralympics. It's also famous for the Rio Carnival.

Demographic

- Brazil contains half of South America's population (210 million in 2016). Its population is young (median age 31.3 in 2015), but ageing. The fertility rate fell from 6 in 1960 to 1.8 in 2015.

Environmental

- Brazil's biodiversity includes 13% of all known species, with a huge range of flora and fauna – especially in the Amazon. It supports global initiatives, e.g. UN Conference on Climate Change, and is a leader in using ethanol.
- However, Brazil also has major environmental issues – deforestation in the Amazon (see Figure 5), illegal poaching, and pollution caused by mining activities and oil spills.

Figure 5 Land clearance and deforestation in the Amazon Basin, Brazil

Russia

Economic

- Russia is the ninth largest global economy, but it's very dependent on oil and gas exports (producing half of its GDP), so it's vulnerable to global price fluctuations.
- Its economy is unbalanced. Under the USSR, it was a big producer of electronics, vehicles, food and medicines. But its manufacturing halved after 1991.
- It's also the most unequal of the developed or emerging nations: 35% of its wealth is in the hands of just 110 people (in 2014); the richest 1% control 71% of its wealth; 94% of Russians have less than US$10 000 in assets. The poorest 20% of Russians share 3% of Russia's GDP.

Political and military

- 'Russian influence' matters to Russians. There has been a reduction in Russia's global influence since 1991, although Vladimir Putin, Russia's President, has sought to rebuild it in recent years, including a substantial role in Syria between 2012 and 2017.
- Although military spending has increased, much of Russia's naval and aircraft stock is ageing, e.g. its one aircraft carrier (see Figure 8) dates from the Soviet era.
- Russia did not support Ukraine's application for membership of the EU and NATO. It still maintains political influence over many of its neighbours, all former republics of the USSR.

Cultural

- Russian is spoken little beyond the borders of the former USSR, but Russia's history is of global significance. It has a large cultural tourist industry. Though 81% ethnic Russian, its diverse population includes Tatars (4%), Ukrainians (1.4%) and Chechens (1%).

Demographic

- Between 1991 and 2015 inclusive, Russia's population declined in 21 of the 25 years, and has never recovered to its 1991 level. Its natural increase is now tiny (0.02 per 1000), and its fertility rate is also low (1.78 in 2015).

Environmental

- Russia has a pollution legacy from industrialisation between 1930 and 1960, which occurred with little concern about the damage caused by deforestation, mining, spillages or toxic waste, and from the Chernobyl nuclear reactor explosion in 1986 (see Figure 6).

▲ ***Figure 6*** *The abandoned nuclear power station at Chernobyl – now part of Ukraine, but in 1986 part of the USSR*

▼ ***Figure 7*** *Traffic problems in New Delhi – part of India's problem with poor infrastructure*

India

Economic

- The Indian economy averaged 7% annual growth – and quadrupled – between 1997 and 2015. However, manufacturing peaked at 17% of GDP in 1995, and is now only 14%.
- Its economic advantages include an English-speaking education system and widespread use of English – leading to the growth of out-sourced industries in IT. Its major universities also have global reputations.
- Indian infrastructure is poor in both energy and water supply, as well as in transport (see Figure 7), and it's a long way behind China. Power cuts are frequent – one cut, in July 2012, affected 620 million people!
- The government is facing large debts, which has led to a reduction in the value of the rupee.
- 20% of Indians live in abject poverty.

Political

- With 672 million voters, India is the world's largest democracy. It was a founding member of the UN and of the G20 grouping of industrialised nations. It also takes part in UN peacekeeping missions.

Military

- *Global Fire Power* ranks India as the world's fourth largest military power in terms of its weaponry (see Figure 8) and personnel.

Cultural

- India was the birthplace of four world religions (Hinduism, Buddhism, Jainism, Sikhism).
- The world's largest film industry, Bollywood, produces 1200 films a year, but without Hollywood's global reach.

Demographic

- At 1.27 billion (in 2016), India has the world's second largest population after China.
- It has a youthful and massive working population (66.2% of India's population is aged 15–64). Its working population may exceed China's by 2020.

Environmental

- India has amongst the world's richest biodiversity; its diversity includes 6% of the world's bird and plant species. However, population and economic growth threaten this.
- India also has the world's worst environmental problems, with serious pollution. It's the world's third largest emitter of CO_2, and has some of the worst urban slums.

China

Economic

- Due to its huge population (1.37 billion in 2016), China's per capita GDP is only 10% of that of the USA, so wealth has yet to spread among its population.
- In 2009, only 2% of China's adult population had graduated from university; 25–30% is usual in developed countries. This affects China's potential in the knowledge economy, limiting its skills in design and research – its industries copy rather than innovate.
- China is a major player in global investment. Its State-run companies and banks all invest heavily overseas (see Section 3.3). However, it also has massive levels of debt.

Political

- Unlike the USA, China rarely gets involved in global crises (e.g. natural disasters, military or political crises). China has an authoritarian, one-party government.

Military

- Although it has the world's largest army, China has little global military reach (see Section 3.2). However, it does have military strengths (see Figure 8).

	Military budget (US$bn)	Aircraft carriers	Submarines		Combat aircraft	Nuclear weapons	Military satellites
			Nuclear	Non-nuclear			
Brazil	$31.9	1	0	5	12	0	0
Russia	$70.0	1	45	22	1337	7700	74
India	$45.2	2	1	13	928	110	5
China	$216.4	1	9	60	2571	260	68
UK	$61.8	1	11	0	278	225	7
USA	$615.5	10	72	0	3680	7100	123
Global total	**$1778.5**	**20**	**148**	**363**	**20 089**	**15 913**	**320**

Figure 8 *The military capability of the BRICs, compared to the USA and UK. All data are for 2015, the latest year for the combined data. You can find 2016 data on military budgets in Figure 5 on page 104.*

Cultural

- Unlike the USA, which dominates, China has few global brands. It also has negligible impacts on global entertainment – 'Western' culture is largely American.

Demographic

- China has a population dependency time bomb. Its former one-child policy has produced an ageing population; in 2015, its median age was 35.2 (compared with India's 27.5). By 2020, 12% of Chinese will be over 65 (compared to India's 6%). Traditionally, many Chinese retire aged 51 (earlier than the legal age) – that's a lot of elderly to support!
- China is isolated in terms of international migration, unlike the USA which attracts global talent. It may need immigration to supplement future recruitment among young people, as only 18% of Chinese were aged 0–14 in 2015 (compared to India's 29%).

Environmental

- China is the world's largest CO_2 emitter; emissions rose 286% from 1990–2013. It produces 33% of global emissions, but in 2016 began to commit to reduction targets.

Explaining changing patterns of power

How is it that some countries rise and fall in power? Three theories help to explain this: Wallerstein's world systems theory (also known as the concept of core and periphery), modernisation theory and dependency theory.

Wallerstein's world systems theory

Wallerstein, an American sociologist and world-systems analyst, developed a theory in 1974 about capitalist world systems and the development gap. He identified two economic areas: **core** and **periphery** (see Figure 9 on page 116) to explain how successful places maintain economic power, and how new centres develop.

Wallerstein claimed that **core regions** drive the world economy. The 'core' developed as the world's first industrial areas during the eighteenth (the UK) and nineteenth centuries (Europe, North America and Japan), financed by capital invested from a wealthy farming sector. He presented these as the first 'core' regions (ignoring that, in 1800, China and India were the world's two largest economies!). Despite the recent global shift to China and India, this western 'core' now owns and consumes 75% of global goods and services. However, due to the global shift into Asia, China and India are regaining their former core status.

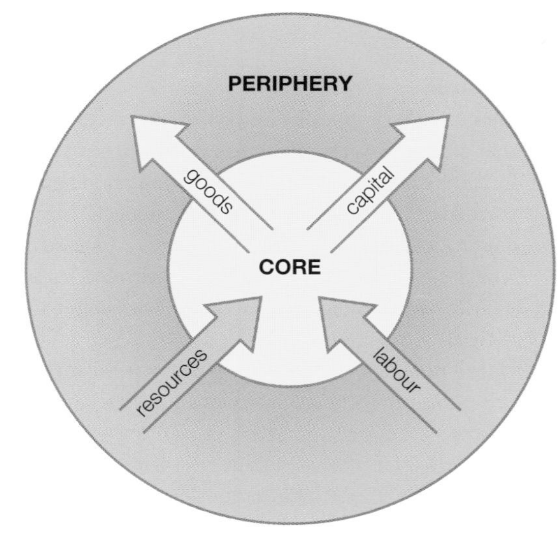

Peripheral areas lie at the other extreme. Distant from the core and lacking capital, they rely on core regions to exploit their raw materials. This has not occurred by accident, but largely results from colonialism (see section 3.3) during which time western superpowers assumed control over areas rich in resources within Africa, Asia and Latin America. Trade between colonial rulers and colonies was unequal – core regions imported, processed, added value to, and profited from processing primary materials from peripheral regions. Populations in peripheral regions were often drafted in as low-cost labour (see Figure 9).

Figure 9 ***A*** *(above) Interactions of capital, goods, resources and labour between core and peripheral areas.* ***B*** *(below) Shanghai – very much part of a major global economic core area.*

Those same trade patterns persist; the economies of developing countries are typically dominated by exports of primary products and imports of manufactured goods. Cores remain dominant because they own production lines and dictate what is produced and by whom. Investment and decision-making therefore remain within the core, maintaining the development gap.

Modernisation theory

Advancing communism in the 1940s caused shockwaves in the USA. By the mid-1950s, Soviet money was pouring into India and Southeast Asia; the US feared further communist expansion. Anti-communism dominated US foreign policy until the USSR collapsed in 1991, and promotion of economic development through modernisation theory dominated its overseas investment. The theory took its name from the idea that, to deliver capitalism, modern institutional reform is central – for example through a structured banking and legal system of currencies and investment loans.

Two organisations, established after the Second World War, helped the USA to achieve this – the International Monetary Fund (IMF) and the World Bank (see section 3.5). Their focus was currency stability (the IMF) and a system of development loans (the World Bank).

Modernisation theorists believed that capitalism was the fundamental solution to poverty. Without reform, they argued:

- poverty would remain a trap or cycle
- traditional family values in poorer countries would hold economies back by preventing geographical mobility.

Investment in countries bordering China and the USSR, they believed, could prevent communism from spreading to – for example – Japan, India, Singapore, South Korea, Taiwan and the Philippines. All of these countries are now major economies. Modernisation policies remained important when the USSR collapsed; investment and aid became a priority for ex-communist countries.

Dependency theory

Dependency theory argues that developing countries remain dependent on wealthier nations, and that their reliance – or **dependency** – on developed economies is the cause of poverty. As with the core and periphery theory, trade patterns involve the exchange of primary exports to developed nations in return for manufactured products. The **terms of trade** remain stacked against them, since tariffs (or duties) are added to any processed imports. This imbalance in the terms of trade remains unfavourable to developing countries.

In this way, poverty is maintained in developing countries, without the opportunity to process or add value to primary goods. The low profit deters investment, and countries become trapped in a vicious cycle (see Figure 10). To develop, countries would have to adopt a virtuous cycle, i.e. retain their primary products and invest in processing and manufacturing – thus adding value and employment. In doing so, they would face tariff barriers in their markets in Europe, Japan or the USA.

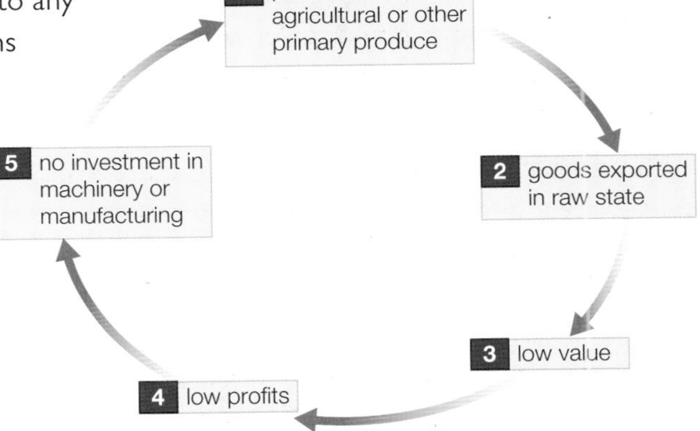

Figure 10 *The vicious cycle of development*

Over to you

1. Working in pairs, pick **one** of Nigeria, Indonesia or the Philippines and research it to explain its anticipated rapid economic growth by 2050, as shown in Figure 2.
2. Still working in pairs, carry out a SWOT analysis (Strengths, Weaknesses, Opportunities, and Threats) for all four BRICs to show economic, political, military, cultural, demographic and environmental factors.
3. **a** Using your SWOT analysis, rank the countries 1-4 in terms of where you think their economic and political futures will lie by 2050. Explain your ranking.
   b How does your ranking compare with the likely ranking estimated by PwC in Figure 2?

On your own

4. Distinguish between the following pairs of terms: (**a**) core and periphery, (**b**) dependency theory and modernisation theory, (**c**) vicious and virtuous cycles.
5. In pairs, assess the strengths and weaknesses of the three development theories (world systems, modernisation, dependency) in explaining which countries become powerful and which do not.

Exam-style question

Assess to what extent China can claim to be a superpower. (*12 marks*)

3.5 Global networking

In this section, you'll learn that superpowers have significant influence over the global economic system.

EQ2 Sections 3.5 to 3.7 will ask what the impacts of superpowers are on the global economy, political systems and physical environment.

SYNOPTIC THEME AND KEY CONCEPTS

- **Players** – the role of TNCs in maintaining power and wealth
- **Causality** – how organisations such as the IMF developed
- **Globalisation** – the role of organisations such as the WTO in globalisation

January, somewhere in Switzerland...

Every January, security agents arrive at Davos in eastern Switzerland, shown in Figure 1. Located in a deep glaciated valley, it's relatively easy to spot who's coming and going in Davos! That's just as well, because 2500 invitation-only VIP guests will shortly be arriving, including Chief Executive Officers (CEOs) of Transnational Corporations (TNCs), government leaders, Hollywood stars (Leonardo DiCaprio attended in 2016 – see Figure 2) and senior academics. They will be arriving to attend the annual meeting of the World Economic Forum (WEF), where the delegates will network, discuss issues, consider decisions and pursue policies.

Figure 1 *Davos, in eastern Switzerland – venue of the annual meeting of the WEF*

How the WEF functions

The World Economic Forum is a Swiss not-for-profit organisation, working across national borders (an **intergovernmental organisation**, or IGO). It promotes public-private co-operation, with its aim *'to improve the state of the world by bringing together business, political, academic, and leaders of society to shape global, regional, and industry agendas'*. It meets annually at Davos, as well as at other forums around the world.

The WEF was founded in 1971 to help resolve disputes and promote global thinking. It discusses issues of corruption and terrorism, together with economic systems and social issues (e.g. health). Its members think internationally, and encourage governments to promote global links. TNCs gain a lot from government policies (such as low taxation), so networking with world leaders is useful for them.

But the WEF is not problem-free. Political scientist Samuel P. Huntington believes that 'Davos Man' (the WEF is mainly men) has *'little need for national loyalty, views national boundaries as obstacles ... and sees national governments as residues from the past whose only useful function is to facilitate the elite's global operations'*. He argues that national voters' instincts can sometimes conflict with the WEF's globalised ideas. For example, in 2016 the UK electorate voted to leave the EU; pro-nationalist views are also growing in many other countries.

Figure 2 *Leonardo DiCaprio receiving an award at Davos in 2016 for his contribution to social issues globally. Whilst there, he also attacked the corporate greed of global oil companies.*

The origins of other IGOs

As Section 3.4 described, a fear of communist expansion after 1945 dominated US foreign policy. American ideology – based on modernisation theory – influenced global economic development and promoted capitalism for six decades. Two organisations, established after the Second World War, helped the USA to achieve this – the International Monetary Fund (IMF) and the World Bank.

The International Monetary Fund (IMF)

The IMF was founded in 1944 at Bretton Woods, USA. Its job was to stabilise global currencies after the 1930s depression and the devastation caused by the Second World War. Forty-four countries initially joined to create a Fund (mostly paid for by the wealthiest nations) to be used for loans to help those countries facing heavy debts, thus helping to stabilise their currencies and economies. The thinking was that poverty – and communism – would be prevented, and capitalism promoted.

By 2016, the IMF had 189 members. However, its members are not all equal – their individual voting rights are proportional to the amounts that they have invested in the Fund. Eight individual countries control 47% of the votes between them; other countries have been grouped together to represent smaller states (see Figure 3). The top ten members in Figure 3 control over 60% of the IMF's total voting rights.

Up to now, most of the IMF's work has reflected US and European policies in managing issues such as international debt. For example, in the 1980s and 1990s, it imposed conditions on many borrowing countries (decided upon by the main donor nations) that forced developing countries, often in Africa, to cut spending on health and education in return for stabilising or extending their debt repayments.

Rank	IMF member countries / country groupings	Voting rights (% of total)
1	USA	16.5
2	Japan	6.2
3	China	6.1
4	Belgium, Netherlands, Israel & others	5.4
5	Germany	5.3
6	Spain, Mexico & some Central American countries	5.3
7	Indonesia, Singapore & Southeast Asian countries	4.4
8	Italy, Greece, Malta & other Mediterranean countries	4.1
9	France	4.0
10	UK	4.0

Figure 3 *Voting rights in the IMF. These are proportional to the funds invested in the IMF by these countries. The eight largest contributors control nearly 47% of the available votes.*

The World Bank

The World Bank was also founded at Bretton Woods in 1944. Its role is to finance development, and its first loan was to France for post-war reconstruction. It also focuses on addressing the effects of natural disasters, as well as on humanitarian emergencies, but its main role has been to help capitalism function – particularly by making loans to developing countries for development projects.

The World Bank gained a bad reputation in the 1970s and 1980s for financing projects that were either environmentally damaging (e.g. rainforest clearance), or so costly that borrowing countries were unable to repay their loans. Now it aims to eliminate poverty and implement sustainable goals. Its decision-making structure is like that of the IMF. In 2016, the USA controlled 16.5% of World Bank votes, and, like the IMF, over 40% of the total votes lie in the hands of eight of the largest contributors.

Figure 4 *Protests against the Belo Monte Dam in the Amazon – the World Bank eventually pulled out of the scheme*

The World Trade Organisation (WTO)

The WTO has the same rationale as the World Bank and the IMF, except that its focus is on trade and its rules. It aims to free up global trade and reduce trade barriers, by negotiating free-trade agreements and ensuring that its members maintain its rules.

Unlike the IMF and World Bank, the WTO operates a system of 'one country, one vote', which in theory is fairer to developing countries. However, no votes have ever been taken at the WTO! Decision-making is by mutual agreement, but most bargaining favours the EU and the USA.

The WTO is currently focused on programmes of poverty reduction, by removing farm subsidies (grants paid to farmers to encourage production) in developing countries to stimulate efficient production. But the result has been that, in many developing countries, cheaper imports then undercut local farmers, who are forced out of business.

Nonetheless, a combination of globalisation (freeing up capital and labour movement) and WTO agreements has led to an explosion in global trade since 1950, as Figure 5 shows. The values shown in Figure 5 are based on the value of trade in 1913 (which has been given the value of 100). Every year shown therefore either below 100 (i.e. a lower value than in 1913) or above it.

Figure 5 *The changing values of global trade, 1800–2014. All values are shown in proportion to the baseline of 100, which represents the value of trade in 1913.*

Year	Value of global trade
1800	2.1
1810	2.5
1820	3.4
1830	5.2
1840	7.1
1850	10.1
1860	16.9
1870	24.7
1880	35.2
1890	48.2
1900	60.4
1910	85.6
1920	90.6
1930	124.5
1950	150.4
1960	315.2
1970	716.3
1980	1194.8
1990	1744.3
2000	3258.9
2010	4928.7
2014	4427.6

The role of TNCs as global players

We think of TNCs as recent features, but in the eighteenth and nineteenth centuries much of India was run by the East India Company. It controlled trade routes and ruled 20% of the world's population. By 2015, there were over 75 000 TNCs; the top 200 produced 25% of the world's economic output by value.

But change is taking place in their distribution:

- In 2006, six of the top ten TNCs by revenue were American. Figure 6 shows that there are now only three US companies in the top ten.
- Some Chinese companies are growing very rapidly.
- American car manufacturers – traditionally in the top ten – have lost ground. Of five companies which dropped out of the top 10 between 2006 and 2015, four (General Motors, Chevron, Daimler Chrysler, Ford) were American motor companies.

The size of such companies is colossal; Walmart (whose UK brand name is ASDA) produces the same revenue as Sweden, the world's 22nd largest economy.

Figure 6 *The top ten TNCs by revenue (or earnings) in 2015*

2006 rank	2015 rank	Company name	Revenue (US$ billions)	Country of origin	Nearest GDP
2	1	Walmart Stores	485.65	USA	Sweden
-	2	Sinopec	433.31	China	Belgium
3	3	Royal Dutch Shell	385.63	UK/Netherlands	Norway
-	4	PetroChina	367.85	China	UAE
1	5	Exxon Mobil	364.76	USA	UAE
4	6	BP	334.61	USA	Egypt
8	7	Toyota Motor	248.95	Japan	Chile
-	8	Volkswagen	244.81	Germany	Chile
-	9	Glencore	209.22	Anglo-Swiss	Portugal
-	10	Total	194.16	France	Vietnam

Most TNCs are publicly owned corporations, with shareholders who receive dividends based on company profits each year. Their desire for profit drives everything. However, in China, for example, TNCs operate differently. They are state-led and operate commercially, but all profits return to the state.

Either way, TNCs are dominant economic forces in the global economy. Each year, the Forbes 2000 ranking lists the world's biggest 2000 companies. When analysing the list, it becomes clear that some countries dominate the world economy and maintain power as well as wealth:

- Figure 7 shows that 75% of the Forbes 2000 companies are based in just ten countries.
- However, the rankings of those ten countries are changing – note the rise of four Asian countries (China, South Korea, India and Taiwan) between 2008 and 2015.

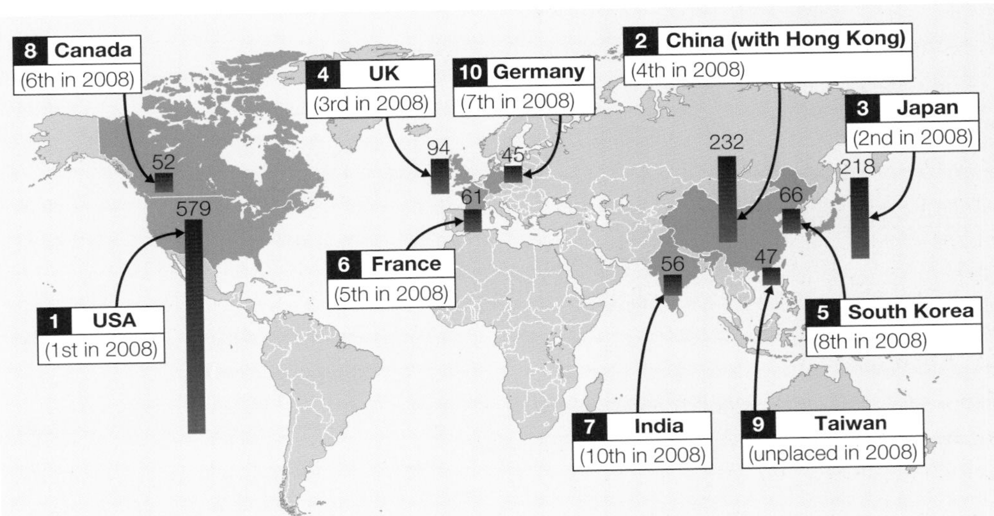

Figure 7 *The ten countries where 75% of the world's 2000 largest companies are based. Each bar has been sized in proportion to the number of large companies in that country. Their 2008 positions in the rankings are given underneath the country names.*

TNCs as players in global trade

TNCs have had huge impacts on global trade. The increases in global trade in Figure 5 show that between 1960 and 2010 trade increased by at least 46% per decade. In the 2000s, global trade increased in value by over 85%!

Part of the reason for this is the global shift in manufacturing to Asia by TNCs. Since 1990, the shift has led to rapid increases in exports from developing countries, a process which speeded up during the 2000s. This has not only shifted economic power away from Western economies into emerging economies, but has also made TNCS extremely powerful. Instead of trade occurring *between* different companies, much of the increase in global trade is *intra-company* – i.e. between different branches or activities of the same company. Much trade now consists of flows of parts or components of goods and services moving between one country and another before a final product is completed. As a result, UNCTAD (United Nations Conference on Trade and Development) estimated in 2013 that TNCs now account for 80% of all global trade – which in 2013 was over US$20 trillion!

Figure 8 *Containerisation at Felixstowe in Suffolk – the means by which trade is maintained. On average, 80% of what is on board this ship will be owned or processed by a TNC.*

TNCs as players in technology

In 1995, the WTO introduced its agreement on Trade-related Aspects of Intellectual Property Rights (TRIPS). It requires all WTO members to protect and enforce their **intellectual property rights** – that is, to register any new technology or process under **patent** law. A patent is the granting of the exclusive right of ownership and possession of intellectual property by a state to an inventor for a fixed period of time. A patent means that anyone else wishing to use this must pay a royalty for doing so.

TRIPS undoubtedly favour TNCs. They spend money on research and innovation – think how much companies, such as Microsoft or Apple, must spend in developing new smart phones, or watches. Part of the high cost of such items lies in the research and development that goes into it, so TNCs feel justified in registering any new technology as theirs. As a result, Figure 9 shows a close link between the number of new patents in 2015 and the location of TNCs throughout the world.

Rank	Country	Number of new patents registered in 2015
1	USA	57 385
2	Japan	44 235
3	China	29 846
4	Germany	18 072
5	South Korea	14 626
6	France	8 476
7	UK	5 313
8	Netherlands	4 357
9	Switzerland	4 280
10	Sweden	3 858

Figure 9 *Top ten countries for new patents registered during 2015*

Two issues illustrate the importance of patents:

- Patents developed by pharmaceutical (drug) companies make many medicines unaffordable to poorer countries. For example, many new treatments for HIV (known as antiretrovirals or ARV) are very expensive. Early ARVs tended to be toxic, so later and less-damaging versions were more desirable – but also more expensive. This has provided a widespread barrier to HIV treatment in sub-Saharan Africa, the worst affected area in the world for HIV/AIDS.
- Genetically Modified (GM) crops are controlled by TNCs, e.g. Monsanto in the USA. Using patent laws, they 'own' every GM plant grown from their seed (like those plants in Figure 10). Some TNCs force farmers to sign contracts to use only their chemicals, or prevent them from saving seed to plant the following year. GM engineers can even stop seeds produced by their crops from germinating – so every year farmers must buy new seed. Over 1 billion of the world's poorest people rely on saved seed, but instead they have to buy new seed every year. Again, TNCs benefit most.

Figure 10 *Field markers in trials of new genetically modified (GM) strains of maize*

Global cultural influences

Whether it's *Strictly Come Dancing* (UK) or *Game of Thrones* (USA), Western culture is global, bringing arts of different forms via the media into homes, theatres or aircraft flying around the world. On 20 November 2015, Adele's third album, *25*, was released globally. Such is media technology and the permeation of TNCs like Apple Music into people's lives, that a release in one country means that it must occur in all countries simultaneously. Extracts from the album's first single, 'Hello', were tantalisingly broadcast in 30-second clips before its release date on global TV channels and YouTube. Programmes such as *The Simpsons* or *Poldark* are available in almost every country, on every airline and on every streaming channel, such as Amazon Prime.

The same globalisation applies with food. As people return from holidays or work trips overseas, wanting the same flavour or experience to remind them of their visit, the influence of international foods in supermarkets in the UK has spread. Chinese, Vietnamese, Italian, Indian ... whatever your taste, the supermarkets have it and TV companies feature chefs cooking it. TV chefs, such as Rick Stein or Madhur Jaffrey, have become global foodie celebrities.

Figure 11 *Indian cookery books on display – but where was the bookshop? You'd be as likely to see this display in Sydney or Buenos Aires as in London.*

Over to you

1 In pairs, draw a spider diagram to consider why the World Economic Forum invites politicians, academics and Hollywood stars – as well as business leaders – to its conferences.

2 Using a Venn diagram, outline the similar and overlapping functions of the IMF, the World Bank and the WTO.

3 a Refer to Section 6.2 'Using linear and logarithmic scales'. Plot two graphs using the data in Figure 5 – the first using a linear scale and the second using a logarithmic scale.
  b Explain why different scales are helpful in displaying data such as those in Figure 5.

4 Using all of the information in this section, discuss in pairs and produce a diagram to show all the ways in which TNCs become dominant economic forces in the global economy.

On your own

5 Distinguish between the roles of the IMF, World Bank, WTO and WEF.

6 Using Figures 6 and 7, describe and explain the changes in location of the world's largest TNCs in recent years.

7 Write a 400-word argument entitled 'Patents – right or wrong?'

Exam-style question

Assess the influence of TNCs over the global economic system. (*12 marks*)

3.6 Players in international decision-making

In this section, you'll learn how superpowers and emerging nations play a key role in international decision-making concerning people and the physical environment.

SYNOPTIC THEMES AND KEY CONCEPTS

- **Players** – the role of powerful countries as 'global police'
- **Actions** – the actions and attitudes of global IGOs
- **Causality** – why global powers become involved in the affairs of others
- **Resilience** – how engagement with other countries is designed to increase resilience

Crisis in Haiti

As if Haiti needed another major disaster, Hurricane Matthew – a devastating Category 4 storm – swept across the country in October 2016. Its impacts were nothing like those of the 7.0 magnitude earthquake of 2010, but Haiti is one of the world's poorest countries, so it has little resilience to disaster. Among many regular donor countries, 'aid fatigue' had begun to set in, so Haiti's appeals for assistance brought in only 25% of the money it needed. It was left to the USA and France to provide 550 personnel, as well as humanitarian aid. NGOs (e.g. the Red Cross) also launched appeals for US$7 million, while IGOs such as UNICEF sought US$5 million from UN funds to provide aid for 500 000 Haitian children.

One way in which superpowers and emerging nations play a key role in global affairs is through crisis response. Poor nations, such as Haiti, look to other countries for help. However, that help can vary – for example, the Nepal earthquake of April 2015 attracted aid from 48 countries, ranging from finance, personnel, emergency supplies and shelter equipment, to materials for rebuilding.

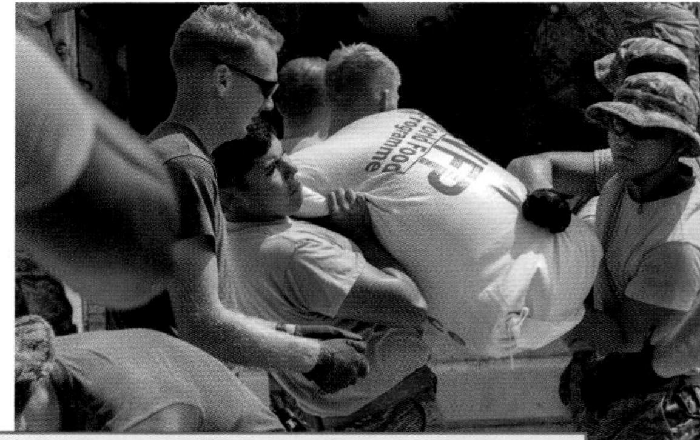

Haiti and Hurricane Matthew

- Over 900 Haitians died.
- Several thousand homes were destroyed.
- An estimated 350 000 Haitians needed aid.
- Within three days of the hurricane, cholera became a threat.

Figure 1 *US forces at Port-au-Prince, the capital of Haiti, unloading aid from the United Nations' World Food Program in October 2016*

Meanwhile in Afghanistan...

As well as responding to crises, superpowers and emerging nations also play a key role in military conflicts – and act as 'global police'. For nearly 40 years Afghanistan has suffered almost constant conflict – from foreign invasion to civil war. **Geopolitics** – that is, political conflict in geographical space – lies at the heart of this.

Afghanistan's geopolitical location and physical landscape is significant. Historically, it linked into the trans-Asian 'silk road'; more recently it has strategic importance for overland trade routes between India and Pakistan into central Asia and Russia. However, its largely mountainous terrain within the high Hindu Kush and Himalayan mountain ranges (see Figures 2 and 3) makes travel difficult, particularly in times of conflict, and strategically its 5500 km mountainous borders with six other countries are hard to defend. Most areas of conflict are challenging to access via mountain routes and passes (often impassable in winter), and opposing forces may be concealed within deep valleys and small isolated communities. Central government control is difficult to maintain.

Afghanistan is also a deeply religious Muslim state, with a 99% Muslim population. However, different Sunni and Shia factions have led to conflict both internally and with some of Afghanistan's neighbours (see Figure 3).

Figure 2 *The Hindu Kush mountain landscape of central Afghanistan*

Understanding the current conflict in Afghanistan

Afghanistan is among the world's poorest countries. Decades of conflict have deterred investment. 35% of people live below the poverty line, and although agriculture accounts for 31% of formal GDP, this excludes illicit opium, the most valuable crop.

In the 1970s, Afghanistan's young king, Zahir Shah, wanted to develop the economy, and allow women greater freedom than traditional Islamic society allowed. This took hold in Kabul, the capital, but failed to reach remote areas. Frustrated by slow economic growth, the Afghan Communist Party seized power in 1978, which in 1979 was supported by invading troops and tanks from the USSR. These troops were resisted by Afghan guerrillas, known as the mujahideen ('Islamic warriors'), provoking conflict between the USSR and USA. The USA supported the mujahideen with weapons and by recruiting Muslim fighters. With American funding, they resisted Soviet troops, which withdrew by 1989.

The Soviet departure left a power vacuum during the 1990s, with two major consequences:

a) By 1995, the Taliban, a militant group among the mujahideen, gained control of much of the country. They enforced programmes of radical Islamic law, or Sharia, including restrictions on women, such as denying them education.

b) The Taliban – hitherto supported by the west – gave protection to Saudi militant Osama bin Laden. Bin Laden had established training camps in Afghanistan with western backing; now he organized attacks against US interests. The most sensational occurred on September 11 2001 (9/11), when two passenger planes were hi-jacked and flown into New York's World Trade Towers, killing nearly 3000 people.

Since the break-up of the USSR, **Russia** no longer has a direct border with Afghanistan, although **Uzbekistan**, **Turkmenistan** and **Tajikistan** (all part of the USSR until 1991) do. All four states fear Islamist uprisings within their own borders (e.g. Chechnya, within Russia), so they are always concerned about the rise of any Islamist groups in neighbouring countries.

China is less concerned about Afghanistan than many of its neighbours, but there is a large Muslim population in western China, so it fears any potential destabilising Islamist threats within Asia.

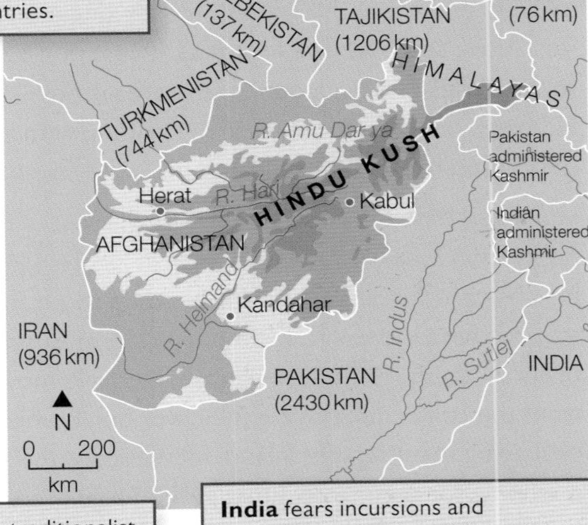

Since 1979, **Iran** has been ruled by a traditionalist Islamic Shia government, and is opposed to the Western-backed Sunni government in Afghanistan. Iran is also regarded with suspicion by many Western governments, who fear its recent attempts to develop nuclear weapons technology.

India fears incursions and destabilisation from fundamental Islamists based in Afghanistan and Pakistan – particularly after previous Islamist attacks, such as on a major Mumbai hotel in 2008. India wants a Western-supported stable government in Afghanistan.

Figure 3 *The geopolitical location of Afghanistan, and the length of its borders with its six neighbours*

The response post 9/11

In response to 9/11, the US led an international military coalition against the Taliban, with forces seeking to destroy training camps, and kill militant leaders, particularly bin Laden. Coalition troops captured Afghan cities, and supported the Northern Alliance, a group of Afghan resistance fighters. A new Afghan president, Hamid Karzai, was installed, easing rules on women's dress and schooling, training an Afghan army, and introducing democratic elections. The continued presence of overseas troops antagonises many supporters of reform. Although bin Laden was killed in 2011, Taliban militants continued to attack forces and government targets.

The challenge of climate change

Superpowers and emerging nations are also being called upon to play a key role in global action against climate change.

In 2002, American writer Curtis A. Moore went in search of Tebua, a small Pacific island. 'But now,' he wrote, 'it's gone, swallowed by the sea.' Tebua was originally to be found off Tarawa Atoll, on the western edge of Kiribati – a nation of widely spaced tiny Pacific islands (see Figure 4). Kiribati consists of low-lying sand and mangrove islands or atolls, mostly one metre or less above sea level (see Figure 5). It covers 2.5 million square miles of ocean, but its land area is tiny – just 720 km^2, one quarter the size of London, with a population of 102 000 in 2016.

Figure 4 *Kiribati and Tarawa Atoll*

However, Kiribati is now disappearing. Most of its population lives on Tarawa (shown in Figure 4). Its beaches are flat, and have now become so eroded by storms that sand has to be imported from Australia to maintain them. Many Tarawan families have moved away from the coast, dismantling their wooden homes and rebuilding them further inland. Increasingly, the people are being squeezed into a thin strip of higher ground. However, many are also leaving the island completely – becoming the world's first environmental refugees.

Tebua's disappearance is the result of a global rise in sea level, brought about by climate change. Since 1920, temperatures in the southwest Pacific have risen about 1°C. Five Pacific nations, including Australia and New Zealand, have warmed by more than 1°C since 1900. In Micronesia, of which Kiribati is a part, sea levels rose by 12 cm in the first five years of the twenty-first century. In addition, increasing tropical storm activity now threatens the region, together with tsunami caused by earthquakes in countries such as Japan.

Figure 5 *An aerial view of Christmas Island in Kiribati*

Attitudes and actions of IGOs towards geopolitical stability

Geopolitical stability has become the responsibility of several inter-governmental organisations (IGOs), particularly the United Nations (UN). The UN and its sub-organisations were formed after the Second World War to provide a peace-making and discussion forum. It had 193 members in 2016, each contributing to its budget. The UN's aims include maintaining peace, promoting human rights, and – through the United Nations Development Programme (UNDP) – social and economic development. It provides humanitarian aid during famine, natural disaster and armed conflict, and it's also involved in relief and aid work through the World Food Program (WFP) and the United Nations Children's Fund (UNICEF).

The UN Security Council and peacekeeping

The UN Security Council is ultimately responsible for preventing conflict. It has 15 members at any one time, although five permanent members have greater influence than the others; these are the USA, UK, France, China and Russia (formerly the USSR). The five permanent members can veto any resolution. During the Cold War, constant vetoes reflected hostility between the USSR and USA, but since 1991 the Security Council has been active in peacekeeping. It has authorized military and peacekeeping missions to conflicts such as Kuwait (1990–94), Bosnia (1998), and the Democratic Republic of the Congo (2004–09).

The International Court of Justice (ICJ)

The ICJ is the judicial branch of the UN, and is based in The Hague in The Netherlands. It settles disputes between UN member countries and advises on international law – and its judgments are generally binding. As Figure 6 shows, the ICJ has 15 judges, who represent different global regions. As with the UN Security Council, five are permanent members from within the allocation of their regions (USA, UK, France, China and Russia). The court deals only with cases brought by individual countries, rather than individual people. So cases against tobacco companies, for example, would not be brought to the ICJ.

The UN and climate change

The annual UN Climate Conferences aim to make progress in managing climate change. Since 1995, each Conference of the Parties (COP) has tried to establish legally binding requirements for all developed countries to reduce greenhouse gas emissions. Between 2011 and 2015, each conference took steps to negotiate an eventual deal, known now as the **2015 Paris Agreement**. This aims to engage all countries in committing to significantly reduced emissions.

Like all global agreements, the 2015 Paris Agreement is as good as its weakest link. Whilst 55 countries (between them responsible for 55% of global emissions) signed the 2015 Agreement, many more did not. Climate change has become a political tool, with climate change deniers in Australia (with the world's largest per capita emissions) and the USA (producing 25% of all emissions) undermining agreements. In 2016, the UK signed the Agreement, but the election that year of US President Trump – an avowed climate change denier – was a setback.

Global region	Number of judges
Western countries	5
Africa	3
Eastern Europe	2
Asia	3
Latin America and Caribbean	2

Figure 6 *The Peace Palace, the headquarters of the International Court of Justice in The Hague, plus the regional allocations of the 15 judges on the ICJ*

International players and global policing

How should the world respond to a situation in which natural disasters (e.g. Haiti), political conflicts (e.g. Afghanistan) and environmental threats (e.g. Kiribati) pose such real challenges? Increasingly, formalised alliances between countries increase interdependence and are important in geo-strategy and global influence. The key players involve alliances of a military, socio-economic and environmental nature.

1 Military alliances

Two international military alliances now dominate, following the dissolution of the Warsaw Pact (of Eastern European previously communist countries) in 1991:

Figure 7 US troops arriving in Riga, Latvia's capital, during NATO exercises in 2014. These were among 600 troops sent to Poland and the Baltic states (Latvia, Lithuania and Estonia) to send a signal of NATO strength to Russian leader, Vladimir Putin.

- The **North Atlantic Treaty Organisation** (NATO); also see Section 3.10. Formed in 1949, at the start of the Cold War, it adopts the guiding principle that an attack on one member is an attack on all. Its members carry out regular military exercises on each other's territory (see Figure 7), but since 1991 and the end of the Cold War, NATO's influence has diminished to such an extent that its role (and cost) is now being questioned, e.g. by US President Trump during his 2016 election campaign. However, Russian military activity in Georgia (2008) and Ukraine and Crimea (2014), as well as Russian naval and air exercises in European waters and airspace in 2016, have brought NATO to the fore again – and led to the decision to base extra troops in Poland and the three Baltic states.
- The **Australia, New Zealand and United States Security Treaty** (ANZUS). This is a 1951 security agreement that binds Australia, New Zealand and the USA to co-operate on military matters in the Pacific and beyond. It has helped the USA to maintain its military presence in the Pacific, and also led Australia and New Zealand to provide military forces for Afghanistan.

2 Economic alliances

- The **European Union** (EU) began as a trading alliance of six countries in 1956. Although enlarged to 28 member states (as of 2016), it remains a free-trade area. However, subsequent agreements extended the EU's remit, e.g. free movement of people (1992), and a common currency for 19 members (the Euro, 1999). Its principle is that economic strength insures against poverty, and it adopts a policy of convergence to reduce inequalities between its richest and poorest members. Its influence also extends into environmental issues, e.g. water quality on beaches. Its social concerns are underpinned by a legal framework established in 1945, the European Convention on Human Rights, which is enshrined in all European law. The UK voted to leave the EU in 2016, and there are increased tensions between those who support greater convergence (e.g. a European defence force), and right-wing political parties calling for separation.

- The **North American Free Trade Agreement** (NAFTA) consists of the USA, Canada and Mexico. Its concerns are economic; there is no free movement of people. It benefits the USA, because labour costs are lower in Mexico, and has therefore led to the drift of manufacturing south into Mexico. However, in his 2016 election campaign, President Trump vowed to tear up the agreement for fear of yet greater loss of employment for US workers.
- The **Association of Southeast Asian Nations** (ASEAN). This comprises ten Southeast Asian nations, and was formed in 1967 to encourage greater cooperation and economic growth between them. Its members are shown in Figure 8, and its aims also include cultural co-operation and common legal frameworks.

Figure 8 *The group of ten nations who comprise ASEAN*

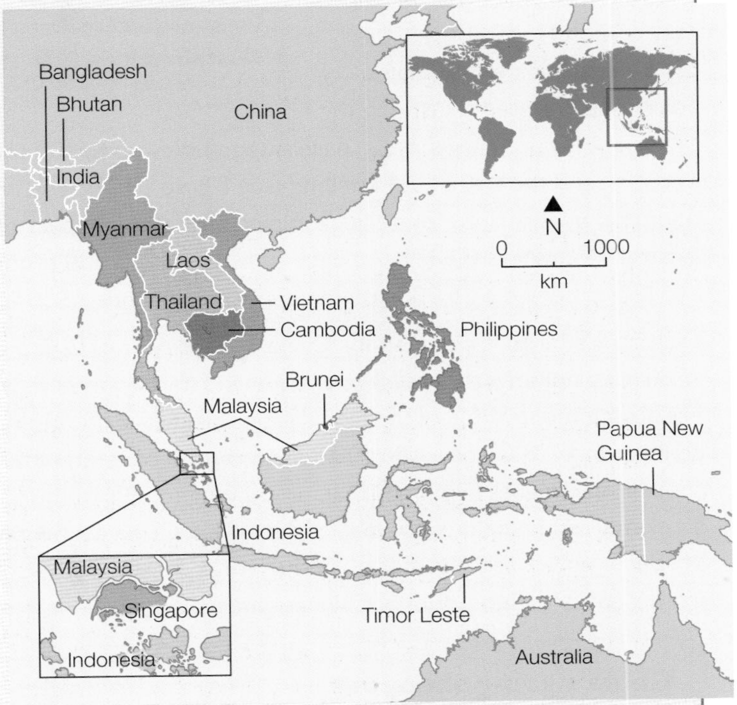

3 Environmental alliances

The **Intergovernmental Panel on Climate Change** (IPCC) was first established in 1988 by the UN. It produces reports which support the main international treaty on climate change, known as the UN Framework Convention on Climate Change (UNFCCC). Its brief is to '*stabilize greenhouse gas concentrations … at a level that … prevents dangerous anthropogenic* [i.e. human] *interference with the climate*'. It does not fund its own research. Instead, it monitors **peer-reviewed** scientific, technical and socio-economic publications, and assembles evidence, enabling UN members to understand the risks created by climate change, and its impacts. Its members represent over 120 countries.

Key word

Peer-reviewed – Publications based on research that has been checked by experts as being valid.

Over to you

1 a In pairs, take each of the three scenarios – Haiti's plea for aid in 2016, the Afghanistan conflict, and rising sea levels in Kiribati. Identify **(i)** which superpowers and emerging nations might play a key role in each scenario, **(ii)** in what ways they might be involved, and **(iii)** why.

b Design a brief presentation on each scenario for your class, and compare your findings with those of other pairs.

c Identify the alliances and IGOs that **(i)** might be involved in each scenario, **(ii)** how they might become involved, and **(iii)** why.

2 a In pairs, research one international event in which the UN and its various organisations has had a significant peacekeeping role. Focus on **(i)** the dispute, **(ii)** the UN role, **(iii)** its degree of success.

b Discuss and decide the extent to which the UN is important to global geopolitical stability.

On your own

3 Assess the fairness of the global representation of judges in the International Court of Justice in Figure 6. How and why could this distribution have occurred?

4 Identify all the major alliances (e.g. NATO) and groupings (e.g. the EU, UN) in this section. Draw up a table of the strengths and weaknesses of each organisation, and include further research if you need.

Exam-style question

Assess the effectiveness of superpowers and emerging nations in playing key roles in international decision-making. (*12 marks*)

3.7 Superpowers and the environment

In this section, you'll learn how global concerns about the physical environment are disproportionately influenced by superpower actions.

And they're away...

SYNOPTIC THEME AND KEY CONCEPT

- **Actions** – the actions and attitudes of different countries in reducing carbon emissions and reaching global agreements on environmental issues
- **Sustainability** – the attitudes of different countries towards climate change

Several times a day, a deafening roar of diesel locomotives can be heard in the town of Tom Price, Western Australia. These are no ordinary trains – each wagon holds up to 105 tonnes of iron ore, and the train is 2.4 km long (see Figure 1)! The line is owned and operated by Rio Tinto for its huge mining operations in part of Western Australia known as the Pilbara. Each train carries 25 000 tonnes of iron ore and leaves behind a 25 000-tonne hole in the ground.

Each train's cargo is destined for China, via the port of Dampier on Australia's northwest coast. China's demand for raw materials is such that it has accounted for 90% of the global growth in sea traffic in the twenty-first century. In 1998 China made 100 million tonnes of steel – 13% of the global total. It now makes five times that, amounting to 33% of the total, with a steel industry four times the size of the USA's. China is now the biggest producer and consumer of steel in the world. Its soaring demand comes from a construction boom in Chinese cities, driven by economic growth.

Figure 1 *An iron ore train travelling across the Pilbara*

China's going shopping

The impact of China's growth on commodity prices – i.e. minerals, foodstuffs such as grain, and fossil fuels – is hard to underestimate. Most commodity prices peaked at the peak of China's growth, during 2008-10; copper prices, for example, doubled in a 12-month period 2007-08. As China's growth has slowed since 2010, commodity prices have fallen back due to the lower demand. Faced with such variable prices, China has tried to guarantee commodity supplies by buying up companies overseas or by investing in sub-Saharan Africa to supply commodities, e.g. iron ore or copper.

China is also trying to guarantee supplies of fossil fuels for itself. In 2007, the government-owned oil company China National Petroleum Corporation (CNPC) became the main shareholder of PetroKazakhstan, a purchase which included a 1000 km oil pipeline into China. Kazakhstan has enormous oil reserves and is one of the world's major producers.

The emerging middle classes

Emerging economies have also led to increased resource consumption, which has exceeded global population growth since 2000 (see Figure 2). China's increased affluence can be shown by the following increases in its consumption:

- **Foodstuffs** – cereal consumption up by 364%, meat by 99%, fruit and nuts by 98%, and coffee and tea by 71%.
- **Consumer goods** – perfume consumption up by 133% and pharmaceuticals by 87%.

As Figure 3 shows, China is now the leading consumer of many commodities.

	2000	2014–15	% increase
Global population	6 billion	7.3 billion	22%
Coal (in tonnes)	2.4 billion	3.7 billion	54%
Fish (in tonnes)	92 million	180 million	96%
Copper (in tonnes)	15 million	23 million	53%

Figure 2 *Increasing global demand for key resources, 2000–2014/15*

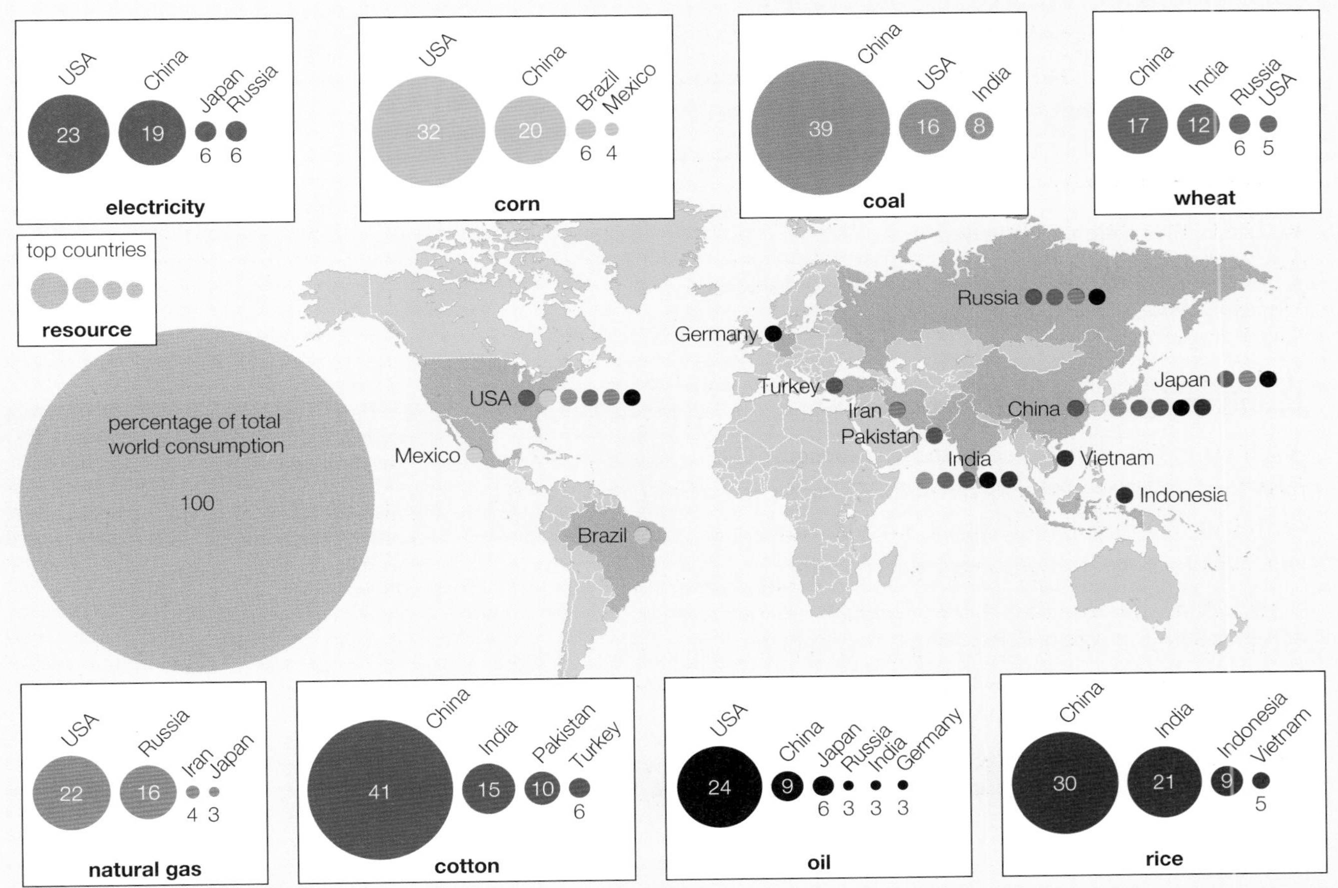

Figure 3 *The main consumers of key commodities in 2012*

The future growth of middle-class consumption in the emerging superpowers has implications for resources. The 'global middle class' has grown rapidly – according to Allianz Financial Services, it grew by 500 million between 2000 and 2014. The main growth areas are economies in Latin America, South and Southeast Asia. The analysts EY estimate that:

- in Mexico, the number of households with annual incomes of over US$50 000 is expected to reach 7 million by 2020 – an increase of 50% since 2010.
- China had 150 million middle-class residents in 2016, which is expected to increase to 500 million by 2020 – and one billion by 2030!

By 2020, more countries will reach what economists call a growth 'sweet spot' – a point when large numbers of people become middle class, and where consumption drives economic growth. Economist Surjit Bhalla estimates that every 10% increase in a nation's middle class produces an extra 0.5% annual increase in economic growth.

Threatened water resources

The World Bank believes that economic growth is pushing China towards a water crisis. China has average renewable freshwater resources of 2000 tonnes per capita, which is double the UN definition of water scarcity. However, its water resources are not evenly distributed. 70% of China's water goes to farming and 20% to the coal industry. Each of these industries is located in northern China – an area of water scarcity – where average water availability per capita is just 200 tonnes. Meanwhile, in Beijing, total consumption exceeded supply by 70% in 2012, as more residents installed showers and flush toilets.

Implications for resources in short supply

Over 1 billion Chinese now own a mobile phone. Internet usage in China reached half the population by 2016. The implications of this for resources are huge, with environmental impacts due to the materials used to make mobile phones:

- Crude oil is used to make plastics.
- Metals used in mobiles include copper, gold, nickel, and zinc. Nickel is already a shortage mineral.
- Phone batteries include several toxic and rare compounds, e.g. lithium-ion, nickel-cadmium, or lead acid. Many are toxic to the environment if buried in landfill.
- Displays on smart phones are made using plastic, glass, liquid crystalline and mercury – almost all of which are non-renewable.

Monitoring the Earth's atmosphere

In July 2014, NASA launched its most advanced CO_2 monitoring satellite. This has allowed CO_2 levels to be measured every second. Figure 4 has collated annual CO_2 concentrations: high concentrations are shown in orange, red and blue, and low concentrations in green. The greatest concentrations are shown in North America, Europe, India and China. These coincide with areas of high population density, and with the developed and emerging economies. This pattern is confirmed in Figure 5, which shows the ten largest emitters of CO_2.

Rank	Country	2013 CO_2 emissions from energy consumption	
		Total CO_2 emissions (Gt – rounded)	Tonnes CO_2 per capita
1	China	9000	6.5
2	USA	5100	17.6
3	Russia	1700	12.6
4	India	1900	1.5
5	Japan	1200	9.3
6	Germany	750	9.2
7	South Korea	610	12.5
8	Canada	560	16.2
9	Iran	550	8.0
10	Saudi Arabia	510	19.7

Figure 5 The 10 countries with the highest CO_2 emissions in 2013 by country and per capita

Figure 4 Concentrations of CO_2 in the atmosphere, averaged over a year

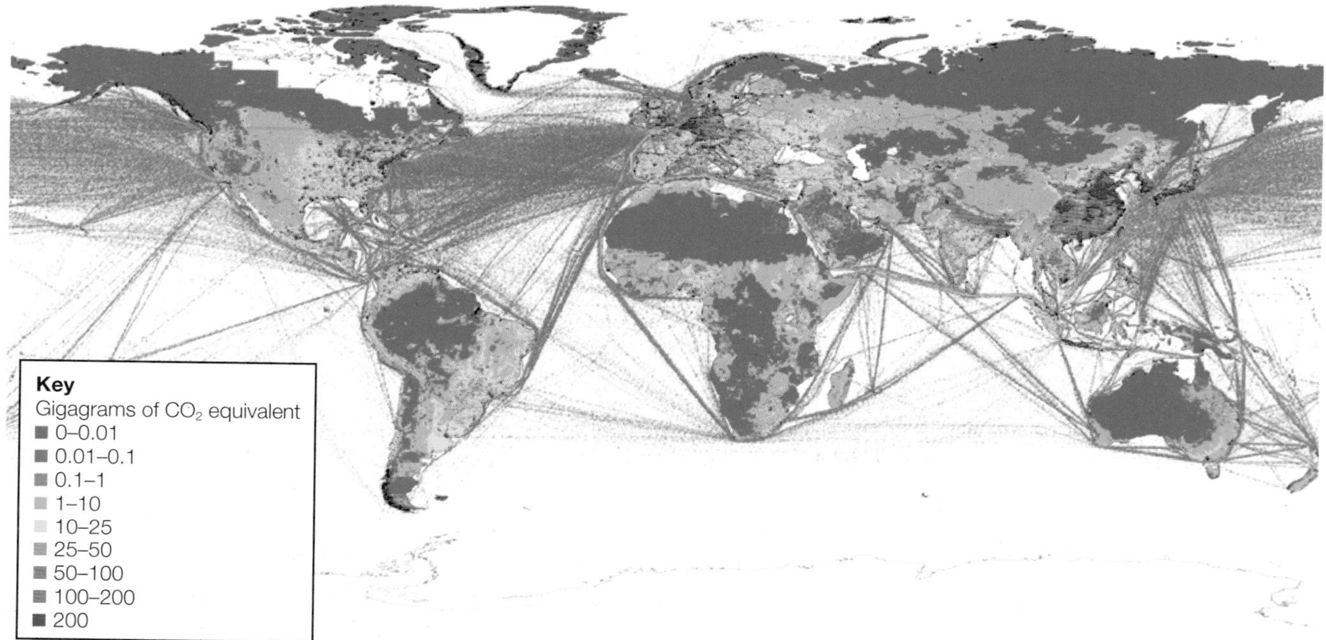

Globally, CO_2 emissions rose by 53% between 1990 and 2013. In that same period, China's emissions increased by 286% – over five times the global rate of increase – making it the world's largest CO_2 emitter, with one third of emissions (see Figure 6).

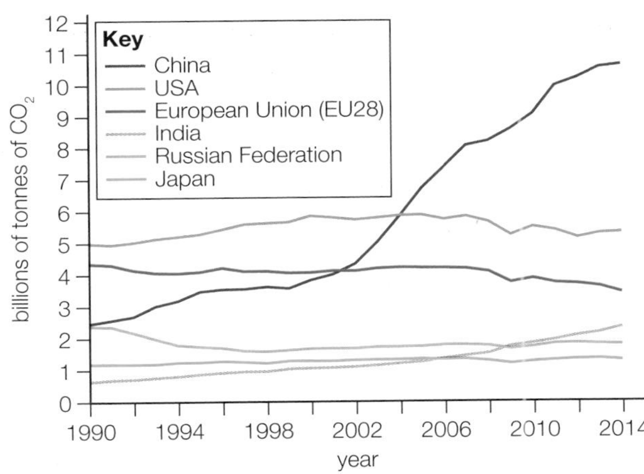

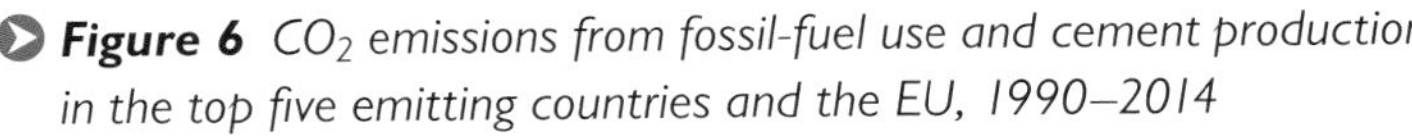

Figure 6 *CO_2 emissions from fossil-fuel use and cement production in the top five emitting countries and the EU, 1990–2014*

Global agreements on CO_2 emissions

Section 3.6 showed how global agreements on climate change involve key players. There is no doubt that superpower resource demands have a disproportionate effect on resource use and greenhouse gas emissions. But there are differences in a willingness to act:

- Any global reduction agreement would be meaningless without China. In 2014 **China** agreed to work towards an emissions peak in 2030, but only committed to any actual targets in 2016. Its current dominance in emissions means that it decides the success or otherwise of any treaties on climate change.
- **The USA** has shown global leadership, and since 2005, has reduced its total emissions most of all. From 2005–15, US wind power tripled in output, and solar energy by ten times. President Obama introduced measures to reduce greenhouse gas emissions through greater energy efficiency, promoting renewable energy, and carbon pollution standards for electricity generation. But attitudes have altered, and President Trump (elected in 2016) disputes the scientific evidence behind climate change.
- **Russia** – like China – supported the 2015 Paris Agreement, to the surprise of many, since it had been sceptical. However, most believe that Russia's attitude towards climate change is unchanged. Its agreement to reduce CO_2 emissions by 30% below 1990 levels could actually allow it to increase emissions! In 2015, these were 35% below 1990 levels (because of Russia's economic collapse after the fall of the Soviet Union in 1991).
- Meanwhile, **the EU** reflects the belief of the majority of Europeans that climate change is the most serious problem. The EU has been at the forefront of climate initiatives, e.g. carbon trading, emissions reductions (working with manufacturers of motor vehicles) and grants to encourage renewable energy. In 1997, it agreed renewable energy policies that cut 12% of total EU energy consumption by 2010, and intends cuts of 20% by 2020.

Exam-style question

Assess the extent to which global concerns about the physical environment can be disproportionately influenced by superpower actions. (*12 marks*)

Over to you

1. In pairs, draw a mind map showing how rising demand from China and other countries for food, fossil fuels and minerals has environmental effects.
2. Explain how far your mind map helps to explain the greatest concentrations of CO_2 in Figure 4.
3. 
   a Using Section 6.4, construct proportional symbols to show the ten countries in Figure 5 (i) by total CO_2 emissions and (ii) per capita.
   b Explain why the two measurements give very different results.

On your own

4. Using Figure 3, explain how far there are 'resource superpowers'.
5. Draw a table giving evidence to show how far the USA, China, Russia and the EU are committed to limiting CO_2 emissions (or not). Add your own research.
6. Write a 750-word report titled 'The middle classes – a threat to the planet?'

3.8 Contested places

In this section, you'll learn how global influence is contested in a number of different economic, environmental and political spheres.

EQ3 Sections 3.8 to 3.10 will ask what spheres of influence are contested by superpowers, and what the implications are.

Tensions over resources

SYNOPTIC THEME AND KEY CONCEPTS

- **Actions** – attitudes and actions of global players in relation to resources
- **Globalisation** – the global nature of trade agreements against counterfeiting
- **Interdependence** – the reliance of countries on the honouring of patents and intellectual property rights

In 2007, a Russian submarine sailed beneath the North Pole and planted a titanium Russian flag on the seabed – staking a claim to ownership of resources there. Other countries have made similar claims. In 2014, Denmark claimed a section of the Arctic – using the UN Convention on the Law of the Sea (UNCLOS), which says that a country can control the seabed (and its resources) within 200 nautical miles of its coastline (called the Exclusive Economic Zone or EEZ). Although Denmark has no coastline bordering the Arctic, Greenland is officially a self-governing part of Denmark, and therefore controls 900 000 km^2 of the Arctic Ocean.

As Figure 1 shows, there are currently several national claims to large parts of the Arctic – some of them overlapping. However EEZs are disputed, which has led to political and military tensions in the region. Since 2002, Canada has carried out military exercises in the Arctic, Norway has expanded its navy, Russia carries out Arctic bomber patrols, and Denmark is creating an Arctic military command and response force.

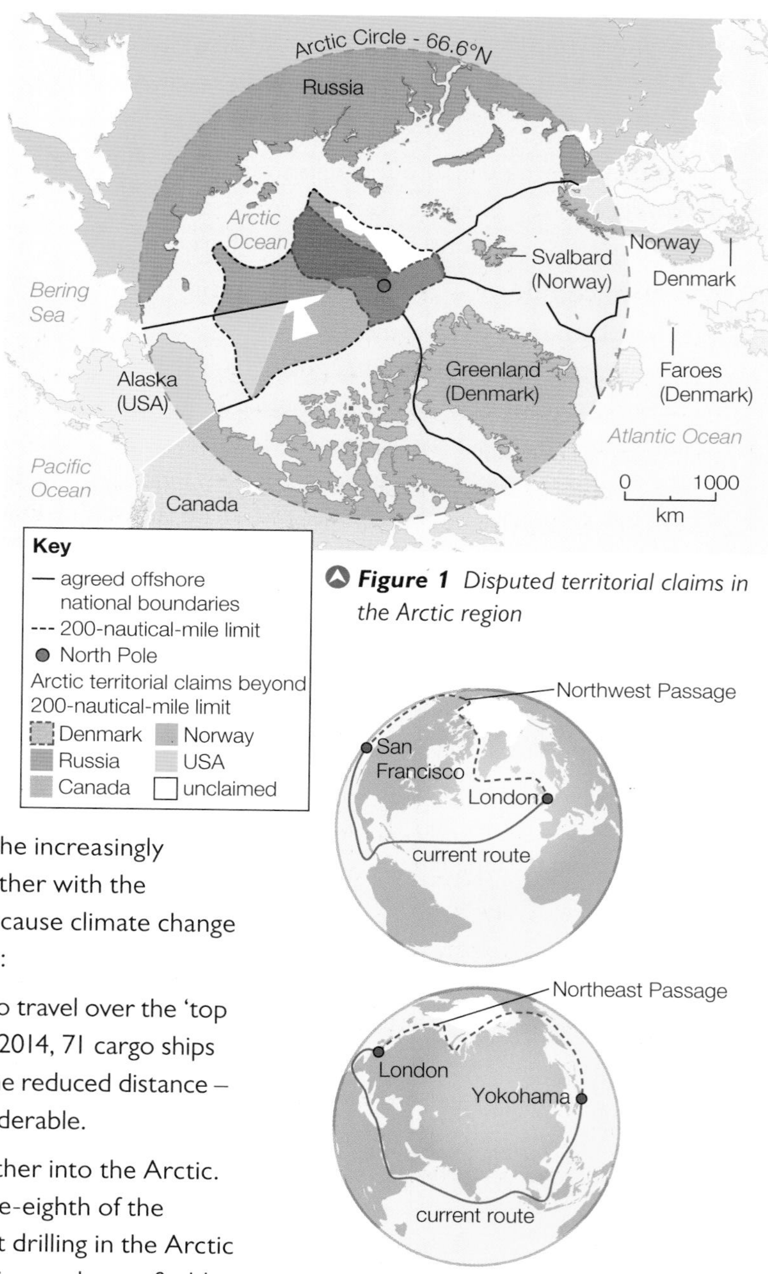

Figure 1 *Disputed territorial claims in the Arctic region*

Figure 2 *The Northeast and Northwest Passages, saving weeks on shipping routes*

The recent political and military tension is due to the increasingly accessible mineral wealth beneath the Arctic, together with the opening up of important new transport routes. Because climate change is thawing more of the Arctic Ocean each summer:

- the melting summer sea ice now allows shipping to travel over the 'top of the world', via the routes shown in Figure 2. In 2014, 71 cargo ships sailed these passages, compared to 46 in 2012. The reduced distance – and time – involved in going 'over the top' is considerable.
- drilling for oil and gas is increasingly possible further into the Arctic. The USGS estimates that the Arctic contains one-eighth of the world's untapped oil and a quarter of its gas. But drilling in the Arctic is expensive and needs high global oil and gas prices to be profitable.

Attitudes and actions in relation to resources

Tensions can arise over physical resources, including water, land and minerals, where ownership is disputed and/or disagreement exists over their exploitation. For instance, in parts of the UK, owning the land does not necessarily mean owning any mineral wealth that lies beneath it. In Cornwall, for example, the Prince of Wales owns all mineral wealth (see Figure 3).

As demand for resources increases, resource disputes are likely to become more frequent. Most are resolved peacefully, by compromise or in the courts. A few become violent, such as where governments are weak or corrupt, or where historic tensions exist. For example, Iraq's oil wealth is hotly disputed between Sunni, Shia and Kurdish regions.

Figure 3 *China clay quarrying in mid-Cornwall – every tonne extracted earns a royalty for the Prince of Wales*

Economic tensions – the world of fake

Each day, at sundown, tables appear on the streets of Bangkok's Patpong district, near the hotel and tourist hotspots. Vans unload their cargo for display on the tables. Soon, thousands of shoppers will appear to buy the cargo – fake, illegal clothes bearing global brand names, together with watches, luggage, jewellery, DVDs and software. Bangkok's counterfeit culture is fun for some; replicas cost a fraction of the normal price. A fake pair of Birkenstocks costs 200 baht a pair (£3.50). Football shirts, handbags, Rolex watches – it's hard to find merchandise that isn't fake. The quality of the workmanship ranges from excellent to poor; some of the best are almost indistinguishable from their real counterparts.

Of course, faking brands is illegal and constitutes an international crime against **intellectual property rights** (IPR) under WTO rules. Part of international trade agreements is the protection of brand names. Countries must reach agreement on intellectual rights – to protect those who have researched, designed, trialled and manufactured successful branded products in international markets. The agreement is known as **Trade-Related Aspects of Intellectual Property Rights** (known for ease as TRIPS), and is part of long-standing attempts to negotiate international rights for companies.

Figure 4 *Street sellers in Bangkok*

The TRIPS agreement incorporates IPR law into international trade. It means that WTO members guarantee copyright protection covering everything from performance rights and designs and trademarks, to confidential information (e.g. recipes for commercially produced drinks and foodstuffs). By protecting **patents** (the legal recognition that a product belongs intellectually to its developer), new innovations cannot be copied and pirated. As Figure 5 shows, the global system of IPR protection is undermined by counterfeiting, which strains trade relations and threatens TNC investment. Thailand has long been accused – rightly! – by the US government of abusing the TRIPS agreement.

IPR Climate in Thailand

Widespread counterfeiting and piracy plague IPR owners in Thailand. Lack of enforcement remains a problem. Counterfeit and pirated products are still readily accessible in retail marketplaces. Although the International Trade Court in Bangkok provides specialised judges to handle IP cases, few recent criminal cases have led to sentencing. The Thai enforcement system remains slow, with lack of consistency and deterrence, creating challenges for rights holders to enforce their rights. Law enforcement authorities are riddled with corruption. Despite assurances by the Thai Government that it will improve, progress on protection and enforcement has not been effectively implemented.

Figure 5 *An adapted statement by the US government agency 'Export.gov' about Thailand's inability to control its counterfeiting industries in December 2016*

Tensions over territory

Political influence often leads to tensions over territory and resources. There are growing tensions between Russia and many Eastern European countries (such as Poland), including former states of the USSR (such as the Baltic states). After the USSR collapsed in 1991, many Eastern European countries felt a desire for independence and to break away from Russia's influence. Many of the Eastern European states closest to the EU looked westwards for economic assistance; eight joined the EU in 2004.

The extent and influence of the EU in 2016 is shown in Figure 6. In the twenty-first century, some former Soviet states – such as Ukraine – have looked towards membership of NATO and the EU, rather than maintaining strong links to Russia, for their future. Europe's economic aid for poorer countries and regions, together with its human rights guarantees (through the European Convention on Human Rights) are attractive influences for many.

However, some countries bordering Russia (e.g. Belarus) are still influenced by Russia in terms of their economy (e.g. trade and energy supplies), culture (e.g. similar languages and social customs), or politics (e.g. similar political systems).

Figure 6 *The political influences of Russia and the EU within Europe in 2016*

Russia has felt this potential loss of influence keenly, and since 2014 has flexed its muscles in a determination to re-establish itself. As Ukraine has sought closer relationships with the EU and NATO, so Russia has opted for direct influence. In 2014, it annexed (took control of) Crimea and has supported separatists fighting in eastern Ukraine. Its armies have carried out combat exercises in the Arctic for the first time since 1991, and it is re-developing former Soviet naval and weapons bases there and testing a new generation of rockets. Its submarines and ships sailed through the North Sea and the Baltic in 2016, and within Swedish territorial waters. The message is clear – Russia wishes to re-establish its influence, using 'hard power' (see Section 3.1).

And as for China?

Until recently, the Chinese influence over global affairs tended to be economic, although that has begun to change since 2010. China has no intention of abandoning its long-held territorial claims over Tibet or Taiwan, and it also seeks to exert wider influence within Asia. For example, using the argument of the extent of its EEZ, China maintains contentious territorial claims in the South China Sea that conflict with the claims of several neighbouring countries. China's claims are based on assertions that the disputed islands are Chinese territory, because they're sitting on an extension of its continental shelf.

Figure 7 *International disputes over islands in the South China Sea*

As Figure 7 shows, areas of the South China Sea (such as the Spratly Islands) are disputed between China, Taiwan, the Philippines, Brunei, Malaysia and Vietnam, and – in recent years – India. The extent of China's territorial claims is shown by the red line on Figure 7, which clearly overlaps with the claims of five other countries. China has responded to the dispute by creating military bases in the Spratly Islands, including a 3 km-long aircraft runway on Fiery Cross Reef. Many countries are worried by this development – including India and US allies such as Japan, Taiwan and Australia.

However, China's ambitions should not be overestimated. Unlike Russia, it is not involved in military conflicts in Syria or elsewhere. It does take part in UN peacekeeping missions, but its military ambitions are focused on supporting its economy, e.g. through anti-piracy measures in 'chokepoints' in the world's shipping lanes (see Figure 4, Section 2.6).

Exam-style question

Using examples, assess the ways in which global influence may be contested politically. (*12 marks*)

Over to you

1. In pairs, study Figure 1 and explain why (**a**) Russia could be considered wrong in claiming the North Pole, (**b**) disputes are likely to persist between Denmark and other Arctic nations.
2. Search online for a map of the Arctic and annotate it to show why (**a**) increased shipping is likely to result in further disputes in the Arctic, (**b**) other countries are likely to become involved in shipping disputes.
3. In pairs, suggest possible reasons why (**a**) IPR are not always defended by consumers, (**b**) Thailand may be unwilling to promote IPR agreements.

On your own

4. Research:
   - **a** **one** dispute involving Russia and either Georgia or Ukraine
   - **b** **one** dispute involving China and one of the five other countries named in Figure 7.

   Research: (**i**) Causes of the dispute, (**ii**) Its economic, environmental or political impacts, (**iii**) Potential for the dispute to escalate, (**iv**) How the dispute is being managed.

3.9 Contesting global influence

In this section, you'll learn how developing nations have changing relationships with superpowers, with consequences for people and the physical environment.

SYNOPTIC THEMES AND KEY CONCEPTS

- **Players** – the role of emerging powers
- **Actions** – contrasting cultural ideologies between the USA and emerging powers
- **Globalisation** – the role of the globalised economy in creating new emerging political players
- **Interdependence** – the increasing interdependence between developing and emerging economies

Tensions over resources

Since 1991, and the collapse of the Soviet Union, the USA has been the only superpower in a uni-polar world (see Section 3.3). However this title is now being contested, with emerging Asian powers such as China and India. China, in particular, has become a major economy – growing from the world's sixth to second largest (behind the USA) between 2000 and 2016. It is expected to overtake the US economy in the coming decades. China's economic growth has also led to greater political influence (see Section 3.8), including within Africa.

China in Africa

As China's economy has grown, its demand for resources has led to increasing trade relations with the developing world, particularly Africa. This has increased interdependence between China and Africa – which, until 2000, was in danger of missing out on global economic growth. China's economic involvement with Africa is focused on trade and investment in infrastructure, e.g. transport links for exporting raw materials. As Figure 1 shows, the bulk of the export trade from Africa to China consists of oil and raw materials. By 2015, China's African trade (i.e. exports to, plus imports from) was worth a total of US$300 billion.

By 2015 China had become Africa's largest trading partner, which has led to US$60 billion in Chinese Foreign Direct Investment (FDI) to boost development in mining and agriculture (to guarantee supplies), and banking and IT (to create secure financial systems). Many sub-Saharan African traders now work in China, while over one million Chinese – mostly labourers and traders – have moved to Africa since 2005. Seen from an African perspective, FDI is important. But from a global perspective, the amounts are tiny; only 5% of global FDI goes to Africa, while about half is in Asia (see Figure 2).

Africa has certainly benefited from Chinese FDI, e.g. the infrastructure investment includes the renewal of the Tazara railway, which links the port of Dar es Salaam in Tanzania with Zambia's inland copper belt. Throughout Africa, China has also built schools, hospitals, anti-malaria centres and agricultural technology demonstration centres – plus trained 40 000 African personnel.

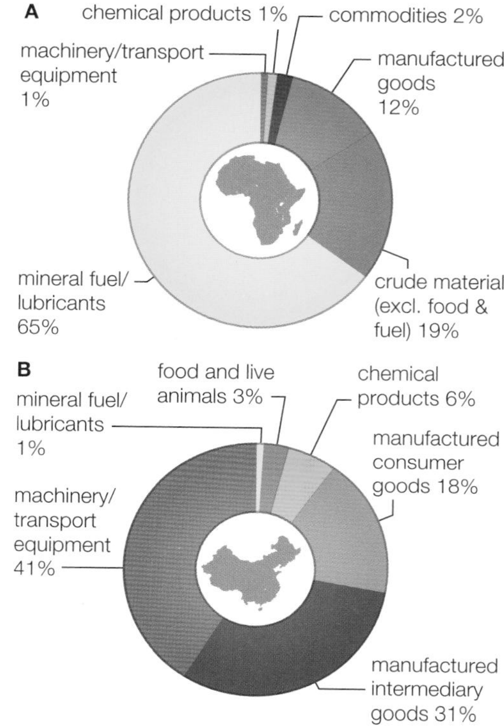

Figure 1 *Trade flows between Africa and China in 2015: (**A**) shows African exports to China and (**B**) shows Chinese exports to Africa*

Figure 2 *Global FDI inflows by amount and destination, 2000–13*

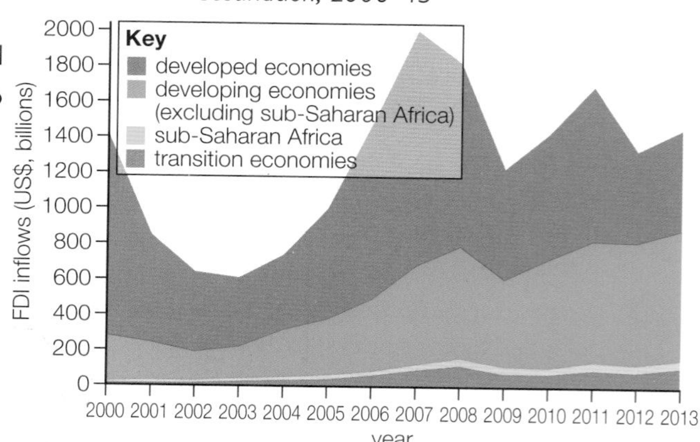

Environmental impacts in Africa

However, development also brings environmental concerns. China's decision to move some industries (e.g. steel, cement and leather tanning) from China to Africa has caused concern in some African countries. In 2014, one Chinese steel company decided to build a steelworks in South Africa – creating employment, but also air and water pollution. China has also invested in Ethiopia's leather industry, which is highly polluting.

Growing tensions within Asia

How will the rise of China and India affect regional dynamics in Asia? Could a combination of crises trigger conflicts based on historical relationships and future ambitions?

China has long-standing political tensions with Taiwan and Tibet, two examples where central Chinese control is disputed:

- **Taiwan.** In 1949, the ending of the Chinese civil war resulted in the establishment of the communist People's Republic of China on the mainland. The opposing government of the Republic of China retreated to the Chinese island province of Taiwan, with Taipei as its capital. Since that time, relations between the two governments have been tense, and no peace treaty has ever been signed. Each government claims to be China's legitimate government, and the communist Chinese government maintains its territorial claim to Taiwan as a Chinese province.
- **Tibet.** Within Tibet and beyond, among its diaspora (people living without a home territory) are those seeking the political separation of Tibet from China. Beijing's communist government is atheist, and is accused by those seeking separation of suppressing Tibetan religion, culture and freedom of expression. Beijing refuses to acknowledge the Dalai Lama, Tibet's traditional spiritual and political leader. In recent years, China has raised tensions by encouraging ethnic Chinese migrants to move to Tibet; building a high-speed rail link between Lhasa and Qinghai (see Figure 3); and investing in Tibetan industry.
- **Japan**. Tensions between China and Japan are historic, although they've improved in the twenty-first century and the two countries now trade extensively. Relations were weak since the mid-nineteenth century, and worsened when US troops were stationed in Japan after the Second World War, during the Chinese civil war. Heavy investment by the USA into Japan to aid its post-war recovery – like the European Marshall Plan in Section 3.3 – increased tensions, as Japan adopted a capitalist, westernised economic recovery.
- **India**. Relations between India and China have been tense, based on historical border disputes between them. Both countries maintain a military presence along their Himalayan borders. India is also suspicious of China's good relationship with Pakistan, and China is equally concerned about India's military interest in the South China Sea (see Section 3.8).

To the above tensions can be added those between India and Pakistan over contested borders in the disputed territory of Kashmir (see Figure 5). The two countries have gone to war several times over Kashmir, and both have now developed nuclear weapons. Tense relations also exist between Bangladesh and India over the extraction of water from the River Ganges.

Figure 3 *The new high-speed rail line between Lhasa in Tibet and Qinghai, which provides the first direct rail link between Tibet and the rest of China. It's the world's highest railway; crossing the Tibetan Plateau, it reaches over 5000 metres above sea level – the train's passengers actually need oxygen masks!*

Key players: the role of emerging powers

Globalisation has altered the geopolitical power of the Asia region, and its influence. Figure 9 in Section 3.2 shows the global economic centre of gravity. It was calculated using GDP from 700 locations, which were then averaged by location. From a mid-Atlantic position in 1980, the economic centre of gravity by 2050 is likely to be between India and China – a shift of 9300 km. Emerging countries are playing an expanding global role, because – increasingly – there is a reversal of FDI flows from emerging to developed countries. For example, in 2016, Indian company Tata's decision to reduce cuts to its UK steel plants, was greeted with relief in towns such as Port Talbot. Asian influences on the global economy are likely to continue.

Figure 4 shows China's 'One Belt, One Road' strategy, developed in 2013, a proposal by China's government to develop connectivity between China, Eurasia, and Africa. The strategy has two components:

- 'One Belt' – countries extending from Russia and Mongolia, through Central Asia, to Western Europe.
- 'One Road' – extending influence into Southeast Asia and India, then to the Middle East and East Africa.

The aim is to form a cohesive economic area by building infrastructure to increase trade and enhance cultural exchanges. This initiative places China firmly on the world stage, and should not be under-estimated – China plans US$46 billion investment in Pakistan alone!

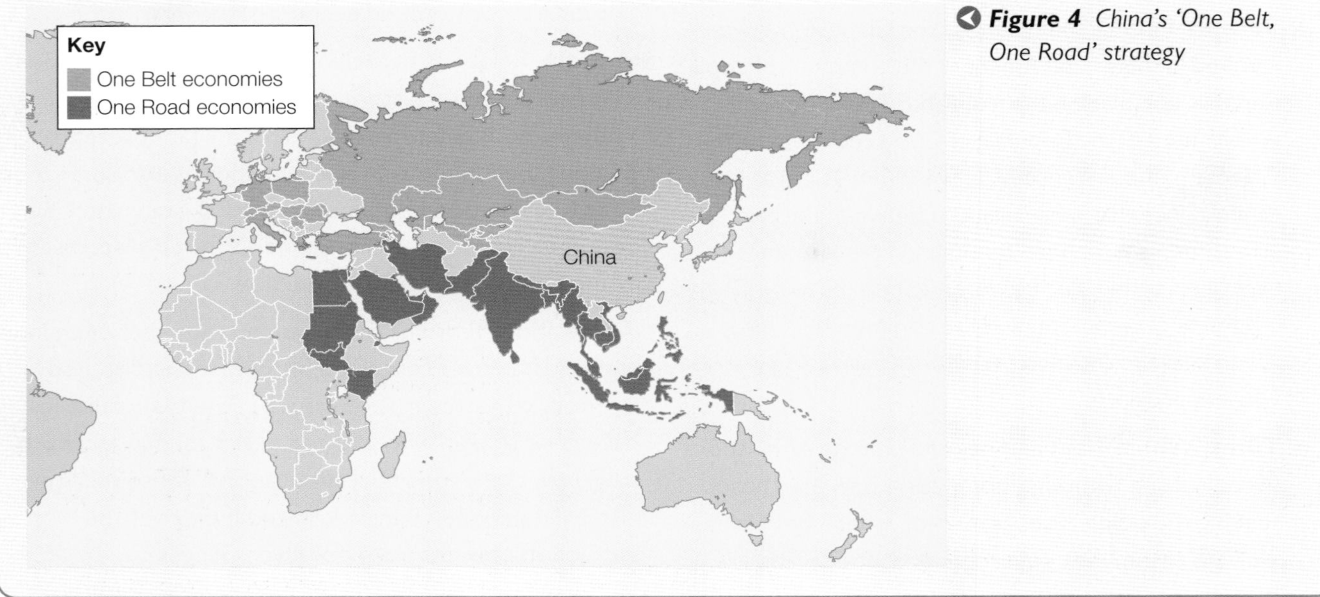

Figure 4 *China's 'One Belt, One Road' strategy*

Attitudes and actions: contrasting cultural ideologies

Tensions in the Middle East present a challenge to global superpowers; caused by complex geopolitical relations on one hand, combined with ensuring supplies of essential energy resources on the other. Figure 5 shows key, long-running trouble spots. Global sensitivities towards trouble spots are reflected in volatile swings in global oil prices that inevitably follow threats of conflict.

Tensions and conflicts in this region can be broadly categorised as:

- **Political.** The state of Israel is contentious for many Arab states, who wish to see a separate state of Palestine alongside the state of Israel. The creation of a Jewish homeland state (Israel) in 1948 politically unified the Muslim Middle East in opposition to it. As a major supporter of Israel (see section 4.7), the USA struggles to maintain a positive influence in the Arab world. In the wider Middle East region, Afghanistan has been unstable since the Soviet invasion of 1979, and has been viewed suspiciously by the USA and its allies for hiding Islamist militant groups responsible for attacks such as 9/11. Russia views any destabilisation of the Middle East caused by Islamist uprisings as a threat which might spread to its own territories in regions such as Chechnya.

- **Economic.** Despite conflict, the wider Middle East region has been an essential supplier of oil from key states such as Libya, Saudi Arabia and the UAE. The rise of ISIS in Iraq since the invasion of Allied forces has focused Western interests on defending the country's oil reserves. Turkey, a long-standing critic of Israeli government policies, nonetheless sells it much-needed water resources.
- **Cultural**, including religious and ethnic tensions. Countries of the Middle East have historical tribal or religious divisions, e.g. between Shia Iran and Sunni Iraq. These include tensions caused by Islamist uprisings, within countries such as Syria and Iraq.
- **Environmental.** Past conflicts have often resulted in economic damage to oil installations, particularly in Kuwait (following the first Gulf War in 1991) and following the invasion of Allied forces in Iraq in 2003.

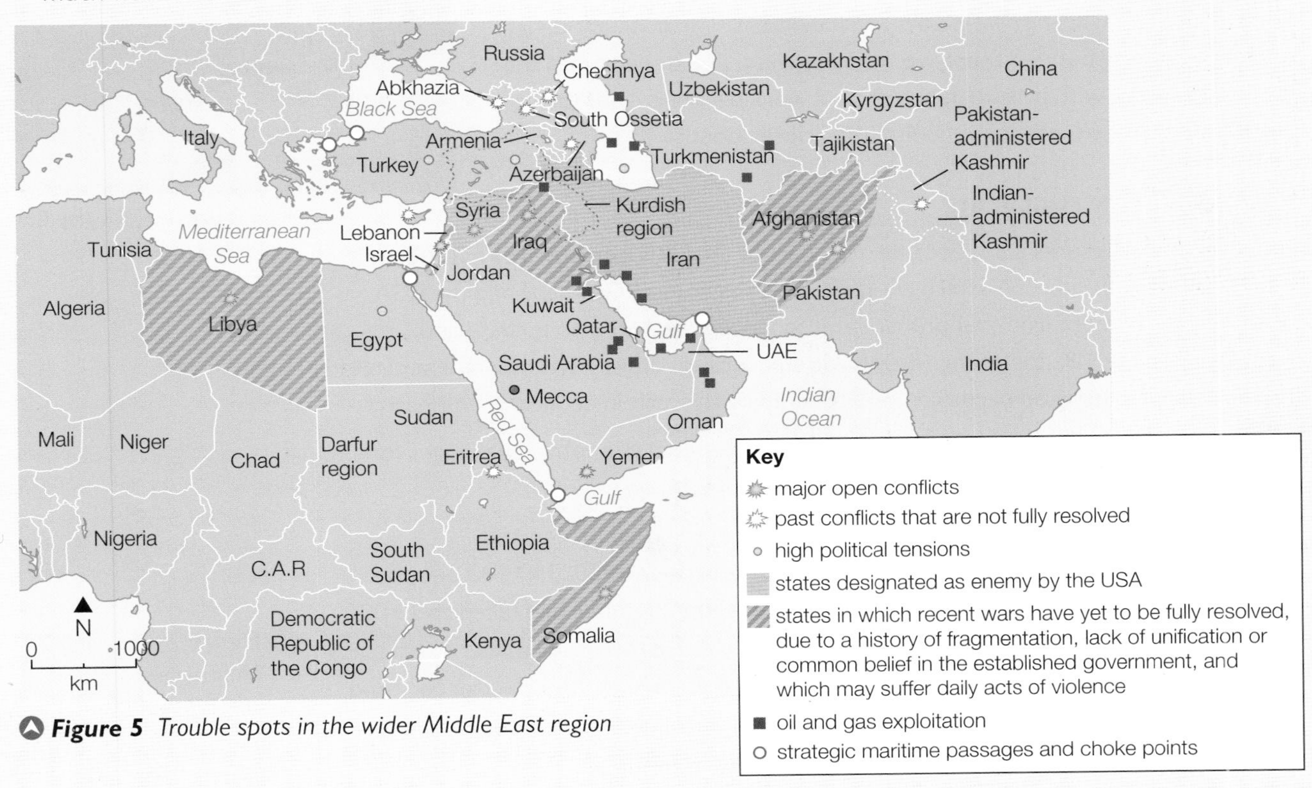

Figure 5 *Trouble spots in the wider Middle East region*

Over to you

1. Using Figure 9 in Section 3.2, and material in this section, plot the changing location of the world's economic centre of gravity on a world map up to 2050.
2. In pairs, select **one** dispute between either China or India and another country of your choosing. Prepare a six-slide presentation explaining (**a**) the origins of the dispute, (**b**) contested territories or ideologies, (**c**) its 'flashpoints' when any conflict was greatest, and (**d**) its likely future at present.

On your own

3. Using Figure 5 to guide you, research **one** wider Middle East conflict between a superpower and an energy producing country or region. Prepare a wall chart explaining (**a**) the basis of the conflict, (**b**) any ideological differences, (**c**) the territories where the conflict has been played out, (**d**) the 'flashpoints' when conflict was greatest, and (**e**) what actions you think are needed for long-term peace to occur.

Exam-style question

Referring to examples, assess the changing relationships between existing and emerging superpowers. (*12 marks*)

3.10 Challenges for the future

In this section, you'll learn how existing superpowers face on-going economic restructuring, which challenges their power.

SYNOPTIC THEME AND KEY CONCEPT

- **Futures** – the uncertainty over future power structures
- **Resilience** – the ability of individual countries to face economic and political risks

The final shift

In December 2015, Kellingley Colliery in North Yorkshire closed (see Figure 1). Opened in 1965, Kellingley was the largest remaining coalmine on the UK's largest coalfield – and the last of the UK's deep pits. At its peak in the 1970s, it employed 2000 miners, at a time when mineworkers were among the UK's highest-paid manual workers. The constant danger involved in mining bonded these workers in ways that extended into the local community, with brass bands and local working men's clubs taking a big part in their lives. Few communities had closer bonds.

Figure 1 *Kellingley Colliery in North Yorkshire*

Economic restructuring

However, mine closures soon became a big part of the UK's **economic restructuring**, which – along with other Western countries, such as France, Germany and the USA – shifted employment from the primary and secondary sectors into tertiary and quaternary. In the UK, the change began with the Conservative government first elected in 1979. Manufacturing, in particular, was affected by this shift in economic emphasis.

The process of economic restructuring created long-term economic challenges for many Western countries:

- **Unemployment** became endemic in the UK's traditional mining and manufacturing regions of the Midlands and the North. In 1980, 240 000 people worked in the UK's coalmines. By the mid-1990s, that number had fallen to 13 000. Europe's other big industrial regions, such as North Eastern France, were also badly affected, together with the 'rust belt' regions of the USA. In the USA, tertiary and quaternary employment has continued to grow in New York and Los Angeles, together with 'sun-belt' regions such as Arizona, while traditional manufacturing cities, such as Allentown, have continued to decline (see Figure 2).
- There were also major **social costs**. Social cohesion was lost in the industrial regions. Films such as *The Full Monty* portrayed northern UK cities where men lost full-time work and faced mental health problems such as depression. People often had to migrate to find work, particularly to London and the South East.

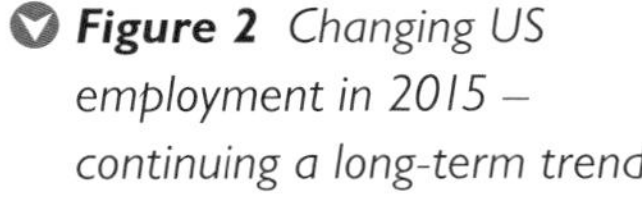

Figure 2 *Changing US employment in 2015 – continuing a long-term trend*

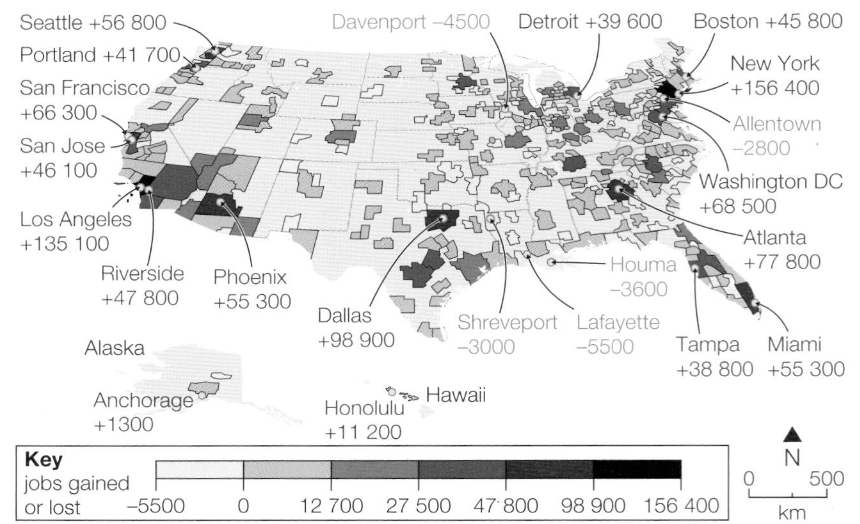

The debt problem and financial crisis

In 2007, queues of people, such as those in Figure 3, began to form outside many branches of the British bank Northern Rock. They had heard, correctly, that Northern Rock had greater debts than assets, and they feared that their savings might be at risk – so they wanted to withdraw all of their money immediately, just in case. Northern Rock had to be rescued by the Bank of England with £3 billion, and then **nationalised** to stop the panic. The government feared that, if it collapsed, the public panic would spread and other UK banks might follow it.

Figure 3 *Concerned customers queue outside the Cambridge branch of Northern Rock in 2007, because they fear their savings might be at risk*

BACKGROUND

Understanding the debt crisis

The global debt crisis arose largely from US and European mortgage-lending markets. Traditionally, funding for mortgages came from savers' invested money, which would then be lent to borrowers by the bank or building society concerned. Interest paid by the borrowers on the mortgage loans would then be used to pay interest to savers and provide the mortgage lender with a profit. Over the period of the mortgage loan (often 25 years), the mortgage lender would hold the legal deeds of the property as security, and count them as part of its **assets**. If the borrower failed to keep up their repayments, the property could then be seized by the lender.

However, debt is also an asset. Including interest, a mortgage of £100 000 can actually cost £200 000 over 25 years; and, as an asset, it can be sold. By selling on a new mortgage of £100 000 for £120 000, a lender can make a quick profit – and the debt purchaser will still collect £80 000 profit over 25 years. Selling debt raises more capital, which can then be lent to others – creating an upward spiral.

The main cause of the 2007 financial crisis was **sub-prime lending** by US banks to low-income earners with insecure jobs, who could never normally afford mortgages. Sub-prime mortgages were a risk; would they be repaid? The solution was to sell on these risky mortgages, packaged and 'hidden' inside other more-secure mortgages that were approved for higher-income earners. However, when the property bubble eventually burst, almost every global bank was affected, because the globalised nature of banking meant that even banks who had not lent sub-prime mortgages had bought debt packages from those who did.

The crisis at Northern Rock became typical in the months that followed. Confidence in the global banking system was shattered. Some of the world's largest banks:

- collapsed, e.g. US investment bank Lehmann Brothers
- were bailed out with government money, e.g. Lloyds
- were nationalised, e.g. the Royal Bank of Scotland (RBS).

The debt levels of many governments, including the UK and USA, increased because of bank bailouts, as shown in Figure 4, and they had to pay an increasing proportion of their GDP to service those debts (pay interest on the debts), e.g. UK government debt more than doubled between 2007 and 2013.

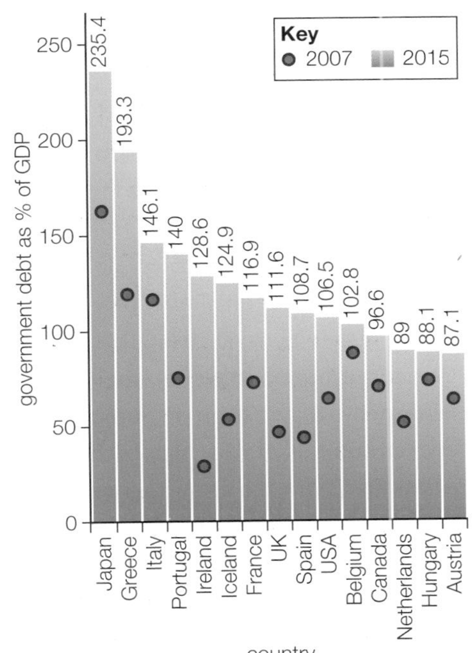

Figure 4 *Government debt as a percentage of GDP in 15 Western countries in 2007 and 2015*

The impacts of the financial crisis

The repercussions of the financial crisis were huge. Without the many bank bailouts, the potential worldwide banking collapse could have caused a global recession like that of the 1930s.

- The US government chose to react to the crisis by increasing national debt to maintain consumer spending and an economic multiplier effect.
- However, centre-right political parties in the UK and Germany favoured a second approach – known as **austerity** – to reduce government spending and debt. Austerity created increased unemployment, as government spending was cut, which led to social tensions and divisions – and bankers became hate figures.
- Elsewhere in the EU, such as Greece, a government debt crisis led to high unemployment, which in turn led to increased hate crimes against immigrants. Support for anti-immigration policies from far-right political parties, such as Golden Dawn, increased tensions.

Figure 5 *Damage caused by protestors in Athens as protests about austerity grew in 2008*

Maintaining global military power

The climate of debt and austerity has called established beliefs and organisations into question. The USA has paid a high price as a uni-polar superpower. When trouble spots have arisen (e.g. the Arab Spring uprisings in 2011), it has been the USA and its allies to whom the world has turned for help and military assistance. Why, some ask, should the USA and its allies always bear these costs?

National defence budgets are usually large. The UK had the world's fifth largest defence budget in 2016-17 (£46 billion or US$56 billion), but that was only the equivalent of 10% of the US defence budget. Within debates about military funding, a question arises – how far should high technology such as unmanned drones meet future challenges, and how far should conventional military power be maintained?

1 Naval power

The desire to expand the British Royal Navy has to be set against a decline in government defence spending; during the Falklands War in 1982, the UK spent 4% of its GDP on defence, which has since been almost halved. The UK's debate about its naval strength is typical – is it better to have a larger number of low-cost ships, providing strength in numbers, or a smaller number of very high-tech ships to act in situations as diverse as anti-piracy operations, hunting drug runners or delivering humanitarian assistance? The Royal Navy's newest Type 45 destroyers use the latest technology (see Figure 6), but the UK had just six of these ships in 2016.

Figure 6 HMS Duncan, *a modern Type 45 destroyer. This is the latest addition to the Royal Navy's 77 sea-going ships. However in 1945 (at the end of the Second World War), the Royal Navy had nearly 900 ships.*

BACKGROUND

NATO – who, when, what?

The North Atlantic Treaty Organization (NATO) was first formed in 1949, after the Second World War. It originally had 12 members and was established to assist Western Europe (in alliance with the USA and Canada) in responding to the threat of the USSR and its allies in Eastern Europe (known as the Warsaw Pact countries). Its guiding principle – an attack on one member is an attack on all – has been invoked just once, after the 9/11 attacks in 2001.

Since 1991, and the collapse of the USSR, the Warsaw Pact has disbanded and NATO has expanded; now it includes many former Warsaw Pact members, such as Poland. As Figure 7 shows, NATO had reached a membership of 28 in 2016.

The funding question

NATO funding is in theory based on GDP per capita and population, so that individual members' shares reflect their national wealth, and therefore their capacity to pay. The US share is calculated using GNI per capita, and is adjusted as the US population increases. Currently the US share of NATO's overall budget is just over 22% (see Figure 7), compared to Germany's 14.7% and France's 10.6%, and so on.

However, NATO's funding is contentious, because only five members actually spend the target of 2% of their GDP on defence – the USA, Greece, the UK, Estonia and Poland. 23 members of NATO do not meet this target, and the median spending in 2015 was only 1.2% of GDP. The five countries that do meet the funding target question why the others do not.

Country	Share of NATO's budget, 2016–17 (%)	Country	Share of NATO's budget, 2016–17 (%)
Albania	0.1	Latvia	0.1
Belgium	1.9	Lithuania	0.2
Bulgaria	0.3	Luxembourg	0.1
Canada	6.6	Netherlands	3.2
Croatia	0.3	Norway	1.7
Czech Republic	0.9	Poland	2.7
Denmark	1.2	Portugal	1.0
Estonia	0.1	Romania	1.1
France	10.6	Slovakia	0.5
Germany	14.7	Slovenia	0.2
Greece	1.1	Spain	5.8
Hungary	0.7	Turkey	4.4
Iceland	0.1	UK	9.8
Italy	8.4	USA	22.1

Figure 7 *Individual member shares of NATO's budget, 2016–17. Decimals have been rounded and therefore may not add to 100% exactly.*

2 Nuclear weapons

The nuclear debate has persisted since 1945 – is it worth possessing weapons which, based on historical precedent, may never be used? Those in favour argue that the possession of such weapons is a deterrent to any major escalation of a conflict. Those against argue that the only beneficiaries of nuclear defence are the (mainly) US defence industries. In 2016, the UK Parliament voted to replace the UK's existing controversial Trident nuclear deterrent (see Figure 8) with an updated version. Trident consists of four submarines that can each carry up to 16 missiles, each one armed with up to eight nuclear warheads.

The cost of the upgraded deterrent is considerable, with estimates varying between £100 billion and £250 billion over 45-50 years. The nuclear weapons themselves are expensive, as are the submarines that carry them, and there are also major costs involved in protecting them when in port and in decommissioning them at the end of their lives.

Figure 8 *Protests against the UK's renewal of its Trident nuclear deterrent in 2016*

3 Air power

The costs of air power tend to be the second highest after nuclear weapons. Current warfare is much more focused on rapid response air power, rather than the size of naval fleets, and the list of the world's ten largest air forces in Figure 9 shows some significant players. The research and development needed to upgrade and maintain combat aircraft means that their cost can increase rapidly when, for most countries, defence budgets are declining. The share of combat aircraft within defence budgets is increasing as the world becomes less peaceful. Challenges so far during the twenty-first century have included bombing in Libya after the Arab Spring of 2011 and the continuing conflict over Syria.

Country	Number of combat aircraft
USA	3318
Russia	1900
China	1500
India	1080
Egypt	900
North Korea	661
Pakistan	502
Turkey	465
South Korea	458
Germany	423

Figure 9 *The world's largest air forces in 2016 by their number of fixed-wing combat aircraft (i.e. helicopters are not included). The UK was eleventh, and France and Saudi Arabia are among the countries just below that.*

4 Intelligence services

Since 9/11 and the subsequent terrorist attacks in Paris, London and elsewhere, government budgets have become increasingly directed towards anti-terrorism work. The war against terrorism is varied – it depends on intelligence derived from on-the-ground surveillance, as well as the electronic interception of mobile phones, email and social media. In spite of the technology, it is still extremely labour intensive – and therefore very costly. However it has claimed many successes, such as the uncovering of terrorist plots across Europe before the terrorists could strike.

5 Space exploration

Only a few countries or partnerships are committed to space exploration – the USA, Russia, the EU, China, Canada, Japan and India. In 2014, the budgets were: in the USA US$17.6 billion, the EU US$5.5 billion, Russia US$5.6 billion, Japan US$2 billion, China US$1.3 billion, India US$1.1 billion and Canada US$0.5bn. The funding is generally used for genuine exploration, rather than military purposes, and it includes joint funding for the International Space Station shown in Figure 10.

However, space budgets are under threat in many Western countries, while Asian countries, such as India and China, have now adopted major space programmes and are able to launch space flights much more cheaply:

- India sent a non-crewed probe to the moon in 2008, and also launched an orbital mission to Mars in 2013. It cost just US$72 million for the satellite and ground tracking and communication infrastructure on Earth.
- China built and launched the Tiangong-1 space station in 2011, and has also landed an exploration rover on the moon.

Figure 10 *The International Space Station, a joint mission funded by the USA, Canada, Russia, Japan and the European Space Agency*

Futures and uncertainties: future power structures

Who will the superpowers of 2030 and 2050 be?

- Will the USA continue to dominate in a uni-polar world?
- Will China overtake the USA's GDP to create a bi-polar world?
- Will an expansionist Russia join China and the USA to create a multi-polar world?

The above questions need informed predictions, but those can still be proved wrong:

- In 2005, the writer Richard Scase predicted that the BRICs (see Section 3.2) would become major economic superpowers by 2020. However, only China is currently realising that prediction.
- In the mid-1980s, economists predicted a time when Japan would overtake the USA as the world's largest economy. However, the Asian financial crisis of 1997 ensured that that prediction never happened.

Now, the data in Figure 11 suggest that China may overtake the USA as the world's largest economy between 2025 and 2030. Will that prediction prove to be accurate?

How well will economies dependent on supplying fossil fuels, such as Russia, face a potential future of precarious economic growth? Much may depend on other factors. For example, during 2015-16, Russia was increasingly interventionist militarily – particularly in Syria – as well as displaying growing confidence along its European borders and in its tense relationship with Ukraine.

Country	2005	2010	2015	2020 est.	2021 est.
USA	13 093 700	14 964 400	18 036 650	21 926 509	22 766 776
Japan	4 572 414	5 498 719	4 124 211	5 506 436	5 603 523
Germany	2 866 308	3 423 466	3 365 293	4 007 765	4 113 869
France	2 207 450	2 651 772	2 420 163	2 850 668	2 941 078
UK	2 511 165	2 431 169	2 858 482	2 927 636	3 022 202
Brazil	891 633	2 208 705	1 772 589	2 213 760	2 314 835
China	2 308 821	6 066 212	11 181 556	16 458 029	18 033 354
India	834 218	1 708 460	2 073 002	3 297 453	3 650 615
Russia	820 568	1 638 463	1 326 016	1 698 192	1 786 240
World	**47 325 751**	**65 643 256**	**73 598 823**	**93 599 266**	**98 632 169**

***Figure 11** Actual GDP 2005–2015 and predictions for 2020–21 for nine of the world's largest economies (in millions of US$)*

Over to you

1 In pairs, construct a mind map with four 'arms' – Economic restructuring, Unemployment, Social costs, Debt. Summarise (**a**) the causes, (**b**) the impacts of each topic on the relevant arm.

2 In pairs, draw up a list of the costs and benefits of naval, nuclear, air power, intelligence services and space exploration in terms of their importance to (**a**) the UK, (**b**) one globally significant country of your choice. You may want to research up-to-date budget data and details about each of the categories.

3 a Using lined graph paper, construct a line graph with dates shown to 2050 to show the past and predicted future GDPs of the countries shown in Figure 11 up to 2021.

b Based on your graph, predict each country's GDP in 2030 and 2050.

c Use the World Bank website to update the data in Figure 11. How far do the new data affect your predictions in part (b)?

On your own

4 a Explain why austerity raises questions about defence spending.

b Outline possible arguments for maintaining or even increasing defence spending in the light of austerity.

5 Write a 750-word report entitled 'Nuclear weapons – a waste of money?'.

Exam-style question

Assess the extent to which the position of the USA as a uni-polar superpower is being questioned. (*12 marks*)

Conclusion – revisiting the Enquiry Questions

These are the key questions that drive the whole topic:

1 What are superpowers and how have they changed over time?

2 What are the impacts of superpowers on the global economy, political systems, and the physical environment?

3 What spheres of influence are contested by superpowers and what are the implications of this?

Having studied this topic, you can now consider some answers to these questions, using the synoptic themes to frame your ideas.

Players – discussion point 1
Working in groups, consider two instances from this chapter where either the roles played by TNCs in their influence over the global economy, or superpowers in their roles as 'global police', have created conflict. Explain your views.

Attitudes and Actions – discussion point 2
Working in groups, discuss and draw a diagram which shows how and why the actions of different superpowers (e.g. towards climate change) may vary.

Futures and Uncertainties – discussion point 3
Working in groups, consider the different scenarios concerning (a) climate change, and (b) the pursuit of resources. Use instances from this chapter to identify the actions that should be taken to manage future global environmental issues and economic growth. Explain your views.

Books, music, and films on this topic

Books to read

1. *Superpower: Three Choices for America's Role in the World* by Ian Bremmer (2015)
   This book gives an insight into why the USA is a superpower and also analyses its foreign policy and global influence.
2. *China Inc.* by Ted C. Fisherman (2006)
   This book assesses how superpower status can be obtained, as well as China's potential as a superpower created by its economic revolution.
3. *Tinker Tailor Soldier Spy* by John Le Carré (1974)
   Set in the Cold War, this book's plot concerns a Soviet mole in the British secret intelligence services.

Music to listen to

1. 'Land of Hope and Glory' (1902)
   Written at, arguably, the peak of the British Empire, it shows how superpowers change over time, and how self-belief influences superpower status!
2. 'Two Tribes' (1984) by Frankie Goes To Hollywood
   This song was released when fears of nuclear war between the USA and USSR were considerable. The video is especially worth watching.
3. 'Cops of The World' (1966) by Phil Ochs
   This song, written during the Vietnam War, is about the influence of the USA as a 'global policeman' on the world.

Films to see

1. *The New Rulers of The World* (2001)
   This is an alternative viewpoint to the mainstream view of power and geopolitics by John Pilger, who explores global power, inequality, and the influence of TNCs on superpower governments.
2. *Superpower* (2008)
   This is an in-depth documentary assessing the USA's emergence as a superpower since 1945 and how it has gained superpower status.
3. *Deutschland 83* (2016)
   A German TV series set in East Germany at a time of tense Cold War relations between the two sides of a divided Germany.

Health, human rights and intervention

4

Chapter overview – introducing the topic

This chapter studies health and human rights, and the reasons why they are contested in different parts of the world – to the extent that military action is sometimes used to defend human rights in some countries.

In the specification, this topic has been framed around four Enquiry Questions:

1. What is human development, and why do levels vary from place to place?
2. Why do human rights vary from place to place?
3. How are human rights used as arguments for political and military intervention?
4. What are the outcomes of geopolitical interventions in terms of human development and human rights?

The sections in this chapter provide the content and concepts needed to help you answer these questions.

Synoptic themes

Underlying the content of every topic are three synoptic themes that 'bind' or glue the whole specification together:

1. Players
2. Attitudes and Actions
3. Futures and Uncertainties

Note that there is no requirement to study the synoptic themes in this topic. However, the synoptic themes are useful in applying your understanding, and the following content areas are relevant to this.

1 Players

Players are individuals, groups and organisations involved in making decisions that affect people and places, collectively known as **stakeholders**. Players can be national or international individuals and organisations (e.g. IGOs like the UN), national and local governments, businesses (from small operations to the largest TNCs), as well as pressure groups and NGOs, together with others.

Players that you'll study in this topic include:

- Section 4.3 – The role played by **governments** in deciding what to spend on health, or, in Section 4.6, in promoting policies that create inequalities.
- Section 4.9 – The role of **national** and **international governments** in condoning military action.

2 Attitudes and Actions

People's attitudes towards health (particularly how it is funded) and human rights vary, together with attitudes about interventions in dealing with human rights (e.g. policies which include military action). People's values and attitudes depend on several factors:

- Their political views (left- or right-wing, for example), and/or their religious beliefs.
- The priorities given to people versus profit.
- The importance of social justice and equality.

Attitudes and Actions that you'll study in this topic include:

- Section 4.3 – How and why governments have different attitudes towards health spending.
- Section 4.8 – The extent to which governments are prepared to offer financial aid to other countries.

3 Futures and Uncertainties

Decisions and actions taken by players today will affect people in the future. For example, is military intervention to defend and assert human rights justifiable, or does it result in opposition to intervention in the affairs of others?

Futures and Uncertainties that you'll study in this topic include:

- Section 4.12 – Why military intervention in some countries that abuse human rights is more likely than in others, who abuse to a similar or greater extent.

4.1 Human development

In this section, you'll learn about concepts of human development and why they are complex and often contested.

EQ1 Sections 4.1 to 4.3 investigate what is meant by human development and why levels of development vary from place to place.

KEY CONCEPT

- **Inequality** – why levels of development vary from place to place

Geography, development and enthusiasm!

Few people have the knack of putting across ideas like Professor Hans Rosling! He was famous for his online lectures, in which he used toy bricks, cardboard boxes, teacups and animated data visualisations (as in Figure 1) to explain statistics on global issues of health, wealth and population.

Figure 1 *Hans Rosling leading one of his famous lectures at the University of Oxford. To actually watch one of these lectures, search for 'Hans Rosling Gapminder' through a search engine or via YouTube. Hans Rosling died in February 2017.*

Rosling used material from his website, Gapminder, which consists of a visual database using UN and World Bank data since 1980. Gapminder presentations are highly visual, and Rosling's message was simple. He argued that the world has made great strides in health, family size and life expectancy since 1980. Those countries that have developed most rapidly (such as South Korea in Figure 2) have improved the most. However, progress has also occurred in the world's poorest countries (such as Malawi in Figure 2) – but Rosling argued that there is still some way to go.

He felt that future goals should be to improve:

- environmental quality, e.g. air and water quality
- the health and life expectancy of the poorest
- human rights, e.g. rights for women.

Rosling believed that economic growth is the most important way of achieving these three goals. But he also argued that human rights, especially property rights, are essential to economic growth, and that human rights cannot exist without good, stable governance – the essence of modernisation theory (see Section 3.4).

Data	Malawi		UK		South Korea	
Demographic indicators	**1980**	**2014**	**1980**	**2014**	**1980**	**2014**
Birth rate (per 1000 people)	53	39	13	12	23	9
Death rate (per 1000 people)	21	8	12	9	7	5
Fertility rate	7.6	5.1	1.9	1.8	2.8	1.2
% population aged 0–14	47	45	21	18	34	14
% population aged 65 and over	2	3	15	18	4	13
Dependency ratio %	99	95	56	55	61	37
Health indicators						
Life expectancy (years)	45	63	74	81	66	82
Infant mortality per 1000 live births	152	43	12	4	12	3
Maternal mortality per 100 000 births	957 (1990)	460	10 (1990)	9	21 (1990)	11

Figure 2 *Comparing changing population and health indicators for Malawi, South Korea and the UK, 1980–2014*

The show goes on ...

By 2014, the global economy had grown in terms of Gross Domestic Product (GDP) for 52 of the previous 53 years (see Figure 3). Countries such as South Korea in Figure 2 have played a big part in this economic growth. The growth trend is likely to continue as more people around the world seek to improve the quality of their lives. The International Monetary Fund (IMF) estimated that global economic growth in 2015 was 3.3% and predicted that this would increase to 3.8% in 2016.

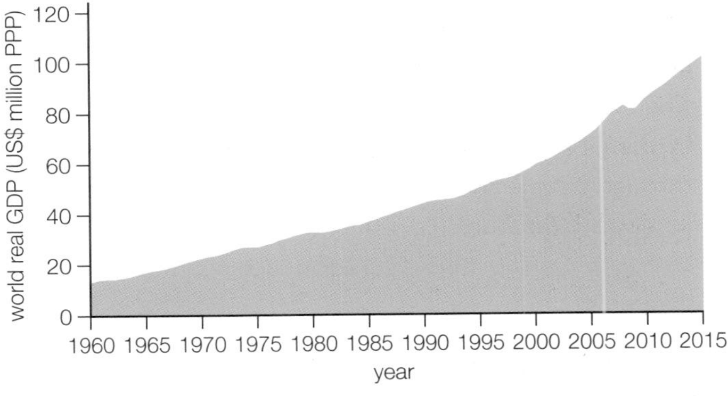

Figure 3 *The growth of global GDP (1960–2015) Note that the only dip on the graph is in 2008–9, after the global financial crisis.*

Measuring economic inequality

Despite overall global economic growth, and the kinds of social progress that Rosling celebrated (see Figure 2), there nonetheless remains great inequality between countries (compare South Korea and Malawi in Figure 2) and within countries. To assess the degree of inequality within any country, an indicator known as the **Gini coefficient** is used. It measures the extent to which income distribution deviates from perfect equality. A Gini coefficient score of 0 indicates perfect equality (everyone has the same income), whilst a score of 1 indicates maximum inequality (one person has all the income). In general, the world's poorest countries are the most unequal, and in recent years, with a few exceptions such as Greece (see Figure 4), wealthier countries have also become more unequal.

Key word

Gross Domestic Product (GDP) – The monetary value of all goods and services produced by a country in a year. It is calculated by combining the value of all of the finished goods produced, together with the value of services (e.g. banking and tourism). GDP is converted to US$ to facilitate comparisons between countries, and may then be divided by the population to give a **per capita** (per person) value.

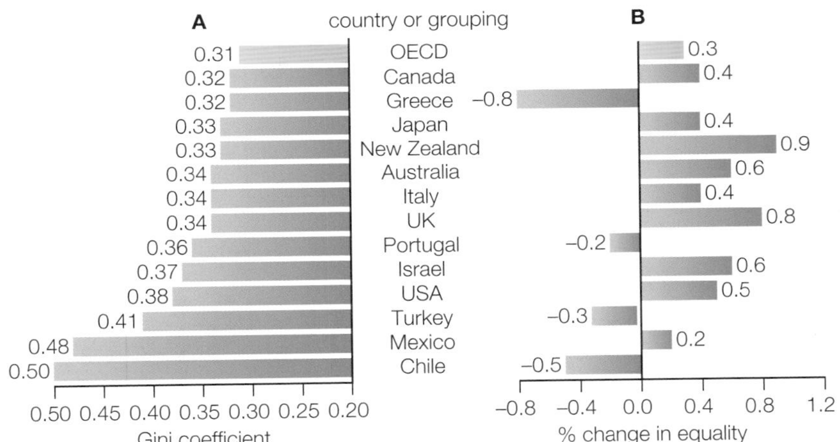

Figure 4 *Changes in the Gini coefficient over time. Graph **A** shows the Gini coefficient for a selection of high- and middle-income countries in 2011. Graph **B** shows the percentage improvement in inequality (countries showing a minus value), or worsening (countries showing a plus value), between the mid-1980s and late 2000s.*

Measuring human development

Development means change for the better – progress sustained over the long-term. However, its measurement is both complex and contested, whether using economic indicators (e.g. GDP), human (e.g. education), and wealth distribution (e.g. the Gini coefficient).

- Economic development is often measured using GDP per capita (or its variants e.g. GNI). But these are crude averages, and mask skews in income distribution, where the majority of incomes fall well below the mean, and a minority of very wealthy raise the average.
- There are few measures concerning the informal economy. Yet in Uganda, the informal economy is estimated to produce 60% of GDP!

However, countries with similar GDP vary in human indicators, such as life expectancy. Development is better considered as the advancement of human well-being through:

- improving people's lives, rather than assuming economic growth leads to greater well-being.
- developing their abilities e.g. promoting higher education, or enabling choices (e.g. through girls' education).

The Human Development Index (HDI)

Measuring human development is complex, because it requires data using both economic and social measures. The **Human Development Index (HDI)** was devised by the UN to simplify the process of showing progress through people and their capabilities. The HDI is a composite measure (i.e. using more than one indicator) to create a single index figure for each country from four data sets:

- Life expectancy
- Education (using two indicators – literacy and average length of schooling)
- GDP per capita (in US$ PPP).

The HDI for each country is calculated by taking these and converting each into an index figure – the value of which ranges from 0 (low) to 1 (high). So the index figure for adult literacy is calculated by taking the literacy rate and expressing it as a figure between 0 and 1 – a 75% adult literacy rate would be 0.75, 50% adult literacy 0.5, etc. The four index figures are then averaged to produce the HDI.

The 2015 Human Development Report shows that, since 1990, 2 billion people have been lifted out of low human development, and that almost every country in the world has seen HDI gains in that period. However, HDI takes no account of environmental quality, democracy or the engagement of voters within it, personal or national security, inequality or freedom of speech.

The Happy Planet Index (HPI)

The **Happy Planet Index (HPI)**, shown in Figure 5, is a measure of sustainable well-being, which shows the extent to which countries deliver long, happy, and sustainable lives for the people who live in them. It is based on three indicators:

- **Life expectancy** – The average number of years that a person born now is expected to live in each country, based on UN data.
- **Experienced well-being** – How satisfied the residents of each country say they feel with life overall, on a scale from 0 to 10, using data collected by Gallup's World Poll.
- **Ecological footprint** – The average impact that each country's residents have on the natural environment, using data collected by the Global Footprint Network (the amount of land required to sustain a country's consumption pattern).

Figure 5 *A Happy Planet Index (HPI) map of the world for 2012 (no country meets the top category)*

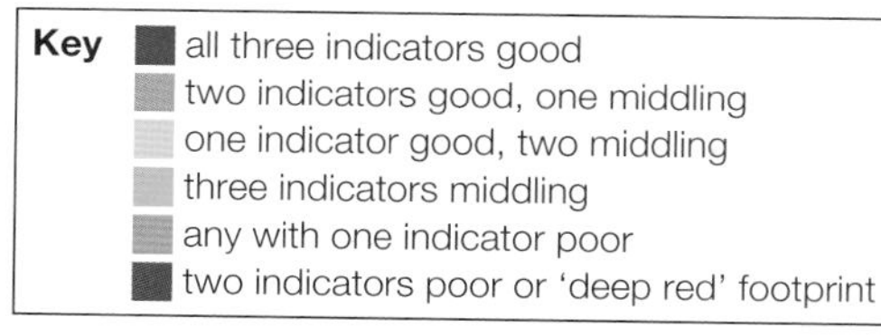

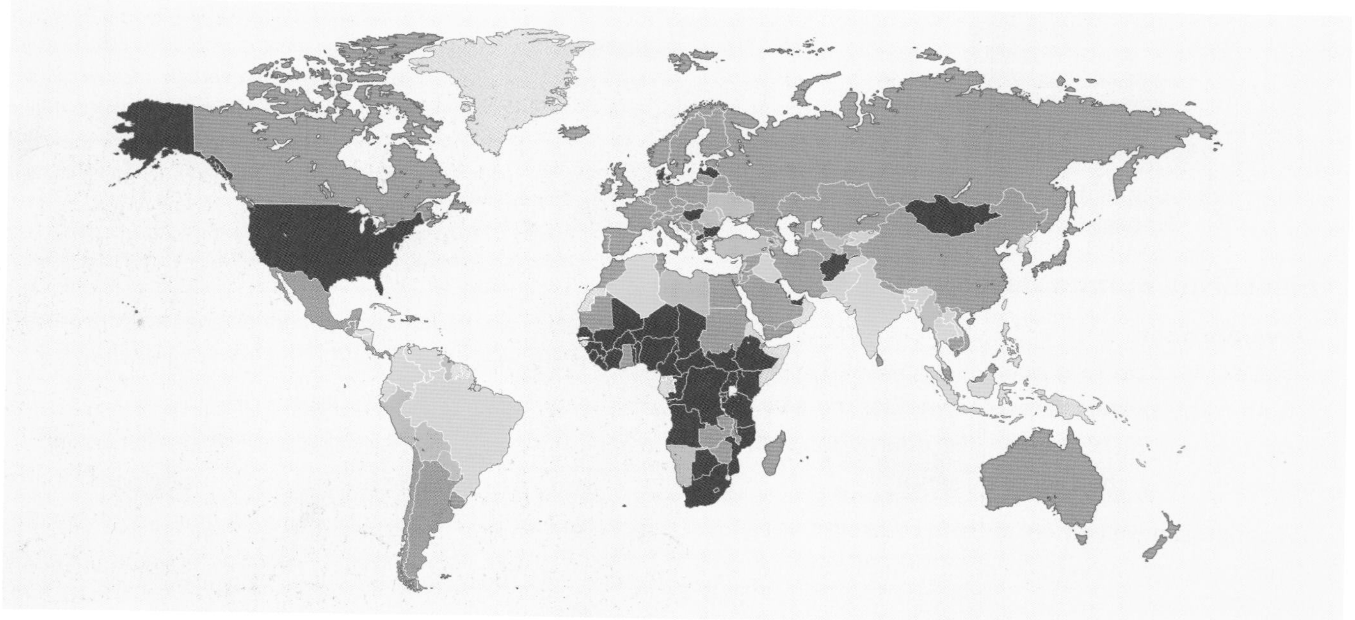

Each country is given an HPI score based on the calculation:

$$\text{Happy Planet Index} = \frac{\text{experienced well-being x life expectancy}}{\text{ecological footprint}}$$

The HPI scores are then adjusted statistically so they lie between 0 and 100. The results of the 2012 HPI report showed that:

- we are still not living on a happy planet. No country achieved high and sustainable well-being, and only nine were close to doing so (eight of which were in Latin America and the Caribbean; see Figure 5).
- the scores of many high-income countries were reduced by their large ecological footprints.
- the USA (with the world's largest economy) was in 105th place out of 151 countries (see Figure 6).

Figure 6 *New York, the largest city in the world's largest economy – but by no means the 'happiest' country*

It's not the only way!

The traditional model of measuring economic growth using GDP is one way of assessing possible improvements in human development. Other approaches contest that model. Two examples are discussed here – the first one, Sharia law, shows the importance of human welfare; the second one, about Bolivia, shows the importance of the intervention of national government.

Sharia law

Sharia law is the law of Islam. It is derived from the actions of the Prophet Muhammad and the words he expressed in the Qur'an. Aspects of a Muslim's life are governed by Sharia. In Islamic tradition, Sharia is seen as nurturing and freeing humanity to realise its individual potential. Muslims believe that God sent prophets and books to humanity to show them the way to happiness in this life, and success in the hereafter, and that the welfare of humans is based on the fulfilment of:

- **necessities** – five things that worldly and religious life depend on. The five necessities are the preservation of religion, life, intellect, lineage, and wealth.
- **needs and comforts** – things that people seek in order to ensure a good life and avoid hardship, even though they are not essential.

Muslims believe that everything that ensures human happiness, within the spirit of Divine Guidance, is permitted in the Sharia.

Figure 7 *Sharia councils in the UK issue Islamic divorce certificates and advice on other aspects of religious Islamic law*

Bolivia under Evo Morales

Juan Evo Morales, a member of the indigenous Aymara group, first became President of Bolivia in 2005 – the first Bolivian President to come from its indigenous majority. His election followed years of excluding indigenous people from Bolivia's political system, an economy with rampant inflation, the selling off of State assets, and high levels of poverty. Evo Morales is an avowed socialist who has combined his left-wing philosophy with traditional Andean values of communal ownership and co-operation.

Bolivia under Morales has been transformed (see page 239). He began by renationalising Bolivia's oil and gas industries. The Morales-led government now uses the revenue from the royalties and profits it earns to fund public works projects and social programmes to fight poverty. Extreme poverty in Bolivia has fallen by 43%. However, despite Bolivia's economic advancements, it remains one of South America's poorest countries, and is still dependent on its natural resources for economic growth.

Figure 8 *Evo Morales has transformed Bolivia, with policies deliberately focused on social gains and reduced inequalities for Bolivians.*

Education matters

Education is central to economic development; a literate population is a population skilled in reasoning and cultural appreciation – and an asset to the economy. Investing in education and health is therefore regarded as investment in **human capital** (the economic, political, cultural and social skills within a country).

Education is also central to an understanding and assertion of human rights, and to democratic participation. The International Covenant on Economic, Social and Cultural Rights (ICESCR) is part of the International Bill of Human Rights passed by the UN, which has been signed by 163 countries since 1948. It recognises the right of everyone to free education at primary level and 'the progressive introduction of free education' for secondary and higher levels. It asserts that education is key to 'the full development of the human personality and the sense of its dignity', and education also enables all people to participate effectively in society.

Variations in education

Despite improvements in the numbers of children attending school worldwide, the United Nations Educational, Scientific and Cultural Organisation (UNESCO) has found that education still remains inaccessible to over 60 million children of primary school age worldwide (see Figure 9). This is often due to continuing inequalities and marginalisation; children often do not have access to basic education because of inequalities such as their gender, health or **cultural identity** (e.g. ethnic origin, language, or religion).

Figure 9 *The number of children of primary school age not attending school in different world regions, 1990–2012*

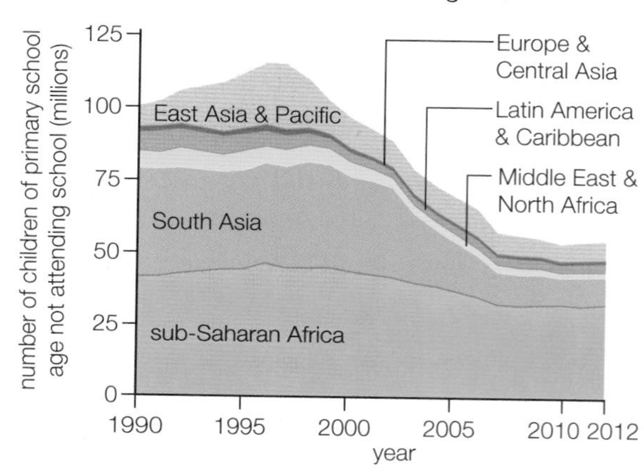

UNESCO has reported that sub-Saharan Africa has the highest number of children without access to education – 32 million children of primary school age remain uneducated in this region. Central and East Asia, as well as the Pacific, are also affected with more than 20 million uneducated children.

Among these countries, **gender imbalance** is significant, because girls make up 54% of the world's non-schooled population. This mainly occurs in Arab states and Asia, and also where culture and tradition give privileged treatment to males, as in many sub-Saharan African countries. Girls' traditional destiny in some cultures is perceived as working in their family home, whereas boys receive a fuller education.

A lack of universal education can have long-term negative impacts on a country. Children vary in educational standards when they leave school – many without having acquired even basic educational skills (as shown in Figure 10). This lack of basic education then hinders the social and economic development of low-achieving countries – providing them with low levels of human capital.

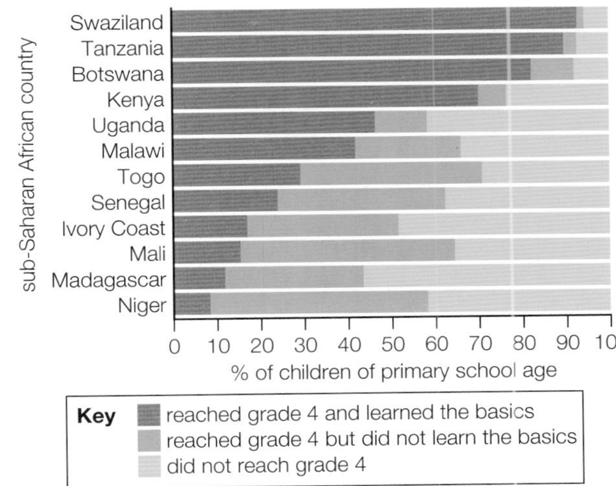

Figure 10 *The percentage of children reaching grade 4 in some sub-Saharan African countries during 2013–14. Grade 4 achievement consists of basic literacy and numeracy skills, equivalent to the end-of-primary basic standards in the UK.*

Over to you

1 a Copy the table on the right and add three extra columns – HDI rank 1-10, Happy Planet Index rank 1–10, and Gini coefficient rank 1–10.

b Research the HDI, Happy Planet Index and Gini coefficient data for each country, then rank them from 1 (best) to 10 (worst).

c Assess the statement that 'high GDP does not guarantee a high level of human development or happiness'.

2 Explain how different models of human development, such as Sharia law or Bolivia under Evo Morales, challenge the accepted views of human development.

3 Explain why sub-Saharan Africa has the highest number of school-age children not in primary education.

Rank	Country	GDP (US$ trillion)
1	USA	17.4
2	China	10.4
3	Japan	4.6
4	Germany	3.9
5	UK	2.9
6	France	2.8
7	Brazil	2.3
8	Italy	2.1
9	India	2.1
10	Russia	1.9

On your own

4 Distinguish between the following measures of human development: HDI, Happy Planet Index, GDP, Gini coefficient.

5 a Study the data below showing GDP and HDI scores for five countries. Add five more countries of your choice and research their data.

Country	Malawi	Egypt	India	France	USA
GDP (US$ trillion)	0.003	0.307	2.067	2.829	17.419
HDI	0.43	0.68	0.58	0.88	0.91

b Produce a scatter graph to display the ten countries from part (a), and then draw a regression (best-fit) line to show their relationship.

c Suggest reasons for the relationship shown.

6 Write 500 words on 'Economic development is the key to improving the lives of the world's poorest people'.

Exam-style question

Explain why levels of education vary both in and between countries. *(8 marks)*

4.2 Variations in human health and life expectancy

In this section, you'll learn that there are notable variations in human health and life expectancy.

Variations in health and life expectancy in Africa

Africa is increasingly becoming a continent of contrasts. Many sub-Saharan African countries had their international debts cancelled under the 2005 Gleneagles Agreement. This means that, in recent years, they have been able to invest much of the money that they previously used to pay debt interest to their international creditors, into improving their economies and their people's lives instead. In 2016, the economies of Kenya, Tanzania, Mozambique and Ivory Coast were all amongst the world's fastest growing.

Despite this progress, considerable variations in both health indicators and average life expectancy still exist across Africa, as shown by the HDI values in Figure 1. There are still big differences between Africa's 56 nations in terms of life expectancy, levels of infant and maternal mortality, and access to food, a safe water supply and effective sanitation.

KEY CONCEPTS

- **Causality** – causes of mortality and differences in life expectancy
- **Inequality** – how and why variations in health and life expectancy exist between and within countries

The Democratic Republic of the Congo

The Democratic Republic of the Congo (or DRC) is one of the world's poorest countries. Its poverty stands out, even within Africa. It is a country where savage conflict has frequently ravaged the land since 1998, and where many of its people live in fear of their lives. Poverty is deeply established, and the DRC was rated among the lowest countries in global HDI rankings in 2014.

The irony is that the DRC is one of the world's richest countries in terms of natural resources. It has vast reserves of gold, silver, copper, cobalt, zinc and diamonds. However, these have been a curse – causing conflict with the DRC's neighbours, which has had a serious impact on food distribution and supply. An estimated 6 million people (half of them children under 5) have died as a result of ongoing conflicts – many due to disease and malnutrition, brought about by a lack of food caused by the distribution issues. Much of this results from unstable governance, civil conflict, controversial election procedures, and power struggles.

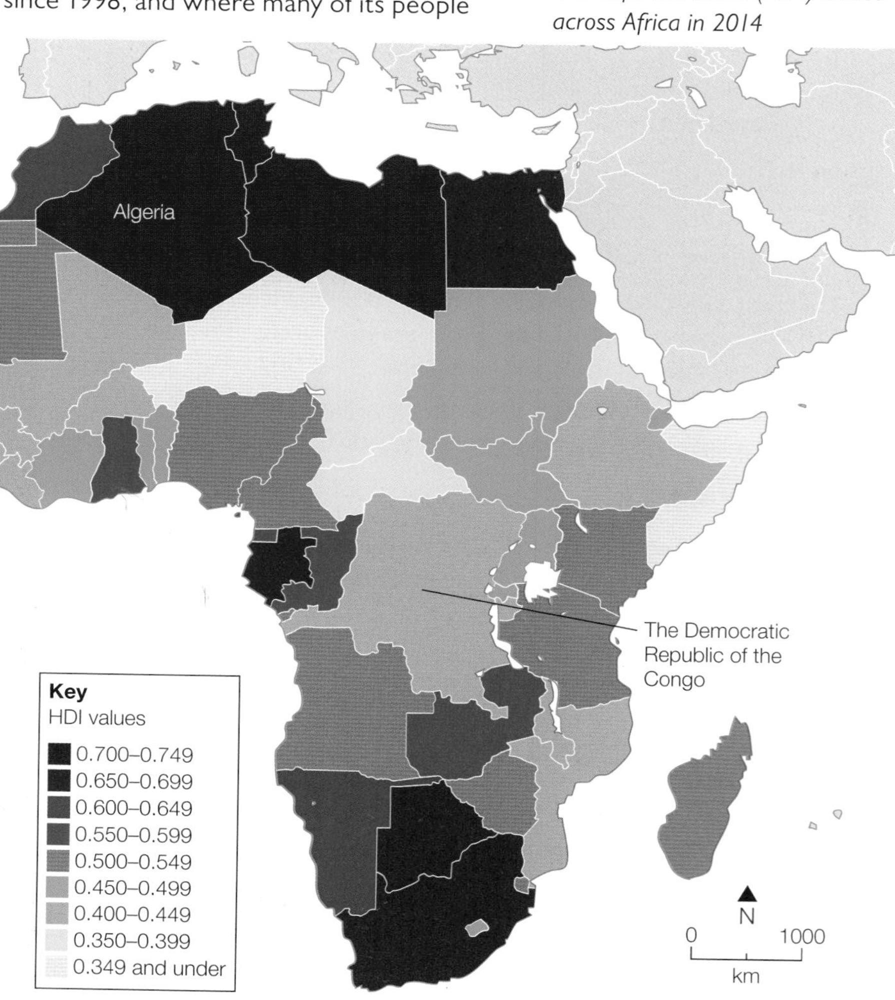

Figure 1 Contrasting Human Development Index (HDI) values across Africa in 2014

Much of the DRC is desperately poor, with average GDP per capita (US$ PPP) estimated to be around US$800, which is the world's third lowest. As a result:

> **Key word**
>
> **PPP (US$)** – Purchasing Power Parity (shown in US$) relates average earnings in a country to local prices and what they will buy. It is the spending power within a country, and reflects local costs of living.

- most of the population lives in a state of moderate to serious food insecurity, and 40% of children under the age of 5 suffer from chronic malnutrition
- 40% of children aged 5-14 are forced to work rather than attend school
- the water supply for 47.6% of the population is classed as 'unimproved' – in other words, it comes from a river, spring or open pond, so water-borne diseases are rife
- the average life expectancy is almost the world's lowest, at just 56 years
- most women have their first child before the age of 20; and infant and maternal mortality rates are the world's highest.

Figure 2 *The average life expectancy in the DRC is very low, because of the high child mortality rate – due in part to 37% of Congolese having no access to medical care, and 47.6% having no access to safe drinking water*

In spite of these indicators, health expenditure as a percentage of GDP is higher in the DRC than in many other African countries. Funding by NGOs, such as Médecins Sans Frontières is high, but progress has yet to show up in the indicators because of the need for long-term solutions.

Although the civil war in the DRC is officially over, fighting still continues in parts of the country. It's a desperate situation, worsened by the extensive migration of young adults to urban areas in search of work. Lacking education and skills, these young migrants pose a threat to future stability if they continue to be poor and unemployed.

Algeria

Algeria has changed considerably in the last 30 or so years. Between 1980 and 2014:

- GDP per capita increased by about 30%
- life expectancy at birth increased by 16.6 years (to 76)
- the expected number of years of schooling increased by 4.5 years
- Algeria's HDI value rose from 0.574 to 0.736, to become one of the highest HDI values in Africa (see Figure 1).

However, Algeria has not made progress in every respect. By many measures it still displays a number of the characteristics of a developing country, including:

- relatively low literacy rates
- 20% of its rural population lacking access to safe sanitation
- 23% of Algerians still living below the national poverty line.

Figure 3 *Inspired by Algeria, and with a nod to Eastern music, the Clash sang 'Rock the Casbah' in their 1982 hit. Situated on a hill in the city of Algiers, the ancient Casbah is an impressive sight that includes many palaces and mosques. In 1992 it became a UNESCO World Heritage Site – but not because of the Clash hit!*

Nonetheless, despite 80% of the country consisting of barren Sahara Desert, Algeria has benefitted from strong leadership and governance, with a series of five-year plans that have enabled it to make significant progress in terms of development. It met and surpassed several of the **Millennium Development Goals** (MDGs) well ahead of the 2015 target, including reducing extreme poverty and hunger by half during the period from 1999 to 2015, and achieving a primary school enrolment rate of 98.16% in 2011 for children aged under 6. Infant and maternal mortality rates have also improved considerably, placing Algeria in the top 100 countries in 2015 for these indicators.

Key word

Millennium Development Goals – These were goals related to different aspects of human development that were agreed by the UN in 2000, and that were to be achieved by 2015. They included reductions in poverty, hunger and infant mortality.

Algeria's progress thus far has been largely due to oil revenues, which generate 98% of the country's export earnings and account for just over 36% of its GDP. Algeria has used much of this oil wealth to drive the public investment that has been integral to the dramatic improvements in development.

Variations in health and life expectancy in the developed world

The Organisation for Economic Co-operation and Development (OECD) is a group of 35 nations from the developed world, which aim to promote policies to improve the economic and social well-being of people around the world. In 2015, the OECD carried out detailed research on the changing average life expectancy in its member countries between 1985 and 2010. The main findings from this research were that:

- the average life expectancy had increased by 5.1 years
- women could expect to live 5 years longer than men
- people with the highest level of education could expect to live 6 years longer, on average, than those with the lowest level
- infant mortality rates had declined sharply in all OECD countries
- those countries in which life expectancy increased the most, varied widely in GDP
- the key factors behind the improving life expectancy were health spending per capita (see Figure 4), economic factors, and two behavioural factors – reduced smoking and calorific intake
- despite a dramatic fall in deaths from cardiovascular diseases (heart attacks and strokes), these still remained the leading causes of death.

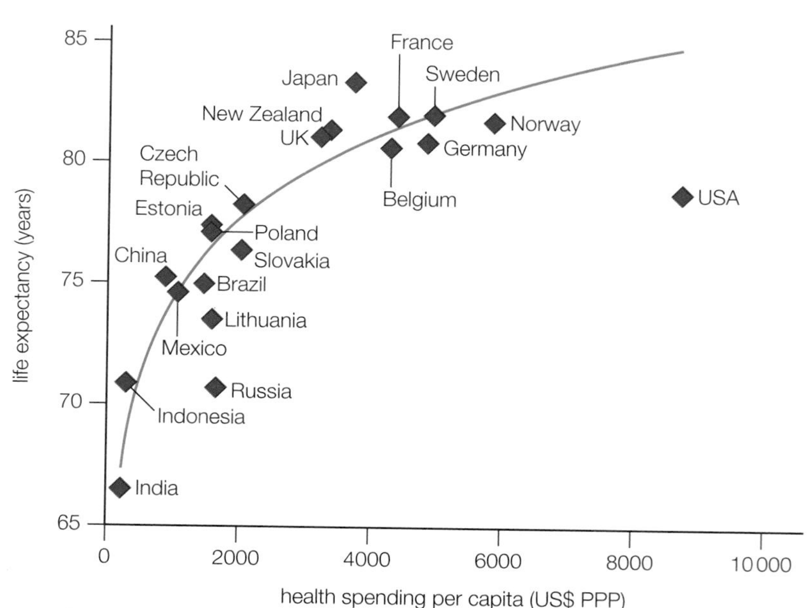

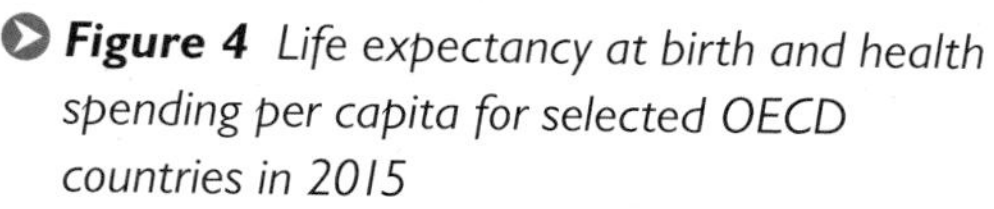
Figure 4 *Life expectancy at birth and health spending per capita for selected OECD countries in 2015*

A key factor in improving the average life expectancy in OECD countries has been the steady rise in health spending, which has tended to grow at a faster rate than GDP. In 1960, health spending accounted for less than 4% of GDP, on average, across OECD countries. But, by 2013, that figure had risen to 8.9%.

However, health spending alone does not explain the improving life expectancy. On that basis, the USA ought to have by far the highest life expectancy of any OECD country. Its healthcare costs – mainly funded through private insurance and run by the private sector – are substantially greater than in the UK, where the NHS delivers State-funded healthcare paid for by taxation revenue. The USA has the highest health spending per capita in the world (see Figure 4), yet its infant mortality rate of 6 per 1000 puts it thirtieth amongst OECD countries!

Figure 5 *An aerial view of Cleveland Clinic hospital in Ohio, USA. US healthcare is privately funded by insurance, so US health spending is the highest in the world. However, health indicators in the USA do not reflect this level of spending.*

Due to their ageing populations, healthcare costs are rising sharply in many developed countries; the average life expectancy for those aged over 60 has risen significantly since 1995. Better medicine is one reason for this, but it comes at a cost. Increased research into expensive new drugs, and more complex surgery, are driving the healthcare budgets for many developed countries upwards at a much faster rate than both GDP growth and general inflation.

Figure 6 *The GlaxoSmithKlein (GSK) research centre at Harlow's New Frontiers Science Park in Essex. This is one of GSK's centres for new drug research, the cost of which helps to make healthcare so expensive.*

BACKGROUND

Factors affecting health and life expectancy

Differences in lifestyles and levels of deprivation – plus the availability, cost and effectiveness of medical care – are all powerful influences on people's health and life expectancy. They are included in a range of factors that are often referred to as **determinants**, because they strongly determine (or influence) health and life expectancy.

Determinants consist of three broad types:

- Wider determinants, e.g. occupation, education, income, housing, etc.
- Lifestyle factors, e.g. smoking, diet, alcohol, drug misuse, etc.
- Preventative healthcare, e.g. immunisation

None of these determinants operates in isolation. They may influence each other:

- *within* categories – for example, low educational achievement can influence employment and income prospects, or
- *between* categories, e.g. high-income earners tend to enjoy much healthier diets.

Therefore, it is important to look at determinants in combination, rather than in isolation. Generally, there are many linkages between different indicators and how they impact on health. Changing trends in one determinant might be caused by, or have implications for, other indicators.

Variations in health and life expectancy within countries

Regional variations in the UK

Current UK estimates from the Office for National Statistics (ONS) for average life expectancy are 82.8 years for women and 79.1 years for men – and, on average, life expectancy at birth is continuing to increase for both genders. However, within this broad picture, there are regional variations across the country:

- For example, people living in South East England have a longer average life expectancy (80.5 years in 2015) than people living in Scotland (77.1 years).
- Research by Age UK in 2016 found that
  - for men at age 65 across the UK the average life expectancy was highest in Harrow (in London), where men could expect to live for a further 21.1 years (compared with 16 additional years for men living in Manchester)
  - for women at age 65, the average life expectancy was highest in Camden (also in London), with an additional 24 years (and lowest in Halton, in North West England, with a further 18.8 years).

The regional variations in average life expectancy are linked to a range of determinants, such as smoking, obesity and income. For example, much of North East England has a below-average life expectancy (see Figure 7) and a much higher death rate – with a higher proportion of those deaths being attributed to smoking and alcohol consumption. The death rates for potentially avoidable causes, such as certain cancers and respiratory and heart diseases, are also significantly higher in the Northern English regions than in the Southern. Spending on fresh healthy foods (such as vegetables, fruit and fish) is also lower in Northern England, because earnings there are often lower and levels of deprivation higher.

Because healthcare across the whole UK has become much more effective in many ways – with early diagnosis of heart disease and cancers, and increased survival rates for almost all cancers – the national average life expectancy continues to rise in the UK. However, there are areas where this trend has stalled. For example, data gathered in 2016 suggest that 21% of local authorities in England saw very small falls in male life expectancy and 28% of local authorities saw falls in female life expectancy. There is also emerging evidence of worsening health for many over-85s in some parts of the UK.

English region	Average life expectancy (male)	Average life expectancy (female)
North East	77.8	81.6
North West	77.7	81.7
Yorkshire and the Humber	78.3	82.2
East Midlands	79.1	82.9
West Midlands	78.7	82.7
East	80.1	83.7
London	79.7	83.8
South East	80.3	83.8
South West	80.0	83.9

Figure 7 *The average life expectancy at birth in 2010–12, by gender and by English region*

Ethnic and regional variations in Australia

Australia has one of the highest average life expectancies in the world – being one of only seven countries with average life expectancies for both men and women of over 80 years; the average life expectancy in Australia is 80.1 years for men and 84.3 years for women. However – just as in the UK – within this overall figure, average life expectancy by gender also varies between states and territories:

- Women in New South Wales (NSW) and the Australian Capital Territory (ACT) have the highest life expectancy (both 84.3 years), whilst it is lowest in Tasmania (82.2 years) and the Northern Territory (79 years).
- There are similar differences for men, with those born in the ACT having the highest life expectancy (80.5 years), whilst those living in the Northern Territory have the lowest (73.3 years).

The main reason for this marked regional variation is the Northern Territory's relatively high proportion of Aboriginal and Torres Strait Islander peoples (see Section 4.6), who have a substantially lower average life expectancy than non-indigenous Australians – as Figure 8 shows. This factor greatly reduces the overall average life expectancy in the Northern Territory in particular.

Nationally, the average life expectancy for indigenous Australians is around 10 years less than for non-indigenous Australians; the average life expectancy for Aboriginal and Torres Strait Islanders is only 69.1 years for men and 73.7 years for women. This is due to:

- relatively high mortality rates in middle age (45–64)
- high rates of chronic disease and injury
- high levels of deprivation
- a higher prevalence of modifiable and behavioural risk factors, such as smoking, drug taking and alcohol abuse
- lower levels of education and employment
- the social disadvantages faced by many indigenous Australians, compared with non-indigenous Australians.

The Australian government launched the Close the Gap initiative in 2009 (see Figure 9). It aims to halve the gap in child mortality by 2018, narrow the divide in reading and numeracy levels, and increase in the proportion of Aboriginal and Torres Strait Islander students completing high school.

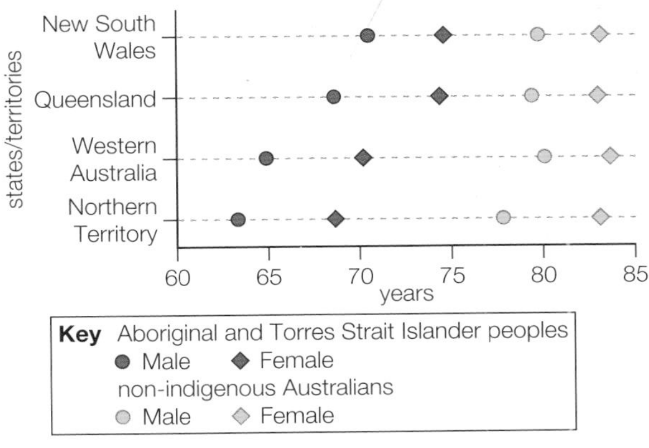

Figure 8 *Variations in average life expectancy between Aboriginal and Torres Strait Islander peoples and non-indigenous Australians, by gender and by selected states and territories (2010–12)*

Figure 9 *The 'Close the Gap' initiative, which was set up in 2009 by the Australian government*

Over to you

1 a Using Figure 1, describe the pattern of HDI values across Africa.

b Using the examples of the DRC and Algeria, discuss in pairs and identify factors that explain why HDI values can vary so much between countries in the developing world.

2 a In pairs, discuss and show on a mind map how and why levels of health and average life expectancy can vary so much between developing countries.

b Now show on another diagram why average life expectancy can also vary within developed countries.

c To what extent are the factors the same for both diagrams? Explain.

3 In pairs, discuss how far you think governments should influence (**a**) wider determinants, (**b**) lifestyle choices. Draw a table to show the main arguments for and against.

On your own

4 Explain how different determinants can impact on people's health outcomes.

5 Research how different OECD countries provide medical care for their citizens, and how effective these models are. Examples could compare the privatised system in the USA with the UK's National Health Service.

Exam-style question

Using Figure 4, explain the relationship between life expectancy at birth and health spending per capita in OECD countries. *(6 marks)*

4.3 Development targets and policies

In this section, you'll learn how governments and International Governmental Organisations play a significant role in defining development targets and policies.

KEY CONCEPTS

- **Causality** – the link between economic development and social development
- **Inequality** – variations in progress with the MDGs
- **Sustainability** – the focus of the SDGs

Figure 1 The opening meeting of the 2016 G20 Summit in China.

Economic and social development

In September 2016, the leaders of 20 of the world's largest economies – known as the G20 (see Section 3.2) – met in Hangzhou, China (shown in Figure 1). A key focus of this meeting was to try to ensure that the global economy continues to grow. The 20 leaders were all united in the fundamental belief that global economic growth will lead to improved conditions for all people – even the poorest!

The G20 is just one of many International Governmental Organisations (IGOs) that play a significant role in defining development targets and policies. However, the relationship between economic development and social progress is often complex. Figure 2 shows how different countries vary in their overall levels of government spending, as well as the priorities they place on where this money should be spent.

Country	G20 Member?	GDP in 2015 ($US billion)	Overall government spending (% of GDP)	Health spending (% of GDP)	Education spending (% of GDP)
Algeria	No	172	40.4	7.2	4.3
Argentina	Yes	972	40.9	4.8	5.3
Bangladesh	No	577	16.0	2.8	2.0
China	Yes	19 390	23.9	5.5	4.2
Congo (DRC)	No	38	29.1	4.3	2.2
France	Yes	2418	56.1	11.5	5.5
Mexico	Yes	2227	26.6	6.3	5.2
Saudi Arabia	Yes	638	29.6	4.7	5.1
UK	Yes	2679	48.5	9.1	6.7
USA	Yes	17 950	41.6	17.1	5.2

Figure 2 Selected countries' spending priorities

How government spending varies – 1 France

France has one of the highest levels of government spending as a percentage of GDP in the G20 – over 56% (see Figure 2).

- Its **healthcare** system, which is predominantly State-funded, requires the fourth highest spending as a percentage of GDP in the G20. Although French residents pay top-up insurance (of about £150 per family per month), the largest proportion of France's health budget is government-funded.
- Government **welfare** and **pension** payments are also high in France. In 2016, someone who had worked full-time for 40 years received about £15 000 in annual State pension. By comparison, UK State pensions will reach about £7500 a year by 2018.
- **Education** spending is also high in France, at about £8500 per student per year in 2015, compared to the UK's top spending of about £7000 per student in inner London and only £3750 in rural areas.

How government spending varies – 2 Saudi Arabia

Saudi Arabia is the G20's most autocratic power – its ruling royal family assumes absolute authority. Oil production (see Figure 3) contributes 97% of export earnings, and is largely owned by the royal elite. They control the Saudi economy, and to some extent the global oil price. When oil prices are high, the government enjoys significant revenue. However, it also becomes burdened with debt when the price falls.

Half of the 10 million employees in Saudi are from overseas (known as **ex-pats**), often on contract work. Everything in the country depends on the decisions of the royal family – from driving bans for women to health spending.

- Saudi Arabia's **healthcare** system is 80% State-funded. Its hospitals are high quality and State healthcare is free.
- **Welfare** and **pension** payments vary. In 2015, a third of working-age Saudis were in work, though the official unemployment rate was just 12% (still high by international standards). The 'hidden' rate is higher, not least because only 22% of Saudi women work. In 2013, Time magazine claimed that 20% of Saudi's population lived in poverty. Half the population is aged 25 or less, with many unemployed. Unemployment pay is £400 monthly, payable for only 12 months. Pensions are low by global standards (£300 monthly), though few retiring ex-pats remain in Saudi Arabia.
- **Education** spending in Saudi Arabia is lower than in France. Education focuses on religious teaching; scientific and technical education are weak, and rote learning dominates. Saudi teachers are poorly trained, and school/college leavers are unable to find jobs in technical and oil industries, or in government departments like defence. Ex-pat workers are skilled and better qualified.

Figure 3 *Oil supply pipelines and waiting oil tankers at Ras Tanura in Saudi Arabia, where the oil industry generates almost all of the country's export earnings*

Promoting development

Section 3.5 outlines the background to the International Monetary Fund (IMF), World Bank and World Trade Organisation (WTO), and why their work is contested. In promoting programmes such as Structural Adjustment (see page 165) they have intervened in the policies of individual governments, in effect cutting education and health programmes, whilst outwardly believing that they are improving the chances of economic growth. Such policies are neo-liberal in nature – based on theories of economic liberalism in which state intervention is reduced, and the workings of the private market are left unregulated – and involve the promotion of free trade, the privatisation of state assets and services (e.g. water provision, or transport), and the deregulation of financial markets (e.g. removing barriers to investment and capital). In this way, their belief is that private wealth 'trickles down' through the economy, and that the poorest people eventually benefit from a strengthened economy.

More recently, these organisations have focused on programmes with a more direct impact on people – such as improving environmental quality, health, education and human rights.

The World Bank, education and the environment

The World Bank is a founding member of the Global Partnership for Education (GPE), which was established in 2002. This partnership was created to help achieve **Millennium Development Goals** 2 and 3; see the Background box below. The GPE invests in early childhood education for all children, and aims to develop a sound educational system for children through developing early reading and numeracy skills. It helps countries to set up early reading assessment systems, so that progress can be measured. The GPE's focus has been on the poorest and most disadvantaged children, including education for girls (see Figure 4), ethnic minorities, children with disabilities, and children in areas affected by conflict. More recent work has focused on secondary and higher education. Between 2002 and 2015, the GPE invested over US$35 billion in its educational programmes.

Figure 4 *The Chair of the Global Partnership for Education (GPE), Carol Bellamy, with schoolgirls at a school in Abidjan during her visit to Ivory Coast in 2012*

In 2016, the World Bank launched a new initiative – the Climate Change Action Plan. This aims to help developing countries, such as India (see Figure 5), to add 30 gigawatts of renewable energy (enough to power 150 million homes) to the world's energy capacity, as well as provide flooding early warning systems for 100 million people and develop investment in agriculture for 40 countries – all by 2020. This is part of the World Bank's new strategy to end poverty. There is an increasing recognition that climate change is a threat to global efforts to end poverty, and that there is an increasingly urgent need to protect poor people and poor countries.

Figure 5 *Renewable-energy generation in West Bengal, India. The World Bank announced in 2016 that it would provide over US$1 billion to support India's plans to increase solar generation.*

BACKGROUND

The Millennium Development Goals (MDGs)

The Millennium Development Goals were a set of goals established by the UN for the new Millennium, to be achieved between 2000 and 2015. The eight broad goals (many of which had sub-targets) were:

- Goal 1: Eradicate extreme poverty and hunger
- Goal 2: Achieve universal primary education
- Goal 3: Promote gender equality and empower women
- Goal 4: Reduce child mortality
- Goal 5: Improve maternal health
- Goal 6: Combat HIV/AIDS, malaria and other diseases
- Goal 7: Ensure environmental sustainability
- Goal 8: Develop a global partnership for development

The International Monetary Fund (IMF) and poverty

The IMF has had its critics in the past three decades. Its role has been to strengthen weakening currencies and foster stronger economic development policies. It has usually concerned itself with heavily indebted countries. In return for re-arranging loans at adjusted rates of interest, and at more affordable repayments, the IMF imposed **Structural Adjustment Programmes (SAPs)** on the indebted countries. These SAPs consisted of a series of conditions that forced the State to play a reduced part in the economy (for example, through the privatisation of State energy or water companies) and in social welfare (with severe reductions in government spending on health or education). The effect of the SAPs was often to reduce education and health provision, and the beneficiaries of privatisation programmes were often TNCs.

However, since 2000, the encouragement for poorer countries to focus on the MDGs has enabled the IMF to shift its attention to global poverty, through the **poverty reduction programme**. Instead of imposed conditions, countries are now required to develop their own medium-term development plans in order to receive aid, loans and debt relief. For example, the IMF is currently working with the government of Haiti to implement development strategies to enable its economy to become more resilient, particularly after Hurricane Matthew in 2016 (see Figure 6) – with the target of making Haiti an emerging economy by 2030. Figure 7 shows that this is no small challenge.

Figure 6 *Damage caused in Haiti by Hurricane Matthew in 2016, after which the IMF contributed emergency funds to help rebuild Haiti's economic capacity*

Figure 7 *These small traders, selling what they can by the side of the road, show the state of Haiti's economy in the aftermath of recent earthquakes and hurricanes that have devastated the country, its infrastructure and economic development*

The World Trade Organisation (WTO) and the environment

WTO policies have encouraged countries to increase trade as a way of promoting economic development and reducing their debts. However, some of the effects of these policies have not always been as intended – for example, they have frequently resulted in environmental degradation, such as rainforest clearance and threats to biodiversity, as forest land has been cleared to grow crops. Particularly culpable have been countries such as Indonesia, where rainforest clearance has led to a rapid growth in palm oil production (see Section 2.7).

Most WTO trade policies now try to tackle environmental problems by:

- restricting the international movement of products or species that are potentially harmful or endangered
- challenging trade agreements where there may be implications for climate change, such as forest clearance.

However, there are clear conflicts of interest between the most powerful countries in the WTO and the limiting of trade that may benefit those countries.

Achievements of the MDGs

Since 2000, significant advances have been made towards many of the MDG targets:

- The number now living in extreme poverty has declined by 56% – from 1.9 billion in 1990 to 836 million in 2015. However, China's economic progress accounts for over 500 million of that fall.
- A dramatic improvement in gender parity in primary school (i.e. ensuring that as many girls attend school as boys) has been achieved in most countries.
- Women have increased their parliamentary representation over the past 20 years in nearly 90 per cent of countries.
- The rate of children dying before their fifth birthday has declined by more than half – from 90 to 43 deaths per 1000 live births since 1990.
- Over 6.2 million malaria deaths were averted through treatment programmes between 2000 and 2015, while TB prevention saved an estimated 37 million lives between 2000 and 2013.
- Worldwide, 2.1 billion people have gained access to improved sanitation.

However, despite these significant achievements, progress has been uneven. The MDGs often fell short for many, particularly the poorest people and those disadvantaged because of gender, age, disability or ethnicity. Critics including Hans Rosling (see Section 4.1) have asserted that all but one MDG concentrate on poverty reduction rather than wealth creation.

Following profound and consistent gains, we now know that extreme poverty can be eradicated within one more generation. The MDGs have greatly contributed to this progress and have taught us how governments, business and civil society can work together to achieve transformational breakthroughs.

Figure 8 *Ban Ki-Moon, UN Secretary-General, speaking in 2015 at the review of the MDGs and the launch of the Sustainable Development Goals (see below)*

Progress in Bangladesh

After China and India, Bangladesh had the world's third largest number of people in poverty. Of its 170 million people in 2014, one third lived below the poverty line. With a large and rapidly growing population, Bangladesh faced by far the biggest challenge in meeting the MDGs (an average annual cost of US$14.5 billion between 2005 and 2015). Despite this challenge, a healthy average 6% GDP growth rate allowed the Bangladeshi government to achieve more than most countries, as Figure 10 shows. However, progress on a wider scale in Bangladesh (Figure 9) and elsewhere (Figure 10) is more variable.

The 2015 Sustainable Development Goals

In September 2015, the UN launched a new set of 17 Sustainable Development Goals (SDGs). These were to be achieved by 2030 as part of a new sustainable development agenda with the aspiration to:

- end poverty
- protect the planet
- ensure prosperity for all.

The SDGs aim to build on the successes of the MDGs by going further to end all forms of poverty. They call for action by all countries – poor, rich and middle-income – to promote prosperity while protecting the planet. Ending poverty must go hand-in-hand with strategies to build economic growth and address a range of social needs including health, education and job opportunities, while also tackling climate change and environmental protection.

However, the SDGs are not legally binding. Governments are expected to take ownership to establish national frameworks for the achievement of the Goals, and then follow-up and review the progress made in implementing them.

Goal	Progress by 2015
1. Eradicate extreme poverty and hunger **Target:** 1.20%	The poverty reduction rate was 1.74%
2. Achieve universal primary education **Target:** 100%	Significant progress was achieved: 97.7% of children were enrolled in primary education (it was 85.5% in 2000)
3. Promote gender equality and empower women **Target:** Gender parity in primary and secondary education	Bangladesh had achieved gender parity in primary and secondary education
4. Reduce child mortality **Target:** 32 per 1000 live births	The infant mortality rate (per 1000 live births) decreased from 58 in 2000 to 38
5. Improve maternal health **Target:** 143 per 100 000 live births	The maternal mortality ratio (per 100 000 live births) fell from 318 in 2000 to 170
6. Combat HIV/AIDS, malaria, and other diseases **Target:** To reduce the prevalence rate of malaria to 310.8 per 100 000	The prevalence rate fell from 441.5 per 100 000 in 2005 to 433.91
7. Ensure environmental sustainability **Target:** 20% of land area to be covered by forest	The land area covered by forest had increased from 11.3% in 2000 to 13.4%
8. To develop a global partnership for development **Target:** US$4.2 billion of Overseas Development Assistance to be received by Bangladesh	The ODA received by Bangladesh rose from US$1.5 billion to US$3.1 billion

Figure 9 *Progress in Bangladesh in achieving the MDGs*

Figure 10 *Global progress in achieving one of the MDGs – Goal 1 – reducing the percentage of people living on less than US$1.25 a day. You can research the achievement of other goals by searching online for 'UN Millennium Development Goals Report'.*

Over to you

1 a Use the data from Figure 2, as well as Section 6.4 and a blank world map, to draw proportional circles to show (**i**) the size of government spending, (**ii**) the share of that devoted to health and education across the countries shown. You will need to calculate government spending in US$.

b Describe the patterns that you notice from your map. How far is there a link between the size of GDP and the proportions spent on health and education?

2 Draw a spider diagram to highlight differences in health, welfare and education spending and service provision in France and Saudi Arabia. You may find other research useful, e.g. the CIA World Factbook on each country.

3 In pairs, review the extent to which the MDGs were met (**a**) in Bangladesh, (**b**) in different parts of the world. You will need to research Goals 2-8 online – search online for 'UN Millennium Development Goals Report'.

On your own

4 Assess the change of focus for the World Bank, IMF and WTO and their engagement with education, poverty reduction and the environment. How successful is each organisation being in this change?

5 a Research and list the SDGs for 2015–2030.

b Research progress on the SDGs. How likely does it seem that these goals could be met by 2030?

Exam-style question

Evaluate the significance of governments and IGOs in defining development targets and policies. (*20 marks*)

4.4 Human rights

In this section, you'll learn how human rights have become important aspects of both international law and international agreements.

EQ2 Sections 4.4 to 4.6 investigate why human rights vary from place to place.

KEY CONCEPTS

- **Causality** – the link between human rights and international justice
- **Inequality** – variations in the implementation of human rights laws

It's against human rights...

In Figure 1, the father of Baha Mousa is shown campaigning outside the UK High Court in 2011. Baha Mousa, an Iraqi hotel receptionist, died in custody at a British army base in Basra, Iraq, after experiencing severe beatings and other harsh interrogation techniques, like sleep deprivation and enforced stress positions. Baha's father maintained that his son's death was a contravention of the UK's 1998 Human Rights Act, as he was held under British jurisdiction when he died.

▲ *Figure 1* *Baha Mousa's father campaigning outside the High Court in 2011*

In 2014, a 250-page report was submitted to the International Criminal Court, by Public Interest Lawyers and the European Centre for Constitutional and Human Rights, alleging that British armed forces subjected over 400 Iraqis to abuses of their human rights during the Iraq War between 2003 and 2008. In its defence, the British government argued that its armed forces are not subject to the Human Rights Act in a combat zone, such as Figure 2 – particularly under Articles 2 (the right to life) and 5 (the right to liberty) of the European Convention on Human Rights (see below). However, despite this, by 2016 compensation payments totalling £20 million had been paid in 326 cases of alleged abuse.

▼ *Figure 2* *British soldiers in Basra, Iraq, in 2003. Questions about whether the Human Rights Act applies in a combat zone are much debated.*

The European Convention on Human Rights (ECHR)

The Council of Europe was formed in 1949 to establish better relationships between European countries following the Second World War. It now consists of 47 member states, including all current 28 EU members. In 1950, The Council of Europe drafted the ECHR as a treaty to protect human rights. All member states now include this within their national laws, so that any human rights case can be heard first within the home country, without having to go straight to the European court. However, the ECHR was only integrated into British law as part of the 1998 Human Rights Act – the delay being caused by resistance within UK political parties to change. The Convention consists of 14 'articles', each protecting a basic right. Together, they allow people in Europe to lead free and dignified lives. The articles include:

- a right to life
- the prohibition of slavery and torture
- the right to a fair trial
- freedom of expression.

The Universal Declaration of Human Rights (UDHR)

Following the many atrocities that occurred during the Second World War, the newly established United Nations set up the Commission on Human Rights – with the task of producing an 'International Bill of Rights'. The result was the 'Universal Declaration of Human Rights', which was signed in 1948 with the aim of providing a common understanding of the rights that every human being should be entitled to, and also to form a basis for freedom, justice and peace. The declaration lists 30 articles that define basic 'human rights', and states that these rights should be protected by law.

The UDHR was originally adopted and signed by 48 nations. Although in itself it is not legally binding, it forms a statement of intent and a framework for foreign policy statements to explain economic or military interventions. It has been accepted as defining the terms 'fundamental freedoms' and 'human rights' as they appear in the UN Charter. In 1968, the UN hosted the 'International Conference on Human Rights', where it advised all member states that the Declaration 'constitutes an obligation for the members of the international community' to all human beings.

The Declaration has since been the basis for two further legally binding UN human rights covenants, both of which came into effect in 1976 and together serve as a legal framework to enforce the UDHR:

- The International Covenant on Civil and Political Rights
- The International Covenant on Economic, Social and Cultural Rights

However, not all countries have signed the UDHR. Those that decided not to sign in 1948 included:

- the Soviet Union – because it considered that the Declaration did not condemn Fascism and Nazism sufficiently
- South Africa – to protect its system of apartheid (see Figure 3), because that contravened almost all aspects of the Declaration
- Saudi Arabia – because of the article that everyone has the right 'to change their religion or belief'. Women's rights are also a controversial issue in Saudi Arabia, as Figure 4 shows.

Figure 3 *South Africa's apartheid system segregated the country's people by skin colour and race, as these two signs show – despite being prohibited under the UN Declaration of Human Rights*

Figure 4 *Segregation is not a thing of the past – Saudi Arabian women are directed to use this separate counter at a fast-food restaurant. They are also not allowed to drive, and were only allowed to vote for the first time in 2015.*

Human rights in the UK

In Britain, most people understand that their 'human rights' are protected by law. This means that, for instance: they cannot be imprisoned without charge; that being gay is not a crime; that they can't assault their children; that employers must respect workers' religious beliefs; and that British soldiers have responsibilities – even on the battlefield.

Had Baha Mousa been arrested for questioning in the UK, regardless of any alleged crime, he would have been protected automatically by the 1998 Human Rights Act (see the summary box opposite). However, despite his arrest being several thousand miles away in Iraq, he was still deemed to be subject to British law, because he was being detained in a British army base when he died.

The 1998 Human Rights Act can be used by every person resident in the UK, regardless of whether they are a British citizen or foreign national, child or adult, prisoner or member of the public. It protects 15 fundamental rights and freedoms, including the right to life, privacy and free speech – all based on articles in the ECHR. It ensures that people can defend their rights in court, and that public and private organisations (e.g. the government, private companies and the police) must treat everyone equally, with fairness, dignity and respect.

Objections to the ECHR

Despite a widespread agreement about 'human rights' in the UK, some of those 'rights' can be questioned by pressure groups and newspapers. They argue that the 1998 Human Rights Act (and therefore the ECHR) is undemocratic, because it threatens British sovereignty and self-determination – i.e. the right of the British Parliament to determine its own laws. Some argue that, under the 1998 Human Rights Act, the British courts are bound by decisions made at the European Court of Human Rights in Strasbourg, and that people have the same rights there, even if they commit serious crimes or perform acts of terrorism.

Figure 5 *The types and numbers of cases brought against the UK to the European Court of Human Rights, 1959–2013*

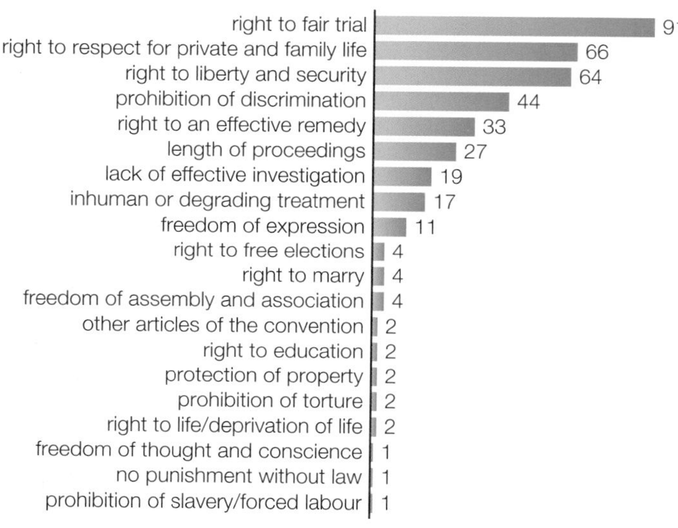

In 2016, following the vote to leave the EU, the British government announced plans to scrap the 1998 Human Rights Act and replace it with a 'British Bill of Rights and Responsibilities'. If passed, it would mean that the European Court of Human Rights would no longer be able to overrule British court judgements – as it had, for example, in 1997 when it ruled that there should be an equal age of consent for gay and straight people. The UK has been deemed in violation of the ECHR in 60% of the cases brought against it to the European Court of Human Rights since 1959 (see Figures 5 and 6). This compares to an average of 83% of ECHR judgements lost across all European states. Five frequent violators – Russia, Turkey, Romania, Ukraine and Hungary – are largely responsible for that high average figure. Many organisations, including the human rights organisation Liberty, are concerned that the abolition of the power of the European Court of Human Rights over British courts could ultimately erode human rights in Britain.

Figure 6 *A summary of the decisions of the European Court of Human Rights in the 499 cases involving the UK, 1959–2013*

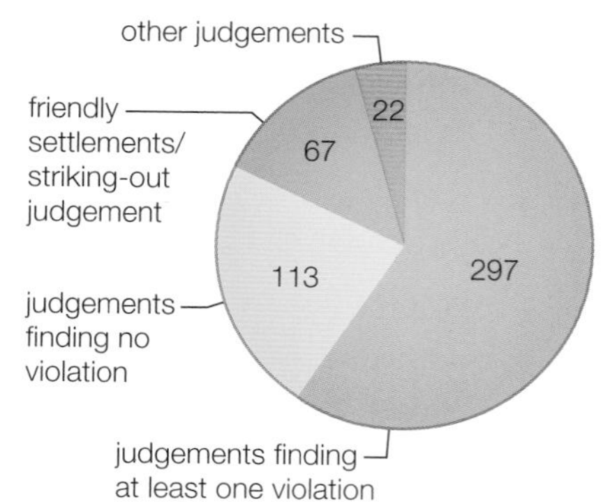

The 1998 Human Rights Act

The 1998 Human Rights Act came into force in the UK in October 2000 (there is almost always a delay between an Act passing and its introduction). It has three areas of focus:

1. It incorporates into British law the rights set out in the European Convention on Human Rights. As a result, if a person's human rights are breached in the UK, they can now take their case to a British court, rather than having to immediately seek justice from the European Court of Human Rights.
2. It requires all public and other bodies carrying out public functions (e.g. courts, police, hospitals and State schools) to respect and protect human rights.
3. Parliament tries to ensure that any new laws it passes are compatible with the ECHR, and that British courts will then interpret those laws in ways that are also compatible with the ECHR.

Figure 7 *Syrian 'White Helmets' trying to find trapped survivors in Aleppo, following a barrel bomb attack by government aircraft. They are listening for any buried survivors' shouts for help.*

A modern tragedy

In 2016, the besieged city of Aleppo in Syria saw some of the worst human tragedies in recent years. Throughout the ruins and the frequent horrible deaths, a group known as the 'White Helmets' (a volunteer rescue service of local people; see Figure 7) ran the gauntlet of bombs, shells and bullets – trying desperately to rescue people buried in the rubble, treat the injured and save lives. It was a never-ending task.

Under the Geneva Conventions (see the next page) the following emergency workers and services are entitled to protection from attack:

- Ambulance services, regardless of their political allegiances.
- Hospitals, so civilians receiving medical treatment are protected from further threats.
- Rescue workers searching in the ruins for the trapped and injured.

Yet news reporters claim that the Geneva Conventions are being abused in Syria by all sides, and are failing to protect those emergency workers from harm. So what happens when the Geneva Conventions are violated? Who is brought to trial, and can nations be 'punished' for such offences?

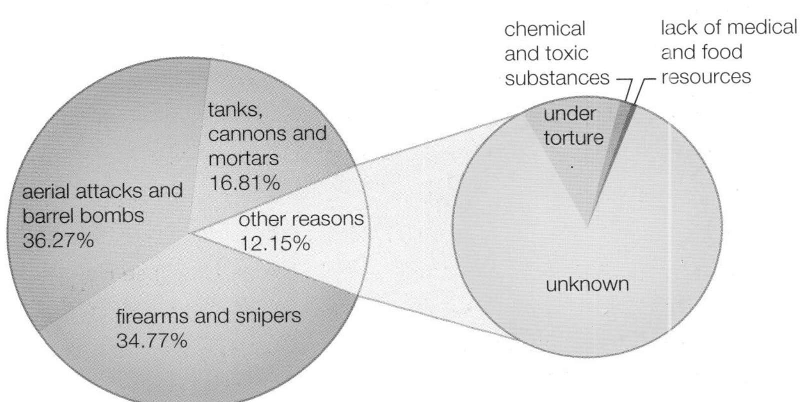

Figure 8 *Causes of death in August 2016, by type of weapon, during the Syrian War. In one month, there were 1737 battle-related deaths.*

The Geneva Conventions

The Original Geneva Convention was established in 1864, following the need for humanitarian protection arising from advances in weapons technology and changes to the nature of armed conflict. Originally, it was concerned only with soldiers wounded on the battlefield. However, following the end of the Second World War, countries around the world adopted the four Geneva Conventions that were expanded to cover anyone caught up in conflict – not just those taking an active part in the fighting. This included members of the armed forces on land and at sea, prisoners of war and civilians.

The four Conventions were designed to be a body of rules that protect civilians and people who are no longer fighting, including wounded and sick military personnel and prisoners of war caught up in conflict anywhere in the world.

Remarkably, the Geneva Conventions have been almost universally ratified – with 196 countries having signed up to them. Britain ratified the four Conventions in 1957. It is now widely considered that the Geneva Conventions apply whether a nation state has signed up to them or not. The Geneva Conventions are also used to determine the definition of what counts as a 'war crime'.

The basic rules of international humanitarian law in armed conflicts, and how they can be defined in the Geneva Conventions, are:

1. Persons out of combat action due to injury or damage are entitled to respect for their lives.
2. It is forbidden to kill or injure an enemy who surrenders.
3. The wounded and sick shall be collected and cared for.
4. Captured combatants and civilians are entitled to respect for their lives, dignity, personal rights and convictions.
5. No one shall be subjected to physical or mental torture, corporal punishment or cruel or degrading treatment.
6. It is prohibited to employ weapons or methods of warfare of a nature to cause unnecessary losses or excessive suffering.
7. Neither the civilian population in general nor individual civilian persons shall be the object of attack.

However, few cases of violations of the Geneva Conventions ever come to trial. In 2014, the human rights organisation Amnesty International's annual report on torture showed that 141 countries still use torture, including the USA. The USA has also been intensively criticised by Amnesty for the continued existence of Camp Delta at Guantanamo Bay in Cuba (see Figure 9), in which terrorist suspects have been allegedly tortured, including by the use of water-boarding.

Figure 9 *American soldiers guarding one of the entrances to Camp Delta, the Guantanamo Bay military prison in eastern Cuba*

Prosecuting 'war crimes'

In March 2016, Radovan Karadzic – a former Bosnian Serb leader in the Yugoslav wars of the 1990s (see Figure 10) – was convicted by a UN tribunal at The Hague of genocide, war crimes and crimes against humanity (see Figure 11). He was then sentenced to 40 years in prison. Among other charges, he was found guilty of the Srebrenica massacre (also see Section 5.8), which aimed to kill 'every able-bodied male' in the besieged town and drive out the entire Bosnian Muslim population living there.

The achievement of the UN in successfully prosecuting one of the leading men behind a systematic campaign of terror against civilians in the deadliest conflict in Europe since the Second World War was considerable. The successful prosecution of countries, organisations or individuals who commit war crimes is rare, because the 'fog of war' can often obscure the circumstances of any crimes or offences, as well as leaving little reliable evidence and few witnesses on which to base any war crimes prosecutions. UN bureaucracy can also hinder the process, which means that many cases never even come to trial.

Figure 10 *Radovan Karadzic, the political leader of the Bosnian Serbs, escorted by his paramilitary bodyguards in 1994*

Figure 11 *Radovan Karadzic, now former Bosnian Serb leader, in court on the first day of his defense against war crimes charges at the International Criminal Tribunal for the former Yugoslavia in The Hague in 2012 – this time escorted by prison guards*

Over to you

1. In pairs, discuss and explain the principles underlying the UDHR.
2. In pairs, research one country which has chosen not to sign the UDHR. Research **(a)** its original decision not to sign in 1948, **(b)** why it persists in not signing. Feed back your findings to the class.
3. Using Figures 5 and 6, explain how far the cases brought before the European Court of Human Rights, and subsequent decisions made by the Court, erode national sovereignty.
4. Using Figures 7 and 8 discuss and assess how far the Geneva Conventions were violated in Aleppo.
5. Discuss as a class: 'Should human rights laws apply to British soldiers engaged in war?' Write a 500-word summary of the discussion.

On your own

6. Select one recent war or dispute (e.g. Syria). Research possible reasons why this war or dispute is unlikely to come to trial under the Geneva Conventions.
7. Research and explain why the Geneva Conventions were signed by 196 countries, while only 48 signed the UDHR.

Exam-style question

Evaluate the importance of both international law and international agreements in protecting human rights. *(20 marks)*

4.5 Defining and protecting human rights

In this section, you'll learn that there are significant differences between countries in their definitions and protection of human rights.

Human rights: the USA and the UN

In 2016, the UN Human Rights Council held its 33rd meeting. Although the USA was taking a mandatory year away from being a voting member throughout 2015-16, it still made several key representations to tackle human rights abuses in the following countries:

- **Yemen.** It ensured that the Council adopted a resolution on Yemen, in order to gather evidence about human rights violations and abuses there.
- **Syria.** It sponsored a resolution to focus on serious Syrian human rights abuses.
- **Cambodia.** It drew attention to human rights abuses in Cambodia, by expressing concerns about a lack of rights involving freedom of opinion and expression, and peaceful assembly and freedom of association (see Figure 1), as well as condemning the escalation of political tensions there.
- **Burundi.** It supported a resolution to investigate alleged violations and abuses of human rights in the country.
- The USA also supported resolutions to ensure the safety of journalists around the world, and also to protect the rights of indigenous peoples.

However, despite being a keen advocate of international human rights, the USA has a mixed history of involvement with the Human Rights Council. It has long been a financial backer of the Council, and has frequently invoked human rights at international forums, but only became an actual member of the Council in 2009 (previous US Presidents had been sceptical of its usefulness).

Economic development vs. human rights: Singapore

Since gaining independence from Malaysia in 1965, Singapore's economy has grown rapidly (see Figure 2). It now has one of the world's highest GDPs per capita. The country depends heavily on overseas trade, in particular through exports of electronic components and refined oil. It also receives a high level of Foreign Direct Investment (FDI), because it's widely regarded as one of the most neo-liberal, competitive and business-friendly economies in the world.

KEY CONCEPTS

- **Causality** – the link between democracy and human rights
- **Inequality** – the different protection of human rights in different countries

Figure 1 A 2015 gathering in Phnom Penh, capital of Cambodia, in which activists demonstrated in support of Human Rights Day there

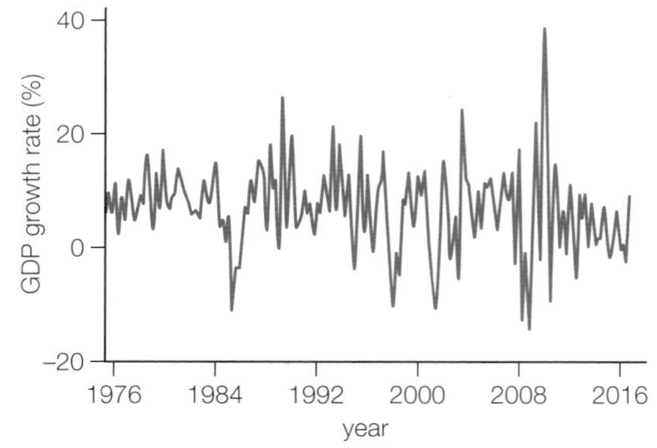

Figure 2 Singapore's GDP growth rate, 1976-2016, which averaged 6.8% over the period – reaching an astounding peak of 37.20% in 2010!

However, Singapore's economic success has come at a cost for human rights. The Singaporean government limits political and civil rights – such as freedom of expression, and peaceful assembly and association – through laws that focus on public order, morality and racial and religious harmony. Singapore still employs the death penalty and has one of the world's highest execution rates per capita. It also enforces corporal punishment, with caning used for many criminal offences. The pressure group Human Rights Watch has expressed concerns about Singapore in relation to its limited press and media freedoms, together with the widespread exploitation of migrant workers, and also human trafficking.

The Singaporean government and its supporters defend their position, by saying that Singapore is 'basically a conservative society' that is intent on preserving the status quo, based on order and stability. They argue that the relative disregard for human rights there has allowed Singapore to prosper since the 1970s (see Figure 2).

Democratic freedom for all?

Over time, some superpowers and emerging powers have moved from more authoritarian governments to greater democracy. However, the level of democratic freedom allowed in each one varies, including free speech and other human rights protections.

Figure 3 shows that, in recent decades, both India and China have undergone remarkable economic growth; together they now account for 16% of global GDP. In 2016, India overtook China as the world's fastest-growing economy – and the Indian economy is likely to overtake those of Japan and Germany by 2019. China continues to grow rapidly (albeit slower than previously), and is now considered to be both an economic and political superpower. However, these two countries have grown by adopting very different economic approaches and political systems, as the two panels below explain.

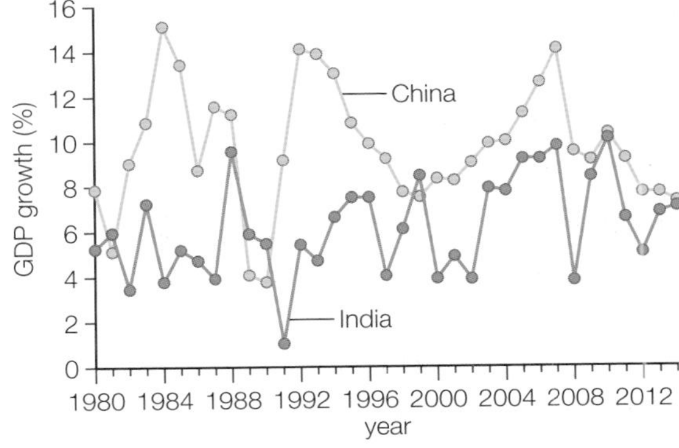

Figure 3 *The annual economic growth rates for India and China, 1980–2014*

Authoritarian government: China

The Chinese Communist Party has governed China since 1949 as a single-party, authoritarian state. There are no general elections, although Local People's Congresses are directly elected – with candidates coming solely from the Communist Party. Political power is concentrated in the hands of the President, who also serves as the General-Secretary of the Communist Party. Human Rights Watch states that China 'curtails a wide range of human rights, including freedom of expression, association, assembly and religion'. Senior Chinese leaders reject the universality of 'human rights' – regarding them as Western ideas and a threat to their power.

However, increasingly the Chinese Communist government is being challenged by China's rapid economic development – with greater wealth, better schooling, and access (albeit limited) to social media – and there are now more frequent calls in the country for greater levels of democratic freedom.

Democratic government: India

Since gaining independence from the UK in 1947, India has become the world's largest democracy. Its Constitution dates from 1950 and consists of 444 articles, which include freedom of speech and religion. India has a federal system of government (i.e. a lot of political power is delegated to individual Indian states), and it has a ceremonial President as head of government. The real power lies in the hands of the *Lok Sabha* (or Lower House of Parliament), whose members decide who will be the country's Prime Minister.

India has a vigorous media and independent judiciary, both of which are important aspects of a free and democratic society. It has also made significant progress in protecting human rights, although Human Rights Watch states that it still has serious concerns about the treatment of minority groups, together with women's rights (e.g. violence against women, such as rape), discrimination over sexual orientation and gender identity, and disability rights. Nevertheless, the Indian government is committed to improving India's human rights further as the economy grows.

Measuring political corruption

Which is the least politically corrupt country? According to the Corruption Perception Index (2015), published by Transparency International (a non-governmental international organisation based in Berlin), the answer is Denmark (see Figure 4A). And the most politically corrupt? Somalia (Figure 4B). According to the data, no single country, anywhere, is corruption-free – and Figure 5 shows that 68% of countries worldwide have serious corruption problems.

Transparency International was formed in 1993 with the mission to combat corruption and prevent criminal activities arising from corruption. The organisation has bases in over 100 countries, and publishes both the Global Corruption Barometer as well as the Corruption Perception Index. It defines corruption as 'the abuse of entrusted power for private gain', which often involves decision-makers who abuse their positions to sustain their power, status and wealth through the manipulation of policies, institutions and rules of procedure in the allocation of resources.

Political corruption in Lebanon

Lebanon was placed 123rd in the Corruption Perception Index for 2015 – below Sierra Leone and only just above Iran. The country is accused of having systemic corruption throughout its State institutions and public services, which often extends into the private sector as well. Among the Lebanese people, it's said to be common knowledge that all major public offices suffer from corruption, which leads to the loss of vast amounts of public money. A UN report in 2001 found that over 43% of companies in Lebanon 'always or very frequently' pay bribes.

One of the major concerns in Lebanon is that it failed to hold a General Election in June 2013, and then again the following year. When the Lebanese Parliament failed to elect a President, it just extended its own term until 2017 – further delaying a General Election. With this political stalemate in place, the Lebanese government has stopped providing basic services, including waste removal services. This has led to a wave of protests, which in some cases were quelled with excessive force – raising questions about human rights protection in the country. There are also wider concerns about human rights abuses in Lebanon, particularly in dealing with Syrian refugees, the prevention of torture, and in the treatment of migrant domestic workers.

A

Rank	Corruptions Perception Index score (2015)	Country
1	91	Denmark
2	90	Finland
3	89	Sweden
4	88	New Zealand
5=	87	Netherlands
5=	87	Norway
7	86	Switzerland
8	85	Singapore
9	83	Canada
10=	81	Germany
10=	81	Luxembourg
10=	81	UK

B

Rank	Corruptions Perception Index score (2015)	Country
158=	17	Haiti
158=	17	Guinea-Bissau
158=	17	Venezuela
161=	16	Iraq
161=	16	Libya
163=	15	Angola
163=	15	South Sudan
165	12	Sudan
166	11	Afghanistan
167=	8	North Korea
167=	8	Somalia

Figure 4 *The top (**A**) and bottom (**B**) countries on the Corruption Perception Index for 2015, based on data from 168 countries. A country's score indicates the perceived level of public-sector corruption on a scale from 0 (highly corrupt) to 100 (very clean). However, like most indices of this nature, some factors are overlooked – such as in Singapore, which has no minimum wage for migrant workers, or legal system in which imprisonment must be determined as legal by a court.*

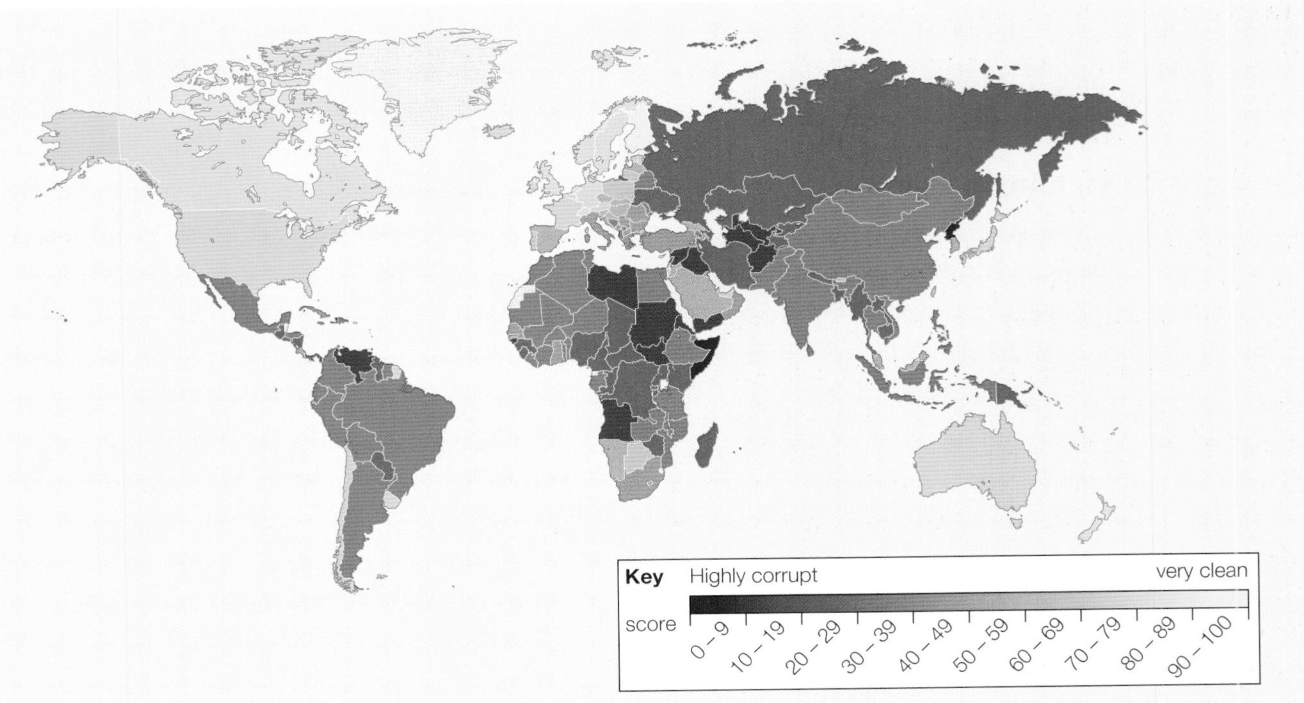

Figure 5 *The Corruption Perception Index (2015), which shows perceived levels of public sector corruption worldwide. Dark red indicates a highly corrupt public sector. Lighter red and orange countries fare a bit better, but corruption among public institutions and employees is still common. Yellow countries are perceived as cleaner, but not perfect.*

Over to you

1 **a** In pairs, brainstorm the list of potential benefits to the USA of promoting human rights in international forums and debates.

b Now consider why other countries (e.g. Singapore) choose to prioritise economic development over human rights.

2 Again in pairs, research two examples of human rights violations in each of India and China. Produce a mind map to show the different ways in which human rights are violated.

3 **a** In pairs, discuss and list ways in which you think that corruption *could* be measured.

b Now study Figures 4 and 5. In pairs, research the (**i**) qualitative and (**ii**) quantitative indicators that could be used to derive an index (or categories) of corruption as shown in Figure 5. Compare this list with your own.

c Using Figure 4, compare variations in levels of corruption with types of government. Research the types of government found in sample countries.

On your own

4 Suggest reasons why the level of protection for human rights can vary between different countries.

5 Research how the protection of human rights and degree of freedom of speech can vary between countries.

6 Suggest ways in which high levels of corruption could threaten human rights.

Exam-style question

Explain why there are differences in human rights between countries.
(8 marks)

4.6 Variations in human rights within countries

In this section, you'll learn that there are significant variations in human rights within countries, reflected in different levels of social development.

KEY CONCEPTS

- **Causality** – links between equality and human rights, health and education
- **Inequality** – variations in human rights within countries

Free speech vs. human rights

It was late 2016 – spring in Australia. Trees were blossoming and it was a warm 25 degrees. For those working in the booming economies of Sydney and Melbourne, the world was good. But *The Australian* newspaper had just found itself embroiled in a human rights controversy over a cartoon it had published. The cartoon depicted a stereotypical indigenous Aboriginal man as drunk and dysfunctional – unable to remember the names of his children.

The cartoon's publication led to allegations of racial hatred under Australia's Racial Discrimination Act. Complaints were also made to the Australian Human Rights Commission, which states that 'it is unlawful for someone to do anything likely to offend, insult, humiliate or intimidate someone because of race or ethnicity'. A big debate ensued over the rights of free speech versus racial discrimination. Does the right of free speech (a human right) allow a newspaper to publish a derogatory cartoon impinging on the human rights of those it insults?

At the heart of this controversy were Australia's indigenous peoples – the Aboriginal and Torres Strait Islanders (ATSI). These indigenous peoples have long been subjected to lower living standards, discrimination and a poorer quality of life than Australia's non-indigenous population (see the text panel on the right). Even Australia Day – 26 January – celebrates the landing of white Europeans in Botany Bay, and completely ignores the long-standing Aboriginal inhabitation of Australia (as illustrated in Figure 1).

ATSI peoples:

- have an average life expectancy which is 10 years shorter than that of non-indigenous Australians (70 years instead of 80)
- have Australia's highest levels of drug and alcohol abuse, as well as homelessness
- are seeing their traditional lifestyles disappearing, with the result that traditional customs, knowledge and beliefs will vanish without some real action being taken to preserve them.

Figure 1 *Welcoming the 43rd Millennium. This cartoon appeared in the* Sydney Morning Herald *on New Year's Day 2000 – a reminder that the world humans know is rather older than 2000 years!*

Aboriginal peoples and the law

Today, ATSI peoples are encouraged to know their rights. The Australian Human Rights Commission (AHRC) has focused on two key aspects:

1 **Preventing racial discrimination**, through the Racial Discrimination Act, which makes racial hatred an offence in Australia and protects indigenous peoples against discrimination in:

- employment (e.g. getting a job, working conditions, promotion, dismissal)
- education (enrolling for or studying a course)
- accommodation (renting or buying a house or apartment)
- getting or using services (e.g. services from banks, insurers, government departments, transport or telecommunication industries, doctors, restaurants or shops)
- accessing public places (e.g. parks, government offices, restaurants, or shopping centres)

2 **Social justice** by recognising the distinctive rights of indigenous Australians, such as the right to:

- a distinct status and culture, through maintaining and strengthening the identity and spiritual and cultural practices of indigenous communities
- self-determination, where indigenous communities take control of their futures and decide how to address issues facing them
- land to provide spiritual and cultural support for indigenous communities.

Although Australian law now protects the ATSI peoples, before 1967 they were not even considered to be Australian citizens. A referendum that year led to voting and citizenship rights for indigenous peoples being written into Australia's Constitution. Before these constitutional changes, ATSI peoples:

- could not vote, gain political representation or participate in shaping the country
- were often forced to live on 'reserves' (for example, Queensland's Aboriginal people could still be forced to live on reserves until 1971, and could not legally own property until 1975)
- often had their children forcibly removed by the Australian authorities to be raised in 'civilised' white-run institutions. The legacy of this policy is known as the '**stolen generations**' and the practice didn't finally end until 1970.

BACKGROUND

Comparing indicators of inequality for ATSI peoples

- In 2011, 43.8% of ATSI peoples lived in remote areas (see Figure 2), compared to 2.2% of non-indigenous Australians.
- In 2014:
  - the national rate of imprisonment for ATSI peoples was 15 times higher than for non-indigenous Australians
  - 41% of ATSI adults smoked, compared to 13.8% of non-indigenous Australians
  - the percentage of unemployed ATSI peoples was nearly three times higher than for non-indigenous Australians.
- In 2015, 30% of ATSI adults lacked basic literacy skills.
- However, there is some cause for optimism. By 2011, 54% of ATSI people aged 20-24 had achieved the Australian equivalent of A level qualifications, so a better-educated generation is beginning to appear.

Figure 2 *Remote areas of Australia are often semi-desert – and those are the lands in which nearly half of ATSI peoples live*

Health issues for ATSI peoples

Past differences in the rights of ATSI peoples are now being reflected in present differences in their health, education and employment opportunities, as shown in a 2016 report by the NGO HealthInfoNet. As well as much lower life expectancy (see Figure 3), this report found that ATSI peoples often lack:

- good (or any) employment opportunities
- safety in their communities
- access to a decent education
- connections to family and friends
- enough money to get by on a day-to-day basis.

The report also found that these factors are all linked to lower life chances, compared to non-indigenous Australians.

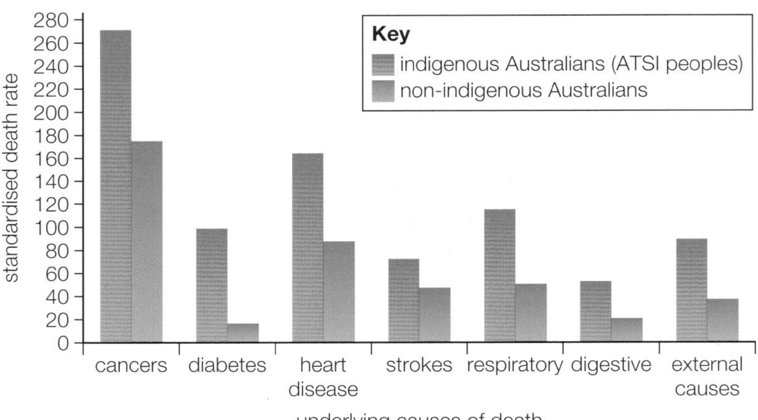

Figure 3 *Selected underlying causes of death for indigenous and non-indigenous Australians in 2011. Note that the term 'standardised death rate' removes those differences between people that might occur as a result of different age groups or socio-economic groupings*

The 2009 'Closing the Gap' initiative (see Section 4.2) is part of the Australian government's commitment to improve the health and quality of life of all ATSI peoples, starting at childhood (see Figure 4). However, progress has been variable:

- Between 2005 and 2012, the life expectancy gap between ATSI peoples and non-indigenous Australians closed by 0.8 years for ATSI men, but by only 0.1 years for women.
- Between 1998 and 2012, ATSI death rates from circulatory diseases fell by 45% and from respiratory diseases by 27%.
- Between 2008 and 2012, the death rates from all avoidable causes were three times higher for ATSI peoples than for non-indigenous Australians.
- Between 1998 and 2012, infant mortality rates for ATSI infants fell by 64%.

Figure 4 *ATSI children at Ramingining preschool in Arnhem Land, learning to clean their teeth with a brush and toothpaste. Education health programmes, like this one, feature as part of the government's 'Closing the Gap' initiative.*

The HealthInfoNet report concluded that the health of ATSI peoples is improving, although more slowly than for non-indigenous Australians. This is linked to factors such as low educational attainment in previous generations, poor employment, low income and socio-economic status, as well as a lack of access to good services or support in remote areas.

Education issues for ATSI peoples

Education data show that 20% of compulsory school-age ATSI children are not enrolled in school, and that many of those who are enrolled do not attend regularly. The previous 'stolen generations' experience has left many ATSI parents deeply suspicious of official institutions, including schools, and they simply refuse to enrol their children in them. In 2015, 78% of ATSI students achieved the required literacy standards at the age of 8 – compared to 95% of non-indigenous students. However, in the Northern Territory – with the highest ATSI population – only 42% of ATSI students reached this standard.

Equal rights for all Australians

In 2016, the Australian Prime Minister, Malcolm Turnbull, presented a motion to the Australian Parliament to promote anti-racism and equal rights for all Australians. It had five components:

1. The entitlement of all Australians to enjoy equal rights and be treated with equal respect, regardless of race, colour, creed or origin.
2. A national immigration policy that is non-discriminatory on the grounds of race, colour, creed or origin.
3. Reconciliation with ATSI peoples, and redress for their past social and economic disadvantages.
4. The maintenance of Australia as a culturally diverse and open society, united by a commitment to democratic institutions and values.
5. Denouncing racial intolerance in any form.

Many ATSI people still believe that they are discriminated against. There are demands for better self-representation, as well as for the restoration of land that was forcibly taken from ATSI peoples, and also cultural awareness programmes such as that in Figure 5.

Gender inequality in Australia

Non-indigenous Australian women won the right to vote in 1902 – 69 years before ATSI women achieved the same right. Yet despite their political rights and equality, many women believe that gender inequality remains a problem in Australia:

- Among their concerns are widespread discrimination and a lack of safety, as well as disrespect at home, online, in public, at work and in relationships.
- Many feel that everyday sexism survives in Australian workplaces.
- Although gender equality has improved, pay equality between men and women in Australia fell between 2015 and 2016.
- While most Australian women say that they have more opportunities than their mothers' generation did, many also claim poor support for working mothers (e.g. parental leave, affordable childcare).

Figure 5 *A cultural centre at Uluru (formerly known as Ayers Rock) run by aboriginal women, an initiative which has proved successful in bringing aboriginal culture to tourists*

Exam-style question

Evaluate the extent to which different levels of social development can be explained by variations in human rights within countries. *(20 marks)*

Over to you

1. In pairs, list the ways in which ATSI peoples in Australia have been, and remain, discriminated against.
2. Using examples from this section, draw a mind map to explain how ethnic or racial discrimination is likely to lead to poorer health and education.
3. In pairs, discuss and list three targets that you believe the Australian government should set itself to bring the health and education of ATSI peoples closer to those of non-indigenous Australians.

On your own

4. Can free speech and racial intolerance ever be compatible? Write 500 words outlining your thoughts.
5. Research (**a**) one country that has made more progress than Australia in achieving equality for women, and (**b**) one which has made less.
6. Research the debate taking place in Australia about whether 'Australia Day' should change date from 26 January.

4.7 Geopolitical interventions

In this section, you'll learn that there are different forms of geopolitical intervention in defence of human rights.

EQ3 Sections 4.7 to 4.9 investigate how human rights are used as arguments for political and military intervention.

Intervention in conflict – is it right?

In 1994, an estimated 800 000 Rwandans were killed in the space of 100 days. The dead were mainly from the Tutsi ethnic group, killed by the Hutu ethnic majority – many believe with the involvement of the Hutu-led government. You can read more about the background to this in Section 5.5. Events such as this act of **genocide** – the mass killing of one particular group – started a debate: does the international community have a right to intervene in a country when the human rights of its citizens are being violated?

That debate has continued. In 2005, the UN passed a resolution stating that each country has a '*responsibility to protect its citizens from genocide, war crimes, ethnic cleansing and crimes against humanity*'. When and if that national responsibility fails, the responsibility then falls to the international community – if necessary, through the use of military intervention. Called the 'Responsibility to Protect' (R2P), this concept was adopted by 150 countries, and has become a key principle of international decisions regarding the protection of human rights around the world (see Figure 1).

KEY CONCEPT

- **Causality** – the reasons why human rights may need to be defended, even to the point of one country interfering in the affairs of another

Figure 1 *African Union (AU) troops from Uganda serving in Somalia in 2012. They were there to boost national security, fight Islamist militants, train Somali security forces, and assist in securing the delivery of humanitarian aid to people displaced by the fighting.*

Geopolitical interventions

Interventions by countries and international organisations to defend human rights, or to address development issues, generally take one of four forms: development aid, trade embargoes, military aid and military action (both indirect and direct).

1 Development aid

Development aid, often called overseas aid or official development assistance (ODA), is financial aid given to developing countries to support their long-term economic, political, social and environmental development (see Figure 2).

Most aid comes from:

- the governments of developed countries, including £12 billion a year from the UK government
- **intergovernmental organisations** (IGOs), such as the UN, the World Bank and the EU
- **non-governmental organisations** (NGOs), such as Oxfam.

The aid may go directly from one country to another (known as **bilateral aid**), or may be channelled through an IGO (known as **multilateral aid**).

Rank	Country	ODA received (in US$ million)
1	Myanmar	4171
2	Afghanistan	4164
3	India	3029
4	Vietnam	2902
5	Indonesia	2061
6	Kenya	1952
7	Ethiopia	1950
8	Pakistan	1896
9	Tanzania	1799
10	Syria	1688

Figure 2 *The ten largest recipients of official development assistance (ODA) from the USA, 2013–2014*

In 1970, the UN General Assembly adopted a resolution under which wealthy countries agreed to commit 0.7% of their GNI each year to development aid. This is a voluntary target, and – as Figure 3 shows – one that most countries fail to meet. In March 2015, the UK government made this commitment a legal requirement, becoming the first G7 country to do so.

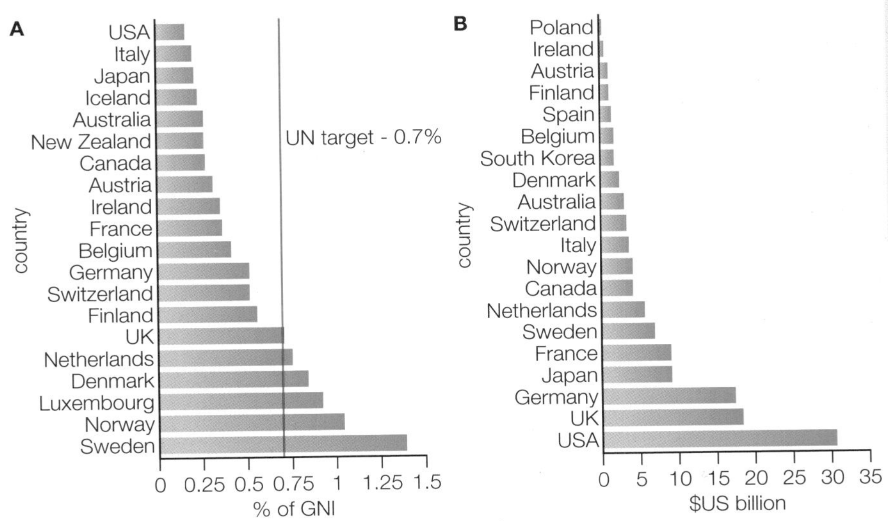

Key words

Geopolitical – The influence of geography (both human and physical) on politics, especially international relations.

Intergovernmental organisation (IGO) – An organisation involving several countries working together on issues of common interest.

Non-governmental organisation (NGO) – A not-for-profit organisation, independent from any government.

Figure 3 *The level of donor countries' ODA as a percentage of their GNI in 2015 (**A**), plus the total amount of ODA by donor country in $US billion (**B**)*

Since 1960, the total amount of global ODA given each year to developing countries has usually risen (see Figure 4). Since 2000, there has been an increase of 82.5% (even including a dip due to the global financial crisis of 2007-8). By 2015, global development aid totalled US$146.68 billion, which was a rise of 6.9% in just one year. However, while the total amount of ODA has steadily increased since 1960, the level of ODA when measured as a percentage of GNI has actually decreased (see Figure 4).

Figure 4 *Total global ODA, shown in both US$ billion and as a percentage of GNI, 1960–2015*

2 Trade embargoes

A trade embargo is a government or international ban that restricts trade with a particular country. It's a political tool, used to encourage a country to change its policies or actions by hindering its economy, or by reducing its access to specific products like military supplies.

Trade embargoes are often used in response to perceived threats to international security, or to force an end to humanitarian or human rights abuses. For example, in the 1980s, the UN imposed an embargo on oil and military supplies to South Africa, in order to pressurise its government into ending the policy of Apartheid.

Trade embargoes can prohibit all trade, or simply ban the trade in certain items (such as weapons), while continuing to allow trade in other items (such as food or medicines). In late 2016, the UK had arms embargoes on 17 countries.

Individual countries can impose embargos, but they are often put in place by IGOs (e.g. the UN and EU), and supported by their member states. For example, in 2011, the UN Security Council imposed an arms embargo on Libya in response to human rights violations.

3 Military aid

Military aid consists of money, weapons, equipment or expertise given to developing countries to help them protect their borders, fight terrorism and combat piracy or drug and people trafficking. Military aid is also sometimes given to opposition groups fighting for democracy against an authoritarian government – for example, the USA and UK have sent vehicles and protective armour to some Syrian rebel groups fighting President Assad.

In 2016, the Organisation for Economic Co-operation and Development (OECD) changed its definition of official development assistance/overseas aid to include some military spending. Donor countries can now use part of their 0.7% aid target to support military forces in developing countries where further economic development or human rights are being put at risk by conflict.

However, this change in aid definition has been controversial:

- The OECD argued that tackling violent extremism was a development activity, with over 90% of militant attacks happening in countries with weak governments and poor human rights records.
- Charities, however, expressed concern that this change would lead to less money being spent on poverty reduction.

The USA is the largest contributor of military aid to other countries. It provides some form of military aid to over 150 countries each year (see Figure 5 for the top 10). Much of this aid is given to protect US interests and security abroad. For example, in 2014, over US$1.3 billion in military aid was given to Egypt, in part to help it fight the so-called Islamic State (ISIS).

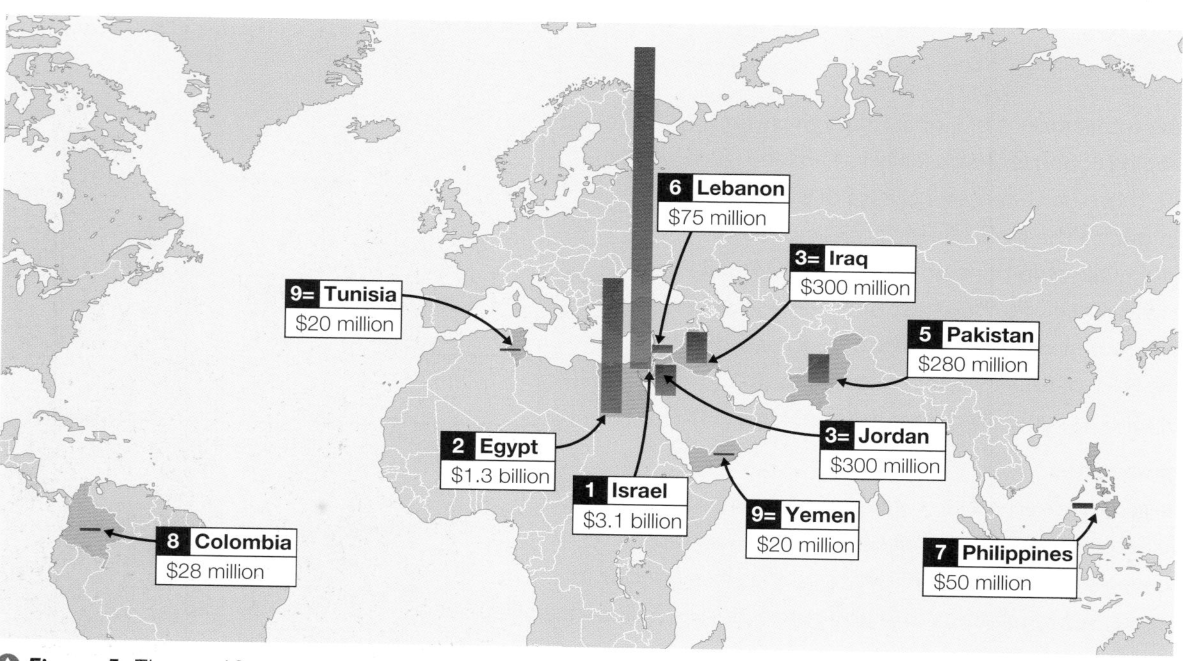

Figure 5 *The top 10 countries, according to the amount of overseas military aid they received from the USA in 2014 (in US$)*

4 Military action

Most governments and IGOs consider the use of military action to be a last resort, after all other pathways (such as embargoes and diplomatic measures) have failed. When used, military action can take one of two forms:

- **Direct action**, e.g. air strikes or troops on the ground. For example, in 2003, the USA and UK were among a coalition of countries who sent troops and carried out air strikes in Iraq against the government of Saddam Hussein.
- **Indirect action**, e.g. providing military and political assistance. For example, in 2017 British army personnel were training Nigerian forces to help them improve the country's security and fight the Islamist militant group, Boko Haram.

Sometimes military action is taken at the request of, or in agreement with, the country concerned. For instance the Nigerian example opposite, or when the government of Mali asked for French help to fight back against Islamist militants who had seized control of large parts of the country in 2013 (see Figure 6).

At other times, military action is taken to protect people from their own government. For example, in 1999, NATO used air strikes in support of the Serbian province of Kosovo, when the Serbian government of Slobodan Milosovic began a brutal crackdown against ethnic Albanian Kosovans and their demands for independence from Serbia. There were accusations of Serbian ethnic cleansing, as there had been in neighbouring Bosnia in the early 1990s.

Figure 6 *French troops helping to fight Islamist militants in Mali in 2013*

The validity of intervention

When situations occur, such as a government systematically abusing its citizens' human rights (as in Kosovo), or militants using child soldiers and attacking schools in an effort to overthrow a legitimate government (as in northern Nigeria and Figure 7), the international community's 'Responsibility to Protect' seems clear. But is it really that straightforward?

Interventions to promote development or protect human rights can come from IGOs, individual countries or NGOs. Sometimes the decision to intervene is supported by the international community, but often there is disagreement about whether the intervention is needed or justified. This difference of opinion can occur because of:

- the different perspectives or aims of the organisations or countries concerned
- the perceived 'real' reason(s) for the intervention, i.e. is it really to stop human rights abuses/promote development, or are the intervening country's self-interests at play? For example, in 2015, research by several UK universities found that overseas intervention in a civil war is 100 times more likely if the country involved has large oil reserves!
- opposing views about whether the stated outcomes are likely to be achieved, or whether any intervention could make matters worse
- concern over a disregard for **national sovereignty** (see the next page)
- disagreements about whether any intervention is proportionate.

Figure 7 *Child soldiers being trained in a militia camp in the Democratic Republic of the Congo*

For example, in Yemen in late 2011, when protests calling for the resignation of President Ali Abdullah Saleh turned violent, Saudi Arabia intervened on behalf of the Yemeni government. The UK government supported the Saudi actions by providing military aid and weapons. But several humanitarian organisations – including Human Rights Watch, Oxfam and Amnesty International – say that Saudi Arabia's actions in Yemen are making the human rights situation there worse, and that British-supplied weapons are being used to destroy medical clinics and charity headquarters.

National sovereignty

National sovereignty is a fundamental principle of international law. The UN states in its charter that '*nothing should authorise intervention in matters essentially within the domestic jurisdiction of any state*'. However, since 2005, instances of governments abusing the rights of their own people through genocide, torture and imprisonment have given increasing weight to the 'Responsibility to Protect' principle – making it clear that the sovereignty of a country has limits. As different situations around the world have shown – e.g. in the following material about Libya – there can be considerable tensions between the two principles of 'national sovereignty' and 'Responsibility to Protect'.

Key word

National sovereignty – The idea that each nation has a right to govern itself without interference from other nations.

National sovereignty, the R2P and Libya

The North African country of Libya, situated on the northern margin of the Sahara (and bordered by the Mediterranean Sea) is almost entirely desert. Its location, as shown in Figure 8, gives it an important geopolitical position in relation to Europe. This geopolitical position is enhanced by the fact that Libya has the world's tenth largest oil reserves. Its capital, Tripoli, was once one of Africa's wealthiest cities (see Figure 9).

Figure 8 *Libya's geopolitical location in North Africa*

However, Libya is perhaps best known for the long rule of Colonel Muammar Gaddafi. The country was under Ottoman Turk and then Italian rule until it gained independence in 1951. Colonel Gaddafi then seized power in 1969 and ruled unchallenged for 42 years. However, in the early part of 2011, many Libyans began to demonstrate against his government, inspired by the 'Arab Spring' that was sweeping across North Africa. When the demonstrators were brutally repressed, with hundreds killed and injured, the UN urged the Libyan government to 'meet its responsibility to protect its citizens'. When it failed to do so, the UN authorised the use of force to protect the civilian population. Bombing raids were then undertaken by the British and French air forces, in support of civilians and rebel forces based in Benghazi, against Gaddafi's Tripoli-based government. This was the first real use of 'Responsibility to Protect' by NATO forces.

Figure 9 *Tripoli, once one of the most developed cities on the African continent – funded by significant oil revenues for over 50 years. However, it has suffered greatly since 2011, due to NATO air strikes to help fight Gaddafi, followed by internal conflicts and ongoing political instability between different Libyan groups*

Over the next few months, arms embargoes and air strikes using aircraft such as the one in Figure 10, supported rebel troops in their attempts to defeat the government forces. By October, Gaddafi was dead and a new government was in place.

Despite the threat to human rights in Libya, the international intervention wasn't widely supported. Five countries on the UN Security Council – Russia, China, Brazil, India and Germany – abstained from the vote. They were concerned that:

- there was insufficient evidence to justify interfering in Libya's national sovereignty
- this action might set a precedent for the international community to have a say in how they treated their own populations, particularly in Russia and China
- the real reason for the intervention was regime change
- intervening in the name of human rights is inconsistent; rich countries often interfere in the affairs of poorer countries, while abuses in powerful Western countries are ignored.

Libya's post-Gaddafi era has been extremely unstable. Many areas of the country are outside official government control, and various Islamist, rebel and tribal militias now control those areas in conflict both with each other and the new government.

Figure 10 *An RAF Tornado based in Malta during operations over Libya in 2011*

Over to you

1. In pairs, use examples from this section to list (**a**) the advantages and (**b**) the risks associated with one country (or IGO) intervening in the affairs of another.

2. **a** Using Figure 2, draw proportional flow lines on a world map to show both the direction and level of aid from the USA to recipients.
   b Research the top ten recipients of aid from one other major aid donor country in Figure 3 (search the phrase 'Top 10 recipients of aid from your chosen country) and draw additional flow lines linking it with these recipients.
3. Using Figure 3 and the material in this section to help you, briefly outline the arguments which show that countries (**a**) should pay at least 0.7% of their GNI in aid, (**b**) should not be forced to pay a target percentage.
4. Complete a table giving reasons why military aid (**a**) should and (**b**) should not be permitted within aid budgets.
5. Using further research where needed, assess the success of the removal of Colonel Gaddafi as leader of Libya by external forces.

On your own

6. Distinguish between the following pairs of terms: (**a**) murder and genocide, (**b**) bilateral and multilateral aid, (**c**) direct and indirect military action.
7. Select one country from Figure 2 and research (**a**) reasons why aid may be needed there, and (**b**) examples of how aid money has been spent.
8. Select one country from Figure 5 and research the reasons for this military aid from the USA.
9. Prepare a 300-word statement for a class discussion titled 'The existence of child soldiers can never be justified'.

Exam-style question

Evaluate the effectiveness of different forms of geopolitical intervention in defence of human rights. (*20 marks*)

4.8 The impacts of development aid

In this section, you'll learn that some development focuses on improving both human rights and human welfare, but other development has negative environmental and cultural impacts.

Types of development aid

Comic Relief is a UK charity event that runs every two years. Like similar annual events, such as BBC Children in Need, it raises public awareness of the need for development aid, and also shows how money raised previously has been spent.

Aid comes in different forms, ranging from charitable gifts to loans. It can also be provided for specific projects (such as rebuilding schools and medical facilities after an earthquake), or for broader development aims. Charitable gifts are funded by **donations** from the public through charities, such as Christian Aid and Oxfam. Sometimes, **governments** support charitable work by matching public donations, such as through 'UK Aid Match', a government programme that works on international development issues.

Most aid is either bilateral or multilateral (see Section 4.7). On average, between 2008 and 2011, 60% of official development assistance (ODA) was distributed bilaterally, and 28% multilaterally. Governments often favour bilateral aid because it:

- provides control over where and how the money is spent
- allows quicker and more flexible action
- encourages long-term trade relationships with recipient countries.

However, multilateral aid is sometimes considered to be more 'legitimate', because for example, NGOs are less tied to political or economic interests. It also allows for pooling resources, which can be more cost-effective when funding larger projects.

KEY CONCEPT

- **Causality** – the reasons why human rights may need to be defended, even to the point of one country interfering in the affairs of another

Haiti

Haiti is at risk from multiple natural hazards, such as earthquakes and hurricanes. It is also very poor; its HDI ranking is 163 out of 188. This country is sometimes called 'the republic of NGOs', because up to 10 000 NGOs may be working there at any one time.

After the 2010 Haitian earthquake, in which over 220 000 Haitians died, IGOs, individual countries and NGOs all responded with different aid projects (see Figure 1). For example:

- US$13.5 billion was donated; 75% from donor countries and 25% from charities
- the US government donated US$1.3 billion in humanitarian assistance, and US$2.2 billion for recovery, reconstruction and development projects
- the charity Oxfam initially focused on humanitarian work (such as rebuilding sanitation systems) and then began to fund reconstruction and growth projects.

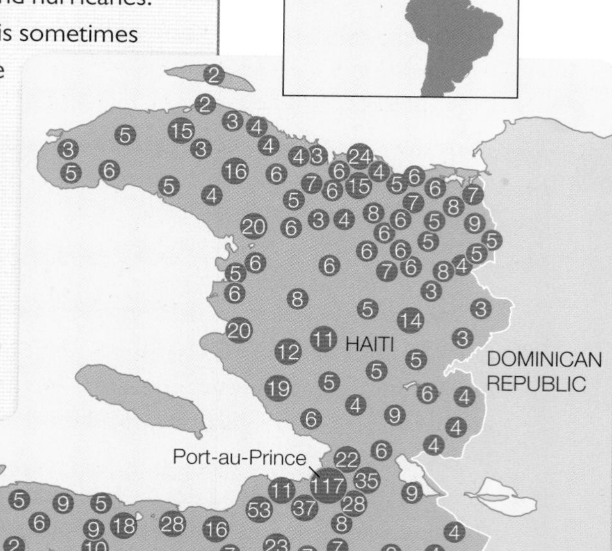

Figure 1 *The widespread locations and numbers of different humanitarian and other aid projects throughout Haiti after the 2010 earthquake – particularly near the capital, Port-au-Prince, which has the highest population density and suffered greatly in the earthquake. In total, there were 373 projects run by 62 organisations.*

Loans

Some IGOs, such as the World Bank and International Monetary Fund (IMF), provide loans and grants to help developing countries reduce their poverty levels and increase their economic growth. Between 2011 and 2015, the World Bank loaned over US$150 billion to developing countries.

Loans, credits and grants are awarded for various development projects, such as reducing poverty, stimulating economic growth, building infrastructure and fighting corruption. They cover areas such as education, healthcare, agriculture, infrastructure and environmental or resource management. For example, in 2015, the World Bank gave Benin in West Africa (166th in global HDI rankings) US$40 million to help with infrastructure improvements, flood-recovery schemes and flood-protection measures (see Figure 2).

Figure 2 *The effects of flooding in rural Benin, where the rural economy can collapse if people are unable to get to local markets. The World Bank has focused on problems like this in recent years.*

However, some concerns have been raised about IGO loans:

- **Conditionality**. Borrowing countries are often told that they must meet certain conditions before they can receive any loans. For example, Uganda (163rd in global HDI rankings) had to meet 197 separate conditions before it was granted World Bank funding!
- **Environmental damage**. Some IGOs prioritise economic development over environmental damage or the displacement of indigenous populations (see Section 4.6).
- **Structural Adjustment Programmes (SAPs)**, like those described in Section 4.3, have led to some countries reducing their public spending on education or healthcare in order to receive loans.

Development aid – a global success?

Since 2000, aid has been particularly effective when related to public health. For example, vaccination programmes have helped to almost eradicate some diseases (such as polio), and have also greatly reduced others (such as measles, which has declined by 79% globally). The improved diagnosis and treatment of other life-threatening diseases (such as malaria) has also helped to save lives.

Fighting successfully against malaria

Malaria is a tropical disease spread by mosquitoes (see Figure 3). It is **endemic** (widespread and part of the natural environment) in many tropical regions. However, as a result of international aid programmes, the global rate of new infections fell by 37% between 2000 and 2015, and mortality rates also fell by 60%.

In 2000, efforts focused on achieving the UN Millennium Development Goals (see Section 4.3), targeted the reduction – and eventual elimination – of malaria. Donor nations increased their funding to provide:

- free insecticide-treated mosquito nets (ITN), so that over half of the population of sub-Saharan Africa had access to an ITN by 2014 (see Figure 4), compared to just 2% in 2000
- free access to new medicines
- better and more widely available diagnosis.

The UN estimates that 6.2 million deaths from malaria have been prevented since 2000.

Figure 3 *Mosquitoes – the cause of malaria. The microscopic protozoan parasite* plasmodium *is transmitted into human bloodstreams when the mosquito bites.*

Figure 4 *A child sleeping under an insecticide-treated mosquito net in South Sudan*

Gender equality

International efforts to protect and improve human rights have also had successes. For example, in many developing countries, women and girls are often disproportionately affected by poverty and human rights abuses. So, in 1975, the UN launched the 'UN Decade for Women' to highlight the issue of gender equality. This, along with more recent initiatives, has moved gender equality up the priority list for attention and funding. By 2014, over US$30 million of aid money was being targeted specifically at programmes with gender equality as their main, or a significant, aim (see Figure 5).

As a result, there have been some notable successes. Maternal mortality rates have fallen, particularly as a result of the Millennium Development Goals (see Section 4.3), with a 44% decline in global maternal death rates since 1990. More girls are also receiving an education (see Figure 6). However, progress is mixed – in developing countries, women and girls still die at a younger age than men, and millions of girls still do not receive an education.

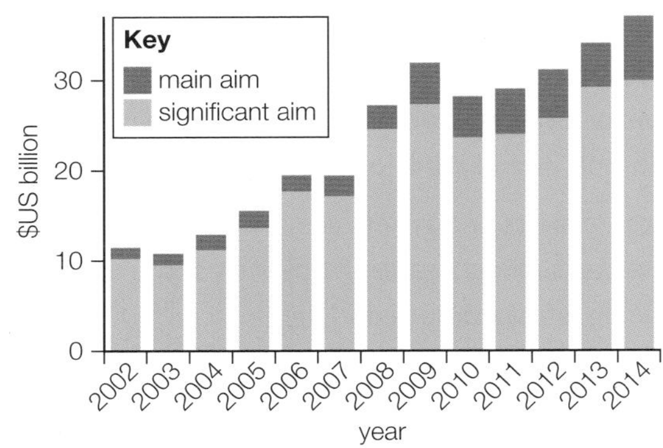

Figure 5 *The annual trend in aid commitments (in US$ billion) to programmes with gender equality and women's empowerment as their main, or a significant, aim*

Figure 6 *Girls on an adolescent programme at a school in rural Uganda. The main reason for girls leaving school early in Uganda is still to marry, but increasingly girls are taking exam qualifications.*

Aid and dependency

How can development aid programmes be harmful? Surely they only provide benefits? In theory this is true, but there are sometimes unintended negative consequences – one of which is **aid dependency**. This refers to the proportion of government income that comes from overseas aid. As Figure 7 shows, in some developing countries this proportion can be significant. A country is considered to be 'aid dependent' if it cannot perform many of the basic functions of government without overseas aid.

Critics argue that aid dependency hinders economic and political development:

- It can become easier for governments simply to rely on aid money, rather than helping local industries and systems to develop.
- Governments may also rely on aid money instead of taking steps to increase the local tax revenue to self-fund development projects.
- Aid goods (i.e. food) can flood the local market, which then drives down prices and reduces the incentive of local farmers to produce enough food themselves.
- Aid dependency can leave the recipient country at risk if that aid is suddenly stopped or reduced.

Country	ODA received as a % of GNI
Afghanistan	23.3
Central African Republic	35.9
Liberia	44.3
Micronesia	33.9
Tuvalu	63.3

Figure 7 *The level of overseas aid received as a percentage of GNI in 2014*

- It can be difficult for recipient countries to plan long-term development projects, if they are unsure about whether the aid money will continue (e.g. after a change of government or policy in a donor country).
- Donor countries often say how and where the aid money should be used.
- Governments that rely on aid can end up becoming more accountable to the donor countries than to their own citizens.

Concern over aid dependency has resulted in efforts being made to reduce the reliance on aid. So, aid dependency is now declining in many countries – on average by a third in the world's poorest countries. For example, aid dependence in Mozambique fell from 67% in 1992 to 12% in 2014. Efforts to reduce aid dependency focus on increasing what is called 'real aid', i.e. aid with few strings attached, which allows countries to lead their own development, and work on projects which may improve infrastructure (see Figure 8).

Figure 8 *A road-construction project in Ghana, funded with Japanese aid. Ghana now has greatly reduced levels of corruption, and rates 64th on the global corruption scale – better than either Italy or Brazil!*

Supporting or promoting corruption

A second criticism of overseas aid is that much of it is lost to corruption – with some people arguing that aid actually fuels or promotes corruption. Many of the countries that receive the most overseas aid are also some of the world's lowest ranking in terms of good governance. These countries are often ruled by dictators, or have government systems that make it easy for aid money to be diverted from its intended use for personal gain (see Figure 9). For example, in 2009, Zambia's former president, Frederick Chiluba, was charged with embezzling US$12 million of aid money. In 2015, the UK donated £128 million to Somalia, despite the latter's ranking as the world's most corrupt country!

Figure 9 *UN Secretary-General, Ban Ki-Moon, speaking about corruption in 2009*

The political elite

A third criticism of overseas aid is that it's sometimes used by the wealthy and political elites to further their own aims at the expense of the general population. Critics suggest that political elites use the money to:

- buy votes to ensure they remain in power
- build a strong military which is then used to repress citizens
- enrich themselves through corruption.

This makes it difficult to hold governments to account for how aid money is spent.

Minority groups in particular, such as the poor and women, pay the price for corruption. It results in fewer opportunities for them and reduced access to jobs, funding and equality. It also undermines human rights, development and democracy.

Development aid versus environmental protection

Sometimes, economic development programmes fail to take environmental issues into consideration. Pollution and the loss of farmland and ecosystems can result – causing both environmental and social/health problems for local communities. Big development projects run by transnational corporations (TNCs) can put traditional cultures and livelihoods at risk – denying local people the right to their land and culture. The discovery of large oil reserves in Nigeria's Niger Delta, and their subsequent exploitation by TNCs, is a case in point.

Oil in the Niger Delta

The Niger Delta is an area of diverse ecological zones, including mangrove forests, freshwater swamps, and tropical rainforest (see Figure 10). The area is home to more than 31 million people and 40 different ethnic groups. It is also rich in oil.

Oil from the Niger Delta accounts for about 75% of the Nigerian government's income, and close to 90% of its export earnings – making Nigeria Africa's largest oil exporter. The enormous wealth brought by the oil industry should lead to economic development for people in the Niger Delta, but the money is not reaching local communities:

- Nigeria earns US$10 billion each year from oil, but over 70% of the people in the Niger Delta live below the poverty line.
- Poorer care is taken of the environment and safety in the Delta region than would be the case in developed nations, where both democracy and effective environmental pressure groups hold companies to account. For example, the situation shown in Figure 11 would never be allowed in the UK.
- Less than 20% of the Delta region is accessible by good roads.
- Local hospitals and schools are under-funded.
- Poor sanitation and pollution make access to clean and safe drinking water a problem.
- Traditional livelihoods in the Delta, such as fishing and agriculture, are being damaged by pollution and the side effects of oil production. This disrupts cultural traditions and also makes people poorer.

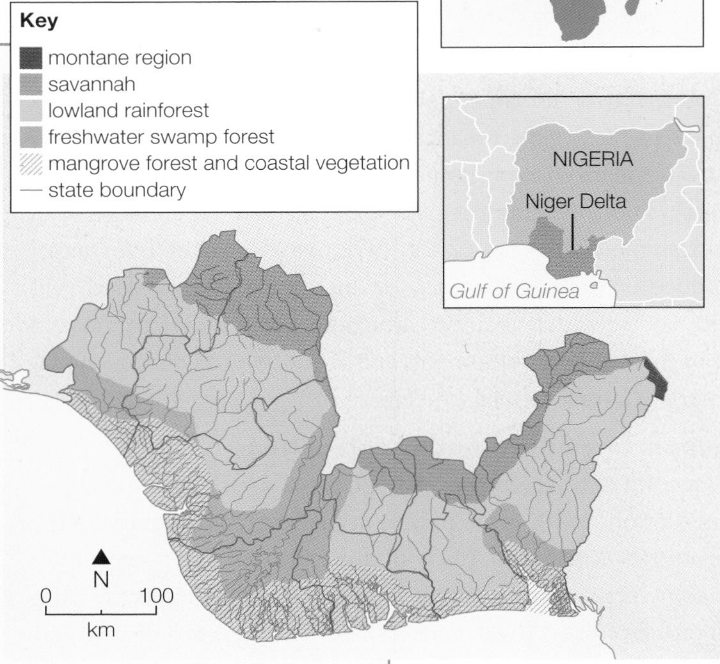

Figure 10 The ecological zones of the Niger Delta, which have been greatly affected by environmental problems resulting from oil extraction

Figure 11 Oil pipelines running right through the middle of a community in the Niger Delta, with local people using the dangerous oil-filled pipes as walkways and places to dry their washing!

> Our only source of drinking water, fishing streams and farmlands covering over 300 hectares of land with aquatic life, fish nets and traps, farm crops, animals … trees are completely destroyed.

Paramount Ruler Chief Clifford E. Enyinda of the Mgbuchi community

Figure 12 *In Rukpokwu, in the Niger Delta, an oil spill and accompanying fire burned for six weeks, destroying local forests and farmland and polluting water supplies. Six months after the spillage, the environmental clean up had still not begun.*

The extraction of oil is having a devastating effect on the Niger Delta's environment (see Figure 12):

- Oil spills are common, which pollute groundwater, surface water and soil. Amnesty International says there were 550 spills just in 2014.
- Mangrove forests and rainforests are frequently damaged or destroyed.
- The burning off of natural gas during oil extraction causes serious environmental and health problems. It produces acid rain, which damages farmland and releases pollutants into the air, causing breathing problems and a higher risk of cancers in local people. It also contributes to global warming.
- The UN says that the oil spills in the Niger Delta over the past five decades will cost US$1 billion and take 30 years to clean up.

Some NGOS argue that a combination of weak governance and a reliance on oil revenue means that the oil companies in the Delta are allowed to do whatever they want, at the expense of the region's minority groups and environment. Feelings of exploitation by local people have begun to build up. Since 2000, the Niger Delta region has been plagued by violence, with frequent attacks on oil pipelines by militant groups.

Exam-style question

Evaluate the statement: 'Some developments improve human rights and welfare, while others have negative environmental and cultural impacts'. (*20 marks*)

Over to you

1 Draw and complete a table to show the advantages and disadvantages of donations and loans as ways of providing development aid.

2 Using examples from this section, discuss in pairs and complete a mind map to show the (**a**) positive, and (**b**) negative aspects of development aid projects.

3 **a** Study Figures 11 and 12. In pairs, research two additional photos to show each of the following aspects of the Niger Delta: (**i**) violence and protests against oil companies on behalf of minority groups, (**ii**) the lawsuit brought in London against Shell Oil.

b Using Sections 6.5 and 6.6 to help you, use all the photos to evaluate the impacts of economic development on the environment lived in by minority groups.

4 Using your answer to question 3b, assess the impacts of TNCs on the environment in the Niger Delta, and the ways in which these impacts affect the human rights of minority groups to land and culture.

On your own

5 **a** Using one development project (such as tackling malaria), research newspaper articles and marketing materials (from drugs companies or development agencies) to determine the impacts of development aid.

b Using Section 6.5 to help, evaluate the materials you have researched. How good an impression of the development project do they give you?

6 Assess the extent to which the exploitation of the Niger Delta has been environmentally and socially beneficial.

4.9 Military action and human rights

In this section, you'll learn that military aid, including both direct and indirect military intervention, is frequently justified in terms of human rights.

KEY CONCEPT

- **Causality** – the reasons why some countries choose to intervene militarily in the affairs of other countries

Military interventions

The decision to intervene militarily in the affairs of another country is one that few governments take lightly. The decision process can be complicated, even at a national level. However – internationally – there are even more issues to consider, because any military intervention must be seen as both justified and proportionate, or it could risk being branded illegitimate and a threat to international security.

Military interventions for solely national interests can be difficult to justify, both at home and abroad. It is much easier to sell an intervention in the name of 'human rights', as explained in Figure 1.

> Power matters … yet many in the United States are … uncomfortable with the notions of power… This discomfort leads to … the belief that the support of many states – or, even better, of institutions like the United Nations – is essential to the legitimate exercise of power. The 'national interest' is replaced with 'humanitarian interests', or the interests of 'the international community'.

Figure 1 *Former US Secretary of State Condoleeza Rice, speaking in 2000*

Libya in 2011 is an example of this (also see Section 4.7). When the Libyan government of Colonel Gaddafi cracked down on pro-democracy protestors (shown in Figure 2) inspired by the 'Arab Spring' demonstrations in neighbouring countries, the UN approved the use of force to counter the actions of the Libyan government. National and international vested interests, such as a desire for regime change and for energy security (Libya is a major oil exporter), were both realistic reasons to justify military intervention, but instead a human rights argument was put forward as justification for international involvement – to defend helpless Libyan civilians from their government.

Figure 2 *Libyan anti-Gaddafi protestors in 2011*

Military aid and poor human rights

Despite the human rights argument discussed above, military aid is often still given to countries with poor human rights records. For example, the USA provides military aid to countries such as Colombia with poor records of human rights abuses (see opposite). The UK's Foreign & Commonwealth Office (FCO) has a watch list of 30 countries that it considers a 'human rights priority' – those where torture and sexual violence occur. Yet, since 2014, the UK has trained security or military personnel in, or from, 17 of those 30 countries (see Figure 3). Critics argue that this willingness to ignore abuses shows that strategic alliances and/or valuable trade deals (e.g. with Saudi Arabia) carry far more weight with governments than human rights concerns.

Figure 3 *British soldiers training security forces in Iraq, one of the countries on the UK human rights abuse watch list*

In 2014, the UK helped to train military or security forces from 17 countries on the UK government's human rights watch list: Afghanistan, Bahrain, Bangladesh, Myanmar, Burundi, China, Colombia, Egypt, Iraq, Libya, Pakistan, Saudi Arabia, Somalia, Sudan, Yemen, Zimbabwe.

Countries that send military aid to governments with poor human rights records argue in turn that to reduce this military aid could risk national interests or global security – and also do nothing to improve the human rights situation in those countries. They argue that by continuing with the military aid, they can pressure the recipient nations to improve their human rights records, e.g. by attaching conditions to the aid (as the USA has done in Colombia; see below).

However, their opponents respond that:

- ignoring human rights abuses is – in effect – condoning them
- continuing to support a government that represses its citizens undermines the basic principle of human rights protection
- some aid (e.g. weapons and training) actually ends up being used to commit further human rights abuses.

Colombia

Colombia has been one of the largest recipients of American military aid for over a decade (with US$10 billion for military and social programmes between 2000 and 2015), yet its record of human rights abuses is poor. NGOs and IGOs have documented the 'widespread and systematic' use of torture by the country's military and paramilitary forces.

- The USA argues that its military aid helps Colombia to maintain peace, tackle illegal armed groups, and fight criminal organisations involved in illegal people or drug trafficking (much of the cocaine that reaches the USA comes from Colombia).
- The US government also argues that it has imposed human rights conditions on aid payments, e.g. by requiring the suspension of military personnel accused of committing human rights abuses. However critics, including NGOs such as Amnesty International, argue that only 25% of the aid is withheld if the human rights conditions aren't met.

Figure 4 *Colombia is located right at the junction of Central and South America and the Caribbean, which makes it an important transit point in the international drugs trade*

The war on terror

As Figure 5 shows, after the attacks on the USA in September 2001 (9/11), President George W. Bush declared a 'war on terror' – a global military, political and legal battle against terrorist organisations and any governments that supported them. During the 'war on terror', the USA justified sending troops into Afghanistan and Iraq as it claimed that these countries supported terrorists (a view which was contested).

The resulting wars and their aftermath were designed to protect the USA and its allies against further attacks, and also ensure global security. However, protecting human rights also became a justification for military action by both the USA and UK. For 15 months leading up to the invasion of Iraq in 2003, the leaders of the USA and UK worked to explain to the UN, other countries, their own governments and citizens, why military action was justified against Saddam Hussein and Iraq – in particular, using the supposed threat of indiscriminate 'weapons of mass destruction' that were allegedly possessed by Iraq.

Our war on terror begins with al-Qaeda, but … will not end until every terrorist group of global reach has been found, stopped and defeated.

American President George W. Bush, September 2001

Figure 5 *The global impact of 9/11*

The use of torture and threats to human rights

For many within the USA and abroad, America's moral position became compromised when it began using **torture** as an interrogation technique. Under both American and international law – including the Declaration of Human Rights (see Section 4.4), which was signed by the USA – the use of torture is illegal. However, the ability of militants to strike in two of the USA's most important cities shook the US government. Stopping any future attacks became both a priority and the justification for a variety of actions, including the suppression of human rights and the use of torture. These actions were viewed as a 'necessary evil', with the need for information to prevent any future attacks outweighing all arguments against the use of torture.

Some other signatories to the Declaration of Human Rights, including the UK, are accused of helping the USA with its '**extraordinary rendition**' programme. Investigators have shown that the UK allowed American aircraft to stop for refuelling at UK airports more than 1600 times, as part of a global network of CIA 'extraordinary rendition' flights (see Figure 7).

However using extraordinary rendition and torture techniques, such as water-boarding, has damaged America's national security and global reputation:

- Organisations such as al-Qaeda, have used it to recruit new members.
- American citizens and military personnel are now at greater risk of being treated more harshly if captured.
- The level of trust between the US government and community-based organisations working to prevent terrorism has been eroded.
- Those countries which helped the USA with its 'extraordinary rendition' programme, have been condemned by human rights groups and the UN. This has harmed their global reputations and ongoing relationship with the USA.

> 11 September [9/11] and its consequences have reoriented world politics, and this is not without implications for human rights policy.
>
> Joschka Fischer, German Federal Minister for Foreign Affairs, 2002

Figure 6 *The impact of 9/11 on human rights*

Key words

Torture – 'Any act by which severe pain or suffering, whether physical or mental, is intentionally inflicted on a person' in order to get information (as defined in the UN Convention against Torture).

Extraordinary rendition – The secret transfer of a terror suspect, without legal process, to a foreign government for detention and interrogation. The interrogation methods often do not meet international standards, and include the use of torture.

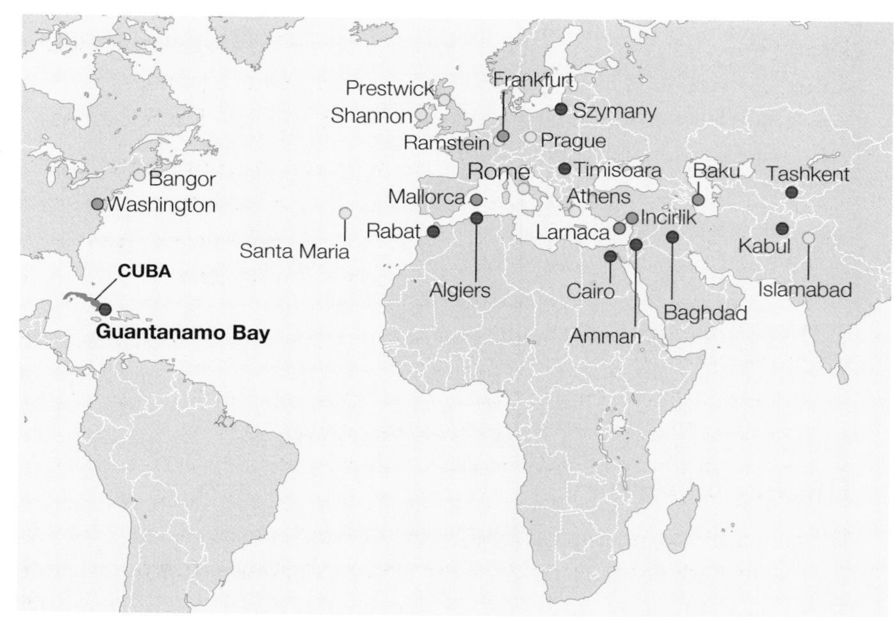

Figure 7 *Airports used by the CIA in the 'extraordinary rendition' of terror suspects*

The USA and Guantanamo Bay

Figure 8 *Detainees at Guantanamo Bay military base, Cuba*

In 1903, the USA established a military base at Guantanamo Bay in Cuba. Since the 9/11 attacks and the war in Afghanistan, this base has been used to hold detainees in the 'war on terror' (see Figure 8). The US administration of George W. Bush argued that detainees at the Cuban base were not on American soil, so were not covered by US laws. They also argued that the detainees' 'enemy combatant' status meant that they could be denied some legal protections. This has allowed detainees at Guantanamo Bay to be held for an indefinite time without access to legal representation or a trial.

In 2004, the International Committee of the Red Cross (ICRC) inspected the camp and found evidence of torture. The US government defended its actions by making a distinction between 'torture' – which it agreed was banned by the American Constitution and international law – and 'enhanced interrogation techniques'. It argued that the methods it was using at Guantanamo Bay were legitimate means to gather information from suspected terrorists in order to prevent future attacks.

In January 2009, President Barack Obama signed an executive order banning 'non-coercive methods' of interrogation, and ordered the camp to close. However, as of February 2017, it still held 41 detainees. In 2014, the American Senate released a report admitting that torture had been used at Guantanamo.

Over to you

1. In Figure 1, Condoleeza Rice spoke about the 'legitimate exercise of power'. In pairs, read through this section and decide (**a**) what is, and (**b**) what is not 'legitimate' in military engagement.
2. **a** In pairs, list arguments justifying why military aid may be given to support countries with questionable human rights records.
   b Select one of the 17 countries listed as part of Figure 3. Research evidence to show why it has a weak human rights record.
3. **a** Research the following aspects of Colombia's drugs trade: (**i**) where it's concentrated, (**ii**) who controls it, (**iii**) its impacts on the Colombian people, (**iv**) why it's linked to Colombia's record on human rights.
   b Research links between the Colombian drugs trade and the USA, and why continued military aid to Colombia might be in US interests.

On your own

4. **a** Distinguish between the terms 'torture' and 'enhanced interrogation techniques'
   b Explain how the two may be connected in the case of Guantanamo Bay.
5. Describe the distribution of airports used by the CIA in the 'extraordinary rendition' process outlined in Figure 7.
6. Explain why the existence of Guantanamo Bay is so (**a**) sensitive, (**b**) contentious.

Exam-style question

Evaluate the justification given for military aid and intervention in the defence of human rights. (*20 marks*)

4.10 Measuring the success of geopolitical interventions

In this section, you'll learn that there are several ways of measuring the success of geopolitical interventions.

EQ4 Sections 4.10 to 4.12 investigate the outcomes of geopolitical interventions in terms of human development and human rights.

KEY CONCEPT

- **Inequality** – ways in which geopolitical interventions can succeed in reducing inequalities in terms of human development and human rights

How successful is geopolitical intervention?

The world is changing. In the 1960s, famine was common in the world's poorest countries. It's now rare – and, when it does occur, it's often the result of political conflicts not drought. Almost all global development indicators show that people now live longer, eat more, go to school and are healthier than they were even in 2000. Most improvements have occurred because of **geopolitical interventions** (the actions of governments, IGOs and NGOs to bring about intended changes). Some of these interventions are the result of global policies, such as the Millennium Development Goals (see Section 4.3). In spite of populist views to the contrary, most refugees are taken in by sympathetic countries and successfully re-housed, e.g. Turkey took 1.6 million Syrian refugees between 2011 and 2015.

However, geopolitical interventions are often politically sensitive, and are also expensive. National opinion polls worldwide routinely show some public unease with overseas interventions. For example, 51% of Americans surveyed in 2016 said that they felt the USA gave too much aid to developing countries (see Figure 1). So it's important for governments, IGOs and NGOs to show that the interventions work. Measuring success demonstrates:

- accountability to taxpayers and voters
- where actions are effective, or can be improved further.

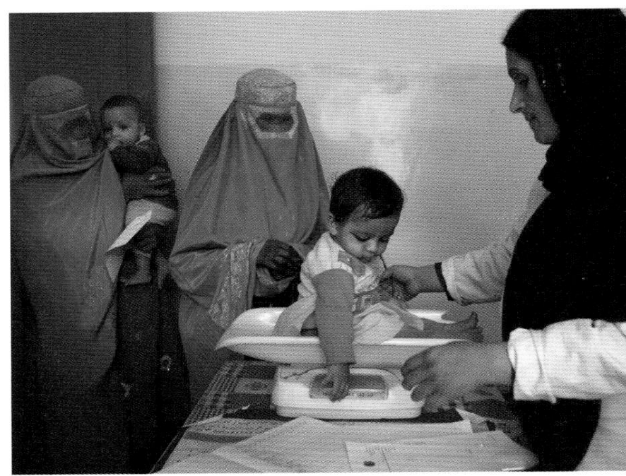

Figure 1 *A US-funded child health programme in Afghanistan*

Most interventions are assessed using 'hard' data (i.e. figures) that measure improvements in areas of human development, such as:

- **health** (see Figure 1), including life expectancy, infant mortality
- **educational** indicators, including literacy, length of schooling
- **wealth**, including GDP per capita.

For example, when the USA claimed that its aid programmes and military presence in Afghanistan had been a success, it cited Afghanistan's human development indicators as proof, such as a 14-fold increase in the number of schools and an increase in Afghan life expectancy of over 20 years. Two developing countries that have definitely made significant advances – according to the data – are shown in Figure 2.

Figure 2 *Indicators of improved health and education in Uganda and Bangladesh between 2000 and 2015.*

Indicator	Uganda		Bangladesh	
	2000	2015	2000	2015
Infant mortality (per 1000 live births)	86	38	61	31
Maternal mortality (deaths per 100 000 live births)	620	343	399	176
Average life expectancy	46	58	65	72
% of literacy among women	50.2 (1995)	71.5	26.1 (1995)	58.5
HDI score	0.393	0.483 (2014)	0.468	0.570 (2014)

However, despite the availability of different forms of hard data, measuring success can be difficult:

- There may be little agreement about how 'success' is defined, i.e. which indicators should be measured or what levels need to be achieved.
- Some countries do not have the facilities to monitor or collect accurate data.
- Many interventions span years (such as the Millennium Development Goals from 2000 to 2015), so they are subject to changing governments and circumstances.
- External factors, such as global food prices or climate changes, can also affect outcomes.
- Data collected can also be interpreted differently by different people, which can lead to the misinterpretation of some results.

'Softer' indicators can also be used to measure success, such as freedom of speech, gender equality (e.g. the part played by women in the economy, or whether they are allowed to vote), and the perceived state of a country's democracy. These softer indicators are hard to 'measure', but their success is important.

Democracy as a measure of success

For many countries and IGOs, such as the UN, the promotion of democratic processes for all people – such as the woman in Figure 3 – is a key goal of intervention. For instance, one of the stated reasons why the USA invaded Iraq in 2003 was to bring about democracy.

The promotion of democracy as an overseas aim is based on the belief that democratic institutions are building blocks for more secure and economically prosperous societies:

- Moving from dictatorship to democracy often leads to other changes, including economic growth and the advancement of women's rights and well-being.
- Democracy can bring about political and social stability, which should then make countries less willing to support militant or criminal organisations. For example, the US government promotes democracy as a long-term solution to the 'war on terror'.
- It's often easier for developed countries to forge military and economic ties with democratic governments.

Figure 3 *In the 2014 general election in Afghanistan, approximately 2.4 million Afghan women voted, which represented 38% of the total turnout*

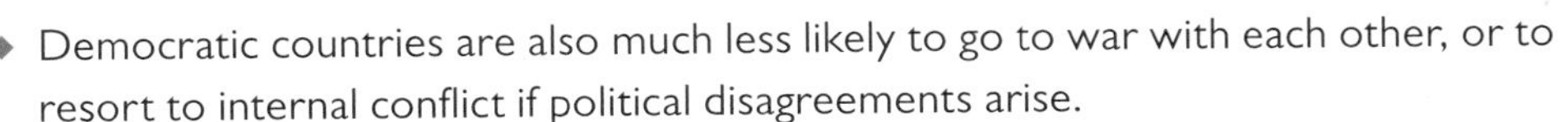

- Democratic countries are also much less likely to go to war with each other, or to resort to internal conflict if political disagreements arise.

Nearly all Western governments now allocate funds for democracy-building – sometimes called '**democracy aid**'. In the late 1980s, less than US$1 billion was spent on this each year, but by 2015 the total was over US$10 billion. Democracy aid tends to focus on:

- supporting crucial processes and institutions, e.g. free and fair elections, the development of political parties, limiting the term of office of a country's leader
- strengthening and reforming government institutions, e.g. parliament and the judiciary
- supporting civil society, e.g. freedom of expression, defending civil and political rights.

Democracy and freedom of expression

Freedom of expression – the right to express one's opinions freely – is a fundamental right, included in the Universal Declaration on Human Rights (see Section 4.4). It guarantees the right to:

- speak and write openly (without government interference or penalty)
- protest against injustice
- criticise a government and its leaders.

For many, freedom of expression is the cornerstone of democracy. It allows citizens to question their leaders, and it allows the media to report openly without censorship. Overseas aid programmes support freedom of expression as part of promoting democracy. For example, the 'Strengthening Freedom of Expression Protection' project in The Gambia works to improve relations between the media and government, and support free expression for journalists. A change of government in 2017 has not as yet led to any changes in this respect.

Democracy aid

Evidence suggests that democracy aid works. 36 out of 57 countries that became democracies between 1980 and 1995 received democracy aid from the USA. For example, between 1996 and 2000, the USA provided over US$18 million in democracy aid for Guatemala, which was then used to train government officers, rebuild the justice system, develop anti-corruption measures, and increase the size of the electorate. As Figure 4 shows, during this period Guatemala officially became a democracy.

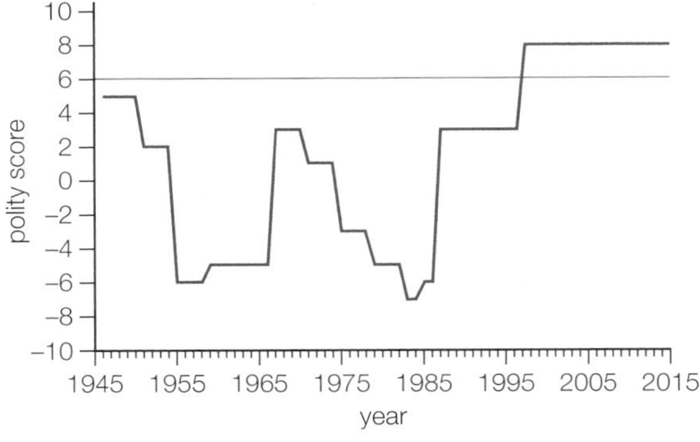

Figure 4 *This graph shows Guatemala's 'polity score' – a measure of how democratic a country is said to be; the higher the score, the more democratic the country. Countries scoring +6 or more are considered to be democracies, which Guatemala achieved in about 1997.*

Economic growth as a measure of success

For some countries, the success of geopolitical intervention is measured by economic growth. A country that prospers economically will gain resources to improve infrastructure, health, education, and environmental protection. For donor nations, a prosperous country often becomes a beneficial trading partner. For example, Taiwan, South Korea and Singapore once received US aid, but they are now among the top importers of US-made goods.

For many countries, promoting prosperity is the key goal of overseas aid. The UK's Department for International Development (DFID) argues that sustained economic growth is 'the single most important way to reduce poverty'. One estimate suggests that a 10% increase in a country's average income reduces poverty by 20–30%.

China's overseas aid policy is largely based on 'Eight Principles for Economic and Technical Assistance', and the focus of its overseas aid is primarily economic development. Benefits from Chinese investment in sub-Saharan Africa have included higher employment and faster economic growth in recipient countries, leading to improved education and health indicators.

Figure 5 *School students in Guatemala City staging an election campaign panel discussion as part of their social studies class prior to the 2011 Guatemalan parliamentary elections*

Aid for trade

A recent international policy shift has been 'aid for trade'. Trade can be a powerful tool for economic growth, but many developing nations lack the knowledge, skills and infrastructure to compete effectively in global markets. To address this, in 2005 the World Trade Organisation (WTO) called for more and better aid for trade. Aid for trade is a WTO initiative to help developing countries to increase the amount they trade. It helps them to:

- develop trade strategies
- negotiate better trade deals
- build infrastructure, such as roads, ports and communications systems.

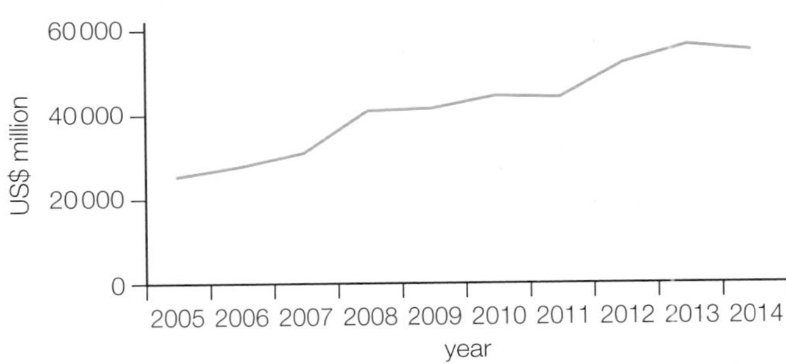

Figure 6 *OECD data from all overseas aid providers shows a steady increase in aid for trade between 2005 and 2014*

The trend for this type of aid is growing (see Figure 6). Aid for trade's share of global official development assistance (ODA) rose from 26% in 2006-07 to 35% in 2010.

As an example of success, Figure 7 shows that aid for trade is working in Uganda. Between 2006 and 2013, 48% of Uganda's ODA was 'aid for trade'. During the same years:

- the export of Ugandan goods increased by 144% and commercial services by 362%
- Uganda's annual GDP per capita increased from US$342 to US$664.
- the number of Ugandans living on less than US$1.25 a day decreased from just over 50% to under 40%.
- Uganda's development indicators also improved, as shown in Figure 2.

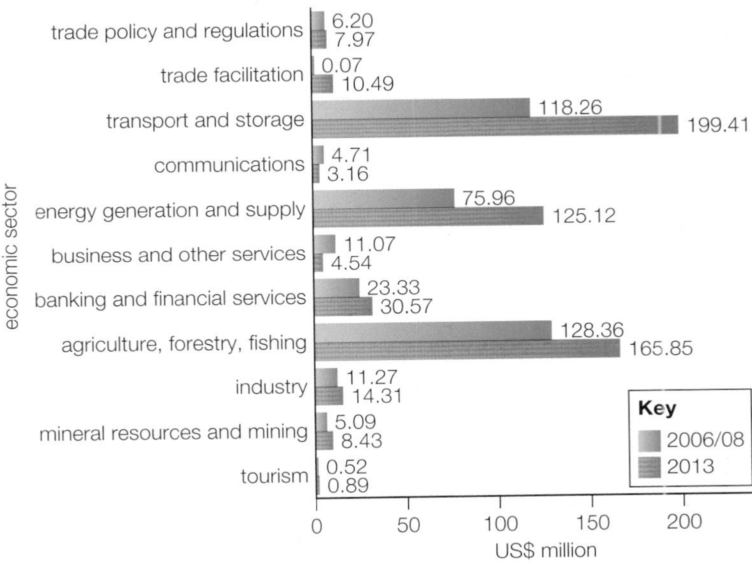

Figure 7 *The distribution by economic sector of 'aid for trade' in Uganda*

Over to you

1 In pairs, list evidence from Figures 1–7 that suggests geopolitical intervention has been successful.

2 a Search for the following article on www.theatlantic.com (a US online magazine): 'Here's the Best Thing the U.S. Has Done in Afghanistan'. Read the article.

b Now search for the following article on www.npr.org (a US news agency): 'Gains In Afghan Health: Too Good To Be True?'. Again, read the article.

c Using Section 6.5 to help you, identify ways in which these two articles show different views about improvements in Afghan health, and suggest reasons why those views may be different.

3 To what extent does the analysis you carried out in question 2 throw doubt on your answers to question 1?

On your own

4 Distinguish between the following pairs of terms: **(a)** hard and soft data, **(b)** geopolitical intervention and democracy aid.

5 a Using Figure 7, outline the key beneficiaries of 'aid for trade' in Uganda.

b Research and suggest reasons why those particular sectors benefited.

Exam-style question

Evaluate the success of geopolitical interventions. *(20 marks)*

4.11 Development aid – a mixed record of success?

In this section, you'll learn that development aid has a mixed record of success.

Development aid – successful?

Development aid is intended to fix a range of complex problems, from long- to short-term, so it's not surprising that its success can vary.

1 Ebola, West Africa – a health success story

The first cases of Ebola were recorded in West Africa in March 2014 (see Figure 1). Within 21 months, 28 616 cases had been reported – 11 310 of whom had died. Yet, by January 2016, the World Health Organisation (WHO) was able to declare the region free of the disease. A co-ordinated local, national and international response had contributed to this notable success in controlling such a deadly disease.

Ebola is a highly contagious and often fatal disease, caused by a virus. When it was diagnosed in West Africa in 2014, the region was unprepared. The affected countries were among the world's poorest and most vulnerable, with weak infrastructure and health services. This allowed the virus to spread, which threatened a global health crisis:

- The outbreak covered a wide area, so it was not easily contained.
- Ebola symptoms can take up to 21 days to appear, so those infected could travel widely and spread the virus. Any city worldwide with an international airport was at risk.
- Overseas volunteer health workers who contracted the virus in West Africa could possibly return home before being diagnosed.

There was a rapid international response, which helped to contain the epidemic:

- The WHO quickly declared the outbreak an emergency, and sent teams of health workers to detect and manage cases.
- Individual countries provided support, such as building treatment centres.
- The UN Security Council called a rare emergency session to assess the implications of the epidemic – announcing its first public health mission as an international response.
- International efforts included longer-term development aid, such as funding general health services.

KEY CONCEPT

- **Inequality** – ways in which aid may or may not reduce existing inequalities

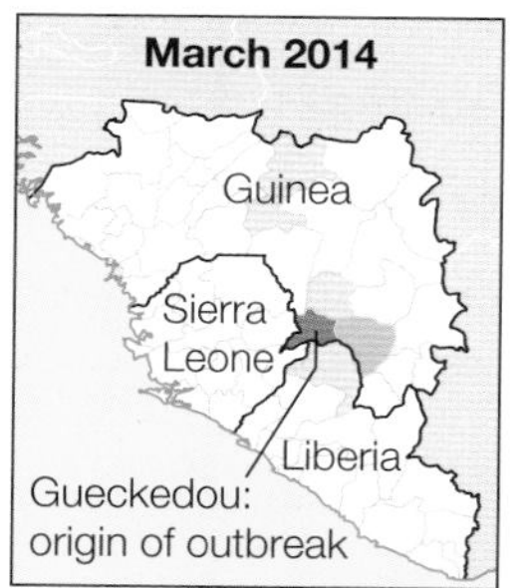

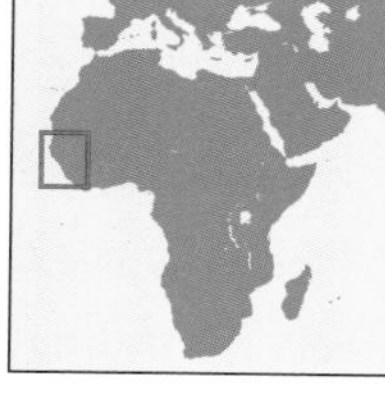

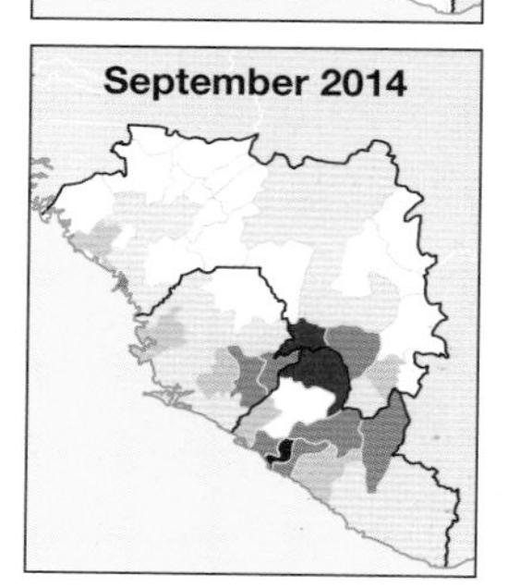

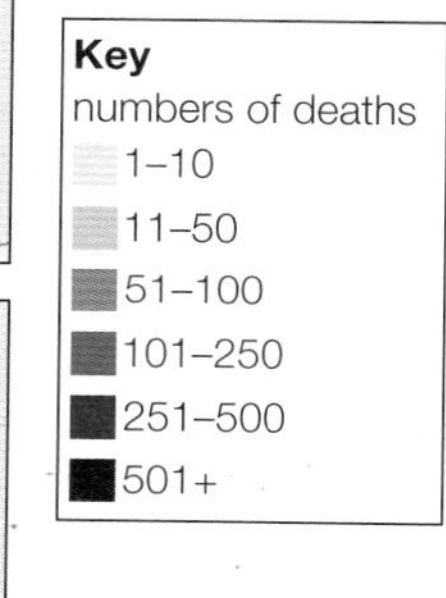

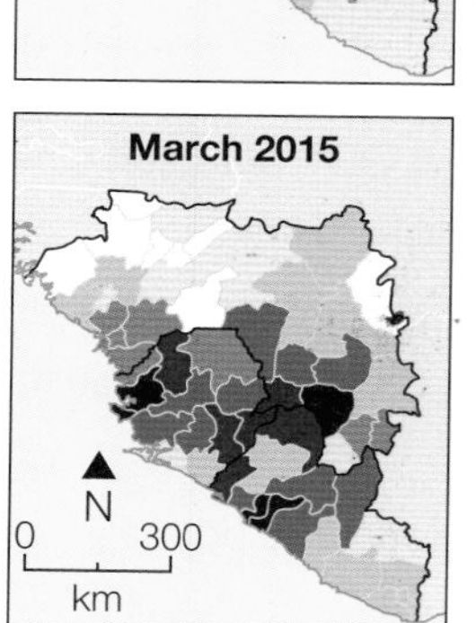

Figure 1 *The Ebola outbreak in West Africa, March 2014 – March 2015. At the peak of the epidemic in autumn 2014, infections were doubling every few weeks.*

2 Haiti – a failed effort?

Despite huge inputs of money and expertise, not all aid succeeds. As Section 4.8 shows, Haiti is vulnerable to threats from multiple hazards, as well as poverty and a reliance on overseas aid (see Figure 2). Despite receiving at least US$38 billion in aid since 1955, Haiti remains one of the world's poorest and worst-governed countries.

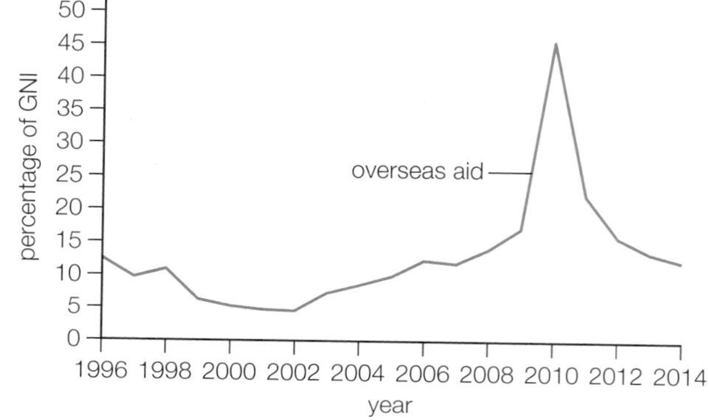

Figure 2 *ODA as a percentage of GNI in Haiti, 1996–2014*

The international response to Haiti's poverty has generally been to provide aid. Yet many experts argue that, despite some successes, aid has created a dependency culture limiting Haiti's progress (see Section 4.8):

- Haiti's governmental systems are weak, because staff from international aid organisations have taken over many jobs best done by local officials.
- NGOs pay higher salaries, so skilled local people work for them instead of Haitian organisations.
- Much of the aid money is spent on contracts with American rather than local companies.
- Haiti is one of the world's most unequal countries, as shown by the **Gini coefficient**. The economic and political elite in Haiti are often more interested in advancing their own interests than in helping Haiti develop.
- Despite the amount of aid, the impact on Haiti's economic development has been small. While global GDP per capita (in US$ PPP) more than doubled between 2000 and 2015, Haiti's only increased by a quarter.
- Human rights are also a problem. In 2015, the pressure group Human Rights Watch reported high numbers of arbitrary arrests and pre-trial detentions by Haitian police.

Figure 3 *Shares of wealth for Haiti compared to the UK. The unequal distribution has led to Haiti's ranking as the world's fourth most unequal country.*

Key word

Gini coefficient – Used to measure inequality between countries. It uses a figure between 0 (wealth is distributed equally) and 1 (where one person has all the wealth). The higher the coefficient, the more unequal the distribution. Section 6.3 has more detail about its calculation and use.

Inequality and development

As Figure 4 shows, all countries experience some degree of inequality. However, developing countries have much wider inequality than developed countries. The map shading is based on the Gini coefficient – the darker the shading, the more unequal the country. The comparison between the UK and Haiti in Figure 3 shows the wide differential between the wealthiest and poorest in Haiti. The data are shown in deciles and quintiles.

Decile/quintile	Haiti % share of national income	UK % share of national income
1st quintile: 1st decile (richest)	48.21	29.93
1st quintile: 2nd decile	16.04	16.61
2nd quintile	18.26	23.39
3rd quintile	9.97	15.57
4th quintile	5.49	9.86
5th quintile: 9th decile	1.43	3.07
5th quintile: 10th decile (poorest)	0.55	1.66

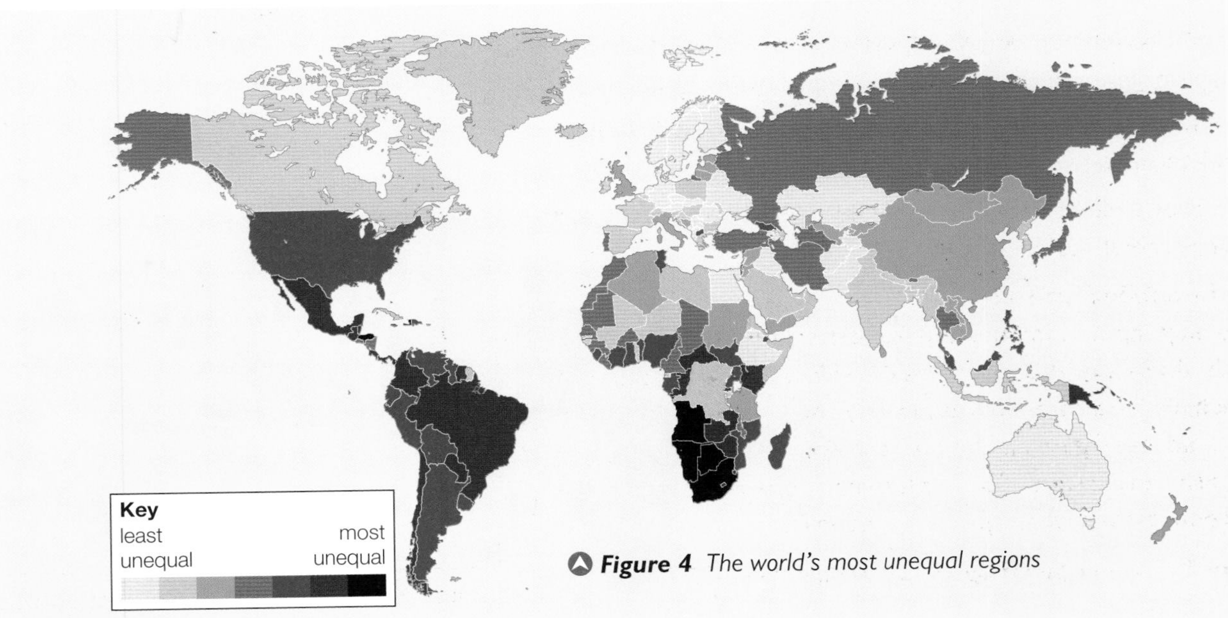

Figure 4 *The world's most unequal regions*

The impacts of inequality

Inequality has several impacts. In countries where inequality is high:

- health indicators are poor. Countries with greater inequality have lower life expectancy and higher infant mortality, because the poorest are least able to afford healthcare. Figure 5 shows the relationship between the Gini coefficient and life expectancy.
- growth in living standards is hindered. A healthy population is more economically productive, and therefore widening inequality harms economic development.

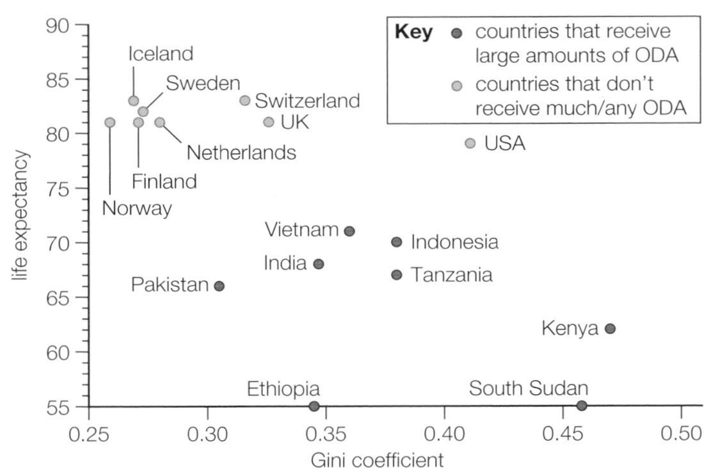

Figure 5 *The relationship between economic inequality (as measured by the Gini coefficient) and life expectancy for selected countries in 2012*

Can aid lead to increased inequality?

It seems counter-intuitive, but inequality has actually increased in some of the countries that receive the largest amounts of development aid. For example, Bangladesh receives billions of dollars of aid money (over US$2.4 billion in 2014), yet its Gini score has gone up (see Figure 6).

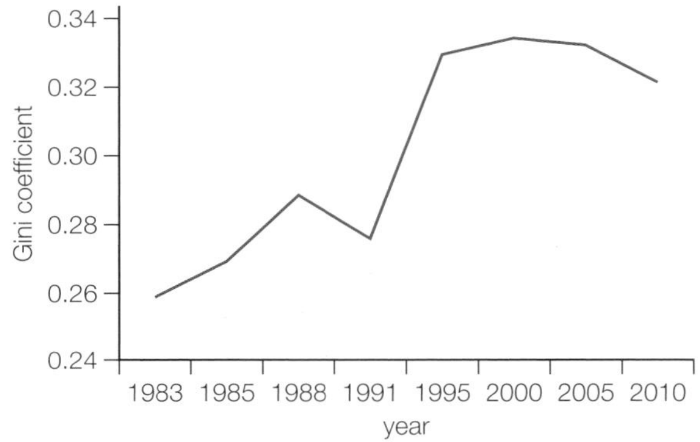

Figure 6 *The Gini coefficient for Bangladesh, 1983–2010*

In those countries where economic inequality is rising in spite of substantial aid, corruption by political and economic elites is often a cause (see Section 4.8). However, the actions of donors can also be a problem:

- Donor countries sometimes act in their own interests when deciding how and where to spend aid money. For example, the decision to improve a country's infrastructure may be influenced by commercial interests – thus concentrating aid in industrial centres rather than remote areas where the poorest people may live.
- Aid agencies sometimes favour large projects that give publicity, even though smaller projects may reduce inequality more effectively.

However, inequality is not increasing in all countries receiving aid. Latin America receives large amounts of overseas aid – about 7% of multilateral overseas aid is given to Latin America and the Caribbean – yet it remains one of the world's most unequal regions (in 2014, the richest decile owned 71% of the region's wealth). That said, income inequality actually decreased between 2000 and 2010 in 16 out of 17 Latin American countries – with the Gini coefficient falling on average by 0.94% each year (see Figure 7 for Columbia). Evidence shows that focusing aid on the poorest, and directing it towards education and health, reduces inequality and has a positive effect on development indicators.

Figure 7 *Improving Columbian health centres resulted in an increased life expectancy at birth of 4 years between 2000 and 2012 – double the global average. This reflects Colombia's improved Gini coefficient from 0.56 in 2008 to 0.535 in 2014.*

Development aid – just an extension of foreign policy?

As discussed in Section 4.7, the goals of overseas aid vary. Many concern poverty reduction and improving human rights in poorer countries. However, donor nations often use aid as an extension of their foreign policies. If the goals of a country's development aid are about promoting its foreign policy, then it isn't surprising that the success of aid programmes – in their eyes – depends on benefits that they receive in return. Three motives tend to dominate:

- **A means of accessing resources**. China has provided funding for the development of resources in sub-Saharan Africa (see Section 3.9), which has involved infrastructure funding (e.g. the Tazara rail link between inland Zambia and Tanzanian ports). In theory, this should be mutually beneficial, but China's demand for raw materials drives its aid and investment policy.
- **Political support in IGOs and NGOs**. India has sought a seat as a permanent member of the UN Security Council since the 1990s. It justifies its case in terms of its population size, the size of its economy (the world's fourth largest in 2017), and its position as a major power in southern Asia (the most populated continent). Its FDI programmes have been targeted at supporting countries that might back it. Similarly, Germany has sought support for its own permanent membership from Kenya, Angola and Nigeria. In return, Germany has offered Nigeria support to develop HEP plants and liquefied natural gas resources.
- **Developing military alliances**. Jordan received over US$750 million between 2014 and 2016 in return for military support against so-called Islamic State. Jordan carries out air strikes, allows the use of its military bases by overseas forces (see Figure 9), and shares intelligence with US and other coalition partners.

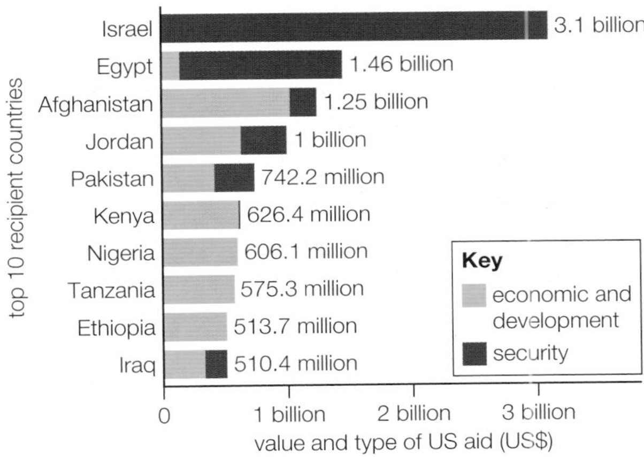

Figure 8 *The top ten recipients of US aid for 2017, by type – development aid and security (including military aid)*

Figure 9 *This air base in northern Jordan is used by US military aircraft for Exercise Eager Lion, an annual two-week multi-national military exercise held there*

Over to you

1. a In pairs, identify the factors which contributed to the speedy response to the 2014 Ebola outbreak in West Africa.
   b Now identify factors to explain why aid has been less successful in Haiti.
2. a Explain the pattern of inequality in Figure 4.
   b Describe the contrasts in wealth distribution between Haiti and the UK in Figure 3, and suggest reasons for the differences.
   c Explain the relationship between inequality and life expectancy in Figure 5.
3. In pairs, identify factors that determine why inequalities may increase in some states that receive substantial development aid, while in others inequalities may decrease.

On your own

4. Prepare a 750-word report entitled 'Aid – just an extension of foreign policy?'
5. a Research source materials which show that the US aid donations in Figure 8 have been 'successful'.
   b Using Section 6.6 to help you, identify possible misuses of data in assessing these 'successes'.

Exam-style question

Evaluate the assertion: 'Development aid has a mixed record of success'. *(20 marks)*

4.12 Military interventions: a mixed success story

In this section, you'll learn that military interventions have a mixed record of success.

KEY CONCEPT

- **Inequality** – ways in which conflict can have mixed consequences for different countries

Military intervention

There is nothing pleasant about war, and military intervention is never an easy option. There are always costs – economic, political, environmental and social.

- **Direct intervention** (sending troops and equipment to fight) inevitably leads to the loss of lives on both sides, as well as physical injuries at the time and often psychological problems afterwards. And it also costs a lot of money; Reuters, a respected news agency, estimates that the 2003 Iraq War cost US$2 trillion. There can also be a political price – Tony Blair, who for years was one of the UK's most popular Prime Ministers, lost his reputation by taking the UK into the Iraq War.
- **Indirect intervention** (providing economic or military assistance without sending troops) offers a preferable option for many governments, particularly because it involves lower risks and costs.

The costs of the Iraq War

In 2003, the US administration of George W. Bush, with coalition allies including the UK, took the decision to invade Iraq to remove Saddam Hussein. In public, the main justification for the invasion was that Saddam was a brutal dictator, who had previously developed, hidden – and even used against his own people – chemical and biological weapons, referred to as 'weapons of mass destruction' (WMD). There was also a lot of evidence that Saddam was systematically violating many Iraqi human rights.

However, many people debate whether Iraq is actually any better post-invasion than before. In the short-term, the military intervention (see Figure 1) did remove Saddam Hussein and his oppressive security forces, although no trace was ever found of WMDs. Some early development efforts also succeeded. For example, a US-funded vaccination programme reduced infant mortality by 75%. And, in 2005, Iraqis voted in the first free election in the country for fifty years.

But the war has also led to heavy costs in the longer-term:

- Critics argue that a lack of understanding and long-range planning by coalition forces left Iraq without the systems it needed to restore security, foster democracy, protect human rights, or grow economically.
- Islamist militant groups like al-Qaeda and IS, who had no presence in Iraq before the US-led invasion, took advantage of Iraq's political instability to establish themselves there. These groups continue to fight for land (see Figure 2), as well as kill and oppress many Iraqi civilians, including members of Iraq's Yazidi minority.

Figure 1 *Many Iraqis welcomed the invading American and coalition troops in 2003*

Figure 2 *Iraqi civilians fleeing Mosul in 2017, as Iraqi government forces (with Western military support) fight to drive out IS militants from Iraq's second-largest city, which they had captured in 2014*

- Animosity between Iraq's Sunni and Shia groups worsened in the aftermath of the Iraq War, which meant that forming a stable and effective national government containing members from all groups became impossible.
- Iraq's political instability has also allowed corruption to flourish. In 2015, it was ranked 161 out of 168 in Transparency International's Corruption Perceptions Index.
- Since the fall of Saddam, human rights in Iraq remain insecure. A 2015 report by Human Rights Watch found evidence of government-sponsored violations, including attacks on civilians by government forces, the kidnapping and killing of Sunni civilians by Shia government security forces, thousands being held in prison without charge, and government restrictions on free expression.

The success of non-military intervention

Military intervention can bring significant long-term costs. Non-military intervention can sometimes be more effective – leading to long-term improvements in human rights and development. For example, diplomacy and other forms of non-military intervention helped Timor-Leste (see Figure 3) gain its independence and end decades of violence and human rights abuses.

Timor-Leste

Timor-Leste (or East Timor) is a small country (one third the size of Wales) in Southeast Asia. For centuries it was a Portuguese colony, before declaring independence in 1975. However, after just nine days, it was invaded by Indonesia. The UN did not recognise the takeover, and called for Indonesia's withdrawal. By 1999, over 200 000 people (25% of the population) had been killed by violence, disease and famine. Human rights abuses, including torture, also occurred routinely.

In 1982, the UN started diplomatic efforts with the Indonesian and Portuguese governments to resolve the conflict. Then, in 1999, it organised a vote on independence (see Figure 4). The result was overwhelming; 78.5% of voters were in favour. However, the vote wasn't universally popular, and an anti-independence militia (supported by Indonesia) started a campaign of violence:

- The UN estimated that 7000 people were killed and up to 400 000 displaced.
- Infrastructure and homes were destroyed.

To pressurise the Indonesian government to end the violence, the USA and UK began arms embargoes against Indonesia. The UN also intensified diplomatic efforts and pressurised Indonesia into maintaining security and distributing humanitarian aid.

Figure 3 *Timor-Leste is located between Indonesia and Australia*

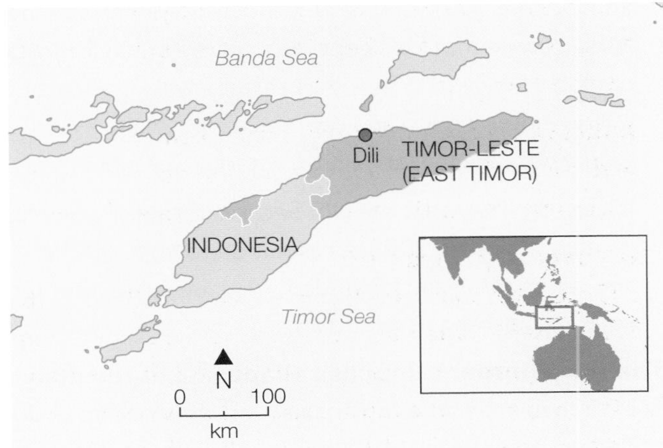

Indonesian forces finally withdrew peacefully. However, their departure left a lack of skilled people to run the country. The UN took control, during the transition to full independence. It set up structures to maintain law and order, and to establish conditions for development. In 2002, Timor-Leste finally became independent. However, human rights remain a concern. Although freedom of speech and the media are protected by law, the legal system deprives citizens of a fair trial, and the police are frequently accused of excessive force.

Figure 4 *UN officials monitoring Timor-Leste's independence vote in 1999*

The effects of no military action

Zimbabwe is a country with a history of systematic human rights abuses against its citizens. Opponents of the government are routinely attacked and imprisoned. Although it's ranked 156 out of 187 on the UNDP Human Development Index, and suffers from great poverty and human rights abuses, the international community has not intervened politically or militarily.

Reasons for the lack of military action in Zimbabwe are:

- Zimbabwe is a former British colony, which fought for its independence (finally achieving it in 1980). Western nations, in particular the UK, are sensitive to claims of intervention linked to colonialism.
- Some countries, including neighbouring African states like South Africa, argue that President Mugabe (shown in Figure 5) is no threat to global peace, and thus they reject any suggestions of political or military intervention and regime change. Many Western governments would not take military action without the support of African nations.
- It's also unlikely that the UN Security Council would agree to military action. In 2008, a resolution to impose an arms embargo and sanctions against President Mugabe failed after China and Russia voted against the resolution.

The environmental, political and social results

The Zimbabwean government's actions have led to economic, social and environmental instability:

- 72% of Zimbabweans live below the national poverty line.
- Rural poverty is increasing, from 63% of the rural population in 2003 to 76% in 2014, with many on seasonal plantation work (see Figure 6).
- The average life expectancy is among the world's lowest – 59 for men and 62 for women.
- In 2014, 82% of the government budget was allocated to government salaries, much of which has been lost to corruption.
- Human rights abuses occur regularly, including violence against and imprisonment of political opponents.
- Deforestation rates are also increasing (see opposite).

The lack of effective international action against Zimbabwe has had global consequences. Although the international community has not responded militarily to the abuses there, the EU did impose an embargo on arms and other military goods in 2002. However, critics say that such sanctions have simply become a propaganda tool – allowing Mugabe to blame Zimbabwe's economic troubles on Western countries trying to enact regime change. The UN and world leaders promote global human rights, but Mugabe's stranglehold on power in Zimbabwe since its independence in 1980 has simply emphasised that the UN and world leaders are prepared to act in some situations but tolerate others.

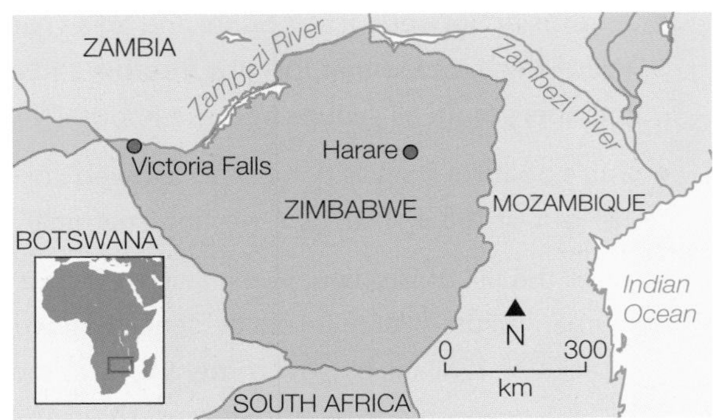

Figure 5 *Zimbabwe is a land-locked country in Southern Africa. The photo shows its President, Robert Mugabe, at the official celebrations to mark his 91st birthday in 2015. Since coming to power in 1980, he has become one of the world's longest-surviving leaders.*

Figure 6 *Plantation wages being handed out on a tobacco farm. Plantations provide employment, but the wages are low and the work is seasonal.*

The loss of forest

Deforestation is occurring in Zimbabwe at a dangerous level. It is one of ten countries recorded as having the largest forest losses between 1990 and 2010. Most of it is due to trees being cut down as firewood by the rural poor, because they have few other options for fuel. Large amounts of wood are also used by tobacco farmers to 'cure' their tobacco leaves. Tobacco farming now accounts for 15-20% of Zimbabwe's yearly deforestation.

Tobacco farming is vital to Zimbabwe's economy:

- In 2015, tobacco accounted for 25% of its exports.
- Tobacco production increased by 30% between 2009 and 2014, providing jobs for the country's poor. 32% of Zimbabwe's tobacco farmers are women.

The Zimbabwean government has passed laws to reduce the environmental damage caused by tobacco farming. However, they are often difficult to enforce, or aren't put into practice. For example, a 1.5% tax was placed on tobacco farmers in 2015 – with the stated intention of using the money to help farmers re-afforest land and re-grow firewood. But two years since the programme was introduced, the tax money – although collected – had still not been distributed to farmers.

Figure 7 *Land in Zimbabwe has been cleared of forest, as people seek firewood and more land on which to farm*

Over to you

1 a In pairs, draw a table to show the economic, social, environmental and political **(i)** benefits, **(ii)** problems created by the regime change in Iraq. You may wish to carry out additional research.

b Based on your completed table, explain whether the invasion of Iraq in 2003 was justifiable.

2 a Draw a spider diagram to show the issues facing Timor-Leste, and their causes.

b Based on your completed diagram, should military action have been approved in Timor-Leste by the UN?

On your own

3 Distinguish between direct and indirect military intervention.

4 a Draw a table to show the economic, social, environmental and political problems faced by Zimbabwe. You may wish to carry out additional research, e.g. socio-economic indicators.

b Identify **(i)** reasons in favour, and **(ii)** reasons against military intervention in Zimbabwe.

Exam-style question

Evaluate the view that indirect interventions are always preferable to direct military interventions. (*20 marks*)

Conclusion – revisiting the Enquiry Questions

These are the key questions that drive the whole topic:

1 What is human development, and why do levels vary from place to place?

2 Why do human rights vary from place to place?

3 How are human rights used as arguments for political and military intervention?

4 What are the outcomes of geopolitical interventions in terms of human development and human rights?

Having studied this topic, you can now consider some answers to these questions, using the synoptic themes to frame your ideas.

Players – discussion point 1

Working in groups, consider instances from this chapter where the actions taken by governments at different levels conflict over issues to do with healthcare and human rights. Explain your views.

Attitudes and Actions – discussion point 2

Working in groups, discuss and draw a diagram which shows how and why people have different attitudes towards healthcare and human rights.

Futures and Uncertainties – discussion point 3

Working in groups, consider different scenarios concerning military intervention in the affairs of another country. Use instances from this chapter either to justify or to reject such intervention. Explain your views.

Books, music, and films on this topic

Books to read

1. *The White Tiger* by Aravind Aviga (2008)

   This novel is based around the Indian caste system, which leads to social, health and economic inequalities.

2. *Poverty and the Millennium Development Goals: A Critical Look Forward* by Cimadamore, Koehler & Pogge (2016)

   An in-depth analysis into progress made towards achieving the UN's MDGs.

3. *The Spirit Level: Why More Equal Societies Almost Always Do Better* by Richard Wilkinson (2009)

   This book assesses the negative impacts of inequality in society, focusing on health.

Music to listen to

1. 'Do They Know it's Christmas' (1984) by Band Aid

   Originally written to raise funds for the famine in Ethiopia. Subsequent versions have included raising money to fight Ebola in 2014.

2. 'Radio Africa' (1985) by Latin Quarter

   This song concerns structural difficulties in African economies in the mid-80s, and how the developed world hinders the development of developing countries.

3. 'Gimme Hope Jo'Anna' (1988) by Eddy Grant

   A song about apartheid in South Africa, where the gap in health and rights led to sharply contrasting lives for different ethnicities.

Films to see

1. *Water First – Reaching The Millennium Development Goals* (2008)

   This film shows how access to clean water in Malawi is vital to improving people's lives and achieving the MDGs.

2. *Millennium Children* (2015)

   A BBC documentary following children's lives and assessing how far they benefit from the MDGs.

3. *Tsotsi* (2005)

   This film concerns a boy living in one of Johannesburg's most deprived areas. It concerns inequality in South Africa and how people become trapped in poverty. It is violent in parts, and not always easy to watch.

Migration, identity and sovereignty 5

Chapter overview – introducing the topic

This chapter studies international migration and identity, how these may change in a globalised world, and the reasons why the sovereignty of nation states may be challenged by processes of globalisation.

In the specification, this topic has been framed around four Enquiry Questions:

1. What are the impacts of globalisation on international migration?
2. How are nation states defined and how have they evolved in a globalising world?
3. What are the impacts of global organisations on managing global issues and conflicts?
4. What are the threats to national sovereignty in a more globalised world?

The sections in this chapter provide the content and concepts needed to help you answer these questions.

Synoptic themes

Underlying the content of every topic are three synoptic themes that 'bind' or glue the whole specification together:

1. Players
2. Attitudes and Actions
3. Futures and Uncertainties

Note that there is no requirement to study the synoptic themes in this topic. However, the synoptic themes are useful in applying your understanding, and the following content areas are relevant to this.

1 Players

Players are individuals, groups and organisations involved in making decisions that affect people and places, collectively known as **stakeholders**. Players can be national or international individuals and organisations (e.g. IGOs like the UN), national and local governments, businesses (from small operations to the largest TNCs), as well as pressure groups and NGOs, together with others.

Players that you'll study in this topic include:

- Section 5.3 – The role played by **governments** in deciding about migration policies, or, in Section 5.6, in promoting policies that create nationalist feelings.
- Section 5.12 – The role of **national** and **international governments** in promoting policies as part of a globalisation agenda.

2 Attitudes and Actions

People's attitudes towards national identity (particularly in the light of globalisation), and globalisation itself, vary – together with managing political issues such as failed states, which may include military action. People's values and attitudes depend on several factors:

- Their political views (left- or right-wing, for example), and/or their religious beliefs.
- The priorities given to people versus profit.
- The importance of social justice and equality.

Attitudes and Actions that you'll study in this topic include:

- Section 5.3 – How and why governments have different attitudes towards migration.
- Section 5.8 – The extent to which IGOs become involved in the affairs of other countries.

3 Futures and Uncertainties

Decisions and actions taken by players today will affect people in the future. For example, is globalisation a cure-all that promotes benefits for all, or does it create losers who suffer as a result? Is international government through organisations such as the EU beneficial, or does it challenge national identity?

Futures and Uncertainties that you'll study in this topic include:

- Section 5.13 – Why nationalism is a preferred option for some, and is seen as a challenge to governmental authority by others.

5.1 A national game?

In this section, you'll learn how the experience of professional club football reflects migration on a wider scale.

A football league of nations?

It was the first Saturday of the new football season, August 2015. Among the English Premier League's 20 teams, only 73 of the 220 players at the kick-off (33.2%) were English-born and eligible to play for England. In the 23 years since the Premier League was launched, that percentage had fallen from 69%. The number of overseas managers in the Premier League had also risen from zero to 55%, and 55% of the Premier League's clubs had been taken over by overseas owners. This change in the structure of top-flight English football was revolutionary, but – as Figure 1 shows – the revolution was repeated across Europe.

The main cause of this revolution was the 1995 Bosman Ruling by the European Court of Justice, which enabled free movement of European football players anywhere across the EU. At the same time, migration laws permit entry to highly skilled individuals from outside the EU with the offer of a job contract, which often includes overseas footballers.

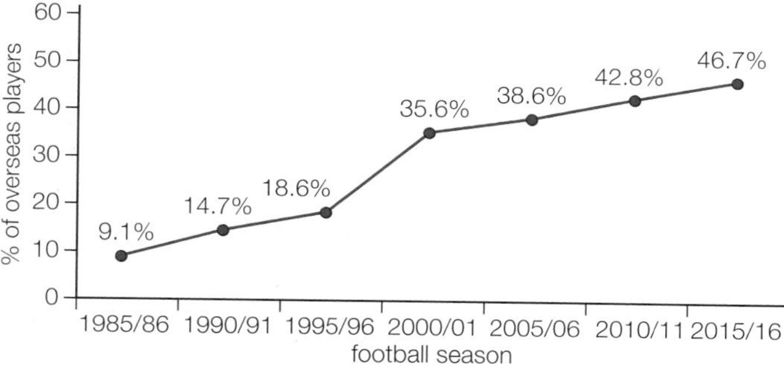

Figure 1 *The rising percentage of overseas players in the big five European football leagues (English, German, Spanish, Italian and French), between the 1985–86 and 2015–16 seasons. Note the big rise after the 1995–6 season, due to the Bosman Ruling.*

The end of English football?

The English Premier League is the world's richest football league. A big prize for those clubs promoted to the Premier League from the Championship is a share of the huge sums earned from global TV rights. The wealthiest clubs pay the highest salaries, so there has been massive salary inflation as clubs try to outbid each other for key players. Because of the high salaries on offer, overseas players often want to sign up to top-flight English clubs. Top Premier League clubs, like Chelsea and Arsenal, sometimes field teams with no British players at all. In reality, a global league has emerged, rather than an English League.

Some argue that the poor performance of the English national team in recent international football tournaments reflects the 'globalisation' of the Premier League. Others believe that overseas players bring more skill, talent and flair to the English game. Either way, domestic players are often squeezed out, and end up playing for lower wages in the lower English leagues. There have been calls for quotas specifying a requirement to field eight British-born players in any team. However, these moves have been opposed by the managers and owners of individual clubs, plus the Football Association (FA).

Football simply reflects what is happening in the global economy, where there are freer flows of labour, capital and power. Most countries have fairly relaxed rules about the migration of highly skilled people. By 2015, players from 64 nations were among the full Premier League squads, and Figure 2 shows where those players came from.

Figure 2 *Where the Premier League squad members came from in 2015*

Globalisation and football

Global media coverage, sponsorship by major TNCs – and very high salaries – all make the top football leagues attractive to world-class players, coaches and managers. Other than contractual factors, the only control on the free movement of players is known as the 'transfer window' – a period of time each year in which football clubs can transfer players to and from other clubs. Work visas are almost never problematic for those players with offers of contracts.

In September 2015, 45 African players played for 17 of the Premier League's 20 clubs – an increase of 25% in a single year. To migrate for a higher income and improved quality of life is normal, although the scale of the migration and the distances involved are increasing. However, another global pattern is now emerging in football – top players are moving to China, where high wages are accompanied by a rapidly growing demand for football.

The globalisation of football has made athletic talent a commodity – lifting barriers to movement and enhancing the lives of those who move. However, like all migrations, there are impacts on the source countries:

- The movement of football players, sometimes called the **muscle drain**, is **deskilling** African clubs of their most talented players.
- However, there are also benefits. Many overseas players send a proportion of their income home as **remittance payments**. For example, Michael Essien of Chelsea bought a house for his parents in Accra, Ghana, and Dwight Yorke of Manchester United funded education projects in his home town in Tobago.

A world without borders?

IT and digital communications systems are now spreading ideas and information faster than ever – helping to create a more connected world in which national borders appear less and less important.

However, there are wider implications of this change to a 'borderless' world.

- Just as Premier League teams have become diversified by the inward migration of overseas players, so wider communities that experience rapid inward migrations are also altered. Globalisation can change the whole cultural and ethnic composition of some communities (see Figure 3), and even whole nations.
- National identities are also affected, because nations and their identities are borne out of complex histories. For example, what does it mean to be 'British', now that so many overseas-born people have come to live and work in the UK?
- Tensions and conflicts can rise as people adapt to a new sense of national identity.

These are just some of the issues that you will learn about as you study this topic.

Figure 3 *Asian-related businesses in Manchester's Chinatown – part of the changing identity of UK cities as overseas-born people establish themselves in the community*

Over to you

1. In pairs, discuss and list the advantages and disadvantages for English football of attracting so many talented overseas players.
2. In pairs, discuss to what extent you think high rates of migration have benefited football, or any other sport you'd like to refer to.
3. As a group, debate (**a**) why immigration is such a sensitive issue nationally, and (**b**) the extent to which you believe migration can dilute national identity.

On your own

4. **a** Research one Premier League football club to develop a factfile on the number of overseas players it employs, and their countries of origin.
   b Collate your data with those of others in your class who researched other Premier League clubs, and generate a migration flow map for the Premier League.
   c Comment on the patterns shown on your flow map.
5. Write 500 words on the extent to which globalisation has benefited football or any other sport.

5.2 Globalisation and migration

In this section, you'll learn that globalisation has led to an increase in migration, both within countries and between them.

EQ1 Sections 5.2 to 5.4 explore the impacts of globalisation on international migration.

Changing patterns of demand for labour

Globalisation works on the principle of free flows of investment capital. Those who decide where to invest and manufacture normally choose the lowest-cost locations. As a result, China, India and Southeast Asia have become manufacturers for the world, because of investment from Western countries. And that has resulted in two processes affecting the demand for labour:

- At a **national** scale, people move from traditional rural economies to work in cities, which have become hubs of industrial activity.
- At an **international** scale, there is easier movement of people; the EU allows free movement, whilst elsewhere most countries readily offer work visas to those with skills and a sponsor.

1 Rural-urban migration in China

The global shift in manufacturing from Europe and the USA to many Asian countries, began in the 1970s and 80s. China's rapid industrialisation has been accompanied by rapid urbanisation, fuelled by rural-urban migration – particularly to the large cities near the coast. Figure 1 shows patterns of internal migration within China, of which there are two main flows:

- One flow is of rural migrants within the rural interior – usually to a small city. Figure 1 shows the example of rural migrants moving to small cities in China's central region.
- A second flow of migrants is from smaller cities to the major east coast cities and industrial areas, e.g. the Pearl River Delta, Guangzhou, Shanghai and Beijing.

In 1980, over 80% of Chinese people lived in rural areas; by 2012, just over 680 million people, or 51% of the population, was urban. Estimates suggest that, by 2025, a further 350 million people will have moved to China's cities – that's more than the population of the USA. However, there are barriers to migration within China, known as the hukou system.

KEY CONCEPT

- **Globalisation** – the impact of globalisation on movements of people

The hukou system

In the 1950s, after the Chinese communist revolution, the new communist government introduced restrictions on internal migration that were designed to keep people in rural areas. These restrictions became known as the **hukou** (household registration) system, where everyone is registered at an official residence. It is very hard for migrant workers from rural areas to change their official residence to a new location. Those moving to cities from rural areas must be 'registered' and buy a permit, which is expensive. Some permits allow permanent migration, but normally only to highly educated workers, or to those who have family already legally resident in the city. Without a permit, hukou workers earn less and their families have no entitlement to schooling or health care. Two-thirds of urban migrants are therefore men, and women and children often remain in rural areas.

Now that China depends so much on the manufacturing and service industries within its cities, the hukou system has become too restrictive. It acts as a barrier to urban integration for many Chinese, and the pressure on the transport system during public holidays is intense – with so many urban workers returning to their rural homes and families.

Figure 1 *Patterns of migration within China*

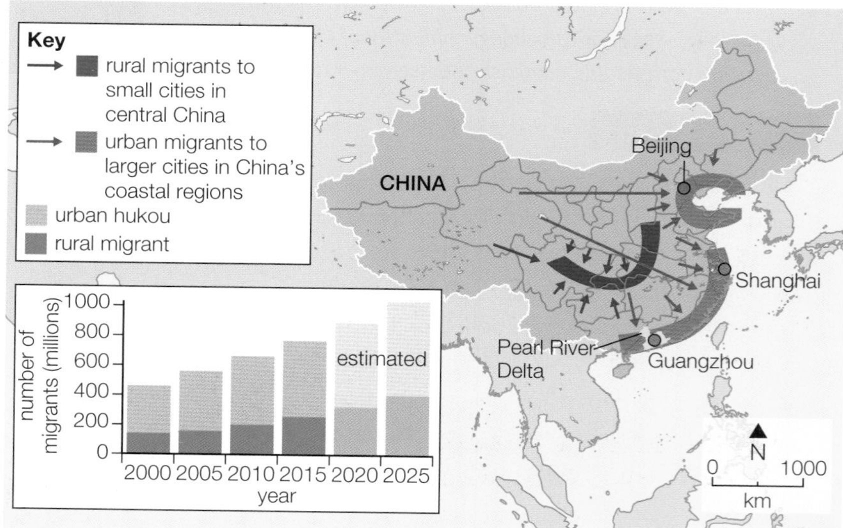

2 The EU – Schengen Agreement

The Schengen Agreement (signed in Schengen, Luxembourg) took effect in 1995 and abolished many of the internal border controls within the EU. This enabled passport-free movement across most EU member states. As Figure 2 shows, there are 26 Schengen countries – 22 EU members and four non-EU members (Iceland, Norway, Switzerland, and Liechtenstein). The UK decided to remain outside the Schengen area, even before its 2016 decision to leave the EU.

Since 1995, millions of EU citizens have moved freely across the Schengen area. This has helped to fill job vacancies in other EU countries. Over 14 million EU citizens now live in another member state – 2.8% of the EU's population.

However, Schengen has been criticised by some people, who claim that it gives easy access to cheaper labour (undercutting domestic workers and lowering wages), as well as allowing free movement to criminals and terrorists. Terrorist attacks, such as Paris in 2015, have prompted a re-think about free movement. In 2016, six Schengen countries – Austria, Germany, France, Sweden, Denmark and Norway – reintroduced internal border controls.

Figure 2 *The extent of the Schengen area in Europe*

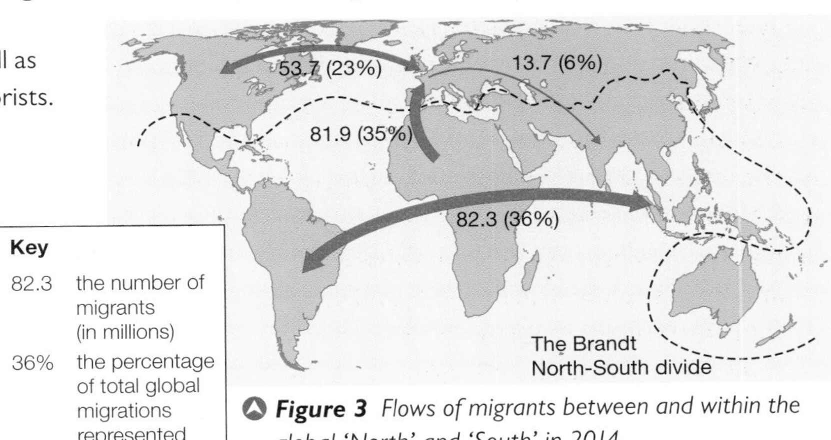

Figure 3 *Flows of migrants between and within the global 'North' and 'South' in 2014*

Trends in international migration

International migration is the movement across national boundaries. Around 4% of the global population – 280 million people – live outside their country of birth. Global flows of migrants are shown in Figure 3, and the countries with the largest number of migrants living abroad are shown in Figure 4.

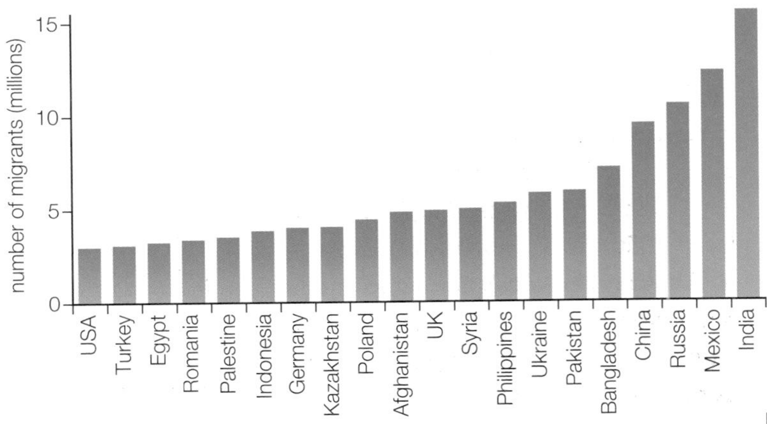

Figure 4 *Countries with the largest number of international migrants living abroad in 2015*

Global variations

People move for various reasons (see Section 5.3). But the proportion of international migrants within each country varies, depending on each country's attitudes and policies towards immigration and engagement with the global economy. Two examples are Japan and Australia.

1 Japan

Japan's population is falling, and 27% are aged over 65. Its median age is 46.5, and its working-age population is predicted to fall to 44 million by 2037 – half the size it was in 2007. Only 1.7% of the Japanese population is immigrant, whereas International Monetary Fund (IMF) research shows that advanced economies typically average 5%. The UN suggests that Japan needs 17 million migrants by 2050 to maintain its population at 2007 levels.

Part of the problem is language; unlike English, Japanese is not a global business language. Japan also has a closed-door policy to immigration (see Section 5.4), and despite concerns about its ageing population, there is little evidence of change in the political mindset.

2 Australia

For four decades, Australia's immigration policy has been skills-based. 70% of immigrants are accepted based on skills shortages where there are insufficient Australian workers (e.g. in medicine or engineering). Almost all immigrants live in big cities like Melbourne (see Figure 5).

Rather than being an economic problem, Australia's immigrants each contribute on average 10% more per capita to Australia's GDP each year than non-immigrants. Between 2015 and 2050, skilled immigrants are expected to add US$1.2 trillion to Australia's GDP. Immigrants are also beneficial demographically. Australia's median age is 37, but migrants tend to be younger; 88% are under 40 (compared to 54% of resident Australians), and 50% are aged 20-34 (compared to 20% of resident Australians). Australia has an otherwise ageing population, and migrants offset the numbers due to retire, which would otherwise place increasing pressure on the costs of medical and social care, as in Japan.

Figure 5 *The expanding CBD of Australia's second largest city, Melbourne. Its population has grown by 50% in three decades as more global companies have located here, bringing employment*

Changing international migration

Migrants move for various reasons, such as in response to changing economic, political or environmental events in their home (source) areas, as well as in their destination (host) areas. Most migrants fall into three categories:

- **Voluntary economic migrants** – moving for work
- **Refugees** – forced to leave their country because of war, natural disaster, persecution
- **Asylum seekers** – fleeing to another country to apply for the right to international protection.

Once migrants are established in their host countries, a fourth group may then follow them – **family members**.

The UK

The UK has two main source areas for international migrants:

- **The Commonwealth.** In 1945, labour shortages in factories, transport (e.g. London's buses) and the newly established NHS led the government to advertise UK jobs overseas. Afro-Caribbean migrants arrived from the West Indies from 1948, followed by those from India and Pakistan.
- **The EU.** EU migration grew after the Maastricht Agreement in 1992. As the EU's second largest economy – with the world's foremost business language (English) – economic migration to the UK has been high, which has helped to fill labour shortages. By 2014–15, nine EU countries were in the top ten source countries for UK immigrants (see Figure 6). Most immigrants are aged 21–35, and consist of both skilled and unskilled workers in equal numbers. However, questions now exist over future migrations after the 2016 referendum decision to leave the EU.

	2004–05		2009–10		2014–15
Poland	62.6	India	75.3	Romania	169.8
India	32.7	Poland	69.9	Poland	128.4
Pakistan	20.3	Lithuania	23.4	Italy	64.4
South Africa	19.3	Latvia	23.2	Spain	58.6
Australia	16.6	Pakistan	23.0	Bulgaria	44.1
Lithuania	15.6	Bangladesh	21.2	India	39.6
France	13.3	Romania	17.7	Portugal	37.5
China	12.6	France	16.5	France	31.0
Portugal	12.2	Nigeria	16.2	Hungary	26.5
Slovakia	10.5	Nepal	14.6	Lithuania	25.0
Total	**439.8**		**572.8**		**917.4**

Figure 6 *The changing pattern of immigration into the UK. This table shows overseas nationals entering the UK and being allocated a National Insurance number between 2005 and 2015 (numbers in thousands).*

Elsewhere

- In **Europe**, 2014-17 saw huge increases in immigration from North Africa and the Middle East, especially Syria. For example, 1.3 million migrants arrived in Germany in 2015-16, as a result of its temporary open-door policy.
- In the **Middle East**, many labourers from India, Pakistan and Bangladesh moved to Qatar temporarily to help build the infrastructure for its 2022 FIFA World Cup, as well as to Dubai to support its rapid modernisation and urban expansion.
- **Globally**, natural hazards have also forced people to move. For example, Haiti's 2010 earthquake displaced 300 000 Haitians, while Hurricane Matthew in 2016 displaced another 55 000.

Over to you

1 In pairs, draw a table to show the benefits and problems for different people created by (**a**) China's hukou system, (**b**) the EU's Schengen Agreement.

2 In pairs, compare (**a**) similarities, and (**b**) differences between international migration to Australia and Japan.

3 **a** Use a world map and the data in Figure 6 to construct proportional flow lines to show migration to the UK in 2014–15.
b Explain the pattern shown on your map.

On your own

4 Distinguish between the following pairs of terms: (**a**) international migration and rural-urban migration, (**b**) economic and family migrants, (**c**) refugees and asylum seekers.

5 Explain why (**a**) urban areas are significant to the global economy, (**b**) the number of people living outside their country of birth varies so much.

6 Research any three countries from Figure 4 to explain why so many people have left.

Exam-style question

Explain why globalisation and increased international migration are linked. *(6 marks)*

5.3 The causes of migration

In this section, you'll learn that the causes of migration are varied, complex and subject to change.

Crossing the Mediterranean

In 2015, just over one million migrants – a record – left North Africa and the Middle East for Europe. A further 340 000 arrived in 2016. They were often fleeing conflict and persecution, or seeking better job opportunities. Most migrants arrived in Europe in boats run by people smugglers, who were paid a fee for every person on board – so it was in their interests to cram in as many people as possible, regardless of safety. As Figure 1 shows, the conditions and experiences encountered by many migrants on their long journeys were dreadful. Some didn't even reach their final destination, because many of the overloaded boats sank at sea and rescuers often couldn't arrive in time to save everyone.

KEY CONCEPTS

- **Causality** – the causes of migration
- **Identity** – the changing identity of populations resulting from migrations of people
- **Globalisation** – the impact of globalisation on movements of people

My father worked in Germany for eight years. When we had a problem in Syria, he would say 'Oh, when I was in Germany it was very good. Good people, good government – everyone respects you. If you go to your job, learn the language and be a good person, you will live a good life there'. So I dream to go to Germany. We know we don't live in a democratic country in Syria. If we talk politics we will go to jail. It's not our fault that we have four years of war.

An unnamed Syrian man, aged 34

I left because of lawlessness and hunger. My mother sold our family home to pay for me to escape. There were 120 people on board the boat – we each paid the smugglers £3000. First they took us to Sudan, where police stopped us at the border. We explained we were escaping war and poverty in Somalia and pleaded with them to let us go. They refused. Some of our group made a run for it and walked for 18 hours.

Fedussa, aged 20, from Somalia

I've chatted every day on social media with a 17-year-old Egyptian friend in Italy. My friend now wears silver chains, attends school, has been adopted by an Italian family and is about to become a legal resident. What could I do earning $4-5 a day sorting dates? If I'd stayed in Egypt, I could never have earned a good living; I could never have got married. My friend now sends money home, and his family's house has a satellite dish, ornate balconies, carved wooden doors and new rooms.

Ashraf Goma, aged 19, from Egypt

Figure 1 *Migrants' experiences in 2015–16*

Many of those leaving the Middle East and Africa were **refugees** fleeing from conflict and poverty. On arrival in Europe, their aim was often to claim **asylum** (apply for the legal right to protection in their destination country). In 2015, half of those arriving in Europe were from Syria. Civil war there led over 2000 people every day to travel by small boat to the Greek islands, a few kilometres from the Turkish mainland, which they had reached overland from Syria (see Figure 2). Other migration routes were from North Africa (often Libya) to Spain, France and Italy.

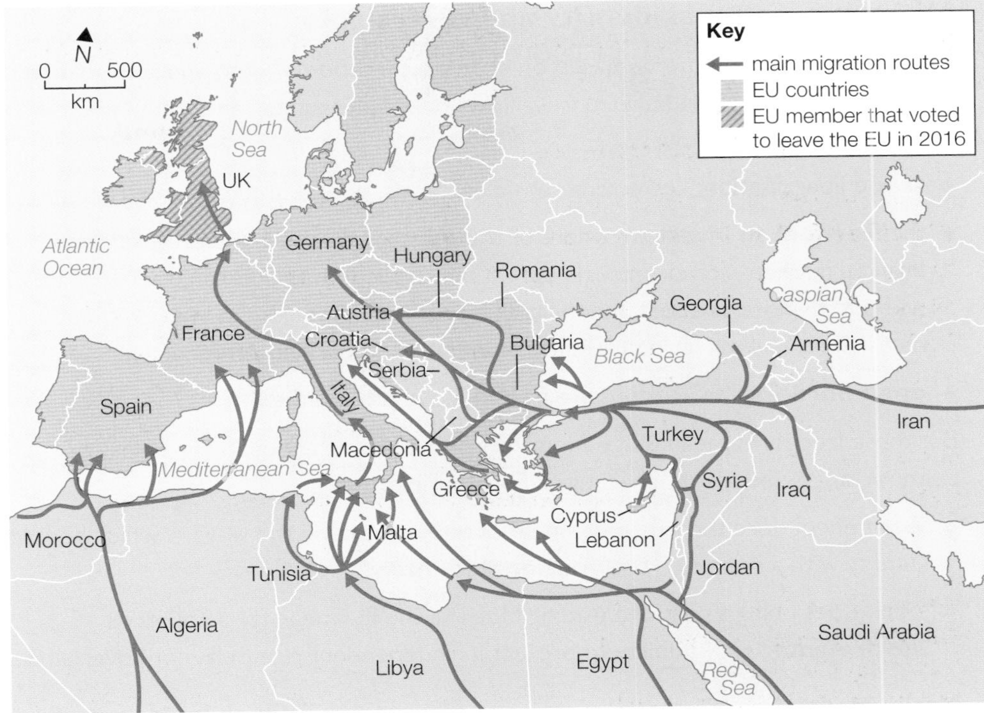

Figure 2 *Migration routes from the Middle East and North Africa into Europe*

EU migration to the UK

Although many migrants are refugees, most are economic migrants – they move for **work**. As Figure 3 shows, most of those who came to the UK from the EU in 2015-16 gave work as their main reason for coming. For those coming from other parts of the world, the highest proportion – nearly half – came to study.

Between 1993 and 2016, 2.5 million EU nationals became resident in the UK. For example, by 2015 about 250 000 French people lived in London. 60% of EU nationals arrived from Eastern Europe after eight countries there joined the EU in 2004. They helped to fill gaps in the UK labour market by working in administration, construction, business and management, hospitality and catering. The high numbers arriving reflected the unemployment figures and low wages in Eastern Europe. Figure 4 shows the effects of international migration across the EU's member states by 2013. In 2016, a further 270 000 EU citizens settled in the UK, whilst 90 000 left – a record net gain of 180 000.

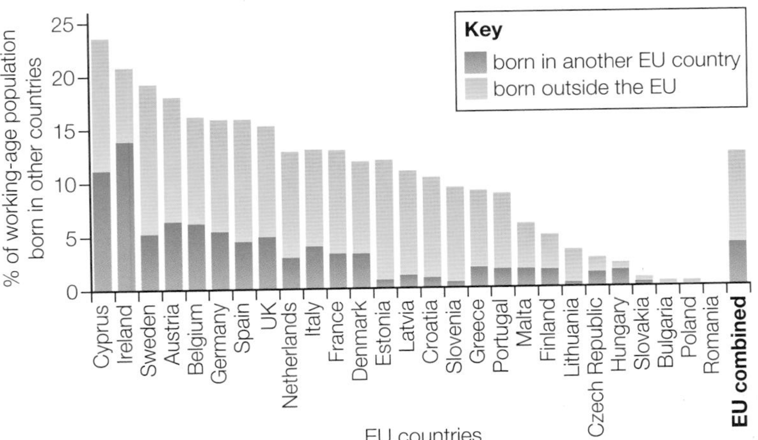

Figure 4 *The percentage of EU member states' working-age populations born in other countries by 2013*

Figure 3 *Reasons given for immigration to the UK up to March 2016. These figures do not include British nationals returning to the UK.*

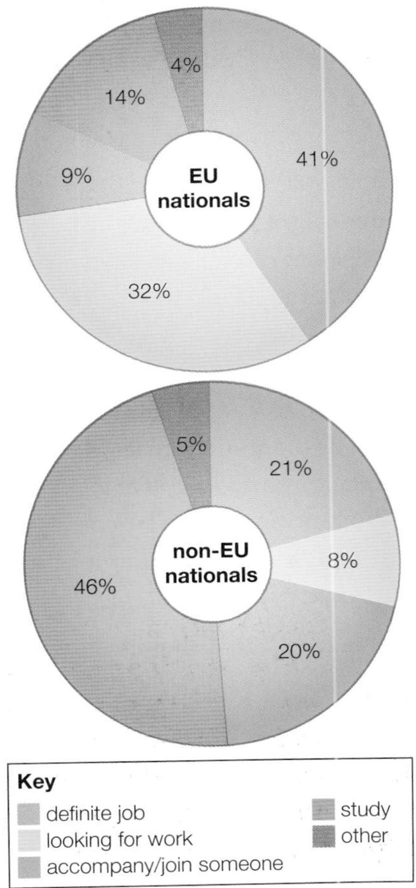

Migration, national identity and sovereignty

The theory of globalisation is based on economic freedoms – known as **liberalism**. Its more recent forms (a belief in freer flows of people, capital, and trade) is known as **neo-liberalism**. It involves:

- **trade** liberalisation – removing subsidies, tariffs, quotas and trade restrictions
- the **freedom to invest** anywhere or transfer capital, known as deregulation of financial markets. For example, in the UK, any bank or individual can trade in shares without having to use the London Stock Exchange. Individuals can invest without restrictions, and any financial institution can trade without government approval.
- **open borders** – EU citizens are free to move around the EU.

But these freedoms mean that national borders become almost meaningless or unimportant, which raises challenges. For example:

- What effect does the free movement of people have on the ways in which people identify with a country – their **national identity**?
- What does being a part of a trading bloc like the EU mean for a country's '**sovereignty**', i.e. its ability to protect its independent rule of law or governance?

National identity

The Oxford English Dictionary defines 'national identity' as 'a sense of a nation as a cohesive whole, represented by distinctive trends, culture and language'. Identity is flexible – if you think of yourself as British, then you are. But the term is complex. It refers to common experiences, beliefs or values, but these are not set in stone. They vary over time (e.g. during the Olympics), in intensity (e.g. during war), or by age group. Migration also affects identity, as different cultures enter a country, bringing different foods, customs and beliefs.

Sovereignty

Definitions of 'sovereignty' include 'supreme power or authority', 'the authority of a state to govern' and 'a self-governing state'. But this term is also complex, and globalisation can reduce its impact. For example, the UK voted to leave the EU in 2016. Among the reasons given by those voting to leave was a loss of sovereignty resulting from EU membership. However, few laws directly originate from Europe, and the UK is more closely bound to a range of international agreements that are not approved by Parliament, such as:

- the European Convention on Human Rights
- the World Trade Organisation (WTO) rules.

Open borders and immigration

Immigration is controversial and can cause resentment within host populations, who may sense threats to their national identities. Some migrants become victims of harassment, abuse, violence and exploitation, or the subject of hostility in the tabloid press. Tensions have risen both within the EU and with its neighbours:

- Extreme political parties are now becoming increasingly significant in Europe (e.g. Golden Dawn in Greece and France's National Front).
- Since 2014, huge numbers of Syrian refugees and economic migrants have caused tensions between Greece, other Balkan countries (the entry points to Northern Europe) and Turkey (see Figure 5).

Figure 5 *The arrival of refugees and economic migrants from Syria and North Africa in Budapest, Hungary, in 2015*

Internal movements within the UK

In any year, about 10% of people in the UK move – some locally, while others move from one region to another, as the data for England and Wales in Figure 6 show. One region's net gain in migration means a net loss somewhere else. This **regional movement** of people is unrestricted and is often linked to the changing labour market.

Reasons for internal migration

- Since the 1980s, de-industrialisation in northern Britain (e.g. steel, textiles) has driven many workers south in search of employment. The growth of footloose industries in the South East (e.g. electrical engineering and IT) has encouraged this, as has the growth of London's knowledge economy (e.g. financial services).
- The regeneration of large cities (e.g. Manchester, London) has led to in-migration of younger people for work, as well as the urban lifestyle. By contrast, many older adults with families move from cities into rural areas, often for lifestyle reasons as well as work.

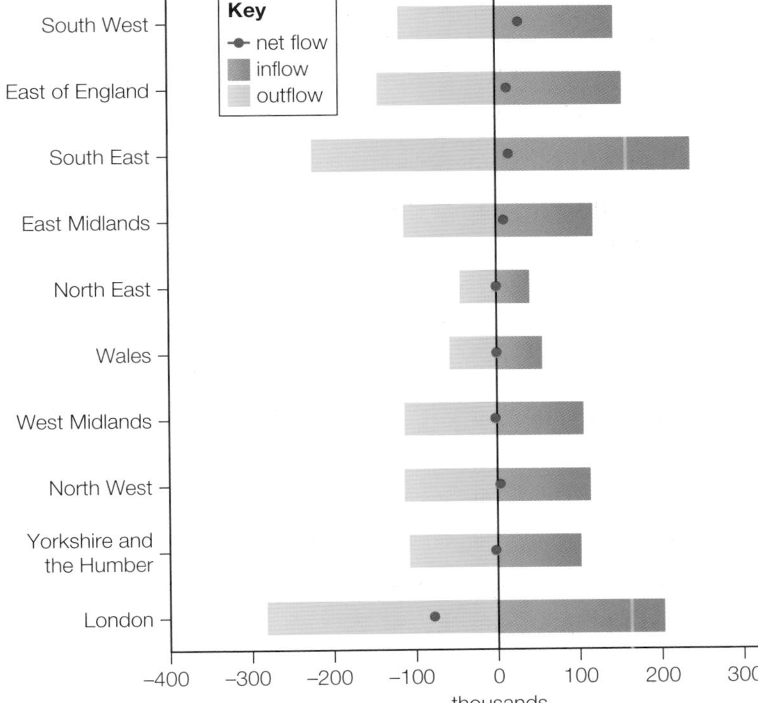

Figure 6 *Internal migration flows for the nine English regions, plus Wales, for the year up to June 2015*

The social consequences of migration

Every migration has social consequences:

- High inward migration can lead to rising house prices, if housing supply fails to meet demand, together with overcrowded schools, strained healthcare provision and falling local wages (because immigrant labour is usually willing to work for less).
- Conversely, large out-migrations from source regions can leave those areas with skills shortages and an ageing population.

Globally, movements of labour *are* restricted, but that doesn't stop migration. Together with those heading for Europe:

- poverty and violence in Mexico and Central America have motivated millions of people to head (both legally and illegally) for the USA
- political upheaval and religious repression in Myanmar is causing people to leave the country, particularly those from the Muslim minority.

Exam-style question

Referring to examples, evaluate the economic, social and political causes of international migration. (*20 marks*)

Over to you

1. In pairs, study the accounts in Figure 1. Draw a spider diagram to show key causes of this particular migration.
2. In pairs, research two source regions for migrant flows shown in Figure 2. Produce a brief PowerPoint presentation about (**a**) the economic, environmental or social causes of migration, (**b**) the pathways used to reach ports, (**c**) migrant experiences on arrival in Europe.
3. Draw spider diagrams to show the impacts of globalisation on (**a**) national identity, (**b**) sovereignty.

On your own

4. Distinguish between national identity and sovereignty.
5. Using Figures 3 and 4, write a 500-word report on the nature of migration to the UK and other EU member states.
6. Draw up a table of costs and benefits to the UK of (**a**) international, (**b**) internal migration.

5.4 The consequences of international migration

In this section, you'll learn how the consequences of international migration are varied and disputed.

All change!

Almost every city in the world now contains mixed ethnicities and distinct cultural communities. Decades of international investment and migration have meant that differences between urban places in different countries are becoming less obvious. However, it is not just street scenes and shop fronts that change (see Figure 3 in Section 5.1); migration can also change the **cultural** and **ethnic** composition of whole countries. The degree of change depends on the rate and level of **assimilation** of migrants into the host nations.

KEY CONCEPTS

- **Causality** – the causes of differing attitudes towards migration
- **Identity** – how the identity of populations changes as a result of immigration

The extent to which migrant groups are assimilated or remain segregated varies within and between countries. In South Africa, for example, nearly three decades of equal rights since the abolition of **apartheid** have hardly altered its **ethnic segregation**; residential areas in both urban and rural locations usually remain differentiated by ethnicity and skin colour.

Even in Western countries, ethnic groups may still be segregated by residence. For example, the segregation of different ethnic groups in London, such as those of Indian descent in Figure 1, is common in many large cities. But, unlike in South Africa, this ethnic segregation usually comes from economic and cultural factors:

- Cheaper rental properties in inner cities have traditionally attracted migrants to settle close to their workplaces. Over time, ethnic **enclaves** (or concentrations) become permanent, such as the Hindu and Sikh communities in Southall, West London. Southall is equidistant between jobs in Central London and at Heathrow Airport, and good job opportunities have enabled these communities to thrive and buy homes and businesses.
- Many West Indian immigrants in the 1950s were recruited to drive London's buses, so many of them settled near to London Transport bus garages, such as Brixton. Many of their descendants still live in the same areas.
- Once established, cultural factors – such as the growth of specialist shops, places of worship and community leisure facilities – help to maintain these separate ethnic enclaves.

Gradually, many ethnic communities have integrated into British economic life, while at the same time retaining their cultural distinctiveness. They have helped to produce the ethnic enclaves shown in Figure 1.

Key words

Assimilation – The gradual integration of an immigrant group into the lifestyle and culture of the host country, sometimes at the expense of their own distinctiveness. This happens over time as migrants become more mobile, have mixed marriages, and adjust to the host nation's way of life.

Ethnic – A social group identified by a distinctive culture, religion, language, or similar.

Culture – The ideas, beliefs, customs and social behaviour of a group or society.

Ethnic segregation – The voluntary or enforced separation of people of different cultures or nationalities.

Apartheid – The enforced segregation of people by skin colour or ethnicity. This policy was used in South Africa between 1948 and 1991.

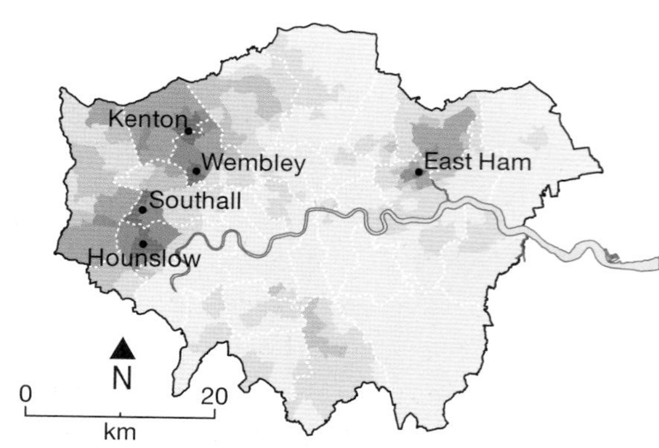

Figure 1 *The clustering into particular London enclaves of Asian / Asian British people of Indian descent from the 2011 Census*

BACKGROUND

Measuring cultural diversity

Most cities in Western countries now have culturally diverse populations. Within the EU, Inner London is Europe's most diverse place, followed by Luxembourg, Brussels and Outer London. However, cultural diversity varies within, and between, nations. Figure 2 shows global diversity on a map of **cultural fractionization**.

This uses an index to measure how diverse countries are. It measures people's attitudes towards, for example, religion, democracy and the law. The index varies between 1 (total diversity) and 0 (no diversity). The global average is 0.53. In Figure 2, darker-shaded countries are more diverse than those shaded lighter.

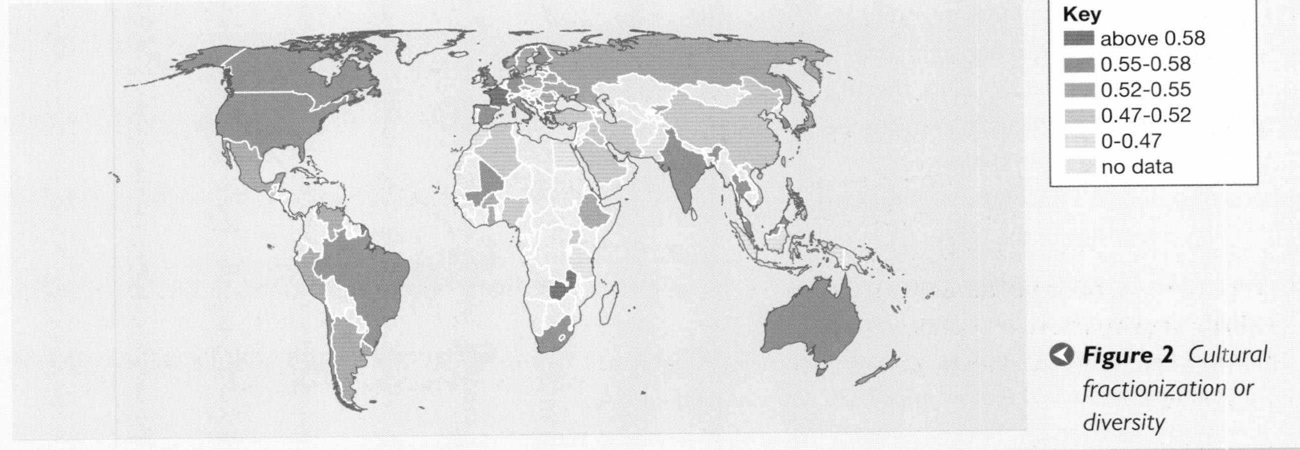

Figure 2 *Cultural fractionization or diversity*

Migration and political tension

1 Japan

Japan's economy is sluggish, and its population is decreasing and ageing (see Section 5.2). A shrinking working-age population means fewer workers, a falling demand for goods, and lower taxation revenue for the government. At the same time, a growing elderly population means increased government spending on health and social care, plus a need for more expensive support services. That combination of demographic factors means increased government debt.

For many countries, immigration would be the answer. However, Japan has a deep-rooted cultural aversion to this solution – only 1.63% of the Japanese population is immigrant, which is among the world's lowest percentages. By contrast, 14.3% of the US population is immigrant.

The Japanese hold the belief that they are a 'homogenous' people. And Japan *is* relatively homogenous – it's one of the few industrialised nations that didn't experience large inflows of migrants after 1945. Japanese people fear that immigrants may disrupt the 'harmony and co-operation' that characterise Japanese society. Politically, the 'no-immigration' principle is widely supported, as the opinions outlined in Figure 3 show.

Figure 3 *The Japanese attitude towards immigration*

The Japanese are increasingly worried about the effects of the declining population. But when asked what should be done to secure the labour supply, the two top answers in a poll were to increase the rate of working women and encourage more elderly to work, rather than increase immigration.

Japan Times

A 2006 Cabinet Office survey found that 84% of Japanese felt public security had worsened, because 'crimes committed by foreigners had increased'. The same survey in 2012 found similar anxiety, but a weakening perception of foreigners as criminals. This reflected the drop in the foreign population since 2009.

Japan Times

Only one out of seven Japanese support the idea of increasing immigration. Nearly half were absolutely opposed. The Japanese unease with foreigners is typically expressed by the word *gaijin*, and is what some people mean when they condemn the Japanese for their *shimaguni-konjo* (their island nation mind-set).

Business website J-CAST's survey, 2012

2 Mexico-USA

Large-scale migration from Mexico to the USA stretches back to the post-First World War economic boom in the USA, on one hand, and economic devastation in Mexico after its political revolution (1910-19) on the other. Figure 4 shows how it has increased, including a big surge from 1970 onwards, with flows of both legal and illegal Mexican immigrants migrating to Californian farms as pickers, and also to US cities. It shows that, by 2015, there were over 11.7 million Mexican immigrants in the USA – making them the largest immigrant group, at 28% of the 42.4 million immigrants then living in the USA.

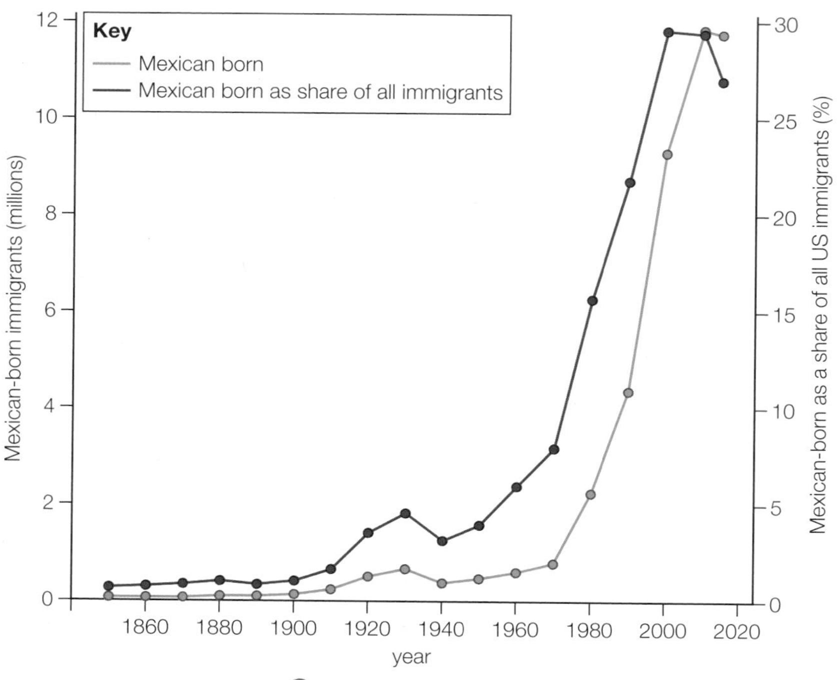

Figure 4 *The Mexican immigrant population in the USA, 1850–2015*

During the 2016 Presidential election campaign, the Republican candidate, Donald Trump, focused on immigration as an issue. Generally, Americans don't see immigration as the most important issue facing the USA, but it is important to them. Their views about immigration vary, often shaped by specific views about immigrants themselves. As Figure 5 shows, when asked in a survey if immigrants were a burden (e.g. taking jobs and services), or whether they strengthened the USA through their hard work and talents, about half of the US voters surveyed (51%) said that immigrants strengthened the country, while 41% felt that they were a burden. As the graph also shows, the views expressed in the survey were largely split along political lines, with Republican voters much more anti-immigrant (63%).

Figure 5 *US voters' views about the impacts of immigrants on the USA, from a survey conducted in May 2015 (18 months before the US Presidential election)*

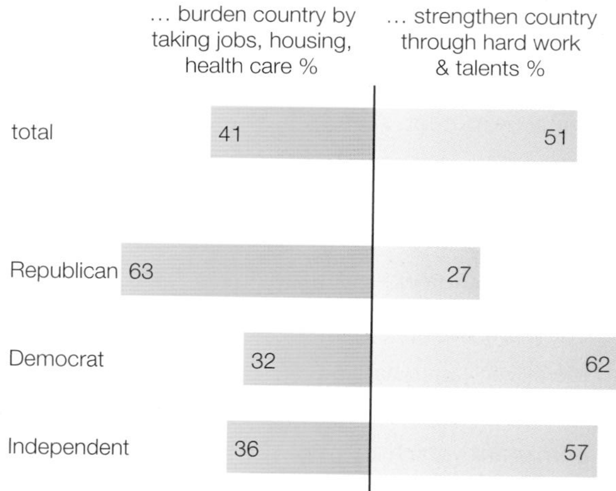

However, as Figure 6 shows, large-scale emigration from Mexico to the USA doesn't just impact on the host country, but also on the source country:

> Martha and Faustino's children, grandchildren and great-grandchildren live in the United States. Martha said: 'We are happy that almost our entire family has a better life in the United States, but we're also sad that our culture and way of life are slowly disappearing from our family as people leave.

Figure 6 *The views of some of those left behind in Mexico (adapted from BBC News online)*

Often during his 2016 election campaign, Donald Trump called for a wall to be built along the entire US-Mexican border – to prevent further illegal immigration. It wasn't a new thought, but a CBS news poll in 2016 showed that 45% of Americans supported it. However, despite that, many Americans actually believe that the main focus should be on developing a plan to manage the Mexican immigrants already living in the USA illegally, rather than trying to halt the flow of illegal immigrants still arriving, which is declining.

Ability and opportunities

The route to a new life in another country can be fraught with difficulties, and is easier to achieve for some than others. For example, it can depend on a person's **skills**:

- Migrants to Australia generally enter as skilled workers (see Section 5.2), but they need a minimum of 65 points in Australia's points-based system. Skilled workers include professional and manual workers, with accountants and mechanics earning 60 points, while those at the lower end of the scale, e.g. youth workers, earn 40 points. Points are awarded depending on age, qualifications and competence in English. Preference is also given to those with an existing job offer.
- Singapore's migration policy divides immigrant workers into 'foreign workers' and 'foreign talents'. The former refers to semi-skilled or unskilled workers, who work mainly in manufacturing, construction and domestic services. In this category, most come from China and Southeast Asia. 'Foreign talent' refers to people with qualifications or degrees who work in Singapore's knowledge economy. People in this category come from Southeast Asia, Europe, Australia, New Zealand and the USA.

Figure 7 *A warning to motorists about smuggling along the US-Mexican border, a crossing point for illegal migrants, usually organised by people smugglers for a large fee*

In other cases, the ease of migration can depend on **existing wealth**:

- For Mexicans, crossing the border into the USA is risky and expensive. Many illegal migrants pay people smugglers (like those referred to in Figure 7) between US$4000 and US$10 000 to cross the border.
- Migrants from North Africa or Syria (see Section 5.3) are also often the victims of organised crime. Gangs in Africa or Central Europe organise the movement of people to Europe for large payments.

The ease of migration can also depend on practical **opportunities**, including:

- the presence or absence of international border controls. So, for example, once within Europe's Schengen area (see Figure 2 in Section 5.2) migrants are able to move unimpeded between the member countries.
- the presence of established and settled family members in the destination country.

Over to you

1 In pairs, devise and complete a mind map to show the social, economic, cultural and demographic impacts of migration (including restricted migration) on Japan and Mexico-USA.

2 **a** Using Figures 3 and 6, analyse the extracts and draw a table to show the causes of, and attitudes towards, migration.
b Research the phrase 'attitudes towards immigration in Japan' (and then the USA and Mexico), and add further details to your table.

3 Prepare a class debate on the motion 'Immigration always brings far more benefits than problems'.

On your own

4 Distinguish between the following pairs of terms: (**a**) assimilation and segregation, (**b**) ethnicity and culture, (**c**) cultural fractionization and cultural diversity.

5 Explain how the following affect people's ability to migrate across international borders: (**a**) work skills, (**b**) wealth, (**c**) language skills, (**d**) border controls, (**e**) any other factors.

Exam-style question

Explain why immigration can cause political tensions. *(6 marks)*

5.5 Nation states and borders

In this section, you'll learn how nation states are highly varied and have very different histories.

EQ2 Sections 5.5 to 5.7 will investigate how nation states are defined and how they have evolved in a globalising world.

KEY CONCEPTS

- **Causality** – the causes of differing degrees of diversity, and how nation states evolve
- **Identity** – how people's identity is bound up with nationality and a sense of belonging

Iceland

Iceland sits in the mid-Atlantic Ocean, astride a plate boundary, hundreds of kilometres from its nearest neighbour, Greenland. Its national characteristics result from: its geographical location; landscape (see Figure 1); dependence on the sea; and isolation. Independence was gained from Denmark in 1944, and Iceland's laws and society fiercely protect its cultural heritage and national identity:

- All children's names must come from an approved list, to preserve the language of Icelandic sagas.
- The national phone book lists subscribers by *first* name, because most Icelandic surnames record the father's name suffixed with either *son* for boys or *dóttir* for girls – a system used since Viking times.
- The Icelandic language has remained unchanged since the 870s AD, although other Nordic languages, plus English and German, are also widely spoken.
- 74% of Icelanders belong to the Evangelical Lutheran Church of Iceland.

- Most of Iceland is completely empty and unsettled.
- Over half of the population of 336 000 live in or close to Reykjavík, the capital.
- The Icelandic population is – by present standards – **monocultural**, with those born overseas constituting only 8.9% of the population in 2015.

Figure 1 *Skaftafell National Park and the Skaftafellsjokull glacier in southeast Iceland*

The Icelandic sagas

The Icelandic sagas are an intrinsic part of Iceland's national identity, and were written by several different authors. They trace the lives and legends of the Viking ancestors of modern-day Icelanders – describing events from the period 950-1050 AD. As well as fantastic stories, such as the fight with the mermaid in Figure 2, the sagas also contain significant historical events, including Norse explorer Leif Ericsson's discovery of North America. They tell stories of farmers, families, warriors and kings, and now inspire music such as the work of modern Icelandic band, Sigur Ros.

Figure 2 *A thirteenth-century illustrated manuscript of an Icelandic saga*

BACKGROUND

The concept of nation states

The concept of a nation, or sovereign state, is one in which the population are united by factors such as language, a common ethnic and cultural background, and customs which bring a sense of national identity. Nation states develop and change over time, and vary with geographical location, historical events and population migrations. Some nations do not exist physically, but their *identity* exists nonetheless, e.g. the Kurdish territories in Turkey, Iran, Iraq and Syria. Dispersed populations of this kind are known as **diasporas**.

Figure 3 *The Sultan mosque in Arab Street, Kampong Glam, Singapore*

Singapore

Singapore – a city-state at the tip of the Malaysian Peninsula – had a population of 5.47 million in 2014, and was first established in 1819, by Sir Thomas Stamford Raffles, as a British colonial trading post. Singapore's subsequent growth was largely due to immigration – particularly from China, but also from India and Malaysia.

Raffles divided Singapore into distinct ethnic areas:

- European Town – for Europeans and wealthy Asians
- Chinatown – for the Chinese majority
- Chulia Kampon – for Indian Hindus and Sikhs
- Kampong Glam – for Muslim Malays and Arabs (see Figure 3).

After brief periods of Japanese and Malaysian rule, Singapore became independent in 1965. Its population today reflects its globalised present (see Figure 4) and its multicultural past – 74% are Chinese, 13% Malay and 9% Indian, with others of European descent or ex-patriots working overseas. This small country possesses a vibrant mix of languages, culture, religions, festivals and food.

But what is it to be Singaporean? Can national identity (see Section 5.3) develop within such a diverse population? The Singaporean government has tried to generate a national identity, largely based on Asian values, but many Singaporeans have their own ideas about this issue that can contradict the government's. This can be problematic, as Figure 5 shows.

Figure 4 *Singapore – a global city skyline*

Singapore's women's table tennis team played China in the final at the 2008 Beijing Olympics. The Singapore team lost, but still won the city-state's first Olympic medal since 1960. However, many Singaporeans were less than enthusiastic about this achievement, because three members of Singapore's Olympic table tennis team, Li Jiawei, Wang Yuegu, and Feng Tianwei, had been deliberately poached from China by the Singaporean government in its bid to attract foreign talent, and had become Singaporean citizens only two years previously.

When Li Jiawei appeared on Chinese TV and spoke of being happy to play on home turf and of being a *Zhongguoren* [Chinese national], it did not go down well in Singapore.

Figure 5 *Does Singapore have a national identity?*

Figure 6 *The Berlin conference of 1884–5 that created Africa's current national borders*

National borders

Borders separate nations and are either natural, have emerged historically over time, or are the result of colonial history or political intervention:

- **Natural borders.** These consist of physical features that once created natural obstacles, such as rivers (e.g. the Niagara River between Canada and the USA), lakes (e.g. the border created by Lake Tanganyika between the Democratic Republic of the Congo, Zambia, Tanzania and Burundi; see Figure 7), or mountains (e.g. the Pyrenees between France and Spain).
- **Colonial history and political intervention.** For example, 14 countries met at a conference in Berlin in 1884-5 to discuss and divide up the continent of Africa (see Figure 6). At that time 80% of the continent was still under indigenous control, but by the end of the conference it had been divided up into 50 separate countries along **geometric boundaries** (formed by arcs or straight lines, e.g. latitude and longitude) – as well as being turned into colonies by the major European powers. The new country borders were superimposed onto the existing indigenous regions of Africa, with no account taken of tribal or linguistic boundaries. Neither the conference, nor any future negotiations, gave African peoples any say over partitioning their homelands and turning them into European colonies.

Rwanda

Before the Berlin conference, Rwanda had been a unified region – home to the Tutsi, Hutu and Twa peoples. The Tutsi were in control of the area, but any problems were resolved through a council of elders that included both Hutu and Tutsi members. However, following the Berlin conference, Germany established colonial rule over the newly created country of Rwanda, which Belgium then took over after Germany's defeat in the First World War. The Belgians favoured the Tutsi minority (14% of the population) with privileges over the Hutu majority (85% of the population) – and, in 1926, they even introduced ethnic identity cards that officially differentiated Hutus from Tutsi.

When Rwanda gained independence in 1962, its government was contested and not seen as legitimate by all. The Hutus had rebelled against the Belgian and Tutsi elite, and thousands of Tutsis fled. The killing of Tutsis occurred throughout the 1960s and 70s. Then, during the 1970s and 80s, the majority Hutus were given preferential jobs in the public services and military. Despite plans to introduce a multi-party government, progress stalled during the early 1990s.

Matters came to a head in April 1994, when the presidents of Rwanda and Burundi were both killed when their plane was shot down. That event led to the **genocide** (mass killing) of an estimated 800 000 Tutsis and moderate Hutus. In July 1994, the Hutu government fled to Zaire (now the Democratic Republic of the Congo; see Figure 7), together with 2 million Hutu refugees, and an interim government of national unity was set up. Later that year, the UN Security Council established an international tribunal to oversee the prosecution of suspects involved in the Rwandan genocide.

Figure 7 *The present-day countries and national borders of Central Africa*

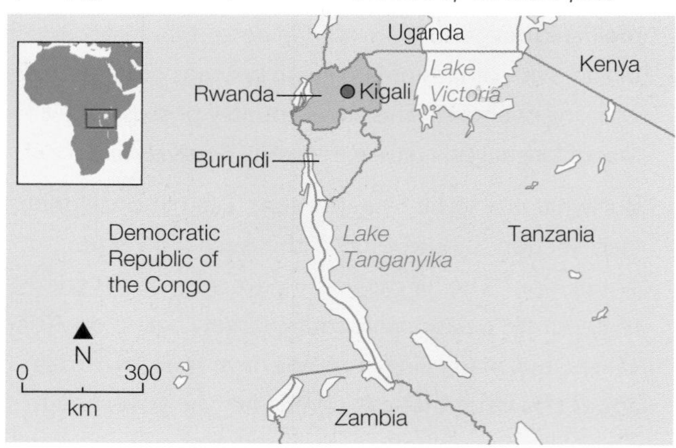

Contested borders

Ukraine and Crimea

The Crimean peninsula stretches from southern Ukraine into the Black Sea. It has a varied population – 58% are ethnic Russians, 24% are ethnic Ukrainians, 12% are Muslim Tatars. It also has a varied history:

- Crimea became part of the Russian Empire in 1783.
- The Germans occupied it for part of the Second World War. In 1944, after being recaptured by the Russians, Stalin exiled the entire population of Crimean Tatars to Uzbekistan on charges of collaborating with the Germans.
- Crimea remained part of Russia until 1954, when it was transferred to Ukraine. At that time both Ukraine and Russia were Soviet republics.
- The break up of the USSR in 1991 created an opportunity for the exiled Crimean Tatars, who began returning.
- Sevastopol (see Figure 8) has long been the base of the Russian Black Sea fleet. After 1991 Russia found itself with part of its navy based in the newly independent Ukraine. In 2010, Ukraine agreed to extend Russia's lease on Sevastopol until 2042 (in exchange for cheaper Russian gas).

But, in 2014, Ukraine's pro-Russian president was driven from power by a new Western-facing government that favoured Ukrainian membership of both the EU and NATO. Russian-backed forces seized control of Crimea, and its Russian-speaking majority voted to join Russia in a snap referendum that Ukraine and the West considered illegal. 850 000 Ukrainians fled Crimea as a result.

Taiwan

Taiwan has effectively been an independent state since 1950, but China still claims sovereignty over it and regards it as a rebel province that should be united with the mainland. China insists that other nations should not have official formal relations (e.g. recognition through embassies and diplomatic services) with both China and Taiwan, so Taiwan has few formal ties with other countries. Despite its diplomatic isolation, Taiwan is one of Asia's economic success stories, and is a top producer of computer technology. Tsai Ing-wen became Taiwan's first female president in 2016. She recognises the importance of Taiwanese identity, but by pursuing its sovereignty and formal independence she risks antagonising China.

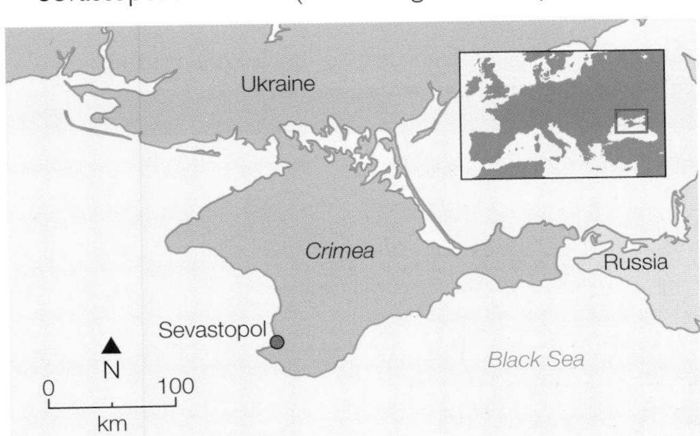

Figure 8 *Ukraine and Crimea*

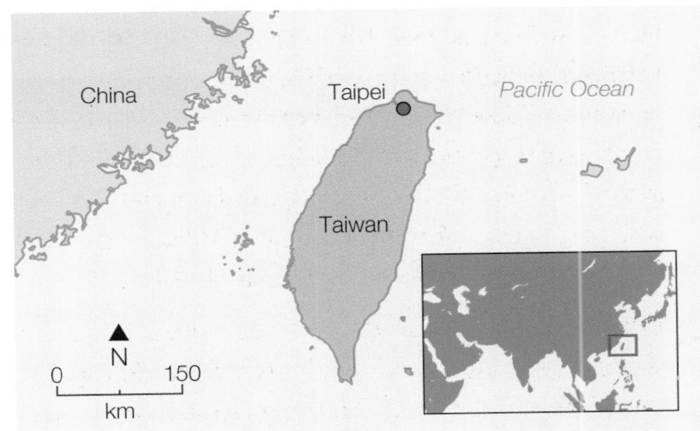

Figure 9 *Taiwan*

Over to you

1. **a** Draw divided bar charts to show the ethnic composition of Singapore and Iceland.
   b Annotate each graph to show how its relative diversity or homogeneity has resulted from geographical factors and past histories.
2. Compare Iceland and Singapore in terms of their **(a)** ethnic, **(b)** cultural and **(c)** linguistic unity or diversity, and research the historical reasons for this.
3. In pairs, select one continent and identify borders within it which are **(a)** based on physical features and **(b)** the result of human intervention. Research examples which illustrate both factors and write a brief report on your findings.

On your own

4. Research either Crimea or Taiwan, and update the state of relations between those who contest sovereignty.

Exam-style question

Evaluate the factors which may lead to national borders being contested. (*20 marks*)

5.6 Nationalism in the modern world

In this section, you'll learn how nationalism has played a role in the development of the modern world.

KEY CONCEPTS

- **Causality** – the complex causes of the emergence of nation states
- **Identity** – how people's identity with a nation state is relatively recent

Where history and geography converge

The idea of a 'nation state' and 'nationality' is relatively new. In Europe before the sixteenth century, people rarely viewed themselves in terms of nationality. Like the fantasy world of *Game of Thrones*, their world was small – maybe just a village – and they associated themselves with their immediate neighbours. Like the communities in *Game of Thrones*, they were controlled by whichever local lord owned their land, and they identified only with their immediate surroundings. Traditions, laws and behaviour varied from one area to another, and few 'rulers' controlled whole countries. 'Territories' were often defined by religion, family dynasties or alliances, the rulers of which considered themselves to be **absolute** – that is, possessing complete power over all. Democracy as an idea wasn't considered.

The emergence of Europe's nation states

Figure 1 provides a very simplified summary of the emergence of Europe's nation states. By the end of the nineteenth century, most of the European states that we know today had emerged in one form or another – only to create closer economic and political ties in the late twentieth and early twenty-first centuries, which has increasingly diluted the importance of national borders. For example, in 2017, 28 EU member states (until the UK leaves) share formal political, legal and economic ties, and their populations can move freely between them. As a result, many EU citizens now consider themselves to be European first and their national identity second.

Figure 1 *The emergence of Europe's nation states*

From your village as the world …	Timeline	Historical context
	Pre-1500s	People lived in small communities and rarely travelled anywhere – their community was their world.
	1485	The ending of the Wars of the Roses at the Battle of Bosworth led to the Tudor dynasty and the emerging idea of an English nation state.
	1492	Spain began to emerge as a global power after Ferdinand and Isabella captured the whole country from the Muslim Moors and began supporting explorers like Columbus.
	1547–1584	Ivan the Terrible, the Russian Tsar, unified local provincial governments and created the first Russian nation state.
	1638–1715	France emerged as a dominant European power during the absolute monarchy of Louis XIV.
	1648	The Peace of Westphalia, which ended the Thirty Years War, made the legal status of the nation state sovereign over other powers.
	1789	The French Revolution led to the modern French nation state. The French monarchy was replaced by a republican government, which led to the growth of nationalist ideas across much of Europe.
	1871	The unification of many small independent states resulted in the formation of the modern countries of Germany and Italy for the first time.
	1919	The Treaty of Versailles, which ended the First World War, led to the break up of the Austro-Hungarian and Ottoman Empires and created many new nation states.
	1945	The United Nations was formed from the pre-war League of Nations.
	1957	The formation of the European Economic Community (the start of the EU) brought six European nations closer together economically.
'… to the world as your village	1993 onwards	The creation of the European Union, and its later expansion to 28 countries, brought closer political ties and a single market, which allowed the free movement of goods, capital, and people between member states.

Nineteenth-century nationalism

'Nationalism' is based on peoples' identification with a 'nation' – in the belief that they share a common identity, language, history and customs that bind them together. They tend to promote their country and are prepared to defend it, even to extend its boundaries. The French Revolution helped to establish nationalism as a force. It removed the absolute power of the French monarchy and instead placed power in the hands of ordinary citizens. A new national government made laws that applied to everyone equally, and a standardised form of French was taught across the whole country to replace local dialects. Loyalty towards France as a nation grew and a new national identity emerged.

Growing tensions across Europe

However, many saw French nationalism as a threat. By 1799, Napoleon Bonaparte was a key national figure. In 1804, he made himself Emperor of France – aiming to extend French control across Europe. His military victories boosted French patriotism, but his belief in expansionism also provoked anger across Europe and led to rising nationalism in countries like Austria and Russia, who sought revenge for French aggression.

In 1800, Prussia was the most powerful German state (Germany as a single country did not yet exist). Prussia's economy was strong, based on coal and iron ore, and it traded with other north German states. Growing German industrial wealth and infrastructure (e.g. railways linking the different German states) encouraged a growing sense of being 'German', with the result that a new combined state (Germany) was created under the Prussian Chancellor Bismarck's national plan in 1871. Bismarck's plan was helped by Prussian rivalries with France that had led to the successful Franco-Prussian War of 1870-71. Prussia and its north German allies took land from France (Alsace-Lorraine), which reduced French influence in Europe and led to the northern and southern German states joining as a united Germany under Prussian leadership.

By now, as Figure 2 shows, the map of Europe had become very complex. Placing borders around states is actually quite complicated, and ethnic, linguistic, religious and cultural aspects may not fit in easily with revised national borders drawn up after conflicts. As Figure 2B shows, this difficulty became even clearer after the First World War, when national boundaries were shifted again and new countries were created from the former Austro-Hungarian and Ottoman Empires (e.g. Hungary, Czechoslovakia, Bulgaria). The map of Europe in 1920 also contained nation states, such as Poland, which had taken over former German territory; ethnic Germans were now scattered in foreign territories such as Alsace-Lorraine (given back to France), the new country of Austria, the Sudetenland (in Czechoslovakia) and Danzig (now surrounded by an expanded independent Poland which completely cut off East Prussia from the rest of Germany). In the period leading up to the Second World War, Hitler re-incorporated most of these territories.

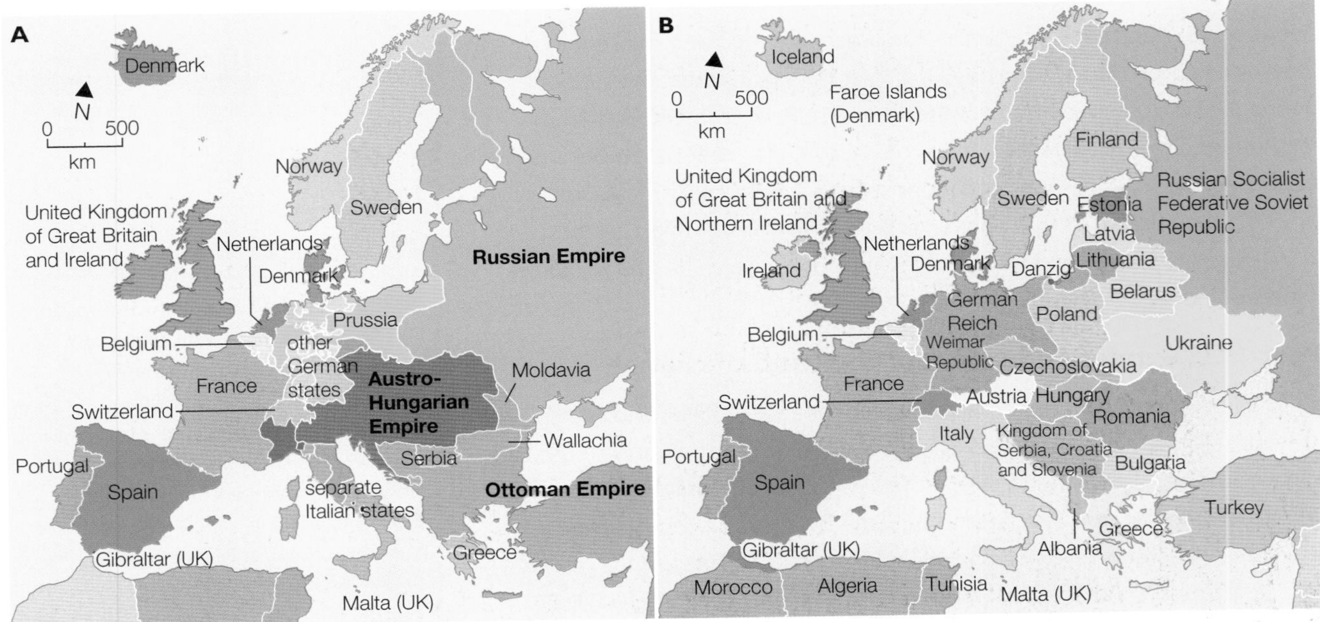

Figure 2 *Shifting European boundaries between 1850 (**A**) and 1920 (**B**). In Map **B**, note that the USSR came into existence in 1922.*

Empires and their consequences

Nationalism also grew beyond Europe in the nineteenth and early twentieth centuries. An age of imperialism and colonialism led to most major European nations extending their overseas interests and colonies. Figure 3 shows the extent of these overseas empires by 1900. Local resistance to this colonisation began to build up and, for example, by 1900 most of Central and South America had won independence from Spain and Portugal, but most of Africa and Asia was still controlled by various European nations.

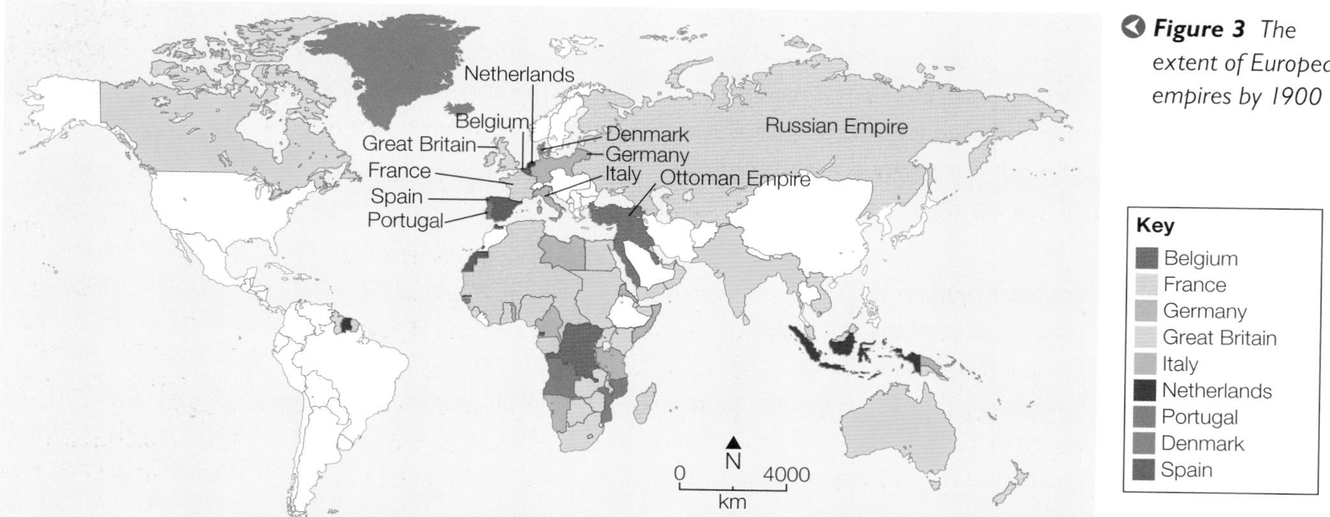

Figure 3 *The extent of European empires by 1900*

'The jewel in the crown'

Trade with, and political influence over, a large part of India by the British East India Company (see Figure 4), eventually led to direct British rule over most of the sub-continent – which became known as the Raj. Wealth and power from its growing empire (of which India was known as 'the jewel in the crown') meant that Britain overtook France and Spain as a superpower (see Section 3.3) – creating international rivalries. Internal tensions within India caused a rebellion against the East India Company in 1857 that led to the British government taking over direct political control.

Between 1857 and 1914, the British Parliament set the rules and sent a Viceroy to govern India. After the First World War, in return for support during the war, Indians were promised some self-government. Demands for independence grew louder and protests by Indian nationalists became more frequent. This resulted in actions such as the Amritsar Massacre of 1919, when British troops opened fire on unarmed Indian protestors, killing several hundred and wounding many more – which helped to fan the flames of Indian nationalism.

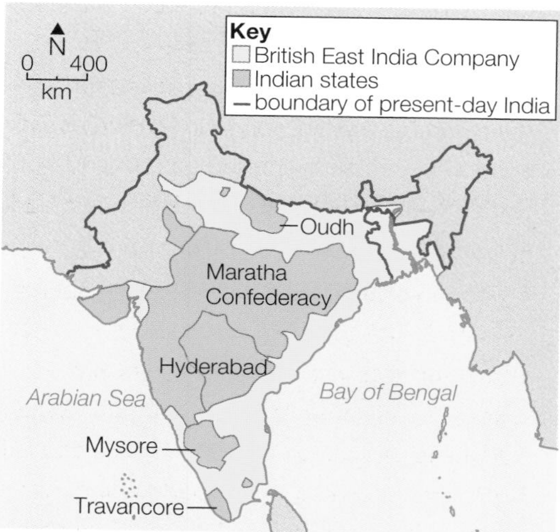

Figure 4 *The extensive influence of the British East India Company in India*

Post 1945 – independence and the wind of change

India was eventually offered complete independence in 1946, and in 1947 – to prevent religious conflict – it was agreed that the former territory of British India would be partitioned to create the new states of Muslim-majority East and West Pakistan (the East later to become Bangladesh) and the Hindu-majority India. Elsewhere, the colonial rulers of sub-Saharan Africa gradually gave up political control to new independent governments. When British Prime Minister Harold Macmillan gave his famous 'wind of change' speech in 1960 (see Figure 5) it was clear that new states were about to emerge.

> … the most striking of all the impressions I have formed since I left London a month ago is of the strength of this African national consciousness. In different places it takes different forms, but it is happening everywhere. The wind of change is blowing through this continent, and whether we like it or not, this growth of national consciousness is a political fact.

Figure 5 *An extract from British Prime Minister Harold Macmillan's speech to the South African parliament on 3 February 1960*

The costs of disintegrating empires

Vietnam – North or South

By 1850, most of Southeast Asia had been colonised by European powers (with the exception of Thailand). The modern countries of Vietnam, Cambodia and Laos were then French colonies in what became known as French Indochina. Much of Southeast Asia's agricultural land was converted to plantations producing rubber (see Figure 6), coffee, tea, rice and tobacco for export to the colonial powers.

Figure 6 *A rubber plantation in French Indochina in the 1930s*

In French Indochina, the society was divided into those with land and those without. The landless classes worked on plantations for overseas landlords, and often lacked food, healthcare and education. As cash crop exports increasingly replaced domestic subsistence crops, the poor became poorer – and hungrier.

After 1945, Vietnamese nationalists increasingly challenged French rule. The French military defeat at the 1954 siege of Dien Bien Phu paved the way for nationalist leader Ho Chi Minh to 'reclaim' Vietnam from France. By then, other colonised Asian states had already gained independence, and the USA was concerned about the spread of communism in Southeast Asia. To reach an agreement between two sides, Vietnam was divided into two along the '17th parallel' (the 17°N line of latitude) – the Vietnamese nationalists, supported by communist China, controlled the north; in the south, independent non-communist rule began, supported by US troops in small numbers until 1961, when more were sent. A long and devastating war then ensued, during which the north Vietnamese nationalists fought to reunify the whole country under their control: 1–4 million Vietnamese were killed, along with 240 000–300 000 Cambodians, 20 000–62 000 Laotians, and 58 220 Americans. The south was finally defeated in 1975 and an independent, united Vietnam emerged.

Timeline Sudan: 70 years of tension

- 1946 – Plans are proposed for a united Sudan
- 1955 – Civil war breaks out, based on internal mistrust and tensions
- 1956 – Sudan becomes independent from Britain and Egypt
- 1956–1972 – Civil wars
- 1983 and 2005 – Civil wars
- 2005 – A political agreement allows South Sudan to form an independent state
- 2011 – Africa's newest country is established, but the presence of 60 different ethnic groups makes central government control difficult
- 2013–17 – Civil war again, with over 2 million people displaced by the conflict
- 2017 – Famine declared, affecting over 1 million people in South Sudan

South Sudan – a new African country (2011)

The major European nations agreed Africa's individual country borders – and which European power would control each country – at a conference in Berlin in 1884-5 (see Section 5.5). Sudan was divided into northern and southern territories, based on ethnic characteristics. Britain and Egypt modernised the mainly Arab north, leaving the mainly black African south to tribal communities. Britain's 'divide and rule' policy pitted the Sudanese people against each other, rather than against the colonial ruler. The north prospered more than the south, where 'indirect rule' created hundreds of tribal chiefdoms and the 'different country' there left people feeling marginalised and left out of Sudan's development.

By 2017, nearly four years of civil war had taken its toll on South Sudan, making it one of Africa's longest-running conflicts. In the north of the country, close to the border with Sudan, lies Unity State, which had seen some of the fiercest fighting. Tens of thousands there had been forced to leave their homes after a government offensive against areas held by the opposition. Food supplies had been cut off, and the World Food Programme and other UN agencies declared a major famine affecting over 1 million people.

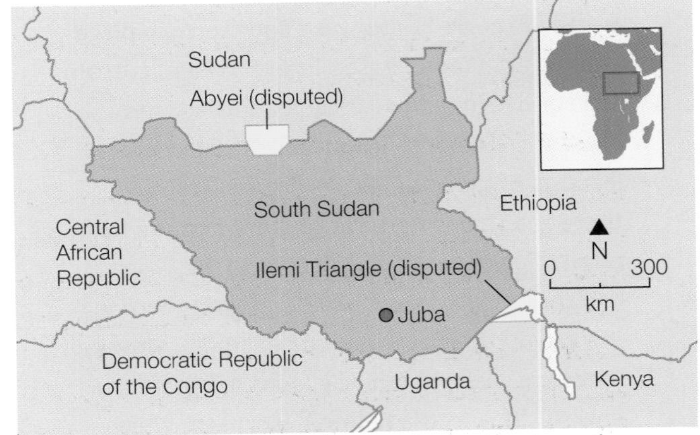

Figure 7 *The newly established country of South Sudan*

Migrations and colonial ties

The years after the Second World War saw a massive increase in labour migration, due to big labour shortages in Western Europe's reviving economies as a result of the US Marshall Plan (see Section 3.3). In 1948, the *British Nationality Act* gave all Commonwealth citizens the right to British citizenship – which meant that they could now legally settle in the United Kingdom. This allowed UK employers to recruit workers from Commonwealth countries, such as India and Jamaica, to fill urgent job vacancies in areas such as transport (e.g. for London's Underground and buses) and the newly founded NHS.

Figure 8 shows the *Empire Windrush* arriving in Britain carrying 490 migrant men (plus two women) from Jamaica and Trinidad, as a symbol of Britain's colonial ties to the Caribbean. These migrants had been educated as though they were British citizens, and they regarded Britain as 'the mother country'. They were usually well qualified and spoke good English, and UK employers actively recruited there.

Figure 8 *In 1948, the* Empire Windrush *brought the first post-war Caribbean migrants to the UK – a turning point in British history*

Changing ethnic composition and cultural heterogeneity

Migrants from India and Pakistan soon followed those from the Caribbean. Again, many were well qualified, including doctors and nurses. Other less-well-qualified migrants were attracted by opportunities in older manufacturing industries, such as textile mills, which were also short of labour in the post-war years. For example, the textile towns of Lancashire and Yorkshire attracted many men from rural Pakistan. As a rule, London and the major conurbations attracted most migrants, because of the wider availability of work and housing.

Migrants from particular countries, or even parts of countries, tend to settle in the same area – due to chain migrations. Examples of this include the Sikh migration to Southall in West London, and the Bangladeshi migrants from Sylhet who settled in the Brick Lane area of Tower Hamlets in East London (see Figure 9).

As the level of international migration increased, a **cultural mosaic** of people from different ethnicities evolved across the country, and the UK's relative homogeneity gave way to a more heterogeneous mix of peoples.

Colonial legacies

British, French, Portuguese and German place names, architecture (see Figure 11) and customs still survive in many African countries, and the former colonial languages often remain as legacies of those times. As Figure 10 shows, there is a strong correlation between the former territories of past colonial rulers (see Figure 3) and the languages still widely spoken there in the twenty-first century. For example, although there are over 40 ethnic groups in Uganda, English remains the national language, which helps with Ugandan trade and development.

Figure 9 *Banglatown – the cultural heritage of generations of Bangladeshi migrants around London's Brick Lane. Pictured are local residents celebrating the Bengali New Year.*

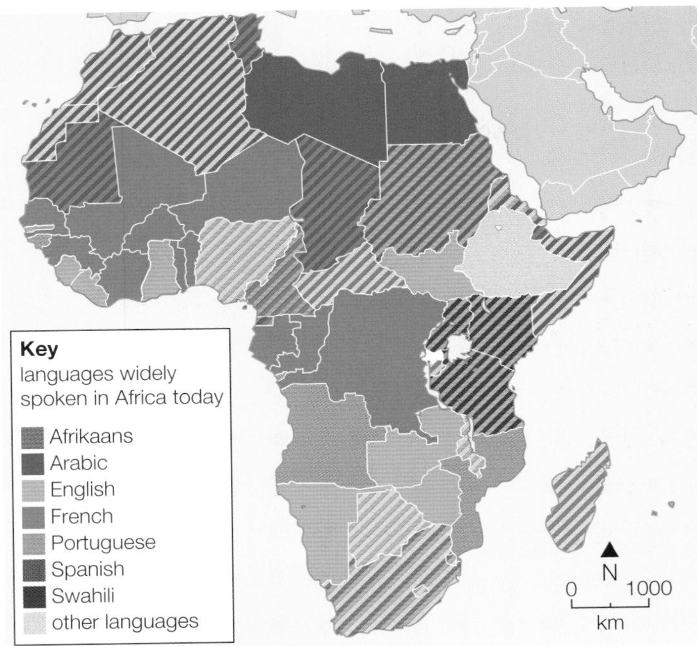

Figure 10 *The colonial legacy of language: several European languages are still widely spoken in former African colonies*

Figure 11 *The colonial legacy of architecture: German-style colonial-era buildings in Luderitz, Namibia (the former colony of German Southwest Africa)*

A very modern world

Now digital languages dominate, and the Internet exists as the most recent example of neo-colonialism. It penetrates wherever there are appropriate connections. Internet activity by users of GoogleChrome is shown by the globe in Figure 12 – each colour represents a different language, and the height of the bar its frequency of use. This image clearly displays English (in blue) as the dominant Internet language, and also shows how disconnected Africa remains, with the entire continent almost completely in darkness. It suggests that the dominance of European languages still lives on in the virtual world.

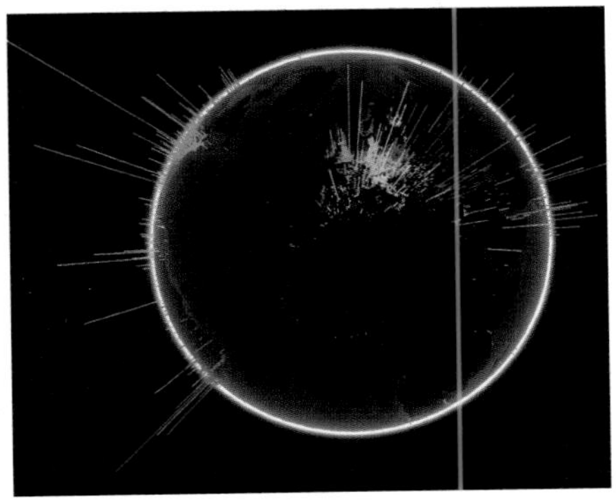

Figure 12 *A digital language use map*

Over to you

1 a Using an atlas, identify physical features of Europe that kept traditional societies from knowing little more than their local region.
  b In pairs, design a mind map to show factors that led to the emergence of different nation states across Europe up to 1920.
  c Produce timelines for any two European countries to show the main events that shaped each nation and its identity.

2 Using Figures 3 and 10 as a basis, research and compare world maps showing (**a**) the distribution of Anglophone (English-speaking), Francophone (French-speaking) and Lusophone (Portuguese-speaking) populations and (**b**) the colonial histories of the UK, France and Portugal to show the relationship between historical background and language use.

3 a Compare the events and problems which led to independence in (**i**) India, (**ii**) Vietnam and (**iii**) South Sudan. Conduct further research if you need to.
  b Explain why conflict emerged in all three cases.

On your own

4 Distinguish between the terms 'nation state', 'nationalism', and 'colonialism'.

5 Explain why 'nationality' is only a recent phenomenon.

6 Draw a table to show the advantages and disadvantages of nationalism, as shown by the examples in this section.

7 Research **one** of India, Vietnam, or South Sudan and produce a six-slide PowerPoint to show colonial influences on the people, environment, economy and culture of the country.

Exam-style question

Evaluate the extent to which nationalism has played a role in the development of the modern world. *(20 marks)*

5.7 Globalisation and the growth of new types of states

In this section, you'll learn how globalisation has led to the deregulation of capital markets and the emergence of new state forms.

New rule – new states

Globalisation has revolutionised global trade, finance and movement of labour. Leading industrialised nations have adopted the **Washington Consensus** – a belief that economic efficiency can only be achieved if regulations are removed. For example, trade liberalisation has lifted many trade regulations, because it is believed that these add time – and therefore cost – to trade.

But globalisation extends more widely than trade. There has also been a reduction in governmental role in in the economy. **Deregulation** became a trend in the 1970s and 80s, with State interference being reduced or removed altogether. National governments used to regulate investment at home and abroad – even restricting how much tourists could take on holiday! However, post-deregulation, capital could be transferred anywhere – freely, cheaply, and (with digital systems) quickly. Globalisation has also led to **privatisation** of government assets in services (e.g. water, transport) or industries (e.g. defence), with ownership often shifting to TNCs and wealthy individuals. Government spending has been reduced, and, as a result, taxation is lower. Several governments have expanded their lack of financial regulation with low income taxes and corporation tax rates, designed to attract wealthy individuals and TNCs to register themselves there. These countries, such as The Cayman Islands, are known as **tax havens**.

KEY CONCEPTS

- **Causality** – the causes of deregulation and its effects on global finance
- **Globalisation** – the impact of the free flow of global capital
- **Identity** – how globalisation affects the identity of places

Figure 1 The small and beautiful Cayman Islands have long been seen as a great place for wealthy individuals and companies to avoid paying taxes

The Cayman Islands

The Cayman Islands (see Figure 1) consist of three neighbouring Caribbean islands with a combined population of just 56 000 – but including within it 100 different nationalities! Settled by the British in the 1730s, they became a Crown Colony in 1962 and are now among the world's most successful financial centres, with over 100 000 registered companies. Financial services now generate 55% of the islands' GDP and employ 36% of the population. In 2015, the average GDP per capita there was US$58 800, which is the world's fourteenth highest.

The Cayman Islands are among the world's largest **offshore** financial centres, which means that they are only permitted to work with businesses resident outside their territory. Forty of the world's top investment banks and insurance companies are licensed there, and, in 2014, the tiny Cayman Islands held US$1.5 trillion in assets! One of the main reasons for the Cayman Islands being such a financial honey pot is their 0% personal income tax rate (see Figure 2) and low corporation taxes, which makes them irresistible for individuals and companies seeking to pay low or no tax.

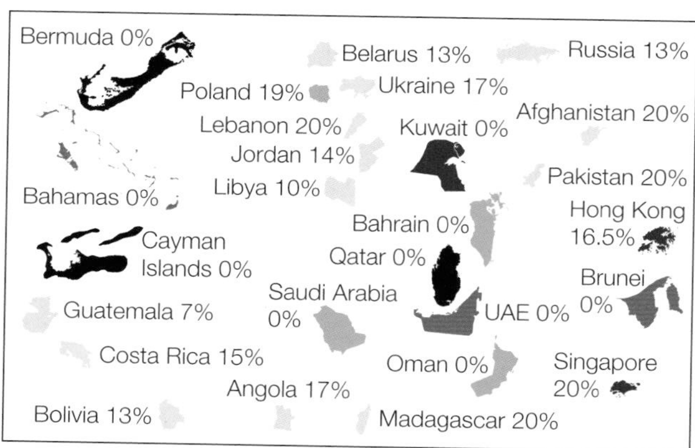

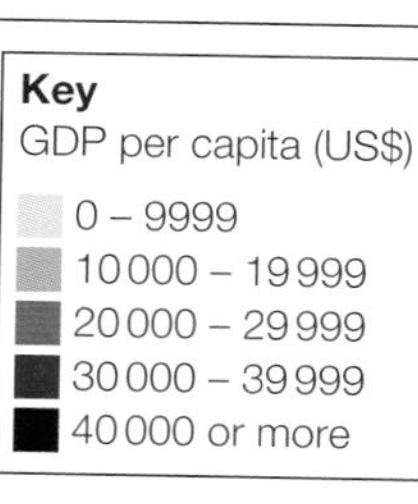

Figure 2 Global tax havens, shaded according to their GDP per capita in US$. Each country has also been sized, not according to its actual physical size, but according to the size of its personal income tax rate – so Russia (with a 13% income tax rate) is shown smaller than The Cayman Islands (with a 0% income tax rate).

What's wrong with avoiding tax?

The Cayman Islands, like other tax havens, offer huge tax advantages to both companies and the super-rich, who stand to gain most by paying low or no taxation on their profits or income. Many of the countries in Figure 2 offer political stability, as well as secure banking and legal systems – and they do not break any rules. However, several do not, and are associated with political and economic instability and corruption. Major TNCs and wealthy **expatriates** (those who live in a country in which they are not citizens) 'rest their cash' in the safer ones. However, doing so is controversial; some argue that companies and individuals are avoiding paying taxes in the very countries that enabled them to earn their wealth in the first place.

Figure 3 suggests that tax havens help companies to avoid paying taxes where they would otherwise be due – in this case, the USA. In 2015, investment bank J.P. Morgan reported that American companies were holding over US$2 trillion in cash overseas. Apple, the leading company in Figure 3, held nearly US$158 billion – or 89% of its total cash – abroad. By doing so, it avoided paying 35% in corporate taxes that would otherwise be due in the countries where its profits were actually being made.

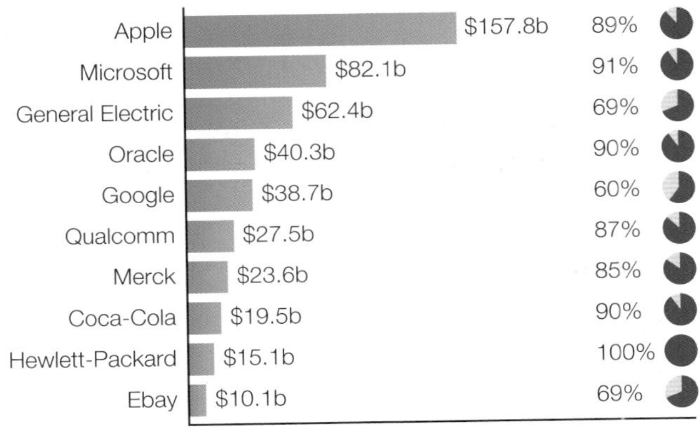

Figure 3 *The percentage of their total wealth held abroad by top US companies in March 2015*

Attitudes towards tax havens

Most governments and IGOs, such as the World Bank, accept the growth of tax havens. National governments seek investment from TNCs to generate employment and wealth, and they have the freedom to set their own tax rates. However, the viewpoints expressed in Figure 4 suggest that this is controversial. Many NGOs have raised objections, and, in 2015, the EU declared that the ability of TNCs to move revenues earned throughout the EU to low-tax member states like Ireland was unfair.

1 Ireland – accused of giving tax breaks

Ireland has been criticised by the EU and the USA for its friendly treatment of TNCs such as Apple, Google, Facebook and Microsoft. Irish corporate tax rates are among the world's lowest at 12.5%.

Adapted from the *New York Times*, October 2015

2 NGOs reveal extensive use of tax havens by French banks

The five French national banks have 16 branches in The Cayman Islands. In 2014, they declared profits of €45 million, without having a single employee there! A discrepancy between their profits and economic activity, points to an abusive use of tax havens to avoid tax. Low-tax havens represent only 25% of their activity, 20% of their taxes and 16% of their employees.

Adapted from Manon Aubry, Head of Tax Justice Advocacy for Oxfam France

3 The UK – ending an era of tax havens

The UK controls about a third of the world's tax havens; the Queen is on the banknotes of countries like The British Virgin Islands, The Cayman Islands and Bermuda. But these are places where billions of dollars are hidden, and the UK has effective control over them. TNCs should publish where they pay their taxes on a country-by-country basis, showing how developing countries are being deprived of tax revenue by tax dodging.

Adapted from Max Lawson, Head of Inequality Policy at Oxfam

Figure 4 *Three viewpoints about tax havens*

Growing inequalities

It's easy to explain why The Cayman Islands attract expatriates – perfect beaches, turquoise seas – but it comes at a cost. Social tensions have increased as incomers outnumber the domestic population and live different lives. There is both a cultural and a generational gap as the islands begin to resemble Florida rather than the Caribbean, changing their identity.

Despite increased wealth since the 1980s, global income growth has not been evenly distributed. Figure 5 shows percentiles of income growth between 1988 and 2008. This graph has also been referred to as 'the elephant graph' because of its shape. Most growth occurred in China as it became the world's workshop, while at the same time outsourcing and offshoring reduced employment and incomes in the USA and Europe. The top 1% – the '**global elite**' in Figure 5 – have gained hugely.

Geographers such as Danny Dorling argue that economic and social stability are threatened by increasing inequality. Dorling claims that inequality is 'more than economics, it is the culture that divides and makes social mobility impossible'. Every step down from the richest to the poorest means reduced life expectancy, education and work prospects, as well as increased mental health problems. It's not surprising that some countries opt for different pathways, as explained below.

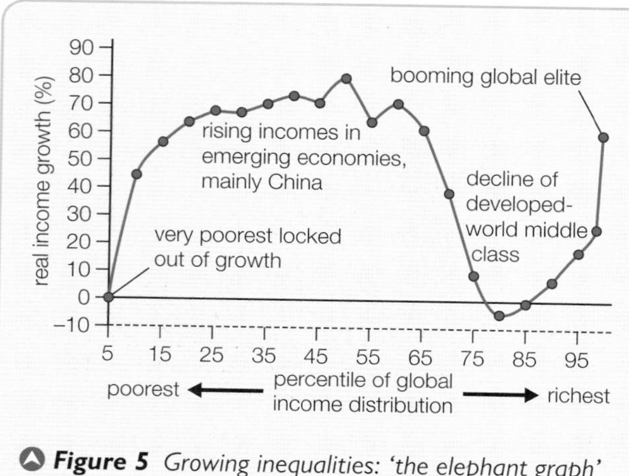

Figure 5 *Growing inequalities: 'the elephant graph'*

> ... the era of globalisation seemed to offer little for people in-between: households in the 75th to 85th percentile of income distribution (who were poorer than the top 15% but richer than everyone else) seemed scarcely better off in 2008 than in 1988. They constituted a decile of discontent, squeezed between their own countries' plutocrats and Asia's middle class. This dramatic dip in the chart seemed to explain a lot. Cue Donald Trump. Cue nationalism. Cue Brexit ...

Adapted from *The Economist*, September 2016

Alternative pathways

Not all countries support the processes of globalisation. In Latin America, in 2010, several governments moved from open-market principles to the left, in order to pursue social justice. As Figure 6 shows, by 2010, eight South American and four Central American countries (five if Honduras is included) had elected left-wing governments. Most have been re-elected since then: although Venezuela, Argentina and Guatemala have elected right-wing governments since 2015, centre-left governments have lasted in Uruguay, Nicaragua, Bolivia and Ecuador, and centre-right governments in Mexico and Honduras lost ground to the left by 2016.

Figure 6 *Latin America turns to the left and towards social justice*

Bolivia

Once referred to as an 'economic basket case', Bolivia is now among the world's fastest growing economies. President Evo Morales was elected in 2006 to turn against neo-liberalism and embark on a programme to undo 20 years' of privatisation and the influence of the IMF. Morales' view was that privatisation had simply resulted in big profits for TNCs, which had then leaked out of the country.

Bolivia established its National Coalition for Change (CONALCAM) in 2007. Its policies:

- nationalised resources (e.g. oil) – with the profits going to the government rather than private shareholders
- reduced primary exports and used these to boost domestic manufacturing of previously imported products (known as **import substitution**)
- redistributed wealth to the *campesino* (peasant classes), by guaranteeing prices for food products.

This economic strategy depended on nationalising Bolivia's oil and gas industries. TNCs had previously claimed 82% of their value – Morales' government took 80%. The State was now the largest player in the economy, with the result that Bolivians began benefiting from:

- increased gas connections (by 835%), electricity (by 150%) and telecommunications (by 300%)
- improved health care, education enrolment, pensions and incomes
- reduced wealth inequalities (see Figure 7) and lower government debt.

The demand for domestically manufactured goods drove sustained annual growth of over 5% between 2006 and 2012. Morales was re-elected in 2014 with over 60% of the vote. There was – and remains – some opposition, but the Morales government claims to 'govern by obeying the people rather than the global economy'.

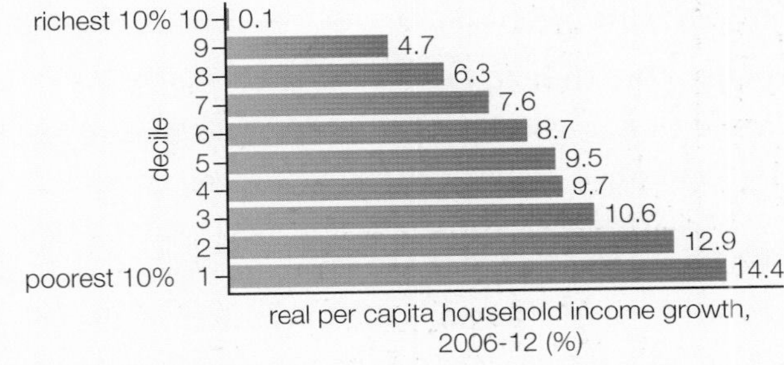

Figure 7 *Bolivia under Morales begins to close its wealth gap*

Over to you

1 In pairs, draw a spider diagram that outlines the links between the Washington Consensus, the deregulation of trade and finance, and low taxation.

2 In pairs, outline the arguments for and against the existence of tax havens. Use the arguments put forward by the following parties to help develop your thinking: (**a**) financial institutions, (**b**) TNCs, (**c**) national governments, (**d**) IGOs, and (**e**) NGOs. Carry out further research to help you if needed.

3 Why should companies such as Apple seek to pay as little tax as possible?

4 **a** Use Section 6.3 (the Gini coefficient) to help you (**i**) describe and (**ii**) explain the income/wealth proportions for deciles of the population in Figure 7.

b Using Figure 7, explain the evidence which suggests that Bolivia managed to reduce income inequalities between 2006 and 2012.

On your own

5 Distinguish between the following pairs of terms: (**a**) Washington Consensus and deregulation, (**b**) offshore finance and tax haven, (**c**) expatriates and the global elite.

6 Research **one** company shown in Figure 3 and the means by which its supposed tax avoidance has taken place.

7 Write a 750-word report entitled: 'Tax havens – the good or bad side of globalisation?'

Exam-style question

Explain how global inequalities may be seen as a threat to the global economic system. *(8 marks)*

5.8 The role and importance of the United Nations

In this section, you'll learn how global organisations have had an important role since the end of the Second World War in 1945.

EQ3 Sections 5.8 to 5.10 will investigate the impacts of global organisations in managing global issues and conflicts.

From League of Nations to United Nations

War is horrifying, and a world war even more so. Each of the two world wars brought out the worst in humans – from the poison gas of the First World War to the Holocaust of the Second. However, these two conflicts did help to create a widespread belief among many nations of the world that war must be avoided whenever possible.

In 1919, after the First World War ended, the League of Nations was established as an American initiative, in an attempt to ensure future global peace. It aimed to give a voice to independent nations, rather than powerful empires, and to open up discussion about conflicts rather than indulge in secret diplomacy. By 1920 it had 48 members. However, the League was unable to challenge the expansionism of either Imperial Japan or Hitler's Germany in the 1930s, and it drifted into relative insignificance in the run up to the outbreak of the Second World War in 1939.

The UN – the first IGO

US President Roosevelt introduced the term 'United Nations' during the Second World War, when, in 1942, 26 nations agreed to work as allies against the Axis powers (see Figure 1). The UN's aims, structure and roles were agreed by the USA, UK, USSR and China in 1944. As allies, they agreed to establish an international organisation – similar to, but more effective than, the League of Nations – that would aim to maintain global peace and security after the end of the Second World War. In October 1945, the UN became the world's first true Inter-Governmental Organisation (IGO), with 50 members. The USA, UK, USSR, China and France became the five permanent members of its Security Council.

KEY CONCEPT

- **Interdependence** – the ways in which global peace and advancement rely on interdependence between countries

Figure 1 *In 1942, 26 nations signed the UN Declaration of Intent in Washington D.C. Each was 'to employ its full resources, military or economic' in 'the struggle for victory over Hitlerism'.*

The role of the UN

The first UN General Assembly met in London in 1946, with a focus on developing the peaceful uses of atomic energy, as well as eliminating weapons of mass destruction. Seven decades later, the UN's work has evolved into a range of functions to help manage global environmental, socio-economic and political issues. For example:

- **maintaining international peace and security** (see Figure 2).
- **promoting sustainable development**, e.g. the 2015 Sustainable Development Goals, the Intergovernmental Panel on Climate Change, gender equality.
- **protecting human rights**, e.g. the International Bill of Human Rights.
- **upholding international law** on trade, the Law of the Sea, justice and information.
- **delivering humanitarian aid**, e.g. to refugees from conflict, the sick from epidemics like ebola, and victims of natural disasters like famine, drought and earthquakes.

Figure 3 lists a number of different UN sub-organisations, such as the WHO and UNICEF, which have been established to deliver these specific roles.

Figure 2 *The UN at work – UN peacekeepers patrolling the disputed Golan Heights on the Israel-Syria border. Israel captured this area from Syria during the Six Day War of 1967, and the Golan Heights have been disputed between the two countries ever since.*

Figure 3 *Defining the role of the UN through its work and the UN sub-organisations that carry it out*

1946 Children's Fund established (UNICEF)
1948 Palestine peacekeeping – UN Truce Supervision Organization (UNTSO)
1948 Universal Declaration of Human Rights (UN)
1956 Suez Canal Crisis – UN Emergency Force (UNEF)
1966 UN Development Programme (UNDP) created
1968 Non-proliferation of nuclear weapons treaty (UN)
1969 The International Convention on the Elimination of Racial Discrimination (ICERD)
1972 Environment conference (UNEP)
1974 Food Conference to eradicate hunger and malnutrition (FAO)
1975 World conference on Women (UN Women)
1982 The Law of the Sea established by the UN Conference on Trade and Development (UNCTAD)
1987 The Montreal Protocol to protect the ozone layer (UNEP)
1992, **2002**, **2012**, **2015** Earth Summits: Rio de Janeiro – Agenda 21 / Sustainable Development
2000 UN Millennium Development Goals (MDGs) are set by the UN Conference on Environment and Development (UNCED)
2014 Emergency Health Mission on the Ebola Crisis (WHO)
2014-onwards The Refugee Crisis stretches UN efforts to support refugees (all organisations)

Personal influences and national disputes

The UN's role in global governance is influenced by the vision of the UN Secretary General:

- In 1974, Secretary General Kurt Waldheim placed hunger on the UN agenda, and he also introduced the Year of Women in 1975.
- After 1992, Secretary General Boutros Boutros-Ghali introduced an agenda for sustainable development.
- In 1996, Secretary General Kofi Annan incorporated UN programmes on gender, health, HIV/AIDs and peacekeeping, and he also established the Millennium Development Goals in 2000.
- In 2006, Secretary General Ban Ki-Moon made climate change a UN priority.

Sometimes national disputes can spill over into UN policy making. For example, the Syrian Conflict has raised ideological differences between the geopolitical visions of two permanent members of the Security Council, with Russia supporting President Assad and the USA backing rebel groups. This kind of ideological conflict was common during the Cold War (see Section 3.3), but it still challenges the UN's key role as peacekeeper.

Using sanctions

Defending human rights is a central pillar of the UN. The Security Council meets to respond to threats, e.g. armed conflict. Sometimes that involves introducing **economic sanctions** against countries where human suffering is prevalent, or even using **direct military intervention** to protect people from conflict or persecution.

A range of possible sanctions exists, which vary according to the country involved and the specific situation being faced. They include:

- **arms embargos** – banning weapons and military supplies
- **trade embargos** – banning specific import items to the country involved (e.g. modern technology), or the purchase of exports from the country
- **restrictions on loans** for development projects
- **freezing assets** (e.g. bank accounts) of specific people or companies
- **travel restrictions** for specific people such as politicians or businesspeople.

Each of the above economic and arms sanctions was applied briefly against Ivory Coast and Liberia in 2015, as a result of suspected war crimes there. Figure 4 shows those countries targeted by UN sanctions at different times. The two examples of Iran and Bosnia on the following page show the variable success of UN actions.

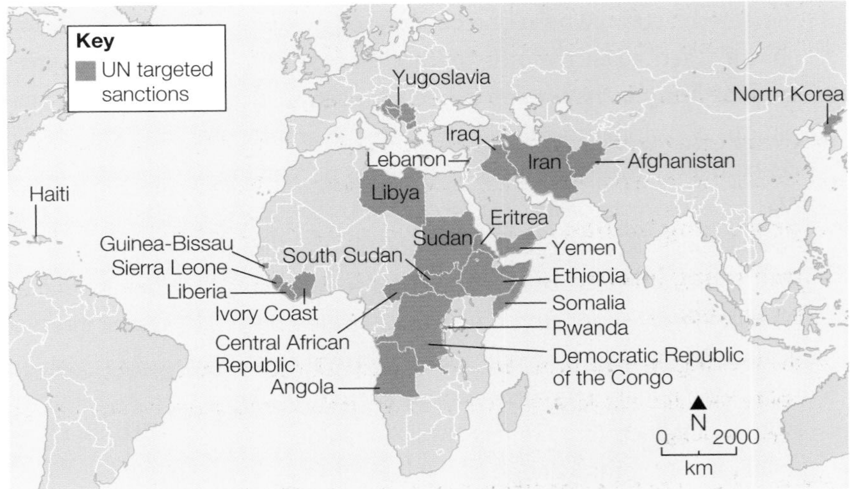

Figure 4 *Those countries affected by UN targeted sanctions at different times*

1 Iran – economic sanctions

A suspicion that Iran – considered by some a 'rogue state' – was attempting to build nuclear weapons, led to the imposition of economic sanctions and financial restrictions by the UN. At the time, Iran was the world's fourth largest oil-exporting country, and influenced global oil prices through OPEC. Figure 5 shows the impact on Iranian oil exports of the trade embargo. Although the UN was shown as willing to act, Iran's annual GDP fell by just 5%.

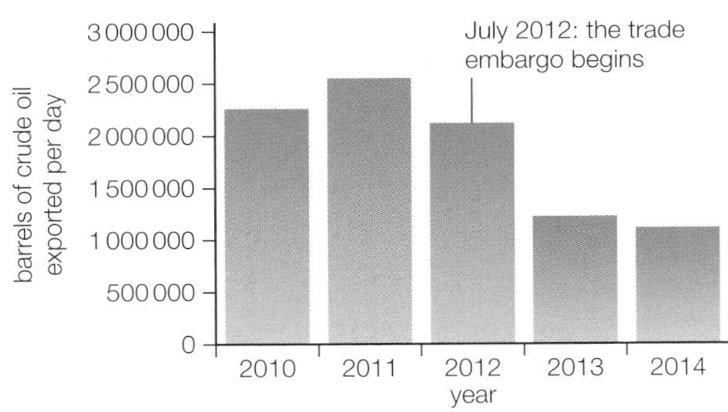

Figure 5 *Iran's crude oil exports between 2010 and 2014, which show the effect of the trade embargo that began in the middle of 2012*

2 Bosnia – direct military involvement

Bosnia is a former part of Yugoslavia (see Figure 4). In 1993, the UN was provoked into action following allegations of **ethnic cleansing** by Bosnian Serb forces against Bosnian Muslims. To protect Bosnian Muslims, the UN designated a safe zone in Srebrenica, a small town in north-eastern Bosnia, protected by a small force of Dutch UN peacekeepers. However, the town was soon put under siege by Bosnian Serb forces. Supplies of food ran low, and many Muslims died of starvation. In 1995, Bosnian Serb forces captured Srebrenica; massacring 8000 Muslim men and boys, and deporting 23 000 women and children, many of whom suffered rape. Dutch peacekeepers were hopelessly outnumbered; several were taken hostage by Bosnian Serbs and threatened with execution if the Dutch interfered. UN Secretary General Kofi Annan described the massacre as a tragedy that would haunt the UN forever.

Figure 6 *Srebrenica, in Bosnia, on 14 July 2014, the anniversary of the massacre there in 1995 of up to 8000 Bosnian Muslim men and boys by Bosnian Serb forces*

Taking unilateral action – the USA

Sometimes UN members take part in **unilateral** (one-sided) action, where one country, or group of countries, acts against another without formal UN approval. This can have deep impacts on geopolitical relations and global stability. An extreme example occurred after the 9/11 attack in 2001. As part of the 'War on terror', a coalition of forces led by the USA, and including UK, Australia and Poland, invaded Iraq in 2003 and deposed Saddam Hussein's government. The UN initially supported the invasion, based on evidence of the existence of Iraqi weapons of mass destruction, which was subsequently proved wrong. In 2004, UN Secretary General Kofi Annan declared the invasion in contravention of the UN charter.

Proposed unilateral action – the UK

In 2013, the UK government sought a resolution of the UN Security Council to condemn the use of chemical weapons by Syrian government forces. This required the backing of the five permanent members – China, Russia, the UK, USA and France. China and Russia have historically vetoed action against Syria, and the vote was unlikely to pass. The UK government argued that it had a legal basis for humanitarian intervention to relieve suffering by deterring further use of chemical weapons. In the event, the UK Parliament voted against intervention in Syria.

Key word

Ethnic cleansing – The deliberate removal, by killing or forced migration, of one ethnic group by another.

Unilateral action against Russia

In 2014 Russian-backed forces seized control of the Crimea region of Ukraine (see Section 5.5), attempting to regain political influence over the country. In protest, during 2014, the EU, USA, Australia, Canada and Norway all imposed sanctions on 23 leading Russian politicians – their overseas financial assets were frozen, and they were also prevented from travelling to those five areas. The USA also led moves towards **sectoral sanctions**, i.e. targeting key areas of the Russian economy (energy, banking, finance, defence and technology) for further sanctions.

The UN General Assembly met in 2014, but not all UN members agreed to act further. 100 member states supported a UN commitment to the 'territorial integrity of Ukraine', but took no action when Russia used its veto. Sanctions were strengthened, but EU member states were reluctant to go too far because of their dependency on Russian gas and oil supplies.

The impacts were substantial – up to a point. US$70-90 billion left Russia as wealthy Russian investors sought secure overseas banks. Russia's currency was also devalued and its international credit rating reduced. But, as often happens with economic sanctions, Russia retaliated, banning imported food from the EU and USA (see Figure 7). The results of these tit-for-tat sanctions included that:

- Russia became less dependent on oil and gas exports, and instead increased the diversification of its economy
- Russian farmers gained larger home markets, because of the restrictions on imported food
- the EU kept importing Russian energy supplies, despite the sanctions
- food exports from the EU and USA were hit; Dutch tomato and cucumber sales to Russia fell by 80%, and Czech and Greek fruit sales to Russia fell by 70% and 50% respectively.

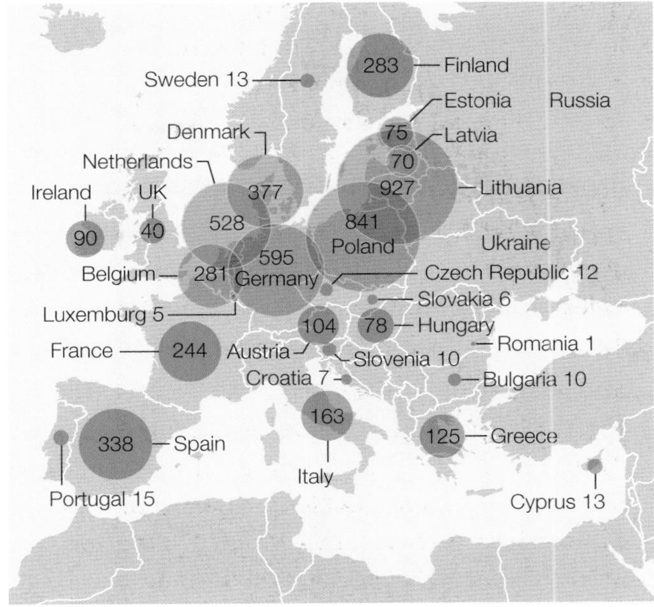

Figure 7 *The lost value of EU food exports to Russia, after Russia introduced a ban on imported EU food in retaliation for EU sanctions in 2014. The individual losses for each country are in million euros; the total value of lost EU food exports to Russia was 5.25 billion euros.*

Over to you

1 In pairs, consider the range of UN activities in Figure 3. Draw a spider diagram to show how each of these activities contributes to achieving world peace.

2 Assess the role played by the UN in each of the examples from this section. Copy and complete the following table:

Example	Social Impacts +/−	Economic Impacts +/−	Political Impacts +/-
Iran			
Bosnia			
Crimea			

3 In pairs, research the work of one social or environmental organisation, e.g. UNICEF. Prepare a six-slide presentation outlining (**a**) its aims and core work, (**b**) where it focuses its efforts in the world, (**c**) examples of its successful work.

4 Search the phrase 'how the UN is financed', and outline some of the funding problems faced by the UN.

On your own

5 Distinguish between the following pairs of terms: (**a**) economic and sectoral sanctions, (**b**) civil war and ethnic cleansing.

6 Draw up a table to explain the arguments for and against economic sanctions by UN members against 'rogue states' or those taking unilateral action.

7 Prepare a 400-word statement for a class debate on the motion 'Despite its weaknesses, the UN is an organisation worth supporting'.

Exam-style question

Evaluate the importance and achievements of one global organisation in the post-1945 world. (*20 marks*)

5.9 The role of IGOs in trade and finance

In this section, you'll learn how IGOs established after the Second World War have since controlled world trade rules and financial flows

KEY CONCEPT

- **Globalisation** – the spread of a global capitalist ideology

International financial organisations

Pennsylvania Avenue, Washington DC, is the address of two of the world's most influential global organisations – the **World Bank** and the **International Monetary Fund** – whose headquarters are shown in Figure 1. Both organisations were established in 1944 at Bretton Woods in the USA, with the aim of stabilising global finances after the Great Depression of the 1930s and the massive costs of the Second World War, which was then drawing to an end.

The philosophy behind each organisation is the **Washington Consensus** (see Section 5.7), which is an ideology about the 'Western way' of organising capitalism. With their headquarters in Washington, and the USA as their largest financial contributor, America remains firmly in the driving seat of global finance. A third body – the **World Trade Organisation**, headquartered in Geneva – is part of the same family of organisations. (You should also read Section 3.5, which explains these three organisations, their roles and how each one works in more detail.)

BACKGROUND

Know your financial IGOs!

- The main purpose of the **IMF** is to ensure global financial stability. Banks and governments (e.g. the US Federal Reserve) in member states pay into a fund, which is then loaned out to help stabilise national currencies.
- Funded in the same way as the IMF, the main purpose of the **World Bank** is to finance global development.
- The main purpose of the **WTO** is to promote global trade by reducing barriers such as tariffs and duties.

Figure 1 *The headquarters of the World Bank (**A**) and IMF (**B**) in Washington DC*

The impacts of the IMF and World Bank

Between them, these IGOs promote **neo-liberalism** as an ideology to deliver economic growth, and some argue, to protect the hegemony of the USA. Broadly, their objectives have been as follows:

- In the 1950s, to support post-war reconstruction among *developed* countries.
- In the 1970s and '80s, to loan money for large development projects in *developing* countries.

However, global interest rates rocketed in the 1980s, making loan repayments unaffordable for many developing countries. Unpaid interest was then added to the remaining loan amounts, increasing the overall debt level so that, by 2000, many developing countries owed more than their original loans. The IMF and World Bank said that helping those countries in difficulty would only occur if they agreed to conditions known as **Structural Adjustment** (see opposite).

Structural Adjustment

If a country defaults on (i.e. cannot repay) its loans, the global banking system is at risk. In the 1980s and '90s, the IMF reorganised many countries' loans to more affordable levels. However, to qualify for this financial adjustment, the countries were told to 'earn more and spend less' – export more goods to earn capital to repay loans, and reduce government spending. These policies were known as **Structural Adjustment Programmes (SAPs)**.

SAPs also required the debtor nations to accept other conditions, without which they would get no further credit. These conditions included:

- **opening up domestic markets** – allowing private companies to develop resources for export
- **reducing the role of the government** – e.g. privatising State industries
- **removing restrictions on capital** – no limits on international investments, or on what foreign companies can own
- **reducing government spending** – cuts to infrastructure projects and welfare
- **devaluing the currency** – to make exports cheaper.

Critics argue that, as a result of the above conditions, many countries sacrificed their **economic sovereignty** as they liberalised their economies – becoming 'trans-nationalised' as TNCs took over privatised services, and increasing their dependency on trade.

The Highly Indebted Poor Countries initiative

In 1996, the IMF and World Bank introduced the **Highly Indebted Poor Countries initiative (HIPC)**, which aimed to reduce national debts by partially writing them off – in return for SAPs. The HIPC initiative affected 36 of the world's least developed countries with the greatest debts, 30 of which were in sub-Saharan Africa.

However, by 2000 – aware of the many problems being created by SAPs – NGOs such as Oxfam and Christian Aid were demanding more concerted action to reduce the debt burden, and they began campaigning for a total debt write-off. In 2005, when the UK held the presidency of the G8 (see Section 3.2), Chancellor Gordon Brown steered the G8 towards the decision to cancel all debts owed to the World Bank and IMF by 18 HIPC – a decision worth US$40 billion, which saved those countries US$1.5 billion a year in debt repayments. However, there were conditions:

- Each country had to show good financial management and a lack of corruption.
- The national governments had to spend the savings gained through the cancelled debt repayments on poverty reduction, education and healthcare programmes.

Figure 2 shows those countries that still qualified for HIPC initiative assistance by March 2016.

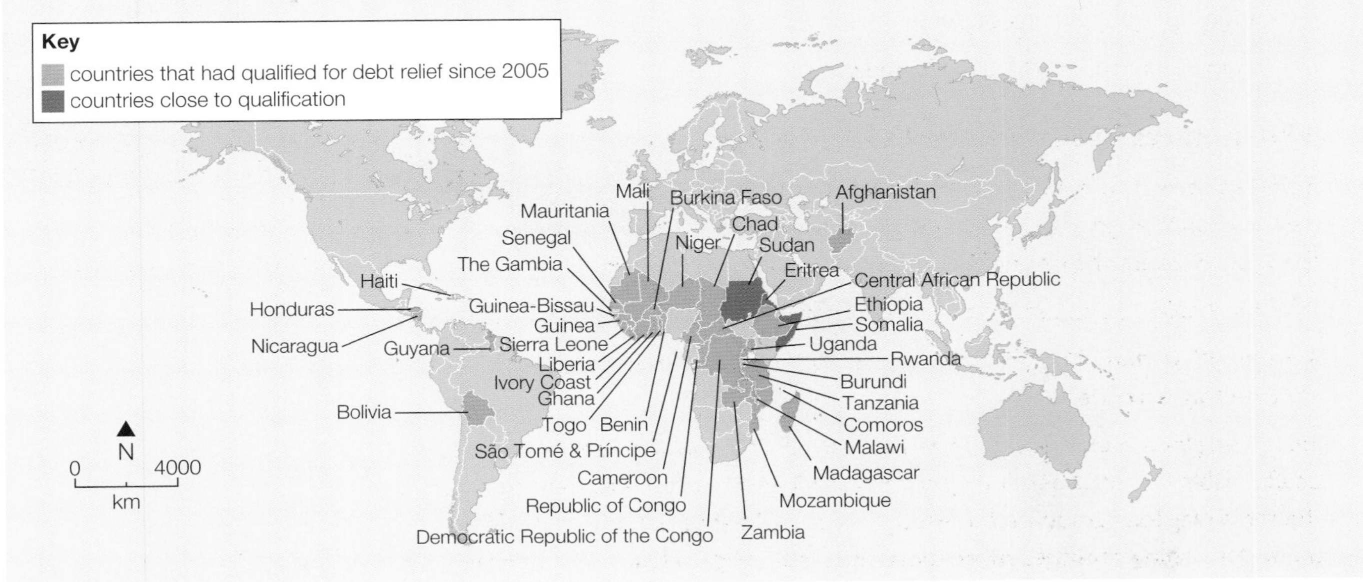

Figure 2 *Those countries that still qualified for, or almost qualified for, HIPC initiative assistance by March 2016*

Uganda and debt

In 1992, Uganda's debts totalled US$1.9 billion. Like many low-income countries, it was unable to repay these. However, in 2000, it was among the first countries to benefit from debt write-offs by the IMF and World Bank through the HIPC initiative. The impacts were immediate:

- Government spending rose by 20% (with 40% more spent on education and 70% more on healthcare).
- Free primary schooling was introduced, which meant that 5 million extra children now attended school.
- Before debt relief, the school enrolment rate was 62%. By 2015, it was 93%.
- Before debt relief, 20% more boys than girls went to school. By 2015, the difference was 2%.

Figure 3 shows other impacts. For example, the impact on Uganda's GDP has been substantial, now that more money is used for investment instead of repaying debts.

	Before debt cancellation	During or immediately after debt cancellation	10–15 years after debt cancellation
GDP (US$)	US$4.3 billion (1990)	US$7.9 billion	US$27.5 billion (2015)
% of people using an improved water source	44 (1990)	60 (2004)	79 (2015)
% of total population undernourished	24 (1990–92)	19 (2002–04)	25.5 (2015)
% of GDP spent on education	1.5 (1991)	5.2 (2002–05)	2.2 (2013)
% literacy rate for those aged 15 and above	56.1 (1985–95 average)	66.8 (1995–2005 average)	78.4 (2015)
% of income from exports spent on debt repayments (debt service ratio)	81.4 (1990)	9.2 (2005)	1.8 (2016)

Figure 3 *The impacts of debt relief on Uganda*

Debt versus prosperity?

At the same time as the introduction of SAPs, the deregulation of financial markets in the 1980s exposed developing countries to free-market capitalism. The easier transfer of capital and services enabled a global shift in manufacturing. TNCs took advantage of relocation and out-sourcing opportunities in Asia, where economic growth was and remains rapid (see Figure 4). Also, just as Uganda's GDP in Figure 3 has shown a rapid growth since its debts were written off, Figure 4 also shows that some of the world's fastest economic growth in the twenty-first century is now occurring in sub-Saharan Africa, particularly East Africa.

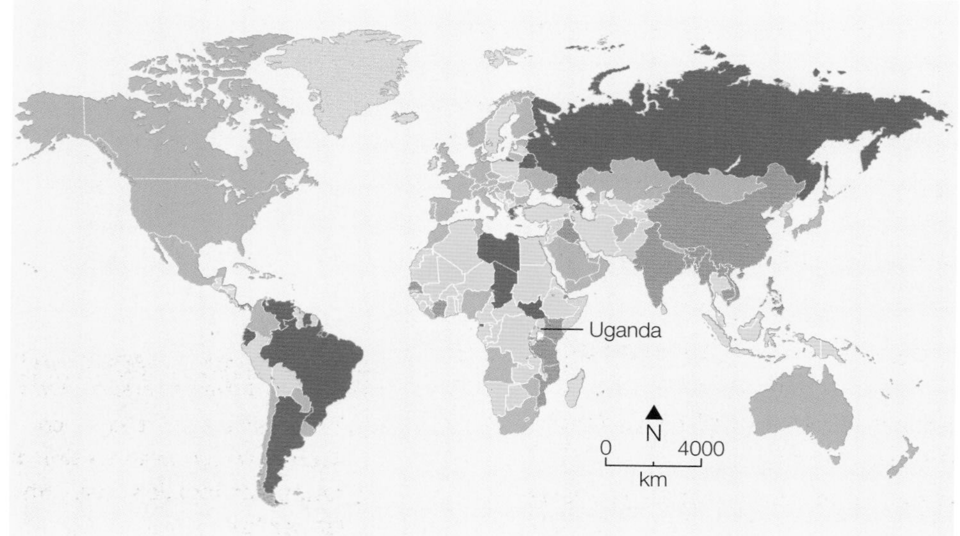

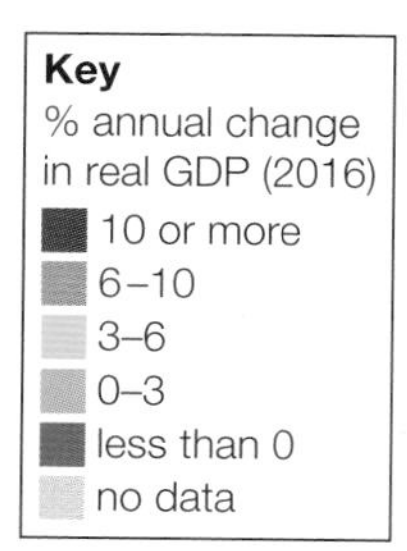

Figure 4 *Economic growth rates around the world in 2016*

Global and regional trade

Membership of the major global trade and financial IGOs is almost universal. WTO members accounted for 96.4% of world trade in 2015 – and 96.7% of global GDP! Over 90% of the world's population are now governed by WTO rules – only 13 members of the UN are not part of this group. Being a member of global organisations provides access to the world marketplace, and a route to economic development through trade.

However, regional trading blocs have also emerged where groups of neighbouring countries now work together on economic decisions – almost as if they are one large country. Regional groups of nations that operate without cross-border taxation (e.g. the USA, Canada and Mexico under the North American Free Trade Agreement), and which permit freedom of movement of goods, services and people (e.g. the EU), are referred to as **single markets**. Such links can extend further – for example, the EU now has its own currency (the euro) for those members who choose it. Some see eventual political union as an ultimate goal of this process, as outlined in Figure 5.

Free trade area
- No internal trade barriers.
- Individual members retain their own currencies and economic policies.

Customs union
- No internal trade barriers.
- Common external tariffs.

Single market
- No internal trade barriers.
- Common external tariffs and free movement of labour.
- A common currency?

Political union
- Total unity – individual nations fuse as one; national boundaries disappear.
- Total freedom of movement of goods, services, labour and capital.
- Common economic and defence policies.

Figure 5 *The development of trading blocs: the progression from a free trade area to possible political union*

Trading blocs – towards political union?

Whether the individual countries in a trading bloc can ever fuse completely and act as one nation probably depends on the internal political will in the member states. **Centripetal** forces, such as the harmonisation of economic policies and even a common currency, draw member states together. But this requires trust and economic consistency at levels not seen before. Sharing laws and ideology (and also language) takes time, and some members may not want union – as the UK's vote to leave the EU demonstrates. Some splintering may also be inevitable, as nationalist forces create **centrifugal** forces that drive organisations or countries apart. The UK has always welcomed the economic benefits of the EU single market, which provides access to 500 million people – but many also worried about diluted UK sovereignty.

Over to you

1 In pairs, discuss and list the factors that have placed the USA in the 'driving seat' of the global economy.

2 Discuss and draw a spider diagram to identify all the features that would show how the 'Washington Consensus' works.

3 In pairs, discuss the extent to which the IMF, World Bank and WTO together lead to an erosion of national economic sovereignty.

4 Draw a table to suggest the benefits and problems caused by (**a**) SAPs, (**b**) the HIPC initiative.

5 Debate the motion that 'the EU should move closer towards political union'.

On your own

6 a Use Section 3.5 to distinguish between the roles of the IMF, World Bank and WTO.

b Distinguish between (**i**) 'Structural Adjustment' and 'HIPC initiative', (**ii**) 'neo-liberalism' and 'Washington Consensus'.

7 Explain how the HIPC initiative might have contributed to the changes in Uganda shown in Figure 3.

Exam-style question

Evaluate the extent to which IGOs may lead to an erosion of national economic sovereignty. *(20 marks)*

5.10 The role of IGOs in managing global environmental problems

In this section, you'll learn how IGOs have been formed to manage global environmental problems – with varying success.

Managing threats to the biosphere

As ecosystems go, few are as important as wetlands. Figure 1 emphasises their beauty too. In 2016, the United Nations Environment Programme (UNEP) stated that wetlands were among the most diverse and productive ecosystems on the planet, yet also among the most threatened by urbanisation and economic development. Tidal marshes, swamps and mangroves are threatened by both direct human activity and also sea level change.

UNEP exists to promote sustainable development and manage the Earth's atmosphere and biosphere. In 2016, it estimated that globally 'over the last 100 years, wetlands have declined by 70%, leaving millions deprived of essential ecosystem services'. In the same year, UNEP's leaders committed to stopping this rapid wetland loss.

Early attempts to conserve and promote the sustainable use of wetlands came in 1971, with the **Ramsar Convention**, an international treaty. Globally, over 2200 Ramsar sites are now managed by national governments, international NGOs (e.g. WWF), and local bodies like Natural England. Although successful elsewhere in the world, wetlands are in significant decline in the UK.

Managing threats to the atmosphere – the Montreal Protocol

The build-up of ozone-depleting substances (ODSs) – chlorofluorocarbons (CFCs), halons, carbon tetrachloride, and methyl chloroform – in the atmosphere increases the amount of harmful UV radiation reaching the Earth's surface from the sun. This UV radiation damages human health (e.g. causing skin cancers), as well as damaging ecosystems, bio-geochemical cycles and air quality. CFCs have already damaged the ozone layer sufficiently to cause the large 'hole' over Antarctica shown in Figure 2B opposite.

To address atmospheric deterioration, the Montreal Protocol on Substances that Deplete the Ozone Layer was signed in 1987. It was a landmark agreement, which stipulated that both the production and consumption of ODSs must be phased out by 2000. By 2009, it was the first global treaty to reach 197 signatories and to have achieved global ratification; by 2010, virtually all countries had phased out ODSs.

KEY CONCEPT

- **Sustainability** – sustainable methods of managing global environmental problems

Figure 1 A photo from the UNEP's Multilateral Environmental Agreements publication on Wetlands in 2016

The Montreal Protocol was successful because:

- there was a definable cause-and-effect relationship
- there was little disputing of the evidence
- funding assistance was given to developing nations
- substitutes for CFCs were already available
- global risks were considered immediate and widespread.

Most ODSs are also greenhouse gases, so the Montreal Protocol's success has also meant reductions in greenhouse gases, and – already! – significant closing of the holes in the ozone layer. Monitoring by NASA shows that levels of ODSs in the atmosphere have declined sharply since the peak of 1989 (see Figure 2A). The global ozone layer should return to pre-1980 levels by 2050, and over Antarctica by 2070.

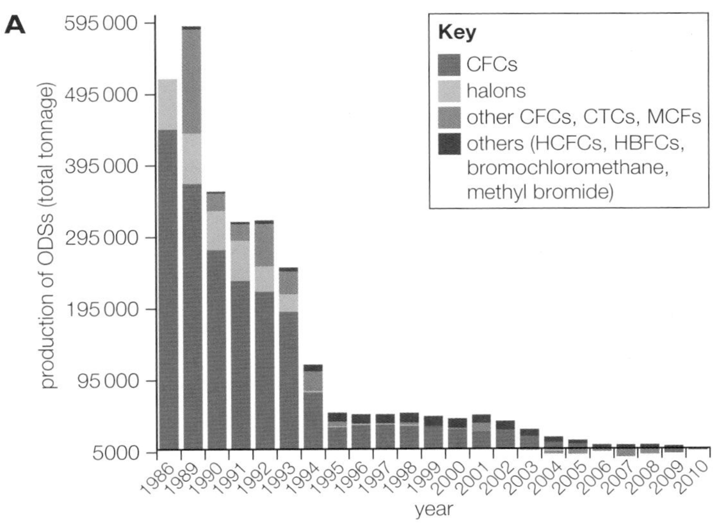

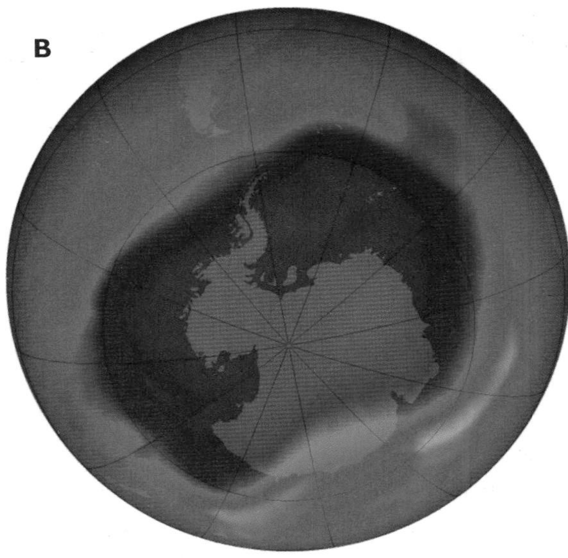

Figure 2 *The reduction in the production of ozone-depleting substances since 1987 (**A**), and the largest recorded Antarctic ozone hole (shown in blue and purple), which was recorded by NASA on 24 September 2006 (**B**).*

Actions by IGOs to protect the environment

Actions by IGOs have helped to establish international co-operation over the environment. The following four actions outline international agreements; **source materials** on pages 250–251 will enable you to evaluate their effectiveness.

1 Convention on International Trade in Endangered Species (CITES)

CITES is an international agreement between governments, aiming to ensure that international trade in wild animal and plant specimens does not threaten their survival. It protects over 35 000 species of flora and fauna. However, it has not been universally successful, because its enforcement has not been strict enough.

2 UN Convention on the Law of the Sea (UNCLOS)

In 1994, 157 countries signed UNCLOS – an agreement defining rights and responsibilities of nations in using the world's oceans. It provided guidelines for managing marine resources, creating Exclusive Economic Zones (EEZs – see Section 3.8) by extending territorial water zones to 200 nautical miles from the coast. Within these, coastal nations have sole exploitation rights over resources, including fishing and minerals.

3 The Water Convention

Also known as the Convention on Protection and Use of Trans-boundary Watercourses and International Lakes, this aims to protect the quantity, quality and sustainable use of trans-boundary water resources by promoting co-operation between countries. 42 nations signed it in 1992.

4 Millennium Ecosystem Assessment (MEA)

The MEA began in 2001, to assess consequences of ecosystem change and actions needed to conserve and use ecosystems sustainably by appraising them and the services they provide (e.g. water, food, flood control and resources).

The MEA is needed. Since 1950, economic development and population growth have caused irreversible ecosystem damage. Half the world's natural habitats have been cleared for human use (mostly agriculture) and up to 1.5% is cleared annually. Current rates of extinction are 100 times faster than natural rates, and species loss is occurring at 30 000 a year, faster than anything known before.

Analysing source materials

Source 1: Overfishing threatens Pacific bluefin tuna

Data from the international scientific committee monitoring tuna in the Pacific show that bluefin tuna stocks are in danger of disappearing [see Figure 4]. Bluefin tuna is prized by Japanese sushi lovers, and has suffered a catastrophic decline in stocks. 90% of specimens currently fished are young fish yet to reproduce. Last week, one fish sold in Japan for £1 million, reflecting the demand across Asia and in high-end Western restaurants. Bluefin tuna is the biggest of the tuna family and a top-of-the-food-chain fish with few natural predators. But industrial fishing has caused its near-extinction.

Adapted from Fiona Harvey, *Guardian* environment correspondent, January 2013

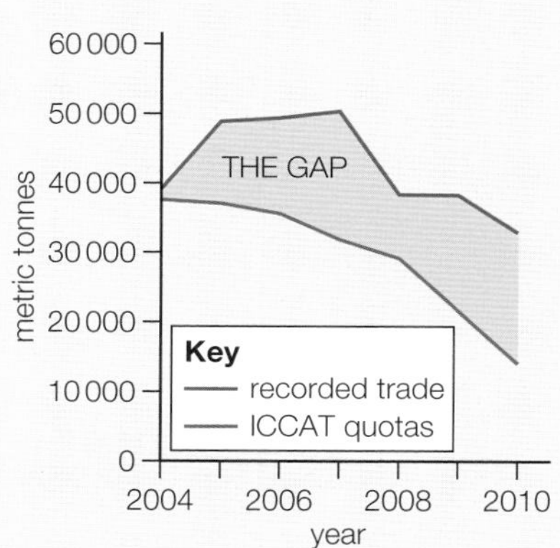

Figure 4 *The overfishing of bluefin tuna, 2004-2010 – even with the International Commission for the Conservation of Atlantic Tunas (ICCAT) quota system in place*

Source 2: 'African elephants could be gone from the wild' Prince William

NEWS

The international trade in elephant ivory is strictly forbidden under CITES rules, but Namibia and Zimbabwe want the ban lifted so that they can sell their stockpiles of ivory seized from poachers to fund community elephant conservation initiatives. This contradicts proposals put forward by 29 other African countries to end ivory trading. Kenya acted in April 2016 by burning 105 tonnes of elephant ivory and 1.35 tonnes of rhino horn recovered from illegal poachers, in order to devalue the stock.

Speaking ahead of the CITES conference, Prince William said personal greed was the cause. 'In 1983, there were one million elephants in Africa. In 2015, the numbers of savannah elephants were 350 000. Rhinos face extinction in our lifetimes. Ivory is a symbol of destruction, not luxury.'

Adapted from BBC TV News, September 2016

Figure 5 *An elephant ivory stockpile destined for destruction to weaken the ivory market in Kenya*

Source 3: Protecting the Antarctic and Arctic environments

Antarctica doesn't have a native population, government or laws. However, as scientific interest there – plus the potential for resource exploitation – increases, management of the region is needed. Twelve countries signed an agreement in 1959, with another 41 signing since then, to create the Antarctic Treaty System. This agreement sets strict rules:

- Antarctica is only to be used for scientific research.
- No military action or equipment is allowed.
- Unlike the Arctic, no territorial claims can be made on the region.
- Under the **Antarctic Protocol on Environmental Protection** (1991), no exploitation of any resources is allowed until at least 2041.

The **Arctic Monitoring and Assessment Programme** was set up in 1991 as an IGO to inform governments about threats to the Arctic in order to inform policy and decision-making.

Source 4: Should Antarctica be protected further?

In 2012, nearly 20 000 people visited Antarctica – scientists, tourists on cruise ships, researchers from countries exploring for resources. These visitors mean disturbances to the fragile Antarctic ecosystem, including introducing pollution and invasive species that significantly affect the delicately balanced ecosystem. Increased shipping means a greater chance of an oil spill. A dozen vessel emergencies have been reported in the Southern Ocean since 2000, including a Chilean vessel that sank in 2007 carrying 190 000 litres of diesel. Fishing boats there target krill and other key species. The Southern Ocean is also vulnerable to acidification, since CO_2 dissolves more quickly in cold water, making it difficult for shell-forming animals to grow.

Adapted from Mahlon Kennicutt, Texas A&M University, 2012

Source 5: Loss of biodiversity

Biodiversity loss faces five major pressures – habitat loss and degradation; climate change; excessive nutrient load and other forms of pollution; over-exploitation; and invasive alien species. Currently, extinction-risks outweigh any conservation successes. Amphibians and corals are most at risk. At threat of extinction are: 1 in 8 bird species, 1 in 4 mammals, 1 in 4 conifers, 1 in 3 amphibians, 1 in 3 corals, and 6 out of 7 marine turtles. Three-quarters of the genetic diversity of agricultural crops has been lost, and three-quarters of the world's fisheries are also over-exploited. Up to 70% of the world's known species risk extinction if the global temperatures rise by more than 3.5°C.

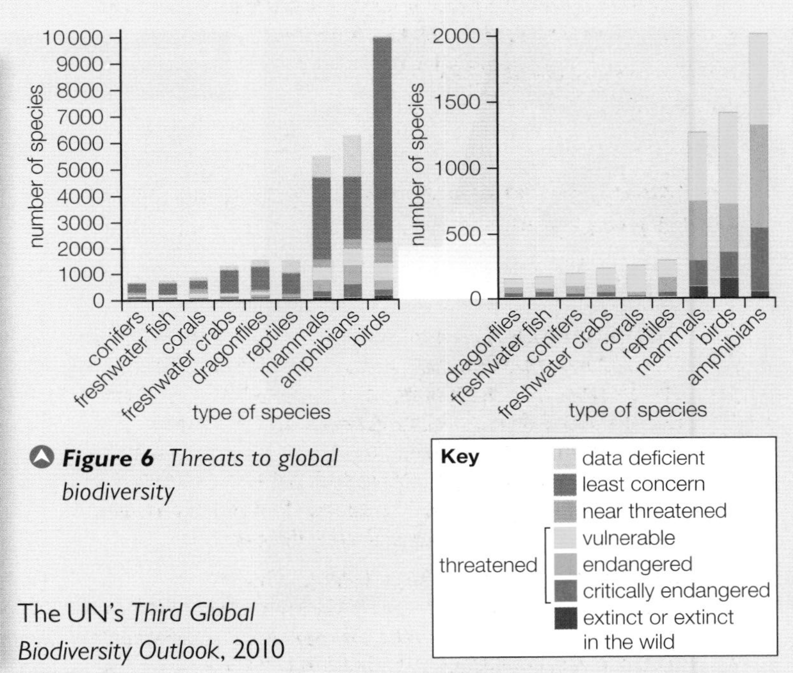

Figure 6 *Threats to global biodiversity*

The UN's *Third Global Biodiversity Outlook*, 2010

Over to you

1 **a** In pairs, list the factors that made the Montreal Protocol so successful.

b Now suggest and discuss reasons why protecting wetlands is unlikely to be as successful.

2 In pairs, research one brief example to illustrate **each** of the four 'Actions by IGOs to protect the environment'. For each example, assess (**a**) one reason for any success, (**b**) one reason for any difficulty in achieving its aim.

3 **a** Study Sources 1-5. For each source, (**i**) identify the key problems, (**ii**) assess the difficulties for IGOs in managing each environmental issue.

b Read Section 1.10 and evaluate difficulties in achieving the aims of the Water Convention on Trans-boundary Conflicts.

On your own

4 Research the work of one pressure group (e.g. Greenpeace) concerning one issue. Compare their work with that of IGOs. What advantages might NGOs have over IGOs?

5 Use the British Antarctic Survey website to justify why the Antarctic Treaty System is crucial for Antarctica's medium- and long-term future.

Exam-style question

Evaluate the success of IGOs in managing global environmental problems. (*20 marks*)

5.11 The concept of national identity

In this section, you'll learn how national identity is an elusive and contested concept.

EQ4 Sections 5.11 to 5.13 investigate the threats to national sovereignty in a more globalised world.

Sport and nationalism

At the 2016 Rio Olympic and Paralympic Games, Team GB's athletes won more medals than in London in 2012. Olympic success saw athletes from many nations wrapping themselves in their national flags (see Figure 1), singing their national anthems, and boosting their nations' rankings in the medals table (see Figure 2). The Olympics are an opportunity to indulge in **nationalism** – a patriotic feeling. International sporting events can nurture national pride, unity and loyalty – even if only briefly – and the effect is often strongest for the host nation. For example, Beijing's 2008 Games allowed China to show itself as a modern power on the world stage.

KEY CONCEPT

- **Identity** – how and why national identity is complex and difficult to define

Figure 1 *British athletes from the gold medal winning women's hockey team celebrating at Rio 2016*

Country	Gold medals	Silver medals	Bronze medals	Total medals
USA	46	37	38	121
Great Britain & Northern Ireland	27	23	17	67
China	26	18	26	70
Russia	19	18	19	56
Germany	17	10	15	42
Japan	12	8	21	41
France	10	18	14	42
South Korea	9	3	9	21
Italy	8	12	8	28
Australia	8	11	10	29

Figure 2 *The top 10 countries in the Rio 2016 Olympic medals table. Team GB won more Olympic medals in Rio than in London, coming second overall in the medals table. The final positions in the medals table relate to the number of gold medals won by a country, so Team GB was placed second ahead of China.*

Education and values

Identifying and believing in what your nation stands for often encourages loyalty and a sense of belonging. UK politicians like to speak about 'British values', but how do you define values that may vary between different people and also evolve over time? Values are rooted in the institutions and history that underpin a nation. Figure 3 lists values identified as 'British' by the *Daily Telegraph*, a traditionalist newspaper. Contrast these ideas with images of the opening ceremony of the London 2012 Olympics, which you can watch on YouTube.

Figure 3 *Core British values and characteristics suggested by the* Daily Telegraph *newspaper*

- The rule of law – the same rules for everybody
- Parliament, the Monarch and the Supreme Court constitute supreme authority
- Tolerance – no one should be treated differently on the basis of belonging to a particular group
- Personal freedoms
- Freedom of speech
- A belief in private property, and the freedom to buy and sell
- Institutions that capture and reflect the British character, e.g. the monarchy, armed forces, Church of England, BBC
- British history and culture
- A love of sport and of fair play
- Patriotism

National flags can be found in classrooms around the world. Some countries (such as the USA) strongly encourage their students to salute the national flag every day, and even to sing the national anthem. National flags also dominate during times of national celebration – and at international sporting events like the Olympics!

Since 2014, English schools have been legally required to promote British values as part of students' Spiritual, Moral, Social and Cultural development. 'Fundamental British values' comprise beliefs and practice in:

- **democracy**, e.g. the right to vote for all aged 18 and over
- the **rule of law**, e.g. the right to trial by jury using laws based either on precedent (i.e. what has gone before) or passed by an elected Parliament
- **individual liberty**, e.g. the right to choose where you live
- **mutual respect and tolerance** of those with different faiths, and those without faith.

Politics and values

In 1997, newly elected Labour Prime Minister, Tony Blair, had a vision of a New Britain – 'Cool Britannia'. Figure 4 explains its purpose. 'Cool Britannia' attempted to persuade Britons to revamp Britain as young and creative. However, it was short-lived – as many brands are – and it didn't focus on Britain's 'core' values.

Politicians usually combine national duty with a political agenda. In 2005, there were protests across China and South Korea in response to the Japanese government's decision to approve school textbooks promoting nationalist views of Japan's history. The writers were accused of ignoring events like the 1937 Nanking Massacre (in which the Chinese government claims 400 000 Chinese civilians were killed by invading Japanese troops), and also of omitting other details about the Japanese occupation of China and Korea in the 1930s and '40s that painted a negative view of Japan. Japan's Prime Minister claimed that their aim was 'to project a country with a proud history'.

In the UK, membership of the UK Independence Party (UKIP) has grown rapidly since 1991. Wanting to 'reclaim the UK's borders' and 'believing in our nation', their first two MPs were elected in 2014. They secured the highest votes (27.9%) in the 2014 European Parliament elections, and collaborated in the successful campaign to leave the EU in 2016. They support citizenship tests for migrants seeking permanent residency. These are supposedly an indicator of willingness to adopt the values and identity of the host country, by knowing something of its history and culture.

Worried by opinion polls suggesting that foreigners regard Britain as backward looking, and keen to burnish its image for dynamism, the Blair government is intent on presenting Britain as a modern type of nation. An international summit was held at Canary Wharf, London's newest skyscraper. The formal dinner was prepared by a young British chef – to emphasise that these days British people can cook! If Britain is regarded overseas as starchy, there is no harm in emphasising a relaxed side to the country; if the rest of the world regards Britain as backward looking, it is less likely to buy British. 'Cool Britannia, Britpop and Chilled' propaganda could work miracles.

Figure 4 *The purpose of promoting 'Cool Britannia' to the world (adapted from an article in the* Economist *in March 1998)*

Figure 5 *Britain's identity in 1997–8 – Cool Britannia*

Distinctive identities

The opening and closing ceremonies of major international sporting events, like the Olympics, are more than just extravagant displays of hi-technology, drama and celebration. They have become opportunities to showcase the host nation's perceived national identity. They set the tone of an event and provide an insight into the character of the host nation – not just what is shown, but the way it has been choreographed and produced too. It was no surprise to watch the light-drum show in Beijing in 2008, with thousands of performers and displays of military precision and timing, nor the rural idyll of bygone Britain portrayed in London 2012 – both shown in Figure 6. The sense of past achievements – and a view of the future direction a nation is taking – combine to present its identity.

Globalisation and identity

Ask ten people to define their country's identity, and you'll get ten different answers! But times change, and identity with, and loyalty to, a home country varies between generations. Occasionally surges in nationalism occur, reflecting the mood of the times.

Although defining what it means to be British, American, or Brazilian isn't easy these days, politicians try to articulate national characteristics and values (see Figure 3, plus Section 5.5 on Singapore).

- France pursues a policy known as *'l'exception culturelle francaise'* to protect its culture, and particularly its language, against influences such as Anglicisation.
- Japan is reluctant to increase immigration in order to protect its culture (see Section 5.4).

But globalisation, with fewer restrictions on movement, trade and investment, and global media, can alter people's views, loyalties and national identities.

Concepts such as tolerance, freedom, respect and fairness are not unique to Britain. And they are certainly as common within migrant communities of all ethnicities living in Britain as they are within British-born individuals and communities. Urban centres usually attract most migrants, and British cities have become centres of mixed populations. Many cities now consist of people of many nationalities, including diverse ethnic groups. London – with people speaking over 200 language groups! – is an example of how globalisation complicates definitions of national identity and loyalty.

Figure 6 *Scenes from recent Olympic opening and closing ceremonies. Military precision and timing dominated Beijing's opening ceremony in 2008 (**A**). London's opening ceremony in 2012 (**B**) began with an idyllic countryside setting, representing Britain's 'green and pleasant land', before its transformation into a gritty industrial landscape. Japanese Prime Minister Shinzō Abe dressed up as Mario at the Rio 2016 closing ceremony (**C**), to provide a taste of the next Olympics at Tokyo in 2020, and also to give a new impression of Japan. Each Olympics ends with the involvement of the next host city – as the baton is passed on.*

London: the face of multi-national Britain

In 2016, Sadiq Khan was elected as London's third Mayor, and its first from an ethnic minority group. London's population at the time was 8.6 million. ONS data show that 3.1 million of those residents were born overseas (see Figure 7), and that 44% of London's population was made up of black and other ethnic minorities (growing from 29% in 2001). That's lower than New York's 67%, but more than Singapore's 26%. The wide ethnic mix makes the identity of both London and the rest of the UK complex. In 2016, the Mayor of London's Office published its vision, entitled *A City for All Londoners*, with the objective to 'celebrate diversity and unite through our unique culture'.

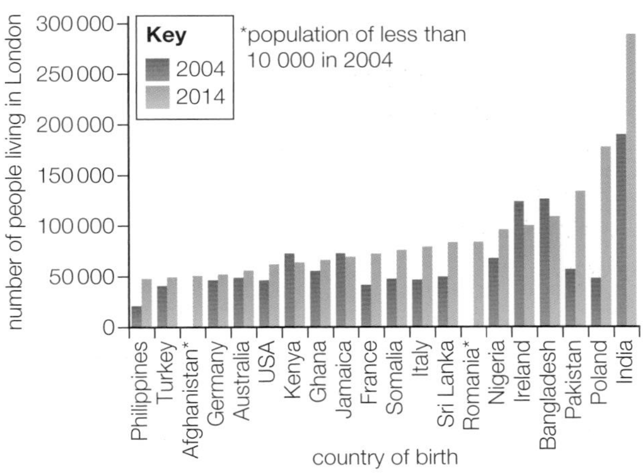

Figure 7 *The top 20 countries of birth of London's overseas-born population in 2004 and 2014*

Questions of national identity and loyalty

For the first time, people's own perception of their national identity was included as a question in the 2011 UK Census. Respondents were asked to indicate their perceived national identity, as well as their birthplace. Figure 8 shows that ethnic minorities often identified more closely with 'Britishness' than their 'white British' counterparts, who more frequently viewed themselves as 'English', 'Welsh', etc. By contrast, a high percentage of 'white other' people – perhaps European, perhaps American – felt little or no connection with 'Britishness', but instead retained their 'overseas' identity.

As an example of individual perceptions, Olympic gold medal-winner Mo Farah – born in Somalia but brought up in London – proclaimed his national loyalty to a journalist after winning gold in 2012. 'Would you have been prouder to have done it for Somalia?' asked the journalist. Farah replied, 'Not at all, mate! This is my country!'

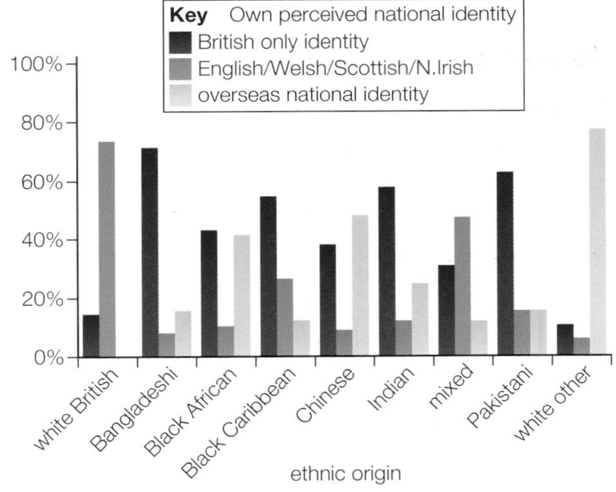

Figure 8 *People's own perceived national identity, as expressed in the 2011 UK Census*

Over to you

1 a In pairs, list all of the things that you believe make up your own national identity. Rank them according to importance.
  b Compare them by ranking the characteristics in Figure 3. Explain any similarities and differences.
  c Watch extracts from the London 2012 Olympic Games opening ceremony (available on YouTube). Compare the British characteristics shown there.

2 How far do you think (**a**) sport, (**b**) education, (**c**) politics can shape national identities?

3 Suggest why different age groups might have different perceptions of national identity.

On your own

4 a To what extent has globalisation made it more difficult to sustain national identities?
  b How far does it matter if our national identities change or become diluted by globalisation?

5 Research the UK government's Citizenship Test. (**a**) See how many questions you can answer, and (**b**) comment on how far you think those questions are good indicators of 'Britishness'.

Exam-style question

Explain why national identity is an elusive and contested concept. *(8 marks)*

5.12 Challenges to national identity

In this section, you'll find out that there are challenges to national identity.

Made in Britain?

Cold meat, pie, or fish and chips – with HP sauce! British food at its best! This famous brown sauce (see Figure 1) was the inspiration of a nineteenth-century Nottingham grocer. It was named HP after he learned that it was eaten in the Houses of Parliament. But, in 2005, the HP brand was bought by Heinz, who are based in the USA. It's one of many British brands to be bought by foreign companies. In 2016, foreign TNCs spent over US$100 billion buying British companies.
For example, while the British car production industry had one of its best years in 2015, producing over 1.5 million vehicles, few of these were made by British-owned companies, as Figure 2 shows.

Manufacturer	Owned by	Location	Number of vehicles manufactured, 2015
Jaguar, Land Rover	Tata Motors (India)	Castle Bromwich / Halewood / Solihull	489 923
Nissan	Nissan Motor Company (Japan)	Sunderland	476 589
Mini	BMW (Germany)	Oxford	201 207
Toyota	Toyota Motor Corporation (Japan)	Burnaston, Derbyshire	190 161
Honda	Honda Motor Company Ltd (Japan)	Swindon	119 414
Vauxhall	General Motors (USA)	Ellesmere Port	85 241
Others			25 142
All makes			**1 587 677**

It's difficult to recognise goods 'Made in Britain', because they might:

- be made by British companies under foreign ownership
- consist of parts made abroad but assembled in the UK.

Figure 3 lists a number of British brands and their foreign owners. In 2013, journalist Alex Brummer wrote how British companies were sold off to overseas owners. However, it works both ways – for example, UK company Serco runs transport in Dubai, and the UK's Vodafone is the world's second biggest mobile phone company.

Global markets encourage mergers and take-overs, and companies achieve economies of scale and efficiency by merging, as well as eliminating a competitor. The UK government rarely intervenes in the sale of UK companies to foreign buyers, unless national security, financial stability or **media plurality** are at risk. Elsewhere, countries like France, Germany and the USA protect certain industries for strategic reasons (e.g. protecting jobs and skills).

KEY CONCEPT

- **Identity** – how and why national identity and culture is challenged by globalisation.

Figure 1 *HP sauce – a classic British brand no longer owned by a British company*

Figure 2 *UK car manufacturing in 2015*

Key word

Media plurality – The ownership of several forms of media by the same company.

British brand	Foreign owner(s)
Scottish Power	Spain's Iberdrola
BAA airports operator	Spain's Ferrovial
Thames Water	German RWE
P&O	Dubai Ports
Abbey National bank	Spain's Santander
Cadbury's	USA Kraft/Modelez
Boots	Italian Equity firm
Harrods	Qatari Investment Bank
Fortnum & Mason	Canada's Weston
British Energy	French EDF
British Steel	India's TATA
National Lottery	Canadian Lottery

Figure 3 *Made in Britain?*

Does company nationality matter?

A company's nationality may not matter, if it provides job security and boosts the economy. Lord Digby Jones, former Director General of the CBI (the representative body of British companies) believes that if companies behave well, then nothing changes. But it's significant nonetheless. Take-overs mean that profits go abroad instead of staying in the UK so corporate taxes are paid overseas, with the UK government losing taxation revenue. For example, the Italian owner of Boots the Chemist moved its headquarters from the UK to low-tax Switzerland in 2014; its new tax bill was £9 million, instead of the £89 million it had paid one year earlier in the UK. Figure 4 shows the value of foreign-owned companies in Britain in 2014.

Sector	Number of businesses	Turnover (£ billions)
Production & agriculture, forestry, fishing	4350	364.2
Construction	1110	22.0
Distribution & transport	6099	596.5
Services (excluding finance)	11 768	319.7
Foreign-owned total	**23 327**	**1302.4**

Figure 4 *Foreign-owned businesses in Britain, 2014*

Westernisation and cultural values

In some ways globalisation is another term for 'cultural imperialism'. Previous generations called it 'Americanisation', 'Westernisation' or 'modernisation'. The global economy has created global brand names like Apple, Vodafone, Coca Cola and Nike. Every year, Forbes (a US company) calculates the brand value of the top 500 companies. Of the top ten in 2015, eight were American.

- In terms of **entertainment**, the programmes we watch on TV, the films we see at the cinema, the music we listen to, and news articles we read, are increasingly provided by a small group of huge companies. For instance, three companies (Sony BMG, Universal Music Group, and Warner Music Group) own 80% of the global music market – all are American. The top four media companies in 2016 were Comcast, Disney, 21st Century Fox and Time Warner, providing both film and TV. In Australia, 70% of newspapers are owned by Rupert Murdoch's News Corporation.
- Westernisation also affects **retailing**. The American model for retail is the mall – enclosed, air-conditioned, and clean, unlike high streets where shoppers battle with traffic and weather. Most indoor centres – e.g. the Trafford Centre in Manchester, Meadowhall (Sheffield), or Westfield (with centres in London and Derby) – are built by large property companies with investment from pension funds and big banks. They change the nature and identity of retail in towns and cities, since they are usually built out-of-town where space requirements, costs, and parking are under less pressure. But within each mall, global brands replace independent businesses, and malls tend to look very similar, as Figure 5 shows.

Figure 5 *Big retail brands create similar place identity. Starbucks' logo is instantly recognisable – the photo could be of the USA or the UK, but it's actually Muscat in Oman!*

A cultural takeover?

Disney owns 40 Spanish-speaking radio stations, plus foreign-language television channels and dozens of international magazines. In China, Disney use leisure and film – Disneyland in Shanghai, with the chance to sing-along to *Frozen*! – to expand their market, and have opened a Chinese-language radio station in Hong Kong. By 2015, they had also opened over 140 learning centres equipped with Disney materials in China, teaching English to 150 000 children (see Figure 6).

Disney promotes a distinctive view of the broader benefits of Western capitalism. It targets the middle classes in China and India, many of whom see Western brands as symbols of economic success and social fluidity. For many, Westernisation represents a bigger picture of social mobility (compared to life in a traditional rural village, for example) and personal freedoms (e.g. freedom of faith, or to choose who to marry, or where to live), as well as purchasing items like cookers or fridges that offer an easier lifestyle.

Figure 6 *Children learning English at a Disney English centre in Shanghai*

Property and land – ownership and identity

In 2013, UK estate agents Knight Frank placed Russians top of the list of foreign buyers of London homes. Non-national investors are also buying into some of London's most recognisable locations – Qatari investors own stakes in the Shard, Canary Wharf, and East Village (formerly London's 2012 Olympic Village).

In 1980, just 8% of the City of London was owned by non-national investors; in 2011 the proportion passed 50%. Between 2008 and 2015, over £100 billion worth of property in London was bought by foreign companies. Purchasers often remain anonymous, but two-thirds of the properties bought were registered to British tax havens such as Jersey, Guernsey, the Isle of Man and the British Virgin Islands. Figure 7 shows the extent of these foreign purchases across Central London.

Figure 7 *Properties owned by foreign investors in Central London in 2015*

Many investment properties remain unoccupied. The owners are not on the electoral register, yet they change the identity of places. London's exclusive Belgrave Square has so many Russian owners that it's nicknamed Red Square; 27 of its 30 properties are owned by foreign nationals. The trend in foreign ownership makes parts of London prohibitively expensive for local people. Many properties become gated compounds, turning public access into private spaces with security guards and CCTV.

Business ownership and identity

Some TNCs have actually altered the way of life in some countries, and even altered national identities. For example, in the 1930s, the American United Fruit Company (now Chiquita) owned over 1 million acres of land in Central America. By the 1950s, it owned over 50% of all land in Honduras, and 75% in Guatemala. It built and ran infrastructure – roads, railways, power stations and port facilities – helping economic growth and fruit exports, especially bananas. Plantations replaced small farms; waged work replaced subsistence farming; and homes, healthcare and education were all provided by the company.

In the UK, the Indian trans-national Tata owns the steel plant in Port Talbot, South Wales. It provides jobs in the area and maintains the historical Welsh association with heavy industry. Tata's publicity claims that they benefit Welsh prosperity, invest in schools, and support local health, safety and environmental policies. But in 2015, when cheap imported Chinese steel threatened Tata's profits, Tata proposed closing the Port Talbot plant. Just as hurricanes can destroy banana plantations in Central America, community futures are at risk when the strong winds of globalisation cause TNCs to change tack.

Figure 8 *A coffee plantation in Honduras, showing how foreign companies can transform landscapes*

Over to you

1. Using examples of goods you research, explain why the label 'Made in the UK' is increasingly complex.
2. In pairs, discuss and suggest ways in which it (**a**) matters, (**b**) does not matter whether British car brands survive under British ownership.
3. Draw a table to show the advantages and disadvantages of foreign ownership using all of the examples in this section.
4. Discuss and explain the potential impacts of losing British film, TV, newspaper and music companies to foreign ownership.

On your own

5. Refer to Section 6.4 to help you.
   - **a** Use the data in Figure 2 to construct proportional circles showing the proportions of cars manufactured by different companies in the UK.
   - **b** Do the same for the data in Figure 4.
   - **c** Comment on what the data show.
6. Using examples, explain how US companies dominate global retail and entertainment, and the impacts that this can have.
7. **a** Study Figure 7 and research current property prices in London.
   - **b** How far do you think foreign ownership should be controlled?

Exam-style question

Evaluate the contribution of globalisation to Western identity. (*20 marks*)

5.13 Disunity within nations

In this section, you'll learn that there are consequences of disunity within nations.

Nationalism versus globalisation

In December 2016, Mark Carney, Governor of the Bank of England, called on policymakers to tackle the causes of a growing sense of isolation and detachment among people who felt left behind by globalisation. He stated that, despite progress, many people faced uncertainty, and felt a loss of control and trust in the system. For them, globalisation meant low wages, insecure employment, faceless organisations, stateless corporations and inequality.

Rising nationalism, as well as calls for independence from regions within countries, has emerged alongside the growing disillusionment with globalisation. However, these nationalist undercurrents are not recent – some have been there for many decades. For example, Catalonia's long-held desire to become independent from the rest of Spain, while remaining in the EU, is similar to the Scottish Nationalist Party's desire to separate from the rest of the UK but remain an EU member – especially since the UK's Brexit decision in 2016, which the majority of Scots voted against.

KEY CONCEPT

- **Identity** – how and why nationalism and globalisation can result in a sense of disunity

Figure 1 The location of Catalonia and its main city, Barcelona

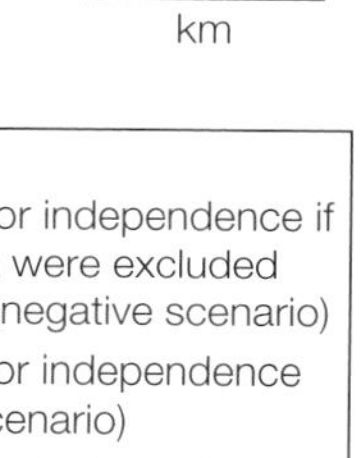

Catalans demand change

Catalonia (see Figure 1) is Spain's wealthiest region, with a population of 7.5 million producing 20% of Spain's wealth. As a separate nation, its GDP would exceed that of Israel, and it would be the world's 34th largest economy.

- As Spain's industrial and economic powerhouse (with textile and, more recently, high-tech companies) it is dominated by Barcelona, the regional capital.
- Since 1978, Catalonia has enjoyed considerable levels of self-government (as in Scotland), with responsibility for education, healthcare, police, prisons and culture.

Many Catalans believe in a pluralistic – i.e. multi-national – Spain with distinctive regions, languages and cultures. Catalonian people who identify themselves as 'Catalans' (rather than 'Spanish') have strong views about independence, as the results of a recent Catalan opinion poll show in Figure 2.

Key
support for independence if Catalonia were excluded from EU (negative scenario)
support for independence (no EU scenario)
support for independence if Catalonia could join EU (positive scenario)

% who support Catalan independence: 100%, 80%, 60%, 40%, 20%, 0%

Catalan respondents' self-identity: only Catalan; more Catalan than Spanish; as Catalan as Spanish; more Spanish than Catalan; only Spanish

Figure 2 The percentage of people in Catalonia who supported Catalan independence under three different scenarios regarding EU membership. The respondents were separated into groups based on self-identity – from 'only Catalan' through to 'only Spanish'. The percentages represent the respondents within each group who supported Catalan independence under the different scenarios.

Figure 3 Barcelona football fans at the Nou Camp stadium, waving the Catalan flag rather than the Spanish national flag

Many Catalans feel that they contribute more than their fair share to the nation's taxes, and also that they subsidise the poorer Spanish regions. By 2010, half of Catalonia's population wanted independence, and the calls for a vote on the matter have grown:

- 2012 – 1.5 million Catalans demonstrated, demanding an independence referendum.
- 2013 – 90 000 attended a 'concert for freedom' at Barcelona's Nou Camp stadium.
- 2014 – A mock referendum was held, with 80% of Catalan voters (on a 40% turnout) wanting separation from Spain.
- 2015 – Pro-independence parties won a majority in regional elections (but with less than 50% of the vote).
- 2016 – The Catalan regional government drew up a strategy to hold a full referendum about eventual independence. Madrid blocked it on constitutional grounds.

What about the EU?

There are many European businesses in Catalonia. Catalan independence could mean the renegotiation of trade deals, as well as changes to tax, regulations and currency, which would create challenges for businesses similar to those of Brexit. Figure 2 suggests that national self-identity is hugely important – the more Catalan or Spanish a person feels, the less likely they are to change their views on independence, regardless of EU membership.

In 2016, Corsica's new nationalist government expressed similar views – to stay in the EU, but to loosen the island's ties with France. Corsica enjoys some degree of self-rule, but seeing moves towards greater autonomy in Catalonia and Scotland, it's now seeking changes. The new nationalist leader addresses the islanders in Corsican rather than French, and crowds wave the traditional 'moor's head' Corsican flag.

Figure 4 *Protests prior to the 2016 Olympic Games in Rio de Janeiro*

Rising tensions in emerging nations

Nationalism often has cultural and historical roots, but it has been strengthened in places where globalisation has created tensions. The BRICS (Brazil, Russia, India, China and South Africa), and other emerging nations, have all seen their GDP grow significantly, but they are also grappling with the consequences of national divisions. Figure 4 shows the 'Exclusion Games' protest, which reflected the resentment felt by many Brazilians about the cost of hosting the 2016 Olympics, when at the same time Brazil was in the throes of a major recession, political strife and a public health crisis (the Zika virus).

There is also a growing political uncertainty in South Africa, as Figure 5 shows. In 2016, the main opposition Democratic Alliance (DA), and the populist Economic Freedom Fighters (EFF), both won parliamentary seats from the ruling African National Congress (ANC) in elections. Cities with a young educated population, and black townships, were losing faith in the ANC after protests over poor services, such as water, electricity and education.

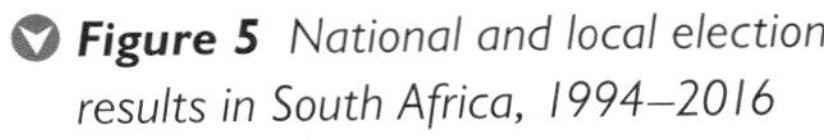

Figure 5 *National and local election results in South Africa, 1994–2016*

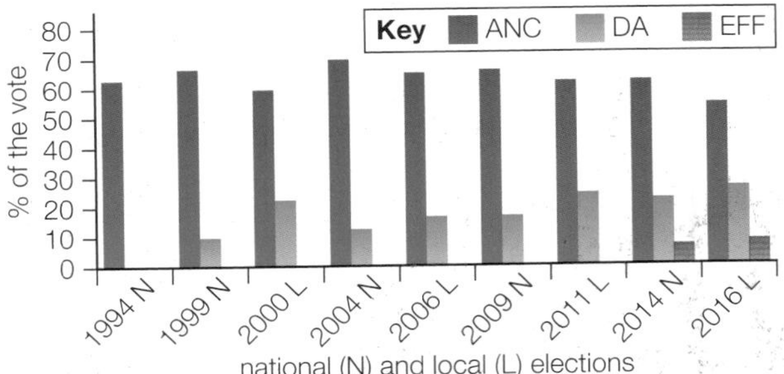

Globalisation and inequality

Globalisation has produced winners and losers. Cheap loans have allowed many to buy cars or property, which, together with the falling prices of many consumer goods, has meant that many people 'feel' better off. However, Figure 6 shows how income inequality (as measured by the Gini coefficient; see Section 6.3) has changed since 1980 for selected nations. Some of the emerging economies are the most unequal, whereas Sweden is the least unequal. Inequality within most countries has grown, although the gap between richer and poorer countries has shrunk.

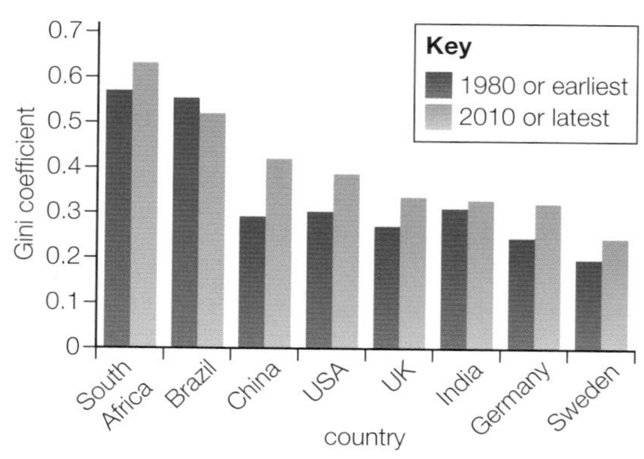

Figure 6 *Income inequality in South Africa and other selected economies in 1980 and 2010. Note that 0 = perfect equality, whereas 1 is perfect inequality.*

Inequality in South Africa

Globalisation has allowed South Africa's manufacturers to gain access to wider markets – exports have grown, as have imports of consumer goods. The gold mines near Johannesburg, wines of the Western Cape, and tourism, have presented the country with economic opportunities and growth. However, the opening up of South Africa to global markets has also meant taking on SAPs (see Section 5.9) and accepting high levels of Foreign Direct Investment (FDI), plus the in-migration of overseas businesses. Some South Africans have undoubtedly gained, but the data in Figure 7 indicate that income inequalities between different ethnic groups in South Africa have actually increased, as have political tensions.

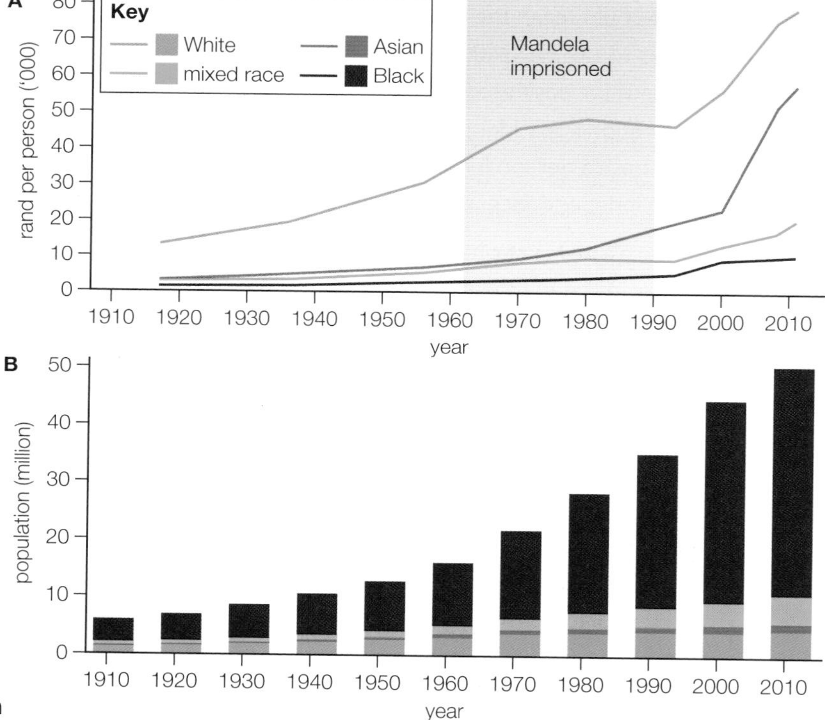

Figure 7 *Average income by ethnic group (**A**) and population by ethnic group (**B**)*

Failed states

The role of the state varies between countries, and national identity is not always as strong as in Catalonia. This is especially true in 'failed states', where there are stark differences between politically and economically powerful elites, foreign investment groups and the wider population. A failed state exists where the political or economic system has become so weak that the national government is no longer in control and cannot maintain security or law and order. Somalia, Yemen, Libya and Zimbabwe are examples of failed states. In these countries, some of the following apply: low life expectancy, undemocratic government, social unrest, widespread poverty, human rights abuses, and poor education, health and welfare. A small elite may wield political and economic power, and any sense of national identity may be weak.

Syria

Civil war in Syria has contributed to its 'failure':

- It has raged since 2011, claiming nearly 500 000 lives and displacing millions of Syrians to other countries as refugees.
- Aleppo, Syria's financial centre and a World Heritage Site, has been reduced to ruins.
- Syria's infrastructure has disintegrated.
- The ongoing conflict involves up to 1000 armed opposition groups, including Islamic Front, Jihadist groups and ISIS, together with the direct involvement of other countries.
- The country is ethnically divided. Sunni Arabs constitute 65% of the population, with Alawis 12%, Christians 10%, Kurds 9%, Druze 3%, and the remainder Bedouin and other ethnic groups.

But the 'failure' of Syria is not new; much of it has been caused by nepotism (the handing of power to family and friends) and corruption. Economic liberalisation in Syria has occurred without the legal basis or rules, checks and balances by which a market economy usually functions. Since 2000, the economy has largely been run by a group of entrepreneurs closely associated with the ruling family. They have become extremely rich in industries such as telecommunications, IT and car dealerships. During privatisation, public services and assets were transferred into the hands of political supporters of the government and those linked by family or clan. Meanwhile, the agricultural sector became neglected. Government ministers were mostly relations of the ruling family. Many established large fortunes by illegal means, corruption and money laundering. One cousin of the President gained a virtual monopoly over mobile phone services, restaurant chains, property and banking.

Figure 8 *Ambulances and buses wait to evacuate people from a rebel-held sector of eastern Aleppo, Syria*

Over to you

1. In pairs, research and prepare a six-slide presentation on Scottish Nationalism. Outline (**a**) its origins, (**b**) its progress since the 1970s as a political force, (**c**) its arguments for a separate Scotland, (**d**) arguments against separation, and (**e**) the extent to which separation is likely and why.
2. Consider the data sources that you used in your research for activity 1. Analyse your source material to identify any misuse of data in assessing how successful the SNP has been in promoting national identity. Use Section 6.6 to help you with analysing this material.
3. Draw a table to show similarities and differences between the desire for, and progress towards, separation in Scotland and Catalonia.
4. Using Figures 6 and 7, assess the extent to which globalisation has benefited (**a**) South Africa, (**b**) other countries (as evidenced by the Gini coefficient). Use Section 6.3 to help you.

On your own

5. **a** Research the Syrian civil war since 2011. Identify its causes, which groups have supported the government and which have rebelled, and why Syria could be considered a 'failed state'.

   b How far has the Syrian government maintained a sense of national identity during the civil war?
6. Consider your research into Syria. Identify possible misuses of data by the Syrian government in promoting support for the government during the civil war.

Exam-style question

Evaluate the consequences of disunity within nations. (*20 marks*)

Conclusion – revisiting the Enquiry Questions

These are the key questions that drive the whole topic:

1 What are the impacts of globalisation on international migration?

2 How are nation states defined and how have they evolved in a globalising world?

3 What are the impacts of global organisations on managing global issues and conflicts?

4 What are the threats to national sovereignty in a more globalised world?

Having studied this topic, you can now consider some answers to these questions, using the synoptic themes to frame your ideas.

Players – discussion point 1

Working in groups, consider instances from this chapter where government policies towards migration conflict over issues to do with sovereignty. Explain your views.

Attitudes and Actions – discussion point 2

Working in groups, discuss and draw a diagram which shows how and why people have different attitudes towards either (a) migration, or (b) the processes of globalisation.

Futures and Uncertainties – discussion point 3

Working in groups, consider different scenarios concerning the challenges presented by nationalism. Use instances from this chapter either to justify increased nationalist feeling against globalisation or IGOs such as the EU, or to reject such feeling. Explain your views.

Books, music, and films on this topic

Books to read

1. *Zebra Crossing* by Meg Vandermerwe (2013)

   This book tells the story of the migration of two siblings who move to South Africa from Zimbabwe to avoid conflict and poverty.

2. *Sovereignty: An evolution of an idea* by Robert Jackson (2007)

   This explores the meaning of sovereignty, its evolution and the challenges created by globalisation.

3. *The No-nonsense Guide to International Migration* by Peter Stalker (2008)

   An analysis of where and why migration takes place, plus its impacts.

Music to listen to

1. 'Borders' (2015) by M.I.A

   This song is about the migrant crisis, and criticises the EU response to the issue. The writer was inspired by her own story, fleeing civil war in Sri Lanka.

2. 'American Oxygen' (2015) by Rihanna

   The song's lyrics are about how immigrants (such as Rihanna) migrated to the USA to 'chase the American dream', and how migration has changed the USA.

3. 'Bengali in Platforms' (1988) by Morrissey

   This song was written about a Bengali boy who migrated to the UK and is struggling to fit into the new culture.

Films to see

1. *Goal!* (2005)

   This is a story of a young Latin American boy, now living in Los Angeles, who migrates to England to become a professional footballer.

2. *Terraferma* (2011)

   A film about an Italian fisherman who is punished for helping illegal immigrants enter Europe.

3. *Winter On Fire: Ukraine's Fight for Freedom* (2015)

   A documentary about the conflict in Ukraine in 2013 and 2014, showing how states want to keep their sovereignty, but that not all countries recognise their borders.

3.1 Complex data sets and scaling

This skill is of particular use for the following topic:

- Superpowers, Section 3.2

Superpower rankings

Based on its economy, the USA is the world's biggest superpower. But which countries come in second and third in the superpower rankings? Assessing the superpower status of powerful nations is complex, because different sets of data can show conflicting patterns. For example, China has increasing economic power – and a huge army – but in terms of military reach it is much less significant than the USA. Russia has the world's largest gas reserves, but that also means that its economy is highly dependent on global gas prices.

Assessing a global superpower hierarchy can be done by comparing the rankings of powerful countries using a wide range of criteria, such as economic power and military strength.

1. Decide which criteria you are going to use to measure each country's power.
2. Research the data for each country (e.g. GDP).
3. Compile a rank order for each set of data. (For example, in Figure 1 the individual rankings of three powerful countries have been worked out using the criteria of physical size, GDP and population – using data from Section 3.2).
4. Add up your completed rankings to calculate a final **index**. The country with the lowest index score will be regarded as the most powerful overall.

Country	Physical size	GDP	Population	Index (the total ranking score)
USA	3	1	3	7
China	4	2	1	7
Russia	1	9	9	19

Figure 1 *A table to compare the different rankings and overall index scores of three powerful countries, using three different indicators of superpower status. The rankings are based on data from Section 3.2.*

Weighted indices

However, countries can end up with the same index score. In Figure 1, the USA and China have the same score of 7, although the USA is generally regarded as more powerful than China overall.

To overcome this problem, rankings can be weighted or **scaled**. In other words, some criteria can be given a greater weighting than others (see Figure 2).

For example:

- You may decide that GDP is more important than physical size, so you could weight it by 3 to show that it's three times more important.
- You then multiply each country's ranking order by the weighting you've decided on for that criteria (in this case 3), so a ranking of 1 becomes 3, and 2 becomes 6, and so on.
- You can also scale downwards. Figure 2 shows the weighting for physical size as 0.5. Remember that you need to decide on your own weightings!
- You can also include any other data that you believe are important. For example, in terms of membership of global organisations, you could give 1 point for OECD membership, 2 for membership of the G8, 3 for the G20, and so on.

Figure 2 *A table for ranking weighted scores to show the comparative superpower status of different countries*

Country	Physical size	Weighting x0.5	GDP	Weighting x3	Population	Weighting x2	Total weighted scores
USA	3	1.5	1	3	3	6	10.5
China	4	2	2	6	1	2	10
Russia	1	0.5	9	27	9	18	45.5

6.2 Using logarithmic scales

This skill is of particular use for the following topic:
- Superpowers, Section 3.5

Logarithmic graphs are used to compare values that vary enormously in size, such as the value of global trade since 1800 (see Figure 5 in Section 3.5). Plotted onto standard graph paper, this data would be a sharp curve (known as a parabola), and any minor differences in the curve would be hard to spot. For example, global trade between 1800 and 1810 grew in value by almost 20% in ten years, but the scale on a standard graph would have to be so compressed to fit in the wide range of values in this particular data set, that the impact of such an increase in the lower values would be lost. Therefore, logarithmic graph paper is used to present this information instead – of which there are two types:

- **Semi-logarithmic graph paper** (see Figure 1) has **arithmetic** values along the x-axis (the independent variable), e.g. for showing a series of regular data such as years (1800, 1810, 1820, and so on). However, the y-axis is **logarithmic** – using a cycle of values, where each cycle increases by a power of 10. Thus the first cycle increases from 1 to 10, the second to 100, the third to 1000 and so on. In this way, the range of values on the vertical scale (the dependent variable) is compressed, allowing greater space for the smaller values (e.g. those for the dates of 1800 and 1810), and reducing the amount of space allowed for the larger values (e.g. those for the dates of 2010 and 2014). It can therefore show relative growth more clearly.
- **Logarithmic graph paper** (see Figure 2) has logarithmic values along both axes. It allows a relationship to be shown between two sets of wide-ranging values. For example, river discharge (in cubic metres per second, or cumecs) along small tributaries where values of discharge would be small, in comparison with discharge further downstream (several hundred miles away) where hundreds of cumecs of water may pass a recording point each second.

Logarithmic scales are also effective when the data being shown uses a very small scale, such as the size of fine sediment – which is measured in fractions of mm – or even microscopic organisms. The scale would still be cyclic, but it might be 0.001 to 0.01 as the first cycle, 0.01 to 0.1 as the second cycle, etc.

Key word

Arithmetic scale – Increasing by a standard value each time – e.g. 2, 4, 6, 8 and so on.

Logarithmic scale – Increasing on a cycle, usually by 10, so that 1 to 10 is the first cycle, 10 to 100 is the second cycle, 100 to 1000 the third, and so on.

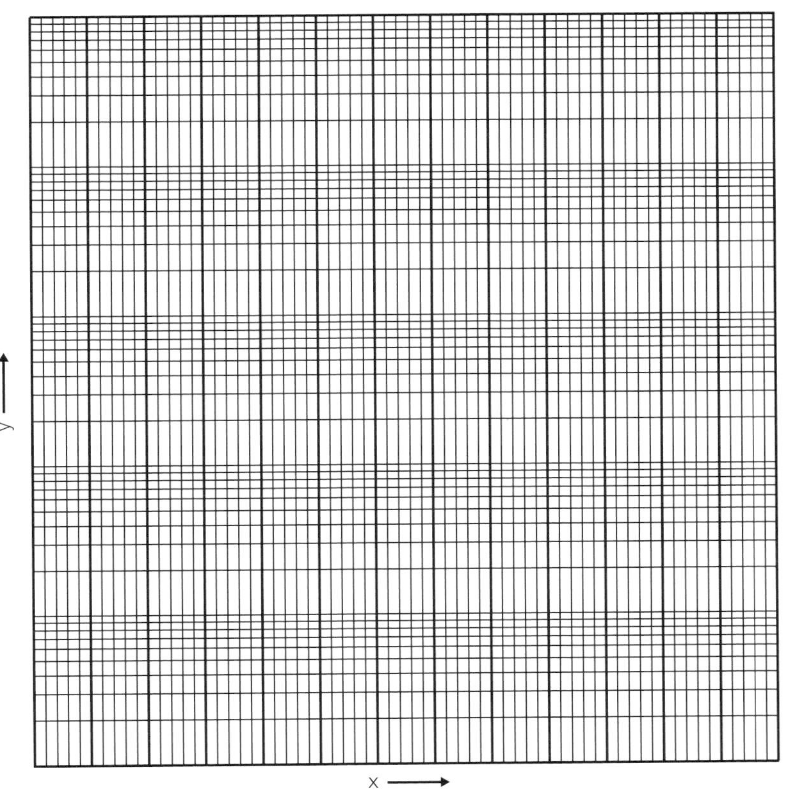

Figure 1 *Semi-logarithmic graph paper – with a logarithmic vertical scale (y-axis), and arithmetic horizontal scale (x-axis). This graph paper allows, for example, population or economic growth to be shown in logarithmic scale on the vertical axis, whilst using an arithmetic scale for regular data – such as years or months – on the horizontal axis.*

Figure 2 *Logarithmic graph paper – with both vertical and horizontal logarithmic scales*

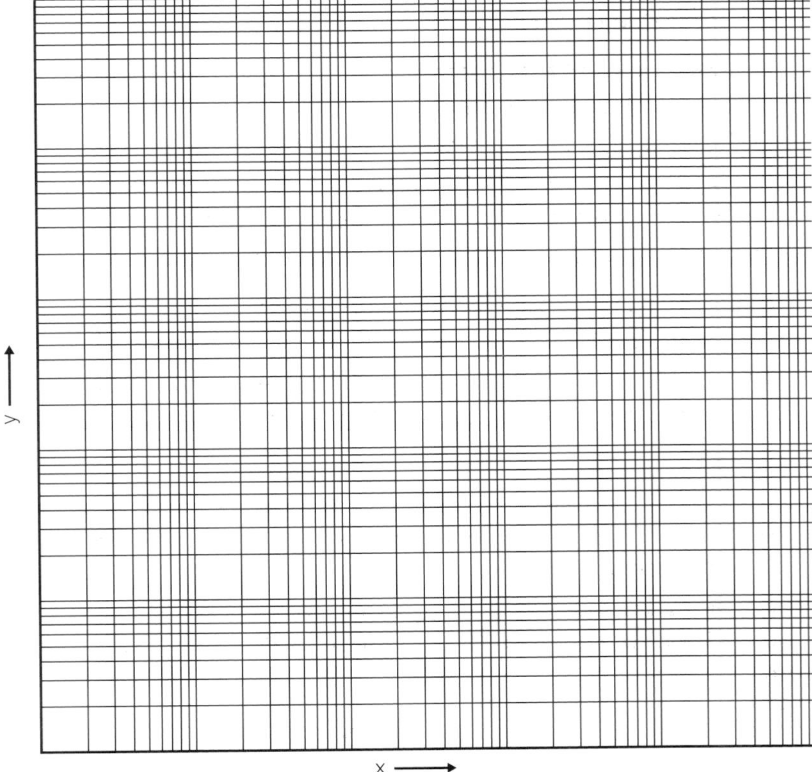

6.3 The Lorenz curve and Gini coefficient/index

This skill is of particular use for the following topics:

- Health, human rights and intervention, Sections 4.1 and 4.11
- Migration, identity and sovereignty, Sections 5.7 and 5.13

The Lorenz curve

Measuring inequality is one of the fundamentals of geography. The Lorenz curve was developed to show and measure any inequality in graphical form. It assumes that – in an equal world – 10% of the population would have 10% of a country's wealth, 20% would have 20% of the wealth, and so on. As Figure 1 shows, this would result in a straight line – i.e. perfect equality. Plotting a Lorenz curve shows how much inequality actually exists in a particular situation. Look at Figure 1. The more the Lorenz curve line bends away from the straight line of perfect equality, the greater the inequality represented will be.

Figure 1 uses income distribution as a measure of inequality. By dividing the percentage of different groups of people by their share of national income, the Lorenz curve shows how relatively wealthy or poor certain sections of the population were. When Figure 1 was prepared in the 1970s, South Africa's 'Black African' population made up over 70% of the total, yet they received just 19% of national income. Meanwhile, the 'White' population represented just 14% of the total, yet they received 73% of national income.

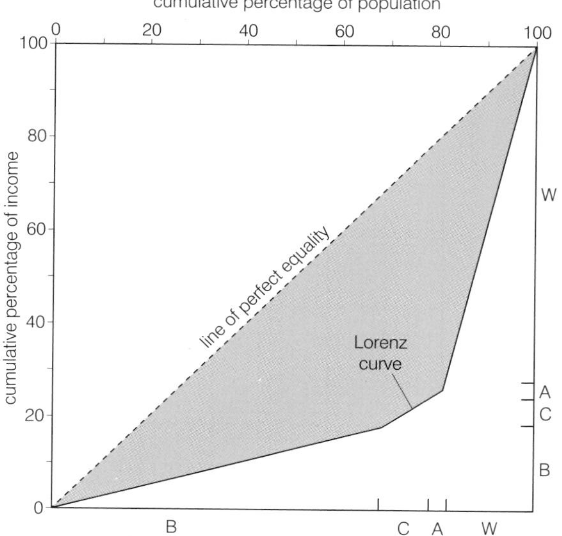

Figure 1 *A Lorenz curve for the distribution of population and national income in South Africa in the 1970s. In the diagram, 'B' means 'Black African', 'C' means 'Coloured' (a term used to describe inter-racial or unregistered people), 'A' means 'Asian', and 'W' means 'White'. The terminology used to describe each population group was a legal classification used in South Africa until the ending of apartheid in 1994.*

Ratios of advantage

By dividing a particular group's share of national income by its percentage of the total population, a **ratio of advantage** can be calculated for each group, which is then used to plot a Lorenz curve.

The graph in Figure 1 was calculated as follows:

- The share of national income of 'Black Africans' in South Africa (the poorest group) was 19% in the 1970s. Divided by their share of the population (75%), this gave a ratio of advantage of 0.25.
- This was then added to for other groups in the population – with the 'White' population added last. Their 73% share of national income was divided by their 14% share of the population – giving a ratio of advantage of 5.2.

Any figure higher than 1 shows advantage, whereas any figure below 1 shows disadvantage. The higher the figure is above 1, the greater the advantage will be.

Drawing a Lorenz curve

A Lorenz curve is plotted on a graph using data showing ratio of advantage. Follow the steps described on the next page (using a graph outline copied from Figure 2) and plot the data for the UK shown in Figure 3. Notice this time that, unlike the South African racial groups used in Figure 1 (which were unequal in size), the data for the UK are divided into equal-sized groups (known as deciles, or tenths).

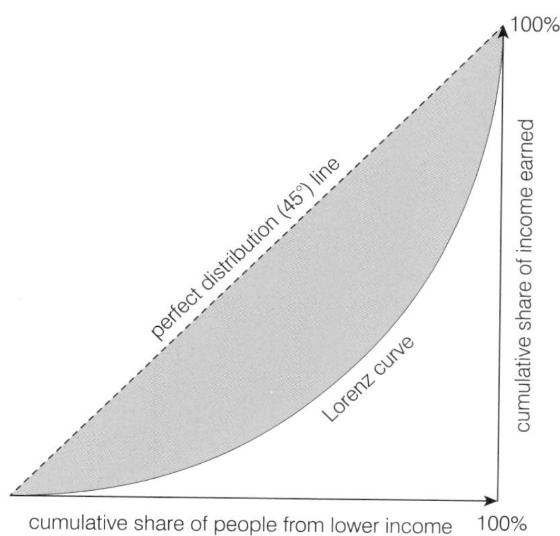

Figure 2 *A Lorenz curve graph outline. To use this to plot your own data, scale each of the axes 0-100% in graduations of 10%.*

- Draw a graph outline and plot a perfect distribution line (as shown in Figure 2).
- Ratios of advantage have already been calculated and ranked in Figure 3, by taking each population decile and its share of national wealth.
- Begin by plotting the group with the lowest ratio – the 'Poorest tenth' in Figure 3. This will be point 1 on your graph.
- Now take the next lowest group. Add its share of wealth and population to those for the 'Poorest tenth' that you have already plotted, and plot these points. In this way, you are plotting cumulative figures.
- Continue to plot the remaining groups in order, adding each one onto the previous cumulative figure – so that the last figure you plot reaches 100%. The last group will be the wealthiest, or most advantaged.
- Join points 1-10 to form a curve, known as the Lorenz curve. The area between the straight line and the curve shows how unequally income is distributed. The more curved the line, the greater the inequality.

Decile of population	% wealth (2012–14)	Cumulative %
Poorest tenth %	0.05	0.05
2nd poorest	0.49	0.54
3rd poorest	1.28	1.82
4th poorest	2.63	4.45
5th poorest	4.25	8.70
6th poorest	6.23	14.93
7th poorest	8.81	23.74
8th poorest	12.52	36.26
9th poorest	18.93	55.19
Wealthiest tenth	44.81	100.00

Figure 3 *Data showing wealth distribution in the UK, 2012–14. Wealth is defined here as the sum total of people's property and pension wealth, added to the total of their other assets (e.g. savings) – minus any debts.*

The Gini index and Gini coefficient

The **Gini index** measures the inequality of wealth distribution. It measures the area between the Lorenz curve and a line of absolute equality (see Figure 2), expressed as a percentage of the maximum area under the line. On graph paper, this would be done by counting small graph squares. It is shown as a value between 0 and 100:

- A lower index indicates more equal distribution, with 0 as perfect equality.
- A higher index indicates more unequal distribution, with 100 corresponding to perfect inequality (where one person has all the income).

The World Bank uses this method to show inequalities globally (the index ranges from 24.9 in Japan to 70.7 in Namibia).

The **Gini index** is sometimes shown as the **Gini coefficient**, which is the same thing except that it's shown as a value between 0 and 1 (i.e. the Gini index divided by 100). An index of 24.9 for Japan therefore becomes 0.249.

The main advantages of either the Gini index or the Gini coefficient are that they:

- measure inequality, rather than presenting a uniform picture of an entire population (such GDP or GNI)
- can be used to compare inequalities of different kinds within a country, e.g. urban areas compared to rural, or comparing different sections of the population
- are easy to use to detect trends over time. In an ideal world, the Gini index would improve as GDP increases, showing that the population shares in increased wealth. If this is not happening, then wealth is becoming more concentrated in the hands of a few.

6.4 Drawing proportional circles

This skill is of particular use for the following topics:

- Health, human rights and intervention, Section 4.3
- Migration, identity and sovereignty, Section 5.12

Proportional circles are sized in proportion to each other, based on particular comparative data (such as the different population sizes of UK cities). They are then placed on a map to show the locations to which they refer, e.g. cities or countries. The size of each circle is proportional to the value it represents.

The data in Figure 1 show the number of vehicles manufactured in the UK in 2015, divided up by manufacturer. Proportional circles can be drawn for these data – each one placed on a map of the UK at the location identified in Column B. In this way, geographical information becomes easier to interpret.

Column A	Column B	Column C	Column D	Column E
Manufacturer	**Location of factories**	**Number of vehicles manufactured in 2015**	**Square root of Column C**	**Diameter of circle**
Jaguar Land Rover	West Midlands (Castle Bromwich, Halewood, Solihull)	489 923	699.9	2 cm
Nissan	Sunderland	476 589		
Mini	Oxford	201 207		
Toyota	Burnaston	190 161		
Honda	Swindon	119 414		
Vauxhall	Ellesmere Port	85 241	291.96	0.83 cm
All makes		**1 587 677**		

Figure 1 *UK car manufacturers, by location and the number of vehicles they produced in 2015*

How to construct proportional circles

1. Take the square root of each value

In Figure 1 the data in Column C range from 489 923 to 85 241. To reduce the range of these values – and make the circles workable – make a copy of Figure 1 and then add the square roots of the remaining four manufacturers to Column D. Work from these smaller figures, instead of the original numbers of vehicles manufactured by each company.

2. Work out the size of the largest circle

The maximum size of circle you want to add to a map will vary, depending on the size of map available to you. For a standard map of the UK on A4 paper, a diameter of 2 cm is probably as large as you want. This figure is shown in Column E in Figure 1.

3. Calculate the size of the remaining circles

Calculate the diameter of the remaining circles in Column E on your copy of Figure 1. Calculate each circle size using the square root data as follows:

symbol size = maximum symbol size x (the value / maximum value)

So for Vauxhall (291.96), the circle's diameter will be:
2 cm x (291.96 / 699.9) = 0.83 cm

4. Draw and place the symbol for each location

If you are drawing circles on a computer, select a circle from the drawing tool menu, and make it into the correct size by pressing the SHIFT key as you drag it to the size you want. Then place it on the map in the correct location.

5. Draw a key

Use the format shown in Figure 2, where the largest circle is 2 cm in diameter. Then draw a horizontal scale, like the one shown. The length of the line should extend from the centre of the largest circle, through the centre of the smallest circle, and then to zero. Although you're using square root values to calculate symbol sizes, label the key with the original real values.

Key:

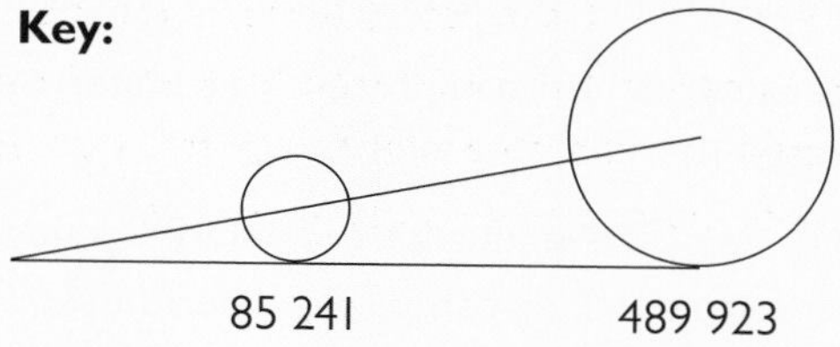

85 241 489 923

Figure 2 *How to draw the key for proportional circles, using data from Figure 1*

6.5 Using source materials critically – text

This skill is of particular use for the following topics:
- Health, human rights and intervention, Section 4.10
- Migration, identity and sovereignty, Section 5.13

Sources and bias

Geographers regularly use a variety of source materials to assess the intentions and impacts of people's words and actions. Both the reliability and the accuracy of those source materials depend on when, by whom and why they were originally written. Any piece of writing reflects the preferences and potential bias of the person or organization that prepared it.

Most bias occurs in sources intended to present a particular viewpoint. For example, UK newspapers generally express the views of their owners. These owners' views – and therefore the opinions expressed in their newspapers – permeate what we read, and may influence what we think. For example, take the topic of attitudes towards immigration:

- If we believe that high immigration has negative impacts on a country (e.g. greater demands for housing and healthcare), then data that show numbers of immigrants increasing will add to our worries.
- However, if immigration data are supported by evidence about the positive impacts that immigration can bring (such as balancing an ageing population), then we may develop different attitudes.

Types of source materials

Source materials come in two broad types – **primary and secondary**.

- **Primary sources** include first-hand reports about an event, persons, place, or set of circumstances. They include legal documents, eyewitness accounts, the results of tests, experiments, statistics, speeches, interviews, surveys, fieldwork, and internet-based information in emails, blogs, social media, audio and video records, plus the Census.
- **Secondary sources** involve processing, interpreting or commenting on primary sources – in the form of discussions, summaries, analyses and evaluations of primary evidence. Articles in newspapers, magazines and journals, as well as TV documentaries and websites presenting cases, depend on processing primary sources – so these are all classed as secondary sources.

The University of California at Santa Cruz offers the following framework for evaluating bias:

1. Authority

- Who published the source, e.g. a university, reputable publisher or government agency?
- What is the purpose of the publication?
- Where does the information in the source come from? Does it appear valid and well researched, or is it questionable and unsupported by evidence? Does it quote and reference its own sources?
- Who is the author? What is their educational background or past writing in this area? Are they an expert whose name is quoted in other sources?
- Is the content a first-hand account, or is it being re-told?

2. Purpose

- What is the author's intention? Is the information fact, opinion or propaganda?
- Is the author's point of view objective and impartial? Is their language free of emotion-rousing words or bias?

6.6 Using source materials critically – data

This skill is of particular use for the following topics:
- **Health, human rights and intervention, Section 4.11**
- **Migration, identity and sovereignty, Section 5.13**

'Lies, damned lies and statistics' – it's a commonly heard phrase. Geographers rely on data for much of their work, so it's important to be aware of any pitfalls that lie in their collection, interpretation and use. Statistical data are a useful source of evidence, so it's essential to be able to interpret such data properly. That means that it's also crucial to know the extent to which they represent any sort of reality.

In 2014, the Scottish Nationalist Party (SNP) – who ran the Scottish government – held a referendum to decide whether Scotland should become independent from the UK. The referendum showed that a majority of Scots were in favour of remaining within the UK. It also showed how data can be misused or misinterpreted, as Figures 1 and 2 show.

Would Scotland benefit from independence? In 2014, the SNP claimed that North Sea oil revenues would sustain Scotland economically for the foreseeable future. Why should Scotland allow profits from oil reserves off the Scottish coast to head south to the London headquarters of UK oil companies like BP, as well as giving oil tax revenue to the UK government?

At the time of the Scottish independence referendum in September 2014, the price of North Sea oil from the Brent oilfield (known as 'Brent crude') was about US$100 per barrel (see Figure 3). However, within four months of the referendum, the price had fallen to less than US$50 a barrel – in effect, halving revenues and making many North Sea oil production platforms uneconomic. Throughout 2016, the fall in global oil prices led to reduced production, the closure or suspension of new drilling – and rising unemployment in Scotland. In addition, it was revealed that a £24 billion clean-up bill would have to be met to cover the costs of closing oilfields down.

Figure 1 *Would Scotland benefit from independence from the UK or not? How short-term data gave a false impression in the 2014 Scottish independence referendum.*

During the referendum, the SNP claimed that Scotland would be an attractive location for FDI from overseas governments and companies. But what benefits does overseas ownership bring? To boost its case, the Scottish government's data showed that 44% of manufacturing businesses in Scotland had overseas owners.

- However, manufacturing is a small part of the Scottish economy. Across the whole Scottish economy, only 5% of Scottish businesses have overseas owners.
- Nevertheless, the influence of overseas companies is extensive. 14% of Scotland's workforce works for overseas-owned companies in the service sector alone. This rises to 42% of employment in oil, gas and other energy companies in Scotland.
- The strength of their economic impact comes from a figure which measures the value added to products or services – known as Gross Value Added (or GVA). Overseas companies accounted for 68% of Scotland's GVA.

Figure 2 *Overseas-owned companies – good or bad?*

Figure 3 *North Sea oil prices (known as 'Brent crude'), September 2014 – December 2016*

Are data to be trusted?

As with text (see Section 6.5), the following framework is useful for evaluating data and their potential misuse:

- Have the data been collected first-hand, or have they come from elsewhere? If they came from Wikipedia, trace the original source.
- Who was the author or organiser of the data collection? What is their educational background or past experience in data collection? Are they an expert whose name is quoted in other sources?
- What is the author's intention? Are the data presented as authoritative (i.e. as fact), as opinion, or as propaganda?
- Is the author's point of view objective and impartial? Is the language free of emotion-rousing words or bias?
- Who published the data? Have they come from a learned institution such as a university, a reputable publisher, or a government agency with a reputation for valid data collection?
- What is the purpose of the data collection? Is it part of a process such as a Census, or have the data been specially commissioned?
- Are the data valid and well researched, or are they questionable? Do the data show trends supported by other sources?

Using data critically in Section 4.11

In Section 4.11, you are asked to identify the possible misuse of data when judging the success of US Aid in countries such as those shown in Figure 8. Remember that government sources and those of the media may present a view of 'success'. That view may be justifiable, but it needs to be checked and not simply accepted as truth. Try to investigate alternative press sources, such as 'Huffington Post' or 'Open Democracy', as well as IGOs such as the UN, NGOs such as the Red Cross, or Amnesty International. If the data from each source match up, then they are probably correct.

Using data critically in Section 5.13

In Section 5.13, you are asked to identify possible misuses of data by the Syrian government in promoting support for the government during the civil war, 2011–17. These might include data on casualties in attacks, or the number of attacks, and on whom they were made. Remember that this conflict involves government sources that may need checking for reliability (e.g. Syria, Russia), as well as those presented by government-sponsored media wishing to portray a particular viewpoint. These views – and any data presented to support them – may be justifiable, but they need to be checked and not simply accepted as truth. Again, try to investigate alternative press sources such as 'Huffington Post' or 'Open Democracy', as well as IGOs such as the UN, NGOs such as the Red Cross, or Amnesty International. If the data from each source match up, then they are probably correct.

6.7 Flow-line maps

This skill is of particular use for the following topics:
- The water cycle and water insecurity, Section 1.2
- The carbon cycle and energy security, Section 2.2
- Health, human rights and intervention, Section 4.7

Using flow lines and arrows

Flow-line maps show movements, e.g. of people or goods. For example, Figure 1 uses arrows of different widths to show population movements from London to the other economic regions in England and Wales.

- The width of each flow line represents a different number of people, using a set scale (e.g. 1 mm = 1000 people).
- The arrowheads on each flow line indicate the direction of movement.

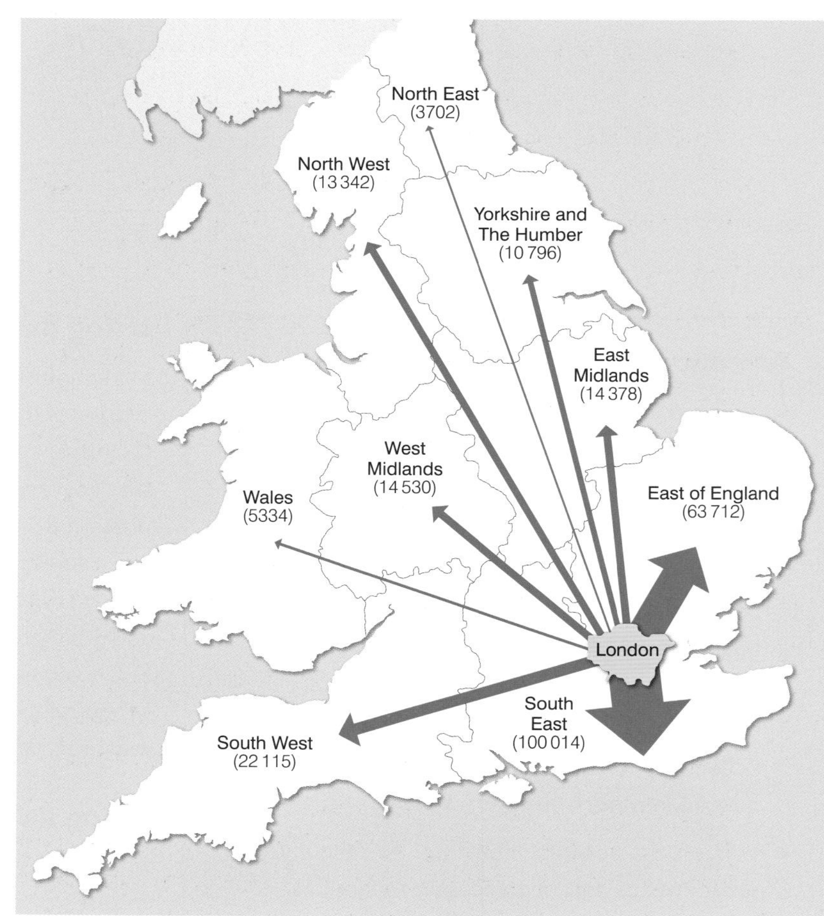

Figure 1 *Flows of people from London to the eight other English economic regions, plus Wales, in mid-2012. The width of each arrow is in proportion to the number of people moving out of London to that region, so the widest arrow is to the South East region and the narrowest to the North East.*

Follow these steps to construct a flow-line map showing the movement of people to the UK:

1. Review the data that you wish to use (e.g. Figure 2) and identify the highest number that you have to show – in this case, India (734 000).
2. Decide on an appropriate width of flow line to show this, e.g. 1 mm = 100 000 people.
3. Now check the minimum value (Nigeria; 181 000) and check that your scale also works for that. (In some cases, flow maps use dotted lines for lower values where the width of the flow is so narrow that it could not be drawn accurately.)
4. Plot the flows on a world map, with arrows leading to the UK (the host country) from the ten major source countries in Figure 2.

Rank	Country of origin	Population
1	India	734 000
2	Poland	679 000
3	Pakistan	502 000
4	Republic of Ireland	376 000
5	Germany	297 000
6	South Africa	221 000
7	Bangladesh	217 000
8	USA	199 000
9	China	191 000
10	Nigeria	181 000

Figure 2 *The top ten source countries for international migrants living in the UK in 2013*

7.1 The synoptic Paper Three

In this section, you'll learn about the synoptic paper and what makes it different from other examinations.

What is Paper Three like?

- Paper Three is a 2 hour and 15 minute exam paper, worth 70 marks, which contributes 20% of the marks towards your final A level grade.
- It is called a 'synoptic investigation' and is designed to draw together your knowledge, understanding, and skills from the two-year A level course.
- It is likely to include short open, open response and resource-linked questions, as well as extended written questions worth 8, 18 and 24 marks.

Paper Three is very different from Papers One and Two (see Chapter 9).

- Instead of focusing on content that you have been taught, it focuses on your ability to handle **unseen** geographical material. Relatively few marks in this examination are awarded for knowledge recall.
- The unseen material consists of a Resource Booklet, and part of your time in the examination should be used to study this - which is one of the reasons why timing is generous – i.e. 135 minutes for 70 marks.
- The Resource Booklet will outline details about a place or issue. Text, statistics, tables of data, and photographs will help you analyse and understand this place and issue more clearly.
- The Resource Booklet is likely to contain details about places with which you are unfamiliar and have never studied. Don't let this put you off; it is your ability to interpret, analyse and make sense of these materials which is being assessed.
- Use your geographical skills in analysing both quantitative and qualitative data. These will include statistical skills (e.g. Spearman's Rank). Note that any formulas and methods for using these skills will be provided, and you may take a calculator into the exam. Your skills should mainly focus on interpreting the *results* of any tests that you perform.

Preparing for Paper Three

The Resource Booklet will be based on **two or more** of the compulsory content areas. Because some of the specification is optional (e.g. Coastal or Glaciated Landscapes), Paper Three can only draw specifically on common topics which have been studied by all students:

- Tectonic processes and hazards (Chapter 1 in Book 1 of this series)
- Globalisation (Chapter 4 in Book 1 of this series)
- The water cycle and water insecurity (Chapter 1 in this textbook)
- The carbon cycle and energy security (Chapter 2 in this textbook)
- Superpowers (Chapter 3 in this textbook).

However, you may use content from any topic to inform your ideas, e.g. Landscape Systems, Processes and Change (Chapters 2 or 3 in Book 1 of this series), Shaping Places (Chapters 5 or 6 in Book 1 of this series), and Global Development and Connections (Chapters 4 or 5 in this textbook).

Synoptic themes across the topics

This specification contains three synoptic themes within the compulsory content areas, that 'bind' or glue the whole specification together.
These themes are:

- **Players**
- **Attitudes and Actions**
- **Futures and Uncertainties.**

These are referred to throughout this student textbook, and you should be clear about their meanings. Paper Three will draw upon these themes and assess your ability to apply them. To help you do this, refer to the following sections:

- Section 7.2 – discusses Players
- Section 7.3 – discusses Attitudes and Actions
- Section 7.4 – discusses Futures and Uncertainties.

Exemplar Resource Booklet

Section 7.5 is an exemplar Paper Three Resource Booklet, complete with exam-style questions. It is based on Tectonics and Energy Security, but you will see that themes such as Globalisation and Superpowers are threaded through it. This should help you to understand how links can be made between different topics you have studied.

More importantly, the booklet should help you to recognise that there is a very wide spectrum of views about geographical issues and that they can be **contested**. You should also be aware that data in all their forms – statistics, photos, text for example – need treating with care and considerable caution. Studying sections 7.2 to 7.4 should help to prepare you for this.

Questions, and what the examiners will look for

The questions in Paper Three will be as follows:

- Questions early in the paper will assess knowledge recall and skills in interpreting geographical information. These are intended to help you to gain an overview of the issue. These questions will generally carry 4 marks. Question 1 in Section 7.5 (page 288) is typical.
- Extended written questions of up to 8 marks may ask you to analyse and explain trends that you see in the data in the Resource Booklet. These are intended to assess deeper understanding, and your ability to apply your knowledge and understanding to analyse new information. Questions 2, and 4 in Section 7.5 (page 288) are typical.
- Finally, two extended essay-style questions, of 18 and 24 marks respectively, will probe your ability to evaluate material in the Resource Booklet. These will draw together your knowledge, your skills in interpreting unseen information, and your ability to analyse and apply this to the framework of concepts and ideas gained from two years of A level study. Questions 5 and 6 in Section 7.5 (page 288) are typical.

To reach the top levels in the mark scheme, you must:

- show accurate geographical knowledge and understanding.
- apply that knowledge and understanding to make logical and relevant connections / relationships to material in the Resource Booklet.
- interpret any data or material coherently, and support any arguments with evidence; so that you write rational, substantiated, and balanced conclusions.
- make valid judgements about the value and reliability of data/evidence.

7.2 Synoptic Links 1: Players

In this section, you'll learn about the importance of players and how to make synoptic links between each of the topics in this specification.

Understanding Players

Think about a particular change that you may have studied in A level Geography.

- At a local scale, the London 2012 Olympic and Paralympic Games brought about regeneration in East London in the early twenty-first century.
- At a national scale, the UK economy has been transformed since the 1980s from one based on primary and secondary activity, to one in which the quaternary, or knowledge, economy dominates.
- Globally, the processes of globalisation have transformed trade, capital flows and investment, and migrations of people.

None of these has occurred by chance; all were planned. The plans in each case have been to develop a specific proposal (e.g. London's 2012 Games), or a long-term programme (e.g. of regeneration), or political strategy (e.g. the UK's economic transformation). The people who have interests in these plans are known as **stakeholders**, whilst those responsible for making decisions about their implementation are known as **players**.

Depending on the topic or issue, players can be categorised into three sectors: private, public, and a third or voluntary sector. It is important to understand how each works, how it is accountable, and to whom.

The private sector

The private sector refers to businesses financed by private capital, ranging from small local companies to large transnational corporations (TNCs). TNCs are fundamental to the concept of 'players'. Being a 'corporation' means that ownership of a company – among its shareholders – is split from management. Managers are legally bound to maximise profits for shareholders, and therefore provide maximum dividend for them. Shareholders hold them to account. Corporations are also bound only by limited liability – i.e. that shareholders share in profits, but are not personally liable for any company debts. So with profit as a key motive, it becomes easy to understand how corporations become significant players in decisions made about people and space.

The public sector

The public sector refers to organisations financed by public sources (e.g. taxation), including government functions such as education, health, social services and defence.

- **Within** a country, governments range from small-scale (e.g. parish councils) to regional (e.g. borough or county councils), and national governments. Their accountability varies, on a spectrum from full democracy (where there are no restrictions on the establishment of political parties, and almost all adults are entitled to vote) to limited (e.g. single party states such as China) through to dictatorship, where there is no accountability.
- **Internationally**, intergovernmental organisations (IGOs) are created when governments collaborate over issues of mutual interest. These include economic or trading unions (e.g. the EU, ASEAN). As yet, only the EU has its own elected government structure.

The 'third sector'

This is the most varied sector, and covers both organisations or individuals.

- Some (e.g. Greenpeace) are pressure groups campaigning on environmental or social issues. Their income is derived from memberships and donations.
- Other larger-scale operations – collectively known as non-governmental organisations (NGOs) – are involved in development work or aid. Their revenue varies, but includes voluntary donations and government-funded programmes (e.g. Oxfam's work in development aid).
- Politically significant players include **think tanks**, which are organisations set up to research and promote particular philosophies. They are usually funded by wealthy foundations – for example the Thatcher Foundation, set up by former Prime Minister Margaret Thatcher, which exists to promote neo-liberal thinking. Its research often supports policies promoted by the UK Conservative Party.

Players in compulsory topics

Tectonic processes and hazards

Tectonic processes and hazards can be found in Chapter 1 in Book 1 of this series. Players include local and national governments, scientists, planners, engineers, NGOs and insurers, who are involved in:

- hazard or disaster relief work
- decision-making which impacts upon policy (e.g. nuclear energy in Japan after the Tōhoku earthquake in 2011)
- hazard management (including prevention strategies, or damage-limitation strategies such as hazard-avoidance, or evacuation procedures)
- hazard prediction.

Globalisation

Globalisation can be found in Chapter 4 in Book 1 of this series. Players include:

- IGOs (e.g. WTO, IMF, World Bank) and trading blocs (e.g. EU, ASEAN)
- individual governments and their policies towards economic liberalisation (e.g. in attracting FDI)
- individual businesses, especially TNCs who account for nearly 80% of world trade
- pressure groups representing those disadvantaged by globalisation.

The Water cycle and water insecurity

The Water cycle and water insecurity can be found in Chapter 1 of this textbook. Players include:

- resource planners in, for example, managing land use or water supply
- governments and investors in large-scale water management projects
- various players in trans-boundary and internal conflicts, e.g. local protest groups, national and state governments.

The Carbon cycle and energy insecurity

The Carbon cycle and energy insecurity can be found in Chapter 2 of this textbook. Players include:

- TNCs and companies which invest in energy reserves, and their views towards climate change
- IGOs (e.g. OPEC), and their role in pricing resources such as oil
- Consumer groups and their views of energy companies
- Governments, and their policies towards energy, sustainable development, or climate change
- Environmental pressure groups and communities affected by e.g. fracking.

Superpowers

Superpowers can be found in Chapter 3 of this textbook. Players include:

- TNCs involved in maintaining power and wealth, and in supporting particular governments and their policies
- Powerful countries, and their role as 'global police'
- Emerging powers in geopolitical change.

7.3 Synoptic Links 2: Attitudes and Actions

In this section, you'll learn about the importance of attitudes and actions, and how to make synoptic links between each of the topics in this specification.

Understanding Attitudes and Actions

Attitudes are the viewpoints that decision-makers and stakeholders have towards economic, social, environmental or political issues; their actions are the ways in which they try to achieve what they want. For example, climate scientists recognising the threats posed by climate change would seek international agreements to mitigate and adapt to its impacts.

You should be aware why attitudes to geographical issues vary so greatly, and how these variations influence actions that are taken – for example, to adopt a policy to combat climate change. Influences on values and attitudes might include political or religious viewpoints, the priority given to profit, the importance of social justice and equality, or views on the natural environment (e.g. sustainability versus a wish to exploit resources). Attitudes are important, because for example, people with certain attitudes towards one issue (e.g. globalisation) *may* have similar views on other issues (e.g. climate change).

Understanding why attitudes differ

For most people, their attitudes towards issues reflect their values. These values may be about economic wealth, issues such as social welfare, or the environment.

As an example, the political plan to transform the UK economy starting in the 1980s has been based upon a belief in **globalisation**. This belief is based on certain assumptions:

- capitalism delivers the greatest good for the majority
- people should generally be responsible for their own lives and not rely on the state
- the private sector delivers goods and services more effectively and cheaply than the public sector
- the private sector does best with few regulations (e.g. on workers' rights, environmental standards) because these add to costs
- governments should promote policies that encourage private companies to invest.

These views lie traditionally on the right wing of politics, and form the underlying basis of **neo-liberalism** (see Section 5.9). They have led to the formation of pressure groups and political parties promoting neo-liberal viewpoints, such as challenging climate change. Many beliefs are explored, researched and promoted by right-wing **think-tanks** – political research groups funded by donors who wish to promote these beliefs. Like all think-tanks, their research should be challenged.

These views can influence governments through persuasion in the following ways:

- through a 'western' capitalist ideology - promoting capitalism as the way forward
- by persuading politicians and decision-makers at national and international levels to pursue policies to encourage the private sector
- by gaining support from the media. Newspapers and some privately-owned television companies support capitalist models and promote them, both among the public and among decision-makers.

Understanding alternative viewpoints

Some groups challenge the assumption that **globalisation** brings prosperity to all. They believe that:

- capitalism results in some individuals or groups becoming immensely wealthy at the expense of others
- society should accept responsibility for those least able to support themselves – and that everyone gains when it does so
- the public sector meets social and economic needs more fairly than the private sector
- a lack of regulation of the private sector leads to reduced workers' rights, and may reduce environmental quality
- governments ought to promote policies that seek the greatest good for the greatest number.

These views lie traditionally on the left wing of politics, and underpin **socialism**. They have led to the formation of pressure groups and political parties who contest the assumption that capitalism provides what is best.

- A few have a specific focus, such as Greenpeace which campaigns for greater environmental protection.
- Others form political parties which campaign across a range of issues. Many of their beliefs are explored, researched and promoted by left-leaning think-tanks – most of whom are funded by wealthy donors, voluntary donations, or by legacies whose funds support left-wing thinking. For example, the Joseph Rowntree Foundation is a British social policy research and development charity, which exists to investigate causes and solutions to social problems such as poverty or housing. Its research informs policies of the UK Labour Party. Like neo-liberal think-tanks, its research needs to be contested before being accepted.

Attitudes and Actions in compulsory topics

Tectonic processes and hazards

There are none required in the specification.

Globalisation

These include:

- actions taken in support of, and against, globalisation
- environmental movements arising from the impacts of globalisation
- viewpoints in favour of, and against, immigration resulting from globalisation
- actions of NGOs and pressure groups, usually in monitoring or opposing globalisation.

The Water cycle and water insecurity

These include:

- contrasting attitudes to water supply (e.g. developing more sustainable schemes of water supply as opposed to hard engineering schemes)

The Carbon cycle and energy insecurity

These include:

- attitudes of global consumers to environmental issues
- attitudes of different countries, TNCs and people towards climate change.

Superpowers

These include:

- actions and attitudes of global IGOs, and different countries towards, for example, globalisation
- attitudes of different players in relation to resources
- contrasting cultural ideologies between different countries and players.

Synoptic Links 3: Futures and Uncertainties

In this section, you'll learn about the importance of futures and uncertainties, and how to make synoptic links between each of the topics in this specification.

Understanding Futures and Uncertainties

Many of the topics that you have studied pose 'big questions' about the future. As global population heads towards 9 billion by about 2050, there are debates about whether the world can provide people with sufficient safe water to drink or for growing food, or whether energy industries can provide for all. What will a global economy look like in 2050, and how might geopolitics play out between the world's major superpowers?

People approach questions about the future in different ways, which can make it seem uncertain. Visions of the future include those who favour:

- business as usual, i.e. letting things stand or function as they are. This might involve doing nothing, or only doing what is necessary when it's unavoidable. In the case of the energy industries, for example, this approach may leave it to private companies to decide on energy futures, by letting supply and demand drive the energy market. Those who believe in the 'fossil fuel society' are likely to support 'business as usual', which means, unless it is challenged, change will never occur.
- more sustainable strategies for future development, such as those who, faced with climate change, might want radical action. In the case of the energy industries, such approaches may require decisions from governments about energy futures, by letting renewable energy sources supply the energy market.

Choice of actions can affect both people and the environment in very different ways (e.g. by adapting to, or ignoring risks of, climate change). We may be unsure about the outcomes of those choices, because uncertainties exist:

- **scientific:** can new energy or water technologies provide for the future?
- **demographic:** will population increase place new demands upon the world's resources such as energy or water?
- **economic:** will even greater pressure come from demands and expectations of rising living standards among the world's largest economies?
- **political:** which political parties will be the decision-makers in 2050? Will these be representative of populations as part of a shift towards greater democracy, or will power lie in the hands of a political or an economic elite?

Sustainability and futures

Sustainability was defined in 1987 by the UN Brundtland Commission as '*development that meets the needs of the present without compromising the ability of future generations to meet their own needs*'. This definition provides a useful framework for assessing sustainability. The sustainability of a proposal can also be measured by:

- The Egan wheel (Figure 1). This judges an idea on its economic, social and environmental outcomes. It is useful for judging specific proposals at a local scale.

Figure 1 *The Egan wheel*

- The sustainability **'quadrant'** (Figure 2) which uses four questions which are 'tests' for sustainability. Ideally, answers to all four should be 'yes' if a development or proposal seeks to be sustainable. This is useful for judging development at a broader scale – for example, resource use.

Equity Does it benefit everyone?	**Futurity** Will it last?
Public participation Is it bottom-up?	**Environment** Is it eco-friendly?

Figure 2 *The sustainability 'quadrant'*

Futures and Uncertainties in compulsory topics

Tectonic processes and hazards

There are none required in the specification.

Globalisation

These include:

- the environmental consequences of resource consumption.

The Water cycle and water insecurity

These include:

- projections of future drought/flood risk
- projections of future water scarcity.

The Carbon cycle and energy insecurity

These include:

- the uncertainty of global projections about climate change .

Superpowers

These include:

- the uncertainty over future power structures as the balance between superpowers changes.

Over to you

Understanding Players

1 Study Section 7.2.
  - **a** In pairs, draw a spider diagram with three spokes – Private sector, Public sector, and Third sector.
  - **b** Build further spokes from each one to show the key players involved in decision-making about Tectonic processes and hazards, Globalisation, Water and Energy insecurity, and Superpowers. Build it further with examples you have studied.

2 Discuss and decide who are the key decision-makers locally, nationally, internationally and globally? Are these private, public or third sector? Are they elected or unelected?

Understanding Attitudes and Actions

3 Study Section 7.3.
  - **a** Review your spider diagram of key players.
  - **b** In different colours, identify and highlight those players who work for a neo-liberal agenda.
  - **c** List and make notes on what these organisations have in common.
  - **d** Now identify those who work for an alternative environmental or socialist agenda.
  - **e** List and make notes on what these organisations have in common.

4 Decide where the global balance of power lies at present.

Understanding Futures and Uncertainties

5 Study Section 7.4. In pairs, identify those players who are:
  - **a** most likely to have a 'business as usual' agenda
  - **b** most likely to pursue a sustainable agenda.

Resource Booklet: Energy futures in Japan

In this section, you'll learn about the role played by nuclear energy in closing an emerging energy gap in Japan, as well as the challenges faced by Japan's nuclear industry from frequent tectonic activity in the country.

- Pages 277–281 are in the format of an unseen Resource Booklet as you would use in Paper Three
- Page 282 includes exam-style questions about this Resource Booklet, of the kind that you could meet in a Paper Three exam.

You are advised to read all five sections before attempting any questions, both here and in the actual exam.

Section A: Nuclear fallout?

In 2010, nuclear energy produced 14% of global electricity. Many countries have regarded nuclear as a 'technological fix' to help close the global energy gap without increasing greenhouse gas emissions. However, 11 March 2011 changed the debate. Following the Tōhoku earthquake (see Figure 1), a tsunami badly damaged Japan's Fukushima Daiichi nuclear plant, which led to the suspension of the Japanese nuclear industry and also caused wider global impacts:

- France, Germany, Italy and Switzerland all abandoned plans to expand their nuclear industries.
- Doubts were also raised over proposed nuclear schemes in the USA, UK and Scandinavia.
- By 2015, nuclear energy had fallen to 10.9% of global electricity production.
- Japan had to resume importing fossil fuels to help meet its energy demands.

Figure 1 *A factfile about the Tōhoku earthquake, and some of its potential implications*

Players
- National government
- International nuclear agencies
- TNCs
- Consumers
- Environmental lobby

Tectonics – the Tōhoku earthquake
- Date: 11 March 2011
- Magnitude: between 9.0 and 9.1
- It was the world's fifth largest earthquake since modern records began in about 1900.
- In Tokyo, less than 200 miles from the epicentre, the shaking lasted for six minutes.
- Parts of the main island of Honshu moved eight metres to the east.

Issues concerning globalisation and Japan

There were impacts on:
- global stock markets
- Japanese GDP
- trade with the rest of the world.

Major TNCs' supply chains were interrupted.

Attitudes and Actions
- Carbon emissions vs. nuclear options?
- Opportunities
- Management

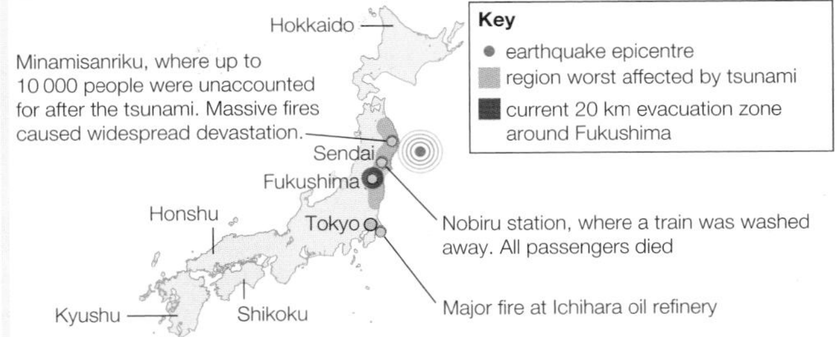

Issues concerning Japan's water security
- Water supplies were contaminated.
- Local ecosystems were threatened by released radioactivity.
- Clouds of radiation spread widely.

Futures and Uncertainties
- Energy security
- Economic growth and stability

Issues concerning Japan as a superpower

Questions have arisen about:
- Japan's status as a leading economic power, as a result of the 2011 earthquake costs
- whether China will take advantage of Japanese economic and political weakness, by exerting power in the disputed waters of the Sea of Japan.

Issues concerning Japan's energy security
- Japan's long-term energy mix could change.
- Negative international reactions.

Section B Reactions to Tōhoku – the background

Japan experiences hundreds of earthquakes each year, and tsunami threats are part of Japanese life. The Japanese government and power industries do apply safety measures, but a 2008 report suggested that Fukushima was at risk from flooding by seawater. It stated that waves of 10.2 metres or higher would breach the sea walls, but the plant's owners regarded such waves as unlikely. However, the Tōhoku earthquake triggered a tsunami of between 13 and 15 metres – much higher than allowed for by the scientific models used to design the coastal defences.

Other organisations had also warned Japan of potential risks, such as the:

- US Nuclear Regulatory Commission (in 2004)
- International Atomic Energy Agency (IAEA) in 2008.

The G8 Nuclear Safety and Security Group (Tokyo) had also advised that earthquakes of magnitude 7.0 or greater posed serious potential problems for Japan.

Figure 2 *Fukushima nuclear power plant in February 2012, almost one year after the earthquake that badly damaged it and forced it to close*

Japan is located at the junction of four major tectonic plates, as well as other minor ones, and is therefore subject to a high level of seismic activity. The 2011 Tōhoku earthquake exceeded the 1995 Kobe earthquake by killing over 16 000 people (compared to Kobe's 6434), and causing an estimated US$236 billion in damage (compared to Kobe's US$102.5 billion). This, according to Credit Suisse, was 3% of Japan's GDP in 2011 (compared to Kobe's 2.5% in 1995).

Context

The timing of the 2011 Tōhoku earthquake occurred when Japan faced several major uncertainties. These included:

- a weakening economy, because globalisation had seen many of Japan's leading export companies lose out to competition from countries in South and Southeast Asia
- stalling domestic demand, due to Japan's ageing population, and reduced spending power among its working-age population due to low economic growth
- a commitment to large reductions in CO_2 emissions at the Paris COP talks.

The Tōhoku earthquake had several short-term implications for Japan:

- It suspended its nuclear power electricity production.
- There was an immediate switch to importing fossil fuels.
- Japan's self-sufficiency in energy fell to 6% – the rest had to be imported.
- Greenhouse gas emissions reached record highs.
- The country faced questions over the potential costs of future earthquakes and tsunami.

Figure 3 *An aerial view of the extensive damage caused to northern Honshu island as a result of the Tōhoku earthquake and subsequent tsunami in 2011*

Section C The economic impacts of Tōhoku

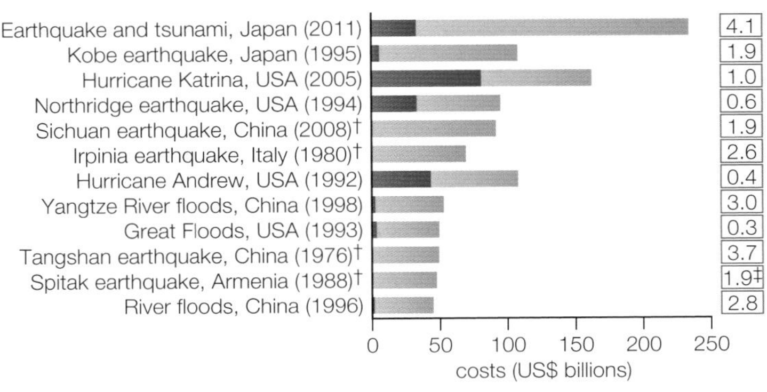

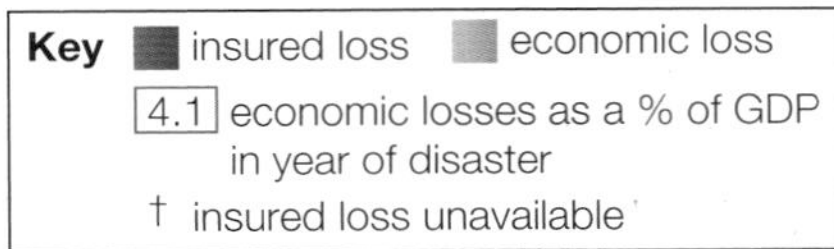

Figure 4 *The world's costliest disasters since 1976*

Figure 5 *The Tōhoku earthquake: companies affected by the disaster*

Estimates in 2011 suggested that insurance claims from the Tōhoku earthquake could reach US$35 billion. Some of the shares most affected were:

Insurance companies and the impact on share prices:

- **Aviva** down 6.77%
- **Beazley** down 8.81%
- **Chaucer** (a specialist in insuring nuclear power plants) down 7.36%

Energy companies and the impact on share prices:

- **Amec** down 7.97%, fearing disruption to UK plans to build new nuclear plants
- **Berkeley Resources** (a uranium mining company) down 37.63%, fearing a global rejection of the nuclear power industry
- **Aggreko** (a mobile / emergency power generation company) up 7.55%, expecting a strong demand for its services

Services / leisure companies and the impact on share prices:

- **Burberry Group** down 9.2%, due to a likely drop in demand for luxury products
- **InterContinental Hotels Group** down 7.34%, with the closure of the Holiday Inn in Sendai, Japan

Industrial / technology companies and the impact on share prices:

- **GKN** (aircraft and car parts producer) down 5.62%; expecting reduced production, because it depends on Japanese customers, who were now unable to take delivery of its products (about 7% of GKN's sales go to Mitsubishi and Nissan)
- **IMI** (supplies the nuclear power industry) down 4.14%

Global connections helped Japan to become the economic success story of the 1980/90s. In particular, its car and electronics industries were poised for global domination, based on reliability and build quality. Economists in 1986 predicted that, by the early 2000s, Japan would be competing with the USA to be the world's largest economy.

However, by 2011, China's economy had overtaken that of Japan. Twenty years of low economic growth in Japan saw major companies there being undercut for price by low-cost Asian rivals. Japan's dependence on exports – the secret of its success – became a problem as overseas demand fell and an ageing domestic population failed to boost sales at home.

Major Japanese brands, such as Sony and Toyota, were also affected by the Tōhoku earthquake. Some production facilities were damaged, and power outages made production difficult. Toyota closed three engine and component factories, with Honda closing two and Nissan four. These factories supplied car assembly plants across the world, so, as Japanese supply lines closed, production in Europe, Australia and the USA also fell.

Figure 6 *The downside of globalisation and Tōhoku for Japanese industries*

Section D The environmental impacts of Tōhoku

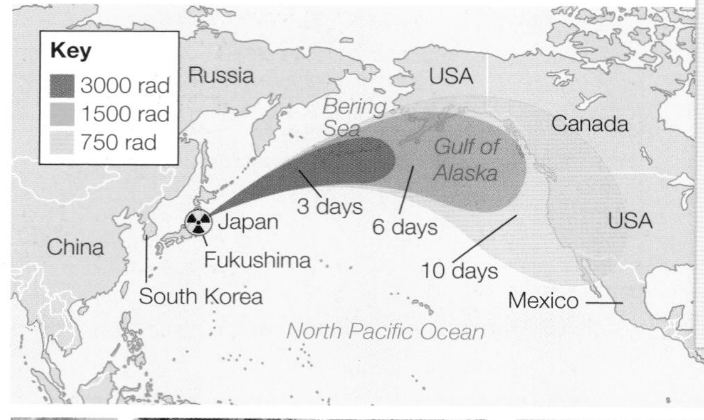

The rad shown in the map key is a unit of absorbed radiation dose. Note that:

- a single dose of under 100 rad typically produces no immediate symptoms, except blood changes
- a dose of 100-200 rad to the body in less than a day can cause acute radiation syndrome, but is not usually fatal
- a dose of 200-1000 rad (delivered in a few hours) causes serious illness, with survival unlikely at the upper end of the range
- a dose of over 1000 rad is invariably fatal.

Figure 7 *How radioactive leaks spread across the Pacific Ocean*

Figure 8 *Local residents queuing for safe water in Fukushima, the day after the earthquake and tsunami*

Figure 9 *Japan's CO_2 emissions hit second highest on record*

Japan's CO_2 emissions hit second highest on record

Already the world's fifth-largest emitter of greenhouse gases, Japan's emissions rose to the second highest on record in the year leading up to March 2014. This reflected a rise in coal-fired power after the immediate and indefinite closure of the country's nuclear power plants.

- CO_2 emissions rose by 1.2% to 1.408 billion metric tonnes of carbon dioxide (CO_2) equivalent from 2012–13, up by 0.8% from 2005 and by 10.8% from 1990.
- In 2012, Japan targeted a 3.8% cut by 2020 from 2005 levels.
- In Paris 2015, Japan agreed to reduce emissions by about 20% by 2030.

Figure 10 *The impacts on Fukushima's fishing industry*

Fukushima's fishing industry is yet to recover

By 2015, Fukushima's fishing industry was still operating at less than 10% of capacity. Highly radioactive water had leaked from the damaged Fukushima nuclear plant into the Pacific fishing grounds. Contaminated seafood has been found to still have radioactive iodine and caesium levels well above Japanese regulatory limits. Restrictions on 32 marine fishery species were still in place in February 2015, as caesium levels in fish remained above 100 Becquerels per kg – 30 times more than someone would consume in an entire year from background radiation levels.

> The number of people who are today willing to buy fish from Fukushima is very low. Wooing back consumers will be a challenge – when we resume full-scale fishing, there may not be people who are willing to buy our fish.

Mr. Kazunori Endo from the Fukushima Fishermen's Cooperative, speaking in March 2015

Section E Japan's energy security

'Security of energy supply is at the top of Japan's political agenda, especially in the aftermath of the country's 11 March 2011 triple disaster (i.e. the earthquake, tsunami, and nuclear meltdown). Having virtually no domestic energy resources and a renewable market still in its infancy, Japan is the world's largest net oil importer.'

'To avoid potential blackouts and overcome this drastic cut in nuclear energy, the share of fossil fuel-based power increased by 25% in 2012, which threatens economic stability and environmental sustainability. Japan needs to move towards a long-term reliable and affordable energy strategy that guarantees security of supply, powers economic growth, supports climate change mitigation policies, and ensures the public's trust.'

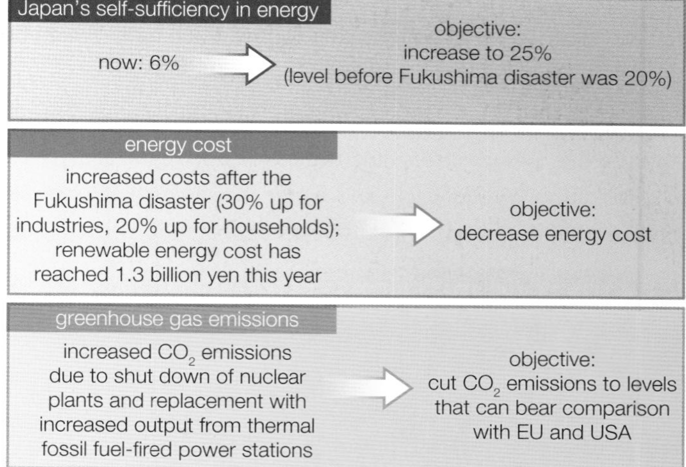

Figure 11 *Two text extracts and an illustration from a publication on academia.edu by Joana Portugal Pereira (United Nations University, Institute of Advanced Studies, Yokohama), and Giancarlos Troncoso Parady and Bernardo Castro Dominguez (University of Tokyo, Graduate School of Engineering) in 2013*

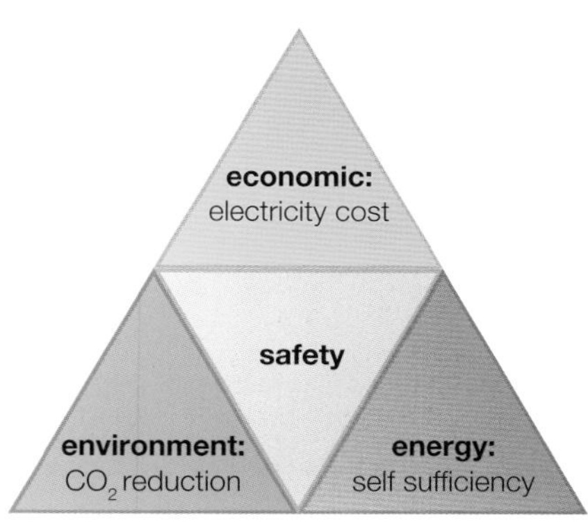

Figure 12a *3E+S – Japanese future policy: securing fossil fuels and expanding renewable energy. Japan's new long-term energy plan is called 3E+S, after the policies shown in the diagram, and it aims to increase energy independence and emphasize safety in a post-Fukushima environment.*

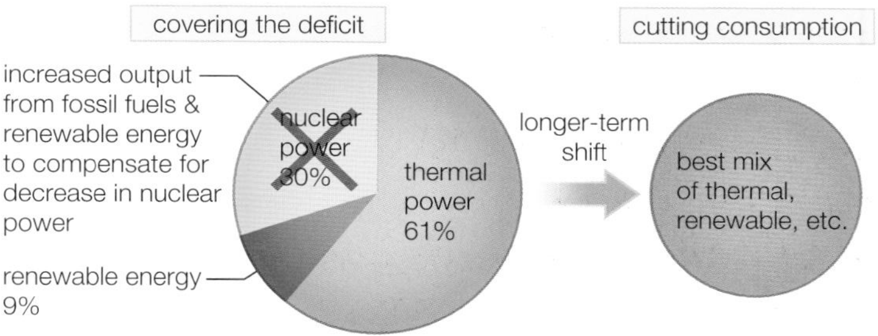

Figure 12b *Japan's energy policy post-2011*

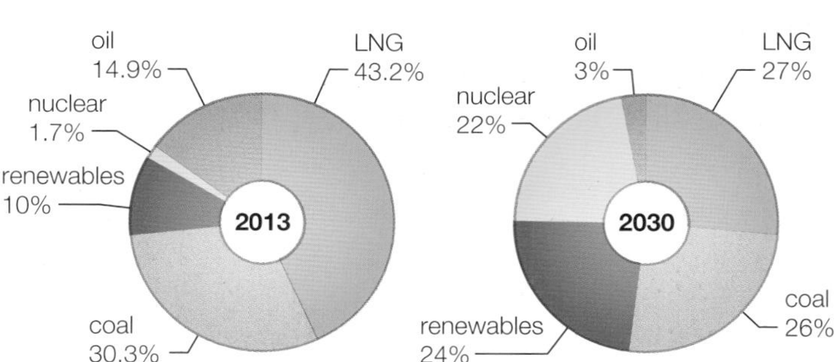

Figure 12c *Japan's proposed energy mix by 2030, compared to 2013. 'LNG' is Liquid Natural Gas.*

Preparing for the exam-style questions

Because this is a practice, Activities **A** and **B** below will help you to prepare in advance for the exam-style questions that follow. Each activity can be done in small groups.

Activity A

Make links between Japan and the Tōhoku earthquake and the five synoptic teaching topics (Tectonic hazards, Globalisation, Water cycle and water insecurity, Carbon cycle and energy security, and Superpowers).

Activity B

Prepare your ideas about the roles of Players (see Section 7.2), Actions (7.3), and Futures and Uncertainties (7.4) in this Resource Booklet. Check the links to these at the start of each section in this book.

Exam-style questions

Instructions:

- Answer ALL questions.
- Use the Resource Booklet provided and your own knowledge and understanding from across your two-year course of study to answer these questions.

1 Explain why nuclear energy is an important contributor to global electricity production. *(4 marks)*

2 Study Sections A and B of the Resource Booklet. Analyse the seriousness of the Tōhoku earthquake for Japan. *(8 marks)*

3 **a** The table below shows total economic and insured losses, plus those losses represented as a percentage of the relevant country's GDP, for 12 natural disasters. It uses data from Figure 4.
The formula for Spearman's rank correlation coefficient value R is given below.

$$R = 1 - \frac{(6 \times \sum d^2)}{(n^3 - n)}$$

Complete the table below and calculate the value of R for the data given. Show your working. *(4 marks)*

b Explain the relationship that you have calculated between total economic and insured losses and those losses as a percentage of GDP. *(4 marks)*

4 Study Section C. Analyse the economic impacts of the Tōhoku earthquake. *(8 marks)*

5 Study Section D. Evaluate the environmental impacts of the Tōhoku earthquake. *(18 marks)*

6 Evaluate the view that the Tōhoku earthquake has compromised Japan's energy policies to deliver the basic principles of sustainable development. *(24 marks)*

Total 70 marks

Natural disaster	Insured plus economic losses (US$ billions)	Rank	Economic losses as a % of GDP	Rank	d	d^2
Earthquake and tsunami, Japan (2011)	236.0	1	4.1	1		
Kobe earthquake, Japan (1995)	102.5	2	1.9	=6	4	16
Hurricane Katrina, USA (2005)	164.0	3	1.0	9	6	36
Northridge earthquake, USA (1994)	93.0	4	0.6	10	6	36
Sichuan earthquake, China (2008)	90.0	5	1.9	=6	1	1
Irpinia earthquake, Italy (1980)	72.0	6	2.6	5		
Hurricane Andrew, USA (1992)	70.0	7	0.4	11	4	16
Yangtze river floods, China (1998)	55.0	8	3.0	3	5	25
Great floods, USA (1993)	50.0	9	0.3	12		
Tangshan earthquake, China (1976)	49.0	10	3.7	2	8	64
Spitak earthquake, Armenia (1988)	47.0	11	1.9	=6		
River floods, China (1996)	44.0	12	2.8	4	8	64
			TOTAL (or $\sum$) d^2			

.1 Introducing the Independent Investigation

In this section, you'll learn about the significance of the Independent Investigation in your A level.

What is the Independent Investigation?

Geography is now one of few A level subjects where coursework is permitted. This means that coursework in Geography – known as the Independent Investigation – will be one of the most advanced pieces of independent work that you will achieve in your school career. This chapter will therefore help you to achieve your best by guiding you through its various stages, and making it clear what you may and may not do according to exam board regulations.

The Independent Investigation is also known as the Non-Examined Assessment (NEA), i.e. it is not assessed by examination! Instead, it consists of a written report. The following guidance is important:

- The report should be about 3000–4000 words long. Although there are no penalties for under- or over-shooting this target, keep it in perspective – you'll need this amount to do a topic justice, but equally to exceed that number of words could be detrimental to your other A level subjects.
- Its title and subject matter must be linked to the A level specification in some way – but that is very broad! It can be a part of the specification that you have not *personally* studied. For example, you may have studied Regenerating Places (Topic 4A) but be interested in exploring an idea in Diverse Places (Topic 4B), which you have not studied. You might even want to cut across topic areas – for example, linking ways in which coastal management (Topic 2B) may affect the nature or identity of a coastal place (Topic 4A).
- It must include fieldwork in which you are involved in collecting primary data (see Sections 8.3 and 8.4). You are required to have four days of fieldwork throughout the A level course, some of which should be used to collect data for your Independent Investigation. You may need more than four days – that is permissible – but you must have four as a minimum.

Deciding on a topic

Although your teachers have probably encouraged you to work independently throughout your school career, the prospect of writing this investigation may seem daunting. Realistically, you'll probably write up most of it in Year 13, after you have completed much of the taught course, so don't expect ideas to occur to you early in the first year of the course. Most likely, ideas will arise during the course, and from fieldwork organised by your teachers. Important in the process is having time to plan and think.

The key thing is to follow an enquiry process, as shown in Figure 1. This means that you should:

- decide on an enquiry **question**, supported by your teacher briefing you
- be fully involved in key decisions about fieldwork **methods** and **data sources**
- process your data fully, making your own decisions about the best ways to **present** data
- independently **analyse** data and reach **conclusions** about your investigation
- consider the validity and reliability of data and the methods you used – known as **evaluation**.

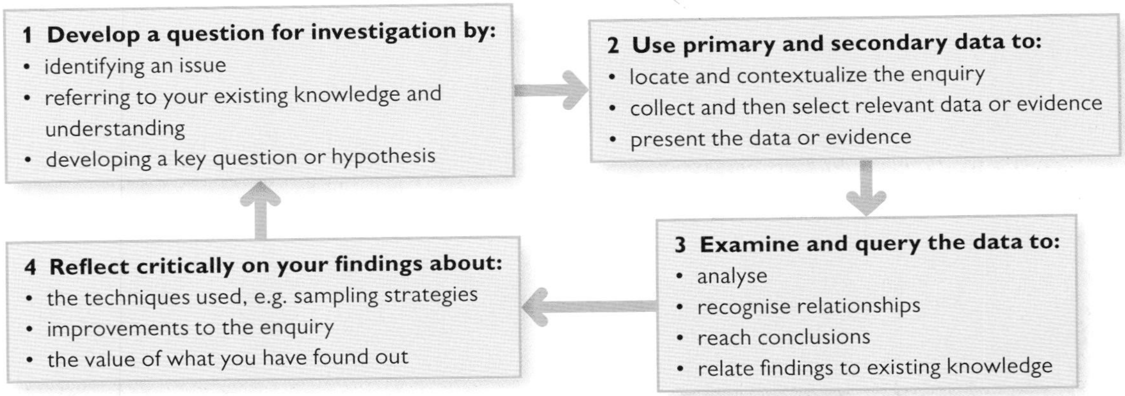

1 Develop a question for investigation by:
- identifying an issue
- referring to your existing knowledge and understanding
- developing a key question or hypothesis

2 Use primary and secondary data to:
- locate and contextualize the enquiry
- collect and then select relevant data or evidence
- present the data or evidence

3 Examine and query the data to:
- analyse
- recognise relationships
- reach conclusions
- relate findings to existing knowledge

4 Reflect critically on your findings about:
- the techniques used, e.g. sampling strategies
- improvements to the enquiry
- the value of what you have found out

Figure 1 *An enquiry model for the Independent Investigation, adapted from Margaret Roberts' book* Geography through Enquiry

While the independent investigation must be based on a question or issue defined and developed by you independently, it doesn't mean that you are completely alone. You will probably have completed fieldwork at GCSE. The structure that you used – defining an aim, setting out methods, presenting results etc. – still applies here. You'll use field data and/or evidence from field investigations, which have been collected individually or in groups. You **can** use group data (see Figures 2 and 4) – it's just the focus and the title that must be your own. You must also use your own research from secondary sources (see Sections 8.3 and 8.4).

Figure 2 *Group working – a more effective way of ensuring that the size of your data sample will be larger. It's permissible – but make sure your title is your own.*

Working independently

Because this is an Independent Investigation, there are restrictions about what your teacher may and may not do. These are summarised in Figure 3, which also refers you to subsequent guidance and support in this chapter.

Stage of investigation	Level of independence
1. Exploring focus	Collaboration with other students is allowed, and teachers may also give a briefing to students.
2. Devising a title, question or hypothesis for the investigation, and the purpose of the investigation	It must be done independently. See Section 8.2 for guidance.
3. Devising methodology and sampling	Collaboration with other students is allowed. See Section 8.4 for guidance.
4. Primary data collection	Collaboration with other students is allowed – not least because it's safer (see Figures 2 and 4). See Section 8.4 for guidance.
5. Secondary data collection (where relevant)	It must be done independently. See Sections 8.3 and 8.4 for guidance.
6. Data/information presentation	It must be done independently. See Section 8.5 for guidance.
7. Data analysis and explanation or interpretation	It must be done independently. However, your teacher could coach you in, for example, a statistical skill that you need. See Sections 8.6 and 8.7 for guidance.
8. Conclusions and evaluation	It must be done independently. See Sections 8.8 and 8.9 for guidance.

Figure 3 *What is and is not allowable in the Independent Investigation*

Figure 4 *Geography fieldwork – always done best in a group for safety's sake, and because you'll collect more data that way*

Devising a focus and title

In this section, you'll learn about devising a title for your investigation.

Thinking of a study topic

It's unlikely that thinking of a study topic will cause you a major problem. Once your teacher has introduced you to some fieldwork, and you have practised data collection, it's very likely that thinking of a topic will be less difficult.

- Your teacher may take you on a field trip to a fieldwork centre, where all students will carry out similar work each day on topics selected by the centre, e.g. investigating features of a coastline.
- Alternatively, you may have carried out some group fieldwork in part of a city, and want to explore that part independently in more depth.
- You might also come up with an idea based on something in your local news (e.g. a proposal for change in a place near you), or based on something you've studied in class (e.g. regeneration) that you could apply to where you live.

However, it's important to remember that your title must be individual, and something devised by you. You can't, for example, select a title from a list given to you by a teacher. However, group work is acceptable if all group members come up with:

- **either** different titles that focus on different aspects of what you have studied (e.g. one person investigates the effectiveness of hard engineering, while another looks at more sustainable methods)
- **or** similarly-worded titles which deal with different areas (e.g. dividing up several beach profiles that you have studied along a stretch of coast)
- **or** the same title but for different areas of a city (e.g. investigating how deprivation varies between different parts of a city)
- **or** the same title and primary data, but using very different secondary sources.

Of course, if you devise your own title anyway, the issue will not arise. Just make sure that it is linked to the specification in some way. Figure 1 may give you some ideas.

Landscape Systems, Processes and Change
- Factors affecting landscapes
- Landform development
- Influence of climate change
- Human impacts on coastal systems

Shaping Places
- How people identify with a particular place
- How a place is represented; place identity
- The players involved in economic change or regeneration, and the impacts on social inequality
- Place-making processes

Global Development and Connections
- Global governance: its impact on places (flows of people or capital)
- Global trade versus local trade
- Human rights issues
- Conflict management

Physical Systems and Sustainability
- An analysis of water / hydrology and carbon / ecological cycles in a locality
- Changes to ecosystems and their impacts on water / carbon cycles
- Changes over time, e.g. climate change
- Links between water and carbon cycles

Figure 1 *Some suggested study areas from core areas of the Edexcel specification*

What makes a good title?

A good title will help to make your investigation successful. Figure 2 shows a very suitable location for geographical fieldwork, and would be likely to lead towards a successful Independent Investigation. But getting the title right is trickier.

Consider these two possible investigation titles for the stretch of coast shown in Figure 2 on page 292:

- How is the coast in Figure 2 managed?
- Do people like the coastal management methods used at Walton-on-the-Naze?

These possible investigation titles could each be answered descriptively. Investigations whose outcome is a description – or that require little more than simple analysis – are generally too closed and simplistic at this level. You should decide whether you wish to use an aim for your title, a question, or a hypothesis – as explained in Figure 3.

Figure 2 *A stretch of coast at Walton-on-the-Naze in Essex – but what would make a good title for an Independent Investigation here?*

Figure 3 *Aim, question, or hypothesis – which is best?*

	Aims	Question	Hypothesis
Meaning	A statement of what an investigation is setting out to achieve.	A title presented in the form of a question linked to the overall focus. Questions have the advantage that they can be split into sub-questions.	A statement or prediction, the accuracy of which is tested objectively using scientific methodology. It's usually used together with statistical tests (e.g. Chi-squared)
Example – physical	*An investigation into the human factors affecting the hydrology of River X in city V.*	*How and why do beach profiles vary between winter and summer at beach N?*	*Shingle beaches have a steeper gradient than sand beaches.*
Example – human	*An investigation into the methods and successes of urban regeneration in X.*	*To what extent has inward migration affected the character of rural area X?*	*There are significant differences in inequality in areas X and Y of Manchester.*

Consider these alternative investigation titles:

- How resilient is the coast in Figure 2 against potential climate change?
- How far do the coastal management methods used at Walton-on-the-Naze affect people's perceptions of this stretch of coast?
- How far have the regeneration strategies in Figure X benefited local people?
- How far have regeneration methods in the area in Figure X affected people's identity with that place?

These titles require complex data and several sources from different people and organisations, because they are open questions. Each title requires an evaluative answer – for example, some people may like the regeneration methods in the area in Figure X, while others may not.

Checklist!

A good Independent Investigation title is therefore:

- not based on a simplistic question that could be answered descriptively. The most successful titles will be open-ended, with several possible answers.
- one that can be answered using a large data sample which draws together varied samples of either things (e.g. coastal sediment) or people (of different ages, gender or background)
- evaluative, involving an assessment of something, e.g. the extent to which regeneration has been a success.
- capable of being answered, even if only tentatively, using a range of data that you or a group can collect over a period of four days or less.

.3 Planning and writing the introduction

In this section, you'll learn how to introduce your investigation – before you've collected any data!

Start writing early!

One of the most helpful processes in clarifying your ideas about what you want to study, and how you will approach it, is to begin writing. Starting the writing process early – before you collect any data – sounds like strange advice. But it can help you to clarify your focus, making a title easier to firm up, and can also help you in planning data collection.

- Begin by firming up a title, while being aware that this might change as you progress.
- Second, decide whether you want to investigate a question (like those in Section 8.2) or a hypothesis. A hypothesis is more likely in a scientific investigation, in which a significant amount of quantitative data will be collected (see Section 8.4), but you do not have to do it this way. Questions or hypotheses are equally suitable – the choice is yours.
- Next, begin some background reading about your topic, and the place where you will carry out your research. This is known as a **literature review**.

The literature review

Your Independent Investigation is likely to be much more detailed than any other study you have done previously in Geography. This textbook will help you with general learning for the A level course, but you also need detailed information about the topic for your Independent Investigation, the factors that affect it, and the place you'll study. This will involve specialist books and information about the background, location and specific processes that might affect your investigation.

The literature review will form a part of your introduction. In total, aim for 600-800 words in this section, covering:

- information about the place and processes you are investigating. For example, a study of hydrology would include data about rainfall, catchment area, slopes, geology and land use.
- specific processes affecting your study. A study of rural regeneration would include details about the place and how regeneration may be changing it. A coastal study could outline past attempts to manage a coast, or the balance of physical and human processes there.

Potential sources

Begin by researching any relevant literature that will provide ideas for fieldwork in the place you're studying. For example, you might look at:

- unique features of the landscape in your chosen location
- the ways in which different players have affected change in the area.

Potential sources could include:

- **specialist textbooks** (see Figure 1), such as those on changing places or globalisation. Your school may have these in the library, or you could request a reader's pass for the library at your nearest university.
- **journals**. Look for journals written for sixth-form audiences (e.g. *Geography Review*) or adult readership, such as the *Economist* or *Nature*; this is the level you should be using.
- **websites**. Use websites of organisations who specialise in the topic or area in which you are interested. This might include the Environment Agency (for hydrology), English Nature (for ecological data), or local authorities for the area you are investigating. Use the local council website for Census data.

Figure 1 *Textbooks or journals like these are the kind of specialist works which you should use for your Independent Investigation*

Keeping track of your sources

Keep a record of the sources used in your literature review, because you will need to list them in your final Independent Investigation:

- in a **bibliography**, which is any source you have used in a general sense to help you
- as **specific references**, which are particular pages or sections of an article or book
- where appropriate, as **footnotes**. If you have not used footnotes before, they are relatively easy to insert using word-processing packages.

References for a **book** should be written as follows:

Author surname(s) and initials or name (plus 'ed.' if this is the editor), date, title of book, place and name of publisher. For example:

Digby, Bob ed. (2017), *A level Geography for Edexcel Book 2*, Oxford, Oxford University Press

References for an **article** should be written as follows:

Author surname(s) and initials or name (plus 'ed.' if this is the editor), date, title of article, name of journal, volume number and edition. For example:

Smith, Gillian ed. (2015), 'Flooding along the River Parrett', in *Journal of River Studies*, Vol. 36 Number 3

Consider, too, the sources of publications – their origin, authority or bias. You should read Section 6.5 to help you.

Checking the mark scheme

Study the mark scheme for the Introduction to ensure that you are maximising your chance of a high mark. The qualities to aim for include:

- accurate, relevant geographical knowledge and understanding of the location where your investigation has been carried out
- appropriate geographical theory about any processes taking place
- relevant links between your investigation and what is happening more broadly
- a wide range of relevant geographical sources to provide accurate geographical information to support your investigation
- a good use of background information to justify your aim, question or hypothesis
- an assurance that your investigation is at a manageable scale
- a logically structured and comprehensive enquiry.

Planning your fieldwork methodology

In this section, you'll consider how to select appropriate methods for collecting your data.

Choosing sources of data

Making choices about which data to collect for your Independent Investigation is difficult – but it must be done well. Your data determine its success, so remember these hints:

- Balance your **primary** data (collected by you) and **secondary** (collected by someone else). You may even use **tertiary** sources (for example, Wikipedia), which draw together several sources. However, when using a tertiary source, use the original references from which it has been drawn – not the tertiary source itself.
- Group data are allowable and can be a real benefit. They provide a sample size and range that you would be unlikely to be able to collect on your own in the time – or in safety. Group data provide levels of data which may have statistical significance.
- Don't rely on single sources of data (e.g. a questionnaire, or pebble sizes on a beach). Use several sources, including secondary data. Secondary data can confirm that what you have collected is correct. They can also provide data that you are unable to collect yourself (e.g. year-round, whereas you have only four days). Remember that unprocessed data collected by someone else still count as primary data.
- Consider when to do surveys – e.g. beach surveys (consider tides and weather), interviews or questionnaires (consider time of day, week or year). Where possible, take samples from different times.
- Ensure that you have done a risk assessment – consider your physical safety when interviewing others, or any risks which may arise from working alone.

Sampling

Rarely is it possible to survey everything in your study area. You couldn't possibly ask every tourist in Blackpool their reasons for coming to visit in the summer season; similarly, it's not possible to survey every pebble on a beach! A method of selection is needed, known as **sampling**. Figure 1 on the next page shows you two possible types of sampling that you could use when collecting data in an area of sand dunes.

Random sampling

Random sampling occurs when each place or person in an area or a population has a mathematically equal chance of being selected. Selections are made using computer-generated random number tables, which are easily available online. Having selected a number, you then apply it to the area or people – e.g. as a grid reference, direction, distance, or person in a sequence.

- **Advantage:** This approach reduces human bias or sampling error.
- **Disadvantage:** It can leave gaps in your sample, or create clusters of data that may not reflect the place or people. It can be time-consuming compared to other sampling methods.

Systematic sampling

Systematic sampling occurs when each sample is selected in a regular manner. In a woodland, you might record vegetation samples every 10 metres (known as a **linear** sample), or perhaps at a series of points located at the intersection of a 10-metre grid (known as a **point** sample), or maybe every tenth customer on a street (a **person** sample).

- **Advantage:** It gives good coverage of a place and is easy to design and undertake.
- **Disadvantage:** You can miss significant points or people if you survey a place or a transect, so certain groups or features in a place might not form part of your sample.

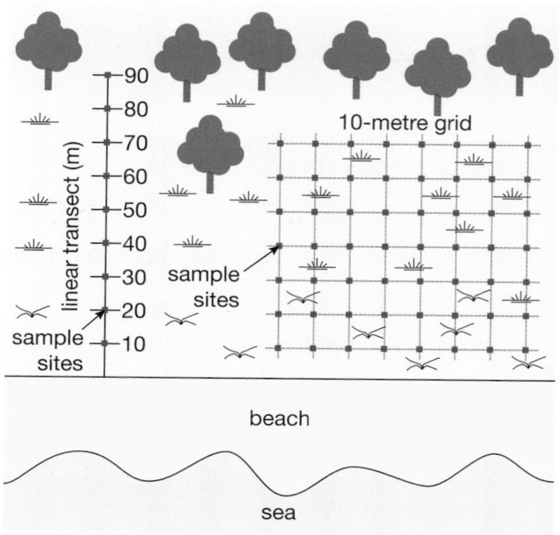

Figure 1 Possible sampling methods in an area of coastal dunes

Stratified sampling

Stratified sampling is used to create a valid sample for a population of people or things with distinguishing characteristics between them. For example:

- On a beach sediment survey, 20% of the beach may be managed while the rest is unmanaged.
- In a survey of an area, 35% of the population may be aged over 65.

Stratified sampling ensures that sample sizes are decided before the survey takes place. For example, you would ensure that 20% of sample points on the beach occur on managed sections, or would ensure that 35% of people surveyed were aged over 65. You would then select the sample in each sub-group using either random or systematic sampling.

- **Advantage:** This approach reduces the potential for bias, but you need to consider the characteristics of the area (e.g. the distribution of sediment) or population (e.g. age balance or ethnicity) in order to make an appropriate selection.
- **Disadvantage:** It can be difficult to get the data that you need to stratify the sample (e.g. if people are at work all day when you collect data).

Checking the mark scheme

Study the mark scheme for Field Methodologies and Data Collection to ensure that you are maximising your chance of a high mark. The qualities to aim for include:

- designing a valid sampling framework appropriate to the geographical focus being investigated
- considering the timing and frequency of observations
- considering ethical dimensions of data collection
- selecting appropriate methods which are relevant to your aim or title.

.5 Presenting your data

In this section, you'll consider how to select appropriate methods for presenting your data.

Types of data

Your data may be quantitative (i.e. statistical – sometimes known as 'hard' data) or qualitative (i.e. impressions, opinions, photos – sometimes known as 'soft' data).

- Quantitative data include measurements of physical features or processes, or results from questionnaires, environmental quality surveys, and Census data.
- Qualitative data include personal evaluations of landscapes, annotations to photos, paintings, music or the use of one-to-one interviews. Before gathering this sort of data, make sure that you read the tinted panel on the next page about considering ethical issues in research.

Your data should also include secondary sources from publications such as newspapers or news organisations (choose a quality newspaper or news outlet, such as the BBC or Reuters), professional journals for adult audiences (e.g. *The Economist*), magazines (e.g. *Nature*). Make sure that you check your sources for bias or imbalanced representation – see Section 6.5 for more about this aspect.

Presenting your data

How you organise and present your data will depend on the type of data collected. You will probably present most primary and secondary data using a combination of graphic (graphs, diagrams, images, tables and infographics) or cartographic (maps) techniques. Figure 1 shows examples of possible techniques that you could consider for each type of data.

Figure 1 *Suggested examples of data presentation, classified as either graphical or cartographic*

Type of data	Suggested graphical (G) or cartographical (C) techniques
Representing sequences of data which change over time (e.g. population, sediment samples)	Line graphs (G) Pictograms (G) Circular graphs / rose diagrams (G)
Data recorded at different places with different categories (e.g. questionnaire data)	Bar charts and histograms (G) Pyramid graphs (G) Pie charts (G) Mirror graphs (G) Multiple / compound bar charts (G)
Measurements of side views (e.g. of a river, glaciated feature, or beach)	Long and cross profiles (G) Cross-sections (G)
Data which show spatial variation (i.e. mappable data such as deprivation data or house prices)	Isopleth maps (C) Dot distribution maps (C) Proportional symbol maps (C) Choropleth maps (C)
Data which require orientation, direction or bearing (e.g. glacier direction or wave data)	Rose diagrams (G) Polar co-ordinates (G)
Continuous data (along a transect), e.g. kick samples in a river, plant data in a woodland, or a sand dune survey	Kite diagram (G) Scatter graph (G) Multiple / compound bar charts (G)
Representing linkage or connections between two sets of data (e.g. infiltration rates related to slope angle)	Scatter graphs (G) Mirror graphs (G)

Considering ethical issues in research

You should ensure that you consider any ethical issues which are likely to arise in any study involving the collection, analysis and representation of any geographical information involving people or physical communities. The most common areas of ethical concern focus on people's informed participation and consent, as well as the safeguarding and confidentiality of any personal information that you collect. Where possible, you should adopt the following approaches:

- All interviews with people, together with any photographs of them or their homes – or detailed descriptions of organisations – should be obtained and used with their consent. Nobody would want to see themselves reported or pictured without their permission.
- Make sure that all interviews or quotes from your interviewees are anonymised – it should not be possible to identify who said what from your presentation, unless the quote has been published already, or the person has given permission for their statements to be used. A good way of seeking this permission is to allow the person or organisation to read what you have written. They may even enhance what you want to say with more!
- When asking people questions, you should display sensitivity to their gender, ethnicity or personal status. For example, if you are male, you should not approach Muslim women.
- Some of the questions in your interviews may uncover offensive statements or viewpoints (e.g. racism or sexism). You need to discuss with your teacher what you should do about this (e.g. according to your school's policy) and whether you wish to include such views in your research.

Checking the mark scheme

Remember that the mark scheme has been set up to reward the most appropriate presentational techniques, not necessarily their degree of sophistication. Study the mark scheme for data presentation to ensure that you are maximising your chance of a high mark. The qualities to aim for include:

- the use of appropriate diagrams, graphs and maps, using suitable technologies to select and present relevant aspects of your data (see Figure 1)
- presenting your data in such a way as to show clearly the patterns revealed and any connections, like the annotated photo in Figure 2, as well as ensuring that your data are presented accurately; their geographical significance must be clear
- a consideration of ethical issues (see above).

Figure 2 *A well-annotated photo of Shadwell in East London*

Analysing data

In this section, you'll consider how to select appropriate methods for analysing your data.

What does analysis involve?

Analysis means picking apart your results in order to find meaning and possible explanation. It therefore involves describing, comparing, explaining and attempting to link different data sets together. Techniques for analysing include:

- **adding annotations to graphs or photos** to describe your data (e.g. *'The largest mean sediment size occurs at the western zone of the beach'*), or compare different locations (e.g. *'Place X has a higher deprivation score than Place Y'*).
- **using analytical text** to explain what you see (e.g. *'The largest sediment size occurs there because…'*), or link one set of data to another (e.g. *'The high level of deprivation in Place X may be explained by its higher unemployment levels'*).

Starting to write

Your analysis should normally be between about 1200 and 1500 words. You should organise it by any sub-questions or sub-hypotheses that you have devised, with the number of words divided roughly equally between them. Begin your writing by giving a brief overview of your findings – notice how the example in Figure 1 begins in this way.

Two processes will add substantially to the quality of your analysis:

- Using data to illustrate your descriptions, e.g. *'The highest mean sediment size (65.8 mm) occurs at the western zone of the beach'*. Notice that Figure 1 gives a good example of how to do this.
- Using detailed analytical methods to give substance to distributions or relationships between sets of data. The methods to be used depend on whether the data are quantitative or qualitative in nature.

My data prove my environmental hypothesis correct because Canary Wharf (which was the major focus for the Docklands regeneration) scored the highest average environmental quality score (average 15.8 out of 34). Shadwell, which until recently has had little regeneration, scored the lowest score (average 1.6 out of 34). Locations within the Isle of Dogs were also part of the regeneration, but not to the same extent as Canary Wharf. These scored an average of 14.8. This proves that environmental quality is higher in areas that have been regenerated. My hypothesis stated that, in regenerated areas, there would be more open space and parkland. This did not prove to be entirely correct, because in Canary Wharf there were almost no open spaces and parks – most available land was used for office space and retail needs.

Figure 1 *A sample of analytical writing about environmental quality in East London. This student studied the impacts of regeneration in the area.*

Methods of detailed analysis

Methods of **quantitative** analysis include:

- using **descriptive** statistics, such as measures of central tendency (mean, median, mode) and of dispersion (range, inter-quartile range, standard deviation)
- using **inferential** statistics, or statistical tests, which explore relationships between sets of data. These include hypothesis testing, levels of significance, student's t-test, Chi-square and Spearman's rank correlation coefficient.

Methods of **qualitative** analysis include:

- using interview analysis and interpretations of images (e.g. photos, advertising material, paintings), music, film, or text.

Beginning to analyse quantitative data

First, describe the patterns revealed by your data. This may include:

- a description of the main patterns and trends
- illustrating any patterns and trends using data from relevant tables, charts or maps
- identifying any anomalies or exceptions which deviate from the main trends.

Next, look more deeply. With quantitative data, the following checklist of questions may be useful:

- What is the range of values?
- Where are most values concentrated? Is there clustering?
- What shape is the distribution of data?
- Are there anomalies or outliers? How separate are these from the range of data?

Analysing qualitative data

Geography is a data-rich subject, often supported by statistics. However, don't let that put you off selecting qualitative methods. Methods such as interviewing people provide detailed in-depth case cases that can help to place human experiences into context (e.g. how regeneration affects people and communities). Interviews help to explore the totality of people's experiences and situations, which can often be supported further by statistical data. Smaller – but focused – samples are used more frequently than large.

The following techniques will help you to analyse qualitative data more effectively:

- Coding (see Section 8.7) is an analytical process in which open-ended questionnaire results or interviews, or blogs, can be categorised in order to help analysis.
- Photograph analysis (also see Section 8.7), or analysis involving any other form of picture (such as paintings), is useful if you wish to interview people to assess their reactions to changes in an area or to local communities. For example, you could compare the impacts of regeneration using photographs of the same place at two different dates, as shown in Figure 2.

A

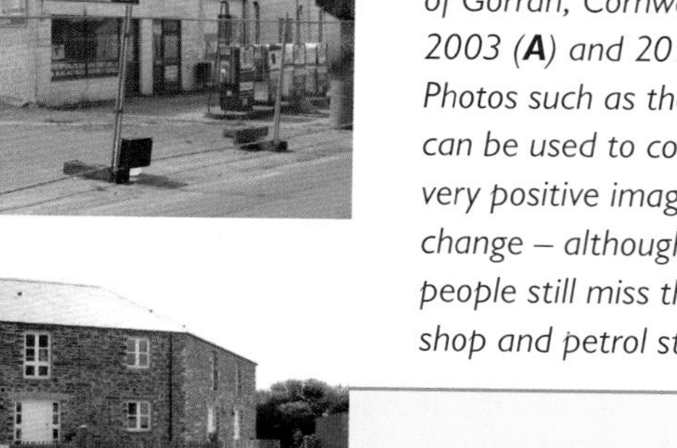

B

Figure 2 *Two photographs of the same view – part of the village of Gorran, Cornwall, in 2003 (**A**) and 2013 (**B**). Photos such as these can be used to convey very positive images of change – although local people still miss their shop and petrol station!*

Checking the mark scheme

The number of marks available for analysis is incorporated within the 24 marks for 'Data Representation, Analysis, Interpretation and Evaluation of Techniques and Methodologies used'. Your analysis should therefore:

- use geographical skills to analyse your data to show connections and accurate statistical and geographical significance of data
- critically examine your data (e.g. you should mention any measurement errors), in order to comment on its accuracy and/or the extent to which it is both representative and reliable
- summarise your findings clearly, to reach evidence-based conclusions (i.e. not the results that you hoped for or hypothesised, but ones for which you have the evidence).

Analysing qualitative data

In this section, you'll consider how to use two qualitative analytical techniques.

1 Coding

Coding is a process by which text data from questionnaires, blogs or interviews can be categorised to make analysis easier. It provides ways of describing and identifying key features of text. Take the following approach:

1. Transcribe each interview, labelling it with the person's name or anonymous number, location and date. Transcribing can be long and tedious, but you can use voice recognition software to help – just be sure to check it for errors!
2. Take each transcript (or blog). As you read, pencil in the margin what is being talked about, e.g. 'housing' or 'neighbours'. Underline key bits. Don't use colour highlighters yet – that comes later.
3. Your notes will give you headings; things you underline are sub-headings. These are called **codes** – like categories. So, someone talking about 'housing' (as a main code or heading) might say something about 'damp' or 'outside toilet' (which are sub-codes, or sub-headings).
4. As you do this, note down your codes (or categories) on a blank piece of paper. You can then change these as you go along.
5. When you read an interview transcript, you may find that the theme of 'housing' occurs many times. This might then become a mega-code!
6. Think about any links between codes. For example, a transcript saying:

   'The house we lived in was old – it was damp and there was mould in the bathroom. My health was poor.' might have these codes:

   - **Mega-code** – housing
   - **Sub-code** – old, damp, mould, poor health, bathroom
7. Start making links between the sub-codes. This could be done as a spider diagram or concept map; Figure 1 shows how.

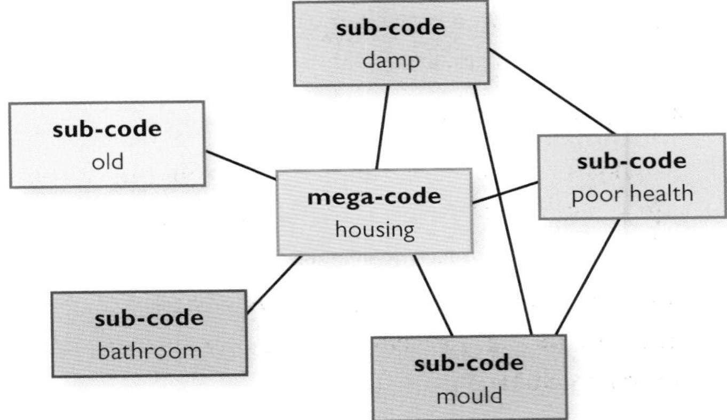

Figure 1 *A spider diagram showing possible codes and sub-codes resulting from an interview transcript*

8. Notice that some points in Figure 1 link up to form a **code map**. This will help you with your analysis. The mega-code – housing – can become a section heading, and the five sub-codes can then be sub-headings. Notice how three of the five are connected – damp, mould, and poor health. You could therefore reduce your sub-headings – the three might become 'The impacts of damp'.
9. Go through other interview transcripts. Compare the code maps, picking out similarities and differences.
10. Now you're ready to begin writing your analysis!
    - **a** Pick out the main points. Summarise if you keep reading the same thing.
    - **b** Pick out any 'wow' quotes! Use these as quotations in your account.
    - **c** Write the whole analysis, then edit it down. Only cut it down when you've done the whole thing and can see the big picture – don't cut as you go.

2 Analysing photographs

Study the photograph in Figure 2. What do you see? If you've studied 'Glaciated Landscapes' as part of your A level course (see Chapter 2 in Book 1 of this series), you will probably look at this photograph with insight; you will have learned previously about glacial features such as arêtes. Therefore, you will be studying the photograph **rationally** – analysing it using your existing knowledge to make sense of it.

However, the same photograph could be viewed differently. To some, the scene portrayed may seem threatening, unwelcoming perhaps. It's a photograph of a dramatic landscape, taken in winter. Some might use words such as 'dangerous'. Such words show that people often react **emotionally** to photographs.

Photographs are therefore powerful tools. In the hands of advertisers, they can carry powerful messages about, for example, the desirability of properties in areas undergoing regeneration – showing how places are being 'improved'. As a possible investigation, you could use official marketing images of an area, and then compare them with interviews with local residents that may reveal negative experiences that happened to real people during the regeneration process – maybe they had to be re-housed, or were evicted against their will.

To analyse photographs, follow these steps:

1 First, describe the technical detail – the location, direction facing, time of day, time of year, weather.

2 Next, describe the scene as objectively as you can – what is there; a description of the subject matter.

3 Consider who took the photograph and why, or who published it. How and why was this image chosen – What is it trying to show? What was its purpose? Does it succeed?

4 Analyse the photograph for emotive content – How do different people react to this image, and why? Show different people the same image to see how they react.

5 Analyse the findings – How have people reacted?

There is further guidance about analysing photographs on the Getty Images website – search 'Getty photo analysis' to find detailed steps in analysing pictures.

Figure 2 *A view from Helvellyn, one of the highest mountains in the Lake District, looking along Striding Edge (an arête), with Red Tarn (a corrie lake) to the left*

8.8 Writing your conclusion

In this section, you'll consider how to write your conclusion.

Writing your conclusion

Your conclusion should provide a summary of all major findings made at different stages of your Independent Investigation. It differs from analysis because you need to return to and focus in on your original aim, question or hypothesis. You should use evidence from your analysis to help you write your conclusion, but no new evidence should be introduced there. The purpose of writing a conclusion is to consider the evidence from your study (both from your own primary fieldwork and from secondary sources), in order to draw out the most significant features from that evidence and arrive at an overall conclusion. In some conclusions, you could justify using a series of final statements – for example, if you examined impacts and find that one (e.g. environmental) must be balanced against others.

Study the mark scheme! This section is weighty and carries 24 marks, the same as your data presentation and analysis combined. Together with your evaluation (see Section 8.9), you should aim to write between 1200 and 1500 words across the two sections.

Distinguishing your conclusion from the analysis

While your analysis focused on your three or four sub-questions, or sub-hypotheses, your conclusion should take your overall aim and provide an answer. For example, a title '*To what extent is there evidence of rural deprivation in north Cornwall?*' requires you to state whether your question can be answered clearly or not, or the extent to which it can be answered. You may find that the question is only partly answerable. You might be better off saying – '*in some parts of the region, there is acute deprivation…*' and then adding later '*while in other ways deprivation is much reduced, for example…*'.

You should then list the main findings from your work. What firm conclusions can you come to? For example, is there evidence of differing levels of deprivation in north Cornwall? Is there a good quality of life there, which perhaps could compensate for some of the economic deprivation? Go through the following stages when reaching and reviewing your overall conclusions:

1. **Reflect on and review** your title and focus. Is your question or hypothesis answerable?
2. **Select** and provide the most important evidence and information that supports or rejects the aim, question or hypothesis.
3. Draw together ideas from **concepts, theories and parallel examples** to develop a logical line of reasoning. To what extent have you discovered something that is either unique, or that fits what happens in other places?
4. **Comment on** how far your results may be inconclusive, and then link this to the strength of your conclusion and how firmly you think it holds.

Messy Geography!

You should also be prepared to accept that your conclusion may be 'messy' – in other words, is not clear-cut. In some cases, your results may also have been 'messy', and perhaps did not work out as you might have expected or hoped. Your conclusion may possibly disagree with a model or theory that you used in your introduction. Don't be alarmed if this happens; in some ways, 'messy' geography is much more like the real world – and has the benefit of giving you much more to write about! Don't worry about the leap between theoretical understanding and evidence from your messy fieldwork – it may be you who is right for this place, at this time, based on the evidence that you collected.

Reading an example

Figure 1 is an extract from the conclusion written about a study of deprivation in north Cornwall. Read it – it is not perfect, and you should be able to see where it could be improved – for example, by adding data to exemplify statements.

***Figure 1** One student's attempt to conclude a study on deprivation in north Cornwall*

The initial question for this study was to investigate the extent to which there is evidence of rural deprivation in north Cornwall. My findings show that in some ways north Cornwall is deprived whilst in others it is not. North Cornwall is certainly not environmentally deprived; all my environmental quality surveys showed strongly positive qualities.

However north Cornwall did prove to be socially deprived, as people often had to travel large distances for basic services that they needed on a weekly or more frequent basis. There was also a lack of opportunities for leisure throughout north Cornwall, with often nothing more than a pub, playground or sports ground in even reasonably sized towns. Social deprivation was most apparent when looking at the age structure of the population in north Cornwall. There were very few young people and a large number of elderly retired people, often on fixed pension incomes.

There was also evidence of economic deprivation though to a lesser extent compared to social deprivation. Economic deprivation in the area does not harm the quality of life, because the environmental quality of the area ensures that it is a very popular area for both tourists and potential property buyers. Although there is a certain level of deprivation, there are also qualities which indicate it is far from deprived. These are shown in Figure 2.

Signs of deprivation	Signs of lack of deprivation
Large numbers of second home owners	High house prices, especially in St Breward
Many people on council tax relief	Low unemployment
Large numbers on housing benefit	Most people feel safe
Long distances (8–15km) to most services	Small distances to some services, e.g. village shop, pub
Very few leisure facilities in most villages	High usage of leisure facilities where they exist
Large number of elderly people on fixed state pensions	High % working population
Few young people aged 15–19 – the 'brain drain'	Clean environment – little litter, no graffiti
Cars essential for accessing services	Some well-planned areas of new housing
Very few new cars, many old ones	Quiet country lanes with little traffic
Many houses lack central heating	Good levels of building maintenance
Many people have part-time jobs	Few people renting social housing
High proportion of un-skilled workers	Very low – minimal! – crime levels
A few areas near the A39 suffer traffic congestion in the tourist season	Poorly served by public transport

***Figure 2** A table summary of the indicators of deprivation in north Cornwall*

8.9 Writing your evaluation and finalising your enquiry

In this section, you'll consider how to write your evaluation.

Writing your evaluation

The evaluation is, for many, the hardest part of the whole Independent Investigation. Dangerously, it is done last – because that's when you may be rushed and tired, either close to the deadline or just eager to hand it in, completed. Yet, combined with the conclusion (see Section 8.8), it takes up 1200-1500 words – up to a third of the study length – and 24 marks (nearly a third of the total!). It is therefore worth doing well.

Your Independent Investigation can be evaluated in terms of its **reliability**, **accuracy** and **validity**:

- **Reliability** means that if you were to carry out the data collection again, the results would most likely be similar.
- **Accuracy** means that the data were gained by methods that were as accurate as it's possible to get. This would consider sampling methods.
- **Validity** means whether the investigation measures what it's intended to measure.

Your evaluation should therefore assess each of the above three elements. The emphasis should be on two things:

- An evaluation of the enquiry itself.
- An evaluation of the geography studied.

Follow the four steps below:

1 Consider your methods

Think about this checklist of questions:

a Did your data collection methods work out well?
b Might your methods have produced anomalous results in any way? Can these anomalies be explained in simple geographical terms?
c Were the results accurate? If so, why? If not, what prevented this? If you went back there at different times, would you get similar data?
d Were your methods the best way of finding out what you wanted?
e Were **enough** data collected?
f Should you have included different weather conditions, days of the week, months of the year, etc.?
g If you have been unable to draw hard conclusions, does it **matter** if no real trends emerged?
h Did any other factors influence your results?

2 Consider the validity of your conclusions

a Based on your methods, are your conclusions valid?
b What has the investigation taught you about the topic, fieldwork, or related issues?
c Would you go about it all the same way again?

3 Consider the usefulness or relevance of the investigation

a What's the usefulness or relevance of your investigation to others?
b Who might be interested in your investigation, and why? What might they do with the information?
c How has your enquiry furthered your understanding of Geography, or of processes or themes in Geography?

4 Consider how the investigation could be extended

a How could your investigation be extended?
b Which aspects might be worth developing further?

Getting your Independent Investigation ready to hand in

Handing in your Independent Investigation will be the last time that you see it, so it is important to make sure that it is readable, tidy, and presentable, Again, follow the four steps below as a checklist:

1 Overall length

There are no penalties for exceeding the recommended 4000 words, but it is worth checking your word count by section, because of the different marks available for each:

- Introduction and aims 400-600 words
- Methodology and data collection 350-550 words
- Data Representation, Analysis, Interpretation and Evaluation of Techniques and Methodologies used 1200-1500 words
- Conclusions and Critical Evaluation of the Overall Investigation 1200-1500 words

2 Methodology

If you have used a table to summarise your methodology, make sure that you:

- outline the places you went to, and why these were selected
- outline the value of these places in terms of your investigation
- outline the stages you went through in data collection, e.g. a pilot study of place X, followed by the development of the real data collection strategies in place Y.
- acknowledge the members of your group in any group collection of data.

Remember to make sampling methods explicit – i.e. random, stratified, or systematic.

3 Presentation

A few handy hints will make your study better organised:

- Make sure that your section headings are identifiable by name.
- Use Figure numbers for all illustrations or data tables. Use either Figure 1, 2, etc. in the introduction and number as the whole study progresses, or number by section – for example, figures in Section 1 Introduction would be numbered 1.1, 1.2, etc.
- Use captions for every Figure number, so that the reader knows what you are showing.
- Refer to all Figures in the text.
- List all Figures in an index at the beginning of your study.
- All photos should be annotated or given captions (e.g. 'This photo shows … *with some indication of the result that it shows*').
- Pagination. **All** pages need to be numbered in sequence. Do this **last**!
- **All** material must be handed in at A4 size.
- Stick down any loose material (e.g. acetate overlays), so they don't fall out.
- Make sure that you acknowledge all sources used in a bibliography at the end.

4 Handing your work in

Your coursework must be handed in as a loose-leaved project in a card or plastic wallet file, with every page in order – don't use ring binders, or individual plastic covers for each page, because that simply adds to the weight and the cost of postage when sent to Edexcel.

9 Exams: hitting the high marks

The A level course is lively and interesting – full of contemporary topics, such as energy security, plus favourites such as superpowers. But exam success is also important: How will you be examined? What kinds of questions might appear? How will you earn marks? That is where this chapter can help.

The A level specification

The A level specification consists of 11 topics, from which you must study **eight**. They have been grouped into four themes, known as Areas of Study.

Area of Study 1: Dynamic Landscapes

Topic 1: Tectonic Processes and Hazards (Chapter 1 in Book 1 of this series). This is compulsory.

Topic 2: Landscape Systems, Processes and Change – you must study **one** of

- **either** Option 2A: Glaciated Landscapes and Change (Chapter 2 in Book 1 of this series)
- **or** Option 2B: Coastal Landscapes and Change (Chapter 3 in Book 1 of this series)

Area of Study 2: Dynamic Places

Topic 3: Globalisation (Chapter 4 in Book 1 of this series). This is compulsory.

Topic 4: Shaping Places – you must study **one** of

- **either** Option 4A: Regenerating Places (Chapter 5 in Book 1 of this series)
- **or** Option 4B: Diverse Places (Chapter 6 in Book 1 of this series)

Area of Study 3: Physical Systems and Sustainability

Topic 5: The Water Cycle and Water Insecurity (Chapter 1 in this textbook). This is compulsory.

Topic 6: The Carbon Cycle and Energy Security (Chapter 2 in this textbook). This is also compulsory.

Area of Study 4: Human Systems and Geopolitics

Topic 7: Superpowers (Chapter 3 in this textbook). This is compulsory.

Topic 8: Global Development and Connections – you must study **one** of

- **either** Option 8A: Health, Human Rights and Intervention (Chapter 4 in this textbook)
- **or** Option 8B: Migration, Identity and Sovereignty (Chapter 5 in this textbook).

Other elements of the course

Three other elements complete the A level qualification: geographical skills, synoptic themes and key geographical concepts, plus fieldwork leading to the Independent Investigation.

Geographical skills (Chapter 6 in this textbook and Chapter 7 in Book 1 of this series). Most geographical skills have been integrated into the main content chapters, but many of those in the two 'Using geographical skills' chapters can be used in more than one topic.

Synoptic themes and **key geographical concepts** have been integrated into every chapter. Chapter 7 in this textbook will help you to prepare for Paper Three, where the synoptic themes are assessed.

Fieldwork (Chapter 8 in this textbook). This chapter will guide your coursework (the Independent Investigation), which is based on fieldwork.

How will you be assessed?

There are three exams for A Level Geography, plus a coursework project known as the Independent Investigation (based on fieldwork). Figure 1 explains what Papers One and Two involve, and Figure 2 on the next page explains Paper Three.

Topics assessed	Assessment information
Paper One	
There is a total of 105 marks for this exam, worth 30% of the A level qualification. **Section A Compulsory** (Assesses Topic 1: Tectonic Processes and Hazards in Question 1) Answer all parts of this question. **16 marks** **Section B Optional** (Assesses **either** Topic 2A Glaciated Landscapes and Change **or** Topic 2B Coastal Landscapes and Change) Answer all questions on the topic that you have studied) **40 marks** **Section C Compulsory** (Assesses Topic 5 The Water Cycle and Water Insecurity and Topic 6 The Carbon Cycle and Energy Security) **49 marks**	**Time**: 2 hours 15 minutes **Sections**: The exam consists of three sections. You answer questions in all three sections, taking care that you select only one option in Section B. You will have a resource booklet and will need a calculator. The exam may include multiple-choice, short open, open response, calculations and resource-linked questions. However, extended written questions dominate this paper – 98 of the 105 marks are for extended writing. The exam includes 6-, 8-, 12-, and 20-mark extended writing questions. • In Section A, Question 1 (Tectonic Processes and Hazards) will include a **12-mark** question. • In Section B, optional Questions 2 (Glaciated Landscapes and Change) and 3 (Coastal Landscapes and Change) will each include two **6-mark**, one **8-mark**, and one **20-mark** question. • In Section C, questions on The Water Cycle and Water Insecurity and The Carbon Cycle and Energy Security will include one **6-mark**, one **8-mark**, one **12-mark**, and one **20-mark** question.
Paper Two	
There is a total of 105 marks for this exam, worth 30% of the A level qualification. **Compulsory Section A** (Assesses Topic 3 Globalisation in Question 1 and Topic 7 Superpowers in Question 2) Answer all parts of both questions. **2 x 16 marks** **Total 32 marks** **Section B Optional** (Assesses **either** Topic 4A Regenerating Places **or** Topic 4B Diverse Places) Answer all questions on the topic that you have studied. **35 marks** **Section C Optional** (Assesses **either** Topic 8A Health, Human Rights and Intervention **or** Topic 8B Migration, Identity and Sovereignty) Answer all questions on the topic that you have studied. **38 marks**	**Time**: 2 hours 15 minutes **Sections**: The exam consists of three sections. You answer questions in all three sections, taking care that you select only one option in each of Sections B and C. You will have a resource booklet and will need a calculator. The exam may include multiple-choice, short open, open response, calculations and resource-linked questions. However, extended written questions dominate this paper – 90 of the 105 marks are for extended writing. The exam includes 6-, 8-, 12-, and 20-mark extended writing questions. • In Section A, Questions 1 (Globalisation) and 2 (Superpowers) will **each** include a **12-mark** question. • In Section B, optional Questions 3 (Regenerating Places) and 4 (Diverse Places) will each include two **6-mark** and one **20-mark** question. • In Section C, optional Questions 5 (Health, Human Rights and Intervention) and 6 (Migration, Identity and Sovereignty) will include one **6-mark**, one **8-mark**, and one **20-mark** question.

Figure 1 *A summary of the Paper One and Paper Two exam requirements*

Topics assessed	Assessment information
Paper Three	
There is a total of 70 marks for this exam, worth 20% of the A level qualification. **ALL** questions are compulsory. The specification contains three synoptic themes within the five compulsory content areas (see below). The synoptic themes are: • Players • Attitudes and Actions • Futures and Uncertainties. The synoptic investigation will be based on a geographical issue within a place-based context that links to the three synoptic themes and is rooted in two or more of the following compulsory content areas: • Topic 1: Tectonic Processes and Hazards • Topic 3 Globalisation • Topic 5 The Water Cycle and Water Insecurity • Topic 6 The Carbon Cycle and Energy Security • Topic 7 Superpowers	**Time**: 2 hours 15 minutes **Sections**: The exam consists of a number of questions based on an **unseen** Resource Booklet. The information in the Resource Booklet will be organised into sections. You have to answer **ALL** questions in the exam. You will need a calculator. The exam may include short open, open response and resource-linked questions, progressing to 8-mark, 18-mark and 24-mark extended writing questions. Extended written questions dominate this paper – 58 of the 70 marks are for extended writing. Shorter questions are likely to appear at the beginning of the exam, asking you: • about the general context of the issue (e.g. the theme or its location • to interpret and analyse information from the Resource Booklet. This could include processing statistical data. Later questions will include two **8-mark**, one **18-mark** and one **24-mark** question. These will test your understanding of the issue in the Resource Booklet, and also allow you to evaluate its wider significance. The examples in Chapter 7 will help you to prepare for these questions.

Figure 2 *A summary of the Paper Three exam requirements*

How are the exam papers marked?

Examiners use **Assessment Objectives** (AOs for short) to assess you. There are three AOs at A level:

- **AO1 Knowledge and understanding**, worth 34% of the A level. These questions test what you know.
- **AO2 Application of understanding**, e.g. interpreting, analysing and evaluating geographical information and issues. This AO is worth 40% of the A level. These questions test what you understand about situations or data that you are presented with.
- **AO3 Geographical skills**, such as handling and processing information in investigating geographical questions and issues (e.g. interpretation, analysis and evaluation of data and evidence), constructing arguments and drawing conclusions. This AO is worth 26% of the A level. These questions test your skills.

Understanding the mark schemes

Examiners use two types of mark scheme, depending on the number of marks allocated for shorter answers (up to 4 marks) and for extended written answers (6 marks or more).

Shorter questions worth 1–4 marks

Questions carrying up to 4 marks are **point marked**. For every correct point that you make, you earn a mark. These may be single marks for a 1-mark question, or more for the development of points, e.g. describing one feature for 2 marks. There are very few point-marked questions at A level.

Extended questions worth 6–8 marks

Questions carrying 6 marks or more are **level-marked**, and are far more common at A level. The examiner reads the whole answer and then uses a set of criteria – known as **levels** – to judge its qualities. There are three levels for questions carrying between 6 and 18 marks, and four levels for questions of 20 or 24 marks. The highest level earns the most marks.

Consider this question:

Explain how the concept of sediment cells enables a clearer understanding of coastal systems. ***(8 marks)***

Examiners would mark this using the mark scheme shown in Figure 3, which consists of three levels. This mark scheme would be identical for all 6- and 8-mark questions in the A level exams that test AO1 (Knowledge and understanding). To reach the highest marks, your answer must match both criteria in Level 3.

Level	Marks	Descriptor
Level 1	1–2	• Demonstrates isolated elements of geographical knowledge and understanding, some of which may be inaccurate or irrelevant. • Understanding addresses a narrow range of geographical ideas, which lack detail.
Level 2	3–5	• Demonstrates geographical knowledge and understanding, which is mostly relevant and may include some inaccuracies. • Understanding addresses a range of geographical ideas, which are not fully detailed and/or developed.
Level 3	6–8	• Demonstrates accurate and relevant geographical knowledge and understanding throughout. • Understanding addresses a broad range of geographical ideas, which are detailed and fully developed.

Figure 3 *The mark scheme for an 8-mark question. These usually assess AO1 questions.*

Extended questions worth 12 marks (Papers One and Two)

12-mark questions also have three levels. However the balance of marks is different, because longer questions assess more than one AO. 12-mark questions are split: 3 marks for AO1 and 9 marks for AO2. To reach the top level, you must:

- demonstrate accurate knowledge and understanding throughout (AO1)
- apply your knowledge and understanding (AO2)
- produce a full interpretation that is relevant and supported by evidence (AO2)
- make supported judgements in a balanced and coherent argument (AO2)

Extended questions worth 20 marks (Papers One and Two)

20-mark questions have four levels. Like 12-mark questions, they assess more than one AO. 20-mark questions are split: 5 marks for AO1 and 15 marks for AO2. The levels are like those for 12-mark questions, except that there is a fourth level worth between 16 and 20 marks. To reach this level, you must – in addition to the best qualities of the 12-mark answer above:

- demonstrate accurate and relevant geographical knowledge and understanding throughout (AO1)
- apply knowledge and understanding of geographical information/ideas to find fully logical and relevant connections/relationships (AO2)
- apply knowledge and understanding of geographical information/ideas to produce a full and coherent interpretation that is supported by evidence (AO2)
- apply knowledge and understanding of geographical information/ideas to come to a rational, substantiated conclusion, fully supported by a balanced argument that is drawn together coherently (AO2)

Extended questions worth 18 and 24 marks (Paper Three only)

18- and 24-mark questions in Paper Three are split by AO. These questions assess all three AOs:

- 18-mark questions are split: 3 marks for AO1, 9 marks for AO2 and 6 for AO3.
- 24-mark questions are split: 4 marks for AO1, 12 marks for AO2 and 8 for AO3.

To reach the top level, you must:

- reach a rational, substantiated conclusion, supported by a balanced and coherent argument (AO2)
- synthesize ideas and concepts from across the course of study throughout the answer (AO2)

Command words

Figure 4 explains the command words used in questions – those words that tell you what you must do.

Figure 4 *Command words for A level*

Command word	Definition
Draw/plot	Create a graphical representation of geographical information. This assesses AO3.
Complete	Create a graphical representation of geographical information by adding detail to a resource provided. This assesses AO3.
Suggest	For an unfamiliar scenario, provide a reasoned explanation of how or why something may occur. This generally assesses AO2.
Explain	Provide a reasoned explanation of how or why something occurs, through the justification or exemplification of points that have been identified. This assesses AO1.
Analyse (Paper Three only)	Break something down into individual components/processes; say how each individually contributes to the question's theme/topic and how the components/processes work together and interrelate. This assesses AO3 (where you use skills to interpret new information), but also AO1 (because you need to understand the significance of what you analyse).
Assess	Use evidence to determine the relative significance of something. Give balanced consideration to all factors and identify which are the most important. This assesses AO1 (because you have to know something), but mainly AO2 (because you must apply understanding and make a judgment).
Evaluate	Measure the value or success of something and provide a balanced and substantiated judgement or conclusion. Review information and then bring it together to form a conclusion, drawing on strengths, weaknesses, alternatives and relevant data. This assesses AO1 (because you have to know something), AO2 (because you are asked to apply understanding and make a judgment), and also AO3 (because you may interpret data using skills to help you).

Figure 5 shows how marks are allocated to questions with particular command words in a standard way.

Figure 5 *Mark allocations to questions with particular command words*

Mark tariff	3	4	6	8	9	12	18	20	24
Calculate		*							
Draw/Plot/Complete		*							
Suggest	*		*						
Explain	*	*	*	*					
Analyse				*					
Assess						*			
Evaluate							*	*	*

Handy hints for high marks!

It's hard to keep cool under exam pressure. However, these hints should help you perform better.

1 Dissect the question

Look at the example below. Try to break up questions like this – it will help to focus you on what the examiner is asking. Figure 6 should give you a clue in response to this question.

Note – assess! You need to make a judgment

The focus for the question – globalisation

Relate everything you say to environmental degradation – and what is causing it

Assess the role of globalisation in creating environmental degradation in developing countries. (12 marks)

'Developing countries' – not developed

12 marks – you only need 4 well-explained examples for full marks

Figure 6 *Urban pollution in Ghana's capital, Accra. Ghana has one of Africa's fastest growing economies – but the environmental cost is high*

2 Choose examples and case studies

Case studies are in-depth examples of particular places, used to illustrate big ideas at localised scales. There are plenty in this book; some examples are a paragraph, while others run to several pages. You should use these to answer the exam questions.

Few questions actually ask for examples. However, you'll get further in answering a question if you quote examples, such as the Ghana example in Figure 6. The following is an example of a question about Superpowers, where good examples are essential to producing a strong answer:

Assess the effectiveness of superpowers and emerging nations in playing key roles in international decision-making. (12 marks)

This would be very dull if written in general terms without reference to examples. Named examples make your answer precise and help you to do as the question asks – that is, be able to assess the role of particular superpowers and emerging nations in international decision-making.

Glossary

A

adaptation strategies – strategies designed to prepare for and reduce the impact of events

afforestation – the re-planting of trees when deforestation has occurred, or establishing forests on land not previously forested

aid dependency – the level to which a country cannot perform many of the basic functions of government without overseas aid

albedo – the amount of heat that is reflected by the Earth

antecedent moisture – water from one storm that has not drained away before more rain arrives

apartheid – the enforced segregation of people by skin colour or ethnicity. This policy was used in South Africa between 1948 and 1991

aquaculture – the breeding and harvesting of aquatic animals and plants

aquifer – an underground reservoir most commonly formed in rocks such as chalk and sandstone

Arctic amplification – the phenomenon where the Arctic region is warming twice as fast as the global average

arithmetic scale – increasing by a standard value each time – e.g. 2, 4, 6, 8 etc

assimilation – the gradual integration of an immigrant group into the lifestyle and *culture of the host country

asylum seekers – people who are fleeing to another country and applying for the right to international protection

austerity – the policy of reducing government spending and debt

B

base flow – also known as *groundwater flow – slow-moving water that seeps into a river channel through rocks

bio-geochemical carbon cycle – the continuous transfer of carbon from one *store to another, through the processes of photosynthesis, respiration, decomposition and combustion

biological carbon pump – where phytoplankton in the oceans sequester carbon dioxide through the process of photosynthesis – pumping it out of the atmosphere and into the ocean *store

biological decomposers – organisms such as insects, worms and bacteria which feed on dead plants, animals and waste

biologically derived carbon – carbon which is stored in shale, coal and other sedimentary rocks

BRICs – the collective term for Brazil, Russia, India and China (and, latterly, South Africa) which were predicted (by writer Richard Scase in 2000) to show rapid economic growth

C

carbon capture and storage (CCS) – the technological 'capturing' of carbon emitted from power stations

carbon fixation – turns gaseous carbon – CO_2 – into living organic compounds that grow

carbon sequestration – the removal and storage of carbon from the atmosphere, usually in oceans, forests and soils through photosynthesis

centrifugal forces – forces which drive people, organisations or countries apart

centripetal forces – forces which draw people, organisations or countries together

channel flow – the volume of water flowing within a river channel (also called *discharge, and runoff)

channel storage – water held in rivers and streams

closed system – where there are no *inputs or *outputs of matter from an external source – i.e. where inputs and outputs are balanced

colonialism – where an external nation takes direct control of a territory, often by force

complex river regimes – where larger rivers cross several different relief and climatic zones, and therefore experience the effects of different seasonal climatic events. Human factors can also contribute to their complexity, such as damming rivers for energy or irrigation

convectional rainfall – when the ground warms up, *evaporation takes place and the air above is heated and rises. The rainfall created is often intense and associated with electrical storms and thunder

coral bleaching – when coral turns white because the water is too warm and algae (which lives in the coral's tissues) are ejected

critical threshold – a point beyond which damage becomes irreversible

cryosphere – the frozen part of the Earth's hydrological system

cultural fractionization – measures how diverse countries are, by measuring people's attitudes towards, for example, religion, democracy and the law

culture – the ideas, beliefs, customs and social behaviour of a group or society

D

democracy aid – the allocation of funds to other countries for democracy-building

dependency theory – argues that developing countries remain dependent on wealthier nations, and that their reliance on developed economies is the cause of their poverty

deregulation – the reduction in government involvement in finance and business

descriptive statistics – measures such as those of central tendency and dispersion which can describe and be used to show patterns in that data

development aid – financial aid given to developing countries to support their long-term economic, political, social and environmental development

diasporas – dispersed populations away from their homeland

discharge – the volume of water passing a certain point in the channel over a certain amount of time

drainage density – describes whether a river has many or few tributaries. Dense drainage networks have many tributaries and carry water more efficiently

E

economic restructuring – the shift in employment from the primary and secondary sectors into tertiary and quaternary

economic sanctions – financial penalties (such as freezing assets or *trade embargoes) which are designed to put pressure on another country to change their policies or behaviour

ecosystem services – a holistic term to describe the services that ecosystems provide such as soil formation, food provision, climate regulation and recreation facilities

El Niño – a situation occurring every 3-8 years where pressure systems and weather patterns reverse

El Niño Southern Oscillation (ENSO) – the change in air pressure between 'normal' years and *El Niño

enclaves – concentrations of particular communities

energy mix – describes the range and combination of sources required to supply a country with energy

energy pathway – describes the flow of energy between a producer and a consumer, and how it reaches the consumer, e.g. pipeline, transmission lines, ship, rail

energy security – being able to access reliable and affordable sources of energy. These may be domestic, but could also include energy sources from 'friendly' countries

enhanced greenhouse effect – the increase in the *natural greenhouse effect, said to be caused by human activities that increase the quantity of greenhouse gases in the Earth's atmosphere

ethnic – a social group identified by a distinctive *culture, religion, language, or similar

ethnic cleansing – the deliberate removal, by killing or forced migration, of one *ethnic group by another

ethnic segregation – the voluntary or enforced separation of people of different *cultures or nationalities

evaporation – the conversion of water to vapour

evapotranspiration – the combined effect of *evaporation and *transpiration

extraordinary rendition – the secret transfer of a terror suspect, without legal process, to a foreign government for detention and interrogation. The interrogation methods often do not meet international standards, and include the use of torture

F

field (or infiltration) capacity – the maximum capacity of moisture that a soil can hold

flash flooding – when dry soil surfaces become waterlogged very quickly, causing rapid *surface runoff

flux – refers to the movement or transfer of carbon or water between *stores

frontal rainfall – formed when warmer moist air meets colder Polar air. The warmer air is forced to rise over the denser colder air, creating low-pressure and rain

G

genocide – the mass killing of a particular group of people

geo-strategic location theory – a theory developed by Halford John Mackinder which argued that whoever controlled Europe and Asia (the world's biggest landmass) would control the world

geological carbon – carbon which results from the formation of sedimentary carbonate rocks – limestone and chalk – in the oceans

geometric boundaries – borders between countries that have been formed by arcs or straight lines

geopolitical – the influence of geography (both human and physical) on politics, especially international relations

Gini coefficient – used to measure inequality between countries. It uses a figure between 0 (wealth is distributed equally) and 1 (where one person has all the wealth). The higher the coefficient, the more unequal the distribution

Gini index – essentially the same as the *Gini coefficient, except the Gini index is a value between 0 and 100 (i.e. the Gini coefficient multiplied by 100)

gravitational potential energy – ways in which water accelerates under gravity, thus transporting it to rivers and eventually to the sea

groundwater flow – also known as *base flow – slow-moving water that seeps into a river channel through rocks

groundwater storage – water held within permeable rocks (also known as an *aquifer)

H

hard-engineering – human-made, artificial structures designed to protect the land from erosion or flooding

hard power – the expression of a country's will or influence through coercive measures, including *economic sanctions and military force or threat

hegemon – a country or state that is dominant over others

Highly Indebted Poor Countries initiative (HIPC) – a policy introduced by the *IMF and the *World Bank which aimed to reduce national debts of the world's least developed countries by partially writing the debts off, in return for *Structural Adjustment Programmes

human capital – the economic, political, cultural and social skills within a country

I

import substitution – boosting domestic manufacturing and production as a substitute for previously imported products

inferential statistics – those which explore relationships between sets of data and can be used to test hypotheses about populations larger than the data set which has been sampled

infiltration – water entering the topsoil. Most common during slow or steady rainfall

input – an input into the system from outside, such as *precipitation into the drainage basin system

Inter-Tropical Convergence Zone (ITCZ) – a narrow zone of low pressure near the Equator where northern and southern air masses converge

interception – temporary storage, as water is captured by plants, buildings and hard surfaces before reaching the soil

intergovernmental organisation (IGO) – an organisation involving several countries working together on issues of common interest

International Monetary Fund (IMF) – a global organisation whose primary role is to maintain international financial stability

J

jet stream – a band of fast-moving air (located 9-16 km above the Earth) which determines the direction of weather systems and their speed of movement

K

Kuznet's curve – the concept that as rapid economic development occurs, environmental degradation increases, but after a certain level of development is reached, action to protect the environment can decrease degradation

L

lag time – the gap between the peak (maximum) rainfall and peak *discharge (highest river level) on a *storm hydrograph

La Niña – when the 'normal' pressure systems and weather patterns intensify and low pressure over the western Pacific becomes lower, and high pressure over the eastern Pacific higher

leaching – the loss of nutrients from the soil by *infiltration

liberalism – the idea that the government's role in business and the economy should be minimal, to allow individual decision-making, a free market and open competition between companies

linear sample – a type of *systematic sampling where a sample is taken at equal points along a line, such as every 10 metres

literature review – the part of the Independent Investigation which involves background reading about your topic and then producing a summary of that information

logarithmic scale – increasing on a cycle, usually by 10, so that 1 to 10 is the first cycle, 10 to 100 is the second cycle, 100 to 1000 the third, and so on

Lorenz curve – used to show and measure inequality in graphical form

M

media plurality – the ownership of several forms of media by the same company

mega-drought – a period of unusually low rainfall, lasting for decades or longer

Millennium Development Goals (MDGs) – goals related to different aspects of human development that were agreed by the UN in 2000, and that were to be achieved by 2015. They included reductions in poverty, hunger and infant mortality

mitigation strategies – strategies which aim to reduce or alleviate the impacts or severity of adverse conditions or events (such as reducing the amount of greenhouse gases that are released)

modernisation theory – a theory that believed that poverty was a trap; traditional family values in poorer countries held economies back; and that capitalism was the solution to poverty

monocultural – consisting of only one *culture

N

national sovereignty – the idea that each nation has a right to govern itself without interference from other nations

nationalise – when a company is transferred from private ownership to ownership or control by the state

nationalism – a patriotic feeling of pride and loyalty to a nation

natural greenhouse effect – the warming of the atmosphere as gases such as CO_2, CH_4 and water vapour absorb heat energy radiated from the Earth

negative feedback – when a change tends to reinforce a system, leading to stability

neo-colonialism – describes how even though less-developed countries may no longer be directly ruled by another, they are still controlled indirectly through economic, cultural and political means

neo-liberalism – a belief in the free flows of people, capital, finance and resources. Under neo-liberalism, State interventions in the economy are minimized, while the obligations of the State to provide for the welfare of its citizens are diminished

non-governmental organisation (NGO) – a not-for-profit organisation, independent from any government

O

ocean acidification – the process of the ocean's pH decreasing as the level of CO_2 in the ocean increases

open system – a system with *inputs from and *outputs to other systems

orographic rainfall – when warm, moist air is forced to rise over upland areas, causing the moisture to condense and create rainfall

out-gassing – when volcanoes erupt, releasing terrestrial carbon (held within the mantle) into the atmosphere as carbon dioxide

output – e.g. from a system, such as *evaporation or *transpiration from a drainage basin system

overabstraction – the removal of too much water from groundwater reserves, leading to rivers drying up

P

2015 Paris Agreement – legally binding global climate deal, adopted by 195 countries at the UN's Paris Climate Conference (COP21) in December 2015

percolation – the downward seepage of water through rock under gravity, especially in permeable rocks e.g. sandstone

person sample – a type of *systematic sampling where a person is selected at regular intervals, such as every tenth one on a street

players – individuals, groups and organisations involved in making decisions that affect people and places, known collectively as *stakeholders

point sample – a type of *systematic sampling where a point is selected at regular intervals, such as a series of points located at the intersection of a 10-metre grid

positive feedback – when a change leads to a decrease within a system and creates instability

potential evapotranspiration (PE) – an estimate of the amount of water lost through *evaporation and *transpiration in any given period, depending on temperature and air humidity

precipitation – moisture in any form, such as rain, snow, sleet and hail

primary consumers – organisms such as bugs, beetles, larvae and herbivores which depend and feed on *primary producers, and return carbon to the atmosphere during respiration

primary producers – green plants that use *solar energy to produce biomass

privatisation – the transfer of state or government assets into ownership by private individuals, companies or shareholders

proxy war – a war instigated by a major power that is not always directly involved in the fighting

Purchasing Power Parity (PPP) – (shown in US$) relates average earnings in a country to local prices and what they will buy. It is the spending power within a country, and reflects local costs of living

Q

qualitative – generates information about thoughts and opinions of people

quantitative – generates numerical data

R

radiative forcing effect (RFE) – the amount that a greenhouse gas affects the balance between the Earth's incoming solar radiation and outgoing long-wave radiation

rain-shadow effect – when *orographic rainfall has occurred over an upland area, the area on the lee side of the hills will receive less rain because the air descends, warms and becomes drier

random sampling – when each place or person in an area or a population has a mathematically equal chance of being selected

re-greening – the conversion of dry landscapes to productive farmland

refugees – people who are forced to leave their country because of war, natural disaster or persecution

remittance payments – income sent home by individuals working elsewhere

resilience – the ability of a system to 'bounce back' and survive

rising limb – the line on a *storm hydrograph which shows the *discharge rise up to its peak discharge

river regime – the annual pattern of flow within a river

S

Schengen Agreement – an agreement which abolished many of the internal border controls within the EU and enabled passport-free movement across most EU member states

sectoral sanctions – penalties that are imposed on targeted key areas in another country, such as energy, banking, finance, defence and technology

simple river regimes – where the river experiences a period of seasonally high *discharge, followed by low discharge

smart irrigation – where drip systems allow water to drip slowly to plants' roots through a system of valves and pipes, reducing wastage and *evaporation

soft power – the power that arises from a country's political and economic influence, moral authority and cultural attractiveness

soft-engineering – attempts to work with natural processes in order to mitigate risks

soil moisture – water held within the soil

solar energy – energy from the sun

stakeholders – the collective name for *players who are individuals, groups and organisations involved in making decisions that affect people and places

stem flow – water flowing down plant stems or drainpipes

store – an accumulation or quantity of, for example, water or carbon, in a system

storm hydrograph – a graph showing how a river responds to a particular storm. It displays both rainfall and *discharge

stratified sampling – a type of sampling which reflects the population being sampled – e.g. if 35% of the population were aged over 65 then 35% of the people surveyed would be over 65

Structural Adjustment Programmes (SAPs) – policies imposed by the *IMF which forced the State to play a reduced part in the economy and in social welfare, in return for re-arranging loans at adjusted rates of interest, and at more affordable repayments

sub-prime lending – the lending by banks to low-income earners with insecure jobs, who could never normally afford mortgages

superpower – a country with dominating power and influence

surface runoff – flow over the surface during an intense storm, or when the ground is frozen, saturated or impermeable. Also called overland flow

surface storage – any surface water in lakes, ponds and puddles

Sustainable Development Goals (SDGs) – a set of goals, launched in September 2015, to be achieved by 2030 and designed to end poverty, protect the planet and ensure prosperity for all

Sustainable Drainage Systems (SuDS) – techniques such as permeable pavements and infiltration basins which reduce *surface runoff produced from rainfall

systematic sampling – when each sample is selected in a regular manner

T

thermohaline circulation – the flow of warm and cold water that circulates around the world's oceans

throughflow – also known as inter-flow; water seeping laterally through soil below the surface, but above the water table

throughput – the quantity of a material, such as water, that flows through a system or *store

tipping point – when a system changes from one state to another, irretrievably

tonnes of oil equivalent – a unit designed to include all forms of energy by comparing them with oil in terms of heat output. It measures each type of energy by calculating the amount of heat obtained by burning one tonne, and then converting it to however much oil would be required to produce an equivalent amount of energy

trade embargo – a government or international ban that restricts trade with a particular country

transit state – a country or state through which goods or people flow (e.g. energy on its way from producer to consumer)

transpiration – water taken up by plants and transpired from the leaf surface

U

unilateral actions – one country, or group of countries, acting against another, for example, without formal UN approval

V

vegetation storage – any moisture taken up by vegetation and held within plants

virtual water – water transferred by trading in crops and services that require large amounts of water for their production

W

Walker Cell – the circulation of air whereby upper atmospheric air moves eastwards, and surface air moves west across the Pacific, causing trade winds

Wallerstein's world systems theory – a theory which claims that core regions drive the world economy and that peripheral areas (distant from the core and lacking capital) rely on core regions to exploit their raw materials. Therefore, unequal trade develops between them

Washington Consensus – a belief that economic efficiency can only be achieved if regulations are removed

water budget – the difference between *inputs of water (such as *precipitation) and *outputs of water (such as *evapotranspiration) in any given area

water insecurity – the state where present and future supplies of water cannot be guaranteed, caused by *water scarcity and *water stress

Water Poverty Index (WPI) – measures how far a community or country meets all the criteria for: the availability of water resources, access to water, handling capacity, use of water, and the ability to sustain nature and ecosystems

water scarcity – there is less than 1000m^3 of water available per person per year. An imbalance between demand and supply of water, classified as physical scarcity (insufficient water to meet demand) or economic scarcity (people can't afford water, even when it's available)

water stress – there is less than 1700m^3 of water available per person per year. If a country's water consumption exceeds 10% of its renewable fresh water supply, including difficulties in obtaining new quantities of water, as well as poor water quality restricting usage

World Bank – a global organisation whose role is to finance development

World Trade Organisation (WTO) – a global organisation which looks at the rules for how countries trade with each other

world water gap – refers to the fact that in many parts of the world there is not enough water to meet demand, whereas wealthy countries are consuming greater and greater quantities of water

Index